The Atlantic World

From about 1400 to 1900, the Atlantic Ocean served as a major highway, allowing people and goods to move easily between Europe, Africa and the Americas. These interactions and exchanges transformed European, African and American societies and led to the creation of new peoples, cultures, economies and ideas throughout the Atlantic arena. *The Atlantic World* provides a comprehensive and lucid history of one of the most important cross-cultural encounters in human history. The European drive to expand, as well as the creative ways in which the peoples living along the Atlantic's borders were able to adapt and co-exist, sustained the growth of empires, economies and trade in the Atlantic World.

The forty maps, sixty illustrations and multiple excerpts from primary documents serve to bring the history to life.

Thomas Benjamin is Professor of History and a member of the Center for Transnational and Comparative History at Central Michigan University. He is Editor-in-Chief of the three-volume *Encyclopedia of Western Colonialism Since 1450* and co-editor of *The Atlantic World in the Age of Empire*.

The Atlantic World

Europeans, Africans, Indians and Their Shared History, 1400–1900

Thomas Benjamin
Central Michigan University

CAMBRIDGE
UNIVERSITY PRESS

CAMBRIDGE UNIVERSITY PRESS
Cambridge, New York, Melbourne, Madrid, Cape Town, Singapore, São Paulo, Delhi

Cambridge University Press
32 Avenue of the Americas, New York, NY 10013-2473, USA

www.cambridge.org
Information on this title: www.cambridge.org/9780521616492

First published 2009

Printed in the United States of America

A catalog record for this publication is available from the British Library.

Library of Congress Cataloging in Publication data

Benjamin, Thomas, 1952–
The Atlantic world : Europeans, Africans, Indians and their shared history, 1400–1900 /
Thomas Benjamin.
    p.   cm.
Includes bibliographical references and index.
ISBN 978-0-521-85099-5 (hardback : alk. paper)
 1. History, Modern. 2. Atlantic Ocean Region – History.   3. Culture conflict – Atlantic Ocean
Region – History.   I. Title.
D210.B46   2009
909′.09821–dc22   2008051266

ISBN 978-0-521-85099-5 hardback
ISBN 978-0-521-61649-2 paperback

This book is dedicated to Leslie B. Rout Jr. (1935–1987),
jazz musician, fiery iconoclast, historian of Brazil and Spanish America,
professor, mentor and friend.

Contents

List of Tables	*page* ix
List of Illustrations	xi
List of Maps	xiv
List of Documents	xvi
Preface	xix
Introduction	xxiii

Part I The Ocean Shall Unloose the Bonds of Things — I

Chapter 1 Antecedents — 6
The Americas, Africa and Europe in the Fifteenth Century

Chapter 2 Commencement — 52
The European Opening of the Atlantic Ocean

Chapter 3 Conquests — 105
Forging the Iberian Empires in Africa and the Americas

Chapter 4 Realms — 161
The Overseas Empires of Spain and Portugal

Part II Europe Supported by Africa and America — 209

Chapter 5 Incursions — 214
The French, English and Dutch Invasions of the Iberian Atlantic

Chapter 6 Engagement — 273
The Entangled Worlds of Indians and Europeans

Chapter 7   Uprooted   326
    West Africa, the Americas and the Atlantic Slave Trade

Chapter 8   Bondage   373
    The Atlantic Plantation Complex and the Cultures of Slavery

Chapter 9   Partners   420
    Women and Men in the Making of the Atlantic World

Part III   A New Order of the Ages   465

Chapter 10   Rivals   472
    Great Britain and France in the Long Eighteenth Century

Chapter 11   Liberty   517
    The Atlantic World in the Age of Revolution

Chapter 12   Equality   567
    The Atlantic World in the Age of Revolution

Chapter 13   Freedom   615
    *The Abolition of the Atlantic Slave Trade and New
    World Slavery*

Epilogue   661
Glossary   667
Select Bibliography   675
Index   699

List of Tables

1.1	Regional Populations: The Americas, c. 1492	*page* 23
1.2	Regional Populations: Sub-Saharan Africa, c. 1500	36
1.3	Population Growth in Western Europe, 1000–1500	38
1.4	Regional Populations: Western Europe, c. 1500	47
1.5	Regional Populations: The World, c. 1500	47
2.1	Total Wealth of World Regions: GDP, 1000–1600	56
4.1	Native Population of the Valley of Mexico, 1519–1800	174
4.2	Population of Spanish America, 1570–1800	185
4.3	Population of Brazil, 1549–1819	202
5.1	National Populations of Western Europe, 1500–1700	224
5.2	Economic Growth in Western Europe, 1500–1700	225
5.3	Europeans on the Move, 1500–1700	259
6.1	European and Euroamerican Populations in the Americas, 1600–1800	274
6.2	Native American Populations, 1492–1996	321
6.3	Indigenous Languages in the Americas, Living and Extinct, 2005	323
7.1	The Atlantic Slave Trade: Arrivals in America, 1510–1870	327
7.2	Atlantic Africa Overseas Trade, 1680–1820	341
7.3	The Atlantic Slave Trade: Arrivals in America by Region, 1451–1700	342
7.4	The Atlantic Slave Trade: Arrivals in America by Region, 1701–1800	342
7.5	The Atlantic Slave Trade: African Origins of Captives, 1662–1867	362
7.6	The African Origins of New World Religions: A Selection	365
8.1	Sugar Production in Atlantic Regions: Tonnage, 1493–1870	391
8.2	Sugar Plantations in Atlantic Regions: Plantations/Mills, 1493–1860	397
8.3	Slaves in Atlantic Sugar Plantation Colonies, 1492–1841	398
8.4	Slave Populations in the Americas, c. 1770	400

8.5	Annual Percentage Decline in Slave Populations: Jamaica and Barbados, 1651–1775	408
9.1	The Portuguese Atlantic: Populations in the Seventeenth Century	437
9.2	Emigration of Spanish Women to the Americas, 1509–1600	444
9.3	British Emigration to America, 1635	458
9.4	French Emigration to Canada, 1670–1729	462
10.1	National Populations of Western Europe, 1700–1800	473
10.2	The Atlantic Contribution to English Trade, 1700–72	490
13.1	Unconditional Emancipation in the Republics of Spanish America, 1823–69	637
13.2	The Slave Population of the United States, 1790–1860	642
13.3	The Slave Population of Cuba, 1795–1860	646
13.4	The Slave Population of Brazil, 1798–1887	649
E.1	Economic Growth of World Regions, 1820–2000	663
E.2	Regional Populations of the World, 1820–2000	665

List of Illustrations

1.1	Theodor de Bry, *Flying Fishes at Sea*	page 2
1.2	Juan de Tovar, *Motecuçuma, the Last King of the Mexica*	13
1.3	André Thevet, *Natives of the African Coast of Guinea*	29
1.4	Theodor de Bry, *Harbor of Lisbon*	43
2.1	Enrico Alberto d'Albertis, *An Astrolabe*	71
2.2	Fracanzano da Montalboddo, *Itinerarivm Portugallensium ex Vlisbona I Indiam*	87
2.3	Enrico Alberto d'Albertis, *The Caravel La Pinta*	92
2.4	Theodor de Bry, *The Atlantic Sphere*	102
3.1	Jean Blaeu, *West Africa from Arguim to Benin*	110
3.2	Jean Blaeu, *The Portuguese Castle of São Jorge da Mina*	111
3.3	Georg Braun and Franz Hogenberg, *Mexico-Tenochtitlan*	138
3.4	Theodor de Bry, *An Imagined Scene of the Spanish Conquest of Cuzco*	148
4.1	Scenographia Americana, *A View of the Market Place in the City of Havana*	168
4.2	Theodor de Bry, *New Spain*	175
4.3	Miguel Suárez de Figueroa, *Franciscan Church and Convent, San Francisco, in Lima*	180
4.4	Pedro Cieza de León, *Mountain of Potosí*	183
4.5	Theodor de Bry, *The Spaniards Cruelly Treated the Indians Who Collapse under Their Loads*	184
4.6	Theodor de Bry, *São Salvador and the Bay of All Saints*	199
5.1	William Blake, *Europe Supported by Africa and America*	210
5.2	Jean Bleau, *The Atlantic Coast of France*	228
5.3	Jean Bleau, *The Dutch Port of Amsterdam*	230
5.4	Theodor de Bry, *Drake's Fleet at Santo Domingo*	233
5.5	Theodor de Bry, *The Arrival of Englishmen in Virginia*	239
5.6	Scenographia Americana, *Miramich, a French Settlement (Habitation) in New France*	246
5.7	Jean Blaeu, *The Dutch Attempt to Conquer the City of Salvador on All Saints Bay*	252

6.1   André Thevet, *Cannibalism Among the Native Brazilians*   276
6.2   Cieza de León, *The Chronicle of Cieza de León*   285
6.3   Theodor de Bry, *The Native Town of Secota in Virginia*   291
6.4   Tiburcio Navarro, *The Franciscan Missionary, Francisco
      Solano, Baptizes Native Americans in Peru*   304
7.1   Atlas Maritimus and Commercialis, *Guinea in the
      Eighteenth Century*   338
7.2   The Uncle Tom's Cabin Almanack, *Slave Barracoon and
      Canoe for Transporting the Slaves from the Barracoon to
      the Ship*   350
7.3   John Atkins, *The Barter Price for African Captives on the
      Coast of Africa*   352
7.4   The Uncle Tom's Cabin Almanack, *Sale of Slaves by
      Native Chiefs*   353
7.5   William Blake, *Group of Negroes, as Imported to Be Sold
      for Slaves*   358
8.1   William Clark, *Slaves Cutting Sugar Cane in the West Indies*   379
8.2   Jean Blaeu, *Pernambuco (Brazilian Engenho)*   387
8.3   Charles de Rochefort, *Figure of a Sugar Mill*   395
8.4   John Knox, *A Scene of Merchants and a Slave in the
      British West Indies*   418
9.1   Theodor de Bry, *The Attack on the Baths of the Inka
      Atahualpa*   440
9.2   B. Cole, *A Spanish-American Lady, Accompanied by
      Two African Servants, Going to Church*   447
9.3   Henry Koster, *A View of a Brazilian Planter and His
      Wife, Attended by African Slaves, On a Journey*   455
9.4   Theodor de Bry, *A Gentle Young Native Lady of Virginia*   457
10.1 The Massachusetts Magazine, *An Allegorical
      Representation of the Liberty of America and Europe in
      the Age of Revolution*   466
10.2 Scenographia Americana, *The French Naval Base and
      Fortification of Louisbourg*   483
10.3 Alexander Tweedie, *The British Warship, the* Formidable,
      in the Eighteenth Century   485
10.4 Scenographia Americana, *Quebec City, the Capital of
      New France*   497
10.5 Bryan Edwards, *The West Indies in the Late Eighteenth
      Century*   507
10.6 Bowle's Chart, *The Atlantic Arena in the Eighteenth Century*   514
11.1 Abbé G. Th. Raynal, *Raynal's Philosophical and Political
      History of the Two Indies*   526
11.2 Paul Revere, *The Boston Massacre, 1770*   529
11.3 Pierre Blin, *A French Allegorical Image Celebrating the
      American Revolution*   543
12.1 Marcus Rainsford, *Toussaint L'Ouverture*   575
12.2 Marcus Rainsford, *Saint Domingue at the Time of the
      Haitian Revolution*   578

12.3 Marcus Rainsford, *The Mode of Exterminating the Black
       Army as Practiced by the French*   582
12.4 The Uncle Tom's Cabin Almanack, *Statue of Toussaint
       L'Ouverture*   587
12.5 M. N. Bates, *Portrait of Simón Bolívar in Military Attire* 608
13.1 A Quaker Anti-slavery Pamphlet, *The Case of Our
       Fellow-Creatures the Oppressed Africans*   622
13.2 Thomas Clarkson, *The Slave Ship, the* Brookes   630
13.3 Thomas Clarkson, *Instruments Used in the Slave Trade*   631
13.4 The Uncle Tom's Cabin Almanack, *Gezo, King of Dahomey*   655

List of Maps

i	The Fifteenth-Century Atlantic	*page* xxv
1.1	The Mexica Empire, c. 1500	11
1.2	The Inka Empire, c. 1500	15
1.3	The Major African Empires, 1000–1500	26
1.4	Late Medieval Europe	44
2.1	The Iberian Peninsula, c. 1492	61
2.2	Atlantic Winds and Currents	69
2.3	The Near Atlantic	74
2.4	The Portuguese Voyages	85
2.5	The Tordesillas Line in the Atlantic	95
2.6	Columbus and the Early Transatlantic Voyages	97
3.1	Guinea in the Early European Era	113
3.2	Central Africa in the Early European Era	116
3.3	Native and Spanish Caribbean	130
3.4	The Valley of Mexico	137
3.5	Early Spanish Overland Expeditions	152
3.6	Native and Portuguese Brazil	154
4.1	Europe in the Age of Carlos V	165
4.2	The Cities and Towns of Spanish America	167
4.3	Iberian Colonies in the Atlantic World, c. 1600	198
4.4	Colonial Brazil	201
5.1	Spain and America: Maritime Routes	218
5.2	North America in the Seventeenth Century	241
5.3	New France in the Seventeenth Century	247
5.4	The West Indies in the Seventeenth Century	258
5.5	The European Seaborne Empires	270
6.1	Indians and Europeans in North America, c. 1660	300
6.2	The Missions of South America	307
6.3	North America in 1750	318
7.1	West Africa in the Era of the Transatlantic Slave Trade	340
7.2	The Transatlantic Slave Trade	343
8.1	African Slavery in the Americas, c. 1770	396

10.1	The Atlantic World, c. 1750	489
10.2	Northeastern North America, c. 1755	492
10.3	The West Indies, c. 1750	498
10.4	The British Atlantic Empire, c. 1763	504
11.1	The Thirteen Colonies	530
11.2	Western Europe in the Age of the French Revolution	562
12.1	Saint Domingue, 1794	576
E.1	The Nineteenth-Century Atlantic	664

List of Documents

1.1 *Popul Vuh*: Maya-Quiché Creation Myth page 8
1.2 How the Spider Obtained the Sky God's Stories: Ashanti
Folktale 30
1.3 The Imitation of Christ 37
1.4 The First Booke of Moses, Called Genesis 41
2.1 The Entire Earth Consists of Three Continents 72
2.2 In Which Five Reasons Appear Why the Lord Infante
Was Moved to Command the Search for the Lands of Guinea 77
2.3 Of the Original Beginning of Christendom in the
Kingdom of Congo, and How the Portuguese Obtained
This Traffic 88
2.4 Mundus Novus 99
3.1 Paulo Diaz in Arms Against the King of Angola 120
3.2 The Warning of the Cacique Hatuey to the Indians of Cuba 131
3.3 The Conclusion of the Conquest of Mexico 142
4.1 Royal Ordinances Concerning the Laying Out of New Towns 176
4.2 The Island of St. Thomas 193
5.1 Royal Patent to the Sieur de Monts 243
5.2 Observations on the Estate and Affairs of Holland 249
5.3 The Buccaneers of America 266
6.1 *De Origine Populi*: On the Origins of the Natives of Virginia 287
6.2 The Lord's Prayer in Nahuatl 303
6.3 The Bloody Victories Obtained by the Iroquois over
Our Hurons 315
7.1 The Manner How the Negroes Become Slaves 333
7.2 Some Account of the Author's Captivity 355
8.1 Of the Manner How Sugar Is Made 377
8.2 Sugar-Canes 392
8.3 The Negroes of Barbados 404
9.1 Concerning Marriage and of Parental Duty 429
9.2 They Love Women Extreamly, and Spare No Charges for
the Setting Out of Their Wives 453

10.1   The Complete English Tradesman   486
10.2   The Late War in North America between France and England   500
11.1   Political Aphorisms   522
11.2   Of Independence, State Constitutions, and the Confederation 536
11.3   The Revolution of America   544
11.4   A Declaration to the French Nation from the National
       Assembly   551
12.1   A Dispatch to Blanchlande, Governor of Saint Domingue   572
12.2   Declaration of the Independence of the Blacks of St. Domingo 584
12.3   Address to the Congress of Angostura   606
13.1   An Exhortation and Caution to Friends Concerning
       Buying or Keeping Negroes   620
13.2   The Origins of Abolitionism in Brazil   652

Preface

My studies have taken me to very interesting places and pasts in the Americas, Africa and Europe. Like many Latin Americans, West Africans, Europeans and Americans today, I am something of a citizen of the Atlantic. That is, I have been crossing the Atlantic by sea and by air for many years to study, visit and live in Latin America, Europe, the Caribbean and, much less, West Africa – at least so far. The idea for this book came from my students when I was Professor of American Studies at the University of Groningen, The Netherlands, in 1989–90. When I returned to Michigan I created a new course called "Atlantic World in the Age of Empire." I taught this course throughout the 1990s and read as much of the abundant historiography and relevant printed primary sources related to these times and places as humanly (meaning matrimonially) possible. In 1999–2001, thanks to a sabbatical leave and a Research Professorship from Central Michigan University, I put together two years of uninterrupted research and writing. Research for and rewriting of this book continued for several more years, and I devoted entire semesters and summers to work on this book in 2004, 2005, 2006 and 2007.

Some brief remarks on terminology are warranted. In this book, I often refer to Europeans, Africans and Indians or Native Americans. Rarely if ever did these peoples think or refer to themselves in those terms. In their perceptions, they were Extremadurans (today's Spaniards), Zealanders (Dutch), Angoumois (French), and so on; they were, at least in European terms, Fante (Gold Coast, today's Ghanaians), Efik and Igbo (Benin, today's Nigerians) and Kongo and Mbundo (today's Congolese and Angolans), to mention only a few; and Mexica or Nahua (today's Mexicans) and Guaraní (today's Brazilians, Paraguayans and scattered other nationals). The term "Indian" or "Indio" is today politically incorrect in many circles. Of course, it is a misnomer, in the sense that Columbus believed the people he came upon in the Caribbean were Asians, that is, what we would call today East Indians. Historians can hardly avoid the term because the documents and printed sources from that past – European sources, to be sure – are suffused with the term. I employ it as well as the term "Native American" and, of course, local and self-descriptive names. We in the United States still live in "Indian Country," if the souvenirs sold in powwows mean anything.

There is a problem in referring to those Africans and their descendants in Africa, the Atlantic islands and the Americas who were so unfortunate to become slaves. This stark word, this adjective, implies that the condition of slavery defined their very being. In fact, these people were captives in Africa and during the middle passage and enslaved Africans on plantations and in cities. Historical sources and documents use many words, terms and names we would never use today. I quote from slave traders and slave masters of centuries past to create some sense of the rough and ugly nature of this age and these people.

I have been working on this book for about ten years, and I have depended upon the kindness of many old friends and quite a few new ones. This history is based on an extensive reading of other books, both the classic histories of the early modern era as well as the most recent relevant scholarship on Europe, Africa and the Americas. I have also examined a considerable number of the printed sources from this era. In my years of reading and research, I have been assisted by the helpful and knowledgeable staffs at the following research institutions: The John Carter Brown Library, Providence, Rhode Island; The William L. Clements Library, Ann Arbor, Michigan; The Clark Historical Library, Mt. Pleasant, Michigan; The Library Company of Philadelphia, Pennsylvania; The Lilly Library, Bloomington, Indiana; The National Library at the National Autonomous University of Mexico (UNAM), Mexico City; The Newberry Library, Chicago, Illinois; and the university libraries of Central Michigan University, Mount Pleasant; The University of Chicago, Hyde Park, Illinois; Michigan State University, East Lansing; the University of Groningen, The Netherlands; The University of São Paulo, Brazil; and The University of Virginia, Charlottesville.

The William L. Clements Library provided historical illustrations for this book. I wish to recognize Director John C. Dann for his gracious welcome and thank Brian Leigh Dunnigan, Head of Research and Publications, and Clayton Lewis, Curator of Graphic Materials, for their invaluable assistance in guiding my research in the Clements Library's magnificent collection. The Clarke Historical Library at Central Michigan University and the John Carter Brown Library at Brown University also provided illustrations and much needed assistance. My thanks to Director Frank Boles at the Clarke and Susan Danforth and Heather Jespersen at the John Carter Brown.

The National Endowment for the Humanities (NEH) helped me create some of the networks of my personal Atlantic World by inviting me to participate in two NEH institutes. The first one, in the summer of 1998, was "Crossroads of Atlantic Cultures: Brazil at 500," in São Paulo, Salvador and Rio de Janeiro. The second, in the summer of 2002, was "Roots 2001: The African Background of American Culture Through the Trans-Atlantic Slave Trade" at the University of Virginia. My thanks go to Professors Phyllis Peres, Daryle Williams and Joseph Miller, the directors of these institutes, for instruction, advice and friendship. Central Michigan University, my academic home for the past quarter century, supported my study in Ghana during the summer of 2001 and provided financial support for research and writing in 1991–2001 and semesters in 2004, 2005 and 2006

My research assistant was Mr. Kwaku Nti, a relentless searcher, invaluable critic and a good guy. Over many years, the students in my course History 562, "The Atlantic World in the Age of Empire," have read earlier versions of this book and have given me many good ideas and some interesting leads. Professor Eric Johnson has spent dozens of hours in conversation and deconstruction in an effort to help me focus the themes and ideas of this book. I have learned much from my colleagues Timothy Hall and David Rutherford, who have written about and teach courses on Atlantic history.

Frank Smith, Eric Crahan, Simina Calin and Mark Fox at Cambridge University Press have supported me and this project for many years. I am most grateful for their patience, expertise and professionalism. I would like to thank the anonymous readers of this book for Cambridge for their careful and serious analysis of the manuscript more than once. Professor Matthew Restall, who withdrew his anonymity, provided remarkably good ideas and suggestions. Midge Benjamin, James Daybell, Timothy Hall, Doina Harsayni, Eric Johnson, Lester Langley, David Rutherford, and Mark Wasserman have read in part, or even sometimes in whole, various versions of this book over the years and have given me good advice. Of course, despite all the help in the world, in the end the omissions and errors in this book are my responsibility.

In his preface to *The Muquaddimah*, one of the great works of history, Ibn Khaldûn refers to his book and its arguments. "I treated everything comprehensively and extensively and explained the arguments and reasons for its existence." He recognized that no author has all the answers. "As a result, this book has become unique, as it contains unusual knowledge and familiar if hidden wisdom. Still, after all has been said, I am conscious of imperfections when I look at the work of scholars past and present. I confess my inability to penetrate so difficult a subject." I, too, am conscious of the imperfections of this book. Like Ibn Khaldûn, I know that the Atlantic World is a vast and difficult subject, and that I have not penetrated all of the important topics, issues and problems of Atlantic history. In history, we have no access to complete truth; as Michael Stanford writes, "we must keep an open mind, recognize the fallibility of our beliefs, be always keen to widen our knowledge, and be ever ready to see the possibility of truth in an unwelcome fact or uncongenial opinion." My wife, Sharon Lee House, recognizes the fallibility of my opinions and truths all the time. Since that Sunday, late last century when we were married in the parish of Saint Michael on the island of Barbados, we have had many occasions when we both needed open minds. Her occasional skepticism and steady emotional sustenance in Barbados, Veracruz, Southampton, Bruges, São Paulo, Accra, Mount Pleasant, Anna Maria Island and other havens and hideaways have helped me chart my course in life.

TB
Anna Maria Island
Summer 2008

Introduction

The idea of an Atlantic World has blossomed in recent decades as a way to encourage all of us in the Americas, Africa and Europe to examine, teach and write about our localities, provinces and nations from wider and comparative perspectives. This is a good idea but we need to remember that the Atlantic World is, in fact, a useful and interesting historical concept more than a self-evident historical reality. Cosmopolitans – that is, the well-traveled worldly type of the early modern era – never employed the term or viewed the societies and peoples perched around the Atlantic Ocean as a larger coherent whole. Yet as the saying goes, what we see often depends upon where we stand. The Chinese published a guide to the Atlantic Ocean in 1701 that described the peoples of Europe, Africa and the Americas as "the people of the Great Western Sea." It is often strangers from afar who see a unity, however tenuous and feeble, that is indistinct to those within.

This book focuses on the connections, interactions and exchanges that crisscrossed the Atlantic Ocean beginning in the fifteenth century. These attachments and engagements transformed European, West African and Native American societies and also created new peoples, societies, cultures, economies and ideas throughout the Atlantic littoral. The past that is under consideration here was vast, protracted, multitudinous and extraordinarily complex. How could it be otherwise, with a historical palette that brings together so many distant lands, so many and various societies and cultures and nearly five centuries of uncountable individuals, events and stories? The past is largely without form or meaning in the absence of historians. They frame the subject, discern patterns, tell a story and give it significance. It is the task of historians to select among the infinite number of facts and abundant accounts to craft a history of past worlds. This history, as all histories, is an interpretation. It defines the Atlantic World and tells its story through the lens of three overarching themes.

The first theme emphasizes the importance of Western Europeans in expanding beyond their homelands into the Atlantic Ocean and onto its many islands and shores. It may seem Eurocentric to some historians and readers to begin on this note as Europe has long been portrayed as the most prominent actor in this drama. But as Philip Curtin, the highly respected historian of Africa, has written, "in fact Europe *was* the most prominent actor." European maritime prowess, according to Curtin, "was the decisive factor shaping the Atlantic world." Europeans were the first to transform the Atlantic Ocean from a great and seemingly impassible barrier into a highway of trade and communication. European mariners and traders as well as colonists, soldiers and missionaries spanned the ocean on behalf of princes, merchants, the church and, of course, their own private interests. Europeans created the shipping lanes, maritime empires and commercial systems that tied every place together. And it was Europeans, and their American cousins, that invented the ideas and led the revolutions to collapse the Atlantic empires.

The second theme argues that the remarkable growth of Atlantic trades, colonies, economies and empires was the result of the creative and adaptive interactions among Europeans, Africans and Indians. As Europeans reached the many shores of the Atlantic Ocean, they would never have thrived, or in many cases survived, without the cooperation, trade, labor and knowledge of Africans and Indians. History can be both cruel and beneficent, noted John Stuart Mill, and in this Atlantic age we see something similar, a paradox of partnership and exploitation. It is a paradox, at least to us in the present, to see partnership and exploitation existing side by side. African princes and merchants raided and captured Africans from other regions and ethnic groups and partnered with European traders to sell them into the Atlantic slave trade. Native American kingdoms and chiefs allied with European war bands to make war against other, more powerful native confederations, states and empires. In most slave societies in the Americas, free men of color served in militias to defend that colony from rival European empires and the greater threat, slave revolts. In Spanish American estates, Hispanicized Africans and blacks supervised the labor of dependent Indian laborers. Unlike Western Europeans, West Africans and Native Americans rarely saw themselves in a manner we would today call a pan-racial or ethnic identity. Africans and Indians many centuries ago lived in worlds of many different groups, languages and cultures and, as a result, it was a dangerous world of enemies near and far. Europeans were willing and able to take advantage of these rivalries. At first, Europeans were relatively weak in Africa and the Americas but in time they became more and more powerful and wealthy, which tilted the balance from partnership to exploitation. However, Africans and Indians were rarely simply victims of Europeans. They resisted and fought back, negotiated the demands put upon them and carved out meaningful lives, whatever the circumstances. Individuals and groups make history acting in their perceived interests, and in the context of specific circumstances that provide limited options. We in the present may not always fully understand or approve of their choices. The English historian Geoffrey Elton was impressed by the "magnificent unpredictability of what human beings may think and do." We all should be.

The third theme maintains that this Atlantic system had a beginning and an end. We might call this pattern, using an old historical figure of speech, a rise and fall. Of course, the rise is easy to recognize and characterize. Prior

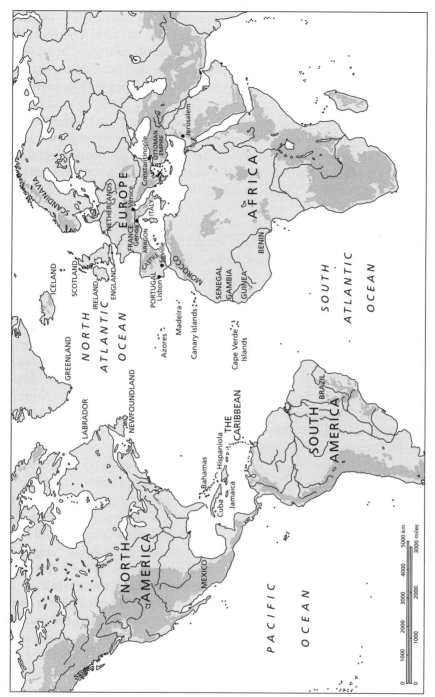

Map 1 The Fifteenth-Century Atlantic.

to the fifteenth century, the peoples, societies and polities in the Americas, Africa and Europe had little or no contact with one another. The European voyages of exploration in the fifteenth and sixteenth centuries, the expansion of transatlantic trade, expeditions of settlement and conquest, along with crucial African and Indian interaction with Europeans, made possible everything that came later. The idea of an end or a fall is more difficult and controversial in several ways. Why should we consider an end to this Atlantic system at all? Goods and people crisscross the Atlantic Ocean today in ships and airliners, and our family and friendship connections, commerce, diplomacy and more are conducted instantaneously from continent to continent by phone, fax and e-mail. If we accept the idea of a limited chronology, then the problem becomes determining the end. Historians have offered different possibilities: was it the American Revolution, the French Revolution, the Haitian Revolution, the Industrial Revolution, the Spanish-American Revolutions, the abolition of the Atlantic slave trade or the end of New World slavery?

It makes sense to differentiate the early Atlantic from our contemporary Atlantic. That earlier Atlantic was tied together in ways that were unique to that age and that no longer exist. Transatlantic empires, the slave trade and a commodities trade made possible by African slaves in New World plantations were just some of the most important connections. In that earlier Atlantic, unlike our Atlantic today, West Africa, South America and the Caribbean were particularly important to the functioning of the international economy and the struggles between the great powers. Four times more Africans than Europeans had migrated – that is, had been transported involuntarily – to the Americas in that earlier Atlantic. In that earlier age, those European immigrants and their progeny who lived in the Americas by and large believed they lived in one of several "New Guineas" – that is, an Africanized part of America – or in "Indian Country."

This earlier Atlantic came to an end over a prolonged period of time as a result of the American Revolution, the French Revolution, the Haitian Revolution, the Industrial Revolution, the Spanish-American Revolutions, the abolition of the Atlantic slave trade and the end of New World slavery. It came to an end also because there were no liberal revolutions in Africa in the eighteenth or nineteenth centuries. "Europe and the Western Hemisphere, profoundly linked to the peoples of West Africa," writes Bernard Bailyn, "have taken different paths in many different spheres since the age of the Enlightenment, and in the course of the nineteenth century they became part of a global world system." Ultimately, that earlier, more coherent Atlantic region came to an end because everything became faster and the world became smaller. Just about everything just about everywhere has become interconnected, intertwined and interactive.

This earlier Atlantic is called the Atlantic World in this book following the lead of the French historian Fernand Braudel. In his classic histories *The Mediterranean and the Mediterranean World in the Age of Philip II* (1949) and *Civilization and Capitalism* (1979), Braudel referred to the Mediterranean as a *Welttheater*, that is, a world-theater. By this, he meant "not merely the sea itself but the whole area stimulated by its trading activities, whether near its shores or far away. I have treated it in short as a world in itself." The Atlantic basin, littorals and substantial parts of adjacent continents were, from the fifteenth to the nineteenth centuries, in many ways a world in itself, and so the term is warranted. After the Second World War, journalists, intellectuals and historians began to refer to a contemporary Atlantic community and look at the past and see an Atlantic civilization. J. H. Elliott employed the term "Atlantic World" in 1970, and he showed a clear appreciation of the wider context of the Atlantic World – Europe, Africa and the Americas – as a whole. Also in the 1970s, the appearance of world-systems theory provided a perspective of a widespread system of interaction, exchanges and information – which embraced regional systems of interaction – that extended beyond the political boundaries of any state or empire.

I would hope that Atlantic World history should give nearly equal weight to Western Europe, West and Central Africa and the Americas, including the Caribbean, and never venture too far from the ocean. Furthermore, this history does not delve excessively into the history of the American colonies, pre-Colonial Africa or early modern Europe. These histories we have in abundance already, and increasingly historians of these regions are writing their histories in light of Atlantic perspectives. We should also realize that this Atlantic World was both a world in itself to some extent and part of the wider world. European mariners reached the edge of the Indian Ocean before they found their way to the Americas. A Portuguese fleet on its way to India reached the coast of Brazil in 1500. The Atlantic World is not all we need to know about the early modern history of the world; it is a part of world history, and it needs to be integrated into the histories of the Indian Ocean, the China Sea and the Pacific Ocean.

More than fifty years ago, Braudel wrote: "I hope too that I shall not be reproached for my excessive ambitions, for my desire and need to see on a grand scale. It will perhaps prove that history can do more than study walled gardens." As someone who has studied my own walled gardens, I developed an irrepressible urge to write a total history of a great ocean and its surrounding peoples, kingdoms, traders, empires and more, something Clifford Geertz has called an "impossible book." So be it. A difficult project for me need not be difficult for my readers to read, understand and, I hope, enjoy. In writing this book, I have been inspired by Pedro de Cieza de León's address to his readers in his 1552 chronicle, *The Discovery and Conquest of Peru*: "And, good and honorable men, this you will comprehend and learn without knowing it when you see the modesty and simplicity of my style, which seeks neither verbosity nor flowery words nor other rhetoric, and only wishes to relate the truth with sincerity because I believe that good writing must be like one person conversing with another – and as one speaks and no more."

This volume is divided into three parts, each with narrative and thematic chapters. Part I, "The Ocean Shall Unloose the Bonds of Things," examines the origins of the Atlantic World in four chapters: Chapter 1 describes the isolated lands and peoples perched around the Atlantic Ocean prior to the European voyages of exploration. Chapter 2 explores the European opening of the Atlantic Ocean in the fifteenth and sixteenth centuries. Chapter 3 analyzes the alliances and conquests that allowed the Iberians to forge empires in Africa and the Americas. Chapter 4 provides an overview of the early Atlantic World, an Iberian Atlantic World, during the sixteenth and seventeenth centuries.

Part II, "Europe Supported by Africa and America," evaluates the more complex Atlantic World of the seventeenth and eighteenth centuries when the French, English and Dutch entered the arena as privateers, settlers, shippers, slave traders, planters and, more than anything else, enemies of Spain. The five chapters of Part II examine some of the most important issues of Atlantic history in some detail. Chapter 5 concentrates on the first battles of the Atlantic, the era when France, England and the Netherlands brought the Iberian dominance of the Atlantic to an end and created their own Atlantic maritime empires. Chapter 6 contemplates how the five European empires, agents, settlers and missionaries in the Americas interacted with the many and very different Native American societies. This chapter investigates how these different Europeans produced different types of colonies and transformed native societies in various ways. Chapters 7 and 8 consider the Atlantic slave trade and New World slavery. These subjects appear in all of the earlier chapters in reference to broader issues, but here they are examined in their own right and, sometimes, in considerable detail. Chapter 9 analyzes the complex relations between men and women – mostly European men and African, Native American and European (and Euroamerican) women – and how these partners created new societies and transmitted many of the basic characteristics of European culture to the Americas.

Part III, "A New Order of the Ages," contemplates the events and persons that brought the dissolution of the Atlantic World in four chapters. Chapter 10 evaluates the struggle for Atlantic – and, indeed, world – supremacy between France and Great Britain during the long eighteenth century. In many ways, this struggle was the mainspring of most of the great events of the eighteenth and nineteenth centuries. Chapters 11 and 12 appraise the Atlantic in the Age of Revolution (1776–1826) and argue, following the lead of earlier historians, that all of these political and social movements were inspired by a common liberal ideology. Their leaders and followers sought liberty and equality, and for these reasons and many others we can call them Atlantic revolutions. Chapter 13 probes the century-long struggle to abolish the Atlantic slave trade and to end New World slavery. This history is not simply a story of white reformers but also one of black runaways, rebels and soldiers. Finally, a short Epilogue considers the end of the Atlantic World and the development of our contemporary modern or global world.

The Pillars of Hercules – the name given to the Rock of Gibraltar and Mount Hacho, facing each other across the Strait of Gibraltar where the Mediterranean Sea ends and the Atlantic Ocean begins – had been known since the days of the ancients as the edge of the known world. To the Greeks and the Romans, the twin rocks were a symbol of the gateway between the inner and outer worlds. The Greek writer Pinder noted that "what lies beyond cannot be approached by wise men or unwise. I shall not try, or I would be a fool." In the ancient and early medieval imagination, the Pillars were a forbidding *non plus ultra*, a warning to mariners not to proceed as there was literally "nothing further beyond." Although some ancient philosophers believed seafaring and connecting the separate regions of the globe were against the natural order, Renaissance mariners transformed the oceans from impassable voids to commercial thoroughfares in the fifteenth and sixteenth centuries and beyond. In 1517, Charles of Ghent boarded a ship in the port of Flushing (Vlissingen) in Zeeland, in what was then the Spanish Netherlands. Charles was on his way to Spain to claim the thrones of Castile and Aragón. The ship in which he traveled had painted its sails with his new personal emblem depicting the Pillars of Hercules with a banner bearing the legend *Plus Outre* – "Further Beyond." In removing the word *Non* – "Nothing" – from the traditional phrase, Charles declared that his empire had already gone beyond the traditional edge of the world and, furthermore, there were no limits to future discoveries and conquests. This idea expressed the self-confidence of the wider Western European culture that expanded into the Atlantic Ocean.

Not quite a century before Charles boarded his ship in Flushing, the Portuguese settled the islands of the Madeira archipelago off the coast of northwest Africa. The first boy and girl born on the main island of Madeira were christened Adam and Eve. These early colonists on Madeira and others throughout the Atlantic World later believed they were beginning the world anew. Following the discoveries of Columbus and the letters of Amerigo Vespucci, European writers and mapmakers began to refer to the Americas as *Novus Mundus*, the New World. The islands and shores of the Atlantic World were not a New World for Europeans only. The arrival of Europeans in West Africa and in the Americas transformed the lives and destinies of Africans and Indians, sometimes for better and more often for worse. To borrow a phrase, the Atlantic World became a New World for all. In all the lands touched by this great ocean, we are today living in the wake of those transformations and revolutions of long ago.

Additional Reading

Jeremy Adelman, editor, *Colonial Legacies: The Problem of Persistence in Latin American History* (New York, 1999).

David Armitage and Michael J. Braddick, editors, *The British Atlantic World, 1500–1800* (New York, 2002).

Bernard Bailyn, *Atlantic History: Concept and Contours* (Cambridge, Mass., 2005).

Bernard Bailyn, *The Peopling of British North America: An Introduction* (New York, 1986).

Thomas Benjamin, Timothy Hall, and David Rutherford, editors, *The Atlantic World in the Age of Empire* (Boston, 2001).

Fernand Braudel, *Civilization and Capitalism, 15th–18th Century*, Volume I: *The Structures of Everyday Life*; Volume II: *The Wheels of Commerce*; and Volume III: *The Perspective of the World*, translated by Sian Reynolds (Berkeley, 1992).

Fernand Braudel, *The Mediterranean and the Mediterranean World in the Age of Philip II*, translated by Sian Reynolds, abridged by Richard Ollard (New York, 1972).

T. H. Breen and Timothy Hall, *Colonial America in an Atlantic World* (New York, 2004).

Paul Butel, *The Atlantic*, translated by Iain Hamilton Grant (London, 1999).

Jorge Cañizares-Esguerra and Erik R. Seeman, editors, *The Atlantic in Global History, 1500–2000* (Upper Saddle River, 2007).

Nicolas Canny, editor, *Europeans on the Move: Studies in European Migration, 1500–1800* (Oxford, 1994).

Alfred Crosby, *The Columbian Exchange: Biological and Cultural Consequences of 1492* (Westport, Conn., 1973).

Philip D. Curtin, *The World and the West: The European Challenge and the Overseas Response in the Age of Empire* (Cambridge, 2000).

Douglas R. Egerton, Alison Games, Jane G. Landers, Kris Lane, and Donald R. Wright, *The Atlantic World: A History* (Wheeling, 2007).

J. H. Elliot, *Do the Americas Have a Common Heritage?* (Providence, 1998).

Alan L. Karras and J. R. McNeill, editors, *Atlantic American Societies: From Columbus Through Abolition, 1492–1888* (London, 1992).

Wim Kloster and Afred Padula, editors, *The Atlantic World: Essays on Slavery, Migration, and Imagination* (Upper Saddle River, 2005).

Franklin W. Knight and Peggy K. Liss, editors, *Atlantic Port Cities: Economy, Culture, and Society in the Atlantic World, 1650–1850* (Knoxville, 1991).

Michael Kraus, *The Atlantic Civilization: Eighteenth Century Origins* (Ithaca, 1949).

Heidi Slettedahl Macpherson and Will Kaufman, editors, *New Perspectives in Transatlantic Studies* (Lanham, 2002).

J. R. McNeill and William H. McNeill, *The Human Web: A Bird's-Eye View of World History* (New York, 2003).

Leonard Outhwaite, *The Atlantic: A History of an Ocean* (New York, 1957).

Timothy J. Shannon, *Atlantic Lives: A Comparative Approach to Early America* (New York, 2004).

Alan Taylor, *American Colonies* (New York, 2001).

James D. Tracy, editor, *The Rise of Merchant Empires: Long-Distance Trade in the Early Modern World, 1350–1750* (Cambridge, 1990).

Part One

The Ocean Shall Unloose the Bonds of Things

There will come an age, in the far-off years
when the Ocean shall unloose the bonds of things,
when the whole, broad earth shall be revealed,
and when Tethys shall disclose new worlds
Thule will not be the Limit of the Land.

Seneca, *Medea*

In retelling the Greek legend of Medea, Seneca "the Philosopher," writing during Rome's Augustan age, foretold that Tethys, the wife of Oceanus, would disclose new worlds. He was referring to maritime exploration and distant seafaring. In the story *Medea*, "a force more evil than the sea" had been brought into the Greek world by way of the first overseas voyage. This raised the question that Seneca wanted discussed: would civilized man be better off with or without the winds of the sea? "Now has the sea grown tame," wrote Seneca in *Medea*, ". . . every small skiff roams at will on the deep." As far as Seneca was concerned, it would only get worse: "The ocean shall unloose the bonds of things." In Seneca's Stoic vision, this future age of discovery would be a cataclysm of moral pollution and decline. "For no purpose did a wise god divide the lands with estranging Ocean," wrote Horace, "if our impious ships nevertheless race across waters [that] should be left untouched; recklessly braving all, the human race rushes through forbidden sin."

X illo tempore. tranquillitate vſi ventoque accommodatiſſi-

Figure 1.1. A fanciful engraving of a *não* or carrack surrounded by flying fishes. *Pisces in mari alati* (Flying Fishes at Sea), from Theodor de Bry, *Americae tertia pars* (Frankfurt, 1592). Courtesy of the William L. Clements Library at the University of Michigan.

What was so threatening? "What of the fact," asked Seneca, "that the winds have allowed all peoples to traffic with one another and has mixed races from disparate locales?" Seneca was concerned as well that crossing the ocean gave an invitation to destruction by enemies because "no land is so far distant that it cannot send out some evil of its own contriving."

At the time of the Columbian voyages, Spanish scholars pointed with pride to the *Medea* of Seneca for two reasons. First, Seneca was a Roman born in ancient Hispania, thus Spaniards claimed him as a fellow countryman even though in his lifetime neither Spain nor Castile existed. Second, Spanish translators found amazing prescience in the words of their "fellow Spaniard." They found greatness in the attainment of the prophecy by Spanish navigators and those sailing on behalf of Spain, particularly Christopher Columbus. For discovery-era Spanish intellectuals, Seneca had prophesied the Spanish Empire.

In the fifteenth and sixteenth centuries, even more than in the Greek age of "impious ships," Western Europeans created ships ever more capable of handling the rough seas of the Atlantic Ocean and sailing around the world. Caravels and *naos* or carracks – like the one so superbly illustrated here by Theodor de Bry – represented the most sophisticated technology of the age. De Bry's *não* shows us the classic design with three masks, two castles extending from the deck and armed for war or carrying merchandise. Europeans were not the only, and not always the most impressive, shipbuilders around the world. However, they were the most persistent, century after century, in constructing more and better ships than any other maritime culture.

Before the ocean – and European ships – unloosed the bonds of things, the lands and peoples surrounding the Atlantic Ocean were separate and mostly unknown one to the other. These distinct worlds are examined in Chapter 1, "Antecedents: The Americas, Africa and Europe in the Fifteenth Century." The peoples and cultures of the Americas and Atlantic Africa are not impeached or idealized but prudently studied and compared. Because late medieval Europe was the culture that unloosed the ocean and expanded into the worlds of the Atlantic, an inquiry into the origins of European expansion is warranted. We see a small promontory of Eurasia – as it became more populous, urban and commercial – begin to colonize itself and its margins before it set out to colonize overseas.

As most schoolchildren know, Portugal and Spain's desire to trade directly with the producers and merchants of Asia for spices, silks, porcelain and other luxury goods aroused the voyages of exploration of the fifteenth century. This is the subject of Chapter 2, "Commencement: The European Opening of the Atlantic Ocean." This chapter considers the significant role that Italian – particularly Genoese – financiers, merchants, navigators, cartographers and other specialists played when they moved their operations to the western Mediterranean and the near Atlantic in the fifteenth century. They offered their talents to the kingdoms of Portugal and Castile (and others) in return for wealth, status and power. The Iberians and the Genoese explored and commercially exploited Atlantic Africa and then attempted to do the same in the Americas. Explorers and navigators were not always looking for a new route to Asia; many maritime expeditions had less grandiose objectives, such as seeking new coastlines, interim profits and an assured way back to where they came.

No one overriding cause or motive drove the expansion of Portugal and Castile into the Atlantic. It was a process of small and generally uncoordinated steps taken over the course of more than two hundred years. Advances were rewarded by profits sufficient to encourage new efforts. Significant payoffs came rather late in the process: only in the late fifteenth century did the gold trade from Africa to Portugal amount to a significant portion of Portuguese overseas trade and to the income of the Portuguese crown; and only in the mid-sixteenth century were the great silver mines in Spanish America discovered that would enrich the Spanish monarchy and the rest of Europe. The European age of exploration and expansion of the fifteenth and sixteenth centuries was a continuation overseas of Europe's internal colonization of its agricultural frontiers during the High Middle Ages and of Christendom's expansion in Moorish Iberia, in Eastern Europe and in the Holy Land during the Crusades.

As it was the Portuguese and the Castilians who led Europeans into the Atlantic in the fifteenth century, they were the first to trade, create colonies and make alliances with and conquer native states in Atlantic Africa and the Americas. Being the first had great benefits in the early Atlantic World. The making of the Iberian Atlantic is the subject of Chapter 3, "Conquests: Forging the Iberian Empires in Africa and the Americas." The Portuguese and the Castilians encountered Africans and Native Americans and required their collaboration to create empires of trade and empires of conquest. In Atlantic Africa, the Portuguese generally obtained African leave to establish trading posts on the coast and, by and large, traded in peace with African chiefs, monarchs and merchants. In the Caribbean, Castilians at first traded peacefully with the Taino. The discovery of gold, and Castilian attempts to force Indians to dig and pan it, led to Indian slavery, resistance and war. The Castilian response was brutal military conquest. While the Portuguese in Africa began and sustained a tradition of peaceful coexistence and trade, the Castilians in America began and continued a tradition of military conquest through a policy of divide and conquer. The Castilians nearly always exploited Indian rivalries and animosities and obtained Indian allies in their military campaigns to conquer Indian states and empires. The Portuguese in Brazil followed the Castilian path rather than their own pattern in Africa. As in the Caribbean, Portuguese efforts to force Brazilian natives to work on sugar plantations prompted Indian rebellions and thus Portuguese reprisals and conquests. The Portuguese in Brazil also followed a divide-and-conquer strategy and obtained Indian allies in their wars against native peoples.

The only sustained Portuguese campaign of conquest in Africa occurred in Angola. There, for more than a century, Portuguese troops and even more African auxiliaries established, with great difficulty, the first European territorial colony in sub-Saharan Africa. Although the Portuguese expected to find wealthy silver mines or to establish a productive plantation sector, neither of these outcomes came to be. For the following three centuries, Angola became the great factory of Portugal's, and later Brazil's, slave trade.

In the fifteenth and sixteenth centuries, the embryonic Atlantic World was Iberian. This emerging world is described and analyzed in Chapter 4, "Realms: The Overseas Atlantic Empires of Spain and Portugal." All of the outposts and colonies spanning the Atlantic at this time were either Portuguese or Spanish. Portugal essentially monopolized trade with Atlantic Africa from its outposts at Arguim, São Jorge da Mina, São Tomé and Luanda. However, Portugal's position on the coast of Africa was thin and tenuous. Angola was its only mainland colony, but even there few Portuguese emigrated and few enterprises other than slave trading prospered. The Iberian presence in the Americas offered a striking contrast. Spanish America became an impressive outgrowth of Europe. Spanish cities were surrounded by vast Indian populations working silver mines and landed estates. The two centers of Spanish wealth and power in the hemisphere, Mexico and Peru, were the restructured societies of the Mexica and Inka Empires. Spanish-American cities were as impressive as their counterparts in the Iberian peninsula: they possessed brilliant viceregal courts in Mexico City and Lima; they had universities, printing presses and theaters; and they were centers of considerable trade and manufacturing. Mines, haciendas and urban workshops created prosperous societies closely tied to metropolitan Spain and regulated by the crown. Portuguese Brazil was a more rural society. Unlike Spanish America, Brazil was a society concentrated on the Atlantic coast, stretching more than two thousand miles from northeast to southwest. The basic economic as well as social and political institution in society was the sugar plantation. The valuable staple sugar contributed to the formation of a dynamic Portuguese colony in the South Atlantic.

This was the early and first Atlantic World, one dominated and nearly monopolized by Portugal and Spain. Atlantic history, as Bernard Bailyn writes, "is the story of a world in motion." This was no static historical unit that existed for three or four centuries. In telling the story of the Atlantic World, Bailyn suggests the historian's job is to describe: "the phasing of the development of this world, its motion and dynamics – to grasp its history as process." The four chapters of Part I seek to do just that. However, as Professor Bailyn notes: "It will not easily be done, the Atlantic world was multitudinous, embracing the people and circumstances of four continents, countless regional economies, languages, and social structures."

Chapter 1

Antecedents

The Americas, Africa and Europe in the Fifteenth Century

Before the fifteenth century, the lands touching the Atlantic Ocean were different worlds, separate and largely isolated, unknown or mostly unknown one to the others. There had been no earlier traveler, no Marco Polo, to demonstrate the connections and networks that could and, in time, would tie these distant lands together. The same ocean that soon became a vast crossroads bringing peoples together had constituted the ultimate barrier for millennia. With the sea at their backs, societies had turned their attention inward, not out. Cultures that one day would cooperate and clash emerged and evolved in different ways on different continents. Their histories followed exceptional courses and their peoples, of course, were unaware of any Atlantic destiny. Out of this diversity, a new circuit would be knitted and forged, the Atlantic World. "The Atlantic, once the end of the world," writes Barry Cunliffe, "was now the beginning." To understand the making of the Atlantic World, we must first examine its components and antecedents. We turn to the distant and separate worlds of the Atlantic rim: the Americas, Africa and Europe on the eve of the European voyages of exploration and expansion.

1.1 The Americas

The very concepts of America, Africa and Europe are products of the Europeanization of world geography. Before the Florentine navigator Amerigo Vespucci lent his name to the northern and southern continents of the Western Hemisphere, the native peoples did not conceive of themselves as Americans or Indians. Identity was local or regional and long it had been. Cultural diversity was the overwhelming reality of the peoples of the lands of the western Atlantic in the fifteenth century. There were at least fifty-nine distinct Native American language families with more than a thousand variations and dialects. Farmers predominated across the landscape but hunters and gatherers persisted in naturally rich environments and in the less hospitable regions that were too cold or too dry to cultivate crops. Some peoples lived in small mobile bands, most in farming villages, others in towns and great cities. There were stateless societies, which became known as tribes and chiefdoms, as well as hierarchical states and empires. For more than ten thousand years, the founders of America made their own history in their own particular and often sophisticated ways.

Native Americans were intelligent and inventive peoples but they were no more or less violent, environmentally destructive or imperialistic than other peoples and cultures around the world. Contrary to popular myths that portray pre-Columbian indigenous peoples as enlightened men and women who lived in peace with one another and in harmony with Mother Nature, Indians shared the same basic human traits possessed by the Chinese, Turks, Ethiopians, Arabs, Europeans and everybody else. They were unimaginably diverse in culture and cultivation, thus making it quite difficult to accurately generalize about Native Americans. One can conclude that pre-Columbian America was no paradise.

By the end of the fifteenth century, two impressive empires, the Mexica and Inka, existed in the Americas and were reaching the crest of their political and cultural development. These two empires were the evolutionary results of ancient civilizations that had seen the rise and fall of several complex cultures over the course of three thousand years. Mesoamerica, homeland of the Mexica, and the Central Andes, cradle of the Inka, witnessed the rise of the first farming villages, labor specialization and social stratification. In these two hearths of civilization, population growth encouraged the development of ever more complex cultures that invented religious ideologies, built cities and monumental architecture and forged complex polities that expanded territorially and ultimately ruled millions of subjects. It is important to realize that what came to know as the New World was, in fact, an old world of ancient civilizations that had risen and fallen before most people in Western Europe had become Christians.

Olmec culture in Mesoamerica and Chavin culture in the Andes are the names scholars have given the first complex societies in the Americas, the "Mother Cultures." During the first millennium B.C.E., peoples of these cultures formed the first urban centers and states that built the first religious monuments. Scholars named the next stage of cultural evolution in Mesoamerica that took place during the first millennium C.E., the "Classic" era. The classic Maya of southern Mesoamerica built dozens of independent city-states and beautiful stone pyramids and palaces. Central Mexico was dominated politically and religiously by the enormous city of Teotihuacan. Post-classic central Mexico was ruled by the Toltec culture from the city of Tula before the rise of the Mexica. In the Andes, the rise and fall of cultures saw first the Moche on the coast and later Tiahuanaco and Wari in the highlands during the first millennium C.E. After the disintegration of these highland states, the Chimu Empire at its capital of Chanchan unified the northern coast of Peru. While these cultures represented the most powerful and influential of their time and place, additional regional cultures in Mesoamerica and the Andes rose and fell as well. The Mexica and the Inka were merely the most recent cultures and states that had arisen from two ancient, sophisticated and prolific civilizations.

Document 1.1
Popol Vuh

Maya-Quiché Creation Myth

In the beginning, everything was in suspense and silence. Only the heavens and waters existed. There were no human beings, animals, birds or fish. There were no valleys, ravines or hills. The surface of the earth was still invisible. But the gods stood out dazzling in clarity against the darkness of the night. And they possessed great sentiments.

The gods conferred and came to a happy agreement. The waters were to remain; they were to irrigate the earth, which was to appear in the form of a plate. Light was to be born in the heavens and on earth, so that food might be planted for the people, who were to express their gratitude for its appearance to the Creators.

The formation of the earth was magical, strange and marvelous. At first, the space was filled with clouds and fog; then the mountains began to appear in the waters; cypresses and pines for the woods, coasts and valleys. Then the gods created the inhabitants for those places.

Afterwards, the Creators talked about their creatures with great satisfaction, designating homes for the animals and the birds. "You, wild beasts of the fields, shall drink from the rivers, sleep in ravines; your bodies shall rest on grass and you shall cohabit and procreate among the banana plants and the bushes; you shall walk on four feet and serve to carry burdens," they were told. "You birds will be in the branches as we are in our houses; there you shall fecundate and multiply." Then they all selected their haunts and shelters; the birds began building their nests.

While everything was being arranged for the birds and beasts, the world was still in silence. Afterwards, the gods said to them, "Shout, howl, chirp; speak to one another; understand one another; don't remain silent. Separate into groups according to your kind and ways. Then say our names, so that we may be honored in heaven, since we are your father and mother."

But they could not speak like rational beings; they only made gestures and sounds; they cackled, bellowed, and chirped without showing any signs of possessing a language.

When the Creators saw that their creatures did not pronounce their names nor recognize them, they were very sad. And they told the creatures that they would be replaced by others because they could not speak; they could not invoke and adore them. "You shall only serve to obey, and your flesh shall be crushed and eaten. That shall be your destiny."

The animals and the birds wanted to recover their preponderance, and tried in a new way to express their adoration. But as the gods were unable to understand them, they did not give them any help. So their fate remained as decreed by the gods; they were to be sacrificed, killed and eaten by the intelligent people.

The Procreators and Engenderers consulted once more and made a second attempt at forming creatures who would be impressed with their greatness. They fashioned them of wet clay, but they soon knew that they were not going to be successful. They dissolved, forming a heap of mire in which could be seen a neck, a very wide mouth, vacant, staring eyes and no head. They could talk but they felt nothing. Because of their constitution, they could not remain in water; they melted immediately; they had no consistency.

The Creators said to the creatures of clay, "Struggle to procreate and multiply but only until the new beings come." They soon fell to pieces, thus undoing the work of their Shapers.

Again the gods consulted and asked one another, "What shall we do to form people who shall see, understand, and invoke us?" And they asked for a new day of creation. They chose one from among them to obtain the presence of the grandmother of the sun, the grandmother of light, as they were told to do by the Creators. Then all met to discuss the kind of people to create, who should adore them as superior beings . . .

From Pazil and Cayali, the places whence come all good things, came the yellow and white ears of maize. The animals that brought the information about them were the fox, the coyote, the parrot and the crow. These four told the gods about the white and yellow maize which was to form the flesh and blood of the new people, and they showed them the way to Pazil.

The gods rejoiced over finding maize, the cacao, fruits and honey. There were also trees and plants growing there for food and beverages.

Immediately they began to plan how to form our first ancestors. The flesh and muscles were made of the products of the yellow and white maize. Only four were made of this food. They had no father nor mother; they were simply called men. They were not born of woman but were children created by the gods. Their creation was the supernatural and marvelous work of the Creators, who endowed them with the presence and likeness to people. Then these men talked and reasoned, they saw and felt, walked and touched. They were perfect of face and of handsome appearance. They saw and understood what was in the heavens and on the earth.

The new people were questioned by two of the gods. "What do you think of the senses that you have received? Do you not see and know that your language is as good as your way of walking? Then open your eyes, let your glances penetrate, and see as far as you can, even into the mountains and the coasts. Whatever you behold, as far as your eyes can see, you will possess it all," they said.

After they had seen everything under the heavens, they showed their gratitude to their Creators, giving them thanks two and three times. "You have given us existence, our mouths, and our faces. We speak, hear, feel, move, talk, and possess the perception to distinguish that which is near and far from us. Because of this we can see the big and the little that exists in heaven and on earth. Thanks to you then, our Makers, for having given us life. You are our grand-parents, our ancestors."

The gods were not pleased; their children knew and saw too much. So they took counsel once more and decided to limit their vision and understanding, for "would not each one in his wisdom want to come to know and do as much as we have made them comprehend, seeing everything!"

So the Creators veiled the eyes of man, covering them as one's breath covers a mirror. Their eyes became clouded and they could only see what was near. And their eyes were the same then as now.

Then women were formed, to be companions for these men. He who sees all fulfilled their wishes. It was in a sort of dream that they received, by their word, women full of beauty. When the men saw them, their hearts were filled with joy because they would no longer be alone, they would have mates.

The *Popul Vuh* has often been referred to as a Maya bible, a redaction of the central myths or beliefs of this culture. The *Popul Vuh*, or the Book of Counsel of the K'iche, was written down sometime in the 1550s. It was derived from a codex written in Maya glyphs. *Source: Popul Vuh. Maya-Quiché Creation Myth* (1927). Manuscrito de Chichicastenango, Guatemala. Edited by C. J. Antio Villacorta and M. Flavio Rodas. From Frances Toor, *A Treasury of Mexican Folkways* (1947), pp. 461–7.

The Culhua Mexica were part of the Nahua, a Nahuatl-speaking people who migrated into the central Valley of Mexico in several waves. (They are better known today as "the Aztecs," which is based on the name of their mythical homeland Aztlán). Over the course of the next three hundred years, these newcomers absorbed the high culture of Mesoamerica, building some fifty city-states in and immediately outside the Valley of Mexico with a population of more than one million. This larger region of the Nahuas was called Anahuac, meaning "in the vicinity of the waters." The most important cities were located on the shore of several interconnected wide and shallow lakes in the southern reaches of the Valley. Tenochtitlan, the largest and most powerful of these cities, was built on marshy islands within Lake Texcoco and populated by the Mexica, the last of the Nahua migrants to enter central Mexico. Tenochtitlan in the early sixteenth century was a city of perhaps seventy thousand to ninety thousand residents covering five square miles. It was divided into four quarters by avenues and canals that converged on a walled sacred precinct containing a great double-stepped stone pyramid, today called the Templo Mayor ("Great Temple"). The ceremonial center contained other temple platforms, a ball court and various shrines and altars. Nearby were the palaces of kings and great nobles. A stone aqueduct carried fresh water to the city from a spring at Chapultepec hill. In the northern district of Tlatelolco, a marketplace held the stalls of hundreds of merchants who traded with thousands of customers. Countless canoes came and went from this city in the lake, making it the hub of trade and communication in the Valley of Mexico (see Map 1.1).

Tenochtitlan, in league with two other city-states, Tetzcoco (today Texcoco) and Tlacopan, formed the Triple Alliance, a confederated empire that dominated much of central Mexico from the Pacific to the Gulf of Mexico.

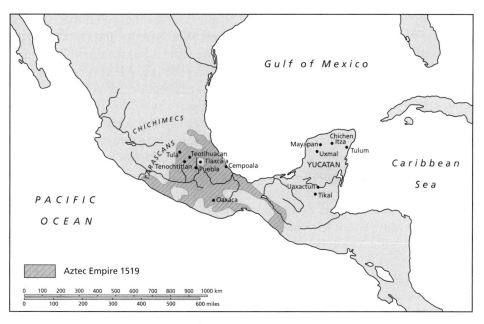

Map 1.1. The Mexica Empire, c. 1500.

Forged over the course of less than a hundred years beginning in 1427, the empire ruled several million subjects, about 450 towns and city-states divided into thirty-eight provinces. An elected hereditary ruler, the Tlatoani or "Speaker," presided over a highly stratified social order that included a warrior nobility, priests, merchants and craftsmen at the top and free commoners, sharecroppers and slaves at the bottom. Conquest meant not the expansion of direct governance but acknowledgment of submission by city-states and local chiefs as expressed through tribute payments. Tribute included maize, beans, chilies and turkeys as well as luxury goods such as cacao beans, jade beads, jaguar pelts and fine feather work. The empire maintained no standing army and no imperial bureaucracy. Conquest without consolidation meant that the empire was vast but control was loose. Rebellion and defiance were frequent, therefore the Mexica were nearly always at war. A few pockets of independent city-states, nearby Tlaxcala most prominently, also existed within the empire, which prompted staged battles – the famous Flowery Wars – to sustain the arts of war and provide captives. The Mexica were intensely militaristic; they fought for power, tribute, honor and most of all because they believed they were a chosen people with a sacred duty. Fray Diego Durán, the sixteenth-century Dominican historian of the Mexica, quoted Tlatoani Moteucçoma the Elder: "You know that our god, the great Huitzilpochtli, was sent to help us conquer the whole world."

Mesoamerican cosmology sustained the belief in cycles of creation and destruction of the world. The Mexica believed they lived in the fifth creation, the "Fifth World," one founded by the sacrifice of a god who immolated himself to become the sun and give light and life to man. In turn, the chosen people of the sun had the duty of supplying their god Huitzilpochtl with vital energy, the blood of captives of war, and thereby they believed sustained the world itself. In the Florentine Codex, the Mexica described their sacred mission: "You have been sent into warfare. War is your desert, your task. You shall give drink, nourishment, food to the Sun and to the Earth." Human sacrifice was an ancient Mesoamerican custom that the Mexica transformed into a massive religious and political cult that demanded tens of thousands of war captives each year and therefore incessant warfare. It is not known when human sacrifice became an imperial duty. Tiçocic, ruler of Tenochtitlan (1479–86) began construction of the great temple to Huitzilopochtli and Tlaloc, which became the central platform for sacrifice in Tenochtitlan, and commemorated his conquests by having sculpted the Sacrificial Stone, an immense vessel for burning human hearts. His successor, Ahuitzotl (1486–1502) reconstructed the Templo Mayor and, in a two-year campaign in Oaxaca, captured and sacrificed twenty thousand warriors. In the time of Moteucçoma the Younger, after a successful campaign, Durán wrote:

> The prisoners taken at Teuctepec were brought out. Motecuhzoma and Cihuacoatl began to sacrifice them, slicing open their chests and extracting their hearts. First they raised the hearts to the sun, then they threw them into the shrine before the gods. The sacrifice began at midday and ended at nightfall. Two thousand and three hundred men were killed, and their blood bathed the entire temple and its stairway. Each time the priests cut out a heart, they rolled the body down the stairs. Every time I describe this my whole body trembles with horror. This is something that nature itself abhors.

Mexica warriors fought to capture their enemy alive and return them to Tenochtitlan (or another ceremonial center). In scheduled ceremonies and on grand occasions, the captives were taken to an altar on the top of the Templo Mayor where priests cut their beating hearts from their chests and tossed their lifeless bodies down the pyramid steps. "The high priest," wrote the Jesuit missionary and chronicler José de Acosta, "used that knife to open his chest with extraordinary speed, tearing out the heart with his hands and holding it up still smoking to the sun, whom he offered the heart's heat and steam." Ritual cannibalism followed to honor the victims, who were then considered gods. Children were also sacrificed to Tlaloc, the rain god, who needed their tears. In Tenochtitlan and other central Mexican cities, human sacrifice became the primary symbol of empire, an act that justified as well as impelled endless war. Mexica sacrificial ceremonies were also demonstrations of state power and terror. The audience was all of central Mesoamerica.

The Mexica Empire did not dominate all of Mesoamerica. In west central Mexico, the Tarascan Empire of the Purépecha people withstood Mexica expansion. The capital Tzintzuntzan, a city of thirty thousand people, presided over more than fifteen cities and some three hundred subordinate towns and villages. This empire was located in what is today the modern Mexican state of Michoacán. Small states in independent enclaves persisted in central Mexico, thus giving the heartland of the Mexica Empire something of a patchwork character. In south central Mexico in what is today the state of Oaxaca, Zapotec and Mixtec peoples were divided into many small states

Figure 1.2. Motecuçuma, the last king of the Mexica. This painting was created by Nahua painters and scribes for the Codex Ramírez. *Motecuçuma 2° deste nombre. Ultimo Rey de los Mexicanos* (Motecuçuma, 2nd of this name, Last King of the Mexicans), from Juan de Tovar, *Historia de la benida de los yndios apoblar a México* (Mexico, c. 1585). Courtesy of the John Carter Brown Library at Brown University.

that fought one another but united from time to time to resist Mexica aggression. In southern Mesoamerica, in the rain-forested lowlands of the base of the Yucatan peninsula, Maya culture had produced numerous city-states that had seen power and glory and experienced military defeat and destruction. By the early sixteenth century, autonomous city-states persisted in northern Yucatan where sixteen warring states jostled for position after the downfall of the Mayapán conquest state. Here, as in central Mexico, war captives were sacrificed by cutting out their hearts, and men and women were thrown into the *cenote* (a large natural sinkhole) at Chichen Itza to communicate with the rain god. In the highlands of Guatemala, some thirty independent city-states existed after the demise of the Quiché Empire.

The other great empire in the Americas in the fifteenth century was the Inka Empire, located in the Central Andes of South America, an immense area of high mountain valleys and arid Pacific coastlands. Similar to the Mexica, the Inka – a Quechua-speaking people – were migrants who settled in a highland valley and founded their city of Cuzco in the early thirteenth century. They absorbed the high culture of Andean civilization and developed into a warlike people to survive and prosper in a competitive and dangerous political environment. This imperial people became known as Inkas after the title of the ruler.

The Inka Empire was founded in the early fifteenth century and, like the Mexica Empire, was successfully expansionist for a little less than one hundred years. Unlike the Mexica Empire, the Inka Empire was a territorial conquest state that consolidated its military aggression. Conquered provinces and local rulers were governed directly from newly constructed administrative centers that sustained military garrisons. These were linked to Cuzco and the rest of the empire by an extensive network of roads and bridges. The Inka state resettled peoples in conquered provinces to enhance security and extend Inka culture. "The Incas called these colonists *mitimaes*," wrote the Spanish chronicler Pedro Sarmiento de Gamboa, "which means 'transported' or 'moved.' Besides this the Inca put garrisons into all the fortresses of importance, composed of natives of Cuzco or the neighborhood, which garrisons were called *michecrima*." Once a province was conquered, the new governor reorganized the existing system of land tenure by dividing the arable land into three parts: one to support Inka priests, a second to support the Inka himself and the imperial state, and a third for the original inhabitants of the land. The imperial state also imposed tribute on conquered peoples in the form of labor services called *mit'a* – farming, soldiering, weaving, masonry and more. This constituted a massive redistribution of energy and resources but not always from the provinces to the imperial center. Andean systems of tribute replaced trade in redistributing goods across diverse ecological zones. A bureaucracy composed of Inka nobles supervised every detail of imperial administration from managing state grain warehouses to maintaining roads and bridges. According to Felipe Guaman Poma de Ayala, there were six *caminos reales*, "royal roads in the time of the Yngas" and fourteen "bridges of great chasms that opened in the time of the Ynga." By the early sixteenth century, the Inka Empire, called Tahuantinsuyu ("Four Quarters of the World") by its subjects, encompassed eighty provinces that extended 2,600 miles from north to south, from modern Ecuador to Chile, containing a population of fourteen million people. Unlike the Mexica, the Inka conquered nearly every people and polity in their world. It was the largest empire in the Americas and one of the most impressive conquest states in the world (see Map 1.2).

In Mexico, imperial tribute existed above and beyond an extensive system of trade and markets. In the Inka Empire, the tribute system was a substitute for long-distance trade. Traditional Andean reciprocity at the local and regional levels was expanded to an imperial scale. The state organized an exchange of goods produced across varied climatic and environmental zones. Tribute generously fed and clothed the royalty, nobility, priesthood and military. It was also redistributed to commoners. Tribute provided famine relief, was used in religious ceremonies and granted as useful public works such as irrigation and terracing. Another view of the Inka tribute system, from the Colonial period, has come to us. From this perspective, the Inka rulers were "exploiters" in the way they took advantage of their vassals. Because of Inka aggression and exploitation, Father Bernabé Cobo wrote, "they built great fortresses, made roads, constructed terraces on hillsides, and made the subjects bring tribute to Cuzco from more than three and four hundred leagues away."

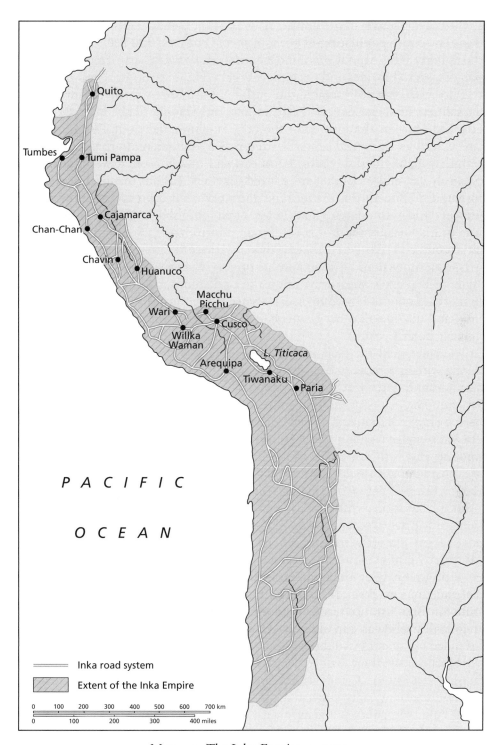

Map 1.2. The Inka Empire, c. 1500.

Cuzco, the "navel of the universe," was a much smaller city than Tenochtitlan. The entire population of perhaps forty thousand had been elevated into the nobility. This capital was almost entirely a showcase city of stone temples, palaces, sacred shrines and open places for ceremonies. Some scholars believe the city was built to resemble the outline of a puma with the great fortress Sacsahuaman suggestive of the head and the Temple of the Sun, the gold-adorned Qorikancha located in the tail. This imperial capital was a sacred site as well as a political center. Cuzco was a monumental urban concentration that highlighted the best of Andean and Inka masonry, which involved precisely carved blocks that were fitted together without the need of cement. Imperial architecture in Cuzco and the provincial centers was intended to impress and intimidate. Tupac Inka Yupanque, who assigned houses and lots to his lineage, the Lords of Cuzco, and to *orejones* or nobles, had the city rebuilt. "He ordered that in this city there be no mixing of people or offspring other than his own and his *orejon* warriors," wrote the chronicler Juan de Betanzos, who drew upon the oral traditions of his Inka wife and her noble family. "He wanted this city to be the most distinguished in all the land and the one all other towns had to serve and respect, like our Rome in ancient times."

The ruler held the title Sapa Inka ("Sole Inka") and was a divine king. Along with his predecessors, he was considered to be a descendent of Inti, the sun god and patron of the Inka state. The ancient Andean cult of ancestor worship was transformed into an imperial institution of great significance as the empire expanded. When rulers died, their royal mummies and their court or *panaca* of kinsmen and advisors maintained their lands, palaces and servants. With one exception, the many royal palaces in Cuzco held the wealth and possessions of deceased kings. According to Garcilaso de la Vega, the historian of Peru who was the son of a Spanish conquistador and an Inka princess, "as soon as the royal owner of a palace died, the apartment in which he used to sleep was shut, with all its gold and silver decorations still inside, as a sacred place, so that no one should ever again enter: this occurred in all the royal houses in the kingdom where the Inca had ever spent a night, even though it were only while on his travels. And they at once built new sleeping quarters for the Inca who succeeded him." The royal mummies were richly dressed and presented with food and drink, sacrifices were made to them and they received visitors and consulted in all matters. Royal mummies attended major state ceremonies together with the reigning monarch, making visible the entire lineage of royal ancestors. However, this royal ancestor cult implied a custom of split inheritance, which greatly influenced the living kings. Each new ruler inherited the power and privileges of kingship but little tangible property and wealth. Lands, houses, clothing and vessels of silver and gold had to be acquired through the conquest of new territories and peoples. Imperial expansion was driven in part by the vested interest of the new king and his *panaca*.

The royal mummies and their houses were missing one thing. In the "tail" of the city, the golden temple of the Sun, the Qorikancha, focused its gilded attention on a golden statue of a young boy on a gold throne. Spaniards in the 1530s observed that this statue received sacrifices of food and drink. The reason for its great status in the greatest temple in the kingdom, Spaniards eventually learned, was that the statue contained the hearts of all of the deceased Inkas.

As part of the religion of the supreme being, the sun, and the royal ancestor cult, blood sacrifice was required. In terms of sheer numbers, Inka society sacrificed multitudes of llama. This society also sacrificed many thousands of children each year, from the age of four years to the age of ten, in a ritual called *capac hucha* or *capacocha*, meaning "royal obligation." Throughout the empire, villages would send two children to Cuzco where they would be received by the Inka and priests, then symbolically married and returned home and sacrificed. These *capacochas* were sacrificed at all of the *huacas*, or sacred places, and temples to ensure the good health of the Inka. They were sacrificed as well upon the death of an Inka and at the accession of a new Inka. Father Cobo noted in his account of Inka religion that during the *capacocha*,

> the things that were to be offered in the sacrifice were brought [to Cuzco's main square] namely, two hundred children from four to ten years of age, a large amount of gold and silver made into tumblers and figurines of sheep [alpacas and llamas] and other animals.

In his history of the Inka Empire, Father Cobo elaborates that not all girls were executed. First of all, more girls were gathered, and of these, "a considerable number" would be killed in sacrifices during the year, others were assigned to the religious houses of *mamaconas* and the most noble and beautiful were given to the Inka or his nobles. "Receiving one of these virgins from the Inca personally," wrote Cobo, "was considered to be an extraordinary favor." Tupac Inka Yupanque ordered that when he died, the Lords of Cuzco "should send out throughout the entire land and have a thousand boys and girls brought. All these children should be from five or six years of age," wrote Betanzos. "These children would be collected from all over the land and would be carried in litters together and by pairs to be buried in pairs with the table service they had been given. They would be buried all over the land in the places where the Inca had established residence." Over the course of the last century, Inka burials of children have been discovered throughout the former Inka Empire with grave goods that match the written descriptions of the *capacocha* ritual. For example, in 1985 Argentine mountaineers discovered the mummy of a young boy on the flank of Aconcaga at twenty thousand feet, the highest mountain in the Western Hemisphere. The boy was richly dressed and wrapped in embroidered blankets and buried with Inka offerings.

For all their apparent differences, the Mexica and Inka Empires shared certain fundamental similarities. Both cultures were heirs of ancient civilizations that transmitted religious concepts, values and practices as well as styles of art and architecture, patterns of governance and much more. Both were cultures based on intensive agriculture, applying significant additional energy to their farming practices to increase output. Both the Mexica and Inka built irrigation and terracing systems. The Mesoamerican peoples invented *chinapa* agriculture, raised and drained garden plots in wetland areas. Both empires had also expanded from single city-states. Only Mesoamerica and the Central Andes generated pristine states in the Americas, leading to complex polities with hereditary rulers at the apex of a system of hierarchical social classes. These states included several levels of administration, a system of law and punishment, an institutionalized religion, centralized control of an economic surplus, the power to organize and construct great public works and the monopolization of military force.

Finally, both were aggressive and expansive imperial states. As Fray Diego Durán concluded regarding the Mexica: "The purpose of this tribute was to show the magnificence and authority of the Aztec nation and so the Aztecs would be held to be Lords of all Created Things, upon the waters as well as upon the earth." Mexica society, writes historian Inga Clendinnen, "was committed to war, not as an occasional heroic obligation, but chronically . . . " The same was true for Inka society. All chronicles and narratives reveal a society that was relentlessly expansionist. Garcilasco de la Vega, offering an idealized portrait of the Inka, viewed Inka imperialism as the gift of civilization to barbaric peoples. According to José de Acosta's sources, Inka imperialism was based on the belief that "they possessed the true religion and knew how God ought to be served and honored, and that therefore they were obliged to teach all the others." The chronicler Juan Betanzos provided a more base interpretation: plunder and tribute. Inka Yupanque ordered his captains "that they bring all the spoils taken in war, including livestock, garments, jewels of gold and silver, Indian men and women, all of which he ordered his captains to distribute among the warriors who had served him on that campaign. First the Inca took what he wanted."

In the fifteenth century, most of the native societies of the Americas were organized as chiefdoms, not states. These were smaller societies with populations ranging from several thousands to tens of thousands. Chiefdoms were sometimes organized as confederations of villages and towns led by a paramount chief that dominated subordinate chiefs. Chiefdoms varied considerably but all were less complex than states in terms of social differentiation, political and religious institutions, economic redistribution and the maintenance of public order. Chiefdoms generally developed with farming, although environmentally rich coastal hunter-gather societies like the Calusas of Florida also organized polities dominated by chiefs. Chiefdoms were widespread in the Caribbean as well as in North and South America.

The Taino people, Arawak speakers, populated the larger islands of the Caribbean, the Greater Antilles. They lived in agricultural villages and larger towns that were organized into regional chiefdoms centered in mountain valleys. The Taino lived in villages of dozens of buildings arranged around plazas, worshiped deities called *zemis* as well as their own ancestors and played a game with a ball on rectangular courts. These increasingly complex political systems built impressive ceremonial centers with plazas and ball courts, which may have channeled the rivalry between chiefdoms into sport. The largest and most densely populated island in the late fifteenth century Caribbean, Hispaniola, contained fourteen *caciques*, or regional chiefs, and five confederations. The Taino cultivated starchy root crops such as cassava and the sweet potato as well as maize, pineapple and tobacco, Their diet also depended on the rich marine environment that provided fish, crabs, turtles and manatee. They built canoes that could hold up to 150 people and carried on trade among the different islands.

There were two other distinct native cultures in the Caribbean. To the west of the Taino, in western Cuba primarily, were the Ciboneys, a hunting, gathering and fishing people who lived in caves and lacked agriculture. To the southeast of the Taino, in the Lesser Antilles, were the Caribs, more recent immigrants from the American mainland. Caribs lived in smaller and more egalitarian societies than the Taino. War chiefs were selected when the need arose. They were renowned for their war-making and seafaring abilities, which were combined in the raiding of Taino villages to obtain wives. The Spanish exaggerated (if not invented) their practice of eating small parts of the flesh of enemy warriors, a relatively common Native American custom, to justify enslaving them. Carib peoples were also settled on the northern coast of South America, the Guiana Highlands and in the Amazon valley.

In North America large, complex chiefdom societies flourished hundreds of years before European contact. In the American southwest, three cultures emerged in succession, Hohokam, Mogollon and Anasazi, by C.E. 700–900. They created semi-urban societies based on intensive agriculture using sophisticated irrigation systems. The Anasazi flourished for five centuries. This culture built multistory apartment buildings, storage houses and circular rooms – *kivas* – for ceremonial and political purposes. In the eleventh century one Anasazi site, Chaco Canyon in northwestern New Mexico, had numerous towns linked together by roadways with a population of approximately five thousand people. Anasazi society disappeared by 1200 due, most likely, to damage to the environment and persistent drought.

Mississippian chiefdoms emerged around C.E. 1000 in the eastern woodlands of what is today the United States. These societies were marked by fortified ceremonial centers containing flat-topped, rectangular earthen mounds, some of which were quite large. The greatest Mississippian city and the most complex polity north of central Mexico was Cahokia. This monumental religious and political center and its surrounding hinterland on the banks of the Mississippi River near the modern city of St. Louis, Missouri, had a population of thirty thousand to forty thousand people at its peak around C.E. 1050–1150. Its principal mound, Monks Mound, was one hundred feet high and more than a thousand feet long; only two pyramids in ancient Mexico were larger. Another one hundred ceremonial mounds were located in the greater Cahokia area and were placed around plazas and ball courts. The paramount chief of Cahokia likely drew tribute from surrounding communities, which were part of a long-distance trade network stretching from the Great Lakes to the Gulf of Mexico and from the Great Plains to the Atlantic Ocean. Cahokia was abandoned in the thirteenth century, and the Mississippian societies and wider culture to the north and east disappeared as well.

Late Mississippian chiefdoms survived into the sixteenth and seventeenth centuries in the southeast. These polities were distinguished by towns and villages that contained ceremonial plazas and mounds. The expedition of Spanish explorer Hernando de Soto in 1541 came into contact with the powerful Pacaha chiefdom. Its likely capital, Bradley Ridge, near Memphis, Tennessee, contained four mounds. At the time of contact, the Pacaha chiefdom was expanding its political and territorial control. Elsewhere, De Soto found densely populated valleys, pyramid mounds, full storehouses and powerful chiefs. Garcilaso de la Vega, in his narrative of the expedition, described one encounter: "The lord of the province, who also had the same name of Guaxule, came out half a league from the pueblo accompanied by five hundred nobles handsomely dressed in rich mantles made of various kinds of skin and wearing long plumes on their heads, in accordance with the common usage of that whole country." He noted furthermore that the lord's house was atop a high mound surrounded by three hundred other houses in the town. The Grand Village of Natchez, near the present day city of Natchez, Mississippi, was another Late Mississippian survivor. Its paramount chief was known as the Great Sun and presided over nobles and commoners. The Coosas of Georgia and the Powhatans of Virginia appeared later, in the sixteenth century. Late Mississippian chiefdoms however, were vulnerable to Old World diseases and thus experienced significant population declines before many European settlers appeared on their lands. Population decline, migration and regrouping led to the newly confederated chiefdoms of the Creeks, Cherokees and Catawbas.

These native chiefdoms and confederations, like most native societies in the Americas, were almost perpetually engaged in conflict with their neighbors. Alvar Nuñez Cabeza de Vaca, part of the Hernando de Soto expedition, was shipwrecked on the coast of Texas. Walking back to Mexico through southwest Texas, he and his companions encountered a considerable number of Indian peoples. "All of them," he wrote in his narrative of the journey, "are warlike and are skillful in protecting themselves against their enemies as if they had been reared in Italy and in constant warfare . . . All of these people, when they have individual enemies, so long as they are not a member of the same family, kill each other at night by lying in ambush and treat each other with the utmost cruelty." The chief Cofaqui informed one of his war captains, as recorded by Garcilaso de la Vega: "You know well the war and perpetual enmity that our fathers have had with the Indians of the province of Cofachiqui." Skeletal remains recovered in pre-contact sites throughout the Americas show that violent trauma killed many young men and women. At one Anasazi site, archaeologists have found that forty percent of skeletal remains provide evidence that suggest massacres and cannibalism. At one site in the central Illinois River valley, one-third of adults died through violence. Similar patterns of embedded projectile points, unhealed fractures, decapitation, nose and tongue removal and scalping appear at sites in Alabama, Michigan, the Great Plains and California. Even today, the Yanomamo of the Venezuelan rain forest have one of the highest homicide rates in the world, four per thousand per annum.

In northeastern North America, native societies of various sizes and organization dominated the landscape in the fifteenth century. Algonquian-, Iroquoian- and Siouan-speaking peoples populated the vast region from the Atlantic to the Great Lakes. The majority were village and town dwellers, peoples who planted maize, beans and squash and who had extensive hunting territories. Some peoples, like the Iroquois south of Lake Ontario, were more sedentary than some and relied on agriculture and food storage. Peoples to the north subsisted entirely upon hunting and fishing and the gathering of tubers, nuts and the making of maple syrup in the spring. In the sub-Arctic and Arctic lands of Canada and Alaska, native groups were also hunters, fishermen and gatherers living in small bands. In these huge territories of the far north, population density was less than anywhere else. All of these peoples were part of a long-distance trading network that exchanged products across different ecological zones. Intergroup conflict was endemic in the northeast, as it was in the southeast. Perhaps for this reason, the chiefs of the five Iroquois chiefdoms in upper New York formed a confederacy sometime around the twelfth century C.E. Modeled metaphorically on a multifamily longhouse, the confederation expanded social boundaries to reduce blood revenge. The People of the Longhouse, the Haudenosaunee as they called themselves, settled disputes through a fifty-member Confederacy Council. This League of the Five Nations was the first of several native confederacies of North America.

The lands touching the southern Caribbean – modern-day Costa Rica, Panama, Colombia and Venezuela – constituted a zone of commercial interaction and cultural diffusion in the fifteenth and sixteenth centuries. In northwest Colombia, in the middle of this zone, several polities – complex chiefdoms or developing states – were clustered together. The Muisca or Chibcha, Tairona and Cenú cultures were stratified societies that depended upon intensive agriculture and maintained urban centers with temples, palaces and warehouses. A 1536 Spanish report described the paramount chief of the Chibcha: "This Bogotá is the principal lord of this land, with many other nobles and chiefs under him. His vassals honor him exceedingly; in truth, the Indians of this kingdom are very subjugated by their lords. He has conquered and tyrannized over much of the land." Elites possessed fine textiles, delicately crafted gold pieces and emerald jewelry, and they collected tribute from commoners. The Muisca domain had a population of perhaps as many as one hundred and fifty thousand people. All of these societies were frequently at war, subduing regional chiefs and their towns. Surrounding these three major polities were dozens of smaller and less complex chiefdoms, some of which dominated a hinterland of allied or subordinate chiefs. These chiefdoms were part of a long-distance trading system like those in many other parts of the Americas.

The native peoples of present-day Brazil lived in relatively small communities at the time of European contact. These communities were governed by councils of elders and generally were only loosely led by chiefs. Sometimes paramount chiefs arose and were given authority or respect in several localities. A shaman or "medicine man" was often the most powerful member of the community. Villages were often temporary and shifting creations based upon slash-and-burn agriculture, gathering oysters on the seashore and moving to richer areas in game or fish according to an annual seasonal cycle. Native Brazilians owned few possessions, including clothing that covered little more than the loins of adult men and women. Intergroup violence or feuding was frequent and larger villages were palisaded. Coastal Tupi practiced ritual human sacrifice of war captives and honorific cannibalism. The Tupinikin Tupinamba, according to the French observer Jean de Léry, "wage deadly warfare against a number of nations in the region . . . But these barbarians do not wage war to win countries and lands from each other, for each has more than he needs; even less do the conquerors aim to get rich from the spoils, ransoms, and arms of the vanquished; that is not what drives them. For, as they themselves confess, they are impelled by no other passion than that of avenging each for his side, his own kinsmen and friends who in the past have been seized and eaten." Tupi-Guaraní speaking peoples occupied most of the Atlantic seaboard and the south bank of the Amazon River. Gê-speaking peoples sparsely populated the vast plateau that dominates the interior of Brazil. There were denser populations situated along the Amazon River that consisted of Tupi and Arawak speakers.

South of Brazil in the Pampas, Patagonia and Tierra del Fuego, small native bands were dependent upon hunting, fishing and gathering. Communities had their own hunting grounds and were quite mobile. Many were skilled warriors like the Mapuche, located on the western side of the southern Andes and who successfully resisted the southward advance of the Inka. Most of these peoples adopted horses after the arrival of the Spanish and, like the peoples of the North American plains, created new cultures centered on the horse.

The greatest population densities in the Americas were located in Mesoamerica and the Central Andes, the two regions where agriculture first developed in the hemisphere. Agriculture was a relatively late development in the Americas. Plant domestication in the Americas appeared approximately five thousand years after it began in the Middle East. Native Americans were handicapped by a smaller availability of wild plants and animals that could be domesticated. Of the five leading cereal crops in the world, only one – maize – was an original American crop. America was even less well endowed with useful animal species capable of domestication. Of the five most widespread domesticated species – cows, sheep, goats, pigs and horses – none were present in the Americas after about 15,000 to 10,000 B.C.E. The turkey and dog were domesticated in Mesoamerica and the llama, alpaca and guinea pig in the Central Andes. The implications of this relatively late and incomplete social and cultural evolution are profound.

Eurasian high cultures had a significant head start and biological advantage. States arose more than three thousand years earlier in Mesopotamia and Egypt than in Mesoamerica. The Chinese were inventing writing fifteen hundred years before agricultural villages even appeared in Mesoamerica and the Central Andes. Without horses or oxen, no wheeled vehicles or any other type of labor-saving technology based on animal power was invented in the Americas. Eurasia's domestic animal species gave their human caretakers infectious diseases such as smallpox, chicken pox, influenza, plague, measles and cholera, which with repeated exposure over millennia gave these populations increased genetic resistance to those same illnesses as they became largely childhood diseases. In tropical Africa yaws, yellow fever, smallpox and the most fatal strain of malaria exposed generations who survived and resisted. However, the peoples of the Americas, without generations

Table 1.1. Regional populations: The
Americas, c. 1492

North America	3,800,000
Mexico	17,200,000
Central America	5,625,000
Hispaniola	1,000,000
The Caribbean	3,000,000
The Andes	15,700,000
South America	8,620,000
Total	53,904,000

Sources: These estimates are from William Denevan, *The Native Population of the Americas, 1492*, second edition (1992). Suzanne Austin Alchon in *A Pest in the Land: New World Epidemics in a Global Perspective* (2003) has studied all of the estimates and the problem of population estimation, and proposes a population range of 46,800,000 to 53,800,000.

of exposure, developed no resistance to these particular deadly diseases, and thus they would be profoundly vulnerable when the Atlantic was finally breached. Although, pre-contact Native Americans were not free of disease. Agricultural peoples, particularly those in densely settled areas, suffered from tuberculosis, pneumonia, hemorrhagic fevers, dysentery, rabies and possibly typhus. "Epidemics, famines, and wars occurred with regularity throughout the hemisphere before the arrival of Europeans, reducing life expectancies and raising mortality rates," writes historian Suzanne Austin Alchon. "In fact, far from an earthly paradise, the profile that emerged of life and death in the New World resembles that of the Old in several important respects."

In 1492, the population of the Americas made up less than one-ninth of the world's population of over 460 million people. During the fifteenth century, the societies of the Old World, from China to Atlantic Europe, were recovering from the enormous population losses of the Black Death – the bubonic plague – which killed perhaps as many as ninety to one hundred million people across Eurasia. Although it is not possible to project with any accuracy or scholarly consensus American populations prior to the sixteenth century, it is most unlikely that the population of the Western Hemisphere experienced any type of crisis like that prior to the sixteenth century. For eighty years, scholars have been trying to calculate the pre-contact population of the Americas. There have been "low counters," who seemingly lacked respect for native social organization and agricultural productivity, and "high counters," who adopted more scientific and quantitative methods but who, it appears, overreacted to the low counts. The following population estimates are beginning to form the basis of a scholarly consensus (see Table 1.1).

America's isolation from the rest of the world and the isolation of significant cultures within the hemisphere, along with late plant and animal domestication, contributed to the absence of iron-ore metallurgy and the late and limited development of literacy. Native Americans worked with soft metals and crafted both luxury and utilitarian objects but otherwise remained in the Stone Age. Stone, wood and bone were the principal materials for tools. The only writing systems in the Americas originated in and remained limited to ancient Mesoamerica. Five related systems – Olmec, Mixtec, Zapotec, Maya and Mexica Nahuatl – evolved and employed pictographs, ideographs and phonetic elements. Writing was confined to a small elite and only marginally facilitated political administration and economic production or exchange. Such limited literacy did not significantly extend and disseminate human experience, and therefore did not yet significantly advance and empower Native American cultures.

Native peoples over thousands of years adapted to immensely diverse natural environments and developed sophisticated societies that would impress and astound European observers. Indians would not, and could not, however, successfully resist European encroachment. Biology and technology greatly disadvantaged this large and isolated branch of mankind occupying one-third of the land surface of the world.

1.2 Africa

The classical geographers generally divided the world into three continents: Europe, Asia and Africa. The region of the Tunisian coast and its interior opposite Sicily had long been part of the ancient Mediterranean World. The Greeks called it Libya. The Roman province of that region was named "Africa." Following Roman rule, North Africa passed to Muslim Arabs who kept an Arabized version of the name, *Ifrîqiyah*. That portion of North Africa across the sea from the Iberian Peninsula became known in the Islamic World for a time as "African Andalusia," named for that part of Spain conquered by Islam. For centuries, the Muslim historian Ibn Khaldûn tells us in 1370, Ifrîquiyah was a province of the Andalusian caliphs. Europeans began the practice of giving the entire continent the name of Africa on their maps and in their books (although "Libya" and "Ethiopia" occasionally appeared as well). By the time of the making of the great Renaissance maps, the continent was generally referred to as Africa.

Sitting off the northwest coast of Africa by about sixty miles are the Canary Islands, seven major and four minor islands. On the eve of the European age of exploration, the islands were inhabited by perhaps as many as fifty thousand people, most likely of North African origin. The native Canary Islanders were farmers and pastoralists who lived in thatched huts and caves and wore little clothing. The people of Gran Canaria, who had the most advanced culture in the archipelago, practiced irrigated agriculture and maintained collective silos. Natives were organized into tribes and redistributive chiefdoms and, on some islands, confederations of chiefdoms. Gran Canaria was divided into two chiefdoms, each governed by a paramount chief and a superior holy man. An assembly of noblemen advised these leaders. Tenerife and La Palma each had nine political communities. Although the Romans had known the island chain, Canarians had no contact with the continent and thus were nearly as isolated culturally as Native Americans.

Northwest Africa, called the *al-Maghrib al-Aqsa* by Arabs, a name derived from Arabic meaning "the far west," had been integrated into succeeding

Islamic empires or caliphates from the eighth century c.e. By the fifteenth century, political power here was fragmented and divided among local Muslim rulers. Europeans had long traded with North African merchants who in turn imported products – gold and slaves being the most important – from beyond the Sahara. The Catalan Atlas of 1375 included a portrait of an African king south of the desert: "This Black lord is called Massa Melly, Lord of the Blacks of Guinea," the Jewish cartographer wrote on the Atlas, referring in fact to the king Mansa Musa of Mali. He continued: "This lord is the richest and most noble lord of all this region owing to the abundance of gold which is gathered in this land." The Catalan Atlas indicated oases, rivers and mountains unlike most other medieval maps that placed monsters, beasts and other grotesque creatures in Africa. Until the Portuguese reached the coast of West Africa in the fifteenth century, Europeans knew little more about this vast continent.

For Muslims, on the other hand, the lands and peoples south of the Sahara were not so mysterious. For over seven centuries, the Islamic World was practically the only extended outside influence on sub-Saharan Africa. North African Moors, Arabs and Berbers crisscrossed the Sahara in caravans with thousands of camels bringing African gold to the Mediterranean. Muslim traders brought with them Islam, a religion and culture that included a written language, Arabic, and the propensity to name places. The land south of the Sahara was called in Arabic *Belad es-Sudan*, "The Land of the Blacks," the origin of the familiar name "Sudan." The northernmost band was named the *Sāhil* or *Sahel*, from Arabic for "The Shore" of the great desert. Arab sources and Muslim travelers chronicled the rise and fall of African empires over centuries in the western Sudan from the Senegambia to the Niger delta.

A vast savanna was located between the Sahara and the Sahel in the north and the tropical forest with its gold fields in the south. It was, and remains, the largest pastoral area in Africa. Rainfall increases as one travels from north to south. Running through the western Sudan from west to east for more than twenty-six hundred miles is the Niger River valley, the hearth of an African civilization that is two thousand years old. This civilization, and the first cities that created it in the early centuries of the first millennium of the Common Era, was based on rain-fed agriculture producing sorghum and millet, livestock herding and the monopolization of trade between the desert and the forest. Horses, books, copper and silk cloth from the Maghrib and salt from the Sahara were traded for grain, kola nuts, ivory, slaves and gold. Trade led to cities, cities developed into states and some of these states became empires (see Map 1.3).

In the fifteenth century, the dominant power in the western Sudan was Songhay with its center at Gao, one of the great trading cities on the Niger. Another such city was Timbuktu, an affluent city of eighty thousand residents, the holy city of the western Sudan with three mosques and 180 Koranic schools. Scholars trained in institutions of higher learning in the Muslim World taught, wrote and debated here. The rise of the Songhay Empire in the fifteenth century accompanied and accelerated the decline of the empire of Mali, the great kingdom that had been famous in the Mediterranean World for its wealth in gold. The world came to know of Mali when

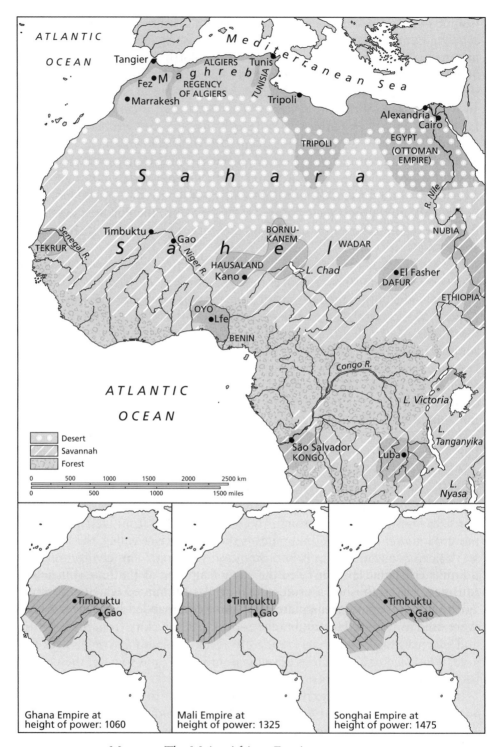

Map 1.3. The Major African Empires, 1000–1500.

one of its kings, Mansa Musa, made a pilgrimage to Mecca in 1324. "He set off in great pomp with a large party, including sixty thousand soldiers and five hundred slaves, who ran in front of him as he rode," wrote the seventeenth-century Timbuktu scholar Abd al-Rahmân al Sa'dî. "Each of the slaves bore in his hand a wand fashioned with 500 mq. of gold... The Easterners who chronicled his visit were astonished at how mighty a ruler he was." The king gave away so much gold that its value declined in the markets of Cairo. In turn, Mali had succeeded Ghana as the great military and economic power on the Niger. Chronicles reported that Ghana was an ancient kingdom, so much so that it had twenty-two kings even before the Muslim era that began in the early seventh century.

Songhay, an empire approximately the size of modern France, stretched from the Atlantic in the west to Kano north of the Niger delta. As was true for Ghana and Mali the Songhay Empire developed in the strategic region that allowed kings and traders to take advantage of the three ecosystems of the desert, the savanna and the forest. Sunni Ali, the eighteenth king, came to power in 1464 and began the systematic conquest of much of the Niger Valley with a fleet of hundreds of boats. In the eyes of the Muslim chronicler Al-Sa'dîs, the unbeliever Sunni Ali was "the great oppressor and notorious evil-doer... he was a man of great strength and colossal energy, a tyrant, a miscreant, an aggressor, a despot, and a butcher who killed so many human beings that only God Most High could count them. He tyrannized the scholars and holy men, killing them, insulting them, and humiliating them." Songhay, like Ghana and Mali before, had begun as a city dominating a confederation of villages – a *kafu* – and a cluster of kafus or chiefdoms. Local chiefs led mounted military noblemen who dominated and drew tribute from agricultural communities. Although the urban elite across the savanna was Muslim, and therefore literate in Arabic, villagers and herdsmen generally maintained their local religion and could neither read nor write. Songhay, like Ghana and Mali, prospered as the major trading center exchanging salt for gold. Sunni Ali's successor, Askia Mohammed, a Muslim, seized power in 1493 and centralized state authority and established courts in the towns to administer Islamic law. He ruled the Niger Valley directly through appointed kinsmen. He established a professional army of mounted warriors of noble birth who wore iron breastplates and were commanded by princes. Slaves were used as infantrymen and archers.

There was no shortage of land in the Niger Valley. However, there was a shortage of labor. Royal and noble estates expanded in number and size under Sunni Ali and Askia Mohammad. They were dependent increasingly on the capture and employment of slaves. There is some doubt among scholars as to whether slavery in Islamic Africa was ever chattel slavery. Peoples who submitted to Islam or Islamic rule were not subject to the type of slavery in which slaves became the property of another person and as property could be bought and sold in markets and treated like farm animals. Archaeological sites in the western Sudan suggest the existence of slavery but not the nature of the slave system. The Niger Valley "plantations" were worked by hundreds of slaves on each and fed a growing empire with rice, millet and sorghum. Slaves were also used as gold miners, salt workers, soldiers and government administrators in West Africa. Slaves were procured as captives of war or unfortunates seized in raids on the lands of the "pagans," that is, non-Muslims. African slavery varied: on the Niger estates, slaves most likely were units of labor with few rights, whereas in the villages and Muslim households slaves were subordinate kin with certain privileges and the possibility of advancement. Timbuktu and other Niger cities had busy slave markets, which were also regularly visited by merchants from north of the desert. When Al-Hasan al-Wazzan, an exiled Spanish Moor today known as Leo Africanus, visited the region in the early sixteenth century, slavery was ever present. He mentioned that Timbuktu had a "great store of men and women-slaves." Gao had many places were slaves were sold and every merchant had a great many servants and slaves. When the Hausa king of Gobir was defeated and slain by the king of Songhay, "most part of the inhabitants were carried and kept for slaves by the said Askia." Slavery, writes the economic historian of Africa Paul Lovejoy, "infected all levels of society and economy."

African slaves were also in great demand in Morocco for work in the sugar cane plantations. The well-to-do in Fez and other Maghrib cities bought slaves to serve as domestic servants. Slaves were also sent in caravans by the thousands to Barca and Tripoli for distribution to Egypt and Turkey on the one hand or to Sicily and Italy on the other. There had been a trans-Sahara slave trade from the ninth century that came under the control of Muslim rulers and traders. "The Arabs and their Muslim allies," writes David Brion Davis, "were the first people to develop a specialized, long-distance slave trade from sub-Saharan Africa."

Early in the fifteenth century, Leo Africanus began his travels to western Sudan and later published an account. "The land of the Negros is divided into many kingdoms," he wrote, "whereof albeit a great part be unknown unto us, and removed far out of our trade; I my self saw fifteen kingdoms of the Negros." On the Niger River, he visited the city of Timbuktu. "The rich king of Tombuto hath many plates and scepters of gold, some whereof weigh 1300 poundes; and he keeps a magnificent and well furnished court...Here are a great store of doctors, judges, priests, and other learned men, that are bountifully maintained at the king's cost and charges...They keep great store of men and women-slaves." The "rich king" in his account was the king of Songhay. The "many kingdoms" referred to other, smaller and less powerful savanna states such as Tekur and Wolof to the west in Senegambia, Diala state and the Mossi Empire in the western Sudan, and the Hausa states and Kanem to the east near Lake Chad. These states, like Songhay, were increasingly dependent upon slave labor captured in war by cavalry forces.

South of the savanna lies a belt of tropical forest that hugs the Atlantic coast from Gambia to equatorial central Africa. The Berbers invented the name *Akal-n-Iquinawen* for the forest and coast, which became known as Guinea in the European era. In the middle of the Guinea coast, just east of the Volta River, a corridor of savanna reaches to the sea called the Togo-Dahomey Gap, a wedge where the savanna peoples could influence the peoples of the forest. The forest received much more rain than the savanna but always had fewer people. An exceptionally hostile disease environment that included malaria, yaws and trypanosomiasis (better known as sleeping sickness) was

Figure 1.3. A view of Africans by a French Franciscan. *Habitas de la Guinée* (Natives of the African Coast of Guinea). From André Thevet, *Les singvlaritez de la France Antarctique* (Paris, 1558). Courtesy of the William L. Clements Library at the University of Michigan.

largely responsible for this population deficit. Trypanosomiasis, carried by the tsetse fly, endemic to the forest, also impeded the spread of livestock. As a result, agriculture was late to develop, therefore state development was slower to arise than in the savanna, states were generally smaller and many societies remained stateless as chiefdoms. For example, the Igbo lived in forest villages, sometimes formed confederations of villages and decided public issues in popular assemblies.

The first states developed here on the forest-savanna edge late in the first millennium c.e. Often they emerged as modest city-states that controlled the trade of forest products to the savanna. One such product, the kola nut, known for its caffeine-like stimulus, was popular in Islamic societies, which prohibited alcohol. More importantly, the forest states generally controlled the production and monopolized the trade of the West African gold fields. However, state formation had various origins. Kaabu, on the coast near the Gambia River, gave Mali an outlet to the sea. Benin may have originally been a religious center. The forest states were therefore as diverse as the reasons for their appearance and growth. Islam did not become a great religious force in this region.

In the fifteenth century when the Portuguese arrived, the Akan and Yoruba kingdoms were the major forest states. The Akan states of Bono and Banda

were located west of the gap in a region the Europeans would name the Gold
Coast. Bono, famous for the wealth of its kings, controlled royal monopolies
of gold mining and trade. On the coast, about a dozen mini-states greeted
the arrival of the Portuguese. The Yoruba states of Benin, Ife and Oyo were
located east of the gap. Benin had been transformed into an empire in the
mid-fifteenth century by warrior kings. Benin City was composed of houses
made of mud walls covered with palm leaves and surrounded by a deep and
wide moat for defense. Monarchs commissioned hundreds of magnificent
ivory, copper and bronze sculptures. The bronzes of Benin and the other
Yoruba cities were the first of African arts to win acceptance in Europe. To
the far west in the Senegambia and along the windward coast, there were
mini-states that had once been part of the Mali and Wolof Empires. Of
course, all of these states looked north toward the Sahara for trade, political
and cultural influence. Until the age of European trade, the Atlantic and the
Gulf of Guinea were barriers, not gateways.

Document 1.2
How the Spider Obtained the Sky God's Stories
Ashanti Folktale

We do not really mean, we do not really mean that what we are going to say is true.

Kwaku Ananse, the spider, once went to Nyankonpon, the Sky God, to
buy the Sky God's stories. The Sky God said, "What makes you think you
can buy them?" The spider answered and said, "I know I shall be able."
Thereupon the Sky God said, "Great and powerful towns like Kokofu,
Bekwai, Asumengya, have come, but they were unable to purchase them,
and yet you who are but a mere masterless man, you say you will be able?"

The spider said, "What is the price of the stories?" The Sky God said,
"They cannot be bought for anything except *Onini*, the python; *Osebo*,
the leopard; *Mmoatia*, the fairy; and *Mmoboro*, the hornets." The spider
said, "I will bring some of all these things and, what is more, I will add
my old mother, Nsia, the sixth child, to the lot."

The Sky God said, "Go and bring them then." The spider came back,
and told his mother all about it, saying, "I wish to buy the stories of the
Sky God, and the Sky God says I must bring *Onini*, the python; *Osebo*,
the leopard; *Mmoatia*, the fairy; and *Mmoboro*, the hornets; and I said I
would add you to the lot and give you to the Sky God." Now the spider
consulted his wife, Aso, saying, "What is to be done that we may get
Onini, the python?" Aso said to him, "You go off and cut a branch of a
palm tree, and cut some string-creeper as well, and bring them." And the
spider came back with them. And Aso said, "Take them to the stream."
So Ananse took them; and, as he was going alone, he said, "It's longer
than he is, it's not so long as he; you lie, it's longer than he."

The spider said, "There he is, lying yonder." The python, who had over-
heard this imaginary conversation, then asked, "What's this all about?"

To which the spider replied, "Is it not my wife, Aso, who is arguing with me that this palm branch is longer than you, and I say she is a liar." And *Onini*, the python, said, "Bring it, and come and measure me." Ananse took the palm branch and laid it along the python's body. Then he said, "Stretch yourself out." And the python stretched himself out, and Ananse took the rope-creeper and wound it and the sound of the tying was *nwenene! nwenene! nwenene!* until he came to the head.

Ananse, the spider, said, "Fool, I shall take you to the Sky God and receive the Sky God's tales in exchange." So Ananse took him off to Nyame, the Sky God. The spider returned and came and told his wife what had happened, saying, "There remain the hornets." His wife said, "Look for a gourd, and fill it with water and go off with it." The spider went along through the bush, when he saw a swarm of hornets hanging there, and he poured out some of the water and sprinkled it on them. He then poured the remainder upon himself and cut a leaf of plantain and covered his head with it. And now he addressed the hornets, saying, "As the rain has come, had you not better come and enter this, my gourd, so that the rain will not beat you; don't you see that I have taken a plantain leaf to cover myself?" All the hornets flew, disappearing into the gourd, and *fom!* the spider covered the mouth, and exclaimed, "Fools, I have got you, and I am taking you to receive the tales of the Sky God in exchange."

And he took the hornets to the Sky God. The Sky God said, "My hand has touched it; what remains still remains." The spider came back once more and told his wife, and said, "There remains *Osebo*, the leopard." Aso said, "Go and dig a hole." Ananse said, "That's enough, I understand." Then the spider went off to look for the leopard's tracks and, having found them, he dug a very deep pit, covered it over, and came back home. Very early next day, when objects began to be visible, the spider said he would go off, and when he went, lo, a leopard was lying in the pit. Ananse said, "Little father's child, little mother's child, I have told you not to get drunk, and now, just as one would expect of you, you have become intoxicated, and that's why you have fallen into the pit. If I were to say I would get you out, next day, if you saw me, or likewise any of my children, you would go and catch me and them." The leopard said, "O! I could not do such a thing."

Ananse then went and cut two sticks, put one here and one there, and said, "Put one of your paws here, and one also of your paws here." And the leopard placed them where he was told. As he was about to climb up, Ananse lifted up his knife, and in a flash it descended on his head, *gao!* was the sound it made. The pit received the leopard and *fom!* was the sound following. Ananse got a ladder to descend into the pit to go and get the leopard out. He got the leopard out and came back with it, exclaiming, "Fool, I am taking you to exchange for the stories of the Sky God." He lifted up the leopard to go and give to Nyame, the Sky God. The Sky God said, "My hands have touched it; what remains still remains."

Then the spider came back, carved an Akua's child, a black flat-faced wooden doll, tapped some sticky fluid from a tree and plastered the doll's body with it. Then he made *eto*, pounded yams, and put some in the doll's hand. Again he pounded some more and placed it in a brass basin; he tied string around the doll's waist, and went with it and placed it at the foot of the odum tree, the place where the fairies come to play. And a fairy came along. She said, "Akua, may I eat a little of this mash?" Ananse tugged at the string, and the doll nodded her head. The fairy turned to one of the sisters, saying, "She says I may eat some." She said, "Eat some then." And she finished eating, and thanked her. But when she thanked her, the doll did not answer. And the fairy said to her sister, "When I thank her, she does not reply." The sister of the first fairy said, "Slap her crying-place." And she slapped it, *pa!* And her hand stuck there. She to her sister, "My hand has stuck there." She said, "Take the one that remains and slap her crying-place again." And she took it and slapped her, *pa!* and this one, too, stuck fast. And the fairy told her sister, saying, "My two hands have stuck fast." She said, "Push it with your stomach." She pushed it and her stomach stuck to it. And Ananse came and tied her up, and he said, "Fool, I have got you, I shall take you to the Sky God in exchange for his stories." And he went off home with her.

Now Ananse spoke to his mother, Ya Nsia, the sixth child, saying, "Rise up, let us go, for I am taking you along with the fairy to go and give you to the Sky God in exchange for his stories." He lifted them up, and went off there to where the Sky God was. Arriving there he said, "Sky God, here is a fairy and my old women whom I spoke about, here she is too." Now the Sky God called his elders, the Kontire and Akwam chiefs, the Adonten, the Gyase, the Oyoko, Ankobea and Kyidom. And he put the matter before them, saying, "Very great kings have come, and were not able to buy the Sky God's stories, but Kwaku Ananse, the spider, has been able to pay the price: I have received from him *Osebo*, the leopard; I have received from him *Onini*, the python; and of his own accord, Ananse has added his mother to the lot; all these things lie here." He said, "Sing his praise." "*Eee!*" they shouted. The Sky God said, "Kwaku Ananse, from today and going on forever, I take my Sky God's stories and I present them to you, *kose! kose! kose!* my blessing, blessing, blessing! No more shall we call them the stories of the Sky God, but we shall call them spider stories."

This, my story which I have related, if it be sweet or if it be not sweet, take some elsewhere and let some come back to me.

The spider-trickster in Ashanti stories outwits the python, the leopard, the fairy and the hornets, and seeks to usurp the Supreme Being, Nyame (Nyankonpon), to gain wisdom. In the West Indies, African slaves told stories of *Anancy* in Jamaica and *Nanci* in Curacao regarding how the trickster fooled others who are more powerful. In the American south, the Trickster became a rabbit, the folkloric Br'er Rabbit. *Source: Akan-Ashanti Folk-Tales*, collected and translated by Captain R. S. Rattray, and illustrated by Africans of the Gold Coast (1930), pp. 54–9.

Large portions of the forest and coast were occupied by mini-states, confederations and chiefdoms. The Niger Delta was and remains a vast region of mangrove swamps, creeks, lagoons and sandbars with no suitable harbors. This natural geography did not encourage large and centralized states. Peoples of the Delta were fishermen, salt collectors and canoe-borne traders. By the fifteenth century, they had formed several kingdoms and many chiefdoms. The small coastal communities here would change significantly with the coming of the Atlantic slave trade. Towns like Bonny and New Calabar would become famous around the Atlantic World.

When the Europeans arrived on the coast of Guinea, they reported that different types and forms of servitude and slavery existed within these African societies. Europeans, to a considerable extent, believed that indigenous slavery morally justified the Atlantic slave trade. Certainly, African slavery existed in Guinea when Europeans appeared on the coast. For example, we know that Africans at São Jorge da Mina imported and purchased slaves that the Portuguese supplied from Benin. This suggests that slaves were used for gold mining in the Akan states. Indigenous African slavery, as it was in the age of the Atlantic slave trade, remains a highly sensitive and controversial subject. Some scholars, in fact, like Joseph E. Inikori, maintain "there was no slavery in the kin-based coastal societies of Western Africa before the Atlantic slave trade." He notes that recent research even questions "whether the servitude that developed in Western Africa as a result of the Atlantic slave trade can be called slavery."

Southeast of the Guinea coast is equatorial Central Africa. This is a region of forest in the northern reaches (from the Niger Delta to the Zaire, or Congo, River) giving way to savanna and dry woodlands to the south (until one reaches the desert at the Kunene River). There were a few states of which the most important was Kongo, a land of half a million people, originally located on the south bank of the Zaire. Its fortified capital of M'banza Kongo was located in the interior highlands. Kongo originated as a conquest state in the late fourteenth century and expanded through military prowess and marriage alliances. Duarte Lopes, a Portuguese chronicler, wrote the first history of the kingdom and noted that by the sixteenth century, there were six provinces controlled by a standing army and administered by royal kinsmen who collected tribute in kind. When the Portuguese arrived on the coast, the kingdom of Kongo was powerful and expansionist. Society was divided into three orders: principal men, freemen and slaves. Iron smelting was reserved for the nobility, who crafted weapons of war that enabled warriors to capture people who would be forced into agricultural slavery on noble and royal estates. As elsewhere in Africa, manpower was the key to wealth.

The Loango kingdom was located north of Kongo on the coast. Lopes wrote: "The King of Loango is in amity with the King of Congo, and the report is, that in times past he was his vassal." The Ndongo kingdom was located south of Kongo near the Kwanza River. The capital, like M'banza Kongo, was far into the interior, a small town with a rich royal compound. "This kingdom of Angola," wrote Lopes, "is full of people beyond all credit: For every man taketh as many wives as he liketh, and so they multiply infinitely."

South of Ndongo, the Kalahari and the Namib deserts extend nearly to the Cape peninsula. To Africans, this was "Thirstland." Europeans named it the "Skeleton Coast" after the many shipwrecks left on the forbidding coast. It was, and is, populated by small groups of Kung! hunters and gatherers. South of the Namib, the Cape peninsula has a Mediterranean-like climate. The largest populations of southern Africa were located in the eastern half where increasing rainfall follows a west to east pattern. In the western half of South Africa, small populations of Khoikhoi, semi-nomadic hunters and pastoralists, fifty thousand or so, lived in chiefdoms when the Dutch arrived in the seventeenth century.

West Africa, like the Americas, developed agriculture and the domestication of livestock thousands of years later than the Fertile Crescent. Fewer indigenous crops originated in Africa, and those viable at one latitude had difficulty moving to another. Bananas and plantains reached Africa by crossing the Indian Ocean from Southeast Asia but not until about 200 C.E. Mediterranean crops, wheat and barley, for example, never reached southern Africa until brought there by European colonists. None of the basic livestock species that provides protein and energy were domesticated in Africa: cattle, horses, pigs and so on were taken later to Africa following their domestications elsewhere. Horses, as an example, reached Egypt around 1800 B.C.E. but did not cross the Sahara for another two thousand years. Surprisingly, none of Africa's big wildlife mammals – zebras, giraffes or elephants, to name just three – are capable of domestication. However, elephants competed with humans for good land and devoured standing crops, which constrained agricultural expansion. In large parts of sub-Saharan Africa, the tsetse fly impeded the spread of livestock or forbade the use of draft animals altogether. As a result, the first cities and states in West Africa appeared more than three thousand years after those in Egypt. While iron making appeared in West Africa during the first millennium B.C.E., writing, wheeled vehicles and the plow did not arise independently in or penetrate the interior of Africa beyond Egypt.

Sub-Saharan Africa's social, economic and political development was constrained by the region's geographical isolation. The Sahara, the world's largest desert, for a long time was as difficult to cross as any ocean. The camel, the great ship of the desert, was not imported to Africa and made available for the caravan trade until about 300 C.E. The Senegal, Niger and Zambezi Rivers are navigable for short stretches, and then only seasonally. The Zaire, although twenty-nine hundred miles long, has waterfalls near the sea, preventing ocean-going ships from entering. The coastline of sub-Saharan Africa has few good harbors and there is, comparatively, not very much of it. The ragged coastline of Western Europe is considerably longer than Africa's. One-third of Western Europe is composed of peninsulas and islands, and thus no part is more than five hundred miles from the sea. Only two percent of the African continent is composed of peninsulas and islands. A very large portion of interior Africa is more than five hundred miles from the sea, and many parts more than a thousand miles. It is not surprising that except in the Mediterranean and in parts of East Africa, Africans did not become seafaring peoples. Although not as isolated as the Americas, sub-Saharan Africa was relatively isolated from Eurasia, and Africans were isolated from each other, as their considerable linguistic fragmentation demonstrates. This isolation delayed and limited the diffusion of ideas, technology and other cultural imports from the great intercommunicating Eurasian zone.

Underpopulation has been sub-Saharan Africa's greatest limitation. Much of sub-Saharan Africa lies in the tropics where more, and more deadly, diseases flourish. The forest zone is the most hostile environment and the home of the tsetse fly, which carries sleeping sickness to livestock and to human beings. Humans generally stayed away from tsetse fly regions and never acquired immunity. The savanna, too, was the home of deadly diseases and parasites. Malaria, likely the biggest killer of humans, was found throughout tropical Africa in the forest and the savanna. Yellow fever, a virus, generally attacked concentrations of vulnerable peoples in towns and cities by means of a particular mosquito. Leprosy was common in equatorial regions, as was yaws. Hookworm anemia, a parasitic illness, is easily transmitted through the foot. Bilhazia or schistosomiasis, also called liver flukes, reached human populations in drinking water and is especially dangerous to children. River blindness, onchocerciasis, has been a common infection. Curiously, the Sahara protected Africa from some Eurasian diseases for a long time: the Black Death, which devastated Europe in the fourteenth century, spared West Africa. On the other hand, the trans-Sahara caravans introduced smallpox, most likely by the eighth century.

Famine has been the next most important obstacle to population growth, a result of drought and locusts. Portuguese records from Angola in the sixteenth century documented that famines accompanied by epidemic disease would occur about every seventy years and kill one-third of the population. Underpopulation limited state formation throughout the continent and placed great value on labor, thus contributing to the widespread practice of slavery. Slavery existed around the world, of course, in the Americas, China, India, the Islamic Empires and Europe, particularly Mediterranean Europe. Scholars have estimated that domestic African slavery fueled a trans-Saharan and Indian Ocean slave trade to the Islamic World that numbered between seven and ten million Africans – primarily women and children – between 770 and 1500 C.E. This eastern slave trade continued as the Atlantic slave trade developed in the west.

In 1500, the population of sub-Saharan Africa composed a little more than one-twelfth of the world's population. Africa's scarcity of people not only promoted slavery but also high levels of polygyny, great competition for women and great significance to fertility and the production of children. "Without children," a Yoruba proverb says, "you are naked." Given its continental size, sub-Saharan Africa in 1500 was unquestionably underpopulated (see Table 1.2).

1.3 Europe

In contrast to the Americas and Africa, Europe was never a well-defined or self-contained landmass. It was not, and still is not, a continent. However, it

Table 1.2. Regional populations:
Sub-Saharan Africa, c. 1500

West Africa	14,000,000
East Africa	12,800,000
Central Africa	8,000,000
Southern Africa	3,500,000
Total	38,300,000

Source: Table 6.1, "African Population, 1–2001
A.D.," in Angus Maddison, *The World Economy:
Historical Statistics* (2003), p. 190.

became a single civilization centered in the west. Historians generally maintain that Europe as a cultural entity emerged by the thirteenth and fourteenth centuries. Christendom was the first name given it, yet the first-century Greek geographer Strabo identified the small promontory on the northwest coast of the Eurasian continent as *Europa*. Charlemagne, the Frankish king crowned Holy Roman Emperor in 800 C.E., called himself *Pater europae*, "Father of the Europeans." The Medieval mappaemundi, world maps, often identified the lands north of the Mediterranean and west of the River Don as Europe. The peoples who came to have a sense of belonging based upon the Roman language, Roman law and Roman Christianity became known as Europeans and their "continent" as Europe. These terms replaced (or at least accompanied) the idea of Christendom only during the fifteenth and sixteenth centuries.

Although there was no single understanding of world geography in late medieval Europe, the Catalan Atlas of 1375 provides an idea of European perceptions. This remarkable map, like those that preceded it, portrayed nothing at all regarding the Americas, naturally, and very little about the Atlantic Ocean, referred to as "the Great Sea." Little or nothing was known in Europe of the early Norse discoveries of Greenland and North America as Scandinavia in 1000 C.E. was not yet fully a part of western Christendom. The Atlas divided the world into Europe, Africa and Asia with Jerusalem at the center of the world and oceans extending off the shores of Europe and Africa in the west and Asia in the east. What would come to be called the Atlantic Ocean was punctuated by islands, some completely imaginary like Brazil and Blest, and some real like the Canary Isles. The Atlantic coast of Africa was very short, and almost nothing was identified. Using the Atlas as a guide, we note that Europeans knew far more about Asia than the interior of Africa. In Africa, the rich king of Mali, Mansa Musa, is pictured in the west. In the center is the "King of Organa," supposedly a Muslim. To the east, we see the King of Nubia and the Emperor of Ethiopia, who belonged to the realm of the mythical figure of Prester John. According to the Atlas, Asia formed the eastern half of the world, no larger than Europe and the Mediterranean together. The text of the map quotes the Book of Isaiah: "I will send to the isles afar off, that have not heard my fame, neither have seen my glory; and they shall declare my glory among the Gentiles."

Europe on the eve of its fifteenth-century expansion into the Atlantic was a civilization just beginning to recover from a century-long crisis. The

Document 1.3
The Imitation of Christ

Thomas Kempis, 1441

"He that followeth me, walketh not in darkness," says the Lord.

These are the words of Christ, by which we are admonished how we ought to imitate his life and ways; if we would be truly enlightened, and be delivered from all blindness of heart.

Let therefore our most earnest study be to mediate upon the life of Jesus Christ.

The teaching of Christ surpasses all the teachings of holy men, and he who has his spirit, will find therein the hidden manna.

But it happens that many who often hear the Gospel, yet feel but little longing after it, because they have not the spirit of Christ.

He, therefore, that would fully and with true wisdom understand the words of Christ, must strive to conform his whole life to that of Christ.

What does it profit you to dispute profoundly of the Trinity if you lack humility and be displeasing to the Trinity?

Surely, it is not deep words that make a man holy and just, but a virtuous life makes him dear to God.

I had rather feel contrition than understand the definition thereof.

If you knew the whole Bible by heart, and the sayings of all the philosophers, what would that profit you without the love of God and grace?

Vanity of vanities, all is vanity, save to love God and to serve him only.

This is the highest wisdom, by contempt of the world to reach forward to the heavenly kingdom.

It is vanity then to seek after perishable riches, and to trust in them.

It is also vanity to covet honors, and to lift up ourselves on high.

It is vanity to follow the desires of the flesh, and to labor for that which will afterward bring heavy punishment.

It is vanity to desire a long life, and to have little care for a good life.

It is vanity to take thought only for the present life, and not to look forward to those things which are to come.

The Imitation of Christ (De Imitatione Christi et contemptu Omnium vanitatum mundi) was the most widely read book in early modern Europe and the colonial Americas after the Bible. *Source: The Imitation of Christ,* edited by Albert Hyma (1927), pp. 3–4.

fourteenth century was marked by famine, plague, invasion, rebellion and war. Failed harvests brought famine in the north in 1315–17 and into the south by 1346–47. A new cooler climate, known as the Little Ice Age, limited the growing season and reduced harvests. At mid-century, the infamous Black Death spread from Asia to the Middle East and then engulfed Europe. The Black Death was a bubonic plague that was, very likely, accompanied by an anthrax-based plague, which helps explain some of the peculiar aspects of the

Table 1.3. Population growth in Western
Europe, 1000–1500

1000	25,400,000
1200	40,900,000
1300	58, 300,000
1400	41,500,000
1500	57,200,000

Source: Table 1-6a, "West European Population Levels, 0–1998, A.D." in Maddison,
The World Economy: A Millennial Perspective,
p. 32. The population growth rate for the period
1000 to 1300 was 0.28. For the century, 1300–
1400, there was a decline of −0.34. Population
growth returned in 1400–1500 with a growth rate
of 0.32. See Table 1-6b, p. 32. M. K. Bennett,
using a different estimation, argued that the population of Europe peaked and began to decline
around 1300 (at 73,000,000), as a result of general and regional famines, prior to the Black Plague
of 1348–51. By 1400, according to Bennett, the
population of Europe stood at 45,000,000. See
Bennett, *The World's Food: A Study of the Inter-
relations of World Populations, National Diets,
and Food Potentials* (1954), p. 5.

mass dying. The plague devastated a European population that had exceeded
its capacity to feed itself and was already in decline. In many regions of Western Europe, disease felled one-third to one-half of the population. Vast populations throughout Eurasia were also decimated. Major epidemics returned
again and again in the second half of the fourteenth century. Small outbreaks then took over: for example, in Barcelona there were eleven "minor"
epidemics between 1396 and 1447. One hundred years would pass before
Europe's population began to recover from this demographic collapse. In the
meantime, fewer people meant less demand for goods, less production and
less trade. This economic crisis became a social crisis as landlords exploited
a smaller peasantry and provoked agrarian rebellions in England, France,
Catalonia and Flanders. Efforts by urban authorities to hold down wages
produced worker and artisan revolts (see Table 1.3).

A different type of menace (from the European point of view), the advance
of the Ottoman Turks throughout the century threatened Europe following
the encirclement of the Byzantine Empire and defeat of the Serbs in Kosovo
in 1389. Wars and brigandage made everything worse. The most severe
and protracted conflict was the Hundred Years War, 1337–1452, between
England and France, which led to increased taxes, disruption of trade and
considerable physical destruction in France, where the fighting took place.

The crisis of the fourteenth century, when seen in a longer perspective,
constituted a temporary setback of a vigorous, expanding and ever more
commercial culture. Between the millennium year (1000) and just before
the mid-fourteenth century Black Death, the total population of Europe
increased from about twenty-five million to nearly sixty million. As both
cause and consequence of population growth, Europeans brought more land

into production, both marginal lands within settled Europe and newly conquered lands on the frontiers. One possible explanation for this agricultural expansion and population growth was a sustained rise in temperature a degree or two that scientists have called the Medieval Warm Period. "The riverbankers conquered the wild wood," as Felipe Fernández-Armesto interestingly phrases it. He sees an "internal exploration" of Europe, "a vast project of the domestication of little-explored and underexploited environments." In the Middle Ages, Europe colonized itself. Forest, swamp, marsh, moor and fen was settled and put into cultivation. In the Low Countries, lakes and shallows were drained in specific areas and plots of land called polders were desalinated, built up and eventually farmed. "God made the world," goes the old saying, "but the Dutch make the Netherlands." A similar process took place in Northern Germany and Eastern England. In the British Isles and on the continent, the primeval forests were felled so fields could be plowed and planted. The Domesday Book indicates that the draining of marshes, a capital-intensive investment similar to polder making, was taking place in England in the late eleventh century. Fishermen expanded fisheries frontiers of cod in Iceland and herring in the Baltic. The increased exploitation of silver, lead, zinc, copper, iron and salt advanced an internal mining frontier. Metallurgy became more exact, ploughs became larger and heavier and crop rotation became more efficient, all of which produced more and better harvests. With an improved collar and iron shoes, horses replaced oxen and provided more productive energy. In time, what had been near universal subsistence agriculture began to give way to more efficient and specialized agricultural practices. The system of fiefdoms allowed feudal warlords – Europe's chiefs – to expropriate the surplus labor of the peasantry as a result of their judicial and military power and authority. As estates began to produce a surplus and sell it to towns, this system of serfdom was gradually modified. Warlords became landlords and peasants became more like tenants rather than the property of their estates.

Western Europe increasingly became receptive to change, particularly in its capacity to assimilate the practical ideas and technology of other cultures, primarily Middle Eastern and Asian cultures. The water mill was an ancient Roman invention borrowed by the Europeans, but during the twelfth and thirteenth centuries thousands of mills were built and applied not only to grinding grain but also to fulling cloth, driving saws, producing iron, manufacturing paper and more. The windmill was borrowed Persian technology and, with European modifications creating a more powerful motor, provided more energy than water mills. From the complicated gearing of water and windmills emerged the first mechanical clocks and the wheel lock mechanism for firearms. Improvements in metallurgy led not only to beautiful knightly armor and weapons but more and better productive instruments like the pitchfork, ax, scythe and harrow.

Expansion of the internal agricultural frontier was accompanied by the expansion of external frontiers. The petty Christian warlords in Iberia made war on the Muslim kingdoms of the peninsula, a conflict that became known as the *Reconquista*, the Reconquest. From the eleventh to the thirteenth century, the emergent Christian kingdoms, military aristocracy and religious orders of Castile ("castle-land"), León, Navarre, Asturias, Aragón and Portugal expanded south, conquered and settled new lands and forced the Muslim population, the Moors, to retreat or become the subordinate population. Crusaders from elsewhere in Europe, notably the knights and nobility of France, led expeditions into Iberia. Aragón moved offshore and conquered Majorca in the 1230s, while Castile, even more ambitious and aggressive, seized Salé on the Atlantic coast of Morocco. The Iberian kingdoms early on had set their sights on the Maghrib, as revealed in the 1291 agreement between Aragón and Castile to partition North Africa at some successful future point.

A French-speaking aristocracy from northern France invaded England, Wales and Ireland and was invited into Scotland in 1066. These Normans assisted the Portuguese, Castilians and Catalans in Iberia and conquered southern Italy and Sicily from Byzantium and Islam. German knights, missionaries and military orders such as the Teutonic Knights expanded into Eastern Europe – Brandenburg, Bohemia, Poland, Prussia, Livonia and Estonia – and colonized new lands. Everywhere expansion took place the European aristocracy built castles, established landed estates, offered land to new settlers, raised churches and founded kingdoms. In medieval Europe, the system of lords, vassals and fiefdoms was nearly always expanding, as was the reach of the Western Christian (Catholic) Church organized from Rome, and thus the boundaries of Latin Christendom expanded and deepened.

The most dramatic European expansion of the eleventh to the thirteenth centuries was called the Crusades, the military expeditions of kings, knights and commoners to the Holy Land of the eastern Mediterranean. These were "holy wars" called by the Roman Church against Muslim occupation of the Holy Land. Crusaders established Latin Kingdoms, crusader states, at Antioch, Jerusalem, Edessa and Tripoli in the lands of modern Syria and Israel. The second and third Crusades attempted, not very successfully, to aid the increasingly beleaguered Latin Kingdoms. The fourth crusade conquered Byzantine Constantinople and created the short-lived Latin Kingdom of Constantinople. None of the Latin Kingdoms of the eastern Mediterranean survived Byzantine or Muslim reconquest. These kingdoms were underpopulated European enclaves in distant and populous lands, and by 1291 they were all gone. Despite their political and military failure, the Crusades were nevertheless impressive demonstrations of the energy and aggression of European civilization.

The dramatic increase in Europe's population, the expansion of its internal and external frontiers and the increase of agricultural production prior to the fourteenth century led to the growth of towns and cities and the expansion of industry and trade. Urban centers attracted migrants from rural areas for a variety of reasons, perhaps especially because towns were less restrictive and hierarchical than the feudal countryside. Towns obtained judicial autonomy from princes, bishops and kings and built ramparts to depend it. *Stadtluft macht frei*, an old German proverb, states, "City air makes you free."

The expansion of commerce in the eleventh to the thirteenth centuries was due more to long distance than local trade. Prior to the Crusades, European merchants were buying spices, silk, porcelain, oranges, dyestuffs, sugar and

Document 1.4
The First Booke of Moses, Called Genesis

The Holy Bible, 1630

Chap. I.

1. In the beginning God created the heaven and the earth.
2. And the earth was without forme, and voide; and darkenesse was vpon the face of the deepe: And the Spirit of God moved vpon the face of the waters.
3. And God said, Let there bee light: and there was light.
4. And God saw the light, that it was good: and God divided the light from the darknes.
5. And God called the light, Day, and the darknesse he called Night: and the evening and the morning were the first day.
6. And God said, Let there bee a firmament in the midst of the waters: and let it divide the waters from the waters.
7. And God made the firmament: and divided the waters, which were vnder the firmament, from the waters, which were aboue the firmament: and it was so.
8. And God called the firmament Heaven: and the evening and the morning were the second day.
9. And God said, Let the waters vnder heaven bee gathered together vnto one place, & let the land appeare: and it was so.
10. And God called the dry land, Earth, and the gathering together of the waters called he, Seas: and God saw that it was good.
26. And God said, Let vs make man in our Image, after our likenesse: and let them have dominion over the fish of the Sea, and over the foule of the ayre, and over the cattell, and over all the earth, and over every creeping thing that creepeth vpon the earth.
27. So God created man in his owne image, in the Image of God created hee him, male and female created he them.
28. And God blessed then, and God said vnto them, Be fruitfull and multiply, and repleneth the earth, and subdue it, and have dominion over the fish of the Sea, and over the foule of the Ayre, and over every living thing that mooueth vpon the earth.

The authorized King James translation of the Holy Bible was finished in 1611. *Source: The Holy Bible.* London: Robert Barker, Printer to the Kings most excellent Majestie: and the assignes of Iohn Bill, 1630.

much more from Muslim and Greek traders in the Levant. Price disparities were the key to success: these luxuries were purchased from Middle Eastern middlemen and sold to the landed nobility and urban elite of the West. Europeans tapped into a rich and sophisticated mercantile economy stretching from Anatolia to India, China and Southeast Asia. This vast network of trade was possible in part because of the Pax Mongolica, the peace and order established by the Mongol Empire along the overland Silk Road from China to the Black Sea. During the Ming Dynasty (1368–1644), China was the greatest economic power in the world. In the early fifteenth century, a European diplomat described the Chinese goods he found in the Central Asian city of Samarkand as "the richest and the most precious of all, for the craftsmen of [China] are reputed to be the most skillful by far beyond those of any other nation." India provided large quantities of manufactured goods for the Indian Ocean trade, the most important being textiles: cottons, silks and muslins. Merchants from the cities of northern Italy, particularly Venice, Genoa and Pisa as well as the more western Mediterranean ports of Marseilles and Barcelona, established trading enclaves and colonies in the eastern Mediterranean and the Black Sea. A few Europeans, like the Venetian Polo family, traveled through central Asia, reaching India, China and the Mongol capital. It was the northern Italian commercial city-states of Venice and Genoa, however, that came to dominate the eastern trades. Italian merchants borrowed, invented or improved upon such fundamental commercial practices as business partnerships, profit-sharing, contract law, double-entry bookkeeping, marine insurance, bills of exchange, currency exchange and the development of capital markets. States tried to protect their merchants at sea and gave guarantees to the enclaves of foreign merchants in their ports, established commercial courts and wrote and enforced commercial codes to set the ground rules of business. "The second half of the thirteenth century," writes Robert Sabatino Lopez, "saw the Genoese fanning out in all directions: they were first in getting the commercial dividends of the Castilians and Portuguese reconquest of the Iberian South, first in establishing direct communications by sea through Gibraltar to London and Bruges, first in opening the western Mongolian states of Persia and South Russia to European trade, and first in numbers if not chronological priority in prolonging that trade to the eastern shores of China."

Italian and Catalan merchants also began to trade and settle in the port cities of the Maghrib in the early thirteenth century. European merchants sold finished textiles to the Barbary and Moroccan merchants and purchased grain, saffron, lavender and, most important of all, gold usually coined in "Moorish ducats." Two-thirds of the gold for European mints came from West African gold fields and the Saharan caravan routes. "Thus the revival of the European economy in the 13th century was signaled by the reappearance of gold coins," writes Edward Ayensu. The emperor Frederick II, for reasons of prestige, issued gold coins in 1231. In 1252 Florence issued the *fiorino d'oro*, or florin, and Genoa the *genovino d'oro*. Venice issued the *ducat* in 1284, France had gold coins by 1330 and the English *noble* dates from 1351.

The expansion of European trade occurred in the Baltic and North Seas as well as in the Mediterranean. The merchants of the German Baltic seaports and other cities, the Hansa or "commercial association," were also pioneers of long-distance trade, in this case from Russia to England. The Hansard merchants exported wheat, timber, furs and salted herrings from the Baltic to the ports of the North Sea. Both the Italians and the Hansards developed early commercial networking, an economic system based more on exchange

Figure 1.4. A view of the harbor of Lisbon. From Theodor de Bry, *Americae tertius pars* (Frankfurt, 1592). Courtesy of the William L. Clements Library at the University of Michigan.

than production that would, in time, put Europeans in all of the major ports of the world and transform the Atlantic basin into Europe's lake.

In between the Hansards in the north and the Italians in the south was Flanders, which specialized in raising sheep. In time, the wool trade developed into cloth manufacturing in the Flemish weaving towns of Ghent and Ypres as well as Lille and Arras in French Flanders. Flemish weavers outstripped local sources and came to import large quantities of wool from England. In the "cloth towns," a vast class of paid workers emerged that had to be fed by local specialized agriculture and with imported grain and fish from Eastern Europe and the Baltic. Halfway between Flanders and Italy was the county of Champagne where, beginning in the twelfth century, international trade fairs were held and Flemings sold their cloth to Italians for spices, silks and other Asian and Mediterranean luxuries. However, late in the thirteenth century Italian seamen opened a trading route from the Mediterranean to the Flemish cities of Bruges and Ghent. Bruges eventually eclipsed the Champagne fairs as the most important market north of the Alps where merchants from across Europe did business. Bruges and the other trading cities of Europe integrated the economy, and culture, of this new civilization. "The unity of the Medieval West was, in part," writes historian Robert Bartlett, "a traders' unity" (see Map 1.4).

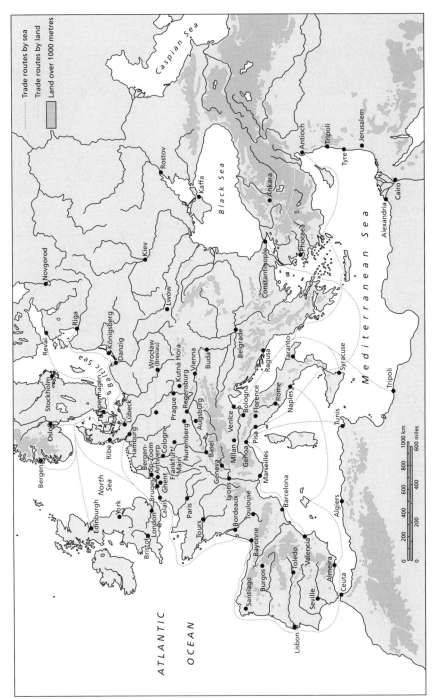

Map 1.4. Late Medieval Europe.

Economic and cultural integration did not bring political integration. The long expectation or hope of a new Roman or Christian empire never fully materialized. Instead, the gradual advance of royal power during the late Middle Ages created, in certain regions of Europe, incipient territorial states and national monarchies. The first of these appeared in England following the Norman Conquest of 1066. The Anglo-Norman monarchy efficiently taxed the realm and created a bureaucratic state that increased its power and authority over the feudal lords. France was created by the Capetian monarchy during the twelfth and thirteenth centuries. Royal government created administrative, legal and financial institutions that began to eclipse the power of the lords. In both England and France, townsmen generally supported the advance of royal power because kings were viewed as less of a threat than local lords and often offered autonomy and certain privileges in exchange for taxation.

The several small kingdoms of the Iberian Peninsula were occupied in fits and starts by the *Reconquista* during the time England and France were creating the foundations of monarchical power. By the fourteenth century, three powerful kingdoms had emerged: Castile, the largest and most powerful; Aragón, which had absorbed Catalonia, was a Mediterranean power; and Portugal on the Atlantic. Portugal was the first of these kingdoms to complete its *Reconquista* and become consolidated as a territorial state with a monarchy. A united Spain did not even begin to emerge until the marriage of Fernando of Aragón and Isabel of Castile in 1479, and Spain as a national monarchy and territorial state began in the sixteenth century.

The wealthy and urban Low Countries – Flanders and Holland – became part of the duchy of Burgundy, an appendage of the French monarchy, as a result of a dynastic marriage and inheritance in 1369. By the mid-fifteenth century, the Burgundian lands stretched from the duchy proper in Middle West France to the county of Luxemburg, the duchy of Brabant and the Low Countries. This constituted a long, narrow dominion between France and Germany. However, this emergent kingdom and empire did not survive the fifteenth century. After a military defeat in 1477, the Burgundian lands were divided between the Habsburgs and France.

Over time, in the territorial states kingship became not only more powerful but more elaborate. Courts became an institution and power-center composed of the nobility and government functionaries. They became larger, more expansive and extravagant to project monarchical power and mystique. As they became tied to one urban center, these new capital cities came to monopolize power and authority with the territorial state. The slow decline of ecclesiastical power, particularly papal authority, and the nationalization of the church enhanced royal authority. Kings developed more complex and elaborate ceremony and rituals, wore special insignia and were identified by the display of certain emblems like the crown, orb and scepter. The idea of an impersonal "crown," a national monarchy distinct from a particular dynasty, gradually gained standing.

Germany and Italy failed to develop national institutions during the late Middle Ages and remained geographical expressions composed of numerous principalities, autonomous city-states and large and small magnates. Despite

Germany's Emperorship, the impressive-sounding Holy Roman Empire, the region was a patchwork of competing jurisdictions. Northern Italy was dominated by the great commercial city-states of Venice, Florence and Milan, which had swallowed up the surrounding territory and smaller cities. Government was in the hands of communes dominated by each city's merchant oligarchy. In Rome and across central Italy, the papacy ruled a collection of small territories. Despite the wealth of the Italian city-states, in time the territorial states of northwest Europe were able to marshal more resources and greater military power even within the Italian peninsula.

In contrast with many parts of the world, and with other civilizations, Medieval Europe was not united nor dominated by an empire but was an arena of discrete and competitive territorial states. These states made war on one another, which advanced princely and royal power and only further consolidated national divisions. To those who dreamed of the order and unity of the Roman Empire, this state system was a sign of chaos and feebleness. It was, in fact, a source of strength and innovation. Competitive states and mercantile wealth produced a dynamic civilization that readily absorbed the knowledge and technology of other civilizations. These states became creative and aggressive and soon expanded into the Atlantic and around the world. The Enlightenment's historian of Rome, Edward Gibbon, argued that Europe had the best of circumstances: both (cultural) unity and (political) diversity, a "happy mixture of union and independence." This civilization, according to Gibbon, was stimulated by competition and emulation. The expansion of the fifteenth and sixteenth centuries was the initiative of a few territorial states and, to a certain extent, a collective European endeavor.

The Atlantic initiatives of the Portuguese and the Castilians in the fifteenth century came from a Western Europe, an Atlantic and Mediterranean Europe that was not only recovering from the Black Death and other traumas of the fourteenth century but also substantially reforming and transforming itself. The European pandemic killed something like thirty million people in Europe as a whole, and as a result land became more abundant for the surviving population. As a result, wages increased and living standards improved. Under these conditions, young people married earlier and produced more children. Population once again began to grow in the fifteenth century, rapidly and substantially, meaning that towns and cities recovered and production and trade expanded (see Table 1.4).

The economic and demographic recovery was not simply a recovery of the old feudal system of servile labor or serfdom within the manorial system control by chiefs or lords. A new economy in some places was arising that created tenants who were paid for their labor or who paid rent for farmland, and farmers who increased productivity to feed townspeople and make money. Higher wages encouraged the development of labor-saving technology and techniques. Agricultural productivity doubled in the fifteenth century in England. Taxation took the place of confiscation, and market prices replaced exchange based on custom. Europe, writes David Herlihy, "emerged from its long bout with pestilence healthier, more energetic, and more creative than before."

Table 1.4. Regional populations: Western
Europe, c. 1500

France	15,000,000
Germany and Austria	14,000,000
Italy	10,500,000
The Spanish Kingdoms	6,800,000
England, Scotland, Ireland	3,900,000
The Low Countries	2,300,000
Portugal	1,000,000
Others	3,700,000
Total	57,200,000

Source: Table 8a, "World Population, 20 Countries and
Regional Totals, 1–2001, A.D." in Maddison, The World
Economy: Historical Statistics, p. 256.

In 1500, Latin Christendom was a minor civilization when compared to
Ming China, Mughal India and the immense but fractured Islamic World.
According to one estimate, Asia (including the Middle East) produced three
times as much wealth annually in the fifteenth century as Europe. In population as well, Asians and the peoples of the Middle East outnumbered
Europeans by a factor of six to one by 1500. The peoples of Europe, Africa
and the Americas constituted less than one-third of the world's population
(see Table 1.5).

Beginning in the fifteenth century Western Europe would become part of
a multi-continental venture (should we say, adventure) to create an Atlantic
World that would begin to surpass these great civilizations in economic
enterprise and wealth, technological innovation, military strength and political power. It is important to realize that the beginning of the "Rise of the
West" preceded the expansion of Europe into the Atlantic. By the early fifteenth century, Western Europe had fifty-six universities, one of the great
European institutional inventions that concentrated intellectual activity. The
mass printing of books began in Europe in 1450 (the Gutenberg Bible was

Table 1.5. Regional populations: The World,
c. 1500

India	110,000,000
China	103,000,000
Other Asia	55,400,000
Western Europe	57,200,000
The Americas	54,000,000
Russia and Eastern Europe	34,000,000
Sub-Saharan Africa	38,300,000
Japan	15,400,000
World Total	467,300,000

Source: This table is from Benjamin, Table 1.1, and
adapted from Table 8a, "World Population, 20 Countries and Regional Totals, 1–2001, A.D." and Table 6.a,
"African Population, 1–2001 A.D." in Maddison, The
World Economy: Historical Statistics, pp. 190, 256.

printed in 1455). By 1500, there were approximately thirty-five thousand separate printed editions of books, that is, thirty-five thousand different books with something like nine million copies of these books in circulation. To place the print revolution in context, we should recall that prior to 1450 there were only about a half dozen important libraries in Europe that contained more than one thousand volumes. Europe began the process of becoming the first mass literate civilization. "The printed book revolutionized the transmission of knowledge," writes Lisa Jardine, "and permanently changed the attitudes of thinking in Europe...The comparative effortless production of multiple copies meant that printed books could disseminate knowledge much more rapidly, widely and accurately than their handwritten antecedents." The printing revolution had a decisive influence on the development of the Reformation, the great schism in western Christianity. Until the printing revolution, manuscript maps and charts were often kept secret so as to maintain an advantage against rival merchants, cities and states. Printed maps and charts led to a process of feedback in which mariners provided new information, allowing cartographers to constantly improve their products. The same was true with published texts on "natural philosophy," that is, observations of nature, experiments, new technology and so on. "As a contemporary of Aldus Manutius [the Venetian printer]," writes Elizabeth L. Eisenstein, "Copernicus had an opportunity to survey a wider range of records and to use more reference guides than had any astronomer before him." Europe became a civilization open to and organized for learning from the classical age, from other civilizations and eventually from ever more sophisticated science and technology.

Late Medieval and Renaissance Europe, although "learning to be civilized," in the phrase of one historian, nevertheless remained, and perhaps became, more violent and brutal. The gradual decline of chivalry, the code of honor among male warriors, was superseded by mercenary armies that often lived off the land and ravaged villages and cities. Rogue war bands destroying both friend and foe sought payment for services and loot. War within and between states became more expensive and bloody. Larger states conquered and digested smaller ones. Armies and fleets became massive and their killing ability became more efficient. Peasant and urban communities often rose in rebellion and were slaughtered. Monarchs, the church and cities were no kinder to their own than to foreign enemies. Torture, maiming and public execution by means of impaling, quartering, burning at the stake, disemboweling and other forms of brutal killing were widely dispensed to rebels, dissidents, heretics, criminals and unlucky, helpless bystanders. To historian J.R. Hale, this was "an age brutalized by a habitual exposure to and indifference towards cruelty."

In the fifteenth century, Western Europe's political fragmentation and the relative freedom of urban communes and their merchants, bankers and other bourgeois tradesmen tied Mediterranean and Atlantic Europe into one vast and diffuse commercial network. "In Bruges," writes Liah Greenfield, "merchants from all over Europe assembled, interacted, traded, and exchanged money year round." More than that, Italian merchants at Constantinople

and in the Black Sea, at Cairo and Alexandria, and at Tripoli and Fez purchased the gold and ivory of West Africa and the spices, silks, tea, porcelain
and textiles from India, China and the Spice Islands. "Europe," continues
Greenfield, "west of Novgorod and Kiev at least, functioned as one economic
system, and represented part of a sprawling commercial network, woven by
Chinese, Muslim, and Italian merchants, which connected the continent to
Asia and Africa." This economic advance occurred prior to any significant
gains from Europe's expansion into the Atlantic. As we have seen, in fact,
European economic development and territorial expansion was well on its
way prior to the crisis of the fourteenth century. Europe's economic growth
and territorial expansion overseas in the fifteenth century was part of a longer
historical pattern.

The peoples of the Americas, Africa and Europe were disconnected from
one another for the most part in 1400. The peoples of the Middle East
set astride the world's most important trade routes, and in three different
waves conquered lands and populations from Iberia in the west to India
in the east. Although China tended to draw away from external influences,
by 1100 Song China had a vibrant economy, considerable manufacturing
and substantial maritime trade. China had the world's largest cities and
the world's largest and most advanced industries, although not the world's
largest merchant class or merchant marine. Chinese culture (or at least the
imperial Chinese bureaucracy) after the voyages of Zheng He in the 1430s
came to disdain trade and officials were not permitted to engage in merchant
activities. Merchants from the other parts of the world, primarily the Indian
and Muslim Worlds, eagerly came to China. The settlement of Muslim traders
along the southern coast of China facilitated trade across the Indian Ocean.
The Silk Road through central Asia brought goods and people on horses and
camels and opened China to the Turks, Persians, Uzbeks and even Europeans.
India, a land of villages and *rajas* – rulers of little kingdoms – had suffered
repeated invasions, sackings, massacres and conquests. It was anything but
isolated, but this was hardly a good thing. It was not until 1525 when Babur
(a descendant of the Mongol Tamerlane) conquered most of the subcontinent
and created the Muslim Mughal dynasty. The Chinese, the Indians, Arabs
and the Turks were each at the center of their worlds. They were great
builders, inventors, manufacturers, merchants and mariners but they were
not explorers or discovers.

The peoples and cultures of the Americas were among the most isolated
in the world. This isolation, in combination with the relative late development of agriculture, produced cultures and civilizations that were biologically
and technologically vulnerable to foreign invasion. The peoples of West and
Central Africa were less isolated. Unlike the empires of Mesoamerica and the
Central Andes, the empires of the Niger Valley possessed iron weapons and
warhorses. They did not have water wheels and windmills, wheeled vehicles,
firearms or ocean-going vessels. The tropical climate of much of sub-Saharan
Africa also gave the area a disease environment that, while deadly to foreigners from a temperate climate like Europe, was very unhealthy for locals.
These basic facts would shape the encounters of Europeans and Indians, and

Europeans and Africans. They also suggest why it was Europeans, not Indians or Africans, who energetically, persistently and aggressively expanded into the Atlantic and advanced upon its islands and distant shores. It was not long before the once poor and relatively backward peoples of the small islands and promontory of Western Europe faced the open Atlantic, "an empty, dangerous place," as Barry Cunliff puts it, "where ships might be becalmed in waters teeming with monsters."

Territorial expansion had become an important feature of medieval European society, and it was briefly delayed by the crisis of the fourteenth century. Motivated by hunger for land, by fear of and competition with Islam, for the profits of trade and the desire to spread the word of God among other reasons, Europeans invaded the Holy Land, reconquered Iberia and expanded east to the plains of Prussia and Poland before the arrival of the Black Death. The motives and energy outlived the crisis. In the fifteenth century, Europeans continued to expand, this time beyond the bounds of continental Western Europe. Europeans borrowed, assimilated and improved maritime technology to go far beyond the shores and the sight of land. At the same time, the Mexica and Inka Empires conquered and expanded in the Americas, and the Mali and Songhay Empires did the same in West Africa. However, none of these empires saw any reason to breach the barrier of the sea. To Europeans, gold, spices and glory beckoned and the Atlantic Ocean stood in the way. What first appeared as an obstacle would become a vast crossroads. Over the next few centuries, writes Fernández-Armesto, "expanding civilizations collided." These communities became joined in conflict, collaboration, commerce, competition, colonization, contagion and – in time – commemoration. "This voyage which I now make," wrote Amerigo Vespucci in 1501, "I recognize is dangerous as to the frailty of this our human life. None the less I make it with a free mind, for the service of God and for the world."

1.4 Further Reading

Janet L. Abu-Lughon, *Before European Hegemony: The World System A.D. 1250–1350* (Oxford, 1989).

Robert Bartlett, *The Making of Europe: Conquest, Colonization and Cultural Change, 950–1350* (Princeton, 1993).

Brian S. Bauer, *Ancient Cuzco: Heartland of the Inca* (Austin, 2004).

Juan de Betanzos, *Narrative of the Inca* [1551], translated by Roland Hamilton and Dana Buchanan (Austin, 1996).

Robert Brown, editor, *The History and Description of Africa and the Notable Things Therein Contains, Written by Al-Hassan Ibn-Mohammad Al-Wezaz Al Fasi, a Moor, Babtised as Giovanni Leones, but Better Known as Leo Africanus* [1526], 3 volumes (London, 1896).

Geoffrey W. Conrad and Arthur A. Demarest, *Religion and Emire: The Dynamics of Aztec and Inca Expansionism* (Cambridge, 1984).

Father Bernabé Cobo, *History of the Inca Empire* [1653]. translated and edited by Roland Hamilton (Austin, 1979).

Barry Cunliffe, *Facing the Ocean: The Atlantic and Its Peoples, 8000 BC–AD 1500* (Oxford, 2001).

Natalie Zemon Davis, *Trickster Travels: A Sixteenth-Century Muslim Between Worlds* (New York, 2006).

Diego Durán, *The History of the Indies of New Spain* [1581], translated, annotated and with an introduction by Doris Heyden (Norman, 1994).

Felipe Guaman Poma de Ayala, *The First New Chronicle and Good Government*, abridged [1615], selected, translated and annotated by David Frye (Indianapolis, 2006).

John O. Hunwick, translator and editor, *Timbuktu and the Songhay Empire: Al-Sa'dis* Ta'rikh al-sudan *down to 1613 and other Conemporary Documents* (Leiden, 2003).

N. Levtzion and J. F. P. Hopkins, translators and editors, *Corpus of Early Arabic Sources for West African History* (Princeton, 2000).

Felipe Fernández-Armesto, *Civilizations: Culture, Ambition, and the Transformation of Nature* (New York, 2001).

Inga Clendinnen, *The Aztecs: An Interpretation* (Cambridge, 1991).

Graham Connah, *African civilizations: Precolonial cities and states in tropical Africa* (Cambridge, 1987).

Jared Diamond, *Guns, Germs, and Steel: The Fates of Human Societies* (New York, 2007).

David Herlihy, *The Black Death and the Transformation of the West* (Cambridge, Mass., 1997).

Charles C. Mann, *1491: New Relevations of the Americas before Columbus* (New York, 2005).

D. T. Niane, *Sundiata: An Epic of Old Mali* (Harlow, 1994).

J. R. S. Phillips, *The Medieval Expansion of Europe*, second edition (Oxford, 1998).

James S. Romm, *The Edges of the Earth in Ancient Thought: Geography, Exploration, and Fiction* (Princeton, 1992).

Marq de Villiers and Sheila Hirtle, *Into Africa: A Journey through the Ancient Empires* (Toronto, 1997).

Bernardino de Sahagún, *Florentine Codex: General History of the Things of New Spain* [1577], translated by C. E. Dibble and A. J. O. Anderson, 12 volumes (Santa Fe and Salt Lake City, 1950–82).

Alonso de Zorita, *Life and Labor in Ancient Mexico: The Brief and Summary Relation of the Lords of New Spain*, translated and edited by Benjamin Keen (New Brunswick, 1994).

Chapter 2

Commencement

The European Opening of the Atlantic Ocean

The Pillars of Hercules, the twin rocks standing on each shore of the Strait of Gibraltar, was the symbol in classical geography of the edge of the known world. They marked the boundary between the "inner" (Mediterranean) and "outer" (Atlantic) seas. Beyond the Pillars and the great island of the earth was the "River Ocean" that encircled the continents. This is portrayed in a Latin map showing the *Aluveus Oceani* (Ocean Riverbed) surrounding the world. Claudius Ptolemy, the librarian at Alexandria and great second-century C.E. mapmaker, noted in his *Geographia*, "the known world extends in a continuous landmass from the western extremities of Europe to the easternmost limit of Asia, and between the two points lays an intervening ocean." In the Medieval period, the idea of the River Ocean was superseded by the belief that a vast open sea lay beyond the Mediterranean. The traditional motto attached to the Pillars was *Ne plus ultra* – "Do not go too far." The great ocean beyond the Pillars had many names over the years – the Great Sea, the Ocean Sea, the South Sea and the Western Ocean. As early as Herodotus its modern name was occasionally used: "the sea outside the Pillars, named Atlantic."

To Arab geographers, the Atlantic was "the Sea of Darkness" and the "Great Green Sea of Gloom." Europeans had a similarly bleak perception of the ocean due to biblical and classical influences. The Bible viewed the oceans as chaos possessed of monsters, like the coiled serpent Leviathan. There was no sea in paradise. Plato wrote in his *Timaeus* that it was not possible "to sail upon that gulf, for the passage was blocked at the Pillars of Hercules," blocked by the continent called Atlantis. In his *Natural History*, Pliny wrote that "the seas that cut off the land split the habitable earth in half, for they cannot be crossed from here, nor from there to here." For ancient writers, the oceans were a dark, sinister force that inspired horror. Monsters like Scylla and Charybdis lived on the seashore. Medieval Europeans firmly believed in sea monsters, and many understood the oceans as the realm of Satan, as in "the Satanic Sea." Some believed that close to the equator, the temperature was so great that the oceans boiled. Late in the first millennium C.E., the ocean brought to the shores of Western Europe the feared Vikings, who killed and plundered from Britain to the Mediterranean. Ships were seen as vile abodes and seasickness only enhanced revulsion of the sea. For Europeans, even mariners, the Atlantic was not approached eagerly or with any romantic sense of adventure. The opening of the Atlantic Ocean in the fifteenth century was difficult and dangerous, both physically and psychologically. After five centuries of maritime trade and navigation along the seacoasts, the opening of the Atlantic constituted a decisive transformation in the expansion of Europe.

European expansion into the far Atlantic began in the ninth and tenth centuries with Irish and, more significantly, Norse voyages to Iceland and Greenland. The early maritime traffic in the North Atlantic appears not to have added any knowledge to Western Europe about the Atlantic and "islands and mainlands" beyond it. The sustained opening of the Atlantic began in the fourteenth century with voyages from diverse Mediterranean and Atlantic countries to the islands of the near Atlantic: the Canary, Madeira and Azores. These islands proved to be useful stopping points to and from the Atlantic coast of Africa in the fifteenth century. Portuguese mariners began to understand to some extent the winds and currents of the North and South Atlantic, which opened the door to Guinea in the 1470s and the Indian Ocean by the end of the century. Castile was hardly a latecomer to the Atlantic; this kingdom claimed and began to colonize the Canary Islands in the fourteenth and early fifteenth centuries. Sustained Atlantic exploration for Castile however, waited upon developments at home and did not even start until the fifteenth century. With Christopher Columbus in 1492, Castile entered the race to the Spice Islands in an important way. Once Columbus discovered the Americas, or as he believed, "the Indies," and discovered the width of the Atlantic, the English, French and Dutch followed. By the early sixteenth century, over the course of a century the North and South Atlantic had been opened for business by European mariners and merchants. According to J.H. Parry, this was "the discovery of the sea, in the sense of the discovery of continuous sea passages from ocean to ocean."

2.1 Europe First Turns West

Why did Europe open the Atlantic? Because the subcontinent not only faced the Atlantic but also jutted into it in various places, exploration was simply a matter of time, motive and method. It would occur in due course. On the other hand, the fifteenth century European age of exploration was contingent upon a few crucial developments. As we have seen, the maritime expansion of Western Europe emerged from a vigorous, commercial and aggressive medieval civilization. Centered on the Mediterranean, this Europe had invested lives, money and centuries into internal colonization and conquests of the outer borderlands and marchlands. As Professor Charles Verlinden expressed so many years ago, here began "the origins of Atlantic civilization."

Late medieval Western Europeans were not the first explorers of the Atlantic from the European subcontinent. Hundreds of years before Prince Henry "The Navigator" and Christopher Columbus, peoples from the western shores had sailed into the ocean. Beginning around 800 C.E., Irish monks discovered Iceland and established a peaceful retreat on that island until Norse voyagers and settlers arrived about 871. From the late eighth century, Norse or Northmen (Norwegians and Danes) maritime raiders – Vikings – looted and terrorized the coastal peoples of Ireland, Britain, France and Spain. A steady stream of poor and land-hungry Norse migrants settled in Iceland, the British Isles and France. Eventually, one Norse sailor over-shot Iceland and found Greenland, this occurring sometime in the early tenth century.

Eirík Raudi, or Eric the Red, created the first settlement in Greenland. Earlier his parents had been banished from Norway for feud killing. A generation later, Eirík was banished from Iceland for the same reason. He fitted out a ship and with family and friends sailed west and covered 450 miles to the southeast Greenland coast, which in that and the next few centuries had a warmer climate during the Medieval Warm Period, safe anchorages, good pasturage and an abundance of land. According to the Saga of Eric the Red, "Eirík sailed to the open sea by way of Snaefekkshijul and made landfall in Greenland at the glacier which is called Blaserk, or Bluesark. From there he headed south, to discover whether more land was habitable there." He named the new country Groenland, meaning "The Green Land," and announced its advantages and thereby encouraged new settlement from Iceland. Eirík's second voyage to Greenland from Iceland in 985 or 986 included twenty-five ships with families and livestock, although only fourteen ships arrived safely. In time, regular voyages were made not only between Iceland and the Greenland settlements but also between Norway and Greenland, the latter voyage extending more than one thousand miles. Two colonies were established inside the only two fjord systems in the south that penetrated far inland and provided flatter land and green pastures. The "Eastern Settlement," located in the fjords in southwestern Greenland not far from the cape, had the most farms and the largest population, about four thousand men, women and children. The "Western Settlement," located in the fjords further north on the west coast of Greenland, was colder and had a shorter growing season, and thus had many fewer farms and a population of only about one thousand persons. Archaeological work by 1990 had registered 444 Norse sites in the Eastern Settlement. Before 1350, perhaps as many as five thousand Norse people lived in Greenland, raised stock, hunted and fished and made butter, cheese and other products for use and trade. These Norse settlements traded with Scandinavian mariners as well as with local natives.

The Norse discovery of North America was, like Greenland, an accident of overshooting. Bjarni Herjólfsson, learning that his father had resettled in Greenland, set out from Norway in the late tenth or early eleventh century, but a foggy northerly blow drove him southwest until he made landfall on a forested land with low hills. Bjarni coasted northward and realized he was on the coast of an island. He turned to sea and sailed north, and in four days found a land with mountains and glaciers but it was not Greenland. He then turned around and sailed east and came to the Greenland cape where his father lived and anchored his boat. Bjarni had sailed directly from Norway to places we now know as Labrador and Baffin Island. His was the first recorded transatlantic voyage and the first European sighting of the mainland of the Americas, although no one understood this geography and the significance of the voyage. Some years later, Eric the Red bought Bjarni's *knörr*, or longboat, and gave command to his son Lief Eríksson, who traced Bjarni's course to the western lands. Lief and his crew named the Labrador and Newfoundland coast Markland ("Forest Land") and wintered further south on the mainland of North America. In the spring, they harvested wild grapes for the return to Greenland, and Lief named this unknown land Vinland ("Pasture Land"). One of the Vinland Sagas provides the first European description of mainland America:

> It seemed to them the land was so good that livestock would need no fodder during the winter. The temperature never dropped below freezing, and the grass only withered very slightly.

The children of Eric the Red made an expedition of exploration and settlement from Greenland to Vinland. These colonists built the base camp that today is known as L'Anse aux Meadows on the north coast of Newfoundland around 1000 C.E. and they came into contact with Native Americans, which the Norse called *skraelings*, or wretches. Conflict with natives influenced several settlers to return to Greenland. The Vinland Sagas describe how the Norse treated the first group of Indians they encountered: they killed eight of nine Indians, leaving one to escape and bring back others to attack the colony. One group of settlers also fought among themselves with one faction massacring the other. It is unlikely that the Norse settlement in North America survived more than ten years. Although the colonists took valuable shiploads of timber to Greenland, the Norse abandoned what was seen as a rich country because, as Eric the Red's saga explained, "though the quality of the land was admirable, there would always be fear and strife dogging them there on account of those who already inhabited it."

The colder climate that emerged with the Little Ice Age and increasingly hostile contact with Greenland's *skraelings* – the Inuit – led to the disappearance of the two Norse Greenland settlements and populations sometime in the fifteenth century. In this first European expansion into the Atlantic, climate change, Indian resistance and Norse unwillingness to learn from the Inuit doomed the efforts. To the Norse for hundreds of years, and perhaps even to early English mariners, Greenland and perhaps other western islands were simply remote extensions of northern artic regions of the (old) world. It was not until the late fifteenth century that mariners figured out the contours of the North Atlantic.

In the early fifteenth century Ming China, not Western Europe, gave all appearances of becoming the civilization that would expand across the world's oceans. Chinese trade in the China Sea and the Indian Ocean in the five hundred years since the tenth century had flourished and Chinese merchants had settled in Southeast Asia. In Table 2.1, we see the enormous size of the Chinese economy from the year 1000 to 1600. In percentage terms, China possessed about one quarter of the world's wealth. If we add India,

Table 2.1. Total wealth of world regions: GDP, 1000–1600

Region	1000	1500	1600
China	26,500,000	61,800,000	96,000,000
India	33,750,000	60,500,000	74,250,000
Africa	13,720,000	19,283,000	23,349,000
Western Europe	10,165,000	44,162,000	65,640,000
World	116,787,000	248,308,000	330,982,000

Note: Figures given in 1990 international Geary-Khamis dollars, a benchmark derived from 1990 GDP levels. Gross domestic product (GDP) is a measurement of the value of all goods and services produced in one area, usually over the course of one year. Historical international income estimates are very difficult to calculate, and different calculation methodology based on limited economic data produces different income estimates. These figures therefore should be viewed as crude but useful estimates that help us better understand long-term and comparative economic change.
Source: Table 8b: World Per Capita GDP in Angus Maddison, *The World Economy: Historical Statistics* (2003), p. 259. Also see Figure 1–4. Comparative Levels of GDP Per Capita: China and West Europe, 400–1998 A.D., in Maddison, *The World Economy: A Millennial Perspective* (2001), p. 42.

these two giants controlled at least one-half of the wealth of the world in the fifteenth century.

In seven state-sponsored voyages between 1405 and 1433, Admiral Zheng He crossed the South China Sea and the Indian Ocean from his base at Nanjing to Vietnam and Java, the Malabar Coast of India and to East Africa. His expeditions were massive undertakings involving hundreds of ships and tens of thousands of sailors and soldiers. Whereas Columbus sailed 2,400 miles on his first voyage to America, Zheng He sailed more than 12,000 miles on one voyage sixty years earlier. These expeditions apparently sought exploration and trade, the collection of rarities and tribute and the announcement – and display – of Chinese power and civilization. As a stele erected in 1432 in Fukien, the center of China's seaborne traders, announced: "In the unifying of the seas and continents the Ming dynasty even goes beyond the Han and the Tang ... The countries beyond the horizon and from the ends of the earth have become subjects." During his powerful maritime expeditions, Zheng He overthrew pirate regimes and set up a transoceanic system of commercial and military allies.

Threats from without and within China beginning in the 1420s led to the abandonment of the powerful fleet in the 1430s. There were new Mongol invasions, problems with Japanese pirates and the rise of local warlords in China. "Symptoms of the naval decline were apparent," writes historian Jung-Pang Lo. "In foreign policy and in strategic outlook, there was a change from offensive to defensive, from advance to withdrawal ... Warships, no longer sent out to sea on patrols, were anchored in ports where they rotted from neglect." It has also been argued that an anti-commercial and anti-foreign attitude became dominant in the Chinese Imperial Court due to a revival of Confucian thought. After the 1430s, all government construction of seagoing ships was ended, all voyages of existing ships were halted and any further maritime trade by Chinese merchants was forbidden.

"Successful private businessmen, frowned on the Confucian prejudice against profit-making," notes Milo Kearney, "were subject to excessive taxation or government take-over of their businesses."

Following the withdrawal of China, Egyptians and Gujaratis of western India became the undisputed trading masters of the Indian Ocean. Arabs and East Indians had established trading colonies in China, on the eastern coast of Africa and in Southeast Asia. In the fifteenth century, the Mamluks of Egypt nearly monopolized the Indian Ocean trade to the Mediterranean World. Their vessels made biannual voyages according to the summer and winter monsoons. Arabian ships, called *dhows*, were highly capable trading vessels. Arab mariners most likely invented the use of triangular (lateen) rigging and sails, which gave ships the ability to sail close to the wind. Arabs were no less advanced in determining their latitude at sea by calculating the attitude of stars and the sun. However, like Europeans Arab mariners believed the navigable ocean had its limits. For them, the seas beyond Madagascar, the island off the coast of southeast Africa, were impassable.

Like the Chinese, these highly capable Arab mariners could have entered the Atlantic, placed commercial outposts on the west coast of Africa and discovered America on behalf of the rest of the world – but they did not. The reason seems to lie in motive more than capability. China saw itself as the "Middle Kingdom," the political, economic and cultural center of the world. Foreign lands, it was widely believed, offered little of real value. Arab merchants and mariners sat astride the world's busiest and most lucrative trade routes. They had no compelling inducement to explore. The late fifteenth and early sixteenth century was one of the peaks of Islamic power. The Ottoman Turks threatened the very heart of Europe. This was when Western Europe turned to the sea. Lûfti Pasha, grand vizier of Süleyman the Magnificent, in the mid-sixteenth century noted the importance of sea power. "The Ottomans," he said, "are everywhere triumphant on the land but the infidels are superior at sea, and this could be dangerous." Of course, he was correct according to Bernard Lewis: "It was European ships, built to weather the Atlantic gales, that enabled the west Europeans to overcome local resistance and establish naval supremacy in the Arabian and Indian Seas."

China turned inward, and the Arabs and Turks dominated the Middle East at the same time Europe began to expand by sea. Europe's advance guard was the small kingdom of Portugal, a country with less than one million people at that time. Whereas China was populous, rich and self sufficient, Portugal was small, poor, short of good land and deficient in grain production from time to time. Whereas Arab and Turkish merchants traded the world's most desirable and valuable luxuries, Portuguese ships brought home grain and fish. The motive for European expansion overseas – a search for land, trade and wealth – was obvious. The means were not.

This was where the Italians entered the picture – *Italiani fuori d'Italia*, Italians beyond Italy. "Italian merchants had traveled throughout the known world for centuries," notes Samuel Hough. "Some of them ventured into areas unknown to all but a very few Europeans, and their reports, reflecting the mercantile virtues of keen observation, bold curiosity, and self possession in the face of adversity and in the midst of alien surroundings, expanded the

geographical knowledge of all Europe and raised questions about what lay
beyond the horizon." In the Middle Ages, as discussed in Chapter 1, Venice
and Genoa were the great rivals in Mediterranean trade. Venice had mercantile colonies throughout the eastern Mediterranean and was particularly
well entrenched in Alexandria, Egypt, where its merchants connected with
the Indian Ocean trades. Genoa also had mercantile colonies and bases in the
eastern Mediterranean, on the coasts of the Black Sea and in Pera, a suburb
of Constantinople. Genoese businessmen traded with Turkish and Arab merchants for the luxuries of Asia: spices, sugar, silk, carpets, vases, porcelain
and numerous additional high-priced goods. Rich Europeans would pay just
about any price for these luxuries, and this created an extremely lucrative
market. This trade with the Orient was possible because of the Pax Mongolica, the pacification of the vast Central Asian steppes by the Great Khans.
When the Polo brothers of Venice traveled in the Empire of the Great Khan
Khubilai in 1261, they were given a *paiza*, a gold tablet that served as a
safe-conduct pass and entitled its holder to use road houses, supplies and
even escorts.

In 1203–4, Venice led an army of Crusaders to attack the richest city in
Europe, the capital of Byzantium – Constantinople. In the past, the Byzantine
monarchy had given little help to crusaders and had even made alliances with
the Turks. Worse still, the Byzantine emperor had for a time ended Venetian
commercial privileges in the port and the Venetians looted the city, and then
established the Latin Kingdom of Constantinople. Venice obtained three-
eighths of the city and key ports and colonies necessary to monopolize the
eastern trade routes. At the same time, the Genoese were dispossessed of their
Byzantine factories and outposts. Not surprisingly, the Genoese assisted the
Greek Byzantines in recapturing their city in 1261, which led to the restoration of Genoa's eastern trading colonies of Pera and Caffa. Conflict and competition with Venice before and after the Fourth Crusade (1202–4) led Genoa
to explore business opportunities in the Western Mediterranean and beyond.

Genoese and Pisan merchants traded with two Muslim Iberian ports,
Malaga and Almeria, that were with the Almorávides of al-Andalus as early as
the eleventh and twelfth centuries. After Seville was taken from the Moors by
Ferdinand of Castile in 1248, the mercantile rights and privileges of Genoa
were reaffirmed and Genoese merchants became established in all Iberian
ports under Christian rule. By the late thirteenth century, Seville had become
the crossroads between the Mediterranean and the Atlantic. As the Catalan
historian Jaime Vicens Vives has written, this was the beginning of "the colonization of Spain by the Genoese." A Genoese captain sailed from Genoa
to Sluys, the port of Ghent in Flanders, in 1277. The following year, two
ships made the voyage from Genoa to London. Thereafter, annual convoys
of Italian galleys were sent from Genoa and Venice to the Low Countries and
England. Genoese and other Italian traders established mercantile colonies
in Castilian and Portuguese ports as well as in France, the Low Countries,
England and Ireland. A Genoese expedition in 1291 by the Vivaldi brothers
attempted to circumnavigate Africa and thereby bring to an end Venice's
monopoly at Alexandria, the only terminus of a sea route to the Orient. The
Vivaldi brothers never returned. Nevertheless, Barry Cunliffe is correct in

pointing out that "the Genoese were the first to take advantage of the freeing of the Straits of Gibraltar."

Trouble began for Italian merchants doing business with India and China through the Middle East in the late thirteenth century. In 1291, the Pope declared a Christian trade embargo on Egypt in retaliation against the Sultan's offensive against the last remnants of the crusader kingdom of Jerusalem. Of course, the embargo was not enforced but it did contribute to the gradual shifting of European commerce to the more northern, and caravan-based, routes. Even Venetians redirected trade away from Egypt for a time. This increased dependence upon the Silk Road was not a problem while the Pax Mongolica continued. However, the peace of the steppes began to disintegrate beginning in the 1330s and 1340s. Word came back from Almalîgh of pogroms against European missionaries and merchants. The Mongolian Empire of Central Asia, Chaghatâï, was divided into two states in 1368: "the western part was ruled by impotent kings while the eastern section fell into anarchy. The *Pax Mongolica* was rapidly approaching its end," writes Robert Sabatino Lopez, "and as a result the overland routes of Asia were being closed to trade one after another."

The growing strength of the Ottoman Empire, culminating in the conquest of Constantinople in 1453, seriously damaged Genoa's trading position. The straits leading to the Black Sea were largely closed to all Europeans. In place of Byzantine commercial intermediaries, Genoese merchants now had to deal with Turkish officials and merchants. But within days of the fall of Constantinople, the Genoese and the Ottomans negotiated a trade agreement by which the Genoese were permitted to ship their cargoes of oriental goods from the colony of Pera, located across the mouth of the Golden Horn at Constantinople, now called Istanbul. However, over the course of only a few decades Turkish conquests eliminated "the entire Genoese colonial galaxy," notes Sabatino Lopez, "with the exception of the island of Chios. The loss of colonies was a most serious blow. It virtually knocked out the Genoese as traders in Oriental spices and silk, for they could no longer compete with the Venetians, whose colonial empire was still almost intact and whose unchallenged predominance among western merchants in Egypt and Syria kept open the greatest spice markets outside the colonies." On the other hand, Venice's trade in oriental goods was dependent upon the Mamluk Egyptians, an old partnership that allowed Venetians to market pepper, spices, sweets, linen cloth, and sugar.

In the fifteenth century, Genoa looked to the western Mediterranean more than ever before for trade and profit. One of the restrictions the Ottomans insisted upon was their monopoly on the production of sugar. As a result, the Genoese shifted sugar cane cultivation from the Levant, Cyprus and Crete to Mediterranean Spain, the Algarve of Portugal and eventually to the Atlantic islands of the Madeira and Canary archipelagos. Genoese merchants established quarters (neighborhoods) in Barcelona, Lisbon and Seville. Before 1480, municipal documents report that sixteen Genoese merchants had been active in Seville. Most likely, this number is far too low. The same documentation reveals that between 1490 and 1515, there were over 430 active Genoese merchants in Seville. We see from the municipal records that a number of Italian families (Castiglione, Marini) had taken Castilian names (Castellón, Marín). Clearly, the Genoese were commercial partners of the Castilian expansion into the Canary Islands and the New World. "As the Spanish were conquering the Americas," writes Thomas Kirk, "the Genoese found their 'America' in Spain." The Genoese monopolized the sugar industry and sugar trade that had developed in the near Atlantic. Genoese merchants and financiers also controlled olive oil, wine, slaves, soap, wheat and spices. Genoese mapmakers and mariners in the Iberian ports were ubiquitous and occasionally prominent. Elected in 1484, Pope Innocent VII was Genoese and referred to by Roman aristocrats as "the Genoese Sailor." At the time of the Pope's election, a genuine Genoese mariner, Cristoforo Colombo (better known today as Christopher Columbus), arrived in Castile to seek royal support for a voyage of exploration to the Indies. "Genoese merchants acted on their own, without consideration of interests at home," writes Hugh Thomas. "That they played such a part in European enterprise in the Atlantic was neither a collective nor a state decision; it derived from the hardheaded calculation of financial advantages by about fifty dynamic families or associations" (see Map 2.1).

The Anonymous Poet of Genoa in the fifteenth century was remarkably good at pointing out the vast and expanding Genoese mercantile network:

> So many are the Genoese
> And so sure-footed everywhere,
> They go to any place they please
> And re-create their city there.

In the fifteenth century, Italians – and the Genoese in particular – moved into the western Mediterranean to assist the Portuguese and the Castilians in opening the Atlantic and to make sugar, to trade in slaves and to find gold. It was during this century that Europe suffered a severe contraction of its monetary stocks. In modern terminology, this was a major liquidity crisis. There was a shortage of gold and silver due, ultimately, to the Black Death. Production of bullion in European mines declined, and thus there was a decline in minting. There was also a decline of deliveries of African gold to Europe by caravan across the Sahara. Portugal did not mint a gold coin from 1383 to 1435. The Kingdom of Navarre did not produce a gold coin for a century after 1382. The minting of coins stopped in Florence in 1392–1404. Wendy Childs notes that the "worst shortage" occurred in the 1450s and 1460s. According to Vitorino Magalhães-Godinho, fifteenth-century Portuguese documents speak of a "gold fever" that became the driving force behind the Portuguese voyages of exploration. In an age that craved gold, Christopher Columbus's obsession with gold in the late fifteenth century makes perfect sense. His patron, King Fernando, commanded those who embarked for the New World to be obsessed with gold: "Get gold, humanely if possible, but at all hazards – get gold."

Europeans had the motive and the means to explore the Atlantic. Unlike the Chinese Empire, Europe was divided into competitive states, and there was no central authority that could halt exploration and expansion. In these competitive states, rulers were forced to search for greater revenue to fight

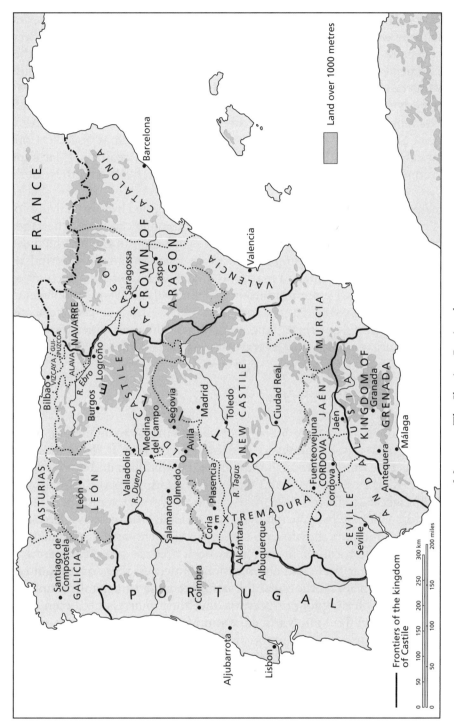

Map 2.1. The Iberian Peninsula, c. 1492.

Land over 1000 metres

Frontiers of the kingdom
of Castile

their wars. They also protected trade and encouraged merchants to seek new markets and expand taxable trade. Unlike Arab merchants, Europeans were many steps removed from the valuable goods of the Indian Ocean. If they could somehow bypass Arab middlemen, the riches of the Orient would be theirs for the taking. "European presence in the east diminished with the loss of the Holy Land and the collapse of the Mongol empire," writes Childs, "but Italians and Catalans remained at the ends of the caravan routes in the Black Sea, Syria and Egypt, and some merchants such as Niccoló Conti still managed to reach India and return in the fifteenth century. Their experience continued to encourage the European desire to trade directly with the east."

The opening of the Atlantic in the fifteenth century, led by Portugal and followed by Castile and later pursued by England, France and the Netherlands, marked the renewal of European expansionism begun in the late medieval age. Mostly economic in nature, motives were concrete and obvious. Italians sought profit backed by Iberian maritime endeavors and organized countless ventures themselves. Exploration itself was relatively slow and evolutionary in nature. One discovery led to another. Profit here encouraged the search for additional profit out there. The arena where these activities took place was the Atlantic Ocean, a barrier transformed into a highway.

2.2 Capitalism and Western Europe

"The year 1492 is as accurate as any to mark the birth of an infant who would grow into a colossus – capitalism," writes Barnet Litvinoff. There has been incessant debate on the meaning and nature of capitalism and its role in the rise of the West as a powerful and wealthy civilization. As the quotation by Litvinoff suggests, numerous historians and historical sociologists believe that the development of Western capitalism accompanied the overseas expansion of Europe beginning in the fifteenth century. Most scholars have argued that capitalism, in one form or another, was both a cause and consequence of expansion, overseas trade and colonization. However, there have been two broadly opposing perspectives on the complex issue of capitalism and the rise of the West. These two perspectives have their genesis in the theories of two great German thinkers, Karl Marx and Max Weber.

An important group of economic historians who have struggled with this problem can be described as Weberians. Weber's seminal study, *The Protestant Ethic and the Spirit of Capitalism* (1904), proposed the theory that the rise of Protestantism was fundamental in the development of a modern industrial economy. "The good Calvinist," Weber wrote, "was thrifty, diligent, and austere." These values and manners in time became secularized and generalized in the Protestant countries and even among Protestants in the Catholic countries of Western Europe. Weber recognized the early commercial and technological achievements of China, India and the Middle East but maintained that the ideological, institutional and legal frameworks that arose in the West gave European countries the decisive edge in creating ever more efficient businessmen, and therefore more productive economies.

Economic historians who follow the Weberian tradition generally have closely studied European business practices, innovations, technological ingenuity and the broader implications of the role of culture. As a result, many of these historians have embraced the idea of European exceptionalism, the idea that of all the cultures of the world European culture uniquely or at least remarkably promoted economic growth and development. The most noted Weberian economic historian of recent times is David S. Landes. In his 1998 study, *The Wealth and Poverty of Nations,* Landes argues, "if we learn anything from the history of economic development, it is that culture makes all the difference." For the West, this meant open societies devoted to work and knowledge, societies amenable to change and, above all, societies devoted to invention and innovation.

The other group of economic historians and historical sociologists who offer a strikingly different analysis of the history of Europe's economic development can be categorized as Marxists and neo-Marxists. Unlike Weber, Marx emphasized social relations (that is, power) and material conditions (conditions of production), and dismissed the role of culture as merely the superstructure resting upon and reflecting the economic base, which he viewed as fundamental. Marx's massive three-volume work, *Capital* (1867, 1883), is primarily concerned with the workings of European economies. He did make a brief foray into world history to condemn the behavior of a predatory Europe. "The discovery of gold and silver in America, the extirpation, enslavement and entombment in mines of the indigenous population of the continent, the beginnings of the conquest and plunder of India; and the conversion of Africa into a preserve for the commercial hunting of black skins," wrote Marx, "are all things which characterize the era of capitalist production. These idyllic proceedings are the chief moments of primitive accumulation." This accumulation of money and wealth through looting, theft and slavery contributed to the preconditions of capitalism according to Marx. However, expansion and colonialism were not the primary causes of capitalist accumulation and the development of capitalism. For Marx and classical Marxists, it was domestic class relations and the expropriation of surplus value from labor within Europe that led to the rise of capitalism and of European wealth and power.

Neo-Marxist scholars begin with the proposition that a precapitalist Europe expanded into the Atlantic and Indian Oceans beginning in the fifteenth century, and its predatory plunder and systematic exploitation of non-Western labor and resources produced the necessary capital accumulation to create modern capitalism. The most important proponent of this neo-Marxist interpretation is Immanuel Wallerstein in his three-volume work, *The Modern World-System* (1974, 1980, 1989). For Wallerstein, Europe expanded overseas to overcome a crisis of feudalism, a classic Malthusian crisis of overpopulation and limited agricultural productivity, by developing and sustaining "a new form of surplus appropriation, a capitalist world-economy," In this new world-economy, the exploited "periphery" – primarily Eastern Europe, the Americas and Africa – employed forced labor to produce grains, silver and plantation crops while the privileged "core" reaped the benefits of capital accumulation and economic development. For neo-Marxists, unlike Marx, it was colonial exploitation rather than the domestic (European) expropriation of labor's surplus value that is the original and fundamental reason for the development of capitalism and the rise of the West. World-systems theory from the 1970s to the present has guided the analysis of a large number of world histories and textbooks as well as Latin American, African, and Asian histories. Furthermore, as Indian and Chinese historians enter the debate they insist that commercial Asian economies before and for some time after the expansion of Europe were more sophisticated and advanced than Europe. They claim Europe's economic development was dependent upon taking advantage of the wealthier Asian markets and gradually upending the terms of trade that had long benefited Asian producers and traders.

Radical neo-Marxist scholars have also made a causal connection between the modern prosperity of the advanced industrial countries of the West and the impoverishment of what used to be called the "Third World." The peoples "who came into the orbit of Western capitalist expansion," noted the economist Paul A. Baran, made the West rich but were themselves impoverished. In his 1972 work, *How Europe Underdeveloped Africa*, Walter Rodney concisely stated his thesis in his title. More recently, J. M. Blaut has argued that "capitalism arose as a world-scale process: as a world system. Capitalism became concentrated in Europe because colonialism gave Europeans the power both to develop their own society and to prevent development from occurring elsewhere. It is this dynamic of development and underdevelopment which mainly explains the modern world."

One of the most important issues highlighted by debates between modern Weberians and neo-Marxists, and within economic history generally, is the significance of endogenous (internal) as opposed to exogenous (external) forces promoting economic growth in early modern Europe. As we have seen, Weberians maintain that it was Europe's internal institutional, legal and cultural advantages, more than anything else, that promoted economic growth and development. On the other hand, neo-Marxists as well as the so called "mercantilist" economic historians have argued that it was overseas commerce and colonization, not Europe's unique cultural superiority, that produced economic growth and development and the widening gap between the West and the rest. Although radical historians emphasize the deployment of political and economic power over non-Western societies, a number of economic historians who are unwilling to accept the world-systems theory argue that European merchants channeled foreign technology and overseas profits into an ever more productive European domestic economy. Europe's commercial, agricultural and industrial economies may have greatly benefited from overseas trade, leading to higher rates of national growth without necessarily and directly undermining the economies of non-Western societies.

These scholarly debates have not produced any clear consensus. Neither a crude Weberianism nor an overly ideological neo-Marxism is tenable. Furthermore, historical research has not reached the point where we can conclude that endogenous or exogenous forces were the fundamental keys to European economic development. Europe's historical comparative advantage in institutional, legal and broadly cultural systems has been largely substantiated by detailed studies, but we cannot today ignore or downplay the role of force and violence in European commercial expansion and colonialism. There is as yet insufficient research of non-Western economies and far too few comparative studies to fully understand the real strengths of European economies and the reasons for the economic dominance of the West by the nineteenth century. On the other hand, world-systems history is far too theoretical and ideological and fails to take into account the considerable historical research on domestic European economic productivity gains.

"Europe invented historians and made good use of them," wrote Fernand Braudel. "Her own history is well lit and can be called as evidence or used as a claim. The history of non-Europe is still being written." If we cannot yet determine the fundamental reasons for the rise of the West, and therefore the full economic significance of the rise of the Atlantic World, we can shed light on the nature of Europe's economic system during the early modern era.

Was early modern Europe capitalist? The meaning of the term "capitalism" depends largely upon the definition one employs. Too few historians who write about the Atlantic World explore the meaning of capitalism in their analyses. On the other hand, too many historians confuse the concepts of commerce and capitalism. If by capitalism we mean the classic (Marxist) definition, the term refers primarily to the organization of production. Capitalists are those who own capital assets and use these resources to hire laborers to produce agricultural and industrial goods for sale in a market to earn a profit. Capitalists reinvest their profits into their enterprises to buy more land, hire more workers or purchase better tools and machines. Competition among capitalists compels them to innovate and reinvest to cut costs and raise productivity. Based on these criteria, medieval and early modern Europe was a commercial civilization very much like the great urban civilizations of China, India and the Middle East. The key operating principle for European merchants was the same as that described by Ibn Khaldûn, the great Arab historian of the fourteenth century: "Commerce is the search for gain by increasing the initial fund when one buys commodities at a favorable prices and resells them at a higher price, whether these commodities consist of slaves, cereals, animals, or textiles. This increase is called profit."

Commercial society in early modern Europe and in the Atlantic World involved the circulation of commodities mediated by money. Merchants and shippers made profits by manufacturing and transporting goods, essentially buying cheap in one market and selling dear in another. The Genoese financed the making of sugar in Madeira and transported it to the sugar-hungry markets of Europe. The Portuguese bartered cheap cloth for expensive gold dust on the coast of Africa. The Dutch built highly efficient ships and transported commodities cheaper than just about anyone else. As Nicolas Baron put it in 1690, "The chief End or Business of Trade, is to make a profitable Bargain: In the making of a Bargain there are many things to be considered: The Ware to be sold, the Quantity and Quality of those Wares, the Value or Price of them, the Money or Credit, by which the Wares are bought, the Interest that relates to the time of performing the Bargain." Merchants quite often sought profit through extra-economic means such as privateering, slavery, trade monopolies and military domination of the seas. Merchants in the market-oriented societies of the Mediterranean and the Atlantic developed a preference for investing in the circulating capital of trade commodities as well as the fixed capital of agriculture and manufacturing. This system of "mercantile wealth" is best referred to as merchant capitalism. It is this economic system that dominated the Atlantic World.

Numerous historians have argued that thirteenth- and fourteenth-century Italian merchants invented (and borrowed from merchants from the Orient) the institutions and mechanisms for a "commercial revolution" and liberated a primitive exchange economy with new credit instruments such as bills of exchange and deposit certificates. Merchant capitalists likewise made trade more dependable, rational and secure through innovations such as business partnerships and companies, contracts and commercial law, marine insurance, deposit banks and factors or commission agents scattered in foreign ports reporting on local market conditions. Merchants became more efficient recording transactions using Arabic rather than Roman numerals and employing double-entry bookkeeping for keeping track of cash and capital, assets and liabilities. Wider social changes were underway in tandem with these specific practices. More Europeans produced for the market, more people were paid in cash and had money to spend, and thus there was rising consumption. The monetarization of European societies – the rise of cash economies – led individuals and families, common, bourgeois and noble, to develop new strategies to earn cash. An increase in labor and business specialization and professionalization accompanied and promoted commercial development. "The key figure in the expanding economy of Europe between 1460 and 1560," writes Eugene F. Rice and Anthony Grafton, "was the merchant."

The creation of the Atlantic economy beginning in the fifteenth and sixteenth centuries furthered the expansion of the commercial societies of Atlantic Europe. "One of the principal effects of those discoveries," wrote Adam Smith in 1776, "has been to raise the mercantile system to a degree of splendor and glory which it could never have otherwise have attained to." A century before Smith's *The Wealth of Nations*, Josiah Child, a British merchant associated with the East India Company, penned *A Discourse of Trade* (1668), which analyzed Dutch commercial success. "The prodigious increase of the Netherlanders in their domestic and foreign trade, riches, and multitude of shipping," wrote Child, "is the envy of the present, and may be the wonder of future generations." He argued the success of Dutch commerce was due to experienced and educated merchants and shippers, well-built and low-cost ships, an unobtrusive government and an uncorrupted court system and, most important of all, a banking system that provided cheap money. Child anticipated Smith's argument that Atlantic markets stimulated agricultural and manufacturing production at home. He stated their commercial success was due to "their exact making of all their native commodities...which they send abroad in great quantities; the consequences of which is, that the repute of their said commodities abroad, continues always good, and the buyers will accept of them by marks, without opening." This early modern European commercial expansion produced what contemporaries called "the mercantile system."

The system of merchant capitalism pushed explorers, traders and colonists into nearly every nook and cranny of the Atlantic World from the early fifteenth to the late eighteenth century. Commerce shaped Portuguese Africa, New Spain, New France and New England and so many other ports, islands, provinces and colonies. Commerce made the Atlantic World through the development of the fur, skin and hide trades, the advance of the plantation system and its valuable staples, the concomitant rise of the Atlantic slave trade and the selling of hundreds of thousands of muskets to American colonists, Native Americans and African merchants and princes. Merchant capitalism produced great transformations throughout the Atlantic World and created wealth for Europeans abroad and at home. Nevertheless, we should be mindful that "until the eighteenth century," according to Daniel Chirot, "Europe was only slightly more powerful than the old Asian centers of civilization, and it was unable to make significant inroads into India, Japan, or China." In fact, by 1820 the collective economies of Western Europe were still smaller in value than the single, if massive, economy of China. By 1820, Western Europe's economies had surpassed that of India but when all of Asia's economies are put together for the sake of comparison, the economies of Western Europe constituted less than half the value of its eastern counterpart. This would change dramatically in the course of the following one hundred years. By 1913, as a result of industrial capitalism, the economies of Western Europe were almost a third larger than those of Asia, including Japan. Far more than the earlier and long-lasting merchant capitalism, industrial capitalism transformed the power and wealth of Europe vis-à-vis Asia.

Near the end of the Second World War, the economist Karl Polanyi made a useful distinction between societies with markets and market societies. Societies with markets, of which much of the world was composed in the fifteenth and sixteenth centuries, were societies in which economic practices and commercial relations were embedded in and dominated by non-economic – that is kinship, communal, religious and political – relationships. Economic activity was motivated by status and communal solidarity as much as by material gain. Long-distance trade was often more in the nature of exploration, hunting, piracy and war, which surely explains why traders in late medieval and early modern Europe were often called "merchant adventurers." On the other hand, market societies – a more modern development – are societies in which traditional social relations are embedded in and dominated by the economy. The mercantile system of Europe from the fifteenth to the eighteenth century increasingly enhanced the market and market institutions, expanded trade, manufacturing and capital itself and ultimately transformed societies with markets into market societies. "From the sixteenth century onwards markets were both numerous and important," wrote Polanyi, "yet there was still no sign of the coming control of markets over human society."

2.3 The Ocean Sea

Although somewhat less than half the size of the Pacific, the Atlantic Ocean is huge, covering more than thirty million square miles. The Atlantic is not an enormous inert body of water. The forces of the earth's rotation, tides, climates and geography itself create complex patterns of surface winds and ocean currents.

The wind flows of the Atlantic, which Europeans came to call the "trade winds" and the "Westerlies," move in opposite circular patterns in the North and South Atlantic. Their names are derived from the direction from which they originated. In the north, the winds move clockwise. The North East, or Portuguese, Trades blow to the southwest beginning around the Iberian Peninsula and cross the ocean between the equator and 30° north latitude. They pushed traders to the New World. When these North East Trades move over waters of changing temperature in the summer, they can bring hurricanes into the Caribbean, Gulf of Mexico and the east coast of North America. The North Atlantic Westerlies blow from west to the northeast. From the Caribbean, they blow to the northeast between 30° and 60° north latitude, and brush northwest Europe and Norway. In the South Atlantic, the South East Trades blow to the northwest up the coast of Africa, west to the bulge of Brazil and then south along the coast of South America. Where countervailing winds meet, calms and variable winds occur. The South East and North East Trades collide near the equator, creating what mariners called the Doldrums. Further north, where the North East Trades intersect the Westerlies, another region of variable or calm winds exist called the Horse Latitudes. The same intersection occurs in the South Atlantic. There are seasonable variations, which slightly modify these patterns but were crucial to sailors.

The Atlantic is also composed of wind-driven currents, which are much like rivers that flow through their channels. As with the wind system, the currents move clockwise in the North Atlantic and counterclockwise in the South. South from the Arctic regions flows the Labrador Current that carries icebergs, cools the shores of northeast North America and stocks the fisheries off Newfoundland and the Grand Banks. Flowing north is the warm Gulf Stream, which originates off the coast of northwest Africa as the Canaries Current and becomes the North Equatorial Current as it crosses the Atlantic. When the Gulf Stream hits the Labrador Current south of New England, it is deflected east to become the North Atlantic Current that, in combination with the Westerlies, warms northwest Europe. For example, Ireland on a latitude north of Newfoundland should be inhospitable to agriculture but the warm waters, winds and rains produce such green fields that it became known as the Emerald Isle. The South Atlantic mirrors the North Atlantic. The cold Falkland Current flows north from the Antarctic along the coast of South America, crosses the ocean and then flows north along the west coast of Africa, becoming the Benguela Current. It turns west when it meets the southern-flowing Guinea Current, a branch of the Canaries Current. It then becomes the South Equatorial Current, which is split by the bulge of Brazil and produces a northward flow across the top of South America and into the Caribbean Sea (ultimately joining the North Equatorial Current to become the Gulf Stream) and a southward flow along the southern coast of South America (see Map 2.2).

In time, this useful information was placed on maritime charts. The first manuscript charts were held as state secrets and later were printed, published and widely circulated. The first printing of Ptolemy's *Guide to Geography*

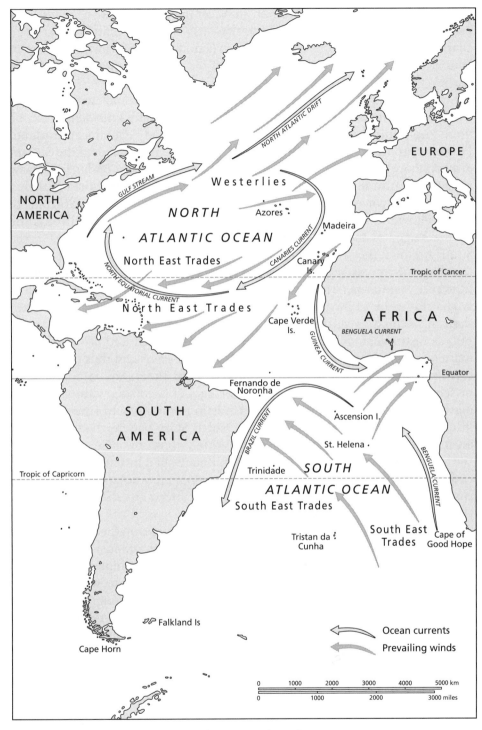

Map 2.2. Atlantic Winds and Currents.

and its world projections appeared in Vicenza, Italy, in 1475. Sea atlases began to be printed and published in the early sixteenth century. Mariner's charts and sea atlases offered sailing instructions that informed mariners of coastal profiles, latitude grids and many of the wind currents in the Atlantic basin.

European mariners learned about the oceanic rivers and winds through trial and error in the fifteenth and sixteenth centuries. This knowledge became more important than ever as ships increasingly sailed beyond sight of land. However, knowing the wind and current patterns was little help if the captain did not know his position north-south and east-west. Sailors had to learn how to find the latitude to catch the wind they wanted and follow the parallel, a maneuver known as "latitude sailing." In the fifteenth century, the Portuguese learned how to read their position without instruments in the North Atlantic by the height of the Pole Star at night and the sun during the day. In the South Atlantic, they found the Southern Cross, a group of six bright stars in the shape of a cross lying on its side, which provided less reliable guidance. However, as mariners approached the equator the Pole Star was too low in the sky to be of any use, and they learned to rely upon the position of the sun. At first, a staff was used for vertical measurement; later a more precise instrument called a nautical astrolabe was employed. To complicate matters, the position of the sun varied with the seasons and thus declination, this variance, had to be taken into account. In the 1480s, a commission of scholars appointed by the king of Portugal created solar tables to assist mariners. The compass was also of great help in sailing out of sight of land, in cloudy weather and in locating the North Star. The magnetic compass, an invention of the Chinese, was first written about by a European in the twelfth century. By the thirteenth century, Italians had invented the maritime compass, a pivoted, magnetized needle placed in a dry box on top of a wind rose, a picture of the sixteen winds of the Mediterranean Sea, with a glass top suitable for use on board a moving ship.

"Degrees of longitude," noted a Portuguese chronicler in the early sixteenth century, "are counted from orient to occident, which the mariners call east and west, and this is difficult to ascertain because they have no firm and fixed point as are the poles for the latitudes..." Position was calculated roughly (very roughly) by a system called "dead reckoning." Navigators kept records as best they could of the ship's speed, direction and time elapsed and then estimated their course on the chart. A precise system and device (an accurate maritime clock) of measuring longitude was not invented until the mid-eighteenth century. In the meantime, "the longitude is a more difficult matter," wrote Amerigo Vespucci in 1501. "Because of this longitude I have lost much sleep and shortened my life ten years."

Seagoing vessels had been tested and improved in the Mediterranean, North Sea and Baltic Sea for centuries. The first regular navigation between these seas began in the late thirteenth century in Mediterranean "great galleys" possessing a square mast and many oars, and in northern cogs with a single square mast and often no deck. By the fourteenth century, ocean-going cargo ships had sternpost rudders and began to be skeleton-constructed, "caravel built," which was far stronger than the "clinker-built" overlapping

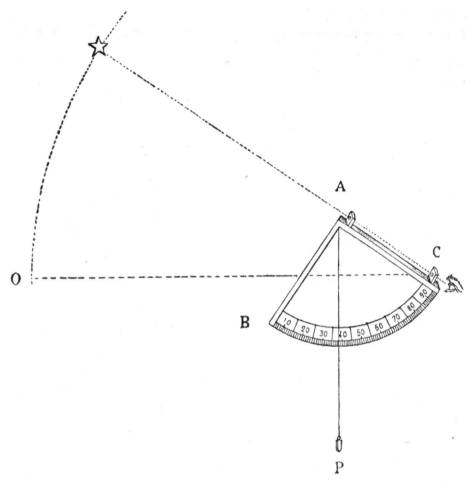

Figure 2.1. An Astrolabe, *Astrolabe*. From Enrico Alberto d'Albertis, *Le construzioni navali e l'arte navigazione al tempo di Cristoforo Colombo* (Rome, 1893). Courtesy of the William L. Clements Library at the University of Michigan.

planking involved in shell construction. These cargo ships could weather rough seas but were heavy, slow moving and deep draft, not the best type of ship for voyages to unknown waters and shores. Smaller, faster and shallow-draft ships were needed for expeditions of exploration, and the Portuguese first employed the sturdy *barcha*, a ship with oars, a single square mast and often no deck. The famous caravel came into service only in the 1440s and was improved through the rest of the century. The fifteenth- and early sixteenth-century expeditions into the unknown Atlantic were made with medieval maritime technology. Improvements did not spur discovery as much as result from trial and error adjustments made in the course of discovery.

2.4 The Near Atlantic

Europeans did not burst into the Atlantic in the fifteenth century. The expansion from the Mediterranean to the Atlantic was gradual or made in fits and

Document 2.1
The Entire Earth Consists of Three Continents

Claudius Ptolemy

We have divided the inhabited regions into three large divisions, as seemed proper to the ancient writers who examined these areas and have left us their conclusions in their commentaries, as we ourselves desire to do, partly from what we have seen and partly from the traditions of others. We have set ourselves to depict such a map of the whole inhabited earth, presenting nothing untried concerning those things which in part are useful and can well fill the mind by giving it something which is historical, arousing and existing it to exercise its powers.

That part of the earth which is inhabited by us is bounded on the east by the unknown land which borders on the eastern races of Greater Asia, namely the Sinae and the Seres, on the south by the likewise unknown land which encloses the Indian sea and which encompasses Ethiopia south of Libya, the country called Agisymba, and on the west by the unknown land encircling the Ethiopian gulf of Libya and by the Western ocean bordering on the westernmost parts of Africa and Europe, and on the north by the continuous ocean called the Ducalydonian and Sarmatian, which encompasses the British islands and the northernmost parts of Europe, and by the unknown land bordering on the northernmost parts of Greater Asia, that is to say, on Sarmatia and Scythia and Serica. The water moreover is much greater in extent than is the land.

Wherefore the entire earth consists of three continents, Asia, Africa, and Europe. Asia is joined to Africa by the part of Arabia enclosed by our sea and the Gulf of Arabia and by the unknown land which is washed by the Indian sea, and is joined to Europe by the land which lies between the Sea (swamp) of Maeotis and the Sarmatic sea in which is the basin of the river Tanis.

Of these three parts of the world, Asia is the largest, Africa is next in size and Europe is the smallest. Of the seas surrounded by land, as has been said before, the first in size is the Indian sea, the second is our sea, the third is the Hyrcanium or Caspian.

Claudius Ptolemy, a mathematician and geographer of second century C.E. Alexandria, invented the system of latitudes and longitudes and catalogued the basic features of the earth. Ptolemy's *Geography* was rediscovered in the fifteenth century and sparked a scholarly interest in geography and cartography that was only reinforced by the European voyages of the fifteenth and sixteenth centuries *Source: Geography of Claudius Ptolemy*. Translated into English and edited by Edward Luther Stevenson. Based upon Greek and Latin manuscripts and important late fifteenth and early sixteenth century printed editions including reproductions of the maps from the Ebner Manuscript, c. 1460, with an introduction by Professor Joseph Fischer, 1932.

starts, with time given to exploring and colonizing a transition zone, what historians have come to call the Atlantic Mediterranean or the Near Atlantic. This intermediate zone refers to the volcanic island groups of the Near Atlantic, the Canary, Madeira, the Azores and the Cape Verde archipelagos. The Canary Islands, which are quite close to the African coast, were known to the ancient world as the Fortunate Isles. Lost or forgotten for centuries, they were rediscovered during Europe's first probes into the Atlantic in the fourteenth century.

The islands of the Atlantic Mediterranean became Europe's first discoveries in the Atlantic after the generally unknown (outside Nordic culture) Norse voyages around the time of the first millennium C.E. These islands most likely were discovered in the search for greater prizes. In 1291, the Vivaldi brothers of Genoa attempted to outflank the Venetians by sailing with a flotilla of galleys to seek "the regions of India by way of the ocean." They disappeared without a trace in the Atlantic. Jaume Ferrer from Majorca set sail for West Africa's "River of Gold" – the assumed source of the Saharan gold trade – in 1346, vanishing like the Vivaldis. Another Genoese mariner, Lanzarotto Malocello, went to look for the Vivaldis in 1312 and rediscovered the Canary Islands, most likely for Portugal. Some of the islands were inhabited and could be raided for slaves, which were an early source of profit. The Canaries also produced useful products, primarily dyestuffs. A Florentine, Angiolino del Teggia, found Tenerife in the Canary chain in 1340 and returned with a cargo of natives for sale. Castile claimed the Canaries as part of the kingdom's Visigothic heritage but sustained and successful colonization was delayed for decades due to Castile's internal and foreign problems and the tenacious resistance of the island's original inhabitants. Meanwhile, the King of Portugal, Alfonso IV, in 1341 declared the Canaries to be Portuguese and sent a slave-raiding expedition.

After the Black Death, the Portuguese and Europeans from many nations "mined" the native Guanche population of the Canaries for slaves in sugar plantations in Cyprus, Sicily and Madeira. In 1404, Portugal granted Giovanni della Parma of Genoa a royal license to establish a sugar plantation in the Algarve, and the Guanche became a primary source of slaves. The Guanche resisted but slave-raiding combined with warfare and disease reduced the population of Lanzarote to 300 by the early fifteenth century.

A Genoese mariner discovered the uninhabited Madeira group in (possibly) 1341. This was the first documented Portuguese expedition to the Atlantic Mediterranean. Named for its wooded shores, Madeira provided hardwood timber to Portugal for shipbuilding and furniture. The Azores, the most distant of the three groups, was probably discovered in the fourteenth century; a definite Portuguese discovery was not documented until 1432. Located near the mid-Atlantic, the nine islands of the Azores became critical ports of call for ships making the return voyage from West Africa. The Portuguese came to control and occupy the Madeira and Azores group and competed with Castile for ownership of the Canaries. Portuguese colonization of the Madeira group began in the 1430s and 1440s, led by a member of Prince Henry's entourage João Gonsalves Zarco.

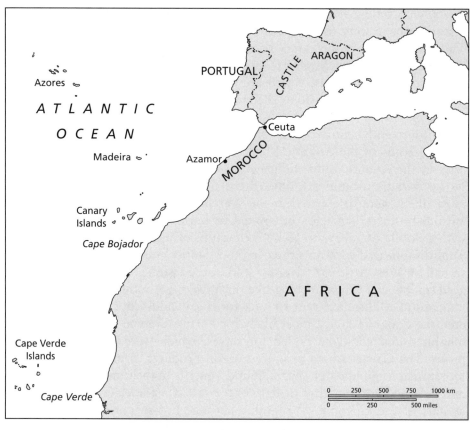

Map 2.3. The Near Atlantic.

Franco-Castilian settlement of Lanzarote in the Canaries began in the early fifteenth century. In his *De Orbe Novo* of 1511, Peter Martyr reported that a Frenchman named Béthencourt in 1405 discovered the island chain, "he took over two of the islands, Lanzelote and Fuerteventura, and civilized them. On his death, his heir offered both islands for sale to Spaniards." In 1424, the Portuguese dispatched a large flotilla of ships and 2,500 men to occupy the Canaries. The definitive Castilian conquest of the Canaries did not begin until the late 1470s. This was soon followed in 1479–80 with the Treaty of Alcáçovas, which settled the claims of the two kingdoms: Castile recognized Portuguese claims to Madeira and the Azores as well as its exclusive rights of trade and navigation in Africa, and Portugal recognized Castile's claim to the Canary Islands. The first step in the conquest was the construction of military towers from which forays would seek and fight natives. For nearly thirty years, Canarians fought Spanish lances and faced European diseases. Conquistadores were organized into freelance companies authorized by royal charters, much as they would be half a century later in the Americas. They exploited internal rivalries between native polities to gain allies in the conquest while native leaders similarly exploited the rivalry between Castile and Portugal to obtain military assistance (see Map 2.3).

In the fifteenth century, the Portuguese and the Castilians planted colonists – not only Portuguese and Spanish but also Flemish, Italian and French settlers – on their islands and introduced livestock, wheat and vines. The islands became important way stations on the way to and from West Africa, and later, America and the Indian Ocean. Genoese merchants introduced sugar cane to Madeira in the 1450s, which produced an explosion of economic growth. Sugar became the first Atlantic product that brought prices as high as the spices from Asia. Dozens of sugar mills produced hundreds of tons of sugar each year in the second half of the fifteenth century. It was reported in 1480 that sixty to seventy ships a year brought cargoes of sugar to Lisbon. A Portuguese historian estimated annual Madeiran production of sugar to increase from 20,000 arrobas in 1470, 80,000 in 1490 and 105,000 in 1494 to 144,000 by 1506. Canarian slaves worked the early plantations at first, but quickly West Africans were brought to the island and forced into slavery. "Madera is the greatest and most principal of all the isles in the Atlantic Ocean," noted Leo Africanus in the early sixteenth century. "It produces infinite store of fruits, excellent wines, and sugars which cannot be matched."

As in Madeira, Genoese capital underwrote settlement and financed agricultural development in the Canary Islands, and something else. Sugar was introduced in the 1480s and production there soon rivaled that of Madeira. Natives were enslaved to work the plantations despite Queen Isabel's prohibition of Canarian slavery. As in Madeira, Africans eventually became the predominant slave population. Portugal and Castile's first overseas colonies were great successes with Canarian and African slavery. The Canary Islands – which, as Leo Africanus recorded, abounded with barley, honey, goats, cheese, hides, meat, sugar, wine and water – "wherefore such ships as go from Spain to Terra firma and 'Brasil,' to there ordinarily provide themselves of fresh food."

The last of the Atlantic islands to be discovered and settled by the Iberians was the Cape Verde archipelago, reached by the Portuguese mariner Dinis Dias in 1441. More than 300 miles from the African coast, the Cape Verde islands like Madeira were granted to Genoese mariners and merchants who were backed by Genoese money in the 1460s. The sugar industry never flourished as it did in Madeira, given the lack of rainfall. However, by the early sixteenth century the Cape Verdes became Portugal's base for commercial and territorial expansion in Africa and America. The Cape Verdeans not only supplied passing ships but sugar planters in São Tomé and slave traders from the Senegambia to Angola.

Columbus sailed west into the Ocean Sea from the Grand Canary and returned with an unplanned stopover in the Azores. In 1497, Vasco de Gama, on his journey to India, spent a week in the Cape Verdes. Pedro Álvares Cabral left the island of Canaria in 1499 for India but came upon the coast of Brazil by accident. To Vespucci, the fleet had begun "at the end of the inhabited Western world at the Fortunate Islands." These mid-Atlantic archipelagoes, writes T. Bentley Duncan, "derive their special character from all four of the continents that rim the Atlantic Ocean. The fifteenth-century Iberian thrust into the Atlantic brought about the utilization of the islands. The growing of special island products, and the evolution of the West African trade, enhanced the economic significance of the archipelagoes."

2.5 The Fabled River of Gold

Many historians have long considered the Portuguese capture of the North African port city of Ceuta near Gibraltar in 1415 as the turning point in Portugal's – and Europe's – overseas expansion. Although it did not mark the beginning of the opening of the Atlantic, it did initiate (indirectly) the first sustained effort of exploration, trade and colonization in the Atlantic to be supported by a European state. As Prince Henry "The Navigator's" biographer, Peter Russell, puts it: "Notice that Portugal was on the move outside its traditional frontiers and was given to a watching but somewhat mystified Europe on Friday, 26 July, 1415, when, amid a blaze of publicity, the greatest fleet and perhaps the largest army ever assembled by a Portuguese king sailed out of the Tagus on a southerly tack."

Of course, for the Portuguese conquest of a Moorish city was hardly unprecedented or unexpected. Europeans saw themselves as combatants in a long and deadly serious "cold war" with the infidel Moslem world that frequently erupted in "hot" armed conflicts. As Castile did not want assistance in its struggle with Granada, the last Moorish kingdom in Iberia, the obvious next step for the crusading Portuguese was across the Strait of Gibraltar. Such a move was not unprecedented. Castile had attacked Salé and Algeciras in the thirteenth and fourteenth centuries. Portugal was at peace and relatively united, and King João I had three sons who recently had attained maturity and sought battle, glory and knighthood. There were economic, strategic as well as personal motives in play. Possession of Ceuta could allow Portuguese merchants to more directly tap into the trans-Saharan caravan trade and its most valuable product, Sudanese gold. It has also been suggested that foreign, mostly Genoese and Florentine, merchants pushed Portuguese expansion at Ceuta and beyond. However, what exactly convinced João I is unknown.

Whatever his motives, conquest brought little strategic or economic gain. Possession of Ceuta hardly injured the Berbers and Arabs of Morocco or enhanced Portugal's power, but it was costly to sustain. Furthermore, Muslim trade with Ceuta, including the Sahara routes, was redirected to other cities of the Maghrib. The brief campaign did mark the entry into public affairs of the Infante Dom Henrique, at the age of 19 years, better known to us today as Prince Henry, one of the king's sons who helped prepare, and participated in, the attack upon Ceuta.

Beginning around 1419, Henrique and his brother Pedro became the sponsors of maritime expeditions to the Atlantic ports of Morocco, the Atlantic Mediterranean and into unknown waters off the African coast. Under Henrique's leadership in particular, the Portuguese competed with the Castilians for control of the Canaries for decades (it was Henrique that dispatched the 1424 expedition) and began the settlement of the Madeira Islands. The remote Azores, 800 miles west of Portugal, were "developed" by Henrique beginning in the late 1420s. Granted royal monopolies of trade and lordship of all of the islands, Henrique sent expeditions and colonists and licensed others to do the same for profit, which was in the beginning very little.

Henrique's chronicler Gomes Eanes da Zurara wrote in 1453 that Prince (often referred to as the Lord Infante) moved to command the search for the lands of Guinea for these reasons:

> He had a wish to know the land that lay beyond the Isles of Canary and that Cape called Bojador; the second reason was that if there chanced to be in those lands some population of Christians, or some havens... many kinds of merchandise might be bought to this realm, which would find a ready market.

Document 2.2
In Which Five Reasons Appear Why the Lord Infant Was Moved to Command the Search for the Lands of Guinea

Gomes Eannes de Zurara, c. 1457–c. 1465

We imagine that we know a matter when we are acquainted with the doer of it and the end for which he did it. And since in former chapters we have set forth the Lord Infant as the chief actor in these things, giving as clear an understanding of him as we could, it is meant that in this present chapter we should know his purpose in doing them. And you should note well that the noble spirit of this Prince, by a sort of natural constraint, was ever urging him both to begin and to carry out very great deeds. For which reason, after the taking of Ceuta, he always kept ships well armed against the Infidel, both for war and because he had also a wish to know the land that lay beyond the isles of Canary and that Cape called Bojador, for that up to his time, neither by writings nor by the memory of man, was known with any certainty the nature of the land beyond that Cape. Some said indeed that Saint Brandan had passed that way; and there was another tale of two galleys rounding the Cape, which never returned. But this doth not appear at all likely to be true, for it is not to be presumed that if the said galleys went there, some other ships would not have endeavoured to learn what voyage they had made. And because the said Lord Infante wished to know the truth of this – since it seemed to him that if he or some other lord did not endeavour to gain that knowledge, no mariners or merchants would ever dare to attempt it (for it is clear that none of them ever trouble themselves to sail to a place where there is not a sure and certain hope of profit) – and seeing also that no other prince took any pains in this matter, he sent out his own ships against those parts to have manifest certainty of them all. And to this he was stirred up by his zeal for the service of God and of the King Edward his Lord and brother, who then resigned. And this was the first reason of his action.

The second reason was that if there chanced to be in those lands some population of Christians, or some havens, into which it would be possible to sail without peril, many kinds of merchandise might be brought to this realm, which would find a ready market, and reasonably so, because no other people of these parts traded with them, nor yet people of any other that were known; and also the products of this realm might be taken there, which traffic would bring great profit to our countrymen.

The third reason was that, as it was said that the power of the Moors in the land of Africa was very much greater than was commonly supported, and that there were no Christians among then, nor any other race of men; and because every wise man is obliged by natural prudence to wish for a knowledge of the power of his enemy; therefore the said Lord Infant exerted himself to cause this to be fully discovered, and to make it known determinately how far the power of those infidels extended.

The fourth reason was because during the one and thirty years that he had warred against the Moors, he had never found a Christian king, nor a lord outside this land, who for the love of our Lord Jesus Christ would aid him in the said war. Therefore, he sought to know if there were in those parts any Christian princes in whom the charity and the love of Christ was so ingrained that they would aid him against those enemies of the faith.

The fifth reason was his great desire to make increase in the faith of our Lord Jesus Christ and to bring to him all the souls that should be saved, understanding that all the mystery of the Incarnation, Death and Passion of our Lord Jesus Christ was for this sole end – namely the salvation of lost souls – whom the said Lord Infant by his travail and spending would fain bring into the true path. For he perceived that no better offering could be made unto the Lord than this; for if God promised to return one hundred goods for one, we may justly believe that for such great benefits, that is to say for so many souls as were saved by the efforts of this Lord, he will have so many hundreds of guerdons in the kingdom of God, by which his spirit may be glorified after this life in the celestial realm. For I that wrote this history saw so many men and women of those parts turned to the holy faith, that even if the Infant had been a heathen, their prayers would have been enough to have obtained his salvation. And not only did I see the first captives, but their children and grandchildren as true Christians as if the Divine grace breathed in them and imparted to them a clear knowledge of itself.

But over and above these five reasons, I have a sixth that would seem to be the root from which all the others proceeded: and this is the inclination of the heavenly wheels. For as I wrote not many days ago in a letter I sent to the Lord King, that although it be written that the wise man shall be Lord of the stars, and that the courses of the planets (according to the true estimate of the holy doctors) cannot cause the good man to stumble; yet it is manifest that they are bodies ordained in the secret counsels of our Lord God and run by a fixed measure, appointed to different ends, which are revealed to men by his grace, through whose influence bodies of the lower order are inclined to certain passions. And if it be a fact, speaking as a Catholic, that the contrary predestinations of the wheels of heaven can be avoided by natural judgment with the aid of a certain divine grace, much more does it stand to reason that those who are predestined to good fortune, by the help of this same grace, will not only follow their course but even add a greater increase to themselves. But here I wish to tell you how by the constraint of the influence of nature, this glorious Prince was inclined to those actions of his. And that was because his ascendant was

Aries, which is the house of Mars and exaltation of the sun, and his lord in the XIth house, in company of the sun. And because the said Mars was in Aquarius, which is the house of Saturn, and in the mansion of hope, it signified that this Lord should toil at high and mighty conquests, especially in seeking out things that were hidden from other men and secret, according to the nature of Saturn, in whose house he is. And the fact of his being accompanied by the sun, as I said, and the sun being in the house of Jupiter, signified that all his traffic and his conquests would be loyally carried out, according to the good pleasure of his king and lord.

Gomes Eannes de Zurara was a courtier and chronicler of Prince Henry of Portugal, the younger brother of the king, or as custom dictated, the Lord Infante. *Source:* Gomes Eannes de Zurara, *The Chronicles of the Discovery and Conquest of Guinea*, translated by C. R. Beezley and Edgar Prestage, 2 vols. (1896 and 1899), Vol. I., pp 27–30.

Henrique wanted the Canaries for two primary reasons. First, slaves captured in the Canaries provided the first, and for a time the only, return on the Prince's maritime investment. Second, the Canaries were the best station on the way to the fabled "River of Gold" – first mentioned in the mid-fourteenth century by the anonymous Spanish author of *The Book of Knowledge* – where it was expected that Portuguese traders could tap into the Saharan gold trade. As Henrique fought the Castilians for the islands, he also began voyages to probe the northwest coast of Africa. Perhaps fifteen voyages over twelve years discovered only desert coastline, and captains proved incapable or unwilling to pass the dreaded Cape Bojador, 120 miles south of the Canaries. Not until Henrique in 1434 sent Gil Eannes, a squire in his household, was the cape doubled and the psychological barrier removed. Thereafter, the pace of new discoveries on the coast of Africa accelerated. A voyage in 1436 reached an inlet a thousand miles south of Bojador, where gold dust could be had in trade, which the Portuguese named the Rio do Ouro, the River of Gold. Merchants now began to apply to Henrique for license to trade in Africa. The historian Marc Bloch, in a celebrated article on gold, argued that the chronic shortage of monetary metals was the most powerful incentive to European expansion.

The slowness of discovery to this point was due to several problems. The desert shore was inhospitable. Reefs extended from the capes and safe landing points were rare. More significantly, wind and current – the Canary Current – favored an outward passage to the southwest but at the same time, it seemed, blocked any easy return or possibly any return at all. The solution, discovered no doubt by accident, was the *volta do mar*, "return by the sea" – sailing northwest out to sea until finding a westerly wind that brought one home. The Canaries, Madeira or finally the Azores would welcome returning mariners, prevent them from going too far like a wide net and allow refreshment and refitting before the final leg home. However, such voyages into the open sea required sturdier ships than barchas. In the 1440s, caravels came into regular use. They were larger and safer than barchas – about fifty tons and sixty to seventy feet long – but still fast, highly maneuverable, drew little water and required only a small crew. Constructed with full decking and a skeleton-first form of construction, caravels could better withstand Atlantic squalls. The Sicilian Nicolò Scillacio in 1494 referred to caravels as "rather small ships, but strong enough for long, rough sailing." With one or two masts with triangular sails called lateen rigging, they could more easily sail into the wind. When provided with an additional square main sail, the *caravela redounda*, as the fully rigged ship was called, became the ideal vessel for long and uncertain exploratory voyages.

The most fruitful expeditions to Africa started in the 1440s. As ships sailed further south, they found local markets to buy gold dust and people they could capture as slaves. With the lure of greater profits, Henrique sent more expeditions and licensed private traders to sail to Africa. Arguim Bay was reached in 1443 – two years later, a trading house was erected on a barren island offshore, the first on the mainland – and the Senegal River – the real river of gold – two years later. The Portuguese were now clearly in the "land of the blacks," which some called "lower Ethiopia." A papal bull in 1442, the first of many, granted Portugal exclusive rights over its African discoveries. By 1448, more than fifty ships had ventured beyond Bojador and nearly a thousand African captives had been taken back to Portugal or to the Atlantic Mediterranean for sale. By the 1550s, the gold trade was in full flourish and some trading ventures brought 800 percent profit (although Henrique himself lost money and accumulated a substantial debt). By Henrique's death in 1460, his ships had discovered the Cape Verde Islands and reached as far south as Sierra Leone on the coast. It was divinely revealed to Prince Henrique, wrote Duarte Pacheco Pereira in the early sixteenth century and who sailed in African waters for the Portuguese, "that in these lands so much gold and other rich merchandise would be found as would maintain the King and people of these realms of Portugal in plenty and would enable them to wage war on the enemies of our Holy Catholic Faith."

In the 1440s, Portuguese mariners and traders began to barter for slaves instead of kidnapping them. Slavery was nearly a universal African custom and a slave trade, across the Sahara, already existed. Muslim merchants and local African rulers accepted cloth, silver, grain and horses in exchange for captives. However, the stateless societies on the coast generally did not trade in people. During the 1450s, at least an additional one thousand Africans were enslaved and sent to Portugal and the Atlantic Mediterranean. Soon thereafter a black community, the Brotherhood of the Virgin of the Rosary, was present in Lisbon. Almost from the beginning, some Portuguese in Africa "went native," joined African societies and took African wives. They and their mulatto offspring, together called *lançados*, became essential middlemen in the slave and other trades.

The first good description of the "land of the blacks" came from the pen of a Venetian merchant, Alvise de C'a da Mosto, called Cadamosto, who made two voyages to Africa in the 1450s and wrote about them and Henry's discoveries in his *Navigazioni Atlabtucge*. On the coast, he found small states and he learned of the great empires of Songhay and Mali located in the interior. Beyond the Senegal, he wrote, "the people should be extremely black, tall, and have large well-formed bodies, and the country is green, fertile, and heavily timbered." He was less impressed with African (Wolof, in this case) culture. The people he noted were poor, badly dressed and lived in straw huts. Their rulers were haughty and abusive.

In 1456, Cadamosto sailed to the Gambia River and met Buttimansa, a tributary lord of the Emperor of Mali. Through a translator, he gave a present to the lord. "The interpreter went with the negro to this lord, and in brief, we treated so with him that when we parted from him we had not only secured his friendship, but had bartered many articles, for which we had received in exchange negro slaves and a certain quantity of gold..." Cadamosto realized that friendship in Africa was the key to any business relationship. "We remained here about fifteen days, and in this time many negroes dwelling on a part of the border of this river came to our ships – some to gaze upon a site so strange to them; others to sell some trifle of theirs, or little rings of gold. The articles they brought were cotton cloth and thread, cotton cloths woven in their fashion, some white, others variegated, white and blue striped, or red, blue, and white, excellently made."

The early sixteenth-century chronicler Durate Pacheco Pereira in *Esmeraldo de Situ Orbis* described only barbarians, cannibals and idolaters. "The negroes of all this coast [West Africa] are naked and are not circumcised, and they are idolaters," wrote Pacheco Pereira. "Sometimes these negroes eat one another, but this is less usual here than in other parts of Ethiopia; they are all idolaters and sorcerers and are ruled by witchcraft, placing implicit faith in oracles and omens...It is possible to buy slaves here...but it is necessary to be on guard against the negroes of this country for they are very evil people and attack our ships." Modern historians and anthropologists seriously doubt that Atlantic Africans were ever cannibals, and recognize that their native religious systems were complex systems of belief and ritual, not the demonized *feitiço*, or witchcraft, as perceived by the Portuguese.

By the time of Henrique's death in 1460, it was clear that his, and Portugal's, persistence had paid off. The Atlantic Mediterranean's sugar and African trade was quite profitable. However, further advance down the African coast still required royal leadership.

2.6 From Guinea to the Cape of Good Hope

For a time after Henrique's death, the Portuguese lost interest in advancing further along the African coast. Trade in gold and slaves had been established and the trading post and fort at Arguim Island was prospering. Royal intervention on behalf of exploration was required.

In 1469, the king awarded (sold, in fact) African trading rights to Fernão Gomes with the proviso that he explore 100 leagues (a Portuguese league was about four miles) of "new" coastline a year. He met his obligation, and then some. As a result of his voyages, by the mid-1470s the Portuguese had explored the entire Guinea coast, from Sierra Leone to the Bight of Benin, and the islands in the Gulf of Guinea: Fernando Po, O Príncipé and São Tomé. Gomes first made his money on the Grain Coast, today Liberia, where he exported malaguetta pepper, "grains of paradise," a cheaper substitute for the real thing. Further east, he found the Ivory Coast where this "white gold" was traded. About halfway across the Gulf of Guinea was the "Costa da Mina" or Gold Coast, modern Ghana, where the gold fields of the Akan forest were and are today located. East of the Gold Coast, now Benin and Nigeria, came the "five slave rivers" region, later called the Slave Coast. It was here where the Portuguese purchased African slaves for sale to African Dyula merchants to be used on the Gold Coast for clearing forestlands, carrying goods and other arduous tasks. The Portuguese sold more than ten thousand slaves to the Dyula between 1500 and 1535. In the early sixteenth century, the Portuguese chronicler Duarte Pacheco Pereira noted:

> In all this country along the coast there is a certain amount of gold, for which we barter bloodstones, yellow and green beads, tin, linen, brass bracelets, red cloth and basins such as barbers use, and we obtain many slaves here in exchange for such merchandise.

The opening of the Guinea coast was of tremendous importance to Portugal. The Portuguese had now begun to outflank Arab and Ottoman traders and the Muslim world. In 1479, the crown refused to renew Gomes' contract so it could directly monopolize trade with Africa. Over the next few decades, the Portuguese on the Gold Coast would divert one-third to one-half of the gold dust from the trans-Saharan caravan trade. By the end of the century, more than twenty thousand ounces of gold annually was carried to Lisbon. The gold Portuguese Cruzado was welcomed throughout Europe. One quarter of the monarchy's revenue derived from the gold trade. Pepper, ivory and especially slaves also made money for the king and Portuguese merchants. In the second half of the fifteenth century, the Portuguese purchased more than one hundred thousand Africans; prior to the discovery of the Americas, the Atlantic slave trade was beginning to compete with the Islamic world's slave trade. Portuguese captains also profited from carrying merchandise and slaves from one African coast to another. The monarchy kept for itself a monopoly on the importing of gold, slaves, ivory and malaguetta pepper, although private trades slipped through the official net. Foreign merchants followed Portuguese expansion: the Genoese, Florentines, Flemish and others.

The diversion of gold to the coast most likely weakened the first Songhay Empire. This polity stood at the crossroads of trade between the forest and the desert. Less gold meant less foreign exchange to buy imports from Maghrib, particularly horses to supply the empire's cavalry, leading to conquest by desert Tuaregs. Elsewhere, Portuguese trade had the opposite effect. In the Senegambia, the Portuguese bought slaves from the Wolof in exchange for horses. Cadamosto noted that the Wolof chiefs had few horses. However, by the end of the century a European observer stated that the Wolof Empire had a cavalry of ten thousand horsemen. Overall, the Portuguese presence on most African polities in the region was negligible or nil.

The discovery and settlement of the islands in the Gulf of Guinea, Fernando Po, O Príncipe and São Tomé, permitted the Portuguese to expand the Madeira model of commercial agriculture. The plantation complex (which combined the expensive technology of the sugar mill with the labor of African slaves and merchant investment and marketing) was transferred to these islands and proved very successful. By the beginning of the sixteenth century, São Tomé had replaced Madeira as Europe's greatest sugar supplier.

In 1479, at the conclusion of Gomes's contract, the trading concession for the islands and the African coast were awarded to the crown prince, the Infante Dom João. When he became João II in 1481, Portugal had a king who was particularly interested in Africa. His first move was to construct a fortified *feitoria*, a trading factory, on the Gold Coast, São Jorge da Mina, later simply called Elmina Castle. This fort was designed not simply to funnel the gold trade to the Portuguese but also, and perhaps primarily, to monopolize it and defend Portuguese traders against Castilian and any other European interlopers.

The construction of the castle meant that trade ships no longer had to wait offshore for weeks or months waiting for African traders to meet them. "Through this fortress," wrote Pacheco Pereira, "trade so greatly increased by the favor of Our Lord that 170,000 doubloons of good fine gold, and sometimes much more, are yearly brought thence to these realms of Portugal; it is bartered from the negro merchants who bring it thither from distant lands . . . " He continued: "We barter cloth, brass, shells, wine, beads . . . our people buy slaves 200 leagues beyond, by rivers and a city called Beny where they are brought to Mina." Although the local ruler on this coast preferred the existing arrangement with what he called the "ragged and ill dressed men," he agreed after some bargaining to the building and operation of the São Jorge castle. "After all," concluded Cadamosto, "if such close neighbors prove inconvenient, the forest is wide and a new village can easily be built elsewhere." In Lisbon, the king set up the Casa da Mina de Guiné, the Guinea Mina House, a regulatory agency that registered all ships that sailed to Africa, acquired the trade goods sent to Africa, warehoused the returning cargoes and collected the crown's revenues. João II then gave himself the title, "Lord of Guinea."

João also hired mariners to lead expeditions of pure discovery. The verb "to discover," *descobrir*, first came into use in the 1470s and 1480s in Portugal. Until this time, it is uncertain whether the Portuguese expeditions had any greater object than to find the sources of the Sudanese gold and, perhaps, to locate the fabled Christian king Prebyter Johannes, Prester John, who would become (it was feverently hoped) an ally against the Ottoman Turks. By the 1480s it was clear that João now sought a passage around Africa into the Indian Ocean. During that decade, the monarchy sponsored expeditions led by Diogo Cão, who explored an additional 1,450 miles of coastline. He carried stone markers in the form of a cross, *padrãoes*, to give notice of Portugal's discoveries. Inscribed on each *padrão* was the announcement, "King João II of Portugal did order this land to be discovered." Cão found the Congo River, at first named Rio Poderoso, "the powerful river" (today the Zaire), and made contact with the Kingdom of Kongo. Its ruler, Nzinga Nkuwu, sent an emissary to the Portuguese king and, in turn, the Portuguese sent missionaries to Kongo. During his second voyage, Cão sailed to a cape on the Namibian coast that he probably believed was the Promontorium

Passum, the point of separation between the Indian Ocean and the Atlantic. After this voyage, the Portuguese envoy to the Vatican stated that Portuguese ships would soon enter the Indian Ocean and find Prester John.

In 1486, João sent João Afonso Aveiro to the Kingdom of Benin. He visited the "great city of Benin," which impressed him, and met the Oba, or king, Ozulua. In Benin, he learned of a great ruler named Ogané, a powerful king and spiritual leader, who could be found 300 leagues to the east. Could this be Prester John? The seriousness of the Portuguese interest in Prester John is demonstrated, among other actions, by the king's preparation some years later of one thousand catechisms as a present to the mythical Christian monarch. In 1487, João dispatched two expeditions out into the world to find Prester John and India. The first was by land: Afonso de Pavia and Pero da Covilhã were directed to find the sources of the spices, and determine if Prester John could help Portugal find the land of the spices. Pavia disappeared on a journey to Ethiopia, whereas Covilhã reached India (and eventually Ethiopia) and sent a report of his findings to Portugal. (It is unknown if that report actually reached the Portuguese court.) second expedition was by sea.: Bartolomeu Dias was given three ships and ordered to round the African continent (see Map 2.4).

The "conquest" of the South Atlantic was an enormous triumph. In 1537, Pedro Nunes commented: "The sea voyages of this kingdom over the last hundred years are greater and more marvelous... than those of any other people in the world. The Portuguese dared to venture fearlessly into the great ocean sea." They also pioneered the caravel and nautical charts. Portolan Charts, Italian *portolani*, perhaps of Roman origin, became more developed and widespread in medieval Italy for Mediterranean navigation. In the fifteenth and sixteenth centuries, secret Portuguese charts superior to Italian *portolani* were guiding ships in African and Asian waters. The magnetic compass, invented by the Chinese, brought west by Moslems and improved by fourteenth-century Italians, was vital to the Portuguese. However, in the South Atlantic pilots discovered that the compass needle pointed away from true north. This reality, called magnetic variation, required the application of other tools. Most important of all was their development of the science of nautical astronomy based on Arab and Jewish scholarship. Jewish astronomers and scientists expelled from or repelled by Castile found a good reception in medieval Portugal, and translated Arabic texts and worked on their own astronomical and mathematical problems. The advantage Portuguese mariners had over all other European mariners was their ability to use the stars and the sun to determine their position on land and at sea. By the time the Portuguese crossed the equator in the 1470s, they were regularly using a land astrolabe to measure the height of the midday sun and therefore their latitude. It was not quite that simple, however. Trigonometric equations were required to calculate the sun's declination for each day during a four-year period. These calculations were translated into latitudes, organized into tables and placed in a handbook printed around 1484 called *Regimento do astrolabio*, or *Rules for the Astrolabe*. Quoting Pedro Nunes again: "It is evident that the discoveries of coasts, islands, continents, has not occurred

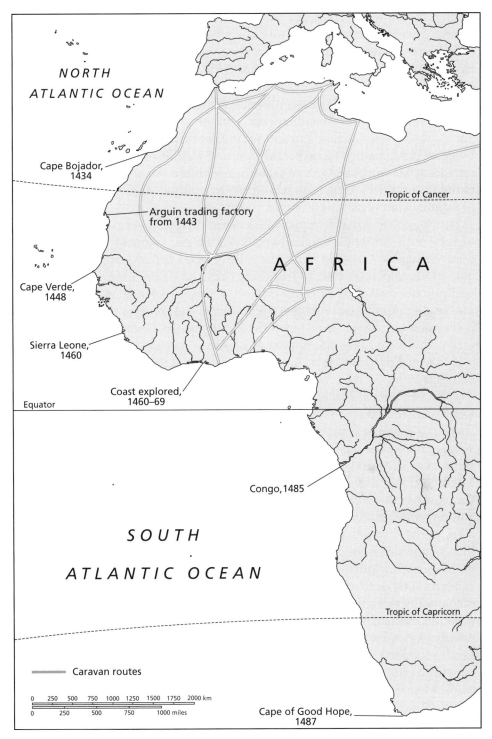

Map 2.4. The Portuguese Voyages.

by chance, but to the contrary, our sailors have departed very well informed, provided with instruments and rules of astronomy and geometry."

Sailing the coast of Africa south of the equator was as difficult as returning from Guinea along the coast of North Africa. The South East Trades blow north along the coast of central and South Africa. In both cases, the solution was to sail out to sea, far beyond sight of land, in order to find winds and a current moving in the direction needed. In the case of the South Atlantic, the South Equatorial Current and the Westerlies flow and blow south from the bulge of Brazil. A bold mariner who turned west at the Cape Verde Islands, instead of east into the Gulf of Guinea, could find the winds and currents to take him south. However, he would be deep in the Atlantic Ocean and out of sight of land possibly for months.

Dias was such a mariner. How he learned this maneuver, the *volta do mar* of the South Atlantic, is unknown. Nevertheless, south of the Congo, at a point he named Capo da Volta, he sailed out to sea and caught the current and winds that took him south. Eventually, he came upon westerly winds and ran east and then northeast. When he sighted land, he was 250 miles east of the Cape of Good Hope. He followed the coast to the northeast and realized he was on the doorstep of the Indian Ocean. Under pressure from his crew, who were homesick and worried about supplies, Dias turned around and returned to Lisbon in 1489 with the news that the two great oceans were connected.

João then directed Dias to build two new ships for an expedition to India. Confusion regarding the voyage of Columbus in 1492, the king's death in 1495 and perhaps waiting for a report from Covihlã delayed the follow-up voyage. João's successor, Manoel I, gave command of an expedition of four ships, two *nãos* and two caravels, to Vasco da Gama. This small fleet left Lisbon in 1497 and at the Cape Verde Islands turned west and out to sea. Da Gama made the *volta do mar*, caught the winds and current heading south and remained at sea for four months. It was the longest oceanic passage yet made in the Atlantic. He rounded the Cape, sailed into the Indian Ocean and then north along the coast of East Africa. At the African port of Malindi, he took on an Indian pilot who directed him across the Indian Ocean to Calicut. Da Gama returned to Lisbon in 1499, after a voyage of 28,000 miles, with spices and knowledge of the Indian Ocean. Manoel, adding to his titles in anticipation of a glorious future, now became "lord of the conquest, navigation and commerce of Ethiopia, Arabia, Persia and India." Pacheco Pereira summed up this amazing discovery: "Our own predecessors and those who lived even earlier in other countries could never believe that a time would come when our West would be made known to the East and to India as it now is."

During the years when the South Atlantic was opened, the Portuguese established themselves all along the Atlantic coast of Africa. This was a trading empire modeled on that of the Venetians and the Genoese in the Mediterranean and Black Sea. Small enclaves of traders and officials dotted the coast from Arguim to Angola. The Portuguese generally did not impose themselves upon Africans; rather, they inserted themselves into existing trading networks and political relationships. The Portuguese were interested in

Figure 2.2. Map of the Portuguese Discoveries in Africa in the Fifteenth and Sixteenth Centuries. Title page from Fracanzano da Montalboddo, *Itinerarivm Portugallensium ex Vlisbona I Indiam* (Milan, 1508). Courtesy of the William L. Clements Library at the University of Michigan.

African societies and wanted to do business with African merchants and kings. Africans had similar interests.

In 1486 King Bemoin, ruler of one of the Wolof kingdoms on the Senegal, petitioned the Portuguese for assistance in a succession dispute. João agreed to help in return for the conversion of Bemoin to Christianity and the friendly reception of missionaries. This affair turned out badly for Bemoin but showed how easily Europeans became involved in African politics. At the invitation of the African king, the Portuguese also became involved in the Kingdom of Kongo. João sent missionaries, craftsmen, masons and farmers to teach the Kongolese European ways. At the Kongo capital of M'banza Kongo, they began to build a town of stone called São Salvador. In 1491, King Nzinga Nkuwu was baptized King João I and several Kongo noblemen followed his example. Portugal's João recognized his counterpart as an ally and brother in arms. African princes and nobles from various kingdoms were welcomed at court in Lisbon, and ambassadors were exchanged whenever possible. It would seem both the Portuguese and the Africans welcomed closer relations and ties of friendship (see Document 2.3).

In the Senegal and the Congo, and many points in between, Portuguese officials and merchants traded with African rulers and merchants. The Portuguese generally had to negotiate treaties with the local ruler and pay some form of tribute to do business. The power of African states, as well as the deadliness of African diseases, kept Europeans away from the interior and on

---

Document 2.3
Of the Original Beginning of Christendom in the Kingdom of Congo, and How the Portuguese Obtained This Traffic

Duarte Lopes, 1588

The K. of Portugal Don Gionanni, the second, being desirous to discover the East Indies, sent forth divers ships by the coast of Africa to search out this Navigation, who having found the Islands of Cape Verde, and the Isle of Saint Thomas, and running all along the coast, did light upon the River Zaire, whereof we have made mention before, and there they had good traffic, and tried the people to be very courteous and kind. Afterwards he sent forth (for the same purpose) certain other vessels, to entertain this traffic with Congo, who finding the trade there to be so free and profitable, and the people so friendly, left certain Portuguese behind them, to learn the language and to traffic with them: among whom one was a Mass-priest. These Portuguese conversing familiarly with the Lord of Sogno, who was Uncle to the King, and a man well up there in years, dwelling at that time in the Port of Praza (which is in the mouth of Zaire) were very well entertained and esteemed by the Prince, and reverenced as though they had been earthly Gods, and descended down from heaven into those Countries. But the Portuguese told them that they were men as themselves were, and professors of Christianity. And when they perceived in how great estimation the people held them, the foresaid Priest and others began to reason with the Prince touching the Christian religion, and to show unto them the errors of the Pagan superstition, and by little and little to teach them the faith which we possess, insomuch as that which the Portuguese spoke unto them, greatly pleased the Prince, and so he became converted.

With this confidence and good spirit, the prince of Sogno went to the Court to inform the King of the true doctrine of the Christian Portuguese, and to encourage him that he would embrace the Christian Religion which was so manifest, and also so wholesome for his soul's health. Hereupon the king commanded to call the Priest to Court, to the end he might himself treat with him personally, and understand the truth of that which the Lord of Sogno had declared unto him. Whereof when he was fully informed, he converted and promised that he would become a Christian.

And now the Portuguese ships departed from Congo, and returned to Portugal: and by them did the King of Congo write to the King of Portugal, Don Gionanni the second, with earnest request, that he would send him some Priests, with all other orders and ceremonies to make him a Christian. The Priest also that remained behind had written at large touching this business, and gave the King full information of all that had happened, agreeable to his good pleasure. And so the King took order for sundry religious persons to be send unto him accordingly, with all ornaments for the Church and other service, as Crosses and Images: so that he was thoroughly furnished with all things that were necessary and needful for such an action.

At the last the ships of Portugal arrived with the expected provisions (which was in the year of our salvation 1491) and landed in the port which is in the mouth of the River Zaire. The Prince of Sogno, with all show of familiar joy, accompanied with all his gentlemen ran down to meet them, and entertained the Portuguese in most courteous manner, and so conducted them to their lodgings. The next day following according to the direction of the Priest that remained behind, the Prince caused a kind of Church to be built, with the bodies and branches of certain trees, which he in his own person, with the help of his servants, most devoutly had felled in the wood. And when it was covered, they erected therein three Altars, in the worship and reverence of the most holy Trinity, and there was baptized himself and his young son, himself by the name of our Savior, Emanuel, and his child by the name of Anthonie, because that Saint is the Protector of the City of Lisbon.

Duarte Lopes, a Portuguese New Christian (converted Jew) served as the ambassador of the Kingdom of Kongo to the Pope in Rome. Lopes endeavored to convince the Vatican that Kongo was a Christian kingdom. The humanist Filippo Pigafetta interviewed Lopes in Rome and published this account in 1591. *Source: A Reporte of the Kingdome of Congo, a Region of Africa, and of the Countries that Border Rounde about the Same.* Drawn out of the writings and discourses of Odordo Lopes, a Portingal, by Philippo Pigafetta. Translated out of Italian by Abraham Hartwell (1597), pp. 118–21.

the coast and the islands in the Gulf of Guinea. For the first time, West and Central Africa was brought into direct contact with Europe. Europeans at first generally approached Africans as equals and partners, and Africans did the same. "Professional merchants could be found in every part of Atlantic Africa," writes John Thornton. "They often formed communities that settled in towns under their own government and linked in networks that Philip Curtin has dubbed a 'trading Diaspora.'"

2.7 Islands and Mainland

As the Portuguese established themselves on the Atlantic coast of Africa and opened the door to the Indian Ocean, they and other Europeans anticipated additional discoveries in the great western ocean. It was widely believed the islands of the Atlantic Mediterranean constituted only some of the many islands of the ocean. Maps and legends referred specifically to Saint Brendan's Isle, Brazil, St. Ursula, Antillia and the Seven Cities and, not so specifically, to islands "not yet discovered." Marco Polo had reported that 1,378 islands lay off the coast of Asia. There surely were islands to the west, and Europeans looked for them.

The port of Bristol, England, and the Portuguese Azores were in the forefront of western exploration. In 1480, a ship set sail from Bristol in search of the "Insulam de Brasylie," the mythical island of Brazil. For nine months, this expedition looked for Brazil, the "Land of the Promise of the Blessed," an Eden long believed to exist west of Ireland. The following year, a second expedition continued the search and, like the first, found only endless ocean and variable winds. Other voyages from Bristol, unrecorded ones, have long been assumed to be made.Some English patriots and scholars have argued that one or more of these voyages must have discovered North America. Between 1462 and 1487, at least eight Portuguese voyages were commissioned to discover new islands in the Atlantic, including Antillia. Three or four of these were by the Genoese merchant Luca de Cazana, who sailed west from the Azores. In 1483 or 1484, an obscure Genoese mariner and mapmaker petitioned João II to finance a venture to sail west and discover the island of Cipango (Japan) and the Antilles. There were others of the same nature. Fernão d'Ulmo, captain of the Azores from the island of Terceira, proposed in 1486 to find "a large island or islands or mainland which is presumed to be the Island of the Seven Cities." João gave his consent and according to one contemporary observer, the voyage was undertaken and it failed.

When Bartolomeu Dias returned from the Cape of Good Hope in 1488, the Portuguese crown had little incentive to continue looking west. However, the kingdom of Castile, prohibited from any further expeditions to Africa (and, by inference, to the south and east) by the Treaty of Alcácovas of 1479, was interested. In the early 1490s, Castile was concluding the conquest of the remaining Canary Islands and Granada, the last Muslim kingdom in Iberia. The fall of Granada would spell the end of that kingdom's tribute in gold to Castile, as well as the end of the *Reconquista* in Iberia. When the monarchs of Castile and Aragon were approached with a proposal for discoveries to the west, they were receptive.

The salesman for such a venture was that obscure Genoese mariner and mapmaker who had earlier approached the Portuguese, Cristoforo Colombo, known as Cristóbal Colón in Spain and Christopher Columbus to us. Columbus was a man with a mission or, as he put it, an "enterprise." He believed he was divinely appointed to open a direct ocean route to Cathay and Cipango (China and Japan) in the Indies, which today we call Asia. He was an experienced sailor in the Mediterranean and the Atlantic. He had sailed to England and quite possibly Iceland in the North Atlantic and Elmina in the South Atlantic, and was quite familiar with Madeira and the Atlantic Mediterranean. He first took his proposal to Portugal, where it was rejected. In Castile he found, after some frustration and delay, royal patronage.

Columbus had a theory that made a voyage across the ocean from Europe to the Indies feasible. His son wrote much later that his father's ideas came from "natural reasons, the authority of writers, and the testimony of sailors." Conventional geographical understanding assumed that the ocean was far too wide to permit any crossing. Columbus's eccentric theory comprised three arguments in favor of a navigable ocean. The first was that the land area of the world was larger than most scholars believed. This meant that Asia extended further east into the ocean and therefore was closer to Europe. The second was that the circumference of the earth was smaller than generally believed. The length of a degree of longitude was shorter, which reduced the width of the ocean. The third accepted Marco Polo's claim that Cipango, or Japan, lay 1,500 miles off the coast of Asia, and thus 1,500 miles closer to Europe, and was among many hundreds of other islands extending far into the ocean. Therefore, according to Columbus's calculations the distance from the Canary Islands to Japan was approximately only 2,400 nautical miles.

Learned commissions considered Columbus's theory in Portugal and Castile and both rejected it. Although his view was unconventional, it was not unheard of. The Florentine geographer Paolo dal Posso Toscanelli, in a letter to the Portuguese king in 1474, maintained that Hangchow on the coast of China was five thousand miles west of Lisbon. Martin Behaim's globe of 1492 pictured the world, and most notably the narrow ocean, as Toscanelli described it and as Columbus theorized. There is some evidence to suggest that Columbus corresponded with Toscanelli. As it turned out, the conventional view was correct. The distance between Portugal and Japan is 10,600 nautical miles, or more than four times the distance calculated by Columbus. However, the distance between the Canaries and the Bahaman islands is approximately what Columbus expected for a voyage to Cipango.

The monarchs of Castile and Aragón, Isabel and Fernando, agreed to authorize and sponsor a voyage of discovery by Columbus immediately after the fall of Granada in 1492. They never explained their reasons, but they must have been impressed by the passion and self-confidence of Columbus. Castile and Portugal had long been competitive in near-Atlantic ventures, and for a time in Africa. Their Catholic Majesties must have been concerned by and envious of Portugal's imminent entrance into the Indian Ocean. Columbus

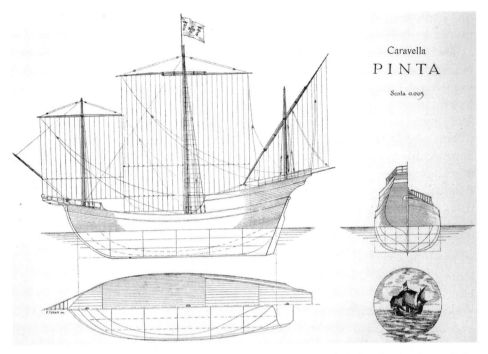

Figure 2.3. A Careful but Imaginative Reconstruction of Columbus's Caravel *La Pinta. Caravella Pinta* (The Caravel La Pinta). From Enrico Alberto d'Albertis, *Le construzioni navali e l'arte navigazione al tempo di Cristoforo Colombo* (Rome, 1893). Courtesy of the William L. Clements Library at the University of Michigan.

offered the possibility of access to the Indies, its riches and trade, or at least additional islands as valuable as the Canaries.

Columbus received his royal commission and was given command of a small fleet of two caravels and one não. All three were small vessels, typical merchant ships. By the late fifteenth century, fully rigged caravels were widely used by the Portuguese and the Castilians. Larger ships called carracks or nãos had come into service as cargo ships in the now-routine African and Atlantic Mediterranean trade. Compared to the sleek caravel, a carrack or não was a larger rounded ship with a high forecastle, a smaller castle in the rear and a deeply cut waist between them. Like the caravela redonda, a carrack or não was fully rigged with three masts and a combination of square and lateen sails. According to Peter Martyr, Columbus received three ships: "one a cargo ship, with a crow's nest, the other two light merchant ships, without crow's nests, which the Spaniards call caravels."

With the royal commission came a negotiated agreement, the Capitulaciones de Santa Fe. The contract between Columbus and the Catholic Monarchs specified that the mariner was setting out at their command "to discover and acquire certain islands and mainland in the Ocean Sea." In return for his services and a successful expedition, the monarchs promised, you "shall be Our Admiral of the said islands and mainland so discovered by you, and shall be Our Viceroy and Governor therein, and shall be entitled to style yourself Don Cristóbal Colón." The expedition cost around two million maravedís, the equivalent of the annual income of a minor landed noble, a substantial but not extravagant sum. Most of the cost was covered by the monarchs – who in turn received the money from interested gentlemen at their court – while Columbus put up half a million maravedis, no doubt borrowed from the Genoese merchant community of Seville. The port of Palos on the gulf of Cadiz was required to contribute two caravels, crews and provisions for four months.

When Columbus set sail in the fall of 1492, he was attempting something that others had tried before. One resident of Palos expected the same outcome as earlier voyages to the west: "There was no land in that part of the world," he stated, "because it had been sought from Portugal many times." If Columbus had set sail from the Azores or even Madeira, he likely would have encountered variable winds and Westerlies, and would have failed as had earlier Azorean voyages. However, by leaving from the southern latitude of the Canary Islands, Columbus caught the prevailing northeast trade winds, which carried him across the ocean at its widest point in thirty-three days. He could not have asked for a better point of departure or a smoother crossing.

For three months, Columbus explored the Caribbean, which he considered an archipelago lying off the coast of Asia. He suspected that Cuba was Cipango. On Christmas Day, he lost one of his ships on a reef off the north coast of the island he named La Isla Española, which came to be called Hispaniola. This island, like the others he found, possessed no sophisticated cities or rich trading ports. Their residents, "Indians," so called by Columbus who thought he was in the Indies somewhere, were unaccountably poor. If these islands were in the Indies, they must be on a distant periphery. According to the Columbus chroniclers Peter Martyr (Pietro Martire d' Anghiera) and Sebastian Münster, the natives of the main islands were tormented by warlike people who arrived in large canoes. According to Münster, these people were "called Canibales or Anthropoghagi, which are accustomed to eat men's flesh." Martyr distinguished the natives of the Caribbean between "these meek and human people" and "the wild and mischievous people called Canibales, or *Caribes*, which were accustomed to eat mans flesh." One discovery made everything worthwhile: the native people of Hispaniola possessed ornaments of gold. Martyr wrote: "Here they found gold, but in no great quantity, not yet that pure. They make of it, certain breast plates and brooches, which they wear for comeliness." However, as far as Columbus was concerned, he could return to Spain claiming he had found the riches of the Indies.

Columbus's first voyage demonstrated how the opening of the Atlantic was a matter of skill and accident as well as learning by trial and error. Departure from the Canaries was perhaps a great inspiration by a close observer of the ocean. Years and perhaps decades before the 1492 voyage, Portuguese marines had sailed west from the Azores to discover nothing, as far as we know, most likely because of winds from the west that prevented any real progress. By beginning his journey much further south in the Canary islands, Columbus picked up the Trade Winds heading west. The return trip revealed a mariner who was learning as he was going. He first plotted a direct course to Spain and ran into the contrary Trade Winds. After fighting headwinds for some days, he took his ships farther north and found the Westerlies that took them to the Azores, Lisbon and then home to Palos. His return on the second voyage encountered a similar problem and solution. Columbus eventually learned the location of the Westerlies, although discovery of the Gulf Stream, and an even swifter return, had to wait for the pilot of Juan Ponce de León two decades later.

Once Columbus had returned, the Catholic Monarchs sought papal recognition of their discoveries and a monopoly of navigation, trade and settlement similar to Portugal's monopoly in Africa. The Pope, Alexander VI Borja, a Spanish Pope, granted Castile all it requested, dominion forever over "all islands and mainland found and to be found, discovered and to be discovered towards the west and south." Of course, this vague grant ran into Portuguese objection. The Portuguese wanted to preserve their monopoly in Africa and their expected and exclusive passage to the Indian Ocean, and they immediately opened direct negotiation with Castile. The Treaty of Tordesillas of 1494, the result of those negotiations, divided the undiscovered pagan world between the two Iberian kingdoms. By this treaty, a line of demarcation from pole to pole was set 370 leagues west of the Cape Verde Islands: "all lands, both islands and mainlands . . . on the eastern side of the said line . . . shall belong to, and remain in the possession of, and pertain forever to, the said King of Portugal and his successors." Portugal's claims in Africa and the South Atlantic were confirmed while Castile's discoveries in the west were recognized (see Map 2.5).

Columbus returned in triumph to Castile, although the rest of Europe paid little attention and, when attention was given, granted little significance to his discoveries. The Portuguese considered that the long awaited Antillia had been found and therefore named the islands As Antilhas, "the Antilles." More islands in the ocean, even if they were near some region of Asia, were hardly a revolutionary discovery in the eyes of many geographers of the day and the Portuguese. To the Italian fellow-Ligurian Michele da Cuneo, who had sailed with Columbus, the new "lord admiral" was a great man. Writing to a Savonese nobleman in 1495, he stated: "But one thing I want you to know is that, in my humble opinion, since Genoa was Genoa there has never been a man so courageous and astute in the act of navigation as the lord admiral, for, when sailing, by simply observing a cloud or a star at night, he judged what was to come, if there was to be bad weather. He himself commanded and stood at the helm."

Columbus made three more voyages to his Indies. The second voyage (1493–6) was a big production: seventeen ships, 1,500 people and enough seed and stock to plant a self-sufficient colony in the Canarian model. The third and fourth voyages were based on the assumption that there was no short cut to Japan and China, and therefore he would have to search for a passage to them much further south and west. The third voyage (1497–1500) sailed on the latitude of the Cape Verde Islands and discovered the northern coast of South America. When Columbus saw the muddy flow of the Orinoco

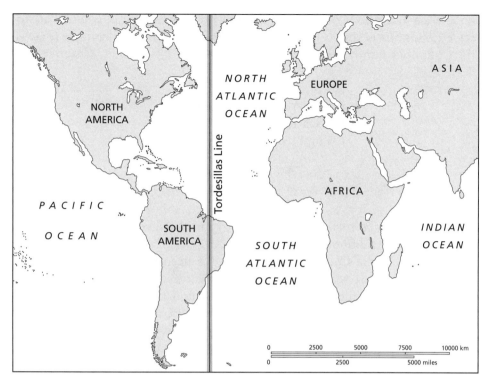

Map 2.5. The Tordesillas Line in the Atlantic.

River into the Atlantic, he realized he had found more than another island: "I believe this is a very large continent," he wrote in his journal, "which until now has remained unknown." The fourth voyage (1502–4) looked for a passage along the Caribbean coast of Central America from Honduras to Panama. This voyage ended badly when Columbus was stranded in Jamaica for a year due to worm-eaten and unseaworthy vessels until he and his crew were rescued.

In Jamaica, Columbus wrote to Fernando and Isabel and summed up his life's work. He told the monarchs that in a dream or vision he heard a voice that told him: "The Indies, which are so rich a part of the world, He [God] gave thee for thine own... Of the barriers of the Ocean Sea, which were closed with such mighty chains, He gave thee the keys; and thos wast obeyed in many lands and among Christians thou hast gained an honorable fame."

Columbus returned to Castile for the last time the same year his patroness, Queen Isabel, died. He was a fairly rich man, although one who felt unjustly under-rewarded and underappreciated. He died in 1506 at the age of fifty-four years, and his death passed almost unnoticed. To the end he still believed, as did many of his contemporaries, that he had taken Castile to the backside of Asia. However, additional voyages across the ocean during Columbus's lifetime added more information to a cloudy picture of the new discoveries. Piece by piece, mariners, geographers and cartographers came to discount the prevailing view and to envision a new world and a new ocean. An inscription on a stone in the floor of the main nave of Seville's cathedral, where Christopher Columbus is supposedly buried, reveals the mariner's epitaph (that is, the Columbus family's epitaph). It reads:

> *A Castilla y León*
> *Nuevo Mundo dio Colón*
> (To Castile and León
> Columbus gave the New World).

2.8 A New World and a New Ocean

After 1492, a race to find the passage to the "civilized" countries of Asia began. Despite Columbus' contractual monopoly of trade and navigation in the Ocean Sea, the Catholic Monarchs gave licenses to Spanish mariners, most of whom were former shipmates of Columbus, to explore to the west. Alonso de Ojeda sailed to the Guiana coast and the Gulf of Venezuela of South America in 1499. He found villages on stilts, which to him seemed like a "little Venice" hispanicized as Venezuela. The same year, Vicente Yáñez Pinzón came upon the Amazon River, which he believed might be the Ganges. Juan de la Cosa sailed to the "Pearl Coast," which had been discovered by Ojeda, to find profit. These and other "minor voyages," as Martín Fernandez de Navarrete called them, were financed by merchant ship-owners of Seville who now began to send vessels to the Indies every year seeking gold, pearls, slaves and other valuables.

Vicente Yáñez Pinzón, who accompanied Columbus on his first voyage, sailed in 1499 with four caravels from the Cape Verde Islands. He made the most southern crossing yet and discovered the bulge of Brazil. He sailed up the Amazon some distance before heading for the familiar Caribbean. Two additional Spanish voyages went to Brazil in 1500, a busy place that year. The French entered the picture with a voyage in 1504 (see Map 2.6).

In 1500, Portugal dispatched a large expedition to follow the successful voyage of Vasco da Gama to India. Commanded by Pedro Álvares Cabral, this fleet followed the now nearly standard maneuver of sailing out to sea near the Cape Verde Islands until finding a southward blowing and flowing wind and current, the famous *volta* of the South Atlantic. Cabral made the *volta* and sailed so far west that he came upon the coast of Brazil south of the bulge, close to the present city of Salvador. He assumed it was an island, which he named Isle of the True Cross, and that it laid within the Portuguese sphere of ownership, which was true. He sent word to Lisbon by one ship of his discovery and directed his fleet on to India.

The Portuguese claimed Brazil on the basis of the Treaty of Tordesillas as well as by right of discovery, and at first considered it valuable as a way station on the route to the Indian Ocean. An expedition to Brazil in 1501 reached the bay at what is today Rio de Janeiro and realized the Isle of the True Cross was, in fact, a vast continent with thousands of miles of coastline. The early Portuguese voyages found a valuable red dyestuff, Brasilwood, which provided a name to the new land and led to the establishment of

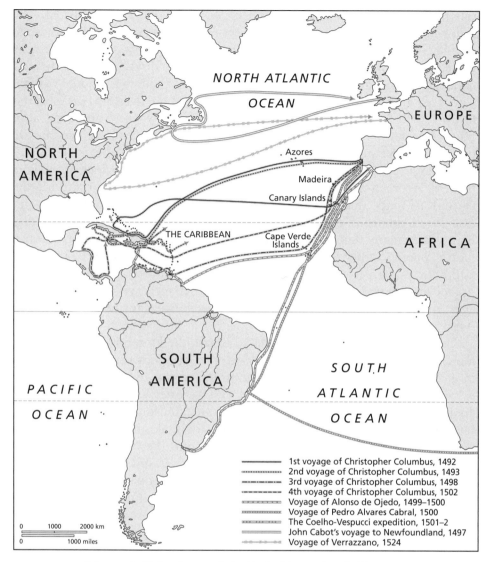

Map 2.6. Columbus and the Early Transatlantic Voyages.

feitorias, trading factories, on the coast. They also found natives. On the second voyage in 1504, at Porto Seguro, according to the Jesuit chronicler José de Anchieta: "The Indian women go about naked and do not deny themselves anything, more than that they are troublesome to men, throwing themselves and ensnaring them for the honor of sleeping with a Christian."

The English joined the action in the 1490s thanks to the ambition of another Italian mariner – a Venetian – Giovanni Caboto, or John Cabot, as the English chronicles spelled his name. Cabot had attempted to sell his own enterprise of the Indies in the Iberian Peninsula as early as 1490. He came to England in 1494 and joined the seafaring community of Bristol. Two years later, the English king approved, but did not finance, a voyage "to find, discover and investigate whatsoever islands, countries, regions or provinces of heathens and infidels, in whatsoever part of the world places, which before this time were unknown to Christians." A 1496 voyage was aborted. The following year, Cabot crossed the North Atlantic to Newfoundland in one ship in thirty-three days, which he believed (like Columbus) was on or near the coast of North Asia. This voyage traversed a distance of 600 to 700 nautical miles, or about one quarter the distance of Columbus's initial voyage. Cabot led a follow-up voyage in 1498, but four of the five ships disappeared in the North Atlantic. A contemporary English historian wrote that Cabot "found his new lands only in the ocean's bottom, to which he and his ship are thought to have sunk, since, after that voyage, he was never heard of more."

However, the North Atlantic was also considered the province of the Portuguese. Azorean mariners and merchants, the brothers Gaspar and Miguel Corte-Real made three or four voyages to the coast of North America and discovered, on behalf of Portuguese fishermen, the rich Grand Banks fishery. Bristol merchants sent the Portuguese sailor and farmer João Fernandes to North America, where his agrarian occupation eventually inspired the name Labrador – "farmer" – to a part of the mainland north of Newfoundland. Bristol maintained its presence in the North Atlantic with additional voyages, one by Sabastian Cabot in 1508–9, seeking a northwest passage to Asia.

On one of the Portuguese voyages to Brazil, the Florentine-born Sevillian merchant Amerigo Vespucci went along. His letters, which were published in 1505, more than any other news propelled the idea that the recently discovered islands and mainlands to the west were new lands, the peoples new peoples and even the heavens new heavens, not extensions of Asia or anything familiar but a new world altogether. In his logbook and letters, Columbus viewed America as some projection of Asia, and the Native Americans as remnants of the Golden Age. On the other hand, Vespucci contradicted the ancients and maintained that these new lands and peoples were not familiar in any way but absolutely different. His letters were the most widely read accounts for decades concerning the discoveries. By 1520, sixty editions and reprints of his letters had been published. Maps began to portray the notion of a new world. Martin Waldseemüller's map of 1507 revealed two continents across the ocean connected by an isthmus. The southern continent was named by Waldseemüller "America," the Latinized name of Amerigo, who considered him to be its discoverer. It was not until the 1538 map of the Fleming Gerhard Kremer Mercator that the name America was also applied to both the southern and northern continents.In an important sense, Vespucci began the intellectual discovery of America in Europe.

In the 1510s and 1520s, new discoveries definitively separated the West Indies from the East Indies. In 1513, Vasco Núñez de Balboa found a land passage through the Antilles across the narrow Isthmus of Panama. He believed another ocean, which he named the South Sea, very likely separated America from Asia. In 1519, the Portuguese mariner Ferdinand Magellan began his voyage on behalf of Spain to find a passage to the Spice Islands in the East Indies. The new Spanish king Charles V wished to believe that the Treaty of Tordesillas placed this valuable archipelago in the Spanish sphere. Magellan discovered a tortuous passage at the southern tip of South America – today named after him – entered the Pacific Ocean, discovered the Philippines and

Document 2.4
Mundus Novus

Amerigo Vespucci, 1503

Albericus Vespucius offers his compliments to Lorenzo Pietro di Medici.

On a former occasion I wrote to you at some length concerning my return to those new regions which we found and explored with the fleet, at the coast, and by the command of his Most Serene King of Portugal. And these we may rightly call a new world because our ancestors had no knowledge of them, and it will be a matter wholly new to all those who hear about them. For this transcends the view held by our ancients, inasmuch as most of them hold that there is no continent to the south beyond the equator, but only the sea which named the Atlantic; and if some of them did aver that a continent there was, they denied with abundant argument that it was a habitable land. But that this their opinion is false and utterly opposed to the truth, this my last voyage has made manifest; for in those southern parts, I have found a continent more densely peopled and abounding in animals than our Europe or Asia or Africa, and, in addition, a climate milder and more delightful than in any other region known to us, as you shall learn in the following account wherein we shall set succinctly down only capital matters and the things more worthy of comment and memory seen or heard by me in this new world, as will appear now . . .

It was on the seventh day of August, one thousand five hundred and one that we anchored off the shores of those parts, thanking our God with formal ceremonial and with the cerebration of a choral mass. We knew that land to be a continent and not an island both because it stretches forth in the form of a very long and unbending coast, and because it is replete with infinite inhabitants. For in it we found innumerable tribes and peoples and species of all manner of wild beasts which are found in our lands and many others never seen by us concerning which it would take long to tell in detail. God's mercy shone upon us much when we landed at that spot, for there had come a shortage of fire-wood and water, and in a few days we might have ended our lives at sea . . .

First then as to the people. We found in those parts such a multitude of people as nobody could enumerate (as we read in the Apocalypse), a race I say gentle and amenable. All of both sexes go about naked, covering no part of their bodies; and just as they spring from their mothers' wombs so they go until death. They have indeed large square-built bodies, well formed and proportioned, and in color verging upon reddish. This I think has come to them because, going about naked, they are colored by the sun. They have, too, hair plentiful and black.

In their gait and when playing their games they are agile and dignified. They are comely, too, of countenance which they nevertheless themselves destroy; for they bore their cheeks, lips, noses and ears. Nor think those holes small or that they have only one. For some I have seen having in a single face seven borings any one of which was capable of holding a plum. They stop up these holes of theirs with blue stones, bits of marble, very beautiful crystals of alabaster, very white bones, and other things artificially prepared according to their customs. But if you could see a thing so unwonted and monstrous, that is to say a man having in his cheeks and lips alone seven stones some of which are a span and a half in length, you would not be without wonder. For I frequently observed and discovered that seven such stones weighed sixteen ounces, aside from the fact that in their ears, each perforated with three holes, they have other stones dangling on rings; and this usage applies to the men alone. For women do not bore their faces, but their ears only. They have another custom, very shameful and beyond all human belief. For their women, being very lustful, cause the private parts of their husbands to swell to such a size that they appear deformed and disgusting; and this is accomplished by a certain device of theirs, the biting of certain poisonous animals. And in consequence of this many lose their organs which break through lack of attention, and they remain eunuchs.

They have no cloth either of wool, linen or cotton, since they need it not; neither do they have goods of their own, but all things are held in common. They live together without king, without government, and each is his own master. They marry as many wives as they please; and sons cohabit with mother, brother with sister, male cousin with female, and any man with the first woman he meets. They dissolve their marriages as often as they please, and observe no sort of law with respect to them. Beyond the fact that they have no church, no religion and are not idolaters, what more can I say? They live according to nature, and may be called Epicureans rather than Stoics.

Amerigo Vespucci, a Florentine navigator, sailed for the Castilians and the Portuguese to the Americas. This letter, on his third voyage, appeared in German in 1505. Within only a few years, forty editions of his letter had been published in Europe. In 1507, the cartographer Martin Wald-seemüller suggested that the land visited by Columbus be called "Land of Americus, or America." *Source:* Amerigo Vespucci, *Mundus Novus: Letter to Lorenzo Pietro de Medici*, translated by G. T. Northrup (1916), pp. 1–4.

eventually his crew reached the Spice Islands. Although Magellan was killed during the voyage, Sebastián del Cano led eighteen survivors and one ship back to Seville in 1522. This first circumnavigation of the world revealed the enormous distance separating South America from East Asia.

French exploration of the Atlantic followed in the wake of the Portuguese, the Spanish and the English. At the beginning of the sixteenth century, Norman and Breton ships were trading for dyewood on the coast of Brazil and fishing for cod at the Grand Banks of Newfoundland. After the Magellan voyage, the merchants of the Atlantic ports of France sought a northwest passage to the Indies. Giovanni da Verrazzano, a Florentine probably born in Lyon, was commissioned by King Francis I to search for such a passage. In 1524, with one ship, Verrazzano searched the North American coastline from Florida to Cape Breton. He mistook the Carolina Outer Banks as a thin isthmus separating the North Atlantic from the "eastern sea" leading to "those blessed shores of Cathay." Little is known of Verrazzano's second voyage in 1526–7, and his third in 1528 was his last. En route to Brazil, France's explorer disappeared.

The French search for a northwest passage was resumed in the 1530s. Beginning in 1534, Jacques Cartier made three voyages of discovery. The first surveyed the Gulf of St. Lawrence. On his second voyage, he explored the St. Lawrence River to the Lachine Rapids. Disappointed that the river could not be the seaway to Asia, Cartier concentrated on finding diamonds and gold on his third voyage in 1541–2. However, the ore he carried back to France was worthless. After a follow-up voyage in 1542–3 led by Juan Francois de La Rocque de Roberval, France abandoned North America and the St. Lawrence for several generations. Although mariners from many countries would continue to search for a northwest passage for centuries, the rough shape and position of the New World of the Americas and the Atlantic Ocean had been made known by the mid-sixteenth century.

It took approximately a century to open the Atlantic Ocean to European traders, conquerors and settlers. This endeavor was a continuation of the medieval expansion of Christendom. The motives and means were essentially the same as before. The expansion of the High Middle Ages was driven by religious fervor as well as a desire for new lands, products and trades. This was the time of the dynamism of European commerce, which was interrupted – not compelled – by the crisis of the fourteenth century. Yet even in the fourteenth century, Europeans explored and began to colonize the islands of the Atlantic Mediterranean. Expansion never ceased. Economic and demographic recovery in the fifteenth century propelled greater efforts in exploration and expansion in the near Atlantic, Africa and eventually the Americas. We see the fruits of pre-sixteenth century economic and commercial expansion in the figures of Table 2.1. In the five centuries before 1500, the European economy expanded more than 400 percent. Its share of world economic wealth doubled in this era before American silver, before the African slave trade and before direct commerce with Asia.

We have seen in this chapter that the main players were Genoese merchants and mariners and Iberian princes, kings and traders. They had modest goals at first and took incremental steps in opening the Atlantic. Until the middle of the fifteenth century, little economic gain was returned from their expansionist efforts. And even in the second half of the century, the trade in gold, slaves and spices were minimal compared to revived intra-European production and trade in textiles, grain, instruments of war and other metal goods. From the conquest of Ceuta in 1415 to the conquest of Mexico in 1521, expansion was profitable for only a few European kingdoms and merchants. It was only in the sixteenth century that the fruits of expansion became widely bountiful, and that is a different question for another chapter.

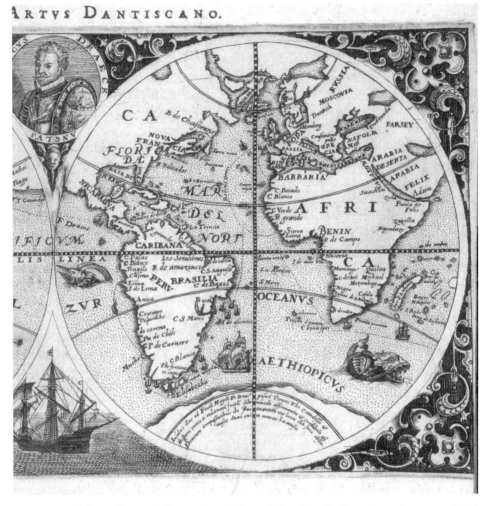

Figure 2.4. The Atlantic Sphere. Detail from Theodor de Bry, *Americae pars VIII* (Frankfurt, 1599). Courtesy of the William L. Clements Library at the University of Michigan.

The opening of the Atlantic, the key to what has been called the European age of exploration, was the continuation of an expansionist impulse that had ebbed and flowed for 500 years. The fifteenth century phase, the last medieval thrust, was as uncoordinated, incremental and limited to only a few players at a time as earlier periods and thrusts. In fact, overseas exploration in the fifteenth century was a minor sideshow in European affairs compared to European diplomacy, alliances and wars. For Europe, this was an age of discovery, not only of new lands and peoples but also of new knowledge, which undermined the venerable tradition that all important truths were found in the books of ancient philosophers, geographers and other scholars. The European expansion into the Atlantic, and especially the existence of the Americas and their native inhabitants, raised questions the ancients did not and could not answer. Referring to his 1497 expedition, Vespucci wrote,

"This voyage lasted eighteen months, during which we discovered many lands and almost countless islands (inhabited as a general rule), of which our forefathers make absolutely no mention. I conclude from this that the ancients had no knowledge of their existence."

In 1537, the Portuguese Cosmographer Major, Pedro Nunes, wrote that the Portuguese had "discovered new islands, new lands, new seas, new peoples, and, what is more, a new sky, new stars." However, this proud statement applies not only to the Portuguese but also to countless and unknown mariners and fishermen from the Azores, Bristol, Rouen and other ports of Atlantic Europe. It applies to Venetians like Alvise da Cadamosto and John Cabot (Giovanni Caboto), Galicians like Juan de la Cosa, Florentines like Amerigo Vespucci and Giovanni Verrazzano, Castilians like Martín Alonso Pinzón, Englishmen like Martin Frobisher and Francis Drake, Frenchmen like Jacques Cartier and Genoese like Christopher Columbus.

2.9 Further Reading

Luis Vaz de Camões, *The Lusíads*, translated by Landeg White (Oxford, 1997).

J. M. Cohen, editor, *The Four Voyages of Christopher Columbus* (London, 1969).

C. R. Crone, translator and editor, *The Voyages of Cadamosto and Other Documents on Western Africa in the Second Half of the Fifteenth Century* (London, 1937).

Bailey W. Diffie and George D. Winius, *Foundations of the Portuguese Empire, 1415–1580* (Minneapolis, 1977).

Gomes Eanes de Zurara, *The Chronicle of the Discovery and Conquest of Guinea* [1454], translated by Charles Raymond Beazley and Edgar Prestage, 2 volumes (London, 1896–9).

Geoffrey Eatough, translator and editor, *Selections from Peter Martyr* (Turnhout, Belgium, 1998).

J. H. Elliott, *The Old World and the New, 1492–1650* (Cambridge, 1970).

Felipe Fernández-Armesto, *Before Columbus: Exploration and Colonization from the Mediterranean to the Atlantic, 1229–1492* (Philadelphia, 1987).

Felipe Fernández-Armesto, *Columbus* (Oxford, 1992),

Anthony Grafton, *New Worlds, Ancient Texts: The Power of Tradition and the Shock of Discovery* (Cambridge, Mass., 1992).

Richard Hakluyt, editor, *Voyages and Discoveries: Principal Navigations, Voyages, Traffiques and Discoveries of the English Nation* (London, 1985).

Gwyn Jones, translator, *Eirik the Red and Other Icelandic Sagas* (New York, 1999).

Louise Levathes, *When China Ruled the Seas: The Treasure Fleet of the Dragon Throne, 1405–1433* (New York, 1994).

Jay A. Levenson, editor, *Circa 1492: Art in the Age of Exploration* (Washington, D.C., 1991).

David Northrup, *Africa's Discovery of Europe, 1450–1850* (Oxford, 2002).

Duarte Pachecho Pereira, *Esmeraldo de situ orbis*, transated and edited by George H. T. Kimble (London, 1937).

J. H. Parry, *The Discovery of the Sea* (Berkeley, 1981).

J. H. Parry, *The Age of Reconnaissance* (Berkeley, 1981).

William D. Phillips and Carla Rahn Phillips, *The Worlds of Christopher Columbus* (Cambridge, 1992).

Philippo Pigafetta, *A Report of the Kingdome of Congo, a Region of Africa, And of the Countries that border rounde about the same*, Drawen out of the writings and discourses of Odoarto Lopes a Portingall, translated by Abraham Hartwell (London, 1597).

Ruth Pike, *Enterprise and Adventure: The Genoese in Seville and the Opening of the New World* (Ithaca, 1966).

Peter Russell, *Prince Henry 'the Navigator': A Life* (New Haven, 2000).

Stuart B. Schwartz, editor, *Implicit Understandings: Observing, Reporting, and Reflecting on the Encounters between Europeans and Other Peoples in the Early Modern Era* (Cambridge, 1994).

John Thornton, *Africa and Africans in the Making of the Atlantic World, 1400–1800*, second edition (Cambridge, 1998).

Chapter 3

Conquests

Forging the Iberian Empires in Africa and the Americas

The opening of the Atlantic brought the Portuguese and Spanish into the lands of Africans and Native Americans. Before these encounters, Portugal and Castile had coexisted and made alliances with, and frequently struggled against, a people close at hand but different in ethnicity, culture and religion. They were the Moors of the Iberian Peninsula and the Maghrib. Alliances were made with Moorish states to gain temporary respite and advantage in fighting other Moorish and Christian states as conditions in the peninsula and the Western Mediterranean dictated. Conquest was also deeply ingrained in Portuguese and Spanish culture, as the *Reconquista* demonstrated. The Iberians entered the Atlantic World seeking partners and allies for conducting trade and making war and conquests. The Iberian "conquests" of indigenous states and societies in Africa and the Americas were incomplete and unfinished for centuries. "But many kingdoms and provinces were not totally or entirely conquered," noted the Spaniard Juan de Villagutierre Soto-Mayor in 1701, "and there were left among other provinces and kingdoms great portions of them unconquered, unreduced, unpacified, some of them not even yet discovered." The conquests were also ambiguous in the way Iberians and indigenous peoples perceived these events. Spaniards and Portuguese took glory in the status of *conquistador*, but native people, for example, rarely saw themselves as "conquered," and many viewed themselves as conquerors alongside their Spanish and Portuguese allies.

Europeans generally approached Africans and Native Americans at first in peace. If Europeans could not attain the wealth they sought through cooperation, they were always willing to use force. Like the Moors, these newly "discovered" peoples were subject to "legitimate conquest" through just war, an important concept in Iberian and European thought. However, unlike the Moors, Africans and Native Americans were generally pagans, people without knowledge of the "one true faith" (not infidels, who were knowledgeable of Christianity but had rejected it). Their subjection to Christian kings, the

Pope and ultimately the Kingdom of God was justified on the basis of evangelization rather than heresy. The Bull of Donation and Demarcation of Pope Alexander VI in 1493 asserted that it was the duty of any Christian king or prince "to lead the peoples dwelling in those lands and countries to embrace the Christian religion; [only then do we] . . . give, grant, and assign to you and your heirs and successors, Kings of Castile and León, forever . . . all rights, jurisdictions, and appurtenances, all islands and mainlands, found and to be found, discovered and to be discovered towards the west and south." The Spanish and Portuguese also believed conquest was justified by virtue of superior culture: they believed they were more refined, advanced, learned – in short, they were civilized. The most compelling argument was based on "the Roman legal claim that the peoples the Spaniards had conquered had never been able to constitute legitimate civil societies," writes Anthony Pagden. "For the Roman jurists, civil society was, by definition, a society based upon property, and property relations were what constituted the basis for all exchanges between truly civil men."

Although one finds alliances and ambivalent conquests on both sides of the Atlantic, the Portuguese generally made alliances and collaborated with local states, chiefs and traders on the coast of Africa, whereas the Spanish generally favored conquest of native kingdoms and chiefdoms in the Americas. These differences were not due primarily to national characteristics: the Portuguese also sought conquest and the Spanish collaborated and avoided war when circumstances made such actions appear to be advantageous or necessary. Nevertheless, one senses that the Portuguese were inclined to made deals and the Spanish were predisposed to make war. In Africa, the Portuguese found networks of trade and, more often than not, cooperative rulers and traders that rendered the wealth they desired peacefully. Alliances with Africans made the most sense. In America, the Spanish found no such readily exploitable business environment. Wealth had to be squeezed and forced from native hands in the Caribbean and looted and plundered from rich kingdoms on the mainland. Nevertheless, the Spanish still found allies. John Hemming's comment about the Portuguese in Brazil applies to all of the European conquests in America: "All the Indian wars exploited fatal rivalries between tribes. No Portuguese ever took the field without masses of native auxiliaries eager to attack their traditional enemies."

On the coast of Africa and throughout the Americas, the Portuguese and the Spanish made alliances and war with African and Native American cooperation and assistance. Forged in the fifteenth and sixteenth centuries, the Portuguese and Spanish empires were not exclusively Portuguese and Spanish constructions. The Portuguese were on the coast of Africa with the forbearance of local African rulers where they traded in gold and slaves with the cooperation and participation of African societies. The Spanish achieved dominion over a few powerful Native American empires thanks to alliances with other Native American states and the arms of Native and African *conquistadores*. They ruled and taxed native societies with the cooperation the native nobility. From the very beginning, the Atlantic World was an ethnically diverse world based on cooperation as much as on force.

3.1 The Canary Islands

The first European colony in the Atlantic was the Canary Island archipelago, lying off the northern coasts of Morocco. Unlike the other islands of the Atlantic Mediterranean, the Canaries were populated by a native people, sometimes collectively referred to as Guanches but should simply be called native Canarians. (Guanches refer specifically to the native people of the island of Tenerife.) In fact, several ethnic groups originally from North Africa with different material, social and cultural structures populated the different islands. For example, on the island of La Palma herding and gathering was the basis of the economy. On Gran Canaria, irrigated agriculture and collective silos were products of a hierarchical social structure and a powerful chiefdom. The island chain had been vaguely known to the ancients as "the Fortunate Isles," and rediscovered by Italians and Portuguese in the fourteenth century. In the second half of the fourteenth century, Catalan-Majorcan missionaries traveled to the islands, trained native missionaries and established a diocese of Fortuna on Grand Canary, which survived from 1351 until 1393. During the late fourteenth and early fifteenth centuries, Portugal and Castile contested each other's claims to the islands.

In 1402, two Franco-Norman knights, Jean de Béthencourt and Gadifer de la Salle, began the conquest and colonization of two of the least populated islands of the Canary chain, Lanzarote and Fuerteventura. As La Salle and sixty Norman warriors pacified the two islands, Béthencourt sought financial support by acknowledging King Enrique III of Castile as his feudal lord. With Castilian assistance, the two knights brought Castilian and Norman settlers to their islands. In 1420, Prince Henrique of Portugal began his life-long obsession to secure the Canary Islands for Portugal. It has often been argued that Henrique sought the island chain as bases for further exploration down the African coast, but at this early date such an ambition had very likely not fully formed in the prince. His motive was simply dominion of territory and the profit of native Canarian slaves and products produced in the land by colonists.

For the next fifty years, the Portuguese attempted to conquer both the native Canarians and the Castilian and French colonists of the island chain. In 1424, Prince Henrique dispatched a force of several thousand mounted and unmounted "crusaders" to conquer Gran Canaria and convert the pagans. This expedition was a military disaster for the Portuguese, who limped back to Lisbon. Ten years later, Henrique sent a fleet to seize Tenerife; it seized 400 captives but also failed to break native resistance and was repulsed. During the next several years, Portuguese attacks on Gomera and La Palma included a new strategy of "divide and conquer," that is, attracting native allies among feuding clans of Canarians. Despite this new approach, both islands remained fully in native control by 1446.

In 1448, Henrique undertook a new type of effort to take control of the Canaries. He bought the feudal rights of lordship of the nephew of the Norman founder of the first colony of Lanzarote, Jean de Béthencourt, and established a new Portuguese administration over the Castilian and French

settlers. In 1450, within a year of the new arrangement, the settlers of Lanzarote rebelled and expelled the Portuguese officials and colonists. The following year, Henrique sent a fleet of five caravels carrying 300 men-at-arms
to retake Lanzarote and invade Gomera and Gran Canaria. This expedition
failed because the settlers and native Canarians of the islands resisted the
Portuguese and because the monarchy of Castile dispatched two caravels to
obstruct the Portuguese. In a letter, the Castilian king complained Henrique's
behavior had involved "a most serious and atrocious injury to us and to the
royal crown of our kingdoms." A quarter century later, the "problem" of the
Canaries was finally settled by war. In 1476, a Castilian force defeated a Portuguese army in the Iberian peninsula, and the resulting Treaty of Alcaçovas
gave Castile title to the Canaries and Portugal its monopoly over African
trade.

Immediately upon the signing of the treaty, Castile began a decades-long
effort to conquer the native Canarians and seize control of their islands. The
wars began in Gran Canaria in 1478–83 by a military governor and partly
at royal expense. The six-year campaign was an unrelenting war of attrition
against ferocious resistance. A Castilian chronicler of Gran Canaria noted
that the natives might not have been subdued if not for their internal rivalries
that the *conquistadores* exploited. The war in Gran Canaria produced great
suffering, slavery and death for the native population, but the peace was
also achieved by negotiation. Native allies, who came to consider themselves
authentic Castilians, were rewarded with land and administrative responsibility. As the "conquest" moved on to other islands, the direct responsibility
of the monarchy receded and wealthy landowners and merchants organized
ad hoc companies of *conquistadores* who fought for themselves, for booty
and for land. Alonso de Lugo was appointed captain-general of Tenerife
and became one of the first Spanish *conquistadores* of the Atlantic. He had
become a sugar planter on Gran Canaria in 1484, made his money and then
sold his mill to finance his expedition, which lasted a total of ten years. His
foray into the island in 1494 with 120 horsemen and 1,000 men on foot
met an ambush in the highlands and hundreds of the invaders were killed.
He returned two years later with more troops and more determination. Peter
Martyr commented that, "Alfonso Lugo had quite some difficulty in finishing
his business; for naked and primitive those people may have been, with only
stones and sticks as weapons of war, yet on one occasion they put his army
to flight and slew about four hundred, before in the end he overcame them."
Two French chroniclers at the beginning of the fifteenth century noted that
the Gran Canarians were so fierce that they earned their name for their valor
and fighting skill.

On the island of Gomera, the dominant landowner, Fernán Peraza,
obtained an alliance with a key indigenous faction, which led to a general peace agreement. Peraza then divided the administration of the island
among nine chiefs. According to the testimony of Antón de Soria, a Castilian
of the age of the conquest, peace agreements lasted "as long as the Canarians wanted." The agreement faltered in 1488 when the native Gomerians
revolted. The resulting war was one in which Castilians and Gomerians both
suffered defeats at times and reached a negotiated settlement in 1489. This

was three years before the mariner Christopher Columbus departed from Gomera on his voyage west to the Orient.

The conquest of the native peoples of the Canary Islands, a people of stone-age technology, lasted more than a century. During the Castilian campaigns, *conquistadores* found Canarians to be formidable enemies and achieved more success and pacification through alliances and negotiation than terror. There is no doubt that Canarians suffered greatly in these campaigns; they were killed, enslaved in their homeland, and enslaved and carried away. However, according to the Spanish historian Antonio Rumeo de Armas, the Christian Church of Castile "prescribed slavery for the infidel neophytes [the newly baptized] and for the aborigines who were being converted." A minority of Canarians, chiefs, allies and collaborators received land, rank and even married into colonial high society. Beginning in 1496 on the island of Tenerife the native population was stricken by an unknown epidemic from Europe. Epidemics soon spread to all of the islands. This gradual depopulation opened the Canaries to greater Castilian and Italian settlement, the rise of a Canarian sugar industry and its development as a staging post for Castilian travel and trade to the Americas. Nevertheless, native Canarians and the descendants assimilated into Spanish colonial society in the islands through intermarriage. They became part of the local economy raising and herding cattle. It was also not long before the Canaries exported the new Canarians, colonial Canarians, to the New World. Castile's first encounter with a native culture in the Atlantic would set a number of precedents.

3.2 Atlantic Africa

The Portuguese reached the shores of tropical Africa when they came upon the Rivers Senegal and Gambia. Between 1440 and 1460, the Portuguese (and the Italian, French, Castilian and Catalan merchants who came with them) sought trade with African brokers from the Senegal River to the harbor of Sierra Leone. In the 1460s and 1470s, all of Guinea's creeks, harbors and beaches were explored. This coast was extremely long and the Portuguese were very few in number. The crown was greatly interested in the gold trade of Guinea, but African colonization at this time and later was never a primary interest. From the beginning, the Portuguese approach to enrichment in Guinea was by means of trade exclusively. The monarchy discouraged European traders from settling on the coast, and did not consider the possibility of building a castle or the establishment of military control anywhere. The gold trade required African cooperation that was often obtained through formal and informal alliances. Because the Senegambia and Guinea coasts were home to numerous small states and chiefdoms (there were approximately forty or fifty states in the backlands of the Gold Coast alone), conquest of one or more must have appeared pointless.

In Upper Guinea, freelance Portuguese traders settled on the coast and upriver along the Gambia. These individuals often "went native" and settled in African villages, took African wives and produced half-caste offspring. The Portuguese called these "outcasts" *lançados*. These traders almost certainly

Figure 3.1. West Africa from Arguim to Benin. Detail from the map *Nigritarum Regio* (Region of the Niger) from Jean Blaeu, *Le Grand Atlas ov Cosmographie Blaviane*, Vol. 10 (Amsterdam, 1667). Courtesy of the William L. Clements Library at the University of Michigan.

gave no thought to conquest. Their activities, and Portuguese trade in general, did have an impact. The number of petty states in the region appeared to have increased local warfare and the taking of war captives expanded, and thus the number of captives sold into slavery swelled. *Lançados* established themselves in Cape Verde, in the Senegambian kingdoms and in Sierra Leone. In time, their trading advantage was so good, or so it seemed to their Portuguese competitors, the monarchy in 1508 and 1514 imposed restrictions upon *lançado* traders and reinforced the monopoly system. Nevertheless, it was too late. *Lançados* were just about everywhere on the West and Central African coast, doing business and making themselves indispensable.

As more and more gold dust – Akan gold from the Akan-speaking people of the forest above what was later named the Gold Coast – was diverted from the trans-Saharan trade, the Songhay Empire conquered Timbuktu from Mali in 1471. This expansion of a powerful inland empire may have prevented Portuguese penetration of the interior and seizure of the mines if, indeed, it was even contemplated, but we will never know because there was no attempt to conquer the mines. However, Songhay's seizure of Timbuktu did not prevent the Portuguese advantage in trade and reverse or even slow the flow of gold dust south to the Atlantic coast. A view from inside the Songhay Empire and court by the Timbuktu scholar and historian al-Sa'dî reveals that throughout the sixteenth century and long into the seventeenth century, Songhay diplomacy, politics, trade, war and religion took no account of the Portuguese. To this great West African empire, the Europeans on the coast were insignificant and essentially invisible.

Figure 3.2. The Portuguese Castle of São Jorge da Mina. Cartouche from *Africa nova descriptio* from Jean Blaeu, *Le Grand Atlas ov Cosmographie Blaviane*, Vol. 1 (Amsterdam, 1663). Courtesy of the William L. Clements Library at the University of Michigan.

Royal Portuguese presence was established on the coast in a few key *feitorias*, or trading factories. Arguim Island just north of the Senegambia region was the first such post in 1445. It was followed by Santiago in upper Guinea, São Jorge da Mina in lower Guinea or the Gold Coast and São Tome, one of the islands in the Gulf of Guinea. (Posts at Accra in 1500, Axem in 1503 and Shama in about 1560, all on the Gold Coast, followed these.) On the Gold Coast, the crown decided that trade should be a state enterprise and monopoly. To keep interlopers off the coast, the King of Portugal, Dom João, ordered the construction of a fortress. São Jorge da Mina castle was constructed in 1482 by D. Diogo de Azambuja and a local chief, whom the Portuguese called Caramansa (perhaps named Kwamina Ansa), agreed to its presence. The Portuguese agreed to annual payments to Caramansa, which they referred to as "gifts" and which the local Africans likely considered rent or tribute. São Jorge and the other forts and trading houses had as their primary purpose the maintenance of the Portuguese monopoly of trade. They were defensible only with local African cooperation – providing access to foodstuffs and military support.

On the Gold Coast, the Portuguese exercised military power but never possessed hegemony. They had military superiority on the coast thanks to ships armed with canon and expeditionary forces armed with firearms. At this early point in European-African relations, Africans had not yet acquired firearms but they did possess iron weapons, javelins and bows and arrows. A contemporary chronicler João de Barrios described Gold Coast African warriors. He wrote, they were "armed after their manner, some with spears and bucklers, others with bows and arrows; and many, in place of helmets, wore monkey skins studded with the teeth of animals." Each village had a militia and inland states possessed small permanent military forces and drafted commoners in time of war. In the seventeenth century, interior states on the Gold Coast could field armies of four thousand soldiers. The Portuguese had cannon and primitive guns, crossbows, pikes and war-horses. In the locality of São Jorge da Mina, the Portuguese faced three small states, the kingdoms of Efutu and Commany on the coast and Akara inland. The Portuguese always had the military support of the nearby Village of Two Parts, where Portuguese soldiers and traders and Africans closely intermingled, sometimes intermarried and even set up households and raised families. The Portuguese frequently launched punitive attacks and expeditions to punish African chiefs and kings who had traded with European rivals. They were nearly always successful, with "success" defined as the burning of a village or town and its canoes. Naturally, this made the Portuguese intensely unpopular among the Mina Africans. One local ruler named Don João, according to an English chronicler, repeatedly "had wars with the Portugals." In 1577–8, the Efutu made an alliance with the Akani confederacy and attacked the Portuguese and their local African allies at São Jorge. Although the Portuguese lost thirty soldiers and the governor himself was killed in the attack, they won the battle.

Africans demonstrated that they could defeat the Portuguese under certain conditions. In 1576, Accra fought back against a punitive expedition that also was charged with transforming the trading house at Accra into a fortification. African soldiers used deception to gain entrance into the half-built fort and, once inside, killed all of the Portuguese and razed the fortification. For the next fifty years, the Portuguese and other Europeans stayed away from this segment of the coast. In 1623, the Portuguese made their first attempt to establish a base in the interior, fifteen miles up river on the Ankobra where they worked their own gold mine. When an earthquake struck in 1636 and collapsed the mine, Aowin villagers buried Portuguese captives alive at the mouth of the mine and drove the few survivors out of the small fort, from where they fled to Azem.

The only major West African kingdom the Portuguese had direct contact with in the late fifteenth and early sixteenth century was Benin, an inland state east of the Gold Coast and located just north of the Niger delta. The Kingdom of Benin was wealthy and militarily powerful and governed by a monarch, the *Oba*, who was supported by a court aristocracy and a bureaucracy. In 1487, the crown secured a foothold at Ughoton, about forty miles from the sea up river but still twenty miles from Benin City. "The Kingdom of Beny," wrote Pacheco Pereira, "is about eighty leagues long and forty wide; it is

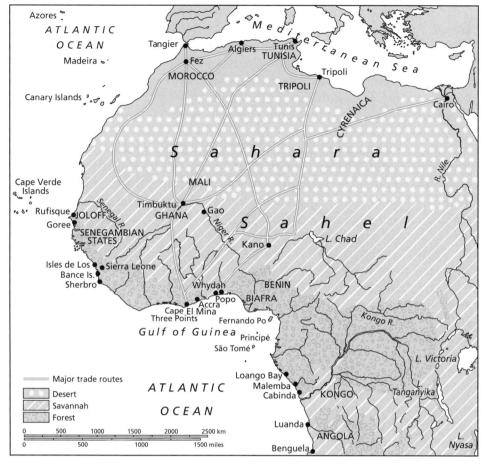

Map 3.1. Guinea in the Early European Era.

usually at war with its neighbors and takes many captives, whom we buy at twelve or fifteen brass bracelets each, or for copper bracelets which they prize more; from there the slaves are brought to the Castle of S. Jorze da Mina where they are sold for gold" (see Map 3.1).

Although the Portuguese possessed military superiority on the coast, the coastline was not subject to Benin and therefore Portuguese power there was peripheral. At Ughoton, the Portuguese were vastly outnumbered and tolerated by the Oba of Benin, Esigie. In 1514, the Oba sent an embassy to Portugal requesting a Christian mission and firearms. He apparently understood that royal policy was to sell arms only to Christian princes. Although the Oba learned to speak and write Portuguese he did not convert, but he permitted his son and several high officials to be baptized. This was not good enough for King Manoel, who explained: "... when we see that you have embraced the teachings of Christianity like a good and faithful Christian, there will be nothing in our realms with which we shall not be glad to favor you, whether it be arms or cannon and all other weapons of war for use against your enemies."

Uncooperative behavior was met with uncooperative behavior. Two years later, the Oba ordered that only female captives be sold into slavery. Opposition of a faction opposed to the Portuguese presence and influence, perhaps, also motivated this action. Not long thereafter, the Oba was poisoned and the new Oba expelled the Christian mission. The Portuguese closed down the trading factory at Ughoton in 1520, and thereafter traded with Benin from São Tomé. In about 1550, Benin ended its participation in the slave trade altogether.

At the same time, the Portuguese cultivated a new state in the Niger delta, Itsekiri Kingdom. The king encouraged Portuguese trade, accepted Christian missions and placed no restrictions on the slave trade. During the second half of the sixteenth century, the Itsekiri rulers became – or so it was reported – enthusiastic converts to Christianity.

Could the Portuguese have conquered the Gold Coast states and Benin like the Spanish conquered the chiefdoms of Española and the more formidable Mexica Empire in 1521? We must remember that prior to the conquest of Mexico, there were approximately ten thousand Spaniards in the Caribbean and the war bands that conquered the mainland states at first numbered several hundreds, quickly reaching a few thousand soldiers. The Portuguese never put anywhere close to that number of people in Guinea. In the late fifteenth century and during the sixteenth century, the garrison at São Jorge da Mina and the other trading factories numbered less than 500 armed men while the civilian population on the coast of Guinea probably was no more than 200 men and a few women. Clearly, the Portuguese did not believe the effort of conquest would equal the reward. African states and chiefdoms were cooperative by and large and, given the very small number of Portuguese traders and soldiers on the West African coast, a policy of trade and peaceful relations made the most sense.

3.3 The Kongo Experiment

Portuguese contact with the Kingdom of Kongo was established after the departure of the exploratory voyage of Diogo Cão from the central African coast in 1483. He had left four Portuguese emissaries on the coast that were taken to the court of the Manicongo at his inland capital, M'banza. At the same time, Cão had seized four Africans who were taken to Portugal and instructed in the Portuguese language, European ways and the Christian religion. When Cão returned to Kongo in 1484 or 1485, his expedition took on the form of an official embassy. The Portuguese king João II sought an alliance with the Manicongo Nzinga Nkuwu as the best approach to penetrate the interior of Africa and perhaps contact Prester John. The return of the four African hostages to M'banza brought detailed information of the power and wealth of the kingdom of Portugal, the friendship and greatness of the Portuguese king and the glory of the Christian religion. Suitably impressed, the Manicongo requested that João send him missionaries, traders and craftsmen, and he in turn dispatched to Portugal several of his own people to be trained in European ways.

In 1490, believing he may have found a Christian ally in Africa, João eagerly complied and sent a fleet of three ships, which transported priests, artisans and samples of European trade goods. The Portuguese considered the Kongolese to be the most advanced of African peoples they had thus far discovered. The Manicongo, his eldest son Mbemba a Nzinga and a number of high nobles were baptized. As told by João de Barros, in early May 1491 the royal baptism took place before one hundred thousand people. In honor of the king of Portugal, the Manicongo was christened D. João de Kongo. The Manicongo then went into battle against some rebellious subjects and, with Portuguese assistance, won a great victory. Little is known about the remainder of the reign of this Manicongo, João I. Traders from São Tomé began to trade with Kongo and at least one other time provided military assistance to the Manicongo in crushing a rebellion. In Lisbon, relations with Kongo and João were neglected at a time when the European kingdom experienced a royal succession and began to open the Indian Ocean trade route.

In 1506, Mbemba A Nzinga, christened as Afonso I, seized the Kongo throne with Portuguese assistance against an anti-Portuguese faction upon the death of his father. Afonso was a sincere Christian and believed in, and cooperated with, the Portuguese experiment of Europeanizing an African state. According to the account of Duarte Lopes in 1597, Alfonso ordered the Lord of his provinces that anyone who had idols or anything else contrary to the Christian religion, and did not deliver them to the Court, "should be burned themselves without remission or pardon. Which commandant was consequently put into execution. And a wonderful thing it is to be noted, that within less than one month, all the Idols, and Witcheries and Characters, which they worshiped and accounted for Gods, were sent and brought into the Court." Two years after Alfonso's accession, a Jesuit mission of some fifteen priests arrived in M'banza at his request. Following the *regimento* or set of instructions of the Portuguese King Manoel in 1512, Afonso and his Portuguese advisors established a European-style royal court, wore Portuguese dress, created a Portuguese table of silver and gold plates and utensils, built a Portuguese-style throne, distributed titles of nobility, attempted to implement elements of Portuguese law and attempted to undermine the Kongo cult of royal graves. M'banza was renamed São Salvador and stone buildings began to arise. In 1521, Afonso's son Henrique returned from Europe as Bishop of Utica *in partibus infidelium* and Vicar Apostolic of the Kongo. The first dictionary in KiKongo was written in 1556, the first catechism in 1556 and the first KiKongo grammar published in Rome in 1659. Despite the best efforts of Afonso, Bishop Henrique and their Portuguese advisors, Afonso remained a Christian king of a mostly pagan land (see Map 3.2).

The alliance and friendship desired by the Portuguese monarchy was steadily undermined by the slave trade directed from São Tomé and, at first, generally for the plantations of São Tomé. Portuguese profiteers and slave trade agents conducted business through subordinate chiefs who increasingly became more independent of the Manicongo. Factions developed

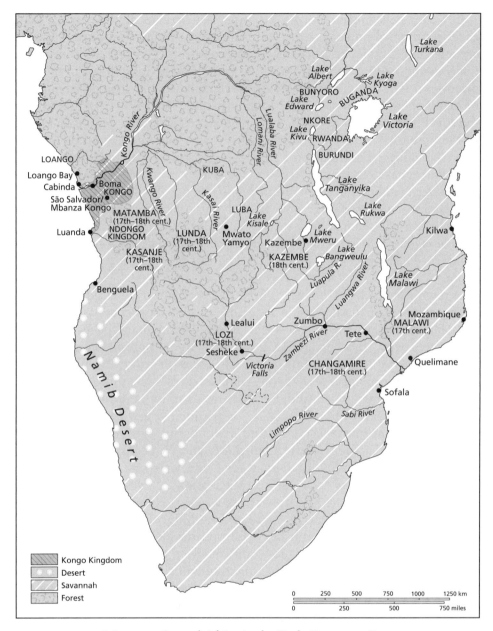

Map 3.2. Central Africa in the Early European Era.

between those in favor and those opposed to the slave trade, with Portuguese residents on both sides. The best indication of this growing menace
is the development of the village of Mpinda (sometimes spelled as Cabinda
on maps) at the mouth of the Congo River, into a major slave port by
1510. Mpinda exported slaves to Lisbon, the Algarve and São Tomé. By the
1520s, the trade had depopulated some areas of the kingdom and created
slave revolts and political turmoil. In a long letter to King Manoel, Afonso
wrote:

Many of our subjects eagerly covet Portuguese merchandise, which your
people bring into our kingdoms. To satisfy this disordered appetite, they
seize numbers of our free or freed black subjects, and even nobles, sons
of nobles, even the members of our own family.

The Portuguese monarchy ignored Afonso's plea and he sought to take
matters into his own hands. In 1526, he established a commission to insure
that captives exported into slavery were true war captives (and thus outsiders) and not free men (or Kongolese). This attempt at a regulation of the
slave trade was greatly resented by the traders of São Tomé and their agents
and mulatto sons in Kongo. However, Afonso used the Atlantic trade and
Christianity to strengthen his kingship and his kingdom. By 1540, his opposition to the slave trade disappeared when Afonso himself had a surplus of
captives from wars to sell to the Portuguese. Afonso wrote, no ruler in Africa
"esteems the Portuguese goods so much . . . as we do. We favor their trade,
sustain it, open markets [for it]."

When Afonso died in 1543, a violent succession crisis arose between
Afonso's son Pedro and his nephew Diogo. Pedro came to power with the
support of Afonso's African and Portuguese supporters. This reign was short-
lived. Those Africans and Portuguese tied to the slave trade, and opposed to
Afonso's policies, revolted and placed Diogo on the throne. Under Diogo,
after 1545 the slave traders were able to establish free and unregulated slaving in the interior. The arrival of a Jesuit mission in 1548 did not improve
matters. After an energetic period of church building and evangelization,
the Jesuits themselves became involved in the slave trade and the political
factionalism of the kingdom. Realizing that evangelization (or political control) was impossible under those conditions, the mission departed in 1552.
A second mission from 1553 to 1555 also ended in failure.

Under Diogo and his successors, the Portuguese experiment in Kongo further unraveled. The kingdom became more fragmented and isolated from
Portuguese culture and Christianity. Diogo himself appeared to revert to
pagan ways. His death in 1561 produced a bloody succession crisis. A
local revolt prevented resident Portuguese from imposing their candidate
as Diogo's successor. Six years later, the Anzico people rebelled, most likely
against excessive slaving. A people nicknamed the "Jaga" invaded Kongo and
defeated the new king Alvaro and the resident Portuguese community who
assisted him in 1568. "For reparation of his state and religion," wrote Leo
Africanus, Alvaro requested Portuguese assistance in 1570. "He had recourse
to Don Sebastian king of Portugall, and obtained of him six hundred soldiers,
by whose valour he drove his enemies out of the kingdom, and within an
year and a half, reestablished himself in his throne." This was the first major
military campaign fought by Europeans in tropical Africa.

The Portuguese crown raised an army to invade Kongo, restore the Christian king and reopen the slave trade. By the mid-sixteenth century, the slave
trade was too important to the Portuguese to let slip away. The captain of
the *conquistadores*, Ferdinand de Mello, the governor of São Tomé and a
slave trader himself, was eager to reestablish the old order in the Kongo.
Despite this dramatic rescue, during the last decades of the sixteenth century

Kongo became increasingly isolated and badly governed. For the most part, the *conquistadores* of 1570 stayed in the kingdom, sired large mulatto families and transformed Kongo into a slave trading state. On the other hand, Kongolese nobles established slave-based plantations on São Tomé as well as in their own land, and occasionally married the daughters of Portuguese planters.

During the seventeenth century, the slave trade and defeat in war led to the further disintegration of the Kingdom of Kongo. By 1670, no central government could hold the kingdom together. Factions fought civil wars while chiefs and provincial nobles became more and more independent. São Salvador was destroyed in 1666 and abandoned in 1678. In 1704, a young female prophet, Dona Beatrice Kimpa Vita, preached a new type of Christianity that rejected missionaries and Europeans. She and her large following brought a new king to M'banza Kongo and attempted to restore the kingdom. However, within a few years the movement failed, Dona Beatriz was burned as a heretic and the Kongo as a political organization disappeared. The Portuguese-Kongolese experiment to create a Christian and Europeanized African kingdom had been an interesting but tragic colonial anomaly. It failed because other Portuguese and Africans, and their mulatto offspring, destroyed it through the trade of people and war.

3.4 The Colony of Angola

Some 500 kilometers south of the Congo River was the Ngola kingdom of the Ndongo. The royal capital was located on a plateau 160 kilometers inland. The king or chief, whose dynastic title was *Ngola*, gave informal allegiance to the Manicongo. As with Kongo, the Portuguese named the country after the title of the ruler.

The Portuguese had explored the coast of Angola during the Cão expeditions and made landfall at the site of the future Luanda, an island north of the Kuanza River. The Ngola, who asked Afonso of Kongo to request the Portuguese on his behalf to send an embassy of traders and priests, initiated direct contact in 1519. King Manuel dispatched an expedition but it was sabotaged by the governor general of São Tomé, who opposed the establishment of royal authority in a land where the trade in slaves was free and unregulated. For the next thirty years, Angola was neglected by the monarchy but not by São Tomé, whose traders intensified the slave trade. In the 1550s, the Manicongo, concerned about the growing independence of Angola, sent an army to re-impose control. With the help of traders from São Tomé, the Ngola defeated the Kongo force, declared his independence and requested direct relations with the Portuguese monarchy and the dispatch of missionaries.

The result was an expedition in 1560 of four Jesuits who traveled in the caravel of Paulo Dias de Novais, the grandson of Bartolomeu Dias, the discoverer of the Cape of Good Hope. When the expedition arrived at the Kuanza River, a new Ngola, one suspicious of Portuguese intentions, refused to accept the mission. Authorities in Lisbon concluded that a policy similar to that pursued in Kongo, one of alliance and assimilation, was not possible in Angola. However, the crown believed that Angola was too important to neglect further. The slave trade here was beginning to surpass that of Kongo and it was believed, erroneously as it turned out, that the interior possessed rich mines of silver. The crown therefore embarked on a radically new African policy.

Jesuits, who had come to believe that peaceful conversion was impossible, advanced the new policy. As one missionary wrote in the 1570s: "Almost everybody is convinced that the conversion of these barbarians is not to be achieved through love, but only after they have been subdued by force of arms and become vassals of Our Lord the King." Unlike Castilian policy in the Canary Islands, although late and inconsistently applied, the Portuguese never saw conversion as a safe-conduct pass for avoiding slavery. As Rumeo de Armas notes, the Portuguese "accepted slavery and conversion of the infidel at the same time, without discriminations or subtleties of any kind."

Two years after the king of Kongo had been restored to his throne by a military expedition, Portugal prepared for a second military conquest. This time it would be a direct conquest following an American rather than an African imperial model. In 1571, the monarchy awarded Paulo Dias de Novais the *donatária* – territorial proprietorship – of Angola. This system was applied in the *Reconquista* of Portugal and during the colonization of Madeira and Brazil. As the *donatory*, or Lord Proprietor, Dias was given the responsibility to settle and defend Angola on behalf of the crown. He was awarded the governorship of Angola for his lifetime, given the power to divide the land among vassals and renters, and granted certain privileges necessary to produce income. In short, the Portuguese for the first time in Africa, authorized the conquest and colonization of an African kingdom.

When Dias arrived on the coast of Angola in 1575, he found a Portuguese population of about fifty men, mostly slave traders dependent on their connections with São Tomé. He founded the city of São Paulo do Assumpção (called Luanda) on the mainland with a company of some 400 Portuguese soldiers and craftsmen, and constructed a fort, church, and hospital. For three years, this small colony was confined to the coast and lived in peace with the Ngola. In 1579, Dias and a military force began a slow advance up the Kuanza, building forts along the way. The first military campaign, which was to last ten years, had begun. Although Dias succeeded in bringing some local chiefs under Portuguese control, and thus African warriors into his army, he was never able to defeat the Ngola. In fact, in several battles, Portuguese forces were routed. Thousands of African bowmen proved to be superior to dozens of Portuguese musketeers. During this decade of conflict, something like two thousand Portuguese were killed in battle or by disease. The Portuguese found the land around Luanda to be too poor and rainfall too precarious to be able to establish profitable plantations after the Madeira and São Tomé model. When Dias died in 1589, the small colony of Angola was little more than a slave-trading outpost.

Document 3.1
Paulo Diaz in Arms Against the King of Angola

Duarte Lopes, 1588

When the trade here beganne thus to increase, and marchaundises were freely carried by the Portingales, & the people of Congo to Cabazo, a place belonging to the Lorde of Angola, and distant from the sea, 150. miles, there to sell and barter them, it pleased his Lordship to give out order, that all the Marchants should be slaine, and their goods confiscated, alleadging for his defence, that they were come thether as spies, and to take possession of his estate: but in truth it is thought that hee did it onely to gaine all that wealth to himselfe, considering that it was a people that did not deale in the habite of warriours, but after the manner of Marchants. And this fell out in the same yeare, that the King Don Sabastiano was discomfited in Barbarie.

When Paulo Diaz understoode of this course, he put himselfe in armes against the King of Angola, and with such a troupe of Portingals as he could gather together that were to bee founde in that countrey, and with two Gallies and other vessels, which he kept in the river Coanza, he went forewarde on both sides of the river conquering, and by force subdued many Lords, and made them his frendes and subjects. But the king of Angola perceyiung that his vassels had yielded to the obedience of Paulo Diaz, and that with all prosperous successe he had gained much land upon him, he assembled a great army to go against him, and so utterly to destroy him. Whereupon Paulo Diaz requested the King of Congo that he woulde succour him with some helpe to defende himselfe withal, who presently sent unto him for aid an army of 60 thousand men, under the conduct of his cosin Don Sebastiano Manibamba, and another captyne with 120. Portingale souldiers, that were in those countries, and all of his owne pay for the atchieving of this enterprise. This was to joyne with Paulo Diaz, and so altogether to warre against the King of Angola: but arriving at the shoare, where they were to passé over the river Bengo. And within 12. miles of Loanda, & where they shoulde have met with many barkes to carry the Campe to the other shore, partly because the said barks had slacked their coming, & partly because much time wold have been spent in transporting so many men, the whole armie tooke their way quite over the river, and so going on forwardes they met with the people of the King of Angola, that were ready to stoppe the souldiers of Congo, from entering upon their Countrey.

The military order of the Mociconghi (for by that terme we do call the naturall borne people of the kingdome of Congo, as wee call the Spaniardes those that are naturally borne in Spaine) and the military order of the people of Angola, is almost all one: For both of them doo usually fight on foote, and divide their armie into severall troupes, sitting themselves according to the situation of the field where they doo incampe, & advancing their ensigns and banners in such sort as before is remembered.

The removes of their armie are guided and directed by certaine severall soundes and noyses, that procede from the Captayne Generall, who goeth into the middest of the Armie, and there signifieth what is to bee put into execution: that is to say, eyther that they shall joyne battell, or els retyre, or put on forward, or turne to the right hand, and to the leaft hand, or to performe any other warlick action. For by these several sounds distinctly delievered from one to another they doe all understande the commandements of their Captayne, as we heere among us doo understande the pleasure of our Generall by the sundrie stroakes of the Drumme, and the Captaines soundes of the Trompet...

In the place above described, there were sundry encounters on the one side and on the other. And in the first battles the people of Congo remained conquerours but afterwards, when they had divers times fought together with great losse on both sides, and victuailes began nowe to faile, and consequently men waxed sicke and died, the Campe of the king of Congo was dissolved, and every man returned to his owne home.

In the meane while Paulo Diaz, though he coulde not joyne his forces with the Armie of his frendes that came to succour him, yet set himselfe forwardes, and passing over the river at Luiola, because it was a place very strong & fit to resist the King of Angola. The situation of Luiola is this: The two rivers Coanza and Luiola do joyne together about 105. miles from the sea shore, and a little above the said joining together, these Rivers doe seaver themselves for the space of an Arcubose shotte, so that they make as it were an Island betweene them: In which Island at the meeting of the two rivers there riseth a hill, which Paulo Diaz surpised and fortified for his better safety. And whereas in times past there was never any habitation there, nowe at this present it is growen to be a pretty countrey inhabited by the Portingalles.

From this place thus surprised by Paulo Diaz, and called Luiola, you may saile along the river with certain small vesselles, even to the sea, and goe by lande without any daunger for the space of one hundred and five miles. Neere there unto are the hilles that are called the hilles of Cabambe, producing infinite store of silver of which the saide Diaz doth every day by little and little endeauour to conquere. And these hils are the graund quarrel betweene him and the people of Angola. For knowing that the Portingalles doe esteeme greatly of these hills, in regarde of the silver pits which are there in great aboundance, they doe use all the force and skill they can to keepe the Portingalles from them. They fight also with them in divers other places: for the Portingalles passing over the river Coanza do continually make inroads into the countries that are subject to the king of Angola...

Now if it shall seeme strange to any man, that so few Portingall souldiours as Paulo Diaz retayneth there with him, and others of the Portingall nation, which traffick into the Realme, & relieve him with succours, being in number but three hundred at the most, accounting their slaves, and also the Malcontentes, the rebelles and fugitives of Angola, which dayly resort unto him, & amount not in all to the quantity of XV. thousand men, should be able to make so gallant a resistance against the innumerable rabble of Negroes, being subject to the king of Angola, which are gathered there together (as it is said) to the number of a Million of soules. I answer, that the great reason may be alleadged for the same. For the armie of Negroes is all naked, and utterly destitute of all provision and furniture for armour of defence: And as for their weapons of offence, they consist onely of bowes and daggers (as I told you). But our fewe Portingalles that are there, are well lapped in certaine jackets that are stuffed and basted with bombast, and stitched and quilted very soundly, which keepe their armes very safe, and their bodies downewardes as lowe as their knees: Their heades also are armed with capes made of the same stuffe, which doo resist the shot of the arrow and the stroke of the dagger: Besides that, they are girt with longe swords, and some horsemen there are among them that carry speares for their weapons. Now you must understand that one man on horsebacke, is of more worth then a hundred Negroes, because the horsemen do affray them greatly: & especially of those that do discharge guns and peeces of artillarie against them, they do stande continually in an extreame bodily feare. So that these few being well armed, and cunningly and artificially ordered, must needes overcome the other, though they be very many in number.

Duarte Lopes and Filippo Pigafetta's account of the early Portuguese campaign of conquest of Ndongo (Angola) refers to the year 1579 when King Alvaro I of Kongo did attempt to assist Paulo Dias de Novais with an army but without success. This account gives this early Portuguese military effort more credit than it deserves, and recounts the false claim of great deposits of silver in the country. *Source: A Reporte of the Kingdome of Congo, a Region of Africa, and of the Countries that border rounde about the same.* Drawn out of the writings and discourses of Odordo Lopes, a Portingal, by Philippo Pigafetta. Translated out of Italian by Abraham Hartwell (1797), pp. 46–55.

In 1591, the Spanish Habsburgs (who had acquired Portugal in 1580) rescinded the donation charter and established a royal colony. A new city, Benguela, was settled 320 kilometers south of Luanda to expand the slave-trading frontier. The new governor arrived with 400 soldiers and 50 cavalry and acquired some fifteen thousand African soldiers, but this renewed conquest was only slightly more successful than the first. The Ndongo kingdom resisted and retreated but withstood conquest. A third attempt at conquest, the most forceful yet with an army of 800 Portuguese soldiers, began in 1602. "In Angola," writes Jeremy Black, "the slow rate of fire of muskets and the openness of African fighting formations reduced the effectiveness of firearms, and the Portuguese were successful only when supported by local troops." This force seized the region where silver was believed to be located, but further expeditions proved that no silver was here. The conquest of Angola to this point had yielded little more than a chain of forts along the Kuanza River.

By 1600, Angola remained what it had been from the beginning, a slave-trading colony centered at Luanda. Portuguese traders and their mulatto sons and business partners traded with chiefs inland and exported approximately ten thousand captives through Luanda. The Portuguese often employed *pombeiros* or mulatto, black or even slave intermediaries who traveled to inland markets (*pumbos*, hence the name) and brought caravans of slaves to the coast. Because African chiefs competed against one another for Portuguese trade and often made war on rivals to obtain captives, the slave trade succeeded without military conquest. During the seventeenth century, the trade devastated the interior of Angola. On the coast in Luanda and Benguela, a Luso-African society developed that was superficially Christian and more mulatto than white. The Jesuits of the colony had little success in evangelization but compensated by becoming rich landowners and slave traders who often lived with African and mulatto mistresses. As in Guinea and Kongo, the trade in slaves in Angola became the most powerful and lasting European impact in Africa.

The Pende people, who originally lived on the Angolan coast in the sixteenth century, preserved in their oral tradition their view of the coming of the Portuguese: "They brought us maize and cassava, knives and hoes, groundnuts and tobacco. From that time until our day the Whites brought us nothing but wars and miseries." A Portuguese observer, Manuel Severim de Faria, offered a similar opinion in the early seventeenth century: "There has been nothing but fighting in Angola from the beginning of the conquest till now, and very little has been done for the conversion of the inhabitants of that great province."

In 1618, a Portuguese campaign broke through onto the plateau, invading the heartland of the kingdom. Success was due in large part to a Portuguese alliance with communities of nomadic warriors, the Imbangala, who lived by plunder and with nomadic people the Portuguese called Jaga. The capital at Pungua Ndongo was burned and the king was forced to flee to the east. Upon the death of the Ngola in 1624, authority was vested in his sister, Nzinga Mbande, who led the anti-Portuguese party. She moved her supporters beyond the range of the Portuguese to Matamba, where a new powerful kingdom was formed. The Imbangala settled down and formed a kingdom named Kasanje. In what remained of the kingdom of Ndongo, the Portuguese bestowed the title of Ngola to the compliant Ari Kiluanji and ruled the kingdom indirectly. The puppet Ngola took the name Dom Felippe, agreed to a tribute of 100 slaves a year and permitted the Jesuits to build a church at Pungua.

The "conquest" of the Ndongo kingdom, such as it had been, had won the Portuguese little. War disrupted peaceful slave trading and convoys – more profitable than the captives taken in periodic campaigns – and simply reduced the numbers of captives dispatched to Luanda. The Matamba kingdom remained hostile to the Portuguese for several more decades, whereas the Kasanje kingdom became an ally of Portugal well into the eighteenth century. As one Portuguese historian concluded, "Angola became a permanent battlefield for the Portuguese." According to the Portuguese historian Fernando Cerviño Padrão, all the Portuguese establishments in Africa "were always sacrifices in relation to the Orient and, later, to Brazil, much less fruitful for the Crown."

When the Dutch seized Luanda in 1641, the Manicongo Garcia II and Nzinga became allies of the Dutch against the precarious Portuguese colony, which had retreated inland to Massangano. The Portuguese kept the support of the puppet Ndongo kingdom and formed an alliance with the Kingdom of Kasanje. This war favored the Dutch until 1648 when a Portuguese-Brazilian force arrived and recaptured Luanda. The victory of the Portuguese led the Manicongo to make peace with the Portuguese and become essentially a tributary to the government at Luanda. Queen Nzinga also signed a peace treaty with the Portuguese, but this peace did not last. In 1671 when a new puppet Ngola demonstrated some independence, the Portuguese occupied the kingdom, overthrew the Ngola and thereafter ruled the kingdom directly. The following year, Nzinga was captured and killed and the Portuguese installed a compliant ruler in Matamba.

The Portuguese pursued the campaigns of conquest in Angola for a century. They always fought with large numbers of African mercenaries or allies. As early as 1585, a Portuguese army had 9,000 African archers and soldiers and only 300 Europeans. As John Thornton writes, "the Portuguese army in Angola was largely an African force under its own command structure, with Europeans simply serving as leading generals." While the military campaigns enriched individual governors who claimed the lion share of the captives, the wars generally disrupted the internal slave trade. The long and difficult conquest of the Ndongo kingdom also spurred, directly or indirectly, the rise of two new kingdoms in eastern Angola, Matamba and Kasanje. Although these new African states eventually became allies and commercial partners with the Portuguese in Luanda, they limited the territorial reach of the colony and its commercial grasp. In the end, the Portuguese still had to do business with independent African states if any profit was to be realized. In Luanda, the original plan to create a settler colony was undermined by slave trading. A small colony did develop around Luanda and, in time, farms and ranches spread along the Kwanza River. In the colony itself, where the Portuguese were supposedly in control, one of the Portuguese officers advised the governor in 1640 that: "Negroes they fear nothing save only corporal punishment and the whip... It is only in this way that the former governors and conquerors kept them in subjection, and only in this way can we keep what we have won by force of arms in these kingdoms."

3.5 Castile and the Americas

In 1492, Castile had reconquered the Moorish kingdom of Granada in the Iberian Peninsula and was nearing the end point of the pacification of the Canary Islands. The most recent campaigns against Granada had taken ten years and required something like twelve thousand knights and forty thousand foot-soldiers. By the end of the fifteenth century, the population of Castile, approximately 4.5 million, comprised more than two-thirds of the peninsular population. The dynastic union of the monarchies of Castile and

Aragón, in the late 1470s under Isabel and Fernando, strengthened Castile. By the sixteenth century, Spain become the most successful expansionist realm in Christendom. A considerable part of this expansion was due to the support of alien minorities and foreign merchants who financed trade and conquest. Castile's resident Jewish merchants like Isaac Abrabanel had financed projects useful to the joint monarchs. After the Granada war when Jewish usefulness was less critical (and their religious and cultural unacceptability more intolerable), Isabel and Fernando, "the Catholic Monarchs," expelled those Jews who did not convert to Christianity. When he abandoned Castile, the merchant Abrabanel had debts of more than one million *maravedís*. More important than Jewish merchants were the Genoese. These foreign merchants in Castile supplied a good part of the support for the campaigns and colonization of the Canary Islands, for the conquest of Granada and later for the voyages to America. The Castile that expanded west into the Atlantic beginning in 1492 was an aggressive crusader state, well financed, with essentially no pause from medieval reconquest and the Canarian campaigns. As Francisco López de Gómera put it in 1552: "Upon finishing the conquest of the Moors, that lasted over 800 years, the one of the Indies was begun so that the Spaniards could always wage war against the infidels."

When the Castilians arrived in the Caribbean, they had two models to follow in dealing with the native Taino people, the first Native Americans they encountered. The first was the older Portuguese tradition of commercial empire on the coast of Africa, which involved settling in enclaves on the coast and trading peacefully with local kings, chiefs and traders. The second was the more recent experience of the conquest of the Canaries. At first, it appears that Castile and Columbus favored the first model because it offered wealth without the considerable effort and cost that accompanied conquest. After all, the conquest of the Canaries had required decades of war. The establishment by the Castilian monarchy of the state trading company, the Casa de Contratación at Seville in 1503, similar to Portugal's Casa de Mina, suggests, as Stanley and Barbara Stein writes, "the initial phase of contact in the Caribbean had generated the vision of a trading post or factory system ... where protected exchange was possible." However, the resistance of the Taino combined with their military weakness, in conjunction with their essentially non-market economy, soon led to the adoption of the conquest model.

3.6 The Devastation of the Indies

In 1492, Columbus approached the Taino in peace, seeking cooperation and trade. He established an alliance with one of the powerful chiefs, or *caciques*, as the Tainos called their leaders, of Española (later called Hispaniola), Guacanagarí. According to most accounts of the first voyage, including Columbus's own journal, the Admiral found on Cuba and Española a generous and kind people. Regarding the island of Española, Columbus wrote Isabel and Fernando that: "Your Highnesses may be assured that there is not upon earth a better or gentler people, at which you may rejoice, for they will easily become Christians and learn our customs. A finer country or people cannot exist, and the territory is so extensive and the people so numerous, that I know not how to give a description of them." During his first voyage and the one following, Columbus and his crew bartered with natives throughout the Greater Antilles, giving glass beads, small bells, cloth and more valuable items to Guacanagarí and receiving in return food, green parrots, precious stones, decorated masks, gold nuggets and fine worked objects. Realizing that success required cooperation, Columbus gave strict orders, according to the summary of his journal by the friar Bartolomé de Las Casas, "that the utmost care should be taken not to give offense to the natives in anything, and that no article should be taken from them without his permission; in this manner they were paid for everything they gave the Spaniards." When Columbus returned to Castile in 1493, he left a small settlement on the north coast of Española, thirty-nine men in the fort and town of La Navidad, and ordered them to do no harm or violence against any Indian, especially the women, and therefore bring no dishonor to the Christians. When Columbus returned to the Caribbean on his second voyage, according a document recorded in the history of the Indies by Las Casas, Isabel and Ferdnando ordered Columbus to bring clerics with him to instruct the natives in the Holy Faith and to treat them very well. "In order to better accomplish this mission," the Sovereigns wrote in their instructions to Columbus, "the Admiral shall take measures and require that, after the armada safely arrives, all who come in it, and those others who come from here later on, treat the Indians very well and lovingly, without offending them in any way. He shall see to it that they have much conversation and familiarity with them, and that they are as pleasant with them as they can be ... If it happens that any person or persons should mistreat the Indians in any way whatsoever, the Admiral, as Viceroy and Governor of Their Highnesses, shall punish them severely, by virtue of the authority that he has from Their Highnesses for that purpose."

This good-neighbor policy began to disintegrate during Columbus's second voyage to the Indies; indeed, its seeds were planted as soon as the second expedition reached the north shore of Española. This large fleet of 17 vessels and approximately 1,500 men reached the settlement of La Navidad in November 1493, that Columbus had established months earlier, and found the site burned down and completely abandoned. According to his friend and ally Guacanagarí, the Christians had quarreled and fought among themselves, taken native women and gold by force, divided their forces and faced attack by the chief Caonabó, of Maguana, who destroyed both factions despite the assistance the Christians received from Guacanagarí. The disaster at La Navidad began a gradual change in attitude between natives and Europeans. Both became more fearful of the other: the natives became less open, generous and trustful of Columbus and the Castilians and, at times, made threatening gestures. The Castilians, and Columbus as well, became more assertive, aggressive and violent.

After the ruin of La Navidad, Columbus chose a new and better site for settlement, about midway across the northern coast of Española, which he named Isabela. There he learned that the interior gold mines were located in a valley and province called Cibao. Columbus and the Castilian Captain

Alonso de Hojeda explored the Cibao, found the gold mines and built a fort, Santo Tomás, eighteen leagues from Isabella, to dominate the mining country. When he returned to Isabela, the captain of the fort reported to Columbus that all the Indians were deserting their villages and that the chief of the province, the already known Caonabó, was preparing to attack the fort. In early April 1494, Columbus ordered Captain Hojeda and four hundred men-of-arms to reinforce the fort. While Columbus set sail on a voyage of discovery in the Caribbean, Hojeda pursued a campaign of terror in the Cibao. To govern his colony in his absence, Columbus chose Mosén Pedro Margarite as captain-general with instructions to patrol the country and compel Indians to obey the Spaniards – especially the province of the Cibao. Unable to get control of the factions in Isabela, Margarite soon left for Castile. With no one in charge, the Castilian colonists, according to Ferdinand Columbus, "each one went where he will among the Indians, stealing their property and wives and inflicting so many injuries upon them that the Indians resolved to avenge themselves on any that they found along or in small groups."

When Columbus returned to Isabela, he found rebellious natives. The Admiral proceeded to subjugate the entire island and in this campaign, the *cacique* Guacanagarí offered to go with him and bring his people to help the Christians. Given Columbus', and the Sovereign's, earlier policy of good relations with the Indians, Las Casas wondered why this policy changed so radically so quickly. Las Casas placed more blame on the Castilians than Columbus. Still, Las Casas maintained that the Admiral's primary concern was to bring all the villages to his obedience in the name of Their Highnesses. According to Las Casas, Columbus "marched through a large part of the entire island for nine or ten months, waging fierce war against all the caciques and villages that did not render obedience to him. During those days or months there was a very considerable destruction or slaughtering of Indians and depopulation of villages." One of the Castilian tactics in this war was to capture the native chiefs. Hojeda turned his ambition upon the chief of the Cibao, Caonabó, one of the fiercest warrior *caciques* of Española. Through a ruse, he was able to handcuff the chief on horseback and bring him back to Isabela alive. Columbus decided to send him to Castile but the small fleet was lost at sea and the great chief presumably drowned. Caonabó's brothers, thus provoked, according to Las Casas, "betook themselves to Arms, and fought means of revenging themselves on their Enemies. The Spaniards attack'd 'em with their Cavalry, which is very formidable to the Indians, whom they soon conquer'd, and made so prodigious a slaughter among 'em, that half the Kingdom was depopulated and became desert after this Defeat."

In 1495, with a semblance of pacification, Columbus imposed a tribute of gold on the surviving chiefs of the Cibao. This tribute was unreasonable and only contributed to great native unrest. Columbus returned to Castile for the period 1496–8 and left his brother Bartolomé Columbus to govern the colony as Adelantado. In 1497, Bartolomé moved the capital from Isabela on the north shore to Santo Domingo on the southern coast, nearer to the mining districts. However, this move provoked dissent within Castilian ranks. The mayor of Isabela, Francisco Roldán, and his faction attempted to seize a gold field in the chiefdom of Xaraguá in the southwest corner of the island. Unable to do so, Roldán and his men sought refuge from Chief Behecchío and his sister Anacaona, the widow of Caonabó. During this Castilian rebellion, a coalition of fourteen native chiefs attacked the primary fort in the Cibao but was defeated by Bartolomé. Many of the chiefs and warriors were captured and enslaved. When Columbus returned to Española in 1498, he believed that one important way to obtain profit from the islands was to send native slaves to Castile. Columbus quickly sent 300 Indian slaves on a return voyage. He also received an offer of negotiation from Roldán, which he accepted. Columbus authorized Roldán to seize the Indians of the chiefdom of Xaranguá and divide them among his followers to use as forced laborers in the gold fields. To divide the faction geographically, Columbus also distributed lands throughout the island as well as Indians, a practice that had occurred during the *Reconquista* called the *repartimiento*.

The transfer of the *repartimiento* to the Indies, a system of tribute and essentially one of feudal labor relations, existed side by side with native slavery. The privileged Castilian who was granted a *repartimiento*, usually called an *encomendero*, had the right to the native labor of the villages assigned to him. The system worked, or worked well, only with native complicity. Pliant *caciques* controlled their populations and organized and mobilized the needed labor. However, in the islands the *repartimiento-encomienda* existed, at most, for only a decade or two before the native population essentially disappeared to be replaced by native slaves from the mainland and by enslaved Africans.

Complaints of how the Columbus brothers misgoverned Española by the Roldán faction and other Castilians, and Queen Isabel's displeasure with the arrival of native slaves from the island, led to the end of any Columbus rule by mid-1500. The first real official governor of the Indies, Nicolás Ovando, arrived in Santo Domingo in 1502 with 2,500 men and 10 Franciscan friars. Among his royal instructions from the king and queen was this familiar pitch: "You will see to it that the Indians are well treated, that they may go safely throughout the land, and that no one may use force against them, or rob them, or do any other evil or harm to them . . . Also: It is Our will and mercy that the Indians pay the tributes and taxes that they must pay Us."

Ovando had no intention of fulfilling either provision. As he saw it, his task was to destroy the remaining independent *caciques* and their chiefdoms. In 1502, the natives of the southeastern chiefdom of Higüey "rebelled" when a Castilian war dog killed one of their chiefs. Sometime later, Indians of the province killed eight unsuspecting Castilian sailors. With this provocation, Ovando invaded the province and rounded up several hundred native rebels and had them slaughtered. Las Casas noted that "in these sallies, it was customary to take along a good number of armed Indians, from among those already conquered, and they fought strenuously, such was their fear of the Spaniards whom they accompanied and their desire to please them; and this custom was generalized later all over the Indies." In the fall of 1503, Ovando paid a visit to the province of Xaraguá, now under the leadership of Chief Lady Anacaona, with an intimidating force of 70 on horseback and 300 on foot. She invited the governor to stay and invited some eighty district chiefs to attend this visit. During a jousting show, Ovando invited all the chiefs to speak with him inside. However, instead of speaking he trapped the chiefs inside the house and then set it on fire, burning alive all those inside. The horsemen then attacked the men, women and children of the town. Those who survived the sword were enslaved. Lady Anacaona was hanged.

In less than two decades, war and forced labor had devastated the Taino of Española. "After these wars had ended, and all the men were slain in them, so that there were generally left only young boys and women and children," Las Casas wrote, "the Spaniards parceled them out amongst themselves." Hardly an unbiased observer, Las Casas maintained a third of the native population died by warfare, starvation and illness as early as 1494 to 1496. Although figures are sketchy, there was a considerable decline of the Taino population on Española from 1492 to 1518. Assimilation played a part in this disappearance: the shortage of European women on the island led to sanctioned marriage with Taino women who were absorbed, with their children, into colonial Spanish society. Smallpox did not arrive in Española until 1518, when the disease spread from a mining camp worked by African slaves into the Indian population. However, it is certainly possible that European diseases had killed natives in the Caribbean long before 1518. For example, from 1502 to 1507, an outbreak of a disease called *modorra* – most likely typhus or influenza – was rampant in Iberia. In 1507, something like one hundred thousand people died in southern Spain due to an outbreak of the plague. It seems unlikely that none of these infections made transatlantic crossings. To replace the dying natives in Española, the Spanish began to raid other Caribbean islands and the mainland to capture Indians and ship them to Española. These expeditions marked the beginning of the conquest of the rest of the Caribbean. The Spanish also began to import African slaves as early as the late 1490s or early 1500s. They became the majority population by the 1520s. Most scholars agree that by the mid-sixteenth century, the Taino population of Española had disappeared (see Map 3.3).

The conquest of Puerto Rico began in 1507. Its conqueror, Juan Ponce de León, found gold on the island, established settlements and assigned *encomiendas*. Two years later, Diego Columbus, son of the explorer and viceroy of the Indies, gave the conquest of Jamaica to Juan de Esquivel. No gold was discovered here but *encomiendas* were established nevertheless, and the island came to produce food and cotton for the other Caribbean settlements. In 1511, Diego Velázquez de Cuéllar began the conquest of Cuba with 330 *conquistadores*. Velázquez led a force into the interior from the southwest coast while his lieutenant Pánfilo de Narváez marched inland from the southeast coast. Referring to Narváez' column, Las Casas remarked: "I do remember with how much spilling of human blood he marked that road." They discovered gold and by 1515 had founded eight towns on the island. All of these islands were depopulated by war, disease and exploitation within a few decades. Animals imported from Europe replaced people: cattle, horses, dogs and pigs. For example, Velázquez informed the king in 1514 that the handful of pigs brought to Cuba in 1509 had become more than thirty thousand four years later.

Map 3.3. Native and Spanish Caribbean.

Slaving expeditions eliminated the population of the Bahamas – approximately forty thousand – in the early sixteenth century. Curaçao, Aruba and the Leeward islands were likewise depopulated in the same way. However, the Windward Islands of the Lesser Antilles, the home of the fierce Caribs, did not suffer the same fate. These islands had no gold and the Caribs were too aggressive. As a result, they were generally left alone until the seventeenth and eighteenth centuries. Slaving on the Central American coast led to the first mainland colony in Panama with the promising name Castilla del Oro, "Golden Castile." Pedro Arias de Ávila took control of the region from Vasco Nuñez de Balboa in 1514 and "pacified" the native population. Here as elsewhere in the Caribbean, the Spanish made effective use of fierce dogs of war to attack and kill natives. The verb *aperrear*, to throw to the dogs, became quite common in the Spanish Indies.

Document 3.2
The Warning of the Cacique Hatuey to the Indians of Cuba

1511

Countrymen and Friends, you are not ignorant of the rumour by which we understand that the Spaniards are come among us, neither am I now to tell you how they have used the inhabitants of Hayti (so they call Hispaniola, in the Indian language) you know it by a sad experience: nor can we hope to find them more merciful than they did.

Then quoth he, Countrymen do you know the Errand which brings them hither? To whom they replyed, that was unknown to them, yet they further replyed, that they were well assured of the cruel nature of the Spaniard. Then quoth he, I'le tell ye the cause of their coming. They do worship some covetous and unsatisfied Deity, and to content the greedy worship of that Celestial Power, they require many things from us, using all their endeavor to murder and enslave us. Which having said, taking up a little Chest filled with Gold, he proceeded in these words: Behold here the God of the Spaniards, and therefore if you think fitting, let us daunce and sing before this their God, Perhaps we may thereby appease his rage, and he will then command the Spaniards to let us alone: Who with an unanimous shout cryed out all, Well said, well said; and so they went to dauncing round this box, not ceasing till they had sufficiently wearied themselves. Then the Lord Hatuey going on with his speech, quoth he, If we do keep this God till he be taken from us, we shall be surely slain, and therefore I think it expedient for us to cast it into the River; so his counsel being followed, the Chest was cast into the River.

A native *cacique* from Hispaniola, Hatuey escaped to Cuba to avoid death or captivity. *Source: The tears of the Indians being an historical and true account of the cruel massacres and slaughters of above twenty millions of innocent people committed by the Spaniards in the islands of Hispaniola, Cuba, Jamaica, &c.* Written in Spanish by Casaus, an eyewitness of those things; and made English by J.P. London, 1656. This is a translation of Bartolomé de las Casas, *Brevísima relación de la destrucción de las Indias* (1542).

Within thirty years of Columbus's first voyage, the Caribbean was a ruined place. The originally numerous Taino had been reduced to a few remnants here and there. The gold fields of Española began to give out in the 1520s, and those of Puerto Rico and Cuba in the 1530s. By this time most Spaniards had departed for the mainland in search of rich Indian kingdoms to conquer and plunder. Those who remained in the islands became ranchers or cultivated sugar cane, a crop that had been transferred from the Canaries.

What Las Casas called the "devastation of the Indies" did not proceed without protest or attempts at reform. In a sermon in 1511, Antonio de Montesinos, a Dominican friar, asked the *encomenderos* of Española to reflect upon their behavior regarding the native people: "You are in mortal sin. You live and die in it, because of the cruelty and tyranny you practice in dealing with these innocent people. Tell me, by what right or justice do you keep these Indians in such cruel and horrible servitude? Are they not men? Do they not have rational souls? Are you not obliged to love them as you do yourselves? On what authority have you waged a detestable war against these people who dwelt quietly and peacefully in their own land?" Protests such as this led to debate regarding treatment of native peoples in the Americas. In 1512–13, a royal commission produced the Law of Burgos, which directed that all Indians should be made Christians and attempted to eliminate abuses and regulate Indian labor.

A second commission confronted the issue of just war and the right of conquest. Conquest was authorized if Indians refused to acknowledge the authority of the Pope and his agent, the king of Spain, and in any way resisted or prevented the preaching of the faith. Prior to hostilities a document called the *Requerimiento*, or Requisition, was to be read to the natives. It contained a brief history of the world and explanation of the papal donation of the Indies to Spain (in the Treaty of Tordesillas of 1494). Natives were then required to accept the two conditions noted within. If they did not comply, conquest, enslavement and robbery of possessions would commence. "And I solemnly declare," the document concludes on behalf of a *conquistador*, "that the deaths and damages received from such will be your fault and not that of His Majesty, nor mine, nor of the gentlemen who came with me."

In the Caribbean, and particularly in the Greater Antilles, the Spanish found societies that had welcomed their arrival but quickly had reservations and fears, which Columbus and the Castilians interpreted as resistance. The Taino were not notably warlike or aggressive even in their own pre-Columbian world. They feared their distant neighbors, the Caribs, and sought to avoid them at all costs. Against the Spanish, the Taino were hardly a match, yet they fought and rebelled until their societies were completely destroyed and they themselves were extinguished. Unlike the Canarians, few Tainos survived to assimilate into Spanish colonial society. However, within a generation the Spanish would come across much more warlike and militarily able peoples on the mainland.

3.7 The Conquest of the Mexica

For nearly thirty years, the Spanish encountered native peoples who had not organized their societies for war. This changed in 1517. In that year, the governor of Cuba, Diego de Velázquez, dispatched an expedition of discovery to the west and found Yucatan. There the Spanish found Maya cities and warriors who attacked landing parties and were able to drive them back to their ships. Intrigued, Velázquez sent a second expedition to Yucatan and into the Gulf of Mexico the following year. Again, the Spanish fought disciplined and aggressive native soldiers and discovered that their own military superiority here could no longer be taken for granted. This expedition found gold for trade as well as some evidence of a great inland kingdom, which was, of course, the Mexica Empire.

In 1519, Velázquez sent a third expedition of exploration and trade under the command of Hernando Cortés. This expedition, the strongest to date, comprised 11 ships and about 450 Spaniards, 200 Cuban natives and several Africans, 16 horses, several canon, crossbows and harquebuses. Although ordered simply to reconnoiter, Cortés left Cuba with a greater ambition in mind: to found a colony on the Gulf coast and to conquer a native kingdom. Cortés informed his expedition: "There we shall do as we see fit, and here I offer you great rewards, although they will be wrapped about with great hardships... You are few, I see, but such is your spirit that no effort or force of Indians will prevail against you, for we have seen by experience how God has favored the Spanish nation in these parts, and how we have never lacked courage or strength, and never shall."

Like the previous two expeditions, Cortés sailed along the coast of Yucatan and at its western base, landed at the Maya city of Champotón and seized the town following two battles. Once Cortés was victorious, Maya nobles presented the captain with gifts of food, clothing, gold and twenty women. One of these women was Malinali, whom the Spanish came to call Doña Marina, a Nahua noblewoman who for one reason or another ended up among the Chontal Maya and spoke both Nahuatl and Maya. Because one of Cortés' soldiers spoke a Maya dialect (having been shipwrecked on the Yucatan coast and integrated into a Maya community for two years before being rescued), the captain now had a way to speak with the peoples of the Mexica Empire. Doña Marina was baptized and in time learned Spanish. She became Cortés' interpreter and mistress as well a trusted advisor.

Cortés proceeded along the Gulf coast until he came upon a natural harbor and disembarked on April 21, 1519. One day later, the local Mexica governor and four thousand unarmed men visited the Spanish camp. The governor presented the Spaniards with gifts of gold objects and information about the Mexica Empire and its ruler, Moteucçoma. He no doubt was ordered to visit the Spaniards to gather intelligence and announce the wealth and power of the empire. He returned a week later with even more lavish gifts and a request from Moteucçoma to proceed no further. Given the wealth that had fallen into his hands so quickly and easily, Cortés decided to stay. Here he and his soldiers founded a city they named Villa Rica de Vera Cruz – the "Rich Town of the True Cross." In doing this, Cortés severed his legal dependence upon the governor of Cuba and became a free agent. To prevent any of his men from betraying him in the name of Velázquez and returning to Cuba, he stripped the remaining ten ships and had them beached.

As was the custom in the islands, Cortés led what was essentially a force of mercenaries. It was a free company that acknowledged the authority of the king and sought a contract giving their commander and themselves the right to a portion of the spoils of war. The Spanish Indies was conquered on behalf of, not by, the king and empire. It was an advantageous arrangement for both parties. To obtain a royal contract, Cortés dispatched Francisco de Montejo to Spain and the "citizens" of Vera Cruz petitioned the king "to order and provide a decree and letters patent in favor of Fernando Cortés, captain and chief justice of Your Royal Highnesses, so that he may govern us with justice until this land is conquered and pacified, and for as long as Your Majesties may see fit, knowing him to be a person well suited for such a position."

At this point, it is not clear what course Cortés planned on taking. At Vera Cruz, he learned of a nearby city of fourteen thousand residents, Cempohuallan (today Cempoala), the capital of the Totonacs and a tributary kingdom under Mexica hegemony. Cortes marched to the city in June and learned for the first time about the discontent that existed among subject peoples of the Mexica. The Totonac ruler complained of Mexica tribute, and Cortés ordered him to cease tribute payments and seize the collector. (As a demonstration of friendship, Cortés later freed him.) In short order, an alliance was forged and Cortés now most likely abandoned the idea of simply establishing a colony confined to the coast. With Indian allies, Cortés greatly augmented his force and decided to march to Tenochtitlan, greet Moteucçoma and – perhaps – divide and conquer. On the march into the Mexica Empire, he remarked: "*Omne regnum in se ipsum divisum desolabitur,*" or "Every kingdom divided against itself will be brought to desolation."

Cortés then began his march inland. He left a garrison at Vera Cruz and took 300 Spaniards, African *conquistadores* and hundreds or perhaps thousands of Totonac porters and warriors on the march. Informed by his Indian allies about the independence of Tlaxcallan (today Tlaxcala), Cortés headed for that kingdom and its central city. However, when the Spaniards approached Tlaxcala, they were attacked by thousands of professional warriors and driven back. The Tlaxcalans later stated that they believed the strangers were Mexica allies and therefore enemies. The Tlaxcalans attacked twice more, killing forty-five of the Spanish force. Without their Totonac allies, Francisco de Solís, one of the *conquistadores*, later testified, "we should not have won." The Spanish now feared defeat and annihilation as the Tlaxcalans appeared unrelenting and the Spanish were running out of lead balls, powder and crossbow bolts. However, at this point the Tlaxcalans sought peace and submitted themselves to the Spanish king and the Catholic faith. Cortés asked the Tlaxcalans if they were subject to Mexico-Tenochtitlan and if they paid tribute. According to the sixteenth-century missionary and historian Fray Diego Durán, Cortés received this reply: "O Great Lord, They answered, we are free men! We do not pay tribute, nor are we vassals of anyone. That great sovereign you mentioned is the king of Tenochtitlan, our mortal enemy, with whom we wage a perpetual war."

On September 23, 1519, Cortés and his *conquistadores* entered Tlaxcala city and were given gifts of food, gold and women. The Spaniards and Tlaxcalans forged an alliance, which must have concerned Moteucçoma greatly. While at Tlaxcala, Cortés received another embassy from the emperor of the Mexica, was given gifts, which the Spaniards interpreted as submission and vassalage, and again Moteucçoma requested that they advance no further.

The passivity of Moteucçoma during the Spanish march into Mexico has long puzzled historians. When the Spaniards had landed in Yucatan and as they approached Tlaxcala, Indian cities and states had shown unprovoked hostility and had attacked the Spaniards again and again. On the other hand, Moteucçoma, ruler of the most powerful state in Mesoamerica, allowed a small alien force, which had abused his provincial authorities and made an alliance with his long-standing enemy, to proceed without opposition despite repeated protests that they stay away. Several explanations of this behavior have been proposed over the centuries, but one has attained special status. Following the conquest, native informants told chroniclers that Moteucçoma believed Cortés to be a returning Mesoamerican god, the Feathered Serpent, called Quetzalcoatl. In fact, if he did believe this, Moteucçoma feared offending a powerful deity. The peoples of Mexico also referred to the Spaniards as *teules*, which the Spaniards interpreted as gods, and they believed the Mexicans viewed them as gods.

There is insufficient evidence to show that the people of Mexico, or natives elsewhere in the Americas, believed that Spaniards or other Europeans were true gods. Castilians brought the idea that natives saw them as gods from the Caribbean. In Mexico, the native reference to the Spanish as *teules* (the Nahuatl plural for god is *teteoh*) could just as likely mean godlike, that is, powerful and privileged rather than divine in any Christian or classical sense. Bernal Díaz noted that the Totonacs "called us *teules*, which is their name for both their gods and evil spirits." However, James Lockhart notes, "all of the Nahuatl texts saying that the Spaniards were called gods were written in a later generation." Franciscan missionaries and, primarily, their indigenous informants and scribes invented the myth of Cortés as the returning god in the 1550s to explain and justify Mexica defeat. One clue that suggests the Quetzalcoatl belief is not true is the Mesoamerican religious tradition that deification was post-mortem. Even Quetzalcoatl himself, in life a priest-ruler, only became a god after he died. As Matthew Restall states, "the Spaniards-as-gods myth makes sense only if natives are assumed to be 'primitive,' childlike, or half-witted."

In Tlaxcala, Cortés learned more about the Mexica Empire and the nearby city of Chollolan (modern Cholula), a Mexica tributary city and the second most populous city in Mexico. Cholula was also the holiest site in central Mexico, center of the cult of Quetzalcoatl with numerous temples and the largest pyramid in Mesoamerica. In October, Cortés marched to this city with his Spanish force and approximately five thousand Tlaxcalan warriors. At the entry way, the Spaniards were invited into the city. Almost immediately, the Spaniards and Tlaxcalans attacked the inhabitants and massacred thousands. According to López de Gómera, the Tlaxcalans warned Cortés that the Cholulans were planning a surprise attack while Mexica warriors waited outside the town. However, the Spanish action in Cholula was not a defensive action (another route to Tenochtitlan was possible). The massacre at Cholula was theatrical terror designed to demonstrate to everyone in central Mexico, and especially to Moteucçoma, the power and ruthlessness of the Spanish. As Inga Clendinnen puts it: "Cortés certainly knew the therapeutic effects of a good massacre." During a two-week residence in Cholula,

Cortés made an alliance with the new leadership of Cholula and met the traditional ally of Tlaxcala, the kingdom of Huejotzingo, and formed another alliance. Thereafter Cortés, his Spanish force, and six thousand Indians from Cempoala, Tlaxcala, Cholula and now Huejotzingo continued the march to Tenochtitlan.

When the Spaniards entered the Valley of Mexico, they encountered a civilization that dazzled them. Years later, Bernal Díaz, one of Cortés *conquistadores*, wrote of his impression:

> During the morning we arrived at a broad causeway and continued our march toward Ixtapalapa, and when we saw so many cities and villages built in the water and other great cities on dry land and that straight and level causeway going toward Mexico, we were amazed and said it was like the enchantments they tell in the legend of Amadis, on account of the great towers and cues [pyramids] and buildings rising from the water, and all built of masonry. And some of our soldiers even asked whether the things that we saw were not a dream.

Cortés and his soldiers realized their expedition and entry into Tenochtitlan was of historic significance. As Díaz crowed: "What men have there been in the world who have shown such daring" (see Map 3.4).

On the causeway, Cortés and his Spanish force (his Indian allies were encamped on the shore) were met by a great delegation of 200 nobles led by Moteucçoma. In his welcoming speech, Moteucçoma stated, according to Cortés: "you are in your own country and your own house, rest now from the hardships of your journey and the battles which you have fought." Cortés interpreted this as an act of submission and vassalage to the king of Spain, Carlos V, an unlikely act. However, it is just as likely that Moteucçoma was simply being polite, proclaiming as modern Mexicans do, "*Mi casa es su casa*," my house is your house. On the other hand, viewed as an act of donation it justified the conquest as a legitimate and just war. When the Mexica later attacked the Spanish, their actions were perceived (in a legal context) not as a legitimate defense of their homeland but as an illegal rebellion against their new sovereign.

Cortés and his men were brought into the city and lodged in the palace of Axayácatl. Following a strategy that had been pursued during the *Reconquista*, the wars in the Canary Islands and in the Caribbean, Cortés seized Moteucçoma and held him captive, and Moteucçoma cooperated with Cortés, gave him more gifts and even defeated a faction that planned to attack the small Spanish force. Within a short time, Cortés accumulated an enormous booty estimated at 160,000 pesos. To put this figure in a Caribbean context, the conqueror of Puerto Rico, Ponce de León, dispatched to the king a tribute of 4,000 pesos during the period 1509–21.

During his residence in Tenochtitlan, in April 1520, Cortés received word from Moteucçoma that a Spanish force had landed at Vera Cruz with instructions to capture the captain and return him to Cuba for trial. Governor Velázquez had organized an expedition of 19 ships and 800 soldiers to defeat

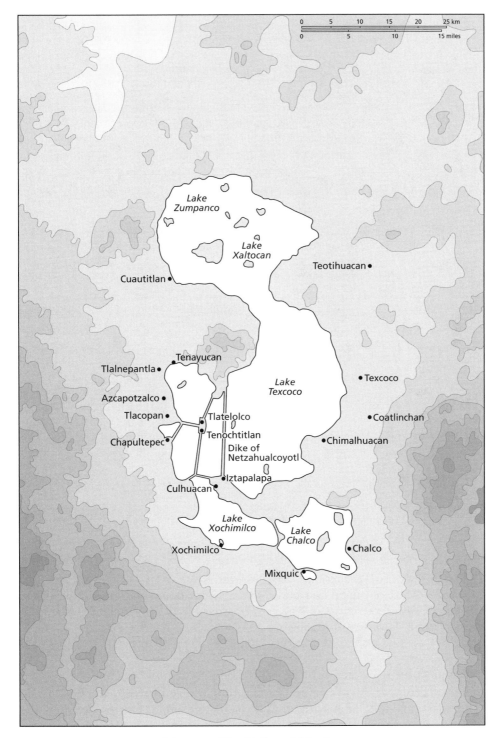

Map 3.4. The Valley of Mexico.

Figure 3.3. Mexico-Tenochtitlan, Based on the Cortés Map, 1524. *Mexico, regia et celebris* (Mexico, capital and famed) from Georg Braun and Franz Hogenberg, *Civitates Orbis Terrarum* (Cologne, 1572). Courtesy of the William L. Clements Library at the University of Michigan.

and punish his wayward protégé. Cortés left eighty soldiers under the command of Pedro de Alvarado in Tenochtitlan and returned to the Gulf coast with the remainder of his force. With skill and guile, Cortés defeated the punitive expedition, thereby augmenting his troops with hundreds of new soldiers.

While Cortés was on the coast, in Tenochtitlan Alvarado took an action that profoundly altered Cortés' plan for peaceful conquest. During the festival of Toxcatl in honor of Huitzilopochtli, Alvarado and his small force attacked and massacred thousands of unarmed Mexica nobles. One post-conquest chronicler estimated that eight thousand to ten thousand Mexica, the political, religious and military elite of Tenochtitlan, were slaughtered. It is unknown whether Alvarado perceived a threat and launched a preemptive attack or was offended by pagan ritual and human sacrifice. Alvarado was later quoted as saying, "he who begins the battle, wins." It is likely that Alvarado, like Cortés at Cholula, was simply following a pattern of seeking submission through the display of violence and terror. Regardless of his motivation, the immediate result was that the surviving Mexica attacked the Spanish, surrounded the palace they occupied and cut off food and fresh water. When Cortés returned to the city, he found a potential disaster. The Mexica allowed his force of 1,300 Spaniards and 2,000 Tlaxcalans to enter the city unopposed where they, too, were besieged.

Cortés and his Spanish and Indian troops remained in the city for another twenty-three days, each one of which witnessed a Mexica attack. During this period, one day Moteucçoma made an appeal to his people from the roof of the palace to cease their attacks and was killed. The Spanish blamed the Mexica and the Mexica blamed the Spanish. Thereafter, the Spanish possessed no bargaining chip, which might have facilitated a peaceful withdrawal. This situation was untenable and Cortés ordered a nighttime retreat. During the early hours of June 30th, the Spanish attempted to escape from Tenochtitlan undetected. This proved to be impossible. During the night, the Mexica rallied and attacked the vulnerable Spaniards fleeing along the causeway to the shore. The Mexica clearly had the advantage as they could attack in canoes from both sides, whereas warriors on the causeway simply had to push a heavily armored Spaniard into the lake where he sank like a stone. This night saw the greatest Spanish defeat by Indian arms since the arrival of Columbus in 1492. Cortés lost 860 Spaniards out of a force of approximately 1,380 (and most of the survivors were wounded, including Cortés) while thousands of Tlaxcalans were killed. Cortés retreated around the northern edge of the lake system to Tlaxcala. The Mexica, no doubt believing the Spanish no longer posed a threat, did not pursue and attempt to destroy the weakened and defeated Spanish force. The Spanish called this nighttime defeat the "sorrowful night," the *Noche Triste*.

At this most dire moment, the fate of Cortés and his diminished, hungry and wounded army lay in the hands of the Tlaxcalans. In his grant of 1525 giving Cortés a Coat of Arms, the Emperor noted that leading *conquistadores* urged the captain to retreat to Vera Cruz. "To this you never gave way," Carlos wrote. Instead, Cortés argued that if they went to the seacoast, "there would be greater opportunity for a confederation of all the natives and if they were in agreement, no force would be adequate for entering among them." Fortunately for Cortés, the Tlaxcalans maintained the alliance, although they negotiated better terms for themselves: fifty percent of all future spoils of war, freedom from Spanish tribute and the independence of Tlaxcala as a kingdom within the Spanish Empire. (The Spanish did not fully honor this agreement.) In Tlaxcala, Cortés decided to conquer the Mexica Empire by force of arms. He confidently informed Carlos V that he would "subjugate them, under the imperial and royal yoke and dominion of His Majesty, to whom, legally, the lordship of these parts now belong." Cortés boasted furthermore that he would gain "the greatest prize and honor that until our times any generation has ever won." To do this, Cortés called upon all Spaniards in the Caribbean to join him. He embarked on the conquest of the towns east of the Valley of Mexico and then the forging of new alliances. He acquired more horses, canon and other arms and directed his Tlaxcalan allies to make thousands of crossbow bolts. At the same time, he had Spanish craftsmen begin the construction of thirteen brigantines, small flat-bottomed ships each to be armed with a canon, to make war and attack Tenochtitlán on the lake itself.

During the fall of 1520 as these preparations were underway, another and much more deadly force attacked Tenochtitlan. When the punitive expedition arrived in Mexico from Cuba in April of that year, one of its members carried smallpox into the country. The disease swept through Indian populations from the coast to the interior and reached Tenochtitlan in mid-October. By the end of the year, perhaps one quarter of the population of the Valley of Mexico had died. Among the hundreds of thousands of victims was Cuitlahuac, the successor of Moteucçoma, who died in December. (Cuauhtémoc succeeded Cuitlahuac in February 1521.) The epidemic not only killed Mexica but also disrupted and weakened Mexica society and its leadership. Naturally, the epidemic also killed allies of the Spanish but Cortés took advantage of this situation by replacing deceased allied rulers with more supportive and dependent Indian kings and chiefs.

In December 1520, Cortés returned to the Valley of Mexico with a force of over 500 Spaniards and approximately 10,000 Tlaxcalans. During the siege of Tenochtitlan, the Tlaxcalan allies sang: "Aid our lords, those who dress in iron, they are besieging the city, they are besieging the Mexican nation, let us go forward with courage!" After the conquest, the Tlaxcalan lords had the right to title themselves *conquistador*. In late 1520, Cortés seized Tetzcoco (today Texcoco), the second city of the empire located on the eastern shore of the lake, and made it his base of operations. Later Texcocans made the claim that they were the most important participants of the conquest. Fernando Alva Ixtlilxochtil, a descendant of the kings of Texcoco, wrote in the seventeenth century that the conquest of Mexico was the result of a partnership. "The first Spaniards who came to these parts achieved little and came off badly." It was the Texcocans, he noted, who had "led the dance and ran the risks." In the following months, Cortés attempted to make alliances with, or if necessary conquer, the city-states in the Valley as well as those in neighboring provinces to the south and west. In this campaign, Cortés was largely, although not entirely, successful. For example, when the Spanish and Tlaxcalans attacked Ixtlapalapan (today Ixtapalapa), a city on the lake, the Ixtlapalapans drew the *conquistadores* into the city and then broke the dikes and flooded the town. The attackers barely escaped annihilation. In April, the captain launched the brigantines on the lake system and began to attack, and be attacked by, Mexica war canoes. In May, Cortés took control of the three cities at the base of the three causeways leading to Tenochtitlán and began a siege.

The assault on the city itself began in late May. By this time, Cortés led a force of approximately 700 Spanish foot-soldiers, 86 cavalry, 118 crossbowmen and harquebusiers and perhaps as many as 75,000 Indian allies. He divided his forces into three armies, not counting the soldiers and sailors on the brigantines, and began the attack on the three causeways. During the day, the Spanish and Indian forces would fight their way along the causeways only to lose ground to the Mexica at night. In one particularly disastrous attack on June 30th, Cortés was wounded and captured for a brief time and eighty-six Spaniards and eight horses were seized and sacrificed. For weeks, the tide of battle ebbed and flowed, favoring the Spanish forces at times and favoring the Mexica at other times. Mexica warriors were hobbled by their requirement to engage in single combat with "prestigious" Spanish or enemy Indian soldiers, with the goal of capturing them alive for sacrifice. Spanish soldiers and their allies had no inhibition against battleground killing. However, by mid-July the attackers were in the city and holding ground in part by having their Indian allies tear down Mexica temples and buildings and fill up the canals with the rubble. At the beginning of August, the Mexica retreated to Tlatelolco where they made their last stand. In mid-August, the Spanish broke through the remaining Mexica defenses. After waiting four days without the city surrendering, Cortés launched another attack, killing, he estimated, more than twelve thousand. Cortés met with some of the lords of Tenochtitlan: "I said many things to persuade them to surrender but all to no avail, although we showed them more signs of peace than have ever been shown to a vanquished people for we, by the grace of our Lord, were now the victors." A few days later, he allowed his Tlaxcalan allies to attack their bitter enemies and a massacre followed. Cuauhtémoc was captured and survivors began to walk out of the city. Writing of the native massacre, Cortés wrote: "No race, however savage, has ever practiced such fierce and unnatural cruelty as the natives of these parts." After three months of siege and battle, the Mexica and their city were utterly devastated. In the end, Cortés informed his emperor: "The people of the city had to walk upon their dead while others swam or drowned in the waters of that wide lake where they had their canoes; indeed, so great was their suffering that it was beyond our understanding how they could endure it."

The conquest of Tenochtitlan had killed more than one hundred thousand Mexica. It was said the lake had turned the color of blood red. Survivors streamed out of the city for three days. The Mexica had put up a heroic resistance, but the smallpox that had attacked the city in late 1520 had brought sickness, weakness, starvation and great death. The preeminent military historian of the Mexica and the conquest, Ross Hassig, concludes: "The Spanish conquest was not one of superior arms and wills but one that took advantage of existing cleavages within the system to split the empire, turn its members on the Aztecs, and rend it asunder." Immediately following the conquest, Cortés and the Spanish looted the city of gold. One Nahua account described the scene: "the Captain, spoke to the rulers, saying to them, 'Where is the gold that was kept in Mexico?' Then they took out of the boats all the gold: the golden banners, the golden miters, the golden armbands, the golden leg bands, the golden helmets, and the golden disks. They laid it all before the Captain, but the Spaniards came to remove it all."

Document 3.3
The Conclusion of the Conquest of Mexico

Bernal Díaz del Castillo, 1568

The detachment of Alvarado continued to advance, and after an engagement of two hours forced the enemy from their barricades in the great square. The cavalry now rendered good service in the open space, and the enemy were driven before us into the temple of the war god. Alvarado divided his forces into three bodies, and while he occupied the attention of the enemy with two, he ordered the third, commanded by Gutierre de Badajoz, to drive them from, and take possession of the great temple. The enemy, headed by their priests, occupied the adoratories or sanctuaries of their idols, and repulsed our troops, driving them down the steps; which being observed by Alvarado, he then sent us to support them, and on our arrival, having ascended to the top, we completely drove the enemy from that post; having done which, we set fire to the images of their false gods, and planted our standard on the summit of the temple. The view of this signal of victory rejoiced Cortes, who would fain have joined us, but he had it not in his power. He was then distant a quarter of a league, and had many ditches to fill as he advanced. In four days from this time, both he and Sandoval had worked their way to us, and the communications to the three posts were opened through the centre of the city of Mexico. This attack upon the temple was truly perilous; the edifice was very lofty, and the enemy numerous; and they continued to engage us on the flat ground at the summit, from the time we had set fire to the idols and their adoratories, until night. The royal palaces were now levelled to the ground. Guatimotzin [Cuauhtemoc] and his troops having retired to a quarter of the city more distant from the centre, and towards the lake.

Still they attacked us in the day, and at night pursued us to our quarters, and thus time passed over, and no proposition was made concerning peace. Our chiefs then proposed a plan of laying ambuscades. Thirty cavalry and one hundred infantry of the prime of our army, together with one thousand Tlascalans were posted in concealment, in some large houses which had belonged to a nobleman of the city. This was done during the night. Cortes with the rest of his troops, in the morning went to attack a post at a bridge, which Guatimotzin had ordered to be supported by a large force. Cortes after his first attack retreated, drawing the enemy after him, by the buildings where the troops were placed in concealment. At the proper moment he fired two shots close together as a signal to us; we sallied out, and the enemy being enclosed between us, our allies, and the party of Cortes which faced about, a dreadful havoc was made of them, and from that time they no more annoyed us in our retreat. Another trap was also laid for them by Alvarado, but not with the same success; I was not present at it, being ordered by Cortes to do duty for that time with his party...

Cortes at this time sent to Guatimotzin requesting him to surrender, under the strongest assurances of enjoying the plentitude of power and honors. He accompanied this embassy with as handsome a present as his situation permitted, of provisions, bread, fowls, fruit, and game. Guatimotzin as he was advised to do by those whom he consulted, dissimulated, and seemed inclined to pacification. He sent four of his principal nobility, with a promise to come to an interview with Cortes in three days. But this was all feigned; he employed the time in fortifying his quarter of the town, and making preparations to attack us. He also endeavored to amuse us by a second embassy, but we were now advised of his schemes. In fact, from what he was told by those about him, and from the example of his uncle Montezuma, he was afraid to trust himself in our hands. But the mask was soon thrown off; we were attacked by great bodies of the enemy, with such violence that it appeared as if all was beginning anew. Having been rather taken by surprise, they did us at first some mischief, killed one soldier, and two horses; but in the send we sent them back with very little to boast of. Cortes ordered his troops now to proceed against that part of the city where the quarters of Guatimotzin were; accordingly we began upon our former styem, and gained grown as we had before done elsewhere. When the king perceived this, he desired an interview with Cortes, on the side of a large canal which was to separate them. To this Cortes readily assented, and it was to take place on the ensuing morning. Cortes attended, but Guatimotzin never appeared; instead of which he sent several of his principal nobility, who said that the king did not think proper to come, from an apprehension that we might shoot him during the parley. Cortes then engaged by the most solemn oaths not to do him any injury whatever, but it was of no effect. A ridiculous farce was played here: two of the nobility who attended on the part of Guatimotzin, took out of a sack, break, a fowl, and cherries, which they began to eat, in order to impress the Spaniards with an idea that they were not in want. Cortes seeing the manner in which he was treated, sent back an hostile message and retired; after this we were left unmolested for the space of four or five days. During this time numbers of wretched Indians, reduced by famine, surrounded our quarters every night. Cortes pitied their miserable situation, and hoping that it might induce the enemy to come into terms of accommodation, order the cessation of hostilities to be strictly adhered to; but no overture of the kind was made . . .

What I am going to mention is truth, and I swear and say amen to it. I have read of the destruction of Jerusalem, but I cannot conceive that the mortality there exceeded this of Mexico; for all the people from the distant provinces which belonged to this empire had concentrated themselves here, where they mostly died. The streets, the squares, the houses, and the courts of the Taltelulco were covered with dead bodies; we could not step without treading on them; the lake and canals were filled with them, and the stench was intolerable.

Bernal Díaz del Castillo accompanied Hernán Cortés to Mexico in 1519. Decades after the events he describes, beyond the age of seventy, Díaz began to write an account of the Spanish campaign in Mexico. This was from his point of view, a "true history," that demonstrated the victory was not due to Cortés solely but was the triumph of ordinary warriors like himself. *Source: The True History of the Conquest of Mexico*, By Captain Bernal Diaz del Castillo, one of the Conquerors. Written in the Year 1568. Translated from the Original Spanish, by Maurice Keatinge Esq. (1800), pp. 307–9, 314.

In 1522, the Emperor appointed Cortés Adelantado, Repartidor [distributor] of Indians and Captain-General and Governor of New Spain, as Mexico was now called. In that same year, Cortés began the reconstruction of México-Tenochtitlan as a Spanish city utilizing the conquered slave labor of tens of thousands of surviving Mexica and Nahua. By 1524, Cortés had granted himself an *encomienda* composed of more than twenty-three thousand Indians, and had distributed much of the population of central Mexico to his *conquistadores* in *encomiendas*. With the arrival of the first priests in mendicant orders, the Franciscans, Augustinians and Dominicans, the Spanish began the destruction of Indian temples and the construction of Christian churches in exactly the same location.

The defeat and total destruction of Tenochtitlan did not result in the conquest of Mesoamerica or even all of the Mexica Empire. The more ambitious *conquistadores*, generally with the permission of Cortés, set off to assert Spanish dominion. These expeditions always took Tlaxcalans, Texcocans, Huejotzincans and other Indian allies as well as African servants, slaves and *conquistadores*. In the early 1520s, Spanish expeditions went in all directions. The Mixtecs and Zapotecs of Oaxaca generally negotiated arrangements with the Spanish due to divisions among them. An expedition further south to Chiapa in 1524 failed, but another one four years later began to establish at least some control over the province. A Spanish expedition was badly defeated in 1522 in the northeastern province of Pánuco by the Huastecas. Cortés then sent the *conquistador* Nuño Beltrán de Guzmán to avenge the defeat. The first Spanish expedition into the Tarascan Empire of west-central Mexico began in 1522 and met no resistance. When the *conquistador* Nuño Beltrán de Guzmán arrived in 1530, he executed the Tarascan king for sedition. Guzmán's brutality and distribution of *encomiendas* produced the massive Mixtón War (1540–1), which defeated three successive Spanish expeditions before the Viceroy Antonio de Mendoza led a force of Spaniards and Indians against the "rebels." As the Spanish moved further north into regions where they found silver mines, they also found intractable natives who resisted these invaders for centuries. In 1524, the lieutenant of Cortés, Pedro de Alvarado, led an expedition of *conquistadores* and Tlaxcalans into western Guatemala, the Kingdom of the Quiche Maya. After a great battle, the Quiche sued for peace. However, fearing treachery, Alvarado captured the Maya lords and burned them and their town. Alvarado then made an alliance with the Cakchiquel Maya to destroy the Tzutuhil, which he did, but in time the Cakchiquel revolted. Other Maya groups inflicted temporary defeat on the invaders. There were more expeditions and campaigns, many of them in northern Mexico where non-sedentary peoples remained unsettled and unconquered until the twentieth century. In the north, center, and south during the following two and a half centuries of colonial rule and throughout the nineteenth century, there were large and small uprisings. In central Mexico, William B. Taylor surveyed 142 local rebellions, most of them occurring in the eighteenth century. Part of native resistance involved not just violent rebellion but also the use of Spanish courts to defend themselves against Spanish abuses. As Susan Schroeder notes, "the numerous instances of ethnic uprisings and large-scale rebellions dramatized a fictive peace in New Spain." It took generations for the Spaniards to subdue Mexico's native populations, and even then protests against Spanish exactions were not at all uncommon in the centuries that followed conquest."

An example of an incomplete conquest in Mesoamerica is Yucatan. For twenty-five years, Spanish expeditions had touched the coast at various points and Maya warriors had driven them back to their ships. During this time, the Spanish had unloosed a devastating plague, smallpox, which had swept through the peninsula killing perhaps hundreds of thousands. In 1527, Francisco de Montejo, another of Cortés' lieutenants, initiated a campaign of conquest in Yucatan. Meeting effective resistance for two years, Montejo withdrew and returned in 1531 with a larger force. This expedition suffered some victories and defeats, and when the news of the discovery and riches of Peru reached Yucatan in 1533–4, many of his men abandoned the campaign and Montejo again withdrew. Montejo's son, Francisco de Montejo the Younger, led the third and final campaign from 1540 to 1547. Nahua fighters and porters accompanied his Spanish *conquistadores* from central Mexico. Montejo found his most important allies in the peninsula. There he discovered rival clans, the Xiu of Mani and the Cocom of Sotuto, involved in a feud that had continued for 100 years. Montejo made an alliance with the noble Xiu and Pech clans. The Pech lords, in their post-conquest annals, perceived themselves as *conquistadores* no less valiant or noble than the Spanish. They saw the struggle as "the history...of how much suffering we went through with the Spaniards because of Maya people who were not willing to deliver themselves to God." To the Pech lords, the pertinent division in the peninsula was not that between Indian and Spaniard but between noble and common and between *conquistador* and conquered. The military campaign of the 1540s was hard fought, and it likely would not have been possible with Mayan allies and old world diseases.

Although the Spanish declared victory in 1547, the fighting never really stopped. The eastern and southeastern regions continued the resist into the nineteenth century. "The Conquest of the peninsula as a whole," writes Matthew Restall, "dragged on for the rest of the colonial period, as the border between the colony and the unconquered territories shifted to the southeast only extremely slowly. These unconquered lands were dubbed *despobaldo*, 'uninhabited,' by the Spaniards, but this was wishful thinking on their part, a euphemism that disguised the incompleteness of the Conquest."

3.8 The Conquest of the Inka

The expeditions that departed from Mexico-Tenochtitlán in search of new conquests found no prizes as rich as the Mexica city. When Cortés returned to Spain in 1528, he met a soldier who had recently returned from Panama,

Francisco Pizarro. As a result of three expeditions down the Pacific coast of South America between 1522 and 1528, Pizarro and his business partners Diego de Almagro and Hernando de Luque had attained definitive proof of the existence of a great Indian kingdom. In Spain, the presence of Cortés and news of the discovery by Pizarro created great excitement. The emperor granted Pizarro a contract authorizing the discovery and conquest of a land called "Peru." Pizarro was named governor and captain-general.

Pizarro returned to Panama in 1530 and at the end of the year left the colony and sailed south. From the beginning, this was an expedition of conquest. Pizarro and his men landed far north of the Inka city of Tumbes, which had been visited during the previous expedition. For the next year and a half, they marched south along the coast and camped on the island of Puná in the Gulf of Guayaquil where the Spaniards suffered from a chronic sickness. In mid-1532, Pizarro founded the first Spanish settlement, San Miguel de Piura, located on the northern coast of Peru. In September, the captain left 60 Spaniards at San Miguel and took 62 horsemen and 106 foot-soldiers into the Inka Empire. Included among this small band were two free mulatto *conquistadores*. "They trusted that God Almighty would be with them," wrote the chronicler of the conquest, Pedro de Cieza de León.

Pizarro arrived in Peru at the conclusion of a great civil war that had bitterly divided the empire. In the mid- to late-1520s, the Inka Huayna Capac had died as a result of an epidemic that had begun in the Caribbean, swept through northern South America and reached Peru years before any Spaniard had set foot in the land. The premature death of the Inka produced a civil war between two half brothers, Atahualpa and Huascar, for control of the empire. By 1532, Atahualpa and his generals from their base in Quito had defeated the forces of Huascar and captured him and Cuzco. Pedro Pizarro later wrote that, "Had Huayna Capac been alive when we Spaniards entered this land it would have been impossible to win it, for he was greatly loved by his subjects." The chronicler Pedro de Cieza de León saw the opportunity for a divide and conquer strategy: "Hence, you see the great calamity of that time in Peru and how apparent it is that God permitted the entry of the Spaniards at a time of such great upheaval never before seen by those born there. The hatred these Indians had for each other was already great." When Pizarro entered the empire, Atahualpa had an army of between forty thousand to eighty thousand soldiers camped at Cajamarca in northern Peru. Atahualpa learned of the presence of these strangers and sent an envoy to investigate. This Inka noble met with Pizarro, gave him gifts and invited him to proceed to Cajamarca and meet Atahualpa.

Pizarro and his small force arrived at Cajamarca on November 15, 1532. This small city was incapable of housing the Inka army, which was camped on a large plain on the outskirts. One of Pizarro's soldiers recorded his impression: "It filled all of us Spaniards with fear and confusion. But it was not appropriate to show any fear, far less to turn back. For had they sensed any weakness in us, the very Indians we were bringing with us would have killed us."

The Spaniards occupied the city and Pizarro sent two of his lieutenants, Hernando de Soto and his brother Hernando Pizarro, and a troop of horsemen to visit Atahualpa. In the Indian camp, the Spaniards shared a drink of *chicha*, a fermented maize beverage, and were told that Atahualpa would come to Cajamarca the following day and meet Pizarro.

The Inka clearly underestimated the Spaniards. Atahualpa did not fear these strangers and planned have them captured and killed. However, first curiosity led him to visit the Spaniards. On November 15th, Atahualpa, carried in a litter by 80 nobles and accompanied by five thousand or six thousand men, entered Cajamarca and saw no Spaniards. He believed the strangers were hiding in fear. However, Pizarro had set a trap. The captain had hidden his soldiers in the houses surrounding the central square of the city. When the Inka arrived in the square, a Dominican friar greeted him, read him the *Requerimiento* in Spanish and then gave him a Bible. After this brief encounter, Pizarro launched his ambush. The Spanish chronicler Juan de Betanzos wrote in his *Suma y naración de los Yngas* in 1557: "The horsemen lanced them and the foot soldiers cut with their swords without the Inca's men putting up any resistance. Given the suddenness of the attack and never having seen a similar thing in all their days, the Indians were so shocked that, without defending themselves and seeing the great slaughter that they were undergoing, they tried to flee."

As in the Canaries, the Caribbean and Mesoamerica, the Spanish in Peru captured the ruler and provided a performance of theatrical violence and terror. The entourage of Atahualpa, which numbered in the thousands, was slaughtered and trampled to death. "They wailed loudly," wrote Cieza de León. "They were shocked by what they were seeing. They asked each other if it was real or if they were dreaming. And the Inca, where was he? More than two thousand Indians died, and many were wounded."

Believing that the Spaniards constituted little more than a raiding party, Atahualpa offered a ransom for his release. He promised one room filled with gold and another twice filled with silver. For eight months, emissaries of the Inka arrived in Cajamarca with objects of gold and silver taken from palaces and temples throughout the empire. The ransom ultimately produced eleven tons of gold ornaments, which were melted into more than 13,000 pounds of gold bars; 26,000 pounds of silver bars were also produced. Horsemen received 90 pounds of gold and 180 pounds of silver, and foot-soldiers received half of that. Pizarro gave himself seven times the amount due a horseman. This booty far exceeded that of Cortés, yet still it marked only the beginning of the plunder of the Inka Empire.

In captivity, Atahualpa still ruled his empire and ordered his armies not to attack the Spaniards. Expecting to be freed eventually, he concluded the last act of the civil war by having Huascar executed. Pizarro, also looking ahead, dispatched an expedition to Cuzco and began his alliance with Huascar's branch of the royal family. This alliance, and the Spaniards' fear that once released, Atahualpa would unleash his fury against them, led to the Inka's execution during the summer of 1533 by the order of Pizarro. Cieza de León noted that the people of Cuzco, oppressed by Atahualpa's followers, "were so pleased when they learned that the Christians were coming to their city that they raised great clamor, praising God because he had remembered them in such a calamitous time. They expected to be revenged on Atahualpa and

Figure 3.4. An Imagined Scene of the Spanish Conquest of Cuzco. *Cuzco, totius regni Peruani* (Cuzco, entire capital of Peru), from Theodor de Bry, *America pars sexta* (Frankfurt, 1596). Courtesy of the William L. Clements Library at the University of Michigan.

his followers by the hand of the Christians." "If the Incas had not favored the Spaniards," noted a contemporary witness, "it would have been impossible to win this kingdom."

In August, Pizarro and his small force began the march to Cuzco. In Cajamarca under Spanish supervision, Huascar's younger brother, Tupac Hualla, was crowned as Inka. This alliance gave Pizarro Indian troops but also strengthened the commitment of Atahualpa's general, Quisquis, to destroy the invaders. Thus, on the march to Cuzco Pizarro's forces were attacked by the Quitan army four times. Although Pizarro was vastly outnumbered, his cavalry proved invincible. Inexplicably, Quisquis also failed to exploit his advantage at the river crossings where the Spanish were most vulnerable. Along the route, Pizarro's force was also greeted and fed by local people who hated the Inka; Pizarro adopted the mantle of a liberator. The Spaniards entered Cuzco on November 15, 1533.

Eyewitnesses later described their prize: "This city is the greatest and finest ever seen in this country or anywhere in the Indies. We can assure your majesty that it is so beautiful and has such fine buildings that it would be remarkable even in Spain." On the march to Cuzco, the Inka Tupac Hualla had died, which meant that Pizarro needed a new ally. In Cuzco, he crowned the twenty-year-old Manco as the new Inka. Encouraged by Pizarro, Manco raised an army which, with Spanish support, attacked Quisquis and his Quitan army and forced him to retreat to the Inka province of Condesuyo. Another of Atahualpa's generals, Rumiñavi, held Quito. The conquest was far from concluded.

In December, the Spaniards looted Cuzco and its palaces and temples without opposition. Five times as much silver and half as much gold, compared to the ransom at Cajamarca, was acquired in Cuzco. Nearly two million gold pesos from Cajamarca and Cuzco, even more than the loot of Tenochtitlán, fell into the hands of the Spanish. "Indeed," according to Cieza de León, "when the Spaniards entered and opened the doors of the houses, in some they found heaps of very heavy and splendid gold pieces, in others large silver vessels . . . the city was full of treasures. In the fortress, the royal house of the Sun, they found unseen and unheard of grandeur because the kings had deposits there of all the things that can be imagined and thought about."

In 1534, an Indian army of twenty thousand men supported by fifty Spanish horsemen undertook the defeat of the Quitan army under Quisquis and the conquest of Condesuyo. At the same time and without authorization, Sebastian de Benalcázar, who had been left at San Miguel after Pizarro had departed for Cajamarca, headed for Quito with 62 horsemen and 200 foot-soldiers. In Ecuador, he made an alliance with the Cañari people, who had sided with the Huascar faction during the civil war, and he joined the campaign with several thousand Indian warriors. In May 1534, Benalcázar attacked Rumiñavi in the greatest battle of the conquest. Although the battle left both armies intact, Rumiñavi and his Quitan army decided to evacuate – but not before burning – Quito. Benalcázar occupied the city and was soon reinforced by Diego de Almagro, who was relieved to find the captain loyal to him and Pizarro.

While the Spanish were in Quito, Quisquis and his army of approximately twenty thousand men, following a retreat of more than a thousand miles, entered Ecuador and threatened the Spaniards. The combined forces of Benalcázar and Almagro, along with their Indian allies, attacked Quisquis and routed his army. His own soldiers, who wished to end the fighting and return home, then killed the Inka general. The Spanish pursued Rumiñavi and his army, defeated and captured him, and put an end to any further resistance. After three years, it seemed the conquest of Peru had been accomplished. "One cannot blame only a handful of foreigners for the downfall of the Inka," write María Rostworowski and Craig Morris. "The end of Tawantinsuyu was also fostered by discontent among subject peoples who saw the arrival of the Europeans as an advantageous time to recover their independence."

Unlike Cortés, who rebuilt Mexico-Tenochtitlán and centered Spanish power in the very center of what had been the Mexica Empire, Pizarro did not make Cuzco his capital. Concerned that the Inka capital was too distant from the sea and the lifeline to Panama, Pizarro founded a city in January 1535 near the coast, Ciudad de los Reyes, later to be known simply as Lima. This meant that Cuzco was essentially left in the hands of Manco and a small Spanish force, which abused its authority. Realizing that the Spaniards were not going to leave and outraged by Spanish insults and mistreatment, in the fall of 1535 Manco decided to destroy the Spanish and force them from his land. Manco described his change of heart this way: "[The Spanish] preach one thing and do another, and they give us so many admonitions, yet they do the opposite. They have no fear of God or shame."

For months, Manco planned the campaign, secretly organized an army, and waited for the rains to end. At Easter 1536, the Inka and his general Quizo Yupanqui, with a force of more than one hundred thousand Indian soldiers, began a siege of Cuzco. Only 270 Spaniards led by Hernando Pizarro defended the city. On May 6th, Manco attacked the city, and after six days forced the Spaniards to retreat to the main square. Facing the real possibility of defeat, Pizarro took a bold step: he divided his forces and seized Sacsahuaman, the great Inka fortress on the edge of Cuzco. This action made it possible for the Spaniards thereafter to adequately defend the city. Manco maintained the siege for a year from his base at Ollantaytambo and dispatched armies to retake the highlands of Peru. Three relief expeditions from the coast were defeated. Manco then turned his attention to Lima, which was attacked by the forces of Quizo.

Francisco Pizarro and the Spaniards in Peru withstood the shock of this enormous rebellion. In November 1536, Pizarro organized a force of 100 horsemen and 450 foot-soldiers in Lima and thousands of Indian allies (who hated the Inka more than they feared the Spanish) and returned to relieve Cuzco. Several months later, Diego de Almagro and a substantial force of Spaniards and Indian allies, who had a year earlier marched south to conquer Chile, approached Cuzco. Almagro defeated Manco's army outside of Cuzco and then found their entry into the city opposed by Hernando Pizarro. However, a number of chroniclers mentioned the miraculous intervention on behalf of the Spanish by the Virgin Mary and Saint James.

There had long been bad blood between Almagro and Pizarro and their factions. Almagro and his supporters believed they had been cheated by Pizarro in Cajamarca and Cuzco, and accorded second-class *conquistador* status because they had not participated in the capture of Atahualpa. Their discontent was only fueled by the disappointing results of the expedition to Chile, which been quite difficult but not very lucrative. Resentment boiled over into civil war in the summer of 1537. Almagro, who had made an alliance with Manco's pliant half brother, Paullu, and thus gained an Indian army of one hundred thousand men, attacked Cuzco and defeated the Pizarrist force. For the next several months, three forces vied for control of Peru: the Pizarro brothers based in Lima and control of the coast, the army of Almagro and Paullo in Cuzco and the surrounding highlands, and the Inka army of Manco now established at Vilcabamba, a wild region east of Cuzco.

In April 1538, Hernando Pizarro and an army of Indian allies invaded the highlands and won a complete victory at the outskirts of Cuzco. Almagro was captured and executed. (Some years later, Almagristas broke into Pizarro's palace in Lima and assassinated him.) Adaptable as ever, Paullu transferred his allegiance to the Pizarros and was crowned puppet emperor with the name and title Paullu Inka Yupanqui. However, the other rebel Inka remained a threat.

In late 1538, Manco initiated a new campaign and organized a series of local rebellions across a thousand miles in the Andes. He had two armies in the field, a northern force in the province of Huánuco under the command of Illa Tupac, and a southern force in Bolivia under the command of Manco's uncle Tiso. Assisted by an army organized by Paullu, the Spanish defeated Tiso in the valley of Cochabamba after a difficult campaign of eight months. However, Illa Tupac resisted the Spanish *Reconquista* in the north Sierra for eight years. Manco and his successors in Vilcabamba fought off Spanish expeditions for decades. The restored neo-Inka state at Vilcabamba was not defeated and occupied until 1571–2. The Spanish had destroyed the Inka state but they had hardly conquered Peru or the Central Andes. Years after the rebellion of Manco, the support of Paullu and other noble lineages permitted the survival of the Spanish in the highlands. Years later, one Spaniard wrote the crown that the Paullu was "a true friend of the Christians and Your Majesty, and it is the truth that he has been a great pillar of support in these parts, for if he had fallen and tried to destroy things, the extinction of all the Spaniards living in Peru, little by little, would have begun." From Peru, expeditions of conquest spun off in all directions (see Map 3.5).

Between 1537 and 1543, six successive expeditions sought the conquest of the central Andes inhabited by the Muisca people, the New Kingdom of Granada, today part of Colombia. Gonzalo Jiménez lost two-thirds of his 600-man force in 1537, the first expedition. In fact, of the nearly two thousand *conquistadores* who signed on to the six expeditions, only 658 survived. In time, the *conquistadores* plundered gold from the Muisica, founded new towns and gave themselves *encomiendas*.

In Chile, the frontier of the Inka Empire extended to the Bio-Bio River. Peoples north of the river had been conquered and had become part of the Inka and later the Spanish Empire. Peoples south of the river, particularly the Araucanians, had not been subdued by the Inka and fiercely – and successfully – resisted Spanish conquest. This was the case in part because Araucanian society was nomadic or semi-nomadic and decentralized. Small groups could be defeated and individuals were captured and enslaved but resistance by numerous independent tribes persisted. After the arrival of the Spanish, Araucanians began to breed horses and established cavalry forces, which eliminated the primary Spanish advantage. On this frontier, war continued for centuries. The first Spanish attempt to found a settlement in the Río de la Plata estuary in 1536 was decisively repulsed by natives the Spanish called the Querandie. It was not until 1580 that another settlement, Buenos Aires, was attempted. By this time, the Querandie were gone, most likely due to the spread of Old World diseases. The previous (temporary) Spanish settlers had abandoned cattle and horses and the Pampas Indians had taken to horseback, which made them unconquerable. The Chocó south of Bolivia was not subdued until the 1680s. The Charrúa of Uruguay remained independent until the nineteenth century. "The so-called 'conquest' of the Americas was never completed," writes Henry Kamen. "For Spanish power in America to become viable, it was essential to work out a system based on collaboration rather than 'conquest.'"

Map 3.5. Early Spanish Overland Expeditions.

3.9 The Conquest of Coastal Brazil

The Portuguese refrained from colonization for about thirty years after their discovery of the coast in 1500. The wealth of the country, Brasilwood, that produced a red dye (and gave the country its name), could be obtained through peaceful barter with the coastal Tupí-speaking tribes. As in Africa, conquest was unnecessary, and perhaps even detrimental, to doing business. Furthermore, innumerable farmers and hunter-gatherers who were often at war with one another populated the coast of Brazil. Brazil was even more decentralized than Yucatan, and therefore conquest would have appeared to be excessively difficult and tedious.

During the decades of coastal trading, the Portuguese were not alone. French traders often appeared on the coast and established good relations with particular Indian peoples. The establishment of a Portuguese coast guard in 1516 and again in 1527 failed to remove the French threat from the three-thousand-mile coast. The obvious solution then was colonization. Only settlement of the vast coastline could guarantee Portuguese control of their New World possession.

Colonization began in 1531 with the crown-supported expedition of Martim Afonso de Sousa and 400 colonists, who founded the colony of São Vicente on the southern coast near present-day Santos. Land was distributed to settlers and the first sugar mill was built in 1533. The following year, following the pattern of colonization of Madeira, King João II divided the coast into fourteen hereditary captaincies granted to twelve individual donatories, who were lord proprietors and usually members of the petty nobility. At their own expense, the donatories were to occupy and settle their domains and were granted the privilege to found towns, distribute lands, levy taxes, retain a portion of the revenue and enslave Indians. The monarchy sought to colonize Brazil at no expense to itself. In one charter, João stated: "To whom it may concern I make it known that I now grant and reward Duarte Coelho, nobleman of my lineage, for him and all his children, grandchildren, heirs and successors, by law and inheritance, forever, the captaincy and territory of sixty leagues of land along my coast of Brazil which begin at the river São Francisco."

The captaincy system was only a partial success. Some donatories made no attempt to colonize their land, whereas others neglected or abandoned their small and isolated settlements. Only de Sousa's São Vicente in the far south and Duarte Coelho's captaincy in Pernambuco, just south of the bulge of Brazil, prospered and survived. One reason for the early success of certain captaincies was the alliances the Portuguese made with native headmen. In the case of the captaincy of Pernambuco, Coelho's brother-in-law married a Tobajara headman's daughter. Similar strategic marriages took place along the coast. In 1549, the king took over the failed captaincy of Bahia and founded the town of Salvador, established at the marvelous Bay of All Saints of the Savior (Bahia de Todos os Santos do Salvador), not quite midway between Pernambuco and São Vicente. This crown captaincy was settled with more than a thousand colonists and became the seat of royal government in Brazil under the first governor-general, Tomé de Sousa (see Map 3.6).

The king informed his governor-general of the purpose of the colony: "The principal reason motivating my decision to settle the land of Brazil was in order that the people of that land might be converted to our Holy Catholic Faith." To further this end, six Jesuits accompanied the 1549 expedition and were followed by more than 125 members of the order in the second half of the century. However, the invasion of Brazil proved to be more violent than spiritual.

Settlers in the captaincies of Pernambuco and Bahia soon found the wealth of Brazil to be located in the stalks of sugar cane, transplanted from Madeira

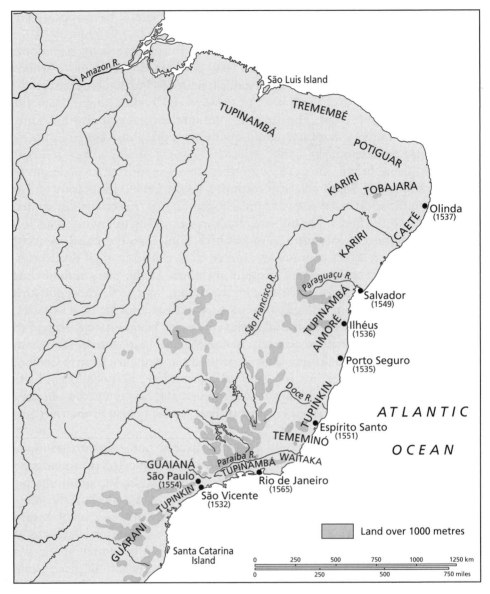

Map 3.6. Native and Portuguese Brazil.

and São Tomé. The cultivation and processing of sugar required significant inputs of labor, which the Portuguese colonists themselves never considered providing. Some Indians at first agreed to work for trade goods, but they soon proved to be unreliable. The solution then was Indian slavery. The unfortunate captives were purchased from the victors of intertribal conflicts or from Portuguese raiding parties who stole men and women from neighboring villages. Slavery soon led to resistance and war, and war, of course, produced more captives and slaves. By the 1560s, there were more than forty thousand Indian slaves in Pernambuco alone. Conquest now became a necessity and proved to be profitable.

In the first decades, the struggle was entangled with the rivalry between the Portuguese and the French, on the one hand, and that between the Tupinambás and Tupiniquins and other native rivalries on the other. The French made allies of the powerful Tupinambás, which forced the Tupiniquins to join with the Portuguese to defend themselves. As elsewhere in the Americas, native peoples viewed their traditional enemies as the primary menace and saw the small number of Europeans as useful allies, not dangerous invaders. Europeans were quite eager and willing to take advantage of native rivalries to augment their forces, attack their enemy and secure their territory.

In southeastern Brazil, Tupinambá groups formed a resistance movement, calling themselves the Tamoio, meaning "ancestor." The Tamoio War involved hostilities between the Portuguese and Tupinikin against the Tamoio. However, in São Paulo in 1562 the Tupinikin rebelled against their Portuguese allies and the Jesuits negotiated a peace agreement with some of the Tamoio groups. "The principal reason that has moved them to want this peace," noted one Jesuit, "was not their fear of the Christians, but their great desire to make war against their Tupi enemies, who until now were our friends, and recently rebelled against us."

Until mid-century, French traders armed and made alliances with natives hostile to the Portuguese all along the vast coast of Brazil. Because the French had not colonized any part of Brazil, it was easier for them to maintain friendly commercial relations with various Indian peoples along the coast. In 1555, the crown established Antarctic France, the first permanent French settlement in Brazil, located on an island at the mouth of Guanabara Bay just of São Vicente in the south. The local Tupinambá, organized as Tamoio, welcomed the 300 colonists. However, they were enemies of the Termimino, another native people of the area who sought the assistance of the Portuguese. In the 1560s, the Portuguese governor-general of Brazil used the Termimino and Tupinambá from Bahia to destroy the French colony, found Rio de Janeiro and establish a new captaincy.

In Pernambuco, the Portuguese settlers menaced the Potiguar to the north and the Caeté to the south of their settlement at Olinda. In 1555, with French support the Potiguar destroyed two sugar mills in the captaincy, thus threatening the economic base of the colony. To survive, the Portuguese required allies. An alliance with the Tobajara people, who were settled near Olinda, was secured by a marriage between the donatory's brother-in-law and a daughter of the local chief. For the next five years, the donatory and his Indian allies extended Portuguese rule over 350 kilometers of the coast with a campaign that proceeded village by village. Beginning in 1569, the next donatory concluded the conquest of Pernambuco with a force of six companies of Portuguese soldiers and an estimated twenty thousand Indian allies. The Indians who were defeated abandoned their coastal lands and fled into the interior. The native allies of the Portuguese were settled in *aldeias*, mission villages, supervised by Jesuits. No independent native chiefdoms and tribes remained in Pernambuco. The Portuguese used native rivalries to advance their conquests and this strategy was indispensable, as a native testament in a 1580 document reveals: "Here the Portuguese sow discord between some (Indian) nations and others, and with slyness we are convinced and confused, so that all of us together cannot meet them."

South of Pernambuco was the captaincy of Bahia. It failed due to Tupinambá hostility, which forced all of the settlers to abandon the colony in 1545. This disaster paved the way for the royal takeover of the captaincy in 1549. Thereafter, Portuguese-Indian relations settled into a familiar pattern. Some natives allied themselves with the Portuguese, who then embarked on campaigns of removal and extermination of other hostile peoples, who often had French assistance. Native tribes that accepted Portuguese authority were settled in mission villages controlled by the Jesuit order and required to assimilate. Military campaigns continued into the late 1580s while small private raiding expeditions persisted much longer. As one native told a Jesuit: "these Portuguese will not leave us in peace. You see how a few of them come among us and are seizing our brothers." Mission Indians lived under Jesuit control and often supported the Portuguese population. According to one Jesuit, "the padres have the Indians always tilling their fields and gathering their food so that, when it is necessary, the Indians, for their own salvation, can help the padres with the Portuguese. It is true that many Portuguese eat thanks to the Indian villages, which is to say that the padres of the Company are fathers to the Indians in both body and soul."

The conquest was not immediately successful across the entire coast. The four captaincies just south of Bahia – Ilhéus, Porto Seguro, Espírito Santo and São Tomé – experienced decades of bloody conflict. The Portuguese and native allies were able to decimate the coastal Tupiniquin people but then faced the inland Gé-speaking tribes, whom the Portuguese called Aimoré. They were hunter-gatherers and fierce guerrilla fighters. By the end of the sixteenth century, the Aimoré were pretty much in control of the captaincy of Ilhéus. Espírito Santo never flourished due largely to Indian attacks. In São Tomé, the nomadic and elusive Waitacá successfully held off expeditions sent against them, and they remained a menace for a century.

On the tip of the bulge of Brazil and in the east-west coast to the north where the captaincies of Paraíba and Rio Grande were located, native peoples successfully blocked Portuguese expansion for a few generations. At one point, the Potiguar people of Paraíba were able put in the field forty thousand warriors in battle. The Potiguar and their French allies confined the Portuguese to a few forts in the captaincy until 1600.

In the mid-sixteenth century, João III issued Portugal's first Indian policy. It was designed to protect peaceful Indians and enslave or destroy those who refused to submit to Portuguese rule and control. The king's *regimento*, or standing orders, on this matter ordered the end of abusive enslaving of oppressed native peoples but recommended enslavement and even the destruction of villages and death for rebellious natives. Jesuits began to establish mission villages, *aldeias*, in the 1550s and 1560s as refuges for the "peaceful" Indians and as a source of free labor. In 1570, the crown prohibited Indian slavery but the institution survived for centuries. Loopholes in the law allowed slavery to persist. Indians captured in a "just war" could be legally enslaved, as could natives rescued from cannibalism. However, these provisions became excuses, and no critic of the stature of Las

Casas arose in Brazil or Portugal to contest these transparent exemptions. As the populations of natives on the coast disappeared, Portuguese raiding parties penetrated the interior to capture Indians and bring them to regular slave markets. These expeditions were often led and manned by half-caste mamelucos and mulattos, rough woodsmen who knew the land and its peoples. In this way, the conquest of Brazil continued throughout the colonial period.

3.10 Morocco and Songhay

The most important and definitive European defeat in the Atlantic in the sixteenth century occurred in Morocco. Europeans had long threatened the Maghrib and the Portuguese, in particular, had attempted to make Morocco a client state. Taking advantage of Moroccan disunity, Portugal had seized the Atlantic ports of Agadir, Safi, Azamor and Arzila. Moroccan recovery followed the rise of a new dynasty, the Sa'dî, who came to power in the early sixteenth century. The Sa'dîs unified the country in the 1520s and 1530s and began to expel the Portuguese in the 1540s. An important element in their success was the adoption of European artillery.

King Sebastian of Portugal, unaware of the achievement of Moroccan military parity, attempted the conquest of the kingdom in 1578. He led an army of twenty thousand soldiers that confronted the Sharif, Abd al-Malik, and his army of seventy thousand. As in many other parts of the emerging Atlantic World, Sebastian had made an alliance with a disaffected faction of Moroccans who were led by the former Sharif. In fact, the former Sharif had requested Portuguese assistance, which gave Sebastian the pretext for the campaign and a tool for controlling Morocco.

The two armies met in the interior of the country at Alcazarquivir. The Portuguese force was not only outnumbered but also unprepared, particularly with regard to cavalry. After several cavalry attacks on the Portuguese army, a powerful, numerous and well-disciplined force of harquebuses on horseback shattered the Portuguese line, which led to the disintegration of the entire army. Most of the army was killed or captured, and Sebastian himself fell in battle. As a result of the battle of Alcazarquivir, Morocco maintained its independence from European control until 1844.

For some time, the Sa'dîs had been gathering intelligence in the middle Niger and sought to plunder the Songhay Empire and control its trade. In 1590, a Sa'dian expedition was dispatched that consisted of three thousand musketeers, both mounted and on foot, and many more support personnel. Although the Sa'dian expedition fought a much larger force defending Gao and Songhay, it triumphed on the field. Songhay's *amîr* Askiya Ishâq offered peace and 100,000 [mq.] of gold and 1000 slaves if the expedition would return to Marrakesh. "This Sa'dian army," according to the Timbuktu chronicler Al'Sa'dîs, "found the land of the Sûdân at that time to be one of the most favoured of the lands of God Most High in any direction and the most luxurious, secure, and prosperous." A military government was imposed on this western Sudanese state and, in time, the expeditionary force became independent of Morocco and ruled the local population into the eighteenth century.

The most important European consequence of the battle of Alcazarquivir was the loss of Portuguese independence. In 1580, Felipe II of Spain claimed the Portuguese monarchy, invaded the country and defeated the Portuguese army. For the next sixty years, the kingdom of Portugal and its Atlantic empire was part of the Spanish monarchy and empire. The age of Atlantic conquests included the conquest of one of the two great Iberian empires by the other. However, this too was an ambiguous conquest. Although Spain now appeared to have the greatest empire ever known in history, the two Iberian kingdoms remained distinct and the administration of the overseas empires remained separate. Felipe II adopted a broader and more ambitious imperial strategy, one that required more war and more silver and that bankrupted Spain four times during the Union of the Crowns.

With the opening of the Atlantic in the fifteenth century, the Portuguese and the Spanish came into direct contact with the peoples in Africa and the Americas. At this point begins the construction of the new Atlantic World, which was at first simply archipelagos of Iberian trading factories and ports. They were joined with, and dependent upon, local peoples and were linked to their European homes by intermittent seaborne reinforcements and commerce. In the beginning, the Iberians came to Africa and the Americas in tiny numbers, ignorant of just about everything of importance regarding these new lands and peoples. As a result, their very survival in the beginning required that they seek and obtain local cooperation and assistance. They found it: Africans and Native Americans supported, traded with and made alliances with the Portuguese and the Spanish based on their understanding of their own self-interest. Africans and Native Americans did not and could not perceive what seems so clear today, that the Iberians were invaders intent on staying in their countries and exploiting their peoples and resources. In the late fifteenth and early sixteenth centuries, "Africa" and "Africans," "America" and "Indians" did not exist in the perceptions of these peoples. Accustomed to centuries of differentiation, divided by language and custom and often at war with one another, the most meaningful distinctions were those between local peoples, for example, between the Mexica and Tlaxcalans. African and Indian alliances with Europeans against local enemies made sense. We also must remember that the Iberians and their motives were complex. Yes, many were greedy, violent and cruel, but there were other Portuguese and Spaniards, significant men as well as common folk, who were noble of spirit, generous, sympathetic, reverential and evangelical. The sixteenth century historian and priest José de Acosta believed the discovery and conquest of the New World was guided by divine providence so that the Indians could receive the Law of Christ; nothing else was important. He spent his life as a cleric and as a writer devoted to this cause. In 1589, he had reasons for sadness and joy. "Surely, those who rule these [native] people both temporally and spiritually ought to treat them as Christ imparted his law, with his easy yoke and light burden." Despite "our sins," noted Acosta, and how ineptly the task of evangelization was carried out, "God's mercy made good out of this evil and caused the subjection of the Indians to be their whole cure and salvation." He continued, "Christianity is undoubtedly increasing and improving among the Indians who have been conquered and is giving more fruit every day, while in other places that have had different beginnings it is declining and threatening ruin."

Using indigenous divisions and such well-worn tactics such as capturing native leaders, employing display violence and terror to intimidate their enemies and forming alliances, the Castilians – and to a somewhat lesser degree, the Portuguese – sought conquest of foreign peoples and lands. Yet definitive conquest was rarely achieved. In Africa and the Americas, the Iberians continued to fight many indigenous peoples for centuries, and when it was possible both sides compromised. The *conquistadores* and their chroniclers only recorded successful conquests. "The reality was more complex," writes Henry Kamen: "there were specific 'successes,' but the general picture was one of a need to adapt to circumstances that were not always favorable."

Here lies the foundation of the Atlantic World, a foundation of Iberian, African and Indian making. Upon this ground, the Portuguese and the Spanish erected more elaborate colonial structures with Indian collaboration and resistance. The first overseas empires stretching across the Atlantic is the subject of the following chapter.

3.11 Further Reading

David Birmingham, *Trade and Conflict in Angola: The Mbundu and Their Neighbors in Angola under the Influence of the Portuguese, 1483–1790* (Oxford, 1966).

Jeremy Black, *War and the World: Military Power and the Fate of Continents, 1450–2000* (New Haven, 1998).

John William Blake, *West Africa: Quest for God and Gold, 1454–1578* (London, 1977).

António de Oliveira Cadornega, *História Geral das Guerras Angolanas* [1683], 3 volumes (Lisbon, 1940).

Inga Clendinnen, *Ambivalent Conquests: Maya and Spaniards in Yucatan, 1517–1579* (Cambridge, 1987).

Pedro Cieza de León, *The Discovery and Conquest of Peru*, translated and edited by Alexandra Parma Cook and Noble David Cook (Durham, 1998).

Cortés: The Life of the Conqueror by his Secretary Francisco López de Gómera [1552], translated and edited by Leslie Byrd Simpson (Berkeley, 1966).

Titu Cusi Yupanquí, *An Inca Account of the Conquest of Peru*, translated by Ralph Bauer (Boulder, 2005).

Hernán Cortés, *Hernán Cortés: Letters from Mexico*, translated and edited by Anthony Pagden (New Haven, 1971).

Bernal Díaz del Castillo, *The Discovery and Conquest of Mexico*, translated and edited by A.P. Maudslay (New York, 1956).

Garcilaso de la Vega, El Inca, *The Royal Commentaries of the Incas and General History of Peru*, edited by Karen Spalding, translated by Harold V. Livermore (Indianapolis, 2006).

Bartolomé de Las Casas, *An Account, Much Abbreviated, of the Destruction of the Indies*, edited by Franklin W. Knight (London, 2003).

John Hemming, *The Conquest of the Incas* (New York, 1970).

John Hemming, *Red Gold: The Conquest of the Brazilian Indians, 1500–1760* (Cambridge, Massachusetts, 1978).

James Lockhart, translator and editor, *We People Here: Nahuatl Accounts of the Conquest of Mexico* (Turnhout, Belgium, 1993).

Laura E. Matthew and Michel R. Oudik, editors, *Indian Conquistadors: Indigenous Allies in the Conquest of Mesoamerica* (Norman, 2007).

Kathleen Ann Myers, *Fernández de Oviedo's Chronicle of America: A New History for a New World* (Austin, 2007).

R. C. Padden, *The Hummingbird and the Hawk: Conquest and Sovereignty in the Valley of Mexico, 1503–1541* (New York, 1967).

Matthrew Restall, *Maya Conquistador* (Boston, 1998).

Matthew Restall, *Seven Myths of the Spanish Conquest* (New York, 2003).

Pedro Sarmiento de Gamboa, *The History of the Incas*, translated and edited by Jean-Jacques Decoster and Vania Smith (Austin, 2007).

Hugh Thomas, *Conquest: Montezuma, Cortés, and the Fall of Old Mexico* (New York, 1993).

John Thornton, *The Kingdom of Kongo: Civil War and Transition, 1641–1718* (Madison, 1983).

John Thornton, *Warfare in Atlantic Africa, 1500–1800* (London, 1999).

Eric Wolf, *Europe and the People without History* (Berkeley, 1982).

Chapter 4

Realms

The Overseas Empires of Spain and Portugal

In the fifteenth and sixteenth centuries, the emerging Atlantic World was Spanish and Portuguese. These innovators constructed the most impressive imperial structures in the West since the Romans dominated the Mediterranean world. For the first time, the Iberian empires connected the peoples of Europe, Africa and the Americas. This connection was commercial, social and cultural as well as political and administrative. Back and forth across the Atlantic in various patterns and networks flowed people, animals, plants, diseases, commodities, manufactures, customs, ideas and much else, which historians have termed the Columbian exchange. Both Spain and Portugal extended their commerce to Asia as well, but it was the Atlantic rim that was Europeanized, albeit a fragmentary and thin veneer overlaying deep African and Indian foundations. Their overseas realms were extensions of European culture but greatly modified extensions, sustained by African and Indian trade and labor and influenced by African and Indian customs. Nevertheless, the empires were inspiring. The Portuguese chronicler João de Barros wrote in 1540: "The Portuguese arms and pillars placed in Africa and Asia, and in countless isles beyond the bounds of three continents, are material things, and time may destroy them. But time will not destroy the religion, customs, and language which the Portuguese have implanted in those lands."

The Atlantic World of the sixteenth century was but one arena of the relatively new dynastic superpower, the Habsburg Empire. In 1516, the grandson of Isabel and Fernando, Charles of Ghent, inherited the thrones of the Spanish realms and in 1520, he was elected Holy Roman emperor. As a Habsburg and as the Emperor, Charles united the central European lands of the Habsburgs, Austria and Hungary, the Burgundian lands that centered on the Low Countries, Franche-Comté and the Spanish monarchy, which brought him the kingdoms of Castile and Aragón, Naples and the Americas. When he was elected Holy Roman Emperor, he assumed his better-known title, Charles V, *Carlos Quinto*. The Spanish-centered Habsburg Empire dominated Western Europe but overwhelmed the capacity of any one ruler to govern wisely and well. For this reason in 1556, Carlos V abdicated and divided his empire. The imperial office and the central European lands went to Ferdinand, brother of Carlos. Carlos' son, Felipe II, inherited the Spanish monarchy, including Milan and Naples, Franche-Comté, the Low Countries and the overseas empire. In 1580, Felipe inherited (or seized) the Portuguese monarchy, which included its empire in America, Africa and Asia. For four decades, Felipe II (1556–98) was the most powerful monarch in Europe. His strength in Europe and the Atlantic was titanic but ultimately overextended.

The sixteenth century marks Spain's Golden Age. Its power and wealth was unrivaled. Poets, dramatists, novelists, theologians and historians made Castilian a great literary language. Artists, architects and sculptors brought Spain respect and recognition in an age dominated by Italian masters. Spanish America was the progeny of a dynamic parent. Spaniards and Spanish Americans, working with the strength and creativity of Indians and Africans, built that era's greatest empire based largely on silver and gold and centered in Mexico and Peru. Great and beautiful cities, no less impressive than many in Europe, stretched across the New World. Universities, libraries, printing presses and theaters enhanced the culture of the American kingdoms. In time, the power and wealth of Spain declined; however, Spanish America remained largely immune. Its population grew, its economy expanded and its regional societies became more complex. The empire as a whole remained mostly secure against powerful rivals and enemies.

Portugal and its empire was part of the Spanish monarchy from 1580 until 1640. This was a dynastic development, not a political revolution. Portugal maintained its distinct institutions and separate privileges, and its empire remained in the hands of Portuguese officials and bureaucrats who answered to Lisbon more than Madrid. But even before Portugal's loss of independence, Portugal had become seriously challenged and overextended. After 1580, Spain's enemies became Portugal's enemies, and the overseas Portuguese empire became the target of many potential looters. And after 1640, when Portugal regained its independence, this small nation still had to face its European rivals and lost a significant portion of its empire. Portuguese Africa and America (not to mention Asia) were then always in a more precarious position than Spanish America. In fact, in the mid-seventeenth century Portugal temporarily lost possession of parts of Brazil and Angola to the Dutch. Portuguese Africa and America – São Tomé, Angola and Brazil – survived and became increasingly more interconnected and less dependent on Portugal.

The Iberian Atlantic was the first layer in the history of the Atlantic World. This chapter considers the Spanish and Portuguese kingdoms and captaincies in the Americas and Africa in the sixteenth and seventeenth centuries. The French, English and Dutch assaults upon the Iberian Atlantic constitutes the next layer in the Atlantic's colossal history.

4.1 Imperium

The Spanish Empire in the sixteenth century was modeled to a considerable extent on the Roman Empire. Carlos I, King of Castile and León and Carlos V Holy Roman Emperor, was addressed as "Your Caesarian Majesty."

Hernando de Acuña reimagined the Roman Empire in the age of Carlos: "One monarch, one empire, and one sword." Even the vocabulary of fifteenth and sixteenth Portuguese and Castilian expansion was Roman: the words *Emperador, res publica, audientia, colonia* and more came from Rome. The *conquistadores*, men of the Renaissance, looked to classical antiquity for models of literary elegance. When Cortés scuttled his ships on the coast of Mexico, his compatriots, according to Bernal Díaz, replied in the words of Julius Caesar when he crossed the Rubicon, *Iacta alea est*, "The die was cast." To the Romans, *imperium* meant law and order. As the Romans expanded territorially, they brought Roman order, law and ethical purpose – in short, *civitas* – to a disordered and barbarian world. When the Roman Empire became Christian, its ethical purpose expanded to include not simply civilizing the world but also Christianizing it. To the Romans and their imitators, the Spanish and other Europeans, the title Emperor meant the ruler of more than more than one city, state or kingdom. The Roman Emperor, in theory and law if not in fact, claimed universal dominion. In time, the *Imperium romanum* developed into the *Imperium Christianum*, which after the demise of the Roman Empire became the responsibility of the Roman Catholic Church and the papacy.

The Christian kingdoms in Iberia (which in medieval times were often referred to as the peoples and territories of "the Spains") fought the *Reconquista* as a Crusade with Papal authority against Moslem al-Andalus. The small and relatively weak kingdom of Portugal had few imperial pretensions; its kings in the thirteenth and fourteenth centuries sought to preserve Portugal's autonomy from its more powerful neighbor, León-Castile. The kings of this realm, the largest in Iberia, did take the title of *Emperador* from time to time. As Castile expanded and brought smaller territories and kingdoms under its authority, the term "monarchy" came to mean political unification under one king. With the marriage of Isabel of Castile and Fernando of Aragón in 1479 and their creation of a united dynasty, a "Spanish Monarchy" under Castilian control only advanced the idea of *imperium* in Castile.

Both Castile and Portugal had designs on overseas conquest and expansion in North Africa. In 1260, the Castilian king Alfonso X sent an expeditionary force to attack and loot Salé in Morocco. As we have seen, it was the Portuguese that seized Moslem Ceuta in 1415 and began serious expansion into the African Atlantic. In the 1450s, the Pope granted the Portuguese crown exclusive rights in African exploration and trade as well as the right to conquer and enslave pagans. In 1430, a royal instruction to the king's captains revealed the nature and understanding of Portuguese *imperium*. Portuguese dominion meant to "take with the intention of obtaining benefit the navigation, trade, and commerce of said lands, places and islands." After the Portuguese had established trading factories in West Africa and sailed into the Indian Ocean with the voyage of Vasco da Gama, Dom Manoel took this new title, which was confirmed by the pope in 1502: "King of Portugal and of the Algarves on this side and beyond the sea in Africa, Lord of Guinea, and the Conquest, Navigation and Commerce of Ethiopia, Arabia and India." As Patricia Seed as observed, this title essentially described the geographic reach of Portuguese vessels. In time, the Portuguese would establish colonies in Brazil and Angola but their imperial ambition never rivaled that of Castile.

The Castilians expanded overseas in the late fifteenth century with papal approval to the Canaries and the islands of the Caribbean under the Catholic monarchs Isabel and Fernando. The papal commission raised a number of legal issues, which were debated in Castile for fifty years. The New World became part of the patrimony of the monarchs of Castile and Aragón, and after 1516, a possession of the Spanish Monarchy. Due to Aragón's dynastic ties to Naples, in the mid-1490s Fernando also claimed, invaded and occupied the Neapolitan kingdom. Isabel and Fernando's grandson (and son of the Habsburg Emperor Maximilian), Charles of Ghent (his Castilian name was Carlos), inherited the Spanish Monarchy of Castile and Aragón upon the death of Fernando in 1516 and arrived in Castile in 1517. Three years later, Carlos was elected Holy Roman Emperor and became Carlos V. Even before his election as Emperor, Carlos told the Spanish that "I was well able to content myself with the Spanish imperium, with the Balearics and Sardinia, with the Sicilian kingdoms, with a great part of Italy, Germany, and France, and with another, as I might say, gold-bearing world." This last reference was to Castile's "islands and mainland" in the New World. At the same time that Carlos became Holy Roman Emperor, Cortés was in Mexico creating a new American kingdom for Castile and Carlos. In fact, Cortés informed the king that in Mexico, "there are so many [lands and peoples] and of such a kind that one might call oneself the emperor of this kingdom with no less glory than of Germany." The idea of universal monarchy, long embedded in the institution of the Holy Roman Empire, began to appear to Castilians and many Europeans as a real possibility under the reign of Carlos V. To the Castilian poet Hernando de Acuña, the appearance of Carlos meant "one monarch, one empire, and one sword" (see Map 4.1).

The establishment of *imperium* in the Americas under the Spanish was very much like the creation of the Roman imperial system. Romans, like Spaniards much later, used a system they called divide and rule, *divide et impera*. Roman generals made alliances with tribes and cities to oppose Rome's enemies and Rome's new allies' ancestral enemies. New lands and peoples were administered with the help of local collaborators who made deals for their peoples in terms of taxes, defense, right of appeal and so on. As we have seen in the previous chapter, Iberians in Africa and the Americas were practitioners of divide and conquer and divide and rule. Romans rarely believed their imperial expansion was aggressive and offensive. The Romans believed that Rome responded defensively to attacks and thus expanded defensively. In a similar manner, the Spanish Empire grew. As he presented it, Hernando Cortés did not seize the Mexica Empire – in 1519 the emperor of the Mexica abdicated in favor of Carlos V. When the Mexica began to fight the Spaniards several months later, Cortés interpreted this action as a rebellion against the legitimate sovereignty of the Spanish monarchy.

Even before the accession of Carlos as king of "the Spains," Spanish *imperium* in the New World had been condemned for its single-minded commitment to the exploitation of Native Americans and their resources. This

Map 4.1. Europe in the Age of Carlos V.

tradition of self-criticism within Castile inspired a "Black Legend" among Spain's European enemies with the aim of de-legitimizing Spanish colonialism in the Americas. Historians of Spanish America in the modern period have generally focused on Spain's economic imperialism. However, under Fernando and Carlos, Spanish *imperium* meant the expansion of law, order and faith above all. The *Requerimiento* of 1512 insisted that Native Americans "recognize the church as the owner and superior of the universal world" and understand that a pope had "made a donation of these islands and mainland of the Ocean Sea to the Catholic kings of Spain." The legitimacy of Spain's possession of the New World was based on the principle of "just war," that is, war intended to save the native peoples from their own barbarism and bring them to the Christian religion. The Spanish humanist Juan Ginés de Sepúlveda wrote that "the Romans, a very civilized people and exalted in virtue, subjected to their rule the barbarian nations." Now God's legate, the pope had chosen the Spaniards to do the same. Bartolomé de las Casas, the great critic of Spanish behavior in the West Indies, believed that God had delivered the New World and its peoples to the Spanish and thus imposed a moral duty to bring the Indians to Christ. Serious conversion efforts began in the 1520s and included the dispatch of missionaries to the New World, the destruction of native temples and rites, the conversion of native rulers and nobles, mass baptisms and the construction of churches throughout the Spanish territories.

The establishment of Spanish *imperium* in the New World involved much more than the effort to evangelize the native people. Like the Romans before them, the Spanish sought to bring *civitas* to their new territories, that is, law and order. To the Romans, the term *civitas* literally referred to the municipality, which was the most important instrument for expanding and imposing law and order. Spanish officials and theorists accepted the same approach. Order was imposed on the "blank" American landscape by the establishment of well-planned Spanish cities. Royal regulations required that Spanish cities in the New World follow basic guidelines: all had to have central plazas, specific placement of the church and other significant structures, a rational grid of straight streets and more. One of the first royal regulations of urban planning stated that "once constructed, the town will appear well-ordered as regards the space designated for the central plaza, the location of the church, and the placement of the streets; because where such orders are given from the outset, orderly results will follow without undue cost and effort, and in other places [without such planning] order will never be achieved." Decrees for city planning included Carlos' 1523 *Ordenanza* and Felipe's in 1573. These and other decrees guided the construction of dozens of cities from north central Mexico to Chile in the sixteenth century alone. In his Latin dialogue, *Life in the Imperial and Loyal city of Mexico* in 1554, Cervantes de Sálazar praised the relatively new city for its stone streets, grand portals, uniform houses, classical proportions and the "artistically made architraves" of the viceroy's palace. In particular, church building was monumental and designed to impress the native peoples and communicate Spanish authority and dominance. Valerie Fraser writes that architecture was "instrumental in the construction and consolidation of the Spanish Empire." One cleric estimated that by the 1620s, some seventy thousand churches, cathedrals, chapels, convents, monasteries, colleges and other religious buildings had been constructed in the Spanish Indies. Over the course of three centuries, the Spanish established something like 900 urban settlements in the Americas. As Richard M. Morse put it, "colonization, then, was largely a labour of 'urbanization,' that is, a strategy of settlement nucleation for appropriating resources and implanting jurisdiction." To George Foster, this was simply "the greatest city-building enterprise ever carried out by any people, nation, or empire in all history" (see Map 4.2).

Map 4.2. The Cities and Towns of Spanish America.

Spanish authorities in the Americas were charged with reorganizing small and dispersed native groups into compact communities. This policy of *reducción*, or *congregación*, was designed to promote Christian conversion and control labor. However, even the new Indian pueblos were required to have a central plaza and a grid pattern of streets, a town hall and an elected municipal government. A Franciscan friar in South America in the 1570s noted that the orderly cities "made their inhabitants worthy of being called men." Whatever the degree of failure, writes John M. Headley, "there can be no doubt as to the presence of the civilizing ideal in the purposes of the

Figure 4.1. A View of the Market Place in the City of Havana. From *Scenographia Americana: Or, a Collection of Views in North America and the West Indies* (London, 1768). Courtesy of the William L. Clements Library at the University of Michigan.

reducción, coexisting along with the religious and the patently economic and administrative."

Imposing *civitas* on the New World included mapping and naming. Of course, both elements denied previous, indigenous ordering of territory. Spanish mapping and naming of the New World legitimized possession and facilitated control and order. The Casa de Contratación as early as 1508 established a department of geography and cartography to create and maintain a master map, the *padrón real*, of Castilian possessions. Carlos and his son and successor, Felipe, ordered maps to help them better understand and rule the regions of their realms. In 1542, Alonso de Santa Cruz drew a world map for the Casa that visualized Spain's domains. Diego Gutiérrez, pilot major and cosmographer of the royal court, published the most detailed delineation of the Americas in 1562 from Greenland to Patagonia. One of the great creations of Spanish cartography was the *Description and demarcation of the West Indies*, produced by Spain's official cosmographer in 1574, which included fourteen maps. "The Indies, the islands and terra firma in the Ocean, which are commonly called the New World," wrote the cosmographer Juan López de Velasco, "are islands and seas which lie within the boundaries of the Kingdom of Castile." He portrayed the world-wide Spanish Empire in cartographic form. At the same time, the royal cosmographer also sought on-the-scene assistance from officials in New Spain to help him better map the Spanish Indies. Most local Spanish officials in Mexico allowed native painters to visually represent indigenous towns and regions which, in effect, re-indigenized the landscape of Mexico. However, in time officials and colonists reestablished the Spanish view of New Spain.

Imperial mapping was also the task of the royal engineers. From the time of Carlos V onward, the Spanish monarchy employed engineers to design, map, construct and maintain fortifications throughout the world. The engineers not only drew plans for fortifications for the ports of Spanish America but also drew larger plans of cities and regions. For example, a 1595 map of Cartagena, which was being fortified against Dutch, French, and English privateers, shows the streets of the city, the surrounding features like the bay and the proposed line of fortifications and bastions. Another map of the same era showed the road from Vera Cruz to Mexico City. The map followed the road, painted as a double line, which began at the bottom of the map and ran to the top, passing by many churches, estates and sugar mills. "Using a map of this kind," writes David Buisseret, "the king could get a good idea of the geographical features of this important communications link."

Just as the Roman *imperium* led to the territorial expansion of the language of the Romans, Spanish *imperium* meant the expansion of the language of Castile. In a famous phrase, Elio Antonio de Nebrija, author of the first grammar of a romance language, *Grammática sobre la lengua castellana*, presented to the Queen Isabel in 1492, noted that "language is the instrument of Empire." In his prologue, Nebrija quoted the Archbishop of Avila, who had informed the Queen, "soon Your Majesty will have placed her yoke upon many barbarians who speak outlandish tongues. By this, your victory, these people shall stand in a new need; the need for the laws the victor owes to the vanquished, and the need for the language we shall bring them with us." This grammar, Nebrija wrote, "shall serve to impart them the Castilian tongue, as we have used grammar to teach Latin to the young." A German Jesuit missionary passing through New Spain to the Marianas Islands in the late seventeenth century noted how "the Spanish in the two Indies, like the ancient Romans, insist that their language together with their authority be perpetuated throughout the world." Of course, the language of Castile did become the language of much of the Americas beginning in 1492 and continuing to the present. It did not completely supplant the indigenous languages of the New World, but over time these languages adopted uncountable Castilian "loan words" and native peoples increasingly became bilingual. For a time, during the age of great Spanish power, Castilian was also one of the dominant languages of Europe. A 1544 book by a Navarrese professor noted "Castilian is understood now in most Christian nations." In 1580, another Castilian stated, "we have seen the majesty of the Spanish language extended to the furthest provinces wherever the victorious flags of our armies have gone." In fact, Castilian, which today is simply called Spanish, became one of the great languages of the world, a language of imperial decrees, of poetry and theater and of innumerable books. And today, Spanish is the principal language of nearly one-fifth of the human race.

Above all, the extension of law and order to the New World meant that colonists and subject peoples were expected to live in *buen policía*. "To live in *policía*, " writes Alan Durston, "required the attainment of the European idea of civility including clothing, food hygiene, etc. but above all, to live an urban life." Royal decrees regulated nearly all aspects of life in the Spanish Indies. For Spaniards and Indians, stone residences were decreed as superior to wood houses, and therefore mandated. Divisions of class and caste were encouraged by law through privileges and restrictions. All people were placed, theoretically and by law, into an elaborate system of hierarchies. Every article of trade in colonial cities was controlled as to price, weight and quality.

Theorizing, projecting and attempting to impose Spanish law and order throughout its new realms in the New World was remarkably ambitious and, of course, never fully or satisfactorily realized. In the late sixteenth century, the Milanese Jesuit Giovanni Botero, in his vast compendium of knowledge of the world, *Relationi universali*, believed that God had never before conceded a greater empire than that granted to Felipe II. Botero argued in the Indies, Spain advanced universal *imperium* by means of Hispanization, Christianization, and – perhaps most important of all – civilization, that is, urbanization, the creation of cities. As for the future, Botero predicted, Spain's geographical location prepared her *per l'Imperio dell'Oceano*, the Empire of the Ocean.

4.2 Spain in America

The most impressive of the European empires of the early modern age was without question the Spanish American empire. Spain had followed Portugal into the Atlantic and at first it appeared that second place was definitely the inferior one in the race for empire. However, with the unexpected, as well as extended and ambiguous, conquests of Mexico and Peru, and the additional mainland conquests and settlements, the Spanish monarchy of Carlos V found itself in possession of an immense, populous and wealthy American empire. Stretching from the Rio de la Plata in South America to the Colorado in North America and encompassing many hundreds of native societies and millions of subjects, the Spanish Indies helped Spain become the greatest power in Europe and the Atlantic basin.

The Spanish American empire was not a pristine construction, and not an exclusively European entity. The conquests of Mexico and Peru gave Spain possession of native empires and subject peoples with a history of submission to centralized authority and administration, as well as a tradition of forced labor and tribute. The Mexica and Inka empires became the double foundation of the American empire, centered in the imperial capitals of Mexico City and Lima. Most of the other Spanish American administrative regions were likewise based on Native American centers of power and population, as the provinces of Guatemala, Quito and Yucatan demonstrate. To a considerable extent, the Spanish adjusted pre-existing empires to their particular customs and needs. José de Acosta made this point with regard to evangelization: "How helpful the greatness of these two empires [the Mexica and the Inka] I have mentioned has been for preaching and the conversion of the people can be observed by anyone who cares to do so by the extreme difficulty that has been encountered in bringing to Christ the Indians who do not recognize an overlord."

But just as the conquests were not purely Spanish military triumphs because native peoples always assisted the *conquistadores*, the new system of empire was based more on collaboration than simple authority or force. Spanish *conquistadores* at first, and imperial officials later, reached agreement with local native rulers regarding tribute payments and labor needs. Native rulers cooperated to protect their communities from excessive exploitation and defend their traditional way of life – and to make themselves more powerful and wealthy. "Spaniards favored those Indian rulers who cooperated," Charles Gibson noted with regard to New Spain, "assuring them of their positions, confirming their titles, and approving their possession of lands, and vassals." Vastly outnumbered and lacking any permanent military forces, notes Alan Knight, "the Spanish elite had to govern with some regard to the wishes of the governed."

In the beginning, the American empire was in the hands of its conquerors, not its emperor. Cortés, Pizarro and dozens of other *adelantados* and governors leading perhaps ten thousand *conquistadores* had conquered in the name of Carlos V. But they, and not the crown's agents, were in control of the lands and peoples on the ground. Cortés, Pizarro and their colleagues had enhanced their possession and power through the distribution of *encomiendas* to their loyal conquistadores. *Encomiendas* permitted their holders and descendants to collect tribute (which otherwise would go to the crown) from a region of native villages, and collect this tribute in coin, produce or labor. By the 1540s, there were approximately 600 *encomenderos* (those in possession of an encomienda) in New Spain and 500 in Peru living off the production and tribute of their Indians. One in four Spaniards held an *encomienda* in New Spain and Peru in 1540. The *encomienda* served the purpose of extending Spanish power across the land and supervising much of the settled population of the native peoples. However, most of these *encomiendas* were negotiated arrangements with local native chiefs. Following the conquest of Mexico, Cortés "obtained" *encomiendas* in Morelos and Oaxaca – he never formally granted anything to himself – and in 1529 Carlos V gave him the title of Marqués del Valle de Oaxaca and formally granted him twenty-three thousand tributary Indian vassals in New Spain. One of Cortés's *encomiendas* (Cuernavaca) was a former Mexica tributary province (Quauhnahuac), whereas his other *encomiendas* were Mexica provinces. His *encomienda* towns had the same nobles and lords as in Mexica times, who took responsibility for the production and gathering of tribute goods and left the task of organizing the required labor services to their *mayordomos* or *tequitlatos*. In the first several years after the conquest, the tribute paid to *encomenderos* like Cortés was delivered according to the old Mexica schedule and the tribute goods of maize, turkeys, cacao, salt, mantas of cloth, grains of gold, bundles of feathers and everything but items for war was the same as before the conquest. "The goods and services secured by these new lords," notes C. Michael Riley, "were not unlike those the peoples of Morelos had earlier rendered the rulers of the Aztec state."

However, the crown wanted to prevent the rise of a new seigniorial (or feudal) class in America and began to restrict and regulate the *encomienda* with the New Laws of 1542. Warnings of a curtailment of conquerors' privileges had been appearing in Spain for several years. Dominican missionaries wrote a bull for the pope condemning Indian slavery in 1537. The New Laws prohibited the enslavement of Indians for any reason in the future. They also essentially abolished the *encomienda* by prohibiting new awards, terminating a number of grants immediately and ordering all other *encomiendas* to return to the monarchy upon the death of their holders. This radically unpopular policy was not enforced in New Spain and led to an armed insurrection in Peru. The Council of the Indies compromised on the *encomienda*. Over the next 300 years, the crown would take back *encomiendas* when possible and converted the decreasing number of *encomenderos* into a privileged but powerless class of state pensioners. A decree of 1549 required all "unemployed" Indians to offer themselves for hire. Out of this decree came the compulsory labor system of *repartimiento* (called *mita* in Peru) by which an Indian town was required to send a proportion of its male population for a fixed period of time out to work. A local magistrate, the *juez repartidor*, allocated the labor for private employers and public works.

The challenge facing the monarchy during the first decades following the conquests was to replace the *conquistador* with the bureaucrat. This process began in the 1530s and the 1540s with the appointment of *audiencias*, courts of appeal and administrative tribunals, which were located in the capitals of the major provinces. Ten were created in the sixteenth century. Although formally courts of law, *audiencias* also exercised executive and administrative authority and represented royal power. The crown created only one office superior to the *audiencia*: the viceroyalty. In the sixteenth and seventeenth centuries, the Spanish Indies was divided into two viceroyalties, one centered in Mexico and the other in Peru. In the city of Mexico and in Lima, the viceroy generally acted as president of the resident *audiencia*. He was military commander of his territory as "captain-general," made appointments to lesser bureaucratic and clerical posts and was in charge of the treasury. As symbol of the crown in America, the viceroy's duties were often more ceremonial than administrative.

Under the authority of the *audiencias* were provincial governors, who were generally the administrators and military commanders of remote frontier regions like New Mexico and Paraguay. *Audiencias* were divided into districts and administered by officials called *corregidores* or *alcaldes mayors* (although the office was uniform, the name varied from place to place). These were the officials who eventually replaced *encomenderos* and supervised Indian communities generally called by the Spanish *pueblos*. By the early seventeenth century, New Spain had about two hundred of these jurisdictions and Peru possessed eighty-six. *Corregidores* and *alcaldes mayors* also supervised Spanish towns and presided over meetings of the *cabildos* (town councils), which were composed of local notables.

This system of government in America was controlled by a centralized agency in Spain, the Royal and Supreme Council of the Indies, which consulted with and acted on behalf of the king. The Council of the Indies made all appointments of bureaucratic and clerical positions in America, made all of the laws for the American empire, served as the final court of appeal and was the central executive and administrative arm of the king in American affairs. All communication with American officials originated from, and returned to, the Council of the Indies. It was the head of a vast bureaucratic body.

Although the government of Spanish America was formally hierarchical and authoritarian, in fact governance was rather flexible and adaptable. Single officials rarely had supreme authority over anything. Viceroys had to work with *audiencias*; *audiencias* were collective bodies that worked best through consensus. Governors and *corregidores* had to contend with bishops, native *caciques* and local Spanish and Spanish-American notables. Every official was subject to official inspections and reviews, and officials at every level could bypass their immediate superior and communicate directly with the Council of the Indies. These checks and balances produced cautious officials who consulted widely before taking any action. Because no official wished to provoke noisy protests, to say nothing of rebellion, this system generally tended to produce conservative paralysis.

The royal government in America was not the only bureaucracy established by Spain. The Spanish Catholic Church was as much a part of the structure of imperial authority in America as the state. The structure of dioceses and parishes, as well as the system of provinces of the regular, or monastic, church, provided a clerical bureaucracy as extensive and influential (if not more so) as that of the royal government. In several papal edicts in the late fifteenth and early sixteenth centuries, the pope essentially gave the Spanish monarchy control of the American church – possession of tithes, right of appointment, veto power over papal dispatches to America and control of the building of cathedrals and other church structures – which was known as the *patronato real*. As a result, church and state in America were virtually one. Of course, royal authority over the American church was based on the duty of the crown to bring the native peoples of America into the faith. To do this, the royal government adopted an innovative policy.

Carlos V believed the enormous task of evangelization was better suited to the regular church, the religious orders of the Franciscans, Dominicans, Augustinians and later the Jesuits, rather than the secular or Episcopal church of archbishops, bishops and parish priests. Several of the regular orders were mendicants, bound by pledges of poverty and service to the poor, the sick and the less fortunate of society. The first Franciscans, who traveled in groups of twelve, arrived in Mexico in 1524. "Do not believe that we are gods," the Franciscans told the native lords of Mexico. "Fear not, we are men as you are. We are only messengers sent to you by a great lord called the Holy Father, who is the spiritual head of the world, and who is filled with pain and sadness by the state of your souls." By mid-century, there were approximately 800 friars in Mexico and 350 in Peru. These missionaries spread across America and attached themselves to communities of Indians. They learned native languages, studied Indian history, culture and religion, built churches and monasteries on the sites of native temples, founded schools for the sons of the native nobility and preached, catechized and baptized. Evangelization was often quite superficial.

Table 4.1. Native population of
the valley of Mexico, 1519–1800

Year	Population
1519	1,500,000
1570	325,000
1650	70,000
1724	120,000
1800	275,000

Sources: Charles Gibson, *The Aztecs
Under Spanish Rule: A History of the
Indians of the Valley of Mexico, 1519–
1810* (1964), pp. 136–65. More than
three decades later, Alan Knight accepts
these figures in his history, *Mexico: The
Colonial Era* (2002), pp. 20–1.

The missionary friars often brought Spanish rule into regions where royal
authority was thin or even nonexistent. The missionaries also provided balance to the potent *encomenderos*; the first generations of friars often sought
to protect Indians from excessive demands of tribute and labor and as a
result, earned the ire of Spanish colonists. However, like the *encomenderos*
the regulars came to be distrusted by the crown for their local influence and
power and, over time, were replaced by seculars.

The imposition of Spanish control over Indian societies by church and
state in the sixteenth century was greatly assisted by the collapse of native
population as a result of repeated epidemics and pandemics, as well as a drop
in births. We have seen that the Taino people of the Greater Antilles essentially disappeared within less than two generations. On the mainland, tens of
millions died during the course of the sixteenth century. Europeans brought
from Eurasia and Africa a range of infectious diseases, including smallpox,
typhus, measles, diphtheria, influenza, typhoid, the plague, pneumonia and
more. It is estimated that the native population of Mexico fell from an estimated 17 million at contact in 1519 to between 3.5 million and 1.1 million
by the end of the sixteenth century. For estimates on native population in the
Valley of Mexico, see Table 4.1. In the Andes, the rate of population collapse
was not as great as in Mexico, perhaps due to the larger population at high
altitudes and colder climates located there.

Despite these enormous losses in Mexico and Peru and throughout Spanish America, natives still vastly outnumbered Spaniards. To better protect,
evangelize and tax native peoples, the crown attempted to implement a policy
of segregation, the creation of two ethnic "republics." Most Spaniards were
forbidden to live in native communities, the *república de indios*. Economic
pressures and race mixing undermined this ambitious design.

Nevertheless, a distinctly separate Indian culture survived conquest and
colonialism. The conquest had largely decapitated native societies by destroying religious leaders and encouraging the nobility to assimilate into colonial
Spanish society. A number of the larger native towns adapted to Spanish governance as native ruling groups elected their own town officials and protected
community interests. In the countryside, what remained of hierarchical native

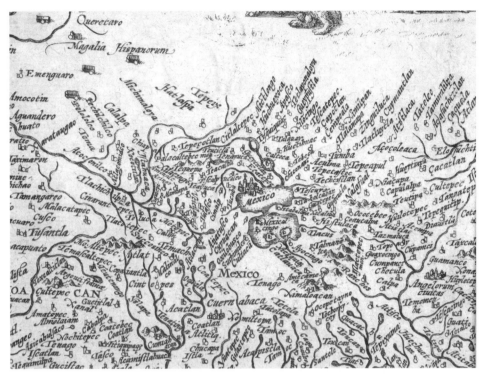

Figure 4.2. The Towns of Central Mexico in the Late Sixteenth Century. Detail from *Hispaniae Novae* (New Spain), from Theodor de Bry, *Americae pars quinta* (Frankfurt, 1595). Courtesy of the William L. Clements Library at the University of Michigan.

societies were masses of Indian peasants. The Spanish attempted to "reduce" the widely scattered Indian hamlets into towns to better tax and control the native population. Indian society became profoundly rural and focused on the village or country town. Local community leaders, called *caciques* and, in the Andes, *curacas*, remained in place as useful intermediaries and agents of Spanish control. Indians were viewed as intellectually inferior to Europeans, although in possession of the ability to learn and advance, much like children, and therefore colonial law was paternalistic.

By the 1570s, approximately 125,000 to 150,000 Spaniards lived in the Indies in some 225 towns and cities. Spanish colonial society was urban and their towns and cities were essentially foreign islands in a vast native sea. Like their Castilian counterparts, Spanish American towns were organized around a central plaza, the *plaza mayor*, where the principal buildings – the church, the municipal hall and the prison – faced. The jurisdiction of these towns extended far into the countryside. The principal cities of New Spain and Peru had their own universities to educate the colonial elite as well as theaters, cathedrals, churches and viceregal courts. The first *corregidor* of Mexico was informed in a verse letter that in Mexico he would find everything there is to be found in Spain – good houses, good horses, beautiful women, wide streets, fine coaches, excellent food, and "you will [also] find a thousand other things besides that are lacking in Spain and that are, to sight and taste, delightful."

Document 4.1
Royal Ordinances Concerning the Laying Out of New Towns

King Philip II of Spain, 1573

110.... After having made the discovery and selected the province, district and land to be peopled and the sites where new settlements are to be founded those who intend to settle are to proceed in the following manner:

On arriving at the locality where the new settlement is to be founded (which according to our will and ordinance must be one which is vacant and can be occupied without doing harm to the Indians and natives of with their free consent) the plan of the place with its squares, streets and building lots is to be outlined by means measuring by cord and ruler, beginning with the main square from which streets are to run to the gates and principal roads and leaving sufficient open space so that even if the town grows it can always spread in a symmetrical manner. Having thus laid out the chosen site the settlement is to be founded in the following form.

111. The chosen site shall be on an elevation; healthful; with means of fortification; fertile and with plenty of land for farming and pasturage; fuel and timber; fresh water, a native population, commodiousness; resources and of convenient access and egress. It shall be open to the north wind. If on the coast care is to be taken that the sea does not lie to the south or west of the harbor. If possible the port is not to be near lagoons or marshes in which poisonous animals and corruption of air and water breed.

112. In the case of a sea-coast town the main plaza which is to be the starting point for the building of the town, is to be situated near the landing place of the port. In inland towns the main plaza should be in the centre of the town and of an oblong shape, its length being equal to at least one and a half times its width, as this proportion is the best for festivals in which horses are used and any other celebrations which have to be held.

113. The size of the plaza shall be in proportion to the number of residents, heed being given to the fact that towns of Indians, being new are bound to grow and it is intended that they shall do so. Therefore the plaza is to be planted with reference to the possible growth of the town. It shall not be smaller than two hundred feet wide and three hundred feet long nor larger than eight hundred feet long and three hundred feet wide. A well proportioned medium size plaza is one six hundred feet long and four hundred feet wide.

114. From the plaza the four principal streets are to diverge, one from the middle of each of its sides and two streets are to meet at each of its corners. The four corners of the plaza are to face the four points of the compass, because thus the streets diverging from the plaza will not be directly exposed to the four principal winds, which would cause much inconvenience.

115. The whole plaza and the four main streets diverging from it shall have arcades, for these are a great convenience for those who resort thither

for trade. The eight streets which run into the plaza at its four corners are to do so freely without being obstructed by the arcades of the plaza. These arcades are to end at the corners in such a way that the sidewalks of the streets can evenly join those of the plaza . . .

120. After the plaza and the streets have been laid out building lots are to be designated, in the first place, for the erection of the main church, the parish church or monastery and these are to occupy respectively an entire block so that no other structure can be built next to them excepting such as contribute to their commodiousness or beauty.

121. Immediately afterwards the place and site are to be assigned for the Royal and Town Council House, the Custom-House and Arsenal which is to be close to the church and port so that in case of necessity one can protect the other. The hospital for the poor and sick of non contagious diseases shall be build next to the church forming its cloister . . .

126. No building lots surrounding the main plaza are to be given to private individuals for these are to be reserved for the church, Royal and Town house, also shops and dwellings for the merchants, which are to be the first erected. For the erection of the public buildings the settlers shall contribute and for this purpose a moderate tax shall be imposed on all merchandise.

127. The remaining building lots shall be distributed by lottery to those of the settlers who are entitled to build around the main plaza. Those left over are to be held for us to grant to settlers who may come later or to dispose of at our pleasure. In order that entries of these assignments be better made a plan of the town is always to be made in advance . . .

134. Settlers are to endeavor, as far as possible, to make all structures uniform, for the sake of the beauty of the town.

These royal ordinances on town planning were part of a much larger royal decree entitled, "Ordinances concerning discoveries, settlements, and pacification," from the royal retreat and monastery, the Escorial. The document was found by Zelia Nuttall in Madrid and published in Spanish and in English translation. The ordinances were translated by an anonymous scholar. *Source:* Zelia Nuttall, "Royal Ordinances Concerning the Laying out of new Towns," *The Hispanic American Historical Review*, 4:4 (November 1921), pp. 249–54, and 5:2 (May 1922), pp. 249–54.

An examination of a Spanish American city and an Indian town shows something of the social framework of colonial society. Lima, actually named La Ciudad de Los Reyes ("The City of the Kings"), was founded by Francisco Pizarro on January 8, 1535. "Pizarro ordered Juan Tello to distribute the plots in the order they were designed in the plan," wrote Pedro de Cieza de León. "And they say that Juan Tello, who was knowledgeable in this, remarked that this land would be another Italy and in trade a second Venice because with such a quantity of gold and silver it was impossible for it to be otherwise." Like all Spanish American cities, Lima had been laid out according to a rational grid system inspired by Renaissance thinking on town planning. At the very center of the city was a public square, the Plaza de Armas, with eight streets running outward from the corners of the square (and one additional street extending from the southern side of the plaza). Around the square were located the cathedral, the viceregal palace and the houses of the municipal government. Proximity to the Plaza de Armas indicated the social prestige of the families who lived in fine houses of two stories. The orderliness of the city demonstrated the Spanish attempt to impose rational European structure upon America. In the early seventeenth century, Garcilaso de la Vega commented, "the city was beautifully laid out, with a very large square, unless it be a fault that it is too big. The streets are broad and so straight that the country can be seen in four directions from any of the crossroads."

Like other Spanish cities, Lima was governed by a *cabildo*, or city council, composed of twelve *regidores* or councilors who took specific posts such as inspector of weights and measures, director of public ceremonies, inspector of public works and so on. The *regidores* elected (from a small list of leading citizens) two *alcaldes* or municipal magistrates. Like Mexico City, Lima became the seat of an archbishop and his cathedral, of a royal *audiencia* that sat in the cathedral and finally of a viceroy and a viceregal palace. During the colonial era, forty-two viceroys occupied the palace originally built by Francisco Pizarro. In 1551, the Council of the Indies established the University of San Marcos in Lima. The first printing press was set up in 1584. In the late sixteenth century, an anonymous chronicler, The Portuguese Jew, described Lima as "an earthly paradise for the lords, parading through the streets on horseback dressed in silk and the finest cloths of Segovia while their wives were carried in sedan chairs to pay social calls."

In 1593, Lima had a population of about 13,000 people. By 1614, the population had grown to 25,454. Africans comprised the largest single ethnic group with 10,386 and with the addition of mulattos, the total exceeded 11,000. Spaniards numbered 9,616. There were 1,978 native Andeans and only 192 *mestizos* (mixed Spanish-Indian offspring). The small number of *mestizos* suggests that many sons and daughters of mixed Indian-Spanish unions lived (and therefore were counted) as Indians or passed as Spaniards. Compared to Mexico City, Lima was a small city but no less rich or monumental. In the mid-sixteenth century, the Spaniards had discovered the mountain of Potosí, the world's largest deposit of silver, which was controlled from Lima. Merchants, agriculturalists and miners like Antonio López de Quiroga, acting as a business agent for others or on his own account, dispatched his money to Lima.

In his mid-seventeenth century *Historia de la fundación de Lima*, Bernabé Cobo wrote of the "trade, splendour, and wealth" of the city. "The commerce and bustle of people which is always to be seen in this square is very great," wrote Cobo, referring to the Plaza de Armas. "The things to be found in this market are all that a well provisioned republic can desire for its sustenance and comfort." There were in Lima fifteen or so *mayorazos*, that is, entailed estates, with fortunes of 300,000 to 400,000 ducats, but that was far exceeded by the total income that flowed annually in salaries to ecclesiastics, bureaucrats and the military. The city's wealth was displayed in churches, houses, luxurious coaches, jewelry, gold and silver plate, tapestries, silks, brocades, fine linens, articles of worship and African slaves.

In 1630, Buenaventura de Salinas y Córdova, a Peruvian Franciscan, could barely control his enthusiasm as he described Lima as:

> A holy Rome in its temples, ornaments and religious cult; a proud Genoa in the style and brio of those who are born in it; a beautiful Florence for its benign climate; a populous Milan because of the crowd of people who flock there from all quarters; a wealthy Venice because of the riches it produces for Spain and prodigally distributes to all, remaining as wealthy as ever; a copious Bologna because of the abundance of foodstuffs; a Salamanca because of its thriving university and colleges.

The most impressive aspect of Lima in the early seventeenth century was the size and splendor of its religious establishment. A contemporary report stated that there were more than 400 secular priests, about 900 friars and 1,366 nuns. They worked and lived in nineteen churches, monasteries and nunneries. This description of Lima by Pedro de León Portocarrero details the numerous religious institutions and impressive architecture. Besides the cathedral and the palace of the archbishop, there were parish churches, monasteries, convents, the house and jail of the Inquisition, separate hospitals for Spaniards and Indians, a hospital for sailors, a house for orphans and another for abandoned women, a doctrinal school for Indians and schools and colleges. The church and monastery of San Francisco, with its beautiful twin towers, conventual buildings and grounds, constituted a city within the city of Lima. In its prime, it housed more than 200 monks with an additional huge staff and slaves. The convent of the Nuns of the Incarnation housed more than 400 nuns. "Many of the rich nobles' daughters come to learn good manners, and they leave it to marry," wrote Pedro de León Portocarrero. "In this convent there are splendid and intelligent women, endowed with a thousand graces, and all of them, both nuns and lay women, have Black women slaves to serve them." The Jesuit College of San Martín enrolled and housed more than 500 students, who were the sons of Spanish Peruvian notables and who were offered "a very elaborate course of studies incorporating many branches of learning." The House of Charity was a religious institution "in which poor sick women are treated and many poor maidens are sheltered until they leave to be married, and where women who live indecently are taken in."

Everyday life in Lima, indeed in every village and town in Spanish America, was regulated by the *Te Deums* (religious services) in the cathedral, solemn processions for religious holidays, the consecration of a bishop, an Inquisition *auto-da-fe*, weddings, funerals, saint's days and calls to worship. The diary of Josephe de Mugaburu, a seventeenth-century Spanish soldier of Lima, observed the dominance of the church in the daily life of the people of Lima. "This City of Lima had a *fiesta* for the beatification of the sainted archbishop, Don Toribio Alonso de Mogrovejo, who had been archbishop of Lima," noted Mugaburu on Tuesday, November 5, 1680. Four years later, he wrote in his diary, "the *fiesta* for the name of Mary was held. In

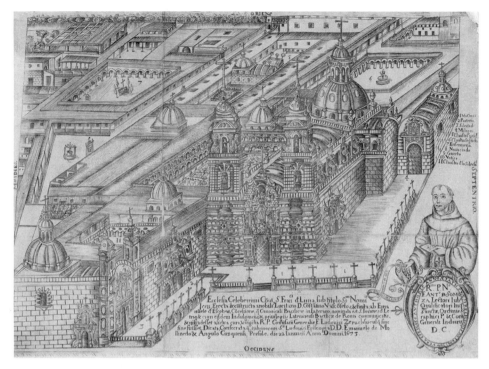

Figure 4.3. The Franciscan Church and Convent, San Francisco, in Lima. From Miguel Suárez de Figueroa, *Templo de N. grande patriarca San Francisco de la provincia de los doze apostoles de le Peru en la Ciudad de los Reyes* (Lima, 1675). Courtesy of the John Carter Brown Library at Brown University.

the afternoon a procession went forth, very resplendent, accompanied by the viceroy, Duke of La Palata, all the gentlemen of the royal audiencia, secular cabildos, and all the nobility of the whole city." The people of Lima came out during the processions of Our Lady of the Rosary, the sermons of the archbishop, the Easter procession of the whole religious order of Saint Francis, the sentencing announcements of offenders by the Inquisition and so on. Religious and church-related events gave meaning and structure to the lives of Spanish Americans, As Mugaburu put it on one occasion, "There was much happiness and consolation for all Christians."

Lima was also a city of manufacturing and commerce. Artisans and merchants tended to concentrate on particular streets according to specialization. There was the street of the silversmiths, the hatters' alley, the street of the mantas (cloaks) and "the main one, that is the Merchants' Street, along which there are always at least forty shops packed full of assorted merchandise." A few years later, the Franciscan Buenaventura de Salinas y Córdova listed twenty warehouses and at least two hundred shops. A nearby street had "many shops with different specialties: chandlers, confectioners, boilermakers who work with a lot of copper, blacksmiths, and other craftsmen." Many seventeenth-century observers described Lima as a city overflowing in wealth. "I am astonished at what they tell me about Castile," noted a Spanish resident of Lima in 1590, "that it is finished, and I believe it from what people say here. Here we go neither hungry nor thirsty, nor do we lack for clothing." Another Lima resident writing home to Spain was upset by the news of "the hardship that you suffer in Spain. Since we want for nothing over here, we can hardly believe it."

The Indian *pueblo* of Texupa in Oaxaca, southern Mexico, revealed another world altogether. When Cortés arrived, the town had a population of 12,000. By 1579, the date of an official report written by the Corregidor of Texupa to the Council of the Indies, there were fewer than 750 natives. "They used to be healthier than they are now," wrote the Corregidor. "It is not known why this should be, but it is thought that by eating less and eating less rich foods they lived longer." The *pueblo* had a monastery of friars of the Dominican Order that instructed the residents. Because this community was not part of an *encomienda*, the residents paid tribute to the monarchy rather than an individual Spaniard. The Corregidor reported that "the trade and produce of the natives of this pueblo amount to the cultivation of their fields. Each married Indian pays a silver peso and one-half fanega [about three quarters of a bushel) of maize in tribute to Your Majesty."

Texupa and thousands of communities like it throughout Spanish America were part of an economy based on exploitation. Indian communities generally paid tribute in produce, labor or coin to an *encomendero* (however, some like Texupa were directly subject to the crown). Because *encomenderos* abused their demand for labor, in the 1540s the crown prohibited personal service and restricted tribute to payments of money. Forced labor became the province of the state. The monarchy required communities to provide laborers on a rotation basis to *corregidores*, who would distribute them to public works projects, the construction of religious buildings, private land-holdings and gold and silver mines. This system, called the *mita* in Peru and the *repartimiento* elsewhere, paid Indians a wage, no doubt a very poor one. Influenced by the moral arguments of the Dominican friar Bartolomé de Las Casas regarding the justice of Spanish rule and settlement in the Americas, in the 1550s Felipe II had a committee of twelve debating whether settlers had the right to use the labor of Indians – in short, was the *repartimiento* legitimate. After the debate, the king wrote, "It appears that a majority from both sides agree that one should and can concede the said *repartimiento* in perpetuity, and that there is no other solution for the security and peace of those lands." American mine-owners and other settlers had offered the crown five million ducats in gold for a positive resolution. "I cannot find supplies anywhere else," Felipe explained to the Council of the Indies, "to pay the great amount that is owed."

The Spanish discovered that tribute and forced draft labor was necessary to obtain anything of value from native communities. Without tribute, communities farmed their own fields and maintained a subsistence lifestyle. On the other hand, with tribute demands communities were forced to produce commodities of some value for trade, and individuals were often forced to sell their labor for a wage to raise the required sum. Some individuals would abandon their communities to escape the burden of tribute and became part of a floating wage-earning population. In the late 1570s, a Spanish judge, Alonso de Zorita, studied Mexica society and the consequences of the conquest. "What I can state with certainty," Zorita wrote in his classic *Breve y*

Sumaria Relación de los Señores de la Nueva España, "is that one Indian pays more tribute today than did six Indians of that time, and one town pays more in gold pesos today than did six towns of the kind that paid tribute in gold." Felipe Guaman Poma de Ayala, a mestizo member of the native nobility of Peru, in his extremely long and illustrated letter to the king of Spain condemned and illustrated the avarice of the conquerors, royal officials, Indian *caciques* and *encomenderos*. "Entrust the poor Indians to the encomendero," Guaman Poma wrote, "and there is no remedy. This realm does not favor justice for these poor Indians and thus depopulates the pueblos. The encomenderos in this kingdom are such absolute lords that they do not fear God nor fairness and give rulings as if they were justice for Indians."

Forced draft labor became particularly important to the crown following the discoveries of rich gold and silver deposits in Mexico, Peru and Colombia in the decades following the conquests. The first significant silver strikes in Mexico came in the 1530s and 1540s. In the Andes, one particular silver strike discovered in 1545 in Potosí and located today in Bolivia produced an enormous quantity of rich ore. From 1550 to 1650, Potosí produced fully one-half of all the silver mined in Spanish America. Gold was discovered across the Andes from central Chile to Popayán in New Granada, today called Colombia. Silver output always far exceeded that of gold in Spanish America. However, the precious metals were worthless without Indians to extract the ore and refine the metal. "From the 1570s on," writes John Wills, "the Spanish authorities required every Indian village in the viceroyalty of Peru to send one-seventh of its male population every year for a four-month term of paid labor in the mines of Potosí, the mercury mines of Huancavelica (in modern Peru), or other public projects. The wages were far below market levels, the work was hard and dangerous (the worst was amid the poisonous mercury ore at Huancavelica) and disease and bad diet contributed to the high death rates. The mita provided only about one-tenth of the labor supply at Potosí, but these laborers did the heaviest and most dangerous work, which no one would do without compulsion, carrying heavy baskets of ore up rickety ladders out of the mines."

The mining centers of Mexico and the Andes required thousands of workers and attracted many thousands of additional opportunists and businessmen looking to get rich. Potosí, Zacatecas, Taxco, Pachuca, Popayán, Chachapoyas and the other mining centers needed food and clothing for its miners, wine for Spaniards and fermented cactus (*pulque*) and maize (*chicha*) drinks for Indians, mules, horses and oxen for transportation and the production of energy, timber, tools, furniture, pottery, leather goods, musical instruments and any number of other useful and luxury products. As a result, Spaniards built agricultural estates in the surrounding countryside, called *ranchos* and *haciendas*, and raised animals and produced commodities for these booming markets. One of the silver refiners at Potosí also built *haciendas* and *estancias* in the surrounding countryside to supply the greatest single urban and industrial market in South America. The *haciendas* and *estancias* of the silver refiner provided Potosí with wine, brandy and jerky as well as leather for containers, rungs of ladders, binding, hinges, clothing and footwear; fat for lubricating wooden machinery; tallow for candles, and

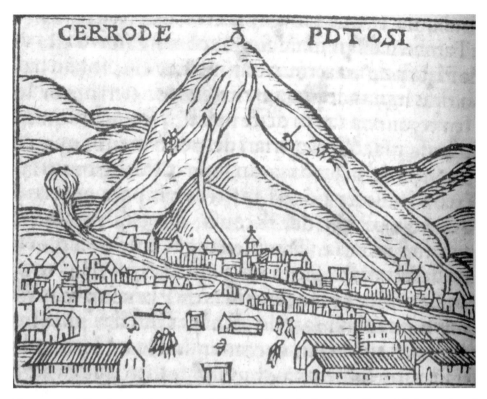

Figure 4.4. The Great Mountain of Silver at Potosí. *Cerro de Potosi* (Mountain of Potosi). From Pedro Cieza de León, *La Chronica del Perv* (Antwerp, 1554). Courtesy of the William L. Clements Library at the University of Michigan.

more. Pedro de Cieza de León remarked in the 1540s that Indians always keep coca in their mouths; "they say it makes them feel little hunger and [at the same time] strong and vigorous." Given the demand for coca in Potosí and throughout the Andes, Spaniards established commercial plantations in the valleys on the inland slopes of the Andes. The *hacienda de coca* of Captain Martín Gonzalez Valero provided Potosí in one-order 12,000 baskets, or some 300,000 pounds, of leaves. At 6 pesos a basket, the order was worth 72,000 pesos.

Sixteenth and seventeenth century Spanish America was a land of opportunity for the lesser nobility, professionals, artisans and even workers and peasants, and they immigrated to America in great numbers. From 1492 to 1570, approximately 226,000 Spanish immigrants sought a better life in America. In the seventeenth century, an additional 450,000 emigrated. Most sixteenth-century emigrants were poor Andalusian men in their 20s and 30s, although more than a few were hard-up gentlemen, *hidalgos*, the younger sons of the nobility. In 1576, Alonso Morales tried to convince his cousin and brother to come to Mexico: "Get my brother Pedro to come with you, and leave that wretched country, because it is only for those who have a lot of money, and here, no matter how poor a man may be, he never lacks a horse to ride and food to eat." America was a haven for Spanish Jews or New Christians, who found refuge and advancement, and who in turn were

Figure 4.5. Exploitation of Native Americans in the Mines of America. *Hispani Indos oneribas succumbentes crudeliter* (The Spaniards cruelly treated the Indians who collapse under Their loads). From Theodor de Bry, *Americae pars sexta* (Frankfurt, 1596). Courtesy of the William L. Clements Library at the University of Michigan.

but also found out and occasionally tormented by the Inquisition. Nevertheless, unlike the rigid aristocratic world of Spain, men from low origins could prosper and rise in society. In 1604, this was perfectly clear to an observer in Mexico City: "It happens that the majority of the people coming to these parts are fetched by poverty and necessity. As this realm has been and is by God's mercy rich, fertile, and abundant, those who come and wish to apply themselves industriously are able to get an honest living by very modest effort." Enrique Otte's study of over 600 letters from the New World to Castile in the late sixteenth century found that the dominant theme was the letter writer's encouragement of family and friends to join him in America where living conditions were better (see Table 4.2).

Spanish immigration to the New World was not a one-way affair. Many emigrants often returned home to Castile for visits, to maintain family ties, to do business and to encourage family members and townspeople to move to their new home in America. As a result, we see family and local networks crossing the Atlantic over long periods of time. Francisco Pizarro, a native of Trujillo in Northern Extremadura, Castile, traveled to Hispaniola in 1502 in the fleet of Governor Nicolás Ovando, who was from a noble family from the neighboring city of Cáceres. Pizarro recruited four brothers and a number

Table 4.2. Population of Spanish America, 1570–1800

Year	Europeans	Mixed and African
1570	118,000	230,000
1650	655,000	1,389,000
1800	3,200,000	6,250,000

Sources: Angel Rosenblat, *La población indígena y el mestizaje en América, 1492–1950*, 2 vols. (1954), Vol. I, pp. 59, 88; Nicolás Sánchez-Albornoz, "The population of colonial Spanish America," Leslie Bethell (ed.), *The Cambridge History of Latin America*. Vol. II: *Colonial Latin America* (1984), pp. 3–35.

of men from Trujillo. Some years later, according to the chronicler Pedro de Cieza de León, "many knights enlisted with Hernando Pizarro, all the very youngest, to come with him to these parts." After the conquest of Peru, Francisco Pizarro had favored the *conquistadores* from his home region with *encomiendas* far in excess of their numbers. Family and homeland counted. Immigrants stayed in touch with family in Castile. In letters home, they often urged family members to join them in America and share in opportunity and good fortune that the New World presented. Not unlike immigrants today, immigrants in the sixteenth century sent home money. Dr. Francisco de Sande, a successful royal official, supported his widowed mother, provided dowries for his sisters to enter a convent and even purchased a city council seat in Cáceres. Immigrants at various income levels sent money to Castile. Finally, because of great success, persistent failure or any number of other reasons, a number of immigrants returned to Castile to stay. This return migration has been estimated to be ten percent, which in the sixteenth century might have been thirty thousand people. Most Castilians in the sixteenth and seventeenth centuries were quite familiar with the Atlantic World. Between 1492 and 1570, it is estimated that 226,000 Spaniards (ninety-five percent of them Castilians) immigrated to the New World. Just about every family in Castile either had a family member in America or knew someone who had emigrated. Castilians were connected to America, and Castilians in America were connected to home. This arrangement benefited both.

As Indian society became increasingly homogeneous, Spanish society in America became more complex and stratified. An American aristocracy arose from the progeny of the conquerors and *encomenderos*, who were joined by wealthy merchants and mine owners as well as the highest-ranking royal officials and clerics. A middle stratum was composed of mostly bureaucrats and clerics, professional people, petty merchants and successful artisans. A lower class developed from the emigration of workers and peasants and the settlement of former sailors and soldiers. Nevertheless, opportunities remained much greater in America than Spain to improve one's station in life. And unlike in Spain, all Spaniards, even the poorest, were exempt from the head tax, and therefore thought of themselves as somewhat special, if not noble.

Another distinction arose among Spaniards in the sixteenth and seventeenth centuries. As families settled in America and women emigrated to find husbands, a population of American-born Spaniards, *españoles americanos*, emerged. Those born in Spain viewed themselves as being purer in blood, and therefore superior. Later, in the eighteenth century American-born Spaniards became known as *criollos*, or creoles, and European Spaniards as *peninsulares*. The growth of American Spaniards is exemplified by New Spain. From 1570 to 1646, the *Americano* population increased from approximately 11,000 to over 160,000. All Spaniards, regardless of wealth or place of birth, saw themselves as superior to the other peoples in their society.

Blacks, mulattos and *mestizos* constituted a category of people the Spanish called *castas*. African slaves had accompanied the conquerors in most expeditions, and were later imported to work the sugar plantations and mines. Over time, some slaves obtained their freedom, and a population of free blacks developed in Spanish American towns and cities. The presence of African and black women as well as Indian women led to race mixing from the beginning of colonization. The children of Spanish and Indian unions, *mestizos*, and those of Spanish and African unions, mulattos, were viewed by Spaniards as inferior people due to their "impure" blood, which supposedly made them lazy troublemakers and misfits. They were discriminated against in law and by custom, and generally relegated to manual and menial labor. All of the *castas*, including slaves, formed part of a European society and culture in America, and generally were considered superior to Indians.

Sixteenth- and seventeenth-century Spanish America was a rich, complex and vigorous new civilization. Spaniards emigrated to America in search of wealth and opportunity and achieved more than they ever could in Spain. They built cities across two continents, sustained by an economy of mines and agricultural estates. Magnificent cathedrals, churches and chapels, monasteries and convents, hospitals and colleges, and official palaces and private houses appeared, all built of stone with elaborate and ornate sculptured facades. Of course, this impressive civilization was based upon the exploitation and collaboration of Indians and Africans. They dug the silver, cut the sugarcane, built the cathedrals and also designed, sculpted and painted many of the baroque masterpieces of Spanish America. In New Spain, Indian art in the service of Christianity involved sculpture, and sculptured facades of convents and churches, mural painting, feather pictures and other featherwork like a bishop's miter. A frieze-like mural in the Augustinian convent in Tlayacapan, Morelos, mixed European and Nahua concepts and artistic styles. However, in one section a Mexica warrior is present, noticeable because of the jaguar skin he wears and the human prisoner he has captured. James Lockhart explains this as follows: "those most exposed to European instruction did the main panels, leaving subordinates or apprentices to do much of the purely ornamental work, in which examination shows a greater preponderance of indigenous technique." The Indian architect José Kondori built baroque churches in Potosí. In the façade of the Church of San Lorenzo, an Inka half-moon coexists with the traditional Mediterranean Corinthian vine. An Indian princess appears as an angel. The contributions of Indians and *castas* were often taken for granted or ignored altogether. The exploitation that Spanish Americans increasingly felt was that of America by Europe, New

Spain by Old Spain. Notice how the seventeenth-century Mexican poetess Sor Juana Inés de la Cruz described the prosperity of her native land:

> Señora, I was born
> in America, land of plenty,
> Gold is my compatriot,
> and the precious metals my comrades.
>
> Here's a land where sustenance
> is almost freely given,
> to no other land on earth
> is Mother Earth so generous.
>
> From the common curse of man
> its sons appear to be born free,
> For here their daily bread
> costs but little sweat of labor.
>
> Europe knows this best of all
> for these many years, insatiable,
> She has bled the abundant veins
> of America's rich mines.

4.3 Portugal in Africa

Portugal's realm on the coast of Africa could not have presented a more different portrait. With the exception of São Tomé and Angola, Portuguese Africa was a string of trade castles and trading houses. No more than a few thousand Portuguese manned this African empire in the sixteenth and seventeenth centuries.

Upper Guinea, that is, the coast from the Senegambia to Sierra Leone, had Portuguese trading establishments from Cacheo, the largest Portuguese settlement on the mainland and the residence of the chief factor of this trade, to some small settlements in Sierra Leone. The merchants of Santiago in the Cape Verde Islands dominated the trade of Upper Guinea. The entire territory of the Guinea coast, that is, from Sierra Leone to Benin, which by the early seventeenth century held some twelve to fifteen trading houses, formed the crown captaincy of Mina. Its capital was at São Jorge da Mina on the Gold Coast. Approximately seventy-five miles to the west of Mina, Axem was the next most important station and the only other castle on the Gold Coast. The castle of São Jorge itself was a rectangular stone fortress containing a large courtyard and defended by towers projecting from two or three corners. It was located on a small peninsula with the African town called the Village of Two Parts situated nearby. In time, the town was enclosed by a separate fortification. The church of São Jorge was built outside the castle presumably so African villagers as well as Portuguese officials and soldiers could attend mass. In 1486, the king granted São Jorge the privileges of a municipality.

Governors were appointed to three-year terms, and their authority covered the other factories at Axem, Accra, Cantor, Shama and elsewhere along the coast. From 1482 until the Dutch takeover in 1637, the Portuguese sent fifty-one governors to São Jorge. Governors commanded the garrison at the castle and the smaller one at Axem. They possessed full civil and criminal jurisdiction, and were responsible for relations with Africans. Subject only to the authority of the king was the royal factor, the official responsible for conducting trade at São Jorge and along the coast. Despite the risk of disease, officials agreed to come to Guinea in the hope of leaving after three years with a respectable fortune. A vicar and one or two more priests from the Order of Christ were stationed at the castle and were little concerned with evangelization among the Africans. For 150 years, the chaplain said mass for Prince Henrique's soul daily. Counting the two senior officials and their staffs, the surgeon, apothecary, smith, cooper and the 20 to 30 soldiers posted to the garrison, São Jorge da Mina counted only 60 or 70 men in the sixteenth century and 300 residents and 200 soldiers by 1621.

The value of the captaincy of São Jorge da Mina (meaning the Guinea coast) was solely in trade. In 1552, João de Barros judged its worth: "As far as the increase of the royal patrimony is concerned I do not know in Portugal of any land-tax, toll, tithe, transfer-tax or any corn tax more certain or one which yields more regular annual revenue with no tenant alleging drought or loss, than what is yielded by the trade of Guinea." The Portuguese were interested primarily in gold but also traded for slaves, malaguetta pepper, ivory and a few other exotic products. A coastal African trade, largely in slaves and cloth, was also profitable. For the precious gold that African traders brought to the coast, the Portuguese bartered cloth, hardware, slaves, shells, beads and wine. The Dutch traveler Pieter de Marees in 1602 noted that the Portuguese "made it customary among the Negroes or Indians not to dare to come to the Castle d'Mina to trade unless between them they had at least four thousand Ducats of Gold (or the equivalent). They would not open their Warehouse before they had received this prescribed sum of Gold, or more, and weighed it."

From 1482 until 1576, the better years of the gold trade, the crown held the trade monopoly on the Guinea coast. After 1576, the monarchy leased the Guinea trade to consortiums of merchants off and on, who maintained the castle, sent the supply ships and returned with the gold. The contractors, who were said to "farm" the coast, in turn sold licenses to private merchants for individual voyages to Guinea. Supervision of the Guinea trade was under the authority of the *Casa de Guiné e Mina*, Guinea House, an administrative body in Lisbon. It granted contracts and collected taxes, appointed and oversaw the officials located in the trading factories, organized annual supply ships to and from Guinea and settled trade disputes. The golden age of Guinea trade was from 1480 to 1530, the period when the African trade was still monopolized by Portugal. After 1530 and the arrival of foreign interlopers – French and English – there was a steady decline in the value of trade until at some point in the late sixteenth century the revenue coming into São Jorge did not cover the expense of the castle and the other stations. There is also evidence that the decline of gold exports at São Jorge da Mina was due to turmoil in the interior, particularly war between Songhay and Mali, which interrupted and redirected the gold trade.

When Portugal and its empire became part of the Spanish monarchy in 1580, São Jorge was reinvigorated. Felipe II dispatched a fleet that carried several hundred soldiers. The castle itself was remodeled and improved. The garrison was enlarged and better armament put in place. The castle came to have twenty-four small bronze and six large iron cannon and an impressive armory of guns, crossbows, lances, halberds and suits of armor. San António de Axem had a garrison of twelve to eighteen soldiers and ten bronze canons. A coast guard was established with the construction of two galleys and the loan of two galleons. However, these improvements could not stop or even diminish for long the arrival of the interlopers.

Next to São Jorge was the African settlement called the Village of Two Parts. Although the town gave allegiance to an African state in 1482, Portuguese policy here at Axem and other coastal towns where the Portuguese traded was one of detribalization, the severing of dependence on African rulers and the establishment of dependence on the Portuguese for protection. This small village grew to nearly one thousand inhabitants by 1600; one or two hundred of the villagers were militiamen who fought for the Portuguese in three companies. In the early seventeenth century, approximately one-half of the villagers were believed to be Christian. Officials, soldiers and merchants sometimes took African wives or mistresses and lived in the village, adopting African customs like tattooing. The mulatto sons of soldiers were often recruited as soldiers themselves when they reached maturity. They were bilingual, with Portuguese as the common language of trade, wore European clothing and practiced a type of Catholicism that embraced African ancestor veneration.

The Portuguese revolutionized agriculture in West Africa with their introduction of new fruits and crops from the Indian Ocean and the Americas. From Asia came oranges, tamarinds, bananas and coconuts. The Americas contributed pineapples, papayas, guava and sweet potatoes. Surprisingly, maize did not become a popular food for a long time whereas cassava or manioc from Brazil became the most important staple.

Beyond the Village of Two Parts, the Portuguese had to do business with three neighboring states, Efutu, Commany and Akan. African gold traders had to travel through their lands and often depended upon local officials to conduct trade with the Portuguese. The governor and royal factor attempted to maintain good relations with the rulers of these states with lavish gifts but sometimes interfered in local politics to advance the interests and power of those closest to the Europeans. When foreign traders appeared on the coast and traded with locals, the Portuguese first warned their African trading partners against such behavior. They later employed military intimidation, including the burning of villages, to stop it. As the presence and power of the Dutch increased in the early seventeenth century, African states allied themselves with the Dutch against the Portuguese. As De Marees commented: "the blacks are deserting the Portuguese more and more every day (since we started trading on the Coast), becoming, on the other hand, more attached to us."

The Gold Coast was home to many more states than the three discussed here. In the sixteenth century, there were approximately forty or fifty states in the interior. Luis Teixeira's 1602 map of West Africa showed thirty towns inland. The much smaller coastal towns and villages were generally subordinate to these major towns. Aside from the small areas surrounding the castles and trading houses, African states and chiefdoms paid little attention to the Portuguese. Politics and war continued unchanged as before the arrival of the Europeans. Interior trade routes paid more attention to the coast and foreign crops, which were spread from people to people, but for the most part the Gold Coast during the Portuguese period changed very little. This European irrelevance was temporary.

In 1506, the gold trade at São Jorge da Mina was as valuable as the new spice trade with Asia. By 1519, the gold trade brought about half the revenue to the crown as the India trade, which reveals the enormous increase in the trade with Asia. And by 1600, the gold trade was less than one-tenth as valuable as the India trade. Trade with Brazil and even the Cape Verdes surpassed that of Guinea. To maintain its position in Guinea in the face of increasing foreign presence on the coast, the Portuguese monarchy debated the advisability of colonization at São Jorge. Given the precarious situation of other imperial possessions like Brazil, and the extreme scarcity of resources and manpower, this option died in conference. When the Dutch seized São Jorge da Mina in 1637, they relieved Portugal of an imperial expense it could little afford.

The captaincy of São Tomé extended from the Volta to the Congo Rivers and included the four islands in the Gulf of Guinea. Originally granted as a private captaincy in the late fifteenth century, it was converted into a crown colony in 1522. This captaincy was little more than São Tomé, the only one of the Gulf islands fully developed by the Portuguese (aside from much smaller Príncipe, which became a crown colony in 1573). In an effort to encourage settlement, in the late fifteenth century the crown granted São Tomé and then O Príncipé the monopoly privilege to trade "in the five Slave Rivers which are beyond our fortress of São Jorge da Mina." However, most settlers to São Tomé were involuntary emigrants: criminals, political exiles and two thousand Jewish children who had been taken from their families and forcibly converted to Christianity. Unfortunately, by 1532 fewer than sixty children had survived the deadly disease environment of equatorial Africa.

As in São Jorge de Mina, the crown appointed a governor and a chief judge to head the captaincy. However, royal authority was weak in the face of entrenched local interests. When the settlement of São Tomé was raised to the status of a city in 1525, residents were given the right to elect a *Senado da Camara*, a city council, which assessed and collected taxes, possessed police power over the entire island and distributed and leased land. The great landowners of the island took control of the *Camara* and converted royal officials into business partners and accomplices. The other center of power on the island was the Catholic Church. The diocese of São Tomé was created in 1533, and thereafter bishops often clashed with governors and the

Camara over petty issues of finance and, at times, the mistreatment of slaves. In fact, politics on the island was marked by constant infighting.

São Tomé's economy was first based on cattle ranching and the provisioning of ships, but the introduction of sugar in the late fifteenth century transformed the island into a booming plantation colony. Portuguese, Genoese and Sicilian merchants transplanted cane and persons skilled in sugar cultivation and milling from Madeira. Settlers and the crown itself created plantations and increased production from 5,000 arrobas in 1530 to 150,000 arrobas by 1550. By 1555, some two-dozen ships filled with sugar supplied Lisbon each year.

However, the value of São Tomé's trade remained less than one-half of São Jorge's. This sugar economy demanded slave labor, and therefore the merchants of São Tomé entered the slave trade to man their own plantations as well as supply slaves to American plantations. The first direct shipment of slaves from the African coast to the New World departed from São Tomé in 1532. These merchants dominated the trade in their protectorate of Kongo and began the trade in Angola. A little before 1550, an unknown Portuguese mariner reported that "the chief industry of the people is to make sugar, which they sell to the ships which come each year, bringing flour, Spanish wines, oil, cheese, and all kinds of leather for shoes, swords, glass vessels, rosaries, and shells... All the population, therefore, buys negro slaves and their women from Guinea, Benin and Manicongo, and sets them to work on the land to grow and make sugar. There are rich men here, who have 150, 200, and even 300 negroes and negresses, who are obliged to work for their masters all the week, except on Saturdays, when they work on their own account."

Brazil's sugar industry eclipsed São Tomé's by the late sixteenth century. Toméan sugar was considered some of the worst on the market because the island's constant humidity made drying quite difficult and incomplete. When cheap high-quality Brazilian sugar began to flood the market, the planters of São Tomé could not compete. The planters were also plagued by slave revolts, attacks from free Africans and later raids by French and Dutch pirates and privateers. A slave revolt beginning around 1544 produced a settlement of free Africans who were almost constantly at war with the Portuguese. These *Angolares*, as they were called, raided plantations and burned fields and mills, captured female slaves for marriage and in 1574 attacked and largely destroyed the city of São Tomé. This war of the backlands continued until 1693 when a Portuguese force invaded the homeland of the *Angolares*, destroyed their settlements and enslaved the survivors. The ongoing war of the *Angolares* and periodic slave revolts, such as the rising of Amador in 1595 (who led a slave army of five thousand men and women), convinced landowners to immigrate to Brazil. "At the conclusion of these events," wrote the Portuguese chronicler of the uprising, "there was sorrow because, seventy-odd sugar mills being burned, there were not enough lashes that could be meted out to the guilty to compensate for it." There were seventy-two large plantations on the island in 1550 but by 1615, fifty-nine had been abandoned. Brazil's production of sugar matched that of São Tomé by 1580.

By 1600 Brazil produced 16,000 tons whereas São Tomé's production had declined to only 960 tons.

As elsewhere in Africa, Portuguese traders and soldiers took African wives and mistresses and produced mulatto offspring. Over time, the merchant class, planters, the military as well as the clergy in São Tomé became mostly Europeanized mulattos and Africans. The great landowners, the *fazendeiros*, in time became virtually African in appearance, although they remained Portuguese in speech and culture. The majority of free islanders were called *filhos da terra*, "sons of the land," descendants of slaves and mixed-race relationships, who were peasants in the countryside and workers in the city. At the height of the sugar regime in the mid-to-late sixteenth century, there were approximately 9,000 to 12,000 slaves on São Tomé.

A long period of economic decline took place in São Tomé during the seventeenth century. The sugar economy suffered from cane disease and competition with Brazil, slave revolts, French attacks and the Dutch occupation of the island in the 1640s. By the mid-seventeenth century, the number of sugar mills had been reduced to only four or five, and royal income from São Tomé had declined more than two-thirds. The slave trade survived the decline of the plantation economy and by the second half of the seventeenth century, the island was little more than a secondary slave *entrepôt* overshadowed by Luanda, Angola and even O Príncipé, where the seat of the captaincy was moved in 1753.

Portugal's only territorial colony on the Atlantic side of Africa was Angola. This colony originally had been granted to Paulo Dias as a private captaincy in 1574. As a system of colonization also employed in Madeira, the Azores, the Cape Verde islands and São Tomé, captaincies were ways to induce individuals to bear the cost of settlement. Donatories were obligated to transport families to the new colonies, distribute land to settlers, establish a military presence and generally create a profitable colony. In return, the crown granted the donatory substantial land grants, ownership of specific resources such as salt mines and a share in taxation.

Dias founded the town of Luanda, São Paulo da Assumpção, and extended Portuguese control only a little into the interior. The conquest of Angola, such as it was, required numerous campaigns stretching over a hundred years. Dias died in 1589, and the crown took over the captaincy in 1592. From that year until 1784, Angola saw fifty governors.

The donatory and the early *conquistadores* had implemented in Angola an unofficial system of rule that resembled the *encomienda* in Spanish America. When new territories fell under Portuguese control, local chiefs and their lands were allocated to soldiers and sometimes to clerics. The African chiefs required their people to provide tribute, goods and labor to the estates of their Portuguese masters. Often this tribute was payable in slaves. Naturally, the monarchy did not approve of this system and only began to abolish it in the later part of the seventeenth century.

Three bodies shared power among the Portuguese in Angola. The first was the royal governor and captain-general, appointed to a three-year term. He collected taxes and the tithe, headed the military garrison at the fortress at São Miguel overlooking Luanda, commanded the local militia and appointed

Document 4.2
The Island of St. Thomas

1670

The Island of St. Thomas, in Portuguese, St. Thomee, because first of all discover'd on that Saints Day; yet Thevet called it Santa Honore, and the Barqarians, Ponkas; it lieth in the Ethiopian Sea, right under the Equinoctial Line, (which comes through the City, and the great Church, and therefore no Latitude hath been ascribed to it) and not far from the Cape of Lopez Gonsalvez. It bears an Oval form about thirty Miles in Circumference, and in length and breadth twelve miles . . .

The Ground is tough, and of a yellowish Russet Colour; and by reason of the many Mists, which fall every Night, it grows soft, like Wax, and becomes fit to produce all sorts of Grain, Fruits, and Plants. The goodness and fertility thereof appears by this; That so soon as a plain Place is left untill'd, or laid waste, Trees grow upon it, and shoot up to a great height in few days, which the Blacks cut down and burn, to plant the Sugar-Canes in their Ashes, which grow every where in the Valleys, but yield less Juyce than those in Brasile.

The Canes Planted in the fore-mention'd Ashes, must have five Moneths time to ripen in: For that which is Planted in January, is Cut in June; and that of February, in July: And in this manner they Cut and Plant all the Year through. The full-grown Canes, when cut, are grownd small in Water-Mills, which the Portuguese call Ingenhas; or by the Labor of Slaves or Oxen, in places where there are no Rivers: Afterwards they put the Juyce into great Kettles, and boyl it over the Fire, to cleanse it; and with the Refuse they feed the Hogs, which eating nothing else, grow exceeding fat, and are esteem'd such wholesome and sweet Flesh, that they Diet therewith the Sick, to recover them to their Health.

Seven Ships Lading of Sugar this Island sends forth every Year; that is, Four for Portugal, two for the Canary and Madera Islands, and one for England: And there might be a great deal more made, and also whiter; but they want Pots and other Necessities to cleanse it, and also Refiners to work it.

The Portuguese have sent for many Articles from the Maderas, to make their Sugar whiter and harder; but could never effect the same, the Air making their Labour fruitless, because it doth not suffer it to dry: And therefore the Sugar-makers are necessitated to set the Loaves upon low Planks inclos'd round, and set them upon Boughs of thick dry Wood, which being set on Fire, make no Flame nor Smoak, but at length glimmer like glowing Coals, and so dry it, as in Stoves. Before the coming of the Portuguese, there grew no Sugar-canes, nor Ginger; but they brought them thither, and planted them.

In the Year Sixteen hundred forty five, there stood on this Island four and fifty Mills, which every one had their Moneths to grind, and could make every Year twelve or fourteen Tun of Sugar. In the Year Sixteen hundred and ten, there were fifty one Mills, which the Hollanders ruin'd;

so that ever since they have for the most part been able to do nothing, for want of Coppers, and Slaves to work....

The Inhabitants are of two sorts: Portuguese, which first found this Island desolate, and inhabited the same; and Blacks, sent thither from Angola to work. Those which are born on this Island, of a Portuguese Father and Mother, though they have liv'd there a long time, are white, like the Portuguese; but the Children of a Portuguese-Man and a Black-Woman, are Brown, or Yellow, and therefore call'd Mulatos. There us'd every Year to be send from Luanda St. Paulo thither, about five thousand young Blacks, for Slaves. The Native Portuguese go clothed like their Countrymen, and the Negro-Merchants with their Families follow the same Mode; but the Slaves, as well Men as Women, go naked, onely with a Cloth of Palmito-Leaf before their Privacies.

The Commodities carried from thence to other Places, consist chiefly in Muscovado-Sugar, yearly made to the quantity of a hundred thousand Arabs, every Arabs being thirty two Pounds, being pack'd in Leaves, and brought over to Europe; the afore-mention'd Cotton Clothes, the Fruit Kolas, and such like. The Merchandise transported thither by the Portuguese, and others, were Linnen of several kinds, all sorts of colour'd Yarn, Says, Silk Stockings, French Serges, mix'd Hair-Says, Axes, Chopping or Hewing-Knives, Iron, Salt, Linseed Oyl, Red Copper in Plates, Copper Kettles, Rosin, Pitch, Tar, Ropes, Earthen Sugar-pots, of bigness to contain twenty or thirty Pound weight; Brandy, and all sorts of Strong-waters, Canary-Wine, Olives, Capers, fine Flow'r, Butter, Cheese, and such like.

The Revenues which the Portuguese have yearly from this Island, amount to a considerable Sum: For all Exported Goods must pay the Tenth of every thing for Custom to the King, either in Ready Money, Sugar, Palm-Oyl, or Clothes. Of Slaves brought from one place to another, they give one out of ten. Those which fish with a Net at the Shore, answer every fifth Fish: And for the Fishing with a Canoe in the Sea, for every eight days they must pay the Value of three Pence: Nay, every Plant which the Country produceth must pay somewhat to the King.

This portrait of the Portuguese African possession of São Tomé reveals a plantation economy that had been surpassed by Brazil but still profitable and important. *Source: Africa: Being an Accurate Description of the Regions of AEgypt, Barbary, Lybia, and Billedulgerid.* Collected and Translated from most Authentick Authors, and Augmented with later Observations: Illustrated with Notes, and Adorn'd with peculiar Maps, and proper Sculptures, By John Olilby, Esq. London, Printed by Tho. Johnson for the Author, M.DC.LXX [1670], pp. 719–25.

capitãos-mores, or captain-majors, to command the inland forts and trading houses in the major African towns. The *capitães-mores* were the backbone of Portuguese authority throughout Angola and were largely responsible for supervising the official slave trade with African rulers in the interior. They often abused their power for personal gain and for this reason, the office was abolished in the eighteenth century. Governors were also at the center of the slave trade in Angola. Besides collecting the tax on each slave, they often held the "slave contract," the official monopoly of the slave trade. On behalf of the crown, governors sold export licenses to individual traders and ship captains. For example, for the period 1603 to 1607 the governor sold more than fifteen thousand licenses to traders to supply the Spanish American market. All royal officials in the colony, neglected and underpaid by Lisbon, participated in some way in the slave trade.

The second source of authority was the municipality of the city of São Paulo de Luanda. This settlement had been granted municipal status in 1576 and 1662, which included certain privileges all cities possessed, including being governed by a council of local notables, the *Camara de Luanda*. The *Camara* occasionally shared authority with governors of the colony and perhaps more often had disputes and even open conflict with governors. To the disgust of governors, the *Camara* discouraged plantation agriculture in Angola and favored policies that only nurtured the slave trade. The third source of authority was the clerical establishment headed by the Bishop of Luanda, who was also given control of the See of São Salvador do Congo in 1676 when that kingdom was breaking apart. The Sacred College of the *Propaganda Fide*, founded in Rome in 1622, sent Italian Capuchins to work in Kongo and Angola who were the most effective missionaries in central Africa. By the end of the seventeenth century, the bishop's clerical establishment in Angola involved about sixty clerics distributed in some twenty-five parishes. The church educated Portuguese and African youths, owned and operated agricultural estates and maintained several impressive churches and a cathedral in Luanda. The church also participated in the slave trade. In fact, the Portuguese monarchy compensated the clergy with a right of priority in the sale of slaves. The Jesuits, the largest religious order in Angola, owned slaving ships that transported Africans to Brazil. "Almost all Portuguese clergy," writes Adrian Hastings, "were effectively dependent upon it for their financial support."

Angola became more of a colony of Brazil than Portugal. After the restoration of Portuguese rule following the Dutch conquest of Angola in 1641–8, many of the governors came from Brazil. Brazil had its own tax on the Angolan slave trade. Brazilian capital, trade goods and ships dominated the Angolan slave trade, which specialized on the Brazilian market.

The port of São Filipe de Benguela, located some 300 miles south of Luanda, prospered in the late seventeenth century as the new frontier of the slave trade. Benguela had been settled by mulattos from Luanda and long remained a haven for undesirables. As military campaigns pushed further into the interior in the eighteenth century and reached more populous regions, the slave trade grew more rapidly, became independent of Luanda, eventually surpassed it and became directed to Rio de Janeiro.

In the beginning, the crown desired the establishment of a prosperous agricultural settler colony much like Brazil had become by the late sixteenth century. This hope proved largely to be illusory. In time, some farms and ranches were created along the Kwanza River and other inland valleys to produce food for Luanda and to maintain the unfortunate captives waiting for transport to São Tomé and the New World. Local subject Africans were forced to work on these farms as well as take part in slave caravans, perform military service, assist in the construction of public works and pay tithes. Where the Portuguese ruled Africans, control was far from subtle. As the seventeenth century Portuguese historian of Angola, António de Oliveira de Cadornega, put it: "it is only by force and fear that we can maintain our position over these indomitable heathen."

The Portuguese population in Angola had little interest in or ability to build small farms or commercial plantations, which required some capital, skills and years of commitment. Officials and soldiers were in the colony for only a fixed term and sought to enrich themselves and get out. A good portion of the population was undesirable, like convicts from Lisbon prisons transported to the colony against their will, hardly good material for yeoman farmers. Even clerics were of low quality. The Bishop of Angola in 1773 described his priests as "greedy, lustful, expatriate, rebellious and libertine men." The business that all could easily tap into was the slave trade. Bento Banha Cardoza, a soldier, wrote in 1622: "because most people being employed in the slave trade, they neglect everything else."

Official policy generally discouraged, and at times prohibited, white Portuguese settlement in the interior. Nevertheless, in Angola as elsewhere in Africa, some adventurous Portuguese settled among Africans, took local wives and mistresses and produced mulatto offspring. Few Portuguese women ever immigrated to Angola, and governors rarely took their wives to their post. Cadornega wrote that most Portuguese arrivals "had accommodated themselves with Mulatas, daughters of worthy men and conquerors who had begotten them on either their female slaves or on free Negro women." Cadornega further described Angola as the country where sons were brown and grandsons were black. In time, these *quimbares*, as they became known, constituted a floating population of traders and caravaneers who were neither Portuguese nor African but uniquely able to function in both worlds and act as intermediaries.

In 1655, the *Camara* of Luanda informed the crown that there were 326 white *moradores*, heads of households, in Portuguese Angola, of whom 132 were citizens of Luanda. In 1680–3, Cadornega wrote that there were some hundreds of households. He also noted the increase of population was caused by soldiers and private persons who, unable to find white ladies, mated with black ladies. By the late seventeenth century, Luanda was more of an African than a Portuguese city. There were fifty thousand blacks, six thousand mulattos and only four thousand whites. In comparison, the leading Brazilian port of Salvador, Bahia, had a similar number of blacks and mulattos but counted five times as many whites. The upper town in Luanda housed the white and mulatto aristocracy who built fine two-story townhouses and dressed in the most costly of imported clothing. The Portuguese attempted to recreate Lisbon at least a little with the fine architecture of the cathedral, other churches and convents and the governor's palace. In his history, Cadornega detailed all of the "sumptuous buildings, which greatly ennoble this city." However, the commercial quarter of the city was a squalid area of slave markets, holding pens or barracoons, and warehouses. Most private houses had an attached enclosure to hold slaves as well. Travelers and residents viewed Luanda as poor and rotten and Angola as a vicious and corrupt colony. For the Portuguese historian E. A. da Silva Correia, Luanda became the haven of the flotsam and jetsam of the Portuguese world, what he called "the monsters of iniquity." The first known Portuguese poetry written in Angola, a seventeenth-century verse by an anonymous poet, provided no heroic portrait of this slave-trading land:

> There is in this turbulent land
> a storehouse of pain and trouble,
> confused mother of fear,
> Hell in life.
>
> Land of oppressed peoples,
> rubbish heap of Portugal
> where she purges her evil
> And her scum.
>
> Where the lie and falsehood,
> theft and malevolence
> selfishness
> Represent vain glory.
>
> Where justice perishes,
> for want of men to understand it,
> where God must be sought
> to achieve salvation...

Portuguese West and Central Africa in the sixteenth and seventeenth centuries was the neglected stepchild of Portugal's Atlantic empire. Aside from São Tomé for a brief few decades, none of Portugal's African possessions promised to become prosperous commercial and agricultural colonies. Angola grew to become the center of Portugal's (meaning Brazil's) Atlantic slave trade. In the long run, the Kongo/Angola coast became the greatest exporter of slaves in the Atlantic slave trade (see Map 4.3).

4.4 Portugal in America

The long Portuguese coast in the New World took a definite second place in the early sixteenth century to the new network of trading factories extending along the coasts of Africa and into Asia. Unlike Africa and Asia, the Portuguese in Brazil did not establish trading posts or factories on the coast but merely sent trading ships from time to time. The crown held the monopoly of the trade of Brasilwood and sold trading licenses to individual traders. However, the presence of more and more French traders on the Brazilian coast forced the monarchy to embrace colonization.

In the 1530s, the Portuguese crown applied to Brazil a colonization technique previously implemented in Madeira and the Azores, São Tomé and

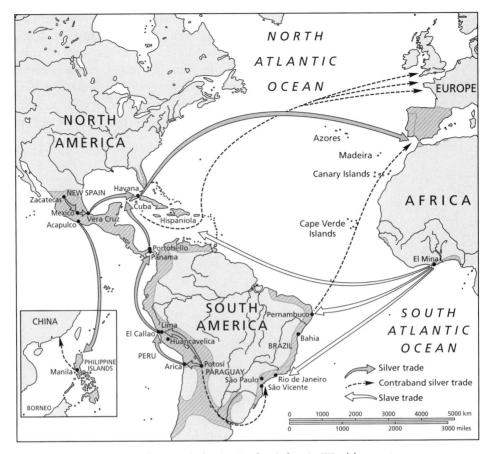

Map 4.3. Iberian Colonies in the Atlantic World, c. 1600.

later in Angola. The coast was divided into fourteen captaincies, of which twelve were granted to individual donatories who would be responsible for the development of their colonies. Some of the captaincies were completely neglected, others got off to a weak start and only two, Pernambuco in the north and São Vicente in the south, grew and prospered. To provide some central impetus and coordination, the crown established the royal captaincy of Bahia in 1549 and dispatched a governor-general and a large colonizing expedition.

Thereafter, Brazil remained a rather decentralized collection of hereditary and royal captaincies. The governor-general in the City of the Savior, Salvador, in the captaincy of Bahia, was largely responsible for matters of defense. During the union of the Portuguese and Spanish crowns from 1580 to 1640, Portuguese administration of Brazil continued uninterrupted and with minimal interference from Madrid. Compared to Spanish America, the colonial government and bureaucracy in Brazil were minimal. Royal centralization was initiated in 1609 when a high court, or *Relação da Bahia*, was established in Salvador with the governor as its president. In time, writes Stuart B. Schwartz, "it was not uncommon for those who served in Brazil to represent colonial interests or to reconcile royal legislation with Brazilian realities."

Figure 4.6. São Salvador and the Bay of All Saints. From Theodor de Bry, *Historia Americae sive Novi Orbis continens in XIII* (Frankfurt, 1634). Courtesy of the William L. Clements Library at the University of Michigan.

In each captaincy, the donatory or royal governor exercised the most effective centralized authority. He usually held the title of captain-general and appointed the local military authorities, the *capitães-mores*, as in Angola. He appointed the local magistrates, made land grants and collected taxes. At the local level, municipal councils composed of local wealthy landholders regulated the most important activities of everyday life and were not always in accord with the policies of the central government of the captaincy or Brazil at large.

In 1620, Brazil was divided into two states for better administration of the distant settlements of the Amazonian region. The *Estado do Maranhão* was formed from the six hereditary captaincies along the northern coast. Because direct communication with Lisbon was more efficient than indirect control through Salvador, its own governor-general governed this new state. The remaining captaincies were grouped into the *Estado do Brazil*.

An episcopate was formed in 1552 with its seat in Salvador. A little more than a century later, the see of Bahia was elevated to an archbishopric and the bishoprics of Rio de Janeiro and Olinda were established subordinate to it. As with government, the bishopric of the *Estado do Maranhão* was dependent on Lisbon rather than Salvador. As in early Spanish America, the religious orders that established themselves in Brazil – the Jesuits, Benedictines, Franciscans and Carmelites – exercised considerable influence over education, care of the sick and poor and relations with Indians.

Administrative supervision of church and state in Brazil was coordinated from Lisbon by a Secretary of State and advised by a royal council, which assumed different names over the years. The Overseas Council, as it was called after 1642, oversaw Portugal's possessions in Africa and Asia as well as Brazil. The Council appointed colonial officials, sold the contracts of monopoly trading privileges and generally set Portugal's colonial policy. However, its duties were far less complex than Spain's Council of the Indies given the small size of the colonial bureaucracy and the decentralized nature of the empire. In short, government was much less important and visible in Brazil as compared to Spanish America. Spain's American empire had a fundamentally urban character, which naturally enhanced the presence and power of government. In contrast, Brazil was profoundly rural. Wealthy landholders, who controlled not only their own properties but also exercised influence over the neighboring small farms and villages, held power. The few underdeveloped towns and cities that arose were the necessary offshoots of estates, which needed ports and centers of distribution. Whereas the wealthiest landholders often owned townhouses, power and status remained decentralized in the countryside. "In sum," wrote João Capistrano de Abreu, one of Brazil's great historians, "centrifugal, dispersing forces held forth in this social system."

Brazil's rural character also derived from the nature of the small, scattered and semisedentary populations of the land's native peoples. In Spanish America, Spaniards naturally settled where the largest Indian towns and cities had been located, and later in mining centers where deposits of silver and gold were found. There were no such native urban centers in Brazil. And as the Portuguese transplanted sugarcane from Madeira and São Tomé in the 1530s, 1540s and after, plantations developed, widely scattered along the vast coast of Brazil, located where the most fertile land and suitable landing points were found (see Map 4.4).

Sugarcane became Brazil's reason for being. During the sixteenth century, sugar was still relatively scarce in Europe and therefore brought a high price. The boom continued into the seventeenth century. The Portuguese had seen the fortunes sugar had created, and the great revenues collected, in Madeira and São Tomé, so its expansion to Brazil was not surprising. Before sugar's migration to Brazil, Spaniards had cultivated it in the Caribbean, Mexico and Peru. However, in Spanish America sugarcane remained a marginal crop, its development often interrupted by gold and silver rushes. Not so in Brazil, where sugarcane had no rival and became king.

Sugarcane was worthless without substantial labor to plant and harvest it and process the cane to produce granular sugar. As shown in the previous chapter, the need for large numbers of laborers led to widespread Indian slavery, native resistance and the campaigns of conquest. Indian slaves remained the predominant labor force on the sugar plantations until the last quarter of the sixteenth century. The epidemics beginning in the 1560s, which slashed the population of coastal Indians, increasingly led Portuguese planters to depend upon African slave laborers. This was a natural development because the Portuguese long before had developed a slave trade on the coast of Africa and purchased Africans for employment in the sugar estates of Madeira and São Tomé. The shipment of increasingly large numbers of Africans to Brazil in the late sixteenth and early seventeenth centuries became routine.

Sugarcane did not prosper along the entire coast of Brazil. It first took root in Pernambuco in the north, which soon became the richest and most populous captaincy and which produced the towns of Olinda and Recife. The other original Brazilian home of sugarcane was São Vicente in the south. From there, it rapidly spread to the region around Rio de Janeiro. With the

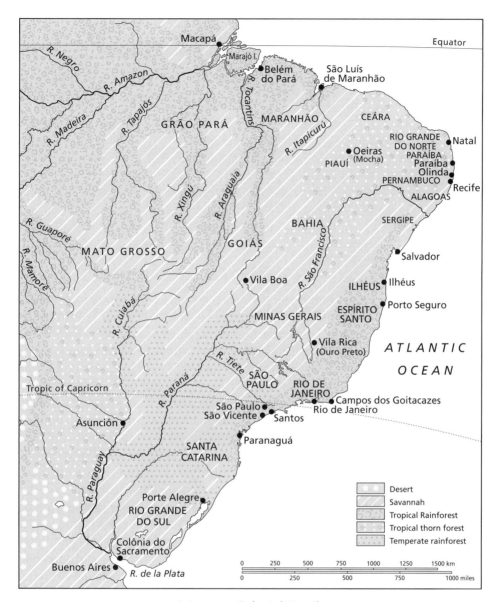

Map 4.4. Colonial Brazil.

establishment of the royal captaincy of Bahia in 1549, sugarcane was transplanted in the rich *recôncavo*, the fertile belt of land around the Bay of All
Saints. By 1584, there were 180 sugar mills – *engenhos* as they were called –
in Brazil, sixty-six in Pernambuco and thirty-six in Bahia. In some years in
the late sixteenth century, more than 100 ships carried sugar to Lisbon annually. By the mid-seventeenth century, sugar constituted over ninety percent of
Brazil's export earnings. An observer in 1573 noted that "[it] is the judgment
of God that, as a result of the money gained in Brazil through sugar and
cotton, wood and parrots, your Majesty's treasury should be enriched with
much fine gold."

Many of the sugar plantations were self-sufficient. They raised cattle,
horses and sheep, farmed corn and wheat, forged iron tools and made leather

Table 4.3. Population of Brazil, 1549–1819

Year	Europeans	Mixed and African
1549	3,500	–
1570	20,000	30,000
1580	30,000	–
1650	70,000	180,000
1798	1,010,000	–
1819	1,302,000	1,107,000*

*The 1819 population figure refers to slaves.
Sources: Angel Rosenblat, *La población indígena y el mestizaje en América, 1492–1950*, 2 vols. (1954), Vol. I, pp. 88, 102; Maria Luiza Marcílio, "The population of colonial Brazil," Leslie Bethell (ed.), *The Cambridge History of Latin America*. Vol. II: *Colonial Latin America* (1984), pp. 37–63.

goods. Specialization in sugarcane produced a market for foodstuffs, which encouraged the creation of farms and ranches – *fazendas* – that fed the plantations and the coastal towns. Artisans and craftsmen immigrated to Brazil's towns where their skills found productive employment. For Portuguese emigrants, Brazil was a land of opportunity. The Jesuit Fernão Cardim in 1600 remarked, "This Brazil is already another Portugal, and not speaking of the climate, which is much more temperate and healthful, without great heats or colds." The only need mentioned by Cardim was the "want of ships to bring merchandise and clothes."

Brazil's attraction to ordinary Portuguese in the sixteenth and seventeenth centuries is demonstrated in its population growth. Neither Africa nor Asia enticed many Portuguese to leave home. Brazil was another matter. Unlike Portugal's other colonial outposts, women and entire families immigrated to America, often from Madeira and the Azores. By 1570, there were approximately 20,700 white settlers in the colony, most concentrated in Pernambuco and Bahia. By 1650, this population had increased to 70,000. "Portugal has no other region more fertile, nor close at hand nor more frequented, nor have its vassals a better or safer refuge than Brazil," noted a Portuguese observer in 1645. "The Portuguese who is overtaken by any misfortunes at home emigrates thither." Portuguese and Iberian Jews generally found refuge in Brazil. In fact, a number of historians believe that Brazil not only became a refuge for Iberian Jews or New Christians but that refugee Jews from Portugal, Madeira and São Tomé transferred sugarcane and milling technology to Brazil and financed sugar estates in the captaincies. Jews became some of the sugar-planting elite in Pernambuco, the *senhores de engenho*. The majority of colonists were seeking opportunity and wealth: laborers, tradesmen, sailors, merchants, minor nobles and debtors. In addition, the crown regularly dispatched convicts called *degredados*. For the humble-born in Portugal, Brazil was a land of opportunity and mobility. The Portuguese had a smaller population at home to send abroad than Spain. In 1650, the white population of Spanish America was nearly ten times that of Brazil (see Table 4.3).

The great sugar planters dominated Portuguese society in Brazil, the *senhores de engenho*, who also controlled the local municipal councils and militias. Dependent on them were the merchants of the ports who exported their sugar and imported their luxuries. Officials of the crown were far fewer and less prominent in Brazil than in Spanish America and, except for the highest officials in Salvador, never attained anything close to the status of the sugar barons. The middle and lower strata of Portuguese-Brazilian society were composed of artisans, shopkeepers and workers in the towns and small ranchers and planters, renters, overseers and cowboys in the country. At the bottom of society were peasants and slaves. A late colonial census in the town of Santana de Parnaíba demonstrated the reinforcement of class and color: ninety-seven percent of the planters appeared as "white" whereas eighty percent of the slaves were denoted as "black." Most laborers, peasants, domestics, mule drivers and artisans were describes as "browns."

Because most migrants over the years were predominantly male, Portuguese men frequently took Indian and African wives and mistresses. Therefore, the rise of a half-caste population was a Brazilian as well as an African development. In the plantation regions of Pernambuco and Bahia, a large mulatto or *crioulo* population arose in the seventeenth century. Colonial legislation harshly discriminated against *crioulos* to ensure that the status of poor white Portuguese were never passed by ambitious mulattos. The largest *mestizo* (Indian-Portuguese), or *mameluco* population as it was called in Brazil, was to be found in and around São Paulo, the inland capital of São Vicente. Of course, *mamelucos* were located everywhere in Brazil, particularly in the backlands, and often participated in the Indian slave trade.

Although many Africans and African-Americans, both slave and free, lived in every province of Spanish America, they were generally concentrated in cities or constituted a minority in a rural population dominated by Indians. However, in the plantation captaincies of Brazil, Africans and African-Americans in the seventeenth century became the majority population on plantations and in plantation zones. In such a potentially volatile situation, the white master class developed tight and often cruel slave codes and systems of control and severely punished runaways and rebels. Nevertheless, the vast interior of Brazil harbored escaped slaves who formed their own communities, which survived on their own for years, sometimes decades. These *quilombos* were based on Central African merit-based, male warrior societies that erased lineage ties called *ki-lombos*. "Many African men," write Arno and Maria Wehling, "likely found these corporate bonds an attractive means of (re)creating identity in the Americas."

Following the conquest of the coastal Indian populations and the repeated epidemics of the late sixteenth century, Indians were not nearly as numerous or important in Brazilian society compared to Spanish America. The Jesuits gathered conquered or "domesticated" Indians into *aldeias*, mission villages, where Portuguese fathers preached the gospel and closely supervised the work and everyday routine of their charges. For example, in Bahia in 1562 more than thirty thousand Indians lived in Jesuit *aldeias*. The vast majority of Brazil's native peoples retreated from the coast or already lived in the interior and tried to have little to do with the Portuguese.

In fact, it was this great Indian population along with the hope of finding rich mines as in Mexico and Peru that first drew Portuguese adventurers into the interior of Brazil. Military companies composed of hardy Portuguese, *mamelucos* and mulattos, called *bandeirantes* after the flags they carried, plunged into the interior to capture Indian slaves. Paulistas from São Paulo were especially well known for their exploratory and slaving expeditions into deepest Brazil. Unlike Spain, which abolished Indian slavery in 1542, Portugal never settled on an unambiguous policy regarding Indian slavery. Although slavery was generally prohibited in theory, loopholes allowed it to thrive. Indians could be legally enslaved if captured during a just war or rebellion, or committed unnatural acts such as cannibalism, or were already slaves of other Indians and then were "rescued" by the Portuguese. The Indians, commented Father Antonio Vieira in 1657, "are the real mines of this state, for the reports of those of gold and silver always served as a pretext for searching for the other mines, which are found in the veins of the Indians, and they were never in those of the earth."

The *bandeirantes* frequently clashed with the Jesuits, who also entered the interior and established mission villages that attempted to protect Indians from the slavers. To prevent the worst outcomes, the Jesuits often would sell the labor of mission Indians for limited periods and under certain conditions. By 1600, the crown had turned over jurisdiction of the Indian population to the Jesuits and guaranteed, for what it was worth, their safety. On the other hand, Brazilian municipal councils constantly sought secular jurisdiction and tried to expel the Jesuits from their captaincies. In the region between southern Brazil and Spanish America, the Jesuit province of Paraguay contained several populous missions and constituted an autonomous theocratic state, which gave voluntary allegiance to the Spanish crown. However, these missions were often the targets of Paulistas and other *bandeirantes* from Brazil.

In time, behind the *bandeirantes* followed Portuguese and half-caste settlers who built small family farms as well as large ranches raising cattle, horses and mules. This agricultural and pastoral frontier made its way up the Rio de São Francisco, the main artery into the interior of central Brazil, as well as up other rivers. Minor discoveries of alluvial gold also encouraged people on the coast to move inland. Eventually, river and mule-train routes began to link the port cities by land for the first time. However, throughout the seventeenth century Brazil remained a coastal society, quite a contrast to Spanish America. During the union of the Portuguese and Spanish crowns, Portuguese settlers, missionaries and government agents moved the frontiers of Brazil west of the Treaty of Tordesillas line. Because all of America was "in the family," so to speak, the Spanish did not object. Thus traders, missionaries and soldiers moved up the Amazon and south along the coast toward the Rio de la Plata. Although some of this expansion was due to earlier momentum, Portuguese officials were also deliberately and preemptively extending the borders of Brazil. By the mid-eighteenth century, Brazil was a vast territory extending thousands of miles along the coast and into the interior beyond the Tordesillas line.

The greatest wave of westward expansion began in the 1690s. Substantial deposits of gold were discovered in the backcountry, northwest of São Paulo and Rio de Janeiro, which sparked the first gold rush in the Americas. During the eighteenth century, Brazil produced two million pounds of gold, or something like eighty percent of the world's supply. In the early eighteenth century, diamonds were also found in the interior. Thousands of would-be miners not only left the coast but also migrated from Portugal. Tens of thousands of black slaves were brought inland to work the streams. The first inland captaincies, São Paulo and Minas Gerais, were formed and quickly populated. Prosperous mining towns like Villa Rica do Ouro Preto popped up while farms and ranches appeared to feed and supply them.

By this time, Brazil's plantation economy was in decline due to soil exhaustion and competition by the more productive sugar islands of the Caribbean. The Brazilian economy revolved around gold during the first half of the century. As the gold boom declined in the second half of the century, plantation agriculture again took first place, located now in the interior as well as on the coast. New plantation crops like tobacco, cotton, rice, cacao and coffee produced a more diversified agricultural economy.

By the eighteenth century, Brazil was the jewel in the crown of Portugal's empire. Most of the empire in Asia was gone. In West Africa, Elmina and the Gold Coast had been lost. Brazil was Portugal's most valuable possession. As large as all of Europe, with more than two million people and holding many of the most valuable plantations and mines in the Atlantic, Brazil provided sixty percent of the exports of Portugal's trade surplus. The metropolis was now dependent on the colony. However, Brazil's wealth, the same as Angola's, was limited in benefit. As one Portuguese resident of Bahia asked, "Why is a country so fecund in natural products, so rich in essence, so vast in extent, still inhibited by such a small number of settlers, most of them poor, and many of them half-starved?"

The Iberian Atlantic World in 1600, in its first and immediate geographical bearing, stretched from Lisbon and Seville to many ports. In the islands of the near Atlantic were the victualing bases and commercial ports of Funchal in Madeira, Angra on Terceira in the Azores, San Sebastián on Gomera in the Canaries and Santiago in the Cape Verdes. On the coast of Atlantic Africa, Portugal possessed (to mention only the main trading factories and ports) Arguim, Gorée, São Jorge da Mina, São Tomé, Luanda and Benguela. In Portuguese Brazil, the major port and capital was Salvador de Bahia, founded when the colony was founded in 1549. A number of other ports appeared on this long coast in the sixteenth century: Santos, Olinda, Recife and Rio de Janeiro. The Spanish created a number of great (and not so great) ports in the sixteenth century, most in the Caribbean: Santo Domingo, Havana, Vera Cruz, Cartagena, Campeche and Nombre de Dios. In South America, Peru's port was Callao, Quito's port was Guayaquil and the Atlantic port of Buenos Aires was refounded in 1580.

The Iberian Atlantic World in 1600 had penetrated the interiors of Africa and the Americas. Aside from the islands in the near Atlantic and in African waters and the hinterland of Luanda, the Iberians in Africa could realistically claim few lands and subject peoples. However, Portuguese cultural influence

and especially trade reached deep into Africa. The Portuguese in Brazil by
1600 had settled the coast and had begun to move into the interior. Their
"conquest" of the coastal native peoples had succeeded to the point that
they were able to establish plantations, but they had not been able to make
the plantation system thrive on Indian slavery. The Spanish had created a
great mainland empire in the New World based on towns and cities by
1600. They were ensconced not only in the great imperial capitals of Mexico
City and Lima but also in Puebla, Mérida, Oaxaca, Guadalajara, Valladolid,
Zacatecas and Santiago de Guatemala in New Spain. In South America, the
Spanish took over Quito, Cajamarca and Cuzco and established Antioquia,
Popayán, Potosí, Santiago and many more.

   These points on a vast map, points of contact, trade and production,
formed the Iberian Atlantic World. This early Atlantic World was composed
of two slender systems of oceanic dominion. Both Iberian empires have been
characterized as merchant empires, which they were. Carla Rahn Phillips has
estimated that in the last of the sixteenth century, Spain sent several hundred
vessels to American each year and more than forty thousand men served
on these fleets. In 1600, Iberians (and various other Europeans) probably
did not add up to more than half a million settlers, traders, bureaucrats,
clerics, soldiers and sailors. They were vastly outnumbered by the locals,
that is, by Africans and Native Americans. By this time, about one hundred
thousand Africans had been transported to Spanish America and Brazil as
slaves, although unlike European emigrants they rarely had children and
therefore were not reproducing their population. This early Atlantic World
was composed of empires of negotiated interdependency. The Spanish and
the Portuguese, so dispersed across these points of contact and so outnumbered, found power and profit primarily in cooperation and partnership with
Africans and Native Americans. In Africa, the Portuguese gold and slave
trades depended upon African intermediaries. Where Iberians sought "conquest," from Hispaniola to Brazil and from Mexico to Angola, Spanish and
Portuguese *conquistadores* were always accompanied by Indian and African
allies. Indian and African labor, forced and enslaved but also negotiated and
purchased, provided the Iberians with their most profitable commodities: silver, gold, sugar, pearls, emeralds and dye-stuffs. As we will see in subsequent
chapters, European, African and Indian alliances, partnerships and cooperation not only led to the formation of the early Atlantic World but to cultural
as well as political, social and economic transformations on all sides.

   At this conclusion of Part I, we need to recall the inequalities of material,
cultural and political resources held by the Portuguese and the Spanish in
their encounters with Africans and Indians in the fifteenth and sixteenth
centuries. Europeans expanded into the Atlantic and forced themselves on
numerous peoples as conquerors, missionaries, bureaucrats and planters.
This was how they arrogantly saw themselves. In 1545, Pedro de Cieza de
León boasted: "Many nations have excelled others and overcome them, and
the few have conquered the many. They say Alexander the Great with thirty-
three thousand Macedonians undertook to conquer the world. So with the
Romans too. But no nation has with such resolution passed through such
labours, or such periods of starvation, or covered such immense distances

as the Spanish have done. In a period of seventy years they have overcome and opened a new world, greater than the one of which we had knowledge, exploring what was unknown and never before seen."

Sources

José de Acosta, *Natural and Moral History of the Indies*, edited by Jane E. Mangan, translated by F. M. López-Morillas (Durham, 2002).

Ida Altman, *Emigrants and Society: Extremadura and America in the Sixteenth Century* (Berkeley, 1989).

Charles R. Boxer, *The Portuguese Seaborne Empire* (London, 1969).

D. A. Brading, *The First America: Spanish Monarchy, Creole Patriots, and the Liberal State* (Cambridge, 1991).

João Capistrano deAbreu, *Chapters of Brazil's Colonial History, 1500–1800*, translated from the Portuguese by Arthur Brakel (Oxford, 1997).

Chronicle of Colonial Lima: The Diary of Josephe and Francisco Mugaburu, 1640–1697, translated by Robert Ryal Miller (Albuquerque, 1975).

Christopher R. DeCorse, *An Archaeology of Elmina: Africans and Europeans on the Gold Coast, 1400–1900* (Washington, D.C., 2001).

Alfred W. Crosby, *The Columbian Exchange: Biological and Cultural Consequences of 1492* (Westport, Conn., 1972).

Ambrósio Fernandes Brandão, *Dialogues of the Great Things of Brazil*, translated and annotated by Frederick Arthur Holden Hall, William F. Harrison, and Dorthy Winters Welker (Albuquerque, 1987).

Henry Kamen, *Empire: How Spain Became a World Power, 1492–1763* (New York, 2003).

Jaime Lara, *City, Temple, Stage: Eschatological Architecture and Liturgical Theatrics in New Spain* (Notre Dame, 2004).

James Lockhart, *The Nahuas After the Conquest: A Social and Cultural History of the Indians of Central Mexico, Sixteenth Through Eighteenth Centuries* (Stanford, 1992).

James Lockhart and Enrique Otte, editors and translators, *Letters and People of the Spanish Indies: Sixteenth Century* (Cambridge, 1976).

David Andrew Lupher, *Romans in a New World: Classical Models in Sixteenth-Century Spanish America* (Ann Arbor, 2003).

Lyle N. McAlister, *Spain and Portugal in the New World, 1492–1700* (Minneapolis, 1984).

Barbara E. Mundy, *The Mapping of New Spain: Indigenous Cartography and the Maps of the Relaciónes Geográficas* (Chicago, 1996).

Anthony Pagden, *Lords of all the World: Ideologies of Empire in Spain, Britain and France, c. 1500–c. 1800* (Cambridge, 1995).

J. H. Parry and Robert G. Keith, editors, *The New Iberian World: A Documentary History of the Discovery and Settlement of Latin America to the Early 17th Century*, 5 volumes (New York, 1984).

J. H. Parry, *The Spanish Theory of Empire in the Sixteenth Century* (Cambridge, 1940).

Angel Rama, *The Lettered City*, translated and edited by John Charles Chasteen (Durham, 1996).

A. J. R. Russell-Wood, *The Portuguese Empire, 1415–1808: A World on the Move* (Baltimore, 1998).

Alan Ryder, *Benin and the Europeans* (London, 1969).

Hugh Thomas, *Rivers of Gold: The Rise of the Spanish Empire, from Columbus to Magellan* (New York, 2003).

John Vogt, *Portuguese Rule on the Gold Coast* (Athens, Georgia, 1979).

Luís Weckman, *La herencia medieval de México* (Mexico City, 1984).

Part Two

Europe Supported by Africa and America

I will now close with an emblematical picture Of *Europe* supported by *Africa* and *America*, accompanied by an ardent wish that in the friendly manner they are represented, they may henceforth and to all eternity be the prop of each other.

John Gabriel Stedman, *Narrative of a Five Years' Expedition*

In the early 1790s, the English artist and poet William Blake provided sixteen engravings, illustrations for John Gabriel Stedman's book, *Narrative, of a Five Years' Expedition, against the Revolted Negroes of Surinam, in Guiana, on the Wild Coast of South America; from the Year 1772 to 1777*. The last engraving in the book was an image conceived and drawn by Stedman and engraved by Blake entitled, "Europe Supported by Africa & America." At the end of his *Narrative*, "after all the horrors and cruelties with which I must have hurt both the eye and the hear of the feeling reader," Stedman explained, "I will close the scene with an emblematical picture of *Europe* supported by *Africa* and *America*, accompanied by an ardent wish that in the friendly manner they are represented, they may henceforth and to all eternity be the prop of each other."

Stedman and Blake's emblematical picture has always been a controversial representation of the Atlantic World. As the title tells us, and the picture itself

Europe supported by Africa & America.

Figure 5.1. Europe supported by Africa and America. Engraving by William Blake from John Gabriel Stedman, *Narrative, of a five years' expedition, against the revolted Negroes of Surinam* (London, 1792). Courtesy of the John Carter Brown Library at the Brown University.

seems to show, white, bejeweled, modest and delicate-featured "Europe,"
obviously superior, is physically supported by the women of color, "Africa"
and "America," wearing slave bracelets. Of course, their support was slavery
and exploitation, looted wealth and even the sensual bodies of native women
themselves. Blake was part of the radical European intelligentsia in the late
eighteenth century that viewed Europe's happiness as destructive of Native
America and Africa. J. H. Bernardin de Saint Pierre summed up this opinion
in his commentary about the evil products, sugar and coffee: "I do not know
if coffee and sugar are essential to the happiness of Europe, but I know that
these two products have accounted for the unhappiness of two great regions
of the world: America has been depopulated so as to have land on which to
plant them; Africa has been depopulated so as to have the people to cultivate
them."

Stedman did not mean for this picture to represent history or present reality. "The friendly manner" in which they appear here, he wrote, represented
for him a wish that "they may henceforth and to all eternity be the prop of
each other." Thus we see three comely and dignified women tenderly embrace
each other and a braid, perhaps representing tobacco, binds them together.
There is a rare hand-colored engraving of *Europe supported by Africa &
America*, from a special edition of the *Narrative*, and a careful examination
of that picture reveals that "Europe" did not wear a string of pearls (they were
simply cheap blue baubles) nor were "Africa" and "America" wearing slave
bracelets but gold arm bands. Stedman and the abolitionist Blake sought to
portray a future Atlantic World in which Europe, Africa and America would
be amicably interdependent, "the prop of each other."

The historical Atlantic World from the discoveries to the eighteenth century was both cruelly exploitative and in many ways amicably interdependent. Stedman and Blake's *Europe supported by Africa & America* is truthful
in its moral ambiguity. A superior Europe (and Europeans) did exploit in the
worst ways Africa and America (and Africans and Indians) for centuries,
and so the "support" portrayed in the engraving appears quite tame. On
the other hand, Africans and Indians cooperated with Europeans in innumerable projects that supported Europe and Europeans as well as their own
self-interests as individual Africans and Indians, and as African and Indian
groups and nations. Long before Stedman hoped it would happen, Europeans, Africans and Indians had become "the prop of each other" throughout
the Atlantic World. It was not equal opportunity interdependence, as wrote
Stedman, "Fortune has not made us equal in authority." There were enormous inequalities in wealth, power and opportunity, and yet there were
still partnerships, alliances, associations, marriages and friendships. Blake
engraved other illustrations for Stedman's book: horrendous images of the
torture of slaves, the inhumanity of the slave trade, the cruelty and corruption
of slavery as an institution and more. Stedman's readers had seen all of these
repugnant images before coming to the last illustration in the book. His readers knew what type of support had been given to Europe in the past. The five
chapters in Part II of this book consider how Europeans exploited Africans
and Native Americans but also how Africans, Indians and Europeans in the
Atlantic World "became the prop of each other."

The first (Iberian) Atlantic World was transformed in the seventeenth century by the incursions of the French, English and the Dutch. This is the subject of Chapter 5, "Incursions: The French, English and Dutch Invasions of the Iberian Atlantic." Although the English and the French had sponsored a few isolated voyages of exploration in the late fifteenth century, they were not sustained or followed up in any substantial way. In the sixteenth century, the English and the French broke into the Iberian monopoly of trade with many scattered voyages. There were also a few early, and famously unsuccessful, attempts to plant colonies in the Americas. Political and economic conditions within England and France were not conducive to any strong and persistent incursion into the Atlantic in the sixteenth century. Furthermore, the Portuguese – and particularly the Spanish – were quite willing and able to defend their trade and territorial monopolies. The sixteenth century brought the English, French and Dutch a wealth of information about the winds and currents of the Atlantic, the basic geography of coastal Africa and the Americas and the rich prizes awaiting commerce raiders and, less frequently, the founders of colonies. In the seventeenth century, the Iberian monopoly was broken in Atlantic Africa and in the Americas. The Atlantic World became not just more conflictive but more complicated, and thus more interesting.

The remaining chapters of Part II focus on significant topics relevant to all of the European empires in Africa and the Americas. Chapter 6, "Engagement: The Entangled Worlds of Indians and Europeans," looks at the many-sided relationships between Indians and Europeans throughout the Americas from 1492 to the mid-eighteenth century. This chapter stresses the mutuality of encounters between Indians and Europeans: they were military allies (as well as rivals and enemies), empire builders, business partners and family members. Indians and Europeans engaged with each other according to their perceived self-interest, which led to all types of complex arrangements. Both Europeans and Indians had to adapt themselves to the other during the colonial centuries. Europeans increasingly gained greater control over the process of adaptation to their New World environments, whereas Indians continued to adapt and engage with a degree of success for some and considerable suffering for many others.

Chapter 7, "Uprooted: West Africa, the Americas and the Atlantic Slave Trade," examines the Atlantic slave trade from its African roots to the middle passage and the African "nations" in the Americas. Because this is an Atlantic history, this chapter on the slave trade emphasizes African participation in the trade and European involvement on the coast of Africa. This chapter relies upon the latest data and calculations on the volume of the trade and employs the W. E. B. Du Bois Trans-Atlantic Slave Trade Database. To bring the slave trade down to more understandable proportions and to view the vast slave trade with its dry statistics on a human scale, this chapter follows the voyage of one slave ship, the *Henrietta Marie*, in 1697–8 from London to the coast of Africa and then to Barbados. Chapter 7 also considers important controversial issues related to the consequences of the Atlantic slave trade.

Chapter 8, "Bondage: The Atlantic Plantation Complex and the Cultures of Slaves," examines the most dynamic economic system of the Atlantic World. At the center of African slavery in the New World and the Atlantic slave trade was the plantation complex. This Atlantic leviathan was an international economic, social and political system that grew sugarcane and other tropical commodities in one continent, purchased and transported labor from another and exported the products to a third. What first developed in the Atlantic World as societies with slaves became, within a generation or two, slave societies, where slavery was the most important form of labor, Africans and their descendants made up most of the population, and slaveholders became the ruling class.

To conclude Part II, Chapter 9, "Partners: Women and Men in the Making of the Atlantic World," considers the most basic relationship in overseas colonization. When Europeans first expanded into the lands of the Atlantic, they explored, conquered and even settled almost entirely without their wives, concubines, daughters and other women from home. As a result, European men took wives or concubines from the native women and created families and children. These cross-cultural partnerships were extremely important for Europeans as well as Africans and Native Americans; they were significant for power, trade, prestige, wealth and other reasons. These partnerships did not sufficiently reproduce European culture in the far provinces of the Atlantic World. The empires and their officials, as well as the overseas colonial elite and gentry, recognized the indispensable requirement of women from the homeland. To "make a good nation," declared the Lord Deputy of Ireland in the 1620s, "it is no great matter of what nation the men be so the women be English."

Stedman's *Narrative of a Five Years' Expedition against the Revolted Negroes of Surinam* was published in a two-volume, leather-bound, gold-toothed edition by Joseph Johnson of London in 1796. There were a total of eighty plates by well-known engravers, sixteen of which were made by Blake. Although this expensive luxury edition was produced initially for only two hundred subscribers, it soon inspired bowdlerized versions and translations into German, Swedish, Dutch and French. For the *finis* page, and following Stedman's specifications, Blake engraved *Europe supported by Africa & America*. "While one hand of Europe limply holds the rope that links the three continents," writes David Hart, "the other more rigorously grasps the hand of the African in sisterly equality. This was a dramatic innovation in the concept of the relationship between the continents, reflecting Blake's abolitionist perspective." For Carolyn Parks, the linking of the arms shows interdependence. "His engraving promotes the image that without Africa and America, Europe is unsupported – therefore, Europe must question the treatment of Africa and America in this cycle." Interdependence and mistreatment, partnership and exploitation – these were the critical elements of the Atlantic World.

Chapter 5

Incursions

The French, English and Dutch Invasions of the Iberian Atlantic

Following Columbus' first voyage to America, the Spanish Pope Alexander VI, in his famous bull *Inter caetera*, confirmed Portuguese possession of West Africa and granted to the crown of Castile all "islands and mainland" to the west of an imaginary boundary in the mid-Atlantic. The monarchies were granted the exclusive right to, and possession of, lands not otherwise held by a Christian prince. Legitimacy of possession was further based on the conversion of native peoples to Christianity. Portugal and Castile adjusted the mid-oceanic boundary and confirmed their respective territorial claims in the Treaty of Tordesillas in 1494. *Inter caetera* and related bulls, collectively referred to as the papal donation, constituted the basic legal claim of the Portuguese and Castilian monarchies to the newly discovered lands of the Atlantic World. Other European monarchs and legal scholars later disputed the legitimacy of Portuguese and Castilian territorial claims. "Show me the clause in Adam's will," proclaimed King François I of France (1515–47), "which gives the king of Spain dominion over half the world."

The French and the English claimed a right to explore where the Portuguese and Spaniards were not settled, and to trade in any seas. In 1534, François I informed the Spanish ambassador that he had not renounced his rights to America. The French protested: "In lands which the King of Spain did not possess [the French] ought not be disturbed, nor in their navigation of the seas, nor would they consent to be deprived of the sea or the sky." Elizabeth I of England argued that if the sea belonged to everyone then "it belongs to me." Like the French, the English also noted, "prescription without possession availeth nothing," in other words, they recognized a legal claim only where there was effective occupation. In 1609, in his treatise *Mare Libervm* the Dutch jurist Hugo Grotius made a legal case against colonial monopolies and against the Spanish concept of a *mare clausum*, or closed sea. "For does not the ocean," Grotius wrote, "navigable in every direction with which God has encompassed all the earth, and the regular and the occasional winds which blow now from one quarter and now from another, offer sufficient proof that Nature has given to all peoples a right of access to all other peoples?"

Portuguese and Spanish territorial and trade monopolies in the Atlantic were ultimately based on their ability to defend them. And in this the Spanish, better than the Portuguese, were able to do for many decades. Mariners explored American shores for the English and the French in the late fifteenth and early sixteenth centuries. Both monarchies made territorial claims in America based on the right of prior discovery. French and English interlopers – that is, contraband traders – were on the coast of Brazil not long after the Portuguese arrived. First French, then English and finally Dutch privateers and pirates attacked Spanish ports in America as well as their trading and fishing fleets in the Atlantic in the sixteenth century. However, despite the increasingly intense onslaught the Atlantic remained Iberian for more than a century. Portuguese and Spanish transatlantic commerce thrived while early French and English attempts to plant colonies in the Americas failed. The Spanish and Portuguese successfully defended their monopolies in the sixteenth century. By the early seventeenth century, the Spanish could no longer prevent or destroy every alien settlement. Remote corners of North and South America were permanently settled and even the "Spanish lake," the Caribbean, saw English, French and Dutch colonies established in the small, unoccupied islands of the eastern Antilles. Sir Walter Ralegh, in one of his poems, perhaps caught the spirit of the incursions: "To seek new worlds, for gold, for praise, for glory."

The battle of the Atlantic in the sixteenth and seventeenth centuries, the first of several struggles for the Atlantic over the centuries, produced a vast arena where five powers competed for wealth and power. The Iberian Atlantic was injured but not annihilated. Despite blatant attempts to steal the empires, the Portuguese and the Spanish managed to hold onto the largest and most important territories of their Atlantic possessions. The weak bases and settlements of England, France and the northern Netherlands in Africa and the Americas in the early and mid-seventeenth century would, in short order, become the basis of new mercantile and territorial Atlantic empires. They would eventually dominate the Atlantic World. The stakes of the first battle of the Atlantic were enormous.

5.1 The Iberian Atlantic

Africa and America produced great wealth for Portugal and Spain during their monopoly eras but ultimately little national development. In the late fifteenth and early sixteenth centuries, the gold trade in Guinea enriched Portugal. Gold from São Jorge da Mina doubled royal revenues during the last two decades of the fifteenth century. The rise of sugar plantations in Madeira, São Tomé and Brazil produced valuable exports and transformed the slave trade into Africa's most important trade by the early seventeenth century. The discovery of gold in the Caribbean, and then enormous deposits of silver in Mexico and the Andes, helped to finance the Habsburg superpower led by Carlos V and Felipe II. From 1503 to 1660, more than thirty-five million pounds of silver arrived in Seville. An additional half a million pounds of gold crossed the Atlantic. "In the last sixty years," wrote Tomás de Mercado in 1569, Spain's trading capital, Seville, had acquired "great riches," and become a "centre for all the merchants of the world."

The Spanish monarchy first brought order to its transatlantic trade in 1503 with the establishment of the *Casa de Contratación*, the House of Trade (whose first administrator was Genoese), in Seville. Henceforth, all trade with the Indies would depart from Seville, the only Spanish port permitted to trade with America. Seville, a city of forty thousand inhabitants in 1500, had a good supply of men to sail the ships, victuals to feed the sailors, money to finance the trade and a commercial distribution network extending to all parts of Europe. Restricting trade to Seville gave Castile the monopoly of American trade. (In 1522, Barcelona's petition to trade with the Indies was turned down.) Seville was forty miles up the Guadalquivir River and thus quite secure from seaborne raiders like the Barbary pirates. The *Casa de Contratación* had the authority to license private merchant vessels that traded with America as well as control immigration to the New World. The *Casa* taxed trade and collected the royal fifth owed the crown in precious metals and jewels. In 1543, with the creation of the merchant guild of Seville, the *Consulado de Seville*, the particular merchant houses that belonged to this privileged association further monopolized trade with the Indies.

The appearance of French corsairs attacking Spanish shipping led the merchants of Seville to ask the king in 1522 for a naval patrol to protect their vessels. To finance the new fleet, the *Casa de Contratación* established an ad valorum tax on merchandise, the *avería*. The first fleet of four warships patrolled the near Atlantic, from the peninsula to the Canaries and the Azores. In 1526, the crown ordered that all trade to the Indies be organized in annual convoys from Seville to Santo Domingo. Additional ordinances required all merchant ships to be armed, to follow a specific schedule and visit only a few restricted ports in the New World. Slave-trading vessels from Africa, as well as dispatch ships – *avisos* – maintained communications between Spain and America between annual fleets and were exempt from the convoy requirement. To supply ports not on the convoy's route, special permits, "single registers," were given to owners and captains of ships, which sailed at their own risk.

With the settlement of Mexico and Peru in the 1520s and 1530s, the *Carrera de Indias* – the Indies Run – became more complicated. From 1543 to 1554, each annual merchant fleet crossed the Atlantic in one convoy and split into two parts once it reached the Caribbean. One part of the fleet continued on to San Juan de Ulúa, an island across the bay from Vera Cruz, the port of New Spain. The entire journey of 4,300 miles took approximately eight weeks. The other part traveled to Cartagena, the port of Tierra Firme (the name the Spanish gave to the northern coast of South America, and which the English called the Spanish Main). From there it traveled to Nombre de Dios, the Caribbean port of the isthmus of Panama (which after 1585 was called Portobello, a marginally more secure terminus). Merchant ships in the Pacific connected Callao, Peru's port on the Pacific, to Panama City, located on the western shore of the isthmus. These Spanish ports in the sixteenth century were slightly populated dismal places composed of humble mud, wooden and thatched houses and located in hot and humid climates thriving with tropical diseases, thus making them graveyards for visiting mariners, merchants and officials.

Vera Cruz counted about 200 Spanish householders in 1570, Cartagena had a population of 250 householders with several thousand black and Indian inhabitants in 1574 and Nombre de Dios was smaller with about 150 houses in 1570. The populations of these towns ballooned when the fleet arrived and collapsed when it left.

In Vera Cruz and Nombre de Dios, the arrival of the fleet each year set in motion trade fairs, which lasted several weeks and allowed merchants to buy and sell European goods and American commodities. With the conclusion of the trade fairs, the fleets would gather at Havana, Cuba, the best port in Spanish America, which possessed a large, deep and well-defended harbor and became known as the "key" to the Caribbean. Like the other ports on the *Carrera de Indias*, Havana was an unimpressive sight in 1570, with about sixty houses made of wood and mud. By 1625 Havana's population had increased to 1,200 Spanish householders and thousands of blacks and mulattos. The return voyage passed through the Bahama channel between Cuba and Florida to catch the Gulf Stream and the Westerlies for the journey to the Azores and, finally, to Seville. The entire circuit could be completed in sixteen to eighteen months, five months of actual sailing time with the additional time devoted to trading and waiting for the fleet to re-gather in Havana.

Beginning in 1555, the *Carrera de Indias* was composed of two separate fleets, which sailed to the Indies on separate schedules. Both fleets sailed in summer or spring to avoid storms and the hurricane season. Sometimes the fleets combined in Havana and returned together in one convoy. More warships than the New Spain fleet, given the rich treasure produced every year at Potosí, generally accompanied the Tierra Firme fleet. By the late sixteenth century, a fleet of six to eight galleons, called the *Armada de la Guardia*, was assigned to guard the Tierra Firme fleet. Once in the Atlantic, the fleets were protected by the *Armada del Mar Océano*, Spain's permanent navy. By the seventeenth century, the Tierra Firme fleet was nicknamed the "*galeones*," while the New Spain fleet was called the "*flota*." In the Caribbean, smaller ships called *permiso* vessels occasionally detached themselves from the fleet to visit settlements in Jamaica or Venezuela, which were off the main routes (see Map 5.1).

The Spanish maintained their commercial contact with their Asian colony of the Philippines through Mexico rather than around Cape Horn. Beginning in 1565, the Manila galleons departed from Acapulco, Mexico, transported American treasure west and returned with silk and other Chinese wares. However, to the Council of the Indies this outlet was draining too much silver. At its peak year at the end of the sixteenth century, twelve million pesos in bullion was sent from Acapulco to Manila, a figure larger than the value of the official Spanish Atlantic trade. In 1592, this trade was restricted to only two ships annually of no more than three hundred tons, and in 1631 direct trade between Peru and Mexico was prohibited. The Acapulco-Manila

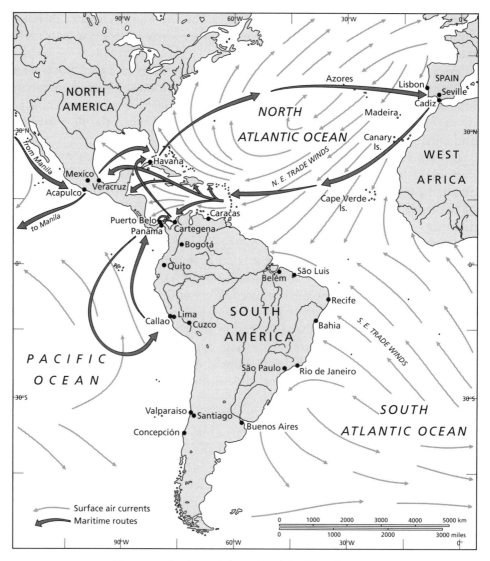

Map 5.1. Spain and America: Maritime Routes.

run was the longest of all the Spanish routes: the return trip took four and sometimes seven months to complete. Over the next two centuries, forty ships were lost in the Pacific.

The volume of trade in the *Carrera de Indias* increased eight hundred percent during the first half of the sixteenth century. In 1506, there were 35 ships participating in the trade, displacing over three thousand tons in total. By 1550, there were 215 ships, displacing more than thirty-two thousand tons. The Atlantic trade experienced a twelve-year recession at mid-century, from 1550 to about 1562, due in part to an increase in privateering and piracy. During the second half of the century, production of the silver mines of Mexico and Peru increased, which also increased the size of the trade fleets. In the ten-year period from 1541 to 1550, 177 tons of silver arrived in Seville. In a later period, from 1591 to 1600, 2,700 tons of silver arrived.

Furthermore, the growing economic maturity of the Spanish Indies produced larger markets for European goods and more enterprises producing a variety of American exports. The great analysts of the Sevillian trade, Pierre and Huguette Chaunu summarized the trend this way: "From 1500 to 1580, the Indies trade is, so to speak, borne up on a rising swell, the rising swell of the sixteenth century which brings an increase in the global volume of outgoing goods from between 3,000 and 4,000 tons in the first years to 30,000 in the record years of the second-last decade of the century . . . The record year, 1608, reaches the impressive figure of 45,078 tons."

The *Carrera de Indias* peaked in the 1590s and the early 1600s, thereafter declining throughout the seventeenth century. The Chaunus discovered that the descent of trade in the seventeenth century was neither rapid nor deep. Although there were fewer ships and less tonnage, these ships were better guarded by armada ships, armed themselves and carried higher-value goods. In the second half of the century sailings became less frequent and less regular: the New Spain fleet sailed on average once every two years, while whereas the Tierra Firme fleet sailed on average once every three years. The *Carrera de Indias* was breaking down by 1700.

The trade fleets were composed of various types of ships. Fully rigged caravels, displacing anywhere between 50 and 250 tons, still sailed the Atlantic. The workhorses of the shipping fleet were carracks and *nãos*. These were large rounded ships with high and protruding aft-castles and smaller forecastles, and a deep-cut waist. Carracks could be huge, as much as 1,000 tons, and were favored by the Portuguese in the East Indies trade. The Portuguese, Swedish, English and French in the sixteenth century commissioned huge carrack warships with guns on multiple decks, which turned out to be sluggish and clumsy. The *não* was generally a smaller version of a carrack and more popular in the Spanish *Carrera de Indias*. For the most part, galleons were warships that were strongly braced for heavy seas and battle, and more heavily armed than most merchant ships. The classic design of a galleon provided a quite different profile from that of a carrack and *não*. The elegant crescent shape of a galleon was due to the high aft-castle and a low, set back forecastle. In the first half of the seventeenth century, the average capacity of a Spanish galleon was 753 tons.

These ships were the most complex and powerful machines of their age. They brought together many of the most sophisticated mechanical inventions of the times: bronze and later iron cannons, apparatuses for astronomical observation, a capstan to move great weights, tillers, whipstaffs, stern rudders, a labyrinth of cables and hundreds of sets of pulleys and more. These machines would work only with the coordination of the efforts of diverse specialists. As traveling warehouses, a ship with a crew of twelve could transport, Adam Smith noted, the same cargo as fifty carts pulled by four hundred horses. As mobile castles, galleons and other types of warships were the most powerful war machines of the day.

Spain's American trade was only part of a larger commercial system, which made Spain one of the most important trading nations in the sixteenth century. Productive shipyards in Spanish America augmented Spain's remarkable shipbuilding industry on the northern coast of the Iberian Peninsula. Spanish ships carried Spanish wool as well as colonial re-exports such as hides, sugar and dyestuffs to Flanders and Italy. A Dominican theologian from Mexico observed the enterprise of one Sevillian merchant family in the early sixteenth century:

> First they deal in all parts of Christendom and even in Barbary. To Flanders they ship wool, oil and wine, and bring there from every kind of haberdashery, tapestries and books. To Florence they send cochineal and hides, and bring back strings of gold, brocades, silks, and from all these countries a great quantity of cloth. At Cape Verde they trade in Negroes, a business which demands large capital and gives considerable returns. To all the Indies they ship great cargoes of every kind of merchandise, and return with gold, silver, pearls, cochineal and hides in vast quantities. Finally, to insure their cargoes (which are worth millions) they have to take out insurances in Lisbon, Burgos, Lyons and Flanders, because so vast are their shipments that neither the merchants of Seville nor of twenty cities like Seville are capable of insuring them.

Portugal was the epitome of a commercial nation. In the early sixteenth century, Portuguese merchant ships crossed both the Indian and Atlantic oceans to bring Asian spices, African gold, Madeiran sugar and Brazilian dyewood back to Lisbon and, ultimately, Antwerp. The Portuguese crown – this monarch was known in Europe as "the grocer king" – had enriched itself substantially by participating directly in trade. For example, the spice trade was a royal monopoly controlled by the *Casa da Guiné e India* (which had replaced the Casa da Mina in 1501). Ships owned and operated by the king plied the seas in convoys and royal factors purchased pepper, cloves and nutmeg in the Spice Islands and sold them in Antwerp. In 1518, nearly forty percent of the crown's income was from profits in the spice trade. The crown obtained nearly a one-hundred percent profit from spices. Gold, sugar, Brasilwood and slaves constituted the next most valuable trades, in that order.

In the Atlantic, the Portuguese monarchy likewise held the monopoly of some of the most valuable trades: Guinea gold, Brazilian dyewood and African slaves. The *Casa da Guiné e India* either organized the actual trading or sold licenses to private traders. Captains, soldiers and civil servants deployed around the Atlantic were permitted to trade in monopoly products to a limited extent. To protect Portuguese traders, the crown deployed squadrons of warships in West African as well as Brazilian waters. From 1530 to 1571, the crown permitted relatively free trade in bulk commodities in the waters under its jurisdiction. Brazilian sugar was transported to Antwerp in Spanish, Dutch, English, Italian, French and even Polish, as well as Portuguese, merchant vessels. Their captains were required to obtain a license to trade and pay the appropriate duties. Before the crown decreed that Portuguese ships had the exclusive right of trade with Brazil in 1571, the Dutch carried the majority of Brazilian sugar.

During the union of the Spanish and Portuguese crowns from 1580 to 1640, the Portuguese system of trade with its empire was tightened. All shipping within the empire had to be in Spanish- and Portuguese-owned ships. The Portuguese monarchy still traded in the most valuable products, when possible, and licensed everything else to private traders. Portuguese colonial markets were not opened to the Spanish but some Spanish American markets were opened to the Portuguese. The contract of supplying Spanish America with African slaves went to the Portuguese. With the right to visit virtually any port in Spanish America, Portuguese slavers also often took the opportunity to sell contraband merchandise. After 1580, Portuguese merchants were doing business throughout the Spanish world, from Seville to Cartagena, Buenos Aires, Potosí and Manila. Portuguese merchants not only replaced the Spanish Empire's earlier dominant core of foreign traders, the Genoese, in the 1580s and 1590s, Portuguese merchant-bankers also supplanted the Genoese banking cartel in Seville. Generally, both trends were welcomed as a way to keep trade and finance within the empire.

Although the Portuguese appeared to receive some commercial benefits from the Union of the Crowns, there were also drawbacks. Perhaps the most important was that Spain's enemies became Portugal's enemies. Hundreds of Portuguese ships were sank or captured by the Dutch during the last twenty years of the Union. Merchants supported the movement for independence in 1640 and welcomed the new Braganza dynasty to power. Within a decade of the discovery of the New World, Castile and then all of Spain was given access to immense new wealth. Yet Spain did not create a vigorous economy or a prosperous country. Why not?

5.2 The Decline of Spain?

Official imports of bullion registered at Seville between 1500 and 1650 counted 180 tons of gold and 16,000 tons of silver. These figures are undoubtedly low as they do not include the quantities of gold and silver involved in the contraband Spanish and foreign trade. It has been estimated that the silver exports from Spanish America between 1500 and 1700 doubled the existing stock of silver in Europe. This infusion of bullion (or coin) into Europe was, by and large, a positive development. For Europe as a whole this flow produced a slow growth of inflation, which furthered the growth of regional economies, promoted monetarized and commercialized production and unleashed trade that was no long stymied by a lack of cash. The infusion of money allowed ambitious and hardworking farmers, manufacturers and merchants to invest and grow more, make more and sell more.

The economic consequences for Spain were also beneficial for a while. The chronicler Florián de Ocampo in 1551 noted the expansion of agriculture: "... even the wilderness disappeared as everything in Castile was dug up for sowing." The Guadalquivir Valley developed into a commercial agricultural area to supply food and goods to Spain and Spanish America. Manufacturing also expanded as the woolen industry in Castile and the silk industry in Granada flourished. One must remember that Castile and much of Spain in the fifteenth and sixteenth century was poor, thus this massive infusion of wealth flooded into a country that needed it but could not adequately absorb or invest all of it. Pierre Vilar notes that many did not know what to do with wealth. He writes that Castilians "spent freely, imported, and lent money for interest; but little was produced. Prices and salaries soared. Parasitism prevailed and enterprise died; only poverty was left for the morrow." As early as 1545, Spanish manufacturers had a six-year backlog of orders from the New World. Unable to make all or even most of these orders, Spanish merchants purchased them from foreigners. "Foreigners who bring merchandise to these realms," complained a politician in 1548, "must give surety to take back merchandise and not money." Another claimed in the same debate, "Spain has become an Indies for the foreigner." What went wrong?

Spain was both unlucky and unwise. Monopolies, privileges, controls and excessive taxes hobbled the commercial and productive enterprises in Castile. The great influx of American bullion produced a bout of inflation in Spain running throughout the sixteenth century. Higher prices in Spain discouraged exports and produced protests at home that led the government to permit the import of foreign-made cloth. Castilian agriculture had been sacrificed to sheep herding and remained underdeveloped and short of labor. In the sixteenth century, Castilian estates and farms could not feed the people of Castile nor supply the new American markets. In the early seventeenth century, Irish wool was displacing Spanish wool, Swedish iron was beating Bilbao's metal and shipbuilding in Spain had slowed to a crawl. By 1702, there were eighty-four commercial houses in Cadiz: twelve were Spanish, twenty-six were Genoese, eighteen were Dutch and Flemish, eleven were French, ten English and seven from Hamburg.

Because of its dynastic empire and possessions, Habsburg Spain in the mid-sixteenth century was Europe's greatest power, and therefore its military expenditures were enormous and excessive. Earl J. Hamilton also suggests that "the illusion of prosperity created by American gold and silver" was also partially responsible for Spain's aggressive foreign policy. Spain fought wars with France in Italy, took up arms for Europe against the Turks on land and at sea, defended the faith in Germany and the Low Countries, provoked the Dutch revolt and then fought the Eighty Years' War, conquered the kingdom of Portugal in 1580 and dispatched a vast armada to invade England in 1588, which was destroyed. Just one campaign, at Metz in 1552, cost ten times the annual silver levies. Because taxes and bullion did not pay for Spain's exercise of power in Europe, the crown resorted to borrowing. It issued interest-bearing bonds and contracted direct loans, secured on the king's share of the treasure fleets, from German, Flemish and Italian bankers. When Carlos V abdicated in 1555, he left a debt that amounted to one hundred times the annual silver revenues. Over the following century, the royal government defaulted on its debts in 1557, 1575, 1576, 1607, 1627 and 1647. "The flood of precious metals from the Indies," writes Paul Kennedy, "it was said, was to Spain as water on a roof – it poured on and then was drained away."

The Habsburg crown's great need of money and rising debt led to a number of unhealthy distortions in the Spanish economy. First of all, the huge public debt itself at very high rates of interest absorbed so much capital that, in modern terminology, it crowded out affordable credit for the private sector. The crown's enormous need for money led it to impose forced loans on government bonds and occasionally seize the silver recently arrived from America. A desperate Carlos V also demanded the seizure of gold and silver from the churches of Castile. Treasure receipts in Seville began to decline in 1600–30. At the end of the reign of Felipe II (1598), the silver remittances to the crown averaged two million ducats a year. In 1620, the figure was eight hundred thousand ducats. The Kingdom of Castile still provided more income to the royal government than American silver and gold ever did, but by the seventeenth century Castilian taxes were paid in a debased copper coinage that could buy very little outside Castile. The economic basis that had once supported Spain's military, political and imperial power was slipping away.

Foreign financiers controlled Spain's debt and trade with the Indies, thus the American commodities and silver sent to Seville actually ended up in Antwerp, Augsburg, Milan, Lisbon and even Amsterdam. "Our Spain," the reformer Martín González de Cellorigo wrote in 1600, "has looked so much to the Indies trade that its inhabitants have neglected the affairs of these realms, wherefore Spain from its great wealth has attained great poverty." He posed a causal relationship: "... if [Spain] is poor, it is because it is rich... One would think that one wanted to make of this republic a republic of enchanted people living outside the natural order."

During much of the seventeenth century, the exports of American silver to Spain declined and Spain debased its currency and prices stagnated. Spain's manufacturing base contracted; over several decades the looms of Segovia fell by two-thirds and the problem only worsened throughout Spanish industry. Shipbuilding slowed to a trickle, producing both a serious commercial and military weakness. Spanish-made goods made up a small portion of exports to the Spanish Indies. Dutch, English, German, Portuguese, Italian and French traders provided the merchants of the Consulado of Seville with their manufactures for the markets of Spanish America. Agricultural productivity in Spain, which had never been very high to begin with, had also slipped. Of the millions of pesos of treasure brought to Spain by the 1670 New Spain fleet, less than half remained in the country after accounts were settled. One Spaniard in 1675 viewed this as a good thing:

> Let London manufacture those fabrics of hers to her heart's content; Holland her chambrays; Florence her cloth; the Indies their beaver and vicuna; Milan her brocades; Italy and Flanders their linens, so long as our capital can enjoy them. The only thing it proves is that all nations train journeymen for Madrid and that Madrid is the queen of Parliaments, for all the world serves her and she serves nobody.

If many Spaniards did not understand the problem, a Moroccan ambassador to Madrid in 1690–1 saw that work was better than wealth and earnings better than riches:

> The Spanish nation today possesses the greatest wealth and the largest income of all the Christians. But the love of luxury and the comforts

Table 5.1. National populations of Western Europe, 1500–1700

Nation	1500	1600	1700
Spain	6,800,000	8,240,000	8,770,000
Portugal	1,000,000	1,100,000	2,000,000
France	15,000,000	18,500,000	21,500,000
British Isles	3,900,000	6,170,000	8,500,000
Northern Netherlands	950,000	1,500,000	1,900,000
Western Europe	57,200,000	62,600,000	81,500,000

Source: Angus Maddison, *The World Economy: A Millennial Perspective* (2003), Table B-10, p. 241.

of civilization have overcome them, and you will rarely find one of this nation who engages in trade or travels abroad for commerce as do the other Christian nations such as the Dutch, the English, the French, the Genoese and their like. Similarly, the handicrafts practiced by the lower classes and common people are despised by this nation, which regards itself as superior to the other Christian nations. Most of those who practice these crafts in Spain are Frenchmen [who] flock to Spain to look for work . . . [and] in a short time make great fortunes.

War, debt, excessive taxation, the conspicuous consumption of the court and the Spanish nobility, the decline of agriculture and traditional industries, the proliferation of priests and monks, the expulsion of the industrious Moriscos, plague, food shortages and famine led to the collapse of industries and cities in Castile. Burgos, Segovia and Valladolid lost up to half of their population between 1599 and 1630. In Valencia and Aragón, hundred of villages were empty. "By 1620," notes C. H. Wilson, "Toledo, once the most important city of Castile, was deserted, its manufactures ruined, its houses shuttered and empty. The surrounding countryside was bleak and depopulated. By 1646 the city's population had fallen to less than half its 1571 figure of over 12,000."

When we look at the larger picture and at the measurable and comparable features of Spain in the early modern period, we see a Spain that is practically stagnant. In terms of national population, none of the five Atlantic powers had such weak population growth from 1500 to 1700 as Spain. For example, the population of France during this period grew by over one-third. The populations of Portugal, the Netherlands and the British Isles each doubled. From 1500 to 1600, the population of Spain increased by over twenty percent. During the next century Spain's population growth barely moved (see Table 5.1). We see a similar trend when we look at per capita economic growth for the period 1500 to 1700. Of the five Atlantic powers, Spain had an annual average compound rate of economic growth of 0.13 percent. Portugal and France, both at 0.15 percent, were not in a significantly improved economic condition. The rate of growth for Britain was 0.31 and that for the Netherlands was 0.52 percent, which means that per capita income in Britain doubled between 1500 and 1700 and it expanded over three times in

Table 5.2. Economic growth in Western
Europe, 1500–1700

Nation	1500	1700
Spain	689	900
Portugal	638	854
France	727	986
Britain	762	1,405
Northern Netherlands	754	2,110
Italy	1,100	1,100

Figures refer to per capita GDP given in 1990
international dollars.
Source: Angus Maddison, *The World Economy:
A Millennial Perspective* (2003), Table 2-22a.
"Levels of GDP Per Capita in European Colonial Powers and Former Colonies, 1500–1998,"
p. 90.

the Netherlands (see Table 5.2). This data provides a preview of the expansion of the North Atlantic populations and economies.

Spanish reformers called *arbitristas* were aware of the problems of their
society and economy and published seemingly endless proposals for new measures in the late sixteenth and early seventeenth centuries. Many of the *arbitristas* in the early seventeenth century were Portuguese merchants, financiers
and political advisors. In 1623, Mendo da Mota, one such Portuguese advisor, pointed out that the Spanish Empire had conquered the entire world by
force of arms but having long neglected matters of trade, it was unable to
maintain that dominion because "it no longer enjoyed the fruits of any of
the World's trades." Da Mota was an advisor of the Count-Duke of Olivares, the principal minister of the king (1621–4), and leader of a reform
movement. At the helm of a state in financial crisis but with endless foreign policy obligations, the Count-Duke sought to preserve the great power
of Spain. To do this, he had learned from the Dutch that power and prosperity were related. Economic reform would then mean "to direct all our
efforts to turning Spaniards into merchants." The reformers, or what one
historian calls the "party of commercial expansion," sought to liberalize and
decentralize the Spanish imperialist mercantilist system. Among the reforms
proposed were to open up imperial trade to more kingdoms and ports of
the monarchy than just Castile and Seville; to open more ports in the Americas, particularly Buenos Aires, to imperial trade; to permit some degree of
intercolonial trade within the empire; to create trading companies that permitted others, like loyal Flemish merchants and financiers, to participate in
imperial trade; to create a national bank to finance industry and commerce;
and more. Entrenched economic interests – the *consulados* of Seville, Mexico
and Lima, the high clergy and the nobility, and royal officials and imperial
bureaucrats in the New World – argued that the imperial mercantilist system
required greater control, great centralization and greater regulation to prevent contraband trade and the slipping away through a thousand rifts and

holes of Castile's gold and silver. To many of these defenders of the imperial trading system, the real threat from within and without was embodied in the Portuguese merchant community.

When the reform movement of Olivares took shape in the 1620s, with the strong support of the Portuguese merchant colony in Spain and the Americas, the Portuguese became a target. From the 1620s to the 1660s, in Seville, Madrid, Mexico, Lima and Cartagena, the tribunals of the Inquisition prosecuted Portuguese merchants and bankers as believing and practicing Jews. There was also a steep rise in prosecutions of members of the Portuguese community before the *Casa de Contratación* for contraband trading and fraud in the 1620s, 1630s and 1640s. Persecution of *Portugueses de la nación*, that is the Portuguese of Spain, did not provoke the uprising of the Portuguese nobility in Lisbon in December 1640 that reestablished Portuguese independence. The separation of Portugal from Spain did lead to the fall of Olivares and thus the reform movement, and to the flight of many Portuguese merchants and financiers to Portugal and Amsterdam. "This year," wrote Olivares at the end of 1640, "can certainly be considered the worst this monarchy has ever experienced." Without reform, the imperial mercantilist system continued its sclerotic degeneration until it essentially broke down in the eighteenth century.

It is an exaggeration to speak of an economic decline of Spain in the seventeenth century. Earl J. Hamilton had it right when he referred to "the illusion of prosperity created by American gold and silver." American treasure and Habsburg power had created a façade of a rich and prosperous Spain in the sixteenth century. Just as there was an illusion of prosperity, there was also "the perception of decline from apparent prosperity and acknowledged grandeur," writes Stanley and Barbara Stein. The Steins argue convincingly, "the construction and preservation of empire in Europe and America progressively drained Castilian Spain of its meager possibilities of growth and development." In fact, as we see in Table 5.2 Spain experienced economic growth from 1500 to 1700, albeit feeble growth.

The wealth of the New World that flowed to Spain in the sixteenth and seventeenth centuries, indeed the wealth of the emerging Atlantic World that was monopolized temporarily by Spain and Portugal in the early modern period, did not bring sustained economic development to these first expansionist empires of Western Europe. However, it did offer a very tempting target. Other nations of Atlantic Europe, motivated by envy and fear of Spain, aggressive commerce and militant Protestantism, and by individuals' daring, greed and opportunism, challenged Portugal and Spain's right to – and control of – this wealth. Among these were French Huguenot corsairs, English West Country men, and the *orang laton*, the sea-gypsies of the west, the Dutch. "Envy of the 'wealth of the Spaniards and Portingals,' which had long spurred the pioneers, now became an immediate stimulus activating every port from London round Bristol, multiplying the nation's ships and fanning the flames of aggressive nationalism," writes Kenneth Andrews. "In the late sixties [1560s] radical, popular and militant Protestantism spread like wildfire as Huguenots, Dutch sea-beggars and English pirates joined forces 'against all Papists.'"

5.3 The Challengers

In the late fifteenth and early sixteenth centuries, the only other areas of Western Europe, besides Spain and Portugal, that were ready to enter the Atlantic in any serious way were France, England and the seventeen provinces of the Spanish Habsburg Netherlands. These three were seafaring nations: they each had a healthy shipbuilding industry, they had several seaports on and close to the North Atlantic and they possessed experienced mariners and merchants who were already sailing the Baltic, the North Sea and the Atlantic route to the Mediterranean. Sweden, a seagoing nation, was focused on dominating the Baltic, which it never quite accomplished. France, England and the Netherlands were the obvious challengers to the Iberian powers in the Atlantic.

At the beginning of the sixteenth century, France was the largest, wealthiest and most populous state in Atlantic Europe. There were more than fifteen million Frenchmen compared to the Spanish kingdoms' nearly seven million people. It could just as easily have been France, rather than Castile, that had sponsored Columbus' voyages to the west and taken the lead in American colonization. France faced the Atlantic seaboard from the English Channel in the north to the Basque lands of the Gulf of Gaston in the south. Norman mariners had pioneered exploration and settlement of the Canaries in the fourteenth and fifteenth centuries. François I, the arch-enemy of the Habsburg Emperor Carlos V, sponsored – and the merchants of Lyon most likely financed – the Florentine Giovanni da Verrazzano's two voyages of discovery in the 1520s to North America. Verrazzano was sent to look for a northwest passage to the East Indies. Jacque Cartier sought the same goal in the Saint Lawrence gulf and river in the 1530s. The western ports of Dieppe, Le Havre, Rouen, St.-Milo, Nantes, La Rochelle and Bordeaux were homes to substantial Atlantic fishing fleets, as well as scores of merchants. As with the ports of the Iberian Peninsula, French ports like Lyon had a substantial Italian community as well as Flemish, German and English merchants. French ports were also home to many Iberian Jews who had been expelled from their homeland in 1492 and were enriching France. "The truth was," writes Bernard Chevalier, "that in important commercial affairs, the French kingdom was dominated by forces outside its boundaries."

France's real strength in the Atlantic lay in the resources of its many and widely dispersed ports. In the first half of the sixteenth century, most of the western ports – Rouen, Dieppe and Cane in Normandy, St. Milo and Vitter in Brittany – became Protestant strongholds. La Rochelle with its royal privileges and liberties was nearly an autonomous Calvinist maritime republic. France's Protestant (Huguenot) mariners and merchants came to be militantly anti-Catholic – and therefore anti-Spanish – thus reinforcing the French monarchy's traditional anti-Habsburg policy. The French then had several motives – mercantile, strategic and religious – behind their invasion of the Iberian Atlantic in the early sixteenth century.

Like France, early sixteenth century England was a relatively consolidated monarchical state. However, there were fewer Englishmen, over four million in the 1540s. The English crown and Bristol merchants had shown interest in

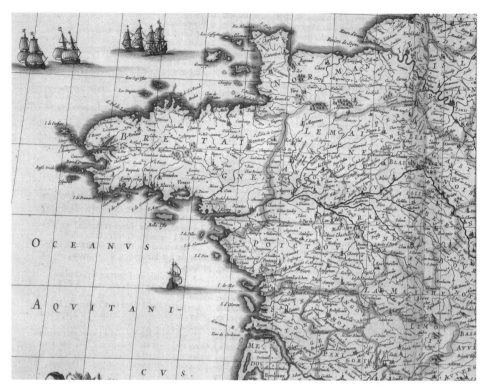

Figure 5.2. The Atlantic Coast of France. Detail of *Gallia vulgo La France* (Gaul, commonly France) from Jean Bleau, *Le Grand Atlas ov Cosmographie Blaviane*, Vol. 12 (Amsterdam, 1667). Courtesy of the William L. Clements Library of the University of Michigan.

the Atlantic in the 1480s and 1490s. Henry VII supported the North Atlantic voyages of discovery of John Cabot. Cabot's son Sebastian remained in English employ. However, the younger Cabot's voyages in the early 1500s did not spark even the slightest interest in the young Henry VIII. John Rut was sent to the coast of North America in the 1520s but there was no follow-up. In the early sixteenth century, interest in Atlantic affairs in England all but disappeared for several decades.

England's ports – London, Southampton, Weymouth, Dartmouth and Plymouth on the English Channel, Lynn, Hull Scarborough and Newcastle on the North Sea, and Barnstable and Bristol facing the Atlantic – were home to a substantial fishing fleet and merchant marine. Fishing near to and trade with Iceland had occupied most of the fifteenth century. English merchants did business in the Mediterranean and the Baltic, as well as in the ports of Spain, Portugal, France and Flanders. Of course, there were also Italian and Flemish merchant colonies in the major English ports. Competition with the Germanic Hanse merchants on the Baltic sharpened the skills of English merchants and mariners. English fishing fleets also visited the cod fisheries off Newfoundland – the Grand Banks – following their discovery in the early sixteenth century.

England had no strategic or dynastic quarrel with Habsburg Spain in the first half of the sixteenth century. The growing population of Protestants in England, particularly strong in the maritime and merchant community, gave a religious tint to the commercial competition with Catholic Spain and Portugal. English attempts to tap into the markets of the Iberian Atlantic at mid-century would sour relations considerably. Spanish military intervention in the Netherlands in the 1560s and 1570s would lead to an anti-Habsburg policy by the crown and eventually to a long and bitter war.

The nearly three million people of the seventeen provinces of the Netherlands in 1550 were the best fed and housed people in Europe. The northern provinces, which would become the Dutch Republic and the greatest thorn in the side of Spain, counted about 950,000 in 1500. Efficient and high-value agriculture, as well as a highly productive textile industry, made this region the economic center of Western Europe. It was also the most urbanized country in Europe. Flemish (southern Netherlanders) and Dutch (northern Netherlanders) mariners and merchants exported their countrymen's cheese and cloth and traded extensively from the Baltic to the Mediterranean and the Levant. In the sixteenth century, the Dutch replaced Hanse dominance in the Baltic and the North Sea in the trade of grain, timber and naval stores. Dutch shippers dominated the Rhine and soon would be swarming in the ports of England, France, Portugal and Spain. Dutch shipyards produced high-quality but low-cost cargo ships that would eventually dominate all European sea lanes. In the mid-sixteenth century, the two hundred or so towns of the Netherlands controlled fifty percent of Europe's commerce.

Flanders and the rest of the Netherlands were part of Carlos V's Burgundian inheritance, and they were transferred to Spanish rule in 1516 when he succeeded to the Spanish throne. The southern provinces were economically dominant during most of the sixteenth century. In the fifteenth century, Bruges was the commercial center of northwest Europe. This town was the meeting-place of Mediterranean and Baltic trades with merchant colonies from Venice, Genoa, Florence, Castile, Portugal, London, the German Hansa and elsewhere. After about 1480, Antwerp became the central distribution center of northwest Europe, particularly, the outlet of what the Dutch called "the rich trades," the luxuries of the Iberian Asian and Atlantic economies. The provinces brought to Spain more bullion in taxes than all of the treasure shipped each year from America to Seville. These rich provinces, particularly the northern provinces, also experienced the growth of Protestantism in the first half of the sixteenth century. Dutch merchants made a considerable amount of money servicing the economies of Spain and Portugal. This marriage of convenience was not lightly dissolved.

The Netherlands was governed by a regent, who represented the Habsburg Emperor and King of Castile, and by the States-General, which represented the provinces and gathered in Brussels. The provinces also had governors, generally called *Stadholders*, who were chosen among the leading nobles. The rebellion of the provinces beginning in the late 1560s constituted a powerful mixture of economic and religious grievances. During the reign of Carlos V, royal revenues from the Netherlands quintupled while prices only doubled.

Figure 5.3. The Dutch Port of Amsterdam. Cartouche from Jean Blaeu, *Le Grand Atlas ov Cosmographie Blaviane*, Vol. 1 (Amsterdam, 1663). Courtesy of the William L. Clements Library at the University of Michigan.

The growth of Calvinism was unacceptable to Carlos V and his son Felipe II. In the defense of local liberties, Dutch nobles and merchants protested and then rebelled. Radical rebels called "the Sea Beggars" began to seize towns in Holland and Zealand in the 1570s. The seven northern provinces successfully made a revolution, resisted Spanish repression and formed a loose federation and republic of sovereign states called the United Provinces. The port of Amsterdam in Holland became rich and powerful. A federal council of state, the States-General, met at The Hague and was chaired by the *Stadholder*, which was held by the House of Orange, and also held the title of Captain-General and Admiral-General. "We have unanimously and deliberately declared, and do by these presents declare," stated the States-General in 1581, "that the King of Spain has forfeited, ipso jure, all hereditary right to the sovereignty to those countries, and are determined from henceforth not to acknowledge his sovereignty or jurisdiction, nor any act of his relating to the domains of the Low Countries."

    In the first half of the sixteenth century, conflict in Western Europe focused on Habsburg Spain and Valois France. These two "great powers" of the early modern age struggled for hegemony in Europe. The theater of conflict in the late fifteenth and early sixteenth century was Italy, where each country defended dynastic claims. François I even saw the Ottoman Turks as a counterweight to the Habsburg colossus and made a tacit alliance with Sultan Süleyman the Magnificent. Conflict was also taken onto the high seas.

French *corsaires* were the first challengers to the Iberian monopoly in the Atlantic. Privateers – raiders authorized by their government to attack, capture, loot and sell enemy ships – were spotted in the Gulf of Guinea in the 1490s and off the coast of Brazil in the 1500s. Corsairs were first active against Spanish trade in the near Atlantic in the 1510s and 1520s. A Norman corsair in 1523 captured several Spanish vessels off the coast of Portugal carrying a portion of the treasure of the Mexica. The French were soon to be found in the Caribbean harassing shipping as well as smuggling. In the 1530s, raids of Nombre de Dios, Cartagena, Santo Domingo and Havana were recorded. Generally, local residents repelled the French, although sometimes, as in 1544 at Cartagena, the raiders would capture a town and demand a ransom for its return. In the larger ports like Santo Domingo, Spanish officials organized militias that defended the port on land and went after the French in armed galleys or caravels. In the first half of the sixteenth century, the Spanish lost hundreds of ships to French corsairs.

The French also became a scourge of the Portuguese in West Africa. Merchants from the ports of Brittany and Normandy outfitted ships to both trade on the coast of Africa (in malaguetta pepper, ivory and gold) and to attack and capture Portuguese ships or their cargo. Early on, French captains often trafficked first on the African coast and then engaged in trade with Brazil. French corsairs reportedly captured more than three hundred Portuguese ships in the African run between 1500 and 1531. The Portuguese responded by ordering that all merchant vessels be armed. Portuguese spies in French ports would also report on the comings and goings of corsairs to send patrols to the right place and at the right time to ambush the interlopers. The Portuguese also began to require that African traders sail in convoy. Irregular naval patrols were dispatched to the African coast to defend Portuguese shipping. In the 1540s, the Venetian ambassador to Lisbon referred to the maritime rivalry between Portugal and France as the "silent war."

By the 1550s and 1560s, the French threat had reached crisis proportions. In 1555, French squadrons, which included royal warships among the ships from various French ports, raided Puerto Rico and Hispaniola and briefly seized Havana. The privateer François le Clerc became famous for his raiding and pillaging throughout the Caribbean. Corsairs also conducted contraband trade whenever and wherever possible. Although the state of war between Spain and France came to an end in 1559 with the Treaty of Cateau-Cambrésis, anti-Spanish Huguenot mariners and merchants, like Admiral Gaspard de Coligny, continued the conflict "beyond the line." In the 1550s and 1560s, Huguenot forces established settlements both in Brazil ("Antarctic France" in the bay of Rio de Janeiro, 1555–67) and Florida (close to the return route of the *Carrera de Indias*, 1562–5). The Iberians forcibly removed both settlements. In Florida, the Captain-General of the *Armada de la Carrera* defeated the French outpost, burned the fort and executed 111 prisoners as heretics. To prevent future incursions in Florida, the crown established the fortress of San Agustín near modern Jacksonville. "I am afraid our eyes are bigger than our bellies, and that we have more curiosity than capacity," wrote Montaigne near the end of the sixteenth century. "For we grasp at all, but catch nothing but wind."

During the last third of the sixteenth century, French activity in the Atlantic diminished. A series of civil wars beginning in 1562 and continuing into the 1590s, the "wars of religion," consumed wealth and energy and distracted the Huguenots of the western ports. Two minors came to the throne during this period, which created a vacuum of leadership. In 1589, Henri of Navarre-Bourbon became king of France, Henri IV, and for the sake of power and peace converted to Catholicism.

Plunder and trade lured the English increasingly into a lucrative Atlantic. A few west-country English merchants had invaded the Iberian commercial sphere in the 1550s. Thomas Wyndham made three voyages to West Africa in 1551–3. With support from the Queen, John Hawkins led or sponsored several voyages to buy African slaves in Sierra Leone and sell them in Tierra Firme and the Caribbean. During his 1567–8 voyage, Hawkins unexpectedly met the New Spain fleet at Vera Cruz, was attacked and escaped with only two ships. In fact, the 1550s witnessed a considerable expansion of English commercial interests. In 1555, merchants established the Moscovy Company to open a northeastern passage to Asia but ended up trading for furs in Russia.

In the 1560s, English smuggling became piracy and privateering. Between 1568 and 1585, there were fourteen known English raids into the Caribbean. One of Hawkins' associates, Francis Drake, led several famous expeditions to attack the Spanish. In 1572–3, "El Draque" (as the Spanish called him) conceived of a plan to steal the annual shipment of treasure from Peru. The English pirate found willing allies among the escaped slaves of the Isthmus of Panama, the *negros cimarrones* – cimarrons or maroons – who had established free and independent communities. Drake, a contingent of cimarrons and some French pirates led by the Huguenot corsair Guillaume la Tetsu marched into the interior of Panama and successfully surprised the mule convoy taking the king's treasure across the isthmus to Nombre de Dios. Every member of Drake's company received enough booty to become rich men for life. Three years later, John Oxenham sought to surpass Drake by crossing the isthmus and building a warship in the Pacific to capture the treasure shipment before it reached Panama. Oxenham lacked Drake's good luck and was captured and hanged in Lima as a heretic. In 1577, Drake raised the stakes even higher by entering the Pacific through the Straight of Magellan. He raided shipping and settlements from Chile to the bay of what would become San Francisco in California. Drake then crossed the Pacific and completed the second circumnavigation of the world.

The English followed the French into African waters in the 1550s. At first, ships from London and Plymouth were interested in the gold, ivory and malaguetta pepper trade but found they were at a disadvantage to the Portuguese who held coastal forts. Although there was discussion about the building of an English castle, it came to nothing as there was no organization, neither the state nor a company, willing to bear the expense. In the 1560s, English traffic to Guinea superseded that of the French, who were involved in

Figure 5.4. Drake's Fleet at Santo Domingo. From Theodor de Bry, *Americae pars octava* (Frankfort, 1596). Courtesy of the William L. Clements Library at the University of Michigan.

their wars of religion. In time, as we have seen, English merchant adventurers like John Hawkins entered the slave trade in Africa and Spanish America. The English generally avoided the Guinea trade after 1571 as relations between England and Portugal improved and Englishmen were allowed to trade with the Madeiras and the Azores.

English raiding and Elizabeth's support for Protestants in France, and then in the Netherlands, worsened England's relations with Spain in the 1560s and 1570s. English intervention in the Netherlands was particularly loathsome to Felipe II of Spain. In 1585 with the Treaty of Nonsuch, the United Provinces essentially became a protectorate of England. English troops intervened on the continent and mariners, like Drake, attacked on the high seas. With an expedition of twenty warships, Drake plundered the Cape Verde islands. An even larger expedition in 1587 attacked Cadiz and then Cartagena and briefly seized Santo Domingo. English raiders also attacked shipping and raided settlements along the coast in Brazil. Every year in the 1580s and 1590s, between one hundred to two hundred ships invaded the Atlantic in search of prizes. To rid himself of the English pest, Felipe II dispatched an enormous fleet of warships, the famous Spanish Armada, to invade England in 1588, a force of 130 ships carrying 18,000 soldiers. The English deflected the Armada in the channel and severe storms scattered it in the North Sea and on the rocky coasts of Scotland and Ireland. "God breathed and they were scattered" (*Flavit et dissipati sunt*), the English commemorative medal stated.

The war continued after 1588. It should be noted that it was often profitable for the English. For example, George Clifford, Earl of Cumberland, financed twelve ventures in the Atlantic to capture Spanish or Portuguese merchant shipping. Merchants contributed shares of investment to outfit a ship, hire a crew, obtain a royal patent and then capture a Portuguese carrack or Spanish *não* and divide the profit. The war stimulated a shipbuilding boom in England leading to the creation of a respectable merchant marine and a body of mariners who became quite familiar with the Atlantic. Sir Walter Ralegh argued in 1596 that the English had to advance into the Atlantic in self-defense: "If the Spanish king can keep us from foreign enterprises, and from the impeachment of his trades, either by offer of invasion, or by besieging us in Britain, Ireland, or else where, he hath then brought the work of our peril in great forwardness."

In the 1590s, Ralegh was issued a royal commission to maraud the Spanish Caribbean and he immediately headed for the already legendary Guiana, seeking the discovery and conquest of an indigenous empire. According to Ralegh, Spanish claims to the New World, particularly in Guiana, were illegitimate due to Spanish atrocities against the Indians. Regarding the chief Topiaware, Ralegh wrote in his 1596 narrative of the expedition, "I made him known the cause of my coming thither, whose servant I was, and that the Queen's pleasure was, I should undertake the voyage for their defence, and to deliver them from the tyranny of the Spaniard." The more strategic goal was, as Ralegh noted, "I will hope that these provinces, and that Empire [of El Dorado] now by me discovered shall suffice to enable her Majesty, and the whole kingdom, with no less quantities of treasure, than the king of Spain hath in all the Indies, east and west." Thus with El Dorado, Ralegh believed, England would have a rich Native American empire, destroy Spain's economic and strategic hegemony in the Atlantic and make England prosperous and invincible. Ralegh's three expeditions to Guiana accomplished none of these aims. His account of his adventures, the *Discoverie*, published in 1596, was an impressive work of propaganda that sought to embolden Queen Elizabeth to dispatch an army and annex this country that supposedly had more cities, temples and treasures than Mexico or Peru. The book was a great publishing success in Europe with many editions in English as well as German, Dutch and Latin. However, neither Ralegh nor any other English adventurers was given command of an army to conquer El Dorado.

Spanish oppression and the Dutch Revolt pushed the Dutch into the Iberian Atlantic. The Union of Utrecht in 1581 united the seven northern provinces to create the United Provinces of the Netherlands. In 1585, Felipe II imposed an embargo on all Dutch ships, forbidding them to trade with Spain and Portugal. The embargo transferred the struggle from Europe to the Atlantic. Dutch privateers had begun to attack Spanish shipping in the late 1560s. The captains adopted a name that the Spanish regent had used to insult the Dutch, *les guex*, meaning "beggars," and so they became the "Sea Beggars." The Sea Beggars raided Spanish and Portuguese shipping in the near Atlantic, in the Gulf of Guinea and in the Caribbean. Unable to obtain Spain and Portugal's "rich trades" in Seville and Lisbon, Dutch traders began to trade directly with the producers in Africa, America and the East Indies. In 1590, the Spanish lifted the embargo but by then it was too late; the United Provinces' merchant marine – the largest in Europe – had begun to penetrate every corner of the Atlantic. More than two hundred Dutch ships were reported on the African coast between 1599 and 1608. The saltpans of Punta de Araya off Tierra Firme were even more popular: between 1599 and 1605, over 768 ships were sighted.

During the 1580s and 1590s, the Dutch, English and sometimes the French were at war with Spain and Portugal. An anti-Spanish alliance of the three countries was agreed to in the Treaty of The Hague in 1596. English raiding of Spanish shipping in the Atlantic reached its peak in the 1590s. Between 1589 and 1591, at least 235 English warships searched the Atlantic for Spanish prizes. In 1596, an English fleet of forty warships with ten thousand English and five thousand Dutch soldiers attacked Cadiz, destroyed close to two hundred Spanish vessels and occupied the city for two weeks. The Spanish responded to the *corsarios luteranos*, the Lutheran corsairs, by putting the first permanent patrols in the Caribbean in 1582. Seven years later, the crown established the *Armada de Barlovento*, the Windward Fleet, a squadron of warships stationed in the Caribbean. In 1586, the Council of the Indies put together a comprehensive plan to fortify the Caribbean. Military engineers were dispatched to Indies. Massive fortifications were installed in the harbors of Havana, Santo Domingo, San Juan (Puerto Rico), San Juan de Ulúa (Vera Cruz), Portobelo (to replace Nombre de Dios in Panama) and Cartagena. New and faster treasure ships, *zabras*, were put into service in 1588–92. In 1605, the Spanish launched a punitive expedition against the Dutch in the Caribbean and, temporarily at least, forced them from the "Spanish sea." A scorched-earth policy was employed in Venezuela where the Dutch had bought local tobacco. To prevent this in the future, the settlements where the Dutch traded were cleared out and the cultivation of tobacco in the region prohibited. To stop smuggling, the Spanish population on the north coast of Hispaniola was forcibly moved to the southern coast. A little later the crown fortified Callao, the port of Lima, and created the *Armada del Mar del Sur*, the South Sea Fleet, to protect Spanish shipping in the Pacific.

An overextended and bankrupt Spain reassessed its position in the late sixteenth and early seventeenth century and sought peace. In 1598, peace was made with France. Peace with England came in 1604, and the Spanish negotiated a cease-fire with the United Provinces in 1607 and a truce in 1609. By 1600, English privateering against the Spanish was essentially over. The Dutch were now focused on the "rich trades" of the East Indies. Directed by the East India Company, established in 1602, the Dutch essentially stole the Portuguese empire of trade in the orient. The Dutch captured the Spice Islands in 1605. Dutch merchants were considering the formation of a similar company to direct Dutch energies in the Atlantic when the truce of 1609 opened the ports of Spain and Portugal once again to Dutch ships.

5.4 Planting Colonies

In 1600, the Atlantic World was still dominated by the Iberians. No
other Europeans had fortifications, settlements and colonies in Africa, the
Caribbean and the American mainland. This would not last much longer.
The age of Spanish hegemony was passing. In the 1590s, a terrible plague
marked the beginning of a century of population recession in the peninsula.
The Spanish added to this deficit in the 1610s when the government expelled
the descendants of the Moors, the Moriscos, one of the most industrious
sectors of the population. The Americas attracted considerable immigration,
further depleting Spanish manpower at home. Spain also suffered from financial chaos and inflation made worse by debasing the coinage. Like his father
Carlos V in 1557, Felipe II upon his death in 1598 left Spain with enormous debts. Unlike mid-sixteenth century Spain, less treasure was arriving
from America: the *Carrera de Indias* overall entered a slump. From 1606
until 1650, the gross tonnage of American trade fell by sixty percent. Spain
had pretty much lost the Spanish American market to the rest of Europe,
even in the legal and regulated trade. In 1686, Spanish manufacturers and
artisans produced only five percent of the exports sent to America in the
annual fleet; France, Genoa, England, Holland and the Spanish Netherlands
provided most of the cargoes. England, France and the United Provinces had
commercial treaties with Spain awarding them "most-favored nation status."
These treaties, write the Steins, "opened the way for both English and French
commercial expansion into Lower Andalusia's colonial trade."

It was not until the early seventeenth century that the French, English and
Dutch were successful in establishing colonies – or what the English called
"plantations" – in America, and somewhat later in establishing trading bases
on the coast of Africa. All earlier colonization attempts had failed. Bad
weather and hostile natives defeated Jacque Cartier's outposts on the St.
Lawrence River. The French settlements in Brazil and Florida in the 1550s
and 1560s had been brutally destroyed by the Spanish. Ralegh's settlement
on Roanoke Island in the Carolina Outer Banks in the late 1580s simply
disappeared. Other French attempts to settle in North America – on Sable
Island, eighty miles east of Nova Scotia, in the Bay of Fundy, and even Cape
Cod in the late 1590s and early 1600s – failed. Several English, French and
Dutch efforts in the early seventeenth century to colonize Guiana, generally
called the "Wild Coast," in northeast South America came to nothing. The
English attempted to establish Sagadohoc colony on the Kennebec River
(today Maine) in 1607 but the colonists all agreed to abandon their settlement
the following summer. All of these efforts demonstrated the great difficulty
of planting permanent colonies in the Americas.

English colonization in the New World was preceded by the Elizabethan
assault on Ireland and the Gaelic Irish beginning in the 1560s. Gentlemen
from the southwestern counties of England, promoters for English trade
and colonization known as "West Country men" – Sir Humphrey Gilbert,
Sir Richard Grenville, Sir Walter Ralegh, the Hakluyt cousins and others –
resumed an earlier English effort at conquest and colonization of Ireland that

had begun in the twelfth century with the Normans. To most English the Gaelic Irish were simply savages, *sylvestres Hibernici*, "wild Irish." Sir John Davies in 1612 stated that the Irish behaved "little better than Cannibals, who do hunt one another, and he that hath most strength and swiftness doth eat and devours all his fellows." Such absurd perceptions and the desire for dominion and wealth led to grants of land to English landlords in the "plantation of Munster" (in southeast Ireland) and in the "plantation of Ulster" (in the northeast). Overseas promotion literature preferred the term "plantation," with its gentler horticultural associations, to the word "colony." The stated policy of the plantations was to civilize Ireland, to "plant civility" by bringing English lords and colonists to the island, introduce English architecture, gardens, schools and language and overcome the "bad weeds." Prior to 1641, approximately one hundred thousand people – some thirty thousand Scots and seventy thousand Welsh and Englishmen – migrated to the Irish plantations. Sir Francis Blundell noted in 1622 that "there cannot be a more easy and honourable way to reduce that kingdom to civility, than by plantation." However, the easy and honorable way was not the only way. The English also executed a number of costly military campaigns to "pacify" Ireland and defeat a Spanish-Papal invasion to "defend the Catholic faith." In 1673, Ireland was described by an anonymous pamphleteer as "one of the chiefest members of the British Empire."

"What exactly was the relationship," asks Andrew Hadfield, "between Irish colonization and the colonization of the Americas?" The English developed the joint-stock principle of colonial development in Ireland and later transferred it to America in the Virginia colonies. The use of fortresses in Ireland, notes Hadfield, influenced the development of the first colonial towns in America. As we see in the language of Sir John Davies previously, Englishmen viewed Irish and Indians in terms of the other. When Davies used the term "cannibal," he was comparing the "savage Irish" to the "savage Indians." As Hadfield states, "English colonialism in Ireland can neither be divorced from nor assimilated to colonialism in the Americas."

Across the Atlantic, the threat to English, French and Dutch colonization remained Spanish power. William Bradford, governor of Plymouth Plantation, warned that in America if the English "should live and do well, the jealous Spaniard would never suffer them long, but would displant or overthrow them as he did the French in Florida." A Dutch pamphlet of 1622 proposing trade and colonization admitted there was opinion in Holland "that the most difficulty will consist in the erecting of certain Colonies in unknown places, our Merchants can have no security of Trade, as you much of force confess, for the King of Spain will not cease, by all the means he can to let and hinder the same." Their new colonies would be planted far from Spanish America in Virginia and Canada in North America and on the "Wild Coast" in South America, and on small and unimportant islands – what the Spanish called the *islas inútiles*, or "useless islands" – in the eastern Caribbean. On the other hand, the merchant adventurers had wildly unrealistic hopes about the profitability of their enterprises. Colonists were dispatched with orders to find a northwest passage to the East Indies or to

find gold and silver mines similar to those of the Spanish. The belief in El
Dorado was alive and well.

Renewed interest in permanent settlements in the Americas motivated the
English and French to act in the early seventeenth century. Merchant adventurers – that is, the same people who invested in privateering – believed there
was profit to be found in American "plantations," and the English monarchy
was quite willing to authorize, although not finance, colonization. English
promoters also played on patriotism. Richard Hakluyt in 1584 wrote that
colonizing America would be "a great bridle to the Indies of the King of
Spain." The French crown was more willing to both authorize and finance
colonization. Merchants in northwest Europe organized trading and plantation companies that were chartered by governments and granted specific
privileges. Trading companies received monopolies in a particular trade (and
a specific territory) while plantation companies were granted the privilege
to apportion land, administer justice, tax settlers and their commerce and
apportion part of their production. The Dutch companies were almost purely
commercial operations and very nearly autonomous states themselves. The
French companies were organized by the government, and therefore were
more directly extensions of state power. Strategic interests were generally
more important than the profit of merchant stockholders. The English companies fell between these two extremes: private profit and state interests were
both objects of these joint-stock companies.

These chartered companies were often joint-stock companies with limited
liability to protect investors and shares offered and sold on a market. They
were often as much military and political organizations as they were commercial. They did not depend upon the modern capitalist methods of making
money, that is, improving efficiency and productivity or becoming more competitive in price and service and so on. While participating in long-distance
trade, these companies also held state monopolies over trades and territories
and appropriated wealth through extra-economic means – looting, forced
labor, slavery and the slave trade. In the early sixteenth century, the Spanish
monarchy subcontracted its imperialism to *conquistadores* and free companies. By the early seventeenth century, the three Atlantic states of northwest
Europe subcontracted their imperialism to chartered companies.

English merchant adventurers set about to colonize America through the
instrument of chartered companies. The second half of the sixteenth century
had witnessed a boom in organized commercial expansion with the establishment of the Muscovy Company, the Turkey Company, the Venice Company,
the Levant Company and the East India Company. Investors from London
and Plymouth received a charter from James I for the Virginia Company
in 1606, which divided the coast of North America, giving the northern
reaches to the Plymouth men and the southern reaches to the Londoners.
The Company first showed interest in Guiana and then New England, where
they sent several expeditions to the coast and even established a settlement
for one year on the coast of Maine. In 1607, the Londoners organized an
expedition that founded a settlement at Jamestown, forty miles up the James
River – hidden from the Spanish, it was hoped – in the Chesapeake Bay area.
When they arrived, the all-male expedition was divided into three crews: one

Figure 5.5. The Arrival of Englishmen in Virginia. From Thomas Harriot, *A Brief and True Report of the new found land of Virginia*, Theodor de Bry edition (Frankfurt, 1590). Courtesy of the William L. Clements Library at the University of Michigan.

to erect a fort, one to plant crops and one to explore the region to find a passage to Asia. Jamestown plantation was very nearly defeated by disease and Indians in its first years. Needless to say, it cost the Company's investors rather than turned a profit. Francis Bacon was accurate in observing in 1625, "You must make account to lose almost twenty years' profit, and expect your recompense in the end."

The settlers started growing tobacco and exports began in 1611. With this staple, the colony found an economic reason for existing, and James I helped the Company by prohibiting the raising of tobacco in England. A tobacco boom immediately took off: exports increased from 20,000 pounds in 1617 to approximately 350,000 pounds by 1621. By 1634, Englishmen in Virginia exported 3 million pounds of tobacco, and by 1672 tobacco exports had climbed to an astonishing 17 million pounds. The tobacco farms required labor and the merchant adventurers transported poor but ambitious Englishmen as indentured servants, who paid for their passage to Virginia by working for a tobacco planter for a period of time, usually five to seven years. Dutch and then English merchants also began to import African slaves. By 1675, there were 38,000 settlers, mostly English, and 2,500 African slaves in Virginia. Virginia Company investors with Sir George Somers formed the George Somers Company in 1612 and planted a colony in Bermuda. By 1622, the island was carved up into tobacco plantations worked by African slaves transported from Africa by the Dutch. By 1625, there were between 2,000 and 3,000 English settlers on Bermuda.

Governance of Virginia was in the hands of the Company, which appointed its governor. After Sir Edwin Sandys came to the leadership of the Virginia Company in 1619, he directed the governor to form an assembly elected from among the settlers so as to give the governor advice and to pass local laws needed to regulate the colony. Such a system would free the company from time-consuming administration. This system was like the governance of a company where all shareholders had a voice and vote, as well as many English towns, which elected a council to run local affairs. The Virginia assembly modeled itself after England's House of Commons in determining its rights and duties. This structure of a governor, an advisory council and an elected assembly was quite natural to Englishmen accustomed to a king, privy council, and Parliament. It spread to the other Anglo-American colonies but was not taken up by the authorities and colonists of other nationalities in their American colonies.

The Virginia Company also granted a charter to Protestant English religious dissidents living in Leiden, in the United Provinces, and these "pilgrims" established Plymouth plantation on Massachusetts Bay in 1620. Another group of religious dissidents, Puritans, who disagreed with the excessive Romanization of the Church of England, found investors and formed the Governor and Company of Massachusetts Bay in 1629. The Puritans settled next to the Pilgrims (and eventually enveloped them) and provided land and freedom to co-religionists who flocked to the colony in great numbers. The "great migration" of the 1630s and 1640s increased the population of Massachusetts Bay colony to 23,000 living in about forty towns by 1650. Dissenters like Roger Williams and his followers established new settlements, in this case in Rhode Island, that peopled the Atlantic shore from Plymouth in the north to the Long Island in the south. These new colonies were without charters and had to devise governing systems on their own. Before long, Massachusetts Bay and the other New England colonies were declared crown colonies, which meant that the king had the right to appoint the governor. Local assemblies survived the transition and a tradition of self-governance developed in the colonies. "Electing people," according to Paul Johnson, "was one of the first things a settler in America learned to do."

Unlike Virginia, Massachusetts had no valuable staple to produce and export. Settlers in New England created small, self-sufficient farms and in time built ships, fished the Grand Banks and organized trade with the British Isles and the other Atlantic colonies. The New England colonies became particularly proficient in supplying provisions to the island colonies in the Caribbean. In the 1630s, the Puritans took over the fur trade of the region, and by the 1640s Massachusetts' furnaces were producing 1,500 tons of iron a year. As early as 1676, English merchants began complaining that New England had supplanted the mother country as "the great Mart and Staple" of the Atlantic World (see Map 5.2).

Sir George Calvert, a courtier at the Stuart court, in the early 1630s converted to Catholicism and sought an American realm where English Catholics could worship as they pleased without discrimination and harassment. Sir George's son, Lord Baltimore, continued the project following his father's death and was granted a colonial charter containing territory northeast of

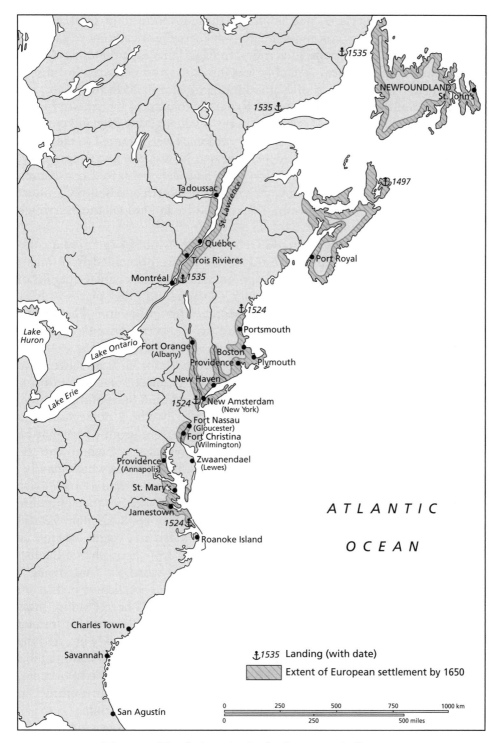

Map 5.2. North America in the Seventeenth Century.

Virginia, called Maryland, one similar to those given to joint-stock companies. This proprietary colony, similar to a Portuguese captaincy, gave the Calverts the right to appoint governors. In Maryland as in the other Anglo-American colonies, a local assembly was instituted and permitted local self-government. Although Catholics immigrated to Maryland in the 1630s, the majority of settlers were Protestants. Religious tolerance, by necessity then, became official policy in Maryland as in the dissident New England colonies like Rhode Island. Additional proprietary colonies were granted to the king's brother, James, Duke of York, which became New York and New Jersey; William Penn, which became Pennsylvania and Delaware; to a consortium of proprietors led by Lord Ashley, which became North and South Carolina; and finally to another consortium, this one led by James Oglethorpe, which became Georgia.

In 1603, the Huguenot Pierre du Gua, Sieur de Monts, organized a company of merchant adventurers from La Rochelle and obtained from Henri IV a ten-year trade monopoly and appointment as Lieutenant General "of the coasts, lands and confines of Acadia, Canada, and other places in New France." In the king's Patent to De Monts, appointing him Lieutenant-General of Canada, Henri IV stated he had two concerns. His first and most important interest was "to cause the people, which do inhabit the Country, men (at the present time) barbarous, Atheists, without faith or religion, to be converted to Christianity." The king's second concern was more down-to-earth. The king had been told "how fruitful, commodious and profitable may be unto us, to our estates and subjects, the dwelling, possession, and habitation of those countries, for the great and apparent profit which may be drawn by the greater frequentation & habitude which may be had with the people that are found there & and the traffic and commerce which may be, by that means, safely treated and negotiated." In 1605–7 and 1610–13, De Monts founded Port Royal on the Bay of Fundy in Acadia but this immature settlement was soon destroyed by an English pirate. In 1608, Captain Samuel de Champlain, a lieutenant of De Monts, commanded an expedition of three ships far up the Saint Lawrence River, and thus far from Spanish and English danger. He built a fort at Québec (an Algonquian word for "narrowing") that survived the winter and became a trading post, buying beaver pelts from the local Algonkian and Huron Indians. Merchants had been sending ships to the Saint Lawrence since the 1580s to trade for furs. A permanent trading post was expected to boost trade and profits. Champlain quickly inserted the French into native politics by militarily supporting the Huron against their enemy, the Iroquois Five Nations south of the river. For nearly two decades, the settlement of Québec stagnated because the merchant adventurers in France focused on the fur trade alone and neglected colonization.

In 1627, the king's first minister, Cardinal Richelieu, established the *Compagnie des Cent-Associes*, the Company of One Hundred Associates, also called the Company of New France, which claimed all lands from the Arctic Circle to Florida. The company was a joint venture that involved both public as well as private investments. Richelieu was more interested in the strategic interest of France in North America than profit, and sought to create a flourishing colony and Catholic preserve as the foundation of a strong north

Document 5.1
Royal Patent to the Sieur de Monts

1603

Henry by the grace of God King of France and Navarre. To our dear and well-beloved the Lord of Monts, one of the ordinary Gentlemen of our Chamber, greeting. As our greatest care and labour is, and hath always been since our coming to this Crown, to maintain and conserve it in the ancient dignity, greatness, and splendour thereof, to extend and amplify, as much as lawfully may be done, the bounds and limits of the same. We being of a long time informed of the situation and condition of the lands and territories of La Cadie [Acadia], moved above all things with a singular zeal and devout and constant resolution which we have taken with the help and assistance of God, author, distributors, and protector of all kingdoms and estates, to cause the people which do inhabit the country, men (at this present time) barbarous atheists, without faith or religion, to be converted to Christianity, and to the belief and profession of our faith and religion; and to draw them from the ignorance and unbelief wherein they are. Having also of a long time known by the relation of the sea-captains, pilots, merchants, and others who of long time have haunted, frequented, and trafficked with the people that are found in the said places, how fruitful, commodious, and profitable may be unto us, to our estates and subjects, the dwelling, possession, and habitation of those countries, for the great and apparent profit which may be drawn by the greater frequentation and habitude which may be had with the people that are found there, and the traffic and commerce which may be by that means safely treated and negotiated. We then for these causes fully trusting on your great wisdom, and in the knowledge and experience that you have of the quality, condition, and situation of the said country of La Cadie: for the divers and sundry navigations, voyages, and frequentations that you have made into those parts and others near and bordering upon it: Assuring ourselves that this our resolution and intention, being committed unto you, you will attentively, diligently, and no less courageously and valorously execute and bring to such perfection as we desire: Have expressly appointed and establish you, our Lieutenant General, for to represent our person, in the countries, territories, coasts, and confines of La Cadie. To begin from the 40th degree unto the 46th. And in the same distance, or part of it, as far as may be done, to establish, extend, and make to be known our name, might, and authority. And under the same to subject, submit, and bring to obedience all the people of the said land, and the borderers thereof: And by the means thereof, and all lawful ways, to call, make, instruct, provoke, and incite them to the knowledge of God, and to the light of the faith and Christian religion, to establish it there: And in the exercise and profession of the same, keep and conserve the said people and all other inhabitants in the said places, and there to command in peace, rest, and tranquility, as well by sea as by land: to ordain, decide, and cause to be executed all that which you shall judge fit and necessary to be done, for to maintain, keep, and conserve the said places under our power and authority, by the forms, ways, and means prescribed by our laws. And for to have there a care of the same with you, to appoint, establish, and constitute all officers as well in the affairs of war as for justice and policy, for the first time and from thence-forward to name and present them unto us, for to be disposed by us; and to give letters, titles, and such provisos as shall be necessary. And according to the occurrences of affairs, yourself, with the advice of wise and capable men, to prescribe under our good pleasure laws, statutes, and ordinances conformable, as much as may be possible, unto ours, specially in things and matters that are not provided by them: To treat, and contract to the same effect, peace, alliance, and confederacy, good amity, correspondency and communication with the said people and their Princes or others having power or command over them: To entertain, keep, and carefully to observe the treaties and alliances wherein you shall covenant with them: upon condition that they themselves perform the same of their part. And for want thereof to make open wars against them, to constrain and bring them to such reason as you shall thing needful, for the honour, obedience, and service of God and the establishment, maintenance, and conservation of our said authority amonst them: at least to haunt and frequent by you, and all our subjects with them, in all assurance, liberty, frequentation and communication, there to negotiate and traffic lovingly and peaceably. To give and grant unto them favours and privileges, charges, and honours. Which entire power abovesaid, we will likewise and ordain that you have over all our said subjects that will go in the voyage with you and inhabit there, traffic, negotiate, and remain in the said places, to retain, take, reserve, and appropriate unto you what you will and shall see to be the most commodious for you and proper to your charge, quality, and use of the said lands, to distribute such parts and portions thereof, to give and attribute unto them such titles, honours, rights, powers, and faculties as you shall see necessary, according to the qualities, conditions, and merits of the persons of the same country or others. Chiefly to populate, to manure, and to make the said lands to be inhabited, as speedily, carefully, and skillfully, as time, places, and commodities permit. To make thereof, or cause to be made to that end, discovery and view along the maritime coasts and other countries of the mainland, which you shall order and prescribe in the foresaid space of the 40th degree, to the 46th degree, or otherwise as much and as far as may be, along the said coast and in the firm land. To make carefully to be sought and marked all sorts of mines of gold and of silver, copper, and other metals and minerals, to make them to be digged, drawn from the earth, purified and refined, for to be converted into use, to dispose according as we have prescribed by edicts and orders which we have made in this realm of the profit and benefit of them, by you or them which you shall establish to that effect, reserving unto us only the tenth penny of that which shall issue from them of gold, silver, and copper, leaving unto you that which we might take of the other said metals and minerals, for to aid and ease you in the great expenses that the foresaid charge may bring unto you. Willing in the meanwhile that – as well for your security and commodity as for the security and commodity of all our subjects who will go, inhabit, and traffic in the said lands: as generally of all others that will accommodate themselves there under our power and authority – you may cause to be built and frame one or many forts, places, towns, and all other houses, dwellings, and inhabitations, ports, havens, retiring places, and lodgings as you shall know to be fit, profitable, and necessary for the performing of the said enterprise. To establish garrisons and soldiers for the keeping of them . . .

   For such is our pleasure. Given at Fountainbleau the 18th day of November, in the year of our Lord 1603, and of our reign the 15th. Signed HENRY: and underneath, by the King, Potier; And sealed upon single label with yellow wax.

Pierre de Gua, Sieur de Monts, was commissioned by the Duc de Montmorency, Admiral of France, to explore and settle the lands of Acadia, including the St. Lawrence as far inward as possible. King Henri IV confirmed the commission in this patent. When de Monts returned to Canada, he was accompanied by one of his associates, Samuel de Champlain. *Source:* Marc Lescarbot, *Nova Francia: A Description of Acadia, 1606,* translated by P. Erondelle, 1609 (1928), pp. 1–6.

Atlantic base. Of all of the European powers in the Atlantic, the government of France was most willing and able to subsidize overseas development. The Company was granted a fifteen-year trade monopoly, perpetual monopoly of the fur trade and the right to grant seigneurial lands and rights to well-to-do proprietors, *seigneurs.* In return, the Company was charged with transporting four thousand settlers, mostly *engagés* – indentured servants – to Canada, as well as subsidizing Jesuit missions to the Indians and defending the colony. New France survived as the beaver trade became big business and expanded west: the Trois Rivières settlement was established in 1634 and Mont-Réal, our Montreal, in 1642. Nevertheless, the harsh climate and the company monopoly of furs attracted few settlers. By 1640, New France had a population of 346 people.

   During the 1640s and 1650s, Richelieu's successor, Cardinal Mazarin, focused France's energies on European affairs and pretty much gave England carte blanche in the Atlantic. Mazarin attempted to develop New France by selling fur trading concessions to sub-lessees and reducing the term of the *engagés* from three years to eighteen months. The five years between 1642 and 1647 brought the most indentured contracts at La Rochelle. The three hundred people of the 1640s had grown to three thousand by the early 1660s. New energy was given to overseas development in the 1660s under the leadership of controller general of the finances, Jean-Baptiste Colbert. The Company of New France was terminated and the crown took direct control of New France in 1663, sending a governor, an intendant responsible for finance and internal administration, and 1,200 soldiers. The colony began to grow, mainly due to natural increase. By 1685, New France had more than ten thousand settlers (see Map 5.3).

Figure 5.6. Miramich, a French Settlement (Habitation) in New France. From *Scenographia Americana* (London, 1768). Courtesy of the William L. Clements Library at the University of Michigan.

During the 1670s and 1680s, explorers from New France enormously expanded the territory in North America claimed by France. In 1673, Jacques Marquette and Louis Joliet, a trader, explored the Fox and Illinois rivers to the Mississippi. At the same time, the governor of New France, Count Louis de Frontenac, founded Fort Frontenac, pushing the limits of New France to Lake Ontario. With the connivance of Frontenac, Robert de La Salle explored Lake Michigan and Illinois country and erected Fort Crèvecoeur near present-day Peoria. In 1682, he traveled south on the Illinois and then the Mississippi River until reaching the Gulf of Mexico. La Salle established trading posts and claimed possession of the entire Mississippi Valley for France. He returned to the Gulf of Mexico in 1684 and landed at Matagorda Bay in Texas with the goal of finding silver or gold mines. In the 1680s, he tried to find the Mississippi River from the Gulf and was murdered by his companions in 1687. At the end of the century, French forces began the colony of Louisiana, which embraced the vast region of the Mississippi Valley to the Great Lakes with a settlement at Biloxi.

During the early years of the seventeenth century, the war between the Dutch and the Spanish had reached a stalemate. Both sides were fatigued and ready to negotiate. With a Twelve Years Truce concluded in 1609, the Spanish recognized the United Provinces of the Netherlands as "free lands, states and provinces," and the English and the French recognized the Dutch envoys in their capitals as ambassadors. The Dutch used the calm provided by the Truce to expand the deployment of their power and commerce around

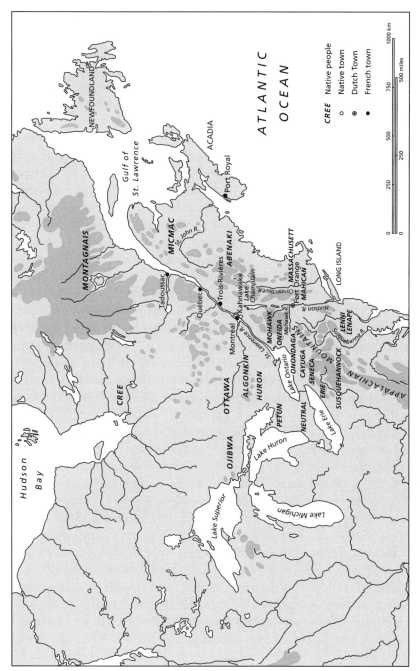

Map 5.3. New France in the Seventeenth Century.

the world. In 1609, the English explorer Henry Hudson, in his one expedition for the Dutch East India Company, crossed the Atlantic seeking a northwest passage. His voyage up the river that bears his name gave the Dutch claim to a portion of North America. Later Dutch voyages up what the Dutch called the North River to trade for beaver pelts led to the formation of a trading company, the New Netherlands Company, which established a trading post/fort called Fort Nassau, close to modern Albany, in 1614.

In 1621, the Dutch and the Spanish decided to go back to war. The Spanish embarked on a vigorous campaign of economic warfare. Spain excluded, embargoed and endeavored to destroy Dutch trade in Europe and the Atlantic. The States General chartered the *West Indische Compagnie* (the West India Company, or WIC), and authorized it to maintain warships and garrisons, sign alliances with native peoples and appoint governors. The Company would replace the separate and competing Dutch companies in African and American seas and become the instrument of the (somewhat) united Dutch mercantile and naval power in the Atlantic. The Charter of the WIC stated: "the navigation, trade, and commerce, in the parts of the West-Indies, and Africa, and other places hereafter described, should not henceforth be carried on any otherwise than by the common united strength of the merchants and inhabitants of these countries." The Company required three years to gather the necessary starting capital to begin its operations. For all intents and purposes, the WIC was the Dutch Republic's instrument for destroying Iberian wealth and power in the Atlantic World (and, in the doing, making profits). In a 1622 pamphlet defending the WIC and the "notable aid to be given them by the general States," the author argued that the only way to preserve Dutch freedom and prosperity, and the only way to be released from continual fear, was "to undermine the foundation of [the King of Spain's] great riches." Backers of the Company believed it would triumph over the tyrannical Spanish in the New World because they would have natural allies, "the assistance of the Indians and revolt of the Negroes."

What was intended to be Spain and Portugal's worst nightmare was also a practical business institution. Merchants and nobles from five leading cities and their provinces – Amsterdam (Holland), Middleburg (Zeeland), Rotterdam (the Mass), Enkhuizen (North Quarter) and Groningen (Groningen) – owned shares of the Company, although the largest investors were recently arrived Flemish southerners from Antwerp who settled in Holland and Zeeland. A federal board of management, the *Heren XIX*, the Nineteen Gentlemen, made policy in coordination with the States General, which also provided warships, munitions and soldiers when needed in wartime. Commanders and governors swore a double oath to the Company and the States General. The WIC was a unique blend of private and state effort to devastate an old and create a new empire in the Atlantic.

The Dutch West India Company invaded the Atlantic with great zeal, once sufficient capital had been raised. During the company's first two decades it had bought or commissioned more than two hundred ships, dispatched some eight hundred trading and war ships, and captured or destroyed more than six hundred Spanish vessels. In a 1633 memorial, the Provincial States of Friesland referred to the WIC as "a pillar of this state" and "a thorn in

Document 5.2
Observations on the Estate and Affairs of Holland

1622

The common opinion is, that the greatest riches of that Trade consisteth in gold and silver Mynes, which are in West India: but it is not so; for the greatest riches at this time consisteth in the severall sourts of Fruits, and other things that grow therein, as Sugar, Ginger, Indigo, Cocheville, and other drugs, as also divers kinds of wood, hides, pearles, and precious stones: and likewise in divers sorts of Manufactures that are carried thether, whereby the Marchants, Saylers, Pesants, and most part of other Handycrafts men live. The gold and silver hath been a great profit to the King, when the Spaniards first entered into those Countries, where they found great quantity of gold, that had beene gathered together by the Indians in a long time: for the which, some millions of poore innocent men, lost their lives in the Mynes, so that the gold at this time is must wasted away, and no more found in so great quantity, and the greateth riches at this day consisteth in the Wares aforesaid that are carried to and fro.

To show this, I will make no long discourse of the riches, (that besides gold and silver) come out of the West Indies, but onely speake somewhat of Brasilia, wherein there is no Mynes of gold or silver, but onely Sugar, Cotton wooll, Brasil wood, Conserves and Ginger: but Ginger may not be brought out of Brasilia into Spaine, because they of St. Domingo (who for the most part get their livings thereby) may not be impoverished. Yet the trade in Brasilia is one of the profitablest trades in West India, whereby the Portugales get most profit, and where they (now they are almost bereft of Guinia and the East Indies, or at least get little by them) maintaine their Trade. For out of Brasilia yearely one with another, there is brought betweene 40. and 50. thousand Chests of Sugar, which my be valued (2. third parts being white, but 1. third part browne Sugar) at 25. pounds Flemish the Chest, which is 48. Tonnes of Golde, not reckning Brasill wood, Cotton wooll, and other wares, which also are of great value: and then the manufactures & other wares, that are carried out of Portugal thether, which also amount unto asmuch as the Sugar. It is true, that there is much mony also carried thither out of Portugal, but that is by reason that there is no other manufactures vied there, then such as the Portugales themselves have need of, but their Slaves, which are many thousands, have nothing, because most of them goe naked, and so get nothing else but their paines for their labours, and of the wilde Brasilians they get no advantage thereby, because they esteeme not of the use thereof. Where to the contrary, if we were there, we would get great furtherance and advantage also by our labours, and thereby trade would bee much increased. By this you may easily perceive, what great riches the wares of West India, altogether amount unto, as also that the wares that are carried thither doe yeeld. For in Nova Spania and Perto, in some places there are some Indians that are polliticke and weare cloathes as we doe. And if the Spaniards, by means of their great strength, had not for the most part rooted out the Inhabitants, where they command, without doubt, they should have reaped more furtherance thereby, then now they doe, for that the Indians would have growne more civill and politicke, and to enjoy the fruits that proceed from labour, would have addicted themselves to labour. But now those Countries for the most part are unpeopled of their naturall Inhabitants, and those that still remaine therein, are had in such subjection that they have neither hearts nor wills, but had rather dye, then live under their government. Thus I have sufficiently shewed, wherein the riches of the West Indian trade most consisteth, that is in the Wares and Marchandizes which are in those Countries, and other Countries have not, yet Golde and Silver is not amisse therewith to encrese and augment Trade.

The means to bee participants in this Trade, is to erect some Colonies there, and the better to doe the same, we must suffer the West Indian Company to proceed in their Trade...

Now if certaine Colonies were erected, by that meanes we would get the most part of the Trade & Traffique in the West Indies into our hands, by reason that we can sell and afford all Manufactures a hundred for one, better cheape then the Spaniards can doe, those Wares that come out of India are better cheape unto us 50. in the hundred, then unto them, because they stand us in so much more, before we can bring them out of Spaine hither, and further our Countrymen by their industry and labour, would advance themselves more then the Spaniards.

This brief for expanding Dutch trade and settlements to the West Indies has been attributed to Willem Usselincx, a merchant capitalist and long-time supporter of an aggressive West India Company. *Source: More Excellent Observations of the Estate and Affairs of Holland. In a discourse, shewing how necessarie and convenient it is for their neighboring Countries, as well as the Netherland Provinces, to Trade into the West Indies.* Faithfully translated out of the Dutch Copie. Printed at London by E. A. for Nicholas Bourne and Thomas Archers, 1622.

the foot of the King of Spain." Between 1624 and 1626, the WIC established trading posts and settlements at New Amsterdam and Fort Orange on the Hudson River in North America. New Amsterdam, on the island the Dutch called Manhattes – today, Manhattan – was originally intended to be a base from which to trade in the New World and from which to strike the Spanish. Within a short period of time, it became a settlement colony composed of *coloniers* from numerous European countries as well as Indians and Africans. One visitor counted eighteen languages being spoken in the 1640s. With the best harbor on the Atlantic seaboard, New Amsterdam soon became one of the busiest Atlantic ports, shipping commodities around the Americas and Africa and to and from Amsterdam. On the upper Hudson, the WIC replaced and relocated Fort Nassau with Fort Orange. Dutch traders allied themselves with the Iroquois – primarily, the Mohawk – to dominate the fur trades in much of the Great Lakes region. In 1624, the WIC exported

4,700 furs down the Hudson River. A little more than thirty years later, the exports had increased to 35,000. Like other Dutch colonies in the Atlantic, New Netherland never attracted many Dutch immigrants. Like Portugal, The Netherlands was a small country with relatively few people. Both of these imperial nations sent tens of thousands of men to sea and to man trading posts and military facilities during their prime. In the case of The Netherlands, perhaps the most prosperous country in Europe, there was little material reason for most people to leave home.

A combination of WIC internal politics and Swedish envy led to the expedition in 1638 that established New Sweden in the Delaware Valley, about one hundred miles south of New Amsterdam. A Dutch merchant unhappy with WIC policy in New Netherland helped created the New Sweden Company, obtained Swedish authorization and financial participation, and recruited Peter Minuit to lead an expedition of colonization to North America. A German native and former governor of New Netherland, Minuit chose a site within the stated boundaries of New Netherlands. Under Minuit's leadership, the settlers established Fort Christina and started trading with the Delaware Indians for furs. Within a few years, the New Sweden Company, essentially a Dutch company, was in financial trouble and the Dutch investors sold out to the Swedish monarchy and its partners. New Sweden under the new company and the governorship of Johan Printz (1643–53) was the destination of twelve Swedish expeditions that carried six hundred Swedes and Finns to the colony. New Sweden not only traded in furs but also became a colony of farms and settlements along both sides of the Delaware River. This slap in the face of the WIC would not long endure. In 1655, New Netherland's most forceful governor, Pieter Stuyvesant, brought a force of seven warships and three hundred soldiers to Fort Christina and demanded the surrender of the colony. The Swedish factor had no choice. As he gave in, he made a prophecy: "Today it's me, tomorrow it will be you."

The primary interest of the WIC was in the South Atlantic. During the Truce, Dutch ships carrying sugar directly from Brazil had supplied the twenty-nine sugar refineries in Amsterdam, and now the source was cut off. To supply its refineries, the Dutch needed sugar – a lot of sugar. However, the Dutch fleets that left the Netherlands in 1623 and 1624 sought empire, not just sugar. An invasion fleet of twenty-three ships in 1624 captured Salvador, Bahia, the principal port and colonial capital of Brazil. An earlier fleet, the first major Dutch offensive against Spain's empire, had set sail for the Pacific. This "most powerful hostile force yet to enter the South Sea" was composed of eleven heavy warships with 294 guns and 1,637 men. Its objective was to capture the silver fleet and, more importantly, as Benjamin Schmidt puts it, "to ignite nothing short of a full-scale revolt in the Americas, an *alteratie* in which a Dutch-Indian alliance would oust the Spanish decisively from the New World." Unfortunately for the Dutch, neither assault succeeded. Shocked by the seizure of the capital of Brazil, the king of Spain put together the largest military force that had ever crossed the Atlantic to that time, an army of 12,500 men, and forced the Dutch garrison in Salvador to yield after holding it for less than a year. The Dutch fleet in the Pacific missed the Spanish treasure fleet and found Spanish power on the mainland well established

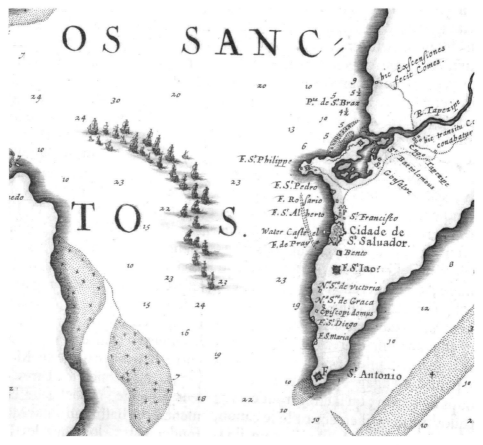

Figure 5.7. The Dutch Attempt to Conquer the City of Salvador on All Saints Bay. Detail of *Sinus Omnium Sanctorum* (The Bay of All Saints). From Jean Bleau, *Le Grand Atlas ov Cosmographie Blaviane*, Vol. 12 (Amsterdam, 1667). Courtesy of the William L. Clements Library at the University of Michigan.

and the possibility of a Dutch-Indian alliance quite remote. The Dutch would return and seek an alliance two more times without success. If the comments of the politician and diarist Alexander van der Capellen were representative, these early setbacks were not without their advantages: "Though we lose our capital, yet the king of Spain suffers thereby."

The WIC was not deterred. In 1628, a WIC fleet led by Admiral Piet Heyn cornered and captured the New Spain treasure fleet at Matanzas, Cuba. Spain's Felipe IV suffered a nervous collapse upon hearing this news and stated, "Whenever I speak of the disaster the blood runs cold in my veins, not for loss of treasure but because we lost our reputation in that infamous defeat, caused as it was by fear and cowardice." Besides reputation, Spain lost nearly one-third of its Atlantic merchant marine. The 12 million florins – about ninety tons of silver and gold – captured in this raid helped to pay for a Dutch new offensive in Brazil. In 1630, an invasion fleet and military forces comprising sixty-seven ships and seven thousand soldiers captured Recife and Olinda, which led to the occupation of the province of Pernambuco. Count Johan Maurits van Nassau-Siegen, the Company's Governor-General of Dutch Brazil – now renamed New Holland – brought six of the fourteen Portuguese captaincies under Dutch rule from 1637 to 1644: Rio Grande do Norte (1633), Paraíba (1634), most of Pernambuco (1635), Ceará and Sergipe (1637–41) and finally Maranhão (1641). In 1638, the Company again tried to take Salvador – and with it the most important remaining sugar plantations in Brazil – without success. Another unsuccessful attempt was made in 1647. In Pernambuco, the Dutch takeover generally led to the confiscation of the sugar *engenhos* of the original Portuguese proprietors and then the selling of many of these properties by the WIC to Luso-Brazilians.

The sugar plantations of Dutch Brazil were worthless without a steady supply of labor. The Dutch had been on the Gold Coast since 1612 with a fort at Mouri, which was named Fort Nassau in 1637. It was located only a few miles away from the capital of the Portuguese captaincy in Guinea. The WIC needed a steady source of labor and in 1637 Maurits organized a military expedition that captured Portugal's principal outpost on the Gold Coast, São Jorge da Mina. The WIC took Chambray and Booty in 1640 and Axem (Fort St. Anthony) in 1641. In that same year, the Dutch also began trading on the coast of the Congo and took São Tomé and Luanda, Angola, away from the Portuguese, making nearly the entire coast of West Africa under their military and commercial dominance. The WIC became involved in one of its most lucrative trades, the slave trade. By 1645, the Heren XIX referred to the slave trade as "the soul of the Company."

Also in Africa, the Dutch East India Company established a colony at the southern cape in 1652. Its function was primarily strategic and logistical, to defend and provision East India Company (VOC) fleets going to and coming from the Indian Ocean. From 1652 to 1700, approximately thirty-three ships a year rounded the cape. Like the WIC in the Hudson River valley, the VOC encouraged Dutch farmers to settle in Cape Colony and by 1685 about one hundred families had emigrated. The Dutch Reform Church established three parishes as the colony expanded: Cape Town in 1666, Stellenbosch in 1685 and Drakenstein in 1691. By 1711, the white burger population of Cape Colony was 1,756 and they owned more than 1,500 African slaves. It became one of The Netherlands' few settlement colonies. Cape Town had become "the Tavern of Two Seas."

The assault of the Dutch West India Company on the Spanish (and Portuguese) empires in the Atlantic in the 1620s and 1630s opened the door of the Caribbean to foreign colonization for the first time. Looking to develop bases for contraband trade and tobacco farms to supply a rapidly growing market in Europe, English and French merchant adventurers and captains began to scout islands the Spanish had ignored for more than one hundred years. The English seized San Cristóbal in the Leeward Islands in 1624 (renaming it St. Kitts) and Barbados in the Windwards – the most easterly of the Lesser Antilles – in 1627. Nevis, Montserrat, Antigua, Tortuga and Santa Catalina (which the English named Providence Island) fell to the English in the late 1620s and 1630s. In 1633, the Dutch took St. Martin and the following year Curaçao, close to the Spanish Main with a splendid harbor and saltpans. Netherlanders soon acquired a few other small specks in the Caribbean. The French shared St. Kitts with the English. The merchants of Dieppe organized an expedition in 1635 that seized Martinique, Dominica and Guadeloupe, rather dangerous islands because they were located on the route of the Spanish treasure fleet where ships stopped for water. During this time, a Spanish observer noted that the West Indies were "sown with French, English and Dutch who could levy thirteen thousand armed men."

The Spanish did not sit by idly: the English and French were expelled from St. Kitts and Nevis in 1629, St. Martin was cleared in 1633, the English were expelled from Santa Catalina in 1641 and in 1635 an expedition from Santo Domingo swept the English off Tortuga. None of these reconquests were permanent. The English, French and Dutch were relentless, and the Spanish were overextended and far too short of ships and soldiers to defend all of their possessions.

The Dutch Antilles, particularly Willemstad on Curaçao, its neighbors Aruba and Bonaire, and the Leeward group, St. Eustatius, Saba, and St. Martin, served largely as provisioning stations and warehouses for Dutch trade to Venezuela, New Granada, Puerto Rico, Santo Domingo and the Anglo-American ports of North America. At its height in the 1680s, Curaçao was the key to and intersection of the Dutch *Grote vaart* (the "Big" or transatlantic trade) and *Klein vaart* ("Small" or local Caribbean trade). Willemstad's local carrying fleet consisted of approximately eight barques, small three-masted ships, each with crews of anywhere between fifteen to eighty men. After 1707, in reaction to privateers and pirates, the WIC organized annual convoys with naval escorts from Amsterdam to Curaçao.

Colonization of Guiana, at the time called the "Wild Coast," proved quite difficult due to the unhealthy climate, hostile Native Americans and Spanish attacks. This South American coastline between the Orinoco River in the northwest and the Amazon in the southeast was approximately eight hundred miles long and was interrupted by some twenty rivers. Charles Leigh, an Englishman, put a settlement on the Wiapoco river in 1604, which lasted only two years. The vice-admiral of Brittany, La Ravardière, put a trading post at Cayenne Island on the eastern side in 1607, which quickly failed. Unsuccessful English colonization efforts were undertaken in 1609–13, 1617–18 and 1619–21. During these years, the Dutch established and maintained several trading posts intermittently to obtain dyes, woods, oil and balsam. The Dutch succeeded in placing the first permanent settlement and military base, Fort Kijkoveral, on the Essequibo River in 1616 and another on the Berbice River in 1624. The Zeeland chamber of the WIC was particularly enthusiastic about business prospects on the Wild Coast and attempted to create its own colony through the WIC – Nova Zeelandia – and gave land grants on the coast to fellow Zeelanders. From 1635 to 1637, the Zeelanders founded seven settlements on the coast, some of which had sugar plantations by mid-century. With the Treaty of Westphalia in 1648, the Spanish recognized the Dutch colonies in Guiana.

While the Dutch were attempting to maintain and grow their colonies on the Essequibo and the Berbice Rivers, the English and French tried again to colonize the coast. Indian and Spanish attacks as well as assaults from each other plagued these new expeditions like their predecessors. Nearly all of the settlements on the coast from the 1610s to the 1670s changed hands, many more than once. In 1651, Francis Willoughby, the governor of Barbados with a proprietary charter in hand, mounted a substantial expedition to plant a settlement on the Surinam River, which is located approximately in the middle of the Wild Coast and between the isolated Dutch colonies. As elsewhere in the Americas, Englishmen poured into this colony, and it prospered with sugar cultivation. This particular colony also attracted English Jews. By 1663, English Surinam had a population of four thousand (including slaves) scattered among some fifty plantations.

At the same time, the English and French moved into the African Atlantic following the Dutch. An English company had been founded in 1618 to trade with "Ginny and Binny" (Guinea and Benin). In 1631, it established a fort at Cormantin on the Gold Coast, but costs exceeded profit and the company went into bankruptcy in the 1650s. The French arrived in Senegal in the 1630s and established Fort St. Louis at Gorée Island, which became the headquarters of their slaving activities in Africa. The Gambia became the preserve of the Baltic Germans for a time, dispatched by the Duke of Courland (Latvia), who fortified an island twenty miles inland in 1651 and thus controlled European trade on the river. The Swedes followed the Dutch and English to the Gold Coast in 1650, founding a trading post at Butre, and the Danes established Fort Christianborg in 1661.

The Dutch West India Company was a holding company that attempted to conciliate the various competing commercial interests in the Dutch Republic. Small and large holdings were apportioned to the different chambers. For example, Amsterdam supervised Curaçao, New Netherland and Fort Orange; Zeeland was entrenched in the Wild Coast; and Groningen administered the Gambia region of West Africa. Only New Holland – Brazil – captured the attention and investments of the company as a whole. To reduce the costs of colonization, the company sold large proprietary patents – patroonships – to individuals or partnerships that were then responsible for settling and developing their territories. These were not unlike the Portuguese captaincies in Brazil and Africa and the English proprietary charters of Maryland and Pennsylvania. Patroons in New Netherland, Berbice and the Wild Coast, and the islands of St. Eustatius, Saba and St. Martin, had the exclusive monopoly on overseas trade and were responsible for justice and government. In time, the Company revoked all of the proprietary patents. Where the Company ruled directly, as at Elmina, New Amsterdam, New Holland and Willemstad on Curaçao, the *Heren XIX* appointed Director-Generals or Governor-Generals who were given full, military-style authority and were advised by a *Raad*, or council, composed of the local military commander, merchants and planters. The Governor-General of New Holland established a representative council – a rudimentary assembly – drawing individuals from both the Dutch and Portuguese populations, but the Portuguese planters never reconciled themselves to Dutch rule.

English colonization of the Caribbean assumed a form similar to the Portuguese captaincy system. Noblemen were awarded islands from the Crown as Lord Proprietors (unfortunately, King Charles granted conflicting patents, which led to legal wrangling and the neglect of colonists). Financed by a syndicate of merchants in London who were also his creditors, the Earl of Carlisle was appointed Lord Proprietor of the Caribbee Islands, which included St. Kitts, Nevis and Barbados. Carlisle appointed the governors of each island and received his rents and dues but left management of trade and production to the merchants and the settlers themselves. However, even more than colonization in North America, Caribbean settlements were also sponsored by competing companies of merchants or religious groups. A company formed by prominent Puritans in 1629 settled Providence Island.

Of all of these new outposts in the Lesser Antilles, English Barbados proved to be the earliest and most spectacular success. As was true on other islands, the English settlers first experimented with tobacco and cotton cultivation but soon turned to sugarcane. The land and climate was perfect and the island attracted many immigrants and indentured servants. By 1643, there were thirty-seven thousand Englishmen in the island. The sugar boom took off in the 1640s, and by 1650 little Barbados – 166 square miles – was most likely the richest plantation economy in the New World. As the plantation system developed, planters required more labor but the island attracted fewer indentured servants. Planters consolidating their ever-larger plantations bought out small landholders. A report in 1667 noted that there were seven hundred considerable proprietors while "12,000 good men formerly proprietors have gone off." The forty thousand white population of Barbados in 1645 had declined to twelve thousand by 1695. For a time, criminals were transported – "Barbadoed" – to the island to finish their terms as virtual slaves. This trickle of laborers proved inadequate but the Dutch, and later English and French traders, brought enslaved Africans. There were only a few hundred slaves on the island in 1640 but by 1705 their number had increased to forty-six thousand. Barbados began a sugar revolution in the Caribbean, which was followed by other English and then French islands.

For nearly fifty years, the development of an English Atlantic empire had been a private and largely inadvertent enterprise. Under the Lord Protector Oliver Cromwell and his Western Design, the British state came to consider colonization and empire as a matter of national interest. In 1654–5, an aggressive England mounted a massive expedition to seize Spanish Hispaniola. The 2,500-man expedition attacked the island and was repulsed. As a consolation prize, the English force invaded and seized the underpopulated and relatively undefended island of Jamaica. Its value, noted an English observer, lay in its location, "lying in the very belly of all commerce." Emigrants from Barbados, former indentured servants and smallholders, largely accomplished the settlement of Jamaica. In time, Jamaica itself became a major sugar producer but it was also large enough to accommodate all types of landholdings. The expansion of the sugar plantation system is shown by population growth and stagnation. In 1673, there were 7,700 whites on the island and about 9,500 black slaves. Fifty years later, the white population had declined to a little over 7,000 whereas the slave population had exploded to 74,000. In the rough interior of Jamaica, communities of escaped blacks, maroon towns, existed and harassed plantations. They had come into existence at the time of the English invasion when the Spanish abandoned the island and their slaves fled into the bush.

French colonization of the Caribbean at first followed the Dutch example by giving full responsibility to a semiprivate company, eventually called the

Compagnie des Isles de l'Amérique, the Company of the Isles of America. However, unlike New France, Frenchmen eagerly indentured themselves to come to the West Indies. By 1645, there were more than 8,500 settlers in the French islands. In 1647, the company sold its privileges to the governors of each island, in effect, creating proprietary colonies. Wars with the Caribs on Martinique, Dominica and Guadaloupe, as well as attacks from the English, retarded development based on tobacco and sugar cultivation compared to the more prosperous English Caribbean. With the defeat of the Dutch in Brazil in 1654, several hundred Dutch planters arrived in the French islands and accelerated the development of a plantation system. Approximately 1,200 Brazilian Dutch with their slaves settled in Martinique and Guadaloupe after the reconquest. With the Dutch providing knowledge, mill technology, credit, slaves and ships to carry their sugar to Amsterdam, the French sugar islands started to boom during the second half of the century (see Map 5.4).

Under Mazarin's leadership, development of the French colony on the Wild Coast, Cayenne, was encouraged but with little success. Under the sponsorship of different and transitory merchant companies, the French sent three expeditions to the Wild Coast from the 1640s to the 1660s, and had to fight the Dutch and then the English more than once to recapture their colony. It was all Colbert could do to simply hang on to the territory. As a result of this conflict and a notable lack of slaves, Cayenne languished. At the time of Colbert's death in 1683, Cayenne had a total population of only eight hundred people, men mostly, which included whites, *métis* and slaves. By comparison, tiny Martinique at the same time had a population of sixteen thousand.

When the successor company of the *Compagnie des Isles de l'Amérique* became bankrupt and was dissolved in 1674, the crown assumed direct control of the islands including western Hispaniola, Saint Domingue. Despite local rebellions, supreme command of all the islands was given to a viceroy-like official, a Governor-General, and each island – as in New France – was governed by governors who held civil and military powers. Somewhat later, intendants and sovereign councils were phased in. Intendants were given authority over finances, administration and economic regulation. A sovereign council was created and headed by the Governor-General and became the civil administration, which was also a court of appeal, and was composed of government officials such as councilors, an attorney general, a recorder and a bailiff. In 1663, there were two sovereign councils in the West Indies at Martinique and Guadaloupe.

English and French colonization of the Lesser Antilles received considerable backing from the Dutch, who operated not only out of Amsterdam and the other Dutch ports but who also possessed merchant colonies in London, Bristol, La Rochelle, La Havre and Honfleur as well. Individual merchants helped finance tobacco and sugar plantations and extend credit. The WIC supplied slaves from Guinea, and the Company eagerly shipped those staples (tobacco and sugar) to Amsterdam. Barbadian Englishmen also traveled to Dutch Brazil to learn the techniques of sugar planting and milling. In his *Description of Barbados*, John Scott in 1650 described the Dutch as "the great assistants to the Plantations since they give large credits to

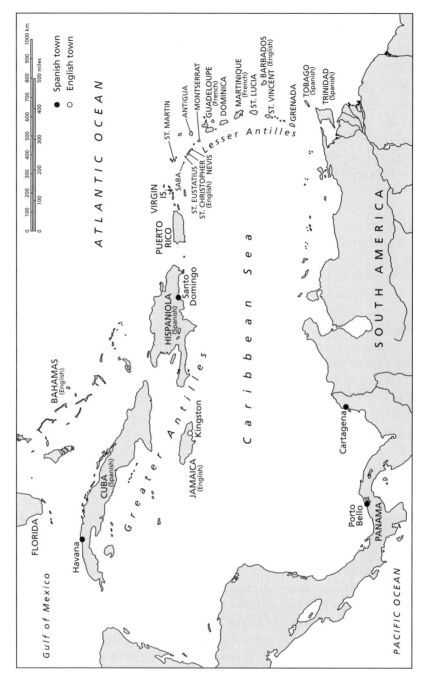

Map 5.4. The West Indies in the Seventeenth Century.

Table 5.3. Europeans on the move, 1500–1700

European movements	Date	Population
Spanish migrants to America	1500–1700	500,000
Portuguese overseas mariners, officials and colonists	1500	10,000
Portuguese in Africa	1650	2,000
Portuguese migrants to Brazil	1500–1700	100,000
British migrants to Ireland	1500–1700	200,000
British migrants to the Americas	1600–1700	390,000
French migrants to the Americas	1600–1700	45,000
Dutchmen employed overseas in commerce and shipping	1670–1688	64,000
Dutch migrants to South America, the West Indies and Africa	1600–1700	15,000

Sources: Woodrow Borah, "The Mixing of Populations," and Magnus Mörner, "Spanish Migration to the New World Prior to 1810: A Report on the State of Research," in *First Images of America: The Impact of the New World on the Old*, edited by Fredi Chiappelli (1976), Vol. II, pp. 707–22, 737–82; A. J. R. Russell-Wood, *The Portuguese Empire, 1415–1808: A World on the Move* (1998), pp. 58–63; Timothy J. Coates, *Convicts and Orphans: Forced and State-Sponsored Colonizers in the Portuguese Empire, 1550–1755* (2001); Robin Cohen (ed.), *The Cambridge Survey of World Migration* (1995); see Part Two: "European colonization and settlement," pp. 11–43; Nicolas Canny (ed.), *Europeans on the Move: Studies on European Migration, 1500–1800* (1994); P. C. Emmer and M. Mörner (eds.), *European Expansion and Migration: Essays on the Intercontinental Migration from Africa, Asia and Europe* (1992); and Jonathan Israel, *The Dutch Republic: Its Rise, Greatness, and Fall, 1477–1806* (1995), pp. 934–45.

the inhabitants and during the misfortune of the civil war in England, they administered all the trade in the western colonies, provided the islands with Negroes, coopers, boilers and many other things."

By the mid-seventeenth century, the Atlantic and Indian Oceans appeared to be Dutch. The Dutch were enjoying the best days of their Golden Age, which coincided with the most prosperous years of the WIC. The population of the United Provinces had grown to nearly 2 million, and Amsterdam, the queen of the Atlantic, had a population of 140,000. When Portugal rebelled in 1640 and regained its independence from Spain, Lisbon and Salvador – despite Dutch occupation of Portuguese territories in Brazil and Africa – were reopened to Dutch shipping. The Spanish fully recognized Dutch independence in 1648 with the Treaty of Münster (thus concluding the Eighty Years War), ended hostilities in the New World and similarly reopened Spanish peninsular ports to Dutch shipping. Just one of the seven Dutch provinces, Holland – albeit the dominant commercial province – possessed a fleet of over 600 fishing vessels and 1,750 merchant ships. The VOC dominated European trade in Asia and the WIC dominated trade in the Atlantic and managed colonies in North America, the Caribbean, South America and trading posts and castles on the coast of Africa. There were not enough Dutchmen to man the scores of outposts and thousands of ships at sea; many of the sixty-four thousand men employed in Dutch shipping were Danes, Norwegians and Germans (see Table 5.3).

After nearly a decade of some uncertainty and preoccupation with European affairs, by the late 1640s the Portuguese were prepared to give up India and concentrate their efforts to save Angola and Brazil. The crown dispatched an armada of some thirty-four ships and six thousand soldiers to

Brazil in 1647 under the command of Salvador Correia de Sá e Benevides, the son of the governor of Rio de Janeiro and the new governor of Angola. The expedition was sent to end a Dutch siege of Salvador but when it arrived, the Dutch had already pulled out. The fleet then recrossed the Atlantic and easily recaptured Luanda and São Tomé in 1648. The force was then redeployed to fight the Dutch in Pernambuco. Three years before, Luso-Brazilians in Pernambuco had rebelled against Dutch rule and begun a grinding guerrilla war. With guerrillas attacking from the interior and Salvador Correia and his armada attacking from the sea, the Luso-Brazilian forces won the first and second battles of Guararapes. Olinda fell in 1648, and finally Recife in 1654. When the Dutch had lost Angola in 1648, "the nerve of Brazil," they lost an assured supply of slaves and thus the lifeblood of the colony. The battle of Brazil was won partially in Africa. As Father Antonio Vieira stated, "Without negroes there is no Pernambuco, and without Angola there are no negroes." However, it was won primarily in Brazil itself. Brazilian sugar financed the War of Restoration, and Luso-Brazilians fought it. This effort and the subsequent shortage of capital compounded by high taxes led to the decline of Brazil's northeastern sugar economy in the second half of the seventeenth century.

Defeated in Brazil, the Dutch redeployed their capital and energy in the Americas. The islands of Curaçao and St. Eustatius became valuable slave trading and smuggling depots while Elmina on the Gold Coast became a center of the Dutch slave trade. A number of merchants and planters from New Holland relocated to the Dutch settlements – Berbice, Suriname, Essequibo and Demerara – on the Wild Coast. Guiana colonies often changed imperial overseers: for example, Surinam was originally settled by Zeelanders, seized by an English force in 1651 and reconquered in 1667. The Society of Surinam, which administrated the colony for the WIC, the city of Amsterdam and a nobleman investor, envisioned the colony as a "second Brazil." By the late eighteenth century, there were approximately four hundred plantations producing sugar, coffee, cotton and cacao with the labor of fifty thousand Indian and, primarily, African slaves. According to Wim Kooster, the planters succeeded "in making Surinam the colony with the highest productivity in the Americas."

Dutch primacy in Atlantic trade in the mid-seventeenth century came to be viewed as a national threat to the English government, and a little later by the French government. Beginning in 1651, the English enacted a series of Navigation Acts intended to take trade out of Dutch hands. For example, the 1651 Act prohibited the importation of goods into England except in English vessels or in vessels of the country producing the goods. This was clearly a commercial attack upon the Dutch, and the Dutch saw it as such and went to war with England to force it to reverse policy. The war of 1652–4 was the first in a series of three Anglo-Dutch wars (the other two were in 1665–7 and 1672–4) concerning the new rules of commerce, which historians have named mercantilism. The English merchant fleet greatly increased in number during the Dutch wars as a result of seizures of enemy vessels, some one thousand ships in the first war alone. The Anglo-Dutch wars weakened and ultimately ended Dutch primary in Atlantic commerce. By the beginning of the eighteenth century, Britain was the rising Atlantic commercial and naval power, with France as its major commercial rival. A popular rhyme in England ran, "Make wars with Dutchmen, Peace with Spain, then we shall have money and trade again."

Louis XIV and his ministers Mazarin and Colbert initiated the French response to Dutch primacy in trade. In 1658, the French began a modest tariff system designed to help French shipping and industry without antagonizing the Dutch. Colbert took a more aggressive program of mercantilist initiatives with the *Exclusif*, a rule allowing only ships from designated French ports to trade with French colonies. In 1664, tariffs were raised on most imports and a prohibitively high tariff levied on imported refined sugar, one of Amsterdam's most profitable trades. A high Dutch official suspected a French intent to "damage the commerce of this state... and divert it there." In 1667, Colbert brought out a second tariff list that was a serious attack upon Dutch commerce: there were significant tariffs on Dutch fine cloth, Delfware, Gouda pipes, East India wares, herring, whale products, tobacco and other imports. Given that France was the Republic's largest market for many of these products, Dutch trade experienced a considerable reduction. Under military pressure in 1678, France canceled the tariff list of 1667 and Dutch trade recovered somewhat in the 1680s. Louis returned to his *guerre de commerce* in 1687, reimposed the 1667 list and added additional provisions such as prohibiting all Dutch textiles and herring. Louis's "commercial war," according to Jonathan I. Israel, marked the turning point in the Dutch overseas trading system. After the 1680s, growth in Dutch trade contracted and eventually trade experienced an absolute decline.

The coast of West Africa became an intense arena of Dutch, English and, to a lesser extent, French conflict in the second half of the seventeenth century. The French focused their limited slave trade in Senegal and the Gambia. The Senegal Company established a fort at Gorée Island in 1671 and Fort Saint Louis on the lower Senegal. There was one post in Guinea. The company was barely a going concern. Colbert was forced to offer special incentives to the company to have it send eight ships a year to Africa. Until the 1690s, Dutch and English traders supplied most slaves purchased in the French West Indies. The English maintained a weak fort in Sierra Leone. Most European trading posts and castles were located in a one-hundred mile strip along the Gold Coast. From the 1630s to the early 1660s, the Dutch West India Company dominated the coast of Guinea with its headquarters at the former Portuguese trade castle São Jorge da Mina, now simply referred to as Elmina. The Dutch maintained other fortified castles at Butre, Shama, Apam, Sekondi, Axim, Mouri, Cormantin and Accra as well as a number of unfortified "strong-houses" and trading posts. The Dutch clearly were the strongest commercial and military power in Guinea from the 1630s until the beginning of the eighteenth century.

Beginning in the 1660s, the English moved into the coast permanently and became seriously engaged in the slave trading business. The Company of Royal Adventurers to Africa was granted a monopoly of the supply of African slaves to the English colonies and needed permanent African bases on the coast to compete with the Dutch. The Company seized the Swedish fort at Cabo Corso in 1664 and ten years later built Cape Coast Castle on that site. It became the headquarters of the English slave trade in Africa and the newly chartered Royal African Company (RAC). Jean Barbot, a Huguenot who sailed for the English, wrote in 1689 that the English castle is "the largest and most beautiful on all that coast next to St. George of Elmina." The RAC also maintained Fort Royal next door to Cape Coast Castle, which it had purchased from Danish slave traders in 1688, Dixcove Fort at Dickie's Cove, Fort English at Anomabu and other fortified stations at Anashan, Egya, Tantum, Winneba, Shido, Accra and Prampram. The RAC maintained a total of seventeen forts and posts in Africa, manned by about two hundred or three hundred employees. "It is evident this [slave] Trade cannot be carried on but by a constant maintaining of Forts upon the place, and Ships of war to protect the ships of Trade," supporters of the Company argued in a 1680 pamphlet. This was the case in part because "the Dutch, Danes, French and other Nations, that likewise Trade in the same Country, are ever more vigilant for their own profit, frequently instigating the Natives against us, as well as by their own force, to extirpate and destroy the English Commerce there."

Other sundry European companies, princes and merchant adventurers also joined in the trade. The Swedes arrived in mid-century but were soon largely bought out or kicked out by the English. The headquarters of the Danish slave trade was located in Christianborg castle beginning in 1661, and remained in business for a century. The governor of Christianborg supervised nine subordinate forts and posts on the Gold Coast. The Great Elector of Brandenburg-Prussia founded the Brandenburg Company in 1683, which maintained the impressive castle Gross-Friedrichsburg. Because this company could find no German merchants experienced in the slave trade, its first governors in Guinea were Dutch slave traders.

The 170 miles that constituted the Gold Coast was home to roughly two dozen fortified castles, trading posts and lesser outposts in the late seventeenth century. Most of the castles and posts were either Dutch or English whose holdings were intermingled. During the Anglo-Dutch wars, each national company tried to capture the castles of the other, and real estate often changed hands more than once. West of the Gold Coast was a long succession of lagoons and swamps, followed by the so-called Slave Coast at the Bight of Benin and Bight of Biafra, bends in the coast on each side of the Niger delta. There Europeans erected no castles but traded at the African towns of Whydah, Bonny and New and Old Calabar. The Kingdom of Benin, which had prohibited the export of male slaves in 1516, continued this policy until the eighteenth century. South of the Bight of Biafra was the island of São Tomé and much further south Angola, both of which remained Portuguese colonies.

The Dutch West India Company was both a product and progenitor of the Dutch Golden Age. Its decline mirrored that of the Republic. Peace with Spain beginning in 1648 did not favor the company, which had profited so much from privateering. War with England from the 1650s to the 1670s overextended its resources, thus making it impossible to hang onto Brazil. In a 1645 report, the Provincial States of Holland accurately predicted, "Without

Brazil all other conquests of the company will be worthless." Ten years after
the loss of Brazil, the English snatched New Netherland in North America.
Commander Richard Nicolls of the conquering force informed Governor
Peter Stuyvesant, "the right and title of His Majesty to these parts of America
is indisputable." On the coast of Africa, the English seized the Dutch posts
at Cape Verde, Gorée and moved into the Gold Coast in force. Only the conquest of English Surinam during the second Anglo-Dutch War, which gave
The Netherlands possession of nearly the entire Guiana coast, brightened
what was generally a slow but inexorable death of the once-great company.
War with France in the early 1670s, an invasion of The Netherlands and a
combined Anglo-French war against the Dutch at sea further weakened the
Republic. In 1674, the WIC declared bankruptcy and dissolved the original partnership. A New West India Company was then established, which
expanded Amsterdam's investment considerably while reducing Zeeland's
stake. The New WIC focused on the slave trade to the Americas and the gold
trade in Guinea and stayed in business until 1791.

By the end of the second Anglo-Dutch War in 1667, European colonial
possessions in the Caribbean were pretty much finalized. During the preceding four decades, nearly all of the English, French and Dutch islands had
changed hands at least one time, and often many more. For example, after
it was initially lost by the Spanish, St. Martin was held by the French five
different times and by the Dutch four different times. There remained certain
"naval forces" in the Atlantic in a state of permanent war against England,
France, The Netherlands, Spain and Portugal. Born in the maritime struggles against the Spanish and Portuguese monopolies, these freelance raiders,
"buccaneers" as they were called, came to be a force to be feared and fought.

5.5 Buccaneers

During the sixteenth and first half of the seventeenth centuries, French,
English and Dutch raiders of Spanish and Portuguese shipping and ports
generally acted under the authorization of their governments. For example,
the English monarch granted merchants and captains "Letters of Marque and
Reprisal" that authorized attacks on Spanish shipping and ports. This legal
document required that the privateer captains deliver to an admiralty court
their captured ships, whereupon everyone would legally carve up a share of
the spoils from king and the admiralty to captain and crew. These privateers
became invaluable military forces in time of war in an age when permanent
navies did not really exist. Until the late seventeenth century, the power of
Europe generally did not recognize truces and peace agreements outside of
Europe, what was called in the Atlantic "beyond the line." Therefore, privateers were tolerated and often encouraged, even in peacetime. In the second
half of the seventeenth century, there was often little meaningful difference
between a privateer and an independent sea raider, that is, a pirate. Letters
of Marque and Reprisal were spread around like candy to spoiled children.

When the French, English and the Dutch were becoming established in the
Caribbean in the early to mid-seventeenth century, privateers were important

naval forces in their own right, allies to vulnerable settlers and often "the great fear that possess'd the Spaniards." Perhaps the first commerce-raiding outpost to appear in the Caribbean arose in mostly French Tortuga, just northwest of Hispaniola. These raiders became widely known as *boucaniers* or buccaneers, after a Tupi Indian word for a smoking frame (*boucan*) or grill used to roast the wild cattle on the island. These raiders were also called "freebooters" in the sense they that soldiered without pay for booty. To the Dutch, a commerce raider was a *vrijbuiter*, which the French translated to *flibustier*. The English and French words "pirate" simply derived from similar Latin and Greek words to handle similar problems in the Mediterranean Sea thousands of years earlier.

In 1630, the same year the Puritan colony of Massachusetts Bay was founded in New England, a second Puritan colony was founded on Providence Island off the Caribbean coast of Nicaragua. To its Puritan founders, the island's main attraction was also its main problem: "it lying in the heart of the Indies & the mouth of the Spaniards." The Providence Island colony had little success as an agricultural settlement, but a change in foreign policy and the issuance of Letters of Marque and Reprisal to the Providence Island Company in 1626 turned the island into a privateering base and a new source of profit (although truth be told, there were already privateers about). Thomas Gage, the English Dominican who traveled through the Spanish world, quoted Spaniards at Cartagena in 1637 as cursing Providence as "a den of Thieves and Pirates." In 1641, the Spanish retook the island. Thereafter, the Spanish and the buccaneers fought over the island, its harbors and inlets for location and control for decades.

After the English seized Jamaica in 1655, that island in the center of the Spanish Caribbean became the center of privateering and privacy. At this time, Tortuga was in Spanish hands, as was Providence Island. To maintain possession of the island, England issued Letters of Marque to French, Dutch, Danish, Italian, Swedish, Portuguese and English captains. One of Jamaica's first historians, Bryan Edwards, noted that it had been observed that "nothing contributed so much to the settlement and opulence of this island in early times, as the resort to it of those men called Bucaniers; the wealth which they acquired having been speedily transferred to people whose industry was employed in cultivation or commerce." But, he continued, these men were not "piratical plunderers and public robbers which they are commonly represented." Because of the Spanish War – a just war, he noted – these buccaneers "were furnished with regular letters of marque and reprisal." The first royal governors of Jamaica established the seaport and capital city of Port Royal, which attracted privateers and pirates as well as merchants, tavern-keepers, runaway servants, prostitutes, slaves, Protestants, Catholics and Jews. Port Royal had five forts, four churches, one synagogue, nineteen taverns and, with nearly 3,000 inhabitants in 1680, was the third largest town in English America. Encouraged by the royal governor, this town sent fleets of privateers between 1665 and 1671 under Henry Morgan to plunder Spanish seaports on the coast of Cuba, Panama, Venezuela and Nicaragua. His raid on Portobelo, Panama, in 1670 was no minor foray: his fleet included thirty-eight ships and had an armed force of more than two thousand Englishmen,

Frenchmen and Anglo-Americans. When he crossed the isthmus, his 175 mules were loaded with silver plate and coin. It was the last great buccaneer raid. Despite England's promise to Spain to end privateering and suppress piracy in the Treaty of Madrid in 1670, not to mention the anti-piracy Jamaica Act of 1683, buccaneers continued to freely operate from Port Royal until the end of the century. Over time the action was better elsewhere. "The scum of the Indies drifted away from Jamaica," writes Violet Barbour, "to Hispaniola and Tortuga where aliens of any nation or reputation were received with obliging catholicity." Port Royal, the Sodom of the English Atlantic World, was swallowed up by a great earthquake in June 1692 that utterly destroyed the port. The government of Jamaica rebuilt a new port on firmer ground, Kingston, across the harbor, and the buccaneers moved to new haunts in the Bahamas, North America and West Africa.

During the second half of the seventeenth century, buccaneers not only attacked Spanish and Portuguese shipping and ports but also English, French and Dutch shipping and American and African ports and posts. When wars erupted between the northern European powers, governments and their colonial authorities began issuing Letters of Marque to captains of just about any nationality so long as the holder was clear who the "enemy" was this time. During the Anglo-Dutch Wars and the Franco-Dutch Wars of the second half of the seventeenth century, the English in Jamaica and the French in Tortuga enlisted buccaneers to cruise against the Dutch. In 1666 when France entered the war on the side of the Netherlands, the Dutch in Curaçao and the French in Tortuga directed buccaneers against English islands and trade. In 1673, the Dutch launched a serious effort to seize the French West Indies and Dutch privateers, assisting the effort, brought more than twenty-five French prizes into Curaçao that year. During the next several years of the war, aggressive Dutch privateers eliminated a few hundred French buccaneers and brought about the decline of commercial traffic from France. While no friend of any government, the buccaneers themselves in the seventeenth century generally preferred to enrich themselves from the Spanish and stay away from English, French and Dutch prizes. The Spanish had more hard money and the buccaneers had more reasons to take vengeance on them. The French buccaneer, the Sieur de Grammont, in 1683 mounted a massive raid on Vera Cruz, the principal port of New Spain, which yielded four days of uninterrupted looting. The Dutch buccaneers Nikolaqas van Hoorn and Laurens de Graaf two years later attacked the city of Campeche, on the eastern coast of the Yucatan peninsula, and left the city in ashes after looting the government treasury, churches and private houses. A Dutch buccaneer known as Roche Brasiliano, originally from the Dutch city of Groningen, provides an example of the buccaneer's basic animosity to the Spanish. A fellow buccaneer described Brasiliano's particularly infamous modus operandi:

> Unto the Spaniards he always showed himself very barbarous and cruel, only out of an inveterate hatred he had against that nation. Of these he commanded several to be roasted alive upon wooden spits, for no other crime than that they would not show him the places, or hog-yards, where he might steal swine.

Document 5.3
The Buccaneers of America

Alex. Olivier Exquemelin, 1684

A certain Pirate, born in Portugal, and from the name of his Country, Called Bartholomew Portugues, was cruzing in his Boat from Jamaica (wherein he had only thirty men, and four small guns) upon the Cape de Corriente, in the Island of Cuba. In this place he met with a great ship, that came from Maracaibo and Cartagena, bound for the Havana, well provided, with twenty great guns, and threescore and ten Men, between passengers and Mariners. This ship he presently assaulted, but found as strongly defended by them that were on board. The Pirate escaped the first encounter, resolving to attacque her more vigorously then before, seeing he had sustained no great damage hitherto. This resolution of his, he boldly performed, renewing his assaults so often, till that after a long and dangerous fight, he became Master of the great Vessel. The Portugues lost only ten men, and had four wounded, so that he had still remaining twenty fighting men, whereas the Spaniards had double the same number. Having possessed themselves of such a Ship, and the wind being contrary to return unto Jamaica, they resolved to steer their course towards the Cape of Saint Antony (which lieth on the Western side of the Isle of Cuba), there to repair themselves, and take in fresh water, of which they had great necessity, at that time.

Being now very near unto the Cape abovementioned, they unexpectedly met with three great Ships, that were coming from New-Spain, and bound for the Havana. By these as not being able to escape, they were easily retaken both Ship, and Pirates. Thus they were all made prisoners, through the sudden change of fortune, and found themselves poor, oppress'd, and stript of all the riches they had purchased so little before. The Cargo of this Ship consisted in one hundred, and twenty thousand weight of Cacao nuts, the cheifest ingredient of that rich liquor called Chocolate, and threescore and ten thousand pieces of eight. Two days after this misfortune, there happened to arise an huge and dangerous tempest, which largely separated the Ships from one another. The great Vessel, wherein the Pirates were, arrived at Campeche, where many considerable Merchants came to salute, and welcom the Captain thereof. These presently knew the Portugues Pirate, as being him who had committed innumerable excessive insolences upon those coasts, not only infinite Murthers and Robberies, but also lamentable *incendiums*, which those of Campeche, still perceived very fresh in their memory.

Hereupon the next day after their arrival, the Magistrates of the City sent several of their Officers, to demand and take into custody, the criminal prisoners, from on board the ship, with intent to punish them, according to their deserts. Yet fearing least the Captain of those Pirates should escape out of their hands on shore (as he had formerly done, being once their prisoner in the City before,) they judg'd it more convenient to leave him safely guarded on board the Ship, for that present. In the mean while they caused a Gibbet to be erected, whereupon to hang him the very next day, without any other form of process, then to lead him from the Ship, unto the place of punishment. The rumour of this future tragedy, was presently brought unto Bartholomew Portugues his ears, whereby he fought all the means he could to escape that night. With this design he took two earthen Jars, wherein the Spaniards usually carry wine from Spain unto the West-Indies, and stopp'd them very well: intending to use them for swimming, as those, who are unskillful in that art, do *calabacas*, a form of pumpkins in Spain: and in other places empty bladders. Having made this necessary preparation, he waited for the night, when all should be at sleep; even the Centry that guarded him. But seeing he could not escape his vigilancy, he secretly purchased a knife, and with the same gave him such a mortal stab, as suddainly depriv'd him of life, and the possibility of making any noise. At that instant, he committed himself to Sea, with those two earthen jars aforementioned, and by their help and support, though never having learn'd to swim, he reached the shore. Being arrived upon the land, without any delay, he took his refuge in the Woods, where he hid himself for three days, without daring to appear, nor eating any other food then wild herbs.

Those of the City failed not the next day, to make a diligent search for him in the woods, where they concluded him to be. This strict enquiry Portugues had the convenience to espy from the hallow of a Tree, wherein he lay absconded. Hence perceiving them to return without finding, what they fought for, he adventur'd to sally forth towards the coasts, called *del Golfo triste*, forty leagues distant from the City of Campeche. Hither he arrived within a fortnight after his escape from the Ship. In which space of time, as also afterwards, he endured extream hunger, thirst, and fears, of falling again into the hands of the Spaniards. For during all this journy he had no other provision with him, then a small *calabaca*, with a little water: Neither did he eat any thing else, then a few shell fish, which he found among the Rocks, nigh the Sea-shore. Besides that, he was compell'd to pass as yet some Rivers, not knowing well to swim. Being in this distress, he found an old board, wherein did stick a few great nailes. There he took and with no small labour, whetted against a stone, until that he had made them capable of cutting like unto knives, tho very imperfectly. With these, and no better instruments, he cut down some branches of Trees, the which with twigs, and Osiers he joyn'd together, and made as well as he could, a boat, or rather a wafte, wherewith he wafted over the Rivers. Thus he arrived finally at the Cape of *del Golfo triste*, as was said before; where he happened to find a certain Vessel of Pirates, who were great Comrades of his own, and were lately come from Jamaica.

Unto these Pirates, he instantly related all his adversities, and misfortunes. And withal demanded of them, they would fit him with a boat, and twenty men. With which company alone, he promised to return unto Campeche, and assault the Ship, that was in the River, by which he had been taken, and escaped fourteen days before. They easily granted his request, and equipped him a boat, with the said number of Men. With this small company he set forth towards the execution of his design; which he bravely performed eight days after he separated from his Comrades at the Cape of *del Golfo triste*. For being arrived at the River of Campeche, with an undaunted courage, and without any rumour of noise, he assaulted the Ship aforementioned. Those that were on board, were perswaded, this was a boat from land, that came to bring *contra banda* goods; and hereupon were not in any posture of defence. Thus the Pirates laying hold on this occasion, assaulted them without any fear of ill success, and in short space of time, compelled the Spaniards to surrender.

Now being Masters of the Ship, they immediately weighed Anchor, and set sail, determining to fly from the Port, least they should be pursued by other Vessels. This they did with extremity of joy, feeling themselves possessours of such a brave Ship. Especially Portugues, their Captain, who now by a second turn of fortunes wheel, was become rich and powerful again, who had been so lately in that same Vessel, a poor miserable prisoner, and condemned to the Gallows. With this great purchase he designed in his mind greater things; which he might well hope to obtain, feeling he had found in the Vessel great quantity of rich Merchandise, still remaining on board although the plate had been transported into the City. Thus he continued his Voyage towards Jamaica for some days. But coming nigh unto the Isle of Pinos on the South-side of the Island of Cuba, fortune suddainly turned her back unto him once more, never to shew him her countence again. For a horrible storm arising at Sea occasion'd the Ship to split against the Rocks or Banks called Jardines. Insomuch that the Vessel was totally lost, and Portugues, with his Companions, escaped in a Canow. After this manner he arrived at Jamaica, where he remained no long time. Being only there, till he could prepare himself to seek his fortune anew, which from that time proved always adverse unto him.

This is one of many pirate yarns spun by the French buccaneer Exquemelin, who first came to the Americas as an indentured servant. Exquemelin's "true account" was apparently first published in Dutch, Spanish and then English. *Source: Bucaniers of America: Or, a true Account of the Most remarkable Assaults Committed of late years upon the Coasts of The West Indies*. Written originally in Dutch, by John Esquemeling, one of the Bucaniers, who was present at those Tragedies; and thence translated into Spanish, by Alonso de Bonne-maison, Doctor of Physick, and Practitioner at Amsterdam. Now faithfully rendered into English. London: Printed for William Crooke, at the Green Dragon without Temple-bar, 1684, pp. 95–103.

Jamaica was not the only colony in the West Indies with buccaneer origins. French buccaneers in Tortuga, known as "the Brethren of the Coast," were quite active during the last three decades of the seventeenth century. One buccaneer captain was so successful in his looting as to invest his wealth in Martinique and become the owner of the largest sugar plantation in the French West Indies. Buccaneers who found a hostile reception in their nation's different *entrepôts* in the Caribbean, or were welcome nowhere else, eventually made their way to Tortuga. It was from Tortuga in the seventeenth century that the French and other buccaneers began to colonize the western end of Hispaniola, which lay just a few miles from each other. In 1669, the governor of French Saint Domingue claimed there were 1,600 freebooters, hunters, settlers and indentured servants on Tortuga and the coast of Saint Domingue. Two years later, a navy captain estimated that about five hundred or six hundred freebooters and about one hundred *boucaniers* lived in the Cul-de-Sac alone, or Western District of Saint Domingue. The successful privateers and petty noblemen established tobacco and, later, sugar plantations. The Spanish officially recognized French possession of its new colony in the Treaty of Ryswick in 1697. During the next fifty years, Saint Domingue would become the most valuable European colony in the Atlantic.

By the late seventeenth century, the English, French and Dutch had achieved the recognition they had long sought from Spain of their New World colonies. The buccaneers that they themselves had commissioned so many times were increasingly not only interfering with but also seriously ravaging Atlantic commerce. The early eighteenth century would see the golden age of piracy and its brutal suppression.

By 1700, a new Atlantic system had been created. The Iberian monopoly of trade and colonization had been destroyed. The challengers of this monopoly – France, England and the Dutch Republic – in the previous two centuries had focused their energies on Spain and its weaker partner, Portugal. These three northwestern European countries confronted the first great superpower in modern European history. They first attacked commerce, then raided port cities, settled in a few distant and unoccupied territories and finally confronted the Spanish in the cockpit of the Americas, the "Spanish lake," at that time called the West Indies and today referred to as the Caribbean. In the sixteenth century, Spanish power was not rashly challenged. Although the power and military forces of the Spanish monarchy were overextended even during its most triumphal years, reprisals were undertaken and many of these were swift, brutal and successful.

In the seventeenth century, the Spanish Empire in the Atlantic was overwhelmed at sea. Even more the English, the French and particularly the Dutch invaded the Atlantic with thousands of merchantmen and warships (often there was no distinction between the two). Spanish shipping was swept from the ocean except for the annual treasure convoy, which was generally, although not always, too formidable to attack. The northwestern Europeans began to challenge the Iberians on land as well as at sea. All three nations cautiously occupied small outposts far from the Spanish in North and South America and on small islands in the Lesser Antilles. Success here led to bolder efforts elsewhere. The French attempted to colonize the Amazon basin and Florida. The Dutch temporarily seized many of the most valuable sugar-producing captaincies of Brazil as well as slave trading depots in Africa. They threw the Portuguese off the coast of Guinea. The English made an effort to seize Hispaniola, but settled for Jamaica instead. This seventeenth-century onslaught on the weakened Iberian powers was rebuffed in the regions of greatest importance. Florida and all of the major

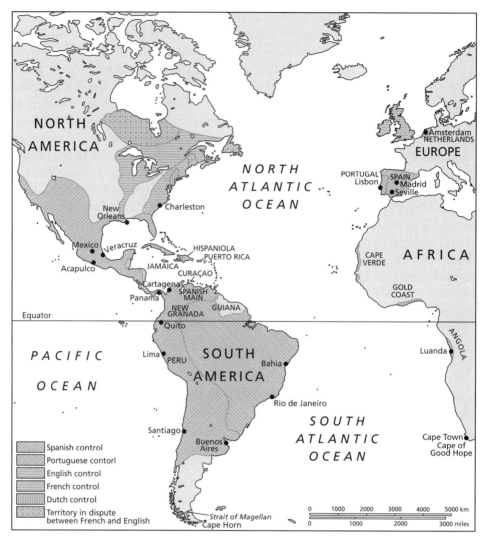

Map 5.5. The European Seaborne Empires.

(Greater Antillean) Caribbean islands and Mexico and Peru remained in Spanish hands. Portugal recaptured Brazil and Angola. The fundamental territorial structures of the Portuguese and Spanish empires in the Atlantic survived, weakened certainly but still intact at the dawn of the eighteenth century (see Map 5.5).

At first, the new American colonies of the French, English and Dutch were insignificant specks of settlements heavily dependent on their oceanic links to their home countries. In the mid- and latter decades of the seventeenth century they grew and prospered against all odds. The key to the success of most of the new colonies was the production and export of a valuable staple, the supply of slaves or the cooperation of Native Americans. In the eastern Caribbean and the Wild Coast of Guiana, that staple was sugar. In Virginia, it was tobacco, whereas in New France and up the Hudson River it was beaver pelts. With the exception of New France and New Netherland, planters believed their economic success and very livelihood was dependent upon a steady supply of African slave labor. Quickly, the English, French and Dutch plantation colonies then became multiracial societies where, in several extreme cases, a small European master class brutally dominated a vastly larger immigrant African population. However, despite similarities each region followed its own path. Brazil, Surinam and Barbados were plantation societies based on slave labor but they were also unique colonial societies. Englishmen streamed into New England, a land mostly devoid of any rich staple, for religious reasons or a desire to elevate one's status in society. In New Netherland, Dutch, Germans, English, French, Danes, Portuguese, Africans, Indians, Protestants, Catholics and Jews immigrated to a colony of great estates and farms, Indian traders, Company men, shippers, merchants, tavern keepers, artisans, slaves and all manner of religious ministers and preachers. Like New England and most New World colonies, New Netherland offered Europeans opportunity and a new beginning. The newly married couple Catalina Trico, a French-speaking teenager, and Joris Rapalje, a Flemish textile worker, sailed to the new Dutch colony on the island of Manhattes in 1624. One year after their arrival in the New World, Catalina gave birth to Sarah, the first of their eleven children. When she was thirty years old, Sarah declared herself the "first born Christian daughter of New Netherland." Joris went to work for the West India Company and, in time, came to own and run his own tavern. As they prospered, they set up a farm in the village of Breuckelen, across the river. In the early 1640s, Joris Rapalje was selected by the residents of New Amsterdam to serve on a council of twelve to advise the governor. In 1639, Sarah married the overseer of a tobacco plantation in a section of New Amsterdam that later became know as Greenwich Village. The descendants of Catalina and Joris Rapalje today, over 350 years later, have been estimated at upwards of one million.

The seventeenth century produced an Atlantic World contested by five powers. European coalitions, wars and peace treaties expanded into the Atlantic. In the second half of the century, England fought the Dutch in three maritime wars. The French also fought the Dutch at sea and on land. By the late seventeenth century, English and French rivalry began a series of wars that would dominate Europe and much of the Atlantic World until 1815. Great power rivalry and conflict, as well as colonization and trade, was complemented and complicated by the interests and actions of other players in the Atlantic: Indians and Africans.

5.6 Further Reading

Kenneth R. Andrews, *Trade, Plunder and Settlement: Maritime Enterprise and the Genesis of the British Empire, 1480–1630* (Cambridge, 1984).

Thomas Astley, *A New General Collection of Voyages and Travels*, 4 volumes (London, 1745–7).

Philip P. Boucher, *Les Nouvelles Frances: France in America, 1500–1815, An Imperial Perspective* (Providence, 1989).

C. R. Boxer, *The Dutch in Brazil, 1624–1654* (Oxford, 1957).

Nicolas Canny, *Kingdom and Colony: Ireland in the Atlantic World, 1560–1800* (Baltimore, 1988).

Nicolas Canny and Anthony Pagden, editors, *Colonial Identity in the Atlantic World, 1500–1800* (Princeton, 1987).

Ralph Davis, *The Rise of the Atlantic Economies* (Ithaca, 1973).

Bryan Edwards, *The History, Civil and Commercial, of the British Colonies in the West Indies*, 2 volumes (Dublin, 1793).

Allan Greer, *The People of New France* (Toronto, 1999).

Hugo Grotius, *The Freedom of the Seas*, translated by James Brown Scott (New York, 1916).

J. I. Israel, *The Dutch Republic and the Hispanic World, 1606–1661* (Oxford, 1982).

Harry Kelsey, *Sir Francis Drake: The Queen's Pirate* (New Haven, 1998).

Kris E. Lane, *Pillaging the Empire: Piracy in the Americas, 1500–1750* (Armonk, 1998).

Marc Lescarbot, *Nova Francia: Or the Description of that part of New France, which is one continent with Virginia*, translated by P. Erondelle (London, 1609).

Richard Ligon, *A True and Exact History of the Island of Barbados* (London, 1657).

D. W. Meinig, *The Shaping of America: A Geographical Perspective on 500 Years of History*, Volume 1: *Atlantic America, 1492–1800* (New Haven, 1986).

Anthony Pagden, *Lords of all the World: Ideologies of Empire in Spain, Britain and France, c. 1500– c. 1800* (New Haven, 1995).

James Pritchard, *In Search of Empire: The French in the Americas, 1670–1730* (Cambridge, 2004).

David Beers Quinn and Alison O. Quinn, editors, *The New American World: A Documentary History of North America to 1615*, 5 volumes (New York, 1979).

Sir Walter Raleigh, *The discoverie of the Large, Rich and Bewtiful Empyre of Guiana*, transcribed, annotated and introduced by Neil L. Whitehead (Norman, 1977).

Benjamin Schmidt, *Innocence Abroad: The Dutch Imagination and the New World, 1570–1670* (Cambridge, 2001).

Captain John Smith, *The General Historie of Virginia, New-England, and the Summer Isles* (London, 1624).

William Strachey, *The History of Travell into Virginia Bratania*, edited by Louis B. Wright and Virginia Freund (London, 1953).

Stanley J. Stein and Barbara H. Stein, *Silver, Trade, and War: Spain and America in the Making of Early Modern Europe* (Baltimore, 2000).

Marcus Rediker, *Between the Devil and the Deep Blue Sea: Merchant Seamen, Pirates and the Anglo-American Maritime World, 1700–1750* (Cambridge, 1993).

Chapter 6

Engagement

The Entangled Worlds of Indians and Europeans

"Atlantic America was the scene of a vast unplanned, uncontrolled, unstable, and unending encounter between European and Indian societies." D. W. Meinig's characterization of European-Indian relations is descriptive and evocative. What began in 1492 was an encounter and collision between Indians and Europeans as well as a sustained engagement among exceedingly diverse peoples for hundreds of years. Engagement meant mutual adaptation and conflict, alliance and conquest, and acculturation as a two-way interaction. Natives and Europeans were entangled with each other, that is, they were intricately intertwined in ways that transformed both. This complex engagement between two diverse groups of peoples over hundreds of years constitutes one of the most important themes in the history of the Atlantic World.

Because Indian populations, cultures and societies varied considerably, as did Europeans and their objectives, Native American and European entanglements were often quite different and distinct from place to place, creating different kinds of outcomes. A few broad patterns emerged. Large and complex native societies such as those in Mesoamerica and the Central Andes experienced military conquests and political subordination. Here Euroamerican conquest colonies incorporated Indian populations and cultures within complex hierarchical and multicultural societies. Where invading agricultural settlers sought the land of small-scale and decentralized native farming societies (generally on the coasts of South and North America), conflict was almost perpetual until the resisting native peoples were defeated, dispersed or placed in "pacified" enclaves within the colonial boundaries. Here Europeans often created frontiers separating themselves and their colonial cultures from independent native peoples. Where Europeans wanted valuable resources, which could be obtained from Indians only through trade, the need for cooperation constrained European behavior. This circumstance led to peaceful relationships shaped by negotiation and based on diplomacy between European and Indian societies. Similar conditions prevailed where rival European powers confronted each other and required Native Americans as military allies. The need for trade and alliances placed Europeans on a more equal footing with

Table 6.1. European and Euroamerican populations in
the Americas, 1600–1800

Region	1600/1650	1750/1800
Spanish America	450,000	3,200,000
Brazil	50,000	1,010,000
British North America	25,000	2,150,000
New France and Canada	3,000	75,000
Non-Spanish Caribbean	75,000	400,000
Totals	603,000	6,715,000

Note: These population figures are rough compilations from different major population centers and, within the two fifty-year time ranges, from different specific years, censuses and estimates.
Sources: Angel Rosenblat, *La población indígena y el mestizaje en América, 1492–1950*, 2 vols. (1954), pp. 88, 102; Nicolás Sánchez-Albornoz, "The Population of colonial Spanish America" and Mariza Luiza Marcílio, "The population of colonial Brazil" both in Leslie Bethell (ed.), *The Cambridge History of Latin America: Volume II: Colonial Latin America* (1984), pp. 3–63; D. W. Meinig, *The Shaping of America: A Geographical Perspective on 500 Years of History. Volume I: Atlantic America, 1492–1800* (1986), Table 4, pp. 288–9, 348; Allan Greer, *The People of New France* (1999), p. 19; The largest European and Euroamerican populations in the Caribbean were in the Spanish West Indies. The first census held in Cuba (1817) counted 291,000 *blancos* (whites). J. H. Parry and P. M. Sherlock, *A Short History of the West Indies* (1957), pp. 142–60, 224.

Indians and created complex alignments among the different European and Indian groups. A few native peoples adopted wild horses and were able to halt European expansion and establish a military frontier that lasted, in some cases, for centuries.

In short, different circumstances produced different new worlds in the Americas. In all of these worlds, Europeans one way or another depended upon Indians and their assistance, knowledge, customs and resources in the creation of their colonial societies. Europeans adopted certain native knowledge, technology, plants, language and more. The Americas experienced the select Indianization of European colonization and a greater Europeanization of native societies. In one direction, the engagement was mostly beneficial and constructive; in the other, it was almost entirely harmful and destructive. Over the long run, one of the most significant influences was the growth of European and Euroamerican populations in the Americas (see Table 6.1). This development occurred alongside the dramatic decline of native populations and, in time, transformed the history of the planet.

6.1 Savages

Indians were savages, barbarians, heathens, pagans and beasts. These characterizations, we assume, is how all Europeans saw native peoples. In 1625 Samuel Purchas, the English promoter who never traveled to America, described the Virginia Algonquian as "so bad people, having little of Humanity but shape, ignorant of Civility, of Arts, of Religion; more brutish than the beasts they hunt, more wild and unmanly than that unmanned wild Country which they range rather than inhabit." It is argued by certain intellectuals that Europeans developed a colonial discourse that denigrated native societies to conquer and exploit them. Indians were defined as barbarous and savage because they were rude and fierce, lawless and wild, naked and lewd. They lacked, Europeans argued, intelligible speech and eloquence, writing and literature, reason and religion, agriculture and property and – above all – civility. Because of their obvious deficiencies, "the Salvages became subject to the English."

Intellectuals, clerics, officials and settlers are on record dehumanizing this branch of the human family. The Spanish theologian Juan Ginés de Sepúlveda in the mid-sixteenth century emphasized Indians' "idolatries and their sins against nature," by which he meant cannibalism and incest. In his view, these sins against nature justified the Indian's status as a "natural slave." A number of Spanish intellectuals and writers debated the nature of barbarism, the different types of barbarians and Indians as barbarians. The first Indians that Europeans saw were often naked, which made them barbarians in the sense of being wild men. To one American bishop, Indians were "wild men of the woods, for which reason they could retain no Christian doctrine, nor virtue nor any kind of learning." Most commentators accepted the humanity of Indians but questioned whether these people were barbarians because they were pagans, uncivilized, without reason or naturally cruel and beastly. To the *conquistador* Hernando Cortés, the Mexica were both sophisticated (in their politics and material culture) and barbarian (in their paganism and fierce customs such as human sacrifice). To the Mestizo historian Garcilaso de la Vega, the Mexica and the Inka represented the highest stage of barbarism in America.

To the French in the sixteenth and seventeenth centuries, Indians were *les sauvages Américains*. In French, the word *sauvage* at this time meant wild or primitive as opposed to cultivated and domesticated. Unlike the Spanish, who adopted the name Indian (*indio*) to refer to the inhabitants of the Americas, the French did not use a specific name for Native Americans. Similarly, the Dutch in the seventeenth century referred to Indians as *wilden*, that is, wild men. However, the rather innocent word *sauvage*, as it came more and more to denote Indians, became more derogatory. "These men may very well and truly be called Wilde (*Sauvage*), " wrote Jacque Cartier, "because there is no poorer people in the world." The *Dictionnaire universal* of 1691 defined a *sauvage* as a man without regular habitation, without religion, law or civility. According to the dictionary, the Americas were peopled with *sauvages*, most of who were naked, shaggy cannibals. However, some French writers like Marc Lescarbot objected to the pejorative understanding of the word. "If we commonly call them Savages," he wrote in his early seventeenth-century history of New France, "the word is abusive and unmerited, for they are anything but that, as well be proved in the course of this history."

The English quickly picked up the word "savage" in reference to Indians, with the connotation of wild, fierce, cruel and barbarous. "Naked" as a

Figure 6.1. Cannibalism Among the Native Brazilians. From André Thevet, *Les singularitez de la France Antarctique* (Paris, 1558). Courtesy of the William L. Clements Library at the University of Michigan.

description became synonymous with savage. Sir George Peckham in 1583 wrote of "these Savages, being a naked kind of people, void of the knowledge of the discipline of war." Purchas argued that the duty of the colonist of Virginia was "not to make Savages and wild degenerate men of Christians, but Christians of those Savage, wild degenerate men." Although Dutch observers of Indians referred to natives as *wilden* and even "Americans," many nevertheless viewed them as barbarous or worse. The preacher Jonas Michaëlius, in a letter from Manhattan, described the natives as "proficient in all wickedness and ungodliness, devilish men, who serve nobody but the Devil."

We should remember that many Europeans of this age were extremely savage to one another, not to mention dogs and cats. From the fifteenth to the eighteenth centuries, European ecclesiastical and secular courts tried, tortured and executed tens of thousands of women (and somewhat fewer men) for the crime of *maleficium*, that is, maleficent magic or witchcraft. That was just in Europe. In the Americas and Africa, Europeans and European-Americans also tortured and executed women for the same reasons. Officials, clerics, soldiers and others tortured fellow Castilians, Rhinelanders, Hollanders, Normans and so on with such cruel and brutal devices as the rack (for stretching), the wheel (for twisting) the pillory (for whipping or holding a person's hands and head for long stretches of time), the scaffold (for lashing, whipping and hanging) and iron gags. Most of these instruments were located in specific dungeons, chambers of horror or public spaces. Europeans also tortured their God-fearing neighbors, fellow countrymen and coreligionists with such barbaric procedures as complete body dismembering by four horses (often called "drawing and quartering"), repeated "buzzings and chuckings" (simulated drowning), castration and the severing of other body parts, and the roasting and burning of parts of the body with boiling oil, sulfur, molten lead and by means of "raking over the coals." The list of tortures is just about endless. There was also the ever popular (I say, only somewhat in jest) burning at the stake. Of course, all of these procedures were applied to the living and produced very entertaining (from the point of view of the spectators) curses, incomprehensible shrieks and howls of pain from the victims, which became the main attraction of these spectacles.

Clearly, Europeans commonly categorized Indians as savages and barbarians in a discourse that sanctioned conquest, slavery, dispossession and exploitation. "Early modern Europe's construction of its collective Other in 'the New World' – its construction of the 'savage' or the 'Indian,'" writes Louis Montrose, "was accompanied by the symbolic and material destruction of the indigenous peoples of the Western Hemisphere, in systematic attempts to destroy their bodies and their wills, to suppress their cultures and to efface their histories." However, there was no one, homogeneous European understanding of Native Americans. There was no singular colonial discourse but a variety of discourses, and they were often discordant and sought diverse outcomes.

6.2 American Ethnography

Almost everything we know today about native societies before 1492 and about relations between Indians and Europeans during the sixteenth and seventeenth centuries are found in texts produced by Europeans, almost always with native guidance and sometimes with native texts. Writing about Indians began with Columbus' letter to Luis de Santángel in 1492. Thereafter, European explorers, conquerors, friars, traders, settlers, many and various others unleashed a flood of reports, accounts and histories about Indians that flowed from the pens and presses for centuries.

This writing can be categorized into a few different types. A part of it can be described as generally superficial and untrustworthy travel narratives or travelogues. Columbus, Amerigo Vespucci, Alvarez Chanca, Michele da Cuneo and Giovanni Verrazzano among others had the disadvantage of being the first, being transitory and being unable to communicate with Indians in any meaningful way. These early travelogues were guided by even earlier literary models of mostly invented travel accounts, some of the most important being Pliny the Elder's *Natural History*, the medieval *The Three Monks' Journey to Paradise* and the celebrated *The Travels of Sir John Mandeville*. The very popular and fictitious Mandeville updated Pliny's "fantastic ethnography" and was printed and translated time and again in the fifteenth century. This

book presented a diverse world of rich kingdoms, strange customs, cannibalistic peoples and monstrous beings like dog-headed men and one-legged
creatures whose feet could be used as parasols.

"We should not underestimate," writes Steven Greenblat, "the cynical
calculation with which the early travel texts were often put together." The
first travelers, explorers and conquerors desired to justify their own efforts
before royal authority, to legitimize possession and conquest, to convince
financial backers and settlers to support colonization and so on. In his letter on the first voyage, Columbus declared his complete success in finding a
corner of the Indies (Asia) in Hispaniola, where "there are many spices and
large mines of gold and other metals." He pretended he and the natives he
encountered could understand each other and that the natives believed the
Europeans had come from the sky. "I have not found the human monsters
which many people expected," Columbus wrote. However, he continued,
he had reports of a "people who are regarded in these islands as extremely
fierce and who eat human flesh." At first, Columbus thought these "canibales" were the soldiers of the Great Khan or Can. However, on his second
voyage he and other travelers such as Dr. Chanca came to believe native
reports that the fierce people of the eastern islands, the Caribs, were man-
eaters, although they never witnessed any acts of cannibalism.

It is difficult to find any truth behind the distinction begun by Columbus
between the cannibalistic Caribs of the eastern Caribbean and the peaceful
Aruaca or Taino of the Greater Antilles. Columbus and other early explorers
maintained that it was the Taino who named their enemies Caribs and who
originally charged them with man-eating. Historians now know that native
peoples across the Americas slandered their enemies to Europeans for various
and obvious reasons. In his new colonial settlement of Isabela on Hispaniola
in 1494, Columbus wrote to the crown recommending that he be allowed
to capture the man-eaters and send them to Castile so that they could learn
the language and be baptized. If the monarch would agree to this, Columbus
then recommended that caravels returning to Spain should carry "cannibal
slaves, a people so fierce, healthy, well-proportioned, and intelligent that,
once rid of that inhumanity, they would make better slaves than any others."
The crown decided that, for the time being, cannibalism was not a sufficient
justification for enslavement. From 1494 to 1503, the Spanish entered the
eastern Caribbean and frequently clashed with Caribs. In this period, the label
justified unprovoked acts of conquest. Europeans did not doubt cannibals
existed in the Caribbean (and, indeed, native cannibals did exist on the
continent) but their accounts of cannibals were always assumed, second-
hand or simply fantastic. With colonial pressure building, Queen Isabel in
a 1503 decree defined all natives who opposed the Spanish as "cannibals"
and further ordered, "They may be captured and are to be taken to these my
Kingdom and Domain and to other places to be sold."

We begin to see the consequences of politicized reporting. The distinction
between Carib and Taino justified a system of Indian slavery that was quickly
entrenched in the Caribbean and spread to the mainland. Indians declared
to be non-Caribs (and thus by definition, non-cannibals) were vassals of the
crown who were required to pay tribute and could be awarded to Spaniards

in *encomiendas*. Official recognition of a people as one or the other was often determined by the shifting power and influence of competing groups of Spaniards. Not surprisingly, slave traders tended to see "Caribs" everywhere. On the other hand, settlers interested in a permanent body of laborers, as well as clerics seeking souls to save, were inclined to see non-Caribs populating their new colonial homelands. As an example, the natives of Trinidad were declared to be Caribs in 1511, non-Caribs following clerical protest in 1518, and Caribs again in 1530. Not until 1542 did the crown prohibit Indian slavery unconditionally.

The accounts of the *conquistadores* – often called *relaciones, crónicas* and *historias* – were not unlike the earlier and contemporary travelogues in their political objectives to convince and persuade. In his letters to Carlos V, Cortés wrote to gain the favor of his emperor and of history itself. He offered the emperor a Mexican kingdom as large, populous and rich as any realm in the world, and in the telling flattered himself as the indispensable knight and future viceroy. His humble comrade-in-arms, Bernal Díaz del Castillo, writing decades later in retirement, presented a *Historia verdadera* ("True History") that emphasized the success of the conquest of Mexico as the result of the heroism and sacrifice of the company of the conquerors and not simply to Cortés alone.

These early chroniclers nearly always got the big picture wrong about native societies and cultures, as historians understand it today. In their time, the unquestioned belief in the reality of Christian eschatology led to broad interpretations about Indian societies being under the power of Satan. Some assumed that Indians were a lost tribe of Hebrews, survivors of Atlantis or remnants of a great flood other than Noah's. However, the *conquistadores*, unlike seaborne explorers, nearly always entered Indian territories with translators, made alliances with native peoples, were keen observers and interrogators of native friends and enemy captives for military intelligence, and most eventually settled among the people they conquered. Thus when the *conquistadores* confronted the more mundane native realities they observed, questioned and analyzed, they often got the details right and their facts straight. And these details and facts have permitted nineteenth- and twentieth-century historians to work on getting the big picture in focus.

In the wake of the voyages of exploration and the conquests came the historians *de segundo mano*, those who wrote from texts rather than from first-hand experience. The first history of the New World was Peter Martyr's "The First Ocean Decade" of *De Orbe Novo* published in 1511. Martyr, a Milanese scholar and courtier in Spain, wrote his account of the discovery of the New World and Castilian exploration and colonization based on contemporary letters and reports from participants who took part in the events about which he writes. Martyr's "The First Ocean Decade" is generally viewed as an apologia of the post-1492 career of Columbus. It is true that Martyr was a friend and partisan of Columbus. He also realized and wrote that the Columbian enterprise of demanding gold from the Indians and seeking to convert them to Christianity was flawed and was leading to disaster. In this first history of the engagement of Europeans and Indians, Martyr was often quite sympathetic to the Indians – there were no *barbari* in the 1511 text – and critical of their exploiters. He was not only able to see the Indian point of view but also, with the report of the Dominican Tomás Ortiz, write a detailed and open-minded account of the daily lives, gender relations, customs, beliefs and more of the natives near Paria on the South American coast, today called the Chiribichi. "Their women," wrote Martyr, "just like our women, rear geese and ducks in their homes." Some of these historians, like the colonial administrator Gonzalo Fernández de Oviedo, in his *Historia general y natural de las Indias* (1526, 1535), wrote to justify all conquests past and future. He viewed Indians as irrational and vicious and useful only as servants and slaves. He declared gunpowder used against Indians should be considered incense to the Lord. Francisco López de Gómera, author of the *Historia General de las Indias* (1552), viewed Indians as little more than foils against which to praise the heroic *conquistadores*. Unlike Oviedo, Gómera never traveled to America. Nevertheless, as Lee Eldridge Huddleston notes, "the author despised Indians and filled his volume with outrageous characterizations of them . . . López de Gómera wrote his book in part 'to persuade the Council of the Indies that they do not deserve liberty' and, consequently, decided they should be enslaved."

The most famous and well-read historian of his own time and later was the Dominican Friar Bartolomé de Las Casas, who lived in Spanish America for most of his life. In a number of histories, pamphlets and polemical tracks circulated and published from the late 1530s to the 1550s, Las Casas used the accounts of explorers, *conquistadores*, clerics and others – as well as his personal experience – to argue for the humanity and rationality of the Indians. From the Taino to the Maya, Las Casas respected native beliefs, rites and customs. He was always more of a polemicist than a scholar. His *Short Account of the Destruction of the Indies*, printed in 1552, focused on the Spanish in the Americas who had become barbarians in their cruel, inhuman, wild and merciless acts against the Indians. Las Casas' most significant work was the *Apologética historia sumaria* ("The Apologetic History of the Indies"), a comparative ethnology of the American Indians. "The ultimate reason for writing this book," noted Las Casas, "was to gain knowledge of the many nations of the vast new world. They had been slandered by people who did not fear God . . . From such slander can come great harm and terrible calamity." Las Casas recognized cultural diversity among the natives of the Americas but he sought to demonstrate that most Indians lived in civil societies, were governed prudently and were wise peoples. They were "barbarians" because they were not Christians and because they lacked certain types of knowledge such as writing. This did not meant that Indians were innately inferior intellectually but that they were a culturally young people, at an earlier stage than Europeans or Chinese in what we would call today cultural evolution.

The Mestizo historian Garcilaso de la Vega wrote a *conquistador* account of the Hernando de Soto expedition in North America of 1539 to 1543 in *La Florida del Ynka*, published in 1605. This chronicle was based on a manuscript by a participant in the *entrada*, Gonzalo Silvestre. It certainly reflected the ideas of the late sixteenth-century Mestizo intellectual as well. "I write from the account of another," wrote Garcilaso, "who saw and took part in these things personally." Both Silvestre and Garcilaso held favorable opinions of Indians. In one encounter during the de Soto expedition, several native war captains and noblemen made elaborate intellectual arguments before "the governor," De Soto. Silvestre commented that their arguments were held by several Spaniards of the expedition to be "too elaborate for barbarous Indians." But not all Spaniards believed this. "Many Spaniards, well read in history, said when they heard them that the captains appeared to have fought among the most famous ones of Rome when she dominated the world with her arms, and that the young lords of vassals seemed to have studied in Athens during her flourishing period in moral letters." Silvestre then commanded Garcilaso to sharpen his pen. "Because of all of this you may write without any scruples what I tell you, whether or not it may be believed; we comply with our obligation with having told the truth as to the things that took place, and doing otherwise would be to injure the parties concerned."

Garcilaso de la Vega and Gonzalo Silvestre, as well as many other Spanish, English, French and Dutch authors who observed, studied and wrote about Indians, believed they could report accurately, meaningfully, indeed truthfully about Indians and that if they were not faithful to truth, the consequences for Indians and for colonial society would be oppressive and malignant. The Spanish Jesuit José de Acosta near the end of the sixteenth century explained the problem of truth or consequences. He wrote that his first aim in writing was "to refute the false opinion that is commonly held about [Indians], that they are brutes and bestial folk and lacking in understanding or with so little that it scarcely merits the name. Many and notable abuses have been committed upon them as a consequence of this false belief."

A third category of texts about native societies and relations with Europeans can be characterized as ethnographies. Although the word "ethnography" was not invented until the nineteenth century, numerous sixteenth- and seventeenth-century writings are ethnographic in the sense that they were based on what is today called fieldwork. There was close participant observation of native peoples by European investigators, often from the perspective of having resided within Indian societies. These early American investigations were also based on informants, that is, natives willing to talk and write about the history and culture of their peoples. These texts face more skepticism today than ever before. The colonial ethnographies, according to recent postcolonial critics, are wholly self-referential. Ethnocentric Europeans may have observed Indians but they invented images of these "Others" not to understand Native Americans but to confirm European misperceptions of the world and advance European power.

It is certainly true that all Europeans who wrote about Indians in the colonial Americas were culturally biased, that is, laden with their own cultural preconceptions. Their narratives were not objective. It would be naïve to believe they were strictly factual. Nevertheless, it also stretches credulity to assert that these early ethnographies were so subjective that they produced no knowledge of native histories, societies and cultures. Many of the investigators of native societies in sixteenth- and seventeenth-century America were Renaissance humanists and Aristotelian empiricists. Like the Jesuit José de

Acosta, they accepted the idea that understanding and knowledge are valid only when it corresponds to the direct evidence of the senses rather than to theories. Aristotle taught by example that investigators should use reason and their senses to understand realities that existed objectively. "Actual knowledge," wrote Aristotle, "is identical with its object." Renaissance humanists found earlier examples of ethnography in the work of ancient historians such as Herodotus and Xenophon, and in such books as Tacitus's *Germania*, a first-century Roman study of the geography, customs and morals of the Germans. Biondo Flavio's mid-fifteenth-century study of ancient Roman culture compared ancient customs and institutions with those of his own time. The Venetian Ermolao Barbaro, in the late fifteenth century in his *Corrections to Pliny*, sorted modern fact from ancient fiction and legend.

When Europeans came into contact with Indians, they were hardly strangers to peoples of various and quite different cultures. As they saw it, barbarians lived in or on the periphery of their own societies: in caves in central Castile, in the wild highlands of Scotland, in the dense forests of central Europe, and in southern Italy. In the mid-sixteenth century, the Jesuits established a mission in Naples that one evangelist referred to as "our Indies." There was just as much need for missionaries in southern Italy as America, wrote the Jesuit Miguel Navarro in 1575, "because there is a great necessity to extirpate many errors, superstitions and abuses of which there are an abundance." Europeans knew about Moors, Turks, Slavs, Persians, Tartars and many others of different colors, faiths, habits and governments. As Europeans expanded into the Islamic Mediterranean, positive images of black Africans began to increase in Western art. Europeans were ethnocentric, but unlike fifteenth- and sixteenth-century Chinese and Muslims, they were not indifferent to other cultures; they were curious. It is not so unimaginable then to think that sixteenth- and seventeenth-century European humanists could attain some understanding of American Indians, particularly when Indians participated in the creation of this knowledge.

The first ethnography of a Native American people, in fact the first book written in America in a European language, was Ramón Pané's *Account of the Antiquities of the Indians* (1498). Fray Ramón, of the Order of Saint Jerome, had been a missionary on Hispaniola since 1493 when he was selected by Columbus, two years later, to live among the Indians and report on whatever he might "discover and understand of the beliefs and idolatries of the Indians." The friar had lived with the Taino in another part of the island and learned of the island's languages when Columbus asked him to make his study in the territory of the native ruler of Guarinonex. Fray Ramón lived in this territory in 1495 and 1496 and had the assistance of native translators, but there is a dispute as to how well he mastered the island-wide language of Taino. Unlike travelogues, Fray Ramón's ethnography is filled with Taino names and terms that later residents in Hispaniola found to be accurate.

Fray Ramón's is a genuine ethnography. Before and long after Fray Ramón's investigation, Spaniards simply assumed that Indians in the Caribbean and in many parts of the mainland were peoples without religion. The friar discovered this not to be true in Hispaniola. He recounted the Taino's origin myths, the separation of the sexes, what became of the souls of the dead, the ceremonies and cures of holy or medicine men, and the worship of *zemis* (stone idols). As a result of the circulation of this early ethnography, later writers were able to draw upon Fray Ramón's pioneering account to provide a comparative anthropological perspective of other native peoples. We see the results of Fray Ramon's investigations in Peter Martyr's "The First Ocean Decade": "I decided to gather together these few facts from the writings of Fray Ramón Pané..." For example, Bartolomé de Las Casas compared the religious errors of the ancients to those of the people of Hispaniola. In support of the dignity of the Indians, Las Casas argued that Fray Ramón discovered that the Taino had faith and knowledge in God but errors intruded because they lacked doctrine and grace. These and other errors, he continued, did not justify torment and cruelty but care and conversion.

The most remarkable ethnographies were created in the aftermath of the conquests of Mexico and Peru. Many of the friars who came to Mexico to convert the Indians also proved to be talented researchers, linguists and anthropologists. The goal was to build a kingdom of God on earth and prepare for the second coming of Christ, and to do this they believed they needed to study the indigenous peoples of New Spain. One of the twelve Franciscan "Apostles" who arrived in Mexico in 1524, Fray Toribio de Benevente, who became known by his Nahuatl name Motolinía ("the poor one"), began the tradition of working in native languages using Nahua scribes and books. He finished his history of the Mexica, *History of the Indians of New Spain*, in 1541, an account of a great civilization corrupted by the Devil. This history traced the origins of the Mexica to 1092 and the construction of Tenochtitlan to 1300 based on Nahua oral tradition and Nahua understanding of the *Tonalpohualli*, the Mexican cosmological calendar. He maintained this calendar system was as sophisticated as any in the world and he argued, on this and other bases, that God had endowed the Nahua with an intelligence superior to that of many other nations.

The greatest scholar among the Franciscans of Mexico was Bernardino de Sahagún, who arrived in New Spain in 1529, mastered Nahuatl and spent the rest of his life researching Nahuatl books, interviewing Nahua lords and nobles, and working with Nahua artists, scribes, informants and assistants. The first drafts of Sahagún's ethnographic collaborative research appeared in 1558–61 as the *Primeros Memoriales*, which consisted of native pictorial images and written text in Nahuatl with comments by the friar in Spanish. Sahagún and his native collaborators produced a Nahuatl-language text of Mexican history, religion, rituals and a native account of the conquest in 1569. The final, massive bilingual text known as the *Códice Florentino* was completed in 1575–6. The twelve books of the *Códice* were eventually published as the *General History of the Things of New Spain*. The Sahaguntine project was not simply the work of a Spanish friar, scholar and ethnographer as much as it was a collaborative effort between the humanist and his native assistants. The books of the *Códice* are the products of native books and oral tradition. Although Sahagún saw the unmistakable influence of Satan on the preconquest Mexica, like Las Casas, he rejected the idea of Indian inferiority or even barbarism. He maintained that the civilization of ancient Mexico surpassed that of Greek and Rome in political and social organization, material achievements and in the arts and sciences. "We may judge what they once were," noted Sahagún, "from what we see of their present capacity for all the mechanical arts."

Contemporary to the work of Sahagún was the Codex Telleriano-Remensis, a product of an intercultural exchange between Nahua artists and scribes who possessed a Mexica manuscript painting and an unknown Spanish friar. This painted book, which includes a ritual calendar, a divinatory almanac and a historical chronicle, was produced under the direction of a friar in collaboration with native scribes who copied prehispanic books and informants who provided information from indigenous oral tradition. As this and other Spanish-Mexican codices demonstrate, natives participated in the production of knowledge about their past and colonial present.

In Spanish Peru as well, postconquest scholars produced histories of the Inka and the Spanish conquest drawn from native oral tradition, native interviews and questionnaires, as well as Spanish accounts and documents. Juan de Betanzos began his career as a Quechua translator. In 1541, he married Doña Angelina Yupanque, a niece of the Inka Huayna Capac and later the wife of Atahualpa. In his *Narrative of the Incas* (1557), Betanzos drew upon Doña Angelina and her noble family as sources of eyewitness accounts and oral tradition. As he informed the Viceroy of Peru when he presented his book, "In order to be a true and faithful translator, I must respect the style and order of the speech of these natives. In this regard, I say that in going over this present writing at times your Majesty may have to strain your eyes to read it. Although it may not be a very elegant work, it has been very difficult. In the first place, in translating and compiling it, I did not limit myself to a single informant; rather I used many of the oldest and most respected I found among these natives." Betanzos' narrative of the conquest presented the Inka point of view that the key to the outcome was the death of Inka Huayna Capac in the early 1530s and the subsequent civil war between his sons, the half-brothers Atahualpa and Huascar.

Pedro de Cieza León, a late-arriving *conquistador* who became a semi-official historian, wrote 8,000 manuscript pages in the 1540s to 1550. He was able to draw upon not only his own limited experience but collect documents and letters from the conquest years of the 1530s as well as interview the surviving Inka lords in Cuzco. As a result, he could tell the story of the conquest of Peru from multiple perspectives. According to Cieza de León, as Pizarro and his company were approaching the first meeting with the Inka Atahualpa at Cajamarca with the plan to capture him, Atahualpa developed a similar plan. He intended to seize the Spaniards, sacrifice the horses and make slaves of the pillaging foreigners. Throughout this chronicle, we see Cieza de León presenting the conquest from the Inka and the Spanish points of view. He also argued that the Spanish and the Inka were similar in a number of ways, as in this example with their hard *real politic*, but also culturally different in so many other ways. For example, in the march to Cajamarca the Andeans were surprised by the European manner of provisioning their soldiers by pillaging fields and villages as Inka armies were provisioned by provincial warehouses of maize, freeze-dried potatoes and other necessities of war.

La Chronica

DEL PERV, NVEVA MENTE ESCRITA, POR Pedro de Cieça de Leon, vezino de Seuilla.

VIRTVS ☉ PIETAS HOMINI TVTISSIMA

EN ANVERS En casa de Martin Nucio, M. D. LIIII. Con preuilegio Imperial.

Figure 6.2. The Chronicle of Cieza de León. Title page from Pedro Cieza de León, *La Chronica del Perv* (Antwerp, 1554). Courtesy of the William L. Clements Library at the University of Michigan.

Betanzos, Cieza de León and other sixteenth-century historians were impressed by the Inka state and empire, and regarded the Inkas as the natural lords of the land and the legitimate sovereigns of their people. These early historians of Peru repeatedly and favorably compared the Inka empire with that of the Romans. Domingo de Santo Tomás, the author of a Quechua grammar, countered the false but relatively common belief that native languages were savage and simple. "My principle objective in offering this little work to your Majesty has been so that it may demonstrate clearly and emphatically how false is the opinion of the many persons who have wished to persuade you that the natives of the kingdom of Peru are barbarous and unworthy of being treated with kindness and liberty as are your other vassals. Your Majesty will clearly understand how false this opinion is when you see by means of this work the great organization that this language has, its abundance in words, and its flexibility."

In his *Natural and Moral History of the Indies* (1590), José de Acosta wrote that much nonsense had been written about the Indians. Those who have lived among them and studied them with "some degree of zeal and consideration," he argued, "well know that it is a common and harmful delusion." These most diligent and learned men, as Acosta referred to the ethnographers, "judge them in a very different way, amazed that there could have been so much order and reason among them." This Renaissance scholar trained in Greek philosophy, Latin rhetoric and Christian theology wrote what is perhaps the most remarkable book about Native Americans during the colonial period. Acosta theorized that the original Indians had migrated across Tartary (Asia) into the Western Hemisphere. Many Europeans of this time and later theorized that the Americans constituted a lost tribe of Israel. Their enormous migrations delayed their settlement for a long time and thus, like Las Casas, Acosta believed the Americans were young cultures making progress in becoming civil, knowledgable and, with Spanish help, Christian.

French, English, Dutch and various other European scholars, artists, soldiers and writers also collaborated with Indians in the sixteenth and seventeenth centuries to produce detailed and empirical accounts of native cultures and European and Indian relations. Jean de Léry, a French Calvinist or Huguenot, accompanied the first Protestant mission to the New World in 1556–8. This French colony, located on Guanabara Bay (today's Rio de Janeiro), brought Léry into a year of intimate association with the local Tupinamba. He wrote self-consciously as a credible witness and sought to demolish the myths and falsehoods that earlier writers had spread about the Brazilians. "I do not endorse the fabulous tales in the books of certain people who, trusting to hearsay, have written things that are completely false," wrote Léry. If it seems like I am showing off, he noted in defense, "I reply that not only are these things with my own subject but also I am speaking out of my own knowledge, that is, from my own seeing and experience."

In fact, Léry's *Histoire d'un voyage fait en la terre de Brésil* (1578) did demolish myths. From Vespucci in the late fifteenth century throughout the sixteenth century, the Tupinamba had been a vessel for Europe's fantasies and nightmares about the Americans. However, Léry described the Tupi as wonderfully human and social. Although he refers to the Tupi as *sauvages*,

Document 6.1
De Origine Populi: On the Origins of the Natives of Virginia

William Strachey, 1612

It were not perhappes too curious a thing to demaund, how these people might come first, and from whome, and whence, to enhabite these so far remote westerly partes of the world, having no entercourse with Africa, Asia nor Europe, and considering the whole world, so many yeares (by all knowledge received, was supposed to be only conteyned and circumscryped in the discovered and traveled Bowndes of those three: according to that old Conclusion in the Scholes *Quicquid praeter Africam, et Europam est, Asia est.* Whatsoeuer Land doth neither appertayne vnto Africk, nor to Europe, is part of Asia: as also to question how yt should be, that they (if descended from the people of the first creation) should maynteyne so generall and grosse a defection from the true knowledge of God, with one kind, as yt were of rude and savadge life, Customes, manners, and Religon? yt being to be graunted, that with vs (infallibly) they had one, and the same discent and beginning from the vniversall Deluge, in the scattering of Noah and his children and Nephewes, with their families (as little Colonies) some to one, some to other borders of the Earth to dwell? as in Egipt (so writing Berosus) Esenius, and his howshold, tooke vp their Inhabitacion: In Libia, and Cyrene, Tritames: and in all the rest of Africa, Iapetus Priscus, Attalaas in East Asia; Ganges, with some of Comerus Galus children, in Arabia-Faelix, within the confines of Sabaea, called the Frankincense bearer; Canaan in Damascus, vnto the vtmost bowndes of Palestyne; etc.

But, yt is observed that Cham, and his family, were the only far Travellors, and Straglers into divers and vnknowne countries, searching, exploring and sitting downe in the same: as also yt is said of his family, that what country soever the Children of Cham happened to possesse, there beganne both the Ignorance of true godliness, and a kind of bondage and slavery to be taxed one vpon another, and that no inhabited Countryes cast forth greater multitudes, to raunge and stray into divers remote Regions, then that part of Arabia in which Cham himselfe (constrained to fly to his father) tooke into possession; so great a misery (saith Boem of Auba) brought to mankind, the vnsatisfyed wandering of that one man: for first from him, the Ignoraunce of the true worship of god took beginning, the Inventions of Hethenisme, the adoration of falce godes, and the Deuill, for he himself, not applying him to learne from his father, the knowledge and prescribed worship of the erternall god, the god of his fathers, yet by a fearefull and superstitious instinct of nature, carried to ascribe vnto some supernaturall power, a kind of honour and reverence, not divout to knowe the essence, and quality of that power, taught his successors new and devised manner of Gods, sacrifices, and Ceremonies; and which he might the easier ympresse into the Children, by reason they were carried with him so young from away from the Elders, not instructed, nor seasoned first, in their true Customes, and religion.

In so much as then we may conclude, that from Cham, and his tooke byrth and beginning the first universall Confusion and diversity, which ensued afterwards throughout the whole world, especially in divine and sacred matters, whilst yt is said agayne of the Children of Sem, and Iaphet, how they being taught by their elders, and content with their owne lymitts and confines, not traveling beyond them into new Countryes as the other, retained still (vntill the coming of the Messias,) the only knowledge of the eternall, and never chaungeable triuth.

In so much as then we may conclude, that from Cham, and his tooke byrth and beginning the first universall Confusion and diversity, which ensued afterwards throughout the whole world, especially in divine and sacred matters, while yt is said agayne of the Children of Sem, and Iaphet, how they being taught by their elders, and content with their owne lymitts and confines, not traveling beyond them into new Countryes as the other, retained still (until the coming of the Messias,) the only knowledte of the eternall, and the never chaungeable truth.

By all which yt is very probable likewise, that both in the travels and Idolatry of the family of Cham, this portion of the world (west-ward from Africa, upon the Atlantique Sea) became both peopled, and in the forme of prophane worshippe, and of an unknowne Diety: not is yt to be wondered at, where the abused truith of Religion is suffred to perish, yf men in their own Inventions, and lives, become so grosse and barbarous as by reading the processe of this history will hardly be perceived, what difference may be betweene them and bruit beasts, sometimes worshipping bruit beasts, nay things more vyle, and abhorring the inbredd motions of Nature ytself, with such headlong and bloudy Ceremonies, of Will, and Act.

But how the vagabond Rance of Cham might discend into this new world, without furniture (as may be questioned) of shipping, and meanes to tempt the Seas, together how this great Continent (devided from the other three) should become stoared with beasts, and some Fowle, of one, and the same kind with the other partes, especially with Lions, Beares, Deare, Wolues, and such like, as from the first Creation tooke begynning in their kind, and after the gererall floud were not anew created, nor have their being or generation (as some other) *ex putredine, et sole*, by corruption and Heate. Let me referre the reader to the search of Acosta in his booke of his morall and naturall History of the West-Indies, who hath so officiously laboured herein, as he should but bring Owles to Athens, who should study for more strayned, or new Aucthority Concerning the same.

Thus much then may be in brief be sayd, and allowed, Concerning their originall, or first begynning in gererall, and which may well reach even downe unto the particular Inhabitants of this particular Region, by us discovered, who cannot be any other, then parcel of the same, and first mankind.

With the European encounter with the Americas and the native peoples of these continents, the question was raised of the origin of these peoples never mentioned in the Bible. Were Native Americans a separate and new branch of humanity? Strachey argued that the Americans were the descendants of Ham (Cham), cursed to be "servants of servants" who wandered to Africa and apparently the Americas. *Source: The Historie of Travell into Virginia Britania* (1612), by William Strachey, gent., Edited by Louis B. Wright and Virginia Freund (1953), pp. 53–5.

in sixteenth-century French the word meant living in a state of nature. Their bodies were normal, even better than normal: strong, healthy and handsome. They went about naked with no shame but also adorned their bodies with inscriptions, scars, body paint, stone inserts and feathers. Unlike many Europeans who saw Indians, and particularly Indian women, as lewd and lascivious, Léry observed a rule-based system that provided marriage customs, forbade adultery and preserved modesty in public. He described the fierce warfare of the Tupi as wars for vengeance and their cannibalism as a ritual social act. Lévy attributed this "cruel" behavior to the Tupi's "fallen state," that is, their ignorance of God and torment by the Devil. Nevertheless, Lévy reminded his readers that far worse behavior had taken place during the French wars of religion.

The French essayist Michel de Montaigne, influenced by Lévy's *Historie*, examined the Tupinamba and attempted to understand and evaluate their culture in comparison to his own. In his essay *Des cannibals* ("Of Cannibals") published in 1580, Montaigne wrote that the Tupinamba were constantly at war and practiced cannibalism. To the writer, it made more sense to eat a man alive as the Tupi did than to tear a body limb from limb by racks and torments as did the French. "We may them call these people barbarous, in respect to the rules of reason," Montaigne wrote, "but not in respect to ourselves, who in all sorts of barbarity exceed them. Their wars are throughout noble and fair pretence, as that human malady is capable of; having with them no other foundation than the sole jealously of valour." Like Las Casas and some others before him, Montaigne was likely following the model of Tacitus, who praised the virtues of the barbarian Germans to highlight the degeneracy of the Roman Empire of his day. This comparative self-criticism has been identified as the "Germania syndrome."

Five years after Montaigne published his essay on cannibals, Sir Walter Ralegh and his syndicate of courtiers planted a colony on Roanoke Island in the Carolina Outer Banks, the first English colony in the New World. Among the colonists on the 1585 expedition was Thomas Harriot, a scientist and mathematician, and John White, very likely appointed as the official artist of the expedition. Harriot learned Carolina Algonquian and thus was able to interview Carolina and Virginia Indians, record their creation story, religious beliefs, governing system and social customs. Not unlike previous ethnographers, Harriot found lessons in native life for Europeans. The Indians were "very sober in their eating and drinking, and consequently very long lived because they do not oppress nature." His conclusion: "I would to God we would follow their example."

The artist John White worked with Harriot to map the region and illustrate Indian material life, culture and bodies. His field sketches, which became finished watercolors in England, detailed Indian villages, agricultural fields, ceremonies, fishing, cooking, men, women, children, chiefs and holy men. His watercolors, and the engravings made by Theodor de Bry from a larger body of White drawings, constitute the most important and accurate illustrations of Native Americans and their way of life in the sixteenth century. Both Harriot and White presented sympathetic portrayals of Native Americans and did so in collaboration with the Indians of the region. "Notwithstanding, in their proper manner (considering the want of such things as we have)," wrote Harriot, "they seem very ingenious. For although they have no such tables, nor any such crafts, Sciences and Arts as we, yet in those things they do, they show excellence of wit."

Numerous French and English accounts of the North American Indians appeared throughout the seventeenth century and, of course, they varied a great deal in quality and bias. "Texts composed during the years from 1584 through the 1630s," writes Nicolas Canny, "indicate that the English then made as genuine an effort as any Europeans to overcome their inherited beliefs and prejudices to accommodate America and its peoples within their world view. This implies that the opinions of Harriot were normative rather than exceptional." The French in North America, particularly Jesuit missionaries, studied native languages, lived in native societies, immersed themselves in native cultures for years and wrote and published yearly reports. These *Jesuit Relations* were partly the result of collaboration and consultation with Algonquians and Iroquoians in describing customs, belief systems and more. As Paul Le Jeune noted in his 1634 report, "All that I shall say regarding the Savages, I have either seen with my own eyes, or have received from the lips of natives." Unquestionably, they are the most important source of information about the Indians of seventeenth-century New France. As the Jesuit Fathers became more and more familiar with native societies, they often became more despairing in their perception of peoples who were slaves to nature and incapable of virtue. However, the French Jesuits also saw God's imprint on the languages and cultures of the Indians. Jérôme Lalemant wrote in 1645, "As regards Intelligence, they are in no wise inferior to Europeans... Why, then, should they be incapable of having a knowledge of a true God?"

The first detailed Dutch account of North American Indians (the Iroquois) was by an employee of the West India Company, Harmen Meyndertsz van den Bogaert. He spent part of the winter of 1634–5 on an expedition into Mohawk and Oneida country and recorded his experience, descriptions and interactions with the natives in his journal. Van den Bogaert was the first Dutchman to see and describe Iroquois villages and longhouses, weapons and shields, curing rituals and more. It is likely that this Dutchman was the first European to make reference to the Iroquois Confederacy in the language of the Mohawk. With his knowledge of at least some of the Mohawk language, he recorded the first listing of the five Iroquois nations. A more impressive work of Dutch scholarship and ethnology came from Adraen van der Donck in 1655, *Beschrijvinge van Nieuw Nederland* ("Description of

Figure 6.3. The Native Town of Secota in Virginia. From Thomas Harriot, *A Brief and True Report of the new found land of Virginia*, Theodor de Bry edition (Frankfurt, 1590). Courtesy of the William L. Clements Library at the University of Michigan.

New Netherland"). Van der Donck had migrated to New Netherland in 1641 and had lived for five years in upcountry Rensselaerswyck patroonship along the Hudson River surrounded by Indians. Through his personal experience with and observation of the natives of the region, and his learning of one Iroquoian language, he became New Netherland's principal negotiator and authority on the Indians. In writing his book on the colony, van der Donck not only relied upon his own knowledge but consulted other authorities and texts. Although his section on the Iroquois and Algonquian constitute only part of the book, he covered a number of topics thoughtfully. He noted their governments were democratic, a good thing, but perhaps too democratic, which made them dependent upon public approval and sometimes paralyzed. Van der Donck wrote that at first sight the Indians appeared "somewhat strange to our people, because of color, speech and dress are so different, but for those who associate with them frequently the strangeness soon passes."

Two of the last great books in the ethnographic tradition were from the colonial soldier Louis-Armand de Lom d'Arce, Baron de Lahontan, and the Jesuit missionary François Lafitau. Lahontan's *Nouveaux Voyages* ("New Voyages") published in 1703 gave an account of his new years in New France and two winters living in Algonquian hunting villages. He discussed natural history, geography and the "customs of the savages" from the perspective of a first-hand witness: "This I have seen so often with my own eyes, that there is no room for the least doubt upon the matter." Lahontan described native life as free and equalitarian where women enjoyed the same liberties as men, children had the same rights as parents and society that was unburdened by the hierarchies of clergy, aristocracy and monarchs. Recalling Montaigne's inversion of savagery and civilization, Lahontan wrote, "The name of savages that we bestow among them would better fit ourselves." Lafitau's *Moeurs des sauvages Amériquains* ("Customs of the American Savages") appeared in 1724. Lafitau, who had been a Jesuit missionary in New France for five years, studied first-hand the "life and customs" of the Iroquois and carefully described their dress, language, habits and – especially – their myths and origin stories. This well-educated Jesuit also read about and included the customs of the Mexicans, Andeans and Brazilians in his analysis. Lafitau maintained that when Europeans sailed to America, they traveled back in time to the *premiers temps* – the first times of man – finding cultures similar to the barbarians of the Old World before the rise of the Greeks. His comparative analysis argued that the Iroquois shared certain beliefs and memories, as well as abilities such as symbolic thought, with the ancient nations of the Old World.

For more than three hundred years, Europeans and European-Americans wrote about and lived among native societies that were among the most libertarian and equalitarian in the world. "Savages" often organized complicated confederations, governed through consensus and highly valued personal autonomy in contrast to the "civilized" European manner of monarchical absolutism, religious intolerance, class-based poverty, institutionalized injustice and the hierarchical and economic demands of deference, dependence and servitude. European writers and philosophers such as Montaigne, John Locke, David Hume, Thomas Paine, Jean-Jacque Rousseau and others drew upon New World ethnography as well as other sources to invent such ideas as the noble savage, the social contract, individual autonomy, religious liberty and natural rights.

6.3 Closely Connected and Interwoven

Everywhere in the Americas from the late fifteenth through the eighteenth century, the critical relationship for native peoples was with colonists and their local governments. "The concerns of this Country are so closely connected & interwoven with Indian Affairs," wrote the governor of South Carolina in 1761, "and not only a great branch of our trade, but even the Safety of this Province, do so much depend upon our continuing in Friendship with the Indians." Colonists, settlers, traders and others who had direct contact with Indians were guided less by any type of ideology than by self-interest. The pursuit of self-interest meant that colonists perceived Indians not in one consistent manner but in a variety of different ways at different times. Depending upon many variables, Europeans treated specific native groups as allies or enemies, partners, teachers, customers and much more. And native peoples, we should remember, were not very different in this respect. They also engaged with Europeans out of self-interest. As D. W. Meinig puts it, Indians and Europeans were "locked together for mutual advantage." However, as Meinig points out, mutual advantage did not even the playing field: Indians and Europeans "were not really on equal terms in a larger sense."

More than anywhere in the Americas, relations between colonists and Indians in Spanish America were regulated by the crown and church. Earlier chapters have discussed several aspects of Spanish-Indian relations but here the objective is to present a more holistic and comparative perspective. The Spanish monarchy in the imperial heartlands of Mexico and Peru attempted to regulate and control Spanish-Indian relations as much as possible. The New Laws of 1542 began the slow and irregular decline of the *encomienda* and outlawed Indian slavery. "We ordain and command," wrote the Emperor Carlos V through the Council of the Indies, "that henceforth and for no cause of war nor any other whatsoever, though it be under title of rebellion, nor by ransom nor in other manner can an Indian be made a slave, and we will that they be treated as our vassals of the Crown of Castile since such they are." To better control and protect Indian communities, the royal government provided a system of government, creating what has been called the *república de indios* – the Republic or commonwealth of Indians. Indian towns were given the legal status of Spanish municipalities with the privilege and responsibility of local self-government. Like Spanish town governments, Indian towns had municipal cabildos or town councils composed of councilmen, notaries, sheriffs and judges. For example, Cuernavaca, just south of the Valley of Mexico, revealed continuous and effective Indian governance throughout the colonial era. Office holding generally remained within traditional ruling groups that learned how to manipulate the colonial system to protect community interests. Indian society was to be separate from Spanish society. Except for clerics, *encomenderos* and select royal officials, Spaniards were prohibited from living in Indian towns. In the principal Spanish towns and cities, Indians were restricted to their own districts. Thus colonial society was officially conceived as two separate and distinct societies or commonwealths, a Republic of Spaniards and a Republic of Indians. However, there was no realistic way to prevent the movement of people and the intermingling of Spanish men and Indian women.

Encomenderos and royal officials became the greatest burden upon Indian communities. All Indians not placed in *encomiendas* had to pay money tribute and provide labor service to the king. Of course, *encomenderos* and royal officials obtained these goods through cooperative native leaders who found it in their best interest to mediate between their communities and the Spanish. Native leaders had their status confirmed by the new system and apportioned for themselves a part of the tribute that went to *encomenderos* or officials. As was true with the military campaigns, Spanish rule was a collaborative endeavor. The Spanish generally respected Indian landholding and the native tradition of communal property. The massive depopulation of Mexico and Peru and other regions of high population density produced a surplus of land for Spaniards and Indians. Communities allotted village land to individual families and made adjustments when necessary. Many native towns and villages were able to maintain their ancestral lands and autonomy until the nineteenth or even the twentieth century. However, throughout the colonial era Indian communities in certain regions lost their lands to aggressive Spanish land grabbers, and Indian villagers found themselves living on private estates, called *haciendas* and *estancias*. They became the *hacienda's* labor force and were forced to obey the wishes of the *hacendado*, the *patrón*.

Direct exploitation of native communities by *encomenderos*, *hacendados* and royal officials was common in Mexico and Peru. *Encomenderos* were infamous for their abuses and extractions in the sixteenth century. Alonso de Zorita, a former judge of the Audiencia of New Spain, informed the king in the mid-sixteenth century that "the encomenderos, their servants, and their Negro slaves trample the Indians' fields and fruit; they prevent them from selling their produce to whom they please and at their own price; they set the Indians bad examples and interfere with their religious instruction by occupying them in their own service. The encomenderos take the Indians' maize and vegetables and force them to serve them, their people, and their horses, all without pay." The growth of *haciendas* often meant the increase of various kinds of native dependence and bondage. In Peru, Indians who left their towns or *encomiendas* and generally found themselves bound to estates were called *yanaconas*. They were part of the property and could not leave or be removed from it. In exchange for a small garden plot, they had to work a certain number of days for the *hacendado*. Local officials often had the most power over Indian communities and therefore the best opportunities to exploit them. Native complaints in the General Indian Court charged the officials forced Indians into personal service, forced communities to purchase Spanish goods and sell them foodstuffs, and punished individual Indians arbitrarily with whippings and confinement.

However, the Spanish colonial system provided commercial and economic opportunities to particularly talented and energetic Indians. In the fertile valleys of Peru, Indian entrepreneurs created *haciendas* to produce coca, wine, maize, hides and vegetables for regional markets. Certain native artisans and merchants learned how to exploit commercial opportunities following Spanish models of economic advancement. Indian *hacendados*, planters and miners – like their Spanish counterparts – took advantage of Indian forced labor, dependent native workers attached to *haciendas*, African slaves and other forms of labor exploitation. Wealthy Indian landowners and merchants became part of the colonial elite and acquired second homes, wore fine clothes, rode the best horses and sent their sons to boarding school run by the Jesuits.

On the peripheries of the Spanish Empire, relations between Spaniards and Indians took on harsher forms than in the imperial heartlands. In these areas where Spanish officialdom was small and weak, the *encomiendas* persisted longer in their original form as an institution of labor service. In New Granada, *encomenderos* used their charges to wash gold in the streams and rivers of the province, while in Venezuela Indians in *encomiendas* were worked in cacao plantations much like slaves. Military campaigns in the far north and far south of Spanish America continued through the seventeenth and eighteenth centuries. Indian slavery also persisted in frontier regions for much of the colonial period.

Portuguese Brazil was more like the frontier regions of Spanish America than the heartlands of Mexico and Peru. This collection of decentralized colonies with a relatively weak and undermanned royal government quickly became a plantation economy dominated by landowners, the Lords of the Sugar Mills. The expansion of the sugar plantation system demanded labor – onerous, dangerous and almost never-ending labor – which Indians would not accede to voluntarily. Thus Indian slavery became the first labor system of Brazil's plantation economy. Although the Portuguese crown, or overseas ministry under the Habsburgs, restricted Indian slavery, they always provided exceptions. Colonists could enslave natives in "just wars" or for reason of rescue and ransom, *resgate*, that is, to save Indians from being eaten by their native enemies.

As a result, military campaigns against native peoples who resisted plantation slavery continued throughout the colonial era. In particular, in the southern captaincy of São Paulo, Paulistas became known for their aggressive slaving expeditions into the interior of Brazil. The Bandeirantes trekked thousands of miles to capture and enslave Indians. They were assisted by *mamelucos*, mixed Portuguese-Indian men, who understood Indian customs, often spoke Indian languages and knew how to survived and hunt in the backlands. The Bandeirantes were also assisted by native allies who, no doubt, believed it was better to enslave others than to be enslaved. One 1629 slaving expedition into the Guaíra region counted among its members 69 Portuguese and Luso-Brazilians, 900 *mamelucos* and over 2,000 Indians. "The entire life of these bandits," wrote one Jesuit, "is going to and from the *sertão* [backlands], bringing back captives with so much cruelty, death, and pillage; and then selling them as if they were pigs."

Paulistas and their *mameluco* and Indian associates in the seventeenth and into the eighteenth century became colonial Brazil's most sought-after Indian fighters. When settlers expanded into the backlands of Bahia, colonizing the region along the São Francisco River and establishing vast cattle ranches, they came into conflict with the natives who they dispossessed. Local authorities and colonists brought Paulistas north to remove or kill, and it worked. By the late seventeenth century, cattle ranches extended almost uninterrupted along two thousand miles of the São Francisco. In 1699, the governor-general of Bahia noted that Paulistas had "left this Captaincy free of all the tribes that oppressed it, extinguished them so effectively that from then until the present you would not know that there were any heathen living in the wilds they conquered."

The interior of Pernambuco and Paraíba in the northeast remained a region of conflict. The Dutch occupation of these captaincies from 1630 to 1654 had halted Portuguese expansion west and given native groups leverage as military allies in the war between the Portuguese and the Dutch. Upon the expulsion of the Dutch, their allies the Potiguar abandoned their homeland and took refuge into the northwest. Portuguese expansion into the interior was resumed and, as in the São Francisco valley, settlers sought vast tracks of Indian land for cattle ranches. In the late 1680s, this expansion provoked Kariri groups to attack the Portuguese frontier in strength and kill settlers in isolated ranches. Again, Paulista Indian fighters were brought to the conflict, the recruited Indian allies, and went to war. (A contemporary reminder of this conflict is the town called Paulista, located about four hundred miles west of Recife.) A three-year campaign produced a stalemate. In 1692, Portuguese authorities signed a formal peace treaty with chief Canindé that recognized the independence of his people as well as the possession of a large territory.

The Portuguese entered the Amazon in the early seventeenth century following the expulsion of the French. A fort was established at the southern mouth of the Amazon delta on the Pará River, which in time became the town of Belém do Pará. On the coast and up the delta rivers and the Amazon itself, Portuguese expansion meant enslavement and led to conflict after conflict. As elsewhere in Brazil, native peoples fought the Portuguese, fought with and for the Portuguese, and many fled into the interior. In 1637, the king awarded an Indian fighter a hereditary captaincy on the north shore of the Amazon in the deep interior, which was essentially a license to capture and enslave Indians. This Amazonian expansion brought enslavement, war, disease and the destruction of many Indian societies. The vicar-general of Maranhão, Manoel Teixeira, estimated that in the thirty years following the settlement of Belém, something in the range of two million Indians had perished. Teixeira attributed all of this death to the few hundred settlers and their "violent labor, exhausting discoveries, and unjust wars." He should have added, as well, repeated epidemics of smallpox and measles.

In English, French and Dutch North America, metropolitan governments and the colonizing chartered companies encouraged settlers to get along with their new native neighbors. However, European-Indian relations in North America were determined less by exhortation than the nature of economic resources and material interests. In some places, particularly English Virginia and New England, settlers established agricultural colonies and therefore needed land. This led to conflict with native peoples who were also settled on the land, practiced agriculture and were willing to defend their homelands. In other places where the resource was peltry and hides, Europeans established trading posts and needed not land but native cooperation. Without Indian hunters and trappers, European traders had no way to obtain the necessary volume of pelts and hides. Here, too, there was conflict, but for a long time it was a conflict driven by native rivalries supported by European allies as suppliers and auxiliaries.

Everywhere, the first colonists, soldiers and traders were ignorant of their new environment and dependent upon the local Indians for food, trade and useful knowledge. Metacom reminded the English at Massachusetts of an earlier time when his father, Massasoit, had been "as a great man and the English as a little child...He give them Corn and Showed them how to plant." William Wood, from the English side, acknowledged native assistance: "Many ways have their advice and endeavor been advantageous to us; they being our first instructors for the planting of their corn." In some places, this goodwill continued; in others, it did not.

In the Chesapeake region and in New England, the English settlers were farmers seeking land and confronting – and eventually displacing – native farmers who possessed the land. In Virginia, this meant conflict with the Powhatan Confederacy time and again during the first half of the sixteenth century. Referring to the Powhatan attack against the English in 1622, Edward Waterhouse clearly attributed the reason to "the daily fear that possesses them, that in time we by our growing continually upon them, would dispossess them of this Country." In New England, where the Pilgrims found deserted native villages as a result of virgin soil epidemics, more than fifty of the first English settlements were established on the remains of once thriving Indian communities. However, the Great Migration of the 1630s brought thousands of land-hungry Englishmen into New England who expanded into the lands of Indian peoples who had survived the early epidemics. The two Puritan "conquests," the Pequot War of 1636 and King Philip's War of 1675–6, were bloody affairs that slaughtered men, women and children and enslaved the survivors. As everywhere in the Americas, the Puritan wars against specific Indian peoples involved Indian allies who fought alongside the English against their traditional Indian rivals and enemies. In the case of the Pequot War, the Mohegan and Narragansett allies of the Puritans were horrified by the English way of war, which produced the virtual extinction of the Pequots.

The French in Quebec, Trois Rivières and Montreal, the three principal settlements of New France, approached the native peoples of Canada quite differently. Apparently, Canada was a land of no mineral wealth as Mexico and Peru and incapable of plantation agriculture as in Brazil and Virginia. Colonial survival had to be based on the region's most valuable resource, furs and hides. The most marketable and luxuriant furs were those of animals found in the coldest northern climates. These included beaver, marten, muskrat, mink, otter and lynx. Hides included deer, elk, moose and bison. The French could obtain furs and hides only if the Indians hunted, trapped and skinned them and brought them to French trading post to be peacefully traded for European goods such as knives, hatchets, cloth, mirrors and other products valued by Indians. Therefore, the relationship between the French and Indians was roughly one between equals, at least at first and for some time to come in the remote backlands.

Given the economic nature of New France, the French generally went along with Indian customs and notions. From the beginning of the founding of Québec, the French acceded to native requests for military assistance. Champlain and two men armed with swords and harquebus joined a war party of the Hurons to attack their foes, the Iroquois. The Hurons made it clear that trade was possible only with French military assistance. The French also accepted the native traditions and rituals of trade. For Indians, trade was essentially a diplomatic occasion that followed a prescribed ritual procedure and emphasized peace and mutual satisfaction. The French, thinking in terms of price and profit, saw no counterpart among their Indian partners. They therefore adapted to Indian customs and smoked the peace pipe, exchanged gifts and made speeches, all in preparation for barter sessions. The closing of a 1633 trading conference was described this way: "Sieur Champlain made his presents, which corresponded in value to those that the Hurons had made him. To accept these presents from the Savages is to bind oneself to return an equivalent."

The Dutch and English traders who participated in the fur and hide trades deviated little from the French model. From the trading post of Fort Orange on the upper Hudson, the Dutch traded with and armed the Mohawks of the Iroquois Confederation. Like the French, the Dutch did business in the Indian way. In 1655, the Mohawk chiefs complained that they were not as well entertained by the Dutch as they entertained their Dutch visitors who came to their villages to trade. As a result, they did not consider Dutch behavior very brotherly. As the Mohawks proposed solutions to this rudeness, they gave the Dutch a belt of *sewant* – small beads drilled for stringing and often made into strings and belts – for each request. In return, the Dutch answered gift for gift. The English also participated in the fur and hide trades from north to south and, like the French and Dutch, depended upon natives for their livelihood. After the English seized New Netherland in 1664, the English moved into the upper Hudson Indian trade. Four years later, the crown issued a charter for what would become the Hudson Bay Company, which brought English merchant adventurers into the fur trade to the north and west of New France.

In the English southeast, primarily Carolina beginning in 1670, English settlers established both a plantation regime and significant trade in hides and

Indian slaves. In fact, Carolinians founded their colony on Indian trade for deerskins and Indian slaves. They had no trouble finding Indian allies who would provide deerskins and slaves in exchange for English metal goods, clothing and guns. During the first fifteen years of the eighteenth century, South Carolinians exported more than fifty thousand deerskins a year. It is also estimated as many as thirty thousand to fifty thousand Indians were sold in the southern Indian slave trade between 1670 and 1715. During the 1690s, Carolinians developed rice as an export crop, thanks to specific techniques learned from West African slaves, and created one of the most important plantation systems in the Americas. With Indian and, increasingly, African slaves, Carolina's rice exports increased from less than half a million pounds in 1700 to 43 million in 1740 (see Map 6.1).

Colonists and their local governments engaged with Indians throughout the Americas in various ways, but almost always through the prism of self-interest. This meant that settlers were guided less by ideology than pragmatism. Under certain circumstances, settlers could be unrestrained in their exploitation and destruction of native societies. On the other hand, when they needed native cooperation, they would assist native allies, sell them arms, trade according to their manner and generally be good neighbors. Indians were equally pragmatic. Balancing concerns about native rivals and enemies, the benefits of European trade goods and the potential and real threats from European colonies and empires, native societies pursued their self-interests as best they could perceive them.

6.4 Sell Them the Pearls of Heaven

All of the European empires acknowledged the overwhelming significance of converting Indians to Christianity. From its founding, the Christian church viewed the conversion of pagans to be one of the fundamental tenets of Christianity. As Europeans began overseas expansion, Pope Innocent VIII in 1486 declared, "Our chief concern and commission from heaven is the propagation of the orthodox faith, the increase of the Christian religion, the salvation of barbarian nations, and the repression of the infidels and their conversion to the faith." Kings and princes, royal officials, explorers, conquerors and merchant adventurers, not to mention the Church in Rome, believed in the mission of overseas evangelization. Commissions, permissions, grants and charters gave priority to the spreading of the faith.

Christianity was not the only militant missionary religion in the early modern world that put forth universal claims. In the seventh century, Arabs burst forth from their peninsula to take their version of ethical monotheism, Islam, to all of mankind. Arab Islamic armies conquered the Middle East, North Africa, Sicily, Iberia, Persia and India. After 1200, the pietistic Sufi movement carried Islam through traders and missionaries to sub-Saharan Africa and the East African coast, southern Russia and central Asia, and into China, the Malay Peninsula and the islands of Southeast Asia. Muslims developed the idea of Holy War, *jihad*, to spread the recitations of Muhammad and

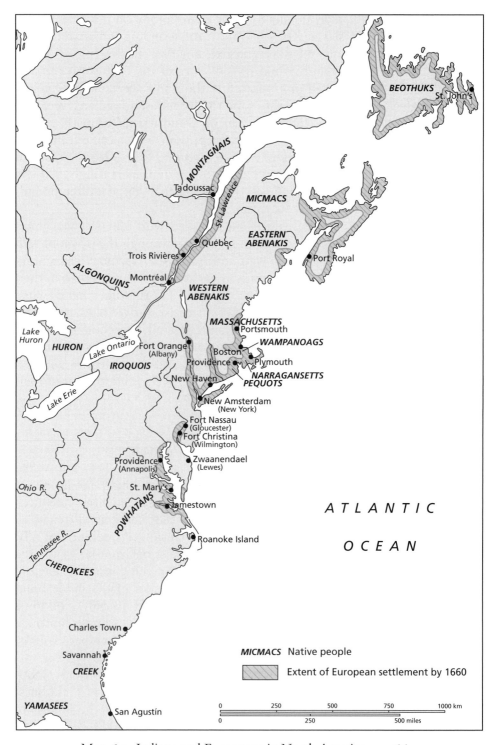

Map 6.1. Indians and Europeans in North America, c. 1660.

Islamic rule and law. Muslims believed they had a religious obligation to convert or subjugate all of mankind. For atheists and polytheists, the choice was conversion to Islam or death. For Jews and Christians, peoples of the Book with incomplete revealed religions, a third option was available: payment of tribute and acceptance of the supremacy of Islam and Muslim power. Muslim societies manifested a religious tolerance that was unknown in European Christian kingdoms in the early modern period. Nevertheless, both Muslims and Christians claimed possession of universal and final truths, and believed it was their divinely ordained task to bring the word of God to the rest of the world.

More than anything else, Christian evangelization was the justification for empire and colonization in the Americas. The Roman Catholic kingdoms of Spain, Portugal and France made the most serious and persistent efforts to convert Indians. There are several reasons for this but certainly the most obvious is that the Roman Catholic church had the institutional structures to best advance serious efforts of evangelization. In addition, Catholic monarchs supported the Church in America politically, militarily and financially. Protestant England and The Netherlands acknowledged the great importance of evangelization but devoted few men and resources to the task. The Protestant nations possessed religious zeal but did not have Franciscans, Dominicans, Augustinians and Jesuits, which could be mobilized for missionary work. The Protestant churches of northern Europe were intensely national and inward-looking, unlike the international and universal Roman Church. Protestant colonists were often concerned about themselves as probationary religious communities, and thus they had little attention to give outsiders. Finally, the Calvinist doctrine of many English and Dutch settlers and ministers may have discouraged substantial missionary efforts on behalf of Indians who (it seemed) were very likely not predestined for salvation anyway. "We should consider the nature of Puritan covenant theology," Diarmaid MacCulloch argues, "which may have inhibited the idea of mission."

Europeans took missionary Christianity to Africa and Asia beginning in the fifteenth and sixteenth centuries. The Portuguese introduced Catholicism to the Kingdom of Kongo and its colonies of Angola and Mozambique. The Jesuits followed the Portuguese and established missions in India, China and Japan. Augustinians, Dominicans and Franciscans took the faith to the Spanish Philippine Islands in the sixteenth century and expanded their mission to China in the early seventeenth century. The Dutch East India Company (VOC) brought their established church, the Reformed Church, to their outposts in South Africa, Ceylon and Indonesia (Batavia). In the late seventeenth and early eighteenth centuries, François Valentijn, a Dutch minister, preached to the Ambonese of the Moluccas and translated the Bible into Ambon-Malay. The British and the Dutch created organized and well-funded Protestant missionary societies in the late eighteenth and nineteenth centuries. The Americas was one "field" in the worldwide mission of European Christianity.

At the beginning of the age of European expansion, the church in Rome gave control of Catholic activity in the overseas empires to the Spanish monarchy by the *Patronato real de indias* and to the Portuguese monarchy by the *Padroado*. This right of patronage gave the Iberian kings the sole responsibility for evangelization and the power to advance this mission. The Spanish crown obtained the tithes and all other income collected in America, which were devoted to the support to the church in America. The crown also had the power to propose candidates for ecclesiastical office, to veto leaders of the regular orders and the control the founding and building of all churches and monasteries. This *regalia* – privilege – gave the Spanish and Portuguese monarchies the power, the means and the inspiration to advance the mission of Indian evangelization.

The Castilian crown authorized religious orders, the regular clergy who were members of religious orders living under vows of poverty, to become the primary instrument of the evangelization of the Indians. The mendicant orders – Franciscans, Dominicans and Augustinians – arrived in the New World to spread the Gospel. As we have seen, many of the missionary clergy studied Indian history and culture, and learned Indian languages to find the best ways to bring Indians to Christ. Friars in the Caribbean and on the mainland sought peaceful and voluntary conversion through instruction and baptism. However, the missionaries were also the new leaders of many communities that had been directly conquered or had felt the effects of Spanish victory and rule. Therefore, the friars could and did order Indians to attend to their lessons, baptize their children and, if baptized, to follow the rituals and schedules of a Catholic life. Towns were the principal units in evangelization. Friars settled in native towns and set about reorganizing native culture. They indoctrinated and baptized the residents, destroyed pagan temples and oversaw the building of churches and cathedrals on top of the temple ruins. The friars forbade pagan rituals and idols, introduced the Christian calendar, organized festivals on holy days and much more. *Cofradías*, or lay brotherhoods, were introduced in Indian towns and were embraced enthusiastically by native men. Native *cofradías* financed and managed religious festivals and charities and provided funeral masses and burials for members. In Mesoamerica and the central Andes, the church contributed to the cohesion of native towns and their survival in the face of epidemics and colonial rule.

The first generation of missionary friars dispersed throughout the imperial heartlands after the conquests of the Mexica and the Inka. In Mexico alone, the missionary clergy numbered fifteen hundred by 1580 and close to three thousand by 1650. For many sixteenth-century missionary friars, particularly Franciscans, Indians offered an opportunity to restore the early Christian church, create a "gospel kingdom" and rapidly advance the Christianization of all of mankind, and thus hasten the final coming of Christ and the end days. This millenarianism helps explain the superficial conversion and mass baptism of Indians. In a 1529 letter, Peter of Ghent claimed that fourteen thousand Indians were baptized on one day, and the Franciscan Toribio de Motolinia reported that by 1536 approximately five million natives had been baptized in central Mexico. One missionary argued the task was essentially completed in Mexico by 1570.

Document 6.2
The Lord's Prayer in Nahuatl

Totatzine, Ilhuicac timoyeztitca, mayectenehualo in Motocatsin; Ma hualauh in Motlatocayotzin, Ma chihualo in Tlalticpan in motlanequi-litzin, in yuh chichihualo in Ilhuicac. Int otlaxcal mo moztlae totech mon-equi ma axcan xitech momauili; ma xitech metlapop huili in to tlatlacol; in yuh ti quin tlapopolhuia: intechtlatla calhuia; macamoxitech momac-ahuili; inic amo ipan tihuetzizque in teneyeyecoltiliztli çanye xitechmo-maquixtili inyhuicpa inamoqualli.

Our revered Father, who heaven in art be praised by name; may come thy kingdom, be done earth above thy will, as is done heaven in; our bread every day to us is necessary today give us; forgive us our sins; as we forgive those who offend; thou not us lead that not in we fall in temptation; but deliver us against from not good.

There are many translations of the Lord's Prayer in Nahuatl. The Francis-cans made the first translations in the mid-sixteenth century. The rather literal translation in English demonstrates how difficult it is to translate religious concepts. This Nahuatl version, of unknown origin, has been slightly revised by Thomas Benjamin. *Source:* Hubert Howe Bancroft, *History of Mexico, Being a Popular History of the Mexican People from the Earliest Primitive Civilization to the Present Time* (1914), p. 88.

Peru and the central Andes presented a different picture. The later con-quest, the Spanish civil war and more recalcitrant Indians were given as reasons for the contrast between Mexico and Peru. The viceroy of Peru also questioned the quality of his clergy: "As the first born, New Spain took the cream from the start, and succeeded both in the choice of Church prelates and of religious, so that all were holy, humble men devoted to implanting the gospel among the natives." The Augustinians arrived in Peru in 1552, the Franciscans in 1563 and the Jesuits in 1569. Unlike Mexico, their smaller number in the Andes meant that missionaries rarely ventured beyond major cities. J. H. Parry writes, "the Quechua people were not effectively evange-lized until the middle of the seventeenth century." Even then, Andeans con-tinued to practice their traditional rites along with Christian ritual. For two hundred years, continues Parry, "ecclesiastical authorities found it necessary to send out periodical *visitadores de idolatría* – inspectors – in a vain attempt to suppress pagan rites." Governor Vaca de Castro informed an assembly of friars in 1565, "out of more than three hundred thousand men who are baptized, no more than forty are truly Christian and as many idolatries exist here as before."

The expansion of the Christian mission across Spanish America was revealed in the construction of large and magnificent church and monastery complexes called *conventos*. These *conventos* along with cathedrals, hospi-tals, nunneries and clerical palaces constituted one of the most impressive

Figure 6.4. The Franciscan Missionary, Francisco Solano, Baptizes Native Americans in Peru. From Tiburcio Navarro, *Triumphus charitatis, siue De vita, virtutibus et miraculis venerabilis serui Dei P. Fr. Francisci Solani* (Rome, 1671). Courtesy of the John Carter Brown Library at Brown University.

building programs in history. The friars built Christian temples on the sites or ruins of former native temples or pyramids. This practice of appropriating the sacred ground was an old if not ancient practice. Castilians had done this during the *Reconquista* and Muslims had done it long before that. The first bishop of New Spain claimed that five hundred ancient temples had been destroyed in Mexico by 1531, only ten years following the conquest of Tenochtitlán. With Indian and European craftsmen, masons, woodcutters, sculptors, painters, gilders and so on, the friars usually built a single-nave church, a one- or two-story monastery around a patio on one side, and a large walled churchyard or atrium in front. *Conventos* were attached to *haciendas* for the production of grain, fruit and livestock and therefore marketable commodities. The Dominicans built the grand *convento* of Santo Domingo in Ciudad Real, in the predominantly Maya province of Chiapa in southern Mexico, beginning in 1551. The church of Santo Domingo has one of the most ornate baroque facades in Mexico. Statues of Dominican saints revered as apostles to distant lands, St. Hyacinth of Poland and St. Peter Martyr, flank the central doorway. Inside the church, the nave is sheathed with gilded relief panels, there are carved and painted side *retablos* and paintings, and an extravagant rococo pulpit and stairway. The two-story monastery included cloisters surrounding an interior garden with a well. By 1574, the Franciscans alone had built 166 *conventos* in Mexico. In Peru, the religious orders constructed impressive churches and *conventos* in cities such as Lima, Cuzco, Arequipa, Potosí, Chuquisaca, Quito and some others. At Copacabana near Lake Titicaca, the Augustinians built the shrine for the Virgin of Copacabana and a *convento* with a church, monastery and a chapel "of the Three Crosses" where religious services could be held outside.

Missionary meddling and coercion in native everyday life and deeply rooted customs, repeated epidemics that killed significant portions of native communities and economic exploitation in the form of tribute and forced labor led to many native rebellions and resistance movements against missionaries and Christianity itself. The Mixtón War of 1541 in north central Mexico was a religious uprising and movement that killed missionaries, burned churches and crosses and spoke on behalf of the god Tecoroli and the ancestors who promised many wives, everlasting life and "suffering no more hardship or pain." The Taki Onqoy ("dance of disease") movement in the central Andes in the 1560s produced native preachers who proclaimed that disease was a sign of the displeasure of the old gods to native conversions to the new religion. Thousands of natives became *taquiongos* and established free and autonomous local societies that rejected Christianity. Taqui Onqoy honored the traditional Andean deities and sought to renew the rites and ceremonies of the Incas. Anti-Christian hatred was the key to many of the major rebellions that upset the *pax colonial* in Spanish America: the Chichimeca War of the 1550s to 1580s in northern Mexico, the Pueblo Revolt in 1680 in New Mexico, the Tarahumara mission uprisings in the 1690s, and the rebellion of the Maya of Chiapa in 1712. A rebel proclamation Maya towns stated, "Ya no hay Dios ni Rey" – "Now there is neither God nor king!" Deadly epidemics, authoritarian missionaries and the rigors of Catholicism, Susan Schroeder notes, "were cause enough for native leaders, many already displaced, to rally forces to prevent further disintegration of their traditions and communities." Interestingly, many rebels "made use of Christian and royal symbols to regain some form of local autonomy."

A number of clerics from the beginning of Spanish colonization in the Caribbean to the eighteenth century realized that peaceful conversion was at risk if Spanish settlers and local officials continued to exploit, enslave and abuse native peoples. Elements of the church in America and Spain became defenders of Indian rights. It was clerical protest that guided the reform and regulatory efforts of the Spanish monarchy. On the peripheries and frontiers of the Spanish Empire in the Americas, clerics often saw evangelization and protection of Indians from settlers as one and the same task. The province of Paraguay, founded in the later 1530s, became an isolated corner of the empire where the *encomienda* and Indian slavery long persisted. The Franciscan order established the first mission communities among the Guaraní in the 1580s to protect natives from *encomenderos* and slavery. In 1610, the Jesuits moved into Paraguay and attracted Indians to their missions who sought relief and security from slavery and forced labor and were attracted by the iron tools, cloth, domesticated animals and other tangible benefits. By 1649, the Guaraní mission population under Jesuit supervision in Paraguay was approximately 30,000. By 1700, there were thirty missions with a total native population of somewhere between 80,000 and 120,000.

The Jesuit missions in eastern Paraguay were located between the Spanish settlement of Asunción in the southwest and Portuguese settlers in Brazil in the northeast. During the first half of the seventeenth century, Brazilian *bandierantes* raided the Jesuit missions for captives. These raids forced the Jesuits to form and arm Indian militias in the 1640s, which were thereafter able to defend the missions. The mission communities themselves were tightly controlled and regulated societies. The Guaraní accepted baptism after indoctrination and observed Catholic rites. The Jesuits exercised considerable authority through native chiefs. The missions were all new towns organized along the gridiron pattern of Spanish towns, with great wooden churches in the center. Indians worked family plots of land as well as communal fields, ranches and in artisan industries such as blacksmithing, shoemaking, weaving and so on. The large herds of cattle provided valuable exports of hides, which the Jesuits used to pay the annual tribute of their charges.

In 1750, following a treaty between Spain and Portugal, seven of the Jesuit missions in Paraguay fell under Portuguese authority. The Jesuits and the Guaraní refused to leave, and in 1754 the Guaraní rebelled and fought a war against a Spanish-Portuguese military expedition. The treaty was nullified in 1761 and the seven Jesuit missions were secure temporarily. Several years later, in 1767 the Spanish crown expelled the Jesuit order from its American empire. The missions, under the jurisdiction of royal officials and inexperienced priests, soon disintegrated (see Map 6.2).

Paraguay was not unique. Religious orders established missions along these lines in the Rio de la Plata frontier, Spanish Amazonia, the plains of Venezuela, the western Guianas, Florida, northern Mexico, New Mexico and California, to name the most prominent regions. Franciscan and Jesuit missions on the edges of the Spanish Empire not only struggled to convert and protect Indians, they also played an important role in the expansion of Spanish dominion beyond Mesoamerica and the Central Andes. Native

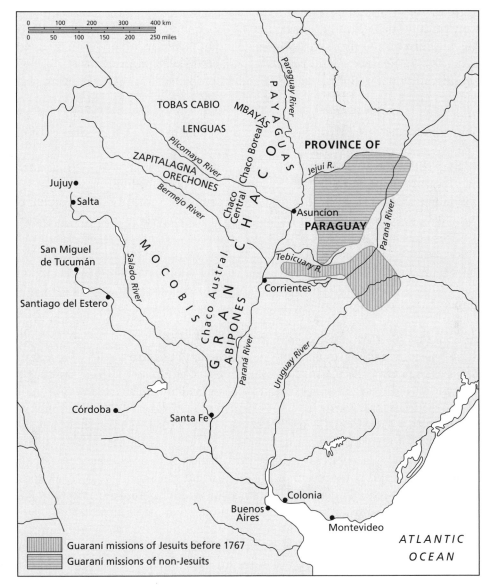

Map 6.2. The Missions of South America.

peoples in some regions resisted and attacked the mission frontier, and other peoples accepted missionization.

Indians in Spanish America who accepted baptism and life under missionary supervision generally were survivors of military campaigns, communities devastated by disease and repeated epidemics, or groups threatened by Spanish authorities and private interests or threatened by more powerful native groups. Missionaries and mission communities offered security, succor, metal tools, pigs and sheep, and the Christian message of hope, love and everlasting life. Indians often explored, considered and incorporated Christian beliefs and concepts into their own, often-flexible systems of belief and spirituality. Native peoples sometimes held new and old religious beliefs side-by-side, introducing Jesus, Mary and the saints into an existing pantheon of spirits, supernatural beings and potent gods. Native peoples also began a process of fusion called syncretism where the new and old overlapped and even merged, where Catholic images and rituals represented aspects of the old cosmology while traditional native images and rituals could be adapted to serve Christian spirituality. Spanish missionaries were rarely satisfied with the faithfulness of Indian Christians, and many clerics viewed Indian converts as frauds, good with the forms of Christianity but incompetent if not indifferent regarding the essentials of the religion.

Regardless of the depth and commitment of native Christianity, the growing number of Indian communities within the church, living under clerical guidance and practicing Catholicism represented a significant development of Indian-European cooperation, interdependence and engagement. Natives as individuals and communities had to give up certain elements of their culture, polygamy for example, to gain specific benefits such as some measure of security, material goods and Old World domestic animals, and thus an enriched diet. Indians decided for themselves whether to accept such cultural bargains and decided how much Christianity and European culture they would accept and reject. In many parts of Spanish America, native communities adopted the Christian calendar and adapted the Virgin Mary and Catholic saints as spiritual guardians. A system of ritual celebration on saints' days, such as the fiesta of San Antonio (January 17), complete with feasts, music, fireworks and a mass, paid for and performed by the native community, became the foundation of a widespread and long-lasting folk Catholicism. In central Mexico, the Virgin Mary took the place of pre-Columbian goddesses, perhaps the Mexica goddess Coatlicue or the older Chalchihuitlicue, both associated with water, fertility and sacrifice. Miraculous images of Saint Mary appeared in native communities, most likely symbolizing Mary's local power as protector and miracle worker and perhaps replacing (or at least giving a new form to) a traditional indigenous goddess.

In late colonial Mexico and Peru, a considerable portion of Indian peoples considered themselves to be Catholic Christians. Their *pueblos* often had Christian churches, they venerated the Virgin Mary and certain saints and the better off contributed time and money to the religious fiestas. "Their conversion the depth of their devotion to Christian values, however," writes Ward Stavig in regard to the Indians of the highland provinces of Quispicanchis and Canas y Canchis, "were tempered by the continued adherence to Andean beliefs, as native peoples accommodated Catholicism to their spiritual and cultural world. The result was a mixture, a syncretic intertwining and blending, of Andean and European religions and beliefs."

The Jesuits began the evangelization of Brazil in 1549. They brought dispersed native peoples and hamlets into mission *aldeias* (villages) and *reduces* (groups of villages or reductions). In their Brazilian missions, Jesuits instructed and baptized their charges, made them attend mass regularly, trained them in useful crafts and arts, and used their labor to farm and ranch to create exports to finance their operations. As in the frontiers of Spanish America, the missionary clergy in Brazil sought to reorganize native life and culture. Permanent settlement replaced a semisedentary way of life. Men were required to work the fields in the European custom, although most native peoples were accustomed to a division of labor by which women were mainly the agriculturalists and men were the hunters and warriors. The decline of coastal forests, the threat of slave raiders and the promise of food and protection attracted many coastal Tupís to the *aldeias* and reductions. However, the missions were never completely secure from slave raiders. In 1580, a Tupinamba leader explained to the Jesuits "we must leave, we must leave before these Portuguese arrive . . . We are not fleeing the Church or your Company, but if you wish to joint us, we will live with you in the forests and backlands."

The efforts by Jesuits to protect Indians from capture and slavery in Brazil made the order despised and hated by settlers. For example, Paulists expelled the Jesuits from their captaincy in 1640–53. In the seventeenth century, the Jesuits established more than fifty missions in Amazonia with some two hundred thousand natives. In Amazonia as in São Paulo, settlers opposed the Jesuits for limiting their supply of Indian slaves. As a result, in São Luis de Maranhão, just southeast of Belém, settlers expelled the Jesuits in 1661. The crown allowed the order to return in 1680 and settlers expelled them again five years later. This time, local authorities and the Jesuits negotiated a settlement. It was acknowledged that the Jesuits controlled the missions, but they had to allow settlers to take their labor for six months each year for payment in cloth. The Jesuits also had to accept, at least formally, the legitimacy of native enslavement in just wars and ransoming.

The most important change in Portuguese-Indian relations in eighteenth-century Brazil took place after 1755 when the crown ended missionary control of the *aldeias* and reductions. Four years later, the Jesuits were expelled from Brazil. *Aldeias* were officially transformed into "free Indian towns" but controlled by officials called directors. The *aldeias* and reductions were opened to forced labor and, as natives abandoned them, they fell apart and were abandoned.

Evangelization was the symbolic fountainhead of New France. The royal patent given to the Sieur de Monts in 1603 stated the King's "singular zeal, and devout and constant resolution" to "cause the people, which do inhabit the Country, men (at this present time) Barbarous, Atheists, without Faith and Religion, to be converted to Christianitie, and to the Belief and Profession of our Faith and Religion: and to draw them from the ignorance and unbelief wherein they are." Champlain began the policy that native trading partners had to accept evangelization. The Jesuits and other religious orders established mission communities they called reserves along the St. Lawrence River and among their principal native allies and trading partners, the Hurons. The Compagnie de St. Sacrement colonized the island of Mont-Réal beginning in 1642, in Iroquois territory, for missionary work. The site was chosen, Father Vimont explained, because it "gives access and an admirable approach to all the Nations of this vast country." Algonquians, Montagnais, Huron and Iroquois attacked by disease accepted baptism and life in reserves. The Jesuits also established Iroquois missions. French policy established that firearms be sold only to converts.

The Jesuits attempted to Europeanize as well as Christianize their native charges. Jesuit frustration with their effort to settle and transform Indian culture, as well as the expansion of the trading frontier, led to a new approach. Jesuits established "flying missions" that traveled to existing Indian towns and offered spiritual guidance to those who would listen. Jesuit fathers in New France, as elsewhere in the Americas, learned native languages and studied native religions to find elements similar to Christianity to better instruct and convert Indians. They traveled unarmed throughout New France and beyond the frontier and accepted and even welcomed martyrdom at the hands of hostile Indians and communities. At first, they were flexible in accepting native customs and beliefs and even adopting certain Indian ways of life. As one Jesuit remarked, "As God made himself man in order to make men God's, a Missionary does not fear to make himself a Savage, so to speak, in order to make them Christians." Nevertheless, the undermanned Jesuit mission in New France over time came to believe the Indians of New France were depraved savages, slaves to corrupt human nature, and thus virtually incapable of conversion. "This censorious Augustinian approach," notes Peter A. Goddard, "was rejected by later missionaries to New France."

By the early eighteenth century, there were only one hundred Jesuits and a few more lay brothers and catechists who supervised approximately thirty-one reserves in New France. During the previous century, the Jesuits had baptized tens of thousands of Indians. However, as the Jesuits recognized, epidemics seemed to kill Christian Indians more than infidels. For many native converts, Christian beliefs were compatible with native spiritual beliefs. For many others, Christianity brought specific benefits in the form of security, firearms, trade goods and other practical gains. An observer in 1750 noted that "there is reason to believe that they only embrace the Catholic faith when they have a reason to do so . . . they practice it in appearance, do what is required, even go to confession, but their shame in avowing their turpitude is false, so that it is apparent they leave without repenting their faults."

Sebastian Rasles, who lived with the Abenaki Indians in Maine for thirty years in the early eighteenth century, testified that their Catholicism was "the bond that unites them to the French." Abenakis in Maine and Québec spoke French, prayed to Catholic saints, adopted French saints' names as surnames and hung wampum belts on Catholic statues. They also maintained traditional rituals and danced to their drums and rattles. The Abenakis rejected English missionary efforts because of their loyalty to the French. "We have promised to be true to God in our Religion, and it is this we profess to stand by." Following the British conquest of Canada in 1763, the Indian reserves maintained the allegiance to the Catholic Church.

By the end of the French regime in North America, there were reserves of Christian Indians at Lorette (the surviving Huron community) near Québec, the Iroquois towns of Kahnawaké and Oka outside Montreal, Odanak or St. Francis in between and others composed of Abenakis, Montagnais and other refugees. They made up perhaps ten percent of the seventy-five thousand inhabitants of New France. These mission Indians were Catholic, self-governing and an important element in the military defense of New France.

Protestant England and The Netherlands prominently claimed the importance of Indian evangelization but their colonizing companies and state churches made little effort on the ground. The 1606 charter of the Virginia Company commended the Company's desire "in propagating of Christian religion to such people as yet live in darkness and miserable ignorance of the true knowledge and worship of God and may in time bring the infidels and *salvages* living in those parts to humane civility and to a settled and quiet government." An advertisement for the Virginia venture four years later proposed a grand bargain between Englishmen and Indians: "[We] do buy of them the pearls of earth, and sell to them the pearls of heaven." Colonists in America, when they did think about religion, were concerned primarily with their own salvation and created local congregations that focused on English lives and souls.

The most serious English missionary effort in seventeenth-century North America was the Puritan missions in New England led by the Reverend John Eliot. Beginning in the 1640s, Eliot organized the surviving native peoples of the region into "praying towns," Indian communities where natives adopted English names, clothing, games, marriages, and hogs and cattle, as well as religious beliefs. Nothing less than cultural suicide was expected and demanded by English missionaries. This generally meant that only those Indian remnant populations in the most vulnerable and dejected state accepted life in the praying towns. By 1674, there were fourteen such towns with some 1,100 inhabitants (and of these, only 199 were baptized). In one of these, Natick, noted Daniel Gookin, the Indians worshipped "with reverence, attention, modesty, and solemnity." In 1663, Elliot sent to Charles II, the King of England, his Holy Bible translated into "the Language of the Natives of this Country." Eliot also founded an Indian college at Harvard to train native ministers. Overall, there were no more than twenty Puritan churchmen who attempted any Indian preaching in the seventeenth century. They were rebuffed by all independent native groups in the region and by many Indian communities among the colonial settlements.

What inspired John Eliot and why did the Puritans not do more? Eliot and other Puritans noted the mission to the Indians was seen as a work on behalf of the glory of God. Eliot also regarded his mission as an act of pity and a way of protecting praying Indians from settlers and marauding Indians. Cotton Mather, the Puritan "divine" and author of *Magnalia Christi Americana* (1702), mentioned the Puritan desire to match the example of the Roman Catholic missions as well as usher in the last days and the second coming of Christ. Puritans generally believed they were creating a Christian commonwealth and extending Christendom by displacing, not converting, Indians. John Higginson declared that the Lord was pleased that "so many Colonies planted, Towns erected, and Churches settled" in places where there "had been nothing before but Heathenism, Idolatry, and Devil worship." Unlike the Catholics who accepted a "blended, mixed worship," explained Mather, Eliot permitted no deviation from biblical Christianity. However, the Indians also stubbornly refused to accept the Gospel.

There were more English and native missionaries in more regions of North America during the eighteenth century. Eliot's students took their ministries to the Indians. The Church of England sent a mission from Scotland to the Mahicans of Stockbridge in 1734. In time, Anglican missionaries were to be found in Iroquois country, Virginia, the Carolinas and Georgia. Eleazar Wheelock's Indian Charity School, which in time became Dartmouth College, educated native preachers. The German mystic Gottlieb Priber took an evangelical Christian spiritualism to the Cherokees in the 1730s and 1740s. Many Indians converted during the evangelical revivalism of the Great Awakening in the 1730s and 1740s. By 1776, there were 133 native preachers in New England. One of these was the Reverend Samson Occom, a Mohegan educated at the Wheelock School, who preached to an Indian congregation at Montauk, Long Island. One of Occom's students, the Mohawk Joseph Brant, assisted an Anglican missionary in the translation of the Gospel into Mohawk. English and American churches became much more serious about evangelization and organized mission societies in the late eighteenth and nineteenth centuries. Before the American Civil War, there were ten societies working among the Iroquois, Cherokees, Chippewas and many other nations. However, the successes were few and minor. Most Indians were uninterested in abandoning their ways and embracing American civilization fully.

The Dutch proved to be better evangelists in Asia than in the Americas. The powerful Dutch trading companies, the East India Company (VOC) and the West India Company (WIC) were required by their charters to promote and protect the established religion, the Dutch Reformed Church, overseas. Although there were only around forty Reformed preachers in all of Dutch Asia by the 1680s, they sought and gained conversions in Ceylon, Taiwan, Malacca and Amboina. Declaring itself the foe of the Portuguese and the Catholic Church, the VOC likely gained converts in the East as it expelled Catholic priests and tolerated greater liberty of worship.

In the Americas, the WIC pledged to bring "the true Christian reformed religion, for the salvation of thousands of souls . . . and to wipe out Papistry and Heathenism." The Dutch expected Indians to convert to Calvinism en masse as they were liberated from Spanish and Catholic tyranny. This theory was to be put to the test in the Dutch conquest of Chile in 1642, but the Dutch could not get the native Araucanians to agree to an alliance. In Brazil (New Holland, 1630–54), the Dutch employed two Brazilian natives trained in The Netherlands to teach religion in the *aldeias*. Not much came of this effort, as might be expected, but in the *Remonstrances* – discourses – of the native allies of the Dutch in Brazil we see a strategy of telling the "High and Mighty Lords of the States General" what they wanted to hear. In your service, wrote one of the Dutch-trained Indians, what was endured and suffered "was not done by a people who still lacked the knowledge of the true God, but by a people who embraced the true Christian Reformed Religion together with their alliance with your High and Mighty."

In North America (New Netherland, 1624–64), the plan was to have Dutch colonists to convert the Indians by example as well as through instruction. However, colonists were busy with other tasks. In the mid-seventeenth century, the patroon of Rensselaerswijck, on the upper Hudson, hired a minister to perform religious services and "to use all Christian zeal there to educate the heathen as well as children in the Christian religion, to practice catechism and teach the Holy Scriptures among the people and to exercise the office of schoolmaster for young and old." However, there is no record of any efforts to educate or convert Indians anywhere in New Netherland. In the Dutch colonies of Curaçao and Surinam in the 1930s, Indians and blacks that claimed attachment to the Dutch Reformed religion constituted less than five percent of the population. There were more Catholics, other Protestants and what the report characterized as "animists."

From the late fifteenth century through the eighteenth century, Europeans struggled again and again to turn Indians into Christians. Native peoples responded to these efforts in many and various ways. Some adopted Christianity along with certain Spanish, Portuguese, French, Dutch or English customs and manners. Over three hundred years, many natives afflicted by conquest and disease tended to find sanctuary, succor and consolation in conversion. To the Huron in 1650, "in the midst of persecution, in the extremity of the evils which assail us and the greater evils which threaten us, we are all filled with joy: for our hearts tell us that God has never had a more tender love for us than now." To the Catawbas, in the Carolina Piedmont, English missionary efforts were met with utter indifference. In fact, Anglican missionaries found only frustration in the backcountry of Carolina. In Spanish America in the sixteenth century and later, many baptized Indians practiced the everyday rituals of Catholicism in front of the friars and worshiped the old gods in caves and secret places. "The great readiness with which these newly converted Indians revert to their idolatries, rites, sacrifices, and superstitions," lamented the bishops of New Spain in 1565, "is notorious." In the long run, the picture is hazy. Some Spanish colonial intellectuals, writes Thierry Saignes, "thought the Indians a flock of sincere and devout believers. Others felt sure their practice of Christianity was superficial and barely concealed fierce attachment to prehispanic beliefs. Present-day historians and ethnographers are equally divided."

6.5 Partners and Allies

The most complex political and commercial relationships between Europeans and Indian peoples anywhere in the Americas existed in North America in the seventeenth and eighteenth centuries. In the northeast as well as the southeast, rival Europeans needed native nations as business partners and military allies. Indians in some regions found themselves in the middle of European commercial and strategic rivalries. Similarly, Europeans found that ties to particular native confederacies and nations brought them into dangerous Indian rivalries and wars. Most Indian groups tried to take advantage of their favorable locations, access to hunting grounds and military prowess to obtain metal tools, firearms and protection from other native peoples. Alliances with Europeans were not always beneficial. Such a relationship could bring military defeat and dispersion instead of security and victory. Some peoples, notably the Five Nations of the Iroquois, successfully played the game of colonial diplomacy and power politics for more than two centuries.

For a few decades, the most important trading partners and allies of the French in Canada were the Hurons (a four-nation confederacy and an Iroquoian-speaking people) located just to the west of the three principal settlements of New France. The arrival of the Dutch on the upper Hudson River in the 1620s transformed the northeastern wedge of North America into a cockpit of both European and Native American rivalry and conflict. The trading post of Fort Orange, located near the present site of Albany, New York, placed the Dutch just east of the Iroquois Confederation, the five nations comprised of the Mohawks, Oneida, Onondaga, Cayuga and Seneca. The Mohawk, "keepers of the western door," became the main trading partners and military allies of the Dutch. When the Iroquois depleted the beaver population in their own territory, they competed with the Hurons for pelts from the north and west. This placed the Iroquois and Huron in direct competition and conflict, and thus the Dutch and French in conflict. For forty years, the "beaver wars" consumed the attention and energy of these four participants facing each other.

The French alliance for the Huron proved disastrous for this native people. The Jesuit missions among them spread disease and severely reduced their population. Their location on the route to the new hunting grounds of the north and west placed them in the path of Iroquois military expansion. The pressure and conflict had been steadily increasing in the 1630s and 1640s. In the winter of 1648–9, the Iroquois attacked Huron towns and destroyed the Huron Confederacy as a political entity. The Iroquois then expanded into the Great Lakes region and attacked, dispersed or incorporated the Petuns, Neutrals, Eries, Susquehannocks, Ottowas and Shawnees. These campaigns had repercussions further west as displaced nations moved into the territory of other people, causing more conflict. Not until they met the Potawatomis in Green Bay, Wisconsin, was Iroquois expansion to the west halted.

Following the destruction of the Huron Confederacy, the French sought to create an anti-Iroquois alliance to contain this threat. However, without English participation, the alliance was stillborn. In 1653, the French agreed not to challenge Mohawk trade and power, hoping to bring an end to the raiding of their Indian allies and French settlements. This uneasy truce held for only a few years, and by 1659 the Mohawk were again raiding Canada. In the mid-1660s, two developments changed the balance of power in the northeast. First, in 1664 the Dutch lost New Netherland to the English and the Iroquois lost, at least for a while, easy access to firearms. Second, in 1665 following the royal government's takeover of New France, France dispatched to Canada 1,200 regular soldiers armed with new flintlock muskets. For the next two years, the French placed forts on the Richelieu River and Lake Champlain frontier and launched a military campaign against the Mohawk. Unable to stop the French raids and facing a defeat and destruction like the Hurons, the Iroquois made peace with the French, which lasted sixteen years. The Iroquois agreed to Jesuit missions as part of the peace agreement, which brought disease and polarized communities into Christian and anti-Christian factions.

Thereafter, the Five Nations of the Iroquois attempted to practice diplomacy as skillfully as they earlier had made war. As a powerful confederation

Document 6.3
The Bloody Victories Obtained by the Iroquois over Our Hurons

The Jesuit Relations, 1649

The 16th day of March in the present year, 1649, market the beginning of
our misfortunes – if, however, that be a misfortune which no doubt has
been the salvation of many of God's elect.

The Iroquois, enemies of the Hurons, to the number of about a thousand
men, well furnished with weapons – and mostly with firearms, which they
obtained from the Dutch, their allies – arrived by night at the frontier of
this country, without our having had any knowledge of their approach;
although they had started from their country in the Autumn, hunting in
the forests throughout the Winter, and had made over the snow nearly
two hundred leagues of a very difficult road, in order to come and surprise
us. They reconnoitered by night the condition of the first place upon
which they had designs – which was well surrounded with a stockade of
pine-trees, from fifteen to sixteen feet in height, and with a deep ditch,
wherewith nature had strongly fortified this place on three sides – there
remaining only a little space which was weaker than the others.

It was at that point that the enemy made a breach at daybreak, but so
secretly and promptly that he was master of the place before people had
put themselves on the defensive – all being then in a deep sleep, and not
having leisure to reconnoiter their situation. Thus this village was taken,
almost without striking a blow, there having been only ten Iroquois killed.
Part of the Hurons – men, women, and children – were massacred then
and there; the others were made captives, and reserved for cruelties more
terrible than death.

Three men alone escaped, almost naked, across the snows; they bore
the alarm and terror to another and neighboring village, about a league
distant. This first village was the one which we call Saint Ignace, which
had been abandoned by most of its people at the beginning of the Winter –
the most apprehensive and most clear-sighted having withdrawn from it,
foreboding the danger; thus the loss of it was not so considerable, and
amounted only to about four hundred souls.

The enemy does not stop there; he follows up his victory, and before
Sunrise he appears in arms to attack the village of Saint Louys, which was
fortified with a fairly good stockade. Most of the women, and the children,
had just gone from it, upon hearing the news which had arrived regarding
the approach of the Iroquois. The people of most courage, about eighty
persons, being resolved to defend themselves well, repulse with courage the
first and the second assault, having killed among the enemy some thirty of
their most venturesome men, besides many wounded. But. finally, number
has the advantage – the Iroquois having undermined with blows of their
hatchets the palisade of stakes, and having made a passage for themselves
through considerable breaches.

Toward nine o'clock in the morning, we perceived from our house
at Saint Marie the fire which was consuming the cabins of that village,
where the enemy, having entered victoriously, had reduced everything to

desolation – casting into the midst of the flames the old men, the sick, the children who had not been able to escape, and all those who, being too severely wounded, could not have followed into captivity. At the sight of those flames, and by the color of the smoke which issued from them, we understood sufficiently what was happening – this village of Saint Louys not being farther distant from us than one league. Two Christians, who escaped the fire, arrived almost at the same time, and gave us assurance of it . . .

In consequence of the bloody victories obtained by the Iroquois over our Hurons at the commencement of the Spring of last year, 1649, and some of the more than inhuman acts of barbarity practiced toward their prisoners of war, and the cruel torments pitilessly inflicted upon Father Jean de Brebeuf and Father Gabriel Lallemant, Pastors of this truly suffering Church – terror having fallen upon the neighboring villages, which were dreading a similar misfortune – all the inhabitants dispersed. These poor, distressed people forsook their lands, houses, and villages, and all that in the world was dearest to them, in order to escape the cruelty of an enemy which they feared more than a thousand deaths, and more than all that remained before their eyes – calculated as that was to strike terror into hearts already wretched. Many, no longer expecting humanity from man, flung themselves into the deepest recesses of the forest, where, though it were with the wild beasts, they might find peace. Others took refuge upon some frightful rocks that lay in the midst of a great Lake nearly four hundred leagues in circumference – choosing rather to find death in the waters or from the cliffs, than by the fires of the Iroquois. A goodly number having cast in their lot with the people of the Neutral Nation, and with those living on the Mountain heights, whom we call the Tobacco Nation, the most prominent of those who remained invited us to join them, rather than to flee so far away – trusting that God would espouse their cause when it should have become our own, and would be mindful of their protection, provided they took care to serve him. With this in view, they promised us that they would all become Christians, and be true to the faith till the death came which they saw prepared on every side for their destruction.

This was exactly what God was requiring of us – that in times of dire distress, we should flee with the fleeing, accompanying them everywhere, whithersoever their faith should follow them; and that we should lose sight of none of these Christians, although it might be expedient to detain the bulk of our forces wherever the main body of fugitives might decide to settle down. This was the conclusion we came to, after having commended the matter to God.

The Jesuit Relations are the reports of Jesuit missionaries in New France from 1632 to 1791. These reports are one of the most important sources of information about the Natives peoples of North America. From Reuben Gold Thwaites, editor, *The Jesuit Relations and Allied Documents: Travels and Explorations of the Jesuit Missionaries in New France, 1610–1791* (1896–1901), Vol. 34, pp. 123–137.

located between New England and New York on one side and New France on the other, the Iroquois realized that they could enhance their bargaining power if they were allied to neither the English nor the French. After making peace with the French in 1677, they turned to the English. In a conference in 1677, the English and the Mohawks created the first "Covenant Chain" treaty in which each side recognized the "subject peoples" of the other and agreed not to treat with them directly. The Five Nations claimed territory from Maine to the Great Lakes and as far south as the Carolinas. In the 1670s, the French had erected forts in the Great Lakes region to secure their trade with the western nations. In the 1680s, the Iroquois attacked French trading partners, the Illinois, Miamis and others. The French responded with more forts and an anti-Iroquois alliance with several native nations. By the 1690s, Iroquois imperialism was thwarted. Indian enemies from the east and west raided the Iroquois homeland, and the French invaded Iroquoia twice. At the same time, the Five Nations were divided by divisions within the Confederacy and within nations regarding strategy and religion. During the 1690s, the total Iroquois population was less than nine thousand. The fighting of that decade led to losses of five hundred warriors out of a total of two thousand. It was time for diplomacy.

In 1701, the Iroquois made their "Grand Settlement." The nations made peace with both the French and the English and pledged their neutrality in future Anglo-French wars. Lands claimed by the French in the west were opened to Iroquois hunting as well as the right to trade at Detroit. There were pro-French and pro-English factions among the Iroquois, and Iroquois leaders used this division to their advantage to gain trade and influence with each power as well as to secure peace. This diplomacy ensured that the Iroquois remained a great power in North America throughout the eighteenth century. The Confederacy was strengthened in 1722 when the Tuscaroras of North Carolina, defeated and driven out of their homeland by settler expansion, moved to New York and were incorporated as the sixth nation in the Iroquois Confederacy. Increasingly in the eighteenth century, developments in the northeast and west shifted from Indian-Indian rivalries and conflicts (with European involvement) to more direct French-English conflict with native participation (see Map 6.3).

In the late seventeenth and eighteenth centuries, the southeast – the Carolinas of England, Spanish Florida and French Louisiana – became another cockpit of native and imperial rivalry and conflict. As in the northeast, European and Indian rivals confronted one another for access to trade as well as strategic position. The Spanish were there first, entrenched in Florida with a few forts, small settlements and mission communities. The English arrived later in the Carolinas and conflict with English slavers and Spanish friars and royal officials erupted from time to time. The French began to settle the lower Mississippi in the early eighteenth century with the aim of containing the Spanish in Florida and the English on the east coast.

The War of the Spanish Succession during the first decade of the eighteenth century set the triangular pattern. The Spanish were allied with the Appalachees, the English with the Creeks and Chickasaws, and the French with the Choctaws. The Creeks with English backing emerged from the war as one of the most powerful Indian confederacies in the southeast. Located

Map 6.3. North America in 1750.

between the English, Spanish and the French, the Creeks realized the neutrality rather than an alliance with any one or another of the European
settlements best served their interests and magnified their influence. Therefore, after the war the Creeks made peace with the French, maintained their
good relations and trade with the English and sent a delegation to Mexico
City to establish peace with the Spanish. The English obtained the support
of the Chickasaws and the French maintained Choctaw allegiance. As in the
northeastern cockpit, developments in the southeast during the eighteenth
century took on a new dynamic as the rivalry between France and Britain
intensified, culminating in the French and Indian War.

Indian trade with the French, Dutch and English produced something of a commercial revolution among trading peoples in seventeenth- and eighteenth-century North America. The native peoples of eastern North America had access to resources, which were very much in demand by Europeans. For example, in 1626 the Mohawk brought some eight thousand beaver pelts to the Dutch at Fort Orange. A little more than thirty years later, forty-six thousand beaver pelts were pouring into Fort Orange annually. In the southeast, natives supplied Charles Town with fifty-four thousand deerskins per year between 1700 and 1715. By the 1740s and 1750s, the deerskin trade of South Carolina had tripled. In return for pelts and hides, Indians obtained an enormous quantity and variety of European trade goods. Indians were most interested in cloth, both cottons and woolens, which was softer, more colorful and washable compared to the hide and fur clothing that was replaced. Natives desired all manner of metal tools such as iron axes, hatchets, knives, fishhooks, hoes, and brass and copper kettles, which replaced bone, stone, wood and copper tools. They also preferred European decorations such as earrings, bracelets, rings, brooches and pins to enhance individual beauty and status. There were no native counterparts for guns, mirrors and alcohol, which proved to be extremely popular consumer items. In particular, guns gave Indian nations an enormous advantage in inter-Indian conflict and permitted Indians to oppose European enemies and aggressive settlers. Guns were so popular among natives, according to historian Michael A. Bellesiles, that by the mid-eighteenth century, the native peoples from Quebec to St. Augustine possessed more firearms per capita than any other society in the world. A Virginia settler in the 1690s wrote that Piedmont Indians "say we English are fools for...not always going with a gun, for they think themselves undressed and not fit to walk abroad, unless they have their gun on their shoulder, and their shot-bag by their side."

Business with Indians was so good in the seventeenth and eighteenth centuries that exports of trade goods became big business in Europe and America. For example, English exports of woolens and metal wares doubled between 1660 and 1700. In one of the last years of the French regime in Louisiana, trade with their native allies involved enormous quantities of cloth, blankets and shirts as gifts. Goods for barter for one year included 17,000 measures of Limbourg cloth, 19,400 blankets, 10,200 men's shirts and 1,700 women's cloth. In 1759, the French expected to trade 4,500 guns, 40,000 flints and fourteen tons of powder.

European traders discovered that they had to respond to native consumer demands and even extend credit when required. South Carolinians believed that by 1715, the Yamasees and their allies had accumulated debts of one-hundred thousand deerskins. Increasingly, natives became more and more dependent upon European goods. Archaeologists have traced the increase of this dependency. In Seneca and Onondaga Iroquois sites, scholars have found that in the early seventeenth century, ten to fifteen percent of artifacts discovered were European in origin. In these same sites, archaeologists have found that fully seventy-five percent of artifacts by 1650–5 were of European origin. Skiagunsta, leader of the lower Cherokees, explained to the governor of South Carolina the significance of trade dependency:

> [I] have always told my people to be well with the English for they cannot expect any supply from anywhere else, nor can they live independent of the English. What are we Red People? The clothes we wear, we cannot make ourselves, they are made [for] us. We use their Amunition with which we kill Deer. We cannot make our guns, they are made [for] us. Every necessary Thing in Life we must have from the White People.

6.6 Death and Life

"Genocide," writes David E. Stannard, "nearly expunged the Western Hemisphere of its people." Stannard and a number of other scholars maintain that the massive decline of native populations that began in the 1490s and continued on a hemispheric level until the nineteenth century was a deliberate genocide, a holocaust, caused by European racism. "Millions of indigenous people died from forced labor, starvation, and disease that were a direct consequence of military invasion, enslavement, and systematic mass murder." Alvin M. Josephy, Jr., writes that "it has been estimated by some demographers that by the seventeenth century, more than fifty million natives of North and South America had perished as a result of war, disease, enslavement, and the careless or deliberate brutality of Europeans – history's greatest holocaust by far." Jayme A. Sokolow argues that "New World military and colonizing expeditions engaged in calculated campaigns of religious and state-sanctioned terrorism against men, women, and children."

These historians are certainly correct in emphasizing that the native population of the Americans collapsed in the centuries following the voyages of Columbus. Historians and social scientists have long debated the size of the contact population in 1492 and the rate and rapidity of population decline. There is no debate regarding the basic facts that there was a large native population before contact and that thereafter, Indian peoples throughout the Americas suffered enormous population losses. The hemispheric picture of native population loss is shown in Table 6.2. This population estimate shows a seventy-five percent decline by 1570 and a more than eighty percent decline by 1650–1700. Of course, Native American population decline was not a homogeneous hemispheric experience. For example, the Valley of Mexico saw a native population collapse from 1,500,000 in 1519 to approximately 325,000 in 1570 and 70,000 by 1650 (see Table 4.1). This constituted a ninety-five percent decline over 130 years. The native population of the Valley of Mexico, indeed the native population of much of Spanish America, began to recover in the late seventeenth century and throughout the eighteenth century. However, the first epidemic among natives of the northern Plains of North America began in 1837. Smallpox spread through Mandan, Arikara and Hidatsa communities and in seven months about seventeen

Table 6.2. Native American populations,
1492–1996

1492	53,904,000
1570	13,507,000
1650–1700	9,359,000
1820	8,470,000
1996	40,000,000

Sources: The population estimate for 1492 is from
Chart I:1, Chapter 1, of this book. The estimates
for 1570 and 1650–1700 are from Angel Rosenblat,
*La población indígena y el mestizaje en América,
1492–1950,* 2 tomos (1954), Vol. I, p. 59, and Peter
C. Mancall, "Native Americans and Europeans in
English America, 1500–1700," Table 15.1, "Indian and
colonist demography, 1500–1700," in Nicolas Canney
(ed.), *The Oxford History of the British Empire. Volume I: The Origins of Empire: British Overseas Enterprise to the Close of the Seventeenth Century* (1998),
p. 331. The estimate for 1820 is from Angus Maddison, *The World Economy: Historical Statistics* (2003),
Table 4.2, "Ethnic Composition of the Americas in
1820," p. 115. The estimate for 1996 is Emma Pearce,
"Appendix 1: Indigenous Population Figures," in Phillip
Wearne, *Return of the Indian: Conquest and Revival in
the Americas* (1996), pp. 204–15.

thousand people died, more than half of the native population of the Upper
Missouri.

The overall native population decline and collapse in North, Central and
South America was primarily the result of epidemic disease. As mentioned
in previous chapters, Native Americans did not have the immunities to such
Eurasian diseases as malaria, yellow fever and smallpox that Europeans and
Africans had acquired over hundreds of generations. Without any understanding of the nature of disease, Africans and Europeans by their very
presence and contact let loose deadly microscopic organisms that caused epidemic diseases to run riot in every part of native America. Diseases in the
Americas were accompanied and made more deadly by war, exploitation,
slavery and missionaries who brought dispersed people together in larger
communities. "The major demographic and epidemiological consequences
of the Atlantic exchange," writes Philip D. Curtin, "thus had their origins
in Africa, though the exchange was made possible by European maritime
prowess and mediated through the slave trade."

The native peoples of the Americas after 1492 were victims of a similar
epidemiological crisis that had struck Asia, the Middle East and Europe in
the fourteenth century. The eruption of the bubonic plague in Asia in the
early fifteenth century was spread to the Crimea by Mongol soldiers in 1347
and to the Middle East and Europe from there. This plague, the infamous
Black Death, killed sixty million Chinese, at least one half of the population,
during the fourteenth century. In Cairo, the world's biggest city at that time,
the plague killed nearly one half of the population, or two hundred thousand

people. During only two or three years at mid-century, the plague killed twenty million Europeans. With the succeeding outbreaks, *pestis segunda* and *pestis tertia* writes David Herlihy, "Europe by about 1420 could have counted barely more than a third of the people it contained one hundred years before." Ibn Khaldûn, the Arab historian, wrote, "Civilization both in East and West was visited by a destructive plague which devastated nations and caused populations to vanish. It swallowed up many of the good things of civilization and wiped them out in the entire inhabited world."

It is likely that the population of Western Europe began a decline in the first half of the fourteenth century as a result of famine. After the outbreaks of 1348–50, which were so devastating, for the next century Europe suffered fourteen additional epidemics. As in the Americas after 1492, epidemics in Europe were accompanied by violence and exploitation – the Hundred Years War, the Peasant's Revolt of 1381 in England and peasant and popular uprisings throughout Europe. Although epidemics of plague as well as smallpox, influenza and dysentery continued to erupt throughout the fifteenth century, Europe's population had likely stabilized by 1400 and increased during the second half of the fifteenth century. By 1500, Europe's population had nearly returned to the level it had reached in 1300.

There was no genocide in Europe in the fourteenth century or in the Americas in the sixteenth through the nineteenth centuries. Although there was massive loss of life, in neither historical case was there intentional mass killing by any kind of perpetrator. Europeans – *conquistadores*, officials and settlers – were not the colonial equivalent of Nazis. While there were many massacres of Indians, from Cortés at Cholula in 1520 to the United States army at Wounded Knee in 1890, there was never any attempt or idea to exterminate Indians as a race. Nor were all European and settler acts of violence and oppression against Indians a form of genocide. Colonialism, not genocide, is the appropriate concept. In both Europe and the Americas, new lethal epidemic diseases were inadvertently spread in vulnerable populations. More people died over a longer period of time in the Americas than in fifteenth-century Europe because it took centuries for various diseases to reach and attack the many different and often isolated native societies of the Americas. Epidemic disease in the Americas, unlike Europe earlier, was accompanied by colonialism. "The violence and social crises that resulted from the imposition of European colonialism," writes Suzanne Austin Alchon, "greatly exacerbated native American mortality." While "epidemic disease accounts for much of that demographic decline," she concludes it was European colonialism "that differentiated the demographic experience of native American populations from that of populations in the Old World."

In both Europe and the Americas, there were population recoveries. However, in Europe there was no Chinese, African or Muslim displacement. In the Americas, disease was more lethal for a longer period of time, and therefore population recovery began later and took longer. In the meantime, during the sixteenth through the eighteenth centuries, Europeans immigrated to the Americas and Euroamerican populations grew through a high birth rate and a low death rate. All the same, as James H. Merrell writes about North

Table 6.3. Indigenous languages in the Americas,
living and extinct, 2005

Country	Living	Extinct	Total
Mexico	287	7	294
Brazil	182	47	229
United States	150	47	223
Peru	91	15	108
Canada	78	4	82
Colombia	74	21	95
Guatemala	51	2	53
Venezuela	37	6	43
Bolivia	34	7	41
Americas Total	1090	194	1284

Note: This table lists all indigenous languages and their dialects, that is, the variations within languages. For example, the 2005 *Ethnologue* lists 25 distinct varieties of Nahuatl in modern Mexico; also 68 Mayan dialects, 60 of Tupi and 45 of Quechua. The *Ethnologue* identifies and classifies 59 Native American language families.
Source: Raymond G. Gordon (ed.), *Ethnologue: Languages of the World*, fifteenth edition (2005). The online version is at http://www.ethnologue.com.

America, "The conquest of the continent was not as swift as the emphasis on depopulation and displacement implies; Indians did not surrender or disappear overnight. Without belittling the devastation wrought by smallpox, militias, or settlers, we need to remember that Indians survived."

One subject that illustrates damage to and survival of Native Americans is that of language. Nicholas Ostler tells us that the rise and fall of empires has great influence on the spread and demise of languages. The success of European languages in the Americas, primarily Spanish, Portuguese, French and English, recalls Nebrija's thesis "that always language was the companion of empire." The destruction of the great native empires in the Americas as well as epidemics and colonialism led to the decline and loss of many Indian languages. Nearly two hundred of these have disappeared over the last five hundred years. But just as Indians survived as peoples, so most of their languages have survived into the present. The tongues of the Mexica and Inka empires are still spoken in Mexico and Peru. According to one count, there are over one thousand Native American languages spoken today (see Table 6.3). One Mexican recently commented, "It is important and at the same time nice to be able to speak Nahuatl because this is the authentic way of talking in Mexico." Another Mexican stated, "There is no way that Nahuatl could disappear because it is the inheritance from our forefathers." Like Nahuatl, Native Americans are not disappearing.

For more than three centuries, Indians and Europeans were closely and profoundly engaged with one another. As we have seen, this engagement did not have the same types of consequences for Indians as for Europeans.

Indian culture was revolutionized by disease, conquest, colonization, evangelization and growing dependence upon European goods. For Europeans and Euroamericans, engagement was more benign. Perhaps no historian has put it better than Francis Jennings:

> In the last analysis, what American society owes uniquely to the Indian component of our matrix is its exploration, development, settlement, and cultivation of the continent. Every European 'discoverer' had Indian guides. Every European colonizer had Indian instruction and assistance. Ethnocentric semantics have hidden the chief role of Indians in the creation of American society by reserving exclusively for Europeans the honorable title of 'pioneer' and contrasting it to the lowly status of 'native,' but the European vanguard were pupils in the Indian school. Indians brought to their symbiotic partnership with Europeans the experience and knowledge of millennia of genuine pioneering. What American society owes to Indian society, as much as to any other source, is the mere fact of its existence.

6.7 Further Reading

James Axtell, *The European and the Indian: Essays in the Ethnohistory of Colonial North America* (New York, 1981).

James Axtell, *Natives and Newcomers: The Cultural Origins of North America* (New York, 2001).

Colin G. Calloway, *New Worlds for All: Indians, Europeans, and the Remaking of Early America* (Baltimore, 1997).

Olive P. Dickason, *The Myth of the Savage and the Beginnings of French Colonialism in the Americas* (Edmonton, 1997).

Charles T. Gehring and William A. Starna, editors and translators, *A Journey into Mohawk and Oneida Country, 1634–1635: The Journal of Harmen Meyndertsz van den Bogaert* (Syracuse, 1988).

Charles Gibson, *The Aztecs under Spanish Rule: A History of the Indians of the Valley of Mexico, 1519–1800* (Stanford, 1964).

P. Hulton, *America, 1585: The Complete Drawings of John White* (Chapel Hill, 1984).

Francis Jennings, *The Invasion of America: Indians, Colonialism, and the Cant of Conquest* (New York, 1976).

John E. Kicza, *Resilient Cultures: America's Native Peoples Confront European Colonialism, 1500–1800* (Upper Saddle River, 2003).

J. C. H. King, *First Peoples, First Contacts: Native Peoples of North America* (Cambridge, Mass., 1999).

Karen Ordahl Kupperman, *Indians and English: Facing Off in Early America* (Ithaca, 2000).

Joseph-Francois Lafitau, *Customs of the American Indians Compared with the Customs of Primitive Times*, edited by William N. Fenton and Elizabeth L. Moore, 2 volumes (Toronto, 1974–7).

Jean de Léry, *History of a Voyage to the Land of Brazil* [1578], translation by Janet Whatley (Berkeley, 1990).

Gary B. Nash, *Red, White, and Black: The Peoples of Early North America*, fourth edition (Upper Saddle River, 2000).

Anthony Pagden, *The Fall of Natural Man: The American Indian and the Origins of Comparative Ethnology* (Cambridge, 1982).

Robert Ricard, *The Spiritual Conquest of Mexico: An Essay on the Apostolate and the Evangelizing Methods of the Mendicant Orders of New Spain, 1523–1572* (Berkeley, 1966).

Daniel K. Richter, *Facing East from Indian Country: A Native History of Early America* (Cambridge, Mass., 2001).

Irving Rouse, *The Tainos: Rise and Decline of the People Who Greeted Columbus* (New Haven, 1992).

Antonio Rumeo de Armas, *Política indigenista de Isabel la Católica* (Valladolid, 1969).

Gordon M. Sayre, *Les Sauvages Américains: Representations of Native Americans in French and English Colonial Literature* (Chapel Hill, 1997).

Ian K. Steele, *Warpaths: Invasions of North America* (New York, 1994).

Steve J. Stern, *Peru's Indian Peoples and the Challenge of Spanish Conquest: Huamanga to 1640* (Madison, 1987).

Reuben Gold Thwaites, editor, *The Jesuit Relations and Allied Documents*, 73 volumes (Cleveland, 1896–1901).

James Wilson, *The Earth Shall Weep: A History of Native Americans* (New York, 1998).

Stephanie Wood, *Transcending Conquest: Nahua Views of Spanish Colonial Mexico* (Norman, 2003).

Chapter 7

Uprooted

West Africa, the Americas and the Atlantic Slave Trade

"To traffick in human Creatures, may at first sight appear barbarous, inhuman and unnatural," wrote Captain William Snelgrave in 1734, "yet the Traders herein have as much to plead in their own Excuse, as can be said for other Branches of Trade, namely, the Advantage of it; and that not only in regard of the Merchants, but also of the Slaves themselves." Snelgrave believed the slave trade benefited the merchant and the slave because enslaved Africans, in his view, lived better lives in their new American country than they did in their old African homeland. By the mid-eighteenth century, as the captain's comment suggests, some Europeans began to question the morality of the slave trade. However, from the fifteenth century into the eighteenth, for most Europeans who thought about the issue the shipping of enslaved Africans across the Atlantic was no more immoral than the shipping of sugar, tobacco and silver. The Atlantic slave trade was simply a business – "the business of kings, rich men and prime merchants," as Jean Barbot put it – that connected Europe, Africa and the Americas. This business was at the core of the Atlantic System, a dynamic commercial economy that connected the Americas, Europe and Africa through the movement of peoples, goods, services, capital and credit. During the seventeenth and eighteenth centuries, the Atlantic System, more than anything else, defined and shaped the Atlantic World.

Across four hundred years, from the mid-fifteenth century until the mid-nineteenth century, Europeans purchased Africans from African rulers, merchants and middlemen and transported the captives to Europe, the islands of the Atlantic Mediterranean and across the Atlantic to the Americas, where they became slaves. The best recent scholarly assessments hold that approximately 12 million captive Africans were exported from the coasts of Africa and that around 10,500,000 were delivered alive to one of many Atlantic (mostly American) slave-trading ports. It required something on the order of thirty-five thousand voyages to transport this many people from Africa to the Americas. Four of every five immigrants to the Americas before 1820 were African captives, that is, there were 8.4 million African involuntary immigrants compared to 2.4 million European immigrants. For a considerable

Table 7.1. The Atlantic slave trade: Arrivals in
America, 1510–1870

Years	Slaves
1510–1600	274,900
1601–1700	1,341,100
1701–1800	5,729,100
1801–1870	2,902,400
Total	10,247,500

Note: It is a generally held that the first direct shipment of enslaved
Africans to the Americas took place in 1510. There some evidence
that such shipments occurred earlier. Prior to 1510, or whenever
the first direct shipment from Africa began, the Spanish (primarily)
brought Africans, slaves and freedmen, from Europe to Hispan-
iola, Cuba and the Spanish Caribbean in general.
Sources: For the period 1451 to 1700, Philip D. Curtin, *The
Atlantic Slave Trade: A Census* (1969), p. 268; for the period 1701
to 1870, David Eltis; revision of Curtin's figures in Eltis, *Economic
Growth and the Ending of the Transatlantic Slave Trade* (1987).
Also see Herbert S. Klein, *The Atlantic Slave Trade* (1999), Table
A-2, pp. 210–11; and David Eltis, Stephen D. Behrendt, David
Richardson and Herbert S. Klein (eds.), *The Trans-Atlantic Slave
Trade: A Database on CD-Rom* (1999).

portion of its post-Columbian era, the Americas were more of an extension
of Africa than of Europe (see Table 7.1).

We should remember that the Atlantic slave trade was not the only slave
trade out of or into Africa. From 1580 to 1680, there were some 850,000
Christians captured by Barbary pirates and enslaved in Muslim North Africa.
One of these slaves, Francis Brooks, wrote about his "cruel bondage" and
"hard Labour" in his 1692 account, *Barbarian Cruelty*. Barbary corsairs continued to enslave European men, women and children through the eighteenth
century, and they enslaved American sailors in the late eighteenth and early
nineteenth centuries until President Jefferson launched four years of naval
assaults against the Barbary ports. Historian Paul Lovejoy has estimated that
more than eleven million captives were carried east to the Muslim world in
the Red Sea, Indian Ocean and Sahara desert trades from 650 c.e. to 1900.
Ralph Austin has placed that number at seventeen million. All of the trans-
African slave trades were based upon a domestic African system of slavery
and slave trading, which underlay and facilitated the transcontinental and
transoceanic slave trades. Indeed, slavery was a part of most African societies
and slave trading was an ancient practice. Berbers and Arabs were connected
to preexisting slave-trading markets and networks. However, the increasing
pace of the Atlantic slave trade in the eighteenth century made slavery and
slave trading much more important in some African societies. The Atlantic
slave trade may have even contributed to the formation of new societies in
Africa as well as in the Americas.

The plantation complex in the islands of the Atlantic Mediterranean and
the New World was the engine that powered the Atlantic slave trade. Most
enslaved Africans – about two-thirds brought to Madeira, the Canary Islands,
São Tomé, Brazil, the Wild Coast of Guiana, Spanish America, and numerous

islands in the West Indies – were shipped and purchased to cultivate, harvest and process sugarcane, the "white gold" of the tropical Atlantic. There were plantations worked by African slaves that produced other luxury or high-value staples: tobacco, indigo, cotton, coffee and rice. African slaves were put to work in Spanish American silver mines and Brazilian gold mines. African slaves nearly everywhere worked as cowboys, mule train drivers, stevedores, shoemakers, stonemasons and house servants. However, sugar and slavery was the magic formula that transformed continents. As the sixteenth-century refrain went, "Whoever says sugar says Brazil, and whoever says Brazil, says Angola."

The Atlantic slave trade began in the fifteenth century, expanded during the sixteenth and seventeenth centuries, and peaked in the eighteenth century. The nineteenth century was the age of the trade's contraction and ultimate demise. Some of these captives went to the plantation islands of the near Atlantic. Naturally, most traffic was directed to the tropical and semitropical plantation zones of the Americas. In most of these regions during the course of the trade, slave populations did not reproduce themselves. Because there were always more men transported than women, in combination with unhealthy disease environments, poor and inadequate nutrition, excessive labor, violent punishment and general mistreatment, plantation regimes could maintain their levels of slave populations only through continuous importation of new slaves.

The ties among Europe, Africa and the Americas were never seen as clearly as in the famous if simplified triangular pattern related to the slave trade. Europeans shipped metal, cloth, guns and other manufactures to Africa and bartered these goods for captives. Commercial and ruling elites on the coasts of Atlantic Africa became integrated into the Atlantic World. They not only became part of Atlantic commercial networks but also sent diplomatic missions to Europe and the Americas, adopted European languages, became literate and numerate, and even accepted Christianity to some extent. Slaves were transported across the Atlantic to the plantations, farms and cities of the Americas in exchange for sugar, tobacco, cotton, indigo and coffee. These valuable staples produced by slaves were then shipped back to Europe. Although only about two-thirds of ships actually made this complete triangular course, people and products did follow this pattern and numerous variations of it. The same merchant capitalism that promoted voyages of exploration and colonialism also underwrote the Atlantic plantation complex and its indispensable characteristic, African slavery. Europeans, Africans and Americans came together across the vast reaches of the Atlantic to make slaves and to make products and, in the final analysis, to make money. The Atlantic System was a system of intercontinental and multicultural collaboration that produced many benefits but also immense exploitation and appalling misery.

7.1 The African Connections

The Portuguese purchased the first captives on the coast of Africa in the 1440s and 1450s. The Portuguese had earlier practiced "man-stealing," the kidnapping of people on the coast (as would other Europeans in the years to come) but traders learned that this was the difficult way of obtaining slaves. Local rulers and merchants were happy to trade slaves for European merchandise. The chronicler Cadamosto noticed, "the [local] King supports himself by raids, which result in many slaves from his own as well as neighboring countries. He employs these slaves...in cultivating the land...but he also sells many to the [Moors]...in return for horses and other goods." King Afonso of Kongo in 1540, after regaining control of his kingdom's trade, wrote that no ruler in Africa "esteems the Portuguese goods so much...as we do." Ivana Elbl has carefully estimated early Portuguese slave trade from 1450 to 1516, and concluded that the Portuguese uprooted and carried away nearly 156,000 Africans.

Nine years after the first Portuguese purchases, a papal bull authorized Portugal to reduce to servitude all heathen peoples. Of course, the church had long accepted slavery in principle, as a necessary part of the world of sin. Until the eighteenth century, the European conscience was more troubled by the enslavement of Native Americans than that of Africans. Iberians would eventually prohibit Indian slavery in law, although these bans were never absolutely enforced. Many Europeans believed that slavery was itself benign. During the age of the slave trade, many good Christians considered slavery beneficial to Africans who were removed from heathen conditions and introduced to the word of God. Francisco de Auncibay in 1592 informed the Spanish Council of the Indies regarding the acceptability of African slavery:

> The negroes are not harmed because it is very helpful to these wretches to save them from Guinea's fire and tyranny and barbarism and brutality, where without law of God, they live like savage beasts. Brought to a healthier land they should be very content, the more so as they will be kept and live in good order and religion from which they will derive many temporal and, which I value most, spiritual advantages.

About a half a century later, a synod of French Protestant churches considered the morality of the slave trade. Here we see a continued acceptance of the legitimacy of African slavery and the slave trade but implicit acknowledgement that the bodies of slaves were abused and their souls abandoned. The synod decreed,

> Though slavery, as it has been always acknowledged to be of the right of nations, is not condemned in the word of God, and has not been abolished in most parts of Europe, by the manifestation of the gospel, but only by a contrary practice, insensibly introduced; nevertheless, since several merchants trading on the coast of Africa and to the Indies, either in exchange, or for money, the possession of whom they transmit to others by formal sales, or exchange; this assembly, confirming the rule made on that subject in Normandy, exhorts them not to abuse that liberty, contrary to Christian charity, and not to dispose of these poor infidels, but to Christians as will use them with humanity; and above all will take care to instruct them in the true religion.

Following an unsuccessful shipboard mutiny of African captives, Captain Snelgrave asked the men what had induced them to revolt. "They answered,

I was a great Rogue to buy them, in order to carry them away from their own Country; and that they were resolved to retain their Liberty if possible." Snelgrave replied with an answer that most Europeans of the age of the slave trade would have accepted. "I replied, that they had forfeited their Freedom before I bought them, either by Crimes, or by being taking in War, according to the Custom of their Country." He noted further, "That if they should gain their Point and escape to the Shore, it would be no Advantage to them, because their Countrymen would catch them, and sell them to other Ships." The moral responsibility for the slave trade, Snelgrave suggested, ultimately rested in African hands.

The historian David Eltis has made the point that many Europeans arrived at a pan-European identity two or three centuries before Africans. Europeans in the age of the slave trade may have believed that Africans enslaved other Africans, but the peoples of this continent did not share this perspective. Generally, those rulers, merchants and middlemen who traded slaves to Europeans did not barter away their own countrymen and women. We begin to see a pan-African identity among those who became the slaves of Europeans and Euroamericans. Quobna Ottobah Cugoano, a former slave from the Gold Coast, noted in the late eighteenth century, "I must own, to the shame of my own countrymen, that I was first kid-napped and betrayed by some of my own complexion, who were the first cause of my exile and slavery." However, Cugoano redirected moral responsibility for the Atlantic slave trade to Europeans with a simple yet profound argument. "If there were no buyers," he wrote, "there would be no sellers."

It is true that Africans came from a continent where slaves were kept, worked and bought and sold. Given the great cultural diversity of sub-Saharan Africa, there was no one type of slavery. There were different levels of servitude, bondage and exploitation. In the Sudanese empires of the Niger Valley, agricultural estates owned by kings and nobility were not unlike Atlantic plantations in their treatment of laborers. Slaves in these estates worked under overseers, and their status and working conditions probably differed little from slaves in Brazilian or Caribbean plantations. A song of the region referred to the families of slaves being split up, children taken away from mothers and wives taken away from husbands. Askiya Dāwôd (1549–83) of the Songhay Empire reportedly had some twenty estates producing rice, with up to one hundred slaves on each. A chronicle of one of his successors reported that after one war, all of the male captives were slaughtered and the women and children enslaved. Sudanese estates worked by slaves cultivated millet, sorghum, wheat and rice; production fed the armies and maintained the privileges and status of the nobility.

It is logical to assume domestic slavery was well established in the Western and Central Sudan before the arrival of the Europeans on the Atlantic coast because this region was the source (and point of trans-shipment) of the trans-Sahara slave trade beginning in the eighth century. Scholars have not been so sure about the existence of domestic slavery in coastal and near-coastal societies. J. D. Fage argues that the type of slave economy that existed in the Sudan spread to the coasts around the Senegal and the coast of Guinea by the fifteenth century. Elbl's research on the early Portuguese slave trade, which considers the first European contacts with coastal African societies, reinforces this interpretation. "The early Atlantic slave trade," as Elbl writes, "tapped into pre-existing patterns of reliance on slaves as sources of wealth and power. Converting slaves into another form of wealth was one possible utilization of slaves as a resource, as opposed to domestic exploitation. The Europeans were seldom the only available buyers, and their success depended very much on their competitiveness and appeal."

Slaves in the gold mines of West Africa performed arduous labor, although they were given certain job benefits. A Portuguese traveler in the sixteenth century noted, "The mines are dug very deeply into the ground. The kings have slaves whom they put in the mines and to whom they gave wives, and the wives they take with them; and they bear and rear children in these mines. The kings, also, furnish them with food and drink." The kings who owned the mines began to buy slaves from the Portuguese not long after they appeared on the Guinea coast, making the Gold Coast the only mainland region that imported, for a time, rather than exported slaves. In the salt works at Teghaza, slaves were also employed in the very difficult job of cutting rock salt. A Dutch observer on the Gold Coast around 1600, before the slave trade became a major force in this region, wrote, "The King of the area keeps many Slaves and trades in them, buying and selling them, by which he makes a profit: in short, one does not find here any Servants who serve people for payment or a salary: all of them are Slaves or Captives who have to spend their life in slavery."

Another region with agricultural estates worked by slaves was Kongo. Captives taken in wars were enslaved on the agricultural estates of the nobility around the capital M'banza Kongo. Kongolese nobles owned sugar plantations in São Tomé and used African slave labor. One Portuguese observer of the Kingdom of Kongo in the 1570s reported, "There are no [free] men who cultivate the ground, nor men who work by the day, nor anyone who is willing to work for a wage. Only slaves labor and serve." Slavery and estate agriculture in Africa differed from European plantations in the Atlantic in terms of their ultimate purpose: whereas plantations exported staples to maintain and expand a large system of merchant capitalism, African estates produced for domestic markets to maintain or support the state and noble class.

Slave markets existed throughout West and Central Africa. In the early sixteenth century, Leo Africanus observed in the city of Gao "a market where many slaves, men and women, are sold every day. A girl of fifteen is worth about six ducats. Little children are sold for about half the price of grown-ups." Of course, in time many markets developed along the coast where Europeans came to purchase slaves. In fact, entire towns appeared on the coast of West Africa in the seventeenth century that were little more than slave markets.

In Atlantic Africa before the great expansion of the European slave trade, slaves were used not only as agricultural laborers and miners but also as skilled artisans, domestic servants, soldiers, state administrators, tax collectors and concubines. Most slaves in most West African societies were forms of property who were integrated into a kinship group or household.

Most wives were a form of property. Domestic slaves added to the wealth and production of the family or clan and could aspire to owning their own slaves. Slaves were valued as dependents and as sources of income. In different societies, there were different levels of servile condition. Most African societies had a form of pawnship, by which an individual would bind himself or a relative to a more prosperous person or clan for a certain sum. "The Slaves found here," wrote Pieter de Marees about the Gold Coast in 1602, "are, firstly, poor people who are enslaved because they are unable to earn a living." A pawned person was a temporary slave who often performed domestic service and could not be sold beyond his or her community. Nicolas Villault noted that these special types of slaves were only permitted to nobles of the Gold Coast, "by which means they are not allowed to entertain any but for their necessary service in their families or fields." Villault went on to report that, "The King has several sorts of Slaves, some like these I have mentioned; others which are forfeited to him for want of paying their Fines, or other penalties imposed for some fault they have committed; They generally use their Slaves very well, seldom or never giving them any correction."

The Africans who were sold to Europeans were captured in Africa for several reasons. Willem Bosman stated, "Most of the slaves that are offered to us are Prisoners of War, which are sold by the victors as their booty." Barbot, also in the late seventeenth century, noted, "The slaves they possess and sell are prisoners of war taken from among their enemies." As European demand increased and Europeans sold guns for slaves, states became more aggressive and more and more slaves were obtained in war. A second group of slaves were victims of kidnapping and slave raiding. One of the more famous kidnapping victims was Olaudah Equiano, who came from the coast of modern Nigeria and later in life wrote about his experiences as a slave. He described the general fear of kidnappers: "Generally, when the grown people in the neighborhood were gone far in the fields to labour, the children assembled together in some of the neighbours' premises to play; and commonly some of us used to get up a tree to look out for any assailant, or kidnapper, that might come upon us; for they sometimes took those opportunities of our parents' absence, to attack and carry off as many as they could seize." The British naval surgeon Alexander Falconbridge in the later eighteenth century argued, contrary to conventional wisdom, "that most of the negroes shipped off from the coast of Africa, are kidnapped." His reasoning was that it could not be wars among the Africans that provided slaves because "I never saw any negroes with recent wounds; which must have been the consequence, at least with some of them, had they been taken in battle." A third category of slaves was those condemned through some type of judicial process. Thieves, adulterers and witches were some of the categories that could lead to slavery. In some African societies, there were additional causes of enslavement. "The Kings are so absolute," reported a European traveler in seventeenth-century Upper Guinea, "that upon any slight pretense of offence committed by their subjects, they order them to be sold for slaves without regard to rank, or profession."

Document 7.1
The Manner How the Negroes Become Slaves

Captain William Snelgrave, 1734

As for the Manner how those People become Slaves; it may be reduced under these several Heads.

1. It has been the Custom among the Negroes, time out of Mind, and is so to this day, for them to make Slaves of all the Captives they take in War. Now, before they had an Opportunity of selling them to the white People, they were often obliged to kill great Multitudes, when they had taken more than they could well employ in their own Plantations, for fear they should rebel, and endanger their Masters Safety.

2*dly*. Most Crimes amonst them are punished by Mulcts and Fines; and if the Offender has not wherewithal to pay his Fine, he is sold for a Slave: This is the Practice of the inland People, as well as those on the Sea side.

3*dly*. Debtors who refuse to pay their Debts, or are insolvent, are likewise liable to be made Slaves; but their Friends may redeem them: And if they are not able or willing to do it, then they are generally sold for the Benefit of their Creditors. But few of these come into the hands of the Europeans, being kept by their Countrymen for their own use.

4*thly*. I have been told, That it is common for some inland People, to sell their Children for Slaves, tho' they are under no Necessity for so doing; which I am inclined to believe. But I never observed, that the People near the Sea Coast practice this, unless compelled thereto by extreme Want and Famine, as the People of Whidaw have lately been.

Now, by these means it is that so many of the Negroes become Slaves, and more especially by being taken Captives in War. Of these the Number is so great, that I may safely affirm, without any Exaggeration, that the Europeans of all Nations, that trade to the Coast of Guinea, have, in some Years, exported at least seventy thousand. And tho' this may no doubt be thought at first hearing a prodigious Number; yet when 'tis considered how great the Extent of this Coast is, namely from Cape Verde to Angola, which is about four thousand Miles in length; and that Polygamy is allowed in general amonst them, by which means the Countries are full of People, I hope it will not be thought improbable that so many are yearly exported from thence.

Several Objections have often been raised against the Lawfulness of this Trade, which I shall not here undertake to refute. I shall only observe in general, That tho' to traffick in human Creatures, may at first sight appear barbarous, inhuman, and unnatural; yet the Traders therein have as much to plead in their own Excuse, as can be said for some other Branches of Trade, namely, the Advantage of it: And that not only in regard of the Merchants, but also of the Slaves themselves, as will plainly appear from these following Reasons.

First, It is evident, that the abundance of Captives, taken in War, would be inhumanly destroyed, was there not an Opportunity of disposing of them to the Europeans. So that at least many Lives are saved, and great Numbers of useful Persons kept in being.

Secondly, When they are carried to the Plantations, they generally live much better there, than they ever did in their own Country; for as the Planters pay a great price for them, 'tis their interest to take care of them.

Thirdly, By this means the English Plantations have been so much improved, that 'tis almost incredible, what great Advantages have accrued to the Nation thereby; especially to the Sugar Islands, which lying in a Climate near as hot as the Coast of Guinea, the Negroes are fitter to cultivate the Lands there, than white People.

Then as to the Criminals amonst the Negroes, they are by this means effectually transported, never to return again, a Benefit which we very much want here.

In a word, from this Trade proceed Benefits, far outweighing all, either real or pretended Mischiefs and Inconveniencies. And, let the worst that can, be said of it, it will be found, like all other earthly Advantages, tempered with a mixture of Good and Evil.

William Snelgrave was a British sea captain from Bristol and a slave trader. He considered himself a humane man and a Christian. From *A New Account of some Parts of Guinea and the Slave-Trade*, by Captain William Snelgrave. London: Printed for James, John, and Paul Knapton, at the Crown in *Ludgate-Street*, MDCCXXIV [1734], pp. 158–61.

Whatever the origin of a slave, whether captive in war, by kidnapping or in some judicial process, no victim considered the process legitimate or the outcome beneficial. Brother Luis Brandaon, a Jesuit stationed in Angola in the early seventeenth century, noted, "I found it true indeed that no negro will ever say he has been captured legally." One hundred and fifty years later, Olaudah Equiano described his capture and then separation from his sister: "I was left in a state of distraction not to be described. I cried and grieved continually; and for several days I did not eat any thing but what they forced into my mouth." Individual African men, women and children obviously did not simply accept the legitimacy of capture and enslavement and, as a result, states, communities and families organized strategies to defend themselves from raiders and traffickers.

In many parts of Africa, communities used natural geography to protect themselves from predatory neighbors. For example, peoples in the lake and lagoon regions of the Bight of Benin built homes and entire villages on stilts at the edge of the lakes or in the lake waters. Villages located in the complex networks of lakes, swamps and lagoons could only be reached by canoe and could only be found by residents. To insure safety, villagers would occasionally relocate their villages. In the area of Lake Chad in central Sudan, peoples and polities protected themselves from conquest and attack by using mountains, cliffs and caves as refuge. In some regions, villagers would create defensive fences of thorny trees and live hedges. Just about everywhere, villages, towns and cities built walls to defend themselves from raiding parties or conquering armies. "The most important defensive strategy in much of Africa," writes Martin A. Klein, "was the construction of walls and the development of architecture that made it difficult for attackers to take prisoners even if they succeeded in entering a fortified village." In the Senegambia, the people of Cayor and Baol often made villages that were easily built and easily rebuilt. In a time of danger, they could burn their houses, escape raiders and rebuild later in safety. In Igboland, as Olaudah Equiano described his own capture, when adults were in the fields, some children took to the trees to look for slave raiders and would give an alarm if any assailant or kidnapper came to the village. Friends and family members frequently paid ransoms to redeem a captive or obtained "replacements," a practice that sometimes meant substituting two or more "inferiors" for a valued kin member. Captive redemption was a practice that existed before the arrival of the Europeans (and thus an African initiative) and one that not only took place directly on the coasts of Atlantic Africa but also in the Americas. John Corrente, the headman of Annamaboe on the Gold Coast, sent one of his sons to Barbados in the early eighteenth century to redeem another son.

Of course, the most radical form of African resistance to the Atlantic slave trade was the use of violence directed against the slaveholding and slave-trading African elite and Europeans on the coast. African captives rebelled during the loading of slave ships on the coast of Africa, onboard ship during the weeks and months the slavers stayed on the coast to continue purchases, and during the middle passage across the Atlantic. Although the records of shipboard rebellions are few, historians suggest revolts may have occurred as many as one slaving voyage in ten. If this figure is anywhere close to the mark, this means there were in the range of three thousand revolts during the age of the slave trade. The implication of this figure, as David Richardson notes, is that one million more African slaves could have been shipped had African captives been more docile when they were loaded on board ship and shipped across the Atlantic.

Once a man, woman or child became a captive, African kings, chiefs and merchants had to determine the slave's trade value. Europeans provided what African consumers wanted and negotiated the quantity or price. If African merchants valued cowry shells, the delicate white shells from the Maldives in the Indian Ocean, then Europeans imported millions of shells each year. If Africans wanted East Indian textiles, guns, shot and gunpowder, rum brandy or molasses-flavored Brazilian tobacco, then European merchants provided them. African consumer preferences dominated the markets. Often captives were bartered for a combination of items that included iron bars, knives and axes, textiles, rum and brandy, guns and gunpowder, and jewelry. Textiles were always the most important and highly valued item of trade even in the eighteenth century when Europeans exported hundreds of thousands of guns each year. "In exchange for these negroes," noted one trader in 1682, "we trade cotton, baft, copper, tin, iron, spirits and a few glass trinkets . . . Often enough, you can get a pretty good slave for four or five jars of alcohol." European slave traders were required to distribute "gifts" to local kings or chiefs in exchange for the privilege of trading. "Customs" and dues were paid in all manner of goods, including slaves. In the Senegambia region, Barbot noted that the Compagnie Français du Sénégal paid "dues and tolls exacted by the black kings which the company conducts trade."

In Africa, the African elite controlled the Atlantic slave trade. One of the obvious signs of African control was the imposition of taxes, duties or simply tribute that local authorities required Europeans pay to trade. Paul Erdmann Isert, chief surgeon at the Danish castle Christianburg, wrote in his account of the slave trade, "The Blacks are difficult to trade with and it requires great effort to reach agreement with them." Willem Bosman, an officer of the Dutch West India Company on the coast for fourteen years, made clear who, ultimately, was in control. "Though the English, Danes and we have Forts here, yet our Authority is very small, and confined within our own Walls: So that the Forts serve to defend our selves; for if we should make any Attempt on the Negroes, they would certainly end in our Destruction."

The British at Cape Coast Castle in the late eighteenth century informed London, "That it is necessary from our present weakness to keep black men of power in our pay, that through their influence, we may live in peace and amity with the natives who would otherwise molest us, knowing we have not a sufficient force to protect ourselves." In the 1760s and 1770s, the British maintained their position and trade on the coast through giving lavish and constant gifts to local African *caboceers*, chiefs or rulers, hiring canoemen, free labors and even paying their castle slaves. From 1770 to 1776. Cape Coast Castle had a total expenditure of £145,460, of which £59,243 was devoted to the salaries of British officials, factors, soldiers and other white men. Africans received, in gifts, rent, wages and more, £47,940, or close to one-third of the total expenditure. This was more than the price of "peace and amity," it was the price of doing business.

Europeans traveled to seven distinct regions in West and Central Africa in search of captives for the Atlantic slave trade. Senegambia, that is, the region of the Senegal River and the River Gambia and points in between, was the home of many ethnic groups such as the Fulbe, Soninke and Bamara – or as the Europeans called them, "Bambara" – all Mande speakers. Bambara slaves were known and desired throughout the Atlantic World. A number of Senegambians from the interior – Fulbe, Mandinka and Hausa – were Muslim and brought Islam to different parts of the Americas. Senegambia came to have a heavily garrisoned coastline in the seventeenth and eighteenth centuries with French and English forts at Saint Louis, Gorée, Saint James, Cacheu and Bissao, among others. The upper (Senegal) coast was one of the centers of the French slave trade; they made their headquarters on the island-castle of Saint Louis. The forty-five acre Gorée Island, located off the coast of Senegal just south of Saint Louis, which had been used as a slave *entrepôt* for the Dutch, English and finally the French, shipped an estimated one hundred thousand African captives from the early sixteenth century to the mid-nineteenth century. The English were more entrenched in the River Gambia region. Only the Gold Coast was more densely occupied by Europeans than Senegambia. Although the Portuguese had been expelled here from all but one of their factories in the seventeenth century, the resident Afro-Portuguese *lançados* and *tangomaos* remained the most common middlemen in the trade, and

Portuguese (or a Portuguese-based creole simply called *crioulo*) remained the language of business on the coast. The early seventeenth-century English trader Richard Jobson found that the Afro-Portuguese mulatto traders were quite willing to do business with other Europeans besides the Portuguese. The Atlantic slave trade and domestic slavery gave rise to political crises and holy wars. In the seventeenth and eighteenth centuries, these conflicts fed the slave trade and gave rise to Islamic states, which were supplied firearms by the slave trade. Overall, Senegambia was one of the least significant sources of supply of the Atlantic slave trade.

Sierra Leone, today Guinea-Bissau, Guinea and Sierra Leone, was a region of considerable political fragmentation in the seventeenth and eighteenth centuries, and remained a backwater of the slave trade until the eighteenth century. Mande speakers in this region included such ethnic groups as the Susu, Kono, Jallonke and the Mende or Mandinka, as they were called in Africa, and "Mandingos," as they came to be known in the Americas. Nicolas Villaut in the 1660s found that the African and Luso-African traders all spoke Portuguese and the king at Boure was a Roman Catholic. The English headquarters on this coast was on Bence Island, and there was an English warehouse on York Island. Similarly, the Dutch had warehouses on the coast. Here, as in Senegambia, Muslim revolutions and the rise of Islamic states in the interior fueled the slave trade. Sierra Leone and Senegambia accounted for less than ten percent of all recorded departures in the slave trade but sixty percent of attacks upon slaving ships by shore-based Africans. This figure may help explain these regions' less than vigorous participation in the slave trade.

Europeans traded on the Windward Coast, which included the Grain and Ivory Coasts – the region between modern Liberia and the Côte d'Ivoire – for pepper, cloth, wood and ivory. "Mandingos," some of them Muslims, were also exported from this coast as well. Local rulers and merchants did not participate in the slave trade in any serious way. "You see all the nations of Europe coming ashore at Sierra Liona, but Frenchmen and Englishmen more than any others," noted Barbot, "either to collect provisions, or to trade in gold, slaves, sandal-wood, and a little yellow wax." Perhaps the most important of the provisioning and trading points on this coast was at the Rio Sestos. "This Coast is called the Coast of Malguette," wrote Villault, "in respect to the Pepper at Rio-Sextos." The Juula revolution of coastal merchants in the late seventeenth century gave rise to the city-state of Bate, which "improved" the slave trade in this region. As in Sierra Leone, Islamic revolutions in the interior in the 1720s to the 1740s produced conflict, and thus captives, which were drawn into the slave trade.

The Gold Coast (modern Ghana) was populated by Akan and Ga speakers. Most captives from this coast were Akan speakers, members of such ethnicities as the Asante, the Fante, Wassa, Ahanta, Nzima, Akeym and others. The Portuguese called all slaves delivered from the Gold Coast "Minas," a name derived from their castle São Jorge da Mina. The English called Gold Coast slaves "Cormantees," "Coromantees" and many similar spellings, a name taken from the English fort and factory of the same name (which was a corruption of the Akan name "Kormantse," a coastal African town). The

Figure 7.1. Guinea in the Eighteenth Century. Detail from Map I-II, *Atlas Maritimus & commercialis* (London, 1728). Courtesy of the William L. Clements Library at the University of Michigan.

Gold Coast had the largest European presence in West Africa. This 175-mile stretch of coast during the eighteenth century counted some two dozen major castles and stone forts and eighty to one hundred factories, trading posts and warehouses. The Dutch had eleven major establishments with their headquarters at Elmina castle since 1637. The Gold Coast saw the appearance of not only Afro-Portuguese mulattos but Afro-Dutch mulattos, called *tapoeijers*, who were some of the richest traders on the coast. The English occupied ten castles with their headquarters at Cape Coast Castle. In the late eighteenth century, the Danes had four castles. For a long time, slaves were not the primary export here. Not until the early eighteenth century did the value of slaves exceed the value of gold exports in the appropriately named Gold Coast. By this time, the influence of the slave trade on local African societies seemed clear. The Dutch director-general on the Gold Coast reported that "the natives no longer occupy themselves with the search for gold, but rather make war on each other to furnish slaves." The rise of Asante, a militarized confederacy in the interior north of Elmina, was built on the sale of African captives and the purchase of European guns. In 1701, Asante defeated Denkyira, its rival that controlled the interior trade routes. By 1727, the three remaining polities that blocked Asante's free access to the coast, Aowin, Wassa and Twifo, were reduced to tributaries. In the 1770s, Asante provided more than one thousand captives annually.

The Bight of Benin, also called the Slave Coast, was a region that greatly influenced the slave trade in the seventeenth and eighteenth centuries. This region – today Togo, Benin and southwest Nigeria – was the home of three major languages and cultures: the Fon, Ewe and Yoruba. The coast was thinly populated before the coming of the Europeans but in less than one hundred years, a network of trading states – Whydah, Jakin or Ardra (Offra), and Porto Novo, to name the most important – had arisen. Europeans built trading lodges rather than stone castles and forts here because the coast was made of endless lagoons. It was also likely that local African states did not permit the construction of stone castles. There were also three powerful states in the interior, Oyo, Allada and Benin. From the sixteenth century, Benin had limited its participation in the slave trade. Such restraint appeared much more difficult to maintain for most other African states, particularly by the late seventeenth century and the early eighteenth century. Oyo's rise in the seventeenth century was indirectly linked to the slave trade. The kingdom's military success was based upon the purchase of horses for its cavalry. Oyo sold captives as slaves to obtain European goods, which were bartered for horses from the Moors of North Africa. The Kingdom of Dahomey had arisen in the hinterland in the seventeenth century, perhaps to defend its people from the wars and kidnappings of the slave trade as well as to fend off Oyo. In the 1720s and 1730s, Dahomey invaded the towns of the coast to expand its power and dominion and to control the trade with Europeans. Dahomey allegedly became an aggressive militarized autocracy that sold slaves to purchase arms, to make war and capture more slaves. By 1730, Europeans were selling around 180,000 guns each year to Africans on the Gold and Slave Coasts.

The Bight of Biafra (today south-central Nigeria), located on the Niger River delta and often called by Europeans the region of the five slave rivers, was home to the Efik, Ijo, Ogoni, Ibibio and the famous Igbo, also called by Europeans "Eboe" and "Ibo." The most wel-known Igbo individual from the age of the Atlantic slave trade was Olaudah Equiano, who was kidnapped as a boy and transported to the British West Indies. There were commercial centers such as New Calabar (Elem Kalabari), Bonny and Aboh but they did not attempt to become territorial states. The region was infested with local warlords. One group, the Aro, began as mercenaries and evolved into merchants as European ships began to appear more frequently on the coast. They created a network of warlord-merchants who obtained captives and routed them to the coast. Because the Aro did not have a state to use to obtain captives, they made use of religious oracles that could use enslavement as a sanction or penalty.

The conflicts among the powerful and aggressive inland states fed captives to the city-states of the Bight of Benin, and the kidnapping system of the Bight of Biafra produced a considerable flow into the Atlantic slave trade. The Slave Coast certainly earned its name, even though the European presence on the ground was weak and thin. One-half of all slave exports from Africa left from the Bight of Benin from 1662 to 1713. Obviously, Europeans did not need dozens of castles and factories to pump the slave trade. They simply needed to appear with empty ships. African merchants in the Bights were organized into dense networks that linked the interior with the coast, and they were in charge. South of the Bights, what is today Cameroon and Gabon, were regions that exported some commodities but few slaves.

Finally, there was West Central Africa – the Loango coast, the Kingdom of Kongo and the Portuguese colony of Angola – the single most important source of captives from the sixteenth to the nineteenth century. Here lived the Kikongo-speaking people of Kongo, the Kimbundu-speaking people called

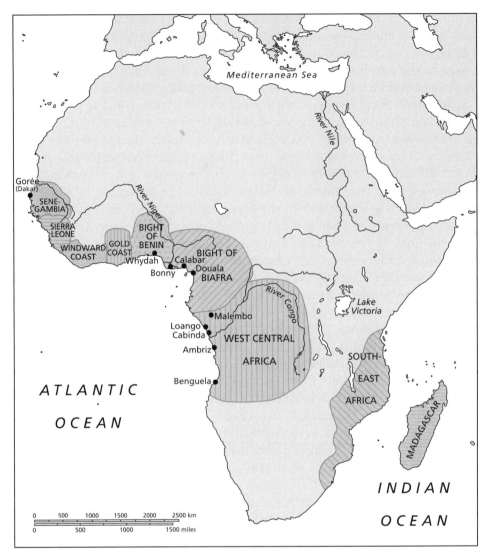

Map 7.1. West Africa in the Era of the Transatlantic Slave Trade.

the Mbundo of Angola, the Ngongo, Maluk, Kete and others. The chaos
that accompanied the decline of the Kingdom of Kongo and the expansion
of Portuguese rule in Angola supplied captives for the Atlantic trade. The
history of the Kingdom of Kongo demonstrated that kings, nobles and merchants could benefit from the slave trade while their societies stagnated or
wasted away. Angola, more of a Brazilian than a Portuguese colony by the
eighteenth century, was a conduit for slaves from the deep interior of the
continent. Angola's capital, the island-city of Luanda, the largest European
city in Africa, generated almost all of its income by the late eighteenth century
from the slave trade, according to a contemporary observer (see Map 7.1).

East Africa was briefly opened to the Atlantic slave trade in the seventeenth
century when the Portuguese had been expelled from Guinea and, briefly,
from Angola. Madagascar and Mozambique participated in the Muslim-
dominated Indian Ocean slave trade. The French had established sugar, coffee

Table 7.2. *Atlantic Africa overseas trade, 1680–1820*

	1680s	1780s	1820s	1860s
Total Imports	£1,700,000	18,500,000	10,600,000	41,300,000
Total Exports	£6,500,000	31,700,000	27,700,000	51,800,000
Slave Trade	50%	90%	60%	2%

Note: Amounts are given in pounds sterling. The slave trade component of total trade is an average of slave imports and exports.
Source: David Eltis and Lawrence C. Jennings, "Trade between Western Africa and the Atlantic World in the Pre-Colonial Era," *The American Historical Review*, 93:4 (October 1988): 936–59.

and indigo plantations on the Mascarene islands in the Indian Ocean and obtained slaves from this region of East Africa. Only in the 1770s did a substantial trade of slaves – roughly 5,400 a year – enter the Atlantic from East Africa.

Paul Lovejoy's estimates of the number of captives exported from the different zones in West and Central Africa in the eighteenth century reveal the dominance of two regions: West Central Africa and the Bight of Benin. Something on the order of three-fifths of the total derived from these two places. Herbert S. Klein, examining the broader period of 1662 to 1867, concludes that these two regions provided approximately sixty percent of the total volume of the Atlantic slave trade.

7.2 The Business of Slaving

The enormous surge in the slave trade during the eighteenth century reflected the increase in the production of slave plantations, plus gold mining in Brazil, which began in the 1690s. In 1620, Brazil produced 15,000 tons of sugar annually. By 1790, the British and French sugar islands were producing 290,000 tons annually. The output of tobacco increased from 20 million pounds annually to over 220 million pounds in 1775. Brazilian gold production reached its peak in 1720–45, where slaves were producing hundreds of thousands of kilograms of gold dust per decade. These productive enterprises, particularly the plantations, were the economic engines that led to the forced immigration of millions of Africans. Table 7.2 shows the growth of trade with Western Africa from the late seventeenth century and how the slave trade came to dominate African trade by the 1780s. The decline of the slave trade in the nineteenth century brought a return to more normal commodity imports and exports.

Where did they go? The largest single flow of the Atlantic slave trade went to Brazil, slightly over 4,029,800 captives during the course of the slave trade. Just about one of every three captives was taken to Brazil. The next three American regions all imported nearly the same number. Spanish America imported 1,662,400 captives over the longest period of any American society. The British sugar islands of the Caribbean imported 1,635,700, and the French sugar islands imported 1,699,700 captives. British North America,

Table 7.3. The Atlantic slave trade:
Arrivals in America by region, 1451–1700

Destination	Slaves
Europe	50,000
Near Atlantic Islands	25,000
São Tomé	100,000
Spanish America	367,500
Brazil	610,000
English Colonies	263,700
French Colonies	155,800
Dutch Colonies	20,000

Source: Herbert S. Klein, *The Atlantic Slave Trade*
(1999), Table A.2, p. 210.

which included the United States after 1776, imported 559,800 captives.
Only six in every one hundred captives were taken to North America (see
Table 7.3, Table 7.4 and Map 7.2).

In 1770, there were about 2.5 million slaves living and working in the
Americas. The largest number of slaves was found in Brazil, which should
not be surprising as it was the destination of the largest number of captives
and the greatest plantation economy in the Atlantic World. In most of the
tropical plantation societies, slaves did not naturally reproduce their populations. The imbalance of the sexes caused by the slave trade was accompanied
by low birth rates and high death rates for enslaved Africans. Large numbers of imports were necessary to maintain a stable population, and even
greater numbers were required to expand slave populations. This meant that
Africa-born Africans populated the plantations of the sixteenth, seventeenth
and eighteenth centuries. North America was the one major exception to this
development. Before any other plantation region, in the early eighteenth century, an American-born or Creole population was arising. Creole populations
had roughly equal numbers of males and females. Were more balanced numbers of men and women delivered to North America? Was tobacco and rice
cultivation less severe and deadly than the cultivation of sugar? Was North
America a healthier disease environment? Something elevated birth and lowered mortality rates. Despite British North America's minor participation in

Table 7.4. The Atlantic slave trade: Arrivals
in America by region, 1701–1800

Destination	Slaves
Spanish America	515,700
Brazil	1,498,000
British Colonies	1,256,600
French Colonies	1,431,200
Dutch Colonies	20,000
British North America/USA	547,500

Source: Herbert S. Klein, *The Atlantic Slave Trade*
(1999), Table A.2, p. 211.

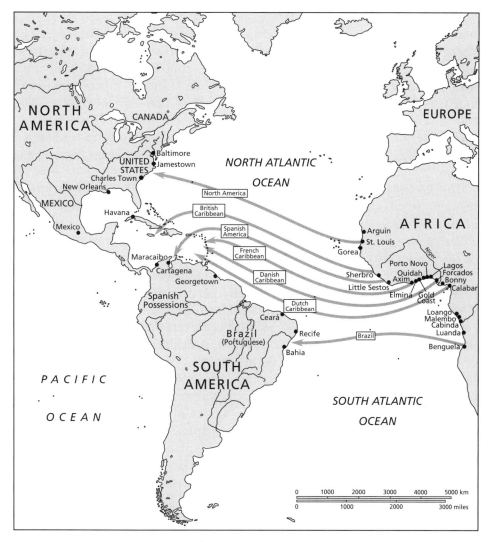

Map 7.2. The Transatlantic Slave Trade.

the Atlantic slave trade, population growth in the eighteenth-century North American slave community produced nearly as large a slave population as in Brazil by the end of the century.

How did enslaved Africans come to the Americas? Europeans organized the business of the trade in two very different ways. The first was through monopoly contracts or monopoly companies, the joint stock chartered companies that appeared in the seventeenth century. The companies had been given monopoly franchise on trade with Africa and to specific colonies or in the entire Atlantic by a monarch or national government. The English charter stated that "trade be confined to a Company by a joint Stock exclusive of all others." For example, the Dutch West India Company (WIC) was given a monopoly in the trade of slaves in Africa and the Americas. The chartered companies were the institutions that built the castles and factories that dotted the coast of the Senegambia and the Gold Coast. The other approach to slaving was simply free trade: independent merchants, or what the British called "separate traders," conducted business under few or no national restrictions and competed among themselves and other nationalities for trade. The chartered companies were responsible for the considerable flow that took off in the seventeenth century. However, the companies could never meet the demand of the American plantations or successfully compete against the independents that were, at first, "interlopers" of one sort or another. The enormous expansion of the slave trade in the eighteenth century was possible because seemingly innumerable companies, partnerships as well as individual merchants and captains, were able to respond to the American demand for slaves.

The Portuguese and the Spanish organized their branches of the trade through royal contracts. The king of Portugal granted (meaning sold) monopoly trade privileges to Portuguese merchants and nobles regarding a certain portion of the African coast for a certain period of time. The holder of the monopoly contract would not necessarily trade in slaves himself but sell shares of the trade to other merchants – in short, subcontract the business. Because the Spanish did not directly participate in the slave trade, the Council of the Indies was required to grant contracts, called *asientos*, to the subjects of other sovereigns. The Spanish contracts purchased units of labor (slaves), which they called *piezas de India*. A healthy male in his late teens or early twenties was judged to be one "piece." Three healthy boys under the age of fifteen constituted two *piezas*. The Portuguese Cacheu Company in 1693 delivered 4,000 captives, or 2,500 *piezas de India*. By the late seventeenth century, the *asiento* had become a prize of considerable importance. The French were awarded the *asiento* in 1702, and the British took it by war and diplomacy in 1713. In the second half of the eighteenth century, the *asiento* system was dismantled bit by bit. In wartime, the slave trade was opened to neutral nations. In 1778, when Spain purchased a few factories on the African coast, the trade was opened to all Spaniards, although a few monopoly contracts continued. Outside the *asiento* system altogether were the interlopers: Portuguese, Dutch, British and French slave traders who took increasingly larger shares of the trade in the eighteenth century.

The great national chartered companies of the seventeenth century were established to break open the Iberian trade monopolies and create new and rich Dutch, French and English monopolies and empires. Founded in 1621, the Dutch WIC was granted monopoly-trading privileges on the coast of Africa, which included the slave trade. However, in the 1620s and 1630s, one of the founders of the WIC was morally opposed to trading in slaves. He steered the company away from the slave trade as much as possible in that complicated and multichambered company. When the WIC seized a considerable portion of Brazil, the company needed a steady supply of slaves, and in 1641 it seized Portuguese Angola and São Tomé for that purpose.

Although the WIC lost its transatlantic empire in Brazil and Angola, it had become a player in the slave trade. From 1630 to 1674, the WIC carried approximately ninety thousand African captives to the New World, and about one-half of that number was smuggled into Spanish America. Curaçao became the Company's principal distribution center, of merchandise as well as slaves. Some of the greatest competition to the WIC came from independent Dutch slave traders who founded rival national slave trading companies for Sweden, Denmark, the Brandenburgers and the Duke of Courland. The Dutch managed more castles on the Gold Coast than was apparent at first glance.

The Swedish African Company established in 1649 was financed by Dutch investment and led by Dutch merchant adventurers under Swedish royal patronage. The Swedish company began building Fort Carolusburg on the Gold Coast and to counter this unwanted competition, the WIC built a fort at nearby Butri. After 1665, the Royal Chartered Danish Guinea Company arrived on the coast and took over the Swedish posts. The Danes built Christianburg Castle at Accra and, beginning in the 1670s, began shipping slaves to their new West Indian colonies of St. Thomas, St. John and, after 1733, St. Croix. The Danes expanded their presence on the Gold Coast with Fort Fredenborg, built in 1736, Fort Kongensteen, and Fort Prindsensteen.In the 1680s, the Germans arrived in the form of the Brandenburg African Company and built Fort Gross Friedrichsburg near Axim, Fort Dorothea at Akwidah, and took over the abandoned Portuguese post at Arguim. Fort Gross Friedichsburg was seized by the German's trusted African broker and trader, John Konny, in 1715. The Brandenburg African Company then sold the castle to the Dutch in 1717, but they were not able to take control of it until 1724.

In 1674, the WIC was declared bankrupt. A new and restructured WIC focused on trade more than empire building. Its only significant remaining trade monopoly was in slaves. In the period 1675–1731, the slave trade was an important profit-making enterprise for the Company but the export of gold from Elmina was considerably more important. Given the makeup of the Company, business was always complicated. Slaving voyages were always planned in a series of nine: Amsterdam received four, Zeeland two and one each for the other three chambers. In 1730–4, the new WIC lost its slave trade monopoly; these trades were thrown open to all Dutch merchants. The Company was left in possession of the costly castles and factories on the Gold Coast. Independent traders who purchased slaves at Company posts had to pay a maintenance fee (which, of course, only encouraged them to trade elsewhere). Increasingly, the Dutch slave trade was in the hands of independent traders. In 1791, the new WIC was abolished and, for the first time, the Dutch republic became a colonial power as it assumed control of the Company's colonies in the Caribbean and Guiana. Long before the formal demise of the Company, the Dutch slave trade was conducted by thousands of independent merchants and captains.

The new WIC held about a dozen castles and forts on the Gold Coast in the late eighteenth century. However, forts had never guaranteed traffic with Africans. The WIC made the error in the early eighteenth century of allying themselves with an African kingdom that was an enemy of a then small and unimportant state called Asante. As Asante power expanded during the course of the century, Dutch influence waned.

The English slave trade was unorganized until 1618, when the first of several companies of "adventurers" was formed and given a monopoly of

African trade. After the restoration of the Stuarts in 1660, the royal family invested in the slave trade through the Company of Royal Adventurers Trading into Africa, which became the Royal African Company (RAC) in 1672. This company was granted a monopoly of African trade for one thousand years, evidence of a long-term business plan. From 1672 until 1713, the RAC controlled at least ten castles and forts from its headquarters at Cape Coast Castle (the original Swedish Fort Carolusburg) on the Gold Coast. It dispatched over five hundred ships to the coast of Africa, which carried 100,000 to 125,000 captives to British ports in the Americas. Naturally, merchants who were not given a share of the trade, and colonists who believed the Company neglected their slave-starved colony, protested the "foul monopoly." However, the RAC provided enough slaves for the plantation revolution to take off in the English sugar islands.

In 1689, the RAC lost its monopoly of trade, one of the after-effects of the Glorious Revolution. The RAC had been too closely aligned with the Stuarts. For about twenty-five years, independent traders paid a commission to the RAC for upkeep of the Company's African castles and factories. After 1712, the slave trade was opened to all British merchants and captains without restriction or fee. The RAC survived for a time because it received, as a subcontractor of the South Sea Company, the Spanish *asiento*, the greatest commercial prize of the Atlantic slave trade. Independent traders took over the slave trade to the British sugar islands, which was many times larger than the trade to Spanish America, and they expanded it greatly in the eighteenth century. The British slave trade during the second half of the seventeenth century carried over 250,000 captives; during the eighteenth century, British slavers carried more than 2.5 million captives. The RAC was dissolved in 1752.

The British presence on the coast of West Africa was unmatched. In a 1709 official report, the RAC listed eighteen establishments. Only the Dutch WIC's Elmina Castle was a rival to the British Cape Coast Castle as queen of the Guinea Coast. The British castle had seventy-four great guns and repositories for at least a thousand captives. British power was also anchored at William's Fort at Whydah and James Fort and Island on the river Gambia. The purpose of the three substantial forts was to prevent rivals from taking trade. William's Fort "situated in the Kingdom of Whidah," the Company reported, "which prevents the Dutch and French from engrossing the whole trade of that Kingdom." Smaller fortifications like Commenda, Succundee, Annamaboe and Dix Cove Forts had repositories for 100 to 150 captives. Unfortified factories like those at Annishan, Agga, Torntomquerry, Shidoe and Alampo on the Gold Coast were "places of Good trade."

The French monopoly companies were organized and financed by the state to better promote French colonial development. The *Compagnie des Indes Occidentales* (CIO), or the French West Indies Company, was established in 1664 with broad privileges and trading monopolies in the Atlantic. The French fleet seized several Dutch factories in the Senegambia, including Gorée Island. The CIO survived only ten years and never made a profit, but it established the French slave trade and redirected most trade with the French Antilles in French ships. In the 1670s, two French slave trading companies were founded: *Compagnie du Sénégal*, headquartered at Gorée, and *Compagnie du Guinea*, which received the Spanish *asiento* in 1702–13. New slave-trade companies with specific privileges and monopolies were chartered throughout the eighteenth century. By 1767, the year when the slave trade was opened to all Frenchmen for a fee, independent traders dominated the trade.

The chartered companies generally were agents of the most important commercial interests in their countries, or the most important political interests, or both. Although they revved up the Atlantic slave trade in the seventeenth century, for the most part they were financial failures. Most independent merchants in the trade were representatives of respectable trading "houses," or they were members of partnerships involving sometimes as many as a dozen investors. In the case of Great Britain, the loss of the RAC's monopoly was also the loss of London merchants and the gain of Bristol and Liverpool merchants. The independents were traders or sea captains directly representing their own interests. Independent traders had to raise the capital to outfit a ship and send it to the coast of Africa and then find African suppliers and barter European goods for African captives, sail to the Americas and find buyers for their human cargoes. If the ship was still seaworthy, it returned to its homeport, sometimes filled with colonial staples, sometimes filled only with ballast. After a voyage of twelve or fifteen months, the independent trader had to cover the costs of the ship and crew, the merchandise carried to Africa, the losses in captives who died during the crossing, and – if fortune smiled – earned a little extra as profit.

African consumers wanted such diverse and quality products that slave traders generally had to outfit a slaving voyage with merchandise from various European, Asian and American countries and colonies. Merchandise constituted fifty or sixty percent of the total cost of a slaving voyage. In the eighteenth century, British traders had access to the best quality merchandise at the lowest possible price, thus giving them an advantage over the Portuguese, French and even the Dutch. The best traders needed to know about the latest African consumer whims and demands. They would inquire of other traders and ships' captains where on the African coast they could find the best and worst trades. The success of a trading voyage, noted John Atkins in the early eighteenth century, "depends at several places on Chance, from the fanciful and various Humours of the Negroes, who make great demands one Voyage for a Commodity, that perhaps they reject the next." During most of the seventeenth, eighteenth and nineteenth centuries, the terms of trade favored African merchants, brokers and princes, that is, over time African traders received more and better goods in trade from Europeans and Americans for the same quantity of slaves, gold and other commodity exports. These favorable terms were the result of intense European competition for Africa's valuable products.

News of war and peace in the kingdoms behind the coast could indicate where to trade or where caution would suggest not going. The best slave traders looked for a good ship, not too big but not too small, one that was swift and could hold about two hundred to three hundred captives. They looked for an experienced crew who knew the various winds and currents of the Atlantic, and knew how to handle the uncooperative "passengers" who would try at any moment to escape, kill the crew or kill themselves. The best independent traders realized that most of their American customers would have to purchase captives on credit or barter them for a quantity of sugar or tobacco. A slaving voyage was never a simple operation. A lot could go wrong, and pretty much everything had to go right before anyone made money. This was the view of Atkins and most of the traders and voyagers to Guinea in the seventeenth and eighteenth century.

Anti-slavery propaganda in the eighteenth and nineteenth century propounded the idea that profits from the slave trade were fabulous, and sometimes they were. There were also financial disasters because of bad weather or epidemics that killed most captives. Most voyages saw neither fabulous profits nor disastrous losses. Various scholarly studies of the slave trade place profits in the broad range of 3.3 to 29.9 percent, with the average pretty close to 10 percent. The chartered companies with their high overhead were great financial failures but the independent traders, who were more flexible and competitive, were often more successful. As more and more merchants and captains entered the slave trade in the eighteenth century, competition intensified and profits became more difficult to find.

The Atlantic slave trade, indeed the entire Atlantic System, was a vast commercial enterprise that was composed of thousands of different and varied active participants in Europe, Africa and the Americas. These businessmen and women located throughout the Atlantic World made many hundreds of thousands of business calculations every year to ship a sufficient number of enslaved Africans, to keep the plantations productive, to increase Europe's imports (and re-exports) of sugar, tobacco, indigo and other plantation commodities, and, finally, to guarantee the bottom line – that is, to keep the profits flowing. According to some historians, the Atlantic slave trade and New World slavery were not simply businesses but the engines and origins of modern global capitalism. What else but immoral and rapacious capitalism would have turned Africans into commodities and plantations into brutally efficient factories? The Atlantic System, while commercially expansive and geopolitically transformative, was not capitalist. The Atlantic slave trade was not completely profit-maximizing because Europeans did not enslave other Europeans. European slaves would have brought lower recruitment costs than African slaves and, as a result, greater profit. Furthermore, the slave trade in Africa was based indirectly on African coercion through war and political power to steal men, women and children from their societies.

In fact, slavery as a form of labor runs contrary to the productive forces of capitalism. "A capitalist society in which free wage labor was not the norm," notes Alan Knight, "is hard to imagine." The most significant investment in any plantation was in slaves. This overcapitalization of slave labor generally led planters to seek to gain efficiencies in production through labor coercion and abuse rather than the capitalist approach and investment in labor-saving technology. The sugar plantations of the late eighteenth century were not all that different from the plantations of the sixteenth and seventeenth centuries. "Great improvements are seldom to be expected from great proprietors," wrote Adam Smith, "they are least of all to be expected when they employ slaves for their workmen." This point was made by Edward Long, a member of the planter elite of Jamaica, in his history of Jamaica in 1774. "The high price and value of Negroes, with other considerations," wrote Long, "should move the planters to try every expedient by machines, or otherwise, for performing that labour which is usually performed by Negroes." The use of a plough, he argued, could do the same labor as one hundred slaves with their hoes in the same time. Why then would the planters not avail themselves of this useful machine? Long mentioned "the force of prejudice and custom" but also the fact (no doubt, an uncomfortable fact to many slaveowners) that "the Negroes will then be able to finish their work in half the time."

The Atlantic System, a system of merchant capitalism, increased economic activity throughout the Atlantic World and led to the development of overseas productive enterprises, ports, cities and entire colonies. The contribution of mercantile profits to European economic growth and capital accumulation and investment from the sixteenth to the eighteenth century was always modest in relation to other sectors of the national economies. Most trade by Europeans during these centuries was intra-European trade, that is, the exchange of English woolens for Dutch linens or something along that line. By 1800, long-distance commerce may have accounted for no more than four percent of Western European annual economic growth. Furthermore, this commerce probably did not contribute more than one percent of capital formation of the West European economies. As for the slave trade, Kenneth Morgan notes that in 1770, profits from the British slave trade (then at its height) amounted to 0.0054 percent of national income. What about sugar? One historian has estimated that sugar production in the British West Indies in 1770 produced a profit of £1.7 million in a national economy valued at over £62 million. The Atlantic trades, including the slave trade, were always more important to the Americas and Africa than Europe.

7.3 The Middle Passage

Slaving voyages on behalf of the monopoly companies only had to sail to one of the company's castles, or to a few factories, and pick up their cargo of captives. The castles contained large dungeons, called *baracoons* by the English and *esclaveries* by the French, where captives were held until the next slave ship arrived. Independent traders often had to sail along the coast of Africa for weeks, even months, buying a few captives at a time here and there. Buyers for independent traders and for the companies inspected the human merchandise for any sickness or defects. The better prepared and organized traders had surgeons (qualified doctors sometimes) who examined the captives. Once certain captives were selected and purchased, they were then often branded to indicate whose property they were during the middle passage.

Both the factors in the castles and individual ship captains needed middlemen who could translate languages and cultures, that is, the meaning of certain arguments and behavior. This role was performed nearly everywhere on the African coast by African merchants and Afro-Europeans who were

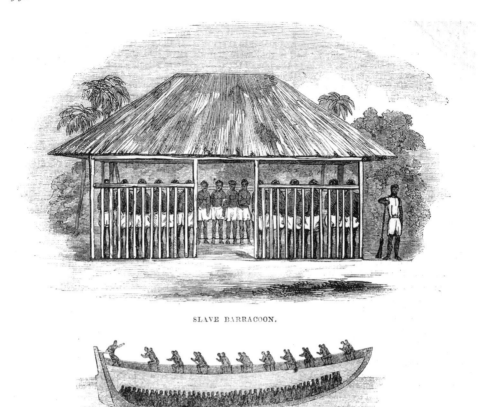

SLAVE BARRACOON.

CANOE FOR TRANSPORTING THE SLAVES FROM THE BARRACOON TO THE SHIP.

Figure 7.2. Slave Barracoon and Canoe for Transporting the Slaves from the Barracoon to the Ship. From *The Uncle Tom's Cabin Almanack* (London, 1853). Courtesy of the Clarke Historical Library at Central Michigan University.

comfortable and conversant among Europeans and Africans. Even ex-slaves who had lived for a time in Brazil or England or the West Indies and returned home became commercial middlemen and slave traders. João de Oliveira was one of these characters. He was born on the Slave Coast and taken to Brazil to be a slave. He was able to return to Africa and settle in Whydah in 1733, set himself up as a fixer for Portuguese traders and sent money back to Brazil to buy his freedom. An official Portuguese source described him as "the greatest Portuguese protector, helping them to carry out trading negotiations speedily with the people or to protect them from suffering from the deterioration and losses to which tobacco is subject in this climate."

Because their captives were "outsiders," African slavers who marched captives from the interior to the coast felt no duty to treat them well. Long lines of captives shackled together called coffles, with sometimes as many as one hundred people, were marched to the coast. Alexander Falconbridge noted that "as soon as the wretched Africans, purchased at the fairs, fall into the hands of the black traders, they experience an earnest of those dreadful sufferings which they are doomed in future to undergo. And there is not the least room to doubt, but that even before they can reach the fairs, great numbers perish from cruel usage, want of food, traveling through inhospitable deserts, etc." One eighteenth-century Portuguese merchant estimated that fully one-half of the captives for the Atlantic slave trade died in Africa before even seeing any Europeans. The average mortality was very likely not this high, as profit depended upon delivering captives alive. Even if the mortality rate was a more modest twenty percent, then all of the figures we use in discussing the Atlantic slave trade should be twenty percent higher. The human costs of the slave trade were high in Africa as well as on the Atlantic and in the Americas.

The captains of slavers, assisted by company factors, African and mulatto brokers, and their own ships' officers and surgeons, picked the best captives available for sale and then got down to the difficult and complex process of bargaining the price. Many Europeans who did business with Africans thought the Africans knew what they were doing and were in control. Again and again, we see comments like those of Bosman, who complained, "The Negroes are all without exception, crafty, villainous, and fraudulent, and very seldom to be trusted." Villault stated that "they are liars to the highest degree, their memory transcendent, and though they can neither write nor read, yet they manage their Trade with the greatest exactness." Although Barbot noted, "now we think it impossible to overcharge any of them the slightest; indeed, as a result of having been cheated, they have become so dishonest themselves that, far from being able easily to impose on them, today you must be thoroughly on your guard lest they in turn cheat you."

Saugnier and Brisson considered the trade at Senegal "extremely complex, and liable to a thousand difficulties." They listed over fifty trade goods they brought to barter on the Senegal River. Here, as just about everywhere else in Atlantic Africa, barter was conducted in the common currency of a real or imaginary gold bar. A cutlass in a red scabbard or an ordinary trade musket was valued at only one bar each. On the other hand, a single or double-barreled bronzed and gilt musket was highly prized and had a value of six bars. A piece of "guinea-blue," a bolt of fine, deep blue cotton cloth manufactured at Rouen, a product in great demand, was worth ten bars. They also traded silver buckles, Virginia tobacco, Bordeaux wines, London scarlets, Brittany linens, Flemish knives and much more. The price of a healthy male in river currency at Galam, far up river on the Senegal, was seventy bars. This meant that for every seventy-bar male, the French had to put together a package of trade goods – guinea-blues, muskets, musket balls, powder, knives, pens and ink, handkerchiefs, buckles, tobacco, brandy, glasses, hats and so on – acceptable to the African traders. Atkins provided a barter list for a seventy-bar male and a forty-bar female at the River Gambia. His list included brandy, guns, powder, beads and cottons.

One of the most desired currencies of Atlantic Africa were cowry shells, brought to Africa from the Maldives Islands in the Indian Ocean in the holds of ships. Bosman called cowries *boesjes*, Isert referred to them as *boss* and snake skulls, and Atkins called the shells *booges* and Whydah currency. In the late seventeenth century, Captain Philip Thomas wrote, "The best goods to purchase slaves here are cowries, the smaller the more esteemed; for they pay them all by tale, the smallest as valuable as the biggest, but take them from us by measure or weight, of which about 100 pounds for a good man-slave." In the eighteenth century, a single male slave could be valued

The Sale of Goods.

At *Sierraleon.*

		Gold Bars.
1 Piece of Planes	———	10
7 77*lb.* Kettles	———	26
3 Pieces of Chintz	———	12
1 Piece of Handkerchief Stuff	——	2
The Price of a Woman Slave	——	50
7 50 *lb.* Kettles	———	20
5 Pieces of Brawls	———	10
1 Piece of Ramal	———	4
1 Bar of Iron	———	1
The Price of a Boy Slave	——	35

At *Apollonia.*

		Accys.
2 Photees	———	14
2 Cotton Ramals	———	8
1 Piece Longee	———	4
2 Sletias	——— ——	5
7 Sheets	—— ——	7
32 Brafs Pans	——— ———	32
A Man Slave	——— ——	70

L 2   At

Figure 7.3. The Barter Price for African Captives on the Coast of Africa. From John Atkins, *A Voyage to Guinea, Brasil and the West Indies* (London, 1735). Courtesy of the William L. Clements Library at the University of Michigan.

at over 150,000 cowries. Around 1720, the European slave-trading nations may have exported around one million pound-weight a year to Africa. This means that some 400 million shells each year were paid for slaves and other commodities. The RAC around 1700 expected to sell an African slave in America at four times the value of trade goods exchanged on the coast of Africa. To a sugar planter in Jamaica, an adult male slave was expected to produce enough sugar to return his purchase price in one year, or at most two.

Although American planters wanted healthy young males and slave trade merchants purchased as many males as they could, slave cargos contained females as well as children. Most African sellers were probably quite happy to provide largely male lots for sale because females were highly valued as workers as well as wives. The slave trade generally carried two or three men for every woman. Even if American conditions were healthy and hopeful, thirty-three females in every group of one hundred slaves did not permit the population to naturally reproduce itself. Of course, conditions were not good. Conditions on plantations included disease, poor diets and malnutrition, excessive work and punishment, and much more that was bad. These led to a low birth rate, a high infant mortality rate and a very high mortality or death rate. Many planters believed it was cheaper to work their slaves to death over a few years than to create the better (and more expensive) conditions that

Figure 7.4. Scene on the Coast of Africa – Sale of Slaves by Native Chiefs. From *The Uncle Tom's Cabin Almanack* (London, 1853). Courtesy of the Clarke Historical Library at Central Michigan University.

would permit slaves to raise families and increase their numbers naturally. Therefore, slave societies in plantation regimes had to ceaselessly replenish their numbers through importation from the slave trade. With each new ship and its unbalanced population, the day when slaves could and would reproduce their numbers was constantly put off. This meant that in nearly all places but North America, natural reproduction was delayed until the end of the slave trade in the nineteenth century.

Ottobah Cugoano was one of only a few Africans who survived the middle passage and slavery and went on to write about his experience. Born about 1757 among the Fante people of the Gold Coast, Cugoano was kidnapped when he was thirteen years old and imprisoned in Cape Coast Castle. In the dungeon, as he later wrote in his autobiography, "the horrors I soon saw and felt, cannot well be described; I saw many of my miserable countrymen chained two and two, some hand-cuffed, and some with their hands tied behind . . . But when a vessel arrived to conduct us away to the ship, it was a most horrible scene; there was nothing to be heard but rattling of chains, smacking of whips, and the groans and cries of our fellow men." On board a British slaver bound for Grenada, Cugoano remembered, "And when we found ourselves at last taken away, death was more preferable than life."

African canoes and canoemen transported captives purchased on the coast to the slave ships. The handlers of the captives had to watch their charges and control their movements at all times in preparation for escape attempts and suicide. Many captives who told their unhappy stories later noted that they and their fellow captives often believed that the strange pale men in ships were taking them to another country and there would eat them. Olaudah

Equiano was held captive with other Africans: "I asked them if we were not to be eaten by those white men with horrible looks, red faces, and long hair?"

Once captives had reached the slaver, they were placed in the slave deck of the hold. The slave deck was usually four or five feet high and usually a half-deck platform around the sides was installed to increase the number of captives that could be shipped. Francesco Carletti, a Florentine merchant, carried slaves from Cape Verde to Cartagena in 1594 and left this observation: "The slaves were placed on the aforesaid ship hired by us, the males being accommodated on it below decks, packed next to one another in such a narrow space that when they wanted to turn from one side to the other they could scarcely do so. The females were in the open all over the ship." Most slavers were ordinary cargo ships converted for use in the slave trade. The *Brooks*, famous for its sketch that is reproduced in many books, had two full decks and two half decks, and was capable of carrying 609 captives. The picture of the ship and its tightly packed cargo inspired a British Prime Minister to say, "In the passage of Negroes from the coast of Africa, there is a greater portion of human misery condensed within a smaller place than has ever yet been found in any other place on the face of the globe."

The slave decks became unspeakably horrid during the course of a voyage. Even with some ventilation from portholes on the side and from vents above, the slave deck was always hot and humid. Buckets were provided as latrines but not everyone could get to them when sea sick or chained together in the dark of night. Dr. Alexander Falconbridge, a ship's surgeon, wrote, "I frequently went down among them till at length their apartments became so extremely hot as to be sufferable for a very short time. But the excessive heat was not the only thing that rendered their situation intolerable. The deck, that is, the floor of their rooms, was so covered with the blood and mucus, which had proceeded from them in consequence of the flux, that it resembled a slaughterhouse. It was not in the power of the human imagination to picture to itself a situation more dreadful or disgusting."

Given such conditions, one would expect the mortality rates of slavers to be horrible, and sometimes they were. Much could go wrong on slaving voyages: disease, bad weather, rebellion and insufficient provisions, to name the most obvious. There are stories of particular voyages when seventy and eighty percent of the cargo died in passage. However, it should be pointed out that the mortality rate of all transoceanic voyages in the age of sail was high. Mortality rates were especially high for the crews of slavers, higher in many cases than the mortality rate for African captives. Crewmen were almost always onboard ship longer than the captive cargo. Insurers were willing to provide policies on slave cargoes but not life insurance for crewmen on slavers. When looking at that part of the trade for which records survived, historians have found that the mortality rate declined over the years, particularly during the eighteenth century. In the sixteenth and seventeenth centuries, mortality rates of about twenty percent were fairly common. The records of 194 voyages in 1680–8 for the English RAC show that yearly averages ranged from a low of 14.8 percent and a high of 29 percent. By the late eighteenth century, rates of about ten percent were standard. By this time, company rules and national

Document 7.2
Some Account of the Author's Captivity

Ottobah Cugano, 1787

The horrors I soon saw and felt, cannot be well described; I saw many of my miserable countrymen chained two and two, some hand-cuffed, and some with their hands tied behind. We were conducted along by a guard, and when we arrived at the castle, I asked my guide what I was brought there for, he told me to learn the ways of the *brow sow*, that is the white faced people. I saw him take a gun, a piece of cloth, and some lead for me, and then he told me that he must now leave me there, and went off. This made me cry bitterly, but I was soon conducted to a prison, for three days, where I heard the groans and cries of many, and saw some of my fellow-captives. But when a vessel arrived to conduct us away to the ship, it was a most horrible scene; there was nothing to heard but rattling of chains, smacking of whips, and the groans and cries of our fellowmen. Some would not stir from the ground, when they were lashed and beat in the most horrible manner. I have forgot the name of this infernal fort; but we were taken in the ship that came for us, to another that was ready to sail from Cape Coast. When we were put into the ship, we saw several black merchants coming on board, but we were all drove into our holes, and not suffered to speak to any of them. In this situation we continued several days in sight of our native land; but I could find no good person to give any information of my situation to Accasa at Agimaque. And when we found ourselves at last taken away, death was more preferable than life, and a plan was concerted amongst us, that we might burn and blow up the ship, and to perish all together in the flames; but we were betrayed by one of our own countrywomen, who slept with some of the head men of the ship, for it was common for the dirty filthy sailors to take the African women and lie upon their bodies; but the men were chained and pent up in holes. It was the women and boys which were to burn the ship, with the approbation and groans of the rest; though that was prevented, the discovery was likewise a cruel bloody scene.

But it would be needless to give a description of all the horrible scenes which we saw, and the base treatment which we met with in this dreadful captive situation, as the similar cases of thousands, which suffer by this infernal traffic, are well known. Let it suffice to say, that I was thus lost to my dear indulgent parents and relations, and they to me. All my help was cries and tears, and these could not avail; nor suffered long, till one succeeding woe, and dread, swelled up another. Brought from a state of innocence and freedom, and in a barbarous and cruel manner, conveyed to a state of horror and slavery: This abandoned situation may be easier conceived than described. From the time that I was kid-napped and conducted to a factory, and from thence in the brutish, base, but fashionable way of traffic, consigned to Grenada, the grievous thoughts which I then felt, still pant in my heart; though my fears and tears have long since subsided. And yet it is still grievous to think that thousands more have suffered in similar and greater distress, under the hands of barbarous robbers, and merciless taskmasters; and that many even now are suffering in all the extreme bitterness of grief and woe, that no language can describe. The cries of some, and the sight of their misery, may be seen and heard afar; but the deep sounding groans of thousands, and the great sadness of their misery and woe, under the heavy load of oppressions and calamities inflicted upon them, are such as can only be distinctly known to the ears of Jehovah Sabaoth.

Quobna Ottobah Cugoano was sold into slavery in 1770 and eventually taken to England. There he was baptized and freed, and he became a Christian anti-slavery advocate and writer much like his contemporary, Olaudah Equiano. *Source: Thoughts and Sentiments on the Evil and Wicked Traffic of the Slavery and Commerce of the Human Species, Humbly Submitted to The Inhabitants of GREAT-BRITAIN*, by Ottobah Cugoano, A Native of Africa. London: Printed in the Year M.DCC.LXXXVII [1787], pp. 16–17.

regulations were in place to reduce the mortality rates of slavers. A study of 522 voyages in the 1790s revealed an average 6.6 percent mortality.

Humanitarians in the late eighteenth century believed that "tight-packing," the practice of putting as many captives in the hold of a ship as possible, contributed to high mortality rates. Laws were passed to prevent or limit overcrowding. Recent studies suggest that the mortality rate of ships with many captives per ton was no more than on ships with few captives per ton. It appears that disease and a dearth of provisions, along with an overly long voyage, were the most important reasons for high mortality. If captives brought yellow fever, malaria, dysentery or simple gastrointestinal disorders on board, or if captains failed to stock enough provisions to feed the captives for the duration of the voyage, the mortality rate increased. If bad weather, poor piloting or war turned an expected five-week crossing into a four-month voyage, the mortality rate increased. Of course, the experienced traders and ship's surgeons had long known this. The surgeon John Atkins noted that the success of a voyage depended on "furnishing proper Food for the Slaves" and "in Dispatch," that is, sufficient provisions and a fairly rapid transatlantic voyage without trouble or revolt.

There are few recorded uprisings by captives on slave ships. Ship captains, like plantation owners, preferred to carry peoples from different African countries and speaking different languages. "The Blacks' . . . different tongues and animosities in their own Country have hitherto kept them from insurrection," noted one English observer in 1668. The Trans-Atlantic Slave Trade Database, which has a record of more than 27,000 voyages, identifies only 383 slave revolts onboard ship and an addition 70 rebellions on the African coast, most occurring in the second half of the eighteenth century. This small number is likely explained by lack of documentation. Given the estimated 35,000 slave trading voyages during the age of the slave trade, it is possible that there were thousands of shipboard plots, aborted revolts and uprisings for which there are no records. To prevent rebellions, captains and crews shackled male slaves, used loyal slaves or "guardians" to control the other slaves and purchased slaves from different parts of the coast speaking different languages.

Once the middle passage was done and the slaver arrived in an American harbor, the captain had three ways of selling his cargo. If the voyage was one for a chartered company or a well-organized merchant house, the captain and a local merchant or agent concluded a private treaty. Captains and investors who operated in a more freelance manner would attempt to sell their captives in a "scramble," seeking out plantation owners or slave brokers directly. The captain and his investors would want to avoid the third option, public auction, because that practice was often known as a method of disposing of poor quality cargo by forcing a buyer to take several weak or sick captives to get a few strong and healthy captives. Once the captives were sold, the captain would purchase colonial staples like sugar or tobacco for sale in his homeport of Amsterdam or Nantes or Liverpool. The French slaver the *Diligent* in 1731–2 transported 247 African captives from the Bight of Benin to Martinique. Some of these slaves were given to local officials while the rest were sold to planters and slave dealers for island products in part and on credit. When the ship returned to France, it carried 251 barrels of white and common sugar, 23 bales of cotton and 13 barrels of rocou paste, a product used to prepare white cloth to receive dyes. For the investors, the costs of outfitting the ship, paying the crew and purchasing the trade goods used to barter for the slaves came to a total of 122,502 livres. The sugar, cotton and rocou that the *Diligent* carried back from Martinique was sold in Nantes for 121,482 livres. This particular triangular trading venture lost money, a little more than 2,000 livres. The investors sued the captain of the *Diligent* in the admiralty court.

About three-quarters of all slave-trading voyages were triangular: merchandise to Africa, captives to the Americas, and staples to Europe. Many voyages ended in the Caribbean with the sale of the ship. In the eighteenth century, few slavers made more than six voyages or were in service for more than ten years. Most of the Brazilian slave trade was bilateral. Because Brazilian and Portuguese traders had easy access to two important trade goods desired by Africans, molasses-flavored tobacco and rum, there was no need for any European leg. Trade between Rio de Janeiro and Luanda was the norm, quite often in Brazilian-built and owned ships. "The Slave Trade is the most important one that the Portuguese have at Congo, and the number, which they send yearly to the Support of their American Colonies, is surprisingly great," wrote Wyndham Beawes in 1761. "And what renders this Business still more advantageous and considerable, is the short Cut from hence to the Brazils, compared with what all other Nations have to run, when carrying these unhappy Wretches to their Plantations."

7.4 *The* Henrietta Marie

A closer look at the story of one slaver helps us understand the vast slave trade on a more individual level. Like most ships, the *Henrietta Marie*

Figure 7.5. Group of Negroes, As Imported to Be Sold for Slaves. From William Blake engraving in John Gabriel Stedman, *Narrative of a five years' Expedition, against the revolted Negroes of Surinam* (London, 1796). Courtesy of the John Carter Brown Library at Brown University.

was not built or intended for the slave trade. She was a French merchantman and privateer until she was captured by the English in the late seventeenth century. Her new London-based owners refitted her for the slave trade. The *Henrietta Marie* would make two voyages in the trade until she was sent to the bottom of the Florida Straits in 1700 by a hurricane.

A consortium of investors owned the *Henrietta Marie*. Thomas Starke, a minor investor, was an absentee owner of five tobacco plantations in Virginia and part owner of several vessels operating in the slave trade. Anthony Tourney, an iron merchant, invested thirty-three tons of iron bars in the second voyage, which would be bartered for captives on the coast of Africa. His stake in the enterprise in current value would be close to £260,000. Thomas Winchcombe was a master pewterer, and his investment in the voyage was a consignment of six hundredweight of pewter bowls, plates, basins and bottles. Robert Wilson's investment was a consignment of 1,200 copper bars, several cases of alcohol and four dozen felt hats. The *Henrietta Marie* also carried such trade goods as bugle beads and English clothe. The ship carried weapons – cutlasses and muskets – for defense or barter, depending on the circumstances. It also carried iron shackles (also called bilbos), large and small, for unruly men, women and children. The investors invited William Deacon, an experienced sailor in his thirties, to captain their ship and carry a share of captives he could sell privately.

In the 1690s, the RAC still retained its charter and monopoly of the English slave trade, and thus the first voyage of the *Henrietta Marie* was as an independent trader and had to pay a ten percent tax on outgoing and incoming merchandise to legally participate in the trade. The *Henrietta Marie* and other "ten-percenters" were highly speculative business ventures and thus potentially extremely profitable, and represented a new and expansive phase in the English slave trade.

The *Henrietta Marie* set sail for the coast of Africa in 1697 with a crew of eighteen to twenty-two men. She went to Madeira to buy wine and then stopped at the Cape Verde Islands to obtain supplies of water and wood. Once the ship was on the Guinea coast, it took a month to reach New Calibar, a traders' city-state in the Bight of Biafra in what is now Nigeria. Captain Deacon very likely obtained permission to trade from the ruler oligarchs of New Calibar and paid a duty in so many captives or in merchandise. He may have found all the captives he wanted to buy in that port or was forced to sail up and down the Rio Real and buy captives in groups of two and three. In the hot and humid climate of the Bight of Biafra and the Bight of Benin, Captain Deacon wanted to do business quickly, for he and his crew probably remembered the seafaring saying, "Beware and take care of the Bight of Benin/for one that comes out, there are forty go in." In fact, of the eighteen to twenty-two men who began the voyage in London, only nine return home alive.

While the enterprise was doing business on the coast of Africa, the crew installed shelves, half decks, along the sides of the cargo deck. A barbed fence was erected amidships to prevent captives from seizing control of the ship when they were topside for air and exercise. The captain also had to concern himself with the purchase of provisions, food and water that could feed the number of captives he hoped to carry for the length of the passage to the Caribbean that he expected. For example, one captain estimated he needed 500,000 yams to feed five hundred captives for two months.

We do not know how many captives Captain Deacon purchased, but we know he delivered 250 Africans in Barbados. Healthy adult males purchased for bundles of goods valued at £3 in Africa were sold in Barbados for £9. After conducting his main business, Captain Deacon purchased 118 hogsheads of muscovado sugar and one of white sugar, and 67 bags of ginger. He was also returning to London with about one hundred elephant tusks. After settling up with the *Henrietta Marie* investment consortium in London, Captain Deacon retired with a small personal fortune, which he promptly invested in the ship's next voyage.

The *Henrietta Marie's* succeeding voyage of 1699–1700 was a disaster almost from start to finish. The vessel's £827 trade goods, not all of which could be bartered, purchased ivory, provisions, and about two hundred Africans. The merchant investors of this voyage had outdated information about market demand in Africa and were unable to sell their pewter or beads. On the middle passage from Africa to Barbados, the new captain, John Taylor, and half of his crew died. Sixteen out of 206 African captives perished as well, a much better survival rate than that of the crew. The surviving crew continued to Jamaica, where the acting captain sold 190 captives and purchased sugar, cotton, indigo and logwood for the return voyage. This time, captives purchased for goods valued at £4 in Africa were sold for between £24 and £30. At the end of June 1700, the *Henrietta Marie* set sail for London. In the Florida Straits between Cuba and Florida, she was brought to the bottom by an early hurricane. In 1983, a graduate student in marine archeology found at the site of a shipwreck an abundance of U-shaped shackles, eighty-one bolts and 165 shackles. Only a slave ship would have carried that many. It was the *Henrietta Marie*. By 1991, most of her artifacts had been found and donated to the Mel Fisher Maritime Heritage Society in Key West, Florida.

7.5 The African Nations of the New World

"One of the greatest achievements of historical scholarship during the past half-century," writes Gordon S. Wood, "has been the imaginative recovery of at least some of the realities of slavery in the New World." As Wood points out, and as we have seen in this chapter, historians now have a better understanding than ever before about the size the Atlantic slave trade, the origins of slave exports from Africa and their destinations in the Americas. Historians know more about the business of slaving among Africans and among Europeans and between Africans and Europeans. However, there is much about the forced African diaspora that remains well out of focus and sustains controversy within the ranks of historians of Africa and the Americas.

These are some of the difficult questions: Did African slaves preserve and transfer African ethnic identities in their forced migration to particular regions of the Americas? If so, did they transfer their languages, customs, beliefs and values to America? Did they implant African culture or cultures in the Americas? Or did the Atlantic slave trade degrade or disintegrate African ethnicity by drawing captives from several different parts of Africa? If the middle passage did disintegrate African ethnicity, did Africans in America create new Creole African-American cultures? Were enslaved Africans, as Charles Joyner has noted, "compelled to create a new language, a new religion, indeed, a new culture"?

There are no clear or easy answers to any of these questions. Some historians, recognizing the cultural destructiveness of the Atlantic slave trade, have emphasized the cultural creativity of African slaves in the Americas in making new religions, new cultures and even new ethnicities. According to Joyner, this process might be called the "creolization" of black culture. It has been argued that ethnically heterogeneous enslaved Africans in the Americas integrated different African cultures and customs to solve ordinary problems, live together as communities and to survive and perhaps even transcend slavery. (This creative process also involved over time African adoptions of specific elements of Native American and European and Euroamerican cultures.) As Sidney W. Mintz and Richard Price explain it, "the Africans in any New World colony in fact became a community and began to share a culture only insofar as, and as fast as, they themselves created them."

Other historians, recognizing that the Atlantic slave trade did not completely randomize the distribution of Africans in the Americas, have pointed out that in quite a few New World colonies, one or two African ethnic groups or ethnic clusters were numerically and culturally dominant within the larger slave population. These ethnicities, or "nations" as Europeans referred to them during the age of the slave trade, spoke their African languages in America and brought to America their knowledge of agriculture, basket weaving, house construction and healing through medicinal plants. They brought to America the spirits of their ancestors as well as particular religious rites and deities. They brought their African names, their African music and their African dancing. They even brought fragments of African institutions, such as the Central African *ki-lombo*, a merit-based male warrior society that found rebirth in the runaway communities or *quilombos* of Brazil. This process might be called the "transplantation of African culture." Historians relying upon more and better data on the slave trade have discovered ethnic clusters in the Americas. David Greggus has found that about thirty percent of the African-born slaves on the sugar plantations of Saint Domingue in the late eighteenth century were "Congos" from West Central Africa. This concentration of Congos was even greater in the colony's coffee plantations. In British North America, two colonies imported most of the region's slaves in the eighteenth century. The largest single group of enslaved Africans to enter Virginia came from the Slave Coast, and most of these Africans – around forty percent – were Igbo. Allan Kulikoff has found that more than fifty percent of the Africans entering Port York, Virginia, from 1718 to 1739 were from the Bight of Biafra. On the other hand, South Carolina imported large numbers of Africans from West Central Africa. About seventy percent of the Africans in that colony were Angolans and Congos until the Stono Rebellion of 1739. After the rebellion, South Carolinians imported more Senegambians and Sierra Leonians. However, by 1800 more than

Table 7.5. The Atlantic slave trade:
African origins of captives, 1662–1867

African region	Slaves exported
Senegambia	599,864
Sierra Leone	756,390
Gold Coast	710,451
Bight of Benin	1,870,620
Bight of Biafra	1,658,152
West Central Africa	3,927,801
Southeast Africa	391,782

Source: Herbert S. Klein, *The Atlantic Slave Trade*
(1999), Table A.1, pp. 208–9.

fifty percent of slaves in South Carolina were still Angolans and Congos
(see Table 7.5).

Ethnic concentration allowed Africans to achieve more than merely save
some culturally diluted customs often called "Africanisms." The African
impact in the diaspora went far beyond "survivals," writes James H. Sweet.
"Africa arrived in the various destinations of the colonial world in all of its
social and cultural richness, informing the institutions that Africans created
and providing them with a prism through which to interpret and understand
their condition as slaves and as freed peoples."

Europeans in the age of the slave trade certainly accepted the idea of African
ethnicity surviving in the New World through the African nations with which
they were all so familiar. John Gabriel Stedman, the English soldier who
fought the Maroon Rebellion in Dutch Surinam in the late eighteenth century,
observed that "the Negroes are composed of different nations or castes, such
as the

Abo	Congo	Loango	Ponbo
Bonia	Gango	N'Zoko	Wanway & c.
Blitay	Konare	Nag	
Coromantyn	Kiemba	Papa	

I have formerly mentioned the names of above a dozen Negro tribes, all
of which know each other from the different marks and incisions made
on their bodies. For instance, the Coromantyn Negroes (who are the
most esteemed) cut three or four long slashes on each of their cheeks, as
I have represented in the face of the armed free Negro or Ranger, and the
Loango Negroes (who are reckoned the worst) distinguish themselves
by puckering, or marking the skin of their arms, thighs, &c. with square,
elevated figures like large dice.

Bryan Edwards of Jamaica noted, after years of experience, "there are
among several of the African nations some striking and predominant features, which cannot easily be overlooked by a person residing in any one of
the sugar plantations." It was said that the Mandingos of greater Senegambia

displayed a gentleness of disposition and demeanor, the Kormanantyn of the Gold Coast were ferocious, courageous, stubborn and honorable, the Papaws of Whydah were the most docile and best disposed, and the Igbos from the Bight of Benin were the most timid and despondent of mind. Congos and Angolas were naturally mild and docile, better fit for domestic service than field labor, and said to be more honest than many other tribes. Like most Europeans who described African national characteristics, Edwards in fact provided trite collective psychological profiles. A Charles Town merchant stated that the "Gold Coast or Gambia's are best, next to them the Windward Coast are prefer'd to Angola's. There must not be a Callabar amonst them." Ira Berlin has called these shallow ethnic stereotypes. In British North America and French Louisiana, these ethnic labels were found in planters' requests for specific types of Africans to slave traders. The Gambians were seen as hard workers, the Bambara and the Coromantees as rebels, the Igbo or Calabars as suicidal and the Angolans as runaways. These slaveholder characterizations were often contradictory. One person's troublesome "Mina" was another's superior "Kormantee." Europeans created these crude stereotypes from collective experience and for the practical purpose of guiding future purchases. They tell us very little about African ethnicity in the Americas.

What makes this issue so difficult for historians is that the ethnicity, culture and religion of Africans was constantly changing within Africa before and during the Atlantic slave trade and remained in flux for enslaved Africans in the Americas. Some scholars doubt the existence of natural ethnic communities. For example, it is likely that the fellow countrymen of Olaudah Equiano did not possess any identity as Igbo before the Atlantic slave trade. The concentration of tens of thousands of people like Equiano in places like Barbados, Jamaica and Virginia began to give them an identity. Equiano learned he was Ibgo most likely after he had become part of the Ibgo diaspora. The process of creolization of culture took place in Africa long before any captive was put onboard a slave ship. For example, quite a few people in Kongo and Angola were Christian in some form and degree, and carried their Catholic faith and rituals to the Americas as slaves and spread their religion to other slaves. African Muslims came from different regions, languages and ethnicities but as Muslim slaves in America, Islam took precedence. Islam was the culture, a synthesized and creolized culture that in Africa had itself been an Africanized rendition of North African and Middle Eastern culture. Africans and Euro-Africans on the coast of Atlantic Africa created and spoke trade languages, Portuguese-based and Dutch-based pidgins. It is not surprising slaves would invent American creoles such as the English-based Gullah, the French-based Kreyòl, the Danish-based Creolsk, the Portuguese-based Papiamento and many others. African ethnicity was not pure or static in Africa. In some cases, as we saw with the Ibgo, there was no ethnic identity until common experiences began to form one. The creation of African ethnicity in the Americas under the adversity of slavery was mangled and always evolving.

In the Americas, individuals from a few dozen or so ethnic clusters were integrated within a spiritual-religious world-view. "Both religion and ethnicity," argues Paul E. Lovejoy, "served to integrate individuals of diverse backgrounds into communities and social networks of interaction that were products of the slave trade." We see identifiable African ethnoreligious patterns moving across the Atlantic and the development in the Americas of religious-based ethnic congeries. The diasporan slave religions, healing practices and divinations – *vodun, obeah, ifá, candomblé, quimbois, gagá* and others – were just such ethnoreligious complexes. In one cultural package, a diasporan religion included theology, cosmology, morality, poetry, magic, healing, pharmacopoeia, music and dance, and more. These African-derived syncretic religions became reborn in America by integrating new African elements as well as European and even, occasionally, Native American elements. They promoted a ritualized union of the people with the spirit world, often through communal rites that brought about spirit possession, that is, direct contact with the deities and ancestral spirits. Through ritual and offerings, the slave community managed threats and dissidents, healed the sick and provided for the necessary human requirements of revenge, justice, harmony and identity.

A selection of ethnic clusters and their associated diasporan religions are listed in Table 7.6. This list might seem like a bewildering number of ethnic groups. "A dozen ethnic concentrations," writes Lovejoy, "compares favorably with the concentration of European populations in the Americas, which included Spanish, Portuguese, English, Dutch, French, Danish, Irish, Scots, and Jews, at least." What is important is that Africans from distinct but similar ethnicities or cultures could rebuild new African ethnicities in the Americas based around some common religious beliefs and practices. Ethnic and religious factors sometimes reinforced community structures, culture and patterns of resistance. "African-born slaves sometimes accused their American descendants of betrayal to European owners, and those born in the Americas could be suspicious of the strange languages and rituals of their African elders," writes Linda M. Heywood. "Yet Creoles, both slave and free, adopted many African values. In their hands, this African heritage underwent further adaptation, melding with European ways to form the dynamic African-American cultures that have come to define Afro-diasporic populations in the Americas. The greatest legacies bequeathed by African-born slaves to their American-born descendants were the religious beliefs and cultural practices they succeeded in preserving."

As an example, Candomblé is the Bahian version of the religion of the Yoruba. In fact, the cult was originally established by a small group of Nago from Ketu from the Agbome Kingdom in Benin. Its early evolution was called *batuque*. Yoruba ethnic groups such as the Egba, Nago, Ijebu and Ife had a pantheon of gods and goddesses known as *orishas*, perhaps more than four hundred in Africa and many more than that in Brazil. The *orishas* were brought to Brazil and invoked and worshiped in ceremonies that involved sacrifices, rhythmic percussion music and dance, spirit possession and a banquet, all of which took place in secret at a temple, that is, a *casa* (house), *roça* (plantation) or *terreiro* (yard). The arrival of Christian slaves from Kongo and Angola, and perhaps Portuguese missionaries as well, influenced the worship of what the Portuguese called *orixas*. African deities became identified with specific Catholic saints: Oxalá, the most respected of the *orishas*, was often represented by the image of Jesus Christ; Iemanjá,

Table 7.6. *The African origins of New World Religions: A selection*

African origins	The Americas
Central Sudan	Bahian (Brazil) Muslim *Mâle* Fulbe Muslims Mandingo Muslims
Senegambia	Fulbe Muslims Mandingo Muslims
Gold Coast	Jamaica: *Obeah* Hausa Muslims
Bight of Benin	Louisiana: *Vodun* Cuba: *Santería* Jamaica: *Myal* Brazil: *Candomblé-Ketu* Saint Domingue: *Vodun-Rada* Afro-Surinam: *Papa-Gadu* Brazil: *Candomblé-Jejé* Cuba: *Ifá* Saint Domingue: *Vodun* Mandingo Muslims Trinidad: Orisha Religion
Bight of Biafra	Ibgo *Jonkonu* British West Indies *Dibia/Obea*
West Central Africa	Saint Domingue: *Vodun-Petro-Lemba* Brazil: *Candomblé-Angola* Brazil: *Calundú* Cuba: *Palo Mayombe* Kongo Christians

Sources: Paul E. Lovejoy, "Trans-Atlantic Transformations: The Origins and Identity of Africans in the Americas," in Wim Klooster and Alfred Padula (eds.), *The Atlantic World: Essays on Slavery, Migration, and Imagination* (2005), pp. 126–46; Gwendolyn Midlo Hall, *Slavery and African Ethnicities in the Americas: Restoring the Links* (2005); Michael A. Gomez, *Exchanging Our Country Marks: The Transformation of African Identities in the Colonial and Antebellum South* (1998); and James H. Sweet, *Recreating Africa: Culture, Kinship, and Religion in the African-Portuguese World, 1441–1770* (2003).

the goddess of the seas, lakes and fertility, was associated with the Virgin Mary, Our Lady of Mercy; Exú, an intermediary to the other *orishas*, one who required sacrifice, became associate with the Catholic Satan. In the cult houses and the black churches, African and Catholic elements were thoroughly mixed to create "god-saints" that were worshipped freely despite ordinances restricting veneration of anything related to *candomby*.

With the arrival of new slaves from the Bight of Benin as well as the Kongo and Angola, new *candombles* developed in Brazil. Besides *candomblé ketu* of Bahia, the Egba, Ife, and Nago created similar cults such as *batuque-de-nação* in Rio Grande do Sul, *tambor-de-mina* in Maranhão, *Xango* of Recife, and *Xanbá* in Alagoas and Pernambuco. Ewe and Fon slaves from Dahomey developed *candomblé jejé* (its deities were called *Vodum* in Portuguese). Other Dahomey-born slaves created *mina jejé* in Maranhão and *babaçuê* in Pará. Slaves from Kongo and Angola created *candomblé bantu* that incorporated local Indian deities, the "*orishas* of the land." The spirits are *caboclos*, Kongoized Native Americans of the backlands and *pretos velhos*, black elders whose names – Pai Joaquim de Angola and Maria Konga – communicate their West Central African origins. As it worked out, Afro-Brazilian slaves came to see themselves divided into three new nations: *Nação Ketu*, *Nação Jejé*, and *Nação Angola*.

7.6 The Impact of the Trade on Africa

How significant was the slave trade to the history of sub-Saharan Africa? There are four main areas of contention in African history: they center on the demographic, economic, political and social consequences of the slave trade. To the uninitiated or the anti-Western ideologue, the natural assumption is that the Atlantic slave trade was an unmitigated disaster for Africa and, indeed, may be the root cause of Africa's contemporary problems. Of course, the slave trade was an unmitigated disaster for the individual Africans who became caught in its grasp. The impact of the slave trade upon African societies, and even Africa itself, is a different matter. For a growing number of writers, like Stephen Small, a Lecturer in Sociology, the answer is obvious: "For the last five hundred years the countries of the West have relentlessly exploited Africa and African people. Millions of Africans were murdered, millions more violently kidnapped and enslaved, women raped and brutalized, and African societies totally ransacked." As Philip Curtin noted in 1969, "the range of opinion runs the gamut from the view that the slave trade was responsible for virtually every unfavorable development in Africa over these centuries, to the opposite position that even the slave trade was better than no trade, that it was therefore a positive benefit to the African societies that participated." My short discussion that follows will not examine the extreme positions of this problem taken for ideological or political reasons but look at the arguments of a number of professional historians and economists who have studied these issues for years and have reached interesting, well-evidenced and logical yet still tentative conclusions.

Although one might presume that the demographic impact of the trade would be the one area with the most consensus among historians, the fact is that there are two opposing interpretations. One group of historians put forward the seemingly obvious conclusion that the removal of 12 million people or more from Africa (and millions more in the Saharan, Red Sea and Indian Ocean trades) had a devastating impact. Historian Paul Lovejoy contends that the removal of so many people, and therefore the removal of their reproductive capacity over many generations, produced centuries of demographic stagnation. According to Patrick Manning, the result is that sub-Saharan Africa's population in 1850 should have been 100 million instead of the 50 million that was counted. Today, we think overpopulation increases underdevelopment; that was not true in the past. In other world regions in the early modern period, population growth spurred intensive agriculture and technological innovation – in other words, economic development. Sub-Saharan Africa did not have that advantage.

On the other hand, another group of historians maintain that scholars do not know what the total population of sub-Saharan Africa was in the fifteenth through the eighteenth centuries, nor do they know the rate of growth. These unknowns make it quite difficult to analyze the effect of the slave trade. A large population and rate of growth would lessen any impact, whereas a smaller population and rate would increase it. In the sixteenth century, the Portuguese introduced two American crops to African agriculture: maize and manioc. These grains were generally introduced to provide a cheap food for the African captives shipped across the Atlantic, which they did, but they also became staples in Africa. The new crops spread throughout Africa, improved nutrition and, by the eighteenth century, were likely producing the first important population growth in Africa in a very long time. Of course, the eighteenth century was also the century of an unprecedented expansion of the Atlantic slave trade. Economic historian David Eltis points out that the slave trade did not draw people from the same region for four hundred years but was constantly moving from one region to another over a long period of time. This lessened the demographic impact in any one region. Eltis has concluded that the slave trade was not large enough to have had more than marginal influence on the population of Africa during and after the slave trade. In addition, J. D. Fage has argued that West African communities knew what they were doing and were not self-destructive. "It seems unlikely," writes Fage, "that African rulers and merchants would have provided slaves for sale to the Europeans, and on the scale that they did, if they had thought that this would lead to demographic catastrophe, to a dramatic reduction in the number of a ruler's subjects and of a society's productive workers."

Scholarly dissension regarding the economic impact of the slave trade mirrors that of the demographic impact. Walter Rodney places his thesis in the title of his 1972 book, *How Europe Underdeveloped Africa*. His view, and that of recent like-minded scholars, is that the slave trade not only removed productive men and women from the continent but also destroyed Africa's nascent industries by trading better-made and cheaper European goods for African people. Fernand Braudel provides a chart showing that from 1680 to 1780, the percentage of gold, ivory and wax as exports decreased while the export of captives increased from fifty-five percent of the total to eighty-six percent. European exports to Africa were mostly luxury goods, which went into the households of the rich and powerful and did not have what economists call "linkage." In short, these goods did not contribute to productivity within Africa in any meaningful way. Africans became dependent upon on the export of captives, which in 1700 constituted ninety percent of African exports. However, slaves were a free good, like fish, as far as the slavers were concerned. There were costs involved for Europeans but nothing like the costs for Africans, the real costs of raising and feeding children and the costs of losing productive labor. For Africa then, the real price of a slave was greatly undervalued.

Another group of historians maintain that the slave trade was too geographically dispersed and marginal in continental terms to have a significant effect on the large, complex, diverse and resilient African economies, most of which were in the interior. According to David Eltis, "the slave trade for most regions and most periods was not a critically important influence over the course of African history." If one takes the value of trade (exports and imports) between Western African regions and the Atlantic World in the eighteenth century, it is clear that trade was economically marginal. From the 1730s to the 1780s, the value of trade for Atlantic Africa more than doubled, from £21 million to £47 million. However, this trade existed in an Atlantic commercial economy that was perhaps five times as large. "In no region could the revenue per person of ocean-going trade have been significant," writes Eltis. The slave trade engulfed Atlantic Africa's commerce in the eighteenth century, "but any plausible numerical assessment indicates a similarly massive dominance of the domestic sector over the external within most African societies."

The third bone of contention concerns the impact of the slave trade upon the African political development. Philip Curtain has identified two positions in this debate. One of them he called the economic model and the other is the political model. Those scholars who have put forward the economic model argue that as the demands of the slave trade grew in the late seventeenth century and throughout the eighteenth centuries, Africans were forced to create more centralized and militarized states to make war to take captives. These states sold these captives to the Europeans in exchange for guns to make war, take captives and sell them to the Europeans. If a state did not do this, a rival state would attack it, capture its people, sell them to Europeans in exchange for guns and remain the dominant, slave-trading state. This is called the "gun-slave cycle." There is considerable anecdotal evidence for this position from Europeans, usually found or written by abolitionists who wanted to highlight the pernicious effects of the trade. A Dutch factor writing in 1730 noted "that part of Africa which as of old is known as the 'Gold Coast' . . . has now virtually changed into a pure Slave Coast; the great quantity of guns and powder which the Europeans have from time to time brought here has given cause to terrible wars." There is also evidence, from European pens, that factors on the coast spurred conflict by arming one people who had a grievance against another. The purpose was to advance English or Dutch interests against their European rivals and, of course, to fill slave ships. In the 1730s, Europeans were exporting about 180,000 guns a year to the Gold and Slave Coasts. Between 1781 and 1789, Danish ships alone carried approximately 90,000 flintlock muskets and 180,000 pounds of gunpowder to the Gold and Slave Coasts.

Those who advance the political model argue that African wars during the age of the slave trade were caused by territorial expansion, state rivalries, control over valuable resources, waterways and seaports, and civil wars. The captives that these wars produced were sold to European slave traders (rather than being killed, as before) and were simply the byproducts of conflicts that would have been fought no matter who was stationed on the coast. The best example of the political model was the rise of Dahomey in the early eighteenth century. In the interior of the Slave Coast, the Kingdom of Dahomey, under the authority of King Agaja since 1708, attacked and conquered Weme, Allada and Whydah. His wars, as European traders noted, did not fill the slave ships but often drove them off. "The King of Dahomey proved almost too martial," writes James Pope-Hennessy. "A professional soldier, he could hardly take time off to organize a competent slave trade on the old lines, and business, in consequence, declined." Later in the eighteenth century, an English factor read the newspaper accounts of the debates regarding the abolition of the slave trade in Great Britain to the new king of Dahomey, Kpengla. In those debates, Dahomey was portrayed as an aggressive, militaristic slave-raiding state concerned, above all, with obtaining more guns. The King demurred: "We Dahomeans are surrounded by enemies who make incursions, we must defend ourselves... Your countrymen, therefore, who allege that we go to war for the purpose of supplying your ships with slaves, are grossly mistaken." He continued, "In the name of my ancestors and myself I aver, that no Dahomean man ever embarked in war merely for the sake of procuring wherewithal to purchase your commodities." We should be aware that this statement was published by a defender of the slave trade. To lend legitimacy to that odious commerce, the supporters of the trade let the public know that Africans believed that the slave trade was honorable.

John K. Thornton argues that because there is evidence for both models, the historical reality must be more complicated than previously believed. Thornton provides a strong case for regional variations. Thornton and Boubacar Barry demonstrate that Europeans were involved in inter-African conflicts as early as 1500 in Senegambia. This region was also the one region closest to Moors of Morocco; their incursions from the sixteenth century to the eighteenth century, as much as anything, required the Senegalese to arm themselves. Kongo and Angola also offer complicated histories. We have seen in an earlier chapter that many of the expeditions involved in the conquest of Angola were little more than slave-raiding outings. Portuguese slave traders from São Tomé interfered in the politics of the Kingdom of Kongo, as did the Portuguese slave traders from Luanda. However, even here the Kongo civil wars that erupted during the seventeenth and eighteenth centuries were primarily motivated by rival groups of nobles seeking control of the crown. And these wars sent slaves into the Atlantic.

A related issue is the impact the Atlantic slave trade had on domestic slavery within Africa. Some historians recently have argued that domestic African slavery before the slave trade was a marginal institution. They contend the slave trade not only captured Africans for American slavery but also captured even more Africans to create slave societies in Africa. As evidence, they present the abundant observations of such men as Robert Norris who, in his 1789 memoir of his stay in Dahomey, noted, "The bulk of the people are slaves to a few freemen; and in some states there is not an individual free but the prince: from every circumstance of intelligence and observation, the general state of the Negro, in Africa, is that of slavery and oppression, in every sense of the word." Norris saw a world of slaves because the Atlantic slave trade (and Muslim commercial expansion) created a slaving frontier that continued to move inland for centuries. Patrick Manning argues that in the period 1700–1850, nine million Africans were transported to the Americas. At the same time, twenty-one million people were captured in Africa: fourteen million were directed to the Atlantic trade and seven million were brought into domestic slavery.

The historical databases and fine historical studies of the Atlantic slave trade give no conclusive answer to the question of how the Atlantic slave trade effected the long-term welfare of Africa and Africans. We have political and ideological answers, not unlike the answers given two hundred years ago by the debate on the abolition of the slave trade. David Eltis and J. D. Fage, among others, pursue a line of argument that contends that the slave trade had marginal impact on Africa. Paul Lovejoy, a scholar in the debate, writes, "this provocative view of African history falls on one end of a continuum. At the other end are those scholars who argue that the Atlantic slave trade had a devastating impact on Africa, particularly in the eighteenth and early nineteenth centuries... Scholars who study slavery in the Americas should read these contributions in the context of an ongoing debate in African history, a debate that is unlikely to be resolved in the near future, if ever."

From its origins in the fifteenth and sixteenth centuries, the Atlantic World was an economy combining European entrepreneurs and markets, fertile American lands and planters, and African slave labor and brokers. Across the Atlantic, writes Robin Law and Kristin Mann, "the commercial links established by the slave trade among ports in West Africa, America, and Europe are well known, but the trade also generated transatlantic social and cultural connections whose importance has been commonly underestimated. The scale and intensity of these bonds were such that the coastal communities of the Slave Coast, or at least their commercial and ruling elites, may be considered as participating in what can reasonably be termed an 'Atlantic community.'" This Atlantic community was not unique to the Slave Coast. From the Senegambia to Angola, African communities were composed of European and American traders, Christian missionaries, Europeanized Africans and the Africanized descendants of European traders and officials and African women, repatriated free slaves and others who became Atlantic-oriented peoples. "Our theme," note Law and Mann, "is the development and maintenance of continuous and commercial, social, cultural links across the Atlantic."

Atlantic slavery and the slave trade not only brought together Europe, Africa and the Americas but constituted a long transit of the plantation complex from the Mediterranean to the near Atlantic of Madeira and the Canary Islands, to São Tomé, then to Bahia and Pernambuco to the West Indies and finally to Louisiana, Tidewater Virginia, and low-country Carolina. The plantation complex was Portuguese, Spanish, Dutch, French and English. It was a symbiosis of a luxury staple like sugar, tobacco, coffee, cacao, indigo, processing technology and slave labor. The plantation complex was the motor of the Atlantic slave trade for four hundred years. As a result of the W. E. B. Du Bois Institute Dataset of Slaving Voyages, we know of 27,233 Atlantic slave trade voyages on record. These voyages most likely represent more than two-thirds of all Atlantic slave voyages. However, as important as the slave trade was in human terms, it formed only a rather small share of the total Atlantic trade of any European power. For example, the busiest single year for the British slave trade was 1792 when 204 vessels comprising 38,099 tons of shipping left England to carry slaves from Africa to the Americas.

Also in 1792, Great Britain registered 14,334 vessels totaling 1.44 million tons of shipping. Slavers accounted for less than 1.5 percent of British ships.

From 1519 to 1867, according to the W. E. B. Du Bois Database, more than 11,062,000 captive Africans departed for the New World. There are disagreements among scholars regarding the numbers of captive Africans who departed for America and those who arrived alive. Not surprisingly, these disagreements are politically charged. Higher numbers for quite a few scholars are signs of commitment to racial justice. Nevertheless, these many millions of captive Africans transported against their will to the Americas represented the largest migration of any group to the New World before 1800. Of the more than six million souls who traveled to the Americas from 1492 until the American Revolution of 1776, only one million were Europeans. Thus in terms of population, the Americas were more African than European until the nineteenth century. Africans built the port cities of Atlantic America, they built the plantations and specialized in complex agricultural and processing techniques, and in some regions they dug and reinforced the mines. Africans became the skilled and unskilled labor in plantation agriculture across the Americas but they also were skilled artisans and unskilled workers in towns and cities. Unquestionably, the importation of enslaved Africans accelerated the economic development of the Americas. Plantation economies came to have the highest income and wealth per white inhabitant.

The Atlantic World as we have seen in Part II was a world of exploitation and interdependence. The Atlantic slave trade would not have functioned without African participation and cooperation. Of course, American slavery was different. This system maintained itself through brute force and violence. However, when one looks closer we see slavery as a negotiated terrain rather than a system of absolute power and authority. The engine of the Atlantic slave trade, the plantation complex and its embedded system of slavery is the subject of the following chapter.

7.7 Further Reading

William Bosman, *A New and Accurate Description of the Coast of Guinea, Divided into the Gold, the Slave, and the Ivory Coasts* (London, 1705).

Boubacar Barry, *Senegambia and the Atlantic Slave Trade* (Cambridge, 1988).

Robin Blackburn, *The Making of New World Slavery: From the Baroque to the Modern, 1492–1800* (London, 1997).

Madeleine Burnside, edited by Rosemarie Robotham, *Spirit of the Passage: The Transatlantic Slave Trade in the Seventeenth Century* (New York, 1997).

Quobna Ottobah Cugoano, *Thoughts and Sentiments on the Evil of Slavery and Other Writings* [1787], edited by Vincent Carretta (London, 1999).

Philip D. Curtin, *The Atlantic Slave Trade: A Census* (Madison, 1969).

David Eltis, *The Rise of African Slavery in the Americas* (Cambridge, 2000).

Olaudah Equiano, *The Interesting Narrative and Other Writings, 1789*, edited by Vent Carrera (London, 1995).

P. E. H. Hair, Adam Jones, and Robin Law, editors, *Barbot on Guinea: The writings of Jean Barbot on West Africa, 1678–1712*, 2 volumes (London, 1992).

Paul E. Lovejoy, *Transformations in Slavery: A History of Slavery in Africa* (Cambridge, 1983).

A. W. Lawrence, *Trade Castles & Forts of West Africa* (Stanford, 1964).

Robin Law, *Ouidah: The Social History of a West African Slaving 'Port,' 1727–1892* (Athens, 2004).

Alexander Falconbridge, *An Account of the Slave Trade on the Coast of Africa* (London, 1788).

A. Van Dantzig, editor and translator, *The Dutch and the Guinea Coast, 1674–1742: A Collection of Documents from the General State Archive at the Hague* (Accra, Ghana, 1978).

Robert Harms, *The Diligent: A Voyage Through the Worlds of the Slave Trade* (New York, 2002).

Herbert S. Klein, *The Atlantic Slave Trade* (Cambridge, 1999).

Kenneth Morgan, *Slavery, Atlantic Trade and the British Economy, 1600–1800* (Cambridge, 2000).

Joseph C. Miller, *Way of Death: Merchant Capitalism and the Angolan Slave Trade, 1730–1830* (Madison, 1988).

Patrick Manning, *Slavery and African Life: Occidental, Oriental and African Slave Trades* (Cambridge, 1990).

Johannes Menne Postma, *The Dutch in the Atlantic Slave Trade, 1600–1815* (Cambridge, 1990).

Edward Reynolds, *Stand the Storm: A History of the Atlantic Slave Trade* (London, 1989).

Walter Rodney, *How Europe Underdeveloped Africa*, revised edition (Washington, D.C., 1981).

Barbara Solow, editor, *Slavery and the Rise of the Atlantic System* (Cambridge, 1991).

Robert Louis Stein, *The French Slave Trade in the Eighteenth Century: An Old Regime Business* (Madison, 1980).

Leif Svalesen, *The Slave Ship Fredensborg*, translated by Pat Shaw and Selena Winsnes (Bloomington, 2000).

Hugh Thomas, *The Slave Trade: The Story of the Atlantic Slave Trade, 1440–1870* (New York, 1997).

Chapter 8

Bondage

The Atlantic Plantation Complex and the Cultures of Slavery

"I do not see how we can thrive until we get into a stock of slaves sufficient to do all our business, for our children's children will hardly see this great Continent filled with people, so that our servants will still desire freedom to plant for themselves, and not stay but for very great wages." Like this seventeenth-century Englishman in North America, many if not most European colonists in the new Atlantic World did not see how they could succeed without some kind of coerced labor.

The New American World had an abundance of good land, and one could not imagine running out or filling it up with people. That was the problem or the opportunity: plenty of land and not enough people to work it voluntarily. With land everlasting but labor scarce, the returns to labor were relatively high. The labor of Native Americans was extracted through forced levies, tribute and outright slavery. Poor Europeans were contracted to work as indentured servants. However, in many tropical and semitropical regions white servants and native slaves proved to be unreliable or simply unavailable. Europeans then turned to Africans. As we have seen, more than ten million Africans were uprooted in Africa and unloaded in the Americas against their will to work in the plantations and workshops of the Americas. Most enslaved Africans, roughly two-thirds in fact, were given to the sugar plantation, an agricultural factory that specialized in the cultivation, harvesting and industrial processing of this one commodity for foreign markets and consumers. By 1700, sugar had become most important and valuable agricultural commodity that the New World sent to the Old. In the West Indies in the late eighteenth century, sugar plantations produced three times more wealth than all other plantations. "The richest of the planters are those who have the most Negroes," wrote Jean-François Robert in 1696, describing the colony of Martinique, "because the more of them they have, the more sugar they can make, and it is only by making sugar that one becomes rich in this country." "Sugar and slavery formed two of the strands that brought together Europe, Africa and the Americas," writes Dale Tomich, "creating at once a new unity and a profound and unprecedented divergence in the paths of historical development of these regions and their peoples." Sugar and slavery, as Sidney W. Mintz puts it quite simply, "traveled together for nearly four centuries in the New World."

The settlement of the Americas and the development of the colonial Atlantic economy were closely associated with the revival of slavery in early modern times. The new slavery was fueled by the production and export of luxury staples like sugar, tobacco, indigo, cacao and coffee. The agricultural factories – called plantations or *ingenios* (by the Spanish), *engenhos* (by the Portuguese), *habitations sucrerie* (by the French) and *suiker molens* (by the Dutch) – that cultivated, harvested and processed these valuable staples demanded and devoured enormous quantities of labor. Because the plantations did not attract or retain voluntary labor, forced labor – bondage – was the solution. Planters engaged the labor of indentured servants (who were usually Europeans), enslaved Indians or enslaved Africans. It was not uncommon to find some combination of all of these categories at work in individual plantations. Over time, Africans became the preferred source of labor in the tropics for economic as well as other reasons. Millions of men, women and children from West and Central Africa became forced immigrants to and involuntary colonists of the New World. In the Atlantic System, slaves were chattel, that is, tangible personal and movable property (compared to real estate). Slaves were not simply forced laborers, they were valuable items of property that could be bought and sold, separated from their kin and had no legal standing as subjects or citizens in any society. Unlike slavery in the ancient world, the new slavery of the Atlantic World became identified with people of color, and Africans became identified with slavery. As slavery became Africanized, racial prejudice unfolded and, over time, racism arose to explain and justify a degrading and brutal system of exploitation. Atlantic slavery became one of the most extreme forms of domination and exploitation in human history.

The expansion of African slavery into the Atlantic World in the beginning created societies with slaves, that is, societies and economies where slave labor was one more form of labor that coexisted with peasant labor, the *encomienda*, indentured servitude and other forms of free and unfree labor. In societies with slaves, slave labor was marginal and slaveowners were another segment of the propertied elite. In certain tropical and semitropical regions, the introduction of sugar, tobacco, rice and indigo cultivation produced plantation revolutions (in sugar colonies, these were called sugar revolutions) that quickly transformed societies with slaves into slave societies. The new slave societies were societies and economies where slave labor was critical to the economy of the entire colony. Because of this, slaves often became the majority population. Slaveowners, who were the plantation elite, became the ruling class. They built Great Houses, controlled the local government and enacted slave codes that granted them absolute legal control over their slaves. The planter elite in slave societies also developed over time a racist explanation for their domination and the subordination of their African and black slaves. The creation of slave societies in many parts of the Atlantic World during the age of the slave trade and the plantation complex was one of the most pernicious developments of European expansion into the Atlantic.

The plantation complex was the masters' economy but slaves were not simply the objects of a regime of absolute power and authority. Africans and their descendants not only survived the day-by-day trauma of slavery, they carved out some autonomy and power to make and shape their own cultures within slavery. Against the odds and under powerful restraints, slaves pushed, schemed, demanded, compromised, resisted, cajoled, sabotaged, flattered, haggled and negotiated with their masters for provision grounds, free time to work them, travel to other plantations and to Sunday markets, and more. On plantations and in towns, slaves recreated and created their own compressed and splintered communities and cultures in the odd hours and days that were available. Where possible, slaves created their own economy, they formed tenuous families and fragile communities, and they followed and transformed African spiritual traditions and rites. Furthermore, slaves shaped their cultures and the Atlantic World also by resisting slavery in countless ways. Slaves resisted slavery by committing suicide and homicide. Slaves sabotaged their assigned work and the master's property. They ran away and formed free communities in the backlands and rebelled and fought for freedom.

Slavery was a brutal and oppressive institution throughout the Atlantic World. Slavery was also an endlessly negotiated association, relationship and engagement that could range from extreme hostility and violence to a rational business relationship, and even to mutual trust and affection. By negotiating for a little time, space and grace, slaves were able to put together some independent creativity, African fragments and European influences to forge something coherent and autonomous. In this way, slaves rose above the dehumanization inherent in their status. Europeans, Africans and African slaves together made the Atlantic World, but slaves did most of the work.

8.1 The Rise of the Plantation Complex

"Roughly one quarter of any major society in antiquity were human chattels – someone's property," Norman Cantor reminds us. Slavery was pervasive and economically crucial in the Greek and Roman worlds. Conquests supplied the Romans slaves from Anatolia to Hispania. For example, after just one battle Julius Caesar sold fifty thousand Gallic prisoners. *Latifundia*, large estates, produced cash crops such as grain and olives and were worked by slave labor. Slaves also mined silver, worked in industry and built public works. One indication of the importance of slavery in Roman society was the slave uprising led by Spartacus in 73 B.C.E. For three years, a slave army marched up and down Italy, attracting nearly one hundred thousand fugitive slaves before it was defeated and the uprising was crushed. Slavery survived the decline and fall of the empire, persisted into the Medieval Age and could be found throughout Christendom.

In Western Europe, slavery declined in the centuries after the empire because, in part, peasant laborers became serfs tied to the land of a lord. By the eighth and ninth centuries, clerics began to denounce the enslavement of Christians. William the Conqueror in eleventh-century England forbade the selling of anyone out of the country. The expansion of Islam under Arab armies in the seventh and eighth centuries in the Mediterranean basin brought new patterns to slavery. Muslims enslaved Christians and other "infidels," and Christians enslaved Muslims, particularly in the Iberian Peninsula where Muslims and Christians faced one another directly. It was through Muslim traders that enslaved black Africans first appeared in the Mediterranean and southern Europe. Nevertheless, the taking and selling of slaves in much of Europe was in decline, and by the fourteenth and fifteenth centuries the institution was essentially extinct in England, the Netherlands and France.

The revival of commerce in medieval Europe involved, among other innovations, the adoption of a crop first brought to the Mediterranean by Arab traders: sugarcane, a giant perennial grass that yields sucrose juice. Until then, Europeans had depended upon honey for sweetness. White crystalline sugar arrived in small, expensive quantities, often dispensed as though it was a rare and precious medicine. At first, Italian merchants purchased sugar from Arabs but over time learned how to cultivate sugarcane and make the refined brown and white crystallized sugar, which the Arabs called *qandi* and *alçucar*. Crusaders planted sugarcane in the Levant and in a like manner, Italians brought cane to Cyprus in the thirteenth century and purchased slaves for the cultivation and milling of cane. The Black Sea factories of Italian merchants not only acquired spices from the Silk Road but also Tartars, Armenians, Bulgarians and other Slavs, who gave their name to bondsman (slave) and bondage (slavery). From the ongoing conflict with Islam came enslaved captives who were Arab, Moor and black African (who were often considered and called Moors and blackamoors by Europeans). Sugarcane and slavery spread under Italian (mostly Genoese) management to Crete, Southern Italy, Sicily, Valencia and the Algarve in Atlantic Portugal. The incipient plantation complex was born in the Mediterranean during the commercial revival of the high Middle Ages.

Sugarcane growers considered slavery particularly well-suited to the requirements of cane cultivation and milling. Holing, planting, weeding and harvesting sugarcane were onerous tasks in the tropics, but there were many industries based on difficult tasks that survived and sometimes thrived without dependence upon slave labor. Sugarcane possessed certain characteristics that required not only very hard work but also very hard work at a rapid pace sustained for long periods of time. The holing and planting of cane cuttings (shoots or ratoons) took most of the summer and fall in the West Indies. The sugarcane got most of its growth during the rainy season, from May to November. We need to remember that sugarcane did not mature in one season or even one year but over the course of fifteenth to eighteen months. Once a cane stalk matured, it had to be cut as soon as possible or the sucrose juice it held would begin to dry, sour or ferment. The cutting of the canes began around January, with the beginning of the dry season, and continued until spring or summer. As a result of this critical timing, growers learned how to plant sugarcane so that fields matured in a particular order, and thus presented harvest workers with recurring deadlines lasting for months. Furthermore, once a cane stalk had been cut, its juice had to be extracted and the process of transforming it into crystalline sugar had to begin relatively quickly or the juice would be ruined and become worthless.

Document 8.1
Of the Manner How Sugar is Made

César de Rochefort, 1666

When the great plenty of Tobacco made at S. Christophers and the other islands had brought down the price of it so low, that it did not turn to accompt, it pleas'd God to put it into the heart of the French General de Poincy, to find out some other ways to facilitate the subsistence of the Inhabitants, and carry on some Trade: He thereupon employ'd his Servants and Slaves about the culture of Sugar-Canes, Ginger, and Indico; and the design met with a success beyond what was expected.

That work is performed by a Machine or Mill, which some call an *Ingenio*, whereby the juice within the Canes is squeez'd out. These Mills are built of very solid and lasting wood, and are more convenient in the Islands then those used to the same purpose at Madera and Brasil: Nor is it to be fear'd in the former, as many times in the latter, that the fire should get to the boiling Coppers, and set all into a flame, to the destruction of those who are employ'd about the work; for the Coppers in these Islands are seen to boil, yet the fire that causes it is made and kept in on the outside by furnaces, which are so well cemented, that neither the flame nor the smoak does any way hinder those who are at work, which they may follow without any fear of danger or inconvenience.

The ordinary way of turning the Mills is by Horses or Oxen; but the French Governour hath one which is turn'd by water, which falling on a wheel sets the whole Machine going.

When the Sugar-Canes are ripe, they are cut somewhat neer the ground, above the first knot which is without any juice; and having cut off the tops, and taken away certain little, long, and very thin leaves, which encompass them; they are made up into bundles, and carry'd to the Mills to be there press'd and squeez'd between two rollers, turning one upon the other

The juice which is squeez'd out of them falls into a great Cistern, whence it is convey'd through long pipes or channels into the vessels appointed for the boiling of it, In great Sugar-works there are at least six Coppers, whereof three very large ones are of copper, about the bredth and depth of those us'd by Dyers, and are to clarifie the juice, which is to be boil'd with a gentle fire, putting in ever and anon a small quantity of a certain very strong Lye, made of water and ashes, commonly call'd Temper, which makes all the filth to boil up, which as it appears is taken off with a great brass skimmer. When the juice is well purify'd in these three Coppers, into which it had been convey'd alternately one after another, it is strain'd through a cloth, and afterwards pour'd into three other Coppers of some other metal, which are very thick, broad enough, and about a foot and a half deep. In these Coppers the Sugar receives its last boiling; for then there is a more violent fire made, and it is continually stirr'd, and when it bubbles up so as that it may be fear'd it should boil over the Coppers, it is allay'd by the casting in of a little sallet-oil; and as it begins to grow thick, it is pour'd into the last of those Coppers, from whence, as it inclines to a consistency, it is dispos'd into vessels of wood or earth, and so carry'd into the Curing-house, where it is whiten'd with a kind of fat earth mixt with water, which is spred upon it; then they open the little hole in the bottom of every vessel or pot, that all the filth or dregs that is about the Sugar may fall into another channel, which conveys it into a vessel prepar'd for that purpose...

The greatest secret in the business of making good Sugar consists in the whitening of it: Those who have it are very loth to communicate it. From what hath been said, it may be easily inferr'd what extraordinary advantages accrue to the Inhabitants of that Island by means of this sweet and precious Commodity, and what satisfaction it brings to their Correspondents in other parts of the world, who have it at so ease rates.

In his history of the "Caribby-Islands," César de Rochefort writes primarily about the French islands and their inhabitants, government, economy and other subjects. He attributes the transformation from tobacco cultivation to sugar not to the Dutch planters abandoning Brazil but to "servants and slaves" who had knowledge of the culture of sugar cane. *Source: The History of Barbados, St Christophers, Nevis, St Vincents, Antego, Martinico, Monserrat, And the rest of the Caribby – Islands, in all XXVIII. In Two Books. [Written by César de Rochefort] Englished by J. Davies of Kidwelly. London, Printed for John Starkey and Thomas Dring, 1666.*

According to one nineteenth-century expert, "The crop being ripe will not wait long without deterioration, and the juice once expressed will not keep twenty minutes without fermenting if proper treatment not be followed."

Once the cane had been cut, mill workers were forced to crush and squeeze the cane stalks between wood, stone or metal presses or rollers at a rapid pace day and night. The cane juice obtained from the mill was transferred to the boiling house where it was cooked and boiled up to six different times in different kettles and at different temperatures to clarify the solution, reduce the water, produce the syrup and begin the process of crystallization. Work in the boiling house was extremely hot, dangerous and continued twenty-four hours, day and night. Hard, fast and long labor were the conditions facing prospective sugarcane workers. "Of all the tropical export crops of this period," writes G. B. Masefield, "sugar cane demanded the most manual labour, especially for harvesting." Cane growers learned that workers had to be forced to work this hard, fast and long if a successful – that is, profitable – harvest could be achieved. Slavery, and the violence that undergirded it, became wedded to sugar. Father Jean-Baptiste Labat, who managed a sugar plantation in the West Indies, wrote, "One can see what the work regimen of a sugar plantation is how difficult it is for the slaves." This conclusion is obvious in the poem of the Cuban slave Juan Francisco Manzano:

> With twenty hours of unremitting toil,
> Twelve in the field, and eight indoors to boil,
> Or grind the cane – believe me few grow old,
> But life is cheap, and Sugar, Sir! – is gold.

Figure 8.1. Slaves Cutting Sugar Cane in the West Indies. From the lithography by William Clark in *Views of sugar production on Antigua* (London, 1833). Courtesy of the John Carter Brown Library at Brown University.

All plantation labor in the Atlantic World was extremely tasking and often brutal for slaves. In the Carolina low country, slaves who worked the rice plantations worked in estuaries, swamps, canals, irrigation ditches and the wet rice fields. They labored in miserably mucky environments. The visitor Janet Schaw noted in 1775 that "the labour required for [rice] is only fit for slaves, and I think the hardest work I have seen them engaged in." Indigo production in the West Indies, Louisiana, South Carolina and elsewhere was a grim affair given the continuous pumping, stirring and beating of rotten, decaying indigo leaves. Indigo processing was not only hard and nasty work; it was also deadly, as indigo paste is toxic. Nevertheless, the slave labor of sugar plantations, as Father Jerome de Merolla noted of Bahia in 1682, was deadly: "Their labor is so hard and their sustenance so small, that they are reckoned to live long if they hold out seven years." Bryan Edwards of Jamaica one hundred years later wrote that labor on the sugar plantations "is unquestionably more severe and constant than that on any other species of landed property in the West Indies."

We have seen in previous chapters that the European expansion into the Atlantic initiated the colonization of the Madeira, Canary and Cape Verde Islands. In 1455, Portuguese planters backed with Genoese capital and assisted by Sicilian technicians began to plant sugarcane on Madeira. The first sugar mill in the Spanish Canary Islands was built in 1484, and the sugar industry took off. With financing from Portuguese, Genoese and German merchants, it prospered. In the Cape Verde Islands, sugar plantations were started at Santiago and Fuego but the dry climate was not conducive to

a thriving sugar industry. "This plant multiplied in the land," wrote Gaspar
Frutuoso, the sixteenth-century chronicler of Madeira, "in such a way that
its sugar is the best that is known in the world and it has enriched many
foreign merchants and a good part of the settlers of the land."

The sugar industry of the Atlantic Mediterranean swelled in the late fifteenth and early sixteenth centuries. The islands' "white gold" was producing
profits in real gold and silver, and lots of it. The crown authorized the first
water-power sugar mill in 1452. Until then, and for long after in many places,
cane was usually and laboriously crushed by a hand press, an *alçaprema*. In
the 1470s, sugar production was starting to compete with Mediterranean
sugar in terms of price, quality and quantity. By the 1490s, Madeira had
over two hundred sugarcane planters, and some eighty sugar mills producing
nearly 1,500 metric tons of sugar a year. These exports were sent to Portugal, Flanders, France, England, Genoa, Venice and even Constantinople. The
sugar business was the main stimulus to population growth and economic
development of the island. At the beginning of the sixteenth century, Spanish
officials on the island of Tenerife, in the Canary Islands, wrote, "sugar estates
are the most important thing on the island." In 1520, this island archipelago
had more than sixty sugar mills. On Gran Canaria alone there were twenty
mills, which were producing about 1,000 tons of sugar a year. By the early
sixteenth century, the booming sugar industry in the Mediterranean Atlantic
had overtaken the decrepit sugar industry of the Mediterranean Sea.

In the Madeira and Canary Islands in the late fifteenth century, the new
Atlantic sugar plantation – in Iberian hands, called an *engenho* or an *ingenio* –
was centered around its namesake: the mill. Mills were machines to crush
sugar canes and squeeze out the liquid sucrose. Over the centuries, the sugar
mill became more technologically complex. The main task remained simple
and straightforward: canes were crushed by two or three grindstones or
cylinders powered by persons, animals, water, wind or, by the nineteenth
century, steam. The three-cylinder sugar mill that developed in Brazil became
the classic form. Once the canes were crushed and the juice was collected,
the plantation needed a boiling house to purge, cook and refine the syrup
into *muscovado* sugars (less-expensive browns and blacks) and "clayed"
sugars (various whites) An *engenho/ingenio* was a sugar mill and boiling
house as well as a sugar estate with the best land for cane fields, pastures for
horses, oxen, cattle and other stock, and some corner set aside for the slave
quarters, the *senzalas*. The center of operations of the *engenho/ingenio* was
the sugar mill but the headquarters of the community was the *Casa Grande*,
the residence of the *Senhor de Engenho*.

In both Madeira and the Canaries, the sugar mill-plantation system that
developed in the second half of the fifteenth century included a class of small
and middle-size cane farmers who owed or rented their land. These *lavradores*
or *labradores* cultivated and harvested sugarcane, often using slave labor,
and sent their canes to the local *engenhos* or *ingenios*, frequently dividing
their crop with the *Senhor de Engenho*. In the late fifteenth century in the
Capitancy of Funchal in Madeira, we see 221 cane growers and 80 *engenhos*.
This system of small cane farmers surrounding and becoming dependent upon
a regional sugar mill-plantation would reproduce itself in the Americas. As

the sugar mill-plantation moved into the Americas and developed along these lines in the seventeenth and eighteenth centuries, it became more than an agricultural or industrial enterprise. The "sugar latifundium," as Fernando Ortiz put it, was a complicated system of land, machinery, transportation, technicians, workers, capital, and people to produce sugar. It was a "complete social organism" and, he argued, it was as "live and complex as a city."

The rise of sugar in Maderia and the Canaries brought the institution of slavery into the Atlantic. At first, and for several decades, slaves in these islands included some Moors, some Europeans, some Africans and a lot of native Canarians. It was the natives of the Canaries who constructed the *levadas*, the irrigation works in Madeira that were carved out of solid rock. The death of Canarians and the expansion of the cane fields led to the importation of enslaved Africans, two thousand laboring in the cane fields of Madeira in the 1490s. In the Canaries, native Canarians remained in service as domestic slaves while African slaves were imported to work the sugarcane. By the early sixteenth century, there were about a thousand African slaves in the Canaries, working with the ever fewer Canarians, Moors, Berbers and even Native American slaves.

Portuguese São Tomé had a total of 325 square miles with rich volcanic soil and heavy rainfall. Sugarcane, Genoese capital and skilled Sicilian sugar technicians were brought to the island from Madeira and by 1510, one visitor noted that sugar estates, called *fazendas*, covered the island. Sugar's "golden age" in São Tomé began in the 1520s and lasted about fifty years. Reportedly, there were somewhere in the range of sixty to eighty *engenhos* on the island in 1522. Within twenty years, production peaked at around 2,250 tons per year (some scholars say twice that amount). Tomean *engenhos* were more productive because just about all of them were water-mills and also because they used African slaves on a new scale. Many *engenhos* had one hundred slaves or more working the cane year round. No plantation system in the Mediterranean Atlantic had ever seen this type of abundance of labor. Reliable figures regarding the population of São Tomé in the sixteenth century are rare. Estimates for the slave population at the height of the sugar regime, around 1550, range from two thousand to nine thousand. A report from an anonymous Portuguese pilot sometime before 1550 observed, "the chief industry of the people is to make sugar, which they sell to the ships which come each year bringing flour, Spanish wines, oil, cheese ... All the population, therefore buys negro slaves and their women from Guinea, Benin and Manicongo, and sets them to work on the land to grow and make sugar. There are rich men here, who have 150, 200 and even 300 negroes and negresses, who are obliged to work for their masters all the week, except on Saturdays, when they work on their own account."

Why was Atlantic slavery Africanized? In the early farms, workshops and plantations of the Atlantic islands, there was a mixed labor force of wage earners, servants and slaves. The Portuguese and the Spanish brought their fellow countrymen and women as servants bound for a length of time because of a debt or a crime. The Mediterranean slave trade also brought to the islands captives of all colors and ethnicities including Arabs, Moors, Canarians, black Africans and, in the 1490s and early 1500s, Native Americans. Canary

Islanders, who had been conquered by the Spanish, constituted a significant slave population in their own islands as well as on other Atlantic islands in the fifteenth and early sixteenth centuries. In 1450, black African slavery would not have appeared to contemporaries as the shape of slavery to come. Fifty years later, things had changed. "Sugar cane and Negro slaves," noted the Cuban historian Ortiz, "arrived together."

The rise of the sugar-centered plantation complex in the Mediterranean had provided energy to the stagnant or declining Western slave trade of the late Middle Ages. The soaring of the plantation complex in the Atlantic islands in the late fifteenth and early sixteenth centuries not only further strengthened the slave trade, it also began to Africanize it. The great need for forced labor by the sugar plantations of Madeira, the Canaries and São Tomé was increasingly met by slaves who were obtained close by, thus keeping the cost down. The budding slave trade along the coast of Africa was in the hands of the Portuguese. Two of the largest markets for slaves in the emerging plantation complex in the Atlantic, Madeira and São Tomé, were Portuguese possessions. The growing reliance upon relatively cheap slaves from Africa made good business sense and was confirmed by hundreds and then thousands of uncoordinated and independent decisions to buy enslaved Africans.

The Africanization of the new Atlantic slave trade at this early point was little more than a question of local supply (Africans on the African coast) meeting local demand (plantations in islands near the African coast). As we will see in this chapter, Atlantic planters also favored enslaved African laborers because they believed they were good workers. Several decades ago in his classic 1944 study, *Capitalism and Slavery*, Eric Williams wrote, "A racial twist has there by been given to what is basically an economic phenomenon. Slavery was not born of racism: rather, racism was the consequence of slavery." David Brion Davis also makes the point that when slavery became indelibly linked throughout the Western Hemisphere with people of African descent, "the dishonor, humiliation, and bestialization that had universally been associated with chattel slavery now became fused with Negritude."

In the mid-sixteenth century, the sugar industries of Madeira and the Canary Islands, and then São Tomé, peaked and began to decline. One of the characteristics of the Atlantic plantation complex was the generation of economic booms and busts. Tomean sugar had brought about the beginning of the end for the first expansion of the Atlantic sugar industry. As would be true in later booms and busts, land was becoming depleted, investors were finding better mills and fields to put their money in and more efficient mill technology was coming into use elsewhere, and so the bottom line was that Madeiran sugar was more expensive and was driven out of the market. In both Madeira and the Canaries, vines replaced sugarcane and wines and liquors replaced sugar exports. Madeiran table wine, simply called madeira around the world, was fortified – made with brandy – to prevent spoilage. It became one of the world's great dessert wines and a pretty good business. The decline of the Tomean sugar industry occurred in the last decades of the sixteenth century for the same reasons as Madeira and the Canaries, with one difference. São Tomé, one of the first slave societies of the Atlantic World, experienced slave rebellions, one after the other (1580, 1595 and 1617) and an almost continuous guerrilla resistance war in the rough interior of the island. The well-endowed slave regime that so benefited the sugar industry during its rise in the late fifteenth and early sixteenth century eventually proved to be the Achilles' heel of the planter class.

Sugarcane crossed the Atlantic Ocean with Columbus in 1493. Columbus was familiar with the business: his father-in-law was Bartolomeu Perestrelo, who founded Porto Santo in Madeira. The Columbus family established the first sugar plantation in Hispaniola in the 1490s, bringing to the New World Madeiran and Canarian technology and quite a few Portuguese sugar technicians. With thirty thousand square miles and a better climate than São Tomé, Hispaniola's future appeared to be "white gold." The first sugar mill was built in 1516 and the first recorded export of sugar was in 1517. Before the end of 1520, there were thirty-four *ingenios* in construction and an additional three watermills and three horse-powered mills grinding cane. "Now sugar is one of the richest crops to be found in any province or kingdom in the world," wrote Gonzalo Fernández de Oviedo in 1546, "and on this island there is so much and it is so good although it was so recently introduced and has been followed for such a short time." The sugar business also spread to Puerto Rico, Jamaica, Central America, the Pacific Coast of Peru and the valleys of Morelos and Chiapa in Mexico.

The rise of the sugar industry in the Spanish West Indies at first depended upon native labor, primarily the *encomienda*. Even during the early years of colonization, when Indians were abundant and African slaves were rare and expensive, Spanish planters almost always preferred Africans because of their skills and dependability. In 1511, a report to the king from Santo Domingo declared that the labor of one black slave was equal to four Indians. The first Africans generally came from Iberia or the Canary Islands rather than directly from Africa. The crown then started granting *asientos* to the Portuguese, Italians and others to ship Africans in larger and larger numbers from the continent to the different ports of Spanish America. By 1542, there were over twenty-five thousand African slaves in Hispaniola, a population twenty times larger than the island's Spanish cane growers, friars, soldiers and government officials. For Fernández de Oviedo, the island was "a new Guinea." The same thing was taking place throughout the Spanish West Indies, although on a different scale. In Puerto Rico, by 1530 the Spanish population was 327 and there were nearly 2,300 African slaves, producing an African to Spaniard ratio of about seven to one.

The sugar plantation complex did not prevail in the Spanish West Indies for two centuries. Beginning in the 1520s and 1530s, upon the discovery and settlement of silver-rich Mexico and Peru, the small Spanish population of the West Indies largely deserted the islands. The collapse of the native populations of Hispaniola, Cuba, Puerto Rico and the others led to Spanish slave raiding of Central America and to the importation of enslaved Africans. The crown controlled the contracts for the slave trade but did not – or could not – send as many slaves as needed or requested for the sugar mills. For example, the sugar elite of Santo Domingo complained to the king, "good slaves were not available at 40 ducats and that those who were available at that price were old, emaciated, or decrepit." An increasing inflexible slave labor supply desiccated the Spanish West Indian sugar industry. The output and number of *ingenios* declined. The sugar industry of Hispaniola began a decline in the 1570s and by the early seventeenth century, only a third as many *ingenios* were in operation as two decades before. In Puerto Rico as well, the *ingenios* began to disappear: the eleven *ingenios* in 1582 had declined to eight by 1602 and to seven by 1747. The export of sugar declined by two-thirds in the late sixteenth century. The Atlantic sugar era that began in Madera and the Canaries should have continued in Hispaniola and Puerto Rico but was thrown off kilter. Later in the sixteenth century, the plantation complex would unfold on the coast of Brazil.

The rise of the first phase of the plantation complex in the Atlantic transformed slavery and the slave trade in the western world. The sugar industry of Madeira, the Canaries, São Tomé, Hispaniola and the Spanish Caribbean required slave labor, and planters preferred Africans. Prior to this development, slavery in the western world, which had been essentially the Mediterranean slave trade, was identified with no one ethnicity, color or religion, and had been stagnant if not in a slow decline. The new Atlantic plantation complex revived, and Africanized, slavery and the slave trade in the West. Beginning in the second half of the fifteenth century, the volume of the African slave trade increased inexorably decade by decade. In the late fifteenth century, Europeans took about a thousand Africans a year from the coasts and made them slaves. By the 1780s, the Atlantic slave trade engulfed about eighty thousand Africans a year.

8.2 The Transatlantic Plantation Complex

The plantation complex first crossed the Atlantic from Madeira and the Canary Islands to Hispaniola in the late fifteenth century. Slave societies in the Spanish West Indies were in the process of formation, which stimulated the Atlantic slave trade and made it transatlantic for the first time. As we have seen, the plantation complex in the Spanish Caribbean faltered and then collapsed in the late sixteenth and seventeenth centuries. The Portuguese had better luck a short time later. The plantation complex was transferred from Madeira and São Tomé to the coast of Brazil about half a century after the Spanish planted sugarcane in Hispaniola. For the first few decades of sugarcane in Brazil, from 1540 to about 1580, Native Americans dominated the labor force of the sugar plantations. By the end of the century, enslaved Africans constituted seventy percent of all plantation workers. Brazil was becoming a slave society and sugar was king. By the early seventeenth century, the plantation complex was thriving on the Portuguese coast of South America.

Slavery first came to the Americas to meet the labor demands of gold and sugar in the Spanish Caribbean. Plantations spread into many parts of Spanish America but the plantation complex never fully developed in any Spanish colony or kingdom. In a few isolated regions – the Chocó of New Granada, the Isthmus of Panama, Morelos, Puebla and Vera Cruz in New

Spain, coastal Peru and a few others – plantations or mines dominated the economy and slaveholders became the local elite. In these regions, enslaved Africans constituted the core of the labor force, and Africans and their Creole cousins, New World blacks, sometimes made up a majority of the population; in short, these regions were small slave societies. However, they were situated within larger colonial societies with many different types of labor, and in colonial societies with a number of different and important economic sectors. For instance, the plantations of Mexico and Peru produced sugar for domestic consumption and regional markets. In Spanish America as a whole, plantations and slavery did not structure the economy and society. They were components of a larger and more complex whole.

The Atlantic slave trade found diverse markets in Spanish America. Enslaved Africans were purchased throughout Spanish America and were found in rural plantations, haciendas, ranches and modest farms as well as in towns and cities. Slaves were employed in field gangs cutting sugar-cane but also tending every type of crop, often unsupervised. They worked on the docks of the great port cities of Spanish America, they made cloth, made shoes, furniture, musical instruments, herded horses and cattle as cow-boys and transported goods in large mule trains. They cared for families as domestic servants, rented their skills to paying customers and thus provided an income to their owner. In the silver mining regions of Mexico and Peru, African slave labor supplemented the dominant Indian labor force. At the peak of the African contribution to mining in New Spain around 1600, slaves constituted perhaps one-quarter of the workforce. Although there came to be many more enslaved Africans employed in Peru's silver industry, they never represented more than ten or fifteen percent of the total labor force. Clearly, in the mining districts of Mexico and Peru Indians were always the numerically dominant labor force. However, Africans often held critical positions as skilled workmen and technicians.

Spanish America was an eager consumer of enslaved Africans for about 150 years. Around 1650, Indian populations began to grow once again. Indians became more mobile and responsive to wage labor, and the demand for enslaved Africans fell. During this century and a half, the Atlantic slave trade transported around three hundred thousand men, women and children to Spanish America. As the slave trade to Spanish America declined in the second half of the seventeenth century, so did the importance of slavery except in a few select enclaves. In Peru, the number of slaves declined from around one hundred thousand in 1650 to ninety thousand by the end of the eighteenth century. In Mexico, the number decreased from thirty-five thousand to less than six thousand.

Spanish America's black slaves increasingly became *ladinos* or *criollos*, that is, Hispanicized Creoles, New World blacks born in the Americas. They were increasingly assimilated into Spanish American society and culture. Slaves directly from Africa, called *bozales*, withdrew from Spanish society and culture. Creoles embraced the dominant culture, economy and society to use it to their advantage, and ultimately to obtain freedom. Creoles spoke Spanish, were to some degree Catholic Christians and often were members of religious brotherhoods called *cofradías*. Many were skilled artisans, familiar with currencies, credit, trade, saving money and were sometimes able to purchase their own freedom. When and where possible, they were members of extended families that guided and helped its members not unlike Spanish American families. New World blacks, slave and free, retained aspects of African culture: Africanisms such as certain religious concepts and rituals, burial practices, music and dance, words and phrases, and more. Compared to most Indians Creoles were part of Spanish society, and the colonial caste system recognized them as members of the familiar Republic of the Spanish rather than the alien Republic of the Indians.

At the same time that Spaniards were attempting to bring the plantation revolution to Hispaniola and the rest of the Caribbean, the Portuguese still viewed Brazil through an African and Asian lens, as a commercial enterprise rather than a settlement colony. Pressure from the French on the coast of Brazil forced the crown to adopt a policy of colonization in 1530, and then to back it up with an official and military presence in 1549. As we have seen, captaincies were granted to wealthy and prominent individuals who were responsible for settling the land and making it pay, one way or another. The establishment of the royal captaincy in Bahia, with the colonial capital at Salvador, reinforced Portugal's commitment to colonization.

For colonization to become self-sustaining, royal officials and the donatory captains needed a profitable enterprise. They would have preferred gold and silver mines, but they experimented with sugarcane brought from Madeira and São Tomé. The crown built the first sugar mills in Bahia in the 1550s, which were called *engenhos*. In other captaincies, the donatory captains invested in *engenhos* as did merchant-backed settlers and religious corporations like the Jesuits, Carmelites and Benedictines. When Indians did not respond to any incentives to work the fields as serfs or wage earners, Portuguese planters tried Indian slavery. In some areas, Indian slavery remained the principal labor force for one hundred years. In the second half of the sixteenth century, the sugar plantation system took off and was most successful and expansive in the captaincies of São Vicente, Pernambuco and Bahia.

The sugar revolution began during the governorship of Mem de Sá (1557–72), who gave out land grants to those willing to grow and mill sugarcane. Sugar prospered in Brazil because of the great expanses of fertile soil, inexpensive enslaved Africans and the fastest sailing times to Europe from the Americas. From the five mills of Bahia in the 1550s, the expansion of the infrastructure of the plantation revolution was remarkable. By 1583, there were 115 mills in all of Brazil, and 350 mills by 1629. As a result, production reached ever-higher records not only because there were more mills but also because the new Brazilian mills were far more productive (some said six times more productive) than the Tomean mills. São Tomé had held the previous record, nearly 5,000 tons in one year. In 1620, Brazil's sugar crop exceeded 13,000 tons. In a few more years, Brazil would reach its maximum of 20,000 tons in one year. Brazil had become the world's largest producer of sugar and the most important supplier of Europe. Brazilian sugar constituted about eighty percent of the European sugar market. Brazil became one of the richest European colonies in the Atlantic.

Figure 8.2. A Brazilian *Engenho* in Pernambuco in the Seventeenth Century. Cartouche from the Map Pernambuco by Jean Blaeu, *Le Grand Atlas ov Cosmographie Blaviane*, Vol. 12 (Amsterdam, 1667). Courtesy of the William L. Clements Library at the University of Michigan.

The transition from Indian to African slavery was determined by a complex interaction of economic, cultural, political and racial forces and motives. In the 1550s and 1560s, there were hardly any enslaved Africans in the plantations of the dynamic northeast. By the mid-1580s, there were about two thousand black slaves in Pernambuco, which constituted about one-third of the total labor force of the captaincy. By 1600, the labor force on the plantations was fairly well balanced between Indians and Africans. By 1620, the majority of workers on most plantations in the northeast were African. The plantation system created greater demand for labor. From 1576 to 1591, it is estimated that about forty thousand Africans were imported into Brazil. From 1600 to 1650, the number of imports has been calculated at two hundred thousand. This was an increase from about 2,500 slaves per year in the late sixteenth century to 4,000 a year in the first half of the seventeenth century.

By 1630, African slavery had become the key to the Brazilian economy. An Italian Jesuit some time later aptly summarized slavery's critical position: "The slaves are the hands and the feet of the sugar-mill owner, because without them it is not possible in Brazil to set up, maintain, and develop a plantation, nor to have a functioning mill." Furthermore, Africans and their descendants had become one-half of the total population of Brazil. In Spanish America by comparison, Africans and their descendants constituted only two percent of the population. Over the span of about five decades, Brazil, which had been a society with slaves, was transformed into a slave society.

Why did Brazilian planters shift from a predominantly Indian workforce to a predominately African workforce? Throughout the transition period, enslaved Indians were far more inexpensive (sometimes on an order of fifteen to one) than enslaved Africans. This price differential was not simply based on the large number of Indians in Brazil and their lower cost of acquisition and transport. Planters in Brazil and throughout the Americas believed Africans were better and more dependable workers than Indians. When enslaved Africans began to increase in numbers in the plantation system, they filled the skilled positions in the milling and boiling houses and only later, as more Africans were available, were they given fieldwork. Admiration of Africans by European planters, rather than disdain, contributed to the transition to some extent.

Africans had other "advantages" that made African slavery the better economic choice. Unlike some other native peoples, Brazil's Indians were unaccustomed to forced labor of any type and, as a result, often refused to cooperate, ran away or rebelled. Enslaved Africans were thousands of miles and one great ocean distant from their kin and communities. They were isolated in another way: other slaves on their plantation were often from other "nations," speaking different languages and following unfamiliar customs. Their color, different from almost all non-slaves, furthermore highlighted their isolation and facilitated the capture of runaways. This isolation did not prevent resistance to slavery but did make substantial resistance more difficult and less frequent.

In the late sixteenth century, Indian slavery in Brazil was adversely affected by several different types of influences. As elsewhere in the Americas, Native Americans died in large numbers when they had contact with Europeans. In the 1560s, the transition to African slavery may very well have begun as a result of a major smallpox epidemic that reportedly killed as many as thirty thousand Indians in *aldeias* and plantations. A Jesuit commented on the many deaths of Indians in the years before 1583 and noted, "Now go take a look at Bahia's farms and sugar plantations. You will find them full of negroes from Guiné, but with very few natives." In 1570, the crown prohibited Indian slavery in Brazil but with the exceptions (capture in just war or rescue from human sacrifice and cannibalism), this had little impact on the institution. With the union of the Spanish and Portuguese crowns in 1580, royal opposition to Indian slavery increased. Although royal policy did not end Indian slavery, its delegitimatization in the late sixteenth century may have influenced planters to believe that an investment in an enslaved African was more secure than one in an enslaved Indian.

Of course, the transition from Indian to African slavery in Brazil was first and foremost an economic decision within an economic system, with profit as the bottom line. Planters bought enslaved Africans instead of enslaved Indians because they believed that, all things considered, Africans were more productive than Indians. Planters held this perception as a result of experience working with both Indians and Africans.

Although African slavery was concentrated in the sugar business in Brazil, slaveholding was widespread in town and countryside. Slaves were employed in just about every occupation and trade, and the renting of slaves became common. A visitor to Bahia at the beginning of the seventeenth century noticed, "There is not a single Portuguese, however poor, man or woman, who does not possess two or three slaves, slaves who earn their masters' living by working a certain number of hours every day and generating sufficient profit to sustain their owners."

The wealth of Brazil attracted a predator. After Portugal became part of the Spanish monarchy in 1580, the United Provinces of The Netherlands turned its seapower against Portuguese shipping. At the end of a twelve-year truce in 1621, the Dutch established the Dutch West India Company (WIC) to raid Spanish and Portuguese shipping in the Atlantic as well as create overseas trading posts and colonies in Africa and America. The forces of the WIC were part of a larger global assault by the Dutch that reached into the Indian Ocean and the Spice Islands. The great prize, which the WIC stalked, was Brazil; the Dutch set out to steal a large and wealthy colony.

During the truce, Dutch shippers transported a good portion of Brazil's sugar output to Amsterdam's sugar refineries. In 1598, there were three such refineries in Amsterdam, but by 1622 the city boasted twenty-nine. The end of the truce meant the reimposition of an Iberian embargo on Dutch shipping. Amsterdam needed raw sugar, and the WIC proposed to get it directly at the source. In 1623–4, the WIC dispatched a twenty-three-ship fleet across the Atlantic and captured Salvador, the capital of Brazil. The Dutch commander of the force noted, "when we entered Bahia we met only blacks, for everyone else had fled from the city."

The WIC held Salvador and the *recôncavo* (the sugar-producing region around the bay) for only one year before a Portuguese-Spanish force recaptured the city. During that year, the Dutch learned of the need to constantly resupply the African labor force. Because the WIC had refused, to that point, to trade in slaves for moral reasons, the company was forced to rethink its policy. In 1626, the Zeeland chamber of the WIC gave permission for the company to trade in slaves.

In 1628, the WIC captured the entire Spanish silver fleet in Matanzas bay in Cuba. This windfall permitted the Company to launch another assault on Brazil. In 1629–30, the WIC organized an expedition composed of sixty-seven ships and seven thousand men. This time, the assault was aimed at the heart of Brazil's sugar industry, Pernambuco. The expedition captured the province's two ports, Recife and Olinda, and it took several additional years to pacify the interior. The governor of New Holland – Dutch Brazil – found that about fifty percent of the *engenhos* had been abandoned or destroyed. The new regime also confiscated *engenhos*. Government auctions allowed Dutch investors to become *Senhores de Engenho*. Over the next two decades, the Dutch population of New Holland rose to about ten thousand, which included hundreds of Jews.

The Dutch now had the plantations but lacked the steady supply of slaves necessary to maintain production. As a 1638 report from Brazil to the WIC's *Heren XIX* stated, in an attempt to explain the declining sugar harvests, "It is not possible to do anything in Brazil without slaves." The new energetic governor of New Holland, Johann Maurits, Prince of Nassau, extended the territory controlled by the company and dispatched a force from Recife to capture Elmina, Portugal's principal outpost on the Gold Coast in 1637. Possession of Elmina and a few other Portuguese trading factories on the Guinea coast allowed the Dutch to import more slaves, about two thousand per year, in the late 1630s but it was still not enough. Seeking more slaves, the WIC attacked and seized Luanda and Benguela on the coast of Angola as well as São Tomé. By 1644, more than five thousand slaves annually were imported at Recife.

In 1640, Portugal rebelled and won its independence from Spain. Five years later, perhaps inspired by a new Portuguese patriotism, some Portuguese Brazilian planters and residents of New Holland initiated a rebellion in the interior of Pernambuco. The rebellion disrupted sugar production and provided an opportunity for slaves to escape, flee into the interior and build free communities. By 1648 and 1649, the planters' rebellion inflicted defeat after defeat upon the Dutch forces and reduced New Holland to a small region around Recife. At the same time, the governor of Rio de Janeiro organized an expedition that recaptured Luanda, Benguela and São Tomé. In 1653–4, the Portuguese took advantage of the Anglo-Dutch War to blockade Recife and finally force the Dutch to capitulate in 1654. For three decades, the Dutch had attempted to steal a European overseas colony; in the end, the WIC and the Dutch Republic had little to show for their enormous investment. Nevertheless, the Dutch withdrawal from Brazil, writes P. C. Emmer, "laid the foundations for the second Atlantic system by forcing the Dutch to offer their expertise in slave trading and transportation to the French and the British."

In the early seventeenth century, the English and French also challenged the Iberian monopoly of the Americas, as we have seen. Encouraged by a weaker Spain and financed by the same merchant adventurers who sent privateers into the Atlantic, chartered companies and individual merchants began to plant colonies in the Americas. In Virginia and Bermuda, the English discovered that tobacco was widely popular at home and developed tobacco farms in the 1610s and 1620s. At the same time, the Dutch founded settlements on the Berbice River on the Guiana coast of South America. The English and the French still feared the Spanish and placed their first colonies in remote regions far from Spanish power. In the West Indies, the Lesser Antilles chain in the eastern Caribbean, which had never been colonized by the Spanish, offered tempting prizes. Perhaps inspired by the Dutch assault on Brazil, perhaps desirous of new tobacco farms, the first English and French settlements began in the mid-1620s. The English and the French both seized San Cristóbal in 1624–5 and shared the island now named St. Kitts (the English portion) and Saint-Christophe (the French). From 1624 to 1635, the English and the French founded ten island colonies. The Dutch seized St. Martin and Curaçao in 1633–4. Although the Spanish fought back and temporarily regained territory here and there, by the 1640s and 1650s, the Lesser Antilles were firmly in English, French and Dutch hands.

In the beginning, the English and French settlers planted tobacco and imported indentured servants from their home countries to work the crop. (The Dutch islands were less suitable for agriculture and were turned into bases for contraband trade with Spanish America.) Although Caribbean tobacco was not as good as Virginian tobacco, the crop still took off but increased production in both regions pushed the price down. On the other hand, the price of sugar climbed in the 1620s and 1630s, stagnated, and

Table 8.1. Sugar production in Atlantic regions:
Tonnage, 1492–1870

Year	Producer	Tonnage
1493	Madeira	1,440
1544	São Tomé	2,250
1570	Hispaniola	1,500
1580	Brazil	5,000
1639	Dutch Brazil	4,000
1670	French Windward Islands	12,000
1670	Brazil	29,000
1680	Barbados	8,000
1767	Jamaica	36,000
1791	Saint Domingue	78,000
1840	Cuba	161,000
1870	Cuba	702,000

Sources: Estimated production in metric tons. Ralph Davis, *The Rise of the Atlantic Economies* (1973), Table 4, p. 257; Philip D. Curtin, *The Rise and Fall of the Plantation Complex: Essays in Atlantic History* (1990), pp. 24–7; and Herbert S. Klein, *African Slavery in Latin America and the Caribbean* (1986), pp. 51, 59, 92–3.

climbed again from 1646 until 1654. The shift from tobacco to sugar was guided by price swings.

Barbados was the first of the English and French islands to take up sugar in the early 1640s. Richard Ligon, who arrived on the island in 1647 and later wrote a history of Barbados, attributed the planting of sugarcane to the influence of the Dutch in Brazil. "Some of the most industrious men," Ligon wrote, "having gotten Plants from Fernambock [Pernambuco], a place in Brasil, and made tryal of them at the Barbadoes, and finding them to grow, they planted more and more, as they grew and multiplyed on the place." The secrets of sugar making, he continued, were discovered by trial and error and "by new directions from Brasil, sometimes by strangers, and now and then by their own people . . . [who] were content sometimes to make a voyage thither, to improve their knowledge in a thing so much desired." Nearly a century later, John Atkins noted, "In the Wars between Holland and Portugal in Brazil, a Dutch-Man arrived here from thence, who taught them the way of Planting and making Sugars." Dutch merchants assisted the English, and later the French, with canes, credit, technology and "the secrets of sugar making." What was in it for the Dutch? They could sell English and French planters slaves and provisions, and ship their sugar to the refineries of Amsterdam. In his mid seventeenth-century book, *Description of Barbados*, John Scott noted that the Dutch "administered all trade in the western colonies, provided the islands with negroes, coopers, boilers and many other things." With the disruption caused by the revolt in Pernambuco beginning in 1645, sugar exports fell and prices rose, which accelerated the sugar revolution in Barbados. By the 1660s, the little island of Barbados, only 166 square miles, 21 miles long and 14 miles wide, was producing in the range of 9,000 to 10,000 tons per year, about one-half of the production of all of Brazil at its peak in the 1620s (see Table 8.1).

Document 8.2
Sugar-Canes

John Atkins, 1735

In the Wars between Holland and Portugal in Brasil, a Dutch-Man arrived here from thence, who taught them the way of Planting and making Sugars. They are set out between August and December, six Inches deep, and do not come to Maturity until one year and a quarter: when ripe, which is known by their Colour, they cut them up with a Bill, and send them to the Wind-mills, which presses out the Juice so clean, the Canes by being an hour or two in the Sun, become fit for Fuel.

The Liquor must not remain in the Cistern above a day, for fear of souring; it is therefore by a Gutter conveyed to the Copper or Boyler, and in the boiling, the Filth scummed off; thence it's conveyed into the second and third, and in the last, called the Tack, is boiled to a Consistency, and turned into a Grain by throwing in of Temper, which is only the Infusion of Lime and Water made strong according to the Goodness of the Cane. Nine Pounds of Juice makes one of Muscovado, and one of Molossus.

From hence it is carried to the cooling Cistern, till fit to put in Pots, which have Holes at Bottom to drain off the Molossus.

Of these Molossus again, they sometimes make another worse Sugar, called Paneels. Of the Scum, coarse Molossus, Washings of the Boilers and Pots, fermented together, is made Rum.

To refine Sugar, is to boil it over again, and clarify with the same Lime-Water and Eggs, reckoned better then the clayed Sugars of this Region, made by putting a clayey Earth mixed with Water to the thickness of a Batter upon them, and repeated three or four times according to the degree of Whiteness design't; both ways carry the Treacle and Molossus downwards, but the former most esteemed, as mixing less, and purging to better purpose. Lime refines from Impurities, and imparts a softer Taste, experienced in throwing it into Wells of hard Water; the best refin'd in Loaves comes back to the Sugar Colonies from England, sell at 50 or 100 per Cent. Advance, and are of common Use; they must be kept dry, a hot and moist Air dissolving them.

John Atkins description of the West Indian sugar business came more than half a century after César de Rochefort's account. Atkins ascribes the origin of sugar making to a Dutchman from Brazil. From *A Voyage to Guinea, Brasil, and the West-Indies; In His Majesty's Ships, the* Swallow *and* Weymouth. By John Atkins, Surgeon in the Royal Navy. London: By Ceasar Ward and Richard Chandler, 1735, pp. 215–7.

Wherever the sugar revolution occurred in the Atlantic, one of the repercussions was the rise of the planter class and its control of power and influence in society. This was one of the characteristics of the transformation from a society with slaves to a slave society. In the census of 1680, after forty years of sugar cultivation, Barbados had a white population of about twenty thousand. Of these, three thousand were landowners and about one thousand were sugar, cotton and indigo planters. However, only 175 planters owned fifty percent of the acreage and more than fifty percent of the slaves. It was this planter elite who also controlled most of the political offices on the island.

Another result of the sugar revolution was the dominance of African slave labor. Prior to 1640, most tobacco farm workers in Barbados were indentured servants from England who obtained passage to the New World in exchange for four to five years of labor on behalf of an American planter. In 1638, there were approximately two thousand servants and only two hundred enslaved Africans. In the 1640s, a servant cost £12, whereas an African slave cost £25. The influence of the Dutch in Brazil convinced many planters that slaves were more cost-efficient than servants. After all, slaves were permanent, could be subject to greater violence and force, and cost less to feed and clothe. The eruption of servant rebellions and conspiracies in the 1640s and 1650s also contributed to the shift. As Richard Ligon tells us, in the early decades of Barbados, "the servants have the worser lives, for they are put to very hard labour, ill lodging, and their diet very slight." The African slaves, he noted, "are kept and preserved with greater care than the servants, who are theirs but for five years, according to the law of the Island." As more and more Africans arrived in Barbados, fewer and fewer English servants desired to go there. After forty years of sugar cultivation, the census of 1680 showed only 2,317 servants but 38,782 slaves on Barbados. Slaves had become the majority of the island's population in 1660. By the 1680s, one planter argued that without slaves, "we must often stand still and could not send out sugar to market."

Every sugar or plantation revolution brought a new and comprehensive set of laws regarding slaves, the slave codes. Slaves were not subject to the same laws other settlers in America were subject. This was due, according to the Barbados Assembly, because these "heathenish, brutish, and an uncertain kind of people" were unfit to be governed by English law. The Barbados code was approved in 1661 and established a severe set of punishments, including execution, to control behavior and protect the masters from their slaves. Repressive rules generally became more severe as the ratio of slave to free population increased. Restrictions intended to protect slaves from cruelty and abuse were almost never recognized or enforced.

France's *Code Noir* ("Black Code") of 1685, like the Spanish laws governing slavery, was not written by planters but by well-meaning legislators in France. The rules were intended to give slaves some protection and rights. Slaves were to be introduced to the Catholic faith and baptized, marriage was to be respected and families were to remain intact, there were no restrictions on manumission and slaves had judicial recourse in cases of mistreatment. Masters were required to provide sufficient food allotments and hours of work and punishments were regulated. However, in everyday life and work, the *Code Noir* was a dead letter according to nearly everyone who witnessed slavery in the French islands. Matbon de la Cour's treatise on the treatment of slaves admitted that the reality of slavery in the islands "allowed all to the master and nothing to the slave." The case of the murderous coffee planter

Le Jeune in Saint Domingue in 1788 revealed the true power of the law. Prosecuted for the murder of four slaves, judges acquitted the planter. As the governor put it, "its seems, in a word that the security of the colony depends upon the acquittal of Le Jeune."

The sugar revolution next spread to the English Leeward Islands and then Jamaica. Production in the Leewards doubled from 1669 to 1683, reaching about a third of Barbados' output. The number of slaves increased from 8,448 in 1678 to over 23,000 by 1708. Jamaica, which had been seized from the Spanish in 1655, began its sugar revolution in the 1670s and 1680s. During this period planters struggled politically with buccaneers for dominance of the island. The planters won and dominated local politics and society by 1700. Production steadily increased throughout the eighteenth century from less than 5,000 tons in 1703 to 78,000 tons in 1808. (Jamaica's production exceeded that of Barbados in 1712.) From 1640 to 1700, approximately 85,000 slaves were imported into Jamaica, compared to over 134,000 to Barbados and 44,000 to the Leeward Islands. The number of slaves increased from 500 in 1662 to over 17,000 in 1673, and to about 40,000 by 1700. A slave majority was in place by 1670. Jamaica and the Leewards adopted slave codes almost identical to Barbados' in the late seventeenth and early eighteenth centuries.

The sugar revolution came to the French Antilles, the Windward Islands of Guadaloupe and Martinique principally, after Barbados, although there were earlier efforts. In 1635, the *Compagnie des Isles de l'Amerique* (Company of the Isles of America) directed settlers to deemphasize tobacco production and "to work their people principally at cotton and at sugar." Little came of this directive, and in 1639 the Company granted to a Dutchman a six-year monopoly of all sugar produced in Martinique if he established a plantation and a mill. Again, not much developed from this contract. In 1644, the Company directly financed the establishment of a sugar plantation on Guadalupe, but as late as 1656 only ten mills existed on the island. The sugar revolution only struck the French islands after the fall of the Dutch regime in Brazil in 1654 when many Dutch refugees and merchants chose these islands to settle (in part because they were more undeveloped but also because the English and Dutch were then at war). Christian Schnakenbourg argues that only with the establishment of the *Compagnie des Indes Occidentales* (French West India Company) did French authorities begin in all seriousness to promote the economic development of the islands. Sugar production in all of the French islands increased from nearly 6,000 tons in 1674 to nearly 9,000 by 1682. By 1700, Guadalupe alone was producing about 10,000 tons.

The western region of Hispaniola had become a base for French buccaneers as early as the 1630s. In 1664, the crown named a governor for the emerging colony, who attempted to transform the privateers into tobacco planters. This worked to some extent, as witnessed by the increase in the French population from about 1,500 in 1665 to 5,000 by 1675. When the Spanish ceded the western part of the island to the French as a result of the Treaty of Ryswick in 1697, Saint Domingue produced tobacco and indigo but little sugar. The sugar revolution began in the two decades after the Treaty of Ryswick. By 1714, French planters produced about 7,000 tons, which increased to 10,000

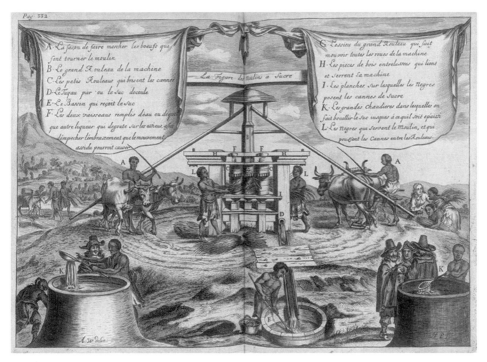

Figure 8.3. A West Indian Sugar Mill Showing the Crushing of the Cane. *La Figure des Moulins a Sucre* (Figure of a Sugar Mill), from Charles de Rochefort, *Histoire naturalle et morale des isle Antilles de l'Amérique* (Rotterdam, 1665). Courtesy of the John Carter Brown Library at Brown University.

by 1720. In time, Saint Domingue became the greatest producer of sugar in the world: By 1764, production had increased to 60,000 tons and then to 78,000 by 1791. The English had been the leading sugar makers from 1680 until about 1735. When the enormous production of Saint Domingue came on line, French sugar became more plentiful and thus cheaper than English sugar (see Map 8.1).

By the 1780s, Saint Domingue was the plantation powerhouse of the Caribbean. The colony counted 655 sugar plantations or *habitations*, 1,962 coffee plantations and 398 cotton or indigo plantations. One-third of the value of France's foreign trade originated in Saint Domingue's plantations. Overall, according to one contemporary observer, "the French islands and colonies form the kingdom's most important branch of commerce" (see Table 8.2).

The sugar revolution in the French islands transformed the labor force. As in the English islands, the first labor force was composed largely of French indentured servants, called *engagés*. The period of the servants lasted longer in the French islands than in the English islands because *engagés* were less expensive than English servants and continued coming to the New World (largely because their terms of service were shorter). By 1655, the Windward Islands still had a white majority with 13,000 Frenchmen and about 10,000 enslaved Africans. By 1700, all of the French island colonies, including Saint Domingue, had about 30,000 slaves (compared to about 100,000 in the

Map 8.1. African Slavery in the Americas, c. 1770.

Table 8.2. Sugar plantations in Atlantic regions:
Plantations/Mills, 1494–1860

Year	Colony	Plantations/Mills
1493	Madeira	80 *engenhos*
1522	São Tomé	60–80 *engenhos*
1530	Hispaniola	30 *ingenios*
1570	Brazil	115 *engenhos*
1630	Brazil	350 *engenhos*
1667	Barbados	175 planters
1689	Brazil	528 *engenhos*
1713	Saint Domingue	138 *sucrières*
1750	Jamaica	535 sugar estates
1767	Guadeloupe	401 plantations
1790	Saint Domingue	793 plantations
1860	Cuba	1,300 *ingenios*

Note: Blackburn notes that there were 211 sugar estates in Madeira in 1500. Blackburn, *The Making of New World Slavery*, p. 109. One of the "sugar lords" of São Tomé owned two *fazendas* and twelve *engenhos*. See Garfield, "A History of São Tomé Island, 1470–1655," p. 40. These planters of Barbados constituted the "plantocracy," according to Beckles, in that they constituted seven percent of all landowners but owned fifty-two percent of all farmland and owned sixty percent of all slaves. See Beckles, *A History of Barbados*, p. 24. According to Thomas Jefferys, 150 of the 401 sugar plantations on Guadaloupe had sugar mills, and therefore were complete *habitations sucrière*. See Jefferys, *The West India Atlas*, London, 1775. The nearly 800 sugar plantations of Saint Domingue in 1790 constituted approximately one-half of the sugar plantations in all of the French West Indies. See Stein, *The French Sugar Business in the Eighteenth Century*, p. 42. The 1,300 Cuban *ingenios* – sugar plantations and mills – possessed fifty percent of the slaves of the country. See Manuel Moreno Fraginals, *El ingenio: Complejo económico-social Cubano del azúcar*, 3 vols. (1978), I, pp. 203–37.

English colonies). In Saint Domingue, the number of enslaved Africans had increased from 3,400 in 1686 to over 47,000 by 1720. By 1740, eighty-two percent of the population in Saint Domingue were slaves and only eight percent were white, leaving the remainder as free men and women of color. By 1791, there were 480,000 slaves, about one-half of all enslaved Africans in the Caribbean; Saint Domingue had become the most extreme slave society in the Americas and the very model of the plantation complex. "Prior to the nineteenth century," notes Richard B. Sheridan, "the plantation islands of the Caribbean were the most-valued possessions in the overseas Imperial world" (see Table 8.3).

The French embarked upon a plantation revolution in Louisiana in the early eighteenth century. It was a revolution that ultimately failed. From 1719 to 1731, over 6,000 enslaved Africans were imported into the colony to work on new tobacco plantations. In this period of time, slaves became the majority population and Louisiana became a slave society. However, in 1729 Natchez Indians and enslaved Africans together rebelled against the rising plantation system and killed two hundred settlers, or ten percent of the population. This scare led to the end of the French slave trade to Louisiana;

Table 8.3. Slaves in Atlantic sugar plantation
colonies, 1492–1841

Year	Colony	Slaves
1492	Madeira	2,000
1522	São Tomé	4,000
1542	Hispaniola	25,000
1580	Brazil	3,000
1630	Brazil	60,000
1680	Brazil	150,000
1685	Barbados	46,000
1740	Martinique	117,000
1760	Jamaica	173,000
1774	Cuba	39,000
1789	Saint Domingue	465,000
1800	Brazil	1,360,000
1827	Cuba	286,000
1841	Cuba	418,000

Sources: Robin Blackburn, *The Making of New World Slavery: From the Baroque to the Modern, 1492–1800* (1997), pp. 109–11, 213, 253, 295; Richard S. Dunn, *Sugar and Slaves: The Rise of the Planter Class in the English West Indies, 1624–1713* (1973), pp. 87, 165; Herbert S. Klein, *African Slavery in Latin America and the Caribbean* (1986), pp. 50–66; and Klein, *The Atlantic Slave Trade* (1999), pp. 32–41.

during the next three decades, only one slave ship arrived in the colony. Due to a chronic shortage of labor, tobacco exports stagnated and then declined, the export economy failed and the plantation complex unraveled. In 1763, France turned over Louisiana to Spain in the aftermath of the Seven Years War. During the Spanish regime, more slaves were imported and more slaves were manumitted than before, creating not only a society with slaves but an increasingly complicated society of masters and slaves and free blacks, mulattos, *mestizos* and Indians.

Although the Dutch facilitated the transfer of the sugar revolution from Brazil to the Caribbean, they did not go into production themselves in any great extent with one exception, Surinam, the Dutch colony on the coast of Guiana. Under Dutch management, the sugar revolution came to Surinam in the late seventeenth century. By 1737, there were more than four hundred plantations situated along the rivers of Surinam. A coffee revolution took off after 1745, and by 1771 the value of coffee exports exceeded those of sugar by five times. Both the sugar and coffee revolutions fueled the African slave trade to the colony. By the early 1770s, there were three thousand Europeans exploiting over fifty thousand African slaves. The ratio of Africans to Europeans in Surinam was extreme: twenty-five to one colony-wide, and sixty-five to one in the plantation districts. Not surprisingly, marauding bands of escaped slaves attacked plantations and the Dutch States-General dispatched a corps of eight hundred professional soldiers to defeat the "revolted Negroes." French Cayenne and British Guiana were late developers in the eighteenth century. Of the two, only British Guiana experienced a dramatic sugar revolution as a response to the slave rebellion in Saint Domingue, which destroyed the plantation complex there and thus ended sugar exports in the 1790s. By mid-decade, British Guiana had a substantial slave population of 120,000 Africans.

The plantation complex followed something of an unusual course in English North America. It began independently in the Chesapeake (Virginia and Maryland) in the early seventeenth century but was taken to South Carolina by planters and merchants, mostly from Barbados, in the late seventeenth century. There, in the coastal plain and swamps, the Low Country, writes Ira Berlin, "rice bankrolled the expansion of the plantation system." A tobacco boom began in Virginia in the 1610s and spread to the Caribbean in the following two decades. Production skyrocketed from 350,000 pounds in 1617 to 17 million by 1672 and 38 million by 1700. On the eve of the American Revolution, production had topped 100 million pounds. Throughout the seventeenth century, North American tobacco farmers employed English indentured servants, who made up eighty percent of all emigrants to the Chesapeake region. Servant labor persisted longer in North America than in the Caribbean because more Englishmen were willing to immigrate to the mainland colonies than to the Caribbean. On the mainland and unlike the Caribbean, servants had a greater opportunity to obtain land.

In the late seventeenth century the flow of servants diminished whereas the availability of African slaves greatly increased and their prices decreased. Virginia planters began to prefer slaves to servants, and they preferred African slaves at that because of their agricultural skill and permanence as a labor force. By 1675, there were 2,500 slaves in Virginia among a total population of 38,000. One indication that a slave society was forming was the appearance of the first comprehensive slave code in Virginia in 1705. By 1720, enslaved Africans and free blacks made up twenty-five percent of the population of the Chesapeake. By 1740, in certain plantation-intensive areas of the Chesapeake, the slave and free-black population made up forty percent of the population. According to William Byrd II in 1736, Virginia had become a "New Guinea."

In the beginning, South Carolina was a colony of a colony. As the sugar revolution on the Barbados led to more and more land concentration and less opportunity for smaller landowners, not to mention servants, Barbadian colonists moved to the mainland and planted rice and indigo. A plantation revolution rapidly took off in the region and by the first decade of the eighteenth century, South Carolina had a black majority. By the 1720s, the lowland region of South Carolina had a two-to-one ratio of slaves to white settlers, and around Charlestown a ratio of three-to-one. South Carolina was the only region in English North America where blacks became a majority, a true slave society. According to one visitor, the South Carolina countryside "look[ed] more like a negro country than like a country settled by white people."

Historians have begun to see that the development of rice horticulture in South Carolina was not a European but an African transplant. Africans from

Table 8.4. Slave populations in the Americas, c. 1770

Region	Slave population	Total population
Spanish America	290,000	12,144,000
Brazil	700,000	2,000,000
British Caribbean	428,000	500,000
British North America	450,000	2,100,000
French Caribbean	379,000	430,000
Dutch Caribbean	75,000	90,000

Source: Robin Blackburn, *The Overthrow of Colonial Slavery, 1776–1848* (1988), p. 5.

Upper Guinea, the "rice coast," had carried rice to Mexico, Peru and Brazil in the sixteenth century. In the late seventeenth century, slaves from the rice-producing areas of Africa were imported into South Carolina. Very likely, their knowledge of cultivation and milling explains the origins of Carolina rice. Low country planters realized that particular slaves grew rice and sought these in the slave trade. A Charleston newspaper in advertising sales of slaves skilled in rice noted 250 slaves "from the Windward and Rice Coast, valued for their knowledge of rice culture."

The early history of Georgia presents an interesting contrast to other plantation colonies. Established in the 1730s as a buffer between South Carolina and Spanish Florida, and as a colony for poor Englishmen, a place to own land and rise in society, the original charter prohibited slavery and all blacks. The colony failed to prosper. By the late 1640s, there were only about four thousand settlers in Georgia practicing subsistence agriculture rather than the more profitable export agriculture. In 1750, the Georgia Trustees who held the charter permitted slavery and, in short order, the institution expanded to support an expanding rice-producing plantation system. By 1776, there were sixteen thousand slaves in this colony where planters were said to be "stark Mad after Negroes" (see Table 8.4).

As in Spanish America, slavery in English North America spread to towns and cities and regions where plantation agriculture did not exist. New England had few slaves but in the Middle Colonies, slaves were widely employed on small and large farms. Urban slaves from Boston to Charles Town (today's Charleston) were found in the skilled trades, labored in ironworks, worked on the docks and spun cotton and wool. Towns and cities offered slaves opportunities for earning money and finding greater freedom than the countryside.

From Madeira and Virginia, the plantation complex expanded into the Atlantic and became the most dynamic economic force in the Atlantic World. It was the prime cause of the forceful removal of millions of Africans from their homeland and thus the foundation of the Atlantic slave trade. It was the masters' economy that created "plantocracies" and their greatest symbol, the Casa Grande, the Great House, the lush and sprawling country mansions of the sugar barons like those who built Freguesía on the shore of the Bahia de Todo os Santos. There were also slaves' economies, and they created very different types of cultures in the niches of slavery and the plantation regime.

8.3 The Cultures of Slaves

Slavery changed and evolved over time throughout the Atlantic as different generations experienced and shaped the cultures of slavery. The first generation or two of slavery in America, prior to the plantation revolutions, saw the appearance of Atlantic Creoles, that is, Africans and a few mulattos from the Iberian Peninsula, the near Atlantic and the Atlantic coasts of Africa. Atlantic Creoles were cosmopolitans, multilingual and had assimilated considerable international culture (Islamic, Iberian, Mediterranean and so on) during a lifetime of travel, pursuing a skill, or just wheeling and dealing. Not all slaves by any means were Atlantic Creoles, and not all Atlantic Creoles were slaves; many of these travelers arrived at their American destinations as servants, sailors or possibly fugitives. These skilled and experienced people helped European colonists transfer crops, handle increasingly large numbers of enslaved Africans, and establish farms and plantations.

With every plantation revolution, slavery in each region became thoroughly Africanized. The African generations of the seventeenth and eighteenth centuries were African farmers and herdsmen brought to the plantations of America. They spoke one or two of a multitude of African languages and accepted the sacred world of the ancestors, the spirits and the gods. They had never been away from home and had never been on a ship, thus they turned protectively and, perhaps, instinctively inward, away from European and Euroamerican culture, religion and everything else. Alexander Garsden was on to something when he observed around 1740 the slaves in the South Carolina low country "twere a Nation within a Nation." These *bozales*, also called "saltwater negroes" and simply "new Negroes," sent away Christian missionaries and sang their own songs, danced their own dances and called to their own spirits. When he arrived in Jamaica in 1750, Thomas Thistlewood wrote in his diary: "the westward of the Town, to see negro Diversions – odd Music, Motions, etc. The Negros of each Nation by themselves." The African generations never integrated themselves into New World societies and thus resistance was an integral part of the cultures of slavery. "New Negros," writes Michael Mullin, "were dangerous." John Gabriel Stedman, who fought "African Negroes" in Surinam, concluded, "no people have greater thirst for revenging an injury . . . The Negroes are spirited, brave, and patient in adversity, while their undaunted fortitude in going to death through every torture approaches even heroism."

The imbalance of men and women and miserable conditions made it difficult for Africans to have children, and thus the plantations had to import more and more Africans to maintain a stable population of slaves. Nevertheless, Africans had some children.A rising population of New World blacks and mulattos was more and more evident by the mid-to-late eighteenth century. Of course, there had always been a small group of New World blacks throughout the centuries of the plantation complex. The Spanish and the Portuguese distinguished between the acculturated *criollo* or *ladino* and the nonacculturated *bozal* or *bossal*. The distinguishing characteristic for the Iberians was culture more than blood. These slaves could be African, mulatto or African-American, none of which was important. What made a *criollo* slave Creole was culture: Spanish or Portuguese language, Roman Catholic Christianity, knowledge of a craft or skill, and that type of thing. On the other hand, *bozales* were Africans who had just made the middle passage and landed in America. Because they were Africans just off the boat, they did not speak Spanish or Portuguese, were "heathens" and they did not, presumably, have any useful skills; they were clearly *bozales*. An Italian Jesuit in 1711 indicated that those slaves "born in Brazil or are brought up from childhood in the home of the white people take on the qualities of their masters and turn themselves to good account, and many of them is worth four new slaves." In time, this sentiment became a popular saying in Brazil: "one creole is worth four bossales." On the plantations across the West Indies during the eighteenth century, there were Caribbean Creoles, a small minority of assimilated blacks who spoke cogent English or French, had families, more and more acknowledged Christ, practiced a skilled occupation and looked after the new arrivals, the "Guineabirds." These men and women were indispensable to the plantation system; their skills and, more importantly, countenance, kept these social machines well greased. Bryan Edwards of Jamaica wrote in the 1790s, "generally speaking, a Creole Negro is considered as worth more than one imported." Pierre Dessalles, a planter in Martinique, made one of them overseer of all operations of his estate, the *Caféière*. "Honoré is very useful to me; he is a good fellow," wrote Dessalles. His slave was also something of a character, apparently, a literate, well-dressed and assertive slave: "Many people," Dessalles continued, "were astonished by his manners, his looks, his pretension, and his language."

In South Carolina in the mid-eighteenth century, Governor James Glen (and, no doubt, quite a few other Carolinians) viewed "country born" slaves as less threatening than "new Negroes." The governor made the distinction between those slaves who "are natives of Carolina, who have no . . . longing after any other country, that have been among white people, and . . . can speak our language" from "new Negroes from Africa." According to the governor, Creole slaves "had no notion of liberty," were "pleased with their masters, contented with their condition, [and] reconciled to servitude." The governor's understanding of who may or may not have possessed notions of liberty may be happily ignored, as we will see in later chapters. However, Governor Glen might be giving us the idea that Creole slaves by the mid-eighteenth century were the first slaves in this region to assimilate to the dominant culture, to learn English and become not "content" or "reconciled" but ready to mediate between the Africans and the masters.

In the Americas, most slaves were plantation slaves, which left anywhere from five to ten percent living in towns and cities. Plantation slaves had their own "slave quarters," which were often described as small African villages by European and American visitors. In Brazil, the slave quarters were called *senzalas*, elsewhere they were called *barracons*, plantation row, the barracks and – again and again – the quarters. They were generally located on the plantation in sight of the Great House (and sometimes, not) and were composed of waddle and daub huts organized as row houses. In the West Indies in the seventeenth and eighteenth centuries, slaves were generally required to make their own houses, and the huts, cottages, cabins and *cabañas* were built around a communal area. The houses were detached, fifteen to twenty feet in length, and divided into two compartments. In one Martinique sugar plantation in the late seventeenth century, all of the houses were round with a pointed roof in the African Mandigo style. The floors of slave cabins, like those in African villages, were made of pounded earth, and sitting around the houses and yards were stools, cooking pots, water jars, wooden bowels, baskets, smoking pipes and drums. Every house had one or two storage pits dug in the ground to keep valuable personal belongings. The log cabins at Carter's Grove plantation in Williamsburg, Virginia, appeared very poor to visitors. "Whatever the arrangement of the buildings," writes Lorena A. Walsh, "the surrounding communal work and living spaces that the slaves fashioned for themselves often closely resembled the layout of a West African compound." It was in the slave quarters, although not only here, that community life took place: dances, weddings, funerals and so on. We see this to some extent in the well-known eighteenth-century watercolor, *The Old Plantation*. The unknown artist illustrates part of the life slaves created for themselves apart from their master. A celebration of some sort is portrayed with some slaves playing music and others dancing. The use by the dancers of a stick and scarves are of African derivation, whereas the clothing (with the exception of the headdresses) reflects eighteenth-century English styles. In the background is a Georgian Great House with outbuildings and the slave quarters.

The masters' economy was relatively similar from region to region, and the organization of slave labor was the master's decision. The plantation system appeared to present two different types of slave labor: the gang-labor system and the task system. In plantation regimes where severe labor requirements were combined with a relatively large slave population, field labor was divided into highly regimented, disciplined and closely supervised work gangs segregated by age, health and sometimes by sex. The first or the "great gang" was composed of young able-bodied workers. It performed most of the field labor, mill work, boiling and distilling, as well as building houses, making roads, cutting irrigation ditches and so on. The second gang was made up of older, less able and less healthy slaves. These slaves were given less physically onerous work such as cleaning young canes, fertilizing the canes and perhaps feeding the cane trash into the boiling house ovens. The first two gangs made up the basic corps of the field workers: they prepared the ground, planted the ratoons and cut the cane. Most, that is, two-thirds or so, members of the first two gangs were women. A slave driver or an overseer who would use his whip to get the job done supervised the field gangs. The third gang was made up, for the most part, of children who were given such work as weeding. Samuel Martin, an agricultural expert, described the plantation in 1754 as "a well-constructed machine, compounded of various wheels, turning different ways, and yet all contributing to the great end proposed." An African slave in Barbados understood the effectiveness of the machine: "The devil was in the Englishman that he makes everything work; he makes the negro work, he makes the horse work, the ass work, the wood work, the water work and the wind work."

Document 8.3
The Negroes of Barbados

Richard Ligon, 1657

The Island is divided into three sorts of men, *vis.* Masters, Servants, and Slaves. The slaves and the posterity, being subject to their Masters for ever, are kept and preferv'd with greater care than the servants, who are theirs but for five years, according to the law of the Island. So that for the time, the servants have the worser lives, for they are put to very hard labour, ill lodging, and their dyet very slight. When we came first on the Island, some Planters themselves did not eat bone meat, above twice a week: the rest of the seven dayes, Potatoes, Loblolly, Bonavist. But the servants no bone meat at all, unless an Oxe dyed: and then they were feasted, as long as the lasted. And till they had planted good store of Plantines, the Negroes were fed with thier kind of food; but most of it Bonavist, and Loblolly, with some ears of Mayes toasted, which food (especially Loblolly), gave them much discontent: But when they had Plantines enough to serve them, they were heard no more to complain; for 'tis a food they take great delight in, and their manner of dressing, and eating it, is this: 'tis gathered for them (somewhat before it be ripe, for so they desire to have it,) upon Saturday, by the keeper of the Plantine grove; who is an able Negro, and knowes well the number of those that are to be fed with this fruit; and as he gathers, layes them all together, till they fetch them away, which is about five a clock in the afternoon, for that day they break off work sooner by an hour: partly for this purpose, and partly for that the fire in the furnaces is to be put out, and the Ingenio and the rooms made clean; besides they are to wash, shave and trim themselves against Sunday. But 'tis a lovely sight to see a hundred handsom Negroes, men and women, with everyone a grasse-green bunch of these fruits on their heads, every bunch twice as big as their heads, all coming in a train one after another, the black and green so well becoming one another. Having brought this fruit to their own houses, and pilling off the skin of so much as they will use, they boyl it in water, making it into balls, and so they eat it. One bunch a week is a Negroe's allowance. To this, no bread or drink, but water. Their lodging at night a board, with nothing under, nor any thing a top of them. They are happy people, whom so little contents. Very good servants, if they be no spoyled by the English . . .

It has been accounted a strange thing, that the Negroes, being more than double the numbers of the Christians that are there, and they accounted a bloody people, where they think they have power or advantages; and the more bloody, by how much they are more fearful than others: that these should not commit some horrid massacre upon the Christians, thereby to enfranchise themselves, and become Masters of the Island. But there are three reasons that take away this wonder; the one is, They are not suffered to touch or handle any weapons: The other, That they are held in such awe and slavery, as they are fearful to appear in any dring act; and seeing the mustering of our men, and hearing their Gun-shot, (than which nothing is more terrible to them) their spirits are subjugated to so low a condition, as they dare not look up to any bold attempt.

Besides these, there is a third reason, which stops all designs of that kind, and that is, They are fetch'd from several parts of Africa, who speak several languages, and by that means, one of them understands not another: For, some of them are fetch'd from Guinny and Binny, some from Cutchew, some from Angola, and some from the River of Gambia. And in some of these places where petty Kingdomes are, they sell their Subjects, and such as they take in Battle, whom they make slaves; and some mean men sell their Servants, their Children, and sometimes their Wives; and think all good traffick, for such commodities as our Merchants send them.

When they are brought to us, the Planters buy them out of the Ship, where they find them stark naked, and therefore cannot be deceived in any outward infirmity. They choose them as they do Horses in a Market; the strongest, youthfullest, and most beautiful, yield the greatest prices. Thirty pound sterling is a price for the best man Negroe; and twenty five, twenty six, or twenty seven pound for a Woman; the Children are at easier rates. And we buy them so, as the sexes may be equal; for, if they have more Men than Women, the men who are unmarried will come to their Masters, and complain, that they cannot live without Wives, and desire him, they may have Wives. And he tells them, that the next ship that comes, he will buy them Wives, which satisfies them for the present; and so they expect the good time: which the Master performing with them, the bravest fellow is to choose first, and so in order, as they are in place, and every one of them knows his better, and gives him the precedence, as Cows do one another, in passing through a narrow gate; for, the most of them are as near beasts as may be, setting their souls aside. Religion they know none; yet most of them acknowledge a God, as appears by their motions and gestures: For, if one of them do another wrong, and he cannot revenge himself, he looks up to Heaven for vengeance, and holds up both his hands, as if the power must come from thence, that must do him right. Chaste they are as any people under the Sun; for, when the men and women are together naked, they never cast their eyes towards the parts that ought to be covered; and those amongst us, that have Breeches and Petticoats, I never saw so much as a kiss, or embrace, or a wanton glance with their eyes between them. Jealous they are of their Wives, and hold it for a great injury and scorn, if another man make the least courtship to his Wife . . .

On Sunday they rest, and have the whole day at their pleasure, and the most of them use it as a day of rest and pleasure; but some of them who will make benefit of that dayes liberty, go where the Mangrave trees grow, and gather the bark, of which they make ropes, which they truck away for other Commodities, as Shirts and Drawers. In the afternoons on Sundays, they have their Musick, which is of kettle drums, and those of several sizes; upon the smallest the best Musitian playes, and the other come in as Chorasses: the drum all men know, has but one tone; and therefore variety of tunes have little to do in this musick; and yet so strangely they varie their time, as 'tis a pleasure to the most curious ears, and it was to me one of the strangest noises that ever I heard made of one tone; and if they had the variety of tune, which gives the great scope in Musick, as they have of time, they would do wonders in that Art . . .

On Sundayes in the afternoon, their Musick playes, and to dancing they go, the men by themselves, and the women by themselves, no mixt dancing Their motions are rather what they aim at, than what they do; and by that means, transgress the less upon the Sunday; their hands having more of motion than their feet, and their heads more than their hands. They may dance a whole day, and ne'r heat themselves; yet, now and then, one of the activest amongst them will leap bolt upright, and fall in his place again, but without cutting a capre. When they have danc'd an hour or two, the men fall to wrestle, (the Musick playing all the while) and their manner of wrestling is, to stand like two Cocks, with heads as low as their hips; and thrusting their heads one against another, hoping to catch one another by the leg, which sometimes they do: But if both parties be weary, and that they cannot get that advantage, then they raise their heads, by pressing hard one against another, and so having nothing to take hold of but their bare flesh, they close, and grasp one another about the middle, and have one another in the hug, and then a fair fall is given on the back. And thus two or three couples of them are engaged at once, for an hour together, the women looking on: for when the men begin to wrestle, the women leave off their dancing, and come to be spectators of the sport . . .

Richard Ligon arrived in Barbados in 1647 and first published his history of the colony in 1657. *Source: Richard Ligon, A True & Exact History Of the Island of Barbadoes Illustrated with a Map of the Island, as also the Principal Trees and Plants there, Set forth in their due Proportions and Shapes, drawn out by their several and respective Scales* . . . (London, 1673).

The task system involved the division of a specific amount of plantation labor to be accomplished in one day – fields to be cultivated or the number of irrigation ditches to be dug – and assignment of a task to every adult slave each day. Each task was assumed to entail a full day's work but once the task was complete, the remaining time of the day belonged to the slaves who could work their own gardens, visit family or just do with it as they pleased. Some masters argued that certain plantation jobs could not be regimented and that the task system encouraged greater productivity of slaves. Others argued that slaves would not do anything productive until an important task was broken down into its simplest motions and slaves were driven by the whip to perform it over and over.

The sugar plantation was generally associated with gang labor, whereas rice plantations in South Carolina, coffee plantations in the Caribbean and even sugar plantations in French Louisiana used the task system. In fact, slave labor in the plantation system was far more complicated than the gang and task classification suggests. For example, in sugar plantations fieldwork was often organized in gangs whereas millwork was divided into tasks. Organized by gang labor, Chesapeake tobacco plantations were faced with individual tobacco plants and delicate leaves that could be easily damaged. As a result, one Virginia planter complained, "All hands at work but so much to do and of such various sorts it is hardly possible to keep much at the hoe." Everything to do with tobacco, noted Fernando Ortiz, "is hand work – its cultivation, harvesting, manufacture, sale, even its consumption." On the largest sugar mills, there were dozens of highly skilled jobs that required specialists such as sugarmaster, purger, mill tender, presser, kettleman and so on. These skills were so valuable and rare that planters often paid wages to these particular slaves. In the end labor productivity was often based not on some type of organizing principle but on violence. A seventeenth-century Portuguese refrain stated, "Whoever wants to profit from his Blacks must maintain them, make them work well, and beat them even better; without this there will be no service or gain."

The historian Richard B. Sheridan has argued, "slavery in the infancy of the sugar industry was considerably milder than it became in a later period of intensive culture." Looking at the West Indies in the seventeenth and eighteenth centuries, Sheridan notes several trends. In the seventeenth century, enslaved Africans were more valuable than indentured servants and, according to Richard Ligon in 1657, better cared for. However, as the plantation revolution took off, and more and more African slaves were imported, the labor became more intense and harsh and their individual value to the planter was less. We see then a rise of mortality as well as a declining birth rate due to the labor regimen, disease, malnutrition, suicide, infanticide and despondency. Sheridan also maintains that slavery in the West Indies became less harsh beginning in the two decades before the American Revolution. In those times, as today, women outlived men. In slave communities, this trend led to a better balance of the sexes and therefore a rising birth rate and an expanding Creole population. To encourage "breeding" as an alternative to purchasing expensive African slaves, planters began to provide better health care, midwives, hospitals, food and clothing to their slaves. When we look at the percentage decline in slave populations in Jamaica and Barbados from 1650 to 1775, it does appear to reflect a slave regime that became more rough and harsh, and then became more pragmatic if not more humane (see Table 8.5).

Planters always wanted to squeeze more labor out of their slaves but they also always wanted to reduce their expenses with regard to feeding and clothing their slaves. Planter policy on provisions, or slave manipulation of planters on what to do about provisions and allowances, was the single most important factor affecting the lives, communities and cultures of slaves. What is called the slaves' economy, the production and marketing of foodstuffs on slaves' provision grounds became the key to the formation of some degree of slave autonomy, family structure and even resistance. Provision grounds and market exchange brought the first taste of independence and self-control. The slave provision ground became, in the expression of Maléurier, the Intendant of Saint Domingue, *une petite Guinée*, a little Guinea.

In the beginning of the Atlantic plantation complex, practically all plantation slaves were given provision grounds and were required to feed themselves based on what they could grow. The point was to save the planter money

Table 8.5. Annual percentage decline in slave
populations: Jamaica and Barbados, 1651–1775

Years	Jamaica	Barbados
1651–1675	2.8	3.8
1676–1700	3.0	4.1
1701–1725	3.6	4.9
1726–1750	3.5	3.6
1751–1775	2.7	3.7

Sources: Richard B. Sheridan, "Africa and the Caribbean in
the Atlantic Slave Trade," *The American Historical Review*,
77:1 (February, 1972), Table 1, p. 29. Also see Sheridan,
*Doctors and Slaves: A Medical and Demographical History
of Slavery in the British West Indies, 1680–1834* (1985).
Michael Craton in "Jamaican Slave Mortality: Fresh Light
from Worthy Park, Longville and the Tharp Estates," *Journal of Caribbean History*, III (1971), pp. 1–27, argues that
natural decrease improved in Jamaica to about 2.0 percent
by 1790 and 0.5 percent by 1830. Barry Higman, Sheridan,
Craton and others show that population increase was a post-
emancipation phenomenon in the larger sugar islands of the
Caribbean.

that would otherwise pay for rations or allowances. Later, when the English
and the French were developing their sugar plantation in the West Indies,
they called the self-provisioning idea "the Brazilian System" or the "Brazilian Custom." It was said that the Portuguese had brought self-provisioning
from São Tomé in the sixteenth century and the Dutch carried it from Pernambuco to the West Indies in the seventeenth century. Observers of the
engenhos of Brazil mentioned that slaves had provision grounds so that they
could cultivate their own food. In 1701, the Portuguese crown noted that
this policy could lead to malnutrition or starvation if done badly. "I have
therefore decided to order you," the King informed the Overseas Council,
"to force the mill owners either to give their slaves the required sustenance,
or a free day of the week, so that they can themselves cultivate the ground,
in the event that mill owners should choose this alternative." It became quite
common for plantation slaves to have provision grounds as well as receive
small weekly allowances or rations from the master of hard to get items like
salt, fish, possibly a little bit of meat as well as clothing, shoes, and pots and
pans. The French *Code Noir* required slaveowners to provide slaves with
provision grounds and Saturdays and a specific minimum diet referred to as
the *ordinaire*. For an adult slave, the *ordinaire* was two and a half measures
of manioc flour and two pounds of salt beef or three pounds of salt fish each
week. Father Jean-Baptiste Labat commented, "slaves who received what the
King's Ordinance authorized were lucky."

Provision grounds and rations at first were often paltry. The land was generally throwaway ground on hillsides or some far away rocky outcroppings.
The rations were commonly discarded food: rotten fruit, yesterday's fish and
a rotting carcass of a cow. This would change if slaves were stubbornly
unproductive, suicidal or found some other suitable bargaining chip. Land
and rations were incentives, that is, bargaining chips in the never-ending

negotiations between slaves and masters. Masters wanted more labor, more control and more power. Slaves wanted more provision grounds, more time of their own, more right to travel and more access to markets – in other words, more independence and self-control. Every negotiation was different and produced different results.

We see this at work with the slaves of the sugar plantation of Pierre Diedonné Dessalles of Martinique in 1840 when news arrived of a royal ordinance requiring the inspection of plantations at the same time that Dessalles' enterprise was failing economically. "My financial trouble is awful," he confided to his diary, and cut cane all day along with his slaves. Yet, he noted, "as soon as the mill starts running, my negroes are exhausted; then they have to be kept going by the whip." He referred vaguely to "unseemly talk," people being "stirred up" and "serious threats," and on the same day wrote, "I gave my negroes all Saturday off in lieu of their food rations." A day later, regarding the royal ordinance on plantation inspection, Dessalles noted in his diary, "The negroes know exactly what is going on; since the arrival of the royal ordinance, I find that mine are less pliable and more difficult to handle." It would seem that Dessalles' slaves, knowing exactly what was going on regarding the royal ordinance, the planter's financial difficulties and his desperate need for making sugar, negotiated a new "contract," Saturdays off to work on their grounds. This type of negotiation was common throughout the slaves' Atlantic World for centuries.

In the seventeenth century, some planters adopted the allowance system completely. In certain flat and dry sugar islands in the West Indies, all land was devoted to sugarcane, and slaveowners purchased foodstuffs and clothing from seaborne traders, often from New England, as allowances to their slaves. Planters or their agents argued that the land was too valuable or the time that slaves' spent in growing their own food was too costly. Therefore, planter allowances were cheap by comparison. Too often we learn that allowances were indecent if not an abomination. In defense against accusations that proprietors in Barbados did not feed or clothe their slaves, John Braithwaite, an agent for the Barbados Assembly, reminded his readers that the Barbadian slave "[eats] from his master's purse, and every mouthful was measured in cash." The allowance system in Barbados may help explain the annual population decline between 1651 and 1775 compared to Jamaica. However, the real reason for the allowance system was planter fear of slave marketing. Throughout the eighteenth century, the Assembly of Barbados attempted to eradicate the commercial activities of slaves. The Assembly passed the 1779 Act "to prohibit Goods, Wares and Merchandizes and other things from being sold, bartered or disposed of . . . from the Traffic of Huckster slaves, Free Mulattos and Negroes." A mid-nineteenth-century Brazilian plantation handbook strongly suggested that the successful planter should provide provision grounds to his slaves. "However, the planter should not allow them to sell their products to anyone else, but only to himself, and he should pay them a reasonable price, to prevent them from going astray and carousing in the taverns." Planters in British North America also adopted the allowance system. Slaves were often given food allowances produced by the plantation itself and were permitted small gardens and the raising of hogs and fowl. For these slaveowners, the issue was control more than anything else. The "planter's custom" in North Carolina was for the slave to raise corn, tobacco and potatoes on their provision grounds. "In some plantations, they have the liberty to raise hogs and poultry, which with the former articles, they are to dispose of to none but their masters (this is done to prevent bad consequences)." The plantation manual by the Virginian John Taylor stated, "One great value of establishing a comfortable diet for slaves, is its conveniency as an instrument of reward and punishment."

Just about everywhere in the Atlantic World, African and Creole slaves produced food and other commodities on their provision grounds. From Brazil to the Bahamas and from Surinam to Saint Domingue, slaves raised maize, potatoes, peas, beans, catalae, plantains, bananas, cassava, yams and more to feed themselves and – more importantly – to take to market. They cultivated and worked sugarcane, tobacco, rice and coffee for their masters, and they did it for their own profit as well. Slaves not only grew their own food on provision grounds but also raised livestock from chickens, goats and hogs to mules, cows and horses. The provision ground was privileged ground, an incentive granted by masters to slaves so they could grow their own food and feed themselves and whatever family they might have. An absentee planter who visited his Jamaican sugar plantation discovered his slaves' provision grounds:

> The provision-grounds of the negroes furnish them with plantains, bananas, cocoa-nuts, and yams; of the latter there is a regular harvest once a year, and they remain in great perfection for many months, provided they are dug up carefully, but the slightest wound with the spade is sufficient to rot them. Calalue (a species of spinach) is a principal article in their pepper-pots: but in this parish their most valuable and regular supply of food arises from the cocoa-finger, or cocos, a species of yam, but which lasts all the year round. These vegetables form the basis of negro sustenance; but the slaves also receive from their owners a regular weekly allowance of red herrings and salt meat, which serves to relish their vegetable diet; and, indeed, they are so passionately fond of salted provisions, that, instead of giving them fresh beef (as at their festival of Saturday last), I have been advised to provide some hogsheads of salt fish, as likely to afford them more gratification, at such future additional holidays as I may find it possible to allow them in this busy season of crop.

Slaves transformed the privilege of cultivating their own provision grounds to feed themselves into the advantage of producing a surplus for market. The slaves of the *engenhos* and cane farms of Brazil "plant their own gardens" as André João Antonil put it in 1711, and gathered at markets (usually against several laws) to barter or sell their produce. During the chaotic decades of Dutch occupation of Pernambuco and the rest of the Brazilian northeast, slaves had achieved more grounds, more production and more marketing. Some slaves turned this confusion into overt resistance and rebellion. In Dutch Surinam and in the plantation-dominated regions of Spanish America, slave-dominated Saturday and Sunday markets became ordinary. In the

West Indies, slaves begged, bartered and beguiled their masters over the years for more provision grounds, for Saturdays and other special days, and for the privilege to travel to other plantations, to town, to the mountains and to the sea. Given a little time and continuity, these privileges of land, time and liberty in the minds of slaves became their property and their rights. On the Caribbean coast of Spanish Venezuela, slaves achieved three days of rest around the summer solstice. Their descendants today in towns like Curiepé and Cumaná celebrate the San Juan festival with days of dancing, drinking, drumming and praying. In British Antigua, planters were apparently stingy about giving slaves Christmas Day as a free day. In 1722, there was a rash of murders and the following year, the Slave Act of 1723 granted slaves Christmas Day and the two days following as free time. Slave protests and threats turned an occasional privilege into a customary right. The Jamaican sugar planter Lewis noted in his journal, "Sunday is now the absolute property of the negros for their relaxation, as Saturday is for the cultivation of their ground." The governor of Jamaica reported, "Every Settlement on the Low Grounds has a Mountain as its appendage, that is parceled out to the Slaves, and every Negro has his particular Lot apportioned to him for raising his Provisions, which is absolutely his Property, and his whole dependence." The market in Roseau, Dominica, had a fish, vegetable and fruit market in the center of a town of five hundred houses. "It was attended by Negros who traveled from as much as eight miles distant. Slaves often earned $3 to $4 and, according to the island's contemporary historian Thomas Atwood, seldom returned home without at least 50 to 60 shillings."

Throughout the slave societies of the Atlantic World, slaves brought produce to Saturday and Sunday markets and fed whites as well as blacks. Bryan Edwards wrote that in Jamaica, "the Negroes make it a practice to enlarge their own grounds, or exchange them for fresh land, every year. By these means, having quicker and better returns, they raise provisions in abundance, not only for their own use, but also a great surplus to sell." It was often the case that women cultivated the grounds and took their melons, manioc, sweet potatoes and such to market while men used their Saturdays to hire themselves out for produce or cash. Slave women in Saint Domingue sold eggs and chickens to ship captains in exchange for cloth, liquor and other goods, which were then bartered or sold to local restaurants. In his history of the French West Indies, Jean-Baptiste Du Tertre noted that planters hired male slaves and gave them tobacco – as good as coin – for wages. In the British Windward Islands (Grenada, St. Lucia, St. Vincent and Tobago), slaves had a monopoly of food, firewood, charcoal and fodder by 1790. The development of the slaves' economy of provision grounds and Sunday markets made slaves less dependent upon their masters in several ways.

What undergirded all slave regimes in the Atlantic World was the assumption that the master had absolute power over his slaves. The African Olaudah Equiano, a slave when he visited Jamaica in the early 1770s, recognized a small fracture in that regime of absolute power. "When I came to Kingston I was surprised to see the number of Africans who were assembled together on Sundays, particularly at a large commodious place called Spring Path. Here each different nation of Africa meet and dance after the manner of their own country. They still retain most of their native customs: they bury their dead, and put victuals, pipes, and tobacco, and other things, in the grave with the corpse. In the same manner as in Africa." These slaves and so many like them in Surinam, Cuba, Brazil, Saint Domingue and elsewhere were wandering across the islands and countryside, engaging in a multitude of economic exchanges, dominating public markets and enjoying being together. Edwards viewed all of this as benign and harmless: the slave, he wrote, "earns a little money, by which he is enable to indulge himself in fine clothes on holidays, and gratify his palate with salted meats and other provisions that otherwise he could not obtain." Planter regimes were less sanguine. All slave peddling, hawking and huckstering was illegal, as was traveling without a pass, assembling in any number, drinking any alcohol, holding a funeral or any meeting at night, and so on. Slaves were prohibited from hawking, peddling or selling without tickets from their masters in Jamaica by law in 1735. The following year, Montserrat restricted slaves from planting indigo, cocoa, cotton and ginger. Naturally, what these and other laws throughout the West Indies meant was that slaves were doing this all the time and that such practices were likely increasing. Slaves were also forbidden from attending public markets on Sundays. The planters of Barbados believed it was slave marketing that led to Bussa's rebellion in 1816. Planters charged that their indulgence regarding slave commerce had "induced the Negroes to assume airs of consequence, and put a value on themselves unknown among the slaves of former periods."

It is likely that the planters of Barbados were right. Provision grounds and Sunday markets gave slaves a little more control over their lives within the system of slavery. Slaves were not supervised, overseen or managed in any way in their work on their own provision grounds. They decided what to grow, how many, by what approach and so on; they were the masters of what they viewed as their family estates. As slaves accumulated livestock, furniture, tools and houses, they became members of society as de facto property owners. Some inherited property from family members rather than obtaining provision grounds assigned by planters. Some came to buy land, even their provision grounds, and a few even purchased slaves and their own liberty when possible. Planter and white society began to make distinctions between rich and poor slaves, and between "Principal Negroes" and "the worthless sort" who worked the grounds of the better sort. These outsider perspectives missed the ties of language, kinship, religion and resistance – the keys to the cultures of the slaves.

The African family was extremely difficult to form and sustain under slavery in the Atlantic plantation complex. The Atlantic slave trade transported more men than women to the Americas, and the horrid conditions of slavery also lowered the fertility rate and increased the infant mortality rate. Chattel slavery allowed for husbands and wives as well as parents and children to be separated and sold to different plantations, not to mention different colonies. Masters frequently raped girls and women on their plantations, which led to the birth of mulatto children to be raised by their mothers and the plantation slave community. There is evidence that women in slavery deliberately avoided pregnancies and used natural abortifacients. Despite these and other detestable conditions, Africans did form families in slavery. In plantation regimes, these families were often centered around and based on provision grounds. A slave household with an assigned plot of land often disguised an extended family that might be dispersed over several plantations. Husbands and wives were rarely married in any formal or legal manner. Indeed, Europeans frequently condemned the "licentiousness" of Africans, not understanding the African tradition of polygamy or the reality of the plantations that women were scarce. Moreau de Saint-Méry's 1797–8 description of Saint Domingue noted, "all the negroes born in Africa are polygamous in Saint-Domingue – and jealous." A male slave with provision grounds, we might say, was a good catch, an attractive candidate for a wife. A female slave with provision grounds would have had suitors from all the plantations in the region. More precisely, plantation slaves practiced polygyny, the custom of having two or more wives or concubines or, for women, several help-mates, at the same time. This flexible strategy of family formation under slavery was an adaptation to the many obstacles slavery presented to Africans in America.

Edward Long viewed the slave family in Jamaica as, among other things, a type of social insurance system: "They are all married (in their way) to a husband, or wife, *pro tempore*, or have other family connections, in almost every parish throughout the island; so that one of them, perhaps, has six or more husbands, or wives, in several different places; by this means they find support, when their lands fail them; and houses of call and refreshment, whenever they are upon their travels." Gathered around provision grounds, which were understood by the slaves as heritable property and passed from generation to generation, often according to the rules of primogeniture, Africans families did their best to hang together under the most difficult circumstances. Father or mother, husband and wives, children, brother, aunt, grandparents, newlyweds, godmother and others rarely lived in the same place but they were tied together by love, loyalty and the family estate.

When Olaudah Equiano discovered a group of Africans in Kingston one Sunday, what he did not tell us is that they were speaking and singing to one another in their own tongues. They were speaking and singing in Cormantee (Twi), Ibo (Ibgo), Congo (Kikongo) and perhaps some other African languages. It is likely that some were also speaking Jamaican Creole. The development of European-derived Creoles, also called pidgins, *patois* and *kréyoles*, were the languages created by African slaves in the Atlantic World. In the British Atlantic World, there were at least twenty-five Creoles: eighteen based on English, two on Dutch and four on French. It has long been assumed that New World Creoles were mixed languages with African grammatical structures and rhythms and mostly European and Native American lexicon. Recent research of French-based Creole languages suggest these languages are considerably more complicated and puzzling than previously believed. It is likely that slaves created a Creole grammar from the *patois* of northern France as well as Ewe, Igbo and Yoruba.

These slave languages show us how the African generations refused to fully acculturate to the second most important European requirement: communication. (We should keep in mind, as well, that Africans spoke their first

languages, African languages, to their fellow compatriots in large numbers.)
What is most interesting is that these were languages for slaves of all African
nations. The Creole languages were utilitarian but also conspiratorial. With
the exception of the Coromantin maroon state in Jamaica, Creole languages
served as the dominant languages for those slaves who fled from their plantations and established rebel communities. Creole was the language of revolt
in Surinam and the West Indies in the eighteenth century, and the language
of most rebels in Saint Domingue in the 1790s.

Africans resisted slavery in many different ways. Rebellion, the most obvious type of resistance, was not as infrequent as logic would dictate, and
even those slave revolts always ended in brutal repression. Slaves could
resist in more subtle ways, using the so-called weapons of the weak. They
slowed down the pace of work and damaged tools and equipment. To Europeans, it appeared somewhat different: "The Africans transplanted to Saint-
Domingue," wrote Moreau de Saint-Méry, "remain in general indolent and
idle." Slaves also destroyed themselves, the most important investment of
the slaveowner. The French planter Dessalles of Martinique noted that he
had twelve mules, ten draft oxen and three cows or heifers poisoned. "Plus,"
he continued, "Bibiane killed herself and Roc hanged himself." A number of
contemporary writers on Jamaican slavery have commented on what appears
to be a high rate of slave suicide, particularly by the extremely painful method
of dirt eating.

One of the most significant forms of slave resistance during the plantation
regime was flight, or marronage, the creation of communities of escaped
slaves called maroons. From sixteenth-century São Tomé, these runaway
communities appeared in nearly every plantation society and by their very
existence confronted the slave regime. Marronage was the product, almost
entirely, of Africans who joined with other Africans of different languages
and nations to resist the plantation and create their own communities and
run their own lives. The first account of a maroon community in the Americas is from the early sixteenth century, a reference to the island of Samaná,
off the northern coast of Hispaniola, which was "inhabited by wild Negroes
who escaped in order to avoid serving the Spaniards." With the expansion
of African slavery to the other Spanish islands of the Caribbean and to the
mainland, there followed an epidemic of slave flight. The Spanish came to
call escaped slaves *cimarróns* (from their term for feral cattle and horses,
hence the term "maroon") and they called runaway communities *palenques*,
because defensive palisades ringed them. From the sixteenth to the eighteenth centuries, African *palenques* were found in Hispaniola, Cuba, Puerto
Rico, Jamaica, New Spain, Central America, modern Columbia, Venezuela,
Ecuador, Peru and elsewhere. In Brazil, runaway communities called *macambos* and, much later, *quilombos*, were present from the beginning of African
slavery. Stuart B. Schwartz has provided a partial list of *macambos* for one
captaincy, Bahia, which counts thirteen such communities for the seventeenth
century alone. A Jesuit wrote in 1619, "this people has the custom of fleeing to
the woods and joining in hideouts where they live by attacks on the settlers,
stealing livestock and ruining crops and cane fields which results in much
damage and many losses beyond that of losing their daily labor." The most

famous of Brazil's *macambos* was the *quilombo* of Palmares. This maroon state located in the hinterland southwest of Recife existed from the beginning of the seventeenth century until its demise in the military campaigns of the 1690s. A Dutch expedition to Palmares in 1645 found a palisaded community with 220 buildings, including a church in the middle. A king ruled Palmares. Over two years later, a Portuguese military expedition learned that besides the main town of Palmares, there were other towns within the orbit of the *quilombo*. After the defeat of the Dutch in Brazil, the Portuguese sent numerous expeditions, sometimes more than one a year, to destroy Palmares. This was finally accomplished in 1694.

In the sugar islands of the West Indies, marronage developed immediately with African slavery. The first governor of French Saint-Christophe in 1639 reported the flight of sixty slaves. French planters described temporary flight, slaves visiting friends and relatives on other plantations without permission, as *petit marronage*. The creation of runaway communities, a more serious matter, was called *grand marronage*. The latter was found in Martinique, Guadaloupe, Grenada during the French regime and Saint Domingue. In the English West Indies, maroons were nearly everywhere: the Bahamas, Dominica, Antigua and particularly Jamaica. When the English seized Jamaica from the Spanish in 1655, African slaves under the Spanish regime fled to the interior of the island and created their own communities. These were the Spanish maroons, according to the English. In the late seventeenth century, Hans Sloane noted, "The same Places remote from Settlements are very often full of run away Negros, who lie in Ambush to kill the Whites who come within their reach." Over the decades, the Spanish maroons made their mountain retreats practically impregnable, attracted new fugitive slaves and occasionally raided plantations. By the mid-1730s, writes Bryan Edwards, the Spanish Maroons "were grown so formidable." There were two powerful resistance bands, one from the center of the island at Trelawrey Town and led by a general named Cudjoe, and the other located in the northeast at Nanny Town and led by Cuffee. In the 1720s and 1730s, the government of Jamaica began a series of military campaigns that came to be called the First Maroon War. By 1737–8, both sides, battered yet undefeated, were willing to agree to a permanent truce. In the Articles of Pacification of 1738, the government of Jamaica recognized the freedom of the maroons and granted territory in perpetuity to the maroon towns. The maroon towns were required to assist the authorities in repelling external enemies, suppressing internal rebels and returning fugitive slaves to their masters for compensation.

In some of the smaller and close-together islands, like the Danish West Indies – St. Thomas, St. John and St. Croix – planters were disconcerted by maritime marronage. Slaves here escaped bondage by building rafts and small boats and fleeing to much larger Puerto Rico, where there were maroon bands. After slavery was ended in the British West Indies in 1838, Danish slaves fled to the British Virgin Islands.

The plantation regimes of the Wild Coast of South America, Guiana, produced numerous and rebellious maroon communities in the backlands. In particular, Dutch Suriname fought a century-long guerrilla war against the

Ndjuka and Saramaka maroons until 1760 and 1762, when peace treaties granted these communities freedom and independence in exchange for peace. Newer maroon communities closer to the coast began raiding plantations, and a new maroon war began. "A most dangerous revolt having broken out in the Colony of Surinam among the Negro slaves who were armed and assembled in the woods threatening immediate destruction to the settlement," wrote the mercenary soldier John Gabriel Stedman in 1790, "the States of the United Provinces determined to sent out a fresh corps of five hundred volunteers in 1772, to act conjointly with the troops already there to quell the insurrection and prevent a general massacre." This war with the Aluku maroons in due course also led to a peace treaty. Six maroon peoples, also called Bush Negro tribes, survived into the late twentieth century.

The plantation system with the least amount of *grand marronage* was that of colonial North America. Runaway groups were found in Spanish Florida, French Louisiana and the southeastern corner of British North America. These often opposing colonial regimes encouraged slave flight in neighboring colonies to undermine their economies and destabilize their societies. Maroon communities survived often with the assistance of plantation slaves who smuggled European goods, including arms, to these fugitive groups. This was possible in the provision ground plantation regimes of Brazil and the West Indies, but in British North America the plantations followed the allowance system and gave their slaves much less leeway regarding marketing and travel. The British in North America used Native American allies to capture and defeat runaway slaves.

The most dramatic, and often suicidal, form of resistance to slavery was violent rebellion. Aside from the maroons who often fought plantation regimes and won their freedom and independence, slave rebellions prior to the Haitian revolution in the 1790s were uniformly and bloodily repressed. Rebellions began in Hispaniola during the governorship of the Columbus family and continued to the end of slavery in the Americas in the 1870s and 1880s. No plantation regime was spared a slave rebellion, and many experienced revolt after revolt. Like maroons, rebellious slaves were generally Africans. In the early years of the plantation regimes, slave rebellions were most likely spontaneous acts of violence by Africans unaccustomed to slavery, hunger, cruelty and similar conditions. However, by the seventeenth and, especially, the eighteenth century, conflict between the Atlantic powers led to incitement of slave flight and rebellion in enemy colonies. In peacetime, the colonial regimes cooperated to suppress slave rebellions. French troops from Martinique in 1733 made it possible for the Danes to put down the slave rebellion on St. John and maintain control. By the last decades of the eighteenth century, Creole slaves began to lead slave revolts. For example, Jamaica witnessed the African Cormantee rebellion of 1760. However, in 1776 a rebellion was started by Creoles who, wrote an island attorney, "were never known before to have been Concerned in anything of this sort." There were fewer slave rebellions in British North America. The largest was South Carolina's Stono Rebellion of 1739, in which about one hundred African slaves fought their way south, seeking Spanish Florida for refuge to no avail. Slave resistance in the last part of the eighteenth century and the early nineteenth century dovetailed with the Atlantic age of revolution that began a process of dramatic political and social change for masters and slaves and everyone in between. We will return to this topic in a later chapter.

The plantation complex of the Atlantic World was the engine that revived slavery in the Western world, Africanized it, Americanized it and transformed it into one of the most important forces of change in the early modern world. The plantation complex in the Americas reached its apogee in the eighteenth century. The production of staple commodities based primarily on African slave labor created slave societies in Brazil, Guiana, the West Indies and in the southern colonies of British North America. Outside this tropical and semitropical plantation zone, African and eventually African-American slaves made significant contributions to the economies of all American colonies. Slavery was responsible for much of the economic development of the New World: slaves not only produced sugar, tobacco, cacao, indigo, rice, coffee and cotton but also maize and wheat just about everywhere. They mined gold in Brazil, raised cattle in Venezuela, built ships in Havana, made clothe in Mexico City, produced wine in Peru and loaded and unloaded ships in New York City. Slaves constituted the majority of unskilled workers in most American cities and were present in most of the skilled trades. Without slavery, the New World outside of Mexico and Peru would very likely had remained vast and scattered frontiers composed of small and poor European outposts.

The plantation – or staple – trades benefited certain European port cities, merchant capitalists and European consumers above all. Competition between staple producers in the seventeenth and particularly the eighteenth and nineteenth centuries led to the almost continual decline in the prices of sugar, tobacco, cacao and coffee. We see the consumption of sugar increase in Britain from approximately four pounds per head in 1700 to twenty pounds per head by 1800. Planters became more and more indebted, and profits were less and less secure. The long-term economic viability of the plantation complex was doubtful. Of the three Atlantic powers that competed for trade and commercial power in the eighteenth century – The Netherlands, France and Great Britain – Atlantic trade appears to have had the most positive effect on Britain. Atlantic staples imported (and often reexported) produced profits and favored consumers, but the commercial revolution of the British Atlantic in the eighteenth century was the result of the expansion of British exports to transatlantic regions. Exports that spurred domestic production, not staple imports, are what energized the British economy.

There should be no illusion about the brutality, degradation and deadliness of slavery for the Africans and their descendants in the plantations, farms, mines, workshops and docks of the Atlantic World. The one-time slave from the Guinea coast, Quobna Ottobah Cugoano, wrote about his own horrifying experience: "Brought from a state of innocence and freedom, and, in a barbarous and cruel manner, conveyed to a state of horror and slavery: This abandoned situation may be easier conceived than described." How do we come to terms with the Atlantic slave trade and plantation slavery in this post-Holocaust age? For some intellectuals, people are morally evil or

Figure 8.4. A Scene of Merchants and a Slave in the British West Indies. From John Knox, *A new collection of voyages, discoveries and travels* (London, 1767). Courtesy of the William L. Clements Library at the University of Michigan.

simply give up on morality and pursue self-interest and group-interest. "This was true," writes James Sterba, "of many Spanish conquistadors, American slaveholders, European settlers, and Nazi SS officers." However, this explanation gives us a static picture of humanity. It does not help us understand the slave trade and slavery because these practices and institutions have very long and complex histories. In most of the world during most of human history, servitude, bondage and slavery were perceived as not only natural and normal but also moral. What history teaches us is that beginning in the eighteenth century, this perception began to change. It was at this point in history that reformers and moralists made slavery into an evil and, within a hundred years, brought it to an end.

We have seen that throughout the Atlantic World, most Africans were sent to the plantations and there, particularly on the sugar plantations, they found the most severe demands for their labor. Plantation slaves were forced to work through violence and threat of violence, and they often were worked until they wore out and were replaced by new Africans. Nevertheless, and quite remarkably, slaves did create lives, spaces and cultures within slavery. We wonder how this would be possible. The historian Peter H. Wood offers an answer: "More important than the pressure of the masters were the desires of the people themselves. The harshness and insecurity of their situation increased the need to share the numerous sufferings and rare pleasures with another person."

8.4 Further Reading

John Atkins, *A Voyage to Guinea, Brasil, and the West-Indies* (London, 1735).

Ira Berlin, *Many Thousands Gone: The First Two Centuries of Slavery in North America* (Cambridge, Mass., 1998).

Judith A. Carney, *Black Rice: The African Origins of Rice Cultivation in the Americas* (Cambridge, Mass., 2001).

Robert Edgar Conrad, editor, *Children of God's Fire: A Documentary History of Black Slavery in Brazil* (University Park, 1994).

Philip D. Curtin, *Rise and Fall of the Plantation Complex: Essays in Atlantic History* (Cambridge, 1998).

Richard S. Dunn, *Sugar and Slaves: The Rise of the Planter Class in the English West Indies, 1624–1713* (New York, 1972).

Elborg Forster and Robert Forester, editors and translators, *Sugar and Slavery, Family and Race: The Letters and Diary of Pierre Dessalles, Planter in Martinique, 1808–1856* (Baltimore, 1996).

Douglas Hall, editor, *Miserable Slavery: Thomas Thistlewood in Jamaica, 1750–1786* (London, 1989).

Gwendolyn Midlo Hall, *Slavery and African Ethnicities in the Americas: Restoring the Links* (Chapel Hill, 2005).

Herbert S. Klein, *African Slavery in Latin America and the Caribbean* (New York, 1986).

Matthew Lewis, *Journal of a West India Proprietor Kept during a Residence in the Island of Jamaica*, edited by Judith Terry (Oxford, 1999).

Edward Long, *The History of Jamaica*, 3 volumes (London, 1774).

Philip D. Morgan, *Slave Counterpoint: Black Culture in the Eighteenth Century Chesapeake and Lowcountry* (Chapel Hill, 1998).

Michael Mullin, *Africa in America: Slave Acculturation and Resistance in the American South and the British Caribbean, 1736–1831* (Urbana, 1998).

Robert Olwell, *Masters, Slaves, and Subjects: The Culture of Power in the South Carolina Low Country, 1740–1790* (Ithaca, 1998).

Fernando Ortiz, *Cuban Counterpoint: Tobacco and Sugar* [1940], translated by Harriet de Onís (Durham, 1995).

Katis M. de Querós Mattoso, *To Be a Slave in Brazil, 1550–1888*, translated by Arthur Goldhammer (New Brunswick, 1986).

Leslie B. Rout, Jr., *The African Experience in Spanish America: 1502 to the Present Day* (Cambridge, 1976).

Stuart B. Schwartz, *Sugar Plantations in the Formation of Brazilian Slavery: Bahia, 1550–1835* (Cambridge, 1985).

Stuart B. Schwartz, editor, *Tropical Babylons: Sugar and the Making of the Atlantic World, 1450–1680* (Chapel Hill, 2004).

Richard Sheridan, *Sugar and Slaves, an Economic History of the British West Indies, 1623–1775* (Aylesbury, 1974).

James H. Sweet, *Recreating Africa: Culture, Kinship, and Religion in the African-Portuguese World, 1441–1770* (Chapel Hill, 2003).

Dale W. Tomich, *Slavery in the Circuit of Sugar: Martinique and the World Economy, 1830–1848* (Baltimore, 1990).

Peter Wood, *Strange New Land: Africans in Colonial America* (Durham, 1996).

Chapter 9

Partners

Women and Men in the Making of the Atlantic World

The making of the Atlantic World was an endeavor accomplished by men and women. Up to this point, few women have been mentioned in this history. This is because few women were sailors and explorers, conquerors and planters, traders, colonial officials, missionaries, and pirates. Women, however, participated in all of these activities and more. As colonists, servants, seamstresses, landowners, cigar rollers, tavern keepers, midwives, market women, and slaves, European, African and Indian women helped make the Atlantic World (literally) work. As the mates of male colonists, women were the irreplaceable partners of men. Founding fathers must have founding mothers. In the early stages of Atlantic colonization, European women tended to stay home. As a result, in many places the founding mothers were African and Indian women. They assisted and resisted Europeans, provided translations, entrée into alien cultures, counsel and guidance. They helped forge diplomatic alliances and business partnerships. African and Indian women in the new Atlantic World gave birth to mulattos and *mestizos* and thus were crucial in the genesis of new peoples and cultures. In time, European women left home and sailed the Atlantic. Far more moved to and settled in the Americas than in Atlantic Africa. European women became partners of their husbands in building farms, estates, businesses and in giving birth to new generations to pass on the hereditary culture. To many contemporaries, women were essential to the making of the Atlantic World. Sir Edwin Sandys, Treasurer of the Virginia Company of London, wrote in 1620, "The plantation can never flourish till families be planted and the respect of wives and children fix the people on the soil." As historian Susan Migden Socolow explains, women in the colonial Atlantic World were a metaphor for rootedness and therefore were seen as carrying the seeds and plants of the Old World to the New. They would "civilize" their men folk and populate the new lands with European Christian offspring.

The expansion of Europeans into Africa and the Americas from the fifteenth to the eighteenth century was, to a considerable extent, an expansion of men and an expansion of a patriarchal (i.e., male-dominated) culture. These European men came into contact with not only different and diverse societies and cultures in Africa and the Americas, but with African and Indian societies with different gender systems. Other societies had different and diverse rules governing the relations between women and men, girls and boys, wives and husbands, and parents and children. European expansion and colonialism created, therefore, what Kathleen M. Brown has called a number of *gender frontiers*, where men and women of very different cultures clashed and collided and also came together. European men and African and Native American women came together to make war and peace, establish political alliances, secure business deals, produce and enhance personal prestige and wealth, form kinship networks, and even create unions and families that satisfied universal emotions for physical desire, personal commitment and children. Brown writes, "By employing the concept of gender frontiers – cultural encounters that extended from Europe, to Africa, across the Atlantic to the Americas – we can begin to appreciate the centrality of gender to colonial exchanges and contests for power."

These gender frontiers, for contemporary intellectuals and scholars, are places of passionate debate and disagreement. One of the most important issues relates to the nature of patriarchy in the different societies of the Atlantic World. Archaeologists and anthropologists have argued that women enjoyed greater equality and power in less complex kinship-based societies. The rise of social stratification, warrior nobilities and complex states, however, gave rise to patriarchal authority and the decline in the power and status of women. A body of recent research, on the other hand, makes a sharp distinction between European patriarchy and gender parallelism and gender complementarity of the native societies of the Americas. These terms refer to gender systems in which men and women lived and worked, and held power and influence, in separate – but equal – spheres. The gender roles of men and women were distinct but complementary. European patriarchy, on the other hand, is presented as an extreme hierarchical gender system that excluded women from power, religion, property and control over their own children. The European family was oppressive and emotionally cruel for wives and children. What is new in the revisionist gender history is the sweeping view of gender parallelism and complementarity. Not only is this gender ideology recognized in the less complex, kinship-based societies of the native Americas, it is also specifically identified in the hierarchical societies of the Mexica, Maya and Inka. The implication of this interpretation is that the colonization of the Americas was not simply a clash of cultures but a collision of two radically different gender ideologies and systems. The result of this collision was a significant decline of status of native noble women in Mexico and Peru and everywhere else in the Americas. A different issue of patriarchy relates to the transmission of the European gender system to the Americas and its evolution and possible liberalization for European women and their Creole daughters. American conditions subverted many European rigidities, conventions and hierarchies. It is not hard to believe that colonial women were not beneficiaries to some extent of Americanization.

A second issue concerns the sexuality of African and Indian women and the nature of their relationships with European men. This subject has a long history. For a long time, many Europeans viewed African and Indian women as licentious. These men came from a Christian tradition and culture that gave great significance to female virginity, chastity and moral restraint. African and Indian women who willingly had sexual relations with European mariners, soldiers, traders and others, it was believed, must be "whores" in a culture of whores. Much later, feminist historians, rereading the self-serving European sources, concluded that all sexual relations between European men and indigenous women, between the colonizer and the colonized, were a form of rape. This issue, not as all encompassing than the problem of patriarchy, poses fewer theoretical problems. We should transcend the whore/victim dichotomy and realize that there were innumerable reasons for European–indigenous sexual relations, cohabitation, trial marriage and legal marriage. These may include rape, kidnapping, sale, prostitution, inebriation, bribery, family or community obligation, economic opportunism, physical attraction, affection and even – dare we think it – love. It is important, however, to keep in mind the early feminists' main point that relations between European men and indigenous women were relations of unequal power. This is true not only in the plantation systems of the Atlantic World, where female slaves were subject to sexual exploitation and abuse, but true throughout the Atlantic World where kings, chiefs and fathers "donated" their young women and daughters to other rulers, chiefs and fathers as symbols of power and hospitality, instruments to forge diplomatic alliances, and vessels to unite families, clans and nations.

A third issue we find on the gender frontiers of the Atlantic World is the problem of the transmission of culture through colonization. The problem of cultural transmission is closely linked to gender systems and particularly to women and mothers as guardians of their hereditary culture and builders of cultural bridges between generations. By briefly looking at the history of the Portuguese, Dutch, French and English in Atlantic Africa, the Spanish in the Philippines, the French in Indochina and the Dutch in The Netherlands Indies we see that European fathers and local, native mothers produced *filhos da terra*, *mulattoes*, *mestizos*, *métisse* and *mengbloeden* – that is, people of mixed descent – who did not acquire the basic characteristics of European culture. In the Americas, on the other hand, European women immigrated in much larger numbers for a much longer time. As a result, in Spanish America, Portuguese Brazil, and the English, French and Dutch colonies, European families created neo-European societies in the Americas that spoke and wrote European languages, practiced and accepted the tenets of Christianity, created economic societies based on European agriculture, private property and a money economy, constructed Portuguese cathedrals, Spanish plazas and English great houses, and generally followed their particular national and local folkways. Rather than focusing on women as the primary carriers of culture, we need to remember that traditional and patriarchal notions of education, moral instruction and guidance on honor, status and wealth – in short, civilizing the brats – were the responsibility of the father. Marriage and child-rearing guidebooks and manuals from the sixteenth to the eighteenth century recognized the father's unique aptitude of authority, education and character.

Recent scholarship also emphasizes the importance of the family itself and childrearing as a partnership shared by mothers and fathers. European mothers and fathers taught their children the most important things, of course, by example. Fathers took a particular interest in the education or training of their sons. They were usually the parent who taught the boys (and sometimes the girls) how to write and how to figure, how to ride and how to fight, and they introduced their sons into the world of their trade, business, profession, arms or power. Mothers taught their daughters, depending on rank, how to keep house in the appropriate Andalusian, Norman or East Anglican manner. Although the guidebooks said it was the duty of the father, mothers often supervised the moral education of both boys and girls.

Men ruled the Atlantic World. Male power was deeply rooted in European culture and it was reproduced and recreated in all of the Atlantic colonies. Overseas conditions, however, created some flexibility here and there at different times, for women and men. Europeans coupled with and married African and Indian women, creating multicultural partnerships. They also brought European women to the Americas (and women sought to go there), which allowed the explorers, conquerors, traders and settlers to recreate and reinvent the cultures of their homelands across the Atlantic.

9.1 Western Patriarchy and Complementarity

In the beginning, or pretty close to the beginning, in the Western tradition, the Lord God said: "*It is* not good that the man should be alone; I will make him an help meet for him." The Western Europe that expanded into the Atlantic in the fifteenth and sixteenth centuries was patriarchal. What this means is that male dominance over women and children in the family and in society in general had become normalized and institutionalized in Portugal, Spain, France and the other countries of Atlantic Europe. In patriarchal societies, political, religious and cultural institutions supported by a system of beliefs, values and unspoken assumptions, allocated power, property and status to men. Western Europe was not unique in this gender system. Patriarchy had historical origins extending into the past at least 4,000 years. It was, furthermore, a social, economic and political system that developed as agricultural-based civilizations arose, reducing women's importance as food suppliers and increasing their significance as mothers of more laborers, warriors and priests. In these societies, men felt the need to ensure that specific women belonged to them and that the children they gave birth to were their biological children. Men also wanted to guarantee, furthermore, that their property was passed on to their "legitimate" sons. As a result of these basic principles, patriarchal societies often prevented or limited women from owning property, allowed men to take multiple wives or created double standards in sexual behavior, severely punished women's sexual offenses, veiled women in public and hid them behind walls at home, and various and numerous ways subordinated women to men. Patriarchal societies were historical and also worldwide, although patriarchal systems from different times and different places were never uniform. Patriarchy developed in ancient Persia, the Greek and Roman worlds, Confucian China and in Hindu India. Chinese patriarchy was a system based not on religion but the Confucian principles of hierarchy and order. Although Confucianism limited men to one wife, low-status concubines as sexual partners were acceptable. Hindu Indian patriarchy developed polygamy and a practice called *sati* (*sahamarana*) that placed social pressure on widows to throw themselves on the funeral pyres of their husbands. This custom was rare but revealing, pointing out the notion that the widow had nothing to live for after her husband died.

Female subordination to men in Western Europe and elsewhere was the result of nature and culture. Men in general have been and remain more aggressive, violent and assertive than women. Male dominance was reinforced by a set of ideas and attitudes that was legitimized by society's acceptance of them. Catholic and Protestant theorists and writers presented the female as the weaker sex, not simply in a physical sense but also emotionally and intellectually. Women needed to be protected from society, and from themselves, as a result of their weak and sinful nature, excessive passions, insatiable sexuality, and extravagant and wasteful ways. Well-to-do women tended to be restricted to the care of the household and the family. The Catholic Church, with its emphasis on virginity and celibacy, not only subordinated women but also had little genuine respect for the family. The medieval church viewed marriage as an inferior (and even sinful) state in comparison to virginity and celibacy. In the sixteenth century, marriage was brought under the strict control of the church and viewed with greater regard. Protestants, meanwhile, exalted the married state. The width of women's hips, according to Martin Luther, was a divine sign revealing that the female was destined to home and childbirth.

European patriarchy has been exaggerated recently in the anticolonial and postcolonial scholarship that has argued that European colonialism intensified, expanded or created anew patriarchal domination around the world. A number of scholars have written about gender systems in Native American societies, as they existed prior to contact with Europeans and after contact, conquest and colonization. Native societies, we are informed, were more sophisticated and complex in their gender relationships and ideologies than European societies. Native societies had systems called gender parallelism and gender complementarity. In a gender-parallel society, writes Karen Vieira Powers, "Women and men operate in two separate but equivalent spheres, each gender enjoying autonomy in its own sphere." In addition to gender parallelism, each gender's role was perceived as equally important to the success of society. "Men's and women's roles were distinct when it involved daily life, but women's roles were not seen as subordinate to or less significant than those to men. Instead, women's and men's contributions were equally valued, considered essential to the other and to the whole of society; that is, they were complementary." Some Renaissance humanists invented Edenic images of the unspoiled Native American world. This tradition, shored up by a different set of assumptions, appears stronger than ever today.

In contrast to the sophisticated native gender systems, European patriarchal relations are summarized and simplified as oppressive and authoritarian. "In the rigidly stratified patriarchal society of the late Middle Ages, women (particularly peasant women) were the most dependent and vulnerable members," writes Irene Silverblatt. "Under common law, a married woman could own no property. Nor were women allowed a voice in either the Church or the state. Woman's chief virtue was silence; her sole duty was obedience to her husband, and her main obligation was to manage the household, under God." Karen Vieira Powers, in her synthesis of Spanish destruction of the balanced and harmonious gender systems of the Mexica and the Inka, argues, "in the political and religious realm, Iberian women were barred from positions of authority. They could not function as bureaucrats, lawyers, judges, or priests and were, therefore, deprived of any meaningful participation in the decision-making process of church and state." In her study of the Huron and Montagnais under French colonialism in the seventeenth century, Karen Anderson notes that one of the issues she wants to address is "woman's oppression in western European culture, at least since the beginning of the seventeenth century."

Gender relations in late medieval and early modern Europe were not quite as simple or oppressive as these and other historians have suggested. Women were not excluded from political power, nor were they lacking any political voice. More women held power in medieval and early modern Europe than at any other time. Matilda of Scotland was Queen of England, Queen Urraca of Aragón and Empress Maud of Germany were all powerful twelfth-century monarchs. Christine de Pisan, a fifteenth-century writer, praised the queens of France for their just and moderate rule. She also wrote a book about military strategy for women and how to command armies. Joan of Aragón ruled in fourteenth century, Margaret of Denmark and Norway (1387–1412), Isabel of Castile (1474–1504), Mary of Burgundy (1477–82), Queen Mary (1553–8) and Queen Elizabeth I (1558–1606) of England, Mary of Guise (1543–1660) and Mary Queen of Scots (1561–7), and Queen Christina (1632–54) of Sweden were each a monarch in her own right. Some of them, in fact, were warrior queens. Women also held power as a result of their relationships with men. Mary, Queen and Regent of Hungary (1531–5) and Margaret of Austria, Regent (1517–30) owed their powerful positions to their brother, Carlos V, Holy Roman Emperor. Similarly, Margaret of Parma, regent of The Netherlands (1559–66), came by her commanding post as a result of her relationship with her brother, Felipe II. Noblewomen participated in positions of command and ordinary women were a normal part of European armies from the fourteenth into the nineteenth century.

Women were viewed by many in the Roman church as the source of sin: one medieval writer painted Eve as the archetypal temptress who led Adam to sin: "Between Adam and God in paradise there was but one woman and she had no rest until she had succeeded in banishing her husband from the garden of delights and in condemning Christ to the torments of the cross." Christianity, however, also recognized the inherent dignity of women and the equality of male and female souls. In the fifteenth, sixteenth and seventeenth centuries there was a spectacular growth of female religious orders. In Florence, the number of nuns rose from 933 in 1427 to 3,400 in 1552 and 4,200 by 1622. In the century after 1545 in Valladolid, Spain, there were five new male monastic institutions founded but no fewer than twelve nunneries established. "The mushrooming of female participation in the religious life was far more than just a cynical development in the economy of wealthy families," argues Diarmaid MacCulloch. "Much of its impetus came from women who wanted to play their full part in the movements of renewal that the Church was fostering. It was a powerful reaffirmation of an independent role for women in the Church." In France, 55 Carmelite convents spread across the country in a "mystical invasion." The Ursulines became the most numerous and influential order, a religious congregation devoted to education. "For France in the seventeenth century," writes Leslie Choquette, "one can speak of a 'feminization' of religious life, in that for the first time female religious outnumbered male." The Ursulines, Chanoinesses and the Hospitalières de Saint-Joseph came to Canada to participate in the evangelization of the Indians uncloistered in the same manner as the Jesuits. "The missionary efforts of women had achieved a remarkable degree of acceptance in Canada."

Women often took the lead in early Protestant movements. In the pre-Reformation Hussite revolution of fifteenth-century Bohemia, Jan Hus encouraged women in religion and public life. In his tract *The Daughter* (1412), he wrote that women were made in the image of God and that they could act with dignity and courage in the movement for reform. Women responded to his call and placed reformers in parishes, wrote tracts and preached sermons. In Switzerland in the mid-1520s, women began to reconstruct Christianity for themselves in spite of Catholic executions of Anabaptists. The women of St. Gallen cut their hair short because they believed it provoked lustful thoughts in men. A servant girl proclaimed herself the New Messiah and gathered disciples. No longer restrained by the Roman church and its institutions, Protestant women led their own sects. Many devoted Christian women married Protestant ministers and as clergy wives became important role models. During a second wave of popular Protestant activism in the 1560s, a number of authors, including women, discussed the idea of women's equality before God and an active and official role of women in the life of the church.

Les femmes, quelle puissance! This comment by the French historian Jules Michelet – 'Women, what strength' – "is not just a tactical maneuver, a sort of consolation prize offered to women," writes the French historian Michelle Perrot and her colleagues involved in the collaborative project on the history of women in the West. "It is also a conviction widely shared by ordinary people of the past and by historians today, persuaded that 'customs,' that is, private life, and civil society, ultimately count more than the political and the state."

Although authority was theoretically and legally vested in the male, a man could seldom take this for granted according to satire and popular art. One of the favorite themes in popular Renaissance woodcuts and engravings was the battle for the trousers. A man and wife wrestled for who would wear the pants and victory usually went to the wife. "Patriarchal authority was more absolute in theory than practice," writes Alison Rowlands. "Sixteenth-century court records show that peasant women had the power to disrupt household harmony and to make their husbands' lives miserable by scolding them or by cooking them inadequate or irregular meals, while praise for their talents as keepers of house and livestock suggests that their contribution to the household economy was so vital that the day-to-day marital relationship was more of a partnership (albeit an unequal one) than a hierarchy." Lloyd Bonfield observes that law may have diverged from practice with a married woman's economic power. "Although the European law was reasonably consistent in manifesting authority in the husband, economic reality frequently required a partnership with the wife (or widow) in control of family property either during the marriage or at its termination." Grandmothers, aunts, widows and sisters exercised considered influence in some families (often well-to-do families) over the marriage partners of youngsters. In Protestant England and Germany in the sixteenth and seventeenth centuries, there is research showing that authority and responsibility was shared by husbands and wives – co-rulers in the household – in their different spheres in the family. The father was the head of the family, certainly, but the perception of the wife as a "deputy husband" in many regions in Europe and America did not mean she was a servile baby-making machine. Although Sir William Blackstone commented that wives had no legal existence, and was subsumed within the legal person of the husband, we are discovering more and more that many husbands and wives in early modern Europe had companionship marriages. And when the marriage didn't work, Protestants could often obtain legal divorce.

In no other culture in the world was there a *querelle des femmes*, a debate about the nature of women and their roles in society. Christine de Pisan in the early fifteenth century attacked the clerical arguments on women's inferiority head on. Women essayists, poets, novelists, dramatists, biographers and other kinds of writers defended women's abilities and reputations against misogynist texts, ancient and modern, secular and scriptural. Women writers often responded to specific, and particularly objectionable, works. The poet Sarah Fyges Egerton, for example, most likely wrote *The Female Advocate* (1686) in reply to the obscene "late satire on women," by Robert Gould. Although quite a number of women authors and their texts have been newly discovered in recent years, this discourse on the roles and rights of women involved male as well as female authors. The famous names are Desiderius Erasmus and Juan Luis Vives. Erasmus praised marriage while Vives favored the education of women, at least those women with the ability to learn and the virtue to know what to do with learning. The *querelle des femmes* obviously did not produce feminism in the seventeenth and eighteenth centuries but it is difficult to imagine the appearance of Olympe de Gouges and Mary Wollstonecraft and "the rights of woman" in the absence of such a literary tradition.

While historians have discovered gender parallelism and complementarity among non-Western societies, the kind of gender relationships described in this literature can also be found in early modern Europe. Feminist scholars, and particularly historians of colonialism, have not looked for gender parallelism and complementarity in early modern Europe because the famous doctrine of separate spheres was so obviously understood to be a nineteenth-century development. This metaphor declared that American women, having adopted a cult of true womanhood, ruled in their domestic sphere while men ruled in the public sphere. Because of the American and French Revolutions, the rise of the idea of "republican motherhood," that is, the requirement of the mother to raise educated and independent citizens, led to the belief that the two spheres, although quite different, were equally important to society. Europeans, however, have been viewing husbands and wives as necessary and complementary, though not equal, partners for more than 1,000 years.

We know very little about real marriages and much more about what marriage experts thought. "There was a flood of publications from the 1530s which idealized marriage and catered for it with advice," notes John Hale. Fray Luis de León's *La perfecta casada* (The Perfect Wife) is a late sixteenth-century series of sermons on the duties of a wife. León began a lengthy tradition in marriage literature in his discussion of the "good woman." His good woman was a woman of God, one who revered her family, loved her children and adored her husband. She was faithful, honest, hardworking and much more. The good woman and the perfect wife, however, was not simply the servant of her husband. "There is nothing richer or happier than good woman," wrote León, "nor any thing worse or more disastrous for her than a marriage that never was." Although León, like most men of his time, viewed women as naturally subordinate to men, he saw marriage as a partnership in various ways. One of the purposes of marriage, he noted, was to create an estate to pass on to succeeding generations. A man by himself was capable of creating an estate but unable to conserve it. A woman by herself, on the other hand, was incapable of creating an estate but was good at conserving one. "We see then," writes León, "nature, in all that it provides, helps each of them to use their own condition to be of use to one another, to conserve together what they cannot conserve when they are apart." Each spouse has different duties and responsibilities but together they are critical to the success of the marriage and to the family.

Montaigne represented a good marriage as a friendship and partnership: "Tis a sweet society of life, full of constancy, trust, and an infinite number of useful and solid services and mutual obligations; which any woman who has a right taste – *Optato quam junxit lumine tæda* (United to a desired object) – would be loath to serve her husband in quality of a mistress." William Seeker's *A Wedding Ring* (1690), an Anglo-American marriage guide, described husbands and wives as two instruments making music, two streams in one current. A Congregationalist minister a few decades later wrote, "Of all the Orders which are unequal [husband and wife] do come nearest to an Equality, and in several respects they stand upon even ground."

Positive views of marriage in sermons, essays, guides and philosophy, of course, do not mean that European husbands and wives necessarily viewed their relationships in the early modern period as partnerships, with each spouse contributing in a very different but still very important way to the family affair. There were plenty of bad marriages and no scholar suggests that men or women generally believed that men were not superior to women in society and or that husbands should not govern the family. It seems clear, however, that the historiography of European women's history, gender history and family history over the past three decades provides a complex portrait that should put an end to the simplistic stereotype of one-dimensional patriarchy. Historians have found, notes Merry E. Wiesner, "Women were

Document 9.1
Concerning Marriage and of Parental Duty

Encyclopedia Britannica, 1768–71

When man arrives to a certain age, he becomes sensible of a peculiar sympathy and tenderness towards the other sex; the charms of beauty engage his attention, and call forth new and softer dispositions than he has yet felt. The many amiable qualities exhibited by a fair outside, or by the mild allurement of female manners, or which the prejudiced spectator without much reasoning supposes those to include, with several other circumstances, point his view and affection to a particular object, and of course contract that general rambling regard, which was lost and useless among the undistinguished crowd, into a peculiar and permanent attachment to one woman, which ordinarily terminates in the most important, venerable, and delightful connection in life.

The state of the brute creation is very different from that of human creatures. The former are cloathed and generally armed by their structure, easily find what is necessary to their subsistence, and soon attain their vigor and maturity; so that they need the care and aid of their parents but for a short while; and therefore we see that nature has assigned to them vagrant and transient amours. The connection being purely natural, and formed merely for propagating and rearing their offspring; no sooner is that end answered, than the connection dissolves of course. But the human race are of a more tender and defenseless constitution; their infancy and non-age continue longer; they advance slowly to strength of body, and maturity of reason; they need constant attention, and a long series of cares and labours to train them up to decency, virtue, and the various arts of life. Nature has, therefore, provided them with the most affectionate and anxious tutors, to aid their weakness, to supply their wants, and to accomplish them in those necessary arts; – even their own parents, on whom she has devolved this mighty charge, rendered agreeable by the most alluring and powerful of all ties, parental affection. But unless both concur in this grateful talk, and continue their joint labours, till they have reared up and planted out their young colony, it must become a prey to every rude invaders, and the purpose of nature in the original union of the human pair be defeated. Therefore our structure as well as condition is an evident indication, that the human sexes are destined for a more intimate, for a moral and lasting union. It appears likewise, that the principal end of marriage is not to propagate and nurse up an offspring, but to educate and form minds for the great duties and extensive destinations of life. Society must be supplied from this original nursery with useful members, and its fairest ornaments and supports.

The connections of neighborhood, acquaintance, and general intercourse, are too wide a field of action for many; and those of a public or community are so for more, and in which they either care not or know not how to exert themselves. Therefore nature, ever wise and benevolent, by implanting that strong sympathy which reigns between the individuals of each sex, and by urging them to form a particular moral connection, the spring of many domestic endearments, has measured out to each pair a particular sphere of action, proportioned to their views, and adapted to their respective capacities. Besides, by interesting them deeply in the concerns of their own little circle, she has connected them more closely with society, which is composed of particular families, and bound them down to their good behavior in that particular community to which they belong. This moral connection is marriage, and this sphere of action is a family....

In order therefore to fit the child for acting his part wisely and worthily, as a man, as a citizen, and a creature of God, both parents ought to combine their joint wisdom, authority, and power, and each apart to employ those talents which are the peculiar excellency and ornament of their respective sex. The father ought to lay out and superintend their education; the mother to execute and manage the detail of which she is capable. The former should direct the manly exertion of the intellectual and moral powers of the child. His imagination, and the manner of those exertions, are the peculiar province of the latter. The former should advise, protect, command, and by his experience, masculine vigour, and that superior authority which is commonly ascribed to his sex, brace and strengthen his pupil for active life, for gravity, integrity, and firmness in suffering. The businesses of the latter is to bend and soften her male pupil, by the charms of her conversation, and the softness and decency of her manners, for social life, for politeness of taste, and the elegant decorums of and enjoyments of humanity; and to improve and refine the tenderness of her female pupil, and form her to all those mile domestic virtues, which are the peculiar characteristics and ornaments of her sex.

From *Encyclopedia Britannica; or, a Dictionary of Arts and Sciences*, By a Society of Gentlemen in Scotland. In Three Volumes. Edinburgh: M.DCC.LXXI, Vol. III: 288–290.

as much a part of structures and events beyond the family as men were, and men just as much family member as women." It is not a great intellectual leap, then, to suggest that in early modern European societies gender roles were both hierarchical and complementary. Complementary gender relations in Europe, similar to what Susan Kellogg attributes to the Mexica, were frequently expressed in parallel structures in which "males and females were conceived of and played different yet parallel and equally necessary roles."

9.2 Africa's Filhos and filhas da terra

The early chroniclers of Portuguese exploration of West Africa commented on how African women affectionately welcomed Portuguese men. "The Joloff women," according to one Jesuit, "they are very good natured and extremely fond of the Portuguese nation, which is not the case of the [African] men." The myth of licentious African women, young and old, married and unmarried, emerged quite early in European-African contact and persisted for a long time. The Dutch trader Pieter de Marees in 1602 referred to the women of the Gold Coast: "From their early years they are very prone to Whoredom, inchastity etc.; for, having gone around for a time with their private parts uncovered." The Muslim ruler of Senegal presented Cadamosto, who sailed with the Portuguese in the mid-fifteenth century, with a 12-year-old girl. Almost two centuries later, the English trader Richard Jobson was offered a "certain young black woman" by an African merchant, which he refused. We know nothing about the emotional states of these comfort women presented to important visitors by their families, masters or rulers.

Later, more discerning European travelers to Atlantic Africa figured out that in many regions there was little taboo against unmarried girls having sexual relations with African boys or Europeans. Paul Erdmann Isert, an agent for the Baltic Guinea Company, noted in his discussion of the Gold Coast that husbands were jealous, adulterers (men and women) were punished and "as restricted as is the life of women, equally unrestricted is the freedom allowed to girls." Beginning with the Portuguese, then, Europeans factors, traders, officials and others had casual liaisons, informal and formal marriages with African women all along the Atlantic African coast. There were several reasons for this cross-cultural mating, but one of the fundamental ones was the extreme reluctance of Portuguese women to reside in Africa. As Marees stated, "Portuguese women do no thrive or flourish here: they are always miserable and ill or unwell, for they cannot get used to the nature of the Country as the Husbands do. That is why the Portuguese do not take many white Women here, since they do not thrive here."

Given the great diversity of societies in Atlantic Africa and the paucity of written sources, it is difficult to describe and generalize about gender relations in the regions Europeans had the most contact with in the centuries of the slave trade. William Smith in the mid-eighteenth century stated that one kingdom on the Gold Coast gave power and high office to a woman to govern. He noted further, "I don't know any other Kingdom in all Guinea where the Supremacy descends to either Sex." Some societies permitted kings and chiefs to take more than one wife, some permitted all men to do so, and others restricted men to one wife. Everywhere marriage was important and children were precious. Adultery was punished in many societies, for women offenders particularly and in many societies for men no less than women were. Men generally hunted, fished, raised livestock and were the masters of long-distance trade. Women not only focused on childrearing and housekeeping but they were the predominant agriculturalists in almost all African societies. Women also grew cotton, spun thread, wove and dyed cloth and made clothing. Women's work, it appears, was not only more labor intensive but had a lower status. Slavery existed throughout Atlantic Africa and women both owned slaves and were slaves. Large portions of the population of women in most societies were in some kind of servitude, pawnship, family service or slavery. African societies, however, valued women and female slaves: we have learned that they generally retained females in the Atlantic slave trade. Paul Lovejoy suggests that in the seventeenth and eighteenth centuries, women made up about thirty-six percent of the total of the Atlantic slave trade. Nevertheless, before 1800 at least four-fifths of the women that crossed the Atlantic to the Americas were African women. It is likely that coastal communities like Whydah during the slave trade had more women than men. Many of the women of the coast were domestic slaves but there were also wives and daughters, local market women, artisans, porters and even a few slave traders.

These same coastal communities, indeed most towns large and small, had small communities of prostitutes; most of whom were also slaves. European visitors and traders frequently mentioned the presence of African prostitutes who, it would appear, were in business to meet the local African demand primarily as well as to "service" European officials, traders and sailors. In many coastal regions prostitution appeared to be regulated as an essential safety valve to prevent rape and protect marriages. Bosman noted that on the Gold Coast if a European factor had a dispute with a prostitute and took her into custody, the local *Caboceros*, or chief men, would urgently do what they could to set her free. They would argue, Bosman wrote, "that during their Imprisonment, those Men who have no Wives, will be put to the utmost necessity for a Woman, and be prompted to run the danger of lying with Mens Wives." Smith, a few decades later, noted the *Caboceros* "provide publick Women in every Town, or the young Man may purchase in the Market a Woman-Slave, cohabit with her as long as he pleases, and then sell her again: So that in this Part of the World, in the Nature of the Thing itself there can be no Temptation to commit a Rape."

This gender frontier in the fifteenth and sixteenth centuries generally brought Portuguese outcasts known as *lançados* and *degredados* together with African women for mutual benefit. It is difficult from our incomplete records today to give evidence of the physical, emotional or simply business attachments that were formed between European men and African women. Certainly, lust drove many Europeans to acquire African wives. The first Portuguese on the coast were said to have taken African wives "often in platoons." We know that Portuguese on the coast found that African wives assisted them as interpreters and as collaborators in commercial exchanges. These women opened doors to individual Portuguese traders to African commercial family networks that were unavailable to outsiders. For Portuguese men, such relations provided a *cuñha*, a wedge, meaning an entrance into a new community. It was not uncommon for important African families to offer a daughter to a Portuguese trader to help them gain particular advantage in trade. Nevertheless, African girls and women also found prestige and power as the wives of Europeans.

From the Senegambia to Angola, and from the Cape Verde Islands to São Tomé, these Portuguese husbands and African wives produced plenty of mulatto progeny called *filhos da terra* (sons of the land) and *filhas* (daughters). Throughout Atlantic Africa, these Luso-Africans became skilled intermediaries for the Portuguese. They were agents, traders, soldiers and *tangomãos*, or slave-dealers. In Senegambia, this Luso-African population spoke Portuguese, worshiped as Christians (or clandestinely as Jews), gave their children Portuguese names, and built their houses and public buildings in the Portuguese style. Diogo Henriques de Sousa of Sierra Leone in the 1570s had built up a trading fleet of 22 vessels, which was inherited by his mulatto son Mateus Fernandes. Barbot in the late seventeenth century described the inhabitants of Cacho in the area of Sierra Leone. He wrote that they "are almost all Portuguese mulattoes [and] entirely supported by the trade they have with these regions. They all live in the Portuguese style and are dependents of the king of Portugal." One of the most famous Luso-Africans on the Senegambia coast was the widow Signorina Cattarina (perhaps Signora Catti), who served as the agent in the slave and salt trade for King Damel, one of the Wolof rulers. Barbot described her as "a black woman, a Portuguese Christian... a woman of high standing among them." At Gorée Island, Froger also met this 'Negro Lady,' "the Widow of a certain *Portuguese*, who had one of the chief Places in the Kingdom: This Lady had excellent Features, who endow'd with a generous Disposition, and of a very obliging Deportment; being of a middle-siz'd Stature, and clothed after the *Portuguese* Fashion." This prominent *filha da terra* was the very representation of European nobility and culture on the coast of Upper Guinea.

Without new reinforcements of Portuguese migrants, however, the Luso-African population and culture became increasingly Africanized. Their spoken Portuguese gradually developed into Crioulo. The first English account of the River Gambia, by Richard Jobson, based on his voyage of 1620–1, described a particular people up the river: "And these are, as they call themselves, *Portingales*, and some few of them seem the same; others of them are *Molatoes* [Mulattos], between black and white, but the most part as black, as the natural inhabitants." Jobson also noted that they reserve "the use of the *Portingall* tongue, and with a kind of an affectionate zeal, the name of Christians, taking it in a great disdain, be they never so black, to be called a *Negro*." About 100 years later, another English voyager, William Smith, described the Gambia: "This Place was first discovered and settled by the Portuguese, whose Progeny are still pretty numerous up in the Inland Country, and drive a very good Trade with the English. Though, to speak Truth, there is but little of the Portuguese to be found in them, beside the Language, being quite degenerated into Negroes, and having but very imperfect Ideas of Christianity. They think of themselves sufficiently qualified for the Title of *Boon Christians*, if they distinguish themselves from the *Pagans*, &c. by wearing a little Crucifix about their Necks." These Luso-African communities in Upper Guinea, which had blended into the local African population by all appearances, maintained their sense of difference, their identity as Portuguese, into the nineteenth century.

The Portuguese on the coast of Guinea, similarly, mated with African women and produced mulatto progeny. Marees, who arrived on the Gold Coast in the early seventeenth century, tells us that the Portuguese bought wives "yet they may consider them to be as much as their own Wives; yet they may separate from them as they please and in turn buy other women whenever it suits them. They maintain these Wives in grand style and keep them in splendid clothes, and they always dress more ostentatiously and stand out more than any other Indigenous women." Barbot noted nearly 70 years later that "the natives of Mina are all either blacks or mulattoes.

Of the latter, there are about two hundred families, and they are baptized and call themselves Portuguese." When he wrote his description in the late seventeenth century, the Portuguese Catholic Church had been gone from Elmina for several decades and the Dutch were in charge. "They all live in an abominable state of idolatry and profound ignorance. The mulattoes, however, are a little more enlightened, for they are half Christian, being born from the union of Portuguese men with indigenous black women." The Dutch called the Luso-Africans on the Gold Coast *Tapæyers*. Bosman noted that "they assume the name of Christians, but are as great Idolaters as the *Negroes* themselves." By the time the Dutch were ensconced in Elmina, most of the men were soldiers for the Castle, "clothed as we are; but the Women prink up themselves in a particular manner: Those of any Fashion wear a fine Shift, and over that a short Jacket or Silk or Stuff, without Sleeves, which reaches from under the Arms to their Hipps, fastened only at the Shoulders."

Most European traders, voyagers and others who visited Guinea and wrote about it expressed the most abhorrent opinions about the Portuguese mulattos. Bosman described the *tapæyers*: "This Bastard Strain is made up of a parcel of profligate Villains, neither true to the *Negroes* nor to us, nor indeed dare they trust one another...I can hardly give them a Character so bad as they deserve. I can only tell you whatever is in its own Nature worst in the Europeans and Negroes is united in them." Smith nearly quoted Bosman word for word in his discussion of the 'Bastard Brood."

When the Dutch and English moved into the Gold Coast in the seventeenth and eighteenth century, they were not shy about taking what was generally called "a temporary wife." These later European occupants of the coast took African wives for the same reasons as the Portuguese. John Atkins, describing the British Director-General of the Royal African Company on the Gold Coast, noted: "The General has taken a *Confa*, which by the *Negroes* is understood a temporary Wife, because she is not obliged to leave the Country, which is looked on as Slavery: She is a *Mulatto* Woman, begot by a Dutch Soldier at *Des Minas*, by whom he has four Children, of fair, flaxen Hair and Complexion. Her *Negro* Friends and Relations add Interest and Power to him, and he again can back their Injustice in the *Pawns* irregularly procured to the Garrison. He dotes on this Woman."Paul Erdmann Isert, the agent for the Baltic Guinea Company in the late eighteenth century, noted that Europeans on the Gold Coast seek a "bed-fellow" and marry daughters of the country, set up house, and pay part of their salary into the Mulatto treasury, which will support his wife and children after he leaves the coast. "The children who are born to such a pair are always christened and instructed in Christianity," writes Isert. "If the child is a boy he will be employed as a soldier in the king's service as soon as he is ten years old, and thus will enjoy a monthly wage of eight *thalers*. Poor girls and boys, as long as they are not otherwise supported, are given one *thaler* from the Mulatto treasury for their sustenance, a sum which is ample for them."

The Gold Coast, as J. T. Lever notes, "never developed a group of mulattos who by their large numbers and cultural cohesiveness could be said to have constituted a distinctive social class." There were, of course, influential mulatto mediators and brokers on the coast. Jan Nieser, whom we know about, was a Dutch mulatto born on the Gold Coast in the mid-eighteenth century who became one of the most important private traders at Elmina and later at Accra. Men like Nieser, however, were unusual. Lever estimates that by the end of the eighteenth century the number of mulattos living around the European castles and trading posts on the Gold Coast may have numbered up to 800. The great majority, however, were likely illiterate and served in humble posts as soldiers or housekeepers. One European observer on the coast noted: "Once the black woman has given [the European] some mulatto children, the white man loves them just as much as a man who cares for his lawfully wedded wife and his children in Europe."

On the Slave Coast, intermarriage between resident Europeans and African women occurred mainly in and around the permanent European forts and factories at Whydah. The Portuguese and Brazilians were still here in the eighteenth century taking local wives and fathering mulatto offspring. Often Portuguese, Brazilian, English and French men of means at Whydah married more than one African woman, fathered several children and sent them back to their European homelands for education. Captain John Adams, who visited the Slave Coast in the late eighteenth century, found that "many of the natives write English, an art first acquired by some of the traders' sons, who had visited England, and which they have had the sagacity to retain up the present period." These mulatto sons also entered the slave trade at Whydah in service either to their fathers or as independent traders. Eventually Euro-Africans had to compete with African ex-slaves who had returned from the Americas and Europe and set themselves up as leading traders and brokers.

São Tomé, an unpopulated island in before the arrival of the Portuguese, became one of the great generators of *filhos da terra* in the age of colonization. In 1493, the Donatory was given permission to carry *degredados*, criminals condemned to jail or exile, in order to create a European population on the island. In the aftermath of the Spanish conquest of the Moorish kingdom of Granada, the Donatory was also allowed to take around 2,000 Jewish children, baptize them and distribute them among the settlers of São Tomé. The crown, however, was not concerned about creating an entirely white population. In the 1490s, the crown imported enslaved African women for the specific purpose of providing a woman for every white colonist. For those men who accepted the gift, formal marriage was optional. This program of government-sponsored miscegenation, as well as the import of Jewish children, demonstrated the great interest in populating the island. A 1515 decree declared that all women slaves brought from Africa for the purpose of breeding, as well as their children, would be free.

The early Portuguese *degredados* in São Tomé did populate the island, largely with mulatto children. When the Jewish orphans reached maturity, noted an observer in 1506, "few of the women bore children of the white men; very many more bore children of the Negroes, while Negresses bore children of the white men." As for the rest of the population, a Portuguese pilot wrote, "It sometimes happens that, when the wife of a merchant dies, he takes a Negress, and this is an accepted practice, as the Negro population is both intelligent and rich, bringing up their daughters in our way of life, both as regards custom and dress. Children born of these unions are of a dark complexion and called Mulattoes, and they are mischievous and difficult to manage."

The "mischievous mulattos," the *filhos da terra*, during the course of the sixteenth century became the majority population. White Portuguese officials and *fazendeiros* constituted the elite of the island, but some sugar-growing and slave-trading mulattos became rich and powerful. The island, in fact, increasingly became mulatto and black in the sixteenth and seventeenth centuries as more and more white sugar growers immigrated to Brazil, and office holders were only temporary residents. Some 300 white residents left São Tomé for Brazil in the early 1640s when the Dutch (temporarily) seized the island. In some parts of the Portuguese empire, Mozambique for example, the crown sought to preserve the white settler population by securing ecclesiastical permission for the marriage of first cousins. This *prazo* system, as it was called, could not stop the disappearance of whites in Mozambique and was never tried in São Tomé. By the early seventeenth century, a small population of white officials governed a black and mulatto population that spoke Portuguese and were nominal Christians. The *filhos da terra* were the majority population of the island and many of these sons of the country were powerful and wealthy landowners, slave owners and slave traders. The term *filhos* by this time had lost its pejorative meaning. In a census of 1621, the island of São Tomé had a population of only 800 white residents out of a total free population of over 15,000. Most of these *moradores* (residents) were *filhos da terra*.

In the Portuguese colony of Angola, as elsewhere in Africa, the Donatory and the Crown found it difficult to populate the land with loyal white Portuguese settlers. Few Portuguese men other than outcasts made their way to Angola and almost no women came here. When the Dutch threat developed, governor-generals of Angola brought numerous soldiers to the colony and most of them were *degredados*. Among the legally degraded were a few white women exiled from Portugal and, more commonly, from Brazil, called *degredadas*. In 1595 twelve ladies from the Pious House of Converted Women in Lisbon (a shelter and reformatory for prostitutes), were sent to Luanda. "These were the first white women to be sent to that colony," wrote the new governor, "and all were to marry during my governorship (1595–1602)." Aside from a few former prostitutes dispatched now and then, called *convertidas*, the Crown also tried to populate and civilize their empire with orphan girls but not just any orphan girls. These *órfãs do rei*, or orphan girls of the king, mostly from the Recolhimento do Castelo in Lisbon (Shelter of the Castle) were special because the crown not only sent these royal orphans overseas but provided them with a dowry of a minor government post. Angola, however, never received many *degredadas*, *convertidas* and *órfãs*.

As a result, Portuguese traders and soldiers married or became intimate with local African women ("married by local custom") and in later decades married Luso-African women. Often there were commercial marriages between Portuguese and African or Luso-African partners in the slave trade. By the latter seventeenth century and the eighteenth century such 'commercial marriages' became more common between Brazilian merchants and

Table 9.1. *The Portuguese Atlantic: Populations in the seventeenth century*

Colonies/Posts	Populations
Brazil (1650)	50,000 Whites
Brazil (1700)	100,000 Whites, one-third of total assimilated population
São Jorge da Mina (1621)	300 Resident Portuguese
	200 Soldiers
São Tomé (1621)	800 Whites
	2,000 *Mestiços*
São Tomé (1650)	400 Families of Portuguese Descent
Angola (1660s)	326 White Households
Cape Verde (1664)	1,240 Soldiers
	(55) White

Sources: Timothy J. Coates, *Convicts and Orphans: Forced and State-Sponsored Colonizers in the Portuguese Empire, 1550–1755* (2001), pp. 179–81; and A. J. R. Russell-Wood, *The Portuguese Empire, 1415–1808: A World on the Move* (1992, 1998), Chapter III, 'Flux and Reflux of People,' pp. 58–122. For purposes of comparison, Portugal's important Asian possessions: were Goa (1635) with 800 'white' families, Colombo (1600), more than 2,500 families of Portuguese descent, and Macau (1640) with 600 Portuguese families and 500 native–born Portuguese families and soldiers.

their Luso-African partners in Angola. As Joseph Miller has found, these business alliances provided African connections, local prestige and working capital to the Portuguese trader, and metropolitan credit, political associations and Atlantic commercial contacts for the Luso-African wife and her extensive slave-trading clan on the coast and in the interior.

The chronicler of the Angolan conquest, António de Oliveira Cadornega, wrote in the early 1680s, "When this conquest began, all the most important conquerors, with the exception of a few who brought their families, accommodated themselves with mulatas, daughters of respectable settlers and conquerors by their female slaves or free concubines."

In the early seventeenth century, a Capuchin friar visited both Luanda (Angola) and Salvador (the capital of Brazil). Although Luanda was the older settlement it had a population of only 4,000 *brancos* (white Portuguese) compared to Salvador's 20,000. In Salvador there was one *branco* for every three *negroes*. In Luanda the ratio was one in ten. Luanda, one of the very few European cities in sub-Saharan Africa, was becoming an Africanized city for want of Portuguese women. A 1776 census of the populations of Angola and Benguela showed a population of 1,700 whites, only 637 mulattos, 50,000 slaves and nearly 500,000 free Africans (see Table 9.1). Over several centuries, *filhos da terra* and many more free Africans create an Africanized Lusitanian culture. They adopted Portuguese names but mixed them with African surnames and titles. Angolan Portuguese was Africanized with the addition of many Kimbundu words while at the same time Portuguese words filtered into Kimbundu. The Catholic heritage of the Portuguese colonists and their Luso-African descendants "underwent a great deal of Africanization during the period." In the 1790s, Silva Corrêa reported that African practices coexisted in the very heart of church rituals: "He noted that most of the population believed equally in 'Jesus Christ and the Moêne-Bengo or other feiticeiros' and observed further that whites had fallen victim to human vice and 'tolerate the primitive rites.'"

A paucity of Portuguese men and women in Portuguese Africa led the crown to programs of forced and sponsored colonization but these efforts went against long-term individual interest and the microbial environment of West and Central Africa. The crown sent *degredados* because Africa almost never attracted free immigration and settlers. Many Portuguese traders and officials in Atlantic Africa viewed their posts as temporary opportunities to make a small fortune and return to Portugal as soon as possible. All Portuguese in Africa felt themselves in a race with the Grim Reaper. Too many were struck down by malaria, yellow fever, sleeping sickness, yaws, bilharzia and smallpox. Building up a European and Europeanized population in Atlantic Africa was essentially impossible so Africa remained African.

The royal policy of sending Portuguese male convicts and female orphans, obviously, did not generate enough colonists. The crown's backup plan to offset the shortage of Portuguese women by encouraging marriages or liaisons with native women did produce a Luso-African population that identified itself as Christian and Portuguese. A. J. R. Russell-Wood notes that sexual relations did not translate into cultural penetration. "In the case of Africa as a whole, but especially markedly in East Africa, the Portuguese had remarkably little cultural impact either in terms of mores or of religion. Indeed, the reverse was more likely to be the case with the Africanization of Portuguese migrants and colonists and their adoption of African customs." In Central Africa, according to Linda Heywood, "the Portuguese, a European people with a western culture, encountered no difficulties in adapting to a dominant African cultural environment."

9.3 Daughters of the Conquistadors

Columbus and those who followed him described native women as both beautiful and hideous. One early chronicler noted that there were some Spaniards who would not marry Indian women "because of the unfitness and ugliness of those women." There were, however, more reports of beauty. Peter Martyr mentioned the ceremonial meeting of Bartolomé Colón and Chief Bechechio Anacauchea in Hispaniola. As the Spaniards approached the royal residence, 30 women met them with dancing, singing and cries. "For the virgins, hair spilling over their shoulders, but their foreheads fastened with a band, conceal no part of their body. They claim that their face, chest, hands and other parts are almost white and very beautiful." We do not know what most men thought but we do know that many if not most Spaniards in the Caribbean during the first decades of colonization had sexual relations with native women. Columbus noted, during his first voyage, that Indian men "make their women hide from the Christians out of jealousy." An incident that occurred in 1493 with Michele da Cuneo might explain the kind of pattern that existed in the early Spanish Indies:

> I laid my hands on a gorgeous Cannibal woman whom the lord admiral granted me; when I had her in my quarters, naked, as is their custom, I felt a craving to sport with her. When I tried to satisfy my craving,

she, wanted none of it, gave me such a treatment with her nails that at that point I wished I had never started. At this, to tell you how it all ended, I got hold of a rope and thrashed her so thoroughly that she raised unheard-of cries that you would never believe. Finally we were of such accord that, in the act, I can tell you, she seemed to have been trained in a school of harlots.

Spanish chronicles often refer to the voluntary submission of native women to Spanish men. Cieza de León reported in the kingdom of Quito that the native girls "were beautiful and not a little lascivious, and fond of the Spaniards." During the Hernando de Soto expedition in North America, the gift of native women was intended to show hospitality and long-term fidelity. In 1541, the caciques of the Cacqui and Pacaha offered de Soto their daughters as wives, noting of one of the caciques: "his greatest desire was to unite his blood with that of so great a lord as he was." We also know about widespread rape of native women from opponents of Spanish colonization (like Bartolomé de las Casas), native accounts of conquest, and occasionally participants themselves. The brutal campaign of Hernando de Soto captured women because, noted Rodrigo Rangel, a member of the expedition, "[the Spaniards] wanted the women in order to make use of them and for their lewdness and lust and that they baptized them more for their carnal inter-course than to instruct them in the faith." The Florentine Codex, a Nahua account of the conquest of Mexico, described the scene following the Mexica defeat: "And [the Spaniards] took, picked out the beautiful women, with yel-low bodies." Theodor de Bry in his *Indiae Occidentalis Historiae* presented an engraving of "The Spaniards Satisfy Their Sensul Lust With the Women they Find." The picture shows Pizarro's men, on the day after the capture of Atahualpa, attacking Indian women in the baths near Cajamarca. Rape of Indian women was the result of war and a conquest mentality, the breakdown of normal morality, and an invader's compulsion for dominance in all ways.

Religious authorities complained about the laxity of morality in the Spanish Indies. "I have often seen encomenderos and caciques," noted a Dominican in Peru, "remove the Indians's sons and daughters. And it is certain that the removal of Indian girls to the house of the encomenderos or of any Spaniard is tantamount to taking them to a house of public prostitution." Bishop Juan de Zumárraga of New Spain, in a similar report, wrote Carlos V in 1529 that "many of those who have Indians have taken from the chiefs of their villages their daughters, sisters, nieces and wives under the pretext of taking them to their homes as servants but in reality for concubines." The crown, like the church, was dismayed by reports of sexual abuse in America. In 1541, the king stated that he had been informed that Spaniards "have a large number of Indian women in their houses in order to carry out their evil wants with them." To end this situation he ordered, "no Spaniard may have in his house a suspicious or pregnant Indian or Indian mother."

Spaniards in the Caribbean and the mainland took women but they were also given women. Native rulers gave the Spaniards gifts of women, appar-ently an established custom, in order to form ties of friendship and alliance. In some cases, Indians also believed, the sons of their daughters and the

Figure 9.1. The Attack on the Baths of the Inka Atahualpa. From Theodor de Bry, *Americae pars sexta* (Frankfurt, 1596). Courtesy of the William L. Clements Library at the University of Michigan.

Spaniards would become great warriors. The Spanish reported this custom throughout the mainland as well as in the islands. When Cortés made peace with the Tlaxcalans in 1519, their leaders gave the Spaniards eight daughters of nobles and "three hundred beautiful and well-adorned slave girls." The captains of the expedition took the highborn women and the foot-soldiers shared the slaves. Earlier in his expedition, Cortés had been given several women from a native chief who wanted peace with the Spanish. One of these was a noble woman named Malinali. She became Cortés' translator and, in time, principal advisor as well as consort. Doña Marina, as the Spanish called her, accompanied Cortés during the conquest and gave him a son, Martín. After the conquest, Cortés married her to one of his soldiers.

What kind of gender frontier was opened when the Spanish entered the empires of the Mexica and the Inka? As we have seen, a number of recent historians argue that in the conquest of Mexico and Peru was a gender collision that annihilated the female political sphere and disenfranchised all Mexica and Inka women of their traditional rights to participate in government. This dramatic representation, we should point out, is not the final word. The impact of the Spanish Conquest on Mesoamerican gender relations, writes

Alan Knight in his history of Mexico, "appears to be a matter of considerable disagreement, but disagreement based, it seems, on a scarcity rather than a surfeit, of hard data and mature debate." There is research that tells us that the Mexica and Inka worlds were men's worlds. The Mexica glorified a cult of male dominance. In the Andean and Inka worlds, maleness was identified with the concept of *hanan*, the cosmological position of "upper" that stood for superiority, and femaleness was identified with *hurin*, the position of "lower" representing inferiority. The fact that the Inka required defeated warriors to parade through the streets of Cuzco in women's dress suggests that femininity was linked to the idea of inferiority and submission. After the conquest, Felipe Guaman Poma, the *mestizo* historian and moral critic, presented the dominant Spaniard in the *hanan* position and put Andean males and females both in the *hurin* position to indicate their new position of inferiority. As Susan Migden Socolow notes, "Men clearly held a superior position in the gender hierarchy. Indeed, although rarely defined in terms of patriarchy, women in pre-Columbian America were, like those in Spain, in a clearly secondary position in terms of social, economic, and political power." As for the later period, James Lockhart writes, "in both Spanish and indigenous cultures during the postconquest centuries, women were subordinated in some ways, able to assert themselves in others."

During the age of the conquests both Spanish and native leaders conducted sexual politics by seeking marriage or simply pairing between leading conquerors and high-status native women. This was a useful policy in its own right but it succeeded all the more in the absence of Spanish women in these early decades. The great insufficiency of Spanish women gave greater value to elite native women, and even to many non-elite women, than normally would have been the case. Spaniards respected nobility, even native nobility, and often sought to better themselves through marriages with native women of noble birth and status. For a time, in fact, this was royal policy: in 1503, Queen Isabella ordered the governor of Hispaniola to arrange marriages between Spaniards and Indians, and in 1516 Cardinal Francisco Jiménez de Cisneros, the archbishop of Toledo, encouraged marriage with the daughters of caciques. It was expected that through the example of monogamous Christian marriage, the Indian tradition of polygamy would disappear. Marriage was also viewed as a tool of assimilation and overlordship. Cortés, who was already married to a Spanish wife, had relationships with two of Moteucçoma's daughters and eventually married them to well-born Spaniards. One of these daughters, Tecuichpotzin, whom the Spanish named Doña Isabel Moctezoma, married Alonso de Grado and, as the wife of a prominent conquistador, she became a proper model of new Indian womanhood after the conquest: Hispanicized and Christian.

Indians, likewise, viewed the paring of a Native woman and a Spaniard as the beginning of an important alliance. Garcilaso de la Vega noted that "in those early times when Indians saw an Indian woman giving birth to the child of a Spaniard, all her relatives joined together to respect and serve the Spaniard as an idol because he had become their kin." Garcilaso himself, also known as El Inca Garcilaso, was the *mestizo* son was Sebastián Garcilaso de la Vega, a captain in Pizarro's army, and Chimpu Oqllo, granddaughter of the Inka Tupaq Yupanqhi, which was a profitable pairing for both the conquistador and the princess. Indigenous women and their families not only obtained a political alliance or the blood of a warrior race in marriage, but also access to the new dominant society through kinship, assimilation, law and politics.

Many daughters of indigenous rulers in central Mexico married high-ranking Spaniards. Doña Leonor de Montezuma married the conquistador Cristóbal de Valderrama. The daughter of the king of Texcoco, Doña Ana, married Juan de Cuéllar. The daughter of the ruler of Teotihuacán married Juan Grande. These women usually brought lands and estates, and sometimes an *encomienda*, into the marriage as dowries. In 1585, the rulers of Tlaxcala reported, "in that province many Spaniards have married women who were the widows of caciques and other rich natives who have left property, houses and other estates." The conquerors of Peru selected Inka princesses as mistresses and wives. All of the daughters of Huaya Capac, the Inka who died on the eve of the conquest, married Spaniards. Francisco Pizarro, a bachelor, lived with Huayna Capac's 15-year-old daughter Quispe Cusi who bore him a daughter and a son. She was later married to one of his soldiers, Francisco de Ampuero, and their descendants became one of the leading families of colonial and modern Peru. Another daughter of Huayna Capac, Marca-Chimbo, became the mistress of Diego de Almagro. The *mestizo* historian Garcilaso de la Vega told a story of one of the princesses who refused to marry Diego Hernández, saying that it was unjust for a daughter of an Inka to marry a common tailor. Gonzalo Pizarro, another brother, developed a liking for Cura Ocllo, the wife of the Inka Manco. Manco attempted to keep his wife out of the hands of Pizarro but failed. He later wrote unhappily, "Gonzalo Pizarro took my wife and still has her."

The native elite survived conquest and colonization as families in Indian towns and Spanish cities. Many fewer elite native men had multiple wives after the conquests than before. It appears Christian marriage had become significant, at least in central Mexico, during the sixteenth century, and with it such practices as free choice of a marriage partner, mutual consent and inheritance rules. Late sixteenth-century Nahuatl testaments show that central Mexican women owned property in their own right and bequeathed it, as they preferred. The elite Nahua family in the colonial era, it appears, was a joint economic venture.

Many Spaniards married non-elite Indian women. There was a tendency among Spaniards to seek their social level when seeking Indian women. Spanish-Indian marriages, at first, were seen as a way to bridge the cultural divide between the two peoples in the Caribbean. The crown ordered Nicolás de Ovando in 1504 to "make sure that some Christian men marry some Indian women and Christian women marry Indian men, so that they will communicate with and teach each other." The Hispaniola census of 1514 showed that 54 of 146 married men had Indian wives. Most of the 60 founders of Vera Paz, Guatemala, according to Bartolomé de las Casas, were married to natives. About 25 percent of the founders of Puebla de Los Angeles, New Spain, were married to native women. Marriage to Indian women was more common for men of lower social rank than high-ranking men. Rodrigo de Albuquerque's sixteenth-century report on *encomiendas* found that out of 692 *encomenderos*, clearly the colonial elite, only 63 had Indian wives. Andrés García, a petty trader in Mexico City in the 1570s, informed his nephew, "I am married here to a woman very much to my taste. And though there in Spain it might shock you that I have married an Indian woman, here one loses nothing of his honor, because the Indians are a nation held in much esteem."

Conquest and colonization, along with Christianization, forced labor and tribute, put a much heavier burden on common women more than noble indigenous women. In Central America, village *Indias* were enslaved, forced to work in *encomiendas*, forced to weave cloth as tribute, and, of course, were subject to molestation and rape by Spanish settlers, friars, officials and *encomenderos*. Indian women often faced a double economic burden: working to sustain their own household as well as to pay tribute to native lords, local *encomenderos* or crown officials. "The tribute that the Indian men are supposed to pay," commented a sixteenth-century observer in the Audiencia of Quito, "is paid by the women through their weaving." In 1575, the viceroy of Peru tried to reduce the burden on Indian women with an order that exempted women married to tributary Indians from paying tribute. He also exempted all Indian women from labor tribute in the mines. The weight of tribute remained, nevertheless. With their husbands away in the mines, the burden still fell on the women. "The [Indian women] are overwhelmed by tribute demands and personal labor service," wrote Felipe Guaman Poma de Ayala, the great Peruvian chronicler of the early seventeenth century. The great burden on village Indian women in the sixteenth and seventeenth century led to a migration of *Indias* to Spanish towns and cities where they could escape community tribute demands and find greater freedom and economic opportunity. In the cities, Indian women became servants, cooks, nursemaids, midwives, sold food in the streets and bought produce from the country and sold it in the market. They were poor then and, remarkably, we see them still today in the modern cities of Latin America doing very much the same things.

Most Spaniards in the Americas wanted Spanish women as wives and partners and their scarcity during the first decades of settlement made such matches extremely desirable. A few women had accompanied some of the early expeditions of exploration and conquest, and there were a few famous accounts of the exploits of these *conquistadoras*. During the first century of immigration from Spain to the New World, most migrants were single young men seeking their fortunes. Husbands and fathers traveled to the Indies as officials, soldiers, merchants or settlers on their own in the expectation of first creating a farm business or some kind of livelihood before sending for the family. In the early decades of settlement, some wives joined their husbands in the New World, as a few daughters, sisters and nieces united with their family members. Most of the female travelers were young single women, many of them servants and most, no doubt, seeking a successful husband. In order to bring order to chaos, the crown organized a few shipments of unmarried women. Until the 1540s, according to official emigration records, however, there were only one or two women who emigrated for every twenty

Table 9.2. *Emigration of Spanish women to the Americas, 1509–1600*

Period	Total women	Total emigration	Percentage women
1509–19	308	5,481	5.6
1520–39	845	13,362	6.3
1540–59	1,480	9,044	16.4
1560–79	5,013	17,580	28.5
1580–1600	2,472	9,508	26.0
1595–98	675	1,909	35.3

Source: Peter Boyd-Bowman, "Patterns of Spanish Emigration to the Indies to 1600," *Hispanic American Historical Review*, 56:4 (November, 1976), pp. 596–601; Boyd-Bowman, "Spanish Emigrants to the Indies, 1595–98: A Profile," in Fredi Chiappelli, ed, *First Images of America: The Impact of the New World on the Old* (1976), II, pp. 723–35; and Nicolás Sánchez-Albornoz, "The population of colonial Spanish America," in Leslie Bethell, ed. *The Cambridge History of Latin America. Volume II: Colonial Latin America* (1984), pp. 3–35. As Boyd-Bowman, Sánchez-Albornoz and other historians have noted, total Spanish migration to Spanish America in the sixteenth century is estimated in the range of 200,000 to 250,000. An additional 195,000 Spaniards immigrated to the Americas in the first half of the seventeenth century. As Boyd-Bowman writes, the extant passenger lists are incomplete and cannot tell us very much about the volume of Spanish emigration to the New World. The detailed records of the lists, however, do help us understand something about the nature and pattern of the immigration stream. Boyd-Bowman notes that the total list for the period 1595–8 is 2,304 individuals. He studied a core of 1,909 emigrants in more detail because more information was available. One of the things we know about this group is that it included 238 'family units,' that is, married couples, about three quarters of whom who took their children with them to the New World and about one quarter who traveled without children.

men. In Spanish Peru in the 1540s, there was only one Spanish woman for every seven or eight Spanish men.

By the mid-sixteenth century, one of the great migrations of the early modern world was in motion. Spaniards, or to be more specific, Andalusians and Extremadurans of New and Old Castile, were leaving their European homes in such numbers that only the English in the seventeenth century would compare. By mid-century, Spanish families were immigrating to Spanish America. By the 1560s and 1570s, women constituted nearly 30 percent of all transatlantic migrants. Over the long term, this percentage was not maintained. It has been estimated that 2,900 women on average migrated to Spanish America per decade between 1500 and 1700. If this figure is accurate, then approximately 58,000 women, out of a total population of 500,000 emigrants, began the cultural re-creation of Spain in America (see Table 9.2).

Marriage *in* the Indies and Hispanization *of* the Indies was encouraged by numerous official policies. For a Spanish emigrant to leave his wife at home, he needed to obtain her written consent and to promise authorities he would return home or take his wife to America in three years. In 1528, the crown ordered that married settlers be favored in the filling of municipal offices. In 1538 and 1539 the crown ordered that new *encomiendas* be awarded solely to married men and that only married men could keep existing *encomiendas*. In 1554, the crown decreed that married men could be in America for no more than two years before sending for their wives, otherwise they were required to return to Spain. Crown policy, however, was often in agreement with personal desires. "Without my wife," wrote a settler in Guatemala, "I am the saddest man in the world." Alonso Ortiz left his family in Spain to find a better life in Mexico City, and he prospered. After a few years, he wrote his wife in 1574 telling her that he and his partner in the tannery business could afford to bring her and their children to Mexico. "So make the decision and come quickly in this very fleet, and let no one hinder you from taking the voyage." Alonso Herojo of New Granada wrote in 1583 that "Everybody says there is not a man who would not bring his wife and children to this country so as to take them away from the want and poverty in Spain, because a single bad day here is worth more than any good day in Castile."

Whether it was policy, or more likely a result of love, loneliness or self-interest, women, wives and families immigrated to the New World. Sometime in the late sixteenth or early seventeenth century, these female migrants, along with the increasing number of American-born daughters of the conquistadors, provided a sufficient number of wives in New Spain and Peru to produce natural population growth. The two great institutions of Spanish America, as William Lytle Schurz saw it, was the family and the church. Women nurtured and managed Spanish American family and they "remained the conservative and stabilizing force in colonial society." Without Spanish women, writes the historian of imperial Spain, Henry Kamen, ""the creation of a productive and organized colonial empire was literally impossible."

The early Spanish American family, of course, was endlessly variable depending upon origin, location, status, wealth and more. It has been calculated that on average the typical Spanish family in the colonial period had six members. If we look at these groups as familial households, what we find is mostly parents and children, but there are a few extended families that included grandparents, aunts and uncles, cousins, godparents and servants. Spanish American households were economic enterprises for the well-to-do, the up-and-coming and the impecunious. Elite women brought a dowry into the marriage for the purpose of attracting a high-status husband as well as enhancing the economic well-being of the family. A dowry, which could be cash, property or material possessions, was entrusted to the husband but remained the property of the wife through the life of the marriage. Doña Lucia Pastene's dowry – *carta dotal* – for her marriage in Lima in 1635 with Don Bernardo de Amara Yturigayen provided, among other things, a cash payment of 7,000 pesos, and an estate with 1,200 head of cattle, 1,000 goats, 6,500 sheep, 12 pair of oxen, 27 slaves, silverware, jewelry and an *encomienda*. It was a kind of insurance policy in case the match failed and the woman was abandoned or widowed. As a result of this custom, Spaniards and Spanish Americans practiced a kind of bilateral inheritance: children inherited the property of the father and the property of the mother and whatever property both parents accumulated together.

Most wives were active in family enterprises. In the 1570s, Isabel Maldonaldo complemented the work of her husband, Antonio Sánchez Navarro, a muleteer-storekeeper. One of their neighbors in Orizaba recalled, "All of their possessions were in common. She used to sell wine and other goods and he used to go with his mules to look for wheat and other things to sell and to stock in their house." When they moved to Vera Cruz, another friend described their partnership. "[Isabel] runs the inn and Antonio goes with his ... mules and brings flour, biscuits, and supplies for the inn and other times he remains at home." The fifth Condesa del Valle de Orizaba, one of the wealthiest women of the wealthiest families of colonial Mexico, managed her own estates and "did not hesitate to correct her husband's business errors in public or to remind the authorities that she, and not he, was in charge." Wives helped with their husbands' businesses by producing and selling goods made in the home when the husband was earning a wage or by supervising the house and estate while the husband was attending the viceregal court. "Marriage," writes Colin MacLachlan and Jaime Rodriguez O., "was more a partnership than is commonly understood. The man and the woman represented their respective families in a new socioeconomic alliance. Unions were based on mutual interests and advantages; women brought with them not only their family names and influence, but also their dowries, which provided them with economic independence."

One of the most important elements in colonization, if not the most important element, was the production of legitimate sons and daughters who were raised in Spanish homes and inculcated with Christian morality and Spanish values. Spanish girls were properly socialized in the home by their mother, and often educated by a tutor, in preparation for marriage with men of their own class. In New Spain, some attended small schools called *escuelas de amigas*, or spent some time in a convent. Marriage was seen, rightly, as the essential foundation of colonization. Spanish fathers in the early years often sent their sons to Spain for their education; they also taught them what their mothers often could not, such skills as writing and making accounts, riding, handling arms, and learning a trade or profession. The continued immigration of Spaniards, and the milieu of the Spanish town and city, further reinforced Spanish culture in each new generation despite the vastly different social circumstances that existed in Spanish America.

The mission of creole women – the daughters of the conquistadors – was to be faithful and obedient wives and bear, primarily, legitimate male heirs in order to perpetuate the lineage. Despite the vital importance of Spanish women to the production of Spanish culture in the New World, sons were preferred to daughters. As Cortés put it, "If I did not have another [legitimate son] and God disposed of the one I have without leaving an heir, what would be the good of what I have acquired since when daughters inherit memory is lost" (see Fig. 9.2).

For the elite, legal marriage was an essential component of social life. Families often arranged the marriage of their children in order to enhance the prestige of the family and to build familial networks of wealth and power. Marriage protected the honor of the husband and his family by ensuring that his fiancée was "pure" (a virgin) and that the mother of his children was faithful and of "pure blood." While honor was a male attribute, shame (*verguenza*) was an essential component of being female. A woman without

Figure 9.2. A Spanish-American Lady, Accompanied by Two African Servants, Going to Church. From the engraving by B. Cole in *A true and particular relation of the dreadful earthquakes which happen'd at Lima* (London, 1748). Courtesy of the John Carter Brown Library at Brown University.

shame (*sinverguenza*) dishonored a father or husband and his family through some act or state of impurity. To avoid a shameless life, then, elite women had to "take a state," that is either marry an honorable man or enter a convent and become, symbolically, a bride of Christ. In both "states," the woman was enclosed and protected from sin and her inherent weaknesses. In marriage, the woman was enclosed in the home whereas as a nun the woman was cloistered within the walls of a convent. In all cases, the family lineage was protected.

Entry into a convent was reserved for the daughters of the elite. Most religious orders required a substantial dowry and sometimes an additional regular payment of support. The first convent of Mexico opened its doors to the descendants of Moteucçoma and in the eighteenth century a few convents in New Spain were founded for "pure blooded" Indian women. Most convents, however, only took elite creole daughters or, wealthy *mestizas* from the best families. There were about 60 convents founded in Mexico from 1550 to 1811. The conquerors of Peru demanded that the option of taking the veil be available to their *mestiza* daughters. As a result, the town council of Cuzco in 1551 became the patron of the city's first convent, Santa Clara. Lima's thirteen convents, at one time, were home to one out of five women in the colonial capital. By the end of the colonial era, only about 6,000 religious women were present in Spanish America and Brazil. These women constituted the elite of the elite and convents became symbols of urban status.

Indian women, as Asunción Lavrin writes, "were a crucial factor in the conquest of America. Liaisons with Indian women provided the first generations of *conquistadores* with allies, interpreters, personal care, and sexual satisfaction." During and after the conquest, "women were pawned by their families in an effort to win friendship and protection of the Spaniards.... Women in Spanish households became socio-cultural mediators between both societies." Indian women, however critical they were to the foundation of Spanish America, were not its procreators. That responsibility fell to Spanish and Spanish American women. They made America Spanish in a way that Portuguese men could never make their African possessions even partly Portuguese. Spanish and creole women "made their most basic contribution to the development of local Hispanic society by educating those around them in the ways of the homeland." Their influence extended, most of all to the second and third generations, the daughters and sons of the conquistadors. "Even in the first generation," writes James Lockhart, "Hispanic society in Peru had enough Spanish women to preclude the simple loss of any important cultural elements."

Over several generations, of course, Spanish American society became increasingly more complicated. The Spanish element was one part among a vastly larger ethnic-racial population that included Hispanicized Indians, culturally unassimilated Indians, African slaves, free blacks, *mestizos*, mulattos, and some non-Spanish Europeans. By the end of the colonial period, the white progeny of the conquistadors and the colonists constituted about one-fifth of the total population of Spanish America. The cultural inheritance and identity of Castile and Spain in the Americas, however, was disseminated beyond these nearly three million men and women. Black slaves and freemen, *mestizos* and mulattos, and Indians, in the millions, also spoke Castilian, worshiped Christ and the Saints, donated wealth to the church in their last wills and testaments, gave their children Christian and Iberian names, lived in municipalities, participated in the legal system and identified with the Spanish crown. Spain in America as it developed and evolved was not a faithful reproduction of European Spain. From the beginning these Spanish American societies, like most American societies that would follow, were less rigid and hierarchal and more flexible and opportunistic. They were ethnically and culturally hybrid societies. In New Spain, for example, Spanish women adopted the pre-conquest Mexica beverage of *cacahuatl* (chocolate), served with sugar now instead of chili. The English Dominican traveler Thomas Gage discovered that in the southern Mexican town of Ciudad Real in the 1620s, Spanish women were so addicted to chocolate that they required "their maids to bring to them to church in the middle of Mass or sermon a cup of chocolate." Chocolate, which had been an elite beverage in the time of Moteucçoma, spread through the households of Spanish Mexico. Every housewife had *jícaras*, lacquerware cups, and copper pots specifically for making and drinking chocolate. Through their recipes, among other ways, the daughters of the conquistadors were Americanizing, as well as Hispanicizing, the New World.

9.4 *Brazil's* Housefuls

Portuguese Brazil has long thought of itself as a racial melting pot. Gilberto Freyre in his classic essay *The Masters and the Slaves* (1933) wrote about a tropical civilization created through European sexual relations with Indian and African women. Freyre called this unique history "a voluptuous contact with the exotic woman." Brazilian society and culture, more than any other colonial New World culture, he argued, was the product of miscegenation, the mixing of the races. To most colonial Portuguese officials, as well as to many scholars and intellectuals at the beginning of the twentieth century, European civilization in Brazil had been cursed and crippled by miscegenation, a corruption of racial purity and cultural integrity. Freyre, however, turned this racist pessimism and stereotyping of Brazil completely around. Freyre accepted the long-standing portrait of Portuguese women as sexually incompetent and woeful, and cloistered in the plantation Casa Grande or Big House, rarely leaving it, it was said, except to be baptized, married and buried. Miscegenation, for Freyre, did not just create Brazil; it was the formula that brought the strengths of Africa and Native America together with the daring of a few thousand Portuguese males to create a (more or less) successful Brazilian civilization in the tropics: "The result took its ideal form in the seventeenth-century slave plantation and its offspring, the mulatto."

Giberto Freyre's sexualized model of the formation of colonial Brazil was an improvement over the racist interpretations of the past. One of the great themes in the correspondence of royal officials in Brazil to the crown during the colonial era was *degeneracy* associated with the Brazilian *filhos da terra*. Portuguese men almost universally had sexual relations with Indian and African women, through rape and donation, made them mistresses, concubines, and wives, and produced *mestizo* and mulatto children in abundance. This was miscegenation on a vast scale but did it produce a culture of miscegenation that from the beginning was more Brazilian than Portuguese?

Perhaps even more than Spanish America, the formation of Brazil in the early and mid-sixteenth century depended upon the partnerships of Portuguese men and native women. The first Portuguese colonizers, for the most part, were outcasts and castaways, *degredados*, shipwrecked sailors, crypto-Jews and other exiles. These throwaways, men like João Ramalho and Diogo Alvares, went native, married Indian women, fathered numbers of children and became influential men in their new native communities. As a result, they became important intermediaries between Indians and the first Portuguese colonists. Ramalho, son-in-law of Tibiriçá, chief of the Guaianá, helped protect the new colony of São Vicente in southern Brazil in the 1530s. Alvares, who in his new Indian life became known as Caramurú, assisted Tomé de Sousa in 1549 in the settlement of the new colony and colonial capital of Salvador Bahia.

As in Spanish America, Portuguese men in Brazil both took women against their will and were given women by native chiefs and rulers. Most Portuguese chroniclers preferred to see Indian women as naturally lascivious.

The Tupinambás, according to Gabriel Soares de Sousa, "are so lustful that there is no sin of lust which they do not commit." In his *Dialogues of the Great Things of Brazil* (1618), Ambrósio Fernandes Brandão wrote that native chiefs provided the Portuguese guest "a damsel or his own daughter as a wife, for him to have her as such as long as he is there. There can be no more barbarous custom than that." Rape by the Portuguese, of course, was ubiquitous. The behavior of the governor of Cearéa in 1626, according to a Franciscan critic, was outrageous: "He always keeps various Indian women as concubines, seizing the wives of some Indians and daughters of others, and threatening them all if they spoke about it or failed to bring them. A mission village that is beside his sugar mill seems more like a harem for him and his men than an aldeia of Christians!" Father Antonio Vieira, in a sermon on mercy, wrote that the Portuguese plantation owner and royal functionary were equally adept at the "conjugation of the verb *rapio*."

However it happened, with force, through gift or by consent, Portuguese men throughout the colonial period had relations with Indian women, sometimes in haremlike abundance. Father Manoel da Nóbrega was appalled by the behavior of the first Portuguese settlers. "Although Christians, they lived like heathen. Their sensual debauchery was extreme. They generally kept their own Indian women as concubines inside their houses whether they were married or single." The creation of a plantation regime within a slave society also led to, as Freyre put it, a "life of Turkish debauchery" as a result of "the provocation of the young Negro and mulatto girls of the household." As late as 1725 the Portuguese Overseas Council complained: "The majority of the [white] residents of those lands do not marry because of the free and easy ways in which they live, it not being easy to coerce them to separate from their black and mulatto concubines." Masters and their sons had absolute control of female slaves and frequently abused it. Father Nóbrega again, this time observing conditions in Bahia, wrote, "with the Christians of this land there is little to be done, for we have closed to them the door of the confessional, on account of the slaves, with which they are loath to part, and for the reason that nearly all of them, married and unmarried alike, are living in concubinage within doors, with their Negro women; and their slaves are all concubines, without their conscience troubling them in the one case or the other; and there are priests who are free with their absolutions and who live in the same manner." He concluded: "The people of the land are living in a state of mortal sin, and there is no one but has many Negro women, who bear them many children, and this is a great evil." Often the slaves themselves, and not their masters, were blamed for lax morality. A Brazilian observer in the late eighteenth century noted: "Negro and mulatto girls, for whom honor is only a chimerical word that signified nothing, when they arrive at adolescence are ordinarily the first to corrupt their adolescent masters, giving them their first lessons in that sexuality which has enveloped the girls since infancy."

The sexual relationships between Portuguese masters and their female slaves, as well as between Portuguese settlers and Indians, produced abundant mixed-race offspring. The Portuguese developed a rather repetitive and confusing terminology to name their mixed-race progeny:

mestiço	"mongrel" or general mixed race
caboclo	copper-colored, or Portuguese-Indian mixture, also a "domesticated Indian"
cabra	offspring of Portuguese, Indian and African
cariboca	offspring of black and Indian
cafuso	offspring of African and Indian, also "slave"
caribocas	generic Portuguese-Indian mixture
mameluco	Mameluke, a slave in Moslem countries; in Brazil an offspring of a Portuguese father and an Indian mother, or generic *mestizo* of all varieties
pardo	colored, or mulatto

There is no question the Portuguese produced a mixed-race population of many colors, particularly in the plantation regions on the coast and the mining districts of the interior, in the three centuries of the colonial era. As in Spanish America, miscegenation was the result of the relative scarcity of Portuguese women at first. In Brazil, however, sexual relations with Indians, Africans, mamelucas and mulattas developed not only from necessity but also from preference. This is the country, after all, that was described as "Hell for blacks, Purgatory for whites, and Paradise for mulattos male and female." When the Dutch conquered Pernambuco in 1637, the wealthy planters fled southward with their pretty mulatta mistresses while their wives struggled barefoot through swamp and scrub. This is no doubt a tall tale, but it is a telling tale. C. R. Boxer writes, "Even when marriageable white women were available, the Portuguese male frequently preferred to live with a mulatta or with a Negress." During the gold rush years of the early eighteenth century, the governor of Rio de Janeiro stated, "There is not a Mineiro who can live without a Negress from Mina, saying that only with them do they have any luck."

Few Portuguese women came to Brazil in the sixteenth and seventeenth centuries. At the time of the founding of the crown captaincy, Father Nóbrega wrote to his superior in Portugal: "I think it would be very good if Your Highness could send here some women who have no chance of getting a husband up there for they would *all* make very fine marriages in the colony even if they are *bad*." During the second half of the sixteenth century, the queen dispatched to Brazil *órfãs do rei* (orphans of the king) from Lisbon. In 1606, the crown pushed a marriage and settlement policy by announcing that minor positions in the high court of Salvador would be awarded to men who married these orphan girls. Female "sinners" condemned by the Inquisition in Portugal were exiled in Brazil. In the seventeenth century, the crown granted permission for families from the overpopulated Azores to emigrate and make Brazil their new home. These and other policies, however, had little to do with the immigration of Portuguese men and women to Brazil.

European immigrants did come to Brazil. During the Union of the Crowns, when Portugal was part of the Spanish monarchy from 1580 to 1640, the gates of Brazil were open to Roman Catholics of any nation. This meant, primarily, Spaniards, of course, but there were also English, French, Flemish, Italian and German as well as Gypsy and Jewish immigrants. By 1580, the

European population of Brazil was approximately 30,000 people, most of them concentrated in the sugar-producing captaincies of Bahia and Pernambuco. Salvador in 1587, the colonial capital of Brazil, had a population of over 12,000 people of which nearly 2,000 were Europeans. Two Inquisition investigations, one in the late sixteenth century and the other in the early seventeenth century, revealed that the European population of Brazil was still predominately male, and more than one-half were migrants born in Portugal or the Atlantic islands.

By the eighteenth century there were, perhaps, as many as 100,000 Luso-Brazilians and Europeans in Brazil. The city of Salvador in 1775 had over 1,500 white married couples in a total white population of nearly 9,000 people. Men still outnumbered women. There were 237 widows compared to 184 widowers. There were almost two times as many bachelors (3,140) as single women (1,803). On the Brazilian frontier, on the other hand, white women outnumbered men. Among the planter class of Santana de Parnaíba in 1775, there was a sex ratio of 84 men to 100 women. Even further west, in Vila Rica, Minas Gerais, the sex imbalance was 79 males for every 100 females in the late colonial period. In addition, way out west, in Goiás near the end of the colonial regime, married and single women were only slightly in the majority. The planters of the coast in the seventeenth and eighteenth centuries dispatched a number of their daughters to Portugal to find suitable husbands or to enter prestigious convents. We also know that the daughters of the planter elite in Bahia shied away from marriage. For the period 1680 to 1795, Susan Soeiro has found that less than fifteen percent of the daughters of the fifty most prominent families of Bahia married. On the frontier like Paraíba and Vila Rica, like all frontiers most likely, families sent their sons to stake out new lands or new mines 'out west.' In general, the Luso-Brazilian colonial family, like the Spanish American family, was a nuclear family and was relatively small, with an average household size of about five members. What this means in both regions, most likely, is that husbands and wives were better able to establish their own households in America and not remain dependent upon their parents' household.

The picture we have of the Portuguese woman and her daughters cloistered in the Big House and dominated by the authoritarian and lascivious *pater familias* is not just incomplete, it is largely inaccurate. Although the harem like seclusion of Brazilian women was famous in its day – and even made fun of by the Spanish – it turns out the voyeurs and wags had a very narrow angle of vision. In the coastal plantation regions from the seventeenth century, Portuguese women and their creole daughters were appearing as managers and owners of sugar *engenhos* and cattle ranches in Bahia, the captaincy we know the most about. These women also instigated judicial proceedings to protect their interests and controlled wealth and property not only as widows but also as nuns. On the frontier in colonial Brazil, women were often a majority of the white population and were critical to elite family continuance and working independently in agriculture, shopkeeping, mining and prospecting, weaving and sewing, washing clothes and prostitution. Around São Paulo, the governor described the women as "beautiful and virile," supervising their households and properties while their husbands were away for years in the backlands.

Document 9.2
They Love Women Extreamly, and Spare No Charges for the Setting Out of Their Wives

The Sieur Froger 1698

As for the City of *St. Salvador*, that is seated upon this Bay, it's large, well built, and very populous; but the Scituation of it is not so advantageous, as could be wished. It's high and low, and scarce one straight Street therein; it's the Capital City of *Brasil*, an Archiepiscopal See, and the Residence of the Vice-Roy: This place is honoured with a Soveraign Council, and in the Privilege to coin Money; where, in order to quicken Trade, they make such sort of Pieces as are current no-where else, but in *Brasil*: They have on the one side the Arms of *Portugal*, and a Cross charged with a Spear on the other, with this Inscription, SUBQ. SIGN. STABO.

This City, to the Seaward, is defended with some Forts, and several Batteries mounted with Cannon, and to the Landward, with earthen Bastions ill made. We saw them law the Foundation of a Fortress, the Governour had ordered to be erected about half a Cannon shot without the Town: The *Dutch* attempted divers times to make themselves Masters of this Place, but without Success, tho' they have taken away two and twenty Ships from thence at one clap.

The Inhabitants, to say nothing of the common People, who are insolent to the highest Degree, are neat, civil, honest, and withal rich, being lovers of Trade, and for the most part are of a Jewish Extract; and this is the Reason that when any one of the Inhabitants is about to make one of his Sons a Divine, he is obliged to prove his Ancestors were Christians, as the Knights of *Malta* are under an Obligation of making our their Gentility, before they enter into the Order. They love Women extreamly, and spare no Charges for the setting out of their Wives, who in respect to all other things, have Cause enough to complain; for they are never allowed to see any Body, and go not out of doors at any other time but on *Sunday* early in the Morning, to go to Church: They are a very jealous People, and 'tis a kind of point of Honour for a Man to stab his Wife, when he can convict here of being unfaithful to his Bed; tho' for all that, this cannot hinder many of them from finding out a way to impart some of their Favours to us *Frenchmen*, whose winning and free Conversation they are mightily in love with.

This French traveler to Brazil in the late seventeenth century takes note of the well-known Brazilian custom of cloistering wives and yet, at the same time, suggests such enclosure cannot kept local women away from the charms of the French. *Source: A Relation of a Voyage Made in the Years 1695, 1696, 1697, on the Coasts of Africa, Streights of Magellan, Brasil, Cayennia, and the Antilles, by a Squadron of French Men of War, under the Command of M. de Gennes.* By the Sieur Froger, Voluntier-Engineer on board the English Falcon. London, Printed for M. Gillyflower in Westminister-Hall; W. Freeman, M. Wotton in Fleet-street; J. Walthoe in the Temple; and R. Parker in Cornhill, 1698.

In the eighteenth century, the Portuguese-Brazilian family was unknow-
ingly described by a contemporary Portuguese dictionary. This dictionary
defined a family as "the people who make up a house, parents, children,
and servants." Antonil noted that "family, sons, and slaves" formed one
unit. This definition is synonymous with the European term *houseful*, which
referred to immediate family members, related dependants and servants and
even some familiar slaves as a meaningful compact. Brazil's housefuls in the
seventeenth and especially the eighteenth centuries came in all shapes and
sizes. The planter elite used their daughters and marital ties to make alliances
with wealthy merchant and powerful officials, and as a means of "consolidating, preserving, and promoting wealth and social distinction." If the best
families of Bahia could not find a suitable match for their daughters, which
was often the case, they sent them to Portugal to enter a convent. In an
attempt to try to prevent this daughter drain, the town fathers of Salvador
constantly sought permission to establish a nunnery in Brazil. Yet, even after
the Convent of Santa Clara do Destêrro was founded in 1677, and others
followed in the eighteenth century, daughters of the Brazilian elite still sailed
for Portugal. Nevertheless, even in Salvador and Bahia, the houseful did not
always reflect the patriarchal ideal. In the parish of São Pedro in Salvador in
1775, women headed over forty percent of the housefuls. Near the end of
the colonial regime, "some of the wealthiest slaveowners of the Recôncavo
were women, especially in the older areas of Santa Amaro and São Francisco
do Conde, where by 1817 ten percent of the cane farmers and over fifteen
percent of the *engenhos* were held by women." These women," notes Stuart
Schwartz, "also owned one fifth of the slaves in the Recôncavo."

In Santana de Parnaíba on the São Paulo frontier, where sons took off to
find new opportunities and stake new claims, daughters became the key to
family survival. Here fathers created fabulous dowries of property, slaves and
goods to attract new blood from coastal Brazil and Portugal. Women headed
one-third of the housefuls in a sample of communities in Minas Gerais. In
Casa Branca, Ouro Preto and Vila Rica, Minas Gerais, women were in charge
of between 37 and 45 percent of all housefuls. These housefuls contained lots
of children, servants and slaves: "Women owned about 40 percent of all the
shops in Vila Rica and comprised at least one quarter of the prospectors and
more substantial miners."

What is interesting about the diversity of the Brazilian family is that both
white and nonwhite women on the coast and in the interior headed a significant portion of housefuls and either managed businesses or worked for
wages. Free nonwhite women, naturally, had a harder course in life. A very
small minority of couples in colonial Brazil, of all ethnicities, became legally
married, a social strategy that suggests husband and wife partnerships were
more common than the patriarchal family that was upheld by law and the
church. Partnerships were necessary for family survival for all but the most
privileged of elite families.

In the end, a Portuguese Brazil was put into formation. "Along the coast
from Pernambuco to Rio de Janeiro, where the sugar plantation system was
created in the sixteenth century," writes Stuart Schwartz, "the European
population was relatively dense, the institutions of government were well

Figure 9.3. A View of a Brazilian Planter and His Wife, Attended by African Slaves, On a Journey. Frontispiece aquatint by Henry Koster, *Travels in Brazil* (London, 1816). Courtesy of the John Carter Brown Library at Brown University.

established, and the social and cultural norms of Portugal were more or less implanted." Elsewhere, except for Mina Gerais – the destination of a great gold rush in the early eighteenth century – the Luso-Brazilian population was much smaller and the level of miscegenation was much higher. Some of these peripheral, less-Europeanized regions and colonies were pulled into the cultural orbit of Portuguese Brazil later in the eighteenth or in the nineteenth centuries, but a considerable portion of Brazil remained outside the imperial Portuguese culture of institutions, law and manners.

9.5 Good Wives and Brave Filles

The English, Dutch and the French arrived in North America in the seventeenth century as groups of men. As everywhere else in the Americas, these northern European male settlers seized native women by force and were given native women by gift and in political and familial alliances. Unlike the French, the English and Dutch developed a reputation for standoffishness with regard to native women. A closer examination, however, reveals that both English and Dutch men in certain circumstances were willing to have sexual relations with and even marry ("according to the customs of the country") Indian women. In plantation regions in North America and the West Indies, when African women were available and relatively powerless, English and Dutch slave owners were notorious for the rape and coercion of slave women.

In the English settlement colonies concubinage and marriage with Indian women was rare. The available historical records, for example, reveal no intermarriage by an Englishman in New England in the seventeenth century. A reticence to establish such a relationship has been attributed to different causes. John Elliott suggested the importance of cultural attitudes. The Spanish and the Portuguese, he argued, had a long history of contact with the Moors, which predisposed them to inter-ethnic marriage. The English, isolated on their island, found a greater cultural divide between Indians and English. The historian David Smits has found that public opinion opposed sexual relations and intermarriage for fear that native women would lure Englishmen into a savage lifestyle. He notes that it was for this reason that the Statutes of Kilkenny in Ireland in 1366 "ordained and established that no alliance by marriage, gossipred, fostering of children, concubinage or amour or in any other manner be henceforth made between the English and the Irish." The Reverend William Symonds preached in 1609 to Virginia's male settlers that Abraham's descendants were enjoined to "keep to themselves. They may not marry nor give in marriage to the Heathen, that are uncircumcised." Richard Eburne recommend that young men be excluded from colonization, fearing that they would marry Indian women "which haply will be nor handsome nor wholesome for them."

Young Englishmen found native women both naturally attractive and intriguing for some and also naturally repulsive for others. The little we know about how native women perceived Englishmen suggests that they made a poor impression. "Our [women] would not live with them," commented one native, "for they have hair all over their faces and we have none there or elsewhere." In Virginia where settlers were barely able to feed themselves, the disdain of native women no doubt contributed to the paucity of intermarriages that took place in the early years of the colony. From the other perspective, notes Brown, "English settlers had little hope of advancing themselves through intermarriage in Virginia. Indian women of the region offered no entrée to lucrative fur trading networks and marrying them did not automatically entitle English men to land. Perhaps most important, Indian women, like their menfolk, had resisted all efforts to conquer them to exploit their labor. English settlers would have had little reason to hope that marriage to an indigenous women would gain them access to Indian labor."

Although Englishmen showed little interest in creating legal or informal unions with Indian women, they generally had no problem having sexual relations with "copper-coloured beauties." This was particularly true on the fur-trading frontiers and was apparently widespread in the southeast where the Indian slave trade was a major business. The leaders of the Lower Creek nation in 1752 met with an agent of the colonial government of South Carolina and "complained very heavily of the white people in general for debauching their wives and mentioned several in particular that were found guilty, and said that if his Excellency would not punish them for it, the injured persons would certainly put their own laws in execution."

Figure 9.4. A Gentle Young Native Lady of Virginia. From Thomas Harriot, *A Brief and True Report of the new found land of Virginia*, Theodor de Bry edition (Frankfurt, 1590). Courtesy of the William L. Clements Library at the University of Michigan.

Although the English colonies of North America in the early seventeenth century started out as male societies, rapid and massive immigration began to balance the sex ratio. At the beginning of the process of populating English America, in 1635, we see that overall less than one-fifth of the immigrants were women. This percentage was even less for Virginia but for New England women constituted almost 40 percent of the total. At this early date, families with children were making the crossing (see Table 9.3). During the seventeenth century, approximately 400,000 Englishmen crossed the Atlantic. The Great Migration of the Puritans to New England in the 1630s brought over 21,000 persons. After 1640, migration abruptly stopped and did not resume to New England for a long time. The great migration, however, provided enough women to double the population every generation for two centuries. By 1700 there were 100,000 Englishmen and women and their descendants in New England and at least one million by 1800. In the seventeenth century, about 40,000 English went to the middle colonies and 120,000 English settled in the Chesapeake colonies of Virginia and Maryland. The migration of women to the south was many fewer than men, and mortality was higher for everyone, thus it took longer for the population of this region to reproduce itself and grow. A 1704 census listed approximately 30,000 English in Maryland, of which only about 7,000 were women. The English in Virginia did not begin to reproduce themselves until the late seventeenth century.

Table 9.3. British emigration to America, 1635

Destination	Travelers	Male percent	Female percent
Virginia	2,009	86.4	13.6
New England	1,169	60.9	39.1
Barbados	983	94.0	6.0
St. Kitts	423	94.8	5.2
Bermuda	218	90.8	9.2
Providence	76	62.7	37.3
North American Total	3,178	73.6	26.4
West Indies Total	1,700	85.5	13.5
Total/Average	4,878	82.2	17.6

Source: Alison Games, *Migration and the Origins of the English Atlantic World* (1999), Table 1.1 and Table 1.2, pp. 21 and 24. These travelers who shipped out from London and, for the first time, were officially registered by clerks at the port of London in 1635 were part of what historians call the 'Great Migration' of some 21,000 Englishmen and women to New England between 1629 and 1640. See David Hacket Fischer, *Albion's Seed: Four British Folkways in America* (1989), pp. 13–17. Games points out that most of these migrants to the British New World were young (the average age was 22) and traveled to American as or to become servants. In individual ships bound for Virginia, New England and Providence Island in 1635, the percentage of servants as part of the total body of passengers was in each case, (to Virginia) 77 percent; (to New England) 39 percent; and (to Providence) 46 percent.

English colonists in the North American colonies took for granted the subordination of women and the idea men and women had different and appropriate roles in the family and the community. As everywhere in the Americas, families differed, and the roles of women differed, according to status and wealth, regional economy and much else. Although in most English families there were different work regimes for husbands and wives, the rough conditions of seventeenth-century America often led women to work beside their husbands in the fields and elsewhere. The "good wives" of New England had a higher status than most women in England. Wives had the right to consent and acknowledge the sale of family property, the right to make contracts and widows had more rights to family estates. The colonial family in Plymouth, according to John Demos, was a self-sufficient business, a school, a vocational institution and a house of correction. A study of court records in Salem in the seventeenth century "reinforce notions of partnership and mutual obligation in marriage that modify the conception of patriarchal deference." Laurel Thatcher Ulrich notes that there was as much variation in seventeenth- and eighteenth-century families as there is today: "Some wives were servile, some were shrews, others were respected companions who shared the authority of their spouses in the management of family affairs." The latter she refers to as "deputy husbands," wives who not only managed the household but also, when asked, assisted in the economic and business affairs of her husband.

The English family in the south, particularly in Virginia and Maryland, was more difficult to get started given the lower rate of female immigration and the higher rate of mortality. Many if not most of the women to travel to the Chesapeake in the seventeenth century were indentured servants who, if they survived their terms of service, married men of property. Serving her indenture brought the woman property in her own right, which often meant these marriages were business partnerships. This first generation of southern wives usually outlived their husbands, inherited the farm or plantation, sometimes married again or became independent and powerful widows. Their daughters in the eighteenth century married younger and lived longer, their marriages lasted longer and more of their children survived to maturity. The small planter elite in the eighteenth century took their wives out of the fields and the kitchen and into brick great houses where they become less "helpmeets" than producers of children and status symbols. With the rising importance of slavery, these husbands and fathers started to see themselves as patriarchs. As in colonial Spanish America and colonial Brazil, most families in colonial British America were nuclear families with three or four children at home. As elsewhere, the clan did not make the transition to America.

Most women in the English colonies in the eighteenth century were not plantation mistresses. Recent research gives us portraits of propertied women throughout the colonies who oversaw farms, pursued businesses and owned slaves with their husbands and on their own. Elizabeth Murray, a Scottish immigrant who arrived in New England parentless at age 14, became a Boston merchant at age 29 and maintained her business through three marriages. During her career, Murray assisted other female merchants, mentored her own female relatives and ensured that upon her death her female heirs received her money. Linda Sturtz gives us a new view of single and married women in Virginia as planters, merchants, tavern and innkeepers and more. Single women often went into marriage with some kind of economic skill or asset with the intention of creating a business partnership. Wives acted as attorneys for their husbands in local courts, kept accounts and established networks of traders. Cara Anzilotti provides a study of women, mostly widows, who owned slaves and property in South Carolina in spite of public condemnation of their remaining single. She shows that these women did not want to relinquish their power.

By the beginning of the American Revolution in 1775, the English and Anglo-American population of the colonies had climbed to over 2.5 million. The colonies were becoming more diverse with the immigration of thousands of Scots-Irish, Irish, Welsh and Germans in the eighteenth century. Nevertheless, given the early dominance of English migrants and migration of women and families, English culture took firm root in British America by the eighteenth century. English America, like Spanish America and Portuguese Brazil, was far from being a copy of England or Britain, but nearly everyone spoke English, lived by British laws, valued their English liberties, were Christian and Protestant, resided in nuclear households and possessed their property under a private ownership system according to English ideas. The sheer fact of leaving home, often an act of self-selection, and the process of surviving in and adapting to America changed Englishmen (and Spaniards, Portuguese and other Europeans) and their Old World cultures in the New World. Colonists sought to conserve tradition and were forced to innovate at the same time. This dialectic produced cultural creativity.

In New Netherland, Dutch fur traders on the upper Hudson took native women as informal wives, following "the custom of the country," in order to facilitate business with local native communities. In New Amsterdam, on the other hand, the Dutch were quite opposed to intermarriage. During the short history of New Netherland, only a few thousand people, not all of them Dutch, immigrated to the colony. The population of the colony in 1645 was only 2,500 and by 1664 it had grown to around 10,000 (7,000 Dutch settlers and 3,000 non-Dutch). As in New England, many Dutch immigrated to North America in family groups. This most likely explains the Dutch disdain for intermarriage, at least in the lower Hudson and New Amsterdam. Under Dutch law, marriage was interpreted as a legal partnership and both partners had an equal claim to their original combined wealth as well as to the wealth acquired during the marriage. The English seized the Dutch colony in 1664, making it the new proprietary colony of New York, and proceeded to Anglicize it over the next several decades. Within a generation, English merchant houses supplanted the Dutch merchant establishment. By 1700, nevertheless, Dutch burghers (townsmen) and boers (farmers) still dominated much of the Hudson Valley. By 1790 about 98,000 people of Dutch descent lived in the United States, still pretty much where the Dutch lived in 100 years earlier. The Dutch dialect survived into the nineteenth century as did the distinctive Dutch architecture and, of course, the reformed church.

The French in North America developed a very different reputation regarding their relations with Indians and native women than the English. The fur-trading economy of New France meant that the French needed Indian cooperation in order to obtain pelts and make any profit. As elsewhere in the Americas, many more Frenchmen immigrated to New France in the seventeenth century and those in the fur trade were notorious for taking Indian women as concubines and wives. Marriages constituted alliances between Europeans and natives, which created "a firm friendship" and were also "a great help in engaging [Indians] in trade."

Marriages in fur trade country were *a la façon du pays*, that is, after "the custom of the country," meaning they were without benefit of clergy or law. Fur traders adopted traditional native marriage rites: They had to obtain parental approval for the match, pay a bride price and usually solemnize the occasion by smoking the calumet. The more important and wealthy traders often kept a number of wives, which impressed Indians who were accustomed to polygamy by chiefs.

Like all Europeans, the French were dismayed by the native "oppression" of Indian women (who appeared to do all of the labor), appalled by their savage customs, and – at the same time – impressed by their abilities. The Jesuit Joseph-François Lafitau observed in the Christian Iroquois community of Kahnawaké that "Nothing, however, is more real than this superiority of the women. It is of them that the nation really consists: and it is through them that the nobility of the blood, the genealogical tree and the families are perpetuated."

The Jesuits focused their proselytizing efforts on men and boys because native women frequently rejected conversion out of hand and maintained their traditional rituals. No one was "more attached to these silly customs, or more obstinate in clinging to this error," wrote the Jesuit Dablon, at Sault Ste. Marie in 1669, "than the old women, who will not even lend an ear to our instructions."

In areas where Europeans and natives traded, a kind of middle ground developed where cultures met and customs clashed and melded. *Nous sommes touts sauvages* ("We are all savages"), noted one French trader in the eighteenth century. In this middle ground traders found native women to be essential as translators and intermediaries. Aside from companionship and sexual favors, translation and cultural mediation, native women dressed the furs, served as guides and porters, and were useful hunters and cooks. A growing presence in the middle ground was the children of French-Indian unions, commonly known as *métis* ("cross-breed"). Once there were a sufficient number of *métis* women, fur traders usually preferred these "daughters of the country."

During most of the seventeenth century, French women were in very short supply in New France. Most of the immigrants to Canada were either soldiers or male engagés. Between 1663 and 1673, the crown subsidized the immigration of the *filles de roi*, the so-called king's daughters, about 770 young women, a majority of them orphans. Within weeks of their arrival, they had chosen mates among the many, many eager bachelors, were married and usually on their way to a farm. The French soldier, the baron de Lahontan, who served in New France for ten years in the late seventeenth century, commented that it was the male colonists who chose the girls: "The Bride-grooms singled out their Brides, just as a Butcher do's an Ewe. The fattest went off best, upon the apprehension that these being less active, would keep truer to their Ingagements, and hold out better against the nipping cold of the Winter." Less than 3,000 French settled in New France between 1670 and 1730. Of these immigrants, over 80 percent were men and less than 20 percent were women (see Table 9.4). These immigrants of 1670 to 1730 represented about one-third of all migrants to New France. Most historians have maintained that over the entire French regime, something like 7,000 to 10,000 migrants settled in New France. More recent historians such as Peter Moogk and Leslie Choquette, however, have argued that far more immigrants went to New France, anywhere from 27,000 to 37,000, but at least two-thirds returned to France. By the 1720s, the ratio of the sexes achieved balance due to natural increase. "There exists no country in the world where the women lead a happier life than in Canada," wrote Pierre Pouchot, a soldier dispatched to New France in 1755. He continued: "The men have a great deal of consideration for them & spare them all the hard work that they can." As a result, perhaps, Canada's French population in the eighteenth century grew vigorously so that by the end of the French regime in 1759–60, New France had a population of 55,000.

Whatever the number of total immigrants, there were remarkably few non-French migrants to New France. Official figures give a number of 40 immigrants and an additional 126 New Englanders and New Yorkers who were granted letters of naturalization in the eighteenth century. These original French immigrants, who came to New France primarily in the seventeenth

Table 9.4. French emigration to Canada, 1670–1729

Period	Total number	Percent men	Percent women
1670–79	429	54.4	46.2
1680–89	483	89.6	10.4
1690–99	490	93.9	6.1
1700–9	283	92.2	7.8
1710–19	293	94.2	5.8
1720–29	420	96.8	3.2
Totals	2,911	82.4	17.6

Source: Hubert Charbonneau and Normand Robert, "The French Origins of the Canadian Population, 1608–1759," in *The Historical Atlas of Canada, Volume I: From the Beginning to 1800*, R. C. Harris, ed. (1987), Plate 45.

century, reproduced French culture, language and religion in North America. They were the progenitors of the six million French Canadians who live in Quebec and Canada today.

To "make a good nation," declared the Lord Deputy of Ireland in the 1620s, "it is no great matter of what nation the men be so the women be English." The European empires that expanded into the Atlantic in the sixteenth and seventeenth centuries confirmed by grand experimentation the truthfulness of this proposition.

In Africa and the Americas, European men created partnerships with African and Indian women. These partnerships undoubtedly promoted European commercial and imperial expansion. They created ties of blood and interest between Europeans and African and Indian polities, trading networks, communities and important families. Europeans certainly understood the nature of strategic marriages as did Africans and Indians, and nearly all involved created them for mutual benefit. Most Euro-African and Euro-Indian partnerships were not sanctified by formal marriage but were dignified by years of devotion and commitment. These African and Indian women and their mulatta and *mestiza* daughters made significant contributions to the formation of the Atlantic World. It is difficult to image the Atlantic slave trade without the *filhos da terra*. "There is an important Indian woman in virtually every major encounter between Europeans and Indians in the New World," writes Clara Sue Kidwell. "As mistresses or wives, they counseled, translated, and guided white men who were entering new territory. While men made treaties and carried on negotiations and waged war, Indian women lived with white men, translated their words, and bore their children. Theirs was the more sustained and enduring contact with new cultural ways, and they gave their men an entrée into the cultures and communities of their own people. In this way, Indian women were the first important mediators of meaning between the cultures of two worlds."

African and Indian women were significant partners in many ways to European explorers, conquerors, traders and settlers but could they, as the Lord Deputy of Ireland put it, "make a good nation"? The answer is found where European males were largely unaccompanied by European females:

Portuguese Africa, the Spanish Philippines and the other Asian colonies of the Europeans. The Lord Deputy understood that the English woman, wife and mother carried English "civility, honesty, sobriety, industry and character" in her and would instill these values and virtues in her children. This was obviously true for all of the European colonizing empires. In the Americas, the Spanish, Portuguese, English, Dutch and French encouraged – to a greater or lesser extent – and at times directly funded, the immigration of their daughters to their colonies. They also strongly pushed their male settlers to marry the women of their homeland. Increasingly, this is what they did. The end result was the substantial Europeanization of most of the Americas in the three centuries from 1500 to 1800.

9.6 *Further Reading*

Asunción Lavrin, editor, *Sexuality and Marriage in Colonial Latin America* (Lincoln, 1989).

Hillary McD. Beckles, *Natural Rebels: A Social History of Enslaved Black Women in Barbados* (New Brunswick, 1989).

Carol Berkin, *First Generations: Women in Colonial America* (New York, 1996).

C.R. Boxer, *Women in Iberian Expansion Overseas, 1415–1815* (New York, 1963).

George E. Brooks, *Eurafricans in Western Africa: Commerce, Social Status, Gender, and Religious Observance from the Sixteenth to the Eighteenth Century* (Bloomington, 2003).

Barbara Bush, *Slave Women in Caribbean Society: 1650–1838* (Bloomington, 1990).

Kathleen M. Brown, *Good Wives, Nasty Wenches & Anxious Patriarchs: Gender, Race, and Power in Colonial Virginia* (Chapel Hill, 1996).

Timothy J. Coates, *Convicts and Orphans: Forced and State-Sponsored Colonizers in the Portuguese Empire, 1550–1755* (Stanford, 2001).

John Demos, *The Tried and the True: Native American Women Confronting Colonization* (New York, 1995).

Gilberto Freyre, *The Masters and the Slaves: A Study in the Development of Brazilian Civilization*, revised 2nd edition, translated by Samuel Putnam (New York, 1978).

Alison Games, *Migration and the Origins of the English Atlantic World* (Cambridge, Mass., 1999).

Ramón Gutiérrez, *When Jesus Came, the Corn Mothers Went Away: Marriage, Sexuality, and Power in New Mexico, 1500–1846* (Stanford, 1991).

Susan Kellogg, *Weaving the Past: A History of Latin America's Indigenous Women from the Prehispanic Period to the Present* (New York, 2005).

Luis Martín, *Daughters of the Conquistadors: Women of the Viceroyality of Peru* (Albuquerque, 1983).

Juan Francisco Maura, *Women in the Conquest of the Americas*, translated by John F. Deredita (New York, 1997).

Alida C. Metcalf, *Family and Frontier in Colonial Brazil: Santana de Parnaíba, 1580–1822* (Berkeley, 1992).

Mary Beth Norton, *Founding Mothers and Fathers: Gendered Power and the Forming of American Society* (New York, 1997).

Steven Ozment, *When Fathers Ruled: Family Life in Reformation Europe* (Cambridge, Mass., 2004).

Ann M. Pescatello, *Power and Pawn: The Female in Iberian Families, Societies, and Cultures* (Westport, Conn., 1976).

Karen Vieira Powers, *Women in the Crucible of Conquest: The Gendered Genesis of Spanish American Society, 1500–1600* (Albuquerque, 2005).

Pierre Ragon, *Les indiens de la déscouverte: evangélisation, marriage, et sexualité* (Paris, 1992).

Susan Schroeder, Stephanie Wood, and Robert Haskett, editors, *Indian Women of Early Mexico* (Norman, 1997).

Susan Migden Socolow, *The Women of Colonial Latin America* (Cambridge, 2000).

Laurel Thatcher Ulrich, *Good Wives: Image and Reality in the Lives of Women in Northern New England, 1650–1750* (New York, 1991).

Silvia Van Kirk, *Many Tender Ties: Women in Fur-Trade Society, 1670–1870* (Norman, 1980).

Part Three

A New Order of the Ages

I saw at that moment that the Revolution in
America signaled the beginning of a new political
era, that this Revolution would necessarily
determine an important progress in World
Civilization, and that before long, it would
cause great changes in the social order which
existed in Europe.

Claude-Henri de Rouvoy
Comte de Saint-Simon

Claude-Henri de Rouvoy, an officer of the Royal-Gatinais Infantry, had his insight regarding the world significance of the American Revolution at the tender age of twenty on the battlefield of Yorktown in 1781. Years earlier, at the beginning of the Revolution, Thomas Paine suggested as much: "We have it in our power to begin the world over again." During the American Revolution a committee of founders created the Great Seal of the United States, which was finalized in 1782. On the reverse side of the seal is an unfinished pyramid and at the base the date MDCCLXXVI (1776) and the motto *Novus Ordo Seclorum*. Chosen by Charles Thomson and borrowed and rephrased from Virgil, the phrase was part of a prophecy about the

Figure 10.1. An Allegorical Representation of the Liberty of America and Europe in the Age of Revolution. Frontispiece from *The Massachusetts Magazine*, Vol. II (1790). Courtesy of the William L. Clements Library at the University of Michigan.

fate of the Roman Empire. Thomson explained: "The date underneath [the pyramid] is that of the Declaration of Independence and the words under it signify the beginning of the new American Era, which commences from that date." This sentiment was portrayed less cryptically than in the reverse side of the motto in the frontispiece of the *Massachusetts Magazine* in 1790. This engraving shows "America" holding a staff with a liberty cap and a shield with the names of America, Europe and Africa inscribed on it, and awakening "Europe" to liberty. At their feet lie a copy of Thomas Paine's *Rights of Man*, and discarded tools of oppression such as shackles, a mask and the keys of the Bastille. In the background obscure figures representing war and want flee into the darkness. Liberty and equality, the rights of the individual and the rights of man, were ideas so revolutionary that contemporaries believed in boundless possibilities, a new era in the annals of mankind.

It is easy to be cynical about late eighteenth-century revolutionary rhetoric and expectations. The eighteenth century witnessed an enormous expansion of plantation slavery and the Atlantic slave trade. Native Americans continued to lose wars, territories and entire peoples in North, Central and South America. Of course, the contradictions between revolutionary principles and the worst American realities were not ignored. The Quaker David Cooper in 1783 declared that slavery was completely contrary with "the principles upon which the American Revolution stands." The English philosopher Richard Price wrote that until they had abolished slavery, Americans would never "deserve the liberty for which they had been contending." David Ramsay in his history of the American Revolution lamented that Europeans had been responsible for the destruction and extirpation of so many of the native inhabitants of America. "That so many tribes should, in so short a time, lose both their country, and their national existence," he wrote, was "an event scarcely to be paralleled in the history of the world." The inconsistency of slavery in a land of liberty, however, brought hope and conviction to many that slavery would end or be ended. Ramsay predicted in 1779 that there would "not be a slave in these states fifty years hence."

The American Revolution was the beginning of what Jacques Godechot and R. R. Palmer called the age of democratic revolution in the Atlantic World. Although both Godechot and Palmer referred specially to the American and French revolutions (and related European revolutions) of the late eighteenth century, this history takes a more expansive view. The American Revolution began a chain reaction of revolutions throughout the Atlantic World that included The Netherlands, France, Saint Domingue, Spain, Spanish America and Brazil. These revolutions were inspired by liberal principles in most cases but were also directed against great inequality and political oppression in some places and times. They were led and fought by European Americans and Europeans as well as by Native Americans, Africans, mestizos and mulattos. Although there was no revolution in Africa itself, the uprising of the slaves in Saint Domingue, the Haitian Revolution, was an African revolution. The age of Atlantic revolutions, from the beginning of the American Revolution in 1776 to the end of the Spanish American War for Independence in 1826, lasted half a century. The influence of the Age of Revolution did not end then and there, however. Embedded in the Age of Revolution were the principles of liberty and equality and a hatred of slavery. Although Great Britain avoided revolution, a good portion of its frustrated revolutionary energy was deflected into the campaigns against the slave trade and colonial slavery. Slavery came under attack by the Atlantic revolutions and was abolished by a few and limited by more. Plantation slavery was tenacious in the southern cotton states of the United States, sugar-producing Cuba, and coffee-growing Brazil. Nevertheless, the revolutionary principles of abolitionists, and the self-liberating actions of slaves themselves, ended slavery in the Americas a little more than a century after the beginning of the American Revolution.

"We have it in our power to begin the world over again," wrote Paine in 1776. A quarter of a century later in 1791, Thomas Paine in his essay on the French Revolution, *Rights of Man*, wrote, "The revolutions of America and France have thrown a beam of light over the world, which reaches into man. The enormous expense of governments have provoked people to think, by making them feel: and when once the veil begins to rend, it admits not of repair." These two revolutions led to the creation of constitutional monarchies and representative republics in Western Europe and the Americas, governing systems in which the rights of citizens were recognized and over time defended and protected. These revolutions led to the dissolution for the most part of the Atlantic empires of Britain, France, Spain and Portugal. In addition, these revolutions began the long and difficult struggle that ended slavery in the Americas, and eventually, in Africa as well.

The broader context of the age of Atlantic revolutions was a titanic contest for supremacy of the Atlantic between France and Great Britain during the long eighteenth century from 1689 to 1815. This is the subject of Chapter 10 *Rivals: Great Britain and France in the Long Eighteenth Century*. Although the revolutions were largely about ideas, they were almost always inaugurated or aggravated by some crisis or resolution of great power politics. The liberal consequences of the Age of Revolution, from rights to republics, founded in the nineteenth century an international system that was dominated by a liberal Great Britain that was, for the most part, more stabilizing than threatening. A comparison with the twentieth century shows how important the international system is for the security and advancement of liberal governments and societies. The dominance of Great Britain in the nineteenth century was also crucial for the abolition of the slave trade and the abolition of New World slavery.

The following chapters of Part III tell the stories of the age of Atlantic revolutions and the abolition of the Atlantic slave trade and American slavery. Chapter 11, *Liberty: The Atlantic World in the Age of Revolution*, considers the American, Dutch and French Revolutions of the 1780s and 1790s. These revolutions emphasized liberty through the ideology of natural rights, although equality was certainly not absent. Long after the American Revolution, American reformers returned to the Declaration of Independence to seek inspiration and support for women's rights, the rights of labor, the abolition of slavery and even the establishment of socialism. Jean Jaurès in France stated that socialism is nothing if it is not republican, and the republic is nothing without the Declaration of the Rights of Man and the Citizen.

The revolutions in Saint Domingue, Spain, Spanish America and Brazil are the subject of Chapter 12 *Equality: The Atlantic World in the Age of Revolution*. All of the revolutions in the Atlantic World were inspired by the principles, as the French phrased it, of *Liberté, Egalité, Fraternité*, and in these later revolutions liberty and natural rights were certainly important. It was in the popular movements of these revolutions, however, particularly in Haiti and Spanish America, that the desire for equality, as well as the fear of equality, was paramount. In Saint Domingue the revolution began as a movement, first, for equality among whites and then, mulattos and whites, and finally freedom and equality for slaves. In Spanish America the revolutions began as movements for equality between creoles and peninsulars and then, in some places, for equality among Indians, blacks and mixed bloods and whites. The leader of the popular revolution in Mexico Miguel Hidalgo was informed in 1810, "since the natives are indifferent to the word 'liberty,' it is necessary to make them believe that the rising is undertaken simply to favor King Ferdinand." The fear of racial equality led Francisco Miranda of Venezuela to proclaim in 1798: "God forbid that these beautiful countries become, as did St. Domingue, a theatre of blood and of crime under the pretext of establishing liberty, let them rather remain if necessary one century more under the barbarous and imbecile oppression of Spain." These revolutions instituted legal equality and sought a degree of compromised social equality that was an ideal to struggle for then and today.

Chapter 13, *Freedom: The Abolition of the Atlantic Slave Trade and New World Slavery*, recounts the struggles, by revolutionaries, anti-slavery movements, and by slaves themselves, to end the Atlantic slave trade and slavery itself. The national and international movements to limit and abolish the slave trade and slavery were all influenced by varying degrees by economic self-interest, party or factional politics, and great power politics. The keys to abolitionist movements everywhere, however, were evangelical Protestantism of the eighteenth and nineteenth centuries that identified the slave trade and slave ownership with the epitome of sin and the revolutionary ideology of natural rights that held that all men were born free and equal and thus had an inalienable right to liberty.

"A New Order of the Ages" did not mean the automatic institution of popular representative governments, which protected the rights and liberty of its citizens throughout Western Europe and the Americas during the nineteenth century, not to mention the larger Atlantic World or the world at large. It did not mean that former slaves became independent farmers and businessmen or that Indian wars came to an end. We should not interpret this phrase or most of the revolutionary rhetoric of the late eighteenth century as millennialist. Their authors did not expect the arrival of some miraculous age of joy, serenity and justice. Under the best circumstances they knew the future would bring hard work, struggle, conflict and even blood, but from such trials over time would come a better world. The essence of these revolutions, writes the Haitian writer Edwidge Danticat, "was not in their instantaneous bursts of glory but in their ripple effect across borders and time, their ability to put the impossible within reach and make the downtrodden seem mighty."

After more than two centuries, the liberal principles of the Atlantic revolutions are, according to Michael Mandelbaum, "The Ideas That Conquered the World." In his book with that title, published in 2002, Mandelbaum argues that at the beginning of the twenty-first century "a world dominated by the East-West conflict had given way to one in which liberal principles were unchallenged." In a 1999–2000 report of Freedom House, an organization that reports on the progress of political liberty in the world, 85 of the world's 192 countries were classified as "free" and 60 more as "partly free." Thus after millennia of societies with autocratic and aristocratic elites and deferential and impoverished masses, a greater portion of humankind today live under constitutional and representative governments than ever before, and this percentage is increasing decade by decade. The countries that have possessed free governments and societies and relatively free economies for more than a few decades are also not by coincidence the most prosperous countries in the world. All of this does not foretell the end of history, as Francis Fukuyama understands it, because we humans have invented the form of government that best suits out nature. Even if this is true, humans are unpredictable, and what is best or right is not always what wins. However, over the last two centuries, with plenty of interruptions and crises, it does appear that history has been progressive and liberal.

The age of Atlantic Revolutions, although undeniably positive for the progress of the world, signified and promoted the decline and ultimate dissolution of the Atlantic World. The Atlantic World had been a world of colonial empires and embedded in most of the revolutions were the first anti-colonial rebellions and wars for independence. As a result the first British Empire was ended in North America in 1783, the French had lost New France earlier in the Seven Years' War in 1763 and lost in revolution Haiti in 1808. The Spanish lost all of its American empire with the exception of Cuba and Puerto Rico, and Portugal lost Brazil in the 1820s. The Atlantic World had also been a world of commodity trades linking Europe, Africa and the Americas with the North Atlantic closely tied to the South Atlantic and the Caribbean as the cockpit of Atlantic trade and politics. The dissolution of the empires, particularly the Spanish and Portuguese empires, along with the abolition of the Atlantic slave trade and New World slavery also began the economic stagnation of the South Atlantic. Decade by decade in the nineteenth century, the economies of the South Atlantic became less important to Atlantic trade than before. Although in the mid- and late nineteenth century most of Africa was carved up into European colonies, Africa became similar to British India and French Indochina. Colonial Africa was not an integral part of a wider oceanic commercial world that depended upon its native traders and exports to keep the larger system viable and growing. That world, the earlier Atlantic World, was gone by the end of the nineteenth century.

It was gone for another reason: the rise of agricultural and industrial capitalism in Great Britain in the eighteenth century and Western Europe and the United States in the nineteenth century. This new economic system transformed an Atlantic commercial system based on transporting expensive goods a long distance and essentially making money by either buying cheap and selling dear or transporting commodities for less. The rise of capitalism turned these Atlantic societies with markets into *market societies*, societies motivated primarily by profit and material gain through the competitive, market requirement to improve labor productivity, lower the costs of production and prevail in price competition. This created a mass market for cheap everyday consumer products, both agricultural commodities and industrial goods, and especially mass markets for manufactured products around the world. The commercial economy of the Atlantic World became obsolete.

A premonition of the dissolution of the Atlantic World is indicated in the engraving that is the frontispiece of the *Massachusetts Magazine*. Although the shield held by "America" is inscribed with the names of the continents of America, Europe, and Africa, the engraving itself shows only two female figures representing "America" the tutor and her apprentice, "Europe." The artist did not expect Africans in the Old World to be awakened to the rights of man. In fact, the absence of liberal revolutions in Africa (until much later), and the European colonization of Africa following the revolutions in the Americas constituted a major desynchronization that also accounts for the decline of the Atlantic World.

Chapter 10

Rivals

Great Britain and France in the Long Eighteenth Century

During the long eighteenth century, from 1689 until 1815, the Atlantic was the arena of a titanic conflict between France and Great Britain. During this second hundred years' war, these rivals expanded their conflicts from Europe itself into the Atlantic and Asia. In the Atlantic, their conflicts had enormous repercussions. France lost its North American Empire during the French and Indian War in the early 1760s while Great Britain sowed the seeds of independence in its North American seaboard colonies. The American war of independence was successful in large part because of an American alliance with France and France's war with Britain. France's debt from this conflict helped provoke the crisis that initiated the French Revolution in 1789, which, in turn, brought more than two decades of war to Europe. The wars of the French Revolution and Empire created the necessary context for the slave revolution in French Saint Domingue in the 1790s and the independence of Haiti in 1804 as well as the revolutions for independence of Spanish America and Brazil. The great Anglo-French wars of the long eighteenth century transformed the Atlantic World.

In this great power rivalry Indians and Africans were often critical participants. The struggle for North America placed Native American nations in the middle of French and British imperial ambitions, which meant that they held the balance of power and, to a considerable extent, could determine who won or lost. Free black and mulatto soldiers fought in colonial militias in the backwoods of North America and manned colored regiments in the sugar islands of the West Indies. African and creole slaves in plantation colonies resisted, ran away and revolted increasingly in the eighteenth century, particularly in the West Indies. The British and the French had to defend their sugar islands not only against each other but also from the enemy within, the large and dangerous populations of slaves. Slave uprisings, and fear of slave uprisings, were as much a part of the imperial struggle as naval strategy and national finance.

Great Britain and France had not always been rivals and enemies. In the seventeenth century, the decline of Spain as a great power left a vacuum to be filled and an American empire to be desired and, perhaps, devoured.

Table 10.1. National populations of Western
Europe, 1700–1800

Nation	1700	1800
Spain	8,770,000	12,200,000
Portugal	2,000,000	2,300,000
France	21,500,000	31,246,000
United Kingdom	8,500,000	21,226,000
The Netherlands	1,900,000	2,355,000
Western Europe	81,500,000	136,900,000

Source: Angus Maddison, *The World Economy: A Millennial
Perspective* (2003), Table B-10, p. 241.

This was the golden age of the Dutch republic, the seven United Provinces.
Spain formally recognized the independence of their former subjects in 1648
and thereafter The Netherlands dominated European overseas commerce and
Amsterdam became the financial capital of Europe. The United Provinces'
commercial hegemony helped spark three Anglo-Dutch wars in the second
half of the seventeenth century as well as two Franco-Dutch wars. The rise of
Louis XIV's France as a continental power made The Netherlands vulnerable
to invasions by land and unable over the long run to maintain its maritime
power.

After years of internal conflicts, France under Louis XIV in the late seventeenth and early eighteenth centuries had become Europe's preeminent land
power. France was Western Europe's most populous nation with more than
twenty million people and its army dwarfed those of any rival. Louis XIV
also built a powerful navy in the late seventeenth century with more ships
of the line in 1689 than Britain. Although Louis never aimed to overrun the
continent, his four major wars inspired alliances to maintain the balance of
power in Western Europe (see Table 10.1).

England during the second half of the seventeenth century was a nation
often divided internally. The English Civil War from 1640 to 1660 saw the
execution of a monarch and the rise of a powerful military regime under the
leadership of Oliver Cromwell. After Cromwell's death and the restoration
of the monarchy in Charles II in 1660, tension between crown and Parliament and between Protestants and Catholics simmered until the Glorious
Revolution of 1689, which established the supremacy of Parliament and the
Protestant succession. From mid-century, however, England was on its way
to become a commercial powerhouse. An expanding merchant marine and a
new permanent Royal Navy helped make Englishmen richer on average than
Frenchmen in 1700.

When the Dutch Stadholder Willem invaded England in 1688 and overthrew his father-in-law, the Catholic James II, the new joint monarchs of
Great Britain, William and Mary, brought Britain and the United Provinces
into a vigorous anti-French alliance. Thereafter the British and the French
fought six major wars. These wars stripped France of nearly all of her American colonies. France was no longer a maritime power nor did it maintain
hegemony of the European continent. By 1815, writes Jeremy Black, "thanks

to the success in war, Britain's maritime strength had brought her the most far-flung empire in the world, and established her in a position with which no European power could seriously compete." The Atlantic was dominated by the Royal Navy, British commerce and London finance. How these wars produced this outcome is the subject of this chapter.

10.1 Prelude

Habsburg Spain dominated Europe and the Atlantic during the sixteenth century. Spain's power was largely based on the large population, productivity and overseas wealth of Castile. All three of these fundamentals went into unmistakable decline in the early seventeenth century. Castile's demographic crisis was due to a weak and backward system of agriculture, a plague and famine at the turn of the century, as well as unwise political intervention with the expulsion of some 270,000 Moriscos between 1609 and 1614. The Spanish economy increasingly became one based on the export of raw materials and the import of manufactures and luxury products. Spain, one of the most conservative societies in Europe, closed itself off to new technologies and techniques in agriculture, industry and shipbuilding. Commercial enterprise was discouraged and even harmed by corrupt and onerous taxes and arbitrary royal confiscations of American silver remittances to merchants in Seville. Finally, the flow of American silver had diminished by the second and third decades of the seventeenth century.

The revival of the Dutch revolt in 1621 (lasting until 1648), the revolt and recovery of independence by Portugal in 1640, a long revolt by Catalonia that also began in 1640, and a war with France during the 1640s and 1650s exhausted Spanish resources and transformed Spain into a second-ranking power in European affairs. During the second half of the century, Spain was the sick man of the Atlantic. The English brazenly seized Jamaica in 1655 and the French simply took over and settled the western third of the island of Hispaniola. Spain's trade with its American kingdoms was largely composed of foreign-made goods, which meant that a good portion of American silver flowed into the accounts of Dutch, French and English merchants. By the late seventeenth century trade fleets sometimes did not cross the Atlantic for years at a time. Naturally this dismal situation encouraged smuggling and the ever-greater economic self-sufficiency of Spanish America.

Once a permanent peace was achieved between Spain and the United Provinces in 1648, Dutch ships flocked to Spanish ports, particularly Seville, and dominated Spanish trade. Dutch ships, in fact, were nearly everywhere. They carried a good portion of the trade of Portugal, England and France, smuggled contraband into Spanish America, dominated the bulk trades from the Baltic, dominated the trade of slaves from Africa and dominated the spice trade from Asia. Most of the American sugar and tobacco shipped to Europe were carried in Dutch bottoms. Dutch commercial success was based on a solid and reliable financial system centered in Amsterdam that provided substantial capital investment, superior coinage, a banking system for the exchange of currencies and the widespread employment of bills of exchange and an excellent system of maritime insurance. It was also dependent upon the reliable and economical *fluyt*, the container vessel of its day. This ship was large, rounded, lightly armed and simply rigged. This meant it could carry more cargo than the heavily armed merchantmen of England and France but required smaller crews, thus cutting costs and enhancing profits.

The United Provinces, the first great maritime power of the modern age, existed by and for trade. Governed by a merchant oligarchy through consultative assemblies, no European country enjoyed such complete liberty as The Netherlands. Peter de Groot during the Dutch Golden Age attempted to sum up his nation's advantages: "What constitutes the wealth of the republic? The opulence of its trade. And what is the source of that trade? Good government. For nothing is more attractive for the whole world than freedom of conscience and security of possessions."

It was Dutch commercial hegemony in the seventeenth century that provoked English and French mercantilist legislation. The French, English and Dutch to this point had attempted to control trade in their favor through the charter of monopoly companies. Now the English and the French would create systems of "imperial preference." England's Navigation Acts of 1651 and 1660 required that all imports be carried in English ships or in the ships of the country of origin. All imports from the American colonies, furthermore, had to be carried in English or Anglo-American ships. American staple exports, finally, had to be shipped to an English port before it could be reexported elsewhere. These acts were designed to take trade from the Dutch and to encourage English shipping and shipbuilding and they were quite successful. The French in 1664 and 1667 relied upon tariffs at first to protect the textile industry from Dutch and English competition. In 1673 all colonial trade was restricted to French ships and imports were given preferential tariff rates. Dutch herring was banned from France unless preserved in French salt. An edit of 1717 established the *Exclusif,* which prohibited the importation of all foreign commodities. English and French legislation, and their systems of mercantilism in general, were designed to ensure that colonies benefited the mother countries and, ultimately, to create a positive trade balance thus producing a net influx of specie and increasing national wealth.

The Dutch, of course, abjured mercantilist precepts. Their prosperity came from organizing and carrying the trade of others, particularly colonial trade. In the second half of the seventeenth century Dutch shipping was more than the combined total of the rest of Europe. As the economic historians Jan de Vries and Ad van der Woude put it, "without question, the Republic's trade and shipping remained, long after 1672, the single greatest concentration of international economic activity in Europe, and its entrepôt function long dominated international markets." Dutch ships and trade presented a tantalizing target.

Intense competition between English and Dutch merchants was the underlying cause of three Anglo-Dutch naval wars between 1652 and 1674. "What matters this or that reason?" noted the English general-at-sea George Monck in 1662. "What we want is more of the trade the Dutch now have." Although many merchantmen on both sides were captured during these wars and both England and The Netherlands were defeated in battle at different times, none of the wars significantly injured or rewarded either one of the combatants. Immediately preceding the second Anglo-Dutch War in 1664 the English seized Dutch forts and posts on the coast of West Africa and captured New Amsterdam and the Dutch colony of New Netherlands, which thereafter was called New York. The Dutch, in turn, took Surinam on the Guiana coast of South America. One of the long-lasting consequences of the first two wars was a transformation in naval battle tactics. Prior to the 1650s and 1660s, better-armed ships charged the enemy in no distinct formation while those less well-armed sought to disable and board enemy ships. In these wars the heavily gunned English fleets, seeking to prevent the Dutch from approaching and boarding, invented fighting in line, that is, organizing warships in a straight line, one after another, and attacking the enemy from a distance with cannonade after cannonade. In short order all of the maritime powers adopted this approach, which dominated naval warfare in the eighteenth and early nineteenth centuries. Line of battle warfare, however, rarely resulted in decisive victory and defeat. Substantial warships became known as "ships of the line" and, depending upon the number of cannon on board, were divided into categories with first-rate warships being the most formidable.

Unlike the insular English, the Dutch faced powerful enemies both at sea and on land. While England wanted to destroy the commercial power of the United Provinces, France wanted possession of the Spanish (southern) Netherlands and the United Provinces were determined at all costs to prevent that. When the United Provinces faced both England and France in war during the 1670s, a French army overran a large portion of the country. The key province of Holland was saved from French occupation by flooding the countryside. Thereafter the Dutch were forced to maintain an expensive army as well as fortresses and a navy. The strain was insupportable and by the early eighteenth century The Netherlands slipped to the status of a lesser power.

The Dutch remained a formidable commercial and industrial nation until the mid-eighteenth century. It was clear by the late seventeenth or early eighteenth century that Great Britain was becoming the new economic powerhouse and London would soon be the new commercial and financial capital of Europe and the Atlantic. Whereas in The Netherlands one branch of trade after another began a slow decline, in Britain all trades were expanding. From the 1660s to the late 1680s England's merchant marine had increased over fifty percent. Although Britain had interests on the continent, its security was dependent more on its growing navy than its relatively small army. As one pamphleteer noted in 1672: "The undoubted Interest of England is Trade since it is that alone which can make us either Rich or Safe, for without a powerful Navy, we should be a Prey to our neighbors, and without Trade, we could have neither sea-men or Ships."

10.2 Round One, 1689–1713

After the Restoration of Charles II in 1660, it was not yet clear that England and France were rivals in any serious way. The two nations went to war against the United Provinces in the 1670s. Charles II, and his brother and successor James II, admired Louis XIV and his absolutist monarchy and viewed France as a needed counterweight against a powerful Netherlands. Louis XIV paid Charles II subsidies to stay out of continental wars in the 1670s and 1680s. In the Caribbean the principal enemy was still Spain and in North America the French and English colonies were still separated by hundreds of miles of wilderness. There were, however, some signs of change.

English Protestants feared that the Catholic monarch James II would make England a client state of Catholic France. French trade was prospering and Louis XIV was building the most powerful navy in Europe. As early as 1673, Sir William Coventry stated what would soon become a basic fact of power politics: "The interest of the King of England is to keep France from being too great on the Continent, and the French interest is to keep us from being masters of the sea."

As far as the Stadholder of Holland was concerned the greatest threat to peace and security was posed by Louis XIV. The Protestant military leader of the United Provinces, Willem III, feared French ambitions in the southern and northern Netherlands and was especially concerned that the Catholic James II would join forces with the Catholic Louis XIV to destroy his country. Encouraged by English Protestants and James II's political and ideological enemies (referred to as Whigs), Willem planned an invasion of England. As nephew of Charles II and James II, and son-in-law of James, Willem had some claim to the throne. In 1688 France had begun to attack Dutch commerce in a prelude to war. To forestall England joining the war in league with France, Willem organized an invasion in late 1688 and marched on London unopposed. Risings by Whig supporters in England secured the success of the invasion and forced James to flee to France. This marked the first successful invasion of England since 1066. In early 1689 the Glorious Revolution was triumphant as Parliament offered the crown to Willem and Mary (known as William and Mary, in English history) jointly. A Declaration of Rights established a constitutional, that is, limited, monarchy that governed the country with a powerful Parliament.

In the spring of 1689 Willem brought England into war against France, joining with Austria, Spain and Brandenburg. This War of the League of Augsburg, better known as the Nine Years' War (1689–97), together with the following War of the Spanish Succession (1702–13), marked round one of the epic Anglo-French struggle of the eighteenth century.

Louis XIV intended to solve his English problem the same way Willem III did: by invasion. With the largest army and navy in Europe, the threat was palpable. In 1690 an English naval force was defeated at Beachy Head and James II led an invasion of Ireland. Willem defeated James in battle on the ground and the deposed monarch returned to France. A second attempt by James and Louis, this time to invade England, was prevented when the English won a decisive naval victory in 1692. After years of an expensive naval buildup, Louis seemed unable to use his navy to gain any strategic advantage. Thereafter the French fell behind England and The Netherlands in ship construction and altered their strategy. No longer would Louis pursue a *guerre d'escadre,* or fleet warfare. Instead, France would rely upon *guerre de course,* or commerce raiding. Privateers now sailed from French ports in France and the West Indies in considerable numbers.

During most of the sixteenth and seventeenth centuries the Americas were rarely tied to European wars in any formal way. The New World, it seemed, existed in a diplomatic state of nature where there was "no peace beyond the line." Europeans felt free to attack one another's shipping and colonies. War was an endemic local condition. Colonies were not included in formal peace treaties. All of this began to change in the second half of the seventeenth century, and dramatically so in the 1690s. Colonies were becoming more important and Atlantic empires were becoming more integrated. The Nine Years' War in Europe quickly became King William's War in America.

In the Caribbean, English and French privateers aided by buccaneers took prizes and occasionally raided undefended islands and plantations. Shipping losses by the English were enormous. Jamaica suffered a natural disaster as well as a military one during the war. In 1692 an earthquake plunged fully one-half of Port Royal, the capital and trading center of the island, into the sea. Two years later French admiral Du Casse, with a force of fifteen hundred men, twenty-three transports and three warships, invaded Jamaica. The French marched inland and burned cane fields, destroyed sugar mills and captured more than two thousand slaves. In the face of English militia and buccaneers, however, the French were unable to keep the island and from 1695 on, the English based a squadron at Jamaica.

In North America conflict developed between the French in Canada and the English in New England and New York. Colonial governors and leaders on both sides proposed ambitious plans to capture entire colonies. An invasion force from France arrived in Quebec too late in the year to undertake any operation. Massachusetts raised seven hundred men and fourteen ships and captured Port Royal in Acadia but left in a hurry when a French warship arrived. One of the most interested parties were the Iroquois, long-time enemies of the French, who launched a large raid in 1689 against settlements near Montreal, destroying fifty-six farms and killing or capturing more than three hundred Canadians. It was the worst massacre in Canadian history. The following year the governor of New France, the Comte de Pontchartrain, launched reprisals against both the New England and New York frontiers. Thereafter the French and the English and their native allies raided frontier settlements, a style of guerrilla warfare the French called *la petit guerre.*

In 1690 an intercolonial conference called for an invasion of New France by land and by sea. A joint expedition of Anglo-Americans and Iroquois warriors against Montreal attacked the small neighboring settlement of La Prairie but turned back after it had been hit by an outbreak of smallpox. The colony of Massachusetts raised two thousand soldiers and gathered thirty-four ships for an assault against Quebec. This expedition reached the capital of New France but was outnumbered by the French, suffered an outbreak of smallpox and then sailed for home without doing any damage. Perhaps the only unequivocal victory in the war was the French capture of York Fort in Hudson Bay.

La petit guerre continued on the New England and New York frontiers year after year. The Iroquois blockaded furs from reaching Montreal and terrorized French farmers. In 1693 Frontenac sent a rather large force against the Mohawk and pillaged their towns. In Maine the French were allied with the Abenakis who attacked settlers and in turn were attacked by expeditions from Massachusetts. In 1693 Frontenac dispatched a force of over two thousand French regulars, militia and Indian allies to invade New York. They advanced into Onondaga and Oneida country and destroyed their villages.

By this time, unhappy with the tepid English efforts against Canada in the war, the Iroquois had begun negotiating with the French. Of all the parties in the war, the Iroquois, with more than thirteen hundred dead and many of their villages destroyed, had suffered the most. Negotiations continued until 1701 when the Grand Settlement established a truce between the French and the Iroquois and promised Iroquois neutrality in any future conflict. For the colonists of New York, this was a disaster.

The Treaty of Ryswick in 1697 formally brought the Nine Years' War to an end. The balance of power in Europe had been maintained and the Glorious Revolution was upheld when Louis XIV recognized Willem and Mary as the legitimate rulers of England. In America all conquests were returned. A treaty between France and Spain legitimized French settlement in the western third of the island of Hispaniola, the colony of Saint Domingue.

A second round of war in Europe soon developed. The issue was the succession to the Spanish throne and the disposition of the Spanish empire. Spain's Carlos II had died in 1700 without a direct heir although his will made Louis XIV's grandson, Philippe of Anjou, the heir. The Duke of Anjou was proclaimed as Felipe V of Spain, which made France and Spain allies. A coalition of powers including England, The Netherlands, Portugal, Prussia and Austria supported the Habsburg (Austrian) heir to the throne and went to war to stop the powerful Bourbon alliance and the possibility that in the future a Bourbon prince could be king of both France and Spain and their overseas empires. The Spanish award in 1701 of the much-desired *asiento* to the French Guinea Company only raised English apprehensions regarding the ultimate control of the Spanish empire. Daniel Defoe expressed a common English fear of French commercial and naval potential at the beginning of the new war: "What is England without trade? Without her colonial trade, her trade in Turkey and Spain? What will become of her when a French garrison is installed in Cuba, when a French fleet returned with Havana silver? What would be the value of the colony at Virginia were the French at liberty to trade from Quebec to Mexico?"

During the War of the Spanish Succession, the maritime powers of Britain and The Netherlands dominated the seas. The British were allowed by their ally Portugal to use the port of Lisbon as the Royal Navy's winter base. To obtain a base in the Mediterranean the British navy seized Gibraltar from Spain. Louis XIV's great navy of 137 ships of the line in 1695 had fallen to only 80 ships by 1715. As in the previous war, the French pursued a *guerre de course*, but the British responded in 1708 with a convoy system to protect their commerce. The British and the Dutch as well attacked French commerce and by 1708 had decimated French industry by creating a shortage of imports and blocking exports. British trade, on the other hand, flourished and was larger at the end of the war than at the beginning.

At the start of the war the British and the French sent naval squadrons to the West Indies. In 1709 Louis XIV wrote, "The principal object of the present war is the commerce of the Indies and the riches they produce." War in the Caribbean followed a familiar pattern. Warships, privateers and buccaneers raided commerce as well as ports and plantations. Slaves proved to be the great booty of war. In 1706 French raiders in Nevis, whose status was uncertain, captured over three thousand slaves who were transported to Martinique. The British stationed a regiment of three thousand soldiers in Jamaica to protect the most important of Britain's sugar islands. The only permanent change of ownership occurred early in the war. British troops from Antigua were sent in 1702 to St. Kitts, the only island in the Caribbean shared by the British and the French, and forced the French commander to surrender. In the peace treaty, France ceded its half of the island to Britain.

More than the Anglo-American colonists in the West Indies, colonists in North America desperately feared the French and their Indian allies. The last war had revealed the vulnerability of the American frontier to French and Indian attacks. Colonists and their colonial governments did not have to be forced by Britain to mobilize for war. The colonial ambition to remove the French entirely from North America had long and old roots.

The best the French could hope for was to confine the populous British colonies to the eastern seaboard. Even before the outbreak of the war, the French founded Mobile and the colony of Louisiana at the mouth of the Mississippi. In the north Fort Frontenac was established on the Detroit River and Fort Pontchartrain on the river connecting Lake Ste. Claire with Lake Erie in order to protect the route between New France and Louisiana. The New York frontier was quiet thanks to the neutrality of the Iroquois.

Queen Anne's War was an Anglo-American war against the French and the Spanish. In the south the governor of Carolina sent a force of colonial militia and Yamasee allies in 1702 to take Fort San Marcos at St. Augustine in Florida. The stone fort held and the attacking force was forced to return north following the arrival of Spanish warships. A second expedition from Carolina the following year attacked the Apalachee missions near Fort San Luis, near present-day Tallahassee, and carried off nearly one thousand Indians as slaves. In the summer of 1706 French privateers carried a force of Spanish soldiers from Havana to attack Charles Town. The attack was repulsed and during the following year in revenge a Carolinian force with hundreds of Talapoosas attacked Fort San Carlos at Pensacola.

On the New England frontier, French and Indian forces resumed their attacks in Maine. The most famous raid of the war came in early 1704 when a raiding party attacked the frontier town of Deerfield, on the Connecticut River in Massachusetts, and killed more than thirty settlers and carried off more than one hundred captives. Border raids like this continued throughout the war.

In 1706 Britain proposed a major invasion of New France and most of the northern colonial governments agreed to supply troops. The plan was for one force to take Port Royal in Acadia and then Quebec up the St. Lawrence while the other force would advance through the Hudson River–Lake Champlain corridor and capture Montreal by land. In 1710 the British-American force from Massachusetts took the weakly defended Port Royal, which was renamed Annapolis Royal. Acadia became Nova Scotia. The following year two armies, one in Albany and the other at Annapolis Royal, were preparing to invade Canada. The invasion fleet ran aground on an island in the St. Lawrence losing more than seven hundred soldiers and sailors and when news of this disaster reached Albany, the invasion force was disbanded. Although the British-American project failed in its grand objective, this campaign marked the first time the British deployed a large force of regulars in North America. Increasingly, the colonies were coming to play an important role in European power politics.

A truce was agreed to in 1712 and peace was made with the Treaty of Utrecht in 1713. Britain recognized Philippe of Anjou as king of Spain, and France assured all of the interested parties of the continued separation of the crowns of Spain and France. The southern (formerly Spanish) Netherlands was transferred to Austria. Spain awarded the *asiento* to Britain along with the right to send one trading ship a year to Spanish America. France ceded Acadia and Newfoundland, as well as St. Kitts and Nevis, to Britain and recognized Britain's claim to Hudson's Bay. The Iroquois were recognized by The French (although not by the Iroquois themselves) as British subjects.

The first round went to the British. In the European struggle Louis XIV had been defeated and bankrupted. The population of France had declined by two million, large sections of industry were ruined and French commerce was greatly damaged. La Rochelle's merchant fleet declined from sixty-five ships in 1687 to less than twenty by 1713. The strength and expansion of British trade was in evidence by the fact that despite the loss or capture of more than four thousand ships to French privateers during the war, Britain had more merchantmen at the end of the war than at the beginning and British commerce was flourishing. The British ended the war with a navy equal to the combined fleets of France, Spain and The Netherlands. During the war the French Secretary of State for Foreign Affairs expressed a fear that would persist throughout the century: "France will become dependent on the English, just as Spain is dependent upon her foreign neighbors for providing what cannot be found within her Realm, in which case our industry and our navigation will die out and England will become strong by the growth of her subjects, her business and her wealth."

The wars of the late seventeenth and early eighteenth century had given employ to many seaborne warriors who drifted into buccaneering. "Privateers in time of War," wrote Daniel Defoe in 1724, "are a Nursery for Pyrates against a Peace." This was the generation of Edward Teach called "Blackbeard" and "Tatch," Bartholomew Roberts or "Black Bart," John "Calico Jack" Rackham, William Kidd and Anne Bonny. The historian Marcus Rediker estimates that there were four or five thousand Atlantic buccaneers after the War of the Spanish Succession. These "Villains of all the Nations" as they were characterized by the law-abiding, terrorized merchant ships throughout the Atlantic Ocean from their ports and bases in the Bahamas and other Caribbean shores, North America, South America, West Africa and Madagascar in the Indian Ocean.

By the second decade of the eighteenth century, commercial interests in London, the West Indies and North America resolved to end the menace. The late seventeenth century act of Parliament "for the more effectual Suppression of Piracy" was renewed in 1715 and again in 1719. The Royal Navy and colonial officials began a campaign of suppression that continued for more than a decade. Crown authorities and colonial governors offered bounties for captured pirates. In 1717 and 1718 George I granted general pardons and about 450 buccaneers surrendered. The Bahamas was brought under control by a special expedition led by Woodes Rogers with four Royal Navy men-of-war. Examples were made of pirates who did fall into the hands of officials. Pirates were condemned and hanged in London, Boston, Cape Coast Castle, Providence, Port Royal, Charles Town, Antigua, New York and elsewhere. "Atlantic piracy effectively came to an end," notes Rediker, by 1726. During the 1730s and 1740s merchant raiding was becoming rather infrequent and only a handful of buccaneers, generally operating from Madagascar, remained in business.

10.3 Interlude, 1713–39

Europe enjoyed its longest period of peace in the eighteenth century in the quarter century following the conclusion of the War of the Spanish Succession. New leadership was installed in both rivals: In Britain, the Hanoverian succession occurred in 1714, and in France, Louis XIV died the following year. Both Britain and France were financially drained and in great debt. France still enjoyed its preeminent position on the continent but it was checked not only by Britain and Austria but also by the up-and-coming great powers, Prussia and Russia. Britain had continental allies that could frustrate France's bids for continental hegemony but France really could depend only upon herself, her own navy (perhaps sometimes aided by Spain), to prevent Britain's mastery of the Atlantic. The Duke of Newcastle noted in 1742, "France will outdo us at sea when they have nothing to fear on land."

Peace was good for French sea power and commerce. Louis XV rebuilt the French navy: from thirty ships of the line in 1723, the navy was expanded to forty-five by 1744 and sixty-three ships by 1756. (The navy of France's Bourbon ally, Spain, doubled in the 1720s and 1740s.) In 1730 France was estimated to possess a merchant marine total of three thousand vessels of all sizes. France's colonial trade expanded significantly. The value of the Canadian fur trade increased from 260,000 livres in 1718 to over 2,000,000 livres in 1727. The value of sugar arriving in French ports increased from 15,000,000 livres in 1730 to 30,000,000 in 1750. The total value of West Indian exports in 1740 exceeded 100,000,000 livres a year. The Comte de Pontchartrain et Maurepas, head of the Ministry of Marine from 1723 to 1749, summed up the significance of commerce to France: "Commerce is the source of a State's happiness, power and wealth.... Wealth and power are the true interests of a nation, and nothing but commerce can procure them both."

Figure 10.2. The French Naval Base and Fortification of Louisbourg. From *Scenographia Americana: Or, a Collection of Views in North America and the West Indies* (London, 1768). Courtesy of the William L. Clements Library at the University of Michigan.

To secure New France, France constructed the fortress of Louisbourg on Ile Royale opposite Newfoundland on the passage into the St. Lawrence, in the years following the War of the Spanish Succession. It was also designed to provide a base for French privateers, protect the fishing fleet and provide a safe place for the dry cod fishery. Maurepas referred to Ile Royale as the *Clef de L'Amérique*, France's Key to America.

The colony of Louisiana was expanded with great difficulty; its unhealthy climate and impoverished economy attracted few voluntary migrants. During the peace the capital of the colony was transferred to New Orleans and after the uprising of the Natchez in 1729–30, Louisiana became a royal colony. During the 1720s and 1730s the French placed forts on the Red River in the west and on the Alabama River in the east to mark the boundaries of the colony. Clashes between French and Spanish forces in western Florida and in eastern Texas and Nebraska stopped further Spanish expansion, which limited Spanish dominion to Texas, New Mexico and California. Forts were also placed and small settlements sprang up on the Mississippi River as far north as Kaskaskia and Cahokia in Illinois country to secure passage. Despite the trade in deerskins and a few plantations, Louisiana never became an economic success and the French crown paid hundreds of thousands of livres each year to maintain this strategic outpost.

Britain certainly understood the increasing significance of naval power. In the 1730s and 1740s Parliament spent anywhere between two to four times the amount of the naval budget of France on the Royal Navy. Britain increased the size of its navy from approximately 100 ships of the line in 1689 to 124 by 1739, almost three times the size of the French navy. It was also during this peaceful interlude that Britain began to formulate and adopt a naval strategy, which came to be called "command of the sea." The Royal Navy established the Western Squadron, Britain's primary fleet, in what was called the Western Approaches, the area west of the English Channel. Here the fleet was better able to protect convoys outbound and homeward bound as well as watch the main French naval base at Brest and intercept ships coming and going. The Western Squadron was first and primarily a defensive shield against any invasion attempt of Britain. In wartime it could shut down the commerce of France's Atlantic ports and interfere with, and keep close to home, the bulk of the French navy. This strategy, in turn, allowed smaller British squadrons in distant waters to undertake operations without any great fear of interference.

As part of the strategy of command of the sea, the British navy also began to seek to control specific stretches of water: besides the Western Approaches this meant the entrance to the Mediterranean, the windward passage in the Caribbean, the straits of Florida, the mouth of the St. Lawrence and others in Asia. The British navy was also large enough now to convoy merchant fleets in time of war as well as maintain its other duties. British naval power in the Atlantic would come to be one of the critical elements, if not the most important one, in the Anglo-French wars of the eighteenth and early nineteenth centuries. In the one war where the Royal Navy failed to maintain command of the sea, the war of American independence, the French navy was crucial to the British defeat and American victory.

Even more important than naval power, however, was the British financial system. As historian Paul Kennedy notes, the Anglo-French wars fought between 1689 and 1815 were struggles of financial endurance; Britain had the greater capacity to maintain credit and therefore build ships, pay armies and raise supplies. In 1694 the Bank of England was established, which meant that loans to the state were guaranteed not by the crown but by Parliament, forming not a royal but a national debt. Because Europe's kings often renegotiated their debts and occasionally declared bankruptcy, royal credit was riskier and thus more expensive. Britain's more secure national debt backed by Parliament's power to tax made government stock more attractive to British and foreign investors and led to steadily dropping interest rates. Britain's flourishing stock exchange and a growing number of county banks increased the supply of money available to both the government and private business. Although the British tax burden was greater than in France, the system of taxation was fairer and more efficient, based on excise duties, customs and a land tax. Britain's ever-increasing trade increased state revenue. Credit was, Bishop Berkeley noted, "the principal advantage that England hath over France."

France had none of these advantages. Partial repudiations of royal debt and other arbitrary actions taken against the holders of short- and long-term debt forced investors and bankers to demand rates of interest far above those charged to the British. During the War of American Independence,

Figure 10.3. The British Warship, the *Formidable*, in the Eighteenth Century. "This view of his Majesty's ship the Formidable of 90 Guns," From Alexander Tweedie, *The naval achievements of Admiral George Lord Brydges Rodney* (Edinburgh, 1782). Courtesy of the John Carter Brown Library at Brown University.

for example, the British government borrowed at a mere three percent rate of interest. This meant that annual payments on Britain's £220,000,000 debt came to £7.3 million. France's payments on its £215,000,000 debt reached £14 million, or nearly double that of Britain's. The French system of taxation, furthermore, was unfair, inefficient, corrupt and chaotic. A number of different bodies, tax farmers and a swarm of small officeholders collected taxes from just about everyone and a good portion of it remained in private hands. Merchants in each of France's ports had different kinds of privileges and faced unequal tax burdens. Britain's financial system permitted the state to pay for its wars and expanded the pool of capital available for investment in trade and industry. In France, high interest rates for government bonds diverted capital from private business.

During this time of peace and throughout the eighteenth century, British merchants flourished. Although there were still monopoly companies and some joint-stock syndicates, most merchants trading overseas operated in small family firms and private partnerships, maintaining merchant counting houses. Merchants owned or rented their own ships, employed captains and sailors, provisioned their ships with supplies and exports, bought merchandise for their overseas clients, imported colonial staples like sugar, tobacco,

Document 10.1
The Complete English Tradesman

Daniel Defoe 1727

The instances which we have given in the last chapter, abundantly make for the honour of the British traders; and we may venture to say, at the same time, are very far from doing dishonour to the nobility who have from time to time entered into alliance with them; for it is very well known, that besides the benefit which we reap by being a trading nation, which is our principal glory, trade is a very different thing in England than it is in many other countries, and is carried on by persons who, both in their education and descent, are far from being the dregs of the people.

King Charles II, who was perhaps the prince of all the kings that ever reigned in England, who best understood the country and the people he governed, used to say, that the tradesmen were the only gentry in England. His majesty spoke it merrily, but it had a happy signification in it, such as was peculiar to the bright genius of that prince, who, though he was not the best governor, was the best acquainted with the world of all the princes of his age, if not of all the men in it; and I take no scruple to advance these three points in honour of our country; viz. –

1. That we are the greatest trading country in the world, because we have the greatest exportation of the growth and product of our land, and of the manufacture and labour of our people; and the greatest importation and consumption of the growth, product, and manufactures of other countries from abroad, of any nation in the world.
2. That our climate is the best and most agreeable to live in, because a man can be more out of doors in England than in other countries.
3. That our men are the stoutest and best, because, strip them naked from the waist upwards, and give them no weapons at but their hands and heels, and turn them into a room or stage, and lock them in with the like number of other men of any nation, man for man, and they shall beat the best men you shall find in the world.

As so many of our noble and wealthy families, as we have shown, are raised by and derived from trade, so it is true, and indeed it cannot well be otherwise, that many of the younger branches of our gentry, and even of the nobility itself, have descended again into the spring from whence they flowed, and have become tradesmen; and thence it is that, as I said above, our tradesmen in England are not, as it generally is in other countries, always of the meanest of our people. Nor is trade itself in England, as it generally is in other countries, the meanest thing the men can turn their hand to; but, on the contrary, trade is the readiest way for men to raise their fortunes and families, and therefore it is a field for men of figure and of good families to enter upon. . . .

It is owing to trade, that new discoveries have been made in lands unknown, and new settlements and plantations made, new colonies planted, and new governments formed, in the uninhabited islands, and the uncultivated continent of America; and those plantings and settlements have again enlarged and increased the trade, and thereby the wealth and power of the nation by whom they were discovered and planted; we have not increased our power, or the number of our subjects, by subduing the nations which possess those countries, and incorporating them into our own; but have entirely planted our colonies, and peopled the countries with our own subjects, natives of this island; and, excepting the negroes, which we transport from Africa to America, as slaves to work in the sugar and tobacco plantations, all our colonies, as well in the islands, as on the continent of America, are entirely peopled from Great Britain and Ireland, and chiefly the former; the natives having either removed further up into the country or, by their own folly and treachery raising war against us, been destroyed and cut off.

Daniel Defoe is well known for his novels *Robinson Crusoe* and *Moll Flanders*. He was also an accountant and businessman who wrote numerous pamphlets on politics, trade, travel and English society in the early eighteenth century. From *The Complete English Tradesman* in *The Novels and Miscellaneous Works of Daniel Defoe*, edited by Sir Walter Scott (1841), Volume 17, pp. 241–6.

indigo and cotton, and traded on their own accounts. British merchants often served as factors for American merchants and planters who consigned their sugar and other staples to the factors to sell in London. Factors also managed the money of their clients, kept their accounts, and collected moneys owed them; factorage was a good business in itself and a complement to merchants' own trading activities. British merchant houses dealt in bills of exchange and granted and received book credit. In time of war merchants obtained Letters of Marque and Reprisal and employed armed ships to capture French and Spanish ships and their cargo. In order to conduct international trade, British merchants built an Atlantic network of employees, correspondents, suppliers, agents and clients.

British merchants often integrated backward into colonial planting and slave trading to promote their principal enterprise, that of shipping and trading. Merchants created or purchased sugar plantations in the West Indies and tobacco plantations in Virginia in order to ensure steady shipments of colonial staples. To provide slaves for their own plantations, as well as to make a profit, merchants entered the African slave trade. In the late 1740s the crown-sanctioned monopoly the Royal African Company had its charter revoked. The African Trade Act of 1750 provided for free trade, which thus permitted merchant partnerships to enter the trade.

French overseas merchants, *armateur-négociants*, operated much like their British counterparts. As in Britain, family firms and partnerships dominated trade; they generally divided both vessel and cargo into fractional shares, thus sharing risk. French merchants went into planting, owned sugar refineries, established small insurance companies, exchanged currency and traded bills of exchange at a discount as well as serving as factors. The Garesché &

Billoteau firm of La Rochelle maintained agents and correspondents in Le Havre, Bordeaux, Nantes, Marseilles and Saintes in France and Au Cap and Port-au-Prince in Saint Domingue. Family members managed two Gareschè plantations in Saint Domingue. Like British merchants, French merchants were merchant capitalists; they brought together merchants and investors, took risks and spread them out over a variety of enterprises, performed specialized functions as factors and insurers, and reinvested returns.

French merchants were generally at a disadvantage with British and Dutch merchants during peacetime. Because of the strength of the British economy and the efficiency of Dutch shipping, their merchants sold goods at lower prices and paid better prices for staples. British and Dutch traders did illegal business with French and Spanish colonies. Smugglers were particularly effective because they usually paid in cash. By the 1780s the French opened their Caribbean islands to foreign slavers and imports in foreign ships.

French merchants were far more vulnerable during wartime than British merchants. Both sides raided commerce during war but because of the strength of the British navy, the British were more effective in privateering and less vulnerable to French privateers. The French also employed convoys but generally their escorts were few and weak. Beginning with the War of the Spanish Succession, each war precipitated an economic crisis in French ports. As mentioned earlier, from 1689 to 1713 La Rochelle lost forty-five of its sixty-five ships. In some wars shipping activity ceased altogether. Because the French were generally unable to supply their American colonies during wartime, the French government opened their colonies to neutral shipping.

British and French, as well as Dutch, Spanish and Portuguese merchants and traders from other nations, increasingly created an integrated Atlantic World during the eighteenth century. There was a dramatic increase in the frequency and quantity of transatlantic voyages in this century. There was an expansion of regular transatlantic postal services within each of the Atlantic empires, which made communication faster and more secure. Transoceanic commercial networks of producers, planters, agents, factors and customers were created by merchants and financiers. They were often responsible for spreading new crops, tools, technologies and ideas throughout the Atlantic World. It was not unusual to find German wares in backcountry Carolina stores and English cloth in Brazil. Despite the series of major wars, and perhaps even because of them, the Atlantic World of the eighteenth century was smaller and more integrated than it had ever been (see Map 10.1).

Most European statesmen believed overseas commerce drove national economic growth and development. "Foreign Trade," argued the British consul at Seville in 1761, "occasions an Employ for all Sorts of Artists, furnishes Work for the Poor, and augments our Manufactures, proving an efficacious Means of enriching the Nation, strengthening the State." This notion, as we have seen, greatly contributed to imperial rivalry and war. A careful examination of broader economic data reveals that commerce was indeed vital to the nations of Western Europe but Asian and even Atlantic trade was far from dominant. English foreign trade records show that the Atlantic component of the nation's trade steadily rose during the first three quarters of the

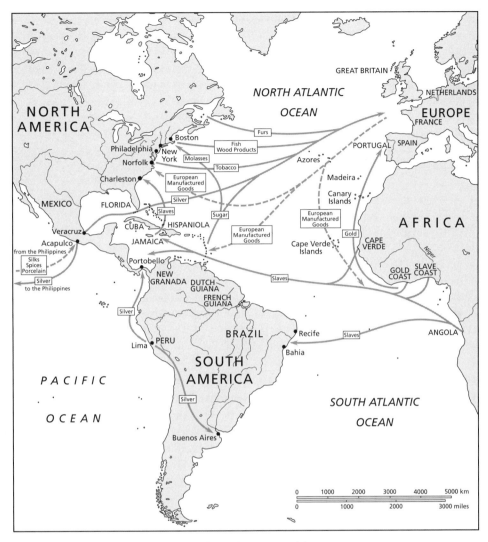

Map 10.1. The Atlantic World, c. 1750.

century. Trade with the rest of Europe, however, always mattered most (see Table 10.2). During the eighteenth century, French trade quadrupled and the Atlantic portion of French imports and reexports was especially important in driving this expansion. Nevertheless, the Atlantic component of French trade by the 1770s and 1780s was about the same for Britain, which is roughly one-third. For the Dutch republic, the East and West Indies trades in the 1780s constituted a little over thirty percent of all Dutch trade. The Atlantic slave trade, massive as it was in the eighteenth century, provided a relatively small benefit to the British and other western European national economies in terms of trade, commodities and profits. At the height of the British slave trade, in the late eighteenth century, only about five percent of the British shipping was involved in the slave trade. The expansion of Atlantic trade promoted – and in turn was itself advanced by – agricultural and industrial productivity in Western Europe, particularly in Great Britain in the eighteenth century. "It would have been surprising," writes Phyllis Dean,

Table 10.2. *The Atlantic contribution to English trade,*
1700–72

	1700–01	1750–1	1772–72
Imports			
Total World	5,819,000	7,855,000	12,432,000
Total Atlantic	1,181,000	2,404,000	4,602,000
Atlantic Portion	20.2%	30.6%	37.0%
Exports			
Total World	6,597,000	12,553,000	15,539,000
Total Atlantic	843,000	2,131,000	5,096,000
Atlantic Portion	12.7%	16.9%	32.7%

Note: Annual figures given in pounds sterling. Import figures include England and Wales. Export figures include totals of home produce and manufactures and colonial reexports. Atlantic trade refers to commerce with
North America, the West Indies and Africa. The contribution of colonial
reexports (sugar, tobacco, rice and others), commodities transported to
England and then reexported to other European countries, is not taken
into account in this table as part of the Atlantic contribution.
Source: Phyllis Deane and W. A. Cole, *British Economic Growth, 1688–*
1959 (1962): 87; and Ralph Davis, "English Foreign Trade, 1700–1774,"
The Economic History Review, New Series, 15:2 (1962) 300–3.

referring to Britain, "if a proportion of the cumulating surplus generated by
three decades [1740–70] of trading prosperity had not found its way into the
manufacturing industries whose products were the merchants' main stock in
trade. With markets expanding, interest rates low, and wage rates tending
to rise, there was a positive incentive to search for and to adopt innovations which saved labour – particularly skilled labor." Merchant capitalism
in eighteenth-century northwest Europe increasingly transformed itself into
industrial capitalism.

10.4 Round Two, 1739–63

During the previous conflicts, war had begun in Europe and spread to America and the Atlantic. Beginning in the 1730s conflict in America began to initiate wars. In international relations the importance of the colonies increased
as the Atlantic became more integrated and the American colonies more
valuable.

Britain and France increasingly gave more importance to colonies and
trade. William Wood in his book *A Survey of Trade*, published in 1722,
reflected this opinion: "Therefore I may safely advance, that our Trade and
Navigation are greatly increased by our Colonies and Plantations, and that
they are a Spring of Wealth to this Nation, since they work for us, and their
Treasure centers all here."

Tension between Britain and Spain increased throughout the 1730s. The
Spanish *guarda costa* in the Caribbean often stopped, searched and captured
British ships suspected of smuggling. The British captain Robert Jenkins was
stopped by the Spanish coast guard in 1731 and lost his ear for violating

Spanish trade law. The new British colony in Georgia, land claimed by the Spanish, established in the early 1730s to check Spanish expansion, added to the growing estrangement between the countries as did British logging camps on the Caribbean coast of Central America. By the late 1730s Spanish attacks on British vessels, and the scandal of Jenkins' ear, which was displayed to a Parliamentary committee in 1738, prompted deafening calls in London for war. Prime Minister Robert Walpole declared in the House of Commons: "This is a trading nation and the prosperity of her traders is what ought to be primarily in the eye of every gentleman in the house." Britain then declared war on Spain.

The War of Jenkins' Ear was the first British war fought exclusively over colonial issues. Pamphleteers and some British strategists believed that the war was one for free trade and that the seizure of important ports would lead Spanish Americans to embrace independence and open the empire to British merchants. They were to be disappointed. In early 1740 British forces seized Porto Bello but later attacks on Cartagena and Santiago de Cuba were repulsed. Spanish Americans remained loyal subjects. That same year General James Oglethorpe of Georgia failed in an attempt to capture St. Augustine but he successfully stopped a Spanish invasion of Georgia. Illegal British trade with Spanish America expanded during the war because warships now convoyed and protected the ships involved in smuggling.

France, unwilling to see the Spanish empire broken apart and seized by the British, assisted the Spanish and inevitably was brought into the war. In the early 1740s both Britain and France were drawn into a war to determine the succession of the Austrian crown. Louis XV's invasion of the Austrian Netherlands, furthermore, reactivated the Anglo-Dutch alliance. France, Spain, Prussia and Bavaria opposed the venerable Anglo-Austrian-Dutch alliance and in 1744 France and Britain began formal hostilities. The War of Jenkins' Ear had merged into the War of the Austrian Succession.

The Royal Navy immediately imposed a blockade upon French commerce, which ended Franco-Spanish trade and nearly cut off France's American colonies from trade and aid. This was a commercial and strategic disaster. France had become the primary supplier of manufactured goods to Spain and her colonies. During the 1730s France's seaborne trade had increased over eighty-five percent, and came close to equaling the value of British overseas trade. This disruption of trade led to the decline of industry in France as well as hunger and civil unrest. The isolation of New France, furthermore, made it more difficult to maintain trade and alliances with native peoples, who demanded quality goods at low prices. Louisbourg, furthermore, was more vulnerable to an Anglo-American assault (see Map 10.2).

King George's War, as it became known in America, fell into a familiar pattern. In the West Indies naval forces and privateers on both sides attacked vulnerable ports and plantations although there was no serious effort to conquer the other's possessions. The purpose of war was to destroy the productive capacity of the enemy by burning cane fields, wrecking milling machinery and carrying off slaves. As Richard Pares put it, "These are the ambitions of the respectable tradesman who hopes to increase his custom, by hiring the racketeer to destroy his neighbor's shop."

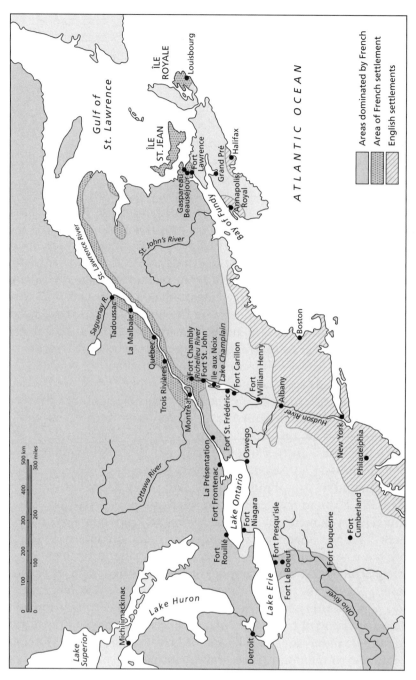

Map 10.2. Northeastern North America, c. 1755.

Legend:
- Areas dominated by French
- Area of French settlement
- English settlements

Labels on map:

Gulf of St. Lawrence

ÎLE ROYALE

Louisbourg

ÎLE ST. JEAN

Fort Lawrence

Gaspareau
Beauséjour

Grand Pré

Halifax

Annapolis Royal

Bay of Fundy

ATLANTIC OCEAN

St. John's River

St. Lawrence River

Saguenay R.

Tadoussac

La Malbaie

Québec

Trois Rivières

Montréal

Fort Chambly
Richelieu River
Fort St. John
Île aux Noix
Lake Champlain

Fort Carillon

Fort William Henry

Fort St. Frédéric

Albany

Hudson River

New York

Philadelphia

Boston

La Présentation

Fort Frontenac

Oswego

Lake Ontario

Fort Niagara

Fort Rouillé

Fort Presqu'isle

Fort Le Boeuf

Fort Duquesne

Fort Cumberland

Ohio River

Lake Erie

Detroit

Lake Huron

Michilimackinac

Lake Superior

Ottawa River

Scale bars:
0 100 200 300 400 500 km
0 100 200 300 miles

The war in the islands favored the British who maintained two naval bases in the Caribbean: Port Royal in Jamaica and English Harbor in Antigua. These naval dockyards were home to a British West Indian squadron, which could effect repairs and dock ships during the hurricane season. Unlike the French who had to send a squadron to the Caribbean from France each year (if possible), the British squadron remained in the region all year. Not until 1784 did the French establish a naval base in the Caribbean in Martinique.

In North America the French and their Indian allies again pursued the *petit guerre*, raiding the frontiers of New England and New York and also attacking Nova Scotia. At the start of the war the governor of Massachusetts proposed an expedition of four thousand colonial soldiers in one hundred transports and supported by fifteen armed ships to assault and capture Louisbourg. The British West Indies squadron sent four warships to assist the New England army. The British navy in command of the sea captured both a supply ship and a warship headed for Louisbourg. Without the possibility of resupply, Louisbourg surrendered to the New England force in June 1745. The following year a French fleet of sixty-five ships with 3,100 troops on board left France with the objective of retaking Louisbourg and burning Boston. The fleet was struck by an epidemic and when storms dispersed it, the decision was made to return to port. Massachusetts also planned the capture of Québec but the failure of British troops to arrive ended the project.

The Treaty of Aix-la-Chapelle restored peace in 1748. Although the victory of Louisbourg was a symbol of American prowess, it was returned to France in exchange for conquests in The Netherlands. This insult to American pride meant that New England would not respond so enthusiastically to an assault on Louisbourg in the next war. As was true after the Nine Years' War, this peace was seen more as a truce than a lasting settlement. Both Britain and France made preparations for a renewal of conflict.

The next war would commence in a remote corner of North America, the upper Ohio Valley. Anglo-American traders had penetrated this region and began to win tribes to their side with the offer of high-quality trade goods and high prices for pelts and skins. The British claimed the region in the Treaty of Lancaster in 1744 in which the Iroquois, who also claimed the territory by right of conquest, sold their rights to the British. In 1749 the Ohio Company of Virginia was formed and was granted 200,000 acres south of the Ohio River with the promise of 300,000 more upon the settlement of 100 families. The Loyal Land Company had obtained a grant of 800,000 acres. In 1750–51 the Ohio Company dispatched an explorer into the region with orders to submit a detailed description of their new land.

The French, who also claimed the Ohio Valley, were determined to prevent the expansion of Anglo-Americans beyond the Appalachians. They intended to join Canada and Louisiana by the Mississippi River as well as by a string of forts and missions across the Ohio Valley. In 1749 a French expedition in Ohio buried lead plates proclaiming French sovereignty and discovered that Anglo-American traders were to be found throughout the region. This prompted the new governor of New France, the Marquis Duquesne, to extend French rule by force: he ordered the construction of a series of forts, Presque Ile (at present-day Erie, Pennsylvania) and Le Boeuf (at present-

Waterford, Pennsylvania). A third fort was to be built at the Forks of the Ohio, where modern-day Pittsburgh is located.

Virginia was not to be intimidated. Lieutenant Governor Robert Dinwiddie obtained royal permission to build forts in Ohio. He chose a young militia officer, George Washington, to carry a warning to the French in 1753 and called out two hundred militiamen to build a fort at the Forks. In the spring of 1754 the French sent a force of more than one thousand men to stop the Virginians and to build their own fort at the Forks, to be called Fort Duquesne. George Washington leading Virginia militia marched into Ohio to stop the French but was badly defeated and limped back to home. Virginia then asked for assistance from London.

In 1755 Britain decided to expel the French from Ohio and made a major show of force. Two regiments of regulars were sent from Britain to spearhead a larger force of militia from several colonies. Under the command of Major General Edward Braddock, this force of 2,500 men was ordered to drive the French from Fort Duquesne and then take Fort Niagara, the gateway of New France to the west. Apparently unprepared for war in the backlands, Braddock was defeated by a force of French and Indians. More than one thousand soldiers were killed or wounded and Braddock himself was killed. From the west, French and Indian forces attacked the frontiers of Pennsylvania and Virginia.

In the northeast, the French intended to restore Acadia, the new British province of Nova Scotia. Two forts were constructed along the neck of the peninsula and the French armed local Acadians. An Anglo-American force from Boston was sent in 1755 to neutralize this threat. The forts were taken, despite more help from Acadians, and this cut off Louisbourg by land from New France. After more than forty years of living in a British province, more than ten thousand Acadians, as well as their Indian allies, were deported from Nova Scotia.

In New York, more than 3,500 New York and New England troops moved north from Albany and erected three forts including Fort William Henry at Lake George. Some 3,200 French and Indians blocked this advance and constructed Fort Carillon (later known as Ticonderoga) on Lake Champlain. The Lake Champlain-Richelieu River corridor had become the most fortified region in North America.

War had begun in America before any formal declarations or fighting in Europe. In 1756 Britain declared war on France, formally beginning the Seven Years' War. In previous wars a coalition of powers were forced to curb the ambitions of France; this time France was determined to curb the ambitions of Britain. Britain was drawn into the war in Europe to protect George II's principality of Hannover, which also brought in Prussia against the alliance of France, Austria, Sweden and Russia. Britain subsidized its ally Prussia so that it could concentrate all of its might against the overseas possessions of France. For Britain, this was a war for empire.

In North America the war began badly for Great Britain and its colonies. In 1757 a large French and Indian force marched south from Canada and captured Fort William Henry on Lake George. In a famous episode after the capitulation, France's Indian allies, unhappy about being prohibited from plundering the fort, massacred more than 250 prisoners and carried another 200 captives away. Except for Nova Scotia, the French were in the ascendancy; they were fully in control in the Ohio Valley, and their destruction of Fort William Henry (in conjunction with the neutrality of the Iroquois) opened the door to an invasion of New York.

Defeat, however, stimulated the government of Great Britain to mount an unprecedented war effort. Secretary of State William Pitt was determined to spend whatever was necessary to rout the French overseas. In North America a four-pronged offensive was planned: an invasion of Canada through the Champlain-Richelieu corridor and the capture of Mont-Réal; an invasion of the Ohio Valley and the taking of Fort Duquesne, Fort Le Boeuf, Fort Presquisle and finally Fort Niagara; an invasion of western Canada through the Mohawk River-Fort Oswego corridor and the taking of Fort Frontenac; and a seaborne amphibious invasion to capture Louisbourg and then Québec. Pitt was prepared to dispatch nearly twenty thousand British regulars to America.

Unlike previous British governments, Pitt treated the Anglo-Americans as full partners rather than subordinates. Pitt agreed to reimburse colonial expenses for the war. American officers, who in previous wars were outranked by all British regular officers, this time were given equal respect and not forced to take orders from junior regular officers. This change of attitude energized the American war effort. Colonial assemblies fully cooperated with the British government and commanders in the field, and raised tens of thousands of troops. Never before were Americans so committed to the cause of the empire.

In the summer of 1758 approximately six thousand regulars and over ten thousand colonials moved up Lake George and attacked Fort Carillon. Casualties were so high that the attack was called off and the force withdrew. In the following year a force from Fort Oswego was more successful and captured and demolished Fort Frontenac. The loss of Fort Frontenac meant that France lost control of Lake Ontario and any ability to easily supply and reinforce Fort Niagara and the forts in Ohio country. Without trade goods and gifts for the Indians of the Canadian West, the French discovered it was nearly impossible to hold on to their native allies. In 1758 a force of nine thousand regulars with only five hundred colonials captured Louisbourg.

The greatest British coup of 1758 was in the area of Indian relations. With the Treaty of Easton, the Indian nations Pennsylvania and the upper Ohio Valley abandoned their alliance with the French and made peace with Britain. The British promised a vigorous trade that the French were incapable of continuing. The natives of Ohio country, nevertheless, were skeptical of British plans: "It is plain that you white people are the cause of this war. Why do not you and the French fight in the old country, and on the sea? Why do you come to fight on our land? This makes every body believe, you want to take the land from us by force, and settle it." Faced with the loss of Indian assistance, and with an advancing colonial force, the French abandoned and destroyed Fort Duquesne. The British erected Fort Pitt on the ruins of Fort Duquesne. At the same time, the Iroquois abandoned their policy of neutrality and began an alliance with the British. The League Council concluded that the Iroquois would not be able to maintain their influence over the Ohio tribes without British cooperation.

In 1759 Major General Jeffery Amherst, commander in chief of British forces in North America, organized a three-pronged invasion of Canada. Amherst with an army of six thousand regulars and colonials would advance up the Champlain-Richelieu corridor. Brigadier General John Prideaux was ordered to ascend the Mohawk River to Oswego with five thousand regulars and colonials and seize Fort Niagara. More than a thousand Iroquois warriors provided assistance. Finally, Major General James Wolfe was given nine thousand regulars to ascend the St. Lawrence and capture Québec. Prideaux took Niagara with Iroquois help while Amherst gained command of Lake Champlain as far as Crown Point and stopped for the season.

Wolfe arrived at Québec in 119 transports and 49 warships. The French secret weapon – seven fire ships – failed to damage the invasion fleet. After confronting French forces at their strongest point below the city for two months, in September Wolfe landed his army above Québec at night and scaled the 175-foot cliff in order to put 4,500 men and two canons on the Plains of Abraham, just outside the walled city. The French commander, Lieutenant Général the Marquis de Montcalm, when informed of this disturbing development concluded: "We cannot avoid action; the enemy is entrenching, he already has two pieces of cannon. If we give him time to establish himself, we shall never be able to attack him with the sort of troops we have." Montcalm then put 4,500 troops on the Plains to attack the British. The French force suffered over 600 casualties while the British lost only 58 men. Both Wolfe and Montcalm were killed. The British army then began a siege of the city. With only three days' rations and its supply line cut, the city quickly surrendered. In 1760 three British forces, one ascending the river from Québec, another marching east from Fort Niagara, and the third marching up the Champlain-Richelieu corridor, converged on Mont-Réal. The Iroquois convinced the Indians still loyal to the French to go home. Cut off from the rest of the world and without any Indian allies, the governor-general of the colony, the marquis de Vaudreuil, surrendered Mont-Réal and New France.

The Seven Years' War was not fought only in North America. In 1758 a British naval squadron and some privateers in two separate operations attacked French slaving stations in West Africa. Fort Louis on the Senegal River was taken in the first raid and Fort Michaels on Gorée Island in the Gambia River was seized in the second. These raids cut off the slave trade to the French West Indies and also captured storehouses rich in gold dust, ivory and slaves. In the spring of 1759 Pitt organized a strong amphibious expedition against Martinique. This force of six thousand troops in sixty-four transports and convoyed by eight ships of the line found Martinique too well defended, and shifted its focus to Guadeloupe, which was taken. In 1761 Dominica surrendered to a North American expedition. In addition, in 1762 Britain, now all-powerful in the Caribbean, returned to Martinique and seized it without difficulty and took St. Lucia, St. Vincent and Grenada as well. Only Saint Domingue remained French. When Spain entered the war in 1762 a powerful British expedition captured Havana and destroyed

Figure 10.4. Quebec City, the Capital of New France. From *Scenographia Americana: Or, a Collection of Views in North America and the West Indies* (London, 1768). Courtesy of the William L. Clements Library at the University of Michigan.

a considerable Spanish naval force and ships from the East Indies captured Manila in the Philippines (see Map 10.3).

The most decisive battle of the war took place not at Québec but near Quiberon Bay on the coast of France in 1759. There the French were concentrating their forces for an invasion of Britain. Late in the year a British fleet destroyed the last effective French naval squadron on the Atlantic. This action prevented an invasion of the home island and also prevented any French attempt to reinforce New France and attempt the recapture of Québec, prevented any assistance of the French West Indies or West Africa, and allowed privateers and the Royal Navy to destroy seaborne commerce at will.

Victory over the French in North America did not immediately bring peace. In 1760–1 the Cherokee confederation, the largest single Indian polity in contact with the British in the southeast, rebelled. During the time when the Cherokee had assisted Virginia in defense of its frontier, hunters and traders from South Carolina crossed into Indian territory, poached Indian game and threatened the Cherokee food supply as well as deer for the skin trade. The Cherokee attacked backcountry trading posts and frontier settlements and the British retaliated by destroying one-half of their villages. The Cherokee then sued for peace.

This victory in the southeast as well as the British victory over the French led Major General Amherst to alter Indian policy. In 1761 Amherst ended the policy of giving gifts to Indian tribes to reinforce peaceful relations and advance trade. "You know how adverse I am," Amherst wrote to Indian

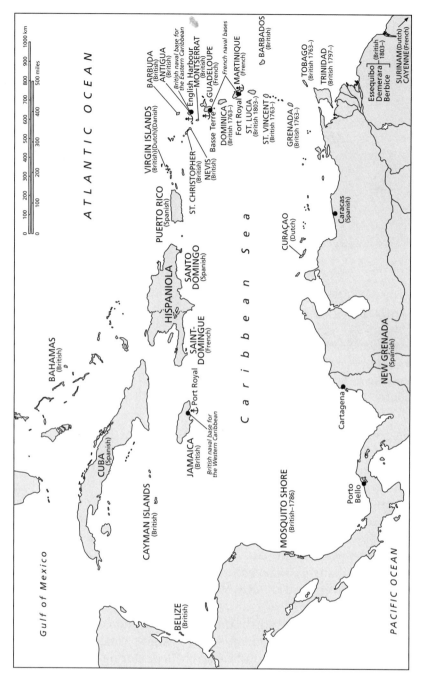

Map 10.3. The West Indies, c. 1750.

Commissioner William Johnson, "to purchasing the good behavior of Indians." Amherst also ordered Anglo-American traders not to trade alcohol, limit trades of powder and shot and to trade with Indians not in their villages but only at approved trading posts. With this change of policy, British–Indian relations began to deteriorate, but it was not the only irritant. When the British made peace with the Ohio tribes they promised an expansion of trade on favorable terms and, at the end of the war, a withdrawal of British military forces. Instead of this, the British placed new restrictions on trade and expanded their military presence by taking over all of the western French forts.

At the same time that relations were worsening, a revitalization movement was sweeping through the native peoples of the west. One of several prophets, Neolin from the western Delawares, was advocating that Indians abstain from alcohol and trade with whites. He also advocated that Indians relearn their ancient ways so that they would no longer be dependent upon whites. This movement coincided with discontent over British policy and helped spark rebellions throughout the Ohio country and the Great Lakes in 1763. Referred to as Pontiac's Conspiracy, after the Ottawa war leader who attacked Fort Detroit, this widespread series of revolts threatened to remove the British from the entire region the French called the *pays d'en haut*. Ottawas, Kickapoo, Chippewas, Shawnees, Mingos, Wyandots, Miamis and other nations were also unhappy about the complete removal of the French from North America and the migration of British settlers into the west. The rebellion sought to defeat the British in order to revive New France. Within a few weeks every British fort and post in the west with the exception of Detroit, Niagara and Pitt had fallen to Indian rebels.

Amherst was prepared to retaliate severely and even ordered the first known effort of biological warfare by giving rebels blankets infected with smallpox. The commander in chief, however, was ordered to return to London and his successor simply did not have the forces to repress the rebellion. The British government responded with the Royal Proclamation of 1763, which created three new provinces (Quebec, East and West Florida) and reserved the territory west of the Appalachians for the Indians. No land grants here were permitted and the territory was closed temporarily to white settlers. Gift giving was resumed and all trade restrictions were lifted. Although scattered resistance continued until 1765, peace agreements restored peace. The British empire, it seemed, could be coerced by determined native tribes.

Peace between the British and the French was restored by the Treaty of Paris in 1763. By this agreement all of Canada and Louisiana east of the Mississippi River, with the exception of New Orleans, was ceded to Great Britain. Cape Breton Island, and Ile Royale the site of Louisbourg, became British. Britain returned Martinique, Guadeloupe and St. Lucia in the Caribbean and Gorée Island in West Africa. Britain demanded the cession of Dominica, Tobago, St. Vincent and Grenada. Free navigation of the Mississippi River was granted to British subjects while Britain conceded fishing rights on the Newfoundland banks. Britain returned Havana and Manila to Spain and Spain ceded Florida to Britain. In a separate treaty, France compensated Spain by ceding New Orleans and Louisiana west of the Mississippi River.

Document 10.2
The Late War in North America Between France and England

Pierre Pouchot 1781

In spite of a century & a half of occupation, France had hardly been able to derive any advantage from that huge country in North America known as Canada. The colony they had founded there was still, so to speak, in its infancy when it passed under a foreign yoke. It could doubtless have emerged from this state of feebleness, or rather prostration, and have become one day very useful to the mother country, if only France had known more about it & had not been so often deceived by those who ought to have provided accurate information. People in France had such false ideas of the country that they considered its usefulness to lie entirely in the fur trade & and failed to distinguish clearly between the colonials and the Indians. In fact, ignorance & blindness were carried to such a degree that some people were even delighted at its loss.

England, in order to prevent its rival from opening its eyes as to the advantages of Canada, began to plan an invasion even in peacetime. The court in London had long repented using up its strength & wealth in vainly expressing its hatred of the French by giving aid to their enemies. Immediately after signing the Treaty of Aix-la Chapelle [1748], she conceived the notion of seizing the French colonies. Canada, or New France, which had to be considered as their most solid bulwark thus became the object of her initiatives. The first step was to extend as far as the St. Lawrence River the settlements she was hastening to found in the region of Acadia. Those which were envisaged, whether in the area of Hudson's Bay, or beyond the Appalachians towards the banks of the Ohio, or on the shores of Lakes Ontario & Erie, were absolutely limitless. The intended consequences of this plan was that what would have remained to France would have been useless to her since entry to the territory would have been blocked.

The Council at St. James fully expected complaints & claims on the part of France, which proposed the appointment of commissioners from each nation to decide upon the boundaries of the respective colonies. This proposal was accepted & it was decided as a first step that there should be no changes to the territories in question. Scarcely had this agreement been signed than England unscrupulously violated it. Her commissioners could never agree with those of France since they had secret orders to raise difficulties & to agree upon nothing. However, Louis XV wished for peace at any price. His ministers believed they could secure its continuance on conditions that England would not have rejected under any other circumstances. But she was by now resolved to use her overwhelming naval strength, to destroy French commercial interests, which, through their vigor, awakened her hatred & aroused her jealousy.

If English aspirations had been fully understood, no one would have been surprised when the English minister only replied to the advantageous proposals made by the Court at Versailles by making unacceptable demands. Despite this, he pretended to negotiate & to desire peace, 'but he had no other aim,' as a judicious statesman observes, 'than to concentrate all his initiatives & to inspire in France a sense of security which would prevent her from preparing the way by dispersing her forces.'

A number of philosophers, or rather men who imagine they deserve the name, every time they can demonstrate the wrong-headedness of princes & can ridicule it, have obstinately declined to perceive the true cause of this war. They have persistently claimed that France only exposed itself to so many setbacks & shed so much blood in order to retain a precarious hold on 'frozen territory.' a few 'savage regions' or 'useless deserts.' Such was the language of cynical ignorance. These are the terms that pride & presumption would dearly like to consecrate as the oracles of sublime reason.

Pierre Pouchot arrived in New France in 1755 with the second battalion of Béarn and served throughout the war in Canada until he was returned to France in 1761. In this introduction to his memoirs, Pouchot blames the British for their commercial and territorial aggression and French ministers and intellectuals for not realizing the value of New France. *Source: Memoirs on The Late War in North America between France and England*. By Pierre Pouchot. [1781] Translated by Michael Cardy. Edited and Annotated by Brian Leigh Dunnigan (1994), pp. 53–5. Permission from Brian Leigh Bunnigan.

Great Britain was the dominant power in the Atlantic World by the end of the Seven Years' War. The war had again devastated French trade while the value of British exports and reexports had risen thirty percent. France's North American empire was gone, "a conquest," wrote Robert Rogers, the leader of Roger's Rangers, "perhaps of the greatest importance that is to be met with in British annals." Many in France, however, including the foreign minister, the Duc de Choiseul, had considered New France and Louisiana a financial albatross and viewed the return of Martinique and Guadeloupe a great victory. The philosopher Voltaire congratulated Choiseul: "Permit me to complement you. I am like the public; I think peace better than Canada and I think France can be happy without Québec."

10.5 Rivalry in South America

The rivalry between Great Britain and France was not the only one in the Americas in the eighteenth century. In South America, Spain and Portugal had a long-standing dispute regarding the southern boundary of Brazil. Unlike the British and French disputes, however, the Spanish and the Portuguese eventually solved theirs through diplomacy.

The Treaty of Tordesillas in 1494 determined the original western boundary of Brazil. This treaty drew a line from north-to-south just west of the mouth of the Amazon River, where the city of Belem came to be located, in the north and about five hundred miles west and more than six hundred miles north of the Rio de la Plata estuary. During the union of the Crowns of

Spain and Portugal (1580–1640) neither Portugal nor Spain worried about any Brazilian boundary, and as a result Portuguese Jesuits and settlers moved northwest and southwest of the Tordesillas line. At the same time, Spanish Jesuits expanded northeast into what is today Paraguay to minister to the Guaraní.

After 1640 the common interest of Spain and Portugal in the Rio de la Plata brought them into conflict. In the same year that Portugal regained its independence, the Portuguese founded the Colonia do Sacramento on the northeastern shore of the Rio de la Plata estuary or what the Spanish called the *Banda Oriental*. The Portuguese were primarily interested in commercial access to the Spanish empire, primarily the silver from Potosí. During the War of the Spanish Succession, Spanish forces from Buenos Aires seized the Portuguese settlement but gave it back at the end of the war. To counter the Portuguese in the *Banda Oriental*, the Spanish built the town of Felipe y Santiago (modern Montevideo) in 1724 and expanded their settlements along this shore north of the Portuguese. Thereafter this region was subject to conflict from time to time. In 1734 the governor of Buenos Aires attacked Colonia do Sacramento and the Portuguese responded by attacking Montevideo. To further advance their claim to the region south of the Tordesillas line, Portugal founded the town of Rio Grande do Sul, north of Montevideo on the Atlantic coast.

Relations between Spain and Portugal entered a new, friendlier phase in 1746 when a Portuguese princess became a Spanish queen. The two governments made a genuine effort to settle the old dispute with the Treaty of Madrid in 1750. This treaty abrogated the Tordesillas line and drew a new boundary between the two American empires. The territory of Brazil expanded west to include the Amazon River and its tributaries and in the southwest expanded west to the Paraná River. Colonia do Sacramento was awarded to Spain and seven Spanish missions and their thirty thousand neophytes northeast of the new boundary were awarded to Portugal. The Jesuits and their charges were required to withdraw from the region. The Treaty of Madrid also put forward the "doctrine of the two spheres" by which both powers agreed that peace should be maintained in South America regardless of any war between them in Europe.

The Treaty of Madrid, however, was never ratified. It aroused opposition in both Madrid and Lisbon and the new Portuguese Secretary of State ignored the provision for the cession of Colonia do Sacramento. At the same time, the Guaraní, encouraged by the Jesuits, resisted the transfer and fought both the Spanish and the Portuguese in the Guaraní War. An intermittent frontier war continued in the 1750s and into the 1760s. The Spanish and the Portuguese fortified the southwestern frontier and the Portuguese built ten forts on the Amazon to ensure their possession. The Treaty of Madrid was formally abrogated with the Convention of the Pardo in 1761.

The Seven Years' War brought conflict again to the region. In 1762 troops led by the governor of Buenos Aires captured Colonia do Sacramento and invaded the Brazilian province of Rio Grande. The end of the war the same year interrupted this colonial conflict and the peace treaty stipulated that all territories be returned. Spain did return Colonia do Sacramento but not Rio

Grande. In 1776 the first viceroy of the Río de la Plata took an expeditionary force of twenty thousand men and captured Colonia do Sacramento. The Portuguese continued to fight for the province and recovered it with the assistance of a British naval squadron.

In 1777 the Spanish and the Portuguese reached a final settlement with the Treaty of San Ildefonso. Both governments agreed to a revised version of the Treaty of Madrid. Colonia do Sacramento and its hinterlands were turned over to Spain and Rio Grande province was recognized as Portuguese. Spain retained the Seven Missions land and the *Banda Oriental*; this boundary remained unchanged until the Portuguese seized the Seven Missions in 1801. The two empires continued to dispute the *Banda Oriental*, as did the new independent nations of Argentina and Brazil in the early nineteenth century. In order to secure peace between their two trade partners, Great Britain brokered into existence the buffer state of Uruguay in 1828.

10.6 The War of American Independence

For fifteen years after the Seven Years' War, Great Britain and France remained at peace and showed little sign of wanting another war. In the late 1770s, however, France saw an opportunity to humiliate its old rival. France signed a formal alliance with the United States, then at war with Great Britain, and was later joined by Spain and The Netherlands. The repression of a rebellion in the colonies had escalated into another imperial war. This was anticipated by William Pitt, now Lord Camden, in 1775: "It is obvious, my lords, that you cannot furnish armies or treasure competent to the mighty purpose of subduing America ... but whether France and Spain will be tame, inactive spectators of your efforts and distractions is well worth the consideration of our lordships."

The War of American Independence grew directly out of the consequences of the Seven Years' War. The removal of the French from North America and thus the disappearance of the French and Indian military threat eliminated one of the most important conditions that Anglo-Americans believed required a powerful British presence in America. With peace it was generally assumed in America that most British troops would be withdrawn. Britain, however, determined that there was a need for a continuing strong military presence in America, particularly in the string of western forts. By 1764 the total cost of administering the North American colonies was £350,000 per year of which nearly two-thirds went to defense against Indians. In addition, it was expected in London that Anglo-Americans would pay at least part of the large expenses of these military forces.

In fact, there was a general consensus in the British government that Anglo-Americans needed to begin to bear more of the cost of empire. During the last war the British national debt had doubled. The tax burden of Britons, however, was many times that of Anglo-Americans who most immediately benefited from the war. Thus two measures were taken to raise more revenue in the colonies. The first was the new Sugar Act, which reduced duties on molasses but tightened enforcement of collection. The second was the

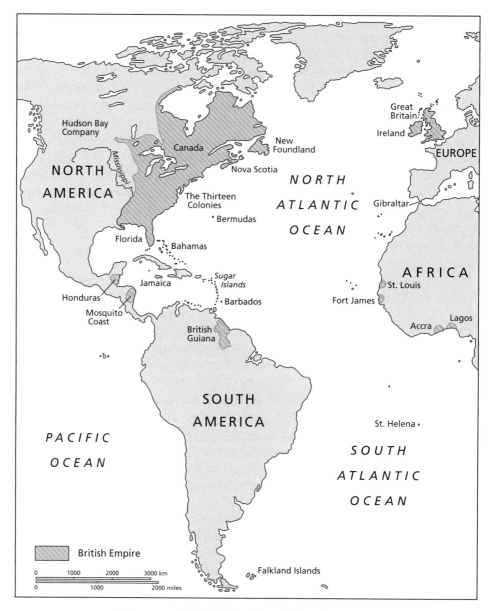

Map 10.4. The British Atlantic Empire, 1763.

Stamp Act, which extended, for the first time, the British taxation system to America. This act taxed all legal and commercial documents as well as newspapers, playing cards and other kinds of paper. Protests in America and plans for an American boycott of British imports created a Stamp Act Crisis and Parliament abrogated the offending act but declared its authority to pass any legislation it thought appropriate for any part of the empire (see Map 10.4).

Some Anglo-Americans informed the government that colonists opposed direct taxation but accepted Parliament's right to regulate trade. Operating with this understanding, Parliament then passed the Townsend Duties, which placed a trade tax on imported paper, lead, paint and tea. These duties were designed to pay the salaries of imperial officials in America and thus make them more independent of the will and wishes of colonial assemblies. By the late 1760s, however, a number of influential Anglo-Americans, particularly those in Massachusetts, were coming to the position that Parliament had no right whatsoever to pass laws for the colonies that were governed by elected assemblies. What began as a dispute over taxation was becoming a constitutional crisis regarding the authority of Parliament in America.

In the early 1770s American protests regarding Parliament's abuse of authority began a spiral of colonial provocations and official punishment and repression. Protests brought the dispatch of British regulars to Boston, which sparked more protests that in one incident led to troops firing on civilians, which locals called the Boston Massacre. The dumping of taxable tea in Boston Harbor by protesters dressed as Indians produced the closing of Boston Harbor, the suspension of the municipal government and the imposition of compensation payments on the population. If the British government could abuse one colony, it was increasingly coming to be understood, it could do likewise in every colony. In response to these "Intolerable Acts," twelve colonies sent representatives to the first Continental Congress. Colonists also began to build up stocks of arms to defend, if necessary, their rights as Englishmen.

The war began in Massachusetts in the spring of 1775. A British force was dispatched to seize military stores in Concord but militiamen put up resistance in Lexington and Concord, and armed colonials forced the British to retreat to Boston. Thereafter colonials besieged British troops in Boston. A Second Continental Congress appointed George Washington as commander in chief of the Continental Army, which at that time meant the disorganized and untrained soldiers surrounding Boston. When Washington placed cannon on Dorchester Heights overlooking Boston in March 1776, the British evacuated the city and withdrew to Halifax, Nova Scotia.

Washington, looking for a dramatic early victory, decided to attack the undermanned British in Canada and capture Mont-Réal and Quebec. One American force advanced up the Champlain-Richelieu corridor and captured Montreal. Another force, led by Colonel Benedict Arnold, chose a novel invasion route, an ascent up the Kennebec River in Maine, and met the victors of Montreal on the outskirts of Quebec. The British force was too weak to present battle and the American force was too weak to undertake an effective siege. An assault on the walls of the city in December failed and Arnold retired to winter quarters outside the city. The arrival of British reinforcements by sea in the spring of 1776 convinced Arnold to retreat to New York by way of Lake Champlain.

When the war began, representatives of the Continental Congress met with French officials seeking an alliance. The Earl of Sandwich at the Admiralty expected the intervention of France and Spain. "At bottom our inveterate enemies," he wrote, " . . . [are] only waiting for the favorite moment to strike the blow." The French, however, waited to see if the Americans possessed the determination to resist the full weight of the British empire. Until they were satisfied, the French beginning in 1776 began to secretly aid the Americans with arms and allowed American privateers to use French ports as bases.

The British also obtained foreign assistance. In treaties with Hesse, Kassel and Brunswick in 1776, the British army secured eighteen thousand German troops. Other small princely states contributed troops and overall nearly thirty thousand Germans would serve in America. The British began 1776 with approximately twenty-five thousand British and German troops.

In 1776 the British captured New York City and, for a time, Philadelphia. The high command organized a campaign for 1777 designed to divide the colonies along the Hudson River and thus isolate New England from the middle and southern colonies. General John Burgoyne was to march an army south from Canada through the Champlain-Richelieu corridor as far as Albany. General Sir William Howe was, according to the plan, to ascend the Hudson from New York and join forces with Burgoyne. The operation, however, did not go according to plan. Howe was diverted to Philadelphia. Burgoyne, inexperienced with warfare in the wilderness of North America, had difficulty moving his army through the lakes and woods of New York and suffered a decisive defeat at Saratoga in October 1777. Short of provisions and unlikely to be reinforced, Burgoyne surrendered his army of seven thousand men to the American General Horatio Gates.

This was the evidence the French wanted to see. In early 1778 France and the United States signed Treaties of Commerce and Alliance. War soon followed between France and Great Britain; Spain entered the war in mid-1779 and The Netherlands in 1780. Since the last war Britain had allowed its navy to decline and because most of its fleet was on station in North America, few ships were left on the Western Approaches. The French, on the other hand, had built up their navy since 1763 and was joined by the Spanish and Dutch navies. The Royal Navy was outnumbered and too widely dispersed, and could not blockade French ports; it no longer had command of the sea in the Atlantic.

For the first time in one hundred years, the French and the Spanish had a superiority of forces in the Caribbean. The British were forced to divert troops from North America to reinforce posts in the West Indies and Florida. During the first year of the war, the quantity of sugar shipped to London fell by half. The French captured Dominica in 1778 but the British replied by taking St. Lucia. The following year the French seized St. Vincent and Grenada. When the Dutch entered the war in 1780 they felt the sting of the Royal Navy. St. Eustatius fell to a British squadron and was soon followed by their three Guiana colonies, Demerara, Essequibo and Berbice. The Dutch lost all but one of their slave-trading stations in West Africa and all of their factories in India and Ceylon. The French recaptured all three Dutch Guiana colonies the following year and also took Tobago. The Spanish operating from New Orleans then took Pensacola and reconquered Florida and then New Providence in the Bahamas. In 1782 the French captured Nevis, St. Kitts and Montserrat.

Entry of France into the war gave the Americans the confidence to reject a British offer that conceded nearly every point of contention except sovereignty. The Franco-American military alliance did not at first appear to be very effective. A combined attack on the British base at Rhode Island in 1778 floundered. A year later, after the beginning of the British southern

Figure 10.5. The West Indies in the Late Eighteenth Century. A map from Bryan Edwards, *The History, Civil and Commercial, of the British Colonies in the West Indies* (Dublin, 1703), Vol. 1. Courtesy of the William L. Clements Library at the University of Michigan.

campaign, a combined Franco-American force failed to take Savannah. Not until 1780 was a French expeditionary force able to land in America, in Rhode Island.

In the west, Indians allied with the British along with loyalist units attacked frontier settlements in New York and Pennsylvania. In Ohio country, Indians unhappy about the streams of settlers coming from the east conducted an unceasing war, which entailed atrocities on both sides. Virginian troops fought Ohioan tribes for Kentucky and southern Indiana. Most Iroquois tribes, particularly the Mohawk, Seneca and Cayuga, joined the British in attacks on rebel towns. The British also obtained the allegiance of some Cherokee. Washington maintained control of Fort Pitt and in 1779 ordered a scorched earth campaign against the Iroquois, burning villages and destroying cultivated fields. Thousands of Iroquois were forced to spend the rest of the war as refugees near the British fort at Niagara. Similar expeditions were sent against the Cherokees.

In late 1778 the British shifted their attention to the southern colonies, which they believed were more loyal. The British army and navy took Savannah and Charles Town with the understanding that they could use these as bases to rally loyalist forces. Lord Charles Cornwallis faced the American

General Nathanial Greene who lost as many battles as he won but wore down the British force. In the spring of 1781 Cornwallis marched his army into Virginia and announced: "I am quite tired of marching about the country.... If we mean an offensive war in America, we must abandon New York and bring our whole force into Virginia."

In New York Washington wished to organize a combined operation, with the Comte de Rochambeau's French army located at Newport, against British forces in the lower Hudson. Washington was also looking for assistance by a large French fleet under Admiral de Grasse that had sailed from France for the Caribbean. Washington, however, heard from de Grasse that he was sailing for the Chesapeake with twenty-nine warships and three thousand troops. At that point Washington realized he had a chance of catching and trapping Cornwallis' army on Yorktown peninsula. By late September 1781 the armies of Washington and Rochambeau, about seventeen thousand troops, had closed in on Cornwallis. De Grasse was in control of the Chesapeake Capes and prevented any reinforcement or supply of the British army. Aware that he was beaten, Cornwallis surrendered his army of seven thousand men on October 19. The government in London, now more worried by the war with France, prepared to cut its losses and make peace with the Americans.

Peace negotiations were begun in Paris. The British agreed to a formal cessation of hostilities with the Americans but war continued with the French. The destruction of de Grasse's fleet in the Caribbean at the Battle of the Saints in 1782 brought the French to the negotiating table. The United States and Britain, however, negotiated a separate peace. The American demand for Canada, naturally enough, fell on deaf ears. The Treaty of Paris of 1783 secured formal recognition of American independence. Britain ceded to the United States the territory east of the Mississippi River and south of the Great Lakes. France recovered Tobago, lost twenty years earlier and Britain recovered Grenada, St. Vincent, St. Kitts, Montserrat, Nevis, Dominica and New Providence. The British ceded Florida to Spain.

Twenty years after the humiliating defeat in the Seven Years' War France had some measure of revenge upon Britain. France had helped dismember part of the British empire and hoped to diminish British trade with America while increasing French trade. The war, and American independence, however, had only interrupted British trade with its former colonies. Britain's trade had declined by one-third and more than three thousand merchant ships had been captured or destroyed. In the 1780s, however, British exports to the United States were booming. For France, the 1778–83 war had cost more than France's three previous wars together. Interest charges on the debt were double those of the British. A financial crisis was looming.

10.7 Round Three, 1792–1815

The French Revolution plunged Europe into one of the most severe crises of its history. The continent was thrown into almost constant war from 1792 to 1815. Three great coalitions were mounted against France in 1793–96, 1799–1802, and 1805–14 by Austria, Prussia, Russia and Great Britain.

The Anglo-French struggle, however, proceeded with only one intermission, 1802–3, for more than twenty-two years. Because the British had command of the sea, the Atlantic was less of a region of contention than it had been in the 1740s and 1750s. Repercussions of the conflict in Europe, nevertheless, produced some significant revolutionary transformations in the Atlantic World.

The financial crisis in France following the War of American Independence led to the calling of the Estates-General in 1789, the body of representatives of nobles, clergy and commoners, which had not met since 1614. This event took place during a period of bad harvests, high food prices, famine, high taxation and general impoverishment, and growing protests regarding social injustice and governmental impotence. The Estates General turned itself into a national assembly, wrote a liberal constitution instituting a constitutional monarchy, agreed to a Declaration of the Rights of Man and the Citizen, and abolished the apparatus of serfdom and noble privilege. Thereafter, a tumultuous, unplanned and unprecedented cascade of events ensued. "The most dangerous moment for a bad government," wrote Alexis de Tocqueville in his *Old Regime and the French Revolution* in 1856, "is generally that in which it sets about reform."

A Parisian insurrection overthrew the monarchy and brought to power a National Convention and the declaration of a Republic. In early 1793 Louis XVI was tried and executed as a traitor. Jacobin Committees of Public Safety used the guillotine to intimidate and eliminate enemies of the Revolution. Perhaps thirty-five thousand Frenchmen and women died by the guillotine, in the hands of mobs, in prisons or in the provinces fighting the revolutionary government. Many more emigrated to avoid such turbulent and uncertain conditions. Political instability produced new constitutions and structures of government. A new assembly and a five-man executive Directory replaced the Convention in 1793. In 1799 a three-man Consulate was established and was dominated by France's most successful general, Napoleon Bonaparte. In 1802 Bonaparte made himself first Consul for life and in 1804 raised himself to Emperor, Napoleon I.

The rest of Europe, particularly its crowned heads, watched events in France with horror. The rulers of Austria, Russia, Prussia, Spain and others favored intervention to rescue Louis XVI. The revolutionaries took the initiative in the spring of 1792 and declared war on Austria and Prussia. Britain, led by William Pitt (the Younger) declared war the following year and organized a coalition of continental powers who one by one dropped out or changed sides, eventually leaving only Britain to confront France.

In 1793 Britain undertook to blockade all French ports, destroy French naval and commercial power and conquer all French colonies in the West Indies. The loss of trade, particularly colonial trade, it was believed in London, would ruin French finances and thus her ability to make war. French royalists assisted the British in the summer of 1793 by handing over the Toulon squadron. Two-thirds of the French officer corps had emigrated, which seriously weakened the navy. During the first thirty months of the war, France lost thirty-two ships of the line by capture or destruction; French naval power never fully recovered. In the fall of 1793 a British fleet with seventeen thousand men sailed to the Caribbean. In 1793–4 the British naval and land forces captured Martinique, Guadeloupe, St. Lucia, Tobago and intervened in Saint Domingue.

The British thought that the disorder in Saint Domingue, and an invitation by French planters to intervene, would make their conquest an easy one. Revolution in France had upset the status quo in Saint Domingue. Artisans and merchants competed with sugar and coffee planters for control of the government. Mulattos, seeking equal civil rights with whites, had taken power in some areas. In addition, in 1791 black slaves arose in rebellion in the north, took control of the interior and allied themselves with the Spanish. In 1793, in an attempt to take control of the situation, a Commissioner from the National Convention exceeded his authority and emancipated the slaves in the north of the island. Into this chaotic colony, the British landed an army. "No one will deny that it was not absolutely necessary for the safety of our colonies," noted a British observer somewhat later, "that a black state not exist in the Western Hemisphere."

One of the reasons for the British intervention in Saint Domingue – to halt the contagion of slave rebellion – was turned around by the French to improve their position. Jacobin Commissions in Guadeloupe and St. Lucia emancipated slaves who then rose up in rebellion against local planters and the British occupying forces. The winds of liberty also blew to Jamaica, where maroons rose in rebellion, and St. Vincent, where Caribs rebelled. In 1795–6 the British sent an army of thirty-five thousand men to Jamaica to force the maroons to surrender and to regain control in Grenada and St. Vincent. These events prevented the British from reinforcing their army in Saint Domingue where conditions were turning against them.

Toussaint L'Ouverture, one of the leaders of the rebellious slaves, defected from the Spanish and made peace with the French Republic in 1794. For the next four years an increasingly powerful Toussaint, appointed lieutenant-governor and then commander in chief of the French republican army in Saint Domingue, fought the British army to a standstill. Yellow fever and battle brought British losses to a staggering fourteen thousand men in 1796. Toussaint's friendship with John Adams enabled him to obtain ships and supplies from the United States to fight the British. In 1797 Toussaint's forces confined the British to a few port towns and in the spring of 1798 Toussaint and the British negotiated a British withdrawal from the island. During the campaign in Saint Domingue, the British lost more than twenty-five thousand men to disease and battle.

In 1801 Toussaint invaded the Spanish part of Hispaniola, which the Spanish had ceded to France in 1795, and unified the French and Spanish parts of the island. In the same year, however, Napoleon decided to reimpose French control over the island. In 1802 an army of nearly sixty thousand French soldiers invaded Hispaniola, quickly capturing the Spanish side of the island and then the French side. Toussaint fell into French hands and was sent into captivity in France where he died. When it became known that Napoleon intended to restore the plantation system, the slave trade and slavery, several of Toussaint's former generals rallied popular support to defend the freedom of their people. When Britain and France went to war in 1803 the British gave military assistance to the black forces. The French spent twenty-one months trying to subdue the former slaves and lost fifty-eight thousand men, including the commander in chief, in the failed attempt. In late 1803 what remained of the French army in Saint Domingue surrendered to the British in Jamaica. In January 1, 1804, General Jean Jacques Dessalines and the other victorious black generals proclaimed the independence of Haiti, the second republic in the New World.

Napoleon's campaign in Saint Domingue was part of a larger effort to rebuild the French colonial system in America. In 1800 France recovered Louisiana from Spain in exchange for a small Italian principality. The failure to regain control in Saint Domingue, however, led Napoleon to give up his dream of a new American empire. "Damn sugar, damn coffee, damn colonies," he is reported to have exclaimed in 1803. As he prepared again to go to war against Britain, Napoleon freed himself of any remaining obligation. In May 1803 France sold Louisiana to the United States for $15,000,000. The western boundary of the new republic now stretched as far as the Rocky Mountains.

The French regime in the Spanish portion of Saint Domingue survived and seemingly provoked the authorities in Haiti by a decree, which permitted slave owners to cross the frontier to obtain slaves for their plantations. Thus in 1805 Haitian armies invaded Santo Domingo and virtually destroyed the properties and fields of the colony. The French military government, with the support of the Spanish inhabitants, pushed the Haitians back. In 1808–9 the Spanish inhabitants rose up against the French regime and forced it to surrender. Both Santo Domingo and Haiti were devastated countries.

When The Netherlands and Spain joined forces with Republican France in 1795, Britain fell upon their overseas possessions. The Dutch colony at the Cape of Good Hope in southern Africa and the three Guiana colonies of Demerara, Essequibo and Berbice were seized. In 1797 the British seized the Spanish island of Trinidad and invaded Puerto Rico but were repulsed. Dutch Surinam fell in 1799, followed by Curaçao in 1800, and French St. Martin's in 1801. Swedish St. Bartholomew and Danish St. Thomas and St. Croix were seized in 1801.

The Treaty of Amiens, concluded between Great Britain and France in 1802, brought peace temporarily to Europe and brought France the return of all of its colonies lost during the previous nine years of war. All of The Netherlands' American colonies were also returned. Spain ceded Trinidad to Britain.

Peace in Europe was short-lived. War between Britain and France began again in 1803 and two years later Britain was joined by Austria, Russia and Sweden. France and Spain opposed this third coalition. Napoleon proved to be unstoppable on the continent but his dream to invade Britain ended with the battle of Trafalgar in 1805 when a British fleet decisively defeated the combined French and Spanish fleets. That same year Napoleon in his Berlin Decree imposed a blockade of Great Britain and closed the continent to British trade, thus inaugurating the Continental System.

When Portugal refused to join the Continental System in 1807, a French army invaded the country and captured Lisbon. One week before the fall of

Lisbon, the Prince Regent João and the royal family, and nearly the entire government of Portugal – some ten to fifteen thousand people in all – sailed under a British escort to Rio de Janeiro, Brazil. The new Portuguese government in exile raised Brazil to a kingdom in status equal to Portugal itself and opened Brazil to the trade of all nations. Prince João (King after 1816) and the government remained in Brazil following the defeat of France and did not return to Portugal until 1821.

In 1808 Napoleon forced the abdication of Spain's Carlos IV and his heir, Prince Fernando, and gave the crown of Spain to his brother Joseph Bonaparte. The majority of the Spanish people, however, did not accept this arrangement and rebelled. A number of provincial juntas and, after a time a central junta led the resistance. This body called together a popular assembly, the General and Extraordinary Cortes, which in 1812 wrote a liberal constitution, which created a constitutional monarchy for Spain. The crisis in Spain led to a crisis of authority in Spanish America and a conflict, in many provinces, between royal officials who wanted to preserve the existing system of government and Spanish Americans who favored self-governing autonomous provinces until the legitimate Spanish king was restored to his throne. Out of this disorder emerged the Spanish American revolutions for independence.

The British intervened with military force in Portugal and Spain in 1808 and fought what came to be called the Peninsular War for six years. Prior to 1808 Britain had viewed Spain as an enemy and Spanish America as fair game. One British military leader, the naval commander of the Cape of Good Hope, on his own initiative attempted to seize Buenos Aires and Montevideo in 1806. Along with the seizure of Trinidad, the British appeared to be interested in taking control of strategic ports in order to break into the mainland market of Spanish America without having the burden of direct rule. Control of Buenos Aires, however, was foiled by a popular uprising, which killed, wounded or captured nearly one-half of the eleven-thousand-man British army.

After 1808 Britain and Spain were allies. Britain did not interfere in the turmoil in Spanish America until after Fernando VII was restored to the throne in 1814. In addition, even after 1814 British policy was officially hands off but London turned a blind eye on the employment of British mercenaries by Spanish American revolutionaries. The most dramatic intervention was the Argentine liberator José de San Martín's employment of British naval officer Thomas Cochrane and seven warships in 1818. This mercenary squadron captured Spain's strongest naval base in the Pacific, established command of the sea and intercepted reinforcements from Spain, and transported San Martín's army from Chile to the coast of Peru.

As the new Spanish American nations threw off Spanish rule, British merchants and bankers moved into the port cities. The new governments obtained British loans and British goods glutted each national market. Boom turned to bust as imported goods piled up unsold and governments had to default on their loans. In time, however, expectations were scaled back, British trade was restored to moderate levels, and Latin America became a semi-colonial economic dependency of Great Britain.

In both the 1790s and the 1800s the United States was neutral and traded with both Britain and France. This brought interference and frequently the capture of U.S. trading ships by both Britain and France who attempted to restrict the commerce of their enemy. In the late 1790s such treatment brought an undeclared naval war between France and the United States. In the mid-1800s the administration of Thomas Jefferson kept the United States out of war by imposing a trade embargo on his own nation. When the embargo was lifted in 1809 British abuses against American trade, including the impressment of Americans to serve in the Royal Navy, continued. By 1812 the United States was sufficiently outraged for President James Madison to declare war on Great Britain. The war itself was a series of military blunders on both sides. The United States failed in its attempts to invade Canada and a British force was unable to advance south through Lake Champlain. Although a small British force captured Washington briefly and burned the White House, an attempt to capture New Orleans in January 1815 was defeated. The peace treaty signed on Christmas Eve 1814 restored the prewar status quo.

When war was renewed with France in 1803 the British again seized all of the French possessions in the West Indies and in Guiana, including Cayenne for the first time, and the Dutch Guiana colonies, Surinam and Curaçao. By the end of 1811 every American colonial possession of France was in British hands. In the final settlement of 1815 the British returned Martinique and Guadeloupe and annexed St. Lucia, Tobago and held onto Trinidad. The British purchased from the Dutch Demerara, Essequibo and Berbice. The twenty-six British colonies of 1792 had become forty-three by 1816.

Britain's long struggle against revolutionary and imperial France resulted in the most complete triumph in the age of European imperial warfare. Britain dominated European trade with the Americas, Africa, the Near East and Asia. During the wars British trade expanded from £78,000,000 in 1796 to £151,000,000 by 1815. The requirements of war had spurred production of iron and steel and thus an industrial revolution in Britain. French trade, with the loss of Saint Domingue and the other sugar islands as well as the loss of the slave trade, was severely damaged. The Atlantic sector of France's economy, so long cut off from the rest of the world, deindustrialized. At the end of the day, concluded General Gneisenau, "Great Britain has no greater obligation than to this ruffian [Napoleon]. For through the events which he has brought about, England's greatness, prosperity, and wealth have risen high. She is mistress of the sea and neither in this dominion nor in world trade has she now a single rival to fear."

For more than 125 years, from 1689 to 1815, Great Britain and France fought a series of wars that determined which power would dominate the Atlantic World and, in fact, the entire world. Until 1814–5, France and her armies were by and large unequaled on the continent whereas Britain and her navy and merchant marine were most of the time unequaled in the Atlantic. Early on in the conflict, Britain played to its strength and sought to maintain command of the sea and use that advantage to promote the growth of overseas trade and the security and prosperity of its overseas empire in the Americas. In turn, trade and colonies enhanced the wealth and power of Great

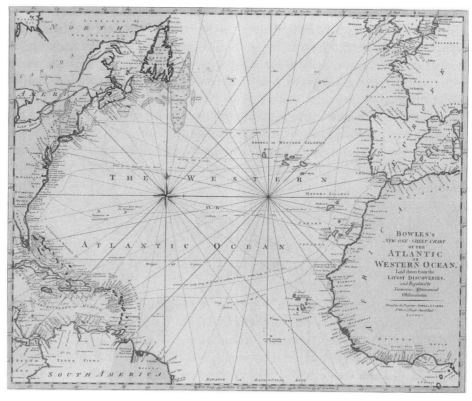

Figure 10.6. The Atlantic Arena in the Eighteenth Century. From Bowles's New One-Sheet Chart of the Atlantic or Western Ocean (London, 1781). Courtesy of the William L. Clements Library at the University of Michigan.

Britain. The turning point was the Seven Years' War at mid-century. In this first of the world wars, Britain threw almost all of its resources into defeating the French overseas. Each war severely damaged French overseas commerce yet her merchants quickly recovered. French overseas trade increased fivefold from 1700–89. French colonial trade, primarily with Saint Domingue and the other sugar islands, increased tenfold during the same interval. Nevertheless, in spite of France's considerable commercial expansion in the eighteenth century, in 1785 the British merchant fleet was more than two times the size of the French fleet, twelve thousand ships compared to five thousand. By 1814 the British merchant marine numbered more than twenty-one thousand ships.

The only strategic victory for France in the eighteenth century was the American war for independence. During this conflict France (along with Spain and The Netherlands), took advantage of Britain's temporary naval weakness and loss of command of the sea, and helped the American rebels dismember part of the British empire. This victory, however, was not an unambiguous one. The destruction of de Grasse's fleet at the Battle of the Saints in 1782 reestablished the perception, and to a great extent the reality, of British naval ascendancy. The independence of the United States did not hamper British trade with America; in fact, it expanded in the 1780s.

France was swept from the Atlantic during the third and last round of the Anglo-French rivalry of the long eighteenth century. The British shut down French overseas trade in the 1790s and 1800s as a result of an effective blockade of French ports. The revolution in Saint Domingue, furthermore, put an end to French ascendancy in the Atlantic sugar trade. France lost her markets in Spain, and therefore Spanish America, while Spain's prostration left no obstacle to British contraband trade with its American empire. After 1807, British ships were Brazil's lifelines to the rest of the world. By the end of the conflict, Britain had seized every one of France's remaining American colonies. Only British magnanimity in the peace negotiations permitted France to retain Martinique and Guadeloupe.

In the interstices of these great struggles for wealth, prestige, land and power during the last decades of the eighteenth century, new kinds of contests for liberty and equality broke out on both sides of the Atlantic Ocean.

10.8 Further Reading

Fred Anderson, *Crucible of War: The Seven Years' War and the Fate of Empire in British North America, 1754-1766* (New York, 2000).

Jeremy Black, *The British Seaborne Empire* (New Haven, 2004).

John G. Clark, *La Rochelle and the Atlantic Economy during the Eighteenth Century* (Baltimore, 1981).

Henry C. Clark, editor, *Commerce, Culture, & Liberty: Readings on Capitalism before Adam Smith* (Indianapolis, 2003).

Peter A. Coclain, editor, *The Atlantic Economy during the Seventeenth and Eighteenth Centuries: Organization, Operation, Practice, and Personnel* (Charleston, 2005).

Ralph Davis, *A Commerical Revolution: English Overseas Trade in the 17th and 18th Centuries* (London, 1967).

Roger Hainsworth and Christine Churches, *The Anglo-Dutch Naval Wars, 1652-1674* (Phoenix Mill, 1998).

David Hancock, *Citizens of the World: London Merchants and the Integration of the British Atlantic Community, 1735-1785* (Cambridge, 1995).

Jonathan Israel, *Dutch Primacy in World Trade, 1585-1740* (Oxford, 1989).

John Keegan, *Fields of Battle: The Wars for North America* (New York, 1996).

Paul Kennedy, *The Rise and Fall of the Great Powers: Economic Change and Military Conflict from 1500 to 2000* (New York, 1987).

Peggy K. Liss, *Atlantic Empires: The Network of Trade and Revolution, 1713-1826* (Baltimore, 1983).

John Lynch, *The Hispanic World in Crisis and Change, 1598-1700* (Oxford, 1994).

A.T. Mahan, *The Influence of Sea Power Upon History, 1660-1783*, twelfth edition (Boston, 1918).

P. J. Marshall, editor, *The Oxford History of the British Empire*: Volume II: *The Eighteenth Century* (Oxford, 1998).

John Robert McNeill, *Atlantic Empires of France and Spain: Louisbourg and Havana, 1700-1763* (Chapel Hill, 1985).

David Ormrod, *The Rise of Commerical Empires: England and the Netherlands in the Age of Mercantilism, 1650-1770* (Cambridge, 2003).

Peter Padfield, *Maritime Supremacy and the Opening of the Western Mind* (Woodstock, New York, 1999).

J. H. Parry, *Trade and Dominion: The European Oversea Empires in the Eighteenth Century* (London, 1971).

Howard H. Peckham, *The Colonial Wars, 1689-1762* (Chicago, 1964).

M. Postlethwayt, *Universal Dictionary of Trade and Commerce*, 2 volumes (London, 1774).

Marcus Rediker, *Villains of All Nations: Atlantic Pirates in the Golden Age* (New York, 2004).

Jan de Vries and Ad van der Woude, *The First Modern Economy: Success, Failure, and Perseverance of the Dutch Economy, 1500–1815* (Cambridge, 1997).

Max Savelle, *Empires to Nations: Expansion in America, 1713–1824* (Minneapolis, 1974).

Stanley J. Stein and Barbara H. Stein, *Apogee of Empire: Spain and New Spain in the Age of Charles III, 1759–1789* (Baltimore, 2003).

Chapter 11

Liberty

The Atlantic World in the Age of Revolution

The fifty years following the American Declaration of Independence constituted the Age of Revolution in the Atlantic World. There were many revolutions on both sides of the Atlantic and several different kinds of revolutions. Artisans, merchants and landowners, commoners and aristocrats, made republican revolutions to make colonies into independent nations and to overthrow absolutism, kings and nobility. Slaves, free blacks, mulattos and peasant villagers organized and fought popular revolutions to overturn deeply entrenched social and political orders. The revolutions had many different causes and many different outcomes but they were all movements of liberation. Liberty was the word on the lips of all revolutionaries, their great motivation and objective. No other region of the world has ever seen such a widespread and sustained period of organized disorder on behalf of an abstract principle. It was an extraordinary period of transformation and it began the dissolution of the Atlantic World. We live in a world still shaped by the principles of these late eighteenth and early nineteenth-century revolutionaries.

So much turmoil in such a compact epoch must have had some common origin or characteristics. Revolutionaries of the age generally shared a political language, democratic republicanism, which had roots in European history and European political thought. This was a radical ideology in the eighteenth and early nineteenth centuries when the governing systems in most countries were monarchies and their social systems were aristocratic and authoritarian. Revolutionary republicanism opposed political and social systems based on the principle that all power and authority was determined by the accident of birth and family rank. It maintained that "the people" were the ultimate authority within a state and that all citizens possessed certain natural rights, which were, or should be, inviolate. It further held that the people had the right and duty to overthrow a despotic ruler or state and the right to create a new system of government that best met their needs; in short they possessed the right to revolution.

Such ideas were discussed and debated by well-educated gentlemen in the late eighteenth century but it was inevitable that people at the lower end of the social system would find them appealing and relevant to their lives. Shopkeepers, artisans and laborers were politicized and participated in revolutionary activities in the United States and France. Slaves in Saint Domingue in the 1790s as well as Indians and *mestizo* peasants in Mexico and Peru in the 1810s sought liberty and equality in their revolutions against a ruling class. In some places democratic pressures from below forced wealthy and powerful elites to construct political systems that gave more authority to ordinary people than ever before in history.

The revolutionary turmoil and institution building of the age was also the result of pollination, sometimes cross-pollination. Earlier revolutions inspired, influenced and even in some cases directly provoked later revolutions, and later revolutions occasionally influenced existing ones. "Let us follow the example of the United States," declared Duke de Montmorency in the debate about a French declaration of rights in August 1789; "they have set a great example in the new hemisphere." The French Revolution permitted and provoked the revolution of the slaves in Saint Domingue, and the new Republic of Haiti assisted the Venezuelan revolutionary Simón Bolívar.

The revolutions of the late eighteenth and early nineteenth century occurred in several slave societies. The contrast between the rhetoric of liberty and the reality of slaveholding was glaring and many people at the time commented on it and in a few cases acted upon it. Many slave owners were revolutionaries who nevertheless never thought their struggle for liberty might inspire or apply to the most unfree among them. The Age of Revolution, however, did begin a general questioning of the justice of slavery for the first time. Elite and popular movements to end the slave trade and abolish slavery were begun at this time and started to produce results here and there. The elimination of slavery everywhere in the Atlantic World except Africa was one of the most important, although delayed, consequences of the Age of Revolution. Because of the complexity of the campaign against the slave trade and slavery, which continued many decades after the last revolution of the age, this subject is taken up in Chapter 13.

The Age of Revolution in the Atlantic World is the topic of the following two chapters. Chapter 11 considers the first and most influential upheavals, the American and French Revolutions, as well as the European revolutions they inspired or spawned in the 1780s and the 1790s. Chapter 12 examines the Haitian Revolution of the 1790s, the Mexican Revolution of the 1810s, and the other revolutions in the Iberian world on both sides of the Atlantic. Both chapters attempt to demonstrate that all of these revolutions were part of a larger and interconnected revolutionary movement that shared many political principles as well as methods of making revolution. These chapters, then, follow R. R. Palmer's lead in arguing that "this whole [Atlantic] civilization was swept in the last four decades of the eighteenth century by a single revolutionary movement, which manifested itself in different ways and with varying success in different countries, yet in all of them showed similar objectives and principles."

11.1 The Age of Reason

"The motto of enlightenment is therefore: *Sapere Aude*! Have courage to use your own understanding." Here Kant in his famous essay of 1784, "What is Enlightenment?" defined the essence of the eighteenth-century age of reason. Modern man, freed from the accumulated prejudices and superstition, in short, the irrationalism of past ages, could apply reason not only to the study of nature but also to human and social affairs. Progress was therefore achievable for society and happiness was possible for the individual.

After the French Revolution a number of writers, most notably Alexis de Tocqueville, identified certain "abstract theories and generalizations regarding the nature of government" as partially responsible for the coming and radicalism of the revolution. This connection between the bundle of ideas and attitudes of certain eighteenth-century intellectuals, which has come to be called the Enlightenment, and the revolutions of the late eighteenth and early nineteenth centuries have long been suggested and debated. There is, however, no simple or direct correspondence between these ideas and the political activities of revolutionaries. Enlightenment writers shared no common political ideology; in fact, they often contradicted each other. Some favored monarchical absolutism, albeit enlightened absolutism, whereas others were constitutionalists and democrats. Few were revolutionaries in thought let alone deed. "The political programs advocated by our eighteenth-century writers," Tocqueville wrote, "varied so much that any attempt to synthesize them or deduce a single coherent theory of government from them would be labor lost."

It is accurate, nevertheless, to call the Enlightenment, as historian Eric Hobsbawm does, a revolutionary ideology. Just as the scientific revolution of the seventeenth century challenged traditional notions of authority and truth about the natural world, enlightenment thinkers questioned traditional notions of authority and truth about the political, social and even religious order of their time. They believed that human reason could understand human problems and offer real solutions to them. They not only wanted to understand the world but through the use of reason and intellect make it better or even create a new world. The Marquis de Condorcet, in his essay on the "progress of the human spirit," presented a picture of humanity casting off the shackles of prejudice and creating a free society where men recognized "no other master apart from their own reason."

A number of Enlightenment thinkers opposed religious zealotry, which they considered just so much superstition, prejudice and bigotry. Voltaire, one of the giants of the Enlightenment, pointed out the irrationality of religious zealotry: "What can we say to a man who tells you that he would rather obey God than men, and that therefore he is sure to go to heaven for butchering you." Fanaticism is to superstition, he noted, "what delirium is to fever and rage to anger." His most famous slogan was *Ecrasons l'infame*: Make War on the Fanatics. Dennis Diderot, coeditor of the most famous publishing venture associated with the Enlightenment, the *Encyclopédie*, saw education not religion as the source of virtue and happiness. A number of Enlightenment thinkers viewed God less as a redeemer or a father and more as a rational creator, like a watchmaker who built the mechanism and then let it run. This theology left humanity with the responsibility for the day-to-day operation of the world. Such a view of religion encouraged many eighteenth-century thinkers to favor freedom of conscience and religious tolerance.

Enlightenment political thinkers, particularly those later consulted by constitutionalists and revolutionaries, condemned arbitrary and despotic government and valued liberty above all. Liberty could best be preserved, the Italian Marquis de Beccaria noted in his book *On Crimes and Punishments*, when society had as few laws as possible and when those who violated law were punished predictably but not excessively. Punishment, he argued, was not an infliction legitimated by divine sanction against sin but a necessary self-defense mechanism by society. The prohibition of cruel and unusual punishment that was established by many new revolutionary states owed its inspiration to this book.

Traditionally Europeans grounded the notion of rights in privilege, the privileges granted to towns, universities, clergy, nobility and so on and thus to members of these corporate bodies. Enlightenment thinkers, however, began to view individual rights as the natural possession of all humanity. All men, in this sense, are born equal. Persons possessed rights not because they had been born with aristocratic status and legal privileges, or were members of corporate bodies, but because they were human. This universalistic idea of rights could be applied in unexpected ways. Women, for example, were perceived by many philosophers like Rousseau as fundamentally different from men whose "nature" made them supposedly emotional, credulous and incapable of reasoning. Mary Wollstonecraft in *Vindication of the Rights of Women* (1791) confronted this contradiction. If women are rational they possess the same natural rights as men. "Contending for the rights of woman," she wrote, "my main argument is but on this simple principle."

One of the most influential political thinkers of the Enlightenment was the late seventeenth-century English theorist John Locke. His two treatises on government introduced radical English Whig political thought to the eighteenth-century Atlantic World. Locke undercut the theoretical foundation of authoritarian government in his first treatise when he argued that paternal and political powers were not the same thing. Subjects were not members of the king's family and household, as was traditionally held, and thus should not be treated like wives and children, beings dependent upon the kindness of the husband and father and without any rights. In the second treatise Locke also discarded the traditional notion that man was basically an evil creature who needed to be restrained by government. To Locke, man was rational and his enlightened self-interest would prompt him to cooperate with his neighbors to create government, usually a monarchy, to restrain violence and settle disputes. This is a social contract, an arrangement binding on every member unless the ruler misuses the authority he is given and creates a breach of contract, which permits members of society to reformulate government. "The end of government is the good of mankind," wrote Locke. "Upon the forfeiture of their rulers, [power] reverts to the society and the people have a right to act as supreme and place it in a new form or new hands, as they think good."

Locke's concept of a social contract included several subversive ideas. He denied the idea of a monarch ruling by divine right. The people and not a king are sovereign and by natural law they possess the rights of life, liberty and property. The social contract implies the principle of consent, that government is the creation of the people and dependent upon their will. Government's most important task is not to constrain men but to safeguard their rights. To protect the people and their rights Locke suggested elections to confirm the consent of the people and advocated the division of power among a legislative, executive and federative authority, the last in charge of foreign policy and war. He favored the toleration of minority opinion in a state and pleaded for religious freedom for all groups except atheists and Catholics. Ultimately the sovereign people retain the power to remove or alter a government if its abuses its trust, they have a right to revolution.

Perhaps the most widely consulted political treatise of the eighteenth century was Montesquieu's *Spirit of the Laws*, first published in France in 1748, and thereafter republished many times although it was placed on the Catholic Church's index of forbidden books. Montesquieu was most concerned about devising a system of government that protected liberty. The political system of Great Britain, he pointed out, was the best system of government in existence because it divided the powers of government, which checked and balanced one another and thus prevented any one man or group of men from possessing absolute power and threatening liberty. Montesquieu admired how the king, representing the monarchical principle, the House of Lords, acting on behalf of the nobility, and the House of Commons, the people's chamber, shared power and acted as an independent check on each other and thus protected the country against tyranny. He also believed the governing system of France had some positive components, particularly such intermediate bodies as the Parlements, a system of provincial courts, which prevented undue concentration of power and often opposed royal decrees.

Montesquieu drew inspiration from not only the British constitution and the Glorious Revolution of 1688 but also from Greek and Roman republicanism. He was no republican, however, and certainly no democrat. He firmly believed in the political value of a hierarchical society, a system of inherited ranks and an aristocratic code of honor. Equality and democracy brought despotism because it concentrated power in the hands of the people. "Monarchical government, by nature," he wrote, "is constituted by dependent and subordinate intermediate powers. The most natural such dependent intermediate power is that of the nobility.... Abolish in a monarchy the prerogatives of lords and clergy, nobility and towns, and soon you will have either a popular or a despotic state."

Montesquieu thus took a rather commonplace eighteenth-century idea, that nobility balanced monarchy to preserve liberty, and transformed it into one of the most influential political principles of the age: separation of powers. He argued that a separation of powers between different estates, that is, social groups, within government and among the executive, legislative and judicial powers of government resulted in a "spirit of moderation" that best prevented despotism and preserved liberty. "When the legislative and executive powers are united in the same person, or in the same body of magistrates,

Document 11.1
Political Aphorisms

John Locke 1691

'Tis plain, from what hath been said, that all Government proceeds from the People. Now I will prove that they have Authority to put back the next Inheritors to Government, when unfit or uncapable to Govern: And also to dispossess them that are in lawful Possession, if they fulfil not the Laws and Conditions by which, and for which their Dignities were given them; and when it is done upon just and urgent Causes, and by Public Authority of the whole Body, and Justice thereof is plain; as when the Prince shall endeavour to establish Idolatry, contrary to the Laws of the Land; or any Religion which is repugnant to the Scripture, as *Popery*, &c. or to destroy the People, or make them Slaves to his Tyrannical Will and Pleasure: For as the whole Body is of more Authority than the Head, and may cure it when out of order; so may the Weal-Public cure or purge their Heads, when they are pernitious or destructive to the Body Politick; seeing that a Body Civil may have divers Heads by Succession or Election, and cannot be bound to one, as a Body Natural is: which Body Natural, if it had Ability to cut off its aking or sickly Head, and take another. I doubt not but it would do it, and that all Men would confess it had Authority sufficient, and Reason so to do, rather than the other Parts should perish, or live in Pain and continual Torment: So may the Body Politick chuse another Head and Governour in the room of its destructive One; which hath been done for many Ages, and God hath wonderfully concurred therein (for the most part) with such Judicial Acts of the Common-Wealth against their Evil Princes; not only prospering the same, but by giving them commonly some notable Successor in Place of the Deprived, thereby both to justify the Fact, and remedy the Fault of him that went before; First, King Saul was slain by the Philistines by God's Appointment, for not fulfilling the Law and Limits prescribed unto him. Ammon was lawful King also, yet was he slain, for that he walked not in the way prescribed him by God, (2 Kings. 21) and David and Sosiah were made Kings in their rooms, who were two most excellent Princes.

In the late seventeenth century, in an age of expanding royal absolutionism, the English philosopher John Locke argues from history and theology that there cannot be any absolute government and that the people can overthrow kings. *Source: Political Aphorisms: Or, the True Maxims of Government Displayed.* The Third Edition [John Locke]. 1691.

there can be no liberty. Again, there is no liberty, if the judiciary power be not separated from the legislative and executive."

Perhaps the most radical of the eighteenth-century political thinkers was Jean-Jacques Rousseau. In his *Discourse on the Origins of Inequality among Men* in 1753, Rousseau emphasized the evils of property and the oppression of the poor by the rich. In *The Social Contract* (1762) he sought the origin of rightful authority and found it not in kings or even government itself but in the people. Like Locke, Rousseau argued that in a state of nature, individuals come together voluntarily to form a political association. "This act of association," he wrote, "creates a moral and collective body.... Those who are associated in it take collectively the name of people, and severally are called citizens, as sharing in the sovereign power, and subjects, as being under the laws of the State." Rousseau's innovation in the theory of popular sovereignty was his argument that the original social contract created the General Will, the whole common force that protected the person and property of each associate. When the citizen places himself under the supreme direction of the General Will he remains free and is, in effect, obeying himself. The subject must be sovereign. Those who obey must command. Thus the government is not the master of men but their servant.

Hereditary aristocracy, in which those who inherit wealth and power also inherit government position, Rousseau argued, is the worst kind of government. The best kind of government is elective, although he denounced representative assemblies as throwbacks to the age of feudalism. He favored the direct democracy of popular assemblies. Citizens cannot delegate lawmaking power because this is a power of sovereignty itself. Citizens cannot turn over their political affairs to a distinct political class and remain free; they must constantly practice the business of politics, that is, attend assemblies, supervise officials and ratify laws. For Locke popular sovereignty came into force only in times of revolution, when a people are forced to change government and reconstitute power. For Rousseau, popular sovereignty required of citizens an active sense of membership and participation.

During the French Revolution certain Enlightenment writers, Rousseau above all, were honored as precursors of the Revolution. They articulated several fundamental principles such as the definition of a natural morality and the reformation of political and social ties on the basis of the idea of liberty. The radical leader Maximilien Robespierre in 1794 had this to say about Rousseau: "Among those who, in times I speak of, stood out in the career of letters and philosophy, one man, by the elevation of his soul and by the grandeur of his character, showed himself worthy of the ministry as preceptor of humankind.... Ah! if he had been witness to this revolution whose precursor he was and that bore him to the Pantheon, who can doubt that his generous soul would have embraced with transport the cause of justice and equality!"

The Spanish world was not generally known for its attachment to Enlightenment thinkers and ideas but reform was in the air in Spain and Spanish America despite the church's ban on books even remotely associated with the Enlightenment. Spain's Locke, Francisco Suárez, advanced the notion of a compact between the people and the king. Francisco Martínez Marina implied that the restoration of a national representative body, an idea and an institution found in Spanish history, was necessary for the restoration of national greatness. José Miranda, the Venezuelan revolutionary of the early nineteenth century, wrote: "The Enlightenment was neither a theory nor a doctrine, but a new way of looking at things and interpreting life.... The

Enlightenment possessed, however, a principle common to the multitude of ideas that sprouted in its bosom: the liberty or autonomy of reason."

Beccaria, Locke, Montesquieu, Rousseau and other Enlightenment thinkers undermined the theoretical underpinning of the absolutist monarchical states of the age. In a continent of monarchies, political theorists saw divine right as a dogma without basis. In the light of reason, reverence and obedience, the traditional props of government held no meaning in an arbitrary or despotic state. Government grew out of nature itself and could be intelligently reformed and even completely reconstituted for the benefit of everyone. The author of the article on government in the *Encyclopédie* summarized some of the most important revolutionary principles of the coming Age of Revolution: "The good of the people must be the great purpose of government. By the laws of nature and of reason, the governors are invested with power to that end. And the greatest good of the people is liberty. It is to the state what health is to the individual."

Why did this intellectual ferment take place in Europe? The Enlightenment was formed in the context of the history of the Atlantic World. The tradition of New World ethnography profoundly influenced thinkers in the late seventeenth and the eighteenth centuries. These writings created the idea of the Noble Savage that forced Europeans to view their own societies and institutions against the idealized portraits of Native American societies. John Locke in the 1680s wrote: "In the beginning all the world was America." These least artificial and most natural of human beings lived in liberty, equality and great happiness, many of the Enlightenment philosophers believed. It was modern or civilized life that was burdened by accretions of generations of irrational artifice, superstition, hierarchy and tyranny. Rousseau argued that Native American societies were guided by a "natural aristocracy" composed of elders and chiefs who were given deference on the rational basis of their experience and skills and not on the irrational – European – basis of inheritance and wealth. The violent conquests of Indian kingdoms and the inhumane slave trade and New World slavery also presented eighteenth-century thinkers with additional failings of European civilization. "The discovery of the New World, in Diderot's view," writes Sankar Mudthu, "promoted crucial advances in moral thought because its diverse practices enabled thinkers to discern what the roots of political injustice, economic exploitation, and social ills were not divinely sanctioned or historically inevitable but 'only the product of time, ignorance, weakness and deceit.'"

The European age of expansion, of course, brought Europeans into contact with societies beyond the Americas. From the fifteenth century on Europeans had numerous travelers' accounts of African societies to read and study. In the seventeenth and eighteenth centuries, furthermore, more Africans lived in Europe as free persons, servants, clerics, musicians, students and scholars. Rare was the noble or royal court that did not display their "exotic" Africans. A few excelled in religion or academia. Anton Wilhelm Amo, born on the Gold Coast, for example, was brought to Amsterdam in 1707 and, with the patronage of a German nobleman, obtained university degrees and pursued a career as a university lecturer. We know much less about the influence that knowledge about Africa and Africans, compared to America and Native

Americans, had on the Age of Reason. All of this accumulated information and knowledge did have consequences. In his contribution to Abbé Raynal's *Philosophical and political history of European settlements and commerce in the two Indies* (1780), Diderot argued that all peoples shared a "general will of humanity" – physical similarities, common challenges, inherent sociability and a universal desire for liberty – but Europeans in their imperial and commercial expansion were blind, self-servingly so, to the unimpeachable evidence "that all men are brothers." The rest of the world as well as Europe needed to learn from Europe's historic mistakes.

11.2 The American Revolution

"The independence of America considered merely as a separation from England," wrote the English revolutionary Thomas Paine in 1791, "would have been a matter but of little importance had it not been accompanied by a revolution in the principles and practice of governments." The revolution spoken of by Paine was the republican revolution that established a completely new form of government in the Atlantic World, the first modern democratic republic, named the United States of America. The American Revolution was a radical revolution in theory and practice. In the name of liberty a monarchical and aristocratic system of government, the prevailing system of government in Europe, was rejected and a system based on the sovereignty of the people was instituted. The American Revolution, however, was not simply theoretically radical. The United States was the first country in the world to bring ordinary people into the affairs of government as voters and rulers.

The American Revolution began in a remarkably republican culture, which explains Americans' rapid conversion to revolutionary principles. Americans rejected monarchy and adopted republicanism, Thomas Jefferson wrote, "with as much ease as would attend their throwing off an old and putting on a new suit of clothes." In the 1770s the thirteen colonies of British North America had a population of 2.5 million free people and slaves, ninety percent of which lived on farms and in country villages. Representative government was established in all thirteen colonies and a majority of adult white males could vote in provincial elections. Two-thirds of American colonists owned land compared to one-fifth of the English population and somewhat more in France. There was no titled nobility or bishops in the colonies or any mass of destitute people aside from slaves. In no European country was social equality so deeply entrenched and widely accepted as in the British colonies of North America.

Before 1763 colonists believed the British system of government to be, as John Adams wrote, "the most perfect combination of human powers in society for the preservation of liberty." Like Montesquieu, Americans praised the British system's ability to balance and check the powers of the monarchy, the nobility and the people. Americans, however, also believed they enjoyed the British constitution in greater purity in America than did the English in Britain. Their colonial charters and provincial governments, they claimed,

H I S T O I R E

PHILOSOPHIQUE

ET

P O L I T I Q U E ,

Des Établiſſemens & du Commerce des Européens dans
les deux Indes.

TOME PREMIER.

A G E N E V E ,

CHEZ LES LIBRAIRES ASSOCIÉS.

M. DCC. LXXV.

Figure 11.1. Raynal's Philosophical and Political History of the Two Indies. From Abbé G. Th. Raynal, *Histoire philosophique et politique, des établissements & du commerce des Européens dans les deux Indies* (Geneva, 1775). Courtesy of the William L. Clements Library at the University of Michigan.

protected their historic rights as Englishmen under the British constitution and their inalienable rights under natural law. For Americans the Lockean idea of government by consent was no theory or abstract doctrine but simply a statement of fact. It was something colonists were willing to defend and preserve even against their beloved mother country.

The great books of the Enlightenment were in the libraries of leading gentlemen and the colonial colleges. "The heart of a Frenchman beats faster," remarked Brissot de Warville when he visited the Harvard College Library, "on finding Racine, Montesquieu, and the Encyclopédie in a place where one hundred and fifty years ago the savage still puffed his calumet." American revolutionaries often couched their arguments in the language of the Enlightenment and adopted specific ideas as if they were tools to build a house. They were, however, far less influenced and guided by Enlightenment writers than the French, particularly the most radical among them. Unlike the French, Americans were able to adjust abstract principles to fit with English political traditions and the long American experience of self-government.

At the conclusion of the Seven Years' War in 1763, American colonists had never felt as free or secure. The war had eliminated the French, their historic and mortal enemy, from the continent, putting an end to a series of bloody colonial wars and opening the west to unfettered expansion and settlement. It was at this moment of supreme triumph, however, that relations between colonists and Britain began to sour. The Proclamation Line of 1763 temporarily prohibited settlement west of the Appalachians. The Sugar Act tightened enforcement of colonial trade regulation. The Quartering Act of 1765 required the colonies to house a standing army. The Stamp Act of 1765 initiated a tax on official papers, newspapers, playing cards and other items to assist Britain in the financial support of the army – of which Americans now saw no need – in America. Decades of benign neglect of North America by the British government came to an end.

The Stamp Act was particularly offensive to colonists. Americans protested that Parliament, a body to which they sent no representatives, had no right to tax them directly. This tax was considered a dangerous precedent because it threatened the authority and independence of their provincial assemblies, the only bodies they recognized that had a right to tax them. The Stamp Act was also seen as a threat to the right of trial by jury, because evasions of the tax were to be punished in Vice-Admiralty Courts. Reaction to the Act was immediate and unequivocal. Revolutionary organizations called the Sons of Liberty appeared in all thirteen colonies, which organized protests, intimidated and forced stamp distributors to resign and prevented the distribution and use of stamps. Nine provincial assemblies passed resolutions condemning the act and defining their rights, and sent representatives to a Stamp Act Congress, which petitioned king and Parliament to repeal the tax. To pressure politicians in Britain, colonists organized a boycott of British imports. This Stamp Act crisis led to the repeal of the offending measure in March 1766. It was also accompanied by the Declaratory Act, which affirmed the right of Parliament to legislate for the colonies "in all cases whatsoever."

During the crisis American spokesmen, including Pennsylvania's delegate in London, Benjamin Franklin, explained that they disputed Parliament's right to levy a direct tax upon the colonies and not Parliament's authority to regulate colonial commerce. Accepting this distinction between internal and external spheres of authority, Parliament passed the Revenue Act of 1767, generally called the Townshend Duties, which imposed import duties on lead, paint, paper, glass and tea. The act also paid fixed salaries on some royal governors and judges to make them independent of the purse of colonial assemblies, and established new Vice-Admiralty Courts. Americans, however, generally viewed the Townshend Duties as taxes disguised as commercial regulation and thus equally destructive of their rights as the Stamp Act. Once again, Americans protested. Pennsylvania's John Dickenson in his influential pamphlet *Letters from a Farmer in Pennsylvania* argued: "Those who are taxed without their own consent, expressed by themselves or their representatives, are slaves. We are taxed without our own consent, expressed by ourselves or our representatives. We are therefore – SLAVES." Americans were coming to the position that Parliament had no authority whatsoever over the colonies.

As before, colonists organized a non-importation movement to put economic pressure on Britain. The first non-importation pact was established in Boston in 1768 and eventually every colony but New Hampshire joined the movement. Colonial imports from Britain fell from over £2,153,000 in 1768 to £1,332,000 the following year. American leaders encouraged domestic manufacturing and the patriotic consumption of American-made goods.

To prevent the kind of disorder that existed during the Stamp Act crisis, Britain placed two regiments of regular infantry (eventually there were four in all) in Boston in October 1768. Two years later these troops fired on some Boston rowdies, resulting in what Bostonians called the Boston Massacre. The imposition of unconstitutional taxes was also accompanied, as Americans saw it, by the establishment of an unnecessary and belligerent standing army among a free people. There seemed to be sufficient evidence of a deliberate assault on liberty in America. In fact, many colonial observers began to see a conspiracy in Britain, which was designed to undermine if not destroy their self-government and ultimately their liberty. At the center of this conspiracy, many believed, was a corrupt assault upon the British constitution in which favorites of the king were coming to control Parliament upset the balance among king, Lords and Commons, and established "ministerial tyrannical authority." In Britain, however, political leaders saw in America an unreasonable and unconstitutional resistance to law and legitimate political authority. Edmund Burke saw a dramatic conflict in perceptions on the opposite shores of the Atlantic: "The Americans have made a discovery, or think they have made one, that we mean to oppress them: we have made a discovery, or think we have made one, that they intend to rise in rebellion against us.... We know not how to advance; they know not how to retreat... some party must give way."

Economic coercion worked once again and Parliament repealed all of the Townshend Duties except the one on tea in 1770 and withdrew the troops from Boston. Relations between the colonies and Britain mellowed for a while until Parliament gave the East India Company a monopoly on the import of tea into the colonies with the Tea Act of 1773, which retained the duty on

Figure 11.2. The Boston Massacre, 1770. From *The Bloody Massacre perpetrated in King Street Boston on March 5th, 1770 by a party of the 29th. REGT.* Printed and sold by Paul Revere (Boston, 1770). Courtesy of the William L. Clements Library at the University of Michigan.

tea. The conspiracy to enslave the colonies, it now seemed, had been revived. In protest of this act, some Boston activists disguised as Indians dumped 90,000 pounds of tea into the harbor rather than allow it to be unloaded. This Boston Tea Party convinced the British government that the supremacy of king and Parliament over the colonies would be lost if it was not asserted and firmly enforced. In retribution Parliament passed the Coercive Acts, which colonists termed the Intolerable Acts, which closed Boston Harbor, curtailed town meetings and altered the Charter of Massachusetts so as to reduce local control of government.

Americans in all of the colonies were outraged. William Henry Drayton of South Carolina asked whether Britain "has a constitutional right to exercise *Despotism* over America." Delegates chosen by provincial assemblies or popularly elected conventions in every colony but Georgia dispatched delegates to a Continental Congress in the fall of 1774. This Congress drew up a Declaration of Rights, which declared that American rights to life, liberty and property were founded upon the colonial charters, the British constitution and

Map 11.1. The Thirteen Colonies.

the law of nature. The colonies acknowledged their allegiance to the crown but argued that they would not accept any acts of Parliament that violated their rights. An "Association," a ban on imports and a future prohibition on exports to Britain if necessary, was agreed to and local committees were established to enforce it. Also in the fall of 1774 the Massachusetts Assembly was dissolved and an extralegal Provincial Congress, essentially a revolutionary government, took its place. This Congress appropriated money for arms and ammunition. Counties began to reorganize their local governments, replacing judges and officials with Patriots, men loyal to the American cause, and reactivate local militias. At the end of the year the king was informed by his government of a plan "for carrying on a War in America." The following spring, British troops were dispatched from Boston to seize a suspected depot of munitions in Concord. Conflict with militiamen at Lexington and Concord began the War of the American Revolution in April 1775 (see Map 11.1).

The Revolution assumed a sense of inevitability in 1775 and early 1776. Royal governors began to flee from their colonies and revolutionary assemblies governed in their absence. In August the king proclaimed that the mainland colonies were in rebellion and that its supporters were committing treason. In November 1775 the royal governor of Virginia called upon the slaves of the colony to rebel and promised them freedom if they joined the British. This declaration destroyed the loyalty of even the most conservative planters in the south. In December 1775 Parliament passed the American Prohibitory Act, which ended all British trade with all of the colonies and put Americans outside of the protection of the king, which meant, among other things, that American ships and cargo were now fair game for the Royal Navy. In January 1776 an English radical named Thomas Paine published a pamphlet called *Common Sense* and within a few months more than 150,000 copies were circulating in all of the colonies. Paine confirmed that a conspiracy was afoot to enslave the colonies and that this crime was the result not of any corruption of the British constitution but because of its very nature. That Constitution was founded on, he wrote, "the base remains of two ancient tyrannies" – monarchy and aristocracy. Reconciliation was unwise and thus Americans had no choice but independence.

In May 1776 the Continental Congress took the essential step to independence by recommending to the thirteen colonies that they adopt governments that best provide for the happiness and safety of their constituents. This resolution required the suppression of all governments deriving their authority from the British crown and their replacement by new governments founded upon the authority of the people. The new states and many localities offered their own declarations of rights and independence. The Committee for the Lower District of Frederick County, Maryland, resolved: "That all just and legal Government was instituted for the case and convenience of the People and that the People have the indubitable right to reform or abolish a Government which may appear to them insufficient for the exigency of their affairs." Congress' Declaration of Independence, written mostly by Thomas Jefferson and approved in July, was a way to announce independence to the American people and encourage commitment to the cause. Like most of the local and state declarations, Jefferson's and Congress' Declaration summarized the abuses by the king and Parliament that made independence necessary. Usually understood as a restatement of Locke's contract theory, the Declaration held that the British government had repeatedly violated the contract with the American colonies. It also eloquently stated the revolutionary principles that undergirded the American movement:

> We hold these truths to be self-evident, that all men are created equal, that they are endowed, by their Creator, with certain inalienable rights, that among these are life, liberty, and the pursuit of happiness. That to secure these rights, governments are instituted among men, deriving their just powers from the consent of the governed, that whenever any form of government becomes destructive of these ends, it is the right of the people to alter or to abolish it....

In 1776–7 new republican constitutions were written in ten states. The essence of republicanism in 1776 was popular sovereignty as stated in the Virginia Bill of Rights: "All power is vested in, and consequently derived from the people," and that "magistrates are their trustees and servants, and at all times amenable to them." Because revolutionaries above all feared the power of executive magistrates, real power was given to popularly elected legislatures and weak governors were established as agents of the legislature. Radicals in Pennsylvania wrote the most democratic constitution of the era. They rejected the principle of mixed government, that is, separation of powers, and established a unicameral legislature whose delegates were elected annually by all male taxpayers. Instead of a governor, the Pennsylvania constitution created a popularly elected executive council headed by a weak president. All bills had to be printed for consideration of the people before they could become law in the following legislative session.

The Massachusetts constitution was more representative of the early American state constitutions with its emphasis on separation of powers. Although less democratic than the constitution of Pennsylvania, it was no less republican. In its preamble, John Adams wrote, "The body politic is formed by a voluntary association of individuals. It is a social compact, by which the whole people covenants with each citizen, and each citizen with the whole people, that all shall be governed by certain laws for the common good." This constitution established a bicameral legislature, an independent judiciary and a relatively strong governor who possessed veto power.

Prior to the revolution only elected legislatures were considered to be the popular or people's branch of government. Britain's House of Commons was generally considered to be the republican element of the British constitution. The American Revolution broadened the meaning of popular sovereignty. "In a free state every officer, from the Governor to the constable," wrote Thomas Tudor Tucker of South Carolina, "is, so far as the powers of his office extend, as truly the representative of the people, as a member of the legislature; and his act, within the appointed limitation, is the act of the people; for he is their agent, and derives his authority from them." In short, every public official and every branch of government was an agent of the people. Popular sovereignty did not simply mean the right of revolution, as Locke had proposed, but the everyday operation of government.

During the early years of the Revolutionary War the states also wrote the Articles of Confederation, which established a "league of friendship" headed by a congress elected by state legislatures. At this time no one conceived of the thirteen states becoming a single republic and most revolutionaries feared a central or national government. Article II of the Articles stated that: "Each State retains its sovereignty, freedom and independence, and every power, jurisdiction, and right, which is not by the Confederation expressly delegated to the United States, in Congress assembled." Congress was given authority to make war and negotiate treaties but commercial regulation and the power to tax remained with the states. Under the Articles, furthermore, there were no central executive or judicial authorities.

The political ferment of the age as well as the war unleashed social forces that radicalized the Revolution beyond what many leading revolutionaries expected or wished. Far more people than ever before, including small farmers, artisans, petty merchants and even laborers, were drawn into politics in local assemblies throughout the colonies to debate and draw up declarations of rights, to elect delegates to provincial legislatures and constitutional conventions, and to advise those delegates on issues of constitutional law and revolutionary principles. The Revolution was as much a democratic movement by "upstarts" and "new men" against American elites, "our gentry" and "nabobs," as one against Britain, king and Parliament. The inhabitants of the western Connecticut River Valley in 1776 proclaimed: "We are contending against the same enemy within, that is also without." The most common allegation by American loyalists during the war was that the Revolution was the work of their social inferiors. And during the course of the war, something like eighty thousand loyalists (who were mostly well-to-do officials, landowners and merchants), left the colonies, over six times as many émigrés per one thousand as fled France during its revolution.

American revolutionary republicanism not only meant popular sovereignty but political and social equality. Many revolutionaries sought not only independence for the country but also independence for individuals, meaning an end to personal dependence and subservience. Traditional deference to well-heeled gentlemen, never very strong in America, began to melt away. After the Revolution Jesidiah Morse described New England as a place "where every man thinks himself at least as good as his neighbor, and believe that all mankind have, or ought to possess equal rights." Equality, said David Ramsay, was the very "life and soul" of republicanism. In a republican system only talent determined advancement. It was now possible, he wrote, "that even the reins of state may be held by the son of the poorest man, if possessed of abilities equal to the important station." In the 1780s a number of leading revolutionaries believed that democratic and egalitarian forces had become too powerful and needed to be restrained. This, of course, proved to be impossible. The property requirements (which restricted voting both before and after the Revolution) were abolished in the early nineteenth century. American officeholders, furthermore, were provided salaries after the Revolution, which opened office holding to all citizens and not just the gentry, who could afford the burden of public service.

The Revolution effected no dramatic liberation or political empowerment of women in American society. It did, however, promote the beginning of political awareness. More than any time before, women became interested in and conversant about politics in the 1760s. The so-called 'Daughters of Liberty' publicly protested the Townshend Duties and actively supported the boycott of British goods. Women's efforts to consume only American goods and to manufacture their own clothes were considered quite significant by some, although not many, men. When the British held Boston in the mid-1770s one observer noticed, "at every house Women & Children making Cartridges, running Bullets, making Wallets, baking Biscuit, crying & bemoaning & at the same time animating their Husbands & Sons to fight for their Liberties."

In 1780 Ester De Berdt Reed published a broadside, *The Sentiments of an American Woman*. In it she asserted that American women wanted to be really useful in the revolutionary struggle and suggested that they renounce expensive clothes and vain ornaments and donate the money saved to General George Washington and the army. She established the Ladies Association in Philadelphia, which ultimately collected and contributed more than 300,000 continental dollars. Other associations did the same in New Jersey, Maryland and Virginia. Most men frowned upon women's politicization. "The men say we have no business with them [politics]," wrote Eliza Wilkinson in 1782, "it is not our sphere."

Only in New Jersey, and then only for about twenty years, did women obtain the right to vote. Generally the effect of the Revolution on the women of America and the relations between the sexes was subtle and personal. After taking over their husbands' farms and businesses during their absence in the war, women earned a new sense of confidence. After the war men generally had more respect for women, particularly in their domestic sphere. "The men possess the more ostensible powers of making and executing laws," noted James Tilton in 1790, but "the women, in every free country, have an absolute control of manners: and it is confessed, that in a republic, manners are of equal importance with laws." In 1799 Abigail Adams wrote, "I will never to consent to have our sex considered in an inferior point of light. Let each planet shine in their own orbit." There was a republicanization of domesticity and motherhood. Women were charged with "planting the seeds of virtue" in their sons and thus preparing them to be good citizens and leaders. To do this, women needed to be educated, and in the new republic public education was extended to boys and girls.

Despite Abigail Adam's request to her husband in 1776 to "remember the ladies" in their deliberations in Congress, the American Revolution did not mark the dawn of a new era of female history. Although some women may have been eager for a reform of their status, male revolutionaries were not. Nevertheless, the egalitarian rhetoric of the Revolution provided a vocabulary for the women's rights movement of the nineteenth century and republican schools produced its first leaders. The women's rights convention at Seneca Falls, New York, in 1848 based their calls for reform upon the Declaration of Independence.

In the 1780s, particularly after the conclusion of the war in 1783, many of the leaders of the revolutionary movement in 1776 became disillusioned with the results of the Revolution. It had gone too far and become too democratic and egalitarian. Critics were particularly concerned about the state governments, which they considered weak and inefficient but also so democratic that they protected debtors against creditors, an abuse of republican liberty. Revolutionaries like Thomas Jefferson assumed the new nation would be governed by well-educated gentlemen, an aristocracy of talent, but in the 1780s it was clear that it was not enough for representatives to be *for the people*, they had to be *of the people*, meaning farmers, artisans, mechanics and shopkeepers. Hugh Henry Brackenridge was concerned that "the common people are more disposed to trust one of their own class, than those who may affect to be superior." John Dickinson was more explicit: "Men of sense and property have lost much of their influence by the popular spirit of the war."

As a result of these concerns a number of leaders sought to reform the Revolution. There was a second wave of constitution making at the state level that reduced the power of the popular legislatures by enhancing the separation of powers, balancing the legislatures with supposedly more elitist upper houses and enhancing the power of governors by giving them the veto and longer terms in office. There was also a movement to weaken the state governments through the creation of a powerful national government. This Federalist movement also believed that the larger electoral districts and the great prestige of the national offices would result in the selection of "the best men in the country."

The Federalist movement produced the Constitutional Convention in Philadelphia in 1787. The Constitution that was written and ratified by state conventions replaced the feeble government of the Articles of Confederation with a national government organized around the principle of separation of powers. The legislative branch of the new government was bicameral, with a House of Representatives representing the people and the upper chamber, or Senate, representing the states. The judicial branch, headed by a Supreme Court whose members held life tenure, was independent of the legislative and executive branches. Many who still believed in the principles of 1776 considered the executive branch established by the Constitution to be the most radical innovation. A powerful magistrate, the president, was given a relatively long-term control of appointments, the power to veto legislation, and was made commander in chief of the military. The Constitution represented a remarkable revision of American republicanism. In 1776 revolutionaries distrusted all executive authority, idolized the people and believed the people and their elected representatives could never abuse their power or become despotic. By 1787 Federalists feared all power, including that of popular legislatures, and wrote a Constitution that divided power to restrain not only executive but also legislative power as well.

In the debates regarding the ratification of the Constitution, Anti-Federalists, those opposed to the new national government and still loyal to the principles of 1776, argued that the new system was aristocratic. As it turned out over the course of a few decades, however, the national government became more and more democratic. Common men were elected to the House of Representatives and the Senate. Over the longer term the Constitution was amended to provide for the direct election of senators as well as the suffrage of women and African Americans.

In response to critics who argued that the Constitution did not protect the rights of citizens from potential abuses of the national government, the first Congress amended the Constitution in order to include a Bill of Rights, which was ratified in 1791. These first ten amendments were hardly an innovation. They included rights that had been recognized in England's Glorious Revolution in the late seventeenth century. These were rights that American colonists had taken for granted many decades before the American Revolution. The state constitutions of the 1770s and 1780s also included Bills of Rights. The state and Federal Bills of Rights ensured freedom of religion, speech, press and the right of the people to assemble in peace and petition the government. They also included the right of trial by jury, protection against unreasonable

Document 11.2
Of Independence, State Constitutions, and the Confederation

David Ramsey 1789

The famed social compact between the people and their rulers, did not apply to the United States. The sovereignty was in the people. In their sovereign capacity by their representatives, they agreed on forms of government for their own security, and deputed certain individuals as their agents to serve them in public stations agreeably to constitutions, which they prescribed their conduct.

The world has not hitherto exhibited so fair an opportunity for promoting social happiness. It is hoped for the honor of human nature, that the result will prove the fallacy of those theories, which suppose that mankind are incapable of self government. The ancients, not knowing the doctrine of representation, were apt in their public meetings to run into confusion, but in America this mode of taking the sense of the people, is so well understood, and so completely reduced to system, that its most populous states are often peaceably convened in an assembly of deputies, not too large for orderly deliberation, and yet representing the whole in equal proportions. These popular branches of legislature are miniature pictures of the community, and from the mode of their election are likely to be influenced by the same interests and feelings with the people whom the represent. As a farther security of their fidelity, they are bound by every law they make for their constituents. The assemblage of these circumstances gives as great a security that laws will be made, and government administered for the good of the people, as can be expected from the imperfection of human institutions.

In this short view of the formation and establishment of the American constitutions, we behold our species in a new situation. In no age before, and in no other country, did man ever possess an election of the kind of government, under which he would choose to live. The constituent parts of the antient free governments were thrown together by accident. The freedom of modern European governments was, for the most part, obtained by concessions, or liberality of monarchs, or military leaders. In America alone, reason and liberty concurred in the formation of constitutions. It is true, from the infancy of political knowledge in the United States, there were many defects in their forms of government. But in one thing they were all perfect. They left the people in the power of altering and amending them, whenever they pleased. In this happy peculiarity they placed the science of politics on a footing with the other sciences, by opening it to improvements from experience, and the discoveries of future ages. By means of this power of amending American constitutions, the friends of mankind have fondly hoped that oppression will one day be no more, and that political evil will at least be prevented or restrained with as much certainty, by a proper combination or separation of power, as natural evil is lessened or prevented by the application of the knowledge or ingenuity of man to domestic purposes. No part of the history of antient or modern

Europe, can furnish a single fact that militates against this opinion, since in none of its governments, have the principles of equal representation and checks been applied, for the preservation of freedom. On these two pivots are suspended the liberties of most of the states. When they are wanting, there can be no security for liberty, where they exist they render any farther security unnecessary.

David Ramsey, a teacher and physician from Pennsylvania, moved to Charleston, South Carolina, before the Revolution and was elected to the state assembly and the Continental Congress. His history of the American Revolution celebrated the principles of revolutionary republicanism, divided powers and representative government. *Source: The History of the American Revolution* by David Ramsay, MD. In Two Volumes. Volume I. (1789), pp. 355–7.

searches and seizures as well as protection against cruel and unusual punishment. These American rights protected individuals and minorities, not the people as a whole, against government and even the people's branch, the popularly elected legislatures. Although these rights were not particularly revolutionary in the minds of Americans, they were revolutionary in most of Europe and the rest of the world. The state and Federal Bills of Rights were translated into European languages and published in several countries.

The thirteen mainland colonies were not the only British colonies in the Americas. The British colonists of the Caribbean colonies shared the same political traditions as the mainland colonists. The Caribbean colonies likewise possessed elected assemblies, which expressed opposition to the Stamp Act and the Townshend Duties. The colonists of the Caribbean did not, however, rebel in the 1770s. The reason lies in the very different social structures of the two sets of colonies and their different levels of dependency upon Great Britain.

The islands had been settled more by wealthy emigrants than religious nonconformists as in some parts of the mainland. Many settlers never made their island their real home; their idea was to make money and return to Britain as wealthy men. One-third of Jamaican planters, for example, were absentee owners by the 1740s. Returning home in combination with high death rates also produced a much smaller colonial population in the islands compared to the mainland. Although there were nearly as many emigrants to the islands as the mainland, by the mid-1770s the mainland had a population of around 2.5 million whereas the islands had fewer than fifty thousand residents. Unbalanced sex ratios in the islands produced fewer families and thus a weaker commitment to create new lives and new societies. A French visitor to America before the Revolution noticed that settlers to the islands regarded their colonies "as a land of exile, never as a place where they plan to live, prosper, and die." North American colonists, on the other hand, he wrote, were "permanent, born in the country and attached to it."

Unlike the mainland colonies, the islands possessed more oligarchical societies where most residents were either very rich or very poor. Fewer colonists owned land in the islands and the few who did owned most of the land. Few colonists, as a result, voted in elections for the island assemblies. Despite the great division between rich and poor, there was greater interclass solidarity in the islands than in the mainland. The overwhelming presence of black slaves and free mulattos in the islands unified whites culturally and politically. Although the poor in the islands were more likely to sympathize with the Patriot cause in the mainland, they held no positions of political power and their sense of deference remained strong.

The political elites of the islands saw themselves as far too dependent upon Britain to consider revolution. Planters and traders sold their sugar almost entirely to Britain, where they found a protected market. Island colonists were also dependent upon British military power to protect them from the French and their own slaves. Although the Seven Years' War freed the North American colonies from further French attacks, the same was not true in the Caribbean. A history of French attacks upon and even seizures of the British islands meant that colonists there depended upon the British navy to protect their interests and lives. The continual threat of slave revolts in the islands also meant that colonists there were dependent upon the presence of British troops. While North American colonists came to see the presence of British troops among them as a threat to their liberty, Caribbean colonists were constantly encouraging British authorities to maintain and enlarge army garrisons in peacetime. Three major slave revolts in Jamaica in the 1760s only heightened the sense of dependence upon Britain.

During the 1760s during the Stamp Act and Townshend Duties crisis in North America, Caribbean colonists and their assemblies often spoke against these taxes but generally did not resist them. Only in the Leeward Islands, which were particularly dependent upon North American exports of food, did colonists riot, intimidate stamp officials and destroy stamps. Most islands were compliant and the Barbados assembly voted to condemn the rebellious opposition on the mainland. In reaction, North Americans complained of the islanders' "base desertion of the cause of liberty, their tame surrender of their rights as Britons, their mean timid resignation to slavery."

During the American Revolution of the 1770s island politicians tried to arrange a reconciliation between the thirteen colonies and Britain but only a minority sided with the American cause. Generally the imperial crisis worsened relations between island and mainland colonists. Island assemblies condemned the Revolution, and local governments authorized privateers to attack American shipping and often arrested American traders as traitors, which officially, they were. The Continental Congress placed a boycott on American trade with the islands that led to malnutrition and even famine among slaves and that in turn increased the threat of slave revolts and that helped precipitate a major rebellion in Jamaica in 1776.

The American Revolution, therefore, bypassed the British colonies in the Caribbean. These colonies even remained loyal in the nineteenth century when Britain ended the slave trade and eventually abolished slavery. It was not until the 1960s, in fact, that some of the British colonies began to achieve independence within the British Commonwealth.

11.3 The Dutch Patriot Revolt

In the 1780s a sizable proportion of the Dutch middle class – lawyers, journalists, professionals and petty and mid-level merchants – organized a revolutionary movement to democratize politics in the Dutch Republic. They
called themselves Patriots after American revolutionaries and adopted the
republican rhetoric of the Enlightenment, the American Revolution and their
own Dutch tradition of Christian egalitarianism and republicanism, which
viewed the Dutch Revolt of the late sixteenth century as a model. Although
Willem V, the Stadholder – an office that made him Captain and Admiral-
General of the United Provinces as well as chief officer for upholding law
and order in each province – was a friend and ally of Great Britain, many
Dutch merchants and politicians supported the American Revolution. Dutch
trade with, and assistance of, the United States during the Revolutionary
War prompted war with Britain in 1780 and a Dutch alliance with the new
American confederation of states. The influence of American ideas in the
Netherlands was contagious. The Declaration of Independence and the Constitution of Massachusetts was translated and published in the country. John
Adams, the American minister to the United Provinces, spoke throughout
the Netherlands explaining and justifying the American cause. "In America,
a holy sun has risen," wrote a Dutch Patriot, "and it will shine on us if we so
will it. . . . America can teach us how to fight against the degeneration of our
national character . . . how to throttle tyranny and how to restore to health
the all but moribund corpse of freedom."

The Netherlands was already an oligarchic republic before the Patriot
movement, ruled by the Stadholder in combination with a hereditary merchant and landowner aristocracy of the towns called regents, a relationship
that was rarely friendly or cooperative. Since 1747–8, as a result of a peaceful
revolution that restored and enhanced the power and authority of the Stadholder following a period of regent supremacy, politics in The Netherlands
had become more and more restricted to and monopolized by a small ruling
class. For the first time the Prince of Orange had become Stadholder in all
seven provinces and strongly influenced, and in some towns and provinces
essentially controlled, appointments to town and provincial government. The
republic was increasingly becoming a constitutional monarchy and the Stadholder an uncrowned king.

The precipitating manifesto of the Patriot movement, *To the People of
the Netherlands*, was published anonymously in September 1781. Written
by Baron Joan Derk van der Capellen, this revolutionary pamphlet was
the first address to the inhabitants of The Netherlands as a "people." Van
der Capellen argued that the House of Orange had conspired to become
a monarchy, imposed its sycophants in the town councils and provincial
assemblies and trampled on the liberties of the people. He also criticized the
regents for becoming a corrupt aristocracy, which monopolized government.
A nation was like a mercantile company, he noted, the people own the society
of The Netherlands just as shareholders owned the East India Company. To
ensure that the powerful listen to the people and respect their rights and

wishes, he advised that the Dutch needed to form popular militias, an idea inspired by American militias. "Assemble in your towns and villages," wrote Van der Capellen. "Meet peaceably, and elect from among yourselves a moderate number of courageous, virtuous and pious men.... Provide for the freedom of the press, the one support of your national liberty.... Arm yourselves, elect those who must command you [in the militias]...and in all things proceed like the people of America, with modesty and composure."

A Patriot press emerged in the early 1780s, adopted Van der Capellen's ideas and suggestions and became more radical and democratic as the decade proceeded. Early Patriot rhetoric held that popular militias would ensure that the Stadholder and the regents would become more responsive to the wishes of the people. As the movement grew and the Stadholder and the regents in some provinces opposed the Patriot movement, demands based on the principle of popular sovereignty were put forward to replace the ruling class by men elected by the people. Patriots, however, were moderate revolutionaries; few sought to transform or abolish the existing institutions of government. Patriots, seeking to restore their provinces to the glory and virtue of the Age of the Revolt against Spain, sought to purify their union through democracy.

Anti-Orange sentiment spread throughout The Netherlands during the early 1780s because of the war with Britain (1780–4), the fourth Anglo-Dutch war. The involvement of Amsterdam merchants in trade with and support of the American patriots produced a British declaration of war in 1780. The prince accused Amsterdamers of provoking an unnecessary war to satisfy their commercial greed. However, once the war was started, it was the responsibility of the Stadholder to lead the fight. He did so, however, in an incompetent manner that produced military setbacks and disasters. The Stadholder had failed in the principal responsibility of his office and his military legitimization disappeared.

The first political move of the Patriot movement occurred in the town of Deventer, which convened a new representative town council in 1782 in defiance of the Stadholder. The real momentum of the movement, however, was propelled by the formation of Patriot clubs and local popular militias called Free Corps. Dordrecht became the first town in January 1783 to establish a Free Corps. Utrecht, which came to be known as the "cockpit of democratic politics," established one of the largest Free Corps. As more and more militias were set up in the rest (although not all) of The Netherlands, they began to send delegates to a series of National Conventions of Free Corps in Utrecht beginning in 1784.

At first the Free Corps in Utrecht and other towns attempted an informal alliance with town regents to oppose the power of appointment of the Stadholder. In 1783 the Free Corps of Utrecht pressured the town council to fill a vacancy without first obtaining the prince's recommendation. As the Free Corps pushed for the popular election of councilors, however, regents in many towns began to back away from the alliance and oppose any real democratization. As a result, the Free Corps in several towns and a few cities began to depose regents and elect new Patriot representatives. By 1785 the Patriot movement had become thoroughly democratic. A radical manifesto from Leiden insisted on the primacy of popular sovereignty and called for the absolute right of free speech, the election of militia officers, and the abolition of all inherited and venal offices. It proclaimed: "Liberty is an inalienable right of all citizens of the commonwealth. No power on earth much less any power derived truly from the people . . . can challenge or obstruct the enjoyment of this liberty when it is so desired. The sovereign is none other than the vote of the people."

By 1786 Patriots had gained control of significant parts of four provinces, Utrecht, Holland, Groningen and Overijssel. Holland deposed Willem from his office of provincial Stadholder and Captain-General and expelled him from his court in The Hague. In the same year the National Assembly of Free Corps and the Assembly of Patriot Regents in Amsterdam jointly published a declaration that proclaimed their objective to be: "the true republican form of government in our commonwealth, namely a government by representation of the people . . . with a Stadholdership subordinate thereto."

By 1787 the Patriot party was in power in many parts of The Netherlands with its main strength concentrated in a military cordon covering Holland, Utrecht and Overijssel in the center of the Republic. Control of the country as a whole and the States-General remained up for grabs with the Patriots firmly controlling three provinces, supporters of the Stadholder in charge of two provinces and the remaining two provinces internally disputed by the opposing parties. Patricians began to flee from Patriot strongholds and call upon Willem's allies, Great Britain and Prussia, to intervene. The Patriots were informally tied to France, The Netherlands' ally in the war of American independence, and were supposedly promised support by Louis XVI. Thus the Patriot revolution became entangled with European great power politics. France desired a Patriot triumph so that The Netherlands would not become a compliant ally of Great Britain. Britain and Prussia, on the other hand, openly deplored and opposed the Patriot movement, in part because of its association with France, and sought a restoration of the authority of the Stadholder. The revolution's fate ultimately depended upon the decisions of foreign powers.

The incident that precipitated the final crisis was the decision by Willem's wife, Princess Wilhelmina, who was also the sister of the King of Prussia, to return to The Hague and rally support for her husband. When she crossed through Patriot territory she was detained, essentially arrested, by the Gouda Free Corps. An outraged King of Prussia sent an ultimatum to the States-General demanding her liberation, reinstatement of the Stadholder and Wilhelmina at The Hague, and punishment of those who held her captive. The French government – deeply in debt from the American war – declined to intervene. On September 13, 1787, an army of 26,000 Prussian soldiers invaded The Netherlands. The Patriot militias were in no shape to resist a professionally trained army. Utrecht was not even defended and a short siege brought about the surrender of Amsterdam.

Willem was restored to authority in The Hague and the Stadholder's forces with the assistance of the Prussian army that purged all Patriot towns and cities. The Free Corps, of course, were disbanded. Thousands of Patriots, perhaps forty thousand, fled south to the Austrian Netherlands (today called Belgium), to France, and even some to America while those who remained were arrested. The Patriot revolution had been crushed by force but it was not destroyed. When a revolutionary French army "liberated" The Netherlands in 1795, Patriots returned to the Netherlands and to power.

11.4 The French Revolution

"The cause of America is in a great measure the cause of all mankind," wrote Thomas Paine in 1776. It was "the concern of every man to whom nature hath given the power of feeling." At the end of the American war for independence Lafayette, in a speech before Congress, declared, "May this serve as a lesson to all oppressors and an example to the oppressed." The American Revolution inspired Dutch Patriots as previously described. In the neighboring Austrian Netherlands, the *Manifeste de Flandres* in 1787 proclaimed the right of the people to declare the independence of the province and quoted from the American Declaration of Independence to advance the cause. The Welsh philosopher Richard Price wrote a book about the significance of the American Revolution and maintained, "Perhaps, I do not go too far when I say that, next to the introduction of Christianity among nations, the American revolution may prove the most important step in the progressive course of human improvement." Accounts of the American Revolution circulated throughout Europe, Spanish America and Brazil. Even a Hungarian newspaper announced in 1789 that "since America became a free society after shaking the English yoke off her neck, all nations are yearning for the same golden liberties."

The American Revolution was particularly attractive to the French. "The American cause seemed our own," wrote the Vicomtesse de Fars-Fausselandry, "we were proud of their victories, we cried at their defeats, we tore down bulletins and read them in all our houses." Some noblemen like the Marquis de Lafayette were attracted to the cause and offered their military assistance. Many officers and ordinary soldiers fought in America in support of their ally and believed the cause of liberty was relevant to their own country. Another high-ranking noble and returning soldier wrote in 1782 that "the freedom for which I am going to fight inspires in me the liveliest enthusiasm and I would like my own country to enjoy such a liberty that would be compatible with our monarchy, our position, and our manners." Thomas Paine viewed these officers and soldiers from the American war as so many revolutionary agents when they returned home. "When the war closed," Paine wrote, "a vast reinforcement to the cause of Liberty spread itself over France, by the return of the French officers and soldiers."

The French had a high regard for America's revolutionary declarations and constitutions. As one of the American envoys to France during the revolutionary war, Benjamin Franklin had introduced American state constitutions and their bills of rights to French political society. The duc de la Rochefoucauld d'Enville, who later sat in the National Assembly in 1789, translated the American Declaration of Independence, the Articles of Confederation, and several state bills of rights and constitutions and published them in a book, *Constitutions des Treize Etats-Unis de l'Amérique* in 1783. Thomas Jefferson

Figure 11.3. A French Allegorical Image Celebrating the American Revolution. The Figure of America, holding a Liberty Cap on a Pole, Stands in Front of a Statue with the Portraits of Louis XVI, Benjamin Franklin and George Washington. *Indépendance des États-Unis* (Independence of the United States), From Pierre Blin, *Portraits des grands homes, femmes illustres et sujets mémorables de France* (Paris, 1786–92). Courtesy of the John Carter Brown Library at Brown University.

translated into French his bill establishing religious freedom in Virginia. In his Paris home, Lafayette placed a copy of the Declaration of Independence in a large frame that was half-empty. The empty space, he often said in the years before the French Revolution, was reserved for a French declaration of rights that would one day be adopted. During the debate on what would become the Declaration of the Rights of Man and Citizen, Duke Mathieu de Montmorency spoke in the National Assembly and implored his fellow deputies: "Let us follow the example of the United States: they have set a great example in the new hemisphere; let us give one to the universe, let us offer a model worthy of admiration."

The American Revolution, of course, did not cause the French Revolution. Both revolutions were part of a revolutionary ferment that existed on both

Document 11.3
The Revolution of America

Guillaume Thomas Raynal 1792

The name of liberty is so sweet, that all they who fight for it are sure to interest our secret wishes. Their cause is that of the whole human race; it becomes our own. We revenge ourselves of our own oppressors, by giving vent, at least, with liberty, to our hatred against those oppressors who cannot punish it. At the sound of breaking chains, it seems as if our own were about to get lighter; and we think for some moments that we breathe a purer air, in learning that fewer tyrants are to be counted in the world. These great revolutions of liberty, moreover, admonish despots. They warn them not to trust too long patience in the people, not to trust to impunity without end. Thus, when the laws of society execute vengeance upon the crimes of private individuals, the good man hopes that the punishment of the guilty will, by its terrible example, prevent the commission of new crimes. Terror sometimes supplies the place of justice to the thief, and conscience to the assassin. Such is the source of the warm interest we feel in all the wars of liberty. Such is that with which we have been inspired for the Americans. Our imaginations have been inflamed in their favour. We seem to be present at, and to feel as they do, all their victories and their defeats. The spirit of justice, which is pleased in compensating past misery by happiness to come, is pleased in thinking that this part of the new world cannot fail of becoming one of the most flourishing countries upon the globe. Nay, it has been even supposed, that there is cause to fear less Europe should one day find her masters in her children. Let us dare to stem the torrent of public opinion, and that of public enthusiasm. Let us not be led astray by imagination, that embellisher of all things, nor by passion, which loves to create illusions, and realizes all it hopes. Our duty is to combat every prejudice, should it be even that which is most comfortable to the wishes of our heart. To be true, above all things, is our chief concern, and not to betray the pure and upright conscience which presides over our writings, and dictates every judgment that we ass. At this moment, perhaps, we shall not be believed: but a bold conjecture, which is verified at the end of many ages, does more honour to the historian, than the recital of a long series of facts which cannot be contested; and I write not only for my contemporaries, who will be some years survive me. Yet a few revolutions of the sun, and they and I shall be no more. But I deliver over my ideas to posterity and to time. It is for them to judge me....

Ye people of North America, let the example of all the nations who have gone before you, and above all that of your mother-country, serve you for instruction. Fear the affluence of gold, which brings with luxury the corruption of manners, the contempt of laws. Fear a too unequal distribution of riches, which exhibits a small number of citizens in opulence, and a great multitude of citizens in extreme poverty; whence springs the insolence of the former, and the debasement of the latter. Secure yourselves against the spirit of conquest. The tranquility of an empire diminishes in proportion to its extension. Have arms for your defence; have none for offence. Seek competency and health in labour; prosperity in the culture of lands, and the workshops of industry; power in manners and virtue. Cause arts and sciences, which distinguish the civilized from the savage man, to flourish and abound. Above all, watch carefully over the education of your children. It is from public schools, be assured, that come the wise magistrates, the capable and courageous soldiers, the good fathers, the good husbands, the good brothers, the good friends, the good men. Whenever the youth are seen depraved, the nation is on the decline. Let liberty have an immoveable foundation in the wisdom of your laws, and let it be the indestructible cement to bind your provinces together. Establish no legal preference among the different forms of worship. Superstition is innocent, wherever it is neither persecuted nor protected; and my your duration, if it be possible, equal the duration of the world!

Guillaume Thomas François Raynal, the Abbé Raynal, in collaboration with Denis Diderot (or perhaps the other way around), condemned European colonialism in his *L'Histoire philosophique et politique des deux Indies* (A Philosophical and Political History of the Settlements and Trade of the Europeans in the East and West Indies), published in several volumes beginning in 1772. Conceived with a new edition in 1780, Raynal's *Revolution d'Amerique* celebrated the American Revolution and its likely impact on history and the world. *Source: A Philosophical and Political History of the Settlement and Trade of the Europeans in the East and West Indies* by the Abbé Raynal to which is added the Revolution of America by the same author, a new translation. 1792, pp. 157–60, 164–5.

shores of the Atlantic. "The French Revolution has often been regarded as a consequence of the American," wrote Alexis de Tocqueville, "and there is no denying that the latter had a considerable influence on it." However, he continued, both revolutions were the result of ideas that were European in origin, many of them French. Americans and Frenchmen acknowledged a common debt to the natural-law school of philosophy. In 1788 the Parlement of Rennes proclaimed, "That man is born free, that originally men are equal, these truths that have no need of proof," a statement that reflected both Rousseau and the Declaration of Independence. "The Americans seemed only to be putting into practice ideas which had been sponsored by our writers," noted Tocqueville, "and to be making our dreams their realities." The American Revolution, according to the historian Simon Schama, gave French patriotism the opportunity to define itself in terms of liberty.

In the 1780s the French lived in a great country that had many doubts about itself. The most populous country in Western Europe, France had a population of over twenty-six million people. Unlike America, France possessed two large and powerful social orders, the nobility that numbered about 400,000 and owned one-fifth of all the land, and the clergy, which numbered about 100,000 and owned over one-tenth of the land. The political heritage of France was monarchical absolutism as expressed by Louis XV in 1766: "The Law is what I say it is." In this aristocratic kingdom, the clergy and the nobility possessed historic political, economic and social privileges, which maintained their status. There was a rising and prosperous, even wealthy, non-noble elite, as well as over twenty million peasants, former serfs, who worked either their own land or that of a lord. American visitors were appalled by the enormous inequality of wealth that was apparent, by the prevalence of abject poverty, wretchedness and despair, which displayed itself in barefoot and hungry beggars amid glittering luxury and opulence. Many French nobles, beneficiaries of the political and social system but often influenced by radical notions regarding rights and equality, were similarly dissatisfied. Their France was a great country with equally great problems.

Perhaps the most critical problem for France in the 1780s was debt. The government had borrowed 1.24 billion livres since 1776, debt service was enormous and short-term loans were too great to pay back. In August 1786 the king's first minister informed Louis XVI that the crown no longer had any money. The current system of taxation – a crazy-quilt system of direct and indirect taxes, internal customs barriers, tariffs, tolls and excises – was unequally applied, unfair and uniformly despised. It did not raise enough money and new loans were not forthcoming while new taxes were politically impossible. It seemed the only solution was to revamp the entire fiscal and administrative structure of the state. The politicization of this money crisis began the French Revolution.

In 1787 the king convened an Assembly of Notables to consider measures to rescue French public finance from bankruptcy. The noblemen who composed this body, considered a radical overhaul of the fiscal system based on the principle of fiscal equality (between nobility and commoners) and political representation. An entirely new fiscal system required ongoing political consultation through elected assemblies at the parish, district and provincial levels. Notables agreed with a rising national call for the meeting of the Estates-General, with representatives from the church (the First Estate), the nobility (the Second Estate) and the commons (the Third Estate), which had not met since 1614. Only the convening of the Estates-General and the creation of a representative regime would generate the public confidence necessary to create a new financial system. As the government suspended treasury payments and the crisis deepened, the crown admitted it could not govern without some sort of representative assembly. The Estates-General was called upon to meet in May 1789.

In the months leading up to the convening of the Estates-General, the people of France met in approximately forty thousand local and provincial meetings and assemblies to select representatives and to draw up a list of grievances. Never had such a populous nation become so thoroughly politicized in such a short period of time. Ordinary Frenchmen were brought into politics for the first time. Moreover, for the crown it was not the best moment to ask what one historian called "the small people in plain occupations" to select representatives and discuss their problems. An economic downturn and poor harvests had resulted in higher unemployment and food shortages and thus high prices. Many delegates sent to the Estates-General were angry men interested in more than fiscal reform. Many of the delegates selected by the nobility and the clergy, furthermore, were disaffected critics of the regime, reformers in many cases and some radicals.

An electorate of some six million people drew up more than twenty-five thousand *cahiers*, documents listing the grievances of the nobility, the clergy and the people. This was an unprecedented act of consultation and representation. Popular *cahiers* attacked grain speculators and tax collectors as well as the effects of the capitalist modernization of late eighteenth-century France. While Enlightenment writers had called for the liberalization of economic forces, peasants, artisans and others of their class wanted an end to the enclosure of common land, less not more mechanization, regulation of prices and wages; in short, control of capitalism. The *cahiers* of the nobility were political, generally demanding the creation of a new representative regime and the end of monarchical absolutism. They mentioned the necessity of an explicit declaration of rights including the right of all Frenchmen to take part directly or indirectly in the government, demands for the abolition of the remains of feudalism, calls for religious toleration and freedom of the press, and the desirability of a constitutional monarchy and the separation of powers. In retrospect it was clear, argued Tocqueville, that what "the authors of these *cahiers* jointly sponsored was one of the vastest, most catastrophic revolutions the world has ever known."

Twelve hundred and one representatives gathered at Versailles as the Estates-General met in May 1789: 300 clergy in the First Estate, 291 nobles in the Second Estate and 610 commoners in the Third Estate. In the run-up to the meeting, the Abbé Sieyes published an influential pamphlet called *Qu'est-ce que la Tiers-Etat?* [What is the Third Estate?] He argued that the two privileged orders were parasites feeding on the nation, they were like a "malignant disease which preys upon and tortures the body of a sick man." Their privileges were usurpations that should be removed. The Third Estate, on the other hand, was not a mere order within society but the nation itself. Although it had been nothing politically speaking, wrote Sieyes, it was everything. Many delegates of the Third Estate shared this perspective, and in June, on a motion by Sieyes himself, the Third Estate with some nobles and clergy present voted to take the title National Assembly. As more and more clergy and nobles joined the National Assembly, the king accommodated himself to a revolutionary situation and urged the privileged orders to unite with the others. When the Estates-General died in late June 1789, royal absolutism went with it to the grave.

The political revolution that was inherent in the creation of the National Assembly was accompanied and accelerated by a popular revolution in Paris in the summer of 1789. This dualism became one of the most important characteristics of the French Revolution: the politician's revolution was again and again radicalized by popular uprisings in the capital. In Paris popular radicals took control of city government and established a new people's militia, called the National Guard and headed by Lafayette, to protect the National Assembly. Fear of a crackdown by royal troops led a Parisian crowd to take twenty-eight thousand muskets from the Invalides and to attack the royal prison called the Bastille, a symbol of despotism, to obtain powder. The fall of the Bastille on July 14 meant that Paris was lost to the monarchy and that the revolution had blood on its hands. The commandant of the Bastille was killed following his surrender and a few days later the Intendants of Paris were murdered by a mob. Two days after the fall of the Bastille, part of the king's court, including his younger brother, fled Versailles and the country. In many provinces across the country municipal revolutions mirrored the situation in Paris, including the creation of local National Guard units.

The National Assembly (which had declared itself a Constituent Assembly on July 9 in order to write a declaration of rights and a constitution) now felt itself secure and free enough to make a real revolution. It abolished the remaining vestiges of feudalism such as personal service, the exemption of nobles to taxation, the different penalties given to nobles and commoners for the same offenses, proprietary offices such as the eleven hundred seats in the Parlements, and similar aristocratic "abuses and outrages." On August 28, the Assembly issued the Declaration of the Rights of Man and Citizen that denied the moral foundations of aristocratic France and provided the death certificate of the Old Regime. The idea of an explicit written listing of rights was probably suggested by the American Bill of Rights, especially the Virginia Declaration of Rights of 1776. Lafayette provided a draft that was annotated by Thomas Jefferson, the American minister. The principles present in the Declaration could be traced to Locke, Montesquieu, and, to a lesser extent, Rousseau and, through them, the European tradition of natural law. Its content, it is clear, was indigenous to France. The preamble of the Declaration announced:

> The representatives of the French people, constituting the National Assembly, believing that ignorance, disregard or contempt for the rights of man are the sole causes of public ills and government corruption, have resolved to set forth, in a solemn declaration, the natural, inalienable and sacred rights of man. . . .

The purpose of such a declaration of rights, the Assembly noted, was to ensure that society and government would always be reminded of them and that laws consistent with them would be "all the more respected." It was also to ensure that the demands of citizens, founded on such simple and incontestable principles, would "correspond to the preservation of the constitution and the happiness of all." The Assembly, concluded the preamble's authors, "recognizes and declares, in the presence and under the auspices of the Supreme Being, the following rights of man and citizen."

> I. Men are born and remain free and equal in their rights. Social distinctions can be founded only on what is useful to all.
> II. The goal of all political associations is the preservation of the natural and imprescriptible rights of man. These rights are liberty, property, security, and resistance to oppression.
> III. The principle of sovereignty resides essentially in the nation. No body, no individual may claim any authority that does not emanate explicitly from the nation.

The first three articles, the most famous ideological statement of the French Revolution, advanced the universal principles of natural rights, the contract theory of government and a kind of popular sovereignty. Article III held that the king was no longer sovereign but neither were, as in America, the people. Article VI, following Rousseau, stated that "law is the expression of the general will" and that all citizens are equal and have the right, directly or indirectly, to take part in its creation. Articles VII and VIII declared that arbitrary arrests and punishments were illegal. Articles X and XI proclaimed religious tolerance and freedom of speech and press. To guarantee the rights of man and citizen, Article XII proclaimed the need for public forces to protect not any private interest but everyone. Running through several of the articles was language that announced that the new age was one of equality with advancement based on virtue and talent, not aristocratic privilege. Unlike the American Bill of Rights, the French Declaration listed the duties of citizens as well as the rights of man. The ultimate duty is to do no harm to others or to society at large. Opinion must not "disturb public order as established by law." Speech and writing that abuse its freedom is restricted by law. Citizens have the duty to pay taxes although they are taxes to which they consent and supervise. In preparing itself to write a constitution for France, the Assembly set two basic guidelines in Article XVI: "Any society in which the guarantee of rights is not assured or in which the separation of powers is not determined, has no constitution."

Revolutionary ideas now began to flow back across the Atlantic to the United States. American newspapers printed English translations of the Declaration of the Rights of Man and Citizen as early as October 1789. Just as the American Revolution had been the topic of topics in France in the 1770s, now the French Revolution dominated conversation among the politically active in the United States. In a few years Americans would become bitterly divided about the French Revolution and the foreign policy implications it involved, which contributed to the formation of the first political parties and further democratization. Revolutionary currents flowed in both directions across the Atlantic.

The Constituent Assembly then began to draft a charter for a constitutional monarchy. In September debate narrowed between a faction called the *monarchiens*, or Anglophiles who were largely guided by the principle of separation of powers, and a faction called Patriots who favored legislative supremacy. The Anglophiles were led by provincial lawyer J. J. Mounier, author of the first three articles of the Declaration of the Rights of Man and Citizen and someone fully familiar with the government of the United States, which he considered the best in the world. The Americans, he explained, had the opportunity to create a completely new government; Frenchmen, on the other hand, had to accommodate an existing system of monarchy. Mounier proposed a bicameral legislature with a strong independent executive, the king. The lower or popular legislative chamber would be balanced by an upper chamber which he called a Senate, to be composed of men of property and high standing. The king, the national executive, would be given an absolute veto. "To defend the independence of the Crown," Mounier said, "is to defend the liberty of the people."

Opponents of this plan led by the Abbé Sieyes argued that a system of separation of powers limited and interfered with the rights of man and the sovereignty of the nation. Some noted that there was no veto in the constitution of Virginia and that there should not be any limitation of the national legislature because its will was that of the nation. A two-house legislature appeared to be a throwback to the time of separate orders. The proposed Senate, in fact, would represent the aristocracy in power. In the end Mounier's proposals lost. A single national assembly was created. The king was granted a suspensive veto, which gave him the power to delay legislation for up to six years but not stop it altogether.

Constituents agreed on a limitation on popular democracy, dividing Frenchmen into "active" and "passive" citizens based on wealth qualifications and restricting suffrage to active citizens. The Constitution created an electorate of about four million Frenchmen, the broadest electorate in European history. As in the American Revolution, however, the French Revolution had begun to liberate the popular – democratic – forces in society regardless what the leaders of the Revolution wanted. The radical journalist Camille Desmoulins asked, "What is this much repeated word *active citizen* supposed to mean? The active citizens are the ones who took the Bastille." A Constituent, a provincial lawyer named Maximilien Robespierre, also wondered, "Is the nation sovereign when the greater part of the persons composing it is deprived of the political rights from which sovereignty derives its essence?"

The king appeared unwilling to agree to the actions of the Constituent Assembly, including the Declaration of the Rights of Man and Citizen. Popular action would change his mind. In October a mob of Parisian women, and a large portion of the National Guard, marched to Versailles to demand bread. Louis then accepted without qualification the Declaration and the other decrees of the Assembly and under popular coercion, agreed to return to Paris. The authority of the king was further eroded. Mounier went into exile and denounced this France as impossibly democratic.

The Constituent Assembly continued to reshape France in fundamental ways in the aftermath of the October Days. The complicated system of tax exemption and privilege was swept away and replaced by a uniform tax structure applicable to all citizens. The traditional provinces were eliminated and replaced by eighty-three departments of about equal size. The old judicial system was swept away and replaced by one with elected judges, trial by jury and a new liberal penal code. Protestants and Jews were granted the same rights as Catholics. To help the government alleviate the financial crisis, the Assembly agreed to sequester the property of the Catholic Church and sell it to the public. The Civil Constitution of the Clergy made the clergy salaried civil servants of the government and mandated that parishes elect their priests and bishops. There was, in fact, a massive expansion of elected offices at the local, district, provincial and national levels. The Assembly abolished all titles of hereditary nobility and all insignia of social superiority. The preamble of the Constitution read: "There is no longer any nobility nor peerage nor hereditary distinctions or orders nor feudal regime nor patrimonial justice nor any title, denomination or prerogative."

Document 11.4
A Declaration to the French Nation from the National Assembly

1790

The National Assembly, as it progresses in its work, is receiving upon every hand the felicitations of the provinces, cities, and villages, testimonials of the public satisfaction and expressions of grateful appreciation; but murmurs reach it as well, from those who are affected or injured by the blows aimed at so many abuses and prejudices. While occupied with the welfare of all, the Assembly is solicitous in regard to individual ills. It can forgive prejudice, bitterness, and injustice, but it feels it to be one of its duties to warn you against the influence of calumny, and to quiet the empty terrors which some are vainly trying to arouse in you. To what have they not resorted in order to mislead and discourage you? They pretend to be unaware of the good that the National Assembly has accomplished; this we propose to recall to your mind. Objections have been raised against what has been done; these we propose to meet. Doubts and anxiety have been disseminated as to what we propose to do in the future; this we will explain to you.

What has the Assembly accomplished? In the midst of storms it has, with a firm hand, traced the principles of a constitution which will assure you your liberty forever. The rights of man had been misconceived and insulted for centuries; they have been reestablished for all humanity in that declaration, which shall serve as an everlasting war cry against oppressors and as a law for the legislators themselves. The nation had lost the right to decree both the laws and the taxes; this right has been restored to it, while at the same time the true principles of monarchy have been solemnly established, as well as the inviolability of the august head of the nation and the heredity of the throne in a family so dear to all Frenchmen.

Formerly you had only the Estates General; now you have a National Assembly of which you can never be again deprived. In the Estates General the several orders, which were necessarily at odds and under the domination of ancient pretensions, dictated the decrees and could check the free action of the national will. These orders no longer exist; all have disappeared before the honorable title of *citizen*. All being citizens alike, you demanded citizen-defenders and, at the first summons, the National Guard arose, which, called together by patriotism and commanded by honor, has everywhere maintained or established order and watches with untiring zeal over the safety of each for the benefit of all.

Privileges without number, irreconcilably at enmity with every good, made up our entire public law. These have been destroyed, and. at the word of this Assembly, the provinces which were the most jealous of their own privileges applauded their disappearance, feeling that they gained rather than lost thereby. A vexatious feudal system, powerful even in its ruin, covered the whole of France; it has now disappeared, never to return. In the provinces you were subject to a harassing administration; from this you have been freed. Arbitrary commands threatened the liberty of the citizens; they have been done away with. You desired a complete organization of the municipalities; this you have just received, and the creation of these bodies, chosen by your votes, offers, at this moment, a most imposing spectacle. At the same time, the National Assembly has finished the task of a new division of the kingdom, which alone might serve to remove the last trace of former prejudices, substitute for provincial selfishness the true love for one's country, and serve as the basis of a just system of representation. . . .

This, Frenchmen, is our work, or rather yours, for we are only your organ, and you have enlightened, encouraged, and sustained us in our labors. What a glorious period is this which we at last enjoy! How honorable the heritage which you may transmit to your posterity! Raised to the rank of citizens; admissible to every form of employment; enlightened censors of the administration when it is not actually in your hands; certain that all will be done by you and for you; equal before the law; free to act, to speak, to write; owing no account to individuals but always to the common will; – what condition more happy? Is there a single citizen worthy of the name who would dare look back, who would rebuild once more the ruins which surround us, in order again to contemplate the former structure.

From "The Assembly Reviews Its Great Work, February 11, 1790," *Histoire parlementaire*, XIX, 9, in James Harvey Robinson and Charles A. Beard, *Readings in Modern European History, Volume I* (1908), pp. 268–2.

The Constituent Assembly finished the Constitution in 1791 but did not submit it to the country for popular ratification. The aristocracy, it was feared, would overly influence the provincial assemblies. Ironically, the Constitution was the result of the work of a number of leading nobles, men who had long sought the end of royal absolutism and the establishment of a rational – enlightened – system of government. The Constitution was a model of late eighteenth-century political thought: it protected the nation against royal despotism, aristocratic privilege and popular licentiousness. When the Constitution went into effect in September 1791, Constituent Robespierre declared that if the Constitution became firmly established, everyone agreed to live under its provisions, and it had no enemies, then "the Revolution is over."

There was a most important flaw in the new system: lack of support by the king. His queen had privately written, "The Constitution is a tissue of impracticable absurdities." He no doubt concurred. In June the royal family attempted to escape from Paris and France and the king left behind a letter that explained: "The King does not think it possible to govern a kingdom of such great extent and importance as France by the means established by the National Assembly." This letter was to be read following the escape by the king, but he did not escape. The royal family was captured and returned to Paris; thereafter the king was a prisoner of his own government. The Emperor of Austria, and the queen's brother, only made matters worse in August when he and the King of Prussia promised in the Declaration of Pilnitz to use force to "affirm the basis of a monarchical government equally suitable to the rights of the Sovereigns and the well-being of the French nation." In September 1791 the king publicly accepted the Constitution and was installed as King of the French, which implied he was a servant of the people rather than his old title, King of France, which implied his ownership of the country. His attempted escape and the counterrevolutionary Declaration of Pilnitz, however, had irreversibly damaged the king's authority and many Frenchmen's faith in constitutional monarchy.

A newly elected Legislative Assembly began its duties in October 1791. Many believed the Revolution was over because France now had a new system of government. It was, in fact, just at the beginning of its most radical phase. The motor of this radicalization was war. Tension with Austria and then Prussia grew in the fall and winter of 1791–2 as many French feared that these monarchs would support aristocratic French émigrés who wanted to restore monarchical absolutism. Politicians pushed for war in France for various reasons. Conservatives thought it would enhance the popularity and authority of the king. Moderates believed war would unite the nation behind the government. Radicals believed it would further undermine the monarchy and lead to the formation of a republic. The radicals were right. After war was declared in the spring and battle after battle was lost, the king became a scapegoat. In the summer of 1792, a Prussian general issued the Brunswick Manifesto, which invited all good Frenchmen to return to their "former fidelity" and demanded "the city of Paris and all its inhabitants, without distinction . . . to submit at once and without delay to the King." If any force or the least outrage was directed at the king, then the Allied powers would "exact an exemplary and forever memorable vengeance by delivering the city of Paris to military execution and total subversion, and the rebels who are guilty of such outrages to the punishments they will have deserved." The Brunswick Manifesto, of course, had the opposite effect.

In August another popular revolution developed in Paris on top of widespread discontent and rioting throughout the country. In the capital, radicals overthrew the municipal government and established a revolutionary Commune. An insurrectionary mob supported by National Guardsmen then attacked the Tuileries, the king's chateau, and massacred hundreds of its Swiss Guards. The monarchy had been overthrown in effect by popular action on August 10, 1792. Following the flight of a number of moderate legislators, a republican mood dominated in the Legislative Assembly, which called upon the country to elect by universal suffrage, a new National Convention. The day after the Convention met in September, it abolished the monarchy and proclaimed the Republic. A new calendar was approved that made 1792 Year One of French Liberty.

By 1792 the constituency in the sixty Paris electoral sections of political radicals and the source of direct actions was a group of people who called themselves *sans-culottes*, spurning the knee breeches of their social superiors. They were artisans, laborers and shopkeepers, women as much as men, who were militantly egalitarian and the voice of the country's democratization.

They belonged to popular clubs in Paris like the Fraternal Society for Patriots of Both Sexes and became especially supportive of the Society of the Friends of the Constitution who met in the convent of St. Jacob and came to be called Jacobins. With the new National Convention the Jacobins became a powerful faction. A group of moderates became known as Girondins and presented themselves as protectors of legality against mob rule. The Jacobins, however, with fierce popular support in Paris and elsewhere, would come to dominate the Convention and its *gouvernement révolutionnaire*.

The first order of business of the National Convention was the trial of the king. The Jacobin Robespierre argued that the people had given their verdict on August 10 and thus the only course was public condemnation and execution. Yet despite the overwhelming sentiment in the Convention that the king was guilty of treason, a trial was ordered and the king was allowed to mount a defense. The final guilty verdict was inevitable. Some Girondins proposed that the verdict be subject to a popular referendum that they hoped would spare his life. This option was narrowly voted down and the king was condemned to death. Louis Capet, the former Louis XVI, was guillotined on January 21, 1793. His wife Marie Antoinette followed him in October. Not content with regicide, the Convention also decreed the destruction of the royal tombs in the Abby of Saint-Denis, the mausoleum of the French kings since the sixth century. The remains of long-dead kings were boiled, burned, and ground up before being scattered and buried in quicklime. The monarchy was exorcised from the soul of the French.

In 1793 the Convention faced the greatest crisis of the Revolution. Virtually all of Europe was at war with revolutionary France. Revolutionaries saw themselves as besieged by enemies without and threatened by traitors within. In some parts of the country, particularly in the Vendée, there were popular uprisings in defense of religion and monarchy: "we want our King, our priests, and the Old Regime," proclaimed the rebels. In the spring the Convention created more efficient institutions of government like the Committee of Public Safety to fight the war abroad and the counterrevolution at home. The Convention also ordered the *levée en mass*, Europe's first conscript army, which eventually created a national army of 600,000 soldiers. The national economy was reorganized in an all-out war mobilization that transformed, for example, metallurgical factories into state munitions enterprises. Price controls were imposed and poor relief extended as a result of forced loans upon the rich.

The Convention wrote a new governing charter during the first half of 1793, the Constitution of the Year One. The Girondin-inspired text created a Legislative Assembly to be elected by direct male adult suffrage. An Executive Committee was to be nominated by the Assembly. A new Jacobin-written Declaration of Rights added new rights to that of 1789. The aim of society was declared to be the happiness of all. Work or financial assistance should be provided for the poorer citizens as a sacred obligation. The last of its thirty-five clauses declared: "When the government violates the rights of the people, insurrection is for the people, and for any portion thereof, the most sacred of rights and the most indispensable of duties." This Constitution of the Year One gave France a system of government that was both republican and democratic. Within months, however, it was shelved for the duration of the war. Elections were suspended and a revolutionary dictatorship came into being.

"What had liberty and the rights of man," asked the American Noah Webster, "to do with this second revolution?" It was a good question. In the late spring of 1793 the Convention was intimidated by a Parisian mob and twenty-two Girondin leaders were arrested and others fled Paris. The assassination of the radical Jacobin journalist Marat led to further purges. The *sans-culottes* again invaded the Convention in September, which led to the passage of the Law of Suspects that gave the Committee of Public Safety sweeping powers of arrest and punishment. In October the Convention declared "the government of France revolutionary until the peace." A delegation from the Jacobin club proposed that "terror be the order of the day." Robespierre maintained that "if the mainspring of popular government in time of peace is virtue, the mainspring of popular government in time of revolution is both virtue and terror: virtue, without which terror is evil; terror, without which virtue is helpless. Terror is nothing but justice, prompt, severe, and inflexible; it is therefore an emanation of virtue."

The Revolution had degenerated into a bloody dictatorship. During the next ten months, a period called "the Terror," more than sixteen thousand citizens were tried and executed. There were an estimated forty thousand victims in the departments. In the Vendée the suppression of the rebellion by the Convention had been accomplished by the deaths of perhaps a quarter of a million people. "There is no more Vendée, Citizens," proclaimed the Committee of Public Safety, "it has perished under our free sword along with its women and children." The region was renamed *Vengé*, "Avenged." As the Terror began, a Girondin representative told the Convention: "it must be feared that the Revolution, like Saturn, successively devouring its own children, will engender, finally, only despotism with the calamities that accompany it." In the name of revolution power overwhelmed liberty, dictatorship trumped constitutionalism and the direct democracy of the crowd overturned representative government. In the American Revolution, Patrick Henry had proclaimed: "Give me liberty or give me death." In the French Revolution, Robespierre proclaimed: "To good citizens revolutionary government owes the full protection of the state; to the enemies of the people it owes only death." Revolution, he contended, "is the war waged by liberty against its enemies." This revolution, as many that were to follow in European and world history, was willing to sacrifice (at least temporarily) its grand principles in order to survive and triumph. The ends justified the means. Many in France and throughout the Atlantic World had come to believe that the Terror proved that a republic was an anarchic, dictatorial and bloodthirsty kind of regime.

Although the Jacobins had come to power with the assistance of direct action by the Parisian *sans-culottes*, they realized that mob democracy was a threat to any government, even their own. "Democracy," noted Robespierre, "is not a state in which the people, continually assembled, itself directs public affairs." Although this fairly described recent politics in Paris, it was not a situation that he wished would continue. "Democracy is a state in which the sovereign people, guided by laws of its own making," he continued, "does for itself what it can do well, and by its delegates what it cannot." This was a plea for delegated authority and representative democracy. To make this possible the Jacobins attacked the popular roots of revolution in Paris. The Terror damaged the machinery of popular insurrection in Paris with executions, spies and trusties. The municipal Commune was purged and militants in the electoral sections scattered across the government. The most radical newspaper was closed and one of the chief rabble-rousers, Desmoulins, was executed. As many as twenty-three thousand Parisians perhaps were absorbed into the army. The National Guard became more of an arm of the Convention than the sections. In short, during 1793 and 1794 the *sans-culottes* as an autonomous movement were weakened and undermined. Louis Saint-Just, Robespierre's colleague, summed it up: "The Revolution has become frozen."

By the summer of 1794 the crises of war and rebellion were past. Yet during June and July 1794 there were some fifteen hundred executions in Paris. Dissidents were regarded as criminals. More and more members of the Convention, even those who were responsible for the Terror, came to fear Robespierre and his closest collaborators. Finally, in late July, Robespierre was denounced in the Convention as an enemy of the people. That same night Robespierre and eighty-three Robespierrists were arrested. Paris did not rise up. The following day Robespierre and his colleagues were executed. The new moderate leadership of the Convention dismantled the Committee of Public Safety, closed the Jacobin club, and executed or deported those who had been associated with the Terror. The basically liberal and constitutionalist ideas of the earlier revolutionary era reasserted themselves.

In 1795 the Convention produced a new constitution, the Constitution of the Year Three. The constitution makers were particularly concerned about preventing a dictatorship and therefore placed great importance on separation of powers. To prevent a legislative dictatorship, the legislative branch was divided into two chambers: the Council of Five Hundred (which initiated bills) and the Council of Ancients (which approved bills sent up from the Five Hundred). The executive branch was confined to a Directory of five members, which was chosen by the Five Hundred. The Directory was not given veto power or the authority to declare war but it did have the constitutional power of conducting diplomacy, supervising the military, making appointments and executing the laws. The members of the Directory were given a magnificent uniform as a protest against the egalitarianism of *sans-culottism*. The franchise was open to anyone who paid a direct tax or who had fought in the armies. These voters, however, selected electors who in turned chose deputies. There were very high wealth qualifications placed on electors, which meant there were only about thirty thousand such men in the country. The delegate who introduced the constitution to the Convention stated, "We must be governed by the best men; those most suited to govern are men of good education and endowed with a great concern for the maintenance of order. You will rarely find such men outside the ranks of the propertied." When the Directory took power it issued a statement that announced their intention of replacing "the chaos which always accompanies revolutions by a new social order."

One month before the Directory was inaugurated, a popular insurrection in Paris erupted with the demand "Bread and the Constitution of '93." The up-and-coming military officer Napoleon Bonaparte repressed the disorder. In the election of 1797 a majority of the new delegates elected to the two Councils were constitutional monarchists. To prevent what they considered a counterrevolution, the Directory initiated a *coup d'état* in September. Elections in forty-nine departments were annulled and the Councils were purged. Opposition journals were suppressed, émigrés were ordered to leave the country and opponents were deported or shot. The coup was successful because of the Directory's reliance upon the military. Within two years this reliance would prove fatal to democratic and constitutional government. Looking back upon these events some years later, Tocqueville wrote, "The nation, at a loss where to turn, began to cast round for a master – under these conditions the stage was set for a return to one-man government." In 1799 General Bonaparte initiated his own *coup d'état* and overthrew the Directory. In its place he created a neo-Roman autocracy headed by three consuls of which he was one. An accompanying proclamation stated: "The Revolution is established upon the principles which began it: it is ended." Soon Bonaparte made himself Consul for life and in 1804 the Senate proclaimed: "The government of the Republic is entrusted to a hereditary Emperor." Napoleon Bonaparte crowned himself Emperor of the French. Absolutist monarchy had been reestablished and an imperial nobility was erected. The French Republic, the first of five, was dead.

Compared to the American Revolution, the French Revolution witnessed a greater radicalization as well as a greater conservative reaction. The same was true in regard to the rights of women and their participation in public affairs. French women, aristocratic women mainly, had occupied a much more prominent place in society before the Revolution than in America. Americans were often shocked at the unusually liberal role of French women and the degree of knowledge of politics that elite women possessed. The arena of women's politicization was the urban *salon*, a kind of court presided over by literate and sophisticated women. These *salonnieres* brought educated men and women together to discuss politics, literature, the arts and much more. Some especially influential *salonnieres* served as promoters and managers of the careers of Enlightenment writers; Mme de Tencin, for example, introduced Montesquieu's *Spirit of the Laws* to society, in part by buying copies of the book and distributing it to influential leaders of society. Mlle de Lespinasse greatly encouraged and disseminated the work of the Encyclopédists. There were women journalists, many of whom wrote for the feminist *Journal des Dames*, which was committed to "a female public's right – and obligation – to be informed about controversial matters." Some Enlightenment writers, even those assisted by *salonnieres*, deplored the influence of these women. Montesquieu's *Persian Letters*, for example, portrayed France from the perspective of a Persian nobleman who deplored how influential women allocated social power to artists, writers and politicians.

With the coming of the Revolution, French women of all classes actively involved themselves in revolutionary politics. In the summer of 1789 Parisian working women frequently sent deputations to the king to express their concerns about bread price. It was armed and militant women who, during the October Days, forced the king and the National Assembly to abandon Versailles and relocate in Paris. Once in the city, women nearly always attended the Assembly, shouting their demands, interrupting debate and voting along with the deputies. By the summer of 1791 women were participating in revolutionary clubs, signing petitions, contributing to newspapers and petitioning the municipal government of Paris and the National Assembly.

In these early days of the Revolution, revolutionaries often portrayed women as heroines and inspirational symbols. One such revolutionary, the Marquis de Condorcet, a liberal and well-educated aristocrat who was married to a well-educated *salonniere*, wrote the essay "On the Admission of Women to the Rights of Citizenship" in 1790. He argued that not only men were created equal by the laws of nature but men and women were equal as rational beings. "Now the rights of men result simply from the fact that they are sentient beings, capable of acquiring moral ideals and of reasoning concerning those ideas," wrote Condorcet. "Women, having these same qualities, must necessarily possess equal rights. Either no individual of the human species has any true rights, or all have the same."

Despite the active participation of women in politics and eloquent arguments for the equal rights of men and women, the Constitution of 1791 did not, for the most part, address the rights of women. All women were assigned to the category of passive citizens, a departure even from the Old Regime when some women in certain jurisdictions voted. The Constitution, however, did advance women's rights in some areas: marriage became a civil contract and divorce was granted on an equal basis to both partners; both men and women upon reaching the age of twenty-one could marry without parental permission; and primogeniture was abolished and more liberal measures on inheritance were established.

Disappointment with Constitution of 1791 prompted three extraordinary pamphlets on women's rights. Olympe de Gouges, a monarchist and daughter of a butcher, wrote "The Declaration of the Rights of Woman" in 1791. Because both men and women possessed reason, she argued, they should possess the same rights such as education for girls, the opening of all careers to women and the establishment of a National Assembly of and for women. "Woman is born free and lives equal to man in her rights." The English writer Mary Wollstonecraft in the same year wrote "A Vindication of the Rights of Woman," which she hoped would influence the National Assembly. Like Condorcet and Gouges, she asked, "Who made man the exclusive judge, if women partake with him the gift of reason?" The third piece, "On Improving the Status of Women" was written in 1792 by the German Theodor Gottlieb. It condemned the new constitution for ignoring fully one-half of the nation. "All human beings," wrote Gottlieb, "have the same rights – all the French, men and women alike, should be free and enjoy citizens' rights."

One female role male revolutionaries could agree upon was republican motherhood. As we have seen, Americans became adherents of this idea. Woman's major political task in life was to instill her children with patriot duty thus making the home the nursery of the state. The liberal revolutionaries of 1789 praised this role: "It is for you to breed [heroes]. Let all the martial and the generous virtues flow together in your maternal milk and in the heart of the nursing women of France." The radical National Convention in 1793 declared the women should not be politically active. "Morality and nature itself," the Convention continued, "have assigned its functions to her: to begin the education of men, to prepare the minds and hearts of children for the exercise of public virtues, to direct them early in life toward the good, to elevate their souls, to educate them in the cult of liberty."

As the Revolution became more radical in 1792 and 1793 so did the working women of Paris. So many women enlisted in the army disguised as men that the Convention officially prohibited this practice. Women's protests escalated, which made it increasingly more difficult for the Jacobins to govern. The first club formed exclusively for women, the Society of Revolutionary Republican Women, more committed to radical democracy than women's issues, became too disruptive of authority in the eyes of Jacobins. In 1793 the Committee of General Security prohibited all clubs and societies of women, which was the first step in the suppression of all popular societies. The editor of one popular newssheet wrote, "It is no longer permitted to women to organize in clubs; they will be tolerated as spectators, silent and modest, in the patriotic societies; in effect women can no more go searching for news outside their homes."

Napoleonic France further degraded the rights of women. The Civil Code of 1804 subordinated women to men and established rigid sexual differentiation. It resurrected unequal standards of divorce; a man, for example, could obtain a divorce if his wife was unfaithful but a woman could not. The Code also denied women the right to own property without their husbands' permission as well as the right to plead in court in their own name. The Civil Code, however, by excluding women from the definition of citizenship, helped to provoke a feminist consciousness. The unfulfilled promise of the Revolution inspired French women in the nineteenth century to demand and struggle for their natural rights. In the Revolution of 1830, women again organized themselves to demand redress. In the Revolution of 1848, there was considerable participation of women in revolutionary events and with the defeat of the Revolution, once again the government banned the participation of women in revolutionary clubs. As in America, the Revolution of the 1790s inspired subsequent generations of women to form a women's movement to obtain suffrage and other political rights.

The French Revolution had a profound impact on the rest of Europe. In some countries the Revolution inspired revolutionaries to make their own revolution; in others the armies of revolutionary France imposed revolution with the assistance of local revolutionaries. "The Declaration of the Rights of Man," noted the American minister in Paris, Gouverneur Morris, "produces the effect of Joshua's trumpets." In the Austrian Netherlands an aristocratic nationalist revolt in 1787 had become a full-scale rebellion in 1789. A Patriot army drove out the Austrians and in January 1790 revolutionaries established the United States of Belgium. As in the American colonies and France, the aristocratic revolt of 1789 had unleashed democratic forces in the country and a popular rebellion in 1790 divided the leaders of the revolution. The Austrians took advantage of the division to reconquer the country and restore the status quo. In Poland revolutionaries compelled the Diet to adopt a constitution similar to the French constitution of 1791. The Diet was declared the representative of the nation and the king's veto was abolished. This outbreak of revolution was also crushed when Russia invaded the country and forced the king to withdraw the constitution. Not long after, Poland was partitioned by its three powerful neighbors and ceased to exist as an independent country.

In Ireland the French Revolution inspired the rebellion of 1794 led by the national independence movement of the Society of United Irishmen. Wolf Tone, a leading revolutionary, wrote that Thomas Paine's *Rights of Man* was the Khoran. The motto of the United Irishmen was: "What have you got in your hand? A green bough. Where did it first grow. In America. Where did it bud? In France. Where are you going to plant it? In the crown of Great Britain." To assist the Irish and primarily to harm Britain, the French twice tried to invade the island. Both attempts failed and the British avoided great danger.

In 1795 the French invaded the United Provinces of the Netherlands and forced the Stadholder to flee to Britain. Dutch Patriots (whose revolution had been crushed by a Prussian army in 1787) came to power and created the first "sister republic," the Batavian Republic. The price of liberation was a treaty that required the Dutch to declare war on Britain, maintain at their own expense a French occupying army and pay to France an indemnity of 100,000,000 florins. In the new republic, politics became a rivalry between democrats who were unitarists and conservatives who were federalists. The popular democrats identified local and provincial governments with elites and thus wanted to establish a new centralized democratic state with uniform rights and based on popular sovereignty. Disagreement among politicians made it impossible to convene a National Convention until 1796. The Convention submitted a constitution for ratification of the Dutch people in August 1797, which was overwhelmingly rejected. A new Convention was elected that same year and in early 1798 an internal *coup d'état* produced a more radical body. This Convention drafted a constitution that was similar to the French Constitution of the Year Three: It established a bicameral legislature with an executive of five directors. It provided manhood suffrage, making it more democratic than the French Constitution, and its most radical measure was the disestablishment of the Dutch Reformed Church.

As French armies advanced across Europe more 'sister republics' were established: the Helvetic Republic in Switzerland as well as the Cisalpine, Ligurian, Roman and Parthenopean Republics in Italy. Between 1796 and 1799 ten constitutions were written and implemented in the new republics. All began with declarations of rights modeled after the Declaration of the Rights of Man and Citizen. All of the republics were based on the sovereignty of the people. Some were more democratic than France, some less. All provided for bicameral legislatures and an executive Directory. As in France the new republics were centralized states. This feature more than any other differentiates the European and American revolutions. In Europe the revolutionary movement favored unitary and centralized government because local power was essentially aristocratic. In America the revolutionary movement arose from local and provincial bases and was profoundly decentralized. Even the American Constitution of 1787, which created the national government, accepted the federal principle as the key component of the new system of government.

In the sister republics, local Jacobins – a label attached indiscriminately by contemporaries to all patriots and revolutionaries – imposed new laws based on the French revolutionary experience. Not only were princes deposed but aristocratic privileges and orders of nobility were abolished along with feudal dues, the tithe, legal inequalities and the remnants of serfdom. Careers were open to all men based on merit and talent rather than birth. Church lands were confiscated and auctioned (see Map 11.2).

The sister republics of the late 1790s reverted to monarchies under Napoleon Bonaparte who imposed family members as kings. The Kingdom of Italy (1805) was given to Napoleon's stepson; the Kingdom of Naples (1806) went to his brother, Joseph Bonaparte, who was also made King of Spain in 1808; the Kingdom of Rome (1811) was bestowed upon the Emperor's son. The Kingdom of Holland (1804) was given to the Emperor's brother, Louis Bonaparte, but in 1810 France annexed The Netherlands. Napoleon Bonaparte, the former Jacobin, turned against democracy and the elective principle when he came to power. He advised Jerome, King of Westphalia: "It is ridiculous that you should quote against me the opinions of the people of Westphalia. If you listen to popular opinion, you will achieve nothing. If the people refuses its own happiness, the people [are] guilty of anarchy and deserved to be punished."

The Napoleonic era, however, was not completely counterrevolutionary. Everywhere French armies advanced in Europe, they carried and imposed the Civil Code, soon to be called the Code Napoleon, which had been drafted in 1804. The codification of revolutionary laws had begun in 1792 and Napoleon's drafting efforts began in 1800. The Civil Code essentially preserved the egalitarian principles of 1789 and rationalized the administration of justice according to Enlightenment principles. Thus the Code established equality before the law, civil marriage and divorce, religious tolerance and secular education; it abolished aristocratic privileges, seigniorial obligations, entail, the tithe and feudal dues. By 1815, there was no country west of Russia where the political and legal institutions had not been changed profoundly by the French Revolution.

The defeat of Emperor Napoleon in 1814–15 led to the restoration, temporarily, of Bourbon absolutism. The coalition of great powers that defeated France was determined to prevent a second French Revolution or, even worse, a general European revolution. The British Foreign Secretary made this clear when he wrote, "The existing concert [of great powers] is their only perfect security against the revolutionary embers more or less existing in every state of Europe; and, . . . true wisdom is to keep down the petty contentions of ordinary times; and to stand together in support of the established principles of social order."

PRUSSIA

BATAVIAN
REPUBLIC

1798

1795

River Rhine

1795

HOLY

ROMAN

EMPIRE

Vienna •
AUSTRIAN
• Leoben

FRENCH

REPUBLIC

POSSESSIONS

HELVETIC
REPUBLIC

SAVOY
1792

VENETIA

CISALPINE REPUBLIC

Venice •
Milan •

1799

PIEDMONT

PARMA

• Genoa

• Bologna

1791

PARMA

Florence •

1793   • Nice

LIGURIAN
REPUBLIC

TUSCANY

ROMAN
REP.

SPAIN

Corsica

Rome •

PARTHENOPEAN
REPUBLIC

Naples •

Annexed (with date)

French republic

French occupation

Sister republic

Sardinia

0	100	200	300	400	500 km
0	100		200		300 miles

Map 11.2 Western Europe in the Age of the French Revolution.

It was impossible, however, to turn back the clock to the pre-1789 era. France experimented again with constitutional monarchy after 1830, republicanism for a brief period at mid-century, a pale imitation of a Napoleonic empire in the 1850s and 1860s, until it finally settled upon a republic after 1870. As Tocqueville put it, "On several occasions during the period extending from the outbreak of the Revolution to our time [1856] we find the desire for freedom reviving, succumbing, then returning, only to die out once more and presently blaze up again. . . . Yet during this same period the passion for equality, first to entrench itself in the hearts of Frenchmen, has never given ground."

Politics and ideology in nineteenth-century Europe were largely shaped by the struggle for and against the principles of 1789 and 1793. A series of revolutions swept through most of Europe in 1848 as governments fell and monarchs and ministers lost their power. Never in European history had revolution been so endemic. In the end the revolutionaries were unable to rally the support of the masses and the revolutions failed. Revolution would continue to shape Europe for the next one hundred years. Aristocratic power was defeated by popular power. Aristocracy or nobility itself was not abolished; instead positions in government and society were opened up to men of talent, to the *parvenu*, the self-made man. In time democratic politics became supreme in constitutional monarchies and republics in Western, and eventually Eastern, Europe.

For all their common ideological roots and manifestations, the American and French Revolutions reveal several interesting differences that highlight certain fault lines in the Age of Revolution. Perhaps the most fundamental was the contrasting definitions of the people and popular sovereignty. At first the Americans conceptualized the people as one and indivisible. By the 1780s and after, however, a pluralistic view came to be dominant. The people were presumed to contain various and differing interests, groups, and factions, and diversity and division were seen as a regrettable but inevitable condition of American life. Some leaders such as James Madison perceived such pluralism as positive, a bulwark against tyranny. A multiplicity of religions, for example, ensured religious tolerance, the freedom of all sects and the dominance of none. Local and provincial interests as well as opposing political factions would check and balance one another. To ensure this, Americans became the supreme practitioners of separation of powers.

French revolutionaries, on the other hand, emphasized again and again the unity of the nation, one and indivisible. Rousseau first developed this idea when he argued that the people possessed one single General Will. True freedom, he maintained, consisted in choosing to obey the General Will. If there was conflict in politics, it was between the people or the nation and something else: enemies, traitors and counterrevolutionaries. "What constitutes a republic," Saint-Just said, "is the total destruction of everything that stands in opposition to it." Instead of separation of powers, the French concentrated the power of the people in one governing institution, the unicameral legislature. In the constitutions of 1791 and 1793 there was one legislative chamber and under the Jacobins it swallowed up all other branches of government. Those who represented the people, those who "thought right" as Sieyes put it, could never accept dissent and opposition. Robespierre once commented that "I am of the people myself," which meant he spoke on behalf of the General Will and therefore could not be wrong. The Convention imposed the death penalty for any attempt to threaten *la République une et indivis- ible*. Whereas Americans feared the potential despotism of the people, or what Tocqueville would later call the "tyranny of the majority," the French, or at least the Jacobins, embraced such an idea. "The Revolution," declared Robespierre, "is the despotism of liberty against tyranny." Here we see the intellectual justification of revolutionary dictatorship and the Terror.

These differing views of the people on opposite shores of the Atlantic produced different ideas about rights. Americans saw the purpose of declared and written rights to protect individuals and minorities against government, even popular government, and even against society or the people themselves. What protected the rights of Americans was not the mere statement of their rights but the separation of powers and limited government itself. For the French, on the other hand, individuals and minorities were potentially disruptive and thus the rights of the people as a whole were more important. What protected the rights of Frenchmen was the concentration of the people's power in unlimited government. We see this in the absence of any right of assembly, which presumably was due to a fear of factions. The rights that are stated are limited by conditions and exceptions such as the prescription not to harm others, to harm society or disturb public order. If Americans wished to protect individuals against government and society, the French were intent on protecting popular government and society from potentially disruptive and divisive individuals and minorities.

The actions and language of revolutionaries of America and France displayed interesting differences. Although both sets of leaders believed in the supremacy of virtue, that is, self-sacrifice on behalf of a noble cause, their public personalities sharply contrasted. The American leaders saw themselves as gentlemen, an aristocracy of merit and talent who thoroughly accepted such values as civility, moderation, self-control and tolerance. George Washington, for example, refused to "set up [my] judgment as the standard of perfection." American revolutionaries maintained strict adherence to parliamentary procedures in their assemblies. Their rhetoric was as moderate and restrained as their actions. Although loyalists were often forced into exile and their property was confiscated, and although mobs sometimes employed violence and imposed vengeance, never did a political trial impose a death sentence. French revolutionaries, even aristocrats, on the other hand, despised the civility and polite manners of the aristocracy and what Rousseau called the "false veil of politeness." The former revolutionary Napoleon Bonaparte belittled George Washington's "moderation, disinterestedness, and wisdom." Revolutionaries ridiculed parliamentary procedures. Revolutionary rhetoric in France was inflammatory. Unlike American rhetoric, it was almost always aimed at arousing the small people in plain occupations to take matters into their own hands. Revolutionary rhetoric encouraged violence and often turned logic and morality upside down. "Terror is an emanation of virtue," Robespierre once said, just one example of the many illogical maxims produced by the French Revolution.

The American and French Revolutions proclaimed the same political principles – popular sovereignty, the rights of man, democratic and representative government – but often gave them different interpretations and institutional manifestations. These two revolutions inspired as well as horrified men and women in other countries and colonies in the Atlantic World. They demonstrated that revolution in the name of liberty could produce freedom and independence but also despotism and conquest. They provided different scripts from which other revolutionaries would improvise. Would future leaders follow the example of Adams or Robespierre, Washington or Napoleon? Regardless of the ideal template, however, future revolutions would take place in very different societies and thus produce different movements and outcomes. Saint Domingue, or as it became known, Haiti, was not France nor was Mexico the thirteen American colonies. Despite echoes of distant struggles and talk of the people and their rights, these revolutions would write their own scripts.

11.5 Further Reading

Bernard Bailyn, *The Ideological Origins of the American Revolution* (Cambridge, Mass., 1967).

Bernard Bailyn, editor, *Pamphlets of the American Revolution, 1750–1776* (Cambridge, Mass., 1965).

Susan Dunn, *Sister Revolutions: French Lightening, American Light* (New York, 1988).

Jacques Godechot, *France and the Atlantic Revolution of the Eighteenth Century, 1770–1799*, translated by Herbert H. Towen (London, 1971).

Patrice Higonnet, *Sister Republics: The Origins of French and American Republicanism* (Cambridge, Mass., 1988).

Mark Hulliung, *Citizens and Citoyens: Republicans and Liberals in America and France* (Cambridge, Mass., 2002).

Joan B. Landes, *Women in the Public Sphere in the Age of the French Revolution* (Ithaca, New York, 1988).

Pauline Maier, *American Scripture: Making the Declaration of Independence* (New York, 1977).

Robert Middlekauff, *The Glorious Cause: The American Revolution, 1763–1789* (New York, 1982).

Baron de Montesquieu, Charles de Secondat, *The Spirit of the Laws*, edited by Anne Cohler, Basis Miller and Harola Stone (Cambridge, 1989).

Mary Beth Norton, *Liberty's Daughters: The Revolutionary Experience of Amerian Women, 1750–1800* (Ithaca, 1996).

Andrew Jackson O'Shaughnessy, *An Empire Divided: The American Revolution and the British Caribbean* (Philadelphia, 2000).

Dorinda Outram, *The Enlightenment* (Cambridge, 1995).

Thomas Paine, *Collected Writings* (New York, 1995).

R. R. Palmer, *The Age of Democratic Revolution: A Political History of Europe and America, 1760–1800*, 2 volumes (Princeton, 1959, 1964).

Richard Price, *Observations on the Importance of the American Revolution* (Boston, 1818).

Abbé G. Th. Raynal, *Historie philosophique & politique des deux Indies*, advertisement et choix des texts par Yves Bénot (Paris, 2001).

Muthu Sankar, *Enlightenment Against Empire* (Princeton, 2003).

Simon Schama, *Citizens: A Chronicle of the French Revolution* (New York, 1989).

Simon Schama, *Patriots and Liberators: Revolution in the Netherlands, 1780–1813* (London, 1977).

Alexis de Tocqueville, *The Old Regime and the Revolution*, translated by Stuart Gilbert (New York, 1983).

Thomas G. West, *Vindicating the Founders: Race, Sex, Class, and Justice in the Origins of America* (Lanham, 1997).

Gordon S. Wood, *The Creation of the American Republic, 1776–1787* (Chapel Hill, 1998).

Gordon S. Wood, *The Radicalism of the American Revolution* (New York, 1993).

Adam Zamoyski, *Holy Madness: Romantics, Patriots, and Revolutionaries, 1776–1871* (New York, 2000).

Chapter 12

Equality

The Atlantic World in the Age of Revolution

From 1811 to 1815 the popular Republic of Cartagena, comprised of the Caribbean port city and its province, became one of the first republics of the hemisphere that guaranteed equal political rights to free *pardos* (blacks and mulattos) and whites. The armed people of the lower-class neighborhood of Getsemaní forced the hesitant Creole elite of the city to declare independence from Spain. Royalist observer Fernández de Santos noted that Cartageñeros had become "enchanted with the promises of happiness and frenetic egalitarianism." The revolutions that continued to break out in the Atlantic World after 1776 and 1789, particularly in Saint Domingue, New Spain and elsewhere in Spanish America, were in substantial part egalitarian revolutions that arose within the basic framework of liberal constitutional revolutions. *Pardos* and Indians claimed and fought for equality with whites. They were inspired by the struggle of white Creoles to attain equality with Europeans. The Spanish American revolutionary Simón Bolívar, however, saw a powerful contradiction at work: "The rich will not tolerate democracy, nor will the slaves and free *pardos* tolerate aristocracy. The rich would prefer the tyranny of a single individual, so as not to suffer the violence of the mob, and also to establish a somewhat peaceful order." In societies of considerable inequality, liberal revolutions faced great obstacles.

The revolutions of the age were unquestionably Atlantic phenomena. The revolution of the slaves in Saint Domingue in the 1790s and early 1800s, the Haitian Revolution, was an unwanted product of the French Revolution. The Haitian Revolution served as a dreadful example and warning to liberal revolutionaries throughout the Americas of the potential danger lurking in any insurrection. It also became a beacon of hope to slaves everywhere in the Americas. Revolutionaries in Spain and Portugal and in Spanish America and Brazil were influenced by the American and French revolutions. "Two great examples lie before our eyes," wrote the Venezuelan revolutionary Francisco Miranda in 1799, "the American Revolution and the French Revolution." These influences and the disruption of the Napoleonic war created the Spanish Revolution, which involved the entire Spanish world from Cadiz to Caracas. The same influences and disruption also sparked the Spanish American autonomy movements that, in time, developed into republican revolutions and wars for independence. Portuguese and Brazilian liberals borrowed from the Spanish Revolution and its Constitution of 1812.

From the early 1770s to the late 1820s revolutionary rumors, rhetoric and ideas, pamphlets and books, declarations and charters, and advice and instructions crisscrossed the Atlantic in every direction with nearly every ship. European and American revolutionaries generally spoke a common political language of popular sovereignty, natural rights and representative government. Revolutionary Atlantic internationalism, however, could never obscure local revolutionary currents, historical sources and popular demands.

The Spanish Revolution in Spain and America had powerful Hispanic as well as American characteristics. Popular sovereignty and representative government were grounded in Spanish history and legal tradition and therefore legitimate even in these profoundly conservative societies. The American and French revolutions were secular and valued religious tolerance whereas the Spanish and Spanish American revolutions were profoundly religious and strictly Catholic. Spanish American revolutionaries were often more conservative than their Spanish counterparts – sometimes becoming authoritarian republicans – for fear of the potential explosiveness of peasants and slaves.

The Age of Revolution in the Atlantic operated at first in a white world and sometimes penetrated into an altogether different world of Indians, mestizos, mulattos and African and creole slaves. In the white world of European and American liberals, moderates and conservatives, revolution was often a struggle about principles that would shape and even invent institutions, influence status and prestige, offer opportunities, especially political office and improve, sometimes radically, the public lives and futures of common people. In the white world of the late eighteenth and early nineteenth centuries, liberty, equality and democracy were principles generally intended to apply to white men exclusively and even in that restricted world they could be quite radical and revolutionary in theory and implementation. However, these principles also inspired nonwhites and inevitably found receptive ears in slave huts and peasant shacks. White revolutionaries could never isolate revolutionary principles that had universal appeal. Nonwhites would also fight and die for liberty, equality and democracy.

Thus, the Age of Revolution, particularly in the Americas, witnessed two very different kinds of revolutionary movements and wars. Those led by white gentlemen were eminently political and sought such strictly political objectives as liberty, representative government and national independence. Those popular insurrections by the most downtrodden, on the other hand, were primarily social revolutions that sought the destruction or radical transformation of the social and economic structure of a colony, which meant more than anything else, equality. The Haitian Revolution, for example, destroyed slavery, the plantation system and even any remaining white presence in the new nation of Haiti. Most popular insurrections were defeated, usually quite violently, although they sometimes prepared the way for the abolition of slavery and the development of more popular and representative governments.

In the early nineteenth century Dominique de Pradt, a French cleric, predicted the independence of the remaining colonies in America: "Independence is innate in the colonies," he wrote, "as the separation of families is in human nature, the first principle of their independence." He then noted that this would rank with the discovery of America as an epoch of transcendental importance. The age of discovery in the fifteenth century gave birth to the Atlantic World. The Age of Revolution in the late eighteenth and early nineteenth century largely ended its imperial and colonial phase in the Americas although not in Africa. The political and mercantilist ties that united European metropolises and American colonies across the Atlantic were permanently broken. This chapter concludes the history of the Age of Revolution with consideration of the Haitian, Spanish and Spanish American revolutions and the independence of Brazil.

12.1 The Haitian Revolution

In 1770 Diderot in the *Philosophical and Political History of the Establishment and Commerce of the Europeans in the Two Indies* attacked slavery as an affront to the universal principle of liberty and prophesied that blacks would rise up and find a leader: "A courageous chief only is wanted. Where is he, that great man whom nature owed to her vexed, oppressed and tormented children? Who is he? He will appear, doubt it not; he will come forth and raise the sacred standard of liberty."

Prior to the Haitian Revolution such a bold prediction would have seemed preposterous. Throughout the Americas and especially in slave societies, slaves were feared but most whites believed that slaves were culturally and intellectually incapable of understanding any political principles and organizing any resistance to slavery. Slavery and slave owning in the Americas became divided into two epochs: the age before the Haitian Revolution and the age after. Before the Revolution slave owners discussed the value of liberty and equality, and even ways and means of implementing these principles, in the presence of their slaves without the least concern. A black revolution was simply unthinkable. That was how self-confident and perpetual the system of black slavery appeared in the Americas before the establishment of the first black republic in the world in 1804.

In the French colonies in the New World, white colonists believed the French Revolution was exclusively their concern. Wealthy planters, referred to as *gran blancs* (big whites), favored autonomy from the metropolis whereas lawyers, petty merchants, artisans and workmen or *petit blancs* (little whites) believed local power should be in their hands, those who constituted the majority of white colonists. Much to everyone's surprise and disgust, however, mulattos and free blacks, called *affranchis*, believed that French declarations of natural rights and decrees establishing legal and political equality applied to them. We are, stated a 1790 pamphlet, "a class of men born French, but degraded by cruel and vile prejudices and laws."

Even among some slaves in Martinique as early as 1789, the influence of the French Revolution was beginning to show itself. "This is no longer a Nation blinded by ignorance and trembling before the lightest punishments," rebellious slaves wrote to the governor, "its sufferings have enlightened it and determined it to shed its blood to the last drop rather than continue to endure the shameful yoke of slavery, a dreadful yoke, condemned by the laws, by humanity, by nature, by the Divinity, and by our good King Louis XVI." This letter revealed awareness by slaves of anti-slavery sentiment in Europe and it repudiated the common colonial view that blacks were ignorant and uncultured beings. The courageous chief foreseen by Diderot would not appear in Martinique but Saint Domingue.

Saint Domingue was the jewel in France's colonial crown and unquestionably the single most valuable plantation colony in the world. This western end of the island of Hispaniola had a population of 24,000 whites, some 20,000 *gens de couleur* (mulattos and free blacks) and over 400,000 slaves. There were more than three thousand sugar, coffee, cotton and indigo plantations. The planter class and merchant elite was dominated by *gran blancs*, naturally, but perhaps one-third of plantation property was owned by *gens de couleur*, some of whom were not only rich but well educated. The majority of whites in the towns and cities of Saint Domingue, *petit blancs*, were middle- and lower-class people who resented the political dominance and aristocratic character of the *gran blancs* and positively hated the wealth and pretensions of equality of the *gens de couleur*. "The French Revolution," wrote an observer, "necessarily produced among the inhabitants of that colony, a diversity of opinion with respect to its effects on their political rights."

Beginning in 1789 the colony became a political cauldron. *Gran blancs* in Saint Domingue and Paris worked to maintain their political dominance and advance their ultimate goal of political and economic autonomy. *Petit blancs*, encouraged by the fall of the Bastille, decided it was their time to rule Saint Domingue and formed their own National Guard to back up their claim. And *gens de couleur* pushed for equal rights, found supporters in France but only obstruction and opposition by whites in Saint Domingue. Each group sought support from the colonial bureaucracy and the regular army and made and unmade alliances as the circumstances warranted. To further complicate the picture, politics tended to follow different courses in the three provinces of the colony: the North, the West and the South.

In the spring of 1790 the National Assembly granted mulattos political rights, which ran into determined opposition in the islands. This unhappy situation led to a mulatto uprising in Martinique in June and several disturbances in Guadaloupe. A rebellion of hundreds of mulattos in North Province in Saint Domingue began in October and these rebels made efforts to recruit slaves to fight for their cause. The rebellion was repressed but violence had begun and slaves were becoming involved. Mulattos and slave or maroon allies in South Province resisted in the mountains against regular troops. In West Province, on the other hand, the collapsing colonial bureaucracy and grand *blancs* allied themselves with mulattos against the revolutionary *petit blanc* patriots. "If for once the slaves suspect that there is a power other than their masters which holds the final disposition of their fates," wrote a perceptive colonist, "if they once see the mulattos have invoked this power and by its aid have become our equals – then France must renounce all hope of preserving her colonies."

By 1791 there was a three-way civil war among *grand blancs*, *petit blancs* and mulattos. In the growing political chaos and violence in Saint Domingue, the opposing parties had largely ignored the slaves. Slaves, however, had not ignored the French Revolution. Slaves had traveled to France with their masters and witnessed firsthand the political ferment. In the Caribbean, slaves got news and political ideas from soldiers and sailors from each ship. Revolutionary literature from the Friends of the Blacks, a French association opposed to the slave trade, had flooded the country. In many ways slaves became aware of the rebellion of the "white slaves" in France and their liberation. Slaves were reported saying, "The white slaves in France had killed their masters and, now free, were governing themselves and taking over the land." That is just what they wanted to do. Rumors spread across the colony of reforms by the king to give slaves three days of leisure and to abolish the hated whip. Local officials and masters, slaves believed, conspired to suppress any news and enforcement of these improvements.

In North Province, the great sugar-producing powerhouse of the colony, the spring of 1791 saw the spread of a slave conspiracy involving blacks in dozens of plantations. Delegates from numerous plantations, usually creoles, artisans, and most importantly, *commandeurs* or overseers, would meet at night under the disguise of vodou ceremonies. Vodou provided a medium for political organization and possibly even a goal; as one vodou chant put it: "We swear to destroy the whites and all that they possess. "It was, in fact, a vodou priest, Boukman Dutty, who organized and led the revolt that began in mid-August. Just before launching the revolt, he made this call to arms: "The god of the white man calls him to commit crimes; our god asks only good works of us. But this god who is so good orders revenge! He will direct our hands; he will aid us. Throw away the image of the god of the whites who thirsts for our tears and listen to the voice of liberty which speaks in the hearts of all of us."

On the night of August 22, 1791, the slaves of North Province revolted. Rebels attacked and destroyed plantations and attracted more and more supporters as the insurrection radiated throughout the fertile north plain. "The revolt had been too sudden, too vast and too well-planned," one colonist later wrote, "for it to seem possible to stop it or even moderate its ravages." Rebels destroyed everything – the great houses, cane fields, sugar mills and tools, even slave quarters. Whites were indiscriminately killed as well as other slaves who remained loyal to their masters. Within eight days the devastation had engulfed seven parishes and nearly two hundred plantations. Early estimates placed the number of rebels at around ten thousand and organized in three separate armies. By September those numbers had risen to forty thousand and then double that by the end of November. Nearly one-half of 170,000 slaves in North Province were in revolt. White survivors retreated to the capital of North Province, Le Cap Francois, the Paris of the West Indies. By the end of the year Le Cap was just about all that remained of white power in the north.

Although the top leadership of the insurrection would be black Creoles (blacks born in Saint Domingue or in the Caribbean), a large portion of the fighting masses were Africans and of those most were from the lower

Document 12.1
A Dispatch to Blanchlande, Governor of Saint Domingue

1791

We have never thought of turning away from the duty and respect that we owe to the representative of the person of the King; but, Just Man! come down to our situation. See this land that we have enriched with our sweat or rather with our blood. The edifices that we have erected! And have we ever obtained any recompense?

Those who should have been to us under God as fathers, were tyrants, monsters, unworthy of the fruit of our labors. And can you wish, Brave General! that we should be like sheep, that we should throw ourselves into the claws of the wolf? No; it is too late. God, who fights for the innocent, is our guide; he will never abandon us. Conquer or die! This is our motto, which we will maintain unto the last drop of our blood. We do not lack either powder or cannon. Hence; Liberty or Death! If God grant that we may obtain it without the effusion of blood, then all our wishes will be accomplished.

Believe us, it has cost much to our hearts to take this way; but do not deceive yourself and think that it is because of weakness on our part. We will never change our motto: Conquer, or die for Liberty!

> Your very humble and very obedient servants,
> Signed: All the Generals and Chiefs of our arms.

This dispatch from the leaders of the uprising is neither signed nor dated. It is likely that it was written and dispatched sometime in September 1791, only about a month after the insurrection began. This dispatch may have been written or dictated by Toussaint Breda, a Catholic. *Source:* T. G. Steward, *The Haitian Revolution 1791 to 1804, Or Side Lights on the French Revolution* (1914), p. 35.

Guinea coast and Angola. The latter were often veterans of the Congo civil wars of the eighteenth century or soldiers, hailing from an African military tradition that was familiar with large formations and guerrilla warfare. Jean-Francois and Biassou described their army as "a multitude of *négres* from the coast [of Africa] who are scarcely able for the most part to say two words of French.... In their homelands, however, [they] had been accustomed to war." This African component, thinks John K. Thornton, a historian of African warfare, is perhaps the best way to explain how the insurgents coordinated large-scale operations during the first weeks of the revolt. The most renowned of the African rebels was Jean-Baptiste San Souci who played an important role in the Haitian Revolution from the first days of the 1791 rising. He not only fought the French but also defended the interests of Africans within the Revolution when creole leaders let them down.

In South Province a rebellion independent of the insurgency in the north also erupted in 1791. Within two weeks ten to fifteen thousand slaves were in rebellion and soon most slaves remaining on the plantations of the region stopped working. One colonist wrote that the slave "has lost the habit of working, and it is thus that he got accustomed to thinking." A coffee planter, revealing what was at stake for slave owners, later wrote to the rebels: "I swear that you will see all my blood flow before I consent to your freedom, because your slavery, my fortune, and my happiness are inseparable."

Were the insurgent slaves inspired by a revolutionary ideology? One captured soldier was found with a French pamphlet proclaiming the rights of man. In September 1791 a rich planter wrote a friend in Paris and described the rising of the "savage beasts." "When they are asked why they have revolted," he noted, "they claim the Rights of Man, or freedom, or three days' holiday a week with pay – or else they say they will do without masters, since the whites have decided to do without kings." In general, however, there was no need for the formulation of revolutionary principles when the principal motivation of most slaves as best as can be determined was vengeance and freedom. Many marched to battle following banners that read "Death to All Whites!" If any political principle appeared to be dominant, it was monarchy rather than democracy. Monarchy was the prevalent form of government in Africa. When insurgents liberated regions they chose kings and queens as rulers. In the first few years of the insurgency, when former slaves chose white allies they selected French royalists. When the French executed their king most insurgent bands joined the Spanish in their war against the republic. A king, some slaves were reported to have said, was the only authority competent to improve the conditions of slaves or to free them altogether.

For a time the insurgency appeared to have little political guidance, unity or even motivation. What were they fighting for? Boukman emphasized revenge and liberty in his call to arms. Following his death early in the fighting, several leaders such as Jean-Francois and Biassou organized bands that controlled certain areas in North Province. When French civil commissioners arrived in late 1791 with six thousand troops, these two black leaders negotiated. They asked for a general amnesty, freedom for themselves and fifty high-ranking subordinates, the abolition of the whip and other reforms in exchange for the return of all remaining insurgents to their former plantations. Jean-Francois commented, "I never claimed to be fighting for general emancipation which I know to be an illusionary dream." Authorities and colonists in Saint Domingue refused to accept any agreement with the insurgents.

One leader emerged, however, who took a firm and consistent position regarding the ultimate objective of the insurgency. This was Toussaint Bréda, a creole black, former slave and steward of Bréda plantation, who joined the insurgency about a month or two after it had begun. He was forty-eight years old when he joined the insurgency; to many rebels he became known simply as "the old man." He became an herbal doctor in Biassou's band and later formed his own. He joined the Spanish when Spain joined the war against the regicide French Republic and obtained arms and supplies. "The Spanish have offered me their protection and liberty for all who fight for the king," Toussaint informed the French, "and having always fought for that same liberty, I adhere to their offer." He had presumed to believe that a government willing to arm former slaves would come in time to free not only the soldiers but all of the slaves. He waited, and hoped, but never saw any progress. Action by the French Republic, however, came to give Toussaint's struggle meaning and purpose.

The Civil Commission sent to Saint Domingue by the French government found chaos and considerable opposition to French Republican rule. Royalist planters welcomed the support of the Spanish and invited Great Britain to send troops to defeat the insurgency and the republican government. The commissioners allied themselves with mulatto forces but this action was insufficient to restore order. Desperate and out of options, the Jacobin commissioner Léger-Félicité Sonthonax called for slaves to join the Republican cause and abolished slavery in the North Province. In his proclamation of August 29, 1793, Sonthonax declared, "Men are born and remain free and equal in rights: that, Citizens, is the gospel of France; it is more than time that it be proclaimed in all the departments of the Republic." He wanted all slaves to understand the role of France: "Never forget...that of all the whites in the universe, only the French of Europe are your friends."

Also in August 1793 Toussaint introduced himself to the blacks of Saint Domingue under the name Toussaint L'Ouverture, the last name meaning "The Opening." In the first of two proclamations Toussaint attempted to take the magic and authoritativeness out of Sonthonax's proclamation. "Having been the first to champion your cause, it is my duty to continue to labour for it. I cannot permit another to rob me of the initiation. Since I have begun, I will know how to conclude." In his proclamation of August 29, intended as a general introduction and invitation, he declared, "Brothers and Friends: I am Toussaint L'Ouverture. My name is perhaps known to you. I have undertaken to avenge you. I want liberty and equality to reign throughout St. Domingue. I am working towards that end. Come and join me, brothers, and combat by our side for the same cause." The Jacobin-led National Convention confirmed Sonthonax's action and abolished slavery in all French colonies in February 1794. In May, Toussaint defected from the Spaniards and joined forces with the French commander-in-chief, General Etienne Laveaux. In a public letter Toussaint complained that the Spanish had not liberated the slaves in Santo Domingo, the Spanish colony in eastern Hispaniola, and that they caused blacks to fight one another. He became a republican and never deviated from the goal of freeing all slaves in Saint Domingue and guaranteeing that slavery was never restored in the colony. From 1793–94 the insurrection of the blacks possessed that transcendent motivation and objective.

Toussaint L'Ouverture was one of the most unusual political and military leaders during the Age of Revolution. He was a humanitarian in a war that produced many monsters on all sides. Toussaint took prisoners, treated them well and opposed any kind of torture. "I have always had a horror of leaders who find satisfaction in shedding blood," he wrote to Laveaux. "My religion whose beliefs I intend to observe forbids it." The religion he referred to was Roman Catholicism, which he practiced assiduously his entire life. "All speak of him as a just man," noted the American Counsel. Bloody and brutal treatment of blacks by British officers offended his sense of decency and

Figure 12.1. Toussaint L'Ouverture. From Marcus Rainsford, *An historical account of the black empire of Hayti* (London, 1805). Courtesy of the William L. Clements Library at the University of Michigan.

honor: "I feel that though I am a Negro, though I have not received as fine an education as you and the officers of his Britannic Majesty, I feel, I say, that such infamy on my part would reflect on my country and tarnish its glory."

Toussaint and the Republican cause confronted a very dangerous situation. In September 1793 a large British army invaded Saint Domingue

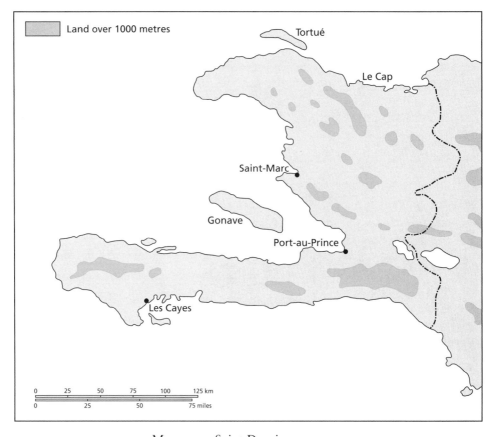

Map 12.1. Saint Domingue, 1794.

and had taken the capital of West Province, Port-au-Prince, by April. The British intended to destroy the insurrection of the blacks, which threatened by example all slave colonies in the Caribbean. Britain was also motivated by their traditional policy of seizing French colonies in wartime and in this war they quickly captured Martinique, Guadaloupe, Tobago and St. Lucia. Aside from Toussaint, most insurgent leaders remained loyal to the Spanish and enemies of the Republic. Toussaint with General Laveaux's assistance soon defeated Jean-Francois and the other pro-Spanish black commanders and made himself the most powerful leader of the blacks. Commissioner Sonthonax and General Laveaux were allied with mulatto forces in the west and south whose most powerful leader was André Rigaud. Toussaint and Rigaud became the principal generals of the Haitian Revolution during the five-year war against the British (see Map 12.1).

During this struggle, in fact, Toussaint and Rigaud became the two most powerful men in Saint Domingue. With insufficient reinforcements from France, General Laveaux became militarily dependent upon his black allies. One of the civil commissioners named Rigaud to be Governor-General of South Province, in effect official recognition of Rigaud's establishment of a mulatto military regime in most of the south. In March 1796 when mulatto forces in Le Cap arrested General Laveaux, Toussaint ordered a large detachment of soldiers to surround the city and obtained the Republican general's release. Once free, Laveaux named Toussaint Lieutenant-General of the Republican army in Saint Domingue. When Laveaux returned to France the following year, Toussaint was named commander-in-chief. Clearly whites no longer controlled the colony. A revolution unlike any in the world had brought blacks and mulattos to power in a former slave plantation colony.

The war against the British dragged on until 1798. Throughout this five-year slugfest the British reinforced their forces several times, ultimately committing more than 100,000 soldiers and ten million pounds. Like all European troops in the tropics, British soldiers were decimated by disease – yellow fever mostly – again and again. Toussaint in the north and west and Rigaud in the south often defeated British forays into the interior and forced them into defensive positions in the cities of the coast. Guerrilla warfare and yellow fever simply wore down the British year after year. New British commanders with new substantial reinforcements periodically went on the offensive. It was simply inconceivable, they believed, that blacks could defeat a well-trained European army. Throughout the war Toussaint remained true to his cause, which he described this way: "To restore men to the liberty which [God] gave them, and which other men would have deprived them." In March 1798 a new British commander, General Thomas Maitland, arrived in Saint Domingue and found a hopeless cause. After five years over twenty-five thousand British soldiers were dead with nothing to show for it. Maitland negotiated a truce with Toussaint in order to permit the withdrawal of his troops to Jamaica. In return for a British promise to trade with the colony, Toussaint agreed not to attack Jamaica or other slave-based colonies in the Caribbean. The British also promised they would support Toussaint if he led Saint Domingue to independence. They wanted to see a French army tied down in an endless colonial war. Toussaint, however, remained loyal to the French Republic.

Following the withdrawal of the last British troops in late 1798, Toussaint, the leader of the blacks, and Rigaud, the leader of the mulattos, completely controlled Saint Domingue. A new French commissioner, as part of a plan to restore French control, created dissention between Toussaint and Rigaud in order to provoke a war. The French decided to help Rigaud defeat Toussaint and suppress the black revolution; then, they believed, they could bring the mulattos under control. Neither Toussaint nor Rigaud needed any outside provocation to destroy the other. Toussaint and the blacks distrusted Rigaud and the mulattos and vice versa. Each leader viewed his rival as the only obstacle standing in the way of the complete control of the colony. The war that ensued, referred to as the War of the Knives, was a brutal and bloody conflict between two popular leaders and between blacks and mulattos.

After putting down a mulatto uprising in the north, Toussaint declared that no mulatto could remain in his territory. "Everyone of that description that could be found," claimed an observer, "was either shot or drowned." Toussaint attacked Rigaud in the south with an army of forty-five thousand blacks. Rigaud and his commanders were surprisingly passive. With the formal support of France, Rigaud fought a defensive war waiting for the arrival of a French army that never came. In mid-1800 Toussaint and his most trusted general Jean-Jacques Dessalines defeated Rigaud in a last series

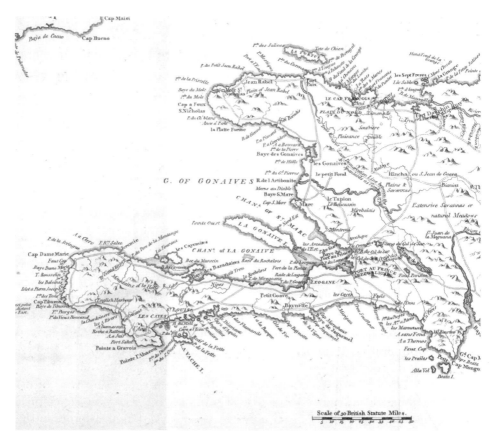

Figure 12.2. Saint Domingue at the Time of the Haitian Revolution. May from Marcus Rainsford, *An historical account of the black empire of Hayti* (London, 1805). Courtesy of the William L. Clements Library at the University of Michigan.

of battles forcing the mulatto leader to flee to France. In 1801 Toussaint dispatched two columns into Spanish Santo Domingo and seized control of the defenseless colony. This former slave now dominated the entire island of Hispaniola. The new government in France, the Consulate, dominated by General Napoleon Bonaparte, recognized Toussaint as Governor-General of Saint Domingue and commander-in-chief of all Republican military forces in the colony. The black revolution and its leader, it now seemed, was unquestionably triumphant.

Even before the expulsion of the British and the defeat of Rigaud, Toussaint had begun to govern the new Saint Domingue. Toussaint's greatest priority was to maintain the plantation system and its exports of sugar and coffee, which brought in the revenues that supported the army and sustained black rule. Upon the withdrawal of the British army Toussaint made this clear: "Learn, Citizens, to appreciate the glory of your new political status. In acquiring the rights that the Constitution accords to all Frenchmen, do not forget the duties it imposes upon you. Be virtuous and you will be Frenchmen and good citizens.... Work together for the prosperity of [Saint Domingue] by the restoration of agriculture, which alone can support a state and assure public well-being."

The restoration of agriculture required the return of white planters who were welcomed back by Toussaint. Plantations were to remain undivided and were to be run by their owners and former managers or black generals who operated them on behalf of the state. The slave trade was reestablished to bring more laborers to the colony, although the slaves were freed upon reaching Saint Domingue. The restoration of agriculture also required the return of black laborers to the plantations. "Field-negroes," Toussaint's regulations stated, "are forbidden to quit their respective plantations without a lawful permission." Cultivators, as the former slaves were called, were forced to work six full days a week for wages. This regime of forced labor was given official status in Toussaint's Constitution of 1801, which formalized the new political and economic regime. Cultivators were guaranteed one-fourth of their plantation's production and were protected from the whip and unnecessary punishment. They were subject to military discipline enforced by local detachments of the army. Only men who had practiced a craft or a trade before the revolution could do so now. 'Cultivators,' in other words, were not free to take up a new line of work. Blacks, not surprisingly, often opposed this system of disguised slavery and really would have preferred to work their own land in their own way. Although blacks were guaranteed freedom in an abstract sense, they were denied any regime that would have given real meaning to their liberty.

A rebellion of rural workers in the north erupted in October 1801, which conspired to overthrow Toussaint, kill all whites, and divide the plantations among the rebels and cultivators. It appealed to all blacks opposed to Toussaint's agricultural code and may have been motivated by rumors that Toussaint planned on restoring slavery. Toussaint's military commander in the north, his nephew Moise, sympathized with the rebels and their goals and refused to repress the movement. "Why should they work on the white man's land?" Moise asked. "Why did not Toussaint allow them simply to work on their own gardens and enjoy the leisurely life that should be the heritage of freedom?" Moise was a great threat to the new regime because he supported the aspirations of the rural masses. Toussaint had him executed, purged his army of sympathizers, and crushed the rebellion before it could become a mass movement.

Toussaint's 1801 Constitution also demonstrated how different the black political revolution was to the other revolutions in the Atlantic World. Written by a small assembly of whites and mulattos without a single black voice, Toussaint was named Governor-General for life and given the authority to name his own successor. An assembly was created but it could not initiate legislation, only approve or delay legislation proposed by the Governor-General. The Constitution gave no political rights to the mass of blacks and mulattos. Not all of his generals approved. Moise asked, "Who does he think he is, King of Haiti?" The Constitution required all citizens to work and all males aged fourteen to fifty-five years old to enroll in the militia. The Catholic Church was declared the official religion and the right to practice vodou was prohibited. Toussaint believed that to rule, men must be lashed and caressed in turn. He was no democrat who saw the need to limit the power of rulers. The black revolution was not a liberal revolution. Toussaint believed that the leader of the new black state needed absolute power to defend it against an absolutely hostile white world.

Toussaint's Constitution said nothing about Saint Domingue's relationship with France. It assumed the island remained a colony or a dominion but a completely autonomous one. Toussaint had been warned that his Constitution would be seen in France as a bid for independence and therefore a provocation. And it was, but Bonaparte had already concluded back in 1799 that France needed not only to restore metropolitan rule but the old plantation system complete with slavery and the slave trade. Planters and merchants lobbied for a complete restoration as did Bonaparte's wife, Josephine, who was a West Indian herself and a plantation owner. Bonaparte was contemptuous of all blacks and firmly believed that one of his armies could easily defeat Toussaint. Peace with Britain in 1801 made a French invasion of Saint Domingue feasible. Thus, in January 1802 an armada of fifty-five warships and transports landed an army of twelve thousand soldiers under the command of Bonaparte's brother-in-law, General Charles Victor Emmanuel Leclerc. Upon seeing this fearful sight, Toussaint was quoted saying, "Friends, we are doomed. All of France has come. Let us at least show ourselves worthy of our freedom."

In Bonaparte's plan of reconquest, deception was to be the key. Leclerc was the first to assure Toussaint that France had no intention of undermining his regime or restoring slavery in order to peacefully land his army and secure key points. Once his army was in place, Leclerc was to arrest Toussaint and his close advisors and ship them to France. Finally, Leclerc was to disarm the black army, return the police and National Guard to white control, and ultimately restore slavery and the slave trade. Bonaparte sought a peaceful restoration of the old regime but he was fully prepared for Leclerc to go to war if necessary. And, as it turned out, it was necessary.

Toussaint had prepared for such an eventuality and had placed hidden arms depots in the mountains. He and his generals destroyed the cities on the coast, retreated into the interior, and began a war to liberate their country once and for all. Although Toussaint called for a general uprising, the black masses were mostly passive. They might have joined with and fought for Moise, a champion of genuine freedom, but Toussaint at this point inspired few cultivators. In fact, he seemed unable to inspire his own army for, within a few months of the invasion, one-half of his eighteen thousand troops had defected. Leclerc, on the other hand, declared that he had no intention to restore slavery, only to restore order and prosperity. Toussaint was not sure what to believe. "Why have so many ships traversed the ocean," he told his soldiers early on, "if not to throw you again in chains?" On the other hand, he appeared to believe that Leclerc simply wanted to restore French rule, not slavery.

Believing, apparently, that the French would never give up and that he and his army faced only annihilation, Toussaint negotiated with Leclerc to find a settlement. Leclerc publicly guaranteed that slavery would never be restored and agreed to recognize the ranks of all of his officers. If Toussaint surrendered, he could keep his staff and a small protective guard and retire to a peaceful life on any plantation he wished. Because Toussaint's officers and soldiers would be incorporated into Leclerc's army, he most likely believed that because the black army remained intact, the French would never be able to restore slavery in the colony. Asked by some blacks if he had abandoned them, he answered, "No, my children, your brothers are armed and all the officers are at their posts." On this basis, Toussaint surrendered in the spring of 1802 and retired to one of his plantations.

Only a few weeks passed before Toussaint was arrested and he and his family placed onboard a ship sailing for France. Once in France Toussaint was sent to a prison cell in Fort de Joux in the Alps where he died less than a year later, a victim of malnutrition and exposure to the cold. Dessalines, Henri Christophe, Charles Belair and the other black generals who had also surrendered agreed, nevertheless, to fight on behalf of General Leclerc against the black forces that opposed the French and still remained in the field. They were sorry to see their old commander forced to leave but glad, perhaps, to have this rival to power removed from the scene. As the months passed, large numbers of French soldiers died of disease as the British troops had before them. Leclerc became ill as well and was dead before the year was out. As he lost his white soldiers, Leclerc came to rely more and more upon his black generals and black troops.

"In overthrowing me," Toussaint had declared when he was arrested, "you have cut down in Saint Domingue only the trunk of the tree of liberty. It will spring up again by the roots for they are numerous and deep." He was right. News of Toussaint's arrest and deportation had shocked the black population and encouraged men to take up arms against the French. In July rumors of the restoration of slavery in Guadaloupe, which had in fact happened, spread through the black population of Saint Domingue and encouraged the spread of the insurrection in the north, west and south. The rumors were accurate and very counterproductive, Leclerc told Bonaparte. "The news of the slavery re-established in Guadaloupe had made me lose a great part of my influence on the blacks." He wrote, "All my army is destroyed.... Every day the blacks leave me." The deportation of Toussaint had accomplished nothing, Leclerc lamented. Even the surrender of Toussaint's generals had not won the war. There were two thousand independent black chiefs in Saint Domingue, many of them Africans who refused to fight under creole blacks, and who fought tenaciously. "These men die with incredible fanaticism," Leclerc wrote, "they laugh at death, and the same is true of the women." The French general in desperation adopted a policy of extermination. He declared that the French needed to kill all blacks over the age of twelve, for they were the ones "infected" with the disease of freedom. Then a new population of slaves, uncontaminated by rebellion and freedom, could be imported from Africa.

When the black insurrection became irresistible by the fall of 1802, Toussaint's generals, Dessalines, Christophe and others, defected from the French and began to organize the rebel bands. Dessalines' prediction at the start of the invasion was coming true. "If Dessalines surrenders to them a hundred times, he will betray them a hundred times. I repeat it, take courage and you will see that when the French are reduced to small, small numbers, we will harass them and beat them.... They will be forced to leave. Then I will make you independent. There will be no more whites amongst us." In November a

Figure 12.3. The Mode of Exterminating the Black Army as Practiced by the French. From Marcus Rainsford, *An historical account of the black empire of Hayti* (London, 1805). Courtesy of the William L. Clements Library at the University of Michigan.

meeting of rebel chiefs recognized Dessalines as the supreme commander of the insurrection and the independence of Saint Domingue was decided.

The war for independence continued for another year. Following Leclerc's death, General Donatien Rochambeau received more than twenty-five thousand reinforcements in two installments and embarked on his own war of extermination. Rochambeau imported from Cuba dogs trained to attack, kill and eat blacks. Dessalines responded with equal ferocity. Neither side took prisoners. Despite great losses to disease, the war seemed to be favoring Rochambeau until May 1803 when Britain again went to war against France. Now Dessalines and the black insurgency in Saint Domingue were unofficial allies of the British. The British shipped arms to the rebels, blockaded France and prevented additional help to go to Rochambeau and even bombarded French positions on the coast. By the fall of 1803 Rochambeau's army was dying, under ceaseless attack and beginning to disintegrate. Since the invasion in early 1802 the French had suffered more than forty thousand casualties out of the sixty thousand soldiers Bonaparte sent to Saint Domingue. In November 1803 Rochambeau began negotiations with Dessalines, asking for a cease-fire to evacuate his eight thousand remaining troops and about eighteen thousand colonists, and send them under British escort to Jamaica.

The war against the French was accompanied by what historians call "a war within the war," the struggle of Dessalines, Christophe and the other black creole leaders against the mostly African chiefs who had fought the French after Toussaint's surrender. Many of these were the same Congos who had made up the rank and file of the insurgency from 1791 on. The chiefs who had fought the French during the darkest days of 1802 were less than enthusiastic about serving the creole generals whose allegiance to the cause of liberty seemed dubious. They were also enemies of the plantation and forced-labor system, which Dessalines and the rest of the creole leadership supported and enforced. They were, in short, obstacles that had to be eliminated; this was true when the creole generals fought on behalf of the French and it was true when they switched sides and fought for independence against the French. Colonel Jean-Baptiste Sans Souci, an African, was one of these unruly chiefs. Even at the war's end he still considered Christophe a traitor and Christophe still considered San Souci a rebel and had him executed.

At the same time as the French withdrawal, rebel chiefs declared independence and selected Dessalines as Governor-General for life. On January 1, 1804, an independent republic called Haiti or Hayti, named after the original Arawak name of the island, was inaugurated. In his Proclamation of Independence, Dessalines made "Eternal hatred of France" the national ideology. The "oath that must unite us," he wrote, is: "Swear to the whole world, to posterity, to ourselves, to renounce France forever and to die rather than live under domination. Swear to fight until the last breath for the independence of our country." The black revolution, the only successful substantial slave insurrection in modern history, triumphed against powerful French, Spanish and British armies after more than twelve bloody years.

Few wars have ever been so completely destructive. All of the cities of Saint Domingue were destroyed, some more than once after periods of rebuilding. Most of the more than three thousand plantations in the colony were also destroyed. What had been the world's greatest producer of sugar in 1789 was, fifteen years later, an economic basket case. One-half of the population of the colony had died or left. After independence had been attained, Dessalines invited "redeemed planters" to return and a few months later killed every white he could find in the country. At first, Haiti's new rulers followed Toussaint's example and maintained the plantation system with forced labor. The mulatto general and president Alexander Pétion and his successor Jean-Pierre Boyer began to give substance to the liberty of the former slaves. The plantations were subdivided and small plots were distributed to the cultivators. The plantation system and export agriculture were replaced by subsistence

Document 12.2
Declaration of the Independence of the Blacks of St. Domingo 1803

Proclamation of Dessalines, Christophe and Clervaux, Chiefs of Saint Domingo.

In the Name of the Black People, and Men of Color of Saint Domingo

The Independence of Saint Domingo is proclaimed. Restored to our primitive dignity, we have asserted our rights; we swear never to yield them to any power on earth; the frightful veil of prejudice is torn to pieces, be it so forever. Woe be to them who would dare to put together its bloody tatters.

Oh! Landowners of Saint Domingo, wandering in foreign countries, by proclaiming our independence, we do not forbid you, indiscriminately, from returning to your property; far from us, this unjust idea. We are not ignorant that there are some among you that have renounced their former errors, abjured the injustice of their exorbitant pretensions, and acknowledged the lawfulness of the cause for which we have been spilling our blood these twelve years. Toward those men who do us justice, we will act as brothers; let them rely forever on our esteem and friendship; let them return among us. The God who protects us, the Good of Freemen, bids us to stretch out towards them our conquering arms. But as for those, who, intoxicated with foolish pride, interested slaves of a guilty pretension, are blinded so much as to believe themselves the essence of human nature, and assert that they are destined by heaven to be our masters and our tyrants, let them never come near the land of Santo Domingo; if they come hither they will only meet with the chains or deportation; then let them stay where they are; tormented by their well-deserved misery, and the frowns of the just men whom they have too long mocked, let them still continue to move, unpitied and unnoticed by all.

We have sworn not to listen with clemency towards all those who would dare to speak to us of slavery; we will be inexorable, perhaps even cruel, towards all troops who, themselves forgetting the object for which they have not ceased fighting since 1780, should come from Europe to bring us death and servitude. Nothing is too dear and all means are lawful, to men from whom it is wished to tear the first of all blessings. Were they to cause rivers and torrents of blood to run; were they, in order to maintain their liberty, to conflagrate seven-eights of the globe, they are innocent before the tribunal of Providence, that never created men to see them groaning under so harsh and shameful a servitude.

In the various commotions that took place, some inhabitants against whom we had not to complain have been victims by the cruelty of a few soldiers or cultivators, too much blinded by the remembrance of their past sufferings to be able to distinguish the good and humane landowners from those that were unfeeling and cruel; we lament with all feeling souls so deplorable an end, and declare to the world, whatever may be said to the contrary by wicked people, that the murders were committed contrary to the wishes of our hearts. It is impossible, especially in the crisis in which the colony was, to be able to prevent or stop those horrors, know that a people, when assailed by civil dissentions, though they may be the most polished on earth, give themselves up to every species of excess, and the authority of the chiefs, at that time not firmly supported, in a time of revolution cannot punish all that are guilty, without meeting with new difficulties.

But nowadays the aurora of peace hails us, with the glimpse of a less stormy time; now that the calm of victory has succeeded to the trouble of a dreadful war, everything in Saint Domingo ought to assume a new face, and its government henceforward be that of justice.

Done at the Headquarters, Fort Dauphin, November 29, 1803.

A convention of generals assembled at Gonaives in January and formally declared the independence of the country and restoring its ancient Carib name Haiti. *Source:* T. G. Steward, *The Haitian Revolution 1791 to 1804, Or Side Lights on the French Revolution* (1914), pp. 235–7.

peasant agriculture. An attempt in the 1820s to revive the plantation system failed when small farmers refused to cooperate and the army refused to enforce the new code. Abandoning cash crops and largely cut off from commerce with the white world, Haiti became the poorest nation in Latin America.

A treaty with France imposed by the threat of bombardment also hindered Haiti's economic progress. In this 1825 treaty, the French government agreed to recognize the independence of Haiti (and thereby remove the threat of reconquest) in exchange for an indemnity of 150,000,000 francs for French losses in the former colony. In order to pay the first installment of the indemnity, the government obtained a loan from a French bank, which exploited Haiti's penury by charging excessive interest rates and commission charges. Inability to pay down the French debt deprived Haiti of long-term financing of public works designed to promote economic development.

The political consequences of independence were equally disappointing. Toussaint had begun a tradition of authoritarian government by a military man and his successors continued it. Dessalines crowned himself emperor, Jacques I, in 1804 but he was assassinated two years later. This prompted a civil war between Christophe, who made himself emperor in the north, and Pétion, who made himself president of a republic in the west and south. After Pétion died in 1818 and Christophe committed suicide in 1820, Jean-Pierre Boyer reunited the regions and took control of Santo Domingo, the Spanish side of the island. Boyer, like leaders before and after him, established a cult of personality and ruled Haiti under the Constitution of 1816, which made him president for life. Politics involved rebellions and coups d'état, which replaced one president by another, often one general by another. Between 1843 and 1915 only two presidents managed to complete their terms in office. A weak tradition of liberalism also emerged. In the 1840s, for example, a Society for the Rights of Man and of the Citizen led an opposition movement composed mostly of mulattos. This so-called Reform Movement denounced the authoritarian Constitution of 1816 and succeeded in removing President Boyer from office. At the same time another tradition was started in Haitian politics, a system called *la politique de doublure* – politics by stand-ins – whereby black generals in the office of the president became the puppets of mulatto political elites backstage. Politics in Haiti became a complicated and endless struggle between soldiers and civilians, authoritarians and democrats, and blacks and mulattos.

Although the political and economic consequences of the Haitian Revolution were disappointing, its significance was, nevertheless, monumental. No other revolution in the Age of Revolution was as revolutionary – as radical – in its motivation and goal. No slave society had ever contemplated the abolition of slavery let alone the political equality of blacks and mulattos with whites. The Haitian Revolution not only abolished slavery but also created a country of blacks and mulattos ruled by blacks and mulattos. Former revolutionaries in the United States were appalled. Many, if not most, French revolutionaries believed the Jacobin-led Convention had gone too far and were not opposed to the return of slavery to French colonies. The Haitian Revolution particularly frightened Spanish American revolutionaries. Their actions would be marked by caution and restraint. In the rest of the Caribbean no other colony sought or achieved independence until many decades later. The radicalism of the Haitian Revolution is confirmed, finally, by the fact that its key tenets were not accepted by world public opinion until after World War II.

The Haitian Revolution created one of the great revolutionary leaders of that age or any age. Diderot anticipated him in 1770: "That great man whom nature owed to her vexed, oppressed and tormented children." There stands this Black Spartacus," General Laveaux declared, "the Negro who Raynal prophesied would avenge his race." Toussaint L'Ouverture demanded the liberty of all slaves early in the struggle when other chiefs sought only their own freedom and reform of the slave system. He created a black army, an army of former slaves (who most Europeans believed would not and could not fight let alone defeat European soldiers), that destroyed armies of the two most powerful states in Europe. He fought at a time when Europe's greatest soldier and ruler Napoleon Bonaparte, and most Europeans generally, believed in "the need to block forever the march of the blacks in the world." The world also came to admire him; the *London Gazette* in 1798 wrote, "Toussaint is a Negro and in the jargon of war he is also called a brigand. But we would like to say that this Negro who was born to avenge the outrage to his race has proved that the character of a man has nothing to do with his colour."

Saint Domingue was not the only slave society in the West Indies affected by the French Revolution. The research of historian David Patrick Geggus has uncovered sixty-two slave conspiracies and rebellions in the greater Caribbean from 1789 to 1815. This list does not include maroon wars and mulatto revolts. Twelve of the sixty-two conspiracies and revolts involved rebellions of 100 slaves or more. Aside from Saint Domingue, the largest

STATUE OF TOUSSAINT L'OUVERTURE.

Figure 12.4. Statue of Toussaint L'Ouverture. From *The Uncle Tom's Cabin Almanack* (London, 1853). Courtesy of the Clarke Historical Library at Central Michigan University.

revolts involving thousands of insurgents were in Guadaloupe in 1793 and Curacao in 1795 and 1800. Thousands of slaves joined the multiclass risings in the British Windward Islands in 1795. Black Caribs made common cause with slaves in a joint war for liberation in Grenada and Saint Vincent in 1795–96.

Why were there so many organized anti-slavery actions in the greater Caribbean during the Age of Revolution? Perhaps they were related to the thousands of slaves who had fought in the American Revolution, some on behalf of the French for the Revolution, others on behalf of the British against the Revolution. These black soldiers, who included Henri Christophe and André Rigaud, were veterans of French regiments deployed in North America, settled throughout the Caribbean and transmitted new ideas and military skills. Angry colonists and slave owners blamed the circulation of anti-slavery and anti-slave trade literature throughout the region. News of the revolution in France was also spread in the Caribbean by letters from slaves in Europe, by black soldiers and sailors, white and mulatto refugees and by slave owners themselves who discussed politics in front of domestic slaves without the least bit of concern. The Coro rebellion of 1794–95 in Venezuela produced a proclamation written by two free blacks that cited the influence of "the law of the French, the republic."

When slaves revolted, however, rarely did they employ the language of French revolutionaries. (The slave revolt in Martinique in 1789, however, is a conspicuous exception.) Mulattos and free blacks, on the other hand, were more likely than slaves to respond to the message of the French Revolution. Everywhere whites noticed greater insolence among slaves, free blacks and mulattos. Slaves in the streets of Kingston, Jamaica, reportedly sang for all to hear: "Black, white, brown. All de same." The governor of Jamaica believed Pandora's box had been opened in the West Indies. He wrote that "a general leveling spirit throughout, is the character of the lower orders in Kingston." Elizabeth Campbell, a slave owner in Jamaica, was concerned that "the free Mulattos [were] reading Cobbett's Register, and talking about St. Domingo."

News of revolution in America and France and knowledge of anti-slavery societies in Europe often produced rumors among slaves. They thought they heard that their king had instituted significant reforms – the abolition of the whip or the granting of three days of leisure per week – which local authorities and their own masters refused to acknowledge and implement. There were also false rumors of emancipation. The authors of the two letters announcing the revolt in Martinique in 1789 noted that slavery was condemned "by the laws, by humanity, by nature, by the Divinity, and by our good King Louis XVI." A number of revolts began peacefully, with their leaders attempting to negotiate better conditions or freedom. Conspiracies and revolts were encouraged by violent conflict among whites, or whites and mulattos, as occurred in Saint Domingue. Slaves also knew about troop movements and variations in the numbers and strength of local garrisons, and timed their revolts when they believed the white establishment was at its weakest.

Some revolts were direct by-products of the Haitian Revolution. "Prepare for flight, ye planters," the whites of Jamaica were warned, "for the fate of St. Domingo awaits you." Saint Domingue mulattos, including Pétion and around 200 officers from Rigaud's army, were behind the invasion of Curaçao by blacks from Guadaloupe. South coast mulattos were also involved in several conspiracies and revolts in the 1790s. Black sailors from Saint Domingue, furthermore, were reportedly the masterminds of the Maracaibo conspiracy. The Haitian Revolution inspired slaves throughout the Caribbean. It certainly influenced José Antonio Aponte, leader of a conspiracy in Havana, who owned portraits of Toussaint, Dessalines, and Christophe as well as one of George Washington. Haitian blacks were instigators of the Marie Galante conspiracy in 1791, the Louisiana uprising in 1811, and the Igbo conspiracy in Jamaica in 1815. The leader of the Martinique rebellion of 1811 had served in the army of Christophe. The most famous example of the influence of the Haitian Revolution occurred in 1816. In that year President Pétion gave the Venezuelan independence leader Simón Bolívar ships, supplies and munitions in return for a promise to liberate the slaves of his homeland. Bolívar kept his promise. The following year Pétion supported the Spanish freedom fighter Francisco Xavier Mina who tried to liberate Mexico but was captured and executed.

Slaves loyal to their masters or fearful of white retaliation betrayed most conspiracies. The British government maintained better control of their Caribbean colonies largely because they maintained high concentrations of troops from 1789 to 1815. Conspiracies and revolts were perhaps fewer in number than they might have been because many slaves were offered and given freedom for service in colonial military units. Thousands of slaves were recruited to defend slavery and the status quo. Much of the fighting in the Caribbean among the British, French and Spanish empires, furthermore, involved blacks in combat against blacks. The Age of Revolution definitely placed Caribbean slavery on the defensive but nevertheless it survived and even thrived. The slave trade continued despite war and revolution and brought perhaps as many as 800,000 Africans to the Caribbean from 1789 to 1815. The Haitian Revolution, by destroying the sugar and coffee industry in Saint Domingue, spurred slave-based plantation production elsewhere – sugar production tripled in Cuba, coffee production expanded significantly in Jamaica and Cuba and there was an agricultural revival in Brazil.

12.2 The Spanish Revolution

In the Spanish world the course and outcome of the Haitian Revolution was followed with horror and, in plantation societies especially, great fear. "I confess to you that just as much as I desire the liberty and independence of the New World," wrote the Venezuelan revolutionary Francisco Miranda in 1798, "I fear the anarchy of a revolutionary system. God forbid that these beautiful countries become, as did St. Domingue, a theatre of blood and of crime under the pretext of establishing liberty. Let them rather remain if necessary one century more under the barbarous and imbecile oppression of Spain." Miranda was also not exactly an admirer of the French Revolution. "Two great examples lie before our eyes," he wrote in 1799: "the American Revolution and the French Revolution. Let us discreetly imitate the first; let us most carefully avoid the disastrous effects of the second." Spanish and Spanish American revolutionaries were politically liberal and often socially conservative. When several European nations experienced revolutions in the 1790s, Spain tried to cut itself off from the rest of Europe and successfully eluded any contagion. Spain, in fact, had avoided or resisted most of the new and progressive ideas that had transformed Western civilization since the Renaissance.

The Spanish world was unreceptive to revolutionary ideas and influences in the 1790s because, in part, it had already experienced a kind of revolution a few decades earlier. The War of the Spanish Succession in the early eighteenth century had replaced the Habsburg dynasty, which had ruled Spain since Carlos V in 1519, by a prince of the French royal dynasty, the Bourbons. Bourbon kings, acting in the best tradition of enlightened despotism, tried to strengthen the monarchy in order to modernize Spain. The Castilian system of administration and justice was extended into Aragón, Valencia and Catalona, creating a more centralized national government. To get around local grandees Bourbon reformers established a professional bureaucracy that was more responsive to the crown. Top-level aristocrats who were already powerful in their own right were excluded in favor of lower-level nobles and middle-rank professional men. Well-paid regional intendants unattached to local merchants and landowners were put in place to implement royal orders. A new level of municipal government was also added in hope of breaking the grip of venal oligarchs. Reformers were opposed to corporate entities outside the control of the crown like the Jesuit order, which was expelled from all Spanish dominions in 1767. This move permitted reforms of the universities and other Jesuit strongholds. The entire educational curriculum was modernized. The military was reformed and reorganized along the lines of the Prussian army. A modern regimental structure was put in place. Four generations of reformers created a revolution in government under the Bourbons. Like all revolutions this one produced opponents, conservatives or traditionalists, who worked to reverse or delay the reforms.

Not all of the modernizing reforms desired by the Bourbons and their lieutenants, therefore, were successfully implemented. A rationalized single tax, payable by all, faltered in the face of vested interests. The same was true for reforms that attempted to roll back some feudal privileges and jurisdictions. The Bourbon reforms, however, had begun a tradition of modernization and reform, a tradition that grew out of the Enlightenment. The Bourbon reformers had begun the modernization of Spain and its empire but they had left many deeply conservative political, social and economic structures in place. A new generation of liberals wanted to finish the job.

These liberals were true children of the Enlightenment. Although the Inquisition had forbidden the *Encyclopédia* and strictly limited the circulation of foreign books, it could not stop the diffusion of ideas. A public press discussed and debated the ideas and principles related to the American and French Revolutions. Economic associations, "Societies of the Friends of the Country," beginning in the 1760s openly discussed modern ideas and reform. Educated Spaniards talked about the ideas of Montesquieu, Locke, Rousseau and Raynal among others. They were also informed and influenced by a Spanish Enlightenment that Hispanicized such concepts as popular sovereignty, natural rights and representative government. Francisco Martínez Marina, for example, Spain's most distinguished legal historian and author of *Theory of the Cortes*, argued that Spain not only had a tradition of representative government in its rarely invoked Cortes (a Spanish Estates-General) but that a modern Cortes organized as a national assembly was necessary to revitalize the monarchy and the nation.

The French Revolution presented both liberals and conservatives with great risks and opportunities. In the year preceding the storming of the Bastille, Carlos III, the greatest of the reforming Bourbon kings, died and was succeeded by Carlos IV who proved to be a weak and ineffectual ruler. For nearly three years the Spanish government tried its best to isolate Spain from the revolutionary contagion. In early 1792 the king appointed a Francophile first minister who opened Spain to most French newspapers, pamphlets and books. Spanish liberals welcomed the change and began to discuss publicly the need for a constitutional monarchy in Spain similar to the one the French were trying to implement. The execution of the French king and the Jacobin reign of terror, however, led Spaniards to loathe the Revolution and join with the monarchs of Europe in a war to destroy the republic and restore the monarchy.

Spain and the Coalition began a series of wars that would throw Europe into turmoil for more than twenty years. For Spain war meant frequent military defeat, great hardship and political confusion. When Spain was defeated by the French Republic, the subsequent treaty of peace forced Carlos IV to become an ally of France and fight Britain and the other members of the Coalition. This new war went no better for Spain. The British Navy blockaded Spanish ports and cut off the metropolis from its overseas possessions. Spain's American trade fell into the hands of British merchants and shippers. Many Spaniards attributed Spain's difficulties to Manuel Godoy, the unpopular secretary of the king. One of the most despised war measures was the 1798 Royal Law of Consolidation (it was introduced to Spanish America in 1804), which required that the Church hand over its lands and wealth to the government in return for interest-bearing bonds. This and other unpopular actions attributed to Godoy led a number of power brokers to favor the Crown Prince Fernando and in 1808 they proclaimed him Fernando VII. Under protest, Carlos abdicated but both father and king asked the French emperor to support their opposing claims.

Both men would soon despair that they ever considered asking Bonaparte to become the arbiter of the Spanish monarchy. In 1808 France had troops in Spain. The year before Bonaparte asked Carlos if he could cross Spanish territory in his effort to defeat Portugal and remove Britain's last ally and trading partner in western Europe. Portugal would then fall under Spanish sovereignty. With the leverage of his army in Spain, Bonaparte invited Carlos and Fernando to a meeting in France. At this encounter the French emperor forced both Bourbons to renounce the throne and recognize him as the legitimate king of Spain. A little later, Bonaparte selected his brother Joseph to become the new Spanish king. In Spain the nobility, bureaucracy, military and upper clergy generally supported the new king. The people, however, generally did not.

On May 2, 1808, the people of Madrid rebelled against the French imposition of a foreign king and their military occupation. Other uprisings spread throughout the country, which permitted the formation of provincial committees of resistance, juntas, to govern parts of the country. The juntas organized resistance in the name of Fernando VII but also maintained that in the absence of the king, sovereignty reverted to the people. The juntas, which were popular governments, asserted that their authority was derived from the sovereignty of the people. In September representatives of the provincial juntas established a national committee, the *Junta Suprema Central y Gobernativa de España e Indias* or simply the Central Junta, to organize the national war of liberation. The Spanish people resisted the French for the next six years. A British army under Arthur Wellesley, the future Duke of

Wellington originally sent to assist Portugal, also fought the French in Spain in what they referred to as the Peninsular War.

It was in 1808 that Spanish liberals seized the initiative. *Liberales*, a term invented by the Spanish at this time, not only wished to liberate their country from the French but also from the great weight of tradition, absolutionism and the Catholic Church. The Habsburgs, many argued, destroyed the feudal development toward representative government in the sixteenth and seventeenth centuries. Now that national sovereignty had reverted to the Spanish people, liberals believed it was time to reform the monarchy. One town demanded of its delegate: "that legislative power be restored to the Nation represented in the Cortes." The first step would be to invite the provinces of Spain and the kingdoms of America to elect representatives to the Central Junta. In 1809, as the French became stronger and the patriots retreated toward the southwest, the Central Junta issued a Consultation of the Nation requesting that all governing bodies, corporate institutions and distinguished individuals recommend the best method of organizing a government. The replies favored the calling of a Cortes.

On January 1, 1810, the Central Junta decreed that elections be held for selecting delegates to the Third, or popular, Estate of the Cortes. Contrary to the imperialist prejudices of most Europeans, Spain's American possessions, and the Philippines in Asia, were entitled to representation. As the French continued to advance, the Central Junta appointed a regency (which was ordered to convene the Cortes) and then dissolved itself to avoid capture. War and chaos in Spain made it impossible to compile a membership role of the clergy and nobility in order to determine who could select delegates to the First and Second Estates. As a result only the Third Estate was convened in September 1810; the Cortes met as one body and became, as in France more than twenty years earlier, a national assembly. About one-sixth of the delegates were nobles, one-third were clergy and one in four represented Spain's American dominions. "The General and Extraordinary Cortes," stated the decree convoking the representative body, "confirm the incontestable concept that the Spanish dominions of both hemispheres form one single and identical Monarchy, one single and identical Nation and one single family."

The Spanish Revolution was on its way. The first step of the Cortes was to declare itself a sovereign body until Fernando VII was rightfully restored to the throne. Its members were recognized as the representatives of the people. A national government for Spain was established that followed the principle of separation of powers: the Cortes was the legislative power while the regency constituted the executive power. Courts and judges were declared independent of legislative and executive authority. When members of the regency objected to the revolutionary assumption of authority of the Cortes, that body arrested the dissidents and appointed a new regency. By this action the Cortes revealed to Spain and the world that it was going to transform politics and government in *la Nación Española*.

During the first period, the Spanish Cortes drafted the Constitution of the Spanish Monarchy, which was approved in March 1812. Because it was written in the city of Cádiz, it has often been referred to as the Constitution of Cádiz. It replaced the federated kingdoms within Spain and throughout the empire with a unitary state united by uniform laws. This decision completed what the Bourbon reformers had begun to do in the mid-eighteenth century. The Constitution eliminated the long reign of Spanish absolutism. The new unicameral legislative body, the Cortes, elected every two years, was given decisive power in making law. Executive power resided in the king who had the power to delay but not absolutely forbid legislation. He could not dissolve the Cortes and needed legislative consent for certain diplomatic acts. The Council of State, a body of forty men selected by the Cortes and the monarch, advised the king on what action he should take on laws passed by the Cortes. The Constitution created a Supreme Court and provincial *Audiencias* and the legislative and executive branches of government were instructed not to interfere with the judiciary.

Bourbon centralization was counteracted in the Constitution by the establishment of two new governing institutions, the Provincial Deputation and the Constitutional *Ayuntamiento*, or Municipal Council. The Provincial Deputation was an administrative body composed of elected delegates and an appointed president. The Constitutional *Ayuntamientos* were elected bodies designed to replace hereditary elites by popularly elected officials. The Constitution guaranteed a free press and abolished the Inquisition. Seigniorial institutions were restricted or abolished, which included in America the end of Indian tribute and forced labor. The system of entailing estates was also abolished as was judicial torture and other cruel punishments. All towns were ordered to establish primary schools and teach science, the humanities and Christian doctrine.

The Spanish Revolution created one of the most democratic systems in the Age of Revolution. Article I of the Constitution of 1812 read: "The Spanish Nation is the union of all Spaniards of both hemispheres." No imperial power before had ever given its American subjects representation in a national legislature. Spaniards were defined as: "First: All free men born and residing in the Spanish dominions and their children." This definition included free blacks and mulattos as well as Indians and *mestizos*. (The United States, to provide some perspective, did not give Indians citizenship until 1924.) Free black and mulatto citizens could vote if they had two Spanish parents, practiced a profession or accomplished some extraordinary deed. There were no literacy or property requirements. Not even Jacobin France had expanded the scope of popular politics this far. The Spanish Revolution was not, however, a radically democratic revolution. A complex system of indirect elections progressively removed the people from the election process: the entire electorate in localities voted for municipal electors who in turn selected local officials. Municipal electors chose provincial electors who in turn elected national deputies.

The Cortes discussed slavery and the slave trade. Father José Miguel Guridi y Alcocer, a deputy from Mexico, declared that slavery was contrary to natural law and repugnant to all enlightened people. He introduced an eight-point proposal that included the abolition of the slave trade, the freeing of all children of slaves at birth and the establishment of a wage system so as to help slaves purchase their own freedom. Augustín Arguelles, a Spanish liberal, presented a bill to abolish the slave trade. Both proposals obtained some support but not enough. The Haitian Revolution still frightened reformers while deputies representing merchant interests and American planters were solidly opposed to them.

The "American Question" during the debates on the Constitution involved the issues of American representation and trade policy. American deputies demanded proportional representation on the basis of population. If this were implemented, there would have been more American deputies than Spanish because there were more Americans (about 16 million) than Spaniards (about 10 to 11 million). Spanish deputies wanted to count only whites, which then gave Spain a larger population. A compromise measure was approved that allowed Americans to count Indians, *mestizos*, and a few 'extraordinary' free blacks and mulattos. With this adjustment Spanish America and Spain then had roughly the same number of people and therefore the same number of deputies. The American deputies also demanded free trade for the overseas territories. "The overseas deputies are just seeking the enjoyment of our rights," declared a Guatemalan deputy, Antonio Larrazábal, "and in no way [are we trying] to hurt or exterminate the peninsula's national trade, as someone has insinuated without reason." Even the most liberal peninsular Spanish deputies, however, were unwilling to consider a policy that was so adamantly opposed by Cádiz merchants. If other peninsular ports were required to trade through the port of Cádiz, continued Larrazábal, "they would shout to the skies complaining of injustice." Yet, he concluded, "this system is the tyrant overseas."

Unlike earlier constitutions in the Age of Revolution, the Constitution of 1812 recognized the Holy Roman Catholic Church as the one true official church and religion of Spain. The Constitution stated that the nation had to protect the church with "wise and just laws." The Constitution also did not provide for religious toleration by the state but instead prohibited the exercise of any other religion. Clergymen were the largest group and they put their stamp on the new order by requiring that elections were held on church property, that masses follow certain electoral acts, and that one priest serve on each local electoral registration committee. The Constitution required that voters had to be "moral and virtuous." The local parish priest determined who could and who could not vote. Four members of the Council of State had to be clergymen. The anticlericalism of the Enlightenment had little influence in Spain where the union between altar and throne was especially intimate. Only the most radical liberals were unhappy with the religious sections in the Constitution. The liberal newspaper published in London, *El Español*, wrote that the article on religion in the Constitution "is a cloud which darkens the light of liberty that is dawning in Spain."

During the sessions of the Cortes, delegates became divided between liberals, that is, the majority who wrote the Constitution, and those called *serviles* who were moderates more than they were conservatives. Their liberal opponents, however, saw them as servile to the crown, delegates who were not absolutely supportive of the constitutional restrictions upon the power of the king. Just about all delegates were committed to the principle of constitutional monarchy. The liberals, however, had not brought along with them most of the Spanish people in their revolution. For one thing, the new system of government had little time to earn the support and loyalty of most Spaniards. By the time the first Cortes elected under the Constitution took office, in October 1813, the Peninsular War was over and Fernando VII was preparing to return to Spain. Everything that had been done during the war, including writing the Constitution, had been done in the name of Fernando, the Desired One, who was beloved but essentially unknown. The real test of the new system of government would begin in 1814 when Fernando was finally restored to the throne. To ensure that Fernando would accept the Constitution, the Cortes decreed: "only after having sworn allegiance to the Constitution in Madrid would he be recognized as Spain's legitimate sovereign."

In the new Cortes most delegates who were either liberals or moderates believed the Revolution had gone far enough. A minority-contingent of *serviles* were convinced it had gone too far. Sixty-nine delegates, ten of them Americans, wrote a manifesto urging Fernando not to accept the Constitution, declaring that it was contrary to Spanish history, tradition and law. They were not opposed to representative government in principle, however, and urged Fernando to call a traditional Cortes with clergy, nobility and commons. Nevertheless, this division among parliamentarians was fatal to the constitutional order. The conservative Duke of Wellington, who had served as Supreme Allied Commander during the Peninsular War, also opposed the constitutional regime. When Fernando began his journey to Madrid in early 1814 he received the manifesto and in Valencia the local military commander offered to support the king should he decide to abolish the Cortes. On May 4, 1814, he did just that – he dissolved the Cortes and abolished all of its acts including the Constitution of 1812. Throughout Spain new men had replaced high-level bureaucrats and traditional elites during the constitutional regime and thus those out of power favored the return of absolutism. The same was true of the professional army, which had been defeated again and again by the French and pushed aside by the irregular guerrilla units. The army welcomed the restoration of absolutism. The guerrillas, on the other hand, were in France fighting Bonaparte in the spring of 1814 and unable to defend the Constitution. Moreover, the people, who retained a strong faith in Fernando, did not rise up to support and defend the Constitution.

The Spanish Revolution was nullified. The army pursued liberals and put, perhaps, as many as twelve thousand behind bars. Many more fled to France, other countries in Europe or Spanish America and remained in exile. They constituted many of the leading men of letters and the best public officials. In America the royalist bureaucracy pursued liberals. The restoration of Fernando turned the tide in Spanish America. Until 1814 American liberals and patriots sought autonomy for their home provinces within the constitutional monarchy. After 1814 repressive policies by the crown transformed autonomy movements into independence movements.

12.3 The Spanish American Revolutions

The abdication of Carlos VI and Fernando VII and the appointment of Joseph Bonaparte to the throne of Spain produced shock and confusion in Spanish

America as it did in Spain in 1808. The revolutionary dynamic of the Spanish American people, however, was different from that of the Spanish people. There were liberals in Spanish America, as in Spain, who favored and helped implement constitutional government in the peninsula and in their American provinces; there were also a small minority of radicals who demanded independence. The overwhelming majority of white Spanish Americans were *criollos*, that is, creoles (Spaniards born in America) and they were divided over the issue of autonomy, free trade and self-government. Many creoles resented the advantages and privileges given to *peninsulares* (peninsular Spaniards) who outnumbered creoles in appointments to high- and even middle-level state and church positions, dominated overseas trade and in many cases had become rich hacendados and mine owners. Many Spanish Americans, almost certainly the majority before 1808, favored the status quo, which meant that the American kingdoms were and should be governed by the royal bureaucracy (most of whom were peninsulars) in America in the name of the king. Other creoles believed that now, in the absence of the king, sovereignty reverted to the people, in this case the Spanish American people, and the people should create autonomous governments staffed by the best creoles and govern their kingdoms or provinces until Fernando was rightfully restored to the throne.

The Spanish American desire for autonomy and self-government had been amplified by the mid- to late-eighteenth-century Bourbon reforms. The centralization of government meant less autonomy and fewer creoles in office. Almost all of the new Intendants, well-paid and powerful provincial administrators, were peninsular Spaniards. "Their [creole and peninsular] mutual antipathy reaches such an extreme," wrote two peninsular bureaucrats in Peru, "that in some ways it exceeds the unbridled fury of two nations, completely at odds, who vituperate and insult each other."

The most important grievance was the transformation of the status of the American possessions. Most creoles, particularly traditionalists, believed the Spanish Monarchy was a federated empire. The American kingdoms, like New Spain and Peru, were equal to the Spanish kingdoms of Castile, Aragón and the others. Only the person of the king united the many kingdoms within the Spanish Monarchy. Many creoles, however, feared that the Bourbons were attempting to reduce kingdoms into dependent and submissive colonies. Many Bourbon reforms, for example, made Spanish America more dependent economically upon Spain. The expulsion of the Jesuits, most of whom were creoles, was an especially unpopular action in Spanish America where the Jesuits trained and educated most young up-and-coming creoles.

All of the reforms, Carlos III stated, were intended "to bring my royal revenues to their proper level." The opening of new Spanish and American ports to trade within the empire revitalized commerce. If a little bit of freer trade was a good thing, most Spanish Americans believed, then unrestricted free trade must be a great thing. In Mexico a scientific and technical college was created to increase the yields of Mexico's silver mines, which it did. Although some regions and occupations benefited economically from the reforms, others regions and groups were hurt by them. Just about everyone paid more taxes and, for the first time, American revenue was not just expended within America for administration and defense; some of the monies went to the central treasury in Madrid. For most creoles the economic reforms simply reinforced the need for autonomous government in Spanish America. Spain was a dead weight around the neck of Americans, which held them back from prosperity and importance. "We were mere consumers," Simón Bolívar noted, looking back upon the colonial past, "confined to the cultivation of indigo, grain [and] mining in the earth to produce gold for the insatiable greed of Spain."

Creoles throughout Spanish America had followed the American and French revolutions and translated and published several of the leading revolutionary declarations and constitutions here and there. A revolutionary conspiracy in New Granada in 1795, for example, issued a translation of *The Declaration of the Rights of Man and of the Citizen*. The Mexican revolutionary Fray Servando Teresa de Mier, one among many Spanish Americans, visited Philadelphia and Washington as well as Paris during the first decade of the nineteenth century. According to the Bishop of Michoacán (Mexico), "the electric fire of the French Revolution has put into movement... an ardent desire for independence." Creoles especially identified with the North American struggle for autonomy and then independence. "The valour with which the English colonies of America have fought for liberty which they now gloriously enjoy," wrote Juan Pablo Vizcardo, an exiled Peruvian Jesuit in 1799, "fills our own indolence with shame."

Creoles had begun in the second half of the eighteenth century to construct an American *consciencia de sí*, self-awareness, based on history and pride of one's homeland. "The New World is our patria and its history is our history," wrote Vizcardo. Alexander von Humbolt, the scientist who had visited Spanish America in the late eighteenth and early nineteenth century, noticed: "The creoles prefer to be called Americans.... Since the year 1789, they are frequently heard to declare with pride, 'I am not a Spaniard, I am an American,' words which reveal the symptoms of a long resentment." One of the most important differences between Americans and Spaniards was that they had different histories.

What made creoles consider themselves Americans? Some creole historians claimed the ancient Indian kings as their particular country's founding fathers. "In our veins flow the pure blood of the native lords of the country," wrote the Mexican theologian Fray Servando Teresa de Mier, "I myself descend from the last [Aztec] emperor, Cuauhtemoc." Other creole historians claimed the *conquistadores* and their Indian wives and allies as the progenitors of their country. Almost all of the historians then described the 300-year interval between the founders and the present as an age of despotism and Spain "an oppressive step mother patria." As several generations of Spanish Americans came to make Mexico, or Guatemala, or Quito their home, these kingdoms, provinces, or intendancies became their real patria, fatherland, homeland, their country. Without thinking about it much, a creole nationalism developed in each 'country,' unified politically by the boundaries of the old jurisdictions and by resentment of or opposition to the royal bureaucracy.

This incipient nationalism was also generated by particular stories about the past, by local newssheets (called newspapers today) and by the open affection of patriots.

The "despotic" Habsburg kings had destroyed the social pact between the founders and the monarchy and between America and Spain. The American kingdoms were supposed to be free and independent of Spain and Spaniards, and obedient and loyal only to the king. Spanish governments had violated the pact over the years and Spanish Americans wanted it restored and revitalized, not destroyed completely. So did liberal Spaniards who as representatives in the constituent Cortes created with Americans a federated monarchy authorized by the Constitution of 1808. However, before that development, before there was a Cortes, in 1808, creoles witnessed the fall of a king and the apparent disintegration of an independent Spain itself. In the absence of the king, sovereignty had returned to the people, and in America that meant first and foremost to the creoles. In addition, they believed they had the right and the duty to form their own governments until Fernando VII was restored to the throne. "With the Monarchy dissolved and Spain lost," wrote a patriot in New Granada, "are we not in the condition of sons who become of age at the death of the father of the family?"

That meant the formation of patriotic American juntas, independent of all royal governing institutions. Creoles in 1808 and again in 1810 did not know if what was left of an independent government in Spain would survive. They were also afraid that royal officials in America might swear allegiance to the new king, Joseph I, if or when all resistance in Spain was exterminated. Creoles here and there, usually from the *ayuntamientos*, began to consider and discuss forming juntas and even took action to establish some. In almost every case royal officials and the peninsular-dominated bureaucracy were opposed to the establishment of creole-dominated juntas. Despite expressions of support like this, peninsular officials and bureaucrats had a profound distrust of creoles and everywhere saw conspiracies plotting independence and even democratic government. The most sophisticated or moderate officials joined with creoles to form hybrid juntas with creoles and peninsulars but ensuring that creole autonomists did not control them. Others simply blocked all creole initiatives. As these officials and bureaucrats put roadblocks in the path of creole autonomists, Americans became slowly but surely more resentful and radical as the months and years passed on.

In Caracas in July 1808, the governor and captain-general convened a council of notables to consider what path to take. The creole-dominated *ayuntamiento* proposed the formation of a local junta to take over government of the city and province. The peninsular-dominated *Audiencia* proposed changing nothing and preserving the status quo. The governor sided with the *Audiencia* and arrested members of the ayuntamiento and other leading autonomists. In Mexico City the *ayuntamiento* declared that sovereignty no longer rested with the king and his viceroy in the Kingdom of New Spain but in the people. Although the *ayuntamiento* asked the viceroy to continue as head of the government provisionally, its creole members in league with other creole conspirators began to make moves to form a more autonomous government. In addition, it appeared that the viceroy approved of what was going on. It was at this point, in September 1808, that Gabriel Yermo and a group of leading Spaniards executed a *golpe de estado*, that is, a coup d'état, perhaps modern Latin America's first. The creole leaders were arrested and an eighty-year-old field marshall was appointed acting viceroy. The *Audiencia* and the archbishop approved the coup. Peninsulars were willing to go to extreme lengths to maintain and preserve their dominance in America.

In New Spain, as just about everywhere else, the cure was worse than the disease. The legitimacy of royal government was shattered and creoles in several towns began to conspire and organize rebellions to throw off the Spanish yoke. Rather than settle things down, the coup provoked an intense politicalization of all classes and colors in New Spain and especially in central Mexico. A December 1809 uprising was exposed and its leaders were brought to trial. In the city of Guanajuato a movement was also exposed but some of the conspirators regrouped and began an uprising in September 16, 1810, in a small town called Dolores. The leaders of the movement, Father Miguel Hidalgo, Ignacio Allende, and other prominent creoles, appealed for support not only to creoles but also to Indians, *mestizos*, free blacks and mulattos. While creoles were concerned about peninsulars and autonomy, poor people, peasants, laborers and *castas* were agitated about food shortages, high prices, French atheism and social justice. Many also believed they were fighting on behalf of good King Fernando. Mexico's own Virgin of Guadalupe became the standard of the rebellion, a symbol of liberation, justice and patriotism. Thousands of people joined within days and constituted a formidable popular insurrection.

This Mexican Revolution is an example of a mass insurrection, a social revolution, being touched off by gentlemen revolutionaries originally concerned mostly about political issues. This soon became the perception of most peninsulars and creoles, especially those well-to-do ones, who believed another Saint Domingue was beginning in Mexico. Hidalgo also appealed to the people by abolishing Indian tribute and black slavery. He ordered the return of lands to native communities although the insurrection was already redistributing wealth and property as it moved across the countryside. As the insurgency grew by the tens of thousands, the rebels almost indiscriminately destroyed property and killed whites. By early November one of Hidalgo's officers informed him, "The Indians are very much out of control. On passing through the village of San Felipe I found three Europeans and a creole torn to pieces, although they held safe conducts from Your Excellency."

A Saint Domingue outcome was not to be. Outside the heartland of the rebellion (a region in center-west Mexico called the Bajio), most Indians and *castas* did not rise in revolt. The conditions were somewhat different because the drought had been less severe outside the Bajio and therefore the problem of hunger was not really an issue. The popular uprising, furthermore, had motivated most creoles and the lower clergy to unite with peninsulars and the royal army and militia units in order to stop this horror in its tracks. Moreover, that very thing happened. Once Hidalgo began to lose battles, his 80,000-strong mob-army started to disintegrate. Hidalgo fled north and eventually was captured, defrocked, excommunicated and executed in 1811.

Although the army was destroyed, the insurgency continued in the hamlets and villages in many parts of Mexico, from the northern frontier to the Gulf of Mexico in the east and the Pacific Ocean in the southwest. Royalists generally held the cities while insurgents dominated the countryside. The insurgents continued, wrote the viceroy, "their system of devouring everything that they encounter." Father José María Morelos in southern Mexico became the most important rebel chief. In June 1813 he convened elections for an insurgent congress, which declared the independence of *América Septentrional*, that is, North America. In Morelos' *Chilpancingo* Congress we are given a chance to see a kind of homegrown Mexican liberalism. In 1814 this Congress drafted a Constitutional Decree for the Liberty of Mexico, which established an independent republic with a strong legislature and a weak plural executive. Representatives of the nation should be paid a "sufficient but not excessive salary" in order to ensure that everyone, not just the rich, could serve in government. This system followed the same outline of the Constitution of 1812 in Spain.

Morelos also issued a more personal declaration of independence, which he called "Sentiments of the Nation." In it Morelos declared the independence of "America" and also confirmed: "the Catholic religion shall be the only one, without tolerance for any other." He asserted that sovereignty "'flows directly from the people," that there should be a separation of powers, and that government posts be held only by Americans. Foreigners were excluded from the country unless they could instruct others in a useful trade. Morelos abolished slavery, torture and all caste distinctions. "Our American," he stated in Article 16, "shall be distinguished from another only by his vices and virtues." Popular Mexican liberalism, it would seem, was profoundly religious, concerned with the vices and virtues of individuals more than individual rights, was humane and egalitarian, and somewhat xenophobic. Although Father Morelos was captured and executed in 1815, the insurrection fought on.

Beginning in 1810 many Spanish Americans, and some peninsulars for that matter, became constitutionalists and implemented the decrees of the Cádiz Cortes. Americans held elections to choose deputies to the constituent Cortes, a process that essentially began the politicization of the American people. Many must have been thrilled to read the February 1810 decree, which stated, "American Spaniards, from this moment you are elevated to the dignity of free men . . . your destinies no longer depend either on the ministers, the viceroys, or the governors; they are in your hands." Under the Constitution of 1812, Americans established many constitutional *ayuntamientos*, far more municipal governments than had existed at any previous time, and elected Provincial Deputations. These institutions further inspired local and provincial patriotism and gave positions of some authority and visibility to creole autonomists. Royal authorities in Spanish America helped implement the Constitution with various degrees of enthusiasm and obstructionism.

In Guatemala City, the captain-general, as well as the *Audiencia*, delayed implementation of the Constitution and obstructed the new institutions at every step. Moreover, he did all of this while also insulting creoles and their institutions. Antonio Juarras, head of the Constitutional *Ayuntamiento*, wrote to the Cádiz Cortes in 1813: "Executives in America have been accustomed to treating these vassals as they might be authorized to do with a colony of slaves." Here in a nutshell was the American grievance: royal officials were local despots, essentially unsupervised by the king when he reigned, and now adamantly opposed to the constitutional monarchy and the new popular and somewhat autonomous institutions of government. The Cádiz Cortes was receptive to American complaints. A new captain-general was appointed to the Kingdom of Guatemala in the fall of 1813. In the spring of 1814, however, the king overthrew the constitutional system in Spain and America, a move that was heartily welcomed by royal officials throughout Spanish America.

The renewed threat of Spanish defeat by French armies and the constitutional awakening in 1810 led to the reemergence of autonomist movements in such cities as Caracas, Buenos Aires, Santa Fé de Bogota, Santiago de Chile and Quito. In several cities constitutional niceties were permitted but autonomist juntas suppressed. In Caracas the leading creoles overthrew the captain-general and established their Supreme Junta. Thus began a revolutionary process that led to a sovereign congress that declared independence and drafted a constitution. Venezuelan liberals led by Francisco Miranda pushed through their program: a federal republic with a strong legislature and a weak executive, legal equality for all free men, the abolition of hereditary privileges and the slave trade. The republic collapsed in July 1812 when a new captain-general accompanied by troops arrived in Venezuela and took over. This official's campaign of repression against liberals and republicans was so offensive that it provoked a new insurgency, which recruited the services of a wealthy young planter and officer, Simón Bolívar. A civil war between royalists and autonomists, in which creoles fought for both sides, continued until 1815 when an army dispatched by the restored absolutionist Spanish Monarchy arrived in Venezuela and, for the most part, restored royal power and authority.

In Buenos Aires in 1810, the capital of the viceroyalty of Rio de la Plata, autonomist creoles backed by popular gatherings in the streets established an American junta and called for a congress. Problems regarding which provinces were part of the revolution delayed the convening of a constituent assembly until January 1813. As in Cádiz and Caracas, liberals dominated the meeting and abolished hereditary privileges, native forced labor, the slave trade and even slavery itself. In an action that began to reveal the difference between South American and Mexican liberalism, the assembly also abolished the Inquisition. Division among the provinces regarding the best way to organize the country delayed the formal declaration of independence until 1816. In July of that year the United Provinces of South America was formed and in 1818 a constitution created a republic, with a constitutional monarchy as a possibility if a suitable prince could be located. By this time liberals had retreated and realists established a strong national government with a bicameral legislature, a popular Chamber of Representatives and an aristocratic Senate. This constitutional system never had a chance to work but not because of any intervention by royalist officials and armies. Of all the autonomous movements that began in 1810, only that of distant Buenos Aires remained free and independent.

The great problem facing the former viceroyalty of the Rio de la Plata was less ideological than geographical. The interior provinces of this proto-country had long histories of separate governmental administration and powerful patriotic sensibilities. Just as kingdoms aspired to autonomy, so did provinces and even localities. Buenos Aires, the city and the province, presumed to lead all of the United Provinces but Buenos Aires had not become the capital and center of the viceroyalty until 1776, quite late in the colonial regime. Thus creole elites in this vast region went to war more than once to impose, or break out of, a centralized or federal system of government. In time some provinces joined with Buenos Aires to create Argentina and others like Uruguay, Paraguay and Upper Peru (today called Bolivia) became independent republics.

The other Spanish American autonomy movements of 1810 fared poorly. Chilean creoles formed a governing junta that convened elections for a congress to take over in 1811. The local *Audiencia* attempted to overthrow the junta and failed; it was then abolished and replaced by a court of appeals. When the congress met it assumed full sovereignty and created a republic within the Spanish Monarchy led by the legislative branch and a weak three-man executive. Liberals finally had their day. They replaced hereditary elites with popularly elected officials, some controls were placed on the Catholic Church, and a "free womb" law began the gradual abolition of slavery. However, in 1813 and 1814 it all came crashing down. The viceroy of Peru sent an army to Chile in 1813 to moderate the Chilean constitutionalist revolution. When Fernando restored absolutism in 1814, the Peruvian viceroy sent another army, dismantled all of the constitutional reforms and structures, and arrested those liberals who did not escape across the Andes into exile. Autonomy movements in Quito and New Granada generally followed similar paths. In Quito, fratricidal divisions among liberals and autonomists led to a royalist triumph two years before the restoration of Fernando to the throne. In New Granada, as in the Rio de la Plata region to some extent, provincial juntas fought each other as well as royalists. A civil war and then an invasion of the kingdom by a royalist army from Venezuela in 1815 brought an end to all constitutional and autonomist hopes among creoles.

Autonomist creoles in Cuzco in 1814 ran into determined opposition by the *Audiencia* and were being imprisoned. As with Hidalgo in Mexico, they asked for the support of Indians and thousands joined the movement. After taking control of Cuzco, the creole revolutionaries dispatched mostly Indian armies to La Paz, which produced a bloodbath, and to Arequipa, and other highland cities. "Thousands of Indians, mobilized with the object of removing these provinces from the rule of Fernando VII, best of sovereigns," the Intendant of Arequipa wrote, reflecting the opinion of most Peruvian Spaniards and creoles, "Then, in satisfaction of their hatred towards the other races, they would exterminate all the other non-Indians of this hemisphere." Another royalist commented on "the support which both Negroes and Indians have given to the rebellion, for their addiction to robbery, pillage, assassination and every kind of disorder make them amenable to its ideas and readily enlists them in its ranks." As in Mexico widespread fear of the black and Indian masses united most Peruvian creole and peninsulars who together repressed this developing popular revolution by mid-1815 and executed the leading rebels.

The restoration of Fernando to the throne in 1814 generally coincided with, and in some cases assisted, the defeat of the last autonomist movements in the New World. The empire in America was intact in 1815–16 with the exception of the Rio de la Plata region. The experiment with constitutionalism was dead and absolutism was restored. Creole liberals and constitutionalists were out of power and in many cases in prison or in flight. In Venezuela alone the Spanish executed five hundred patriot leaders. The monarchy had determined to use military force to repress all autonomist movements and in 1815 sent an army of ten thousand soldiers to Venezuela, the largest army ever shipped to America. Creole autonomists throughout Spanish America, realizing that conciliation and compromise were impossible, now embraced independence. Fernando lost the empire when he lost the confidence and loyalty of a significant portion of the basically conservative creole elite. Reflecting the views of more and more Spanish Americans, a Buenos Aires newspaper wrote in 1816, "In 1810 we only wished to preserve freedom against foreign domination.... But the Spaniards began to make war on us and tried to impose despotism on America. We still placed all our hopes in Fernando. But these hopes were destroyed when he actually reached the throne, for he waged bloody war against America. And we began to detest so unjust a king."

The struggle in Spanish South America involved numerous campaigns and years of war and destruction. The United Provinces and exiled Chilean patriots supported José de San Martín and his Army of the Andes, which crossed the mountains in 1817 and liberated Chile in 1818. San Martín and his backers realized the key to Spanish power in South America was Peru and organized an expedition that successfully landed on the Peruvian coast in 1820. The following year Spanish forces withdrew to the highlands and the creole elites of Lima proclaimed the independence of Peru. The other theater of war was the Spanish Main. The Venezuelan patriot Simón Bolívar returned to his homeland in 1815–16 thanks to Haitian support and an army of foreign mercenaries. He secured the lower Orinoco region in 1818–19 and from 1819 to 1821, won battles that gave him control of New Granada and then all of Venezuela. In 1821–22 Bolívar liberated Quito. After San Martín withdrew from the war in 1822, Bolívar accepted the invitation of Peruvian creole elites and went after the Spanish armies in Andean highlands. Victories in 1824 and 1825 ended nearly three hundred years of Spanish rule in South America.

The revival of the Spanish Revolution beginning in 1820 accelerated the divorce of Spain and America. The rebellion of an army waiting in Andalucía for transport to America that year led to the restoration of the Constitution of 1812. Spanish liberals, however, were no more willing to grant autonomy to the American kingdoms and provinces than Bourbon monarchists were. As a result, few Americans participated in the Cortes this time around. This revolutionary revival was short-lived; in 1823 a French army restored

Fernando to absolute power and again, as in 1814, he abolished the Cortes, nullified the Constitution and imprisoned liberals.

The brief rebirth of the Spanish Revolution and the prospect of a new era of instability and even liberal anticlericalism gave conservative Mexican creoles an excuse to separate from Spain and at the same time bring the ten-year-old insurgency to an end. Colonel Agustín de Iturbide, an officer in the royal army, made a deal with the most important insurgent leader and together they issued the Plan of Iguala in early 1821 that declared independence. They agreed the new government would be monarchist and headed by Ferdinand VII or another member of the Spanish royal family, that the Catholic religion would remain the official and only tolerated religion of the nation, and that there would be absolute equality between Spaniards and Americans. A year later, unable to find a suitable Spanish prince, a congress proclaimed Iturbide to be Mexico's first emperor.

Liberals and federalists overthrew Agustín I in 1823 and elected a constituent convention, which established a republic and wrote a federal constitution in 1824. The new constitution, which was modeled on the Constitution of 1812 and the American constitution of 1787, established a rather weak executive and a strong legislative branch. It created nineteen states, which were given substantial autonomy and rights. Catholicism was established as the official religion. Guadalupe Victoria, a military man and former insurgent, was elected Mexico's first constitutional president.

An assembly of notables in Guatemala approved Iturbide's Plan of Iguala and declared the independence of Central America in September 1821. For a short time, many Central Americans believed federation with Mexico would promote the economic development of their provinces. After Iturbide's fall, however, all of the provinces save one decided to establish their own republic and in 1823 the United Provinces of the Center of America was founded. Central American liberals wrote a constitution closely based on the Constitution of 1812.

The independence wars of Spanish America were complicated civil wars and social conflicts. Creole patriots fought royalist creoles in just about every province but these were not just wars of Europeans and Americans. Both the Spanish and the patriots recruited free blacks and mulattos for their armies. At certain times and places both sides promised freedom to slaves who joined their cause and fought for a specific period of time. In San Martín's Army of the Andes, for example, nearly one-half of the soldiers were former slaves. Most of the soldiers in Bolívar's armies and those of his lieutenants were *castas* or *pardos*. Indians seemed to be particularly partial to royalism and composed significant portions of the Spanish armies in Peru. They also fought in patriot armies, however, as was true in the Cuzco rebellion of 1814–15.

The racial composition of the armies had revolutionary consequences. In 1815 a royalist general noted, "the darkest Pardo became accustomed to giving orders to whites and to treating them on at least equal terms." Spanish and Spanish American liberals had been unwilling to extend civil and legal equality to all blacks and mulattos in the Constitution of 1812. The everyday equality experienced by *castas* and *pardos* in the armies, however, created a new American egalitarianism that was backed up by the various declarations and constitutions of the new nations. The legal caste system of the Spanish empire in America was destroyed by the wars for independence.

Spanish American revolutionaries also advanced the rights and interests of Indians and black slaves. The wars had recruited soldiers from both groups and given them a taste for equality. Revolutionary ideology also encouraged creole patriots to promote liberty and equality. As a result, revolutionaries across the two American continents abolished Indian tribute and forced labor. Most revolutionary leaders or governments also abolished the African slave trade at the time of independence or soon thereafter. Slavery itself was weakened and placed on the defensive. Where it was not abolished outright, gradualist emancipation laws brought it to an end. Although most creole patriots did not seek to alter the social structures of their countries, they did enact and create some limited but still revolutionary changes of society.

Were the wars political revolutions as well as movements for national independence? Almost all creole patriots were liberals in that they supported natural rights, representative government, separation of powers and legal equality. They were part of the same tradition that produced the Spanish Revolution and the Constitution of 1812. More than a few, like General San Martín, were constitutional monarchists. Because no legitimate Spanish (or any other) prince offered his services to Spanish American monarchists, this type of government became quite rare in Latin America. Only a few creole patriots were democrats, that is, leaders willing to extend the vote and active citizenship to all men regardless of wealth and education. The founding fathers of the new Latin American states were conservative republicans: they supported self-government by property-owning and educated men.

As in the United States and France, the roles and rights of women in Spanish America were little changed as a result of the revolutionary movements and wars. Elite and lower class women participated in the insurrectionary movements; some even took up arms and fought for the cause. Neither participation nor ideology, however, promoted any significant change for women. In some countries the new civil codes tended to somewhat curtail the rights of women. In others there appear to have been some modest gains. In Mexico, for example, the age of majority of single female daughters was lowered and widows were given control of the legal affairs of their children. There has been very little research on the 'women's question' and the Spanish American revolutions and as a result we simply do not know how the revolutions affected the roles and rights of women.

Within the emerging Latin American liberal tradition there was room for political variation. Many of the new national leaders and constitution makers were direct heirs of the constitutionalism that produced the Constitution of 1812. They established political systems with powerful, even dominant legislatures and weak executives. Leaders, who thought of themselves as realists, favored governing systems with strong executives. Often wartime conditions produced situations where the dominant military leader assumed presidential or dictatorial powers. The new national leaders were also divided into centralists and federalists. Centralists followed in the Bourbon tradition of a central government, usually located in the largest city (and former colonial capital), governing directly all of the provinces. Federalists, inspired by the

Document 12.3
Address to the Congress of Angostura

Simón Bolívar, 1819

Happy is the citizen who, under the shield of the armies he commands, has convoked national sovereignty to exercise its absolute will! I, therefore, place myself among those most favored by Divine Providence, for I have had the honor of uniting the representatives of the people of Venezuela in this august Congress, the source of legitimate authority, the custodian of the sovereign will, and the arbiter of the Nation's destiny. . . .

The continuation of authority in one individual has frequently been the undoing of democratic governments. Repeated elections are essential in popular systems, because nothing is so dangerous as to permit a citizen to remain long in power. The people get used to obeying him and he gets used to commending it, from which spring usurpation and tyranny. . . . We have been subjected by deception rather than by force. We have been degraded by vice rather than by superstition. Slavery is a child of darkness: an ignorant people becomes a blind instrument of its own destruction. It takes license for freedom, treachery for patriotism, vengeance for justice. Liberty is a rich food, but of difficult digestion. Our weak fellow citizens must greatly strengthen their spirit before they are able to digest the wholesome and nutritious bread of liberty. The most perfect system of government is the one that produces the greatest possible happiness, the greatest degree of social safety, and the greatest political stability.

In republics, the executive must be the stronger, because all conspire against him: while in monarchies, the legislative power should be the stronger, because all conspire in favor of the monarch. The splendor of the throne, of the crown, of the purple: the formidable support given to it by the nobility: the immense wealth which generations accumulate in the same dynasty: the fraternal protection which kings mutually enjoy, are considerable advantages which militate in favor of the royal authority and make it almost boundless. These advantages show the need of giving a republican executive a greater degree of authority than that possessed by a constitutional prince.

A republican executive is an individual isolated in the midst of society, to restrain the impulses of the people toward license and the propensities of administrators to arbitrariness. He is directly subject to the legislative power, to the people: he is a single man, resisting the combined attack of opinion, personal interests and the passions of society. . . .

The government of Venezuela has been, is, and must be republican: its foundation must be the sovereignty of the people, the division of powers, civil freedom, the proscription of slavery, the abolition of monarchy and of privileges. . . . Unlimited freedom, absolute democracy, are rocks upon which republican hopes have been destroyed. Look at the old republics, the modern republics, and the republics now in process of formation: almost all have aimed to establish themselves as absolutely democratic, and almost all have failed in their just desires. . . . Angels only, and not men, could exist free, peaceful and happy, while all of them exercise sovereign power.... Let the legislative power relinquish the attributes belonging to the executive, but let it acquire, nevertheless, new influence in the true balance of authority. Let the courts be strengthened by the stability and independence of the judges, by the establishment of juries, and of civil and criminal codes, not prescribed by ole times, nor by conquering kings, but by the voice of nature, by the clamor justice and by the genius of wisdom.... Humankind cries against the thoughtless and blind legislators who have thought that they might with impunity try chimerical institutions. All the peoples of the world have attempted to gain freedom, some by deeds of arms, others by laws passing alternately from anarchy to despotism, from despotism to anarchy. Very few have contented themselves with the moderate ambitions constituting themselves in conformity with their circumstances. Let us not aspire to impossible things, lest, desiring to rise above the region of freedom, we descend to the region of tyranny. From absolute liberty, peoples invariably descend to absolute power, and the means between those two extremes is social liberty.... In order to constitute a stable government, a national spirit is required as a foundation, having for its object a uniform aspiration toward two capital principles: moderation of popular will and limitation of public authority.

Source: From "Address Delivered at the Inauguration of the Second National Congress of Venezuela at Angostura," February 15, 1819, excerpts translated by Guillermo A. Sherwell, in *Simón Bolívar: A Sketch of His Life and Work* (1930), pp. 111–17.

United States, favored a system of government in which provinces governed themselves and a national government of limited power conducted foreign policy.

The constitutionalism of Simón Bolívar reflected the deep conservativism of a considerable portion of the elite. He believed neither the American Constitution of 1787 nor the Spanish Constitution of 1812 offered a suitable model for the new nations of the former Spanish American empire. He referred to the United States as a "republic of saints" where liberal governing institutions were successful because of the Americans' long tradition of self-government, not to mention their prosperity and widespread education. Bolívar's Americans, as he saw it, were unprepared for representative government. "Subject to the threefold yoke of ignorance, tyranny and vice," he declared in 1819, "the [Spanish] American people have been unable to acquire knowledge, power or virtue." With such unpromising raw material, he believed, self-government would quickly produce anarchy and then despotism. "Perfectly representative institutions," Bolívar cautioned, "are not suited to our character."

The constitutions crafted by Bolívar established powerful presidents and centralized governments. The Constitution of 1821 of Colombia divided authority between a powerful president and a conservative senate. The Constitution of 1826 of Bolivia (formerly Upper Peru) provided for a president

Figure 12.5. Portrait of Simón Bolívar in Military Attire. An engraving derived from the engraving by M. N. Bates (London, 1810). Courtesy of the John Carter Brown Library at Brown University.

with life tenure and a subordinate legislative branch with three houses for tribunes, senators and censors. Because most positions in government were appointed and the electorate was quite restricted, elections were of minor importance. By this point whatever faith Bolívar once had had in republicanism was gone: "I am convinced to the very marrow of my bones that only a clever despotism can govern in America." Three years later when he surveyed Latin America he saw only disorder: "Constitutions [are] mere books, elections open combat; liberty is anarchy, and life itself is a torment. America is ungovernable to us. He who serves the revolution ploughs the sea."

Revolution in the Spanish world did produce chronic political instability for decades. Generally this was simply part of the price of nation building. Spain, Mexico, Venezuela, Chile and the others were confronting new problems and challenges and experimenting with political solutions. It took time to create stable governing institutions and positive traditions. We need to remember that France was also politically unstable during a good portion of the nineteenth century and the United States fought a very bloody and costly civil war that almost destroyed the political nation. The nations of the Spanish world over the long run remained faithful to their revolutionary heritage and ideology. Spain became a constitutional monarchy and the Spanish American countries remained republics with representative governments. Like the United States and France most have become modern democracies with universal suffrage, political equality, a free press and free and fair elections.

Historians of Latin America have long argued that the wars and revolutions for independence here changed society very little. The struggles gave political power to creoles but left the lower classes impoverished and powerless. This contrasts with the American Revolution, which began a truly democratic revolution that in a rather short time gave the vote, and thus power, to all white men regardless of wealth or education. Recent research, however, has begun to reveal that poor whites, Indians and *mestizos*, and even in some cases blacks and mulattos, exercised their citizenship rights after independence and participated in and influenced to some extent provincial and national elite politics. In Mexico, for example, lower-class popular groups joined and supported the liberal and federalist faction, which not long thereafter was led by a full-blooded Indian who came to be elected president of Mexico. It seems that the Mexican Revolution and other Spanish American revolutions were also democratic revolutions to some extent that opened politics to men who had been excluded from public life during the colonial regime. Much more historical research is needed to uncover the populist outcomes of these revolutions and how popular groups participated in politics in the post-independence era.

12.4 The Independence of Brazil

Spanish American patriots in some regions fought for independence for more than a decade. In 1822 Brazilian independence was attained relatively quickly and peacefully. Long before independence Brazil had superseded the metropolis in wealth and promise. During the Napoleonic wars the Portuguese crown made Brazil the center of the empire and granted it de facto independence. Brazilians were united in large part because a branch of the Portuguese royal dynasty remained in Brazil and gave legitimacy to the new nation and its political institutions. Portugal, on the other hand, lacked the resources, and perhaps the will, to recolonize Brazil and resist independence. Thus Brazil attained independence without a revolution, establishing America's only long-lasting monarchy of the nineteenth century. Over time liberal principles guided Brazil's political development but in the beginning Brazil was the great exception to the revolutionary rule.

Brazil was not immune to the revolutionary infections of the age. A number of Portuguese American elites, influenced by the American Revolution, organized an independence movement in the gold-rich province of Minas Gerais in 1789. They wanted to establish a republic with a constitution modeled on the American Constitution of 1787. The movement was aborted when authorities discovered the movement. A more popular rebellion composed of artisans, workers, sharecroppers and soldiers – white and mulatto – broke out in Bahia in 1798. In this case independence and republicanism became identified with social equality and social reform. This movement was also repressed, savagely. It reminded too many Brazilian elites of the disaster of Saint Domingue and perhaps made them more politically cautious and loyal to Portugal than they might have otherwise been.

As it turned out, however, Brazil and Portugal followed a most unusual course. In 1807 French Emperor Bonaparte invaded Portugal, Britain's last continental ally and trading partner. To avoid capture and coercion, the royal family, the court and most of the governing bureaucracy – some ten to fifteen thousand people – boarded a Portuguese fleet and protected by British warships set sail for Brazil. Prince Dom João VI, regent since 1792 when his mother the queen was declared insane, established the new government of the Portuguese empire in Rio de Janeiro. It was the first time the head of a European state was transplanted in America.

Once in Brazil Dom João made Rio capital of the worldwide Portuguese empire. The Portuguese reestablished significant institutions such as the national bank and the national library in Brazil. Two medical schools were founded as well as a military and a naval academy. Brazil's first printing presses were set up by the Portuguese in 1808 and were soon printing Brazil's first newspapers. Dom João opened Brazil to the trade of friendly nations, in effect establishing free trade. Decrees prohibiting manufacturing in Brazil were revoked and subsidies for certain new industries were granted. As far as Brazil was concerned the colonial system had come to an end. Brazil's new status was recognized juridically in 1815 when Dom João made Brazil a kingdom, the equal of Portugal.

Although Portugal had been liberated by British troops and the war in Europe was ended by 1814, Dom João remained in Brazil. Upon the death of the queen he became king in 1816 and stayed in his tropical capital. A republican rebellion in Pernambuco in 1817 revealed some Brazilian disaffection but most of the Brazilian planter and merchant elite supported the Portuguese regime in Rio. Real disaffection was growing in Portugal. The commander-in-chief of the Portuguese army, an Englishman, essentially ran the country and the nobility wanted the monarchy back. Portuguese manufacturers and traders were unhappy about Brazil's economic independence. In addition, they wanted their king back. By 1820 disaffection had developed into rebellion.

The rebellion initiated a Portuguese revolution. Liberal revolutionaries came to power in the *Junta Provisória* and called a Cortes to write a constitution. Portuguese revolutionaries followed the script of the Spanish Revolution in creating a constituent assembly that seated representatives from every part of the empire. Their constitution would be modeled after the Spanish

Constitution of 1812. The revolutionary junta also demanded the return of the king and in April 1821, after thirteen years in Brazil, Dom João and about four thousand Portuguese traveled to Lisbon. The king left his son, Dom Pedro, in Rio as prince regent.

In 1821 and 1822 the Cortes drafted a constitution for a constitutional monarchy for Portugal and the empire. Like the Spanish charter of 1812, the Portuguese constitution of 1822 created a powerful unicameral legislature and a relatively weak executive, the king, who could delay but not stop legislation. Unlike the Spanish constitution, the Portuguese document authorized religious toleration. Brazilian deputies attempted to have the constitution recognize Brazil's political and economic equality but failed. The Cortes instead took steps to recolonize Brazil politically and economically. In early 1822 the Cortes ordered the return of Dom Pedro. Each action convinced the Brazilian elite that the time for independence had come. They asked Dom Pedro to stay and on September 7, 1822, he declared the independence of Brazil. In December he was crowned Dom Pedro I, emperor of Brazil, in Rio de Janeiro.

Pedro thought of himself as a liberal and in May 1823 inaugurated a constituent assembly. (In Portugal a military coup in May abolished the Cortes and the constitution. Portugal would have to fight a civil war in the 1830s in order to reestablish constitutional government.) Pedro's assembly, however, turned out to be too liberal for his taste. The Brazilian liberals favored a constitution that limited the power and prerogatives of the emperor more than the emperor thought was wise. In November 1823 he dissolved the assembly and sent several leaders to jail or into exile. Pedro then ordered his advisors to draft a constitution. This document, which became the Constitution of 1824, created a bicameral legislature, a Chamber of Deputies, whose members were indirectly elected, and a Senate whose members served for life and were selected by the emperor. The emperor controlled all appointments and could veto legislation. He was advised by a Council of State composed of counselors who were appointed for life by the emperor. He could dissolve the Chamber of Deputies and call new elections when he felt it was necessary. He left day-to-day governing to an appointed cabinet and intervened as a moderating power when he determined it was necessary. The constitution created a centralized state: presidents appointed by the emperor headed the provinces. Catholicism was declared the religion of state and the emperor was made head of the church. This constitution survived sixty-five years until the monarchy was abolished in 1889.

The independence of Brazil was perhaps the most conservative political development in the Age of Revolution in the Atlantic. A creole elite led by a European prince determined that it was necessary for a colony to separate from its metropolis. The separation was almost entirely peaceful and thus did not involve the recruitment and participation of the masses. The prince then drew up his own constitution to govern the new nation. The birth of Brazil, although not revolutionary itself, reflected revolutionary principles and developments. Dom Pedro and his Brazilian supporters understood that an absolutist monarchy was out of the question. Brazil's constitutional monarchy included features that other peoples had fought and died for: representative government, separation of powers and individual rights. There were, furthermore, a substantial number of liberals within the Brazilian elite who participated in national politics and constantly pushed for reform, political and social. Eventually they created the republic of Brazil. The formation of the independent nation of Brazil was not an anomaly in the Age of Revolution. The leaders of this new state were the heirs of the American, French and Spanish revolutions. Brazilian planters, not unlike revolutionary Virginian and Venezuelan planters, wanted liberty and self-government without upsetting the social order, which included slavery.

From the mid-1770s to the mid-1820s the Atlantic world was shaken and transformed by revolution after revolution. Revolutionaries fought monarchical absolutism and regimes of feudal and aristocratic privilege. They replaced sovereign monarchs with popular sovereignty: the people were now in charge, which meant self-government, individual rights, elections, representative institutions, separation of powers and more. In the Americas political revolution generally meant the breakup of empires. In the American Revolution popular sovereignty was anti-imperialist. The Spanish Revolution, however, attempted to revolutionize not only the monarchy but also the empire itself. The Constitution of 1812 accepted the Spanish American interpretation of the empire as a federated empire and created a legislature that counted elected representatives from every province in the Spanish world. Even more significant, this legislature contained no fewer American representatives than peninsular representatives. The Spanish Revolution nevertheless could not preserve the empire because it failed to control and moderate royal officials in America who opposed, often with force, creole autonomy movements. The restoration of royal absolutism in 1814 only strengthened the repressive attitude and actions of royal officials in America. Like American patriots in Philadelphia, creole patriots in Spanish America came to see popular sovereignty as a principle that required independence.

The Age of Revolution produced the dissolution of an important portion of the Atlantic empires. Only the Caribbean colonies of Britain, France, Spain and a few others remained loyal or dependent by the 1820s. The revolutionary principles of the age were not inherently anti-imperialist. The Spanish Revolution, in fact, tried to show that imperial bonds were irrelevant to the revolutionary formation of a new state and political culture. The revolutions, nevertheless, became anti-imperialist and revolutionary principles came to serve the cause of separation and independence. Americans identified despotism with the metropolis whereas liberty signified independence. Sovereignty of the people meant Virginians, Mexicans and Chileans, among others, had the right of revolution, the right of self-government, and so on. In the Americas, therefore, revolution overlapped with independence and revolutionaries created new systems of politics and new nations. The most important consequence of the Age of Revolution many historians often claim was the establishment of more than a dozen new American nations by the mid-1820s. We should remember, however, that almost all of these nations were republics with representative governments and democratic, or potentially democratic, political cultures. What was revolutionary about the Age of Revolution was the transformation of the exercise of political power, not the establishment of home rule itself.

Despite the uniform underlying principles that shaped the Age of Revolution in the Atlantic, the revolutions produced considerable political and constitutional variety. Constitutional republics coexisted with constitutional monarchies. European revolutionaries had to adapt revolutionary principles to reality, which meant monarchy. American revolutionaries were less constrained by existing institutions and traditions and could remake their political world almost entirely. Americans, therefore, were more republican than Europeans were. Radicals generally created powerful unicameral legislatures whereas moderates or conservatives, who believed the separation of powers diluted the potentially despotic power of the people, established bicameral or even tricameral legislatures with strong executives. Some revolutionaries were democrats and granted the vote and privilege of holding public office to all men regardless of wealth and education, even color in some places. Most were not. These non- or antidemocratic revolutionaries believed self-government worked only when the active citizens were men of property (who had a stake in society, and thus something to conserve) who were educated and virtuous. Even the most radical revolutionaries, oftentimes those who believed in the sovereignty of the people, favored restricting the franchise with property or income, and literacy, qualifications. Democratic revolutionaries were usually men who started out life as, or were still, artisans, wage earners and renters, that is, men from the ranks of the common people.

The greatest contradiction of the Age of Revolution was the persistence of the slave trade and slavery itself in the face of sincere protestations of liberty and equality. Men of the age, even slave owners, realized the hypocrisy of making revolution while preserving slavery. For the first time in Western civilization, however, slavery and the slave trade came under serious and persistent criticism. Revolutionaries frequently called for the end of the slave trade and the immediate or eventual abolition of slavery. Revolutionary governments sometimes acted upon these generous sentiments: the trade was terminated in several countries and while some nations abolished slavery outright or began gradual abolition. The Age of Revolution, thus, was largely but not successfully anti-slavery. It began the effort to abolish the slave trade and slavery in the Atlantic but could not finish the job. Slavery and the slave trade, after the achievement of independence by the American nations, remained the last transoceanic sinews of the age of empire in the Atlantic. The struggles and campaigns to rid the Atlantic of these related evils is the subject of the following and concluding chapter.

12.5 Further Reading

Charles Arthur and Michael Dash, editors, *Libete: A Haitian Anthology* (Princeton, 1999).

Madison Smart Bell, *Toussaint Louverture: A Biography* (New York, 2007).

Nettie Lee Benson, editor, *Mexico and the Spanish Cortes, 1810–1822: Eight Essays* (Texas, 1966).

Simón Bolívar, *Selected Writings of Bolívar*, 2 volumes, translated by Lewis Bertrand, selected and edited by Vicente Lecuna and Harold A. Bierck, Jr., (New York, 1951).

David Bushnell, *Simón Bolívar: Liberation and Disappointment* (New York, 2004).

Laurent Dubois, *A Colony of Citizens: Revolution & Slave Emancipation in the French Caribbean, 1787–1804* (Chapel Hill, 2004).

Laurent Dubois, *Avengers of the New World: The Story of the Haitian Revolution* (Cambridge, Mass., 2004).

Bryan Edwards, *An Historical Survey of the French Colony in the Island of St. Domingue* (London, 1797).

Carolyn E. Fick, *The Making of Haiti: The Saint Domingue Revolution from Below* (Knoxville, 1990).

David Barry Gaspar and David Patrick Geggus, editors, *A Turbulent Time: The French Revolution and the Greater Caribbean* (Bloomington, 1997).

David Geggus, editor, *The Impact of the Haitian Revolution in the Atlantic World* (2002).

A. Goodwin, editor, *The New Cambridge Modern History*: Volume VIII: *The American and French Revolutions, 1763–93* (Cambridge, 1965).

C. L. R. James, *The Black Jacobins: Toussaint L'Overture and the San Domingue Revolution*, revised 2nd edition (New York, 1989).

Lester D. Langley, *The Americas in the Age of Revolution, 1750–1850* (New Haven, 1996).

Kenneth Maxwell, *Conflicts and Conspiracies: Brazil and Portugal, 1750–1808* (New York, 2004).

Médéric L. E. Moreau de Saint-Méry, *Description topographique, physique, civile, politique et historique de la partie francaise de l'isle de Saint Domingue*, 2 volumes (Philadelphia, 1797–8).

Michael A. Morrison and Melinda Zook, editors, *Revolutionary Currents: Nation Building in the Transatlantic World* (Oxford, 2004).

Thomas O. Ott, *The Haitian Revolution, 1789–1804* (Knoxville, 1973).

Wenda Parkinson, *This Gilded African: Toussaint L'Ouverture* (London, 1978).

Marcus Rediker, *The Many-Headed Hydra: Sailors, Slaves, Commoners, and the Hidden History of the Revolutionary Atlantic* (Boston, 2000).

Jaime E. Rodríguez O., *The Independence of Spanish America* (Cambridge, 1998).

Jaime E. Rodríguez O., editor, *Mexico in the Age of Democratic Revolutions, 1750–1850* (Boulder, 1994).

Mario Rodríguez, *The Cadiz Experiment in Central America, 1808–1826* (Berkeley, 1978).

Martin Ross, *Night of Fire: The Black Napoleon and the Battle for Haiti*, translated by Karin Ford-Treep (London, 1994).

Robert Louis Stein, *Léger Félicité Sonthonax: The Lost Sentinel of the Republic* (Cranbury, New Jersey, 1985).

Chapter 13

Freedom

The Abolition of the Atlantic Slave Trade and New World Slavery

The empires and economies of the Atlantic World had been built to a great extent upon the slave trade and American slavery. By the late eighteenth century some sixty to seventy thousand Africans each year were dragged from their homelands and transported to the Americas. They joined the 2.5 million black slaves who produced the valuable commodities – sugar, tobacco, coffee, cacao, indigo, cotton and more – of the plantation complex. African slavery was ubiquitous throughout the Atlantic World. It was present in Europe, Africa and the Americas, it had expanded for hundreds of years and appeared to be everlasting. Beginning in the 1770s and 1780s, however, an international anti-slavery campaign attacked the morality and legitimacy of the slave trade and of slavery itself. During the course of about a century, the Atlantic slave system was destroyed by European, American and some African reformers and by the actions of the slaves themselves. The fall of black slavery and the Atlantic slave trade was a transformation as significant and dramatic as the destruction of the Atlantic empires.

The rise of anti-slavery sentiment in the eighteenth century was related to both a religious reevaluation of slavery and the rationalist questioning of tradition, which was an important part of the Enlightenment. Beginning in the 1770s, anti-slavery became part of the ideology and program of the Age of Revolution. The first official abolitionist legislation in the world came in the United States during the American Revolution. Inspired or perhaps compelled by the slave rebellion in Saint Domingue, French revolutionaries abolished slavery in their colonies in 1794, temporarily as it turned out. Spanish American revolutionaries in the 1810s and 1820s abolished the slave trade and put slavery on the path to abolition. Neither the slave trade nor slavery, however, was completely or even substantially done away with during the Age of Revolution. The revolutionary generation condemned slavery and began to tear it down, generally where it was weakest. Slavery and the plantation complex as a whole were too entrenched, too profitable and too powerful to destroy quickly or easily.

Anti-slavery forces first targeted the slave trade for abolition. The movement began in Great British in 1787 with the formation of the Society for the Abolition of the Slave Trade. British abolitionists brought to life the first popular campaign to influence Parliament and ended the British trade in 1808. The United States abolished its slave trade at the same time. Over the next twenty years the British government used its power and influence to convince or pressure the other European and American participants to abolish their slave trades. Once the entire Atlantic slave trade was illegal by 1830, British influence and naval power was directed toward getting nations to enforce their prohibitions, or doing it for them. The illegal Brazilian slave trade was not suppressed until 1850 and the illegal United States and Cuban trades survived until the early 1860s. Overall, the nineteenth century slave trade still transported more than three million Africans to the Americas.

In the late eighteenth and early nineteenth century, the first anti-slavery activists believed that the abolition of the slave trade would inevitably lead to the contraction and demise of slavery itself. By the 1820s that early optimism was generally viewed by the activists as unrealistic and perhaps even incorrect. The British anti-slavery movement was revived and pressured Parliament to abolish slavery in the British West Indies in 1833. The French abolished colonial slavery a second time in 1848 during another revolution. By mid-century, slavery in the Americas was not only surviving but also thriving in three prosperous plantation economies: the southern United States, Spanish Cuba and the empire of Brazil. In these regions commercial agriculture experienced new vigor and expansion in the early and mid-nineteenth century. Because of the cotton boom in the United States, the sugar boom in Cuba and the coffee boom in Brazil, slavery remained a powerful institution in the Americas. Abolitionist movements, pressure from without, civil or international wars and the actions of the slaves themselves led to emancipation of the slaves in the United States in 1863 and 1865, Cuba in 1886 and Brazil in 1888.

The end of slavery in the Americas did not mean the end of slavery throughout the Atlantic. The abolition of the slave trade and the rise of "legitimate trade" increased the number of slaves, the internal slave trade and the importance of slavery in Africa. Britain brought its anti-slave trade campaign to Africa and negotiated treaties with local states and rulers to bring it to an end in the African ports. With the effective end of the Atlantic slave trade in the 1860s, anti-slavery activists then turned their gaze on African slavery. All of the European powers offered the abolition of slavery as a rationale for colonial expansion in the 1880s and 1890s. Anti-slavery legislation, missionary work and slave resistance and flight brought an end to most African slavery by the 1930s.

The fall of slavery signified the freedom of millions of Africans and African Americans. In the Americas this meant for many (although not all) the strengthening or unification of fragile families, the rejection of fieldwork by sisters, wives and mothers, the end of supervised gang labor and whipping and the possibility of leaving the plantation and even the area. Populations that had previously declined now began to increase because more babies were born and survived, and men and women began to live longer. Some plantation economies disintegrated and former slaves became peasant farmers. Where the plantation system survived many former slaves continued working the same fields for a small cash wage. Freedom for most former slaves in the Americas was real and not an illusion. Freedom, however, did not often bring full independence, prosperity, justice or civil rights. In their different national homes, the former slaves and their progeny were generally desperately poor and occupied the bottom rung of society's ladder. Vagrancy laws, taxes or simply severe poverty itself forced blacks into labor contracts that paid below-market wages. Without the vote or basic rights, they were almost powerless to defend their interests in society. In short, for the former slaves freedom marked the beginning of a new, difficult and long struggle for dignity and justice, a better life, and a higher position in society.

13.1 Anti-Slavery Thought and Opinion

Until the mid-eighteenth century, slavery was accepted nearly universally as part of the natural order of things. Slavery was regrettable in the same way that poverty or illness was regrettable. It was perceived as a permanent element of human life not unlike kingship or war. Slavery had existed in the ancient world and had been justified by the ancient philosophers. It existed in the Holy Land in the age of the Old Testament and the New, and Christians had long cited biblical passages that seemingly justified slave holding and trading. The enslavement of Africans was widely considered acceptable behavior because African slaves had already been enslaved by their own kind in their own country and removed from that "savage continent" and brought to "civilized" and Christian lands. Prior to the eighteenth century, public attacks upon slavery and slave trading, like those of Jean Bodin in the sixteenth century and António Vieira in the seventeenth, were rare.

All of this changed in the eighteenth and nineteenth centuries. The leading European philosophers argued that slavery was an unnatural, illegitimate and even anachronistic institution. Theologians and religious leaders began to condemn slave holding and slave trading as sinful, the corrupt products of irreligion. Anti-slavery crusaders attacked traditions, laws and governments that permitted, and sometimes encouraged, slave trading and slave holding. Governments eventually outlawed slave trading and slavery itself. From the formation of the first abolitionist society in 1787 to the emancipation of the last slaves in the Americas in Brazil in 1888, the great anti-slavery crusade in Europe and America achieved its goals in only one century. Why was slavery transformed from a normal, acceptable and legitimate practice and institution into an unacceptable, immoral and ultimately illegal and unconstitutional practice and institution?

Most observers and scholars have attributed the great anti-slavery crusade to a revolution in moral perception that began in the eighteenth century. Thomas Clarkson, one of the leaders of the British anti-slavery movement, argued in his 1808 book *History of Abolition* that many "springs and rivulets" of anti-slavery thought and action, each marked with the name of a thinker or statesman, converged, eventually "swelling the torrent which swept away the slave-trade." The anti-slavery crusade to many was an intellectual, moral and altruistic campaign against the dark forces of sinfulness, materialism and avarice. Slavery's forced demise represented the decisive triumph of humanity's idealistic nature.

In the 1940s the Caribbean scholar Eric Williams put forth an altogether different explanation in his book *Capitalism and Slavery*, 1944. According to Williams, the Atlantic slave-based plantation and the slave trade financed the Industrial Revolution, and mature industrial capitalism then helped destroy the slave system. Williams attempted to show that by the late eighteenth and early nineteenth century the British West Indian plantation system was inefficient, unprofitable and in decline. Slavery was abolished because its time had passed and it was becoming unprofitable, unnecessary and an obstacle to modern capitalist development. The moral crusade of the abolitionist forces was a diversion, Williams believed, one of the greatest propaganda movements of all time. Slavery was abolished not so much by the actions of some extraordinary activists and statesmen, the so-called Saints as they became known, but by the inevitable forces of capitalism and history.

Beginning in the 1970s several historians, particularly economic historians, seriously undermined the Williams thesis. We have learned from their research that the West Indian plantation system generally, and slave labor in particular, was productive and very profitable to the end. Slavery, in short, was not a dying institution obstructing capitalism. The abolition of slavery in the British West Indies in the 1830s seriously injured a prosperous and powerful plantation system and was, in the words of Seymour Drescher, an example of econocide. More recently, scholars working in the Williams tradition have maintained that it is surely no accident that the abolition of slavery coincided with the Industrial Revolution in the Atlantic World. The growth and success of industrial capitalism was both accompanied by and gave rise to a new value system that portrayed slavery as outmoded, inefficient, irrational and unnecessary.

Before any moral or philosophical attack of slavery could have influenced parliaments, congresses and assemblies, the universal understanding of slavery as a permanent and natural part of the world had to change. If slavery was viewed in the same way as war, deplorable but eternal, it mattered little what most people thought about it. Ethics implies optionality. Unprovoked violence by an animal predator is neither good nor bad; it simply is. Unprovoked violence by an aggressive human being is murder, it is bad and it is outlawed. In the eighteenth century, slavery was transformed from a perceived fact of nature into an object of debate, reform and ultimately, abolition. The tremendous economic growth of Great Britain, the northern states of the United States and France, based on wage labor and freedom, raised the idea that slavery was not economically necessary and therefore not necessarily permanent. A part of the world could get along just fine, indeed, better than fine, without slavery. Slavery became optional.

The rise of anti-slavery thought and opinion in the eighteenth century was in part an illusion. There was a deep and widespread popular anti-slavery current in the Atlantic World even before the eighteenth century. Ordinary people, generally, accepted the *idea* of slavery but disliked the reality of slavery. No one, of course, wanted to be a slave and those who witnessed slave trading and plantation labor firsthand realized how undesirable these activities were. Jean Bodin in 1576 noted that servitude was contrary to nature according to "common sense and capacity of the people." The humanitarian founders of Georgia banned slavery and the slave trade, and poor Scottish immigrants to Georgia in the early eighteenth century had this opinion of slavery: "Its shocking to Human Nature." Popular anti-slavery sentiment was often inspired by fear of slave rebellions and resentment against arrogant and powerful slaveholders. Popular anti-slavery sentiment was also generally racist; people disliked and even hated Africans and blacks at the same time they found slavery and the slave trade distasteful. The rise of religious and philosophical anti-slavery traditions in the eighteenth century developed on top of a popular culture that was already anti-slavery to a considerable extent.

Quakers were the first religious group to pronounce and act upon their anti-slavery sentiments. Quaker William Edmundson in 1676 wrote that slavery should be unacceptable to Christians and cited the Golden Rule as the best reason. Central to Quaker thought was the concept of equality before God and the brotherhood of man. In this spirit, the Germantown, Pennsylvania, Quakers in the late seventeenth century composed and advanced anti-slavery petitions to the representative assembly of the colony. The annual meeting of the Society of Friends in Philadelphia in 1711 gave advice to fellow Quakers to stop buying and selling slaves. A 1716 Quaker tract written in Massachusetts criticized the slave trade and maintained that slaves had a right to liberty. Anti-slavery sentiment became important in the Quaker sect to a great extent because many successful Quakers were slave owners or deeply involved in the slave trade. The purity of the church was in question. Popular and religious anti-slavery sentiment became abolitionist for the first time.

In 1754 the Society of Friends in Philadelphia pronounced that slavery was inconsistent with Christianity and common justice. By 1758 the Society stated that no Quaker could keep a slave without risking damnation. Slave owners and traders were prohibited from attending Society business meetings. In that same year the London Quakers condemned slavery and the slave trade. They ruled, a few years later, that slave-trading members should be disowned. The Philadelphia Quakers condemned everyone involved in the slave trade in 1763 and four years later the Boston Quakers presented an anti-slave trade petition to the Massachusetts Assembly. Beginning in the 1770s the London Quakers helped put the abolition of the slave trade on the national political agenda of Great Britain.

Anti-slavery also developed out of the new evangelical Protestant movement of the eighteenth century, which disassociated for the first time black

Document 13.1
An Exhortation and Caution to Friends Concerning Buying or Keeping Negroes

George Keith, 1693

Seing our Lord Jesus Christ hath tasted Death for every Man, and given himself a Ranson for all, to be restituted in due time, and that his Gospel of Peace, Liberty and Redemption from Sin, Bondage and all Oppression, is free'y to be preached unto all, without Exception, and that *Negroes*, *Blacks* and *Taunies* are a real part of Mankind, for whom Christ hath shed his precious Blood, and are capable of Salvation, as well as *White Men*; and Christ the Light of the World hath (in measure) enlightened them, and every Man that cometh into the World; and that all such who are sincere *Christians* and true Believers in Christ Jesus, and Followers of him, bear his Image, and are made conformable unto him in Love, Mercy, Goodness and Compassion, who came not to destroy mens Lives, but to save them, nor to bring any part of Mankind into outward Bondage, Slavery or Misery, nor yet to detain them, or hold them therein, but to ease and deliver the Oppressed and Distressed, and bring into Liberty both inward and outward.

Therefore we judge it necessary that all faithful Friends should discover themselves to be *Christians* by having the Fruits of the Spirit of Christ, which are *Love, Mercy, Goodness, and Compassion* towards all in Misery, and that such Oppression and severe Usage, so far as in them possible to care and relieve them, and let them free of their hard Bondage, whereby it may be hoped, that many of them will be gained by their beholding these good Works of sincere *Christians*, and prepared thereby, through the Preaching the Gospel of Christ, to imbrace the true Faith of Christ. And for this cause it is, as we judge, that in some places in Europe Negroes cannot be bought and sold for Money, or detained to be slaves, because it suits not with the Mercy, Love & Clemency that is essential to *Christianity*, nor to the Doctrine of Christ, nor to the Liberty the Gospel calleth all men unto, to whom it is preached. And to buy Souls and Bodies of men for Money, to enslave them and their Posterity to the end of the World, we judge is a great hinderance to the spreading of the Gospel, and is occasion of much War, Violence, Cruelty and Oppression, and Theft & Robbery of the highest Nature; for commonly the Negroes that are sold to white Men are either stolen away or robbed from their Kindred, and to buy such is the way to continue the evil Practices of Man-stealing, and transgresseth that Golden Rule and Law, *To do to others what we would have others do to us*.

Therefore in true *Christian Love*, we earnestly recommend it to all our Friends and Brethren, Not to buy any Negroes, unless it were on purpose to set them free, and that such who have bought any, and have them at present, after some reasonable time of moderate Service they have had of them, or may have of them, that may reasonably answer to the Charge of what they have laid out, especially in keeping Negroes Children born in their House, or raised in their House, when under Age, that after a reasonable time of service to answer that Charge, they may set them at Liberty, and during the time they have them, to teach them to read and give them a Christian Education.

This pamphlet reveals that some Quakers, nearly a hundred years before British Quakers formed a committee to agitate against the slave trade, opposed slavery, particularly slavery practiced by members of their own denomination. *Source:* George Keith, *An exhortation & caution to Friends concerning buying or keeping of Negroes.* Printed by William Bradford, 1693, pp. 1–2.

slavery from the Christian ideal of servitude. Slavery and the slave trade, for many evangelicals, was the epitome of sin. It was a threat to the religious purity of a congregation and society at large. They generally indicted the wickedness and vanity of slaveholders. John Wesley, the founder of Methodism, published *Thoughts upon Slavery* in Philadelphia in 1774. He called the slave trade "that execrable sum of all villanies" and warned slave owners and slave traders "Thy hands, thy bed, thy furniture, thy house, thy lands are at present stained with blood." In 1785 the General Committee of Virginia Baptists condemned slavery as "contrary to the word of God." Abolitionists in Great Britain and the United States came disproportionately from the ranks of the Quakers and other Protestant sects and their rhetoric was largely the language of sin and salvation. Evangelical Christianity called for the eradication of this evil.

It is sometimes proposed that a cult of moral sensibility, an ethic of benevolence, developed from British Protestantism in the eighteenth century. This tendency also had, clearly, French roots. The Abbé de Saint-Pierre coined the word *bienfaisance* (benevolence) to describe the disinterested impulse to promote the happiness of others. Tocqueville credited eighteenth-century France with having "propagated, led, and illuminated that unselfish but passionate love of humanity which suddenly made Europe alive to the cries of slaves." John Wesley in his 1774 book demonstrated the moral sensibility he expected of Christians and even captains of slave ships: "Is there no such principle as compassion there? Do you never *feel* another's pain? Have you no sympathy? . . . no pity for the miserable?"

Several Enlightenment thinkers, who generally questioned tradition and long-established institutions, questioned and condemned slavery. Montesquieu began the trend in 1748 when he ridiculed many of the traditional justifications given by the ancient philosophers. He pronounced that slavery "is not good by its nature; it is useful neither to the master nor to the slave; not to the slave, because he can do nothing from virtue; nor to the master, because he contracts all sorts of bad habits from his slaves, because he imperceptibly grows accustomed to failing in all the moral virtues, because he grows proud, curt, harsh, angry, voluptuous, and cruel." In 1761 George Wallace, influenced by Montesquieu, concluded that "[a]n institution so unnatural and so inhuman as that of slavery ought to be abolished." The article "Esclavage" in Diderot's *Encyclopédie* in 1755 credited Montesquieu with exposing the irrationality of human bondage.

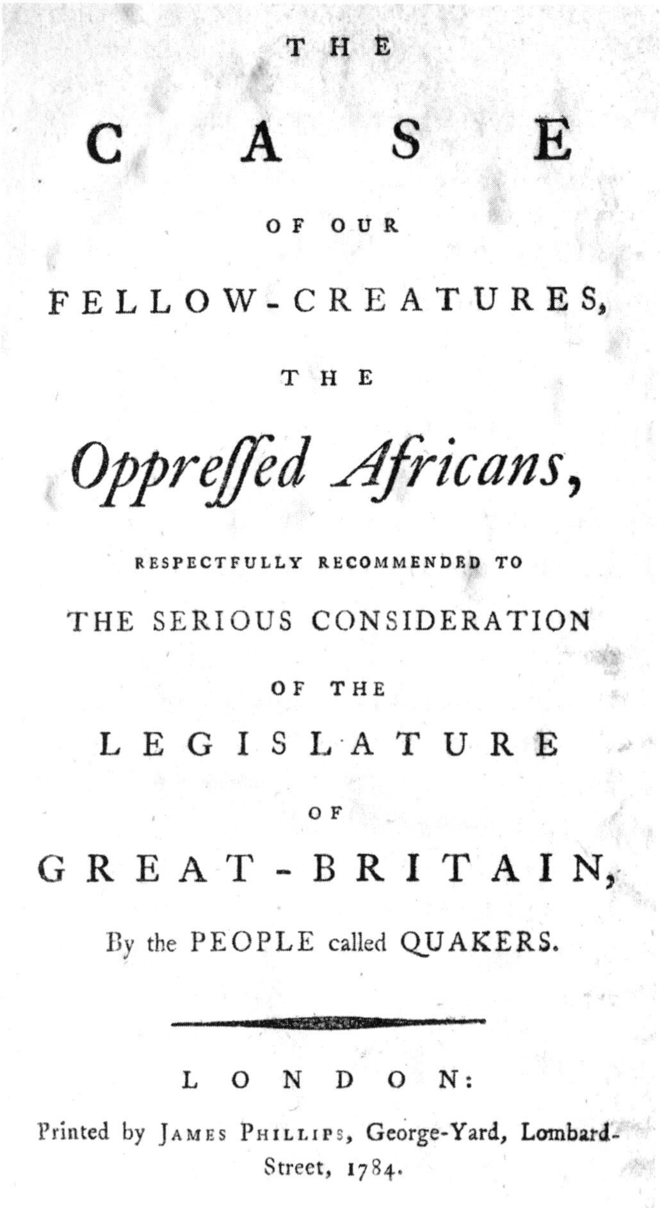

THE

CASE

OF OUR

FELLOW-CREATURES,

THE

Oppreſſed Africans,

RESPECTFULLY RECOMMENDED TO

THE SERIOUS CONSIDERATION

OF THE

LEGISLATURE

OF

GREAT-BRITAIN,

By the PEOPLE called QUAKERS.

LONDON:

Printed by JAMES PHILLIPS, George-Yard, Lombard-Street, 1784.

Figure 13.1. A Quaker Anti-slavery Pamphlet. From *The Case of Our Fellow-Creatures the Oppressed Africans* (London, 1784). Courtesy of the Clarke Historical Library at Central Michigan University.

Enlightenment writers often made the Lockean argument that because man was born free and equal, slavery violated man's natural rights. Rousseau noted that slavery could be justified by no principle or right and thus was based simply on force and violence. Francis Hutcheson in 1755 wrote that nothing "can change a rational creature into a piece of goods void of all rights." In 1765 a French Encyclopédist maintained that a slave possessed natural rights and "he had the right to demand that others allow him to enjoy those rights." Anthony Benezet, a Philadelphia Quaker, linked Quaker sentiments with Enlightenment notions of natural rights in a number of writings from 1759 to 1771. Abbé Raynal's *Histoire des deux Indes*, published in 1770, brought together many of the anti-slavery ideas of the age. Over the next thirty years this book appeared in fifty-five editions in five different languages and in every edition slavery was condemned as inherently unnatural and unjust.

Enlightenment thinkers also criticized slavery as an economic institution, seeing it as not only a moral wrong but a utilitarian wrong as well. Benjamin Franklin in 1751 wrote that slave labor deprived the poor of employment and thus impeded the growth of the population. He perhaps invented the argument that slave labor was costly but essentially inefficient and underproductive. Mirabeau in 1756 maintained that slavery was unprofitable and economically unhealthy for society. He and later *physiocrats* noted that slaves had no motive to work hard and efficiently but tied up valuable capital that could be employed more productively. In his famous *Wealth of Nations*, Adam Smith in 1776 wrote that slavery was the most costly and least productive form of labor. Free labor was good for the employer and beneficial to society. These political economists demonstrated to many across the Atlantic World that slavery was not simply an evil but also an economic anachronism, and that its abolition was motivated by self-interest as well as altruism.

In the mid- to late eighteenth century, at the height of the Atlantic slave trade, slavery was intellectually discredited by many of the leading philosophers in Europe and morally condemned by a growing number of religious sects and denominations. There had been a long popular anti-slavery tradition and now it was reinforced in religious thought and secular philosophy. Slavery was widely denounced as evil and unnatural, a position increasingly adopted by gentlemen and ladies, aristocrats, the educated and well-bred. It was even taken up by some high-minded, plantation-owning slaveholders. This constituted a revolution in the moral consciousness of mankind, and like the slave system it condemned, this revolution was an Atlantic development. It was as American as it was European.

In both the religious and secular arguments, slavery was harmful not only to the slave but to the slaveholder and the wider society. In the religious view, the slaveholder and his society were guilty of the sins of avarice and pride. Slavery corrupted the slaveholder but it also corrupted society at large. In Enlightenment philosophy the slaveholder tied himself to an inefficient, underproductive and ultimately unprofitable form of labor. Society was denied social, economic and even political progress and modernity by the anachronism that was slavery. Slavery's threat to society transformed anti-slavery thought and opinion into abolitionism, commitment to the cause of abolishing the slave trade and emancipating the slaves. Abolitionists were often concerned about the welfare and justice of the African and black American slave, but their concern about the moral, political and economic health and well-being of society constituted the fundamental motive and drive of the abolitionist movement.

13.2 Revolutionary Abolitionism, 1770s–1808

The rise of anti-slavery thought in the north Atlantic occurred at the same time as the American Revolution. The Revolution's natural rights ideology and rhetoric was similar if not identical to some anti-slavery arguments. The guiding principle in both camps was liberty. Revolutionaries often, although certainly not always, adopted anti-slavery positions, and anti-slavery advocates often became revolutionaries. The American Revolution offered anti-slavery visionaries the first opportunity to take political action against the slave trade and slavery. Beginning with the American Revolution, anti-slavery became allied with revolution throughout the Atlantic World.

"How is it that we hear the loudest yelps for liberty among the drivers of Negroes?" Samuel Johnson's famous quip underscored the fact that the American Revolution took place within a society with slaves. Indeed, certain Virginia planters and slaveholders were among the first ranks of the revolutionary leadership. Although slavery was not directly related to British oppression or the rebellion, revolutionaries could not ignore slavery because the principles they proclaimed to the world conflicted with the institution that underpinned the economy of the colonies. In 1776 the New York House of Representatives resolved that slavery was "utterly inconsistent with the avowed principles in which this and other states have carried on their struggle for liberty." Some years later the American Convention of Abolition Societies noted, "The fundamental principles of our government, as well as the progressive and rapid influence of reason and religion, are in our favor."

American revolutionaries, perhaps caught up in the fever of revolution, were not shy in condemning slavery and the slave trade. In 1775 one of the Darien Resolutions, from the people of Darien, Georgia, proclaimed: "We hereby declare our disapprobation and abhorrence of the unnatural practice of Slavery in America." The citizens of Worcester County, Massachusetts, in 1775 called for the abolition of slavery: "Resolved, that we abhor the enslaving of any of the human race, and particularly of the Negroes in this country." They noted that "we will use our influence and endeavor that such a thing [emancipating the Negroes] may be effected." Even American slaves petitioned colonial authorities for freedom. "The divine spirit of *freedom*," wrote four Massachusetts slaves in 1773, "seems to fire every humane breast on this continent." In a clause that was ultimately deleted from the Declaration of Independence, Thomas Jefferson described the slave trade as a "cruel war against human nature itself." He criticized the King of England for "violating [nature's] most sacred rights of life & liberty in the persons of a distant people who never offended him."

From the pen of this distinguished revolutionary came the memorable declaration that defined the American Revolution: "We hold these truths to be self-evident, that all men are created equal, that they are endowed, by their Creator, with certain inalienable rights, that among these are life, liberty, and the pursuit of happiness." This principle implicitly condemned slavery, as most revolutionaries in that day realized, although today we are often taught that Jefferson and his fellow revolutionaries really meant that all *white* men are created equal. All of the leading American founders expressed their judgment that slavery was wrong, to a great extent because the institution violated the universal principles proclaimed by the Revolution. The preamble to Pennsylvania's 1780 emancipation law stated the religious principle behind Jefferson's declaration: "It is not for us to inquire why, in the creation of mankind, the inhabitants of the several parts of the earth were distinguished by a difference in feature or complexion. It is sufficient to know that all are the work of the Almighty hand." Certainly American slavery was the great contradiction but the first actions taken to restrict and abolish slavery and the slave trade came during the American Revolution and because of the Revolution. The revolutionary principles had anti-slavery consequences.

The first Atlantic polity to abolish slavery was Vermont in 1777 when provincial revolutionaries included the anti-slavery clause in the state's constitution. New Hampshire followed in 1779. In 1780 Pennsylvania passed the first emancipation law in the Americas, a gradual abolition that freed all of the children of slaves after 1781 but required their continued service until age twenty-eight. Judicial action freed the slaves in Massachusetts in the 1780s. Rhode Island and Connecticut passed gradual emancipation laws like Pennsylvania's in 1784; New York followed in 1799 and New Jersey in 1804. Revolutionaries placed slavery in the northern states, where it was weakest, on the road to extinction. New Jersey's abolition law was so conservative and gradual, however, that there were still "apprentices," freed slaves who owed service as late as 1860.

There were also petitions and proposals to abolish slavery in the southern states. Jefferson proposed a gradual emancipation bill for Virginia in 1779. Two Virginia counties petitioned the state legislature to abolish slavery in 1787 saying that such an act was required by the principles of the Revolution. There were also debates regarding abolition in Delaware, Maryland and Kentucky in the 1780s and 1790s. There was generally broad agreement in the southern states that slavery was wrong. In the 1790s and early 1800s there were more anti-slavery societies in the south than in the north. In addition, in 1818 the Mississippi Supreme Court held that: "Slavery is condemned by reason and the laws of nature." During the era of the American Revolution southerners were ashamed of slavery, not enough to abolish it, but ashamed nevertheless.

The Continental Congress and all of the new states suspended the Atlantic slave trade to the United States. This action was not always motivated by anti-slavery sentiments. The suspension by the Congress in 1774 and 1776 was part of the commercial embargo aimed against Great Britain. The suspension of the slave trade by the southern states was generally motivated by fear of too many Africans and of slave uprisings. Even so, South Carolina relapsed in 1803–07, which shocked the country. Because the American south was unique among plantation societies in possessing a slave population that naturally reproduced itself and even grew in numbers, American slaveholders were not particularly dependent on the slave trade. In 1806 President Jefferson proposed the permanent abolition of the American slave trade. The bill was passed in Congress and it took effect on January 1, 1808.

The American Revolution and the war for independence began to dissolve the bonds of slavery to some extent. The northern abolition laws and judicial decisions freed slaves. There was also a dramatic increase in manumissions and runaways. Five thousand slaves fought for the patriot cause and obtained freedom as a result. For these reasons Georgia lost one-third of its prewar slave population, South Carolina lost one-fourth. In the colonies as a whole, before 1776 there were only a handful of free blacks, a few thousand at most. By the time of the first United States census in 1790 there were 59,000 free blacks and by 1810 there were 186,000. Some scholars have called the American Revolution the greatest slave uprising in the history of North America because of the considerable increase in the number of free men.

The American Revolution, however, did not liberate all or even most American slaves. Slavery was simply too important to the economies of the southern states, especially those in the deeper South. As Charles Cotesworth Pinckney of South Carolina acknowledged, "South Carolina and Georgia cannot do without slaves." Those northern revolutionaries who wanted to abolish the slave trade and implement a plan for the gradual emancipation of the slaves at the constitutional convention in 1787 discovered that these actions, if pursued and enacted, would led to the secession of the southern states. The Constitution prohibited Congress from abolishing the slave trade before 1808 and implicitly recognized slavery by permitting the states to count slaves as three-fifths of a person for purposes of representation in the House of Representatives. Many in the revolutionary generation, however, believed slavery was on the road to peaceful, gradual extinction; slavery was doomed, it was only a question of when and how it happened, not if. These optimists did not foresee the tremendous expansion of the southern plantation economy and of slavery itself in the early nineteenth century. The 237,000 slaves in 1750 would grow to nearly 700,000 by 1790s and over 4 million by 1860.

The French Revolution was both more and less anti-slavery than the American Revolution. The *Société des Amis des Noirs* (the Society of the Friends of the Blacks) was founded in Paris in 1788, only one year after the founding of the first British anti-slave trade society. The French Society never developed a popular following and was never very influential. In 1790 the Amis proposed the abolition of the slave trade before the National Assembly and rested their case upon the universal principles found in the 1789 Declaration of the Rights of Man and Citizen, particularly the first, which stated "men are born and remain free and equal in rights. Immediate emancipation, it was noted, would be fatal to the colonies and a "deadly gift for the blacks." Defenders of the slave trade argued that five million Frenchmen depended economically on colonial commerce, and that slavery and the slave trade were essential to the prosperity of France. When the proposal was defeated, anti-slavery advocates changed targets.

In 1791 the Amis and anti-slavery revolutionaries convinced the National Assembly to condemn slavery in principle, the first such condemnation by any European legislature. The Amis then pressed for full civil and political rights for free blacks and mulattos. After some vacillation, a law with this provision was passed in March 1792. "The fears of our colonists are therefore well-founded in that they have everything to fear from the influence of our Revolution on their slaves," noted an anti-slavery advocate during the debate in the National Assembly. "The rights of man overturn the system on which rests their fortunes." The agitation of mulattos for their rights in Saint Domingue, of course, had been one of the tremors that shook up the slavery regime and precipitated the uprising of the slaves on the north plain in 1791. By 1793 France was facing the loss of the colony altogether as rebel slaves joined France's wartime enemies, Spain and possibly Great Britain in the near future, who provided the slaves with weapons and other kinds of assistance.

In August 1793 the Jacobin Civil Commissioner of the National Convention in North Province, Saint Domingue, Léger Felicité Sonthonax, issued a proclamation that freed all of the slaves in his jurisdiction. The Commissioner in West Province did the same in September. The National Convention was left little choice but to endorse this revolutionary emancipationism, and on February 4, 1794, voted to formally abolish slavery. The decree stated: "The National Convention declares the abolition of Negro slavery in all the colonies; in consequence it decrees that all men, without distinction of color, residing in the colonies, are French citizens and will enjoy all the rights assured by the Constitution."

The Jacobin delegate George Jacques Danton declared on emancipation day that "until now we have decreed liberty as egotists for ourselves. However, today we proclaim universal liberty.... France, until now cheated of her glory, repossesses it before the eyes of an astonished Europe." Throughout France there were celebrations and the decree inspired anti-slavery songs, poems and engravings. Certainly the delegates who voted for emancipation in 1794 were influenced by revolutionary principles, but this abolition had less to do with anti-slavery conviction than military necessity. By the time of the official emancipation most of the members of the Amis des Noirs had fled the country, were in prison or were dead. By 1794 the slaves of Saint Domingue had freed themselves by force of arms. French revolutionaries endorsed abolition in order to convince armed blacks, and particularly Toussaint L'Ouverture and his army, to join the French Republic and save Saint Domingue from the British invasion.

Copies of the emancipation decree and the Declaration of the Rights of Man and Citizen were now introduced to all parts of the Caribbean. A French military expedition to the West Indies in the spring of 1794 liberated Guadaloupe from the British and freed the slaves on the island. Former slaves were formed into military units called Légion d'Egalité. In March 1795 black Caribs on St. Vincent joined the French republican cause and drove out the British there and in Grenada.

The uprising of the slaves in Saint Domingue and the official abolition of slavery in the French colonies in 1794 constituted a tremendous blow against slavery in the Americas. Its influence was felt far from Saint Domingue and Paris. In 1794 copies of Sonthonax's proclamation circulated in Charleston, South Carolina, and a newspaper reported: "The S. Domingue negroes have sown those seeds of revolt." A group of "citizens of color" of Philadelphia wrote a letter to the French Convention that thanked them for "breaking our chains" with "the Immortal Decree wiping out all trades of slavery in the French colonies." The governor of Cuba reported that among slaves "the rumor is too widespread that the French desire that there be no slaves, and that [the French] will make all of them free." From Caracas to Philadelphia, the waterfront, where slaves and black sailors traded news and documents, became a cauldron of revolution.

Among slaveholders and their defenders, indeed for many whites throughout the Atlantic, the French emancipation set back and discredited revolutionary anti-slavery. The 1794 decree, considered just one among numerous appalling radical Jacobin actions, set back the anti-slavery movement in Great Britain. The slaveholding class in all of the American colonies became much more cautious and conservative; revolutionary ideas were considered simply too dangerous to even debate in the colonial slave societies.

In time this conservatism returned to the leadership of France. General and First Consul Napoleon Bonaparte expected to defeat Toussaint and his armies of former slaves in Saint Domingue and restore the slave trade and the slave regime in all French colonies. In 1802 the emancipation decree was nullified and slavery was restored in Guadaloupe. News of this reverse revolution influenced and motivated Toussaint's generals and the rank and file to resist the invading French and eventually expel them from the island. In 1804 the former slaves proclaimed the independence of the Republic of Haiti, the second independent state in the Americas and the first to outlaw slavery. Slavery ended in Haiti but in Martinique and Guadaloupe and the rest of the French colonial empire the institution was given a new lease on life. Like the American Revolution, the French Revolution attacked slavery and advanced the day when slavery would come to an end everywhere in the Atlantic World.

In Great Britain anti-slavery forces drew their strength, at first, as much from religion as revolution. In the mid-eighteenth century Horace Walpole, a member of the British oligarchy, noted in private correspondence that "it chills one's blood" to think of the number of Africans in the British slave trade. He implied that the slave trade should be especially distasteful to the British and, "*we*, the British Senate, that temple of liberty, bulwark of Protestant Christianity." British anti-slavery always drew inspiration and strength from the belief that Britain was the temple of liberty in the world and the bulwark of Protestant Christianity. Anti-slavery advocates argued that slavery unjust, unprincipled, ungodly and even unproductive but in the final analysis it was, above all, un-British.

The British anti-slavery campaign began effectively in 1787 when a group of Quakers and other social reformers formed the Society for Effecting the Abolition of the Slave Trade. Although devout Quakers were always the backbone of anti-slavery organization in Britain, there was also a strong anti-establishment (quasi-revolutionary) element to British anti-slavery in the 1780s and the 1790s. Anti-slavery ideology was part of a wider egalitarian and liberalizing reform movement that pushed for broader suffrage, the elimination of rotten boroughs and more effective representation by Parliament, religious liberty and the separation of church and state, and more. The Manchester Abolition Committee began a petition campaign that was led by radicals who were inspired by Tom Paine's *The Rights of Man*, 1791. The Society for Constitutional Information, one of many reform organizations in Britain in the late 1780s and early 1790s, pushed for social and political reform in Britain and the abolition of the slave trade.

The anti-slavery campaign publicized the evils of slavery and the slave trade. The campaign highlighted the Zong affair to raise public indignation. This was the scandal of a Liverpool slaver in 1783 in which the captain threw 133 slaves into the sea and to their deaths in order to obtain compensation from the insurance company. Activists also encouraged Olaudah Equiano, an African and a former slave, to write an autobiography that gave the evil slave trade a sympathetic human face. *The Interesting Narrative of the Life of Olaudah Equiano* was published in 1789 and became a bestseller. Equiano portrayed Africans as innocent victims and the white slavers as the uncivilized ones. "The white people looked and acted," he wrote, "as I thought, in so savage a manner." Thomas Clarkson publicized the inhumanity of the slave trade by sketching the sardine-like condition of slave stowage of the slave ship, the *Brookes* of Liverpool. His diagram inspired William Grenville to remark: "In the passage of the negroes from the coast of Africa, there is a greater portion of human misery condensed within a smaller place than has ever yet been found in any other place on the face of this globe."

Unlike the United States and France, the anti-slavery campaign in Great Britain became a popular movement throughout the country. Activists organized local anti-slavery societies, held mass public meetings and pushed anti-slavery petitions. Josiah Wedgewood's anti-slavery emblem – a kneeling African in chains saying, "Am I not a man and a brother" – was distributed throughout the country on cups, plates, broaches and pendants. In 1788 Parliament received 102 petitions supporting the abolition of the slave trade. It received 508 petitions in 1792 and one of them, the Manchester petition, was signed by over twenty thousand of the city's sixty thousand inhabitants. The anti-slavery campaign influenced Parliament to reform the slave trade and even won the support of the Prime Minister, William Pitt the younger. He described the trade as "the greatest practical evil which has ever afflicted the Human Race." Anti-slavery sentiment also developed in Canada where the Parliament of Upper Canada adopted gradual emancipation in 1793. Abolition of the trade, however, was staunchly opposed by the King, the House of Lords, a majority in the House of Commons, and by the British oligarchy in general.

When Parliament defeated abolition in 1792 and Britain went to war against revolutionary France in 1793, the anti-slavery movement began to decline. If Jacobin France was in favor of abolition, if (as seemed likely) there was an intrinsic connection between radical republicanism and abolition, then, many in the public believed, abolition must be unwise, even unpatriotic. The war also brought government repression at home. British reformers, dissenters and republicans were expelled from the country or imprisoned. The Coercion Acts of 1794 allowed the government to stamp out unauthorized political meetings and publications. Pitt's "reign of terror," supplemented by local magistrates, just about destroyed radicalism in Britain in the 1790s and the anti-slavery movement was weakened in the process. The National

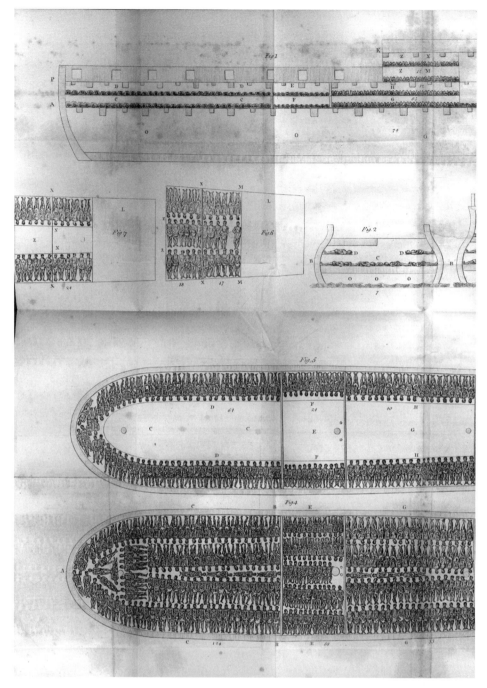

Figure 13.2. The Slave Ship, the *Brookes*. From Thomas Clarkson, *The History of the Rise, Progress, and Accomplishment of the Abolition of the African Slave-Trade by the British Parliament* (London, 1808), Volume 2. Courtesy of the Clarke Historical Library at Central Michigan University.

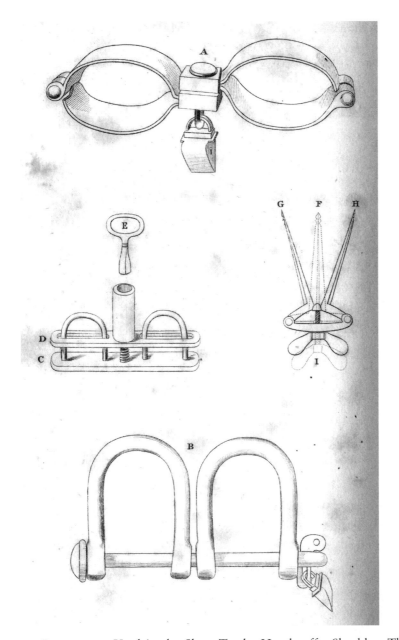

Figure 13.3. Instruments Used in the Slave Trade: Hand-cuffs, Shackles, Thumb-screw, and Speculum Oris for Forced Feeding. From Thomas Clarkson, *The History of the Rise, Progress, and Accomplishments of the Abolition of the African Slave-Trade by the British Parliament* (London, 1808), Volume 2. Courtesy of the Clarke Historical Library at Central Michigan University.

Committee of the Society for Effecting the Abolition of the Slave Trade (generally called the Abolition Society) did not even meet from 1797 to 1804.

After the rise of Napoleon and France's restoration of slavery and the slave trade, anti-slavery again became popular and patriotic in Britain. The Abolition Society revived the popular anti-slavery campaign. Anti-slavery activists advanced humanitarian reasons but also argued that it made no sense to fill the colonies with dangerous and resentful 'savages' who could destroy Jamaica like similar slaves destroyed French Saint Domingue. For the British establishment, abolition of the slave trade was the least radical element of the reform agenda and therefore acceptable. In 1807 Parliament voted to abolish the British slave trade beginning in 1808. This constituted a significant victory for the anti-slavery cause. Britain was the foremost slave-trading nation in the world. In 1800 nearly one-third of all Africans transported in the Atlantic slave trade were shipped in British bottoms. Thomas Clarkson, one of the leaders of the British campaign, wrote a history of the movement in 1808 and declared that the slave trade was the root evil of Atlantic slavery. Abolition of the slave trade, he and many others believed, would set in motion forces that would lead to reforms that would improve the conditions of slaves, prepare them for freedom and gradually but eventually emancipate all slaves.

After 1808 Great Britain worked to convince and pressure the other nations that transported slaves to also abolish the slave trade. As the most influential and powerful nation in the Atlantic to emerge from the European wars that came to an end in 1815, Britain had a lot of clout. In 1810 Portugal signed an agreement with the British committing it to the gradual abolition of the slave trade. At the end of the war Britain returned Surinam, Curaçao and Java to the Netherlands on condition that its slave trade would not be renewed. The Congress of Vienna in 1815, upon the initiative of Britain, issued a declaration that condemned the slave trade. In 1817 Portugal agreed in a treaty with Britain to abolish its slave trade north of the equator. In a similar treaty in 1817, Spain agreed to abolish its slave trade in 1820. Following the independence of the Latin American republics in the 1820s, Britain pushed such treaties on these new states. When Britain pressured Brazil to abolish the trade in 1831, the entire Atlantic slave trade became illegal although far from truly abolished. The British stationed anti-slave trade squadrons on the African coast and treaties often gave British warships the right to stop likely slave ships and search them, try them before judicial commissions, and sell the ships as prizes and free the captives.

Slaves freed by the British navy were relocated to Sierra Leone on the upper Guinea coast. Beginning in 1787 this slice of Africa had been used by private organizations to receive poor black Londoners, former loyalist slaves from the North American colonies, and even 550 Jamaican maroons in 1800. In 1808 Sierra Leone became a dependency of the crown and the headquarters of Britain's anti-slaving activities in Africa. Up to 1840, the British navy escorted 425 slavers (slave ships) to Sierra Leone and freed some 160,000 African captives. By 1850 about one thousand freed captives or former slaves coming from the Americas arrived in Sierra Leone each year. In the 1820s the American Colonization Society began to ship American blacks as well as former slaves to a region sixty miles south of Sierra Leone. Established officially as Liberia in 1823, this semi-colony also received captives freed by the United States Navy.

From the 1770s to the early nineteenth century, the anti-slavery efforts by American, French and British activists and governments constituted the first organized and substantial attacks upon slavery in the Atlantic World.

This first wave of anti-slavery activity was an integral part of the Age of Revolution. Revolutionary anti-slavery ideology was built upon Enlightenment natural rights philosophy and influenced revolutionaries and liberals not only in the United States, France and Britain but also in the Netherlands, Spain, Portugal, Mexico, Venezuela, Chile, Argentina and other countries in Latin America. Revolution and war motivated slaves to resist and flee slavery as was demonstrated in the United States and Saint Domingue. The revolutionary attack on slavery thus came from within the slave system as well as without, by slaves and free blacks as well as white revolutionaries and reformers. The revolutionary generation, of course, did not destroy slavery. Its actions did mark the beginning of the end.

13.3 Spanish American Anti-Slavery, 1810s–50s

Spain and Spanish America were swept up in the Age of Revolution and as a result slavery came under direct attack in most of the new nations of Latin America. Slavery in this part of the Atlantic World was not only undermined by the principles of the Spanish American revolutions but also by the bitter and prolonged wars, which were fought in the 1810s and 1820s. Because both patriots and loyalists enlisted large numbers of slaves in their armies, military manumission reduced the slave population. The disruption of war permitted or incited slaves to flee slavery and even rebel. After the wars the new nations abolished the slave trade and put the institution of slavery on the path of abolition and eventual destruction. The struggle against New World slavery expanded to include a new culture and region in the 1810s and 1820s. After Haiti, the first independent American nations to legislate full and immediate abolition of slavery were Latin American nations.

Iberian culture in Europe and the Americas did not possess an anti-slavery tradition like that of the Quakers in Britain and America and the natural rights philosophers and physiocrats of France. In the mid-eighteenth century Frei Manuel Ribeiro de Rocha, a Portuguese cleric, condemned slavery and the slave trade "as a deadly crime against Christian charity and common justice" but such attacks were extremely rare. The Catholic Church had a mixed record with regard to the African slave trade and slavery. Pontiffs had strongly and consistently opposed Native American slavery from the sixteenth century, and in the eighteenth century two popes, Clement XI and Benedict XIV, specifically condemned African slavery. The church accepted Africans as men who possessed mortal souls and strongly encouraged the evangelization of black slaves. The church also legitimated slave marriages and provided slaves with religious brotherhoods and associations. It was not until Pope Gregory XVI in 1838, however, that a papal bull prohibited Christians from taking part in the African slave trade on pain of excommunication. Religious orders in Spain and Portugal, and Spanish America and Brazil, furthermore, owned African and African American slaves and worked them in their New World plantations.

Prior to the revolutions and wars for independence, slavery in Spanish America was an institution that was in decline and that had never been of enormous value or importance in the first place. The only true slave society was Cuba; the mainland colonies of Spain were societies with slaves, which in the late eighteenth century counted no more than 250,000 slaves. The slave trade to the mainland colonies was often interrupted by war in the 1790s and 1800s, and generally was in decline. The growth of the Indian population along with *mestizos*, mulattos and free blacks, and Creoles in the eighteenth century, furthermore, meant there was less and less need for slave labor. In some countries slavery had gradually slipped into insignificance. The 200,000 African slaves imported into Mexico in the sixteenth and seventeenth centuries had pretty much disappeared into the much larger population of Indians and *mestizos*. By 1810 there were only about six thousand slaves remaining and these were concentrated around Veracruz and Acapulco. All of Central America had fewer than five hundred slaves by 1810.

The Age of Revolution was anti-slavery in the Iberian world as well as the Anglo-American and French worlds. The revolutionary Cortes of Cádiz, which wrote the first constitution for Spain and established representative government in 1811–12, also debated the legitimacy of the slave trade and slavery itself. One of the delegates from New Spain, a Mexican priest, declared that slavery was opposed by natural law and was repugnant to all enlightened people. He proposed the immediate abolition of the Spanish slave trade and gradual emancipation of slavery by means of a free-birth law. A very cautious Cortes, responsive to the concerns of Cuban sugar planters and reminded that it was metropolitan reform and meddling that sparked the slave uprising in Saint Domingue, refused to alter the system of slavery. The Cortes did incorporate racial discrimination in the Constitution of 1812. In Article 22, mulattos and free blacks were excluded from the status of citizenship.

The first outbursts of revolution in Spanish America were more anti-slavery than those in America in 1776 and France in 1789. The popular Mexican revolution that exploded in 1810 and was led by the priest Miguel Hidalgo was fundamentally anti-slavery. Hidalgo not only proclaimed the abolition of Indian tribute but also ordered all masters to free their slaves within ten days on pain of death. José María Morelos, who took command of the insurgency following Hidalgo's defeat and execution, issued a formal declaration of independence in 1813, which confirmed the abolition of slavery. The revolutionary juntas of Caracas, Buenos Aires, Bogotá and Santiago, Chile, prohibited the "vile traffic" of the slave trade in 1810–12. A constituent assembly in Buenos Aires in 1813 was the first Latin American government to enact a free womb law, a measure that freed all children born to slave mothers but required these *libertos* to work for their mothers' masters until they reached the age of twenty.

Almost all of the new nations of Latin America abolished the slave trade for a variety of reasons. Political leaders were influenced by the anti-slavery sentiments present in the Age of Revolution. In Latin America as in the United States, leaders also wanted to cut off the flow of "dangerous" Africans who were potential rebels who could arise and destroy the plantation system as they did in Haiti. There was also pressure by Great Britain, the great commercial and military power of the nineteenth century. The Duke of Wellington in 1822 made plain Britain's stand on the slave trade: "No state in the New World will be recognized by Great Britain which has not frankly and completely abolished the trade in slaves." Few Latin American countries needed any more motivation than this.

From the beginning to the end, the wars for independence in Spanish America attracted slaves for military service and often forced slaves to become soldiers. As early as 1811 Chilean patriots drafted slaves, gave them military pay and directed one-half of their pay to the former owners in compensation. In 1812 Francisco Miranda in Venezuela offered freedom to slaves who served in the patriot army for ten years. José Miguel Carrera in Chile in 1814 decreed freedom for slaves who volunteered for the patriot forces. Beginning in 1816 both General Simón Bolívar and José de San Martín authorized detachments to seize able-bodied slaves (to be paid for by promissory notes) and offered freedom to slaves who fled their masters and volunteered to serve in the army. In fact, both patriot and royalist armies were composed of former slaves who gained their freedom as a result of military service. Tomás Boves, the Spanish commander in Venezuela, drafted slaves belonging to patriot creoles. About one-half of the soldiers in San Martín's Army of the Andes who invaded Chile in 1817 were former slaves. "The best infantry soldier that we have," San Martín once remarked, "is the Negro and the mulatto." During one battle, however, he threatened the former slaves with reinslavement if the battle was lost. Bolívar asked, "Is it fair that only free men should die for the liberation of slaves? Is it not proper that the slaves acquire their rights on the battlefield?"

Military manumission freed many thousands of slaves in the 1810s and 1820s. Continued political instability after independence in several countries meant that slaves continued to be drawn into military service. A few former slaves rose to become generals, and one became an admiral, while hundreds became officers and noncommissioned officers. The wars also disrupted and destroyed large numbers of haciendas and plantations, which permitted and even encouraged slaves to abandon their masters and flee to maroon communities or to towns and cities. By the late 1820s, slavery in the new Spanish American republics was both a smaller and a weaker institution. Some military leaders became committed to abolition, like Bolívar who had accepted assistance from Haiti for a promise to abolish slavery once the revolution had triumphed. In the constitutions he wrote for the lands he liberated, particularly Gran Colombia and Bolivia, Bolívar abolished the slave trade and enacted free womb laws. San Martín, Protector of Peru in 1821, banned the slave trade, immediately freed the slaves of all Spaniards and royalists and enacted a free womb law.

At the time of independence a few of the new nations, those with particularly small slave populations, enacted immediate and total emancipation. In 1823 the Chilean government emancipated the approximately four thousand slaves who were said to have "honest occupations." Slavery was abolished totally in the Constitutions of 1825, 1829 and 1833. The constituent assembly of the United Provinces of Central America decreed the unconditional emancipation of the region's five hundred or so slaves in 1824 and when the federation dissolved in the late 1830s the constitutions of each republic abolished slavery. Mexico prohibited the slave trade in 1824 and abolished slavery in 1829.

In all of the other Spanish American republics, independence brought the abolition of the slave trade and legislation and constitutions that put the institution of slavery on the road to extinction. That road in most countries was a long one. Political instability in the new republics often delayed the effective abolition of the slave trade and interfered with enforcement of emancipation laws. Changes in regimes in Argentina from 1813–39 led to the slave trade being officially turned off and on several times. In Uruguay a free womb law was enacted in 1825, slavery was unconditionally abolished in 1842, abolished by a new president in 1846 and abolished once again in 1853. These numerous "abolitions" suggest the survival of the institution because of political instability, frequent regime changes and the weakness of government enforcement. Bolivia, despite its very small population of slaves, saw a prolonged abolition of slavery beginning with Bolívar's free womb decree in the late 1820s, the inclusion of a free womb provision in the Constitution of 1831, the abolition of slavery in a treaty with Great Britain in 1837 and a decree of total abolition in 1861.

The free womb laws that were enacted by most of the Spanish American republics delayed the final abolition of slavery for decades. The 1828 Constitution of Peru, for example, declared, "no one is born a slave in the Republic." The free children of slave mothers, called *libertos* and *manumisos*, were required to give service to the masters of their mothers for fifty years. The Constitution permitted the sale of services of *libertos*. Most free womb laws limited the time of service of *libertos* to twenty-one years or a little more. Final abolition in Peru came in 1854 during a civil war when both sides needed to attract slaves and *libertos* into their armies. The free womb law, for what became the republic of the United Provinces of Argentina, was first implemented in 1813. Libertos were required to work for the masters of their mothers until they were fifteen years old and then work an additional five years for payment of one peso a month. The on–again, off–again pattern of the slave trade meant that slavery could last indefinitely. The Constitution of 1853 abolished slavery unconditionally. The emancipation of *libertos* who were forty years old revealed the lax enforcement of the old system.

Fully one-half of all of the slaves on the mainland of Spanish America were located in Gran Colombia, which in the 1830s broke up to form the three republics of Venezuela, Colombia and Ecuador. Venezuela had a substantial plantation sector that held most of the slaves while in Colombia most slaves were located in the provinces with the gold fields. All three countries retained Bolívar's free womb law. In Venezuela the term of service of *manumisos* was increased three years, from eighteen to twenty-one years, and in 1840 the age was again increased to twenty-five years with the four additional years disguised as an 'apprenticeship' program. In 1854 unconditional emancipation was decreed, freeing over twelve thousand slaves and over eleven thousand *manumisos*. The term of service for *manumisos* in Ecuador was raised and then lowered in the 1840s and final abolition came in 1851 with the emancipation of approximately five thousand slaves and *manumisos*. In Colombia an 1836 census counted nearly thirty-nine thousand slaves. In

Table 13.1. Unconditional emancipation in
the Republics of Spanish America, 1823–69

Nation	Date
Chile	1823
Central America	1824
Mexico	1829
Colombia	1851
Ecuador	1851
Argentina	1853
Uruguay	1553
Venezuela	1854
Peru	1854
Bolivia	1861
Paraguay	1869

Source: Robin Blackburn, *The Overthrow of Colonial
Slavery, 1776–1848* (1988): 331–79; and Leslie B. Rout,
Jr, *The African Experience in Spanish America: 1502 to
the present day* (1976), see Part II.

1850 a liberal regime came to power and condemned slavery as "a barbarous legacy, incompatible with the philosophy of the century and the dictates of Christian brotherhood." The following year, close to twenty thousand slaves and an unknown number of *manumisos* were granted unconditional emancipation.

The abolition of slavery in the Spanish-speaking republics of Latin America took a long time. All of the nations undertook abolition measures in the 1810s and 1820s. Where slavery was most important economically and most numerous, Venezuela, Colombia, Ecuador, Peru, Argentina and Uruguay, slavery persisted in the 1830s and 1840s and was not finally abolished until the early 1850s. By this time slavery was disintegrating as a result of frequent slave revolts and a significant rise in the number of runaways. War and military necessity rather than good intentions also brought about the end of the institution. Generals and politicians, in need of soldiers and fearful that their enemies would abolish slavery and pick up valuable support, finally acted and brought the institution to an end. The end of slavery in Paraguay came at the conclusion of a disastrous war when the Brazilian commander of the occupying force abolished slavery by fiat (see Table 13.1).

Slavery in Spanish America in the early nineteenth century was about as important as slavery in New England or as slavery in Pennsylvania, New Jersey and New York. Like New England, countries where slavery was relatively insignificant such as Chile, Mexico and Central America abolished the institution without conditions and at an early date. In addition, like Pennsylvania, New Jersey and New York, countries where slavery constituted about five percent of the total population enacted free womb laws that extended the life of slavery for an additional thirty years at least.In the slave society of Cuba where sugar plantations constituted the most important sources of wealth, slavery survived unhampered. Spain held onto only two colonies in the Americas, Cuba and Puerto Rico, protected their plantation economies from anti-slavery forces, and reaped substantial revenues as a result. In this case slavery was maintained and defended by colonialism. Slave systems also survived in the British, French, Dutch and Danish colonies in the Caribbean.

13.4 British and French Emancipations, 1830s–48

British anti-slavery activists in 1808 believed that the abolition of the British slave trade would set in motion forces that would lead West Indian planters to treat their slaves better and to accept gradual emancipation. The news from the Caribbean in the early 1820s, however, revealed that little had changed. Slave populations in the British colonies still did not naturally reproduce themselves as a result of low fertility and high mortality. Reports from the islands indicated that conditions for slaves were as bad as ever, something that James Stephen documented in *The Slavery of the British West Indian Colonies Delineated,* which was published in two volumes in 1824 and 1830.

Discouraging news demonstrating that slavery was neither improving nor disappearing led British abolitionists to revive the anti-slavery movement. In 1823 activists founded the Society for Mitigating and Gradually Abolishing the State of Slavery throughout the British Dominions. Even more than the campaign against the slave trade, the campaign of the 1820s and 1830s was motivated by religion and led by devout Christians. James Stephen was a member of the evangelical Clapham sect. James Cropper was a devout Quaker as well as a disciple of Adam Smith. The leader of the campaign in Parliament, Thomas Fowell Buxton, was an evangelical Anglican. Like the earlier campaign this one was propelled by hundreds of local anti-slavery societies that attracted public interest and support with mass meetings, anti-slavery pamphlets and books, and petition drives.

By the 1820s and 1830s the system of slavery in the British West Indies was under attack from within and without. From without came evangelical missionaries, Moravians, Methodists, Baptists and independents, to convert slaves and free blacks. The London Missionary Society was founded by abolitionists and brought the evangelical movement and its anti-slavery sentiments to the islands. Although missionaries usually said that they preached humility and obedience to the slaves, their real effect was subversive. Most missionaries believed that slavery was incompatible with Christianity. Slaveholding planters, managers and colonists realized the danger posed by missionaries and tried to prevent them from coming, harassed them in the colonies, blamed them for slave conspiracies and revolts, and attacked them when slaves were rebellious. By 1833 it was estimated that there nearly 150 missionaries and at least 47,000 slave members of the sectarian churches.

The system of slavery was also under attack from within by the slaves themselves. The 1810s to the 1830s witnessed numerous slave plots and conspiracies as well as many small and some large-scale revolts. Some slave restiveness was clearly derived by missionary activity. Quamina, a black deacon of Reverend John Smith's Baptist chapel, for example, led the Demerara Insurrection of 1823. Colonists referred to the Jamaican uprising of 1831 as the Baptist War because so many Baptist converts and deacons were involved. Slave restiveness was also due to spreading news and rumors within the slave community of anti-slavery sentiment, arguments and campaigning in Britain. Some rebel slaves in Demerara in 1823 told the British governor: "God had made them of the same flesh and blood as the whites, and that they were tired of being Slaves to them, that their good King had sent orders they should be free and they would not work any more." In 1833 Buxton realized that slavery would soon be brought to an end: "I know our power of emancipating in one way or another is fast drawing to a close. I mean [the slaves] will take the work into their own hands."

Popular support in Britain for abolition became overwhelming in the aftermath of the Jamaican rebellion of 1831. As was almost always the case, the repression was bloodier than the rebellion itself. Two hundred slaves were killed during the rebellion and another 312 were executed later. Colonists also burned nine Baptist and six Methodist chapels and jailed a number of missionaries. One missionary was tarred and feathered and one was expelled from the colony. This religious persecution inflamed not only abolitionists but also British churchgoers in general. The Jamaican Assembly further inflamed opinion in Britain when, invited to introduce its own ameliorative regulations, debated a ban on the indecent flogging of female slaves (that is the whipping of women naked above the waist) and decided in the end to continue to permit the practice. The people led the abolitionists in demanding immediate emancipation.

In the early 1830s the anti-slavery cause was intertwined with parliamentary reform. A small landed oligarchy and powerful vested interests dominated the unreformed Parliament and a strong reform movement wanted to make the House of Commons more representative of the new industrial cities and Britain's middle class. Supporters of reform were also usually abolitionists whereas opponents of reform were usually opponents of abolition. When the aristocratic and oligarchic House of Lords defeated the second reform bill the country entered a prerevolutionary crisis. Thomas Babbington Macaulay noted in the Commons: "All history is full of revolutions, produced by causes similar to those which are now operating in England." His advice to the king and the oligarchy was "reform that you may preserve." That is exactly what the king did by appointing enough new Lords to pass the third reform bill in June 1832. Elections in December reduced the West Indian lobby in the Commons and brought to office over one hundred Members of Parliament pledged to immediate emancipation. In 1833 the Grey ministry proposed an emancipation bill that attempted to satisfy abolitionists and their followers as well as West Indian planters. The Abolition of Slavery Act provided for gradual abolition by which the former slaves, now called apprentices, were required to work for their former masters for six years. The act also appropriated £20,000,000 to compensate former slaveholders.

With more and more news from the islands of abuses of apprentices, anti-slavery activists launched a new national campaign to end the apprenticeship system immediately. Abolitionists again organized a massive popular movement in Britain and for the first time took the campaign to the slaves and free blacks. Fearful of strikes and revolts and seeking abolitionist support for maintaining the islands' protected market for sugar in Britain, all of the colonial assemblies ended the apprenticeship system between March and July of 1838. Two years ahead of schedule, the 376,000 slaves in Jamaica and tens of thousands more in the other islands and British Guiana were free. The abolition of slavery in the British colonies was the most important blow to Atlantic slavery since the slaves of Saint Domingue liberated themselves in the 1790s.

British emancipation inspired Victor Schoelcher and other French abolitionists to found the *Société pour l'Abolition de l'Esclavage* in 1834. Unlike British abolitionists, Schoelcher and French activists generally were not particularly involved in or motivated by religion. French abolitionists also did not attempt to bring to life a mass popular movement as in Britain but rather campaigned to gain the support of "the foremost citizens." The French movement was also given impetus by the July revolution of 1830, which gave the crown to the ex-Jacobin Louis Philippe, the Citizen King, and power to French constitutionists who began to effectively police and repress the illegal French slave trade. The new king also pledged to abolish slavery.

After the founding of the French Abolition Society, abolitionists worked to ameliorate slavery in the colonies. In the 1820s the *Société de la Morale Chretienne* had sought the protection of family life among slaves, regulation of punishment, the promotion of religious education and more but had few results to show for its efforts. Not until 1845 did a comprehensive ameliorative measure, the Mackau Law, pass in the Assembly. This law banned the whipping of female slaves, it required that families be given separate quarters, required masters to provide land for gardens and a free day to cultivate them and more. The following year the king freed all slaves belonging to the royal domain.

As in the British colonies, French slaves advanced the end of the slave system through resistance and violence. Plots, strikes, riots and revolts became more common after 1815 and especially after 1834. When the British abolished slavery completely in 1838 thousands of slaves from the French islands fled to the British islands. The rise in the number of free blacks (in Martinique the free population doubled in the 1830s) reflected the demoralization of French planters who manumitted many slaves and the determination of slaves who fled their plantations and blended into the free population in the towns.

In France, as in Britain earlier, the anti-slavery cause was intertwined with larger political issues. In Britain the foremost issue was parliamentary reform. In France, home of the frustrated revolution, liberal reformers also wanted to extend the franchise and establish a democratic republic. In February 1848, radicals and a large number of students, upset by a conservative government that refused permission to the last of a series of public political banquets, launched protests that quickly snowballed into a revolution that forced the abdication of the king. The Revolution of 1848 brought Victor Schoelcher into the new republican government as Undersecretary of the Navy for the Colonies. This appointment signified that the government backed the abolition of slavery in the colonies. Before any emancipation decree could be passed and implemented, however, the system of slavery disintegrated completely as slaves stopped working and abandoned the plantations. The municipal governments in the islands recognized reality and proclaimed unconditional emancipation. In 1849 the National Assembly voted to compensate the former slaveholders. Fifteen years after the British abolition, the third great mass emancipation in the Atlantic World was effected.

The French emancipation encouraged slaves in the Dutch Lesser Antilles – St. Martin, St. Eustatius and Saba – to abandon slavery and the Dutch government quickly ratified this self-liberation with an official abolition decree. News of the Dutch emancipation then reached the nearby Danish Virgin Islands. The year before, the Danish government had begun to implement a free womb law, which provided for a twelve-year apprenticeship. In 1848, however, the Danish slaves emancipated themselves and the governor endorsed it. The king later ratified the governor's decree and provided compensation to the former slaveholders. The French, Dutch and Danish emancipations, as well as the earlier British abolition, put pressure on the Spanish American republics to finally bring an end to their lingering slave systems, which most did in the early 1850s.

From the early 1830s to the late 1840s most of the slave systems of the Caribbean, the center of the New World plantation complex, were destroyed by European reformers and by the slaves themselves. The Spanish American republics ended slavery in the early 1850s with the exception of Bolivia and Paraguay where slavery persisted into the 1860s. Thus by mid-century American slavery had been severely crippled and isolated. Three booming plantation economies, however, preserved slavery and the leaders of these societies expected their "peculiar institution" to survive into the twentieth century. These three societies and economies – the southern states of the United States, the Spanish colonies of Cuba and Puerto Rico and the independent empire of Brazil – possessed millions of slaves who were considered absolutely necessary to their prosperity. The slavocrats of the American south, Cuba and Brazil were not about to give up their slaves.

13.5 The Demise of American Slavery, 1860s–80s

The three plantation economies in the Americas, where slavery not only persisted but also thrived in the mid-nineteenth century, were beneficiaries of the Industrial Revolution. Cuba was the first plantation economy that saw the application of steam engines. Brazil's coffee was the Industrial Age's quintessential stimulant. In the case of the southern states of the United States, the cotton boom, which began in the early nineteenth century fueled, and was fueled by, the textile manufacturing revolution in Britain. The mechanization of spinning and weaving increased production of low-cost cloth. As more people in Britain, Europe and around the world were able to afford cheap cotton fabrics and clothing, the market expanded enormously, which stimulated higher production that in turn stimulated greater imports of raw cotton. Cotton came to be cultivated in most plantation zones around the world but the first world-class plantation economy based almost entirely upon cotton was the United States.

Table 13.2. The slave population of
the United States, 1790–1860

Date	Population
1790	717,021
1810	1,192,486
1820	1,538,145
1840	2,487,439
1860	3,953,760

Source: Ira Berlin, *Generations of Captivity:*
A History of African-American Slaves (2003):
Table 1, pp. 272–5.

Cotton had been a secondary crop in British North America and the United States until the early nineteenth century. The invention of the cotton gin, a machine for cleaning cotton fiber, allowed cotton farmers to produce and sell more cotton. The gin also encouraged successful commercial cultivation of cotton in the interior. High British demand and rising prices also motivated more farmers to take up cotton. From 1810 to 1840 cotton production in the United States increased tenfold. In the 1840s it flattened out but during the 1850s total production doubled and by 1860 amounted to over 4.5 million bales. The cotton boom took off during the expansion of the frontier in the old southwest. Cotton cultivation, originally centered in South Carolina and eastern Georgia, gradually moved west into Georgia, Alabama, Mississippi, Louisiana and eventually into Texas.

The cotton revolution in the southern states was dependent upon slave labor. In 1800 cotton plantations accounted for 11 percent of American slaves; at this time the overwhelming proportion of slaves were engaged in tobacco, sugar and rice production. By 1850, however, the proportion of slaves engaged in cotton plantations had risen to 64 percent. The westward shift of cotton cultivation also produced a westward shift in American slavery: from 1790 to 1860 some 835,000 slaves were moved from the old tidewater south into the cotton states of the deep south.

The economic and geographic expansion of cotton cultivation was made possible in the first place by an increase in the number of American slaves. The unusually high rate of natural increase of the African American population in the United States almost doubled the number of slaves from 1830 to 1860. One of the smaller slave populations in the Americas in the mid-eighteenth century had become the largest slave population in the hemisphere one hundred years later. Contrary to what some optimists had thought at the time of the American Revolution, American slavery had not withered away (see Table 13.2).

The American Revolution had generated the first anti-slavery movement in the country as we have seen. By 1804 nine states north of Maryland and Delaware had either freed their slaves or adopted gradual-emancipation plans. For a time anti-slavery activists in the north and south channeled their energy into the colonization movement, an effort to transplant American blacks on the coast of Africa or Haiti. By the 1830s, however, only about fifteen hundred American blacks had been resettled in Liberia.

The American anti-slavery movement was reborn in the 1830s in the wake of the failure of colonization. Inspired by the abolition of colonial British slavery in the 1830s, American abolitionists believed their task was to mobilize national opinion against slavery as their counterparts had done in Britain. Thus abolitionists published newspapers, wrote pamphlets and books and organized petition campaigns. There were black abolitionists as well as white. Frederick Douglass, a former slave, published his inspirational autobiography in 1845, *Narrative of the Life of Frederick Douglass, An American Slave*, and became a leader in the anti-slavery movement. In 1839 the abolitionist movement was energized by the Amistad affair. Activists obtained the liberty of a shipload of African captives who had rebelled against their Cuban owners on the high seas and who were later captured by the United States Navy.

By the late 1830s the American Anti-Slavery Society had 1,346 local associations with over 100,000 members. In one campaign the Society had published and distributed one million pieces of anti-slavery literature. In 1838–9 abolitionists had gathered two million names in a petition drive. A British-style movement and campaign, however, could not succeed in the United States. Unlike the British case, slavery in the United States was a domestic institution that was deeply embedded in southern society. The abolitionist campaign of moral persuasion was not only ineffective in the south, it also provoked a proslavery backlash. Beginning in the 1830s southern leaders argued that their paternalistic system of slavery was beneficial to the slave. In 1837 Senator John C. Calhoun of South Carolina declared that slavery was "a good – a positive good." The other important American contrast to Britain was the decisive national political power possessed by the cotton-producing and slave-owning south. Unlike the West Indian lobby in London, America's slave states had the institutional and constitutional power to defend slavery against all threats. Southerners generally dominated the federal government before 1860. Most presidents and Supreme Court justices had come from the south. The Missouri Compromise in 1820 regularized the equilibrium in the number of slave states and free states, which made the Senate the great defender of southern interests. Thus opposition to slavery became political opposition to the south. Anti-slavery moved into politics.

Despite the efforts of the abolitionist movement in the 1830s, most northerners and westerners were uninterested in the abolition of slavery. Indeed many were racists who were hostile to abolitionism. If there was a popular anti-slavery sentiment, it was related to the issue of slavery in the west. Many wanted to keep slavery out of the territories. The Missouri Compromise in 1820, which had divided the Louisiana Purchase at 36° 30′ latitude, had solved this problem but the Mexican War in 1846–8 and the annexation of new lands reopened it. Some northerners, in fact, perceived the conflict as a southern war of aggression, which was designed to expand the territory of slavery. In 1848 anti-slavery Democrats and 'conscience Whigs' joined with political abolitionists to form the Free Soil Party. Free Soilers wanted the abolition of slavery in the District of Columbia and the exclusion of slavery from all Federal territories. Although the Free Soil Party lost the election, its formation marked the beginning of a sectional, political revolution.

In the 1850s more and more northerners and westerners came to fear a Slave Power conspiracy, a southern plot to take complete control of the national government, seize foreign lands through war and aggression, extend slavery into the western territories and the new acquisitions and subvert America's republican principles and institutions. The Fugitive Slave Act of 1850 required all citizens to assist law enforcement in the capture and return of runaway slaves. The Kansas-Nebraska Act of 1854 repealed the Missouri Compromise and permitted the expansion of slavery in the territories on the basis of popular sovereignty, that is, the will of a majority of residents in a territory. Some southerners began to question the termination of the slave trade. A grand jury in South Carolina in 1854 declared, "The Federal law abolishing the African Slave Trade is a public grievance." The Dred Scott decision of the Supreme Court in 1857 ruled that Congress did not have the authority to prohibit slavery in the territories. The Chief Justice, the son of a wealthy planter, viewed abolitionism, not slavery, as a crime. The Illinois politician Abraham Lincoln in 1858 expressed a growing concern when he said he believed there was "a conspiracy to perpetuate and nationalize slavery." The feeling was growing deeper in the northern heart, wrote *The New York Times* in 1858, "that our character, our prosperity, and our destiny are more seriously involved in the question of the perpetuation or extinction of slavery in those States."

Growing fear and apprehension of a frightening Slave Power strengthened the political anti-slavery movement in the north. The Republican Party, formed in the mid-1850s, represented a coalition of Free Soilers, northern Whigs, Jacksonian and anti-slavery Democrats, Know-Nothings or nativists, colonizationists and radical abolitionists. The Party focused its platform on one issue more than any other: implacable opposition to the expansion of slavery into the territories. Republicans began to elect an anti-slavery bloc in Congress in 1856 and 1858. In the election of 1860 the Republican candidate Abraham Lincoln attained the presidency by winning all of the free states (but not one southern state) and 40 percent of the popular vote.

To most southerners the election of Lincoln was simply unacceptable. Although northerners had become increasingly apprehensive of a vast and sinister Slave Power conspiracy, southerners believed in a northern pro-Negro, race mixing and abolitionist conspiracy and believed Lincoln and the Republican Party was at its head. Although the Republican platform in 1860 had disavowed any intention of interfering with slavery where it currently existed, many southerners assumed that the 1860 election began the process of transferring control of the national government to radical abolitionists and enemies of the south. As a result, seven slave states seceded from the Federal Union and in 1861 formed the Confederate States of America. "Its foundations are laid, its cornerstone rests," noted the new Confederate Vice President Alexander Stephens, "upon the great truth that the negro is not equal to the white man; that slavery . . . is his natural and normal condition. This, our new government, is the first in the history of the world based upon this great physical, philosophical, and moral truth."

President Lincoln was unwilling to assent to southern secession and therefore war came. Lincoln and the postsecession Republican-dominated Congress were definitely anti-slavery, if not yet abolitionist, and acted on their convictions. The administration put teeth into the enforcement of the ban on the slave trade and finally brought the illegal American trade to an end. Congress abolished slavery in the District of Columbia and the territories. Congress also ended the Fugitive Slave Law of 1850, emancipated slaves confiscated by Union soldiers, and authorized blacks to serve in the military. In the fall of 1862 the president proposed a limited abolition if the secessionists did not return to the national fold. Although Lincoln justified it in military terms, his Emancipation Proclamation freed all of the slaves in rebel territory beginning on January 1, 1863. This act, he stated, was "an act of justice, warranted by the Constitution, upon military necessity." A northern publisher stated that the Emancipation Proclamation added "an incalculable element of strength to the Union cause" and that it "perfects the purposes of the Declaration of Independence."

Although the south seceded and rebelled to preserve slavery, the war hastened and ensured its complete demise. At the beginning of the war Frederick Douglass realized, "He who faithfully works to put down a rebellion undertaken and carried on for the extension and perpetuity of slavery, performs an anti-slavery work." It would be impossible, he said, to separate victory of the union from freedom of the slave. Free blacks and slaves realized this and did their part to affect both. Slaves hastened the demise of slavery by running away or refusing to work without pay. Thousands from the beginning of the war claimed their freedom by fleeing to the protection of Union armies. The Emancipation Proclamation encouraged resistance and increased the number of runaways. In 1863 the War Department approved the formation of black regiments and within a year there were more than 100,000 black men in uniform serving in more than sixty regiments. Black soldiers from northern states constituted almost 50 percent of all black men ages eighteen to forty-five. These soldiers fought in 449 battles and ultimately 37,000 black patriots lost their lives. The Confederacy refused to arm blacks and slaves. Confederate General Howell Cobb of Georgia remarked, "The day you make soldiers of [negroes] is the beginning of the end of the revolution. If slaves will make good soldiers our whole theory of slavery is wrong."

In 1864 Republicans proposed an amendment to the Constitution to emancipate all of the slaves and to forever abolish slavery. In April, the Thirteenth Amendment passed the Senate but was defeated by Democrats in the House of Representatives. If Lincoln had lost the election that November the amendment would not have been revived. Lincoln's reelection and the Republican victory in 1864 led to passage in both houses by a two-thirds majority in January 1865 and ratification by the states by the end of the year. With this amendment came the end of slavery in the United States:

Article XIII.

Sec. 1. Neither slavery nor involuntary servitude, except as a punishment for crime, whereof the party shall have been duly convicted, shall exist within the United States, or any place subject to their jurisdiction.

Table 13.3. The slave population
of Cuba, 1795–1860

Date	Population
1795	84,000
1810	212,000
1845	324,000
1860	370,000

Source: Herbert S. Klein, *African Slavery in Latin America and the Caribbean* (1986): 95.

After 1865 slavery survived in Brazil and the Spanish Caribbean, meaning Cuba and Puerto Rico. During most of the colonial period the Spanish Caribbean had been relatively poor because the sugar revolution had mostly bypassed Puerto Rico, Santo Domingo and Cuba. The Seven Years War and British occupation in 1763 began the economic rebirth of Cuba. In the 1790s the slave rebellion in Saint Domingue brought French sugar planters to Cuba, a total of twenty to thirty thousand refugees altogether. Cuban sugar plantations became more productive and began to seriously compete in a world market left wide open after the collapse of the sugar industry in Saint Domingue. By 1815 Cuba was producing 42,000 tons a year, a little more than one-half of the quantity produced by Jamaica. Within a few years Cuba was the world's largest producer of sugar; in the late 1860s Cuba produced more than 700,000 tons, which represented about 40 percent of the world market.

This late sugar boom in Cuba brought a vigorous slave trade to the island. In 1792 the island counted about eighty thousand slaves. Thereafter Spain removed all restrictions on the slave trade and from 1790 to 1810 about 150,000 slaves were imported into Cuba. After 1820, the year the slave trade to Cuba was formally abolished, the now illegal slave trade continued to prosper. In 1837 alone, more than twelve thousand slaves were imported. More than 600,000 slaves were imported during the illegal trade era until the United States Navy shut down the Cuban trade in the early 1860s. As a result the slave population boomed. The 1817 census revealed a quarter of a million slaves in Cuba in a total population of 630,000 people. By 1841 the slave population had risen to over 430,000. Thereafter the slave population declined as the trade was unable to replace all of the slaves who died. By 1862 the slave population was 368,000 in a total population of over one million (see Table 13.3).

In Cuba, slavery survived with colonialism. As in the other plantation colonies of the Caribbean, the Cuban planter class was more afraid of its slaves than interested in independence. Slave rebellion in Saint Domingue inspired political caution among the Creole population. During the Spanish American revolutions and wars for independence on the mainland, Cuba had served as the center of Spanish military activities and was the principal Spanish naval base in the Americas. The island, as a result, was heavily garrisoned in the 1810s and 1820s. The Cuban creole oligarchy also realized that their island's great wealth gave them considerable political influence in Spain. Cuba in the 1820s and 1830s became Spain's cash cow and thus the Spanish government did pretty much what Cuban sugar planters wanted it to do. There was little opportunity or reason for Cubans to seek independence.

During the sugar boom years there was little opposition to slavery in Spain or Cuba. The American Civil War stimulated the first abolitionist movement in Spanish culture in 1864 when a Puerto Rican founded the Spanish Abolitionist Society in Madrid. Since the Spanish revolution in the early nineteenth century, abolitionism had been linked to liberalism. The liberal revolution that triumphed in 1868 led to the formation of a Spanish republic that was anti-slavery in principle. Segismundo Moret, the minister of colonial affairs and an abolitionist, introduced an abolition law into the Cortes in May 1870. This Moret Law, as it came to be called, was a free womb law that created an apprenticeship system for the liberated children or *patrocinados*. They were required to give service to the masters of their mothers until the age of eighteen and work for half-wages until the age of twenty-one. The law also freed all slaves over the age of sixty-five.

At the same time that the Spanish revolution overthrew Queen Isabel II and established a liberal republic, a rebellion for independence began in Cuba. The rebellion was inspired by a rising Cuban nationalism as well as a new system of direct taxes that seemed most burdensome to small planters, farmers and shopkeepers. The rebels had not arisen from the planter oligarchy, which meant that the rebellion was both a civil war as well as a struggle for independence. The movement was anti-slavery to some extent. Its chief, Carlos Manuel de Céspedes, freed his personal slaves and enlisted them into his army at the beginning of the rebellion. In 1869 a rebel assembly officially freed the slaves but bound them to their masters for an indefinite period. The rebels encouraged slaves on the plantations of loyalists in the west to revolt and promised that those who joined the rebel army would be freed.

The Moret Law of 1870, therefore, was not simply inspired by the principles of Spanish liberalism. In order to prevent the rebels from attracting and arming tens of thousands of slaves, the Spanish government was forced to disarm the incentive of freedom. Fearful that the anti-slavery governments of Great Britain, France and the United States might assist the rebels in return for an abolition decree, the government preempted the rebels and officially "abolished" slavery. The abolition law, however, maintained the support of the sugar barons by putting off the effective date of emancipation for decades. The Moret Law of 1870 was important as a symbol but it freed very few slaves.

The independence rebellion in Cuba, which was the result of a guerrilla war in the two mountainous provinces in the eastern zone of the island, continued until 1878. This Ten Years War dismantled slavery in the east and left it more concentrated in the dominant plantation regions in the western provinces. The war also cut the ranks of slavery by freeing the thousands of slaves who had fought for the rebels and for the government. With the effective end of the slave trade in the 1860s and the continued inability of the slave population to replace itself, the slave population was naturally decreasing. During the

1870s the slave system further disintegrated as slaves, inspired by the talk of abolition but frustrated with the survival of the institution, increasingly abandoned the sugar plantations and joined the free population. In 1869 there had been 360,000 slaves; ten years later there were about 230,000. Some masters began to offer wages to their slaves in order to keep them on their plantations.

Slavery was dying. Not only was there increasing desertion but also slaves were also burning cane fields and resisting masters and overseers with violence. In 1879 another brief rebellion called the Guerra Chiquita erupted. There were so many free blacks and slaves in the rebel army that the Spanish government called it a "race war." In order to better control the situation, the Spanish government in 1880 abolished slavery and offered conditional freedom. Slavery was replaced by a *patronato* system that would last for eight years. Masters became patrons and the slaves were transformed into wards, *patrocinados*, who could still be whipped, locked up, bought and sold. For the masters, this allotted eight years of labor was their compensation for abolition. For the slaves, or former slaves officially speaking, this eight-year period was supposed to assist them in preparing for "responsible freedom."

Slavery continued to disintegrate. Slaves abandoned the plantations and between 1881 and 1886, over 35,000 slaves were freed unconditionally by their masters with mutual-accord agreements by which workers promised to continue working for their former masters for an agreed-upon period of years and an agreed-upon wage. An additional eight thousand slaves successfully challenged rightful ownership or purchased their freedom. By 1886 there were, supposedly, only about twenty-five thousand slaves in Cuba. In that year the Spanish government, with the agreement of Cuban planters, abolished the *patronato*. Slavery had finally and completely come to an end in Cuba.

Slavery survived in Cuba until the last quarter of the nineteenth century because of the labor requirements of a rich and expanding plantation economy. It survived because an imperial government placated the interests of a rich and powerful colonial oligarchy. It also survived because a popular and determined abolitionist movement never developed in Spanish culture. To some Spanish liberals, the blame for this last failing was due to Catholicism. "I will say that we have had nineteen centuries of Christianity, and still there are slaves," exclaimed Emilio Castelar in 1870, "nineteen centuries of Christianity, and there are still slaves among Catholic peoples! One century of revolution, and there are no slaves among revolutionary peoples."

During the preceding decades the Cuban planter class and the Spanish government had attempted to begin the transition to wage labor in the sugar industry. The Spanish government provided free passage and land to white immigrants to Cuba. By 1861 over 100,000 Spaniards had been attracted; by the 1880s tens of thousands arrived each year. From 1847 to 1874, over 125,000 Chinese workers, "coolies," had been imported. These new workers, in conjunction with the gradual abolition of slavery, meant that sugar production was not disrupted. Masters successfully evolved into employers. Slaves evolved into individual wage workers or *braceros*, skilled workers and operatives of various kinds or *operarios*, day workers and contract laborers,

Table 13.4. The slave population
of Brazil, 1798–1887

Date	Population
1792	1,582,000
1818	1,930,000
1864	1,715,000
1874	1,540,000
1884	1,240.000
1885	1,133,000
1887	723,000

Source: Robert Conrad, *The Destruction of Brazilian Slavery, 1850–1888* (1972): 47.

hired mobile work gangs and so on. Some developed into peasant farmers or even small cane farmers called *colonos*. As a result, sugar production fell somewhat in the 1880s but climbed in the 1890s. In some years Cuba's sugar mills produced more than one million tons.

Cotton in the United States and sugar in Cuba was matched by coffee in Brazil. Brazil's nineteenth-century coffee boom was sparked by Haiti just as Cuba's sugar boom. Prior to the slave rebellion, Saint Domingue produced one-half of the world's supply of coffee. The Haitian Revolution, which destroyed the island's coffee plantations and thus opened the market, and Brazilian planters took full advantage of the opportunity. By 1820 Brazilians exported 5,500 tons of coffee, which represented a little less than 20 percent of all Brazilian exports (compared to sugar, which was almost one-third). By 1850 coffee constituted over 40 percent of Brazilian exports and over 60 percent by 1890. Total production increased from less than 200,000 sacks of coffee beans in 1822 to over five million sacks by 1889. In the nineteenth century, Brazil became the world's largest producer of coffee just as the United States became the world's largest producer of cotton and Cuba became the world's largest producer of sugar.

Like cotton and sugar, coffee production was dominated by slave labor. Coffee cultivation (and the cleaning and processing of the beans) was labor intensive. One visitor to the Paraiba Valley in the mid-nineteenth century, the center of Brazil's coffee industry, recorded that on one coffee fazenda, slaves provided "seventeen hours of almost uninterrupted labor." Centuries before slavery in Brazil had been intimately associated with sugar. In the nineteenth century, noted Senator Silveira Martims, "Brazil is coffee and coffee is the Negro."

Brazil, of course, had been a slave society long before the nineteenth-century coffee boom. The slave trade continued legally to 1831 and illegally until the early 1850s. In 1800–50, about 1,600,000 Africans were imported into Brazil. At the time of independence in the early 1820s there were nearly two million slaves in a total population of 3.8 million. By the 1870s the slave population was approximately 1,500,000. Only the United States, until 1863–5, had more slaves in the Americas than Brazil (see Table 13.4).

During the first half of the nineteenth century, Brazilian slavery was geographically reoriented. The decline of the sugar industry in the northeast and the rise of the coffee industry in the south and south-center required a labor adjustment. An interprovincial slave trade moved people from north to south. The effective suppression of the slave trade in the 1850s turned the inter-provincial trade into a torrent. From 1852 to 1862 more than thirty thousand slaves were transferred from the north to Rio de Janeiro. By 1874–84, the south-central provinces of São Paulo, Minas Gerais, Espírito Santo and Rio de Janeiro obtained nearly ninety thousand slaves in the interprovincial trade. By 1885 the north and northeastern provinces possessed over 300,000 slaves while the southern and western provinces had nearly 800,000.

Brazilian slavery survived the independence period unscathed. The country was not pressured to abolish the slave trade until 1831 and even then there was no interest in enforcing the ban. It was not effectively ended until 1850 when the British navy entered Brazilian ports to flush out slavers and establish a blockade, which forced Brazil's leaders to enact a law that finally ensured the enforcement of the abolition. Before mid-century few Brazilians questioned the legitimacy of slavery.

The abolition of slavery in the United States put anti-slavery on the agenda in Brazil. The Civil War, noted one observer, "reverberated in the Empire like an immense and frightful thunderclap." The British Minister in Rio in 1865 reported "a rapidly growing feeling among the leading men of the necessity of the abolition of slavery." The Paraguayan War of 1865–70 also raised the issue of slavery because thousands of slaves were recruited for the army. Political opponents of the war were also critics of slavery. Not until the late 1860s did a strong anti-slavery movement emerge. Abolitionists wrote and published polemical articles, pamphlets and books, organized clubs and held meetings. They raised money to purchase the freedom of individual slaves. Liberals began to take up the anti-slavery cause; the Liberal Center, a group of senators, proposed a free womb law in 1868. The enactment by Spain of a free womb law for Cuba in 1870 put further pressure on Brazil, now the only "Christian nation" to maintain slavery. "How can Brazil, isolated and only of its kind on the globe," asked the abolitionist José Tomaz Nabuco, "resist the pressure of the entire world?"

In 1871 a Conservative government enacted a free womb law intended to satisfy world opinion and domestic abolitionists while at the same time delaying the effective abolition of slavery for several more decades. The Rio Branco Law, named for the leader of the ministry, freed all newborns of slave mothers. The free children, called *ingenuos* and sometimes *riobrancos*, were to be maintained by the masters until age eight when the slave owner decided either to accept indemnification in bonds or in labor. If they chose the latter, the *ingenuos* had to provide labor for the masters of their mothers until the age of twenty-one. One abolitionist opponent of the law argued that a slave born on September 27, 1871, one day before the law took effect, could conceivably still be a slave at the age of eighty in 1951. Despite the very moderate nature of the law and the grumblings of some abolitionists, there was still considerable opposition to the measure by slaveholders, particularly coffee planters. One slavocrat worried that the law would "completely rupture the ties of subordination ... " and thus make it impossible to "continue under the system of passive obedience."

The government succeeded. In time slaveholders came to view the Rio Branco Law as an effective delay of abolition and an instrument that pre-served the status quo. The law deflected international pressure and criticism and the domestic anti-slavery movement stagnated and declined for a while. During the 1870s some coffee planters nevertheless began to prepare for the end of slavery and turned to European immigrants and labor contracts to meet their needs. In the 1850s and 1860s some coffee planters began to recruit European peasants, a process eventually taken over by the Brazilian government who paid the passage. From less than five thousand immigrants a year in the early 1850s, the number had reached eleven thousand in the late 1860s and really took off in the 1870s. By 1880 over thirty thousand immigrants entered the country.

Anti-slavery sentiment started to rise again in the late 1870s. The Liberal Party returned to power in 1878 and began to discuss new abolitionist mea-sures. Increased unrest by slaves on the plantations, assassinations and even revolts put slavery on the agenda. Slavocrat planters and politicians talked about strengthening the repressive powers of the state. Abolitionists argued that emancipation, not more repression and punishment, would solve the problem. "Everyone knows it," remarked a professor, "Brazilian society is sitting on a volcano, let us not delude ourselves." The anti-slavery move-ment began to revive as it became apparent slavery was as strong as ever: new abolitionist societies were formed in the capital and the provinces, abo-litionist newspapers appeared and books were published, and professional groups embraced abolitionism. In 1881 the Fourteenth Army Battalion at Fortaleza declared itself an abolitionist society. For the first time the Brazil-ian anti-slavery movement became a widespread, decentralized and popular or mass movement not unlike the earlier British and American anti-slavery movements. Local societies organized mass meetings and parades to gather support for the immediate and unconditional abolition of slavery.

The anti-slavery movement confronted a divided slaveholding class. "There is a fair indication that the old-fashioned slaveholding element will rule the country with but little opposition," reported a Rio de Janeiro newspaper in 1880. The slaveholding element, however, did not defend slavery like the North American slavocrats. Northeast planters had been disinvesting in slavery for several decades. Even some coffee planters had begun the transition to free labor. Unlike the American south, Brazilian slaveholders did not have the widespread support of non-slaveholders. Although the slavocrats controlled certain provincial governments and were a powerful force in the national Imperial government, they understood they could not defend slavery politically to the same extent that their counterparts in the United States had done.

The revived anti-slavery movement of the early 1880s sought municipal and provincial victories. As an essentially urban movement, abolitionist soci-eties began to liberate slaves in major sections of certain cities and declare some cities completely slave free. In Belem abolitionists liberated the city block by block. The provinces of Amazonas and Ceará abolished slavery. The anti-slavery movement also had some political victories: the emancipation of sexagenarians, the abolition of the interprovincial trade, and the prohibition

Document 13.2
The Origins of Abolitionism in Brazil

1879

While there have always been some philanthropic men amongst the Portuguese and their descendants, who deplored and denounced as a cruel wrong the African Slave-trade, domestic slavery and the former treatment of Indians, but few had the courage or the influence to make their opinions felt, either in Portugal or Brazil.

It was early understood that the present Emperor was in favor of some mode of emancipation, and the subject became a matter of study, after the African Slave-trade was broken up in 1815. From time to time his sentiments and that of the leading statesmen of Brazil became known, and in 1865, there was quite a spirited debate on this subject in the Brazilian Senate when passing resolutions on the reception of the news of the death of President Lincoln. At the request of Professor Laboulaye of Paris, I furnished both him and M. Cochin that discussion, and statistics of slavery in Brazil. The result was some most able articles on the subject by Professor Laboulaye in the *Journal des Débates*. In 1864, when at Rio de Janeiro, I was almost implored by some of the members of the Brazilian Parliament – amongst whom was the late A.C. Tavares Bastos – to send to Brazil works on emancipation. The same request also came from higher quarters. Through some of the leading journals of the United States I made an appeal for works bearing on the subject of slavery. The response was generous in the three cities of New York, Boston and Providence, and there volumes were gratefully received both in the palace and in the homes of eminent Brazilians. I recall that the works, which were the most impressive in their effects, were those of the late George Livermore, of Cambridge, Mass. (on the status of the negro as the slave, the citizen, and the soldier), and the tracts and pamphlets of Mrs. Lydia Maria Child. The collapse of slavery in the United States, in 1865, had also a powerful effect in directly the minds of the Brazilian leaders on this subject. Silveira de Motta, the senator from Goyaz, immediately brought in a bill to limit slavery. This senator, though a 'great talker,' was neither an eloquent nor an impressive speaker, but the debate evoked by his bill brought into the arena men like the late Visconde Jequitinhonha (Montezuma), who spoke forcibly on the question. It was on this occasion, that Mr. Livermore's book (which had only been four weeks in Rio), was freely quoted on both sides. The Paraguayan war, which began in 1865, and did not end until March 1870, absorbed the attention of the nation almost to the exclusion of any other subject; but notwithstanding this, there were Brazilians (and amongst them Dom Pedro II), who did not forget the subject of slavery. In 1868, the question of emancipation took a more definite form in the expressions of the emperor. It was the knowledge of this, that caused the 'Quaker' poet, Whittier, to write his spirited verses entitled, 'Freedom in Brazil,' in which he spoke words of encouragement to the 'great-hearted ruler' of whom he said: -

Crowned doubly by man's blessing and God's grace,
Thy future is secure;
Who frees a people makes his statue's place
in Time's Valhalla, sure.

James C. Fletcher and D. P. Kidder had twenty years' experience traveling about and residing in Brazil. Few outsiders had more intimate knowledge of Brazil in this century than these two authors. *Source:* James C. Fletcher and Rev. D. P. Kidder, *Brazil and the Brazilians Portrayed in Historical and Descriptive Sketches*, Ninth Edition (1879), pp. 582–3.

of the whip in the punishment of slaves. Even the Catholic Church became a late convert to anti-slavery: bishops condemned slavery and religious orders finally freed their slaves. Still, slavery persisted and slavocrat power fought back with a tough fugitive slave law.

During the 1880s the anti-slavery movement became more and more radical. "No one is obligated to respect slavery," declared the abolitionist José do Patrocinio, a former slave, in 1886. "On the contrary, it is the duty of every citizen to fight it by every means." Abolitionists began to call for direct action: activists and citizens were called upon to take the anti-slavery message to the slaves on plantations and encourage them to stop working, run away, damage the property or even resist with violence. Now that some cities and provinces had abolished slavery and were free territory, abolitionists set up the "underground railroad" complete with escorts, railroad passes, hiding places in the cities and forged certificates of freedom. Abolitionist societies trained specialists, called *caiphazes*, who secretly slipped into rural plantations at night, read anti-slavery literature and urged slaves to flee, and then escorted them to places of refuge in towns and cities. Shantytowns called *quilombos*, inhabited by hundreds and then thousands of runaway slaves, grew up on the edges of cities. A group of 150 slaves – men, women and children – armed with guns, knives and machetes fought a police force sent to return them and overwhelmed their pursuers, stripped and beat them. Groups of sympathizers sometimes attacked policemen who were returning runaway slaves.

Although the police and planter armed forces attempted to hold the slave system together, Brazil's army decided not to interfere. Many soldiers viewed slave catching as undignified and dangerous, and realized that the public opposed it. In 1887 the unofficial Military Club petitioned the Princess Regent requesting that the army not be required to chase fugitive slaves. With the military unwilling to prop up the slave system, slavery could not be preserved any longer.

In São Paulo province, flights by slaves began in 1886 and accelerated in 1887. The provinces of Rio de Janeiro and Minas Gerais were next. Freedom became infectious and spread from plantation to plantation. The rapid collapse of slavery in 1887 and 1888 astounded slaveholders and abolitionists alike. "The disorganization of agricultural labor threatens to spread over the entire province," declared the Paulista Senator Antonio Prado in December

1887, "producing results more to be feared than those caused by any natural disaster." In order to keep their workers on their plantations, slaveholders made agreements with slaves to free them in the near future or immediately if they promised to stay and work for a wage. In March 1888, one planter wrote, "Since the first of January I have not possessed a single slave! I liberated all of them, and bound them to the property by means of a contract identical to the one that I have with the foreign colonists."

By the spring of 1888 the system of slavery in Brazil had disintegrated. When Parliament opened in May the Conservative government presented a proposal for immediate and unconditional emancipation. During the debate over the law, one deputy stated that "already slavery does not exist in the Empire; what exists is an apparition of slavery." What became known as the *Lei Aurea*, the Golden Law, was approved by the politicians and sanctioned by the Princess Regent Isabel on May 13. Article 1 read: "From the date of this law slavery is declared extinct in Brazil." With this law the last holdout of slavery in the Americas had come to an end. An era as old as European colonization of the New World was over. Slavery still survived in the Atlantic World, however; it persisted and thrived in Africa.

13.6 Africa and Anti-Slavery

The campaign against the slave trade and slavery itself came to Africa in the nineteenth century. Both institutions were deeply ingrained in African life, politics and economy. Aside from the slaves themselves, few Africans opposed slavery. The Enlightenment and native evangelical Protestantism had bypassed the continent, thus the traditional intellectual bases of anti-slavery were missing in Africa. Europeans, then, mainly the British and the French, brought the idea and practice of anti-slavery to the Africans.

The first African consequences of European and American anti-slavery were the territories established to take in free blacks and liberated slaves. Sierra Leone, set up in 1787 to provide a home for the black poor of London, in time became the place for the reception and settlement of slaves captured at sea by the British navy. Eventually, nearly 160,000 liberated slaves were settled in Sierra Leone. In time it became the British Protectorate of Sierra Leone. The American Colonization Society established a similar settlement in 1822, at Cape Mesurado, just south of Sierra Leone. Liberia, as it became known, had nearly five thousand settlers who declared independence in 1847, creating the first republic in Africa. The new nation adopted as its motto, "The love of liberty brought us here." In 1849 the French navy established Libreville at the Gabon estuary facing São Tomé as a refuge for freed slaves.

After the Anglo American abolitions of their slave trades in 1808, and as more and more empires and nations legally abolished the trade, Britain attacked the problem from the African side. The British navy maintained squadrons on the coast to intercept slavers and liberate their cargo. Britain endeavored to sign treaties with coastal towns and rulers that banned the trade. The rulers of the two leading towns in Old Calabar, for example, abolished their slave trade in return for ƒ2,000 a year for five years. In 1840

GEZO, KING OF DAHOMEY.

Figure 13.4. Gezo, King of Dahomey. From *The Uncle Tom's Cabin Almanack* (London, 1853). Courtesy of the Clarke Historical Library at Central Michigan University.

the British approached King Gezo of Dahomey who was asked to give up the slave trade. He refused. "The slave trade has been the ruling principle of my people," he replied. "It is the source of their glory and wealth." The Obi Osai of Aboh was more accommodating: "Hitherto, we thought that it was God's wish that black people should be slaves to white people; white people first told us that we should sell slaves to them, and we sold them; and white people are now telling us not to sell slaves. . . . If white people give up buying, black people will give up selling."

The abolition of the slave trade on the African coast took a long time and varied from region to region. The Gold Coast, the prime supplier of the British trade, dropped out of the slave trade almost entirely after 1808. Sierra Leone reduced its exports considerably, from seventy thousand in the pre-1808 decades to a few thousand in the 1820s and 1830s and a few hundreds thereafter. Pressure on the trade in West Africa pushed slave traders to Central Africa and led to the rebirth and enormous expansion of the Atlantic trade in southeast Africa. The southeast African trade increased from less than 10,000 in 1810–15 to a peak of 99,000 in 1836–40. In general, the African suppliers continued selling until the 1860s when the slave trade declined to negligible levels.

As Africans moved out of the slave trade they embraced what was called the legitimate trade. There was no powerful causal link, however, between the two. European markets in the late eighteenth and early nineteenth century created a demand for such products as palm and peanut oil, gum, beeswax, hides, timber and more. Palm oil exports from West Africa to Great Britain from the 1820s to the 1850s increased from 1,000 tons a year to 30,000 tons. Not all of the regions that had benefited most from the slave trade benefited from the new legitimate trade. There was also a shift within African societies of who profited from the different kinds of trade. Militaristic oligarchies lost revenue and power with the decline of the slave trade whereas merchant classes continued to take advantage of and benefit from Atlantic trade, and African producers of the new exports obtained a share of the profits. By the 1840s and 1850s the value of legitimate trade exports in West Africa had completely replaced the slave trade in importance. Legitimate trade earned more foreign exchange than the slave trade had earned at its height in the late eighteenth century. The economic transition for Africa had not been particularly difficult and was quite advantageous for some regions and groups.

European involvement and presence in Africa did not decline as the slave trade declined but increased and expanded. Africa's legitimate trade brought much more European entanglement than the slave trade that, in Africa, had been almost completely in African hands. The new use of steamboats extended direct European trading up the navigable rivers, permitting Europeans to penetrate deeper into Africa than ever before. Armed steamboats also expanded European power and influence. New kinds of weapons, repeating rifles and machine guns, also permitted Europeans to expand into Africa and overpower, for the first time, the great states and empires of the interior. A medical revolution dramatically increased the number of Europeans who could safely reside in Africa. Before 1850 and the introduction of quinine treatment for malaria, the annual mortality of newly arrived Europeans varied between 250 and 500 per 1,000. In the second half of the nineteenth century, death rates for Europeans dropped to about 50 per 1,000. All of these improvements paved the way for the European conquest and colonization of Africa in the late nineteenth century.

The rise of legitimate trade and the decline of the Atlantic slave trade increased the importance of slavery within Africa. European demand for the new trade items led to new and larger plantations dependent upon slave labor. Surplus slaves, who were not sold to Atlantic slave traders, were not emancipated but redeployed in the local economy or sold to other regions. In the 1870s the population of the Kumasi area, in Asante, was reported to be equally slave and free. In the area around Abomey, the capital of Dahomey, about one-third of the inhabitants were slaves in mid-century. In the late nineteenth century the estimated slave population of Senegal constituted over

30 percent of the total population. Some commercial centers in the Sudan had 80 percent slavery. Slave raiding and trading in the interior of equatorial Africa continued until the twentieth century. Africa had several kinds of slavery with varying degrees of dependency and coercion, and all of the different varieties of slavery, especially slaves committed to plantation labor, expanded in the nineteenth century. The African social order by the late nineteenth century, according to Paul Lovejoy, a leading historian of African slavery, was more closely tied to slavery than ever before.

The rise of European political influence and then colonization in Africa promoted coerced labor but undermined slavery. European authorities needed construction workers, porters and soldiers, and established systems to conscript African men. All five European powers involved in Africa – France, Belgium, Portugal, Germany and Great Britain – designed taxation and labor policies, which forced Africans to work for the authorities or for particular companies. The French, for example, required men to work unpaid for up to twelve days a year. The British required chiefs to deliver coerced laborers. During the First World War, about half a million Africans were drafted and taken to the battlefields of Europe. Europeans embraced and expanded systems of forced labor but opposed slavery.

Europeans went after slavery in different ways. In West Africa the British and the French at first abolished slavery in their small – precolonial – trading-post towns. The French in 1849, for example, liberated over twelve thousand slaves in Saint Louis and about five thousand in Gorée. The British and the French later withdrew official recognition and legal support for slavery. When the British annexed several coastal states and created the Gold Coast Colony in 1874, slavery lost its legal status. British authorities now did nothing to assist masters recover runaways; slaves were free, in short, to liberate themselves but colonial officials did not actively undermine slavery. "Slavery is not recognized in the Soudan," noted the British governor of the Sudan in 1899, "but as long as service is willingly rendered by servants to masters it is unnecessary to interfere in the conditions existing among them." The French abolished the legal status of slavery in their colonies and territories in 1903. Slaves in the Sudan in the hundreds of thousands took advantage of British and French policies and quit their masters. The collapse of Sudanese slavery in the 1890s and 1900s represented one of the largest slave revolts in the history of the world.

Conquest and colonization in the late nineteenth century was justified, among other reasons, as a way to end slavery in Africa. The General Act of Brussels of 1890 committed the European powers involved in Africa to act against slavery. The five powers officially abolished slavery in their colonies (although not in their protectorates). Portugal, for example, abolished slavery outright in 1875, again in 1910, and finally in 1961. Sierra Leone did not abolish slavery until 1926. The repetition of official abolitions in Portuguese colonies as well as in all the others indicated the deep resistance of African slavery to the pronouncements of governments. Colonial governments did not have the personnel or the commitment to abolish slavery completely. Slavery ceased to exist in many regions in West and Central Africa in the early twentieth century when slaves themselves took the initiative and abandoned their masters. Historians generally maintain that slavery in most parts of Africa had declined to insignificance by 1930.

Slavery in Africa, however, did not disappear. Pockets of slavery survived throughout the continent and new ones appeared from time to time. Unlike the Americas, colonial governments did not actively enforce abolition and African authorities and the general population did not repudiate slaveholding. A 1954–5 survey suggested that there were over 200,000 slaves among Fulbe speakers in French West Africa. A United Nations inquiry on slavery in 1963 found the institution alive and well in several countries. Newspaper reports today often highlight the existence of slavery here and there in Africa. One such report in 1980 stated that ninety thousand black Africans were said to live as slaves to Arab masters in Mauritania.

The abolition of the Atlantic slave trade and slavery was one of the most important developments in history. It has often been remembered and characterized as either incredibly noble and consequential or ingloriously spurious. The British campaign against slavery, noted the nineteenth-century Irish historian W. E. H. Lecky, "may probably be regarded as among the three or four perfectly virtuous pages comprised in the history of nations." Former Brazilian slaves, however, lamented:

> Everything in this world changes,
> Only the life of the Negro remains the same:
> He works to die of hunger,
> The 13th of May fooled him!

Historian Rebecca Scott argues that slave emancipation was neither a transcendent liberation nor a complete swindle. Freedom was significant to those who were liberated and liberated themselves. The mere fact that slaves had risked their lives to rebel against slavery, and that nearly everywhere slaves were at least partially responsible for destroying the institution, tells us that slavery was a despised condition. Slavery had separated families and freedom brought them and kept them together. Slavery created conditions that reduced populations of slaves whereas freedom brought higher fertility and lower mortality. Slavery had imposed upon slaves whipping and other forms of violent discipline and punishment whereas freedom brought release from systematic and brutal violence. Slavery had generally prevented literacy and education but freedom brought opportunity for self-improvement. The list goes on demonstrating what should be obvious, that slavery was relentlessly bad and freedom brought considerable improvement.

The end of slavery, however, did not mean the end of subordination, inferiority, discrimination or poverty for most former slaves. In the Americas, although several governments provided compensation for former slaveholders, none compensated the former slaves or provided any kind of assistance to help them become independent and productive citizens. Former slaves faced a variety of legal and political systems. Except in Haiti, however, former slaves and their descendants found themselves politically powerless and generally on the bottom rung of civil society with few rights and privileges. Emancipation brought a variety of working and living conditions for former slaves. Many men continued to work on plantations although women often dropped out of fieldwork. Many entered into contracts that legally bound them to their plantation for a specified number of years. There were enough dropouts in the plantation zones of the Americas, however, to force planters and their governments to import hundreds of thousands of contract laborers from Europe, India, China and elsewhere. Some former slaves became semi-independent farmers as renters and sharecroppers working someone's land. In some regions the plantation system did not survive slavery and the former slaves became subsistence peasant farmers who remained dirt poor. In Jamaica where the plantation system continued for a time, there were an estimated fifty thousand new small farmers by 1865. Some former slaves abandoned their plantations and joined the impoverished underclass in the towns and cities where they could only take the most undesirable jobs when jobs were available. Two former slaves in Brazil remembered: "The [Italian] immigrants were in the factories and in commerce. The only work left for the blacks was to clean houses and offices, cart wood, and other chores. We were all underemployed."

Emancipation did not deliver the Promised Land. It marked the beginning of a new struggle for dignity, equality and prosperity.

13.7 Further Reading

Roger Anstey, *The Atlantic Slave Trade and British Abolition, 1760–1810* (London, 1975).

Robin Blackburn, *The Overthrow of Colonial Slavery, 1776–1848* (London, 1988).

Thomas Clarkson, *The History of the Rise, Progress, and Accomplishment of the Abolition of the African Slave-Trade by the British Parliament* (London, 1808).

Robert Conrad, *The Destruction of Brazilian Slavery, 1850–1888* (Berkeley, 1972).

David Brion Davis, *The Problem of Slavery in the Age of Revolution, 1770–1823* (New York, 1975).

David Brion Davis, *Slavery and Human Progress* (Ithaca, New York, 1984).

Seymour Drescher, *Econocide: British Slavery in the Era of Abolition* (Pittsburgh, 1977).

Seymour Drescher, *The Mighty Experiment: Free Labor Versus Slavery in British Emancipation* (Oxford, 2002).

W. E. B. Du Bois, *The Suppression of the African Slave-Trade to the United States of America, 1638–1870* (Cambridge, Mass., 1896).

David Eltis, *Economic Growth and the Ending of the Transatlantic Slave Trade* (New York, 1987).

Mose Elias Levy, *A Plan for the Abolition of Slavery* (London, 1828).

Michael A. Gomez, *Reversing Sail: A History of the African Diaspora* (Cambridge, 2005).

Adam Hochschild, *Bury the Chains: Prophets and Rebels in the Fight to Free an Empire's Slaves* (Boston, 2005).

Martin A. Klein, editor, *Breaking the Chains: Slavery, Bondage, and Emancipation in Modern Africa and Asia* (Madison, 1993).

Robin Law, editor, *From Slave Trade to 'Legitimate' Commerce: The Commercial Transition in Nineteenth-Century West Africa* (Cambridge, 1995).

Suzanne Meiers and Richard Roberts, editors, *The End of Slavery in Africa* (Madison, 1988).

John Newton, *Thoughts upon the African Slave Trade* (London, 1788).

Cassandra Pybus, *Epic Journeys of Freedom: Runaway Slaves of the American Revolution and their Global Quest for Liberty* (Boston, 2006).

Benjamin Quarles, *The Negro in the American Revolution* (Chapel Hill, 1961).

Simon Schama, *Rough Crossings: Britain, the Slaves and the American Revolution* (New York, 2006).

Julius Sherrard Scott, III, "The Common Wind: Currents of Afro-American Communication in the Era of the Haitian Revolution," Ph.D. dissertation, Duke University, Durham, 1986.

Rebecca J. Scott, *Slave Emancipation in Cuba: The Transition to Free Labor, 1860–1899* (Princeton, 1985).

Robert Brent Toplin, *The Abolition of Slavery in Brazi* (New York, 1975).

James Walvin, *An African's Life: The Life and Times of Olaudah Equiano, 1745–1797* (London, 1998).

Eric Williams, *Capitalism & Slavery* (Chapel Hill, 1994).

Epilogue

The Atlantic World was a bounded world, one limited in space and time. The collapse and disintegration of the fundamental structures that connected and defined the Atlantic World began in the late eighteenth century and required another century to complete. During this same period the economic, technological and organizational capabilities that Western Europe first developed in the Atlantic were unleashed across the globe. A fragmented world of more or less autonomous cultures, societies and states gave way to an increasingly connected, interdependent and uniform world. To put it simply, the fall of the Atlantic World and the rise of the modern world is one of the most important transitions in history.

The processes of dissolution and formation took place roughly at the same time. In this book, the demise of the key connections entwining the Atlantic World is shown to have taken place beginning in the 1770s and extending into the 1880s. In his history of the origins of the modern world, C. A. Bayly directs his attention to the period from 1780 to 1914. These large and complex transitions are very closely related, much like the two faces of a coin. The downfall of the European empires in the Atlantic took place as a new surge of European imperialism and colonialism swept over Africa, Asia and the Pacific. The winding down of merchant capitalism as the economic adhesive holding together all of the ports, hinterlands and societies around the Atlantic World occurred as revolutions in agricultural and industrial productivity were ramped up. The primacy of high-value luxury commodities in world trade would soon be eclipsed by increasing quantities of affordable manufactures that would flood the markets of just about every commercial society in the world. The abolition of the Atlantic slave trade and New World slavery took place as plantation agriculture expanded significantly into Africa and Asia. Indentured workers from India, China and Japan, bound by their indentures and debt, were sent to the plantations around the world. This replacement of the Atlantic slave trade produced what one British prime minister called a "new system of slavery." Great transitions in history have often been portrayed as the unwinding and recharging of epochal cycles. Of course, this is a metaphor but it is a powerfully suggestive and popular metaphor that has guided our thinking about the past for many generations. "Everything disappears and is replaced," as one eighteenth-century philosopher put it, "but nothing perishes." History is change and continuity.

The societies perched around the Atlantic Ocean began to break out of a long pattern of rough cohesion and synchronization starting in the 1770s and 1780s. Forces of divergence and globalization began to bring to an end the patterns of coherence and congruity that make it possible to speak of an Atlantic World in the first place. The wealth and power of the states and regions of the North Atlantic began to far outpace those of the South Atlantic. Some of the most important, productive and wealthy spots in the Atlantic World in the seventeenth and eighteenth centuries – Upper Peru, Saint Domingue and South Carolina – had become some of the most impoverished societies by the dawn of the twentieth century. At the beginning of the eighteenth century, the extremely small plantation colony of Barbados (counting both Englishmen and African slaves) had a per capita income higher than Great Britain. Such an absurdity could only exist during an age when plantations produced the agricultural equivalent of silver and gold. In contrast, relatively neglected and undeveloped regions and colonies – New England, Canada and Argentina – were transformed into dynamic and wealthy societies by the end of the nineteenth century. During the nineteenth century, the national economies of the North Atlantic increasingly constructed a system of mature capitalism that created wide gaps between a few rich countries and all of the rest. "By 1913 the income level in Western Europe and its Western Offshoots," writes Angus Maddison, "was more than six times that in the rest of the world."

During the nineteenth and twentieth centuries, the growing divergence between the North and South Atlantic was not simply an economic matter. While European and American societies created nation-states, almost all regions in Africa were reduced to the status of colonies. The relative success of constitutional systems of government in Western Europe and North America was contrasted by difficulties in establishing political stability and representative governments in Latin America. The enormous productive capacity and growing wealth of the North Atlantic states has meant that the capitals that counted diplomatically, financially and militarily were London, New York, Washington, Paris, Berlin and even Moscow, not Havana, Mexico City and Rio de Janeiro or Lagos, Brazzaville and Luanda. The partition and colonization of Africa in the late nineteenth century brought more than ten million square miles and one hundred million people under the control of just eight European empires. However, despite the best efforts of colonial exploitation, Africa never became economically or strategically important to Europe. In 1890, Sir John Pope-Hennessy, a former British governor of the Gold Coast, was asked, "Is Central Africa worth having?" He answered emphatically, "No." There was no scramble for Latin America following the African model, although North Atlantic powers occasionally intervened and even invaded a few countries. Financiers in London, New York and Paris invested many millions in copper mines and rubber plantations, ports, railroads and government bonds. The United States became jealous and, at times, quite

Table E.1. Economic growth of world regions, 1820–2000

	1820–1900	1900–1950	1950–2000
OECD	1.2	1.3	2.6
Latin America	0.6	1.7	1.5
Asia	0.2	0.1	3.5
Africa	0.4	1.0	1.0
World Average	0.8	1.1	2.5

Average annual percentage growth of per capita gross domestic product (GDP). OECD is the Organization of Economic Cooperation and Development, the so-called club of rich counties that includes North America, Western Europe, Japan, Australia and New Zealand. Because Japan is included in the OECD group, it is not part of Asia in this accounting.

Source: Bill Emmott, *20:21 Vision: Twentieth-Century Lessons for the Twenty-first Century* (2003), p 326; Stanley L. Engerman and Kenneth L. Sokoloff, "Factor Endowments, Institutions, and Differential Paths of Growth Among New World Economies."

paranoid about Old World interests and interference in Latin America and often made itself a bossy neighbor. Nevertheless, in the two centuries since the collapse of the Spanish and Portuguese empires the great powers never fought a war over territory, resources or the allegiance of Latin America or any of its nations.

Over the past two centuries, the economies of Latin America and Africa have simply not kept up with those of North America and Western Europe or the "tigers" of Asia. By and large, the countries of Latin America and Africa have created some of the slowest rates of economic growth in the world. Over the period from 1820 to 1998, Latin American economies grew on average 1.2 percent a year while those in Africa created a 0.7 percent annual increase. In comparison, the United States economy expanded at a 1.7 percent annual average. What this means in dollars and cents is that African economies saw a three-fold expansion since 1820, Latin American economies grew approximately ten-fold and the United States economy increased almost twenty-five-fold during this same period. In our modern era even more than in the past, sustained economic growth and development signifies and sustains military strength, strategic power and ideological allure. Long-term economic growth trajectories, as displayed in Table E.1, shaped the unequal distribution of power and wellbeing across the globe.

This desynchronization within the Atlantic basin was pushed along by the acceleration of global integration. Clipper ships and steamships, transcontinental railroads, telegraph lines and cables, interoceanic canals, new massive streams of immigrants and, in time, radio, television, airplanes and satellites brought more societies into closer contact than ever before (see Map E.1). European imperialism as well as Western philosophies, institutions, technologies, styles and even certain values became truly global phenomena. In the nineteenth century and even more in the twentieth century, nonwestern (Japan and Turkey, for example) and postcolonial (Brazil and South Africa) societies began to pick and choose what appeared to be the most useful western exports to "progress" and "modernize." Governments and nationalist

Map E.1. The Nineteenth-Century Atlantic.

movements began to address the rift in wealth and power between western and nonwestern, or perhaps more salient between Northern and Southern, societies. To catch up, the most independent nonwestern and postcolonial societies embraced western technology, economic practices and educational institutions by the late nineteenth and early twentieth centuries. Latin American countries invited European military missions to professionalize their armies. Chinese reformers adopted western institutional and managerial models and skills. In the 1890s, the government of Japan required its bureaucrats and officials to adopt western dress. Elite and popular movements in colonies, many of which were energized by western ideologies, began to demand reform and to resist colonial rule. In Africa, Asia and the Middle East, nation-states arose in the second half of the twentieth century out of the territorial husks of empire.

Rapid population growth in Europe and in its overseas settler societies in the eighteenth and nineteenth centuries led to a world where more than one of every four inhabitants of the globe in 1900 was European or of European descent. The power and reach of Western culture, when viewed from this demographic perspective, is perhaps more comprehensible if not necessarily

Table E.2 Regional populations of the world, 1820–2000

	1820	1913	2000
Europe	190,000,0000	480,000,000	729,000,000
Latin America	21,700,000	81,000,000	531,000,000
North America	11,000,000	107,000,000	314,000,000
Africa	74,000,000	125,000,000	821,000,000
World	1,000,000,000	1,800,000,000	6,100,000,000

Source: Angus Maddison, *The World Economy: Historical Statistics* (2003), see Table 7a; and *The New York Times Guide to Essential Knowledge* (2004), p. 173.

agreeable. After 1820, over sixty million Europeans left home seeking better lives in the United States and Canada, Latin America, Australia and New Zealand as well as in colonies and enclaves in Africa and Asia. This European diaspora increased the diffusion of western institutions, religion, technology, manners and more around the world. As Europe became more wealthy and urban, birth rates fell and population growth slowed. In the first half of the twentieth century, war and disease killed over fifty million Europeans. With the expansion of affordable medicines and public health regimes throughout Latin America and Africa, mortality began to decline and population growth accelerated. During the twentieth century, the countries of the South Atlantic raced ahead of those in the North Atlantic in terms of population, as Table E.2 shows, even as they lagged behind in terms of economic development. One of the consequences of this turn of events was the new reverse flow of immigrants from Asia, Africa and Latin America to Western Europe and North America.

The fall of the Atlantic World does not mean that the deeply rooted habits and arrangements did not influence what came after. We can trace many contemporary developments – certain problems as well as distinct benefits – to their origins in the Atlantic World. The spread of epidemic disease from the Old World continued in the nineteenth and twentieth centuries. "Wherever the European has trod," noted Charles Darwin, "death seems to pursue the aboriginal." Modern "scientific racism" appeared as a result of centuries of enslavement of Africans and conflicts with Native Americans. Nationalism and its attendant vices of imperial expansion and ethnic cleansing began during the death throes of the Atlantic World. The expansion of liberal principles and constitutional systems of government around the world started with the Age of Revolution in the Atlantic World. This matter of change and continuity is one of the quandaries of history that often leads to heated disputes.

Some recent scholars are inclined to believe that the worst elements of that earlier world – colonialism, slavery, fanaticism and bureaucracy – became the keystones to modernity and, in time, produced the horrors of the twentieth century. For these postcolonialists, there is a straight line from the Inquisition to Auschwitz. The colonial/modern dichotomy that has long structured our sense of history supposedly is a myth that empowers contemporary forms of domination and exploitation. "Globalization and neoliberalism are new names, new forms of rearticulating the colonial difference," writes

Walter D. Mignolo. "The colonial period may have ended, but the coloniality of power continues to order planetary relations." Certainly, the modern world has seen plenty of atrocities and too much hatred and savagery disguised as the price of progress. However, the fantasy that European blood and culture was superior to all others should not be replaced by the equally spurious conceit that the West is the font of all modern evil. To take this leap, one needs to believe that the basic human flaws that have led to war, slavery and conquest in all cultures in the past are of a fundamentally different character than those that produced European imperialism. Of course, this brief concluding essay is not the place to engage in any comprehensive manner this type of historical problem. I must leave this problem to other historians and their books. Here I can only affirm a relatively optimistic outlook based on years of reading, travel and conversation.

I would like to believe that same sentiments and principles that brought down empires, monarchies and slavery are requisite in the struggle against racism, poverty and oppression. One of the most important improvements over the past two centuries is that our standards for decent behavior are much higher than before. Today we no longer have to argue against chattel slavery and caste hierarchies. The battle has moved on to decent wages, safe working conditions and the opportunity for women and men as well as people of all backgrounds, religions and colors to work and achieve all that their efforts and talents can provide. Colonialism and tyranny are unacceptable, even in the guise of democratization or people's republics. "It is good that we thus agitate for further progress," Robert Wright proclaims, "and all the signs are that this agitation goes with the flow of history."

However, whether this is true or not does not affect the fact, or perhaps I should say the argument, that the most important systems and structures that long ago distinguished the Atlantic World no longer exist today. We have a powerful Atlantic alliance, billions of dollars of cross-Atlantic commerce and much more contact and communication between Europe, Africa and the Americas than ever before. All of these new Atlantic connections and relationships are part and partial of wider, multitudinous and global networks of diplomacy, business, science, travel, entertainment and so on. The Atlantic World existed in a bigger and more jagged world when there were great moats and walls. When the world became smaller and the walls were gradually dismantled – as the world became flat, as Thomas Friedman has put it – the Mediterranean, Atlantic and Indian Ocean Worlds and any others dissolved into the modern, or should we call it, the universal world.

Glossary

aldeias   A Portuguese term referring to mission villages of native Americans supervised by Portuguese clergy, generally, Jesuits; similar to Spanish *reducciónes* and French *reserves*.

anker   Liquid measure equal to approximately ten gallons of wine (38.4 liters).

arroba   As a Spanish weight, an *arroba* equals about twenty-five pounds; as a Portuguese weight, it comes in at about thirty pounds.

asiento   A Spanish term referring to the trading contract and official license awarded to kingdoms and charter companies to supply African slaves to Spanish America.

astrolabe   An astronomical instrument used to measure the height above the horizon of celestial bodies. The mariner's astrolabe was a device to measure the altitude of the sun or a star to determine one's approximate latitude.

bandeiras   A Portuguese term referring to the flags carried by military companies that marched into the backlands of Brazil to capture and enslave native Americans.

bandeirantes   Participants – Portuguese, African, Indian, Mameluco, mulatto or some other racial mixture – in a *bandeiras*.

bossal/bozal   A slave brought directly to the New World from Africa and therefore speaks no European language, has no knowledge of Christianity and is outside of civilization.

Brasilwood   *Caesalpina echinata*, a hard red wood found in South America, among other places, and used for making red dye.

buccaneer   Another term for pirate, a word derived from the French *boucan*, or grill for cooking the wild cattle that roamed the islands of the Caribbean. The French also employed the term *flibustiers*, the Dutch called them *zee-rovers* and the Spanish used the word *corsarios*.

cacique	An Arawak term originating in the Caribbean for an hereditary Indian chief or ruler. The Spanish adopted this term and used it throughout Spanish America.
capitão-mor	A Portuguese term meaning "captain-major"; a civil and military officer in overseas Portuguese territories. In Angola, *capitães-mors* commanded inland forts or trading factories.
captaincy	A grant of dominion in the overseas territorial empire of Portugal to a private individual, a *donatorio*, who is given the authority to govern, assign land and profit from the territory.
caravel	A type of Europe ship of the fifteenth and sixteenth centuries characterized by its small rounded size, skeleton-framed hull and three masts usually carrying one or more lateen sails. A *caravela redonda* was a fully rigged ship with a square main sail and a triangular (lateen) sail at the mizzen mast.
careen	The operation of laying a wooden sailing ship down on one side ashore for the purpose of exposing the opposite side and the bottom so that it could be cleaned of weeds and barnacles and make repairs. This practice was common for most trading vessels throughout the Atlantic World.
carrack	Carrack is a term used to describe the new three-masted ocean traders of the sixteenth and seventeenth centuries. In time, this type of ship was identified by large forward and aft castles. Also see *não*.
Carrera de Indias	A Spanish term meaning the "Indies Run" and referring to the tightly controlled and regulated system of annual trade convoys between Spain and Spanish America.
casta	A term for all persons of mixed blood, including freed blacks, in Spanish America.
Cathay	The name by which China was known by Europeans, beginning in the thirteenth century. Marco Polo made it famous, and its derivation comes from the Mongal *Khitai*, the name of the tribe that founded the Liao Dynasty (916–1125 C.E.).
chip log and reel	A device for measuring the speed of a vessel through the water. It consisted of a triangular piece of wood weighted on one side and attached to a line with marked (knots) lengths. When thrown from the stern of a vessel, the line was allowed to run out for a specified time. The number of knots that had come off the reel determined the vessel's speed.
cimarrónes	A Spanish term meaning "wild" or "shy" and originally applied to wild horses or cattle, and then quickly thereafter to fugitive slaves or runaways.
cofradía	A Spanish term for a lay brotherhood or religious confraternity. In Spanish America (as well as Portuguese Brazil), there were *cofradías* of Spaniards and Spanish-Americans, Native Americans, African slaves and African Americans. The Portuguese term is *irmandades*.

compass	An instrument whose magnetized metal needle aligns itself with the magnetic fields of the earth. This causes one end of the needle to point north. Mariners used this device to navigate ships.
concubine	A woman who lives with a man to whom she is not legally married.
coureurs de bois	A French term for backwoodsmen who traveled into the interior of New France to trade with Native Americans.
criollo	A Spanish term for a Spaniard born in America; the English equivalent is *creole*. The Spanish also used this term to refer to African American slaves who were American-born and acculturated into Spanish American society. The equivalent Portuguese word is *crioulo*.
dead reckoning	Estimating the location and speed of a ship at sea using deductive reasoning and a variety of methods including wind, waves, bird sightings and current.
degradados	A Portuguese term that refers to convicts or exiles, most often men who were banished from Portugal by force as punishment for a crime.
doctrina	An Indian parish administered by friars.
dollar	From the German *Taler,* or *Joachimstaler*, a coin of the sixteenth century made of silver from a mine in St. Joachim's valley, a town in northwestern Bohemia. (In Low German, a *taler* is a *daler*.) By 1581, the use of the term "dollar" was recorded in English for the Spanish *peso* or piece of eight. In 1785, the Continental Congress established the dollar as the currency of the United States.
donatório	A Portuguese term meaning "donatary," or lord-proprietor, a person granted land and lordship or judicial authority over it.
engagé	A French term referring to an indentured servant who contracted to work a certain number of years for payment of passage to New France or another French colony.
engenho	A Portuguese term – literally, "engine" – that came to refer to a sugar mill and the entire plantation. *Engenhos* were found in Portuguese Madeira, São Tomé and Brazil.
encomienda	A Spanish term for a royal grant of the tribute or labor of a population of native Americans to a private individual, an *encomendero*, usually as a reward for service to the crown in a military campaign.
entrepôt	From the French verb *entroposer*, "to store." The historical meaning of this word refers to a commercial distribution center, usually a port city, where goods were shipped and deposited for export later to other countries. In the seventeenth century, Amsterdam was the most important *entrepôt* in Europe, a distribution center for commodities from the Americas, Africa and Asia.

estancia   A Spanish term for a ranch.

fathom   A unit of measure. The term is from Old English, *fæthm*, meaning the length of the outstretched arms. The figurative meaning is to get to the bottom of or understand fully, from the literal sense of to take soundings. As a measurement, a fathom is six feet.

fazenda   A Portuguese term for a landed estate or cattle ranch, similar to the Spanish term *hacienda*. In São Tomé, a *fazenda* was a sugar plantation.

fetitço   A Portuguese term meaning fetish. Beginning in the fifteenth and sixteenth centuries, it referred to the Portuguese and general European understanding (or misunderstanding) of West African religion. "Fetish" referred to charms or material objects in which a spirit or spirit dwells and may be used for magical purposes, and to magic and sorcery in general.

feitoria   A Portuguese term for a factory, trading post or commercial-military outpost headed by a *feitor*, or factor.

filhos da terra A Portuguese term meaning "sons of the country, land, or soil." The term in Africa generally referred to Portuguese-African mulattos.

florin   Gold coin produced by the mint in Florence for the Habsburg empire. Later synonymous with the Dutch guilder and source of the Dutch monetary symbol *f*.

fluyt   A Dutch merchant vessel, also spelled *fluit* and known to the English as a "fly-boat." This cargo ship was inexpensive to build and because it was lightly armed, if at all, and possessed a simple three-masted rig, it required a small crew. The Dutch dominated Atlantic commerce in the seventeenth century with this economical vessel.

galeón   This vessel evolved from carracks in the sixteenth century. *Galeóns* or galleons were longer and slimmer vessels than carracks and had smaller fore- and aft-castles. Galleons could be trading ships or warships.

gens de couler A French term meaning "people of color" and referring to mulattos in the French West Indies. Another term meaning the same thing in the eighteenth century was *affranchis*.

grand blanc   A French term meaning literally "great white" and referring to the plantation owners, wealthy merchants and high government officials in the French West Indies in the eighteenth century.

habitant   A French term designating landowning farmers in New France and plantation owners in the French West Indies.

habitation   A French term for house or residence, which came to mean farm or plantation in the West Indies.

hacienda   A Spanish word referring to a diversified agricultural estate in Spanish America; similar although not exactly the same as the Portuguese *fazenda*.

hogshead	A measure of 6 ankers, or 60 gallons (of wine); equal to 230 liters. An English hogshead of sugar contained approximately 1,600 pounds.
Huguenot	French Protestants and the Protestant movement in the sixteenth century.
ingenio	A Spanish term for a sugar plantation and mill.
ladino	A Christianized African slave who spoke Spanish or had some knowledge of Spanish culture.
lançado	A Portuguese term for an "outcast" or exile who tended to settle in the Senegambia in Africa and on the coast of Brazil in the sixteenth century.
lateen rigged	A triangular sail set at an angle to a short mast. Lateen rigging was pioneered on caravels in the fourteenth and fifteenth centuries. Northern Europeans who went to the Mediterranean named this technology after the culture they observed using it, "latin."
latitude	Imaginary lines that run east to west on the surface of the earth. The latitude determines location north or south on the globe.
lavradores de cana	A Portuguese term meaning "workers of the cane" and referring to small cane farmers, either landowners or renters, who grew their own cane and processed it for a fee, or a share of the crop, at the local *engenhos*.
legua	One Spanish *legua* or league is a measure of distance equal to approximately three and a half to four miles.
league	One English or French league is equal to approximately three miles.
longitude	Imaginary lines that run north to south on the surface of the earth. The prime meridian is 0° and each degree of longitude is equal to one hour of time.
malaguetta pepper	Red or cayenne pepper found on the coast of West Africa. This valuable spice was called by contemporaries "grains of paradise," for which the "Grain Coast" of Guinea was named.
mameluco	A Portuguese term referring to the offspring of Portuguese and Indian parents.
maravedí	A Spanish copper coin of small value. There were 450 *maravedis* in a silver *peso*, or piece of eight.
maroon	From the Spanish word *cimarróm* (wild) for runaway slave. A *maroon* is both a runaway slave and a community of runaway slaves.
mestiço	A Portuguese term that, in Africa and the islands of the near Atlantic, referred to mulattos.
mestizo	A person of mixed Spanish and Indian heritage, usually someone with a Spanish father and an Indian mother.

mit'a/mita   A Quechua term for draft rotation labor tribute in the Inka state. The Spanish adopted this term for forced Indian labor to the mines of Potosí in the post-conquest period.

mulatto   A derivation of the word *mulo*, which refers to the hybrid offspring of a horse and a mule. It became a term used to designate a person of mixed blood, usually someone with a Caucasian father and an African or African-American mother.

não   A Spanish term, taken from the Portuguese word *nau*, that refers to a large cargo or warship, a carrack. One of Columbus' three ships on his first passage to the New World was a *não* – the flagship, *Santa María*, a ship estimated to have been 120 tons. The other two smaller ships were caravels.

nau   A Portuguese term for a large sailing ship, a mid-to-late fifteenth century Portuguese carrack.

pardo   A Spanish term meaning literally "brown" or "dark," which in Spanish America generally referred to a mulatto. A dreaded *pardocracía* referred to a state or society under *pardo* rule.

patroonship   An Anglicized Dutch term referring to a grant of land and political authority (a fief) awarded to an individual, a *patroon*, who had the obligation to settle fifty colonists within four years.

Paulistas   The residents of São Paulo, Brazil, famous in the colonial era for their "talent" as Indian fighters.

petit blanc   A French term meaning literally "small white" and referring to the white laboring and artisan class in the French West Indies in the eighteenth century.

pirate   An oceanic outlaw who sailed with a like-minded crew and raided commerce for booty; a similar term was buccaneer.

plantation   From Middle French *plantation*, and directly from Latin *plantātiõnem*, a "planting." The English referred to colonies as plantations in the seventeenth century. An early eighteenth-century English dictionary (Philips' *Dictionary*, 1706) defined a plantation as a large farm or estate on which cotton, tobacco or other crops are grown.

portolano   An Italian term that denotes a manuscript pilot book that provided detailed guidance for sailing specific coasts. Also called *portolan* and *portulan* charts, the first such charts were Venetian and Genoese charts that sketched the outline and geography of the coasts of the Mediterranean in the late Middle Ages.

provision   Gardens maintained by slaves on lands provided by a
  grounds   plantation owner. In the West Indies, the provision grounds are usually in the mountains, some distance from the plantation. Slaves cultivated fruits and vegetables for sale and profit during Sunday markets.

quadrant	An instrument for determining the altitude of heavenly bodies and the latitude of ships. It is a quarter of a circle with a plumb bob suspended from its apex. Held vertically and aligned with the sun or a star, the plumb line (a string with a weight on it) falls across the scale of degree markings from 0–90 degrees on the curved edge, indicating the angle of elevation.
quintal	A Spanish weight of 100 pounds. A quintal is also a traditional English weight for salt fish equal to about 112 pounds.
quipo\u	A knotted-string mnemonic device used for large quantities.
Peninsular	A Spaniard born in the Iberian Peninsula who settled in Spanish America. In Mexico, *Peninsulares* were called *gachupins* ("spurs"), whereas in Peru they were called *chapetones* ("greenhorns").
privateer	A ship's captain and crew that had legal authorization ("Letter of Marquee and Reprisal") to attack the shipping of an enemy nation.
regular clergy	In the Roman Catholic Church, the regular clergy refers to those clerics who live by their own rules (*reglas*) in religious orders. Examples include Franciscans, Dominicans, Augustinians and the Company of Jesus, or Jesuits.
reserve	A French Jesuit mission community for Native Americans in New France; similar to the Portuguese *aldeia* and the Spanish *reducción*.
secular clergy	In the Roman Catholic Church, the secular clergy refers to those clerics who "live in the world" (*seculum*) such as parish priests and bishops.
seigneur	A French term meaning "lord" and in America referring to those who were granted *seigneuries*.
seigneuries	A French term meaning "fiefs," or large tracts of land, in New France granted to favored individuals, usually nobles or ecclesiastical bodies, who promoted colonization and collected rent from their "vassals" or *habitants*; similar to Dutch patroonships and, on a smaller scale, English proprietary colonies and Portuguese captaincies.
ship of the line	A European warship with mounted guns designed to fight in a line of battle. These large and complex warships with 100 guns or more dominated the navies of the maritime powers during the eighteenth century.
tithe	The obligatory religious tax, one-tenth of the increase of goods or money.
ton	A short ton equals 2,000 pounds. A ton is also the traditional estimate of the displacement of a ship, originally the space to put a *tun* (wooden container, equivalent to eight barrels) of wine, e.g., a 100-ton ship would not carry 100 tons of salt cod. Cargo tonnage was less than cubic capacity.

volta do mar A nautical maneuver invented by the Portuguese involving a ship sailing far west into the South Atlantic to catch a southern-blowing wind to reach Guinea or South Africa, and thus the sea route to the East Indies.

wampum White and purple shell beads used by American Indians in belts for ceremonial diplomatic purposes and for money and exchange.

Select Bibliography

Primary Sources

de Acosta, José, *Natural and Moral History of the Indies*, edited by Jane E. Mangan, translated by Frances López-Morillas (Durham, NC: Duke University Press, 2002).

Adair, James, *The History of the American Indians* (London, 1775).

Adams, Captain John, *Sketches Taken During Ten Voyages to Africa Between the Years 1796 and 1800* (London: Hurst, Robinson and Co., 1800).

Astley, Thomas, *A New General Collection of Voyages and Travels*, 4 volumes (London, 1745–7).

Bailyn, Bernard (ed.), *Pamphlets of the American Revolution, 1750–1776* (Cambridge, MA: Belknap Press, 1965).

de Betanzos, Juan, *Narrative of the Inca*, translated by Roland Hamilton and Dana Buchanan (Austin: University of Texas Press, 1996).

Blake, John W. (trans. and ed.), *Europeans in West Africa, 1450–1560*, 2nd series, volumes 18–87 (London: Hakluyt Society, 1942).

Bosman, William, *A New and Accurate Description of the Coast of Guinea, Divided into the Gold, Slave, and the Ivory Coasts*, 2nd edition (London, 1721).

Brown, Robert (ed.), *The History and Description of Africa and of the Notable Things Therein Contains, Written by Al-Hassan Ibn-Mohammed Al-Wezaz Al-Fasi, A Moor, Babtised as Giovani Leones, but Better Known as Leo Africanus. Done Into English in the Year 1600 by John Pory* [1526], 3 volumes (London: Hakluyt Society, 1896).

de Bry, Th., *Conquistadores Azteken en Inca's*, gravures van Th. De Bry (Amsterdam: Van Hoeve, 1980).

de Bry, Th., *De Ontdekking van de Nieuwe Wereld*, gravures van Th. De Bry (Amsterdam: Van Hoeve, 1979).

Burke, Edmund, *An Account of the European Settlements in America*, 2 volumes (London, 1770).

Cadornega, António de Oliveira, *História Geral das Guerras Angolanas* [1683], 3 vols. Anotado e corrigido por José Matias Delgado (Lisboa: Divisão de Publicações e Biblioteca, Agência Geral das Colónias, 1940).

Cabeza de Vaca, Alvar Nuñez, *Castaways*, translated by Francis M. López-Morillas, edited by Enrique Pupo-Walker (Berkeley: University of California Press, 1993).

Cabeza de Vaca, Alvar Nuñez, *The Narrative of Cabeza de Vaca*, translated and edited by Rolena Adorno and Patrick Charles Pautz (Lincoln: University of Nebraska Press, 1999).

de Charlevoix, P., *Journal of a Voyage to North-America: Undertaken by Order of the French King*, 2 volumes, edited by Louise Phelps Kellogg (Chicago: Caxton Club, 1923).

Child, Lydia Maria, *An Appeal in Favor of That Class of Americans Called Africans* (Boston, 1833; reprinted by Amherst: University of Massachusetts Press, 1996).

de Cieza de León, Pedro, *The Discovery and Conquest of Peru: Chronicles of the New World Encounter*, translated and edited by Alexandra Parma Cook and Noble David Cook (Durham, NC: Duke University Press, 1998).

Clarkson, Thomas, *The History of the Rise, Progress, and Accomplishment of the Abolition of the African Slave-Trade by the British Parliament* (London, 1808).

Clayton, Lawrence A., Vernon James Knight, Jr. and Edward C. Moore (eds.), *The De Soto Chronicles: The Expedition of Hernando de Soto to North America in 1539–1543*, 2 volumes (Tuscaloosa: University of Alabama Press, 1993).

Cobo, Father Bernabé, *History of the Inca Empire: An Account of the Indian's Customs and Their Origin Together with a Treatise on Inca Legends, History, and Social Institutions* [1653], translated and edited by Roland Hamilton (Austin: University of Texas Press, 1979).

Conneau, Captain T., *A Slaver's Logbook or Twenty Year's Residence in Africa* (Englewood Cliffs, NJ: Prentice Hall, 1976).

Cortés, Hernán, *Letters from Mexico*, translated and edited by Anthony Pagden (New York: Orion Press, 1971).

Crone, Gerald R. (ed.), *The Voyages of Cadamosto and Other Documents on Western Africa in the Second Half of the Fifteenth Century*, 2nd series, volume 80 (London: Hakluyt Society, 1937).

Cugoano, Ottobah, *Thoughts and Sentiments on the Evil and Wicked Traffic of the Slavery and Commerce of the Human Species, Humbly Submitted to the Inhabitants of Great-Britain, by Ottobah Cugoano, a Native of Africa* (London, 1787).

Cunningham, J., *An Essay on Trade and Commerce* (London, 1770).

Defoe, Daniel, *A General History of the Robberies and Murders of the Most Notorious Pirates* [1724] (New York: Carroll and Graf Publishers, 1999).

Díaz del Castillo, Bernal, *The Discovery and Conquest of Mexico*, translated and edited by A.P. Maudslay (New York: Farrar, Straus and Girous, 1956).

Díaz del Castillo, Bernal, *The True History of the Conquest of Mexico, written in the Year 1568*, translated by Maurice Keatinge (London: High Street, 1800).

de Diereville, Sieur, *Relation of the Voyage to Port Royal in Acadia or New France*, [1708] (Toronto: Champlain Society, 1933).

Douglass, William, *A Summary, Historical and Political, of the First Planting, Progressive Improvements, and Present State of the British Settlements in North America* (Boston, 1749).

Dunn, Oliver and James E. Kelly, Jr. (eds.), *The Diario of Christopher Columbus's First Voyage to America, 1492–1492: Abstracted by Fray Bartolomé de Las Casas* (Norman: University of Oklahoma Press, 1991).

Durán, Fray Diego, *The History of the Indies of New Spain*, translated by Doris Heyden (Norman: University of Oklahoma Press, 1994).

Eatough, Geoffrey (trans. and ed.), *Selections from Peter Martyr*, Volume V of Repertorium Columbianum (Turnhout, Belgium: Brepols, 1998).

Edwards, Bryan, *An Historical Survey of the French Colony in the Island of St. Domingue* (London, 1797).

Edwards, Bryan, *The History, Civil and Commercial, of the British Colonies in the West Indies*, 2 volumes (Dublin: Luke White, 1793).

Encyclopaedia Britannica; or, A Dictionary of Arts and Sciences, 3 volumes (Edinburgh, 1768–71).

Equiano, Olaudah, *The Interesting Narrative and Other Writings* [1789], edited by Vincent Carretta (London: Penguin Classics, 1995).

Equiano, Olaudah, *The Interesting Narrative of the Life of Olaudah Equiano, or Gustavus Vassa, The African, Written by Himself*, edited by Werner Sollors (New York: W. W. Norton, 2001).

Esquemeling, John, *The Buccaneers of America* [1681] (Glorieta, NM: Rio Grande Press, 1992).

Fernandes Brandão, Ambrósio, *Dialogues of the Great Things of Brazil* [1618], translated by Frederick Arthur, Holden Hall, William F. Harrison and Dorothy Winters Welker (Albuquerque: University of New Mexico Press, 1986).

Gamble, David P. and P. E. H. Hair (eds.), *The Discovery of River Gambia by Richard Jobson, 1623* (London: Hakluyt Society, 1999).

Garcilaso de la Vega, Inca, *Comentarios Reales de los Incas*, 2 tomos, Edición, índice analítico y glosario de Carlos Araníbar (Lima: Fondo de Cultura Económico, 1991).

Goss, John (ed.), *Blaeu's The Grand Atlas of the 17th Century World* (New York: Barnes and Noble Books, 1997).

Guaman Poma de Ayala, Felipe, *El Primer Nueva Corónica y Buen Gobierno* [1615], 3 volumes, translated by Jorge L. Urioste, edited by John V. Murra and Rolena Adorna (Ciudad de México: Siglo Veintiuno, 1980).

Grotius, Hugo, *The Freedom of the Seas*, translated by James Brown Scott (New York: Oxford University Press, 1916).

Hair, P. E. H., Adam Jones and Robin Law (eds.), *Barbot on Guinea: The Writings of Jean Barbot on West Africa, 1678–1712* (London: Hakluyt Society, 1992).

Hair, Paul (ed.), *Barbot on Guinea: The writings of Jean Barbot on West Africa, 1678–1712*, 2 volumes (London: Hakluyt Society, 1992).

Hakluyt, Richard, *Voyages and Discoveries: The Principal Navigations, Voyages, Traffiques and Discoveries of the English Nation* (London: Penguin Books, 1985).

Hall, Douglas (ed.), *In Miserable Slavery: Thomas Thistlewood in Jamaica, 1750–1786* (London: Macmillan, 1989).

Historia General de Las Cosas de Nueva España, Que en Doce Libros y Dos Volumenes Escribió El R. P. Bernardino de Sahagún, Dala a Lux con Notas y Suplementos, Carlos María de Bustamante, 3 tomos (México, 1829).

La Historia General de las Indias con todos los descubrimientos, y con las notables que han acaefcido en ellas, dende que fe ganaron hafta agora, efcrita por Francisco Lopez de Gomera, clerigo. En Anvers. Año M.D. LIII [1553].

Howard, Thomas P., *The Haitian Journal of Lieutenant Howard, York Hussars, 1796–1798*, edited by Roger Norman Buckley (Knoxville: University of Tennessee Press, 1985).

Insert, Paul Erdmann, *Reise nach Guinea und den Karibäischen Inseln in Columbien* (Copenhagen, 1788).

Johnson, Charles, *A General History of the Pyrates* [1724] (London: J. M. Dent, 1972).

Kalm, Pehr, *The America of 1750: Peter Kalm's Travels in North America*, 2 volumes, edited by Adolph B. Benson (New York: Dover, 1966).

Keen, Benjamin (trans. and ed.), *Life and Labor in Ancient Mexico: The Brief and Summary Relation of the Lords of New Spain by Alonso de Zorita* (Norman: University of Oklahoma Press, 1994).

Keen, Benjamin (trans. and ed.), *The Life of the Admiral Christopher Columbus by his Son* (New Brunswick, NJ: Rutgers University Press, 1959).

Lafitau, Joseph-Francois, *Customs of the American Indians Compared with the Customs of Primitive Times*, 2 volumes, edited by William N. Fenton and Elizabeth L. Moore (Toronto: Champlain Society, 1974–7).

Baron de Lahontan, Louis-Armand de Lom d'Arce, *New Voyages to North-America*, 2 volumes, edited by R. G. Thwaites (Chicago: A. C. McClurg, 1905).

de Las Casas, Bartolomé, *The Devastation of the Indies*, translated by Herma Briffault (Baltimore, MD: Johns Hopkins University Press, 1992).

de Las Casas, Bartolomé, *History of the Indies*, translated and edited by Andrée Collard (New York: Harper Torchbooks, 1971).

Levy, Mose Elias, *A Plan for the Abolition of Slavery* (London, 1828), edited and reprinted by Chris Monaco (Micanopy, FL: Wacahoota Press, 1999).

Lewis, Matthew, *Journal of a West India Proprietor during a Residence in the Island of Jamaica*, edited by Judith Terry (Oxford, UK: Oxford University Press, 1999).

de León, Fray Luis, *La perfecta casada*, undécima edición (Madrid: Espasa-Calpe, 1980).

de Léry, Jean, *History of a Voyage to the Land of Brazil*, translation and introduction by Janet Whatley (Berkeley: University of California Press, 1992).

Lescarbot, Marc, *Nova Francia: Or the Description of that part of New France, which is one continent with Virginia*, translated by P. Erondelle (London, 1609).

Leslie, Charles, *A New and Exact Account of Jamaica* (Edinburgh, 1739).

Ligon, Richard, *A True and Exact History of the Island of Barbadoes* (London, 1657).

Lockhart, James (trans. and ed.), *We People Here: Nahuatl Accounts of the Conquest of Mexico*, Volume I of Repertorium Columbianum (Berkeley: University of California Press, 1991).

Lockhart, James, Frances Berdan and Arthur J. O. Anderson (trans. and eds.), *The Tlaxcalan Actas: A Compendium of the Records of the Cabildo of Tlaxcala, 1545–1627* (Salt Lake City: University of Utah Press, 1986).

Long, Edward, *The History of Jamaica or, General Survey of the Ancient and Modern State of That Island*, 3 volumes (London: T. Lowndes, in Fleet-Street, 1774).

López de Gómera, Francisco, *Cortés: The Life of the Conqueror*, translated by Leslie Byrd Simpson (Berkeley: University of California Press, 1964).

Manzano, Juan Francisco, *Autobiography of a Slave*, translated by Evelyn Picon Garfield, edited by Ivan A. Schulman (Detroit, MI: Wayne State University Press, 1996).

de Marees, Pieter, *Description and Historical Account of the Gold Kingdom of Guinea (1602)* translated and edited by Albert van Dantzig and Adam Jones (Oxford, UK: Published for The British Academy by Oxford University Press, 1987).

Markham, Sir Clements (trans. and ed.), *History of the Incas by Pedro Sarmiento de Gamboa and The Execution of the Inca Tupac Amaru by Captain Baltasar de Ocampo* (Cambridge, UK: Hakluyt Society, 1907).

McCalman, Iain (ed.), *'The Horrors of Slavery' and Other Writings by Robert Wedderburn* (Edinburgh: Edinburgh University Press, 1991).

de Medina, Pedro, *A Navigator's Universe: The Libro de Cosmographia of 1538*, translated and edited by Ursula Lamb (Chicago: University of Chicago Press, 1972).

Baron de Montesquieu, Charles de Secondat, *The Spirit of the Laws*, edited by Anne Cohler, Basis Miller and Harola Stone (Cambridge, UK: Cambridge University Press, 1989).

More Excellent Observations of the Estate and Affairs of Holland, Faithfully Translated out of the Dutch Copie (London, 1622).

Moreau de Saint-Méry, Médéric L. E., *Description topographique, physique, civile, politique et historique de la partie francaise de l'isle de Saint Domingue*, 2 volumes (Philadelphia, 1797–8).

Newton, John, *Thoughts upon the African Slave Trade* (London, 1788).

Niane, D. T., *Sundiata: An Epic of Old Mali* (Harlow, UK: Longman, 1994).

Olilby, John, collected and translated, *Africa: Being an Accurate Description of the Regions of AEgypt, Barbary, Lybia, and Billedulgerid* (London, 1670).

Pacheco Pereira, Duarte, *Esmeraldo de Situ Orbis*, translated and edited by George H. T. Kimble, 2nd series, volume 79 (London: Hakluyt Society, 1937).

Paine, Thomas, *Collected Writings* (New York: Library of America, 1995).

Pané, Fray Ramón, *Relación Acerca de las Antigüedades de los Indios*, Nueva version con estudio preliminar, notas y apendices por José Juan Arrom (Ciudad de México: Siglo Veintiuno, 2001).

Pigafetta, Philippo, *A Reporte of the Kingdome of Congo, a Region of Africa, And of the Countries that border rounde about the same*, Drawen out of the writings and discourses of Odoarto Lopes a Portingall, translated by Abraham Hartwell (London: John Wolfe, 1597).

Price, Richard, *Observations on the Importance of the American Revolution* (Boston, 1818).

Raleigh, Sir Walter, *Judicious and Select Essays and Observations* (London, 1667).

Raleigh, Sir Walter, *The discoverie of the Large, Rich and Bewtiful Empyre of Guiana*, transcribed, annotated and introduced by Neil L. Whitehead (Norman: University of Oklahoma Press, 1977).

Raynal, Abbé G. Th., *Historie philosophique & politique des deux Indies*, Avertissement et choix des texts par Yves Bénot (Paris: La Découverte, 2001).

Raynal, Guillaume-Thomas, *Histoire philosophique et politique des établissements et du commerce des Européens dans les deux Indes*, 6 volumes (Amsterdam, 1770).

Raynal, Guillaume-Thomas, *A Philosophical and Political History of the Settlements and Trade of the Europeans in the East and West Indies*, 3rd edition, 5 volumes (London, 1777).

Riemer, Johann Andreus, *Missions-Reise nach Suriname und Barbice* (Zittau-Leipzig, 1801).

Rotker, Susana (ed.), *The Memoirs of Fray Servando Teresa de Mier*, translated by Helen Lane (New York: Oxford University Press, 1998).

Rousseau, Jean-Jacques, *The Social Contract and other later political writings* (Cambridge, UK: Cambridge University Press, 1997).

Robertson, William, *The History of America*, 2 volumes (London, 1777).

de Sahagún, Bernardino, *Florentine Codex: General History of the Things of New Spain*, translated by C. E. Dibble and A. J. O. Anderson, 11 volumes (Santa Fe, NM: School of American Research, 1950–69).

de Sahagún, Fray Bernardino, *Historia general de las cosas de Nueva España*. Versión íntegra del texto castellano del Manuscrito conocido como *Códice florentino*, Estudio introductorio, paleografía, glosario y notas, Alfredo López Austin y Josefina López Quintana, 3 tomos (Ciudad de México: Cien de México, 2000).

Smith, Adam, *Wealth of Nations* (New York: Prometheus Books, 1991).

Smith, Captain John, *The General Historie of Virginia, New-England, and the Summer Isles*, Divided Into Six Books (London, 1624).

Smith, William, *A Natural History of Nevis and the rest of the English Charibee Islands...* (Cambridge, UK, 1745).

Snelgrave, William, *A New Account of Some Parts of Guinea and the Slave Trade* [1734], reprint (Edinburgh: Gordon Wright Publishing, 1978).

Stedman, John Gabriel, *Narrative of a Five Years Expedition against the Revolted Negroes of Surinam – Transcribed for the First Time from the Original 1790 Manuscript*, edited by Richard Price and Sally Price (Baltimore, MD: Johns Hopkins University Press, 1988).

Van der Donck, Adriaen, *A Description of the New Netherlands*, edited with an introduction by Thomas F. O'Donnell (Syracuse, NY: Syracuse University Press, 1968).

Vespucci, Amerigo, *Mundus Novus: Letter to Lorenzo Pietro de Medici*, translated by G. T. Northrup (Princeton: Princeton University Press, 1916).

Vaz de Caminha, Pero, *The Voyages of Pedro Alvares Cabral to Brazil and India*, 2nd series, volume 81 (London: Hakluyt Society, 1937).

Vaz de Camoes, Luis, *The Lusíads*, translated by Landeg White (Oxford, UK: Oxford University Press, 1997).

Volney, C. F., *The Ruins: Or, A Survey of the Revolutions of Empires* (London: J. Johnson, 1795).

Williams, Roger, *A Key into the Language of America* (London, 1643).

Wood, William, *A Survey of Trade* (London, 1722).

Wright, Louis B. (ed.), *A Voyage to Virginia in 1609* (Charlottesville: University of Virginia Press, 1964).

de Xerex, Francisco, *Verdadera relación de la conquista del Perú*, edited by Concepción Bravo (Madrid, 1985).

Collected Documents

Arthur, Charles and Michael Dash (eds.), *Libète: A Haitian Anthology* (Princeton, NJ: Marcus Wiener, 1999).

Biggar, Henry Percival (ed.), *A Collection of Documents Relating to Jacques Cartier and the Sieur de Roberval* (Ottawa, ON: Public Archives of Canada, 1930).

Blassingame, John W. (ed.), *Slave Testimony: Two Centuries of Letters, Speeches, Interviews, and Autobiographies* (Baton Rouge: Louisiana State University Press, 1977).

Bolívar, Simón, *El Libertador: Writings of Simón Bolívar*, translated by Frederick H. Fornoff, edited by David Bushnell (Oxford, UK: Oxford University Press, 2003).

Bolívar, Simón, *Selected Writings of Bolivar*, 2 volumes, translated by Lewis Bertrand, selected and edited by Vicente Lecuna and Harold A. Bierck, Jr. (New York: Banco de Venezuela, 1951).

Boyer, Richard and Geoffrey Spurling (eds.), *Colonial Lives: Documents on Latin American History, 1550–1850* (New York: Oxford University Press, 2000).

Conrad, Robert Edgar (ed.), *Children of God's Fire: A Documentary History of Black Slavery in Brazil* (University Park: Pennsylvania State University Press, 1994).

Curtin, Philip (ed.), *Africa Remembered: Narratives by West Africans from the Era of the Slave Trade* (Prospect Heights, IL: Waveland Press, 1997).

Davenport, Francis G. (ed.), *European Treaties bearing on the History of the United States and its Dependencies*, 4 volumes (Washington, DC: Government Printing Office, 1917–37).

Donnan, Elizabeth (ed.), *Documents Illustrative of the History of the Slave Trade to America* (New York: Octagon Books, 1965).

Eltis, David, Stephen D. Behrendt, David Richardson and Herbert S. Klein (eds.), *The Trans-Atlantic Slave Trade: A Database on CD: ROM* (Cambridge, UK: Cambridge University Press, 1999).

Forster, Elborg and Robert Forster (trans. and eds.), *Sugar and Slavery, Family and Race: The Letters and Diary of Pierre Dessalles, Planter in Martinique, 1808–1856* (Baltimore, MD: Johns Hopkins University Press, 1996).

Greer, Allan (ed.), *The Jesuit Relations: Natives and Missionaries in Seventeenth Century North America* (Boston: Bedford/St. Martins, 2000).

Hakluyt Society, *Spanish Documents Concerning English Voyages to the Caribbean* (London: British Library, 1928).

Hargreaves-Mawdsley, W. N. (ed.), *Spain Under the Bourbons, 1700–1833: A Collection of Documents* (Columbia: University of South Carolina Press, 1973).

The Harkness Collection in the Library of Congress: Manuscripts concerning Mexico, with selected transcriptions and translations by J. Benedict Warren (Washington, DC: Library of Congress, 1974).

Hopkins, J. E. P. and Nehemia Levtzion (eds.). *Corpus of Early Arab Sources for West African History* (Princeton, NJ: Marcus Wiener, 2000).

Hulton, P., *America, 1585: The Complete Drawings of John White* (Chapel Hill: University of North Carolina Press, 1984).

Hulton, Paul and D.B. Quinn, *The American Drawings of John White, 1577–1590*, 2 volumes (Chapel Hill: University of North Carolina Press, 1964).

Hunt, Lynn (ed.), *The French Revolution and Human Rights: A Brief Documentary History* (Boston: Bedford St. Martins, 1996).

Hunwick, John, *Timbuktu & the Songhay Empire: Al-Sa'dî's Ta'rîkh al'sudan down to 1613 and other Contemporary Documents* (Leiden, The Netherlands: Brill, 2003).

Israel, Fred L. (ed.), *Major Peace Treaties of Modern History, 1648–1967*, 4 volumes (London: Chelsea House, 1967).

Jameson, John Franklin (ed.), *Privateering and Piracy in the Colonial Period: Illustrative Documents* (New York: Macmillan, 1923).

León-Portilla, Miguel, *The Broken Spears: The Aztec Account of the Conquest of Mexico*, translated from Nahuatl into Spanish by Angel María Garibay, and from Spanish into English by Lysander Kemp (Berkeley: University of California Press, 1992).

Lockhart, James and Enrique Otte (eds.), *Letters and People of the Spanish Indies: Sixteenth Century* (Cambridge, UK: Cambridge University Press, 1976).

Mills, Kenneth and William B. Taylor (eds.), *Colonial Spanish America: A Documentary History* (Wilmington, DE: S. R. Books, 1998).

Museu Aberto do Descobrimento: O Brasil Renasce Onde Nasce (São Paulo, Brazil: Fundacao Quadrilátero do Descobrimento, 1994).

Otte, Enrique (ed.), *Cartas privadas de emigrantes a Indias, 1540–1616* (Seville, 1988).

Parry, John H. and Robert G. Keith (eds.), *New Iberian World: A Documentary History of the Discovery and Settlement of Latin America to the Early Seventeenth Century*, 5 volumes (New York: Times Books and Hector and Rose, 1984).

Quinn, D. B. (ed.), *New American World: A Documentary History of North America to 1612*, 5 volumes (New York: Arno Press, 1979).

Rhodchannel, John (ed.), *The American Revolution: Writings from the War of Independence* (New York: Library of America, 2001).

Sanderlin, George (trans. and ed.), *Bartolomé de las Casas: A Selection of his Writings* (New York: Alfred A. Knopf, 1971).

Scheer, George F. and Hugh F. Rankin, *Rebels and Redcoats: The American Revolution Through the Eyes of Those Who Fought and Lived It* (New York: De Capo Press, 1957).

Schwartz, Stuart B. (ed.), *Victor and Vanquished: Spanish and Nahua Views of the Conquest of Mexico* (Boston: Bedford/St. Martin's, 2000).

Symcox, Geoffrey (ed.), Luciano Formisano (textual ed.), Theodore J. Cachy, Jr. (trans., Italian texts) and John C. McLucas (trans., Latin texts), *Italian Reports on America, 1493–1522: Accounts by Contemporary Observers*, Repertorium Columbianum, Volume XII (Turnhout, Belgium: Brepols, 2002).

Thatcher, Oliver J. (ed.), *The Library of Original Sources*, volumes IV–VI (Milwaukee, WI: University Research Extension Company, 1907).

Thwaites, Reuben Gold (ed.), *The Jesuit Relations and Allied Documents*, 73 volumes (Cleveland, OH: Arthur H. Clark, 1896–1901).

Tyson, George F., Jr. (ed.), *Toussaint L'Ouverture* (Englewood Cliffs, NJ: Prentice-Hall, 1973).

Secondary Sources

de Abreu, Joáo Capistrano, *Chapters of Brazil's Colonial History, 1500–1800* (New York: Oxford University Press, 1997).

Abu-Lughod, Janet, *Before European Hegemony: The World System, A.D. 1250–1350* (Oxford, UK: Oxford University Press, 1989).

Adams, Richard E. W., *Ancient Civilizations of the New World* (Boulder, CO: Westview, 1997).

Adelman, Jeremy (ed.), *Colonial Legacies: The Problem of Persistence in Latin American History* (New York: Routledge, 1999).

Alberro, Solange, Alicia Hernández Chávez and Elías Trabulse (eds.), *La Revolución francesa en México* (Ciudad de México: El Colegio de México, 1992).

Altman, Ida, *Emigrants and Society: Extremadura and Spanish America in the Sixteenth Century* (Berkeley: University of California Press, 1989).

Altman, Ida and James Horn, *'To Make America': European Emigration in the Early Modern Period* (Berkeley: University of California Press, 1991).

Anderson, Fred, *Crucible of War: The Seven Years' War and the Fate of Empire in British North America, 1754–1766* (New York: Alfred A. Knopf, 2000).

Andrews, Kenneth R., *Spanish Caribbean: Trade and Plunder, 1530–1630* (New Haven: Yale University Press, 1978).

Andrews, Kenneth R., *Trade, Plunder and Settlement: Maritime Enterprise and the Genesis of the British Empire, 1480–1630* (Cambridge, UK: Cambridge University Press, 1984).

Andrews, Kenneth R. et al. (eds.), *The Westward Enterprise: English Activities in Ireland, the Atlantic and America, 1480–1650* (Detroit, MI: Wayne State University Press, 1979).

Andrien, Kenneth J. and Rolena Adorno (eds.), *Transatlantic Encounters: Europeans and Andeans in the Sixteenth Century* (Berkeley: University of California Press, 1991).

Anstey, Roger, *The Atlantic Slave Trade and British Abolition, 1760–1810* (London: Macmillan, 1975).

Axtell, James, *Beyond 1492: Encounters in Colonial North America* (New York: Oxford University Press, 1992).

Axtell, James, *The Europe and the Indian: Essays in the Ethnohistory of Colonial North America* (New York: Oxford University Press, 1981).

Axtell, James, *The Invasion Within: The Contest of Cultures in Colonial North America* (New York: Oxford University Press, 1985).

Axtell, James, *Natives and Newcomers: The Cultural Origins of North America* (New York: Oxford University Press, 2001).

Bailyn, Bernard, *Atlantic History: Concept and Contours* (Cambridge, MA: Harvard University Press, 2005).

Bailyn, Bernard, *The Ideological Origins of the American Revolution* (Cambridge, MA: Belknap Press of Harvard University Press, 1992).

Bailyn, Bernard, *The Peopling of British North America: An Introduction* (New York: Vintage Books, 1988).

Bailyn, Bernard and Philip D. Morgan (eds.), *Strangers within the Realm: Cultural Margins of the First British Empire* (Chapel Hill: University of North Carolina Press, 1991).

Banks, Kenneth J., *Chasing Empire across the Sea: Communications and the State in the French Atlantic, 1713–1763* (Montreal, QC: McGill-Queen's University Press, 2002).

Barry, Boubacar, *Senegambia and the Atlantic Slave Trade* (Cambridge, UK: Cambridge University Press, 1988).

Bartlett, Robert, *The Making of Europe: Conquest, Colonization and Cultural Change, 950–1350* (Princeton, NJ: Princeton University Press, 1993).

Bastide, R., *African Civilizations in the New World* (New York: Harper and Row, 1971).

Bastide, Roger, *Les Religions africaines au Brésil, Vers une sociologie des interpénétrations de civilsations* (Paris: Société de l'Histoire des Colonies Francaises et Librairie Larose, 1952).

Beckles, Hilary McD., *Natural Rebels: A Social History of Enslaved Black Women in Barbados* (New Brunswick, NJ: Rutgers University Press, 1989).

Beckles, Hilary McD., *White Servitude and Black Slavery in Barbados, 1627–1715* (Knoxville: University of Tennessee Press, 1989).

Bell, Madison Smart, *Toussaint Louverture: A Biography* (New York: Pantheon Books, 2007).

Bernard, Antoinette (ed.), *Le Grand Atlas des Esplorations* (London: HarperCollins, 1991).

Bender, Gerald R., *Angola Under the Portuguese* (Berkeley: University of California Press, 1978).

Benson, Nettie Lee (ed.), *La diputación provincial y el federalismo mexicano* (Ciudad de México: El Colegio de Mexico, 1955).

Bergquist, Charles, *Labor and the Course of American Democracy: US History in Latin American Perspective* (London: Verso, 1996).

Berkin, Carol, *First Generations: Women in Colonial America* (New York: Hill and Wang, 1996).

Berlin, Ira, *Many Thousands Gone: The First Two Centuries of Slavery in North America* (Cambridge, MA: Belknap Press of Harvard University Press, 1998).

Berlin, Ira and Philip D. Morgan (eds.), *Cultivation and Culture: Labor and the Shaping of Slave Life in the Americas* (Charlottesville: University Press of Virginia, 1993).

Bethell, Leslie, *The Abolition of the Brazilian Slave Trade* (Cambridge, UK: Cambridge University Press, 1970).

Bethell, Leslie (ed.), *The Cambridge History of Latin America*, volumes I–II (Cambridge, UK: Cambridge University Press, 1984–5).

Birmington, David, *A Concise History of Portugal* (Cambridge, UK: Cambridge University Press, 1993).

Birmingham, David, *Portugal and Africa* (London: Macmillan Press, 1999).

Birmingham, David, *Trade and Conflict in Angola: The Mbundu and Their Neighbors under the Influence of the Portuguese, 1483–1790* (Oxford, UK: Clarendon Press, 1966).

Black, Jeremy, *War and the World: Military Power and the Fate of Continents, 1450–2000* (New Haven, CT: Yale University Press, 1998).

Blackburn, Robin, *The Making of New World Slavery: From the Baroque to the Modern, 1492–1800* (London: Verso, 1997).

Blackburn, Robin, *The Overthrow of Colonial Slavery, 1776–1848* (London: Verso, 1988).

Blake, John W., *West Africa: Quest for God and Gold, 1454–1578* (London: Curzon Press, 1977).

Boucher, Philip P., *Les Nouvelles Frances: France in America, 1500–1815: An Imperial Perspective* (Providence, RI: John Carter Brown Library, 1989).

Boxer, C. R., *The Dutch in Brazil, 1624–1654* (Oxford, UK: Clarendon Press, 1957).

Boxer, C. R., *The Dutch Seaborne Empire, 1600–1800* (London: Penguin Books, 1973).

Boxer, C. R., *Four Centuries of Portuguese Expansion, 1415–1825: A Succinct Survey* (Johannesburg, South Africa: Witwatersrand University Press, 1965).

Boxer, C. R., *The Golden Age of Brazil, 1695–1750* (Berkeley: University of California Press, 1962).

Boxer, C. R., *Portuguese Society in the Tropics* (Madison: University of Wisconsin Press, 1965).

Boxer, C. R., *Race Relations in the Portuguese Colonial Empire, 1415–1825* (Oxford, UK: Clarendon Press, 1963).

Boxer C. R., *Salvador de Sá and the Struggle for Brazil and Angola, 1602–1686* (London: Athlone Press, 1952).

Boxer, C. R., *Women in Iberian Expansion Overseas, 1415–1815* (New York: Oxford University Press, 1975).

Brading, D. A., *The First America: The Spanish Monarchy, Creole Patriots, and the Liberal State, 1492–1867* (Cambridge, UK: Cambridge University Press, 1991).

Braudel, Fernand, *Civilization and Capitalism, 15th–18th Century. Volume I: The Structures of Everyday Life*, translated by Sian Reynolds (Berkeley: University of California Press, 1992).

Braudel, Fernand, *Civilization and Capitalism, 15th–18th Century. Volume II: The Wheels of Commerce*, translated by Sian Reynolds (Berkeley: University of California Press, 1992).

Braudel, Fernand, *Civilization and Capitalism, 15th–18th Century. Volume III: The Perspective of the World*, translated by Sian Reynolds (Berkeley: University of California Press, 1992).

Braudel, Fernand, *The Mediterranean and the Mediterranean World in the Age of Philip II*, translated by Sian Reynolds (New York: HarperCollins, 1972).

Bridenbaugh, Carl, *Mitre and Sceptre: Transatlantic Faiths, Ideas, Personalities, and Politics, 1689–1775* (New York: Oxford University Press, 1962).

Bridenbaugh, Carl and Roberta, *No Peace Beyond the Line: The English in the Caribbean, 1627–1690* (New York: Oxford University Press, 1972).

Brinley, Thomas, *Migration and Economic Growth: A Study of Great Britain and the Atlantic Economy* (Cambridge, UK: Cambridge University Press, 1984).

Brown, Kathleen M., *Good Wives, Nasty Wenches, and Anxious Patriarchs: Gender, Race, and Power in Colonial Virginia* (Chapel Hill: University of North Carolina Press, 1996).

Bulmer-Thomas, Victor, John H. Coatsworth and Roberto Cortés Conde (eds.), *The Cambridge Economic History of Latin America*, volumes I–II (Cambridge, UK: Cambridge University Press, 2006).

Burnside, Madeleine and Rosemarie Robotham, *Spirit of the Passage: The Transatlantic Slave Trade in the Seventeenth Century* (New York: Simon and Schuster Editions, 1997).

Bush, Barbara, *Slave Women in Caribbean Society, 1650–1838* (Bloomington: Indiana University Press, 1990).

Butel, Paul, *The Atlantic* (London: Routledge, 1999).

Cabral de Mello, Evaldo, *Olinda Restaurada: Guerra e Açúcar no Nordeste, 1630–1654*, 2a edição revista e aumentada (Rio de Janeiro: Topbooks, 1998).

Calloway, Colin G., *New Worlds for All: Indians, Europeans, and the Remaking of Early America* (Baltimore, MD: Johns Hopkins University Press, 1997).

Cambell, Mary B., *The Witness and the Other World: Exotic European Travel Writing, 400–1600* (Ithaca, NY: Cornell University Press, 1988).

The Cambridge History of the Native Peoples of the Americas, volumes I–III (Cambridge, UK: Cambridge University Press, 1996–2000).

The Cambridge Modern History, volumes I–VI (Cambridge, UK: Cambridge University Press, 1902–9).

Canny, Nicolas, *Kingdom and Colony: Ireland in the Atlantic World, 1560–1800* (Baltimore, MD: Johns Hopkins University Press, 1988).

Canny, Nicolas and Anthony Pagden (ed.), *Colonial Identity in the Atlantic World, 1500–1800* (Princeton, NJ: Princeton University Press, 1987).

Carneiro da Cunha, Manuela (ed.), *História dos indios no Brasil* (São Paulo, Brazil: 1992).

Castro y Rossi, Adolfo, *Cortes de Cádiz* (Madrid: Imprenta de P. Pérez de Velasco, 1913).

Chaunu, Huguette and Pierre Chaunu, *Séville et l'Atlantique (1504–1650)*, 13 volumes (Paris: S.E.V.P.E.N., 1955–60).

Chaunu, Pierre, *Conquete et exploitation des Nouveaux Mondes* (Paris, 1969).

Chaunu, Pierre, *European Expansion in the Later Middle Ages* (New York: North-Holland, 1979).

Chiappelli, F. (ed.), *First Images of America: The Impact of the New World on the Old*, 2 volumes (Berkeley: University of California Press, 1976).

Cipolla, Carlo M., *Before the Industrial Revolution: European Society and Economy, 1000–1700*, 3rd edition (New York: W. W. Norton, 1993).

Cipolla, Carlo M., *Guns, Sails, and Empires: Technological Innovation and the Early Phases of European Expansion, 1400–1700* (New York: Minerva Press, 1965).

Clark, John C., *La Rochelle and the Atlantic Economy during the Eighteenth Century* (Baltimore, MD: Johns Hopkins University Press, 1981).

Clendinnen, Inga, *Aztecs: An Interpretation* (Cambridge, UK: Cambridge University Press, 1991).

Clendinnen, Inga, *Ambivalent Conquests: Maya and Spaniard in Yucatan, 1715–1570* (Cambridge, UK: Cambridge University Press, 1987).

Collier, George A., Renato I. Rosaldo and John D. Wirth (eds.), *The Inca and Aztec States, 1400–1800: Anthropology and History* (New York: 1982).

Connah, Graham, *African Civilizations: Precolonial Cities and States in Tropical Africa: An Archaeological Perspective* (Cambridge, UK: Cambridge University Press, 1987).

Conrad, Robert, *The Destruction of Brazilian Slavery, 1850–1888* (Berkeley: University of California Press, 1972).

Conrad, Robert, *World of Sorrow: The African Slave Trade to Brazil* (Baton Rouge: Louisiana State University Press, 1986).

Conrad, Geoffrey W. and Arthur A. Demarest, *Religion and Empire: The Dynamics of Aztec and Inca Expansionism* (Cambridge, UK: Cambridge University Press, 1984).

Cook, Noble David, *Demographic Collapse: Indian Peru, 1520–1620* (Cambridge, UK: Cambridge University Press, 1981).

Corbin, Alain, *The Lure of the Sea: The Discovery of the Seaside in the Western World, 1750–1840* (Berkeley: University of California Press, 1994).

Cordingly, David, *Under the Black Flag: The Romance and the Reality of Life Among the Pirates* (San Diego, CA: A Harvest Book, 1998).

Couto, Jorge, *A Construção do Brasil: Amérindos, Portugueses e Africanos, do inicio do povoamento a finais de Quinhentos* (Lisboa: Edições Cosmos, 1998).

Cronon, William, *Changes in the Land: Indians, Colonists, and the Ecology of New England* (New York: Hill and Wang, 1983).

Crosby, Alfred W., *The Columbian Exchange: Biological and Cultural Consequences of 1492* (Westport, CT: Greenwood Press, 1972).

Cunliffe, Barry, *Facing the Ocean: The Atlantic and its Peoples* (New York: Oxford University Press, 2001).

Curtin, Philip D., *The Atlantic Slave Trade: A Census* (Madison: University of Wisconsin Press, 1969).

Curtin, Philip D., *Cross-Cultural Trade in World History* (Cambridge, UK: Cambridge University Press, 1984).

Curtin, Philip D., *Economic Change in Precolonial Africa: Senegambia in the Era of the Slave Trade*, 2 volumes (Madison: University of Wisconsin Press, 1975).

Curtin, Philip D., *The Rise and Fall of the Plantation Complex: Essays in Atlantic History* (Cambridge, UK: Cambridge University Press, 1990).

Curtin, Philip D., *The World and the West: The European Challenge and the Overseas Response in the Age of Reason* (Cambridge, UK: Cambridge University Press, 2000).

Curtin, Philip D. et al., *African History: From Earliest Times to Independence* (London: Longman, 1995).

Davidson, Basil, *The African Slave Trade* (Boston: Little, Brown, 1980).

Davidson, Basil, *West Africa before the Colonial Era: A History to 1850* (London: Longman, 1990).

Davidson, David M., "Rivers and Empire: The Madeira Route and the Incorporation of the Brazilian Far West, 1737–1808," Ph.D. dissertation, Yale University, New Haven, CT, 1970.

Davies, K. G., *The North Atlantic World in the Seventeenth Century* (Minneapolis: University of Minnesota Press, 1974).

Davis, David Brion, *Inhuman Bondage: The Rise and Fall of Slavery in the New World* (Oxford, UK: Oxford University Press, 2006).

Davis, David Brion, *The Problem of Slavery in the Age of Revolution, 1770–1823* (New York: Oxford University Press, 1999).

Davis, David Brion, *The Problem of Slavery in Western Culture* (Ithaca, NY: Cornell University Press, 1966).

Davis, David Brion, *Slavery and Human Progress* (New York: Oxford University Press, 1984).

Davis, Ralph, *The Rise of the Atlantic Economies* (Ithaca, NY: Cornell University Press, 1973).

Davis, Ralph, *The Rise of the English Shipping Industry in the 17th and 18th Centuries* (London: Newton Abbot, David and Charles, 1962).

DeCorse, Christopher R., *An Archaeology of El Mina: Africans and Europeans on the Gold Coast, 1400–1900* (Washington, DC: Smithsonian Institution Press, 2001).

De Pauw, Linda Grant, *Founding Mothers: Women of America in the Revolutionary Era* (Boston: Houghton Mifflin, 1975).

Denevan, William M. (ed.), *The Native Population of the Americas in 1492* (Madison: University of Wisconsin Press, 1976).

Diamond, Jared, *Guns, Germs, and Steel: The Fates of Human Societies* (New York: W. W. Norton, 1997).

Dickason, Olive P., *Canada's First Nations: A History of the Founding Peoples from Earliest times* (Norman: University of Oklahoma Press, 1992).

Dickason, Olive P., *The Myth of the Savage and the Beginnings of French Colonialism in the Americas* (Edmonton: The University of Alberta Press, 1997).

Diffie, Bailey W. and George D. Winius, *Foundations of the Portuguese Empire, 1415–1580* (Minneapolis: University of Minnesota Press, 1977).

Dobyns, Henry F., *Their Number Become Thinned: Native American Population Dynamics in Eastern North America* (Knoxville: University of Tennessee Press, 1983).

Doggett, Rachel (ed.), *New World of Wonders: European Images of the Americas, 1492–1700* (Washington, DC: Folger Shakespeare Library, 1992).

Drescher, Seymour, *Econocide: British Slavery in the Era of Abolition* (Pittsburgh, PA: University of Pittsburgh Press, 1977).

Drescher, Seymour (ed.), *From Slavery to Freedom: Comparative Studies in the Rise and Fall of Atlantic Slavery* (New York: New York University Press, 1999).

Du Bois, W. E. B., *The Suppression of the African Slave-Trade to the United States of America, 1638–1870* (Cambridge, MA: Harvard University Press, 1896).

Dubois, Laurent, *Avengers of the New World: The Story of the Haitian Revolution* (Cambridge, MA: Belknap Press of Harvard University Press, 2004).

Dubois, Laurent, *A Colony of Citizens: Revolution and Slave Emancipation in the French Caribbean, 1787–1804* (Chapel Hill: University of North Carolina Press, 2004).

Duffy, James, *Portuguese Africa* (Cambridge, MA: Harvard University Press, 1968).

Duncan, Bentley, *Atlantic Islands: Madeira, the Azores and the Cape Verdes in Seventeenth-Century Commerce and Navigation* (Chicago: Chicago University Press, 1972).

Dunn, Richard S., *Sugar and Slaves: The Rise of the Planter Class in the English West Indies, 1624–1713* (New York: W. W. Norton, 1973).

Dunn, Susan, *Sister Revolutions: French Lightening, American Light* (New York: Faber and Faber, 1999).

Eccles, William J., *The French in the Americas* (East Lansing: Michigan State University Press, 1998).

Elliot, J. H., *The Count-Duke of Olivares: The Statesman in an Age of Decline* (New Haven, CT: Yale University Press, 1986).

Elliot, J. H., *Empires of the Atlantic: Britain and Spain in America, 1492–1830* (New Haven, CT: Yale University Press, 2006).

Elliot, J. H., *Imperial Spain, 1469–1716* (New York: Mentor Books, 1966).

Elliot, J. H., *The Old World and the New, 1492–1650* (Cambridge, UK: Cambridge University Press, 1970).

Elliot, J. H., *Spain and its World, 1500–1700* (New Haven, CT: Yale University Press, 1989).

Eltis, David, *Economic Growth and the Ending of the Transatlantic Slave Trade* (New York: Oxford University Press, 1987).

Eltis, David, *The Rise of African Slavery in the Americas* (Cambridge, UK: Cambridge University Press, 2000).

Emmer, Pieter, *The Dutch in the Atlantic Economy, 1580–1880* (Aldershot, UK: The Ashgate Variorum Collected Series, 1998).

Encyclopédie coloniale et maritime, 10 volumes (Paris: Encyclopédie Coloniale et Maritime, 1944–51).

Fage, J. D., *A History of Africa* (London: Routledge, 1988).

Farris, Nancy M., *Maya Society under Colonial Rule* (Princeton, NJ: Princeton University Press, 1984).

Fernández-Armesto, Felipe, *Before Columbus: Exploration and Colonization from the Mediterranean to the Atlantic, 1229–1492* (Oxford, UK: Oxford University Press, 1987).

Fernández-Armesto, Felipe, *The Canary Islands after the Conquest: The Making of a Colonial Society in the Early Sixteenth Century* (New York: Oxford University Press, 1982).

Fernández-Armesto, Felipe, *Civilizations: Culture, Ambition, and the Transformation of Nature* (New York: Free Press, 2001).

Fernández-Armesto, Felipe, *Columbus* (Oxford, UK: Oxford University Press, 1992).

Fernández-Armesto, Felipe, *Millennium: A History of the Last Thousand Years* (New York: Scribner, 1995).

Fick, Carolyn E., *The Making of Haiti: The Saint Domingue Revolution from Below* (Knoxville: University of Tennessee Press, 1990).

Fischer, David Hackett, *Albion's Seed: Four British Folkways in America* (New York: Oxford University Press, 1989).

Foster, George M., *Culture and Conquest* (Chicago: University of Chicago Press, 1960).

Freyre, Gilberto, *The Mansions and the Shanties: The Making of Modern Brazil* (New York: Alfred A. Knopf, 1963).

Freyre, Gilberto, *The Masters and the Slaves: A Study in the Development of Brazilian Civilization*, revised 2nd edition, translated by Samuel Putnam (New York: Alfred A. Knopf, 1978).

García-Baquero González, Antonio, *Cádiz y el Atlántico, 1717–1778: El comercio colonial español bajo el monopolio gaditano*, 2 volumes (Sevilla: 1976).

Garfield, Robert, "A History of São Tomé Island, 1470–1655," Ph.D. dissertation, Northwestern University, Evanston, IL, 1971.

Gaspar, David Barry and David Patrick Geggus (eds.), *A Turbulent Time: The French Revolution and the Greater Caribbean* (Bloomington: Indiana University Press, 1997).

General History of Africa, volumes IV–V (Paris: United Nations Educational, Scientific and Cultural Organization, 1992).

Genovese, Eugene D., *From Rebellion to Revolution: Afro-American Slave Revolts in the Making of the Modern World* (Baton Rouge: Louisiana State University Press, 1979.

Gerbi, Antonello, *The Dispute of the New World* (Pittsburgh, PA: University of Pittsburgh, 1973).

Gibson, Charles, *The Aztecs under Spanish Rule: A History of the Indians of the Valley of Mexico, 1519–1810* (Stanford, CA: Stanford University Press, 1964).

Gibson, Charles, *Spain in America* (New York: Harper Torchbooks, 1966).

Godechot, Jacques, *France and the Atlantic Revolution of the Eighteenth Century, 1770–1799* (New York: Free Press, 1965).

Godinho de Magalháes, V., *A economia dos descobrimientos henriquinos* (Lisbon: Sá da Costa, 1962).

Gomez, Michael A., *Exchanging Our Country Marks: The Transformation of African Identies in the Colonial and Antebellum South* (Chapel Hill: University of North Carolina, 1998).

Goslinga, Cornelis Ch., *The Dutch in the Caribbean and on the Wilde Coast, 1580–1680* (Assen, The Netherlands: 1971).

de Graff, N. J., *Nederlanders Over de Zeeën* (Utrecht, The Netherlands: Uitgeversmaatschappij W. de Hann, 1955).

Gray, Richard (ed.), *The Cambridge History of Africa*, volumes 3–4 (Cambridge, UK: Cambridge University Press, 1975–7).

Greene, Jack P., *The Intellectual Construction of America: Exceptionalism and Identity from 1492 to 1800* (Chapel Hill: University of North Carolina Press, 1993

Greenblatt, Steven, *Marvelous Possessions: The Wonder of the New World* (Chicago: University of Chicago Press, 1991).

Greer, Allan, *The People of New France* (Toronto: University of Toronto Press, 1999).

Gutiérrez, Ramón, *When Jesus Came, the Corn Mothers Went Away: Marriage, Sexuality, and Power in New Mexico, 1500–1846* (Stanford, CA: Stanford University Press, 1991).

Hainsworth, Roger and Christine Churches, *The Anglo-Dutch Naval Wars, 1652–1674* (Phoenix Mill, UK: Sutton Publishing, 1998).

Hale, J. R., *Renaissance Europe: Individual and Society, 1480–1520* (Berkeley: University of California Press, 1977).

Hall, Gwendolyn Midlo, *Africans in Colonial Louisiana: The Development of Afro-Creole Culture in the Eighteenth Century* (Baton Rouge: Louisiana State University Press, 1992).

Hamilton, Earl J., *American Treasure and the Price Revolution in Spain, 1501–1650* (Cambridge, MA: Harvard University Press, 1934).

Hampson, Norman, *The Enlightenment* (Harmondsworth, UK: Penguin Books, 1968).

Hancock, David, *Citizens of the World: London Merchants and the Integration of the British Atlantic Community, 1735–1785* (Cambridge, UK: Cambridge University Press, 1995).

Hanke, Lewis, *The Spanish Struggle for Justice in the Conquest of America* (New York: Little, Brown, 1965).

Hannay, David, *The Great Chartered Companies* (London: Williams and Norgate, 1926).

Hanson, Marcus Lee, *The Atlantic Migration: A History of the Continuing Settlement of the United States* (Cambridge, MA: Harvard University Press, 1940).

Haring, Clarence H., *Empire in Brazil: A New World Experiment with Monarchy* (Cambridge, MA: Harvard University Press, 1958).

Haring, Clarence Henry, *Trade and Navigation between Spain and the Indies in the Time of the Hapsburgs* (Cambridge, MA: Harvard University Press, 1918).

Hassig, Ross, *Aztec Warfare: Imperial Expansion and Political Control* (Norman: University of Oklahoma Press, 1988).

Hassig, Ross, *Mexico and the Spanish Conquest* (London: Longman, 1994).

Hemming, John, *Red Gold: The Conquest of the Brazilian Indians, 1500–1760* (Cambridge, MA: Harvard University Press, 1978).

Hemming, John, *The Conquest of the Incas* (New York: Harcourt Brace, 1970).

Herlihy, David, *The Black Death and the Transformation of the West* (Cambridge, MA: Harvard University Press, 1997).

Hobhouse, Henry, *Seeds of Change: Five Plants that Transformed Mankind* (London: Sidgwick and Jackson, 1985).

Hobsbawm, Eric, *The Age of Revolution, 1789–1848* (New York: Vintage, 1996).

Hugill, Peter J., *World Trade since 1431: Geography, Technology, and Capitalism* (Baltimore, MD: Johns Hopkins University Press, 1993).

Huppert, George, *After the Black Death: A Social History of Early Modern Europe*, 2nd edition (Bloomington: Indiana University Press, 1998).

Iliffe, John, *Africans: The History of a Continent* (Cambridge, MA: Cambridge University Press, 1995).

Inikori, Joseph E. and Stanley L. Engerman (eds.), *The Atlantic Slave Trade: Effects on Economies, Societies, and Peoples in Africa, the Americas, and Europe* (Durham, NC: Duke University Press, 1992).

Innis, H. A., *The Fur Trade in Canada: An Introduction to Canadian Economic History* (Toronto: University of Toronto Press, 1970).

Israel, Jonathan I., *The Dutch Republic: Its Rise, Greatness, and Fall, 1477–1806* (New York: Oxford University Press, 1995).

Israel, J. I., *The Dutch Republic and the Hispanic World, 1606–1661* (Oxford, UK: Oxford University Press, 1982).

Israel, J. I., *Dutch Primacy in World Trade, 1585–1740* (Oxford, UK: Oxford University Press, 1989).

James, C. L. R., *The Black Jacobins: Toussaint L'Ouverture and the San Domingue Revolution*, revised 2nd edition (New York: Vintage Books, 1989).

Jardine, Lisa, *Worldly Goods: A New History of the Renaissance* (New York: Doubleday, 1996).

Jennings, Francis, *The Ambiguous Iroquois Empire: The Covenant Chain Confederation of Indian Tribes with English Colonies from its Beginnings to the Lancaster Treaty of 1744* (New York: W. W. Norton, 1984).

Jennings, Francis, *The Invasion of America: Indians, Colonialism, and the Cant of Conquest* (New York: W. W. Norton, 1976).

Julien, Charles-André, *Les Français en Amérique pendant la premiere moitié de XVIe siecle* (Paris: Presses Universitaires de France, 1946).

Kadish, Doris Y., *Slavery in the Caribbean Francophone World: Distant Voices, Forgotten Acts, Forged Identities* (Athens: University of Georgia Press, 2000).

Kamen, Henry, *Philip of Spain* (New Haven, CT: Yale University Press, 1997).

Kamen, Henry, *Empire: How Spain Became a World Power, 1492–1763* (New York: Harper-Collins, 2003).

Karras, Alan L. and J. R. McNeill (eds.), *Atlantic American Societies: From Columbus Through Abolition, 1492–1888* (London: Routledge, 1992).

Kelsey, Harry, *Sir Francis Drake: The Queen's Pirate* (New Haven, CT: Yale University Press, 1998).

Kemp, Peter (ed.), *The Oxford Companion to Ships and the Sea* (New York: Oxford University Press, 1988).

Kennedy, Paul, *The Rise and Fall of the Great Powers: Economic Change and Military Conflict from 1500 to 2000* (New York: Random House, 1987).

King, J. C. H., *First Peoples, First Contacts: Native Peoples of North America* (Cambridge, MA: Harvard University Press, 1999)

Van Kirk, Sylvia, *Many Tender Ties: Women in Fur-Trade Society, 1670–1870* (Norman: University of Oklahoma Press, 1980).

Klein, Herbert S., *African Slavery in Latin America and the Caribbean* (New York: Oxford University Press, 1986).

Klein, Herbert S., *The Atlantic Slave Trade* (Cambridge, MA: Cambridge University Press, 1999).

Klein, Herbert S., *The Middle Passage: Comparative Studies in the Atlantic Slave Trade* (Princeton, NJ: Princeton University Press, 1978).

Klein, Martin (ed.), *Breaking the Chains: Slavery, Bondage and Emancipation in Africa and Asia* (Madison: University of Wisconsin Press, 1993).

Klein, Martin, *Slavery and Colonial Rule in French West Africa* (Cambridge, UK: University of Cambridge Press, 1998).

Klooster, Wim, *The Dutch in the Americas, 1600–1800* (Providence, RI: John Carter Brown Library, 1997).

Knight, Alan, *Mexico: From the Beginning to the Spanish Conquest* (Cambridge, UK: Cambridge University Press, 2002).

Knight, Alan, *Mexico: The Colonial Era* (Cambridge, UK: Cambridge University Press, 2002).

Knight, Franklin and Peggy Liss (eds.), *Atlantic Port Cities: Economy, Culture, and Society in the Atlantic World, 1650–1850* (Knoxville: University of Tennessee Press, 1991).

Kraus, Michael, *The Atlantic Civilization: Eighteenth Century Origins* (Ithaca, NY: Cornell University Press, 1949).

Kupperman, Karen Ordahl, *Indians and English: Facing Off in Early America* (Ithaca, NY: Cornell University Press, 2000).

Landes, David S., *The Wealth and Poverty of Nations: Why Some Are So Rich and Some Are So Poor* (New York: W. W. Norton, 1998).

Landes, Joan B., *Women and the Public Sphere in the Age of the French Revolution* (Ithaca, NY: Cornell University Press, 1988).

Lane, Kris E., *Pillaging the Empire: Piracy in the Americas, 1500–1750* (Armonk, NY: M. E. Sharpe, 1998).

Larner, John, *Marco Polo and the Discovery of the World* (New Haven, CT: Yale University Press, 1999).

Lavrin, Asunción (ed.), *Latin American Women: Historical Perspectives* (Westport, CT: Greenwood Press, 1978).

Lavrin, Asunción (ed.), *Sexuality and Marriage in Colonial Latin America* (Lincoln: University of Nebraska Press, 1989).

Law, Robin, *The Slave Coast of West Africa* (Oxford, UK: Oxford University Press, 1991).

Law, Robin (ed.), *From Slave Trade to 'Legitimate' Commerce: The Commercial Transition in Nineteenth-Century West Africa* (Cambridge, UK: Cambridge University Press, 1995).

Lawrence, A. W., *Trade Castles and Forts of West Africa* (London: Jonathan Cape, 1963).

Leonard, Irving A., *Baroque Times in Old Mexico: Seventeenth-Century Persons, Places, and Practices* (Ann Arbor: University of Michigan Press, 1959).

Leonard, Irving A., *Books of the Brave: Being an Account of Books and of Men in the Spanish Conquest and Settlement of the Sixteenth-Century New World* (Cambridge, MA: Harvard University Press, 1949.

Levenson, Jay A. (ed.), *Circa 1492: Art in the Age of Exploration* (Washington, DC, and New Haven, CT: National Gallery of Art and Yale University Press, 1991).

Lewis, Bernard, *Cultures in Conflict: Christian, Muslims, and Jews in the Age of Discovery* (New York: Oxford University Press, 1995).

Linebaugh, Peter and Marcus Rediker, *The Many-Headed Hydra: Sailors, Slaves, Commoners, and the Hidden History of the Revolutionary Atlantic* (Boston: Beacon Press, 2000).

Liss, Peggy K., *Atlantic Empires: The Network of Trade and Revolution, 1713–1826* (Baltimore, MD: Johns Hopkins University Press, 1983).

Litvinoff, Barnet, *1492: The Decline of Medievalism and the Rise of the Modern Age* (New York: Avon Books, 1991).

Livermore, H. V., *A New History of Portugal* (Cambridge, UK: Cambridge University Press, 1976).

Lockhart, James, *The Men of Cajamarca: A Social and Biographical Study of the First Conquerors of Peru* (Austin: University of Texas Press, 1972).

Lockhart, James, *The Nahuas After the Conquest: A Social and Cultural History of the Indians of Central Mexico, Sixteenth through Eighteenth Centuries* (Stanford, CA: Stanford University Press, 1992).

Lockhart, James, *Nahuas and Spaniards: Postconquest Central Mexican History and Philology* (Stanford, CA: Stanford University Press, 1991).

Lockhart, James, *Spanish Peru, 1532–1560: A Colonial Society* (Madison: University of Wisconsin Press, 1968).

Lockhart, James and Stuart Schwartz, *Early Latin America: A History of Colonial Spanish America and Brazil* (New York: Cambridge University Press, 1983).

Lopez, Robert S., *The Commercial Revolution of the Middle Ages, 950–1350* (Englewood Cliffs, NJ: Prentice Hall, 1976).

Louis, Wm. Roger (ed.), *The Oxford History of the British Empire*, 5 volumes (Oxford, UK: Oxford University Press, 1998–9).

Lovejoy, Paul E., *Transformations in Slavery: A History of Slavery in Africa* (Cambridge, UK: Cambridge University Press, 1983).

Lovejoy, Paul E. (ed.), *Africans in Bondage: Studies in Slavery and the Slave Trade* (Madison: University of Wisconsin Press, 1986).

Lovejoy, Paul E. and Nicholas Rogers, *Unfree Labor in the Development of the Atlantic World* (Essex, UK: Frank Cass, 1994).

Lynch, John, *Spain under the Habsburgs, Vol. I: Empire and Absolutism, 1516–1598* (New York: New York University Press, 1981).

Lynch, John, *Spain under the Habsburgs, Vol. II: Spain and America, 1598–1700* (New York: New York University Press, 1984).

MacCulloch, Diarmaid, *The Reformation: A History* (New York: Viking 2003).

MacLachlan, Colin M., *Spain's Empire in the New World: The Role of Ideas in Institutional and Social Change* (Berkeley: University of California Press, 1988).

MacLachlan, Colin M. and Jaime E. Rodríguez O., *The Forging of the Cosmic Race* (Berkeley: University of California Press, 1980).

MacLeod, Murdo J., *Spanish Central America: A Socioeconomic History, 1520–1720* (Berkeley: University of California Press, 1973).

Maddison, Angus, *The World Economy: A Millennial Perspective* (Paris: Development Centre of the Organization for Economic Cooperation and Development, 2001).

Maddison, Angus, *The World Economy: Historical Statistics* (Paris: Development Centre of the Organization for Economic Cooperation and Development, 2003).

Magnusson, Magnus and Harmann Palsson, *The Vinland Sagas: The Norse Discovery of America* (Baltimore, MD: Penguin, 1965).

Maier, Pauline, *American Scripture: Making the Declaration of Independence* (New York: Vintage Books, 1997).

Mann, Charles C., *1491: New Revelations of the Americas Before Columbus* (New York: Alfred A. Knopf, 2005).

Manning, Patrick, *Slavery in African Life* (Cambridge, UK: Cambridge University Press, 1990).

Mannix, Daniel P. and Malcolm Cowley, *Black Cargoes: A History of the Atlantic Slave Trade* (New York: The Viking Press, 1962).

Marques, A. H. de Oliveira, *History of Portugal, Vol. 1: From Lusitania to Empire* (New York: Columbia University Press, 1972).

Martín, Luis, *Daughters of the Conquistadors: Women of the Viceroyalty of Peru* (Albuquerque: University of New Mexico Press, 1983).

Mattoso, Kátia M. de Queirós, *To Be a Slave in Brazil, 1550–1888*, translated by Arthur Goldhammer (New Brunswick, NJ: Rutgers University Press, 1986).

Maura, Juan Francisco, *Women in the Conquest of the Americas*, translated by John F. Deredita (New York: Peter Lang, 1997).

Mauro, Frédéric, *Le Portugal et l'Atlantique au XVlle siecle (1570–1670). Etude économique* (Paris: S.E.V.P.E.N., 1960).

Mauro, Frédéric, *L'expansion européenne (1600–1870)* (Paris: Presses Universitaires de France, 1967).

McAlister, Lyle N., *Spain and Portugal in the New World, 1492–1700* (Minneapolis: University of Minnesota Press, 1984).

McCuster, John, *Money and Exchange in Europe and America, 1600–1775: A Handbook* (Chapel Hill: University of North Carolina Press, 1978).

McCusker, John and Russell Menard, *The Economy of British America, 1607–1789* (Chapel Hill: University of North Carolina Press, 1985).

McNeill, John Robert, *Atlantic Empires of France and Spain: Louisbourg and Havana, 1700–1763* (Chapel Hill: University of North Carolina Press, 1985).

McNeill, William H., *Plagues and Peoples* (Garden City, NY: Anchor Books, 1977).

Meinig, D. W., *Atlantic America, 1492–1800* (New Haven, CT: Yale University Press, 1986).

Merriman, Roger B., *The Rise of the Spanish Empire in the Old World and the New*, 4 volumes (New York: Macmillan, 1918–34).

Metcalf, Alida C., *Family and Frontier in Colonial Brazil: Santana de Parnaíba, 1580–1822* (Berkeley: University of California Press, 1977).

Middlekauff, Robert, *The Glorious Cause: The American Revolution, 1763–1789* (New York: Oxford University Press, 1982).

Miers, Suzanne and Richard Roberts (eds.), *The End of Slavery in Africa* (Madison: University of Wisconsin Press, 1988).

Miller, Joseph C., *Way of Death: Merchant Capitalism and the Angolan Slave Trade, 1730–1830* (Madison: University of Wisconsin Press, 1988).

Mintz, Sidney W., *Sweetness and Power: The Place of Sugar in Modern History* (New York: Viking, 1985).

Moreno Fraginals, Manuel, *The Sugar Mill: The Socioeconomic Complex of Sugar in Cuba, 1760–1860* (New York: Monthly Review Press, 1976).

Morgan, Edmund S., *American Slavery, American Freedom: The Ordeal of Colonial Virginia* (New York: W. W. Norton, 1995).

Morgan, Kenneth, *Bristol and the Atlantic Trade in the Eighteenth Century* (Cambridge, UK: Cambridge University Press, 1993).

Morgan, Philip D., *Slave Counterpoint: Black Culture in the Eighteenth-Century Chesapeake and Lowcountry* (Chapel Hill: University of North Carolina Press, 1998).

Morineau, Michel, *Incroyables Gasettes et Fabuleux Métaux: Les Retours des Trésors Américains d'apres les Gazettes Hollandaises (XVIe-XVIIIe siecles)* (Cambridge, UK, and Paris: Cambridge University Press, 1985).

Morison, Samuel Eliot, *The European Discovery of America, Vol. I: The Northern Voyages, A.D. 500–1600* (New York: Oxford University Press, 1971).

Morison, Samuel Eliot, *The European Discovery of America, Vol. II: The Southern Voyages, 1492–1616* (New York: Oxford University Press, 1974).

Morner, Magnus, *Race Mixture in the History of Latin America* (Boston: Little, Brown, 1967).

Morris, Roger, *Atlantic Seafaring: Ten Centuries of Exploration and Trade in the North Atlantic* (New York: International Marine, 1992).

Mullin, Michael, *Africa in America: Slave Acculturation and Resistance in the American South and the British Caribbean, 1736–1831* (Urbana: University of Illinois Press, 1992).

Munford, Clarence J., *The Black Ordeal of Slavery and Slave Trading in the French West Indies, 1624–1715*, 3 volumes (Lewiston, NY: Edwin Mellen, 1991).

Murphy, Joseph M., *Santería: African Spirits in America* (Boston: Beacon Press, 1988).

Musgrave, Peter, *The Early Modern European Economy* (New York: St. Martin's Press, 2000).

Nash, Gary B., *Red, White, and Black: The Peoples of Early North America*, 4th edition (Upper Saddle River, NJ: Prentice Hall, 2000).

The New Cambridge Medieval History, Volumes VI–VII (Cambridge, UK: Cambridge University Press, 1998).

The New Cambridge Modern History, Volumes I–IX (Cambridge, UK: Cambridge University Press, 1957–70).

Newton, A. P., *The European Nations in the West Indies, 1493–1688* (London: A. & C. Black, 1933).

Norton, Mary Beth, *Founding Mothers and Fathers: Gendered Power and the Forming of American Society* (New York: Vintage Books, 1997).

Norton, Mary Beth, *Liberty's Daughters: The Revolutionary Experience of American Women, 1750–1800* (Ithaca, NY: Cornell University Press, 1996).

O'Gorman, Edmundo, *The Invention of America* (Bloomington: Indiana University Press, 1961).

de Oliveira Lima, Manuel, *The Evolution of Brazil Compared with that of Spanish and Anglo-Saxon America*, edited by Percy A. Martin (Stanford, CA: Stanford University Press, 1914).

de Oliveira Lima, Manuel, *El movimiento de independencia, 1821–1822* (São Paulo, Brazil: Companhia Melhoramentos de São Paulo, 1922).

Olmos, Margarite Fernández and Lizabeth Paravisini-Gebert (eds.), *Sacred Possessions: Vodou, Santería, Obeah, and the Caribbean* (New Brunswick, NJ: Rutgers University Press, 1999).

Olwell, Robert, *Masters, Slaves, and Subjects: The Culture of Power in the South Carolina Low Country, 1740–1790* (Ithaca, NY: Cornell University Press, 1998).

O'Rourke, Kevin H. and Jeffery G. Williamson, *Globalization and History: The Evolution of a Nineteenth-Century Atlantic Economy* (Boston: Massachusetts Institute of Technology, 1999).

O'Shaughnessy, Andrew Jackson, *An Empire Divided: The American Revolution and the British Caribbean* (Philadelphia: University of Pennsylvania Press, 2000).

Outram, Dorinda, *The Enlightenment* (Cambridge, UK: Cambridge University Press, 1995).

Ott, Thomas O., *The Haitian Revolution, 1789–1804* (Knoxville: University of Tennessee Press, 1973).

Padden, R. C., *The Hummingbird and the Hawk: Conquest and Sovereignty in the Valley of Mexico, 1503–1541* (New York: Harper Colophon Books, 1967).

Padfield, Peter, *Maritime Supremacy and the Opening of the Western Mind: Naval Campaigns that Shaped the Modern World* (Woodstock, NY: The Overlook Press, 1999).

Pagden, Anthony, *European Encounters with the New World* (New Haven, CT: Yale University Press, 1993).

Pagden, Anthony, *The Fall of Natural Man: The American Indian and the Origins of Comparative Ethnology* (Cambridge, UK: Cambridge University Press, 1982).

Pagden, Anthony, *Lords of all the World: Ideologies of Empire in Spain, Britain and France, c. 1500 – c. 1800* (New Haven, CT: Yale University Press, 1995).

Pagden, Anthony, *Peoples and Empires: A Short History of European Migration, Exploration, and Conquest, from Greece to the Present* (New York: Modern Library, 2001).

Pagden, Anthony, *Spanish Imperialism and the Political Imagination* (New Haven, CT: Yale University Press, 1990).

Palmer, Colin A., *Human Cargoes: The British Slave Trade to Spanish America, 1700–1739* (Urbana: University of Illinois Press, 1981).

Palmer, Colin A., *Slaves of the White God: Blacks in Mexico, 1570–1650* (Cambridge, MA: Harvard University Press, 1976).

Palmer, R. R., *The Age of the Democratic Revolution: A Political History of Europe and America, 1760–1800. Vol. I: The Challenge* (Princeton, NJ: Princeton University Press, 1959).

Palmer, R. R., *The Age of the Democratic Revolution: A Political History of Europe and America, 1760–1800. Vol. II: The Struggle* (Princeton, NJ: Princeton University Press, 1964).

Paquette, Robert L. and Stanley L. Engerman (eds.), *The Lesser Antilles in the Age of European Expansion* (Gainsville: University of Florida Press, 1996).

Pares, Richard, *Merchants and Planters*, revised edition (Cambridge, UK: Cambridge University Press, 1970).

Parker, Geoffrey, *The Dutch Revolt* (London: Penguin Books, 1988).

Parkinson, Wenda, *'This Gilded African': Toussaint L'Ouverture* (London: Quartet Books, 1978).

Parry, J. H., *The Age of Reconnaissance* (Berkeley: University of California Press, 1981).

Parry, J. H., *The Discovery of the Sea* (Berkeley: University of California Press, 1981).

Parry, J. H., *The Spanish Seaborne Empire* (New York: Alfred A. Knopf, 1966).

Parry, J. H., *The Spanish Theory of Empire in the Sixteenth Century* (Cambridge, UK: Cambridge University Press, 1940).

Parry, J. H. and P. M. Sherlock, *A Short History of the West Indies* (London: Macmillan and Company, 1957).

Patterson, Orlando, *Slavery and Social Death: A Comparative Study* (Cambridge, MA: Harvard University Press, 1982).

Pauketat, Timothy R., *The Ascent of Chiefs: Cahokia and Mississippian Politics in Native North America* (Tuscaloosa: University of Alabama Press, 1994).

Paz, Octavio, *Sor Juana or, The Traps of Faith* (Cambridge, MA: Harvard University Press, 1988).

Padrão, F. Cerviño, *A Colonizacão do Sur de Angola, 1485–1974* (Lisboa: Gráfica Europam, 1997).

Penrose, Boies, *Travel and Discovery in the Renaissance, 1420–1620* (Cambridge, MA: Harvard University Press, 1952).

Pérez-Mallaína, Pablo E., *Spain's Men of the Sea: Daily Life on the Indies Fleet in the Sixteenth Century*, translated by Carla Rahn Phillips (Baltimore, MD: Johns Hopkins University Press, 1998).

Perkins, Edwin J., *The Economy of Colonial America* (New York: Columbia University Press, 1980).

Pescatello, Ann M., *Power and Pawn: The Female in Iberian Families, Societies, and Cultures* (Westport, CT: Greenwood Press, 1976).

Phelan, John L., *The Millennial Kingdom of the Franciscans in the New World* (Berkeley: University of California Press, 1970).

Phillips, Carla Rahn, *Six Galleons for the King of Spain: Imperial Defense in the Early Seventeenth Century* (Baltimore, MD: Johns Hopkins University Press, 1986).

Phillips, J. R. S., *The Medieval Expansion of Europe*, 2nd edition (Oxford, UK: Clarendon Press, 1998).

Phillips, William D., Jr. and Carla Rahn Phillips, *The Worlds of Christopher Columbus* (Cambridge, UK: Cambridge University Press, 1992).

Pike, Ruth, *Enterprise and Adventure: The Genoese in Seville and the Opening of the New World* (Ithaca, NY: Cornell University Press, 1966).

Pirenne, Henri, *Economic and Social History of Medieval Europe* (New York: A Harvest Book, 1937).

Pirenne, Henri, *Medieval Cities: Their Origins and the Renewal of Trade* (Princeton, NJ: Princeton University Press, 1969).

Pires, Fernando Tasso Fragoso (ed.), *Antigos Engenhos de Açúcar no Brasil* (Rio de Janeiro: Editora Nova Fronteira, 1994).

Postma, Johnannes, *The Dutch in the Atlantic Slave Trade, 1600–1815* (Cambridge, UK: Cambridge University Press, 1985).

Powers, Karen Vierira, *Women in the Crucible of Conquest: The Gendered Genesis of Spanish American Society, 1500–1600* (Albuquerque: University of New Mexico Press, 2005).

Price, Jacob M., *Capital and Credit in British Overseas Trade: The View from the Chesapeake, 1700–1776* (Cambridge, MA: Harvard University Press, 1980).

Price, Jacob M., *France and the Chesapeake: A History of the French Tobacco Monopoly, 1674–1791, and of Its Relationship to the British and American Tobacco Trade* (Ann Arbor: University of Michigan Press, 1973).

Price, Richard, *Maroon Societies: Rebel Slave Communities in the Americas*, 3rd edition (Baltimore, MD: Johns Hopkins University Press, 1996).

Priestley, Herbert I., *France Overseas: A Study of European Expansion* (New York: Appleton-Century, 1938).

Pritchard, James, *In Search of Empire: The French in the Americas, 1670–1730* (Cambridge, UK: Cambridge University Press, 2004).

Quarles, Benjamin, *The Negro in the American Revolution* (Chapel Hill: University of North Carolina Press, 1961).

Quinn, D. B., *England and the Discovery of America, 1481–1620* (London: George Allen and Unwin, 1974).

Ragon, Pierre, *Les indiens de la désouverte: evangélisation, marriage, et sexualité, Mexique XVIe siecle* (Paris: L'Harmattan, 1992).

Rediker, Marcus, *Between the Devil and the Deep Blue Sea: Merchant Seamen, Pirates and the Anglo-American Maritime World, 1700–1750* (Cambridge, UK: Cambridge University Press, 1993).

Reinhardt, Steven G. and Dennis Reinhartz (eds.), *Transatlantic History* (College Station, TX: Texas A&M University, 2006).

Restall, Matthew, *The Maya World: Yucatec Culture and Society, 1550–1850* (Stanford, CA: Stanford University Press, 1997).

Restall, Matthew, *Maya Conquistador* (Boston: Beacon Press, 1997).

Restall, Matthew, *Seven Myths of the Spanish Conquest* (Oxford, UK: Oxford University Press, 2003).

Reynolds, Edward, *Stand the Storm: A History of the Atlantic Slave Trade* (London: Allison and Busby, 1989).

Ribeiro, René, *The Afrobrazilian Cult-Groups of Recife: A Study in Social Adjustment* (Evanston, IL: Northwestern University Press, 1969).

Ricard, Robert, *The Spiritual Conquest of Mexico: An Essay on the Apostolate and the Evangelizing Methods of the Mendicant Orders of New Spain, 1523–1572* (Berkeley: University of California Press, 1966).

Rich, E. E. and C. H. Wilson (eds.), *The Cambridge Economic History of Europe, Volumes III-IV* (Cambridge, UK: Cambridge University Press, 1967),

Robertson, Claire C. and Martin A. Klein (eds.), *Women and Slavery in Africa* (Madison: University of Wisconsin Press, 1983).

Robinson, D. J. (ed.), *Migration in Colonial Spanish America* (Cambridge, MA: Cambridge University Press, 1990).

Rodriguez, Mario, *The Cádiz Experiment in Central America, 1808 to 1826* (Berkeley: University of California Press, 1978).

Rodríguez O., Jaime E., *The Emergence of Spanish America: Vicente Rocafuerte and Spanish Americanism, 1808–1832* (Berkeley: University of California Press, 1975).

Rodríguez O., Jaime E., *The Independence of Spanish America* (Cambridge, UK: Cambridge University Press, 1998).

Romm, James S., *The Edges of the Earth in Ancient Thought: Geography, Exploration, and Fiction* (Princeton, NJ: Princeton University Press, 1992).

Ros, Martin, *Night of Fire: The Black Napoleon and the Battle for Haiti*, translated by Karin Ford-Treep (London: Sarpedon, 1994).

Rose, J. H. (ed.), *The Cambridge History of the British Empire*, 8 volumes (Cambridge, UK: Cambridge University Press, 1929–59).

Rouse, Irving, *The Tainos: Rise and Decline of the People Who Greeted Columbus* (New Haven, CT: Yale University Press, 1992).

Rout, Leslie B., Jr., *The African Experience in Spanish America: 1502 to the Present Day* (Cambridge, UK: Cambridge University Press, 1976).

Rudé, George, *Revolutionary Europe, 1783–1815*, 2nd edition (Oxford, UK: Blackwell Publishers, 2000).

Rumeo de Armas, Antonio, *Política indigenista de Isabel la Católica* (Valladolid, Spain: 1969).

Russell, Peter, *Prince Henry 'the Navigator': A Life* (New Haven, CT: Yale University Press, 2000).

Russell-Wood, A. J. R., *The Black Man in Slavery and Freedom in Colonial Brazil* (New York: St. Martin's Press, 1982).

Russell-Wood, A. J. R., *The Portuguese Empire, 1415–1808: A World on the Move* (Baltimore, MD: Johns Hopkins University Press, 1998).

Russell-Wood, A. J. R. (ed.), *From Colony to Nation: Essays on the Independence of Brazil* (Baltimore, MD: Johns Hopkins University Press, 1975).

Ryder, Alan F. C., *Benin and the Europeans, 1485–1897* (New York: Humanities Press, 1969).

Sacks, David Harris, *The Widening Gate: Bristol and the Atlantic Economy, 1450–1700* (Berkeley: University of California Press, 1993).

Salomon, Frank, *Native Lords of Quito in the Age of the Incas* (Cambridge, UK: Cambridge University Press, 1986).

Sanchez Albornoz, Nicolas, *The Population History of Latin America* (Berkeley: University of California Press, 1974).

Sánchez Agesta, Luis, *Historia del constitucionalismo español* (Madrid: Instituto de Estudios Políticos, 1955).

Sauer, Carl Ortwin, *The Early Spanish Main* (Berkeley: University of California Press, 1966).

Sauer, Carl Ortwin, *Sixteenth Century North America: The Land and the People As Seen by the Europeans* (Berkeley: University of California Press, 1971).

Savelle, Max, *Empires to Nations: Expansion in America, 1713–1824* (Minneapolis: University of Minnesota Press, 1974).

Scammell, G. V., *The World Encompassed: The First European Maritime Empires, c. 800–1650* (Berkeley: University of California Press, 1981).

Schama, Simon, *Citizens: A Chronicle of the French Revolution* (New York: Vintage Books, 1989)

Schama, Simon, *Patriots and Liberators: Revolution in the Netherlands, 1730–1813* (New York: Vintage Books, 1977).

Scott, Julius Sherrard, III, "The Common Wind: Currents of Afro-American Communication in the Era of the Haitian Revolution," Ph.D. dissertation, Duke University, Durham, NC, 1986.

Scott, Rebecca J., *Slave Emancipation in Cuba: The Transition to Free Labor, 1860–1899* (Princeton, NJ: Princeton University Press, 1985).

Scott, Rebecca J. et al., *The Abolition of Slavery and the Aftermath of Emancipation in Brazil* (Durham, NC: Duke University Press, 1988).

Schlesinger, Roger and Arthur P. Stabler (eds.), *André Thevet's North America: A Sixteenth-Century View* (Kingston, QC: McGill's Queen University Press, 1986).

Schmidt, Benjamin, *Innocence Abroad: The Dutch Imagination and the New World, 1570–1670* (Cambridge, UK: Cambridge University Press, 2001).

Schumpeter, E. B., *English Overseas Trade Statistics (1697–1808)* (Oxford, UK: Oxford University Press, 1960).

Schwartz, Stuart B., *Slaves, Peasants, and Rebels: Reconsidering Brazilian Slavery* (Urbana: University of Illinois Press, 1992).

Schwartz, Stuart B., *Sugar Plantations in the Formation of Brazilian Society: Bahia, 1550–1835* (Cambridge, UK: Cambridge University Press, 1985).

Schwartz, Stuart B. (ed.), *Tropical Babylons: Sugar and the Making of the Atlantic World, 1450–1680* (Chapel Hill: University of North Carolina Press, 2004).

Searing, James, *West African Slavery and Atlantic Commerce: The Senegal River Valley, 1700–1860* (Cambridge, UK: Cambridge University Press, 1993).

Shepherd, Verene and Hilary McD. Beckles (eds.), *Caribbean Slavery in the Atlantic World: A Reader* (Kingston, QC: Ian Randle, 2000).

Silverberg, Robert, *The Realm of Prester John* (Athens: Ohio University Press, 1996).

Slenes, Robert W., "The Demography and Economics of Brazilian Slavery, 1850–1888," Ph.D. dissertation, Stanford University, Stanford, CA, 1975.

Smith, Abbot G., *Colonists in Bondage: White Servitude and Convict Labor in America, 1607–1776* (Chapel Hill: University of North Carolina Press, 1947).

Smith, David G., "The Mercantile Class of Portugal and Brazil in the Seventeenth Century: A Socio-Economic Study of the Merchants of Lisbon and Bahia, 1620–1690," Ph.D. dissertation, University of Texas, Austin, TX, 1975.

Smith, Roger C., *Vanguard of Empire: Ships of Exploration in the Age of Columbus* (New York: Oxford, 1993).

Socolow, Susan Migden, *The Women of Colonial Latin America* (Cambridge, UK: Cambridge University Press, 2000).

Solow, Barbara L. (ed.), *Slavery and the Rise of the Atlantic System* (Cambridge, UK: Cambridge University Press, 1991).

Sowell, Thomas, *Conquests and Cultures: An International History* (New York: Basic Books, 1998).

Spalding, Karen, *Huarochirí: An Andean Society Under Inca and Spanish Rule* (Stanford, CA: Stanford University Press, 1984).

Spell, Jefferson R., *Rousseau in the Spanish World before 1833: A Study in Franco-Spanish Literary Relations* (Austin: University of Texas Press, 1938).

Spurlin, Paul M., *Montesquieu in America, 1760–1801* (Baton Rouge: Louisiana State University Press, 1940).

Stannard, David E., *American Holocaust: The Conquest of the New World* (New York: Oxford University Press, 1992).

Steele, Ian K., *The English Atlantic, 1675–1740: An Exploration of Communication and Community* (New York: Oxford University Press, 1986).

Steele, Ian K., *Warpaths: Invasions of North America* (New York: Oxford University Press, 1994).

Stein, Robert Louis, *The French Slave Trade in the Eighteenth Century: An Old Regime Business* (Madison: University of Wisconsin Press, 1980).

Stein, Robert Louis, *The French Sugar Business in the Eighteenth Century* (Baton Rouge: Louisiana State University Press, 1988).

Stein, Robert Louis, *Léger Félicité Sonthonax: The Lost Sentinel of the Republic* (Cranbury, NJ: Associated University Presses, 1985).

Stein, Stanley J. and Barbara H. Stein, *Apogee of Empire: Spain and New Spain in the Age of Charles III, 1759–1789* (Baltimore, MD: Johns Hopkins University Press, 2003).

Stein, Stanley J. and Barbara H. Stein, *Silver, Trade, and War: Spain and America in the Making of Early Modern Europe* (Baltimore, MD: Johns Hopkins University Press, 2000).

Stern, Steve J., *Peru's Indian Peoples and the Challenge of Spanish Conquest: Huamanga to 1640* (Madison: University of Wisconsin Press, 1982).

Stern, Steve J., *Resistance, Rebellion and Consciousness in the Andean Peasant World (18th to 20th Centuries* (Madison: University of Wisconsin Press, 1987).

Sutherland, D. M. G., *France 1789–1815: Revolution and Counterrevolution* (New York: Oxford University Press, 1987).

Thomas, Hugh, *Conquest: Montezuma, Cortés, and the Fall of Old Mexico* (New York: Simon and Schuster, 1993).

Thomas, Hugh, *Rivers of Gold: The Rise of the Spanish Empire, from Columbus to Magellan* (New York: Random House, 2003).

Thomas, Hugh, *The Slave Trade: The Story of the Atlantic Slave Trade, 1440–1870* (New York: Simon and Schuster, 1997).

Thornton, John K., *Africa and Africans in the Making of the Atlantic World, 1400–1800*, 2nd edition (Cambridge, UK: Cambridge University Press, 1998).

Thornton, John K., *Warfare in Atlantic Africa, 1500–1800* (London: UCL Press, 1999).

Thwaites, Reuben G., *France in America, 1497–1763* (New York: Harper, 1905).

Tibbles, Anthony (ed.), *Transatlantic Slavery: Against Human Dignity* (London: National Museums and Galleries on Merseyside, 1995).

de Tocqueville, Alexis, *The Old Regime and the Revolution*, translated by Stuart Gilbert (New York: Anchor Books, 1983).

Tomich, Dale W., *Slavery and the Circuit of Sugar: Martinique and the World Economy, 1830–1848* (Baltimore, MD: Johns Hopkins University Press, 1990).

Toplin, Robert Brent, *The Abolition of Slavery in Brazil* (New York: Atheneum, 1975).

Toussaint-Samat, Maguelonne, *History of Food*, translated by Anthea Bell (Oxford, UK: Blackwell, 1992).

Townsend, Richard, *The Ancient Americas: Art from Sacred Landscapes* (Chicago: Art Institute of Chicago, 1992).

Tracy, James D. (ed.), *The Political Economy of Merchant Empires: State Power and World Trade, 1350–1750* (Cambridge, UK: Cambridge University Press, 1991).

Tracy, James D. (ed.), *The Rise of Merchant Empires: Long-Distance Trade in the Early Modern World, 1350–1750* (Cambridge, UK: Cambridge University Press, 1990).

Trudel, Marcel, *An Atlas of New France* (Sainte-Foy, QC: Les Presses de l'Université Laval, 1968).

Usner, Daniel H., Jr., *Indians, Settlers, and Slaves in a Frontier Exchange Economy: The Lower Mississippi Valley before 1783* (Chapel Hill: University of North Carolina Press, 1992).

de Vaissiere, Pierra, *Saint-Domingue. La société et la vie creoles sous l'ancien régime, 1629–1789* (Paris: Perrin, 1909).

Verger, Pierre, *Bahia and the West African Trade, 1549–1851* (Ibadan, Nigeria: 1970).

Verlinden, Charles, *The Beginnings of Modern Colonization: Eleven Essays with an Introduction* (Ithaca, NY: Cornell University Press, 1970).

Verlinden, Charles, *Les Origines de la civisation atlantique* (Paris: 1966).

de Villers, Marq and Sheila Hirtle, *Into Africa: A Journey Through the Ancient Empires* (Toronto: Key Porter Books, 1997).

Viola, Herman J. and Carolyn Margolis, *Seeds of Change: A Quincentennial Commemoration* (Washington, DC: Smithsonian Institution Press, 1991).

Voeks, Robert A., *Sacred Leaves of Candomblé: African Magic, Medicine, and Religion in Brazil* (Austin: University of Texas Press, 1997).

Vogt, John, *Portuguese Rule on the Gold Coast, 1469–1682* (Athens: University of Georgia Press, 1979).

de Vries, Jan and Ad van der Woude, *The First Modern Economy: Success, Failure, and Perseverance of the Dutch Economy, 1500–1815* (New York: Cambridge University Press, 1996).

Wallerstein, Immanuel, *The Modern World-System. Vol. I: Capitalist Agriculture and the Origins of the European World-Economy in the Sixteenth Century* (New York: Academic Press, 1974).

Wallerstein, Immanuel, *The Modern World-System. Vol. II: Mercantilism and the Consolidation of the European World-Economy, 1600–1750* (New York: Academic Press, 1980).

Walton, Timothy R., *The Spanish Treasure Fleets* (Sarasota, FL: Pineapple Press, 1994).

Walvin, James, *The Slave Trade* (Guernsey, UK: Sutton Publishing, 1999).

Watts, Sheldon, *Epidemics and History: Disease, Power and Imperialism* (New Haven, CT: Yale University Press, 1997).

Weber, David J., *The Spanish Frontier in North America* (New Haven, CT: Yale University Press, 1992).

Weckman, Luis, *La herencia medieval de México* (Ciudad de México: El Colegio de México, 1984).

Wehling, Arno and Maria José C. de Wehling, *Formação do Brazil Colonial* (Rio de Janeiro: Editora Nova Fronteira, 1994).

West, Thomas G., *Vindicating the Founders: Race, Sex, Class, and Justice in the Origins of America* (Lanham, MD: Rowman and Littlefield, 1997).

Westergaard, Waldemar, *The Danish West Indies under Company Rule, 1671–1754* (New York: Macmillan, 1917).

Whitfield, Peter, *New Found Lands: Maps in the History of Exploration* (New York: Routledge, 1998).

Whitaker, Arthur P. (ed.), *Latin American and the Enlightenment* (Ithaca, NY: Cornell University Press, 1942.

White, Deborah Gray, *Ar'n't I a Woman? Female Slaves in the Plantation South* (New York: W. W. Norton, 1985).

White, Richard, *The Middle Ground: Indians, Empires, and Republics in the Great Lakes Region, 1650–1815* (Cambridge, UK: Cambridge University Press, 1991).

Williams, Eric, *Capitalism and Slavery* (Chapel Hill: University of North Carolina Press, 1994).

Wilson, James, *The Earth Shall Weep: A History of Native America* (New York: Atlantic Monthly Press, 1998).

Wilson, Samuel M., *Hispaniola: Caribbean Chiefdoms in the Age of Columbus* (Tuscaloosa: University of Alabama Press, 1990).

Wolf, Eric, *Europe and the People Without History* (Berkeley: University of California Press, 1982).

Wolf, Eric R., *Sons of the Shaking Earth* (Chicago: University of Chicago Press, 1970).

Wood, Betty, *The Origins of American Slavery: Freedom and Bondage in the English Colonies* (New York: Hill and Wang, 1997).

Wood, Gordon S., *The Creation of the American Republic, 1776–1787* (Chapel Hill: University of North Carolina Press, 1998).

Wood, Gordon S., *The Radicalism of the American Revolution* (New York: Vintage Books, 1993).

Wood, Stephanie, *Transcending Conquest: Nahua Views of Spanish Colonial Mexico* (Norman: University of Oklahoma Press, 2003).

Wood, Stephanie and Robert Haskett (eds.), *Indian Women of Early Mexico* (Norman: University of Oklahoma Press, 1997).

Wrong, George M., *The Rise and Fall of New France*, 2 volumes (New York: Macmillan, 1928).

Wyndham, H. A., *The Atlantic and Slavery* (London: Oxford University Press, 1935).

Wyndham, H. A., *The Atlantic and Emancipation* (London: Oxford University Press, 1937).

Zamoyski, Adam, *Holy Madness: Romantics, Patriots, and Revolutionaries, 1776–1871* (New York: Viking, 2000).

Zavala, Silvio, *The Colonial Period in the History of the New World* (Ciudad de México: Instituto Panamericano de Geografía é Historia, 1962).

Zavala, Silvio, *El mundo americano en la epoca colonial*, 2 volumes (Ciudad de México: Editorial Porrua, 1967).

Zerubavel, Eviatar, *Terra Cognita: The Mental Discovery of America* (New Brunswick, NJ: Rutgers University Press, 1992).

Index

Abenakis, 310
Acadians, 243–245, 494
Acosta, José de, 281, 286
Adams, Abigail, 534
Adams, John, 435, 525, 539
Address to the Congress of Angostura, 606–607
Africa, 24–35
  agriculture, 24, 25
  Akan kingdom,
  animal domestication, 34
  arts, 30
  Berbers in, 25
  Canary Islands chiefdom (*See* Canary Islands)
  colonization, 662
  Dyula, 82
  early descriptions of, 80–81
  economic/political development in sub-Saharan, 34–35
  endemic disease, 28–29, 35
  equatorial Central Africa state development, 33
  European disease, 35
  famine, 35
  forest-savanna edge state development, 28–29
  Ghana empire, 27
  hearth of civilization, 25
  herding in, 25
  hunting/gathering in, 33–34
  Igboo, 29
  Kongo kingdom (*See* Kongo kingdom)
  Koranic schools, 25
  literacy, 27
  Loango kingdom, 33
  Mali empire, 25–27, 81
  Moors in, 25

  Muslims in, 24–25
  Niger Delta chiefdoms, 33
  plant domestication, 34
  savanna state development, 25–28
  slaves, indigenous
    agricultural, 33
    as infantrymen/archers, 27
    as laborers, 27–28
  slave trade, indigenous, 28, 33, 35
  Songhay (*See* Songhay)
  South Africa chiefdom, 34
  Thirstland, 33–34
  trade in, 25, 29
  tribute systems, 33
  underpopulation, in sub-Saharan, 35
  Wolof, 81, 82
  Yoruba kingdom, 30. *See also* Angola, and Portugal; antislavery, and Africa; gender relations, in Africa; Portuguese imperium, in Africa; slavery; slave trade; West Africa
African Trade Act, 487
Africanus, Leo, 28, 75, 117, 331
Age of Reason. *See* Enlightenment
Age of Revolution
  Dutch patriot revolt, 539–542
    crushing of, 541–542
    Free Corps (popular militias), 540–541
    precipitating manifesto, 539–540

    independence of Brazil, 609–612
    inspiration of early revolutions, 518
    reasons for anti-slavery actions in Caribbean, 587–589
    revolutionary republicanism, 517
    and slavery, 518, 613. *See also* American Revolution; Enlightenment; French Revolution; Haitian Revolution; Spanish America revolutions
agriculture
  expansion in 14th-century Europe, 38–39
  in pre-contact Africa
    irrigated, 24
    rain-fed, 25
  in pre-contact Americas, 19, 21
    chinapa, 17
    plant domestication, 22
    slash-and-burn, 21
Ahuitzotl, 12
Aimoré, 156
Akan kingdom (Africa),
Alaska, pre-contact sub-arctic/arctic, 21
Álavres Cabral, Pedro, 96
alcaldes mayors, 172
aldeias, 203–204, 308, 667
Alexander VI (pope), 214
Alfonso I (Kongo; Mbemba A. Nzinga), 115–117
Alfonso IV (Portugal), claims Canary Islands, 73
Alfonso X (Castille), 163

Algonkian Indians, 242
Algonquian, 20–21
  ethnography on, 289–290,
    292
Allada, 339
Allende, Ignacio, 599
Almagro, Diego de, 150
Alvarado, Pedro de, 138–139,
  144
Alvares, Diego, 449
American Revolution, 503–508,
  525–538
  anti-Federalists, 535
  Articles of Confederation,
    532
  beginning of, 505, 530
  Bill of Rights, 535–537
  Boston Massacre, 505, 528,
    529i
  Boston Tea Party, 528–529
  British diversion in West
    Indies/Florida, 506,
    537–538
  Continental Congress,
    505–506, 529–530, 531
  Declaration of Independence,
    531
  difference from French
    Revolution, 563–565
  dispute over taxes, 503–505
  Enlightenment influence on,
    527
  Federalist movement, 535
  foreign assistance, 505–507
  impetus for, 503–505,
    527–528
  Intolerable Acts, 505
  Native American assistance,
    507
  non-importation pact by
    colonists, 528
  peace negotiations, 508
  and political/social equality,
    533
  Proclamation Line of 1763,
    527
  Quartering Act, 527
  as radical, 525
  republicanism, 531–532
  rights of women, 533–534
  separation of powers, 532
  in southern colonies, 507–508
  Stamp Act, 503–504, 527,
    537
  Sugar Act, 503, 527
  surrender of British, 508
  as too democratic/egalitarian,
    534–535
  Townshend Duties, 504–505,
    528, 533, 537
Americas, pre-contact, 6–24
  agriculture, 17, 19, 21, 22

animal domestication, 22
  Chavin culture, 7
  chiefdoms in, 18–22
    Anasazi, 19
    Carib, 19
    Cenú, 21
    Chibcha, 21
    Ciboney, 19
    conflict among, 20, 21–22
    Hohokam, 19
    Mississipian, 19–20
    Mogollon, 19
    Muisca, 21
    native Brazil, 21–22
    Pacaha, 19–20
    Taino, 18–19
    Tairona, 21
  Chimu Empire, 7
  confederacies, 21
  disease, 23
  fishing, 19, 21, 22
  gathering, 19, 22
  hunting, 19, 20–21, 22
  Inka empire, 7, 13–17
    ancestor worship, 16–17
    child sacrifice, 17
    Cuzco, 16–17
    tribute system, 14
  Mapuche, 22
  Maya, 7
  metals, 23
  Mexica Empire, 7, 10–13
    cosmology, 11–12
    Flowery Wars, 11
    human sacrifice, 12
    social stratification, 11
    Teotihuacan, 7, 10–11
    Triple Alliance, 10–11
  Moche culture, 7
  Native American languages, 6
  Olmec culture, 7
  population, 22–23
  population, regional c. 1492,
    23t
  similarity between
    Inka/Mexica Empires,
    17–18
  Tiahuanaco culture, 7
  Toltec culture, 7
  tools, 23
  trade, 10, 19, 21
  tribute system, 11, 14, 19
  Wari culture, 7
  writing/literacy, 23–24
Amherst, Jeffery, 496, 497–499
Amistad affair, 643
Amsterdam
  port of, 230i. See also United
    Provinces of the
    Netherlands
Anahuac (in the vicinity of the
    waters), 10

Anasazi, 19
  violence among, 20
Anderson, Karen, 425
Anglo-Dutch wars, 260–261,
  475–476
Anglo-Norman monarchy, 45
Angola
  Dutch defeat in, 259–260
  intermarriage in, 436–437
Angola, and Portugal, 192–197
  agriculture, 195–196
  clerical establishment, 195,
    196
  as colony of Brazil, 195
  council of local notables in,
    195
  donatório awarded, 119
  Dutch invasion, 124, 195
  government, 192–195
  Imbangala, 123
  Jesuits in, 123
  Luanda, 118, 122–123, 124,
    195
  military conquest of, 119,
    123–124
  missionaries, 118–119
  mulattos, 196
  Pende on arrival of
    Portuguese, 123
  puppet ruler, 123, 124
  slave trade, 118, 122–123,
    195, 196–197
  Spanish Habsburgs establish
    royal colony, 122
  tribute, 192
Angolares, 191
animal domestication, in
    pre-contact Americas, 22
anker, definition of, 667
antislavery, and Africa,
  654–658
  abolishment of legal status of
    slavery, 657
  British efforts to abolish
    slavery, 654–655
  economic consequences,
    656–657
  forced labor, 657
  increase in Central/southeast
    trade, 655–657
  slow demise of slavery/slave
    trade, 655–656, 657–658
  territories for liberated slaves,
    654
antislavery, British and French,
  638–641
  abolition by Britain, 639–640
  antislavery movement in
    France, 640
  Dutch and antislavery, 641
  emancipation and French,
    640–641

religious motivation in
Britain, 638
slave revolts and Britain,
638–639
slave revolts and French, 640
antislavery, demise of American
slavery, 1860s–1880s,
641–654
Amistad affair effect on, 643
antislavery movement in
United States, 643–645
black soldiers in Civil War,
645
in Brazil, 649–654
Civil War, 644–645
consequences of election of
Lincoln, 644
cotton and, 641–642
cotton boom effect on
slavery, 641–642
and Cuban independence,
646–648
Dred Scott decision, 644
Emancipation Proclamation,
645
formation of Confederate
States of America, 644
Fugitive Slave Act, 644, 645
industrial revolution effect on
slavery, 641–642
Kansas-Nebraska Act, 644
Lincoln and, 644, 645
Missouri Compromise, 643,
644
Moret Law, 647
resettlement of slaves in
Africa/Haiti, 642–643
Slave Power conspiracy, 644
Spanish Abolitionist Society,
647
Thirteenth Amendment, 645
antislavery, revolutionary,
1770s–1804, 624–633
American Revolution,
624–626
abolition of slave trade,
625
early emancipation laws,
625
founding fathers and
antislavery, 624–625
slaves as soldiers in, 626
southern states and
antislavery, 625
antislavery in Great Britain,
628–632
abolishment of slave trade,
631–632
emergence of antislavery
movement, 628–629
freed slaves shipped to
Sierra Leone, 632

influence of other nations
on abolishment, 632
popular support for
antislavery movement,
629
and Quakers, 628
weakening of antislavery
movement, 629–631
Zong affair effect on, 629
French Revolution, 626–628
emancipation decree, 627
Society of the Friends of the
Blacks, 626–627
antislavery, Spanish American,
1810s–1850s, 633–638
abolition of slave trade,
634–636
and Catholic Church, 633
and Cortes of Cádiz, 634
free womb laws, 634, 635,
636–637
lessening need for slave labor,
633–634
and Mexican Revolution, 634
and slaves as soldiers,
635–636
slow rate of emancipation,
637–638
survival of slave systems,
637–638
antislavery thought and
opinion, 617–623
capitalism effect on, 618
Enlightenment philosophers
on, 621–623
moral consciousness,
617–618, 623
political economists on, 623
Protestants on, 619–621
Quakers on, 619, 620–621,
623
slavery as not
permanent/natural,
618–619
slavery harm to
slaveholder/society, 623
Antonil, André Jaão, 410, 454
Anzico, 117
Anzilotti, Cara, 459
aqueduct, stone in Teotihuacan,
10
Arab astronomy texts, 84–86
Arab mariners, 57
Arabs, 25, 327
Arawak speakers, 18–19, 22
arbitristas (Spanish reformers),
225
Armas, Rumeo de, 119
Aro, 339
arroba, definition of, 667
Articles of Pacification, 415
Aruba, 130

asientos, 344, 383, 667
Askia Mohammed (Muslim
king), 27
astrolabe, 70, 71i, 667
Atahualpa, 146–148, 284, 439
Atkins, John, 347, 351, 356,
391, 392
Atlantic, first forays, 53
Eric the Red, 54, 55
into Greenland, 54
into Iceland by Irish monks,
53–54
into Labrador and Baffin
Island, 54–55
Norse raiders/settlers, 54
into North America by Norse,
54
Atlantic Africa Overseas Trade,
1680–1820, 341t
Atlantic Mediterranean. See
Near Atlantic
Atlantic Ocean, 67–71
early charts/maps of, 68–70
map of Near Atlantic, 74, 74i
maritime technology for
exploring, 70–71
Near Atlantic, 71–75
reasons for opening of,
101–103
wind-driven current system,
68
winds and currents map,
69m, 70
wind system, 68
Atlantic System, 326
Atlantic World
fall of/rise of modern world,
661–666
growth as result of
European/African/Indian
interactions, xxii
Iberian/Native alliances,
158–159
importance of Western
Europeans in, xxi–xxii
rise and fall of, xxii–xxiv
shipping routes, c. 1750, 488,
489m
audiencias, 172
Augustinians, 301
in Mexica, 144
in Peru, 303
in Philippines, 301
Austrian Netherlands, French
Revolution influence on,
559–560
Aveiro, João Alfonso, 84
Ávila, Pedro Arias de, 130
Azores, 73
Aztecs. See Nahua

Bacon, Francis, 239

Bahamas, 129–130
Bahia capitancy, 156, 386, 388–389
Balboa, Vasco Núñez de, 98
ball courts, 18, 19
Baltic Germans, 255
Banda (Africa),
bandeirantes, 204, 667
bandeiras, definition of, 667
baracoons, 349, 402
Barbados
  account of Negroes of, 404–406
  annual percent decline in slave populations, 408t
  indentured workers in, 256
  Jews in, 255
  planting English colony, 256, 257–259
  reaction to American Revolution, 538
  sale of African slaves in, 359–360
  sugar industry in, 256, 391–393
Barbot, Jean, 262, 337, 351, 433–434
barcha (ship with oars), 71
Barry, Boubacar, 369
Battle of Jenkins Ear, 491
Bayly, C.A., 661
Bay of All Saints, 199i
Beccaria, Marquis de (Cesare), 520
Bemoin (King), 88
Benalcázar, Sebastian de, 149
Benedictines, 199
Benevente, Toribio de, 283
Benguela Current, 68
Benin, 29, 30, 33, 84, 112–114
  Bight of Benin, 262, 334, 338–339, 357, 359, 365
Berbers, 25, 28, 76, 327
Berbice, 260, 511–513
Bermuda, tobacco farms in, 239
Betanzos, Juan de, 16, 17, 18, 284
Biafra, as slave source, 262, 339, 359
Bight of Benin, 262, 334, 338–339, 357, 359, 365
Bight of Biafra, 262, 339, 359
Black, Jeremy, 473–474
Blackstone, William, 427
Blake, William, 207
The Bloody victories Obtained by the Iroquois over Our Hurons (Jesuit Relations), 315–316
Bodin, Jean, 619
Bolívar, Simón, 597, 601

Address to the Congress of Angostura, 606–607
  constitutionalism of, 607–608
  and liberation of slaves, 588–589, 603
  portrait of, 608i
  on revolution, 567
Bolivia (Upper Peru)
  end of slavery in, 641
  independence of, 602
Bonaparte, Joseph, 512, 561, 595–596
Bonaparte, Napoleon, 509, 510–511, 557, 561, 591
Bono (Africa),
Bosman, Willem, 332, 336, 351, 432, 434
bossal/bozal, 401, 402, 667
Boston Massacre, 505, 528, 529i
Boston Tea Party, 528–529
Botero, Giovanni, 170
Bourbon reforms, 589–590, 596–597
Boxer, C.R., 451
Boyer, Jean-Pierre, 583–585
Braddock, Edward, 494
Bradford, William, 237
Braithwaite, John, 409
Brandão, Ambrósio Fernandes, 450
Braudel, Fernand, xxiv–xxv, 65, 367
Brazil, 197–205
  administrative supervision of church/state, 199–200
  African slave labor, 200
  Aimoré, 156
  Bahia capitancy, 156, 386, 388–389
  Bahia capitancy, 198, 200–201
  bandeirantes, 204
  bilateral pattern of slave trade, 357
  candomblés in, 364–366
  coffee economy, 649
  conquest of coastal, 152–157
  crioulos (mulattos), 203, 204
  crown capitaincies, 153
  discovery of bulge of, 96
  division into states, 199
  Dutch defeat in, 259–260
  Dutch efforts at religious conversion, 312
  episcopate, 199
  ethnography on, 286–289
  French in, 153, 154–155, 197
  gold, 204, 205
  government, 197–199
  hunter-gatherers, 156
  Ilhéus capitaincy, 156

  immigration to, 202
  independence of, 609–612
    created without revolution, 609
    Dom João VI as ruler, 610
    Dom Pedro I as emperor, 611–612
    Portuguese revolution and, 610–611
    repression of independence movements, 609–610
  Indian slave labor, 153–154, 156, 200, 204
  intermarriage, 153, 155, 203
  Jesuits in, 153, 155, 156, 199, 203–204, 309–310
  Jews in, 202
  lurid scene of cannibalism, 276i
  mamelucos (mestizos), 203, 204
  map of colonial, 201m
  map of Native and Portuguese, 152m
  missionaries, 203–204
  Paraíba capitancy, 156
  Paulistas, 204, 295–296
  Pernambuco capitancy, 155
  Pernambuco capitaincy, 198, 200
  plantations, 200–202, 205
  population of, 202t
  Portuguese alliances with Natives, 155, 156
  Portuguese claim to, 96–97
  Portuguese colonization, 153
  Potiguar, 155, 156
  pre-contact, 21–22
  quilombos (runaway slave communities), 203
  Rio Grande capitancy, 156
  royal governors, 198–199
  royal Indian policy, 156–157
  São Paulo capitancy, 295
  São Tomé capitancy, 156
  São Vicente capitaincy, 198, 200
  slavery, 649
    abolitionism in, 652–653
    delaying abolition with Rio Branco Law, 650–651
    emergence of antislavery movement, 650
    geographic reorientation of, 649–650
    revived antislavery movement, 651–653
    slave population, 1798–1887, 649, 649t
    social class system, 202–203
    sugar economy, 153–154, 191, 200–202, 295–296

Tupinambá, 154–155, 286–289
Tupiniuin, 154–155
westward expansion, 204–205. See also gender relations, in Brazil
Brazilian engenho (sugar mill), 200–201, 387i
brazilwood (red dyestuff), 96–97, 152, 197, 667
Bristol, England, 97–98
British Guiana, 398–399
Brooks, Francis, 327
Brown, Kathleen M., 421
Bry, Theodor de, 439
bubonic plague, 321–322
buccaneers, 263–271, 667
    Dutch, 265
    French, 268–269
    in Jamaica, 264–265
    and Providence Island colony, 264
The Buccaneers of America (Exquemelin), 266–268
Buenos Aires, 151, 205, 225, 502, 512, 601–602
buen policía (law and order), 169–170
Bull of Donation and Demarcation, 106
Burke, Edmund, 528

Cabeza de Vaca, Alvar Nuñez, 20
caboclo, 450
Cabot, John, 97–98, 228
Cabot, Sebastian, 228
cacahuatl (chocolate), 448
cacique, 175, 668
Cadamosto, 80–81, 83
Cadornega, António de Oliveira, 437
cafuso, 450
Cahokia, 19
Cajamarca, 149
Cakchiquel Maya, 144
calba, 450
Calhoun, John C., 643
Calusas, of Florida, 18
Camara de Luanda, 195
Canada
    French emigration to, 1670–1729, 462t
    gradual emancipation in, 629
    Jesuits in New France, 309–310
    pre-contact sub-arctic/arctic, 21
    Québec, 242, 478, 496, 497i, 505
    Seven Years War and, 494, 496–497, 502

Canary Current, 68, 79
Canary Islands, 73, 107–109
    Castile claim to, 73, 74
    Castile conquest of, 74, 107, 108–109
    Castile control of, 73, 76
    chiefdom, 24
    claims to control of, 73–74, 76, 107–108
    diversity among, 107
    epidemics in, 109
    Fuerteventura, 107
    Gomera, 107–109
    Gran Canaria, 107–108
    Lanzarote, 73–74, 107–108
    La Palma, 107
    missionaries, 107
    pre-contact, 24
    slaves in, 73, 75, 79, 381
    sugar production, 75, 380
    Tenerife, 107, 108
    Treaty of Alcáçovas, 74, 90, 108
candomblés, in Brazil, 364–366
cannibalism
    lurid scene from Brazil, 276i
    in travel narratives/travelogues, 278
canoe-building, by Taino, 19
Cantor, Norman, 375
Cão, Diogo, 83–84, 114
Caonabó (chief), 126, 127
capac hucha/capacocha (royal obligation), 17
Capetian monarchy, 45
Cape Verde Islands, 75, 80
capitalism
    defining, 65. See also capitalism, and western Europe
capitalism, and western Europe, 62–67
    industrial, 67
    Marxists/neo-Marxists, 63–64
    merchant capitalism, 65–67
    significance of endogenous/exogenous forces, 64–65
    society with market/market society, 67
    Weberians, 62–63, 64
capitão-mor, definition of, 668
Capitulaciones de Santa Fe, 92–93
captaincy
    in Brazil, 386
    definition of, 668
caravels, 71, 79–80, 219, 668
careen, definition of, 668
cargo ships, ocean-going, 70–71

Caribbean
    African slaves in, 129
    Cuba, 125, 129
    devastation of, 131
    disease in, 129
    emancipation of slaves in, 627
    map of Native and Spanish, 130m
    nonindigenous animals, 129
    protests against devastation of, 131
    right of conquest in, 132. See also Columbus, Christopher; individual country
caribocas, 450
Caribs, 19, 130, 278–279
Carlos I (Spain), 161–162
Carlos III (Spain), 590, 596
Carlos IV (Spain), 590
Carlos V (Spain), 139, 146, 171, 222, 223, 229–230
Carlos VI (Spain), 595–596
Carmelites, 199
carracks, 92, 219, 668. See also nãos
Carrera de Indias, 216–217, 218–219, 668
Cartier, Jacque, 101, 227, 236, 275
Casa de Dontratación, 216
castas, 186, 599, 604–605, 668
Castile
    and Caribbean, 125
    claim to Canary Islands, 73, 74
    conquest of Canary Islands, 74, 107, 108–109
    control of Canary Islands, 73, 76
    dynastic union with Aragón, 124–125
    financial support for expansion, 125
    state trading company at Seville, 125. See also Spanish imperium, making of
Castillo, Bernal Díaz del, 279
Catalan Atlas, 24–25, 36
Catawbas, 313
Cathay (China), 91, 668
Cayenne, 257, 398–399
Central Africa, in Early European era, 116m
Central Mexico
    late 16th-century towns, 175i
    Spanish in, 144, 145
Cenú, 21
ceremonial mounds, Cahokia, 19
Chaco Canyon, 19

Champlain, Samuel de, 242,
　298, 309
Chanchan, 7
Charles II, 477
Charles of Ghent, xxvii
Charles V (Holy Roman
　Empire), 98–100,
　161–163, 166
Charrúa, 151
chartered companies, 238
Chavin culture, 7
Chiapa, 144
Chibcha, 21
Chichen Itza, 13
Child, Josiah, 66
Chile, 150
Chimu Empire, 7
China
　invention of magnetic
　　compass, 70, 84
　maritime expeditions, 55–57
　slavery in, 35
　trade and,
chinapa agriculture, 17
Chipango (Japan), 91
chip log and reel, definition of,
　668
Chocó, 151
Chollolan, massacre at,
　135–136
Chontal Maya, 133
Choquette, Leslie, 426, 461
Christophe, Henri, 585, 587
Chronicle of Cieza de León,
　285*i*
Ciboney, 19
Cieza de León, Pedro, 284
cimarrónes, definition of, 668
circumnavigation, first, 98–100
Clarkson, Thomas, 617–618,
　629, 632
Classic Era, in pre-contact
　Americas, 7
Clerc, François de, 231
cloth, 65, 81
Cobo, Bernabé, 17, 178
coca crop, 183
Cocum, 145
Code Noir, 393–394, 408
Codex Telleriano-Remensis,
　284
Coelho, Duarte, 153
coffee
　in Brazil, 649
　in Haiti, 649
cofradías, 302, 385–386, 668
Colbert, Jean-Baptiste, 245,
　257
Colmobo, Cristoforo. *See*
　Columbus, Christopher
Colonia do Sacramento,
　502–503

colonial/modern dichotomy,
　665–666
colonies, planting, 236–263
　Anglo-Dutch wars, 260–261
　Baltic Germans and, 255
　Cayenne, 257
　chartered companies, 238
　Company of New France,
　　242–246
　Danish slave trade,
　Dutch and, 246–254,
　　259–261
　Dutch Brazil, 251–252, 253
　Dutch defeat in Brazil and
　　Angola, 259–260
　Dutch East India Company,
　　253, 259
　Dutch New West India
　　Company,
　Dutch West India Company,
　　248–253, 255, 259
　English and, 238–242, 254,
　　255
　English and Virginia
　　Company, 238–240
　English Barbados, 256,
　　257–259
　English colonization of
　　Ireland, 236–237
　English in Caribbean,
　　255–256
　English proprietary, 240–242
　failed colonies, 236
　French and, 242–246, 255,
　　256–257
　indentured servants in
　　Virginia, 239
　Jamaica, 256
　Jamestown settlement,
　　238–240
　Louisiana, 246
　Maryland, 240–242
　Massachusetts Bay colony,
　　240
　New Amsterdam, 250
　New Holland (Brazil), 255
　New Netherlands Company,
　　248
　New Sweden, 251
　Plymouth plantation, 240
　Port Royal, 242
　Providence Island colony,
　　264
　Québec, 242
　Rhode Island, 240
　slave labor in Virginia, 239
　Surinam, 260
　Swedes and, 255
　tobacco farms in Bermuda,
　　239
　tobacco farms in Virginia,
　　239

Columbus, Christopher, 60,
　91–96
　brings sugarcane to
　　Hispaniola, 383
　complaints about
　　misgovernment, 128
　death of, 95–96
　destruction of La Navidad,
　　126
　on Española during first
　　voyage, 126
　finds gold mines at Cibao,
　　126–128
　first voyage, 93–94
　fourth voyage, 95
　imposes tribute, 127
　royal commission, 92–93
　second voyage, 94
　settlement at Isabella, 126
　slave trade and, 127–128
　theory of, 91
　third voyage, 94–95
　writings about Indians, 278
Columbus, Diego, 129
Columbus, Ferdinand, 127
Company of New France,
　242–246
Company of the Isles of
　America, 394
compass, 70, 669
*The Complete English
　Tradesman* (Defoe),
　486–487
"Concerning Marriage and of
　Parental Duty", 429–430
concubines
　among plantation slaves, 413
　children of, 437, 449
　definition of, 669
　Indian women as, 439, 460
　native women as, 207
　slaves as, 331
Condorcet, Marquis de, 519,
　558
Consulada de Seville (merchant
　houses), 216
Continental Congress, 505–506,
　529–530, 531
Cooper, David, 467
Coosas, of Georgia, 20
Corrêa, Silva, 437
corregidores, 172
corsaires
　Barbary, 327
　French corsaires and
　　Portuguese, 231
　French corsaires and Spanish,
　　231
　French Huguenot, 226
　Lutheran and Spanish, 235
Corte-Real, Gaspar, 98
Corte-Real, Miguel, 98

Cortés, Hernando, 133–144
  alliance with Texcoco, 140
  alliance with Tlaxcala, 134,
    139
  alliance with Totonacs, 134
  arms and ships, 140
  booty, 136
  disease effect on enemies,
    140, 141
  encomienda distribution, 144
  encomiendas, 171
  entry into Valley of Mexico,
    136
  gold looting, 141
  Indian allies of, 135–136,
    139, 140, 141
  Indian women as gifts to, 440
  at Ixtlapalapan, 140
  massacre at Chollolan,
    135–136
  Moteuççoma pays tribute to,
    133
  myth of, as god, 135
  native massacre at
    Tenochtitlán, 141
  personal view of Mexica,
    275
  rape of Indian women by men
    of, 439
  and results of massacre by
    Alvarado, 138–139
  royal contract, 133–134
  Tenochtitlán
    native massacre at, 141
    rebuilding of, 144
    resides at, 136
    siege/conquest of, 139–141
    temporary defeat at, 139
    wounding/capture of, 141
  writings on Indians, 279
Cosa, Juan de la, 96
cosmology, in Mexica Empire,
    11–12
coureurs de bois, definition of,
    669
Coventry, William, 477
Covilhã, Pero da, 84
creoles, in plantation complex,
    401–402
criollos, 186, 596, 669
Cromwell, Oliver, 256
Crusades, 40, 58
Cuba, 125, 129
  Chinese workers in, 648
  Havana marketplace, 168i
  independence of, 646–648
  patronato system in, 648
  slave population, 1795–1860,
    646t
  as Spanish port, 217
  wage labor in sugar industry,
    648–649

warning letter to Indians of,
    131
Cugano, Quobna Ottobah, 330,
    353, 355–356, 417
Cuneo, Michele de, 438–439
Curaçao, 130, 254, 260,
    586–587
curacas, 175
Curtin, Philip, 366
Cuzco, 16–17
  ancestor worship at, 16–17
  architecture at, 16
  imagined scene of conquest,
    148i

da Gama, Vasco, 86
Dahomey kingdom, 339,
    368–369
da Mota, Mendo, 225
Darwin, Charles, 665
dead reckoning, 70, 669
Dean, Phyllis, 488–490
de Cieza, Pedro, xxv
A Declaration to the French
    Nation from the
    National Assembly 1790,
    551–552
Declaration of the
    Independence of the
    Blacks of St. Domingo
    1803, 584–585
Defoe, Daniel, 481, 486–487
degradados, 202, 432, 435,
    436, 669
de Gua, Pierre, 243–245
de la Vega, Garcilaso, 16, 20
Demerara, 260, 511–513, 639
Demos, John, 458
De Origine, Populi: On the
    Origins of the Natives of
    Virginia (Strachey),
    287–289
de Rochefort, César, 377–378
de Rouvroy, Claude-Henri, 465
Desmoulins, Camille, 550
de Soto, Hernando, 19–20, 439
de Sousa, Martim Afonso, 153
de Sousa, Tomé, 153
Dessalles, Pierre, 402, 409, 414
dhows, 57
Dias, Bartomomeu, 84, 86, 192
Diaz, Paulo, 120–122
Díaz del Casillo, Beranl,
    142–144
Diderot, Dennis, 519, 524, 525,
    569
disease
  Black Death in pre-expansion
    Europe, 37–38, 46
  in Canary Islands, 109
  in Caribbean, 129
  endemic in Africa, 28–29, 35

epidemics in 19th/20th
    centuries, 665
  European, in Africa, 35
  leprosy in Africa, 35
  Native American lack of
    resistance to, 22–23
  of pre-contact Native
    Americans, 23
  schistosomiasis (liver flukes),
    35
  smallpox epidemic in Valley
    of Mexico, 140, 141
  smallpox in Africa, 35
  smallpox in Brazil, 388
A Dispatch to Blanchlande,
    Governor of Saint
    Domingue 1791, 572
doctrina, definition of, 669
Doldrums, 68
dollar, definition of, 669
Dominicans, 301
  Bartolomé Las Casas, 126,
    127, 129, 166, 280
  on Indian slave labor,
    131–132, 172
  in Mexico, 144, 181, 305
  in Philippines, 301
Dona Beatrice (Kimpa Vita),
    118
donatório, 119, 669
Douglass, Frederick, 643, 645
Drake, Francis, 232, 233
  fleet at Santo Domingo,
    233i
Dred Scott decision, 644
Durán, Diego, 11, 18
Durston, Alan, 169–170
Dutch
  Anglo-Dutch wars, 260–261,
    475–476
  commercial success, 66
  defeat in Brazil and Angola,
    259–260
  Dutch patriot revolt, 539–542
  invasion of Angola, 124
  invasions of Iberian Atlantic,
    234–235
  planting colonies, 246–254,
    259–261
  rise and fall in New World,
    474–476
  view of Indians as wild men,
    275
  in West Indies, 249–250. See
    also United Provinces of
    the Netherlands
Dutch Brazil, 251–252, 253
Dutch East India Company
    (VOC), 66, 235, 248,
    253, 259, 301, 312
Dutch New West India
    Company,

Dutch Reformed Church,
312–313
Dutch West India Company
(WIC), 312, 389–390,
674
Atlantic slave trade, 344–345
and planting of colonies,
248–253, 255, 259
Du Tetre, Jean-Baptiste, 411
Dyula, 82

East India Company (VOC), 66,
235, 248, 253, 259, 301,
312
Eburne, Richard, 456
ecomiendas, 171, 294–295
economic growth
North/South differences, 662,
663
Western Europe, 1500–1700,
225t
of world regions, 1820–2000,
663
economy
total wealth of world regions,
GDP, 1000–1600, 56,
56t. See also capitalism
Ecuador, 149
Edwards, Bryan, 362–363, 379,
402, 411, 412, 415
Egerton, Sarah Fyges, 427
Egypt
Christian trade embargo on,
59
mariners from, 57
Eighty Years War, 259
Elbl, Ivana, 329, 330–331
Eliot, John, 311
Elizabeth I (England), 214
Elliott, John, 456
Eltis, David, 367–368, 370
Emancipation Proclamation,
645
Emerald Isle, 68
encomendero, 128
encomiendas, 129, 669
distribution by Cortés,
144
The End of the Conquest of
Mexico (Díaz del
Casillo), 142–144
engagés, 245, 669
engenho (sugar mill), 200–201,
387i, 669
England
Atlantic contribution to trade,
1700–1772, 490, 490t
Bristol, 97–98
colonization of Ireland,
236–237
interventions in Netherlands,
233

invasions of Iberian Atlantic,
232–234
in Africa, 232–233
in Caribbean, 232
in Guiana, 234
and New World
arrival in Virginia, 239i
British Atlantic empire,
1763, 504, 504m
in Caribbean, 255–256
colonies planted by,
238–242, 254, 255
early voyages to New
World, 97–98
emigration to America,
1635, 458t
on late war with France,
500–501
ports of, 228
view of Indians as savage,
275–276. See also
Europe, pre-expansion;
France and Great Britain,
in long 18th century;
gender relations, in New
England/New France
English and Virginia Company,
238–240
English Barbados, 256,
257–259
English Carolinas, 298–299
English proprietary, 240–242
Enlightenment, 519–525
and greater good, 524
and individual rights, 520
influences on, 524–525
and popular sovereignty,
522–523
and punishment, 520
and religion, 519–520
as revolutionary ideology,
519
and rights of women, 520
and separation of powers,
521–522
and social contract, 520–521
and Spain, 523–524
Enrique III (Castille), 107
The Entire Earth Consists of
Three Continents
(Claudius Ptolemy), 72
entrepôt, 475
definition of, 669
slave, 192, 336
epidemics. See disease
Equiano, Olaudah, 332, 334,
335, 339, 353–354,
411–412, 413, 629
Erasmus, Desiderius, 427
Eric the Red, 54, 55
Eríksson, Lief, 55
esclaveries, 349

Española, 125–128
devastation of Taino, 129.
See also Columbus,
Christopher; Hispaniola
Essequibo, 260, 511–513
estancia, 182–183, 294, 670
ethnographies, on Indians,
281–292
Acosta, José de, 286
Algonquian, 289–290, 292
artist John White, 289–290
Benevente, 283
Betanzos, 284
bilingual, 283–284
in Brazil, 286–289
on cannibals, 289
Cieza de León, Pedro, 284
Codex Telleriano-Remensis,
284
Harriot, Thomas, 289–290
on Inkas, 284–286
on Iroquois, 290–292
Jesuit Relations, 290
Lafitau, 292
Lahontan, 292
Léry, Jean de, 286–289
Montaigne, 289
Nahua, 283–284
New France, 292
New Netherland, 290–292
Pané, first ethnography,
282–283
Sahagún, 283–284
Santo Tomás, 286
van den Bogaert, 290
van der Donck, 290–292
working with native
languages, 283
Europe, pre-expansion, 35–50
agricultural expansion,
38–39, 46
Anglo-Norman monarchy,
45
Black Death in, 37–38, 46
Capetian monarchy, 45
Crusades, 40
expansion of external
frontiers, 39–40
famine, 37
fiefdom system, 39, 40
fishing, 39
Germany, 45–46
gold coins, 42
Iberian peninsula, 39–40, 45
Italy, 45–46
lack of political integration,
43–46
Low Countries, 43, 45
metallurgy, 39
mining, 39
population, growth in
Western, 1000–1500, 38t

population, regional in Western, c. 1500, 47t
print revolution, 47–48
Reconquest, 39–40
slavery in, 35
technological change, 39
tenant sytem, 46
trade, 40–43, 48–49
university system, 47
urban expansion, 40
violence and brutality, 48
wars, 38
wool trade, 43
European exceptionalism, 63
European expansion, motives for, 57, 60–62
European migration, 1500–1700, 259t
European seaborne empires, 270m
"Europe Supported by Africa & America" (engraving), 207
An Exhortation & Caution to Friends Concerning Buying or Keeping Negroes (Keith), 620–621

Fage, J. D., 367, 370
Falkland Current, 68
famine, in Africa, 35
Faria, Manuel Severim de, 123
fathom, definition of, 670
fazendas, 201–202, 436, 670
feitoria (trading factory), 83, 96–97, 110–111, 670
Felipe II (Spain), 158, 162, 166
dispatches Spanish Armada, 233
imposes embargo on Dutch ships, 234
Felipe V (Spain), 479
Fernández de Oviedo, Gonzalo, 280, 383
Fernando Po, 82–83
Fernando VII (Spain), 82–83, 591, 592, 595–596, 603
Ferrer, Jaume, 73
fetitço (witchcraft), 81, 670
fiefdom system, 39, 40
filhos da terra, 192, 432–433, 435, 436, 437, 462, 670
The First Booke of Moses, Callled Genesis, The Holy Bible, 1638, 41
First Maroon War, 415
fishing
Ciboney, 19
in pre-expansion Europe, 39
Taino, 18–19
Flanders, wool trade in, 43

florin, definition of, 670
Flowery Wars, 11
fluyt, 475, 670
Fortunate Isles. *See* Canary Islands
France
Atlantic coast of, 228m
in Brazil, 153, 154–155, 197
colony planting by, 242–246, 255, 256–257
invasions of Iberian Atlantic, 227
defeat in Florida, 231–232
French corsaires and Portuguese, 231
French corsaires and Spanish, 231
in New World
early voyages to New World, 96
emigration to Canada, 1670–1729, 462t
on late war with England, 500–501
ports of, 227
view of Indians as savages, 275. *See also* France and Great Britain, in long 18th century; French Revolution; gender relations, in New England/New France
France and Great Britain, in long 18th century
American Revolution, 472, 514
Battle of Jenkins Ear, 491
British debt, 484–485
British in South America, 512
British naval power, 483–484
British triumph, 513–514
Cherokee Rebellion, 496–497
Continental System, 483–484
effect of Dutch commercial hegemony on, 475–476
England, internal division in, 473
English-Indian relations, 497–499
English merchants, 485–487
France as preeminent land power, 473
French and Indian War, 472
French debt, 484–485
French merchants, 487–488
French Revolution, 472
interlude, 1713–1739, 482–490
King George's War, 491–493
Louisiana colony, 483
Napoleon overtakes Spain, 512

Ohio Valley war, 493–494, 495–496
Peninsular War, 512
privateers/piracy, 481–482
Queen Anne's War, 480
round one, 1689–1713, 476–482
round three, 1792–1815 (French Revolution), 501–508
round two, 1739–1763, 490–501
Seven Years War, 494, 496–497, 502
value of French colonial trade, 482
war in New England, 478–479
war in New France, 478, 480–481
war in West Indies, 479–480, 509–511, 513
War of 1812, 512–513
Franciscans, 144, 173–174, 199, 301, 303, 306–307
Francis I (France), 101
François I (France), 214, 227
Franklin, Benjamin, 527–528, 542, 623
free womb laws, 634, 635, 636–637
French and Indian War, 318
French Revolution, 542–565
Brunswick Manifesto, 553
Civil Code of 1804, 559, 561
convening of Assembly of Notables, 546
convening of Estates-General, 547
and Declaration of Rights of Man and Citizen, 543, 548–549
difference from American Revolution, 563–565
Directory takes over, 556, 557
drawing up of cahiers, 547
early political activism, 546–547
early work of Constituent Assembly, 550–552
fiscal problems, 546
influence of American Revolution on, 542–545
influence on Europe, 559–561
Louis XVI becomes King of the French, 552–553
Napoleon becomes absolute monarch, 557
and National Assembly, 547–549

French Revolution (*cont.*)
and National Convention,
553–555
population make-up,
545–546
and rights of women,
557–559
separation of powers issue,
549–550
sister republics, 560–561
suffrage limitations, 550
the Terror, 555–556
trial/execution of king and
queen, 554
uprisings in Paris, 547–548,
550, 553–554, 556–557
French West India Company,
394
Freyre, Gilberto, 449, 450
Friedman, Thomas, 666
Froger (Sieur), 433, 453
Frontenac, Louis de, 246
Fuerteventura, 107
Fugitive Slave Act, 644, 645
fur trade, 232, 242, 248,
250–251
European-Indian cooperation,
319

galeóns, 219, 670
Gao (Songhay Empire), 25, 28
Garsden, Alexander, 401
Geggus, David Patrick, 586
gender relations, 420–463
in Africa, 420, 430–438
African prostitutes, 432
commercial marriages,
436–437
degredados, 432, 435, 436
Dutch men and African
women, 434–435
English men and African
women, 434
intermarriage in Angola,
436–437
intermarriage on Gold
Coast, 434–435
intermarriage on São
Tomé, 435–436
intermarriage on Slave
Coast, 435
Luso-Africans, 432–433,
436–437, 438
multiple wives, 435
myth of female
licentiousness, 430–431
Portuguese men and
African women,
432–434, 435–436
Portuguese women and
girls sent to Angola, 436
prazo system, 436

sexual conduct of
unmarried girls *vs.*
married women, 431
women slaves, 431–432
in Brazil, 449–455
activities of Portuguese
women, 452
Crown policy on orphan
Portuguese girls, 451
dowries, 454
European immigrants in
Brazil, 451–452
Indian women as naturally
lacivious, 449–450
legal marriages, 454
nunneries, 454
Portuguese-Brazilian
family, 454
preference for native mates,
451
rape by Portuguese, 450
sex ratios of Europeans,
452
terminology for mixed-race
offspring, 450
ways to obtain Indian
women, 449–450
women as heads of
households, 454
childbearing and family as
partnership, 422–423
cultural transmission, 422
European creation of gender
frontiers, 420–421
Indian women, 420
in New England/New France,
455–463
activities of English wives,
457–458, 459
Dutch and intermarriage,
459–460
English culture, 459
English families, 458–459
English reticence toward
intermarriage, 456
English sexual relations
with Indian women, 456
English women
immigrants, 456–457
French and intermarriage,
460–462
French women immigrants,
461
Indian women opinion of
English men, 456
métis, 461
sexuality of African/Indian
women, 421–422
gender relations, in Spanish
America, 438–448
burdens on village Indian
women, 443

Christian marriage, 442
convents, 447–448
Crown policy on wives left in
Spain, 444–445
daughters of indigenous
rulers, 442
dowries and inheritance, 445
impact of Spanish Conquest
on Mesoamerican gender
relations, 440–443
importance of legal marriage,
446–447
Indian view on marriage to
Spaniard, 441–442
Indian women as gift in
Spanish Indies, 439–440
legitimate children, 446
marriage as socioeconomic
alliance, 445–446
marriage with non-elite
Indian women, 442–443
rape of Indian women in
Spanish Indies, 439
Spanish American families,
445–448
Spanish view on marriages to
elite native women, 441
taking of Indian women in
Spanish Indies, 439
gender relations, Western patri-
archy/complementarity,
423–430
destruction of gender system
of Mexica/Inka, 425
literature on marriage, 428
migration of women/families
from Spain, 443–444
overview of gender
parallelism/
complementarity, 424
overview of patriarchy,
423–424
patriarchy in late medieval
Europe, 424–425
patriarchy in theory and
practice, 426–427
power of women in late
medieval/early modern
Europe, 425
proliferation of women
religious orders, 425–426
Protestant women, 426
querelle des femmes, 427
republican motherhood,
427–428
Roman Catholic Church and
women, 425–426
separate spheres, 427–428
Genoa/Genoese
attempt to circumnavigate
Africa, 58
loss of colonies, 59

mercantile colonies, 58
mercantile expansion into
  Spain, 58
recapture of Constantinople,
  58
sugar production/trade, 75
support of Castile expansion,
  125
and trade, 58–59, 75. *See also*
  Columbus, Christopher
gens de couleur, 570, 670
Germany, and slave trade, 345
Gê speakers, 22, 156
Gezo (Dahomey), 655*i*
Godoy, Manuel, 591
gold
  in Brazil, 204, 205
  in Caribbean, 130
  in Iberian Atlantic, 215–216
  imports, and decline of Spain,
    221, 222
  mining in Spanish America,
    182
  in Yucatan, 132–133
Gold Coast, 82, 83, 434–435
gold coin minting, decline in,
  60
gold dust, 65
Golden Age of Spain, 162
Gomera, 107–109
Gomes, Fernão, 81–82
Gottlieb, Theodor, 558
Gouges, Olympe de, 558
Grain Coast, 81–82
gran blancs (big whites), 569,
  570, 670
Gran Canaria, 107–108
Grand Banks fisheries, 98, 228
Grand Village of Natchez, 20
Great Awakening, 312
great galleys, 70
Great Migration (1630s), 297
Grenada, revolt in, 586–587
Groot, Peter de, 475
Grotius, Hugo, 214
Gua, Pierre du (Sieur de Monts),
  242, 243–245
Guacanagarí, 125, 126
Guadaloupe
  emancipation of slaves in, 627
  revolts in, 570, 586–587
Guaman Poma de Ayala, Felipe,
  182
Guanche, 73, 107
Guaraní mission, 306
Guiana, 254–255, 260
Guinea
  in Early European era, 113,
    113*m*
  in 18th century, 338*m*
Guinea Current, 68
Gujaratis mariners, 57

Gulf Stream, 68, 217
gun-slave cycle, 368
Guzmán, Nuño Beltrán de, 144

habitant, definition of, 670
habitation, definition of, 670
haciendas, 182–183, 670
Hadfield, Andrew, 237
Haitian revolution, 511, 567,
  568, 569–578, 589
  affranchis, 569
  and aftermath at Saint
    Domingue, 578–585
  agriculture restoration,
    578–579
  and Rigaud, 576–578, 587
  and Britain, 577
  and Leclerc, 580–581
  and Christophe, 585, 587
  coffee plantations, 649
  and Dessalines, 581–585
  destructiveness of, 583–585,
    649
  economic consequences of,
    585
  and France, 577–585
  gens de couleur, 570
  gran blancs, 569, 570
  influence of, 588–589
  influence of French
    Revolution on, 569–570,
    571, 573
  in North Province, 570,
    571–572
  petit blancs, 569, 570
  political consequences of,
    585–586
  and Rochambeau, 582–583
  and Saint Domingue,
    570–578
  in South Province, 570,
    572–573
  Toussaint L'Ouverture role
    in, 573–581, 586
    arrest of, 581
    1801 Constitution,
      579–580
    efforts to overthrow, 579
  War of the Knives, 577
  in West Province, 570
Hakluyt, Richard, 238
Hale, John, 428
Hamilton, Earl J., 222, 226
Hansa, 42–43
hardwood timber, from
  Madeira Islands, 73
Hasburg Empire, 161–162,
  222–223
Haudenosaunee, 21
Havana, Cuba, 217
Hawkins, John, 232, 233
Hemmings, John, 106

Henry "the Navigator"
  (Portugal)
  attempts to conquer Canary
    Islands, 76, 107–108
  at Ceuta, 76
  and Madeira/Azores, 76
  reasons to search for lands of
    Guinea, 76–79
  sends expeditions down coast
    of Africa, 80
  sends expeditions to
    northwest coast of
    Africa, 79
Henri IV (France)
  and colonization, 242,
    243–245
  converts to Catholicism, 232
Henry VII (England), 228
Henri VII (France), 243–245
Henry VIII (England), 228
Heywood, Linda M., 364, 438
Hidalgo, Miguel, 599
Hispaniola
  Columbus brings sugarcane
    to, 383
  sugar industry on, 383, 384
  Taino on, 18
Hobsbawm, Eric, 519
hogshead, definition of, 671
Hohokam, 19
Hojeda, Alonso de, 127
Holland
  colonies, planting
    Danish slave trade,
hookworm anemia, in Africa,
  35
Horse Latitudes, 68
horses
  in Africa, 82
  in Caribbean, 129
  in post-conquest Americas,
    22
  in pre-Expansion Europe, 39
*How the Spider Obtained the
  Sky God's Stories*
  (Ashanti Folklore),
  30–32
Huascar, 146, 147
Huastecas, 144
Hudson, Henry, 248
Hudson's Bay Company, 298
Huejotzingo, 136
Huguenots, 226, 231, 671
Huitzilpochtli (Mexica god),
human sacrifice
  among Maya, 13
  in Mexica Empire, 12
  in pre-contact Brazil, 21–22
Humboldt, Alexander von, 597
Hundred Years War, 38
hunting, in pre-contact
  Americas, 20–21

hunting-gathering
    Ciboney, 19
    Kung!, 33–34
Huron Indians, 242, 298, 313,
    315–316
Hus, Jan, 426

Iberian Atlantic, Spanish,
    215–221
    Carrera de Indias (Indies
        Run), 216–217, 218–219
    defense of trade monopolies
        in, 214–215
    extent of imperium, 205–206
    gold in, 215–216
    interdependency among, 206
    map of, 198*m*
    New Spanish fleet, 217
    and Portuguese, 220
    protection against French
        corsair attacks, 216
    Reconquest in, 39–40, 45
    resource inequity between
        Europeans/Natives,
        206–207
    ship types, 219
    Spanish crown authority over
        trade, 216
    and Spanish/Portuguese
        union, 220–221
    Tierra Firme fleet, 217
    trade decline, 219
    trade fairs in Americas, 217
    trade growth, 218–219, 220
    trade with Philippine colony,
        217–218. *See also* Brazil;
        Portuguese imperium, in
        Africa; Spanish imperium
Ife, 30
Ilhéus capitaincy, 156
Imbangala, 123
The Imitation of Christ
    (Kempis), 37
Imperium Christanum, 162–163
Imperium romanum, 162–163
indentured workers, 373
    Asian, 661
    in Barbados, 256
    engagés, 245, 669
    in Virginia, 239, 399
India, slavery in, 35
Indian Charity School, 312
Indian/European entanglements
    broad patterns in, 273–274
    closeness of connection,
        293–299
        in Dutch fur trade, 298
        in English Carolinas,
            298–299
        in English fur trade, 298
        in English Virginia and
            New England, 297

in French Canada, 297–298
in French fur trade, 298
in Portuguese Brazil,
    295–297
self-interest role in,
    293–299
in Spanish America,
    293–295
death and life, 320–324
    epidemic disease, 321, 322
    languages, 323
    Plains native population
        decline, 320–321
    population recovery,
        322–323
    smallpox epidemics,
        320–321
    Valley of Mexico native
        population decline, 320
ethnographies, 281–292
    Acosta, José de, 286
    on Algonquian, 289–290,
        292
    artist John White, 289–290
    Benevente, 283
    Betanzos, 284
    bilingual, 283–284
    on Brazil, 286–289
    on cannibals, 289
    Cieza de León, 284
    Codex
        Telleriano-Remensis, 284
    Harriot, Thomas, 289–290
    on Inkas, 284–286
    on Iroquois, 290–292
    Jesuit Relations, 290
    Lafitau, 292
    Lahontan, 292
    Léry, 286–289
    Montaigne, 289
    Nahua, 283–284
    New France, 292
    New Netherland, 290–292
    Pané, first ethnography,
        282–283
    Sahagún, 283–284
    Santo Tomás, 286
    van den Bogaert, 290
    van der Donck, 290–292
    working with native
        languages, 283
Europeans as savages,
    276–277
European view of Indians as
    savages, 274–277
partners and allies, 313–320
    Chickasaws, 318
    Choctaw, 318
    Covenant Chain treaty, 317
    Creeks, 317–318
    Dutch and Mohawk, 314
    English and Mohawk, 317

French and Hurons,
    313–314
French and Iroquois, 317
Iroquois Confederation,
    314–317
trade and, 318–320
relaciones/crónias/historias,
    279–281
    Acosta, José de, 281, 286
    Garcilaso de la Vega,
        280–281
    historians *de segundo
        mano* (writing from
        other texts), 279–281
    Las Casas, 280
    López de Gómera, 280
    Martyr, first history of
        New World, 279–280
    Oviedo, 280
religion and, 299–313
    Anglican missions, 312,
        313
    Calvinism, 301
    Catholicism, 301–310
    Catholic missionary friars
        in Caribbean and
        Mexico, 302
    Catholic missionary friars
        in Peru and central
        Andes, 303
    Catholic missions, 301
    conventos, 303–305
    conversion to Christianity,
        299
    Dutch Reformed Church,
        312–313
    entwined beliefs, 308,
        310
    Jesuits missions in Brazil,
        308–309
    Jesuits missions in New
        France, 309–310
    Jesuits missions in
        Paraguay, 306
    life at missions, 307–309
    missionary efforts to
        protect Indians,
        305–307, 309
    Protestantism, 301,
        310–313
    Protestant missions, 301
    Puritan missions, 311
    resistance to Christianity,
        305
    revivalism, 312
    spiritualism, 312
travel narratives/travelogues,
    277–279
    cannibalism, 278
    by Columbus, 278
    writings about Indians,
        277–293

Indies
  devastation of (*See* Cuba;
    Española)
  emigration of Spanish women
    to, 1509–1600, 444t
indigenous languages, living and
  extinct in Americas, 323t
industrial capitalism, 67
ingenios, 374, 380, 383, 671
Inka Empire, 7, 13–17
  ancestor worship, 16–17
  Charrúa, 151
  child sacrifice, 17
  civil war in, 146
  conquest of, 145–151
  Cuzco, 16–17
  ethnographies of, 284–286
  Musica, 151
  in pre-contact Americas, 7
  Querandie, 151
  similarity to Mexica Empire,
    17–18
  size of army, 146
  tribute system, 14
Inter caetera (papal bull), 214
Intolerable Acts, 505
Inuit, 55
*In which five reasons appear
  why the Lord Infant was
  moved to command the
  search for the lands of
  Guinea* (Zurara), 77–79
Ireland
  English colonization of,
    236–237
  influence of French
    Revolution on, 560
Iroquois, 298
  chiefdoms of, 21
  ethnography on, 290–292
Iroquois Five Nations, 242,
  315–316, 478–479
Isabel and Ferdinand (Spain),
  91–93
  on treatment of Caribbeans,
    126, 128
Isert, Paul Erdmann, 351, 431,
  434
Islam, spread of, 299–301
Islamic slave trade, 35, 82
The Island of St. Thomas,
  193–194
Italy
  Christian trade embargo on
    Egypt, 59
  invention of maritime
    compass, 70
  motives for expansion,
    57–58, 60
  nautical charts, 84. *See also*
    Europe, pre-expansion;
    Genoa/Genoese; Venice

Itsekiri kingdom, 114
Iturbide, Agustín, 604
Ivory Coast, 82
Ixtlapalapan, 140

Jaga, 117, 123
Jamaica, 129, 256
  annual decline in slave
    populations, 408t
  French and England at war
    in, 478
  runaway slaves in, 415
  slave family in, 413
  slave rebellions in, 416, 538,
    588, 638–639
James I (England), 238, 239
James II (England), 473,
  476–478
Jamestown settlement, 238–240
Jefferson, Thomas, 525,
  542–543, 548, 624–625
Jenkins, Robert, 490–491
Jennings, Francis, 324
Jesuit Relations, 290, 315–316
Jesuits
  in Angola, 123
  in Asia, 301
  boarding schools, 295
  in Brazil, 153, 155, 156, 199,
    203–204, 309–310
  college in Peru, 179
  efforts to protect Indians,
    305–307, 309
  expulsion from Spanish
    dominions, 590, 596
  flying, 310
  in Kongo Kingdom, 115, 117,
    118–119
  in Naples, 282
  in New France, 309–310,
    460–461
  in Paraguay, 204, 306,
    501–502
  in Peru, 303
  and slave trade, 195, 387
Jews
  astronomers in Portugal,
    84–86
  in Barbados, 255
  child immigrants in Africa,
    190
  in colonial Brazil, 202, 389
  expelled from Spain, 125
  as New Christians, 183–184
  orphan children on São
    Tomé, 435
Jiménez, Gonzalo, 151
João I (Portugal), 76, 83–84
João II (Portugal)
  and African trade, 83
  and Bemoin, 88
  and Brazil, 153, 156–157

and India, 86, 88, 90
and Japan, 90
and kingdom of Kongo,
  114–115
and Prester John, 83–84
Jobson, Richard, 433
Johnson, Samuel, 624
Joliet, Louis, 246
Joseph I (Spain), 598
Joyner, Charles, 361
just war principle, 105–106,
  132, 136, 156, 165–166,
  204, 295, 388–389

Kamen, Henry, 445
Kansas-Nebraska Act, 644
Keith, George, 620–621
Kellogg, Susan, 430
Kennedy, Paul, 484
Khoikhoi, 34
KiKongo language, 115
King Philip's War, 297
King William's War, 478
kivas, 19
Klein, Herbert S., 341
Knight, Alan, 440–441
kolo nut, 29
Kongo kingdom, 33, 83, 88,
  114–118
  under Alfonso I, 115–117
  Anzico, 117
  Christianity in, 115
  under Diogo, 117
  disintegration of, 117–118
  European-style royal court in,
    115
  Jaga, 117
  Jesuits in, 115, 117, 118–119
  literacy, 115
  missionaries in, 117
  under Nzinga Nkuwu,
    114–115
  Portuguese military conquest,
    117
  slaves on agricultural estates,
    331
  slave trade, 115–118
  succession crisis in, 117
Koranic schools, in Africa, 25
Kung!, 33–34

Labat, Jean-Baptiste, 378,
  408
Labrador, discovery of, 98
Labrador Current, 68
ladinos, 385–386, 401, 671
Lafayette, Marquis de, 542,
  543, 548
Lafitau, François, 292
Lafitau, Joseph-François, 460
Lahontan (Louis-Armand de
  Lom d'Arce), 292

lançados, 80, 109, 336–337, 432, 671
Lanzarote, 73–74, 107–108
La Palma, 107
La Salle, Robert de, 246
Las Casas, Bartolomé, 126, 127, 129, 166, 280
lateen rigged, 57, 671
The Late War in North America Between France and England (Pouchot), 500–501
Latin America
  Early Spanish overland expeditions, 152m
  lack of scramble for, 662–663
latitude
  calculating, 57, 84
  definition of, 671
latitude sailing, 70
lavradores de cana, 671
Lavrin, Asunción, 448
Law, Robin, 370
league, definition of, 671
League of the Five Nations, 21
Leclerc, Charles Victor Emmanuel, 580–581
Leeward Islands, 130, 538
legua, definition of, 671
León, Cieza de, 439
León, Luis de, 428
leprosy, in Africa, 35
Léry, Jean de, 22, 286–289
Lesser Antilles, 19, 130
Letters of Marque and Reprisal, 263
Lever, J.T., 434–435
Liberia
  freed slaves shipped to, 632
  liberated slaves in, 654
Ligon, Richard, 391, 393, 404–406, 407
Lima
  founding of, 149–150, 177
  government of, 178
  manufactures and commerce, 180–181
  population of, 178
  religious establishments, 179
  social framework of colonial society in, 177–181
  wealth of, 178–179
Lincoln, Abraham, 644
literacy, in Muslim Africa, 27
Little Ice Age, 37
Loango kingdom, 33
Locke, John, 520–521, 522, 524, 548
Lockhart, James, 441
Long, Edward, 349, 413
longitude, 70, 671

Lopes, Duarte, 33, 88–89, 115, 120–122
López de Gómera, Francisco, 280
The Lord's Prayer in Nahuatl, 303
Louisbourg, French naval base and fortification, 483, 483i
Louisiana, 246
Louis XIV (France), 477–478, 479–480, 481
Louis XV (France), 482
L'Ouverture, Toussaint, 575i, 582–587
Lovejoy, Paul E., 341, 363–364, 366, 370, 431–432, 657
Low Countries. *See* Dutch; Europe, pre-expansion
Luanda, 118, 122–123, 124, 260
Lugo, Alonso de, 108
luxury goods, from Orient, 58

macambos, 414–415
MacCulloch, Diarmaid, 425–426
MacLachlan, Colin, 446
Maddison, Angus, 662
Madeiras, xxvii, 73
  sugar production, 75, 379–380
Magellan, Ferdinand, 98–100
magnetic compass, 70, 84
malaguetta pepper, 82, 188, 231, 671
malaria, in Africa, 28–29, 35
Maldonaldo, Isabel, 445–446
Malinali (Doña Maria), 133, 440
Malocello, Lanzarotto, 73
mameluco (mestizo), 203, 295, 450, 671
Manco (Inka), 148–149, 150
Mann, Kristin, 370
The Manner How the Negroes Became Slaves (Snelgrave), 333–334
Manning, Patrick, 366, 369
Manoel I (King of Portugal), 86, 113
  and Angola, 118
  and Kongo kingdom, 115
Mapuche, 22
maravedí, 92–93, 671
Marees, Pieter de, 431, 433
Margarite, Mosén Pedro, 127
Marina, Francisco Martínez, 523, 590
maritime compass, 70
maritime routes, Spain and America, 218m

market society *vs.* society with market, 67
maroon, definition of, 671
Marquette, Jacques, 246
marronage (running away), 414–416
Martinique, 357, 373, 570, 588
Martyr, Peter, 92, 93, 108, 438
Martyr, Peter, first history of New World by, 279–280
Maryland, 240–242
Masefield, G.B., 378
Massachusetts Bay colony, 240
Massa Melly (African king), 25
Mather, Cotton, 311
Maya
  Cakchiquel, 144
  Chontal, 133
  classic, 7
  Quiché Empire, 13, 144
Mazarin, Jules (Cardinal), 245, 257
Medea (Seneca), 1–2
Medieval Warm Period, 39
Mediterranean Europe, slavery in, 35
Mello, Ferdinand de, 117–118
mendicant orders
Mercator, Gerhard Kremer, 98
merchant adventurers, 67, 238
merchant capitalism, 65–67, 661
Merolla, Jerome de, 379
mestiço, 450, 671
mestizos
  definition of, 671
  in Spanish America, 186
metallurgy, in pre-Expansion Europe, 39
Mexica Empire, 7, 10–13
  conquest of, 132–145(*See also* Cortés, Hernando)
  cosmology, 11–12
  Flowery Wars, 11
  human sacrifice, 12
  in pre-contact Americas, 7
  similarity to Inka Empire, 17–18
  social stratification, 11
  Teotihuacan, 7, 10–11
  Triple Alliance, 10–11
Michelet, Jules, 426
Mignolo, Walter D., 665–666
Miller, Joseph, 437
mining
  Native labor in Americas, 184i
  in pre-expansion Europe, 39
Miranda, Francisco, 567, 589, 601
Miranda, José, 523–524
missionaries, 107

baptism in Peru, 304i
  in Brazil, 153, 155
  in Kongo kingdom, 117. See
    also Augustinians;
    Carmelites; Dominicans;
    Franciscans; Jesuits
missions, in South America,
  307i
Mississipian, 19–20
Missouri Compromise, 643,
  644
mit'a/mita, 14, 172, 181, 182,
  672
Mixtecs, 12–13, 144
Mixtón War, 144, 305
Moche, 7
Mogollon, 19
Mohawk language, 290–292,
  312
Monck, George, 475
Mongolian Empire, 59
Monks Mound (Mississipian),
  19
Montaigne, Michel de, 289, 428
Montcalm, Marquis de, 496
Montejo, Francisco de, 145
Montesinos, Antonio de,
  131–132
Montesquieu, 521–522, 548,
  557, 621
Montevideo, 512
Moogk, Peter, 461
Moors, 25, 39–40, 58, 105
Morelos, José María, 600
Moret, Segismundo, 647
Moret Law, 647
Morocco
  European defeat in, 157
  slaves in, 28
Moscovy Company, 232
Moteucçoma, 133, 134–135,
  136, 139
Mother Cultures, in pre-contact
  Americas, 7
Mounier, J.J., 549–550
Mozambique, prazo system in,
  436
Mudthu, Sankar, 524
Mugaburu, Josephe de,
  179–180
Muisca, 21
mulattos
  in Brazil, 203
  definition of, 672
  in Kongo, 118
  in Spanish America, 186
Mullin, Michael, 401
Mundus Novus (Vespucci),
  99–100
Musica, 151
Muslims
  enslavement by, 327, 376

  in Northwest Africa, 24–25

Nahua
  definition of, 672
  ethnography of, 283–284
  Lord's Prayer in Nahuatl
    language, 303
  origins of, 10
nãos, 2–3, 92, 219, 672
Narrative of a Five Years
  Expedition (Stedman),
  207
Native American languages, in
  pre-contact Americas, 6
nau, definition of, 672
nautical astronomy, 84–86
Navigation Acts (England), 475
Ndongo. See Angola, and
  Portugal
Near Atlantic, 71–75
  Azore Islands, 73
  Canary Islands (See Canary
    Islands)
  Cape Verde archipelago, 75
  Madeiras, 73
  map of, 74, 74i
The Negroes of Barbados
  (Ligon), 404–406
Netherlands
  economic strength of,
    229–230
  government of, 229–230. See
    also Dutch; United
    Provinces of the
    Netherlands
New Amsterdam, 250
New England. See gender
  relations, in New
  England/New France
Newfoundland, discovery of, 98
New France
  Jesuits in, 309–310, 460–461
  Miramich settlement, 246i
  in 17th century, 247m. See
    also gender relations, in
    New England/New
    France
New Holland (Brazil), 255
New Netherland, Dutch efforts
  at religious conversion,
  312–313
New Netherlands Company,
  248
New Sweden, 251
New World religions, African
  origins of, 365t
Nieser, Jan, 434–435
Niger Delta chiefdoms, 33
Nine Years War, 477, 478
Nkuwu, Nzinga, 114–115
Nóbrega, Manoel de, 450, 451
Normans, 40

Norris, Robert, 369
North America
  Indians and Europeans, c.
    1660, 300i, 307i
  map, 1750, 318m
  in 17th century, 241m
North Atlantic Current, 68
North Atlantic Westerlies, 68
Northeastern North America, c.
  1755, 491, 492m
North East (Portuguese) Trade
  winds, 68
North Equatorial Current, 68
northwest passage, 101
Novais, Paulo Dias, 118
Nova Scotia, 494
Novus Mundus, xxvii
Nunes, Pedro, 84–86

Oaxaca, 144, 181
Observations of the Estate and
  Affairs of Holland,
  249–250
Of Independence, State
  Constitutions, and the
  Confederation (Ramsey),
  536–537
Of the Manner How Sugar is
  Made (de Rochefort),
  377–378
Of the Original beginning of
  Christendom in the
  Kingdom of Congo, And
  how the Portuguese
  obtained this traffic
  (Duarte Lopes), 88–89
Ojeda, Alonso de, 96
Oliviera, João de, 350
Olmec culture, 7
O Príncipe, 82–83
The Origins of Abolitionism in
  Brazil 1879, 652–653
Ortiz, Fernando, 382, 407
Ottoman Turks, 38, 57, 59
Ovando, Nicolás de, 128–129,
  184, 442
Oxenham, John, 232
Oyo, 30, 339

Pacaha, 19–20
Pacheco Pereira, Duarte, 80, 81,
  82, 83, 86, 112–113
padrão (stone marker), 83
Paine, Thomas, 465, 468, 525,
  531, 542
palisaded villages, in
  pre-contact Brazil, 21
Palmer, R. R., 518
Panama, 130
Pané, Ramón, 282–283
Pánuco province, 144
papal bulls, 80, 214

papal donation, 214
Paraguay
    end of slavery in, 637, 641
    independence of, 602
    Jesuits in, 204, 306, 501–502
Paraguayan war, 650, 652
Paraíba capitancy, 156
pardos, 450, 567, 604–605, 672
Parma, Giovanni della, 73
Parry, J.H., 303
patroonships, 255, 292, 672
Paulistas, 204, 295–296, 672
Paullu (Inka), 150–151
Paulo Diaz in Arms Against the King of Angola (Duarte Lopes), 120–122
Pavia, Afonso de, 84
pawnship, 332
Pax Mongolica, 42, 58, 59
Pech, 145
Pende, 123
peninsular, 186, 673
Peninsula War, 592
People of the Longhouse, 21
Pequot War, 297
Peraza, Fernán, 108–109
Pernambuco, 155, 260
Perrot, Michelle, 426
Peru
    church and convent, 180i. See also Inka Empire; Lima; Pizarro, Francisco
Pétion, Alexander, 583–585, 588–589
petit blancs (little whites), 569, 570, 672
petit *vs.* grand marronage, 415
peublos, 172
Pillars of Hercules, xxvi–xxvii, 52
pirates, 672
    Barbary, 216, 327
    Dutch, 191
    end of Atlantic piracy, 481–482
    English, 232
    French, 191
    in Jamaica, 264–265
    Japanese, 56. See also buccaneers; corsaires
Pisan, Christine de, 427
Pitt, William, 495, 503, 629–631
Pizarro, Francisco
    alliance with Cuzco, and Almagro, 150
    arrival in Peru, 146
    capture of Inka leader, ecomiendas, 171
    founds Lima, 149–150, 177
    granted contract to conquer Peru, 145–146

and Manco, 148–149, 150
marches on Cuzco, 146, 150
ransom offered by Inka leader,
recruits men from Trujillo, 184–185
size of Inka army, 146
slaughter of Inkas,
Pizarro, Hernando, 185
plantation, definition of, 672
plantation complex
    Africans as preferred labor source, 374
    creoles, 401–402
    cultures of slaves and, 401–419
        African generations, 401
        allowance system, 409–410
        assumption of master absolute power, 411–412
        Atlantic creoles, 401–402
        on Desalles plantation, 409
        gang-labor system, 403
        marronage (running away), 414–416
        provision grounds and rations, 407–409, 410–411, 412
        resistance to slavery, 374–375, 414–417
        slave families, 412–413
        slave languages, 413–414
        slave suicide, 414
        Sunday market, 410–411, 412
        task labor system, 406
        violent rebellions, 416–417
    in Gulf of Guinea, 82–83
    plantations as labor intensive, 374
    rise of, 375–384
        and Africanization of slave trade, 381–382
        indigo production, 379
        in Mediterranean, 382
        rice in Carolinas, 379
        sugarcane in Canary Islands, 380–381
        sugarcane in Europe, 376
        sugarcane in Madeiras, 379–381, 382
        sugarcane in New World, 376–378, 379
        sugarcane in São Tomé, 381, 382–383
        sugarcane in Spanish West Indies, 383–384
    slave quarters, 402–403
    societies with slaves *vs.* slave societies, 374
    sugar plantations, 373–374

trade in staples, 417. *See also* colonies, planting; plantation complex, transatlantic
plantation complex, transatlantic, 384–400
    African slaves, 393, 395–397, 399–400
    coffee and sugar in Surinam, 398
    decline of African slave trade in Spanish Ameria, 385
    French and English in lesser Antilles, 390–391
    French in Louisiana, 397–398
    indentured servants, 395, 399
    New World blacks (creoles), 385–386
    rice in Georgia, 400
    rice in South Carolina, 399–400
    rise of planter society, 392–393
    slave codes, 393–394
    sugarcane in Barbados, 391–393
    sugarcane in Brazil, 384, 386–390
        Dutch in Brazil, 389–390
        Indian slavery, 386
        productivity, 386
        transition from Indian to African slavery, 386–389
    sugarcane in Jamaica, 394
    sugarcane in Leeward Islands, 394
    sugarcane in Saint Domingue, 394–397
    tobacco in Caribbean, 390–391
    tobacco in Virginia, 399
    types of work slaves performed, 385
    urban slaves, 400
    West India Company, 389–390
plant domestication
    n Africa, 34
    in pre-contact Americas, 22
Plymouth plantation, 240
Poland, influence of French Revolution on, 560
Polanyi, Karl, 67
polders, 39
Pole star, 70
Political Aphorisms (Locke), 522
polygyny
    on plantations, 413
    in sub-Saharan Africa, 35
Poma de Alaya, Felipe Guaman, 441, 443

pombeiros (slave trade intermediaris), 123
Ponce de León, Juan, 129
Pope-Hennessy, James, 368–369
Pope-Hennessy, John, 662
Pope Innocent VIII, 299
Popol Vuh, Maya-Quiché Creation Myth, 8–10
population
  Americas, regional c. 1492, 23t
  Brazil, 202t
  European and Euroamerican, 1600 and 1800, 274t
  national of Western Europe, 1700–1800, 473, 473t
  national populations of Europe, 1500–1700, 224t
  Native American, 1492–1996, 321t
  Portuguese Atlantic, 17th century, 437, 437t
  sub-Saharan Africa, regional c. 1500, 36t
  world regional, 1820–2000, 665t
  world regional c. 1500, 47t
Portocarrero, Pedro de León, 179
Portolan Charts, 84
Port Royal, 242
Portugal
  alliance *vs.* conquest, 106
  Atlantic Africa and, 109–114
  Cape Verde archipelago as base, 75
  capture of Ceuta, 76
  claim to Brazil, 96–97
  control/occupation of Azores, 73, 74
  control/occupation of Madeiras, 73, 74
  and control of Canaries, 73, 74, 76
  discoveries in Africa, 86, 87m
  discovery of Grand Banks fishery, 98
  expeditions from Guinea to Cape of Good Hope, 81–90
  and fabled river of gold, 79
  feitoria establishment, 83
  and gold from Africa, 82
  importance of opening Guinea coast, 82
  islands and mainland, and making of imperium, 163–164
  map of voyages, 84, 85m
  maritime technology, 71, 79–80, 84–86

nautical charts, 84
  overextension of empire, 162
  Overseas Council, 199–200
  pure discovery voyages by, 83–84
  reaches India, 84, 86
  reasons for expansion, 57
  regulatory house in, 83
  and slave trade, 73, 75, 79, 80, 82. *See also* Angola, and Portugal; Brazil; Henry "the Navigator" (Portugal); Portuguese imperium, in Africa; West Africa, Portugal in
Portuguese imperium. *See* Brazil; Portuguese imperium, in Africa
Portuguese imperium, in Africa, 187–197
  agricultural revolution, 189
  Angola (*See* Angola)
  Angolares, 191
  Catholic Church, 190–191
  coast guard, 189
  disease in, 190
  Dutch and, 189, 190, 191
  economic decline, 192
  French and, 191
  Gold Coast, 189–190
  gold trade, 188–189, 190
  government, 187–188, 190–191
  inter-African rivalries, 189–190
  intermarriage, 189, 192
  Jewish children in, 190
  language, 189
  Mina captaincy, 187
  mulattos, 189, 192
  relations with natives, 189
  religious establishment, 188
  São Jorge de Mina capitaincy, 187, 188, 189, 190
  São Tomé capitaincy, 190–192
  slave trade, 191–192
  sugar economy, 191
  supervision of trade from Lisbon, 188
  trading establishments, 187
  Village of Two Parts, 189
Portuguese imperium, in America. *See* Brazil
Potiguar, 155, 156
Potosí, 182–183
  Silver Mountain, 183i
Pouchot, Pierre, 500–501
Powers, Karen Vieira, 424, 425
Powhatan, of Virginia, 20
Pradt, Dominique de, 568–569
prazo system, 436

Prester John (fabled Christian king), 83, 84, 114
Price, Richard, 542
Prideaux, John, 496
print revolution, 47–48
privateers, 673
  Dutch, 215
  French, 231. *See also* buccaneers; pirates
Proclamation Line of 1763, 527
Promontorium Passum, 83–84
Protestant ethic, 62–63
Providence Island colony, 264
provision grounds, 407–409, 410–411, 412, 672
Ptolemy, Claudius, 52, 72
Puerto Rico, sugar industry on, 384
Purépecha, 12
Puritans, 297, 301

Qorikancha (Inca temple of the Sun), 16–17
quadrant, definition of, 673
Quakers, 619, 620–621, 623, 628
Quartering Act, 527
Quauhtemoc, 140, 141
Québec City, New France, 242, 478, 496, 497i, 505
Quechua, 13, 303, 673. *See also* Inka Empire
Quechua grammar, 286
Querandie, 151
querelle des femmes, 427
Quetzalcoatl, 135
Quiché Empire, 8–10, 13, 144
quintal, definition of, 673
quipo/u, definition of, 673
Quisquis, 148–149
Quito, 149, 602, 603

Ralegh, Walter, 234, 236
Ramalho, João, 449
Ramsay, David, 467, 533
Ramsey, David, 536–537
Raynal, Guillaume Thomas, 544–545
Reconquista, 39–40, 105, 124
reducción/congregación policy, 166–168, 308
Reed, Ester De Berdt, 533–534
regular clergy, 173–174, 673
religion, and Indian/European entanglements, 299–313
  Anglican missions, 312, 313
  Calvinism, 301
  Catholicism, 301–310
  Catholic missionary friars in Caribbean and Mexico, 302

religion, and Indian/European
    entanglements (*cont.*)
  Catholic missionary friars in
    Peru and central Andes,
    303
  Catholic missions, 301
  conventos, 303–305
  conversion to Christianity,
    299
  Dutch Reformed Church,
    312–313
  entwined beliefs, 308, 310
  Jesuits missions in Brazil,
    308–309
  Jesuits missions in New
    France, 309–310
  Jesuits missions in Paraguay,
    306
  life at missions, 307–309
  missionary efforts to protect
    Indians, 305–307, 309
  Protestantism, 301, 310–313
  Protestant missions, 301
  Puritan missions, 311
  resistance to Christianity, 305
  revivalism, 312
  spiritualism, 312
repartimiento (forced labor),
    128, 172, 181
Republic of Cartagena, 567
Requerimiento (Requisition),
    132
reserves, 309–310, 673
The Revolution of America
    (Raynal), 544–545
Rhode Island, 240
rice farming, in Carolinas, 299
Richelieu, Armand Jean du
    Plessis de (Cardinal),
    242–245
Rigaud, André, 576–578, 587
Rio de Janeiro, 96
  emancipation, 653–654
  founding, 155
  gold in, 204–205
  Protestant missions in, 286
  slave trade, 195, 357, 650
  sugar industry, 200, 454–455
Rio Grande capitancy, 156
river blindness (onchocerciasis),
    35
River of Gold, unsuccessful
    expedition to find, 73
Robespierre, Maximilien, 523,
    550, 555–556, 564
Rochambeau, Donatien,
    582–583
Rodney, Walter, 367
Rodriquez, Jaime, 446
Rogers, Robert, 501
Roldán, Francisco, 127–128
Rome, slavery in ancient, 375

Rousseau, Jean-Jacques,
    522–523, 524, 548, 549,
    622
Rowlands, Alison, 426–427
Royal African Company (RAC),
    262, 346, 347, 352,
    354–356, 359–360, 487
Royal and Supreme Council of
    the Indies, 172–173
*Royal Ordinances Concerning
    the Laying Out of New
    Towns* (Philip II),
    176–177
*Royal Patent to the Sieur de
    Monts*, 243–245
Russell-Wood, A.J.R., 438
Rut, John, 228

Sabatino Lopez, Robert, 42, 59
Sa'dîs expedition against
    Songhay Empire,
    157–158
Sahagún, Bernardino de,
    283–284
St. Domingo, 572, 584–585
Saint Domingue, 511
  map of, 576m
  slave uprising in, 627, 628
  at time of Haitian Revolution,
    578i
Saint-Méry, Moreau de, 413,
    414
St. Thomas, literary description
    of, 193–194
Saint Vincent, 586–587, 627
Salinas y Córdova,
    Buenaventura, 179, 180
Sandys, Edwin, 420
sans-culottes, 555, 556
Santo Tomás, Domingo de, 286
São Jorge da Mina (Portuguese
    castle), 83, 111, 111f,
    114, 187
São Paulo capitancy, 295
São Salvador, 199i
São Tomé
  capitancy of, 156, 190–192
  intermarriage on, 435–436
  Jewish children on, 435
  and Kongo kingdom, 115,
    118
  Portuguese recapture of, 260
  slave trade and, 115–117, 118
  sugar estates on, 82–83, 381
  sugar productivity in, 386
Sapa Inka (Sole Inka), 16
Schama, Simon, 545
schistosomiasis (liver flukes), 35
Schurz, William Lytle, 445
Schwartz, Stuart, 454–455
scientific racism, 665
Scott, John, 391

Scott, Rebecca, 658
Sea Beggars, 234
Sebastain (Portugal), 157
Secota, Virginia, 291i
secular clergy, definition of,
    673
Seeker, William, 428
seigneuries, 245, 673
seigneurs, 245, 673
Seneca, 1–2
Senegambia, 82, 432–433
Seven Years' War, 494,
    496–497, 502
shaman, in pre-contact Brazil,
    21
Sheridan, Richard B., 397, 407
ship of the line
  definition of, 673
Sierra Leone
  liberated slaves in, 654
  Luso-Africans in, 433
Sieyes, Abbé, 549–550
Silk Road, 59
silver
  imports, and decline of Spain,
    221, 222
  mining in Spanish America,
    178, 182
  in Peru, 178
Silver Mountain, 183i
Silverblatt, Irene, 424–425
Siouan-speaking, 20–21
Slave Act of 1723, 411
slave barracoon, 350i
Slave Coast, 82, 359, 365
  Bight of Benin, 262, 334,
    338–339, 357
  intermarriage on, 435
Slave Power conspiracy, 644
slavery
  in Africa, 80
  annual percent decline in
    Jamaica/Barbados, 408t
  in Brazil, 649
    abolitionism in, 652–653
    African slave labor, 200
    bilateral pattern of slave
      trade, 357
    delaying abolition with Rio
      Branco Law, 650–651
    emergence of antislavery
      movement, 650
    geographic reorientation
      of, 649–650
    Indian slave labor,
      153–154, 156, 200, 204
    revived antislavery
      movement, 651–653
    slave population,
      1798–1887, 649, 649t
  in Canary Islands, 73, 75, 79,
    381

concubines
    among plantation slaves,
        413
    slaves as, 331
emancipation of slaves in
    Caribbean, 627
forced labor *(repartimiento)*,
    172, 181
freed slaves shipped to
    Liberia, 632
gun-slave cycle, 368
in India, 35
map of African slavery in
    Americas, 396*m*
in Mediterranean Europe, 35
in Morocco, 28
by Muslims, 327, 376
in pre-expansion Europe, 35
slave population in U.S.,
    1790–1860, 642*t*
slave populations in
    Americas, c. 1770, 400*t*
slaves after abolition,
    658–659
in West Africa, 340*m. See
    also* antislavery, and
    Africa; antislavery,
    demise of American
    slavery, 1860s–1880s;
    plantation complex
slave trade
    abolition of, 615–616
    African indigenous, 28, 33,
        35
    Angola and Portugal, 118,
        122–123, 195, 196–197
    barter price for African
        captives, 352*i*
    Biafra, as slave source, 262,
        339, 359
    Caribbean, 129–130
    Central American coast, 130
    Dutch, 260
    and Germany, 345
    instruments used in, 631*i*
    Kongo kingdom, 115–117
    markets in Timbuktu, 28
    sale of African slaves in
        Barbados, 359–360
    sale of slaves by native chiefs,
        353*i*
    and São Tomé, 115–117,
        118
    slave-raiding in Canary
        Islands, 73
    transatlantic, 340*m*, 343*m*
slave trade, Atlantic
    African connections, 328–341
    African elite control of, 336
    African nations of New
        World, 360–366
    candomblés, 364–366

creolization of black
    culture, 361, 363
    ethno-religious patterns,
        363–366
    names of nations, 362
    slavehold national
        characteristics of natives,
        362–363
    transplantation of African
        culture, 361–362
African view on morality of,
    330
African violent resistance to,
    335
arrivals by region,
    1451–1700, 342*t*
arrivals by region,
    1701–1800, 342*t*
arrivals in America,
    1510–1870, 327*t*
asiento system, 344, 346
Bight of Benin (Slave Coast)
    as source for, 338–339
Bight of Biafra as source for,
    339
bilateral pattern of, 357
Brandenburg African
    Company, 345
Brazil as destination, 341,
    342
British North America as
    destination, 341–343
British sugar islands as
    destination, 341
business of slaving, 341–349
captive redemption in Africa,
    335
capture in war as cause for
    enslavement, 332
chartered companies, 343,
    344–345, 347, 348, 357
determining trade value of
    slave, 335–336
Dutch West India Company,
    344–345
East Africa as source for,
    340–341
European view on morality
    of, 329–330
French sugar islands as
    destination, 341
French West Indies Company,
    346–347
Gold Coast as source for,
    337–338
Henrietta Marie, 357–360
impact on Africa, 366–371
    demographic, 366–367
    domestic slavery in Africa,
        369
    economic, 367–368
    political, 368–369

social, 369–371
independent traders,
    343–344, 346, 347, 348,
    357
judicial process as cause for
    enslavement, 332
kidnapping as cause for
    enslavement, 332
levels of servile conditions in
    Africa, 331–332
merchandise traded to
    Africans for slaves, 347
Middle Passage, 349–357
    cowrie shells as currency,
        351–352
    gender discrepancy,
        352–353
    gold bar as common
        currency, 351
    middlemen, 349–350
    mortality rates, 354–356
    selling slaves in New
        World, 357
    slave auctions, 357
    slave decks, 354
    uprisings on ships,
        356–357
mortality rate of captives in
    Africa, 350–351
as not capitalism, 348–349
number of Africans *vs.*
    Europeans in Americas,
    326–327
origins of captives,
    1662–1867, 362*t*
pawnship in Africa, 332
Portugal and, 328–329
profits/losses, 348
protecting selves from slavers
    in Africa, 334–335
Royal African Company
    (RAC), 345–346,
    354–356
Royal Chartered Danish
    Guinea Company, 345
royal contracts, 344
Senegambia region as source
    for, 336–337
Sierra Leone as source for,
    337
slaves in African mines,
    331
slaves on African agricultural
    estates, 330, 331
Spanish America as slave
    destination, 341
sugar plantation slaves,
    327–328
Swedish African Company,
    345
triangular pattern of, 328,
    357

slave trade, Atlantic (*cont.*)
    West Central Africa as source
        for, 339–340
    Windward Coast as source
        for, 337
Sloane, Hans, 415
Small, Stephen, 366
smallpox, 141
    in Africa, 35
    in Brazil, 388
    epidemic in Valley of Mexico,
        140, 141
Smith, Adam, 66, 348–349, 623
Smith, William, 431, 432, 433
Smits, David, 456
Snelgrave, William, 326,
        329–330, 333–334
Society of the Friends of the
    Blacks, 626–627
society with market *vs.* market
    society, 67
Socolow, Susan Migden, 420,
    441
Soeiro, Susan, 452
Solano, Francisco, 304*i*
solar tables, 70
*Some Account of the Author's
    Captivity* (Cugano),
    355–356
Songhay chiefdom, 27
Songhay Empire, 25–27, 82,
    110
    Sa'dîs expedition against,
        157–158
Sonthonax, Léger-Félicité, 574
South Africa chiefdom, 34
South East Trade winds, 68, 86
South Equatorial Current, 68,
    86
Southern Cross, 70
Spain
    alliance *vs.* conquest, 106
    claim to Portugal, 158, 189
    Council of the Indies,
        199–200
    early voyages to New World,
        96
    emigration of Spanish women
        to Indies, 1509–1600,
        444*t*
    expels Moors, 236
    and first circumnavigation,
        98–100
    Golden Age of, 162
    shipbuilding industry,
        219–220. *See also*
        Spanish America;
        Spanish imperium,
        making of
Spain, decline of, 221–226,
    269–270, 474

agriculture/manufacturing,
    221–222
conspicuous consumption,
    223–224
depopulation, 224
economic reform attempts,
    225–226
effects of gold and silver
    imports, 221, 222
excessive taxes, 222, 223
military expenditures,
    222–223
per capita economic growth,
    224–225
persecution of Portuguese in
    Spain, 226
public debt, 222, 223
uprising of Portuguese
    nobility in Spain, 226
waning hegemony in Atlantic
    World, 1600s, 236
Spanish Abolitionist Society,
    647
Spanish America
    African slaves in, 186
    agricultural estates, 182–183
    art/architecture by Indians,
        186
    audiencias, 172
    basis of administrative
        regions, 170–171
    Catholic Church authority in,
        173
    checks and balances system,
        173
    city planning, 175
    class system, 185
    coca crop, 183
    control from Spain, 172–173
    control through ecomiendas,
        171
    corregidores/alcaldes mayors,
        172, 178
    disease in, 174
    ecomiendas, 171
    ecomiendas, Crown
        restriction of, 172
    extent of, 170
    forced labor, 172, 181
    gold mining, 182
    health of Indians, 174, 181
    immigration/emigration by
        Spanish, 183–185
    manufactures and commerce,
        180–181
    map of cities/towns of, 167*m*,
        170–187
    missionaries, 172, 173–174,
        181
    native cooperation in, 171
    New Laws of 1542, 172

population of, 1570–1800,
    174, 185*t*
provincial governors, 172
pueblo life, 181–183
race mixing in, 185–186
religious establishments, 179
royal government, 172–173
segregation in, 174
separate Indian culture in,
    174–175
silver mining, 178, 182
social framework of colonial
    society (Lima), 177–181
tribute, 181–182
unconditional emancipation
    in, 637*t*
viceroys, 172. *See also* gender
    relations, in Spanish
    America
Spanish America revolutions,
    595–609
    and ayuntamiento, 598–599
    in Buenos Aires, 601–602
    in Central America, 604
    in Chile, 603
    and conservative
        republicanism, 605
    and Constitution of 1812,
        600–601, 612
    coup d'etat by Audiencia, 599
    and creole juntas, 598
    and creole nationalism,
        597–598
    criollos/peninsulares, 596
    in Cuzco, 602–603
    Indian/black slaves interests,
        605
    influence of American/French
        revolutions on, 597
    influence of Bourbon reforms
        on, 596–597
    Mexican Revolution,
        599–600, 604
    in New Granada, 602, 603
    in Peru, 603
    political consequences of,
        605–609
    populist consequences of, 609
    in Quito, 602, 603
    racial composition of armies,
        604–605
    and restoration of Fernando
        VII, 603
    and rights of women, 605
    variety of political outcomes,
        612–613
    in Venezuela, 601, 603
Spanish Armada, 233
Spanish-as-god myth, 135
Spanish imperium, making of,
    164, 165*i*, 170

city planning, 166, 167*i*
divide and rule strategy, 164
expansion of Castillian
    language, 169
extension of law and order,
    169–170
imposition of civitas,
    166–169
mapping/naming conventions,
    168–169
reducción/congregación
    policy, 166–168
religious justification,
    165–166
royal engineers, 169
self-criticism of, 164–165
Spanish Revolution, 567–568,
    589–595
and Bonaparte, 591
Bourbon reforms prior to,
    589–590
and Central Junta, 591–592
Constitution of 1812,
    592–595
and Cortes, 592–595
and free trade, 594
liberals *vs.* serviles, 594–595
and religion, 594
representation for American
    subjects, 593, 594
resistance by juntas, 591–592
and slavery, 593–594
and Spanish Enlightenment,
    590
and war with France,
    591–592
spice trade, 220
Stamp Act, 503–504, 527,
    537
Stannard, David E., 320
Stedman, John Gabriel, 207,
    362, 401, 416
Stephens, James, 638
Sterba, James, 418
Stono Rebellion, 416–417
Strachey, William, 287–289
Stuyvesant, Pieter, 251
Suárez, Francisco, 523
Sugar Act, 503, 527
sugar cane
    crushing of, 395*i*
    making sugar from, 377–378,
        392
    slave cutting in West Indies,
        379*i*
Sugar-Canes (Atkins), 392
sugar production/trade, 59, 60,
    65
    in Atlantic Regions,
        1492–1870, 391*t*
    in Barbados, 256, 391–393

in Brazil, 153–154, 191,
    200–202, 295–296
in Canary Islands, 75, 380
in Caribbean, 257
and Genoa, 75
in Madeiras, 75, 82–83,
    379–380
plantations in Atlantic
    regions, 1494–1860,
    397*t*
slave labor, 73, 75, 398*t*
wage labor in Cuba, 648–649
Sunni Ali (Muslim king), 27
Surinam, 260, 415–416
Swedes and, 255
Symonds, William, 456

Taino, 18–19, 125, 129, 132,
    278–279. *See also*
    Columbus, Christopher
Tairona, 21
Tamoio War, 155
tangomaos, 336–337
tapoeyers, 434
Taqui Onqoy, 305
Tarascan Empire, 12, 144
Taylor, John, 410
Templo Mayor (Great Temple),
    10, 12
Tenerife, 73, 107, 108
Tenochtitlán, and Cortés
    Cortés resides at, 136
    defeat of Cortés, 139
    native massacre, 141
    rebuilding of, 144
    siege/conquest of, 139–141
    temporary defeat at, 139
Teotihuacan, 7, 10–11, 138*m*
Texcoco, 10–11, 140, 144
Texupa, 181
They love Women extreamly,
    and spare no Charges for
    the setting out of their
    Wives (Sieur Froger), 453
13 colonies, map of, 530*m*
Thirteenth Amendment, 645
Thislewood, Thomas, 401
Thomson, Charles, 465–466
Thornton, John K., 90, 124,
    369, 572
Tiahuanaco, 7
Tiçocic (ruler of Tenochtitlán),
    12
Timbuktu, 25, 28, 110
tithe, 173, 188, 192, 196, 302,
    561, 673
Tlacopan, and Triple Alliance,
    10–11
Tlaloc (rain god), 12
Tlatelolco, 10
Tlatoani speaker, 11

Tlaxcalan, 134, 144
tobacco farms
    in Bermuda, 239
    in Virginia, 239
Tocqueville, Alexis de, 519,
    545, 563, 621
Togo-Dahomey Gap, 28
Toltec culture, in pre-contact
    Americas, 7
ton, definition of, 673
tools, in pre-contact Americas,
    23
Toscanello, Paolo dal Posso, 91
Totonac, 134
Toussaint, L'Ouverture, 510
Townshend Duties, 504–505,
    528, 533, 537
trade
    in Africa, 25, 29
    Americas, pre-contact, 10,
        19, 21
    Atlantic Africa, 1680–1820,
        341*t*
    Atlantic contribution to
        English, 1700–1772,
        490, 490*t*
    China and,
    Christian embargo on Egypt,
        59
    Dutch-West Indies, 249–250
    Europe, pre-expansion,
        40–43, 48–49
    fur trade, 232, 242, 250–251,
        319
    Genoa and, 58–59, 75
    gold trade, 188–189, 190
    Portugal-Africa, 83, 188–189,
        190
    Portugal-West Africa, 109
    Spanish Revolution and free
        trade, 594
    spice trade, 220
    sugar production/trade, 59,
        60, 65
    supervision from Lisbon, 188
    by Taino, 19
    in Valley of Mexico, 10
    value of French colonial
        trade, 482
    wool trade, 43. *See also* slave
        trade
Trade fairs, 43
trans-African slavery, 327
Treaty of Aix-la-Chapelle, 493
Treaty of Alcáçovas, 74, 90, 108
Treaty of Cateau-Cambrésis,
    231
Treaty of Madrid, 502
Treaty of Nonsuch, 233
Treaty of Paris, 499
Treaty of Ryswick, 479

Treaty of San Ildefonso, 503
Treaty of The Hague (1596), 235
Treaty of Tordesillas, 94, 95*i*, 96, 214
Treaty of Utrecht, 481
tribute system
　in Inka Empire, 14
　in Mexica Empire, 11
　Mississippian, 19
Triple Alliance, 10–11
trypanosomiasis (sleeping sickness), 28–29, 35
Tula, 7
Tupac Hualla (Inka), 148
Tupac Huascar (Inka), 148
Tupi, 21–22
Tupi-Guaraní speakers, 22
Tupinambá, 154–155, 286–289
Tupiniuin, 154–155
Tuscaroras, 317
Twelve Years Truce, 246–248

Ulrich, Laurel Thatcher, 458
United Provinces of the Netherlands
　Atlantic slave trade, 344–345
　claims in North America, 246–248
　commercial treaties with Spain, 236
　creation of, 230, 234–235
　influence of French Revolution on, 560
　merchant marine, 235
　planting colonies, 246–254, 259–261
　as protectorate of England, 233
　truce with Spanish, 235, 474–476. *See also* Dutch
Upper Guinea, 187, 433
Uruguay, 151, 602

Valley of Mexico
　Cortés entry, 136 (*See also* Cortés, Hernando)
　map, 137*m*
　mendicant orders in, 144
　native population collapse in, 320
　native populations of, 1519–1800, 174*t*
　smallpox epidemic in, 140
　trade at Tlatelolco, 10
van den Bogaert, Harmen Meyndertsz, 290
van der Capellen, Joan Derk, 539–540
van der Donck, Adraen, 290–292

van der Woude, Ad, 475
Vega, Garcilaso de la, 280–281, 441–442
Velázquez, Diego de, 132–133, 136–138
Velázquez de Cuéllar, Diego, 129
Venezuela, 96, 588–589
Venice
　Crusade against Constantinople, 58
　mercantile colonies, 58, 59
Verrazzano, Giovanni da, 100–101
Verrazzano, Giovanni [Same person as next entry?], 227
Vespucci, Amerigo, 70, 98, 99–100
Viceroyalty of Rio de la Plata, 601–602, 603
Vieira, Antonio, 204, 450
Villaut, Nicolas, 337, 351
Virginia
　arrival of Englishmen, 239*i*
　indentured servants in, 239
　on origin of natives of, 287–289
　slave labor in, 239
　tobacco farms in, 239
Virginia Company, and Christian mission, 311
Vitclupuchtli (Mexica god), 8
Vives, Juan Luis, 427
volta do mar, 79, 86, 96–97, 674
Voltaire (François-Marie Arouet), 519
Vries, Jan de, 475

Waitacá, 156
Waldseemuller, Martin, 98
Wallerstein, Immanuel, 63
Walpole, Robert, 491
wampum, 310, 674
Wari, 7
The Warning of the Cacique Hatuey to the Indians of Cuba, 131
War of Spanish Succession, 317, 477, 479, 589
War of the Knives, 577
War of the League of Augsburg, 477
Washington, George, 505, 564
Weberians, 62–63
Webster, Noah, 555
Wedgewood, Josiah, 629
Wesley, John, 621
West Africa

map from Arguim to Benin, 110*m*
Songhay Empire, 25–27, 82, 110. *See also* Africa; West Africa, Portugal in; individual country
West Africa, Portugal in, 109–114
　Accra, 112
　Akara, 112
　arms/warfare, 111–112
　Benin, 84, 112–114
　Commany, 112
　converts to Christianity, 113, 114
　feitorias (trading factories), 83, 96–97, 110–111
　Gold Coast, 82, 83, 110, 111–112
　gold mining, 29–30, 42, 110, 112
　Grain Coast, 81–82
　Guinea, 33
　Itsekiri kingdom, 114
　Ivory Coast, 82
　Portuguese arrival, 29–30
　settlers, 80, 109, 671
　Slave Coast, 82
　slave trade in, 113–114, 340*m*
　trade, 109
　Upper Guinea, 109–110
Westerlies, 86, 217
westernization, of Southern global societies, 663–665
West Indies
　Dutch in, 249–250
　late 18th-century map, 506, 507*m*
　map, c. 1750, 497, 498*m*
　in 17th century, 258*m*
　war between France/Great Britain, 479–480, 509–511, 513. *See also* plantation complex; individual country
West Indische Compagnie. *See* Dutch West India Company (WIC)
White, John, 289–290
Wiesner, Merry E., 428–430
Wild Coast (Guiana), 207, 236, 254–255, 257, 260
Willem III (Holland), 477, 541
Williams, Eric, 382, 618
Williams, Roger, 240
Windward Islands, 586–587
Wolfe, James, 496
Wollstonecraft, Mary, 520, 558
Wolof, 81, 82, 88

Wood, Gordon S., 360
Wood, William, 490
world-systems theory, xxv, 64,
    65
Wright, Robert, 666
writing/literacy, in pre-contact
    Americas, 23–24

Xiu, 145

Yáñez Pinzón, Vicente, 96
Yanomamo, homicide rate
    among, 20
yaws, 28–29, 35
yellow fever, 35

Yoruba kingdom, 30
Yucatan, 132–133, 145

Zapotecs, 12–13, 144
Zong affair, 629
Zorita, Alonso, 181–182
Zurara, Gomes Eannes de, 77–79